A Critical History and Philosophy of Psychology

In line with the British Psychological Society's recent recommendations for teaching the history of psychology, this comprehensive undergraduate textbook emphasizes the philosophical, cultural, and social elements that influenced psychology's development. The authors demonstrate that psychology is both a human (i.e., psychoanalytic or phenomenological) and natural (i.e., cognitive) science, exploring broad social-historical and philosophical themes such as the role of diverse cultures and women in psychology, and the complex relationship between objectivity and subjectivity in the development of psychological knowledge. The result is a fresh and balanced perspective on what has traditionally been viewed as the collected achievements of a few "great men."

With a variety of learning features, including case studies, study questions, thought experiments, and a glossary, this new textbook encourages students to critically engage with chapter material and analyze themes and topics within a social, historical, and philosophical framework.

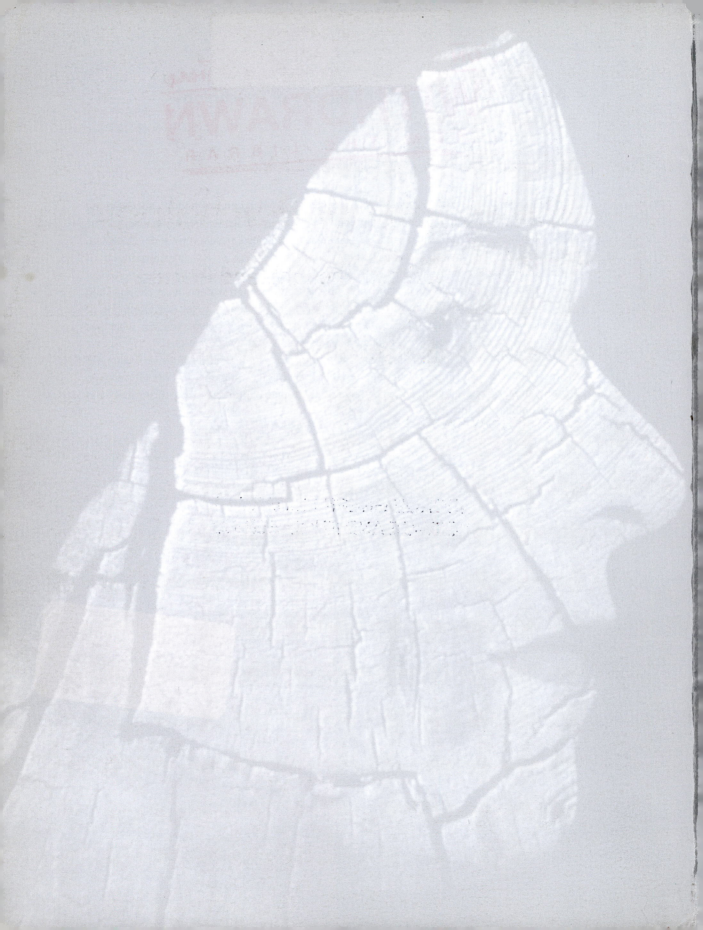

A Critical History and Philosophy of Psychology

Diversity of Context, Thought, and Practice

RICHARD T. G. WALSH

THOMAS TEO

ANGELINA BAYDALA

CAMBRIDGE
UNIVERSITY PRESS

CAMBRIDGE
UNIVERSITY PRESS

University Printing House, Cambridge CB2 8BS, United Kingdom

Published in the United States of America by Cambridge University Press, New York

Cambridge University Press is part of the University of Cambridge.

It furthers the University's mission by disseminating knowledge in the pursuit of education, learning, and research at the highest international levels of excellence.

www.cambridge.org
Information on this title: www.cambridge.org/walsh

10 07237013

First published 2014

Printing in the United Kingdom by TJ International Ltd. Padstow Cornwall

A catalogue record for this publication is available from the British Library

Library of Congress Cataloguing in Publication data
Walsh, Richard T. G., 1942–
A critical history and philosophy of psychology : diversity of context, thought, and practice /
Richard T.G. Walsh, Thomas Teo, Angelina Baydala.
  pages cm
ISBN 978-0-521-87076-4 (hardback) ISBN 978-0-521-69126-0 (paperback)
1. Psychology – History.   2. Psychology – Philosophy.   I. Teo, Thomas, 1963–
II. Baydala, Angelina.   III. Title.
BF81.W296 2014
150.9–dc23   2013022559

ISBN 978-0-521-87076-4 Hardback
ISBN 978-0-521-69126-0 Paperback

CONTENTS

FIGURES

TABLES

BOXES

PREFACE

In this textbook on the history and philosophy of Psychology our intention is to provide a comprehensive but accessible account with international content suitable for a one-term or two-term, advanced undergraduate course in which the instructor aims to foster critical thinking about the discipline's intellectual and social development. Below we describe our intellectual approach, text structure and chapter content, and the educational intent and pedagogical features of our text.

The distinctive **characteristics of the text** are as follows:

- Integrates the history and philosophy of Psychology.
- Distinguishes between natural-science and human-science Psychologies.
- Relies on current scholarship in the history and philosophy of Psychology.
- Takes an international and contextualized approach to psychological ideas.
- Includes applied and professional psychology, current developments in the discipline, and Psychology's research traditions.
- Fosters students' critical thinking about the history and philosophy of Psychology.
- Facilitates instructors employing a different order of presenting the twelve chapters, because they are relatively self-contained, yet thematically linked.

Intellectual approach

As teachers and authors of works on historical and philosophical issues in Psychology, we were dissatisfied with the coverage of these issues in the available textbooks. Whether these works were primarily historical, theoretical, or an integration of both, the authors seemed to be relatively uncritical and to take for granted psychologists' standard concepts, theories, research findings, methods, and professional practices, all of which have a history and philosophical content. Writing from a standpoint of Anglo-American nations, the authors tended to celebrate the achievements of mainly White men, universalized across times, places, and persons (Brock, 2006a).

However, the Psychology typically practised in the USA, which has prevailed internationally since World War II, represents one perspective, *Psychology as a natural science*. As we note throughout this textbook, another perspective, *Psychology as a human science*, has flourished simultaneously since the discipline's formal inception, if in circumscribed ways and contexts. Arguably, then, diverse philosophical positions best characterize Psychology's history (G. Richards, 2010; R. Smith, 1997).

Here we describe the particular emphases that we place in practising our intellectual approach, our conception of historical scholarship (i.e., historiography), and the critical standpoint that we adopt.

Emphases

In integrating the history and philosophy of Psychology we assume that any history of a discipline presupposes theoretical and philosophical content. Correspondingly, all theoretical and philosophical content has a history, because it is a human creation subject to contingencies of time and place. Accordingly, our intellectual approach is less chronological and less centred on "great men," while more philosophical than the standard text.

We concentrate on the connections among the psychological ideas of key individuals in their social-historical context and underscore the diversity of thought and practice in Psychology's history internationally. This approach of intellectual history situated in social context is congruent with the recommendations of the British Psychological Society for a course in the history and philosophy of Psychology.

Our intellectual approach also is partially *thematic* in that we address broad issues and debates that shift across historical eras and that link earlier and later historical figures. These **themes** include:

- The emergence in European and Anglo-American nations of individualism and administrative management of individuals, two historical trends that made Psychology possible and sustain and shape it.
- The place of women and diverse cultures in Psychology.
- The relationship between objectivity and subjectivity in making psychological knowledge.
- The historical relationship between science and Psychology, on the one hand, and philosophy, spirituality, and religion, on the other hand.

Such themes link past, present, and future concerns of psychologists to the multiple contexts in which the issues have been embedded.

Historiography

Writing history necessarily entails a process of selection; historians include some aspects of the past, while excluding other aspects (Weimer, 1974). But there are consequences of any selection-bias. If authors' frame of reference is exclusively Psychology as a natural science steadily progressing from functionalism through behaviourism to cognitive and behavioural neuroscience, which is the standard account of US Psychology, then authors will ignore Psychology as a human science and the historical trajectories of Psychologies in other nations.

Many history of Psychology textbooks begin with the discipline's emergence in nineteenth-century Germany, concentrating on nearly 150 years of Psychology's development. But we decided to examine psychological thought dating back to ancient times for two reasons. First, scholars might discern partial historical continuity of psychological ideas posed in previous eras. Although these ideas arose from particular existential conditions and are unique to their historical context, one can sense similarities based in common human conditions. Secondly, earlier psychological thought can inspire new ways of thinking about contemporary issues in Psychology. Instead of taking for granted accepted meanings associated with standard practice, scholars can refigure present meanings in the light of past representations.

When we reviewed current textbooks on the history of Psychology, we resolved to write one that acquaints students with the roots, concepts, and practices of both natural-science and human-science Psychology for the central purpose of fostering critical thinking about the origins, present, and future of the discipline. Accordingly, by adopting a social con-textual and critical orientation, we highlight the diversity of context, thought, and practice in Psychology's history.

Contextualizing is important, because Psychology has taken different forms in diverse national contexts. If students are exposed to only one national perspective, they are likely to assume that no alternative perspectives have existed. To cite just two national examples, the US American cultural mentality led to functionalist and then behaviourist psychologies, while the contemporary German mentality led to a rather different approach, Gestalt psychology, in which the active perceiving mind was pivotal. In fact, there are numerous examples of the different forms that Psychology has taken historically in diverse contexts (Jansz & van Drunen, 2004).

The forerunners for our intellectual approach include Canadian historian of Psychology, Kurt Danziger (1979, 1990, 1997, 2008), who examined the origins of the discipline's conceptual and investigative traditions in social context, and Dutch authors Jeroen Jansz and Peter van Drunen (2004). Our standpoint also reflects the influence of two British historians of Psychology: Graham Richards (2010) and Roger Smith (1997). In addition, we have incorporated much of the new literature on the history and philosophy of Psychology published in recent decades.

Critical standpoint

The distinction between a critical approach to the history and philosophy of Psychology and the traditional approach deserves explanation. According to the latter, psychologists regard psychological objects as if they are permanent entities, unaffected by social-historical context, objectively knowable as truths, and equivalent to the natural objects that natural scientists study. Authors of traditional histories of Psychology compose a narrative by which the present state of the discipline upholds the truth, while "the past becomes the story of how this truth triumphed and error was defeated" (Danziger, 2008, p. 12).

However, the traditional standpoint on the history of Psychology is problematic for several reasons. Current critical histories of science and philosophy have broadened and deepened the literature on the key figures, intellectual movements, and social conditions that laid the foundation for Psychology's formal emergence in the late nineteenth century. Consequently, rather than using outdated sources and possibly perpetuating misconceptions about Psychology's scientific and philosophical origins, we relied on current historical and philosophical scholarship.

In a *critical* approach to Psychology's history and philosophy, every aspect of psychologists' activities has a social history. Scholars operating from this orientation believe that one can use the past to examine the discipline's truth-claims in the light of social-historical contingencies. Therefore, by adopting a critical historical and philosophical approach we attempted to practise two important intellectual values: explicating the characteristics of the past and showing "the impermanence of human constructions," including psychological concepts (Danziger, 2008, p. 15).

In our experience, Psychology scholars who practise a critical approach to the discipline are rather dissatisfied with the traditional approach to the history of Psychology. Critical thinkers seek a text that is international in scope and contextualized, and integrates the history of Psychology with its philosophical foundations. This search is what inspired us to produce our text.

Furthermore, psychological bodies of knowledge, such as theories of mental processes, are as much social institutions as the university system, parliamentary democracy, and financial systems are, because the relevant collectives of people attribute institutional status to them (Kusch, 1999). Consequently, theories of mental processes are subject to influence from social institutions other than academic disciplines. Thus, our historical account of psychological thought and practice includes societal influences.

Text structure and chapter content

Our intellectual approach informs the text's structure and content. We proceed chronologically from ancient civilizations to the nineteenth century, but when describing Psychology, we divide our coverage into natural-science and human-science domains. Furthermore, we devote an entire chapter each to applied and professional psychology, the history of psychologists' ideas about how to conduct research, and current reflections on Psychology's philosophy and history. Thus, our approach is more philosophical and critical than the standard account.

The *content* of our twelve chapters is as follows. In **Chapter 1** we discuss the diverse meanings for the terms "history," "psychology," "science," and "philosophy." Then in **Chapters 2** and **3** we review how scholars in previous civilizations up to the nineteenth century dealt with psychological ideas. However, we caution our readers that modern psychological terms and concepts are not linear extensions of centuries of previous "psychological" thinking. We describe in **Chapter 4** the philosophical and scientific context for the discipline's formal emergence.

In **Chapters 5**, **6**, and **7** we discuss the development of natural-science Psychology. But our approach, although chronological, is thematic, because our interest is in comparing different schools of thought. Also, our scope is international, because natural-science and human-science Psychology took different forms in different nations.

Students in a history of Psychology course commonly ask, "How did Psychology get to be this way?" We believe that, to best appreciate the origins of psychological ideas and practices, they need a sense of the "big picture" of the discipline's *present* status. Thus, Chapter 7 also contains a review of the current state of natural-science Psychology to enable students to integrate what they have been learning about Psychology in other courses and then situate that learning in historical and philosophical context.

In **Chapter 8** we cover applied and professional psychology, although nearly all Psychology has practical intentions. In this chapter we describe historical applications of Psychology to industry, business, the military, education, and mental health, as well as newer specialty areas such as community, environmental, and health psychology.

Then we address human-science psychologies: psychoanalysis in **Chapter 9** and hermeneutic, phenomenological, existential, humanistic, and transpersonal psychologies in **Chapter 10**. Historically, human-science psychologies have been marginalized relative to natural-science psychologies. Despite their marginalization, human-science psychologies remain relevant to any scholarly account of the discipline's past, present, and anticipated future. This is the case particularly for some international psychologists who have not found behaviourism and neobehaviourism convincing and who preferred psychoanalysis and humanistic-existential psychologies.

The heart of Psychology always has been its claim to be a legitimate science, grounded in empirical research. Accordingly, we devote **Chapter 11** to a historical review of the multiple foundations of human and animal research in Psychology. We describe the origins of the relationship between investigators and animal subjects and research participants, research methods, and quantitative and qualitative methods.

We conclude in **Chapter 12** by returning to the present, where we reflect on the value of critical, philosophical, feminist, and postcolonial perspectives for the future of scientific and professional Psychology. In addition, we review the conceptual themes of the preceding chapters and discuss our concluding theme, Psychology as a problematic science. We end by encouraging student reflection on the discipline's future.

Educational intent

Although the historical and philosophical issues that we discussed above are central to how we wrote and structured this text, its *educational* purpose takes priority. By "education" we mean instructors fostering students' active learning about the past, present, and anticipated future of Psychology's diverse contexts, thought, and practice. Consequently, we attempt to avoid training or indoctrination in "one best way" to think and behave as a psychologist. Our intention is to provide instructors and students with intellectually respectable stimulation to facilitate student reflection and critical consciousness about the field and yet to avoid the pitfalls of dogmatism.

Besides encouraging student-readers to engage in critical thinking about Psychology, we adopt international perspectives rooted in respect for human diversity. In our account, we strive to contextualize the story of Psychology by describing its diverse theories, concepts, and terms, and varied applications to research and community practice. Thus, we resituate women in science and Psychology, and adopt a multicultural scope. We trust that women and students from culturally diverse backgrounds will recognize their heritage, at least partially. However, given the limits of our knowledge, our approach is the story of primarily Western cultures' attempts to explain psychological experience scientifically.

Pedagogical features

Here we explain the pedagogical features that we employed.

Context and background

Throughout this textbook we frequently use the key terms "context" and "background." *Context* refers to both material substances and immaterial phenomena that interact with and influence the activities of individuals, groups, societies, and cultures. Material substances include social institutions, such as governmental sources of and eligibility criteria for research funding. Immaterial phenomena include culturally shared assumptions, such as the strong preference in the Western world over several centuries for scientific "facts" and against philosophical, spiritual, and religious knowledge.

Background refers to substances and phenomena with which individuals, groups, societies, and cultures have not interacted. The artificial background (e.g., a sunny beachfront) introduced by a portrait photographer does not interact with the subject of a portrait, but an actual background, that is, the *context*, clearly influences the individuals situated within it.

Structure and style

We follow the same organization in each chapter: **outline** and **introduction**, including specific **chapter aims**; two **boxes** in which we provide case examples; two images that convey context not easily accessible in words; **thematic review** of the significant historical issues and philosophical ideas discussed; **chapter summary**; **sample essay questions**; and **recommended reading**, including online resources.

At the end of the text are a **Timeline** depicting the societal and scientific contexts, the institutionalization of Psychology, and the principal schools of thought, a **Glossary**, **References**, **Name index**, and **Subject index**.

By using **bolded** section-headings and suggesting questions or issues for **small-group discussion**, two per chapter, we signal some of the important issues that link individuals and contexts. Furthermore, in sections where we discuss a particular issue or historical figure we provide a critical review of what we have just described, entitled **Section conclusion**. In addition, where relevant, we discuss the relation of the issue or historical figure to gender, ethnocultural, and ethical–political matters.

Whenever the name of a key figure whose work we describe at some point in the text appears for the first time, we **bold** that person's name. We provide the individual's years of birth and death when we first identify them.

We employ **Canadian English** (e.g., "behaviour") rather than US spelling.

In addition, we use "USA" as a noun and "US" as an adjective rather than "America" and "American," because there are dozens of nations in the Americas. We also use the term "European and Anglo-American nations" rather than "Western culture" to be more precise in our characterizations.

We use the term *sic*, which means "thus," in brackets to indicate where an original text includes language that in current discourse is questionable practice.

Lastly, in the **References** we include an author's, editor's, or translator's first given-name so as to recognize women's contributions where possible.

ACKNOWLEDGMENTS

The following former students reviewed previous drafts and made helpful recommendations concerning content and format: Marissa Barnes, Jason Goertzen, and Sarah Wallace. In addition, Nicole Abbott, Colleen Canivet, Ravi Gokani, Brian Hoessler, Steve Kearns, Annette Penney, Amanda Peters, Melissa St. Germaine-Small, and Megan Snoyer completed valuable tasks. We thank them all.

The following colleagues offered helpful advice on specific aspects of content: Ben Harris, Christian Jordan, Mark Pancer, Mike Pratt, and Pamela Sadler. We thank them too.

Colleagues David Checkland, Kurt Danziger, William Smythe, and Hank Stam offered helpful comments on portions of the text. Graham Richards also graciously facilitated the development of our work. We, of course, are solely responsible for the text.

Lastly, we are very grateful to Cambridge University Press staff Hetty Marx and Carrie Parkinson for their professional guidance and support and to the copy-editor, Kay McKechnie, for her expertise.

ABOUT THE AUTHORS

Dr. Richard T. G. Walsh(-Bowers) is Professor of Psychology at Wilfrid Laurier University. In Laurier's undergraduate programme he has taught abnormal psychology, clinical psychology, community psychology, group processes, drama and human development (a course he created), a seminar in personality and abnormal psychology focused on feminism and gender issues, the history of psychology, and introductory psychology at an aboriginal college. He also contributes teaching and thesis supervision to Laurier's MA and PhD programme in community psychology. In 1999 he received his university's Outstanding Teacher Award. His interests are in the history, philosophy, and ethics of psychology; community psychology; and electoral politics.

Dr. Thomas Teo is Professor of Psychology at York University. His research areas and publications include the intellectual history of philosophical psychology; history of German psychology in the nineteenth century; the historical, epistemological, and methodological foundations of critical and human-scientific psychology; and the history and theory of race and racism. Dr. Teo has taught undergraduate courses on history of psychology, theories of human nature, alternatives for contemporary psychology, and graduate courses on historical and theoretical foundations of contemporary psychology, history of psychological practice, and on race and racism in the human sciences.

Dr. Angelina Baydala is Associate Professor and Registered Clinical Psychologist in the Department of Psychology at the University of Regina. She provides thesis supervision to students in the MA and PhD programme in clinical psychology. Her areas of research and publications include history and theory of psychotherapy, critiques of psychological research methods, hermeneutics and narrative research, cultural psychology, and socio-political implications of psychological belief systems. She teaches undergraduate courses in the history of psychology, systems of psychology, theories of personality, and yoga psychology (a course she created), as well as a graduate course on theories and practices of psychotherapy.

1 Introducing the history and philosophy of psychology

Chapter outline

Introduction

In this chapter we begin a journey through the vast and varied terrain of the history of psychological topics by attempting to clarify what the terms "psychology," "history," "science," and "philosophy" mean. We discuss some central ideas underlying a critical history and philosophy of psychological topics. Then we place the work of scientists in context and describe social realities that influence scientists' attempts to be objective and unbiased. As such, we propose a view of science as socially embedded.

Because the discipline and professions of Psychology as practised currently are indebted to both ancient and modern philosophy, we examine domains of philosophy that seem most relevant to Psychology. Our view is that a philosophical outlook on psychological issues strengthens systematic critical inquiry. By "critical" we mean an approach that not only examines what psychologists are doing, but also why they are doing what they are doing. This approach includes an analysis of the implicit assumptions as well as the contexts in which psychological thinking and practice are embedded.

The **aims** of this chapter are to describe:

- Different definitions of psychology and how they have changed historically.
- Different definitions and types of history, the crucial role that interpretation plays, and different assumptions about historical change.
- How to practise the history of psychology with relative objectivity.
- Different definitions of science, basic assumptions of the natural-science approach, and assumptions about how science changes.
- What a critical approach to the history and philosophy of any science entails when practising science.
- The value of philosophical questions and critical thinking for understanding the history and philosophy of psychology.
- Four interrelated themes that summarize the main issues discussed in this chapter: multiple psychologies, reflexive historiography, intersubjective science, and critical thinking.

Part 1   What is psychology?

Before we can explore the history and philosophy of psychology, we need to clarify what we mean by the term "psychology." The questions "what is psychology?" and "what are the discipline and professions of Psychology?" are best answered as: "It depends on history!" Although authors of current introductory textbooks typically define psychology as the *study of behaviour and mental processes*, in the past, psychologists did not share that definition.

History of definitions

Diverse definitions of psychology have been the historical norm. For instance, **Friedrich Beneke** (1798–1854), a German philosopher-psychologist who understood his own personal psychology as *the new psychology* of his time, published a book, *Textbook of Psychology as a Natural Science*. Students of philosophy and education and interested laypersons studied it. In it Beneke (1833/1845) defined psychology as the *natural science of inner experience*. He suggested that psychology was everything that one apprehended through *internal perception* (perception of one's own thinking, feeling, and willing). For Beneke the subject matter of psychology was "what you find in yourself" (p. 1) and this definition complemented his particular natural-scientific approach.

Wilhelm Wundt (1832–1920), the famous German psychologist who is considered one of the founders of the discipline, defined psychology's subject matter as the *total content of experience in its immediate character* in his *Outlines of Psychology* (1896). **William James** (1842–1910), considered one of the pioneers of US Psychology, defined topics of psychology in his 1890 book *The Principles of Psychology* as the *science of mental life, both of its phenomena and of their conditions*. Clearly, Beneke's, Wundt's, and James's psychological terminology and theoretical and methodological frameworks differ from those of present Psychology.

An analysis of more than 200 introductory textbooks, published between 1887 and 1987, showed that prior to 1930, definitions of Psychology included the concepts of *mind*, *consciousness*, or *mental activity* 67 per cent of the time, whereas *behaviour* was only used 14 per cent of the time (Henley, Johnson, E. Jones, & Herzog, 1989). But from 1930 to 1969 terms referring to the mind were only mentioned 7 per cent of the time, while use of the term "behaviour" escalated to 68 per cent. Then, in the 1980s, terms referring to the mind increased again to 33 per cent, even while "behaviour" climbed to 79 per cent, indicating that later authors tended to use both sets of terms (behaviour and mental activity).

There is a tendency for current definitions of Psychology in Anglo-American nations (Australia, Canada, New Zealand, the UK, and the USA) and in many non-anglophone nations to abide by twentieth-century "American" definitions of natural-scientific Psychology. The natural-science perspective was influenced briefly by Wundt, then dominated by earlier and later forms of *behaviourism* (the science of behaviour) and more recently by *cognitivism* (the study of mental processes) and *neuroscience* (the science of brain–behaviour relations). Changing definitions of Psychology reflect dominant research programmes in particular times and places.

European psychologists, however, especially before World War II, generally did not share the natural-science view. But after the war, a process termed the *Americanization of psychology* reflected the expansion of US economic power, and with the increasing global dominance of US Psychology the US terms became the norm.

From a theoretical perspective, it is curious that, when US psychologists expressed a preference for studying *behaviour* or *mental processes*, they did not discuss how these two domains interact. Yet, why not assume that Psychology is the study of behaviour, cognitive processes, and their interaction? One answer is because, historically, this interaction was not considered a primary research problem. Academic communities at different times have developed different definitions of what Psychology should be, and these definitions themselves depend on the story of Psychology in specific cultural contexts.

So far we have covered a few definitions of psychology from the nineteenth and twentieth centuries. But the issue becomes more complicated when we examine even earlier times. In the eighteenth century, German philosopher **Christian Wolff** (1679–1754) divided psychology into *rational* and *empirical psychology*. *Rational psychology*, for him, was the science of what was possible by the human *soul*, which included the mind. Within rational psychology Wolff discussed the soul's substantiality, simplicity, immateriality, immortality, and the mind–body problem.

By contrast, the aim of Wolff's *empirical psychology* was to identify psychological principles with the aid of concrete experiences of what actually happens in the human soul. His use of the term "empirical" did not mean what it suggests today, but something that one can attain through direct human experience rather than through reason. Within his empirical psychology Wolff discussed the soul's ability to know and desire, the interaction of soul/mind and body, and the soul/mind's "faculties" (capacities).

Outside the history of psychology and theology it might be difficult to understand what Wolff intended. However, his psychology was the culmination of centuries of thought on the soul, which traditionally scholars have claimed originated with the ancient Greeks (see Chapter 2), specifically **Aristotle** (384–322 BCE).

Although most psychologists today do not discuss the soul and they understand the mind as material, historically psychology remained the *study of the soul* until the nineteenth century with few exceptions. Then in the second half of that century, German philosopher **Friedrich Lange** (1828–1875) proclaimed a *psychology without a soul*, which reinforced the movement towards a natural-science definition of psychology (see Chapter 12). This and other developments led to the formal emergence of scientific psychology. But the term "behaviour," which emanates from late nineteenth-century biology, would have been foreign to Psychology's predecessors.

Did Lange, Wolff, James, Wundt, and Beneke mean the same thing when they defined "psychology?" Clearly, although there is some overlap among their definitions, the general framework, meaning, and purpose of Psychology have changed rather significantly over time. Accordingly, it is important to distinguish **four different domains** when considering the history of psychology:

- *Psychological topics*. Scholars, philosophers, poets, etc. have studied certain psychological topics for millennia. For instance, Aristotle discussed memory, recall, and recollection. However, he did not study IQ, stereotype-threat, or mirror-neurons, nor did he use the term "psychology."
- *Psychology as a separate field of study*. Although there is controversy on this issue, Psychology as a distinct field of study independent of philosophy did not exist before the eighteenth century (Danziger, 1997b). In 1590 Rudolf Goclenius (1547–1628), a German professor of physics, mathematics, logic, and ethics, used the term "*psychologia*" (psychology) in a book title. Evidently the term was used sporadically even earlier, but psychology was not yet a separate field.
- *Psychology as an institutionalized discipline*. Psychology as a formal discipline of research and teaching at universities did not exist before the nineteenth century. So, when did the *institutionalization* – meaning establishing an academic discipline that follows institutional rules – of Psychology occur? One might claim 1824 as its birth-year, when Prussia established psychology as an examinable discipline at its universities where professors of philosophy were required to teach courses on psychology and pedagogy to high-school teachers-in-training (Gundlach, 2004). Customarily, however, authors of histories of Psychology cite 1879 as the discipline's birth-year, when Wundt began to conduct experiments in his psychological laboratory in Leipzig.

- *Psychology as a profession*. Although one could consider local events of professionalization occurring at different times in different nations, Psychology as a profession and an expert occupation emerged only in the twentieth century (Ward, 2002). This fact means that in 1850 our ancestors were unable to go to a psychologist for assessment or treatment. Furthermore, Psychology's professionalization was linked to the development of other institutions in a given society. For instance, German psychology was professionalized in the context of Nazi militarization beginning in the 1930s (Geuter, 1984/1992), whereas in the USA after World War II the Veterans Administration was an important factor in the establishment of clinical psychology as a profession (R. Baker & Pickren, 2007).

Part 1 conclusion

It is difficult to attribute the birth of a discipline to a single event. The evidence suggests that the institutionalization of Psychology occurred at different times in different geographical or national contexts. In this sense it is difficult to write the history of Psychology according to a single narrative (R. Smith, 2005). Instead of a solitary global event of institutionalization, one finds many local ones. Psychology originated in Germany differently than in Brazil, China, or South Africa, for example.

Furthermore, the term "psychology" has been ambiguous historically. British historian of Psychology Graham Richards (2010) deals with this ambiguity by using Psychology (with an upper-case *P*) to mean the *discipline* as a science (and later as a profession). The discipline of Psychology is a construction of nineteenth-century European scientists that has flourished ever since in Western societies and currently pervades popular consciousness. Richards uses psychology (with a lower-case *p*) to mean psychological subject matter with aged roots, practised in diverse cultures through philosophical inquiry or self-reflection. Accordingly, in this textbook we use the generic term "psychology" to encompass psychological subject matter and topics and psychology as an independent field of study. We reserve the specific term "Psychology" for the academic scientific discipline and its professional and applied branches.

Finally, as British historian Roger Smith observed (1997), the discipline is so diverse in its theoretical positions that multiple psychologies prevail rather than one unitary Psychology. Thus, we do not accept the claim that Psychology is exclusively a natural science. Despite the efforts of many psychologists to convey a public image of uniformity, conceptual diversity has been the historical norm in the discipline (see Chapter 7).

Regardless of intellectual boundaries concerning what is and is not legitimate Psychology, definitions of the discipline always have been contestable, because what constitutes "psychology" varies significantly over time and culture. Accordingly, we attempt to account for the range of definitions and conceptual approaches to Psychology. In addition, we do not share *a priori* (as an assumption that is not tested) the view that the latest is also the best Psychology. There is an inherent problem in such an idea of progress: if the latest is always the best, then the present Psychology cannot be the best, because it will be outdated tomorrow.

In sum, psychology as a subject of inquiry has had different definitions over the thousands of years that human beings have thought about their own and others' experiences. The term psychology has meant the study of the soul, consciousness, behaviour, the mind, or the brain, depending on the era and cultural context investigated.

Similarly, psychologists have defined the focal points of their studies quite differently. Psychologists with a **natural-science** orientation typically emphasize the prediction and control of behaviour; in more recent decades they added mental processes, meaning cognitive and brain functions, to their definition. Psychologists with a **human-science** orientation generally stress *subjectivity* (i.e., personal experiences of thinking, feeling, and willing, and the meanings that human beings attribute to these experiences) and making one's intentions known to oneself or others in a context of meaningful action and reflection. In subsequent chapters, we distinguish between natural-science and human-science Psychology.

> **Small-group discussion.** Based on your understanding of the current definition of Psychology, how valid might this definition be in 25 or even 100 years?

Part 2   What is history?

Before we can explore the origins of different theoretical perspectives and describe influential scientific psychologists and practitioners, we should define what we mean by "history," describe how historians construct interpretations of the past, examine underlying assumptions about historical change, and discuss the ways in which scholars understand history as a discipline. These are all issues of *historiography*, which means the philosophy, history, and methods of history as a scholarly pursuit.

Different definitions and the problem of interpretation

As with "psychology," different definitions of "history" are possible. A *basic definition* of history suggests that history is the record or chronicle of past events. But what events should a history record?

Imagine that you have to write a chronological account of the daily events in your life. What is important to *you* might not be important to your mother, friend, teacher, or (if you have one) your psychotherapist. You would have to select certain events as *significant and relevant* for documentation yet neglect other events. Thus, in history, a complete chronological account is impossible. Moreover, one always filters events through cultural–historical lenses. This statement means that selecting meaningful events depends on both objective and subjective criteria.

Philosophically, historians' procedures of *selecting* and *interpreting* events and objects do not differ qualitatively from psychologists' investigative procedures. Researchers do not *just* observe, because they always observe something that interests them. Making sense of observations without a meaningful context is impossible psychologically. Moreover, what is considered an important observation or interpretation often is based on the *consensus* of experts, which itself entails subjectivity.

Another way to appreciate the historical dimensions of significance and relevance is to consider that what nineteenth-century scholars regarded as important might be insignificant presently. Many peers regarded **Johann Friedrich Herbart** (1776–1841) as one of psychology's most important innovators (see Chapter 4). Yet today his name is hardly known outside the history of Psychology.

You can see, therefore, that interpretation plays a significant role in choosing a chronicle of past events and giving them meaning. This conclusion leads us to a second definition of history: the interpretation of the record of past events in order to understand them. But, as we explain in Part 3, interpretation always depends on the interpreter's present horizon of understanding (i.e., on the extent of one's own current perspective).

This point, in turn, points us to the issue of the relationship between objectivity and subjectivity. For us, objectivity and subjectivity are located on a continuum. Complete subjectivity produces *solipsism*, the philosophical notion that nothing beyond "me" exists and that everything else in the world is "my" invention. Of course, clinical psychologists today might characterize such thoughts as psychopathological.

On the other hand, complete objectivity is impossible, because any record of past events is inherently too complex, and the selection and interpretation of past events to understand their importance always entail subjectivity. Nevertheless, objectivity as an ideal, in the sense of attempting to do justice to the complexity of past events and objects, remains a valid goal, if it is combined with reflexive knowledge about the limitations of all interpretations. Yet, we would argue, better and worse interpretations do exist. Moreover, objectivity itself has a history and differing ideas of what constitutes this ideal have been proposed (Daston & Galison, 2007).

The hermeneutic circle

As the above discussion indicates, data and interpretation are significant elements of historians' work. Historical data consist of published works, letters, archival material, oral records, objects, instruments, films, etc. Interpretation refers to the art of understanding such material.

The discipline in which scholars develop understandings of interpretations is *hermeneutics*. For Emilio Betti (1890–1968), an Italian hermeneutic scholar, interpretation is the procedure that evokes understanding. One pioneer of hermeneutics in historiography was the German scholar **Wilhelm von Humboldt** (1767–1835). He believed that history is the description of what has taken place, but this description is only partially accessible through the historical material itself. How one makes sense of that material involves interpretation.

German scholar **Friedrich Schleiermacher** (1768–1834) called the complex procedure of interpreting data the *hermeneutic circle*. Each selection can be understood only within the whole to which it belongs, and vice versa. In order to understand the meaning of a fact in history you have to understand the context to which it belongs. But the whole context can only be understood based on the parts that make up the whole.

Classical types of interpretation

Emphasizing the historical method of *understanding*, **Johann Droysen** (1808–1884), a German historian, specified **four types of interpretation** (Droysen, 1858/1967):

- *Pragmatic interpretation* organizes the basic historical material and provides a sketch of the factual context. This form resembles what is known as *chronological history*, for example, a history of all the important events in **Sigmund Freud's** (1856–1939) life. Interpretation is involved in selecting and organizing this material.

- *Interpretation of the conditions* involves analyzing the factors that influence a historical event, object, or person, such as space, time, economy, technology, religion, etc. This form resembles what is known currently as *social history*. We could study the religious, technological, economic, and social contexts during Freud's life and their influences on his theory.
- *Psychological interpretation* means biographical reconstruction with a special focus on psychodynamic interpretations of personal actions. In Freud's biography we would try to understand his relationship with his parents and colleagues in order to understand his theory. Interpretation involves arguing that his relationship with his mother or his drive for success influenced the form and content of his theories.
- *The interpretation of ideas* means analyzing what ideas were dominant at a certain point in time. For instance, the notion of unconscious processes was not new at all when Freud originated psychoanalysis. In fact, in his era there were different conceptions of "the unconscious" (see Chapter 9). Thus, one could argue Freud gave specific meaning to an existing idea. This form of interpretation is now known as *intellectual history*. A similar term is *zeitgeist* (a German noun meaning literally "the spirit of the time"), which refers to the intellectual and cultural climate of an era.

A working definition

The definition of history that we prefer is: *the interpretation of past events from multiple perspectives in order to understand their meaning*. Interpretation is pivotal. That is, historians construct a plausible vision of the past, based on data, but this vision inevitably is selective, based on how they organize the available evidence. *How* humans construct historical events and objects (e.g., documents) is crucial. Events and objects are not simply discovered in nature, but are the social consequences of humans embedded in culture and historical time.

In our definition of history we stress fostering multiple perspectives, which facilitates a more differentiated understanding of historical events than does operating from a single frame of reference. Another interpretive safeguard is to report "the informed judgment of others" (Barzun, 2000, p. x). As a scientific principle, it is important to focus on *confirming evidence*, yet it is also wise to report *disconfirming evidence*.

Interpretations themselves derive from a more or less explicit theoretical framework, embedded in history, culture, and personal preferences. Thus, in our working definition, history and philosophy of psychology are intertwined. As the historian of psychology **Kurt Danziger** (b. 1926) argues, there is no scientific theory without personal and social history and no personal and social history without theory. Philosophy and history complement each other in that philosophy contributes to answering current historical problems, while history allows for a more adequate understanding of philosophical-psychological issues. Accordingly, in this textbook, we try to examine individual dimensions and social forces as well as ideals that incline people to action (Brinton, 1963). In this sense, history is the story of ideas in social context with predominant ideals and material factors.

Understanding the past in this way means that historical explanations comprise both *reasons* and *causes*. Historical figures might give reasons for their ideas, but their ideas are also the consequence of unconscious motives and social factors. For example, a scientist might propose a new concept that has rational value, but he or she also might be impelled to propose the idea, because of competition with a rival scientist and the desire to win the race to claim discovery of the concept.

Types of history

Answers to the question of what historians study are quite varied, because there are many types of history.

Biography of "great men"

Biographical history, or the "*great man*" (*sic*) approach, focuses on the life and works of individuals who are considered to have significantly shaped the outlook of a given field. In this genre, historians usually emphasize the individual more than the social context. Biographical history also is termed *personalistic theory* of history. Biographical history includes "psychobiography" wherein the historian applies psychoanalytic concepts to understand a "great man's" internal conflicts, as in the 1958 study by **Erik Erikson** (1902–1994) of the Protestant reformer **Martin Luther** (1483–1546).

Some historians of Psychology focus on eminent researchers and their "discoveries." These individuals are termed "great psychologists" (Watson & Evans, 1991) or "pioneers of psychology" (Fancher & Rutherford, 2012). A review of this type of history in Psychology appears in Box 1.1.

Box 1.1 "Great psychologists"

Based on the nature of their discipline, psychologists often focus on individual greatness (e.g., Simonton, 1994). Some have researched whether "great" people differ from the rest of us in terms of specific personality traits that predispose them to become world leaders, scientific geniuses, and athletes, while the rest live ordinary lives. Psychologists adopting this standpoint have examined genetic inheritance, intuition, aesthetic appreciation, birth order, formal education, sexual orientation, aging, IQ, and substance abuse.

But the question remains how a conception and orientation towards history with an exclusive focus on people and personalities can be integrated with the social context within which the individual lived and that influences what an individual does and is able to do. Would calculus have been developed if German philosopher Gottfried Leibniz (1646–1716) had died as a child? The answer is "yes," because Isaac Newton (1642–1727) was working on calculus simultaneously. For another example, it is very likely that the theory of evolution would have come to prominence had **Charles Darwin** (1809–1882) never lived.

As such, to be most comprehensive about a psychological topic under investigation, it is important for historians to focus on ideas, theories, or systems of psychological thought, while acknowledging individual and social contexts.

From the zeitgeist to social history

Those historians who emphasize the zeitgeist concentrate on the intellectual, cultural, and sometimes technological atmosphere of the era in which their subject lived. In scientific psychology, historians attempt to elucidate the zeitgeist of a particular pioneer during which he or she developed new theories, methods, and practices. From this perspective, psychoanalysis, for example, was inevitable in the social climate of late nineteenth-century Vienna.

Robert Watson (1977), an early US historian of psychology and Psychology, asserted that psychological works are embedded in the social context from which they emerge. Thus, for him, history is neither chronology nor biography, but the study of cultural trends. However, the disadvantage of an exclusive focus on the zeitgeist is that such reconstructions lack specificity; for example, in what ways, concretely, does the zeitgeist influence a psychologist?

Consider that **Plato** (429–347 BCE) and Aristotle were central figures in ancient Greece (see Chapter 2). They lived in roughly the same zeitgeist and drew upon common extant ideas, but they produced different understandings. Social conditions and the zeitgeist were the background for, but did not *determine*, their ideas.

An approach related to the zeitgeist approach is *social history*, a very broad term, in which scholars focus on social developments, including political-economic and legal aspects. This approach expanded in the 1960s, using local studies of concrete activities of everyday life, in solidarity with people who have been marginalized in society, to give a vision of the larger society (e.g., Zinn, 1985). Using a kind of "bottom-up" narrative, social historians study the ordinary lives of people excluded from the mainstream due to gender, class, ethnocultural status, religious beliefs, sexual orientation, etc. In the field of Psychology, for example, instead of asking who invented critical psychology, social historians would examine underlying socioeconomic and political developments, the students and faculty members, and institutional and educational developments that led to the emergence of critical psychology and its different expressions in various countries.

In social histories of science scholars situate scientific activity in the everyday world of socioeconomic and political contingencies. Rather than ignoring the context, social historians of science investigate such factors as the exclusion of women from science, the dependence of many male scientists on networks of socially subordinated groups (e.g., women), and the shift of scientific practice from private homes to institutions during the seventeenth century (Fara, 2004).

Feminist history

Feminist accounts emphasize women's stories in areas such as philosophy, science, and scientific psychology. Feminist historians claim that women's contributions to the history of ideas and science, such as those of **Anne Conway** (1630–1679) and **Emilie du Chatelet** (1706–1749), were excluded systematically. The societal consequence of maintaining the invisibility of women and ignorance of their contributions is entrenchment of patriarchal domination intellectually (Spender, 1983).

The exclusion of women from history occurs in several ways. Until recent decades, the founding scientists and subsequent generations were almost entirely men.

Traditionally, men communicated ideas about nature and human nature only with other men. This androcentric pattern of scientific practice led historians, intentionally or not, to shunt women's contributions to the margins. As British historian Patricia Fara (2004) stated:

In conventional versions of science's history, women are either absent, or else feature as useful appendages of a famous man – the admiring wife, the helpful sister, the docile pupil. This is partly because stories about science have been written like schoolboy adventure novels. Bristling with the vocabulary of warfare and competitive sport, they feature scholarly gladiators triumphantly battling against the forces of nature … Such glorified visions of the past are updated versions of classical myths. Stepping into the sandals of the gods, scientists have become the super-heroes of the modern age. (pp. 23–24)

Another way of keeping women's ideas and women's contributions invisible is for men to discredit the quality of women's ideas because of alleged personality deficiencies and mental health problems of the female theorists. For example, some thinkers responded to the criticisms by British author **Mary Wollstonecraft** (1759–1798) of women's status in society by claiming that she was mentally ill. How could scholars take her provocative ideas seriously if she were emotionally disturbed?

Feminist histories of science emerged in the 1970s. Initially, they consisted of biographies of prominent female scientists such as British biologist **Rosalind Franklin** (1920–1958), the unacknowledged co-discoverer of DNA (Sayre, 1975), and US biologist **Barbara McClintock** (1902–1992), who received a Nobel Prize for medicine (E. Keller, 1983). Subsequently, feminist scholars have produced histories of forgotten female practitioners of science from ancient times to the modern period, situating their stories in the context of gender bias in society (Alic, 1986; M. Rossiter, 1982; Schiebinger, 1989).

Later feminist scholars question the advisability of projecting a modern definition of science onto earlier historical eras, despite the fact that the conventional story of science has been constructed around the achievements of "great men" (Hunter & Hutton, 1997). One distortion of women's importance, apparent in early feminist accounts of women's contributions to science, consists of exaggerating their scientific activities or their personal sacrifices and depicting them as solitary fighters, who struggle against gender oppression. Recent feminist historians of psychology discuss the need to understand the complexities of political and academic life (Rutherford, Vaughn-Blount, & L. Ball, 2010). The feminist project of the 1970s itself has become an object of historical inquiry.

Acknowledging the key contributions of female scientists is important. But it is insufficient, because science always has been embedded in contemporary social contexts not only of gender but also of social class, occupational roles, and political contingencies (Hunter & Hutton, 1997). All these social dimensions have functioned as the underlay for scientific activity. For example, instrument makers, technicians, and educators have been essential for the development of science. Nevertheless, we agree with Fara (2004):

Science's history is about far more than equations, instruments and great men – it is about understanding how a huge range of practical as well as scholarly activities became the foundations of our scientific and technological society. Women played vital roles in that transformation. (p. 22)

Intellectual history

This type of history deals with the written ideas and symbols that people and societies use to give meaning to their world. One can study Psychology's history in terms of ideas or intellectual problems that are considered relevant in non-academic and academic psychology (D. N. Robinson, 1976).

Traditionally, the focus of intellectual history has been more on the ideas of "special" thinkers and writers, whereas in the new *cultural history* the focus is more on ideologies and cultural values popular in a given era. Both approaches are concerned also with the reciprocal relationship between ideas and the social context that evokes ideas (L. Hunt, 1989; Iggers, 1997).

In *problem-oriented history* one can examine the development and suggested solutions to basic intellectual problems. One can consider the development of Psychology as a progression of ideas, answers, and solutions to problems raised in the discipline (Pongratz, 1984).

Intellectual history, however, is different from the history of *institutions* or *scientific organizations*, like the sensory deprivation lab at McGill University in Montreal in the 1960s or the development of the Australian Psychological Society (APS). One also could study the history of *scientific instruments*, like the Skinner box, or the history of research methods and statistical techniques. In short, historians are aware that individual, social, and theoretical contexts shape the development of any technique, method, instrument, organization, or institution.

Other histories

Modern historians often have been *determinists*. That is, they have understood historical events to be inevitable, assuming that effects follow causes. In this regard, they apply a natural-science notion of determinism to interpretations of events. Advocates of *counter-factualism*, however, argue that historians should consider alternative possibilities to actual events, speculating on what *might* have happened *if,* while mindful of plausible dimensions of character, time, and place (Ferguson, 1997; Roberts, 2004). An actual event is only one of several possible outcomes, perhaps not even the most likely one. For example, what if the USA had won rather than lost the war of 1812 with Britain?

The counter-factual approach emanates from a *skeptical* orientation to reality and truth and is indebted to modern developments in natural science. Counter-factualist historians argue that, although there are "laws" that can explain the workings of the world and historical events, the phenomena that these laws describe are so complex that it is extremely difficult to make deterministic predictions.

In addition, histories can be divided into *periods*, say, a history of France from the French Revolution to the revolutionary upheavals of 1848. We can write a history of *places*, as in urban history (e.g., Beijing), regional history (e.g., the Atlantic provinces in Canada), nations (e.g., the Netherlands), or continents (e.g., Africa). We also can write a history of human *groups* such as children, Jews, or the labour movement. We can write histories of *social institutions* such as the Roman Catholic Church or the welfare state. We even can divide history by the different historical *methods* employed, for example, oral history (i.e., insights about history obtained by asking individuals about their experiences) or archival history (i.e., based on documents).

Assumptions about historical change

Creating histories of any science rests on certain assumptions about how historical change occurs and entails certain methodological problems. Just as there are diverse focal points for history in historiography, so there exist different ideas about how historical change proceeds. All historians, including historians of Psychology, at least implicitly, operate from one of **five assumptions about historical change**:

- The most popular assumption about historical change is that of inevitable *progress* whereby history is regarded as a pattern of unilinear growth. Historians of Psychology implicitly express this progressive view when characterizing the discipline as built on incremental improvements in its scientific foundations. For example, if you claim, "Aristotle was wrong, Wundt was wrong, James was wrong, Freud was wrong, **B. F. Skinner** (1904–1990) was wrong, but we cognitive psychologists are right," then you have adopted a "progressive" view.
- Some historians of Psychology explicitly apply *evolutionary* concepts and suggest that present Psychology is best, allegedly because unfit psychologies did not survive. The issue here is whether concepts developed in the biological sphere apply equally to human institutions. For instance, some psychological studies that reflect scientific racism persist, despite the challenges to the concept of "race." In addition, what US psychologists for over fifty years considered the fittest school of thought, behaviourism, expired. Could this fate await the cognitive school of thought in current Psychology?
- According to the *cyclical* assumption, history proceeds through alternating periods of growth and decline, as in the cliché about political and military history, "history repeats itself." However, this assumption is rare in Psychology.
- Perhaps a more useful schema for Psychology is the *spiral* assumption about historical change by which there is circularity of growth and decline, but change is ultimately progressive as a result of human "discoveries." Indeed, the history of science and scientific psychology has shown that "the latest" is not always "the best" and discoveries can alter scientific directions significantly.
- The *dialectical* assumption is that history is a process of clashes and conflicts of opposing positions. According to German philosopher **Georg Wilhelm Friedrich Hegel** (1770–1831), a *thesis* and its opposite, an *antithesis*, produce a *synthesis* that sooner or later divides into new clashes, and so on. For example, one could argue that Wundt's thesis, a focus on consciousness, was opposed by behaviourists' antithesis, a focus on observable behaviour, which was followed by cognitive psychologists' synthesis which adopted aspects of both programmes. Although Psychology's history is complex, the dialectical schema can serve as a starting point for historical inquiry.

Part 2 conclusion

Central to the study of history is the role of interpretation. In addition, historians emphasize the necessity of a comprehensive perspective. These two scholarly dimensions also suggest that history and science should be integrated not segregated, because, as noted earlier, the conduct of historical inquiry, that is, employing systematic procedures of *selecting* and *interpreting* events and objects, does not differ qualitatively from the selection and interpretation of data that scientific inquiry entails.

Although in the following chapters we include brief accounts and case studies of influential figures in psychology, our approach follows more an intellectual and social-historical approach than a biographical one. Accordingly, we place the contributions of individuals in their intellectual and social contexts. Our view is that history as a discipline can enrich psychologists' understanding of their science and profession, inasmuch as its subject matter, the mental life of humans and other sentient beings, is historically and culturally constituted and embedded.

Part 3   Practising the history and philosophy of Psychology

When investigating Psychology's history, ideally scholars not only are mindful of the reasons why historical inquiry is valuable and of the limited support within the discipline for studying its history, but also they are aware of contested applications of historiography. In this part we discuss practical issues in investigating the history and philosophy of Psychology. Then we specify concrete steps that you can take to practise sound historical inquiry on the background of philosophical reflexivity.

Reasons for studying the history and philosophy of Psychology

There are important intellectual, even moral reasons for understanding the history and philosophy of our science and profession beyond pragmatic considerations of students' degree requirements. Studying the history and philosophy of Psychology provides a sense of perspective on current research issues. In this regard, many of the concerns of today's psychologists are expressions of ideas that investigators grappled with in previous decades or centuries.

Students also can derive a deeper understanding of the subject matter by evaluating the significance of new movements in Psychology, which in turn can help us to avoid past mistakes. Studying the discipline's history and philosophy, for example, can yield a valuable reservoir of ideas to explore topics using non-experimental methods that some early psychologists pursued. Lastly, reflecting on Psychology's past, including figures who struggled with intellectual and professional problems, might facilitate your developing a personal identity in the discipline, your choice of vocational directions, and understanding your motives for majoring in Psychology.

From a critical perspective, studying the history and philosophy of Psychology supports and enhances analytic and integrative thinking. Just as courses on research methods enable students to evaluate the strengths and weaknesses of empirical studies, so studying the discipline's history and philosophy aids evaluating the trajectory of diverse psychological worldviews, theories, concepts, methodologies, the meaning of psychological research, and professional practices. Appreciating the history and philosophy of Psychology not only enhances comprehending the "big picture" of intellectual and professional practices, but it places current research in its historical context and facilitates thoughtful assessments of the discipline.

But before proceeding it is important to consider the disciplinary and cultural obstacles that have militated against a critical study of Psychology's history and philosophy and to examine the kind of history of Psychology that was normative until recently. Inhibitions against exploring the discipline's history and philosophy and its subject matter include an ahistorical cultural disposition towards the past and celebrating the "progressive" present and future. Another source of inhibition is one's personal experience with patriotic-history courses in primary and secondary schools, in which teachers drilled students in names and dates of battles, laws, and leaders without connecting these facts with any contexts or concrete experiences.

For its first century, Psychology was similarly ahistorical. For example, of all the articles published in the discipline's major journals for the twenty-year period from 1938 to 1957, only 1 per cent was primarily historical (R. Watson, 1977). Beforehand, research articles generally contained lengthy historical introductions. But thereafter, to save space and publish more empirical articles in the same issue, journal editors directed authors to abbreviate historical discussions in their introductions. Although there is now greater receptivity to historical studies of scientific psychology, exploring the history and philosophy of the discipline remain somewhat marginal.

In addition, many psychologists tend to regard history and philosophy as irrelevant to their research, because of their identification with the natural sciences. They tend to believe that the psychological objects they study are equivalent to the natural objects that natural scientists study, which presumably are devoid of social-historical context (Danziger, 1997b). Thus, because for natural-science psychologists psychological concepts and methods are not historically situated objects, as scientists they need not be concerned with history, let alone philosophy. If history has any use for many psychologists at all, it is to celebrate the progress of its "discoveries." But other psychologists believe that studying the discipline's history and philosophy enhances Psychology's contributions to knowledge.

Philosophical issues in historiography of Psychology

Researching and writing on the history of Psychology and its subject matter entail confronting key interpretive issues in historiography: presentism, progress and celebration, continuity or discontinuity, and overcompensation for marginalization.

Presentism

Let's begin with an analogy. *Ethnocentrism* is the tendency to use one's own culture or ethnicity as the criterion to judge all other ethnocultural groups. A similar problem occurs in historiography, which can be called *time-centrism* (Teo & Febbraro, 2003). This term means that our own time is the criterion for all other times and that we judge the past based on current standards. In everyday life humans do this routinely, but this habit is problematic if scholars wish to understand the past.

Historians have created the term *presentism* for this attitude, which means that one interprets the past from a current perspective or one interprets the past primarily in terms of its value for the present. In the nineteenth century, Droysen argued that there is a danger in historiography, when one voluntarily or involuntarily brings views and presuppositions of the present into the process of understanding the past. As a counter-measure, he recommended cautious, methodical interpretation that measures the past according to its own standards. Droysen labelled this approach, which potentially can overcome presentism, as *historical objectivism*, for which some historians use the confusing term "historicism." It means interpreting the past from the perspective of the past.

But historical objectivism has had opponents. German philosopher **Hans Gadamer** (1900–2002) contended that understanding and interpretation of historical objects and events are always subject to people perceiving events and objects from different viewpoints (see Chapter 10). Gadamer argued that rather than pretending that we are outside of a perspective, we must acknowledge that we are part of a tradition that makes knowledge possible. This notion applies to studying the history of psychological subject matter and to empirical research in general.

From a critical perspective, too, complete historical objectivism is not workable, because it is impossible to eradicate current horizons (i.e., the extent of your own perspective) from historical or empirical research and because questions and interests emerge from the present. However, in Gadamer's language, a *fusion of horizons* (i.e., an encounter between the current horizon and the past horizon of the interpreted) of the past and present is possible. This stance is the basis for reflecting on how deeply presentism has invaded our historical interpretations.

Take the case of **Galileo Galilei** (1564–1642), the seventeenth-century Italian scientist (see Chapter 3). Some historians in the eighteenth and nineteenth centuries interpreted his work to mean that he relied only on experimentation, when in fact he only hypothesized some experiments. Yet some historians in the twentieth century depicted him as so confident in his mathematical reasoning that he did not need to do experiments.

Galileo both experimented and theorized. So, why did these different interpretations occur? Some earlier historians wrote for a context in which concrete, sensory experience was important, so they emphasized experiments, while some later historians wrote in a context that embraced rational mathematical analysis, so they stressed theorizing. Which of Galileo's activities is regarded as more important depends on interpretations favoured in a given epoch.

Another strong bias to overcome in constructing a history of any science or subject matter is "the temptation to scour the past for examples or precursors of modern science" (Lindberg, 1992, p. 3), as if previous discoveries or viewpoints are "anticipations" of current theory and practice. For example, some historians of Psychology have suggested that **René Descartes** (1596–1650) was a precursor of behaviourism as well as cognitive psychology and neuroscience. However, such reconstructions do not do justice to the complexity of Descartes' thought, which is embedded in his place and time.

Presentist historians assume that historical change inherently is progressive and that science develops in cumulative progression; both assumptions are debatable. Presentist historians also might neglect the evidence for cyclical and revolutionary change in science, suppress theoretical and interpersonal conflicts, ignore social contextual influences, and celebrate and privilege the successes of dominant groups and ideas (Weimer, 1974). The appropriate safeguard for this inclination is to adopt a broad and inclusive approach and respect how preceding generations of sociolinguistic communities (e.g., the ancient Greeks) wrote about nature and human nature in their own language and on their own terms.

Scholars in earlier eras did not focus on scientific problems peculiar to later eras. Rather, they were preoccupied with a problem of their own – namely the need to comprehend the world in which *they* lived, within the bounds of an inherited conceptual framework that defined the important questions and suggested useful ways of answering them. (Lindberg, 1992, p. 363, author emphasis)

Progress and celebration

In the nineteenth century under the influence of scientific discoveries and Darwinian theory, but also Hegelian and Marxist ideas of development (see Chapter 4), historians produced interpretations of events that reflected Western societies' faith in the reputedly unstoppable march of progress. The "good news" from this type of history was that historians attempted to create historically accurate accounts. The "bad news" was that they believed that the *latest* events represented humankind's highest achievements. This approach to histories of science is *progressive* in the sense that some historians regard science as beginning with the "Scientific Revolution" of the sixteenth and seventeenth centuries and as inevitably progressing since then in a series of triumphs.

In the 1930s, British historian Herbert Butterfield (1931) coined the term *Whig history* (from the British Whigs [liberals] who opposed the Tories [conservatives]). His purpose was to describe historians who characterized British history as a steady march of progress leading inevitably to constitutional monarchy, regarded as the highpoint of human political development. In effect, Whig history was an account of constant improvement in which its supporters were heroes and its opponents were villains. When in thrall to this interpretive bias, scholars wrench historical actions from their context and evaluate them in terms of how they illustrate progress.

However, any history of science is contingent upon historians' interpretations of scientists' accounts of their scientific work. Moreover, scholars' notions of progress are themselves sociohistorical products. In Western culture the modern concept of change emerged in the mid sixteenth century: "Change came to be judged a move forward or backward, the latter being pointless. This in time generated the familiar labels progressive, conservative, and reactionary" (Barzun, 2000, p. 74). The latest product became the best (Stocking, 1965), a viewpoint that has persisted for centuries and is expressed in a bias towards progress. The term "modern" similarly connotes praiseworthy ideas or activities.

In Psychology, Whig history is a celebratory approach to interpreting the past as a linear path of rational progress to our present scientific state. For example, it has been commonplace to consider Freud one of the villains who interrupted the progress of a truly natural-scientific Psychology. But instead, we could understand him as one who attempted to develop a psychology of unconscious processes in individuals.

Many past and present authors of Psychology textbooks have tended to express the biases of presentist and progressive history by celebrating "classic" experiments in Psychology that purportedly "established the organizing concepts and objective methods of the discipline as a science" (R. Smith, 1997, p. 26). Such authors seem to have assumed that the story of scientific psychology is the most recent, advanced unit of unbroken evolution dating from the ancient Greeks to the present-day discipline in an incrementally progressive march towards increasingly sophisticated, scientific truth that reveals pre-existing, universal "laws" of behaviour. In this celebratory or triumphalist view of history, "the present is the inevitable and desirable outcome of the past" (R. Smith, 1997, p. 26).

For example, the US historian of experimental psychology **Edwin Boring** (1886–1968), whose 1950 textbook was standard fare in US Psychology graduate programmes for decades, created a distorted picture about Wundt as a pure experimentalist in conformity with Boring's own experimentalist orientation (Danziger, 1979). But Wundt did *not* use the experimental method to study higher human functions, like language; for these psychological phenomena he advocated historical and observational methods instead (see Chapter 5).

A celebratory history also tends to focus on individuals as determining social and historical events. This conventional approach, described by US historian of Psychology Laurel Furumoto (1989) as "old" history, focuses on distinguished contributors or on influential schools of thought, such as behaviourism. Of course, to include historical agents is important, because historical changes in Psychology do not occur in isolation from individual psychologists and their social circumstances. Nevertheless, the appropriate focus is not the personality characteristics of the authors of particular psychological concepts, but rather the nature of their concepts and the connections of those concepts within a web of scientific and professional discourses, practices, and materials (e.g., instruments). Moreover, honouring psychologists' achievements should not preclude examining the possible weaknesses of their ideas.

Continuity or discontinuity

Closely related to the issue of progress and the conflict between presentist and contextualized approaches in historiography is the question of the continuity or discontinuity of historical change.

Let's use a metaphor for this problem: is the history of Psychology best represented by building a house where each generation adds a new floor so that the house gets taller and taller over time (continuity)? Or is it a building on which several generations worked and which, after it did not fulfill its purpose anymore, was abandoned, and a new generation started to build a new house somewhere else (discontinuity)? Or was the house abandoned by one generation and several generations later a new generation started to pick up the pieces and reconstruct a better structure on top of the old house (discontinuity *and* continuity)?

Historians of science have asked, for example, whether medieval and Renaissance science resembles early modern science. Also, they have questioned what durable influence earlier scientific practices had on the so-called "Scientific Revolution" and modern science (Lindberg, 1992). British scholar **Francis Bacon** (1561–1626), writing at the dawn of modern science (see Chapter 3), claimed that the "new science" that he helped instigate was indebted to the ancient Greeks and the Renaissance but that the Middle Ages produced no memorable scientific contributions. Bacon implicitly took the position of discontinuity of historical change.

A sound answer to the continuity–discontinuity debate should specify the criteria and dimensions of scientific practices that are investigated. If historians focus on broad developments in science, then the emergence in the sixteenth and seventeenth centuries of the "Scientific Revolution" provides ample evidence of fundamental discontinuity in terms of a new worldview of nature and new scientific methodologies. However, if historians concentrate on developments within particular fields of study, such as physicists' study of falling bodies, then there *is* evidence for continuity between the medieval and the early modern periods.

It is important to understand that psychology of the classical periods was not the same as it is today. There are some continuous developments in topics (e.g., the concept of memory) but also discontinuous developments (e.g., the concept of IQ, which did not exist until the twentieth century). After all, Psychology as a distinct discipline did not emerge until the late nineteenth century.

Overcompensation for marginalization

While critiquing the assumption of traditional historians, critical historians of Psychology should not be exempt from reflecting on their own historical context and premises (Lovett, 2006). Critical historians, for instance, could misuse history by attempting to overcompensate for conventional historians' bias of viewing the past from the perspective of the rich, the famous, and the successful. Thus, critical historians of Psychology could distort history by inflating the contributions of marginalized groups, such as the influence of humanistic psychology.

Disciplinary support

Histories of psychology have been published in German for over 200 years (Teo, 2005). A Canadian scholar, George Brett (1962), published *A History of Psychology* in several volumes between 1912 and 1921. But the most influential English-Language history was Boring's *A History of Experimental Psychology*, originally published in 1929 with a second edition in 1950. Yet the history of Psychology as a formal subdiscipline was not institutionalized until later.

In 1965 the *Journal of the History of the Behavioral Sciences* was inaugurated. In 1966 the American Psychological Association (APA) established a History of Psychology division. In 1969 the International Society for the History of the Behavioral and Social Sciences was organized. There are now two other English-language journals that specialize in the history of Psychology: *History of Psychology* and *History of the Human Sciences*. There are also history of Psychology journals in German, Spanish, Italian, and other languages.

Internationally, the Canadian Psychological Association has a section on the History and Philosophy of Psychology, and York University and the University of Calgary offer History and Theory options in their Psychology graduate programmes. The British Psychological Society includes a History and Philosophy Section and has established The History of Psychology Centre, which is the main repository for its archive collections.

Critical history

Critical history draws on a variety of sources, but two highly influential thinkers from the nineteenth century helped to shape critical thought: **Friedrich Nietzsche** (1844–1900) and **Karl Marx** (1818–1883) (see Chapter 4). Two recent scholars also had an impact on how to practise history critically: **Michel Foucault** (1926–1984) (see Chapter 12) and **Thomas Kuhn** (1922–1996). Feminist history and postcolonial theories also provide critical inspiration (see Chapter 12).

In his essay, *On the Use and Abuse of History for Life*, Nietzsche ([1873–1876] 1983) divided history into **three programmes**:

- *Monumental history* focuses on the history of powerful people (a "great man" approach).
- *Antiquarian history* is celebratory. For instance, if you are an admirer of Skinner you would collect relics of his past (books, letters, photographs, signatures, etc.).
- *Critical history* breaks with the past, interrogates one's roots, and exposes embarrassing issues of the past, without hesitating to question them. For example, we could examine the sexism, racism, and Eurocentrism of founding psychologists, although we would have to be mindful of a presentist bias in doing so.

For his part, Marx argued that society's dominant ideas are also the ideas of the dominant social class (e.g., Marx & Engels, [1845–1846] 1964). Related to historiography, one could argue that histories are written and interpreted in ways that express and serve the interests of the powerful. Applying Marx's perspective to the history of Psychology, one could suggest that psychologists compose history to make the current, dominant school of thought, cognitive neuroscience, appear as the best and logical outcome of a historical trajectory.

Marxist theory is also important in underscoring the primacy of economics. The basic premise is that changes in economic realities lead to changes in intellectual and research programmes. From this perspective historians could analyze the role of funding (research grants) in shaping research questions and outcomes, or they could study the impact of the publish-or-perish ethos on research content and investigative conduct with participants in psychological research (e.g., Walsh-Bowers, 2002).

Foucault provided various historical studies on the human sciences (e.g., psychiatry, the prison system, and sexuality). Suggesting a close relationship between power and knowledge, he argued that hierarchical power relations, endemic to modern institutions such as medicine and the criminal justice system, made the subject matter of scientific psychology possible.

Foucault ([1975] 1977) argued, for instance, that abolishing physical punishment and torture in Western prison systems was not due to a progression of enlightenment. Rather, power found a more efficient and effective way of controlling prisoners: centralized surveillance via a *panopticon*. This is an architectural design whereby the guard tower located in the middle always allows guards to observe prisoners in their cells unobtrusively and without their knowing when they are being observed, thereby advancing power over prisoners by cultivating their own self-surveillance and distrust of everyone else. Many prisons, including the Kilmainham Gaol in Dublin, Ireland (see Figure 1.1), are constructed in this way. For a critical history it is important not only to reflect on the power expressed by subjects but also on power expressed in objects. For example, the architecture of institutions shapes our actions and mental life.

Foucault also suggested that power operates in all social institutions, such as Psychology. For example, psychologists have taken for granted the "rules" for writing a scientific paper, contained in the APA's *Publication Manual* (see Chapter 11). Yet critical history shows that these prescriptions, known as "APA style," have a social history emanating from a dominant view of what constitutes acceptable research in the discipline (Walsh-Bowers, 1999).

New histories of the natural sciences, such as Kuhn's famous book, *The Structure of Scientific Revolutions* (1962), showed that changes in science occur discontinuously. A common interpretation of Kuhn is that standards of scientific certainty are not immutable but

Figure 1.1 Kilmainham Gaol can be understood as a panopticon to shape prisoner self-surveillance

are socially constructed. His critical approach was very influential in new histories of Psychology that challenged traditional assumptions about constructing histories of any science. Kuhn argued that the natural sciences (specifically physics) might be non-cumulative, which reveals the problem of discontinuity, and might be "non-rational," meaning influenced by social, emotional, political, group, or random factors (not to be confused with "irrational," meaning unreasonable).

Critical historiography

Some practical implications flow from our discussion of critical history. Practising critical historiography involves particular approaches to historical sources, methodological attitude, and reflexivity.

Primary vs. secondary sources

Like the practice of law, historical research begins with examining evidence. In sound historical inquiry historians assess testimony, investigate the causes and effects of human events, evaluate and assign responsibility, and reconstruct an authoritative, plausible account of events. Of course, like any discipline, historical scholarship is subject to human error and systematic bias.

Historians distinguish between *primary sources* (e.g., Wundt's own writings, preferably in the German original) and *secondary sources* (e.g., Boring's interpretations of Wundt). Critical historians privilege studying the original material. Obviously, this expectation can be difficult to meet if one does not read the language of the primary source. A preference for primary sources also means studying archival material.

Concerning Psychology, authors of textbook-histories commonly use interpretations from established authors for their own interpretations, for example, relying on Boring's (1950) account of Wundt's Psychology. In law, such a practice is referred to as "hearsay," meaning an account that consists of what others have said. However, hearsay might not be reliable. Thus, it is problematic to base an interpretation of a person or issue on someone else's interpretation.

Academic sources often are considered reliable, but experts do make mistakes. Accordingly, the critical historian attempts to understand experts' perspectives to assess the quality of their interpretations. It is important to realize that all textbooks in our discipline are secondary if not *tertiary sources* (i.e., textbook authors' interpretations of historians' interpretations of secondary sources). Accordingly, these interpretations must be treated cautiously. This caveat also applies to our own textbook and to our critical perspective.

Methodological attitude

Earlier we discussed *presentism* versus *historical objectivism*. Here we distinguish **four methodological attitudes** located along a continuum (Teo, 2005):

- At one extreme is *pure historical objectivism*. This attitude is an unachievable ideal, because it is impossible to eradicate current horizons from research or because questions and interests emerge from the present. Thus, we cannot imagine that we are living in the nineteenth century without the benefit of hindsight.
- At the opposite extreme, describing and evaluating the past in terms of present perspectives constitute *naïve presentism*. Within this perspective scholars are not aware of the problem of time-centrism and behave as if there were no difficulty with a presentist reconstruction. Although commonly adopted by directors of Hollywood "historical" movies, naïve presentism is unacceptable academically.
- Located between naïve presentism and pure historical objectivism, *sophisticated presentism* enables historians to do justice to the past but also to discuss the contemporary significance of past discourses. In this approach scholars use historical material to elucidate current perspectives. This type of presentism is "sophisticated" or "critical," because historians who adopt it are aware that, although presentism is problematic, it can be theoretically useful.
- In *critical historical objectivism* scholars attempt to do justice fully to historical perspectives but are aware that present horizons infiltrate historical studies. Educationally, such accounts might be less interesting to students than sophisticated-presentist interpretations, because they require more training in past thought systems.

From our perspective, sophisticated presentism and critical historical objectivism are the most appropriate methodological attitudes for studying the history and philosophy of psychological topics and Psychology. The challenge in constructing the discipline's history is to strike a balance between telling an accurate story of the past with accessible, modern language, on the one hand, and inadvertently creating a misleading impression about the past because of the language that one employs to describe that past.

Reflexivity

For historians to practise reflexivity means acknowledging openly in their writing how their personal biases and "social locations" (backgrounds) might have shaped their interpretations. For example, Dale Spender (1983) disclosed her perspective as a White, middle-class woman in her treatment of the experience of nineteenth-century African American women, like Sojourner Truth (c. 1797–1883), who agitated for ending racism and sexism. Spender acknowledged that she engaged in a process of selective editing to construct her accounts.

As noted above, the complex act of interpretation is at the heart of critical history. Interpretation encompasses a reflection on five points discussed below: one's goals, objects, focus, conception of reality, and linearity. Reflexivity always means asking, "How did 'I' bias my work with regard to these issues?"

Goals Critical historians strive to avoid historical distortions by comparing historical figures with their predecessors, not with present figures. They also strive to guard against constructing celebratory histories of Psychology. We agree that historical inquiry should not serve as the intellectual and moral equivalent of a domestic servant for aggrandizing a scientific discipline (R. Smith, 1997). This stance does not mean that celebration is impermissible in history, but it is a minor aspect of a large network of issues. Furthermore, critical historians investigate not only achievements but also the problems that historical actors have caused, for example, psychologists promoting *scientific racism* (i.e., scientific rationales for marginalizing an ethnocultural group or people) (see Chapters 5 and 6) or contributing to torture (see Chapter 8).

Objects Critical historians might study personalities and theories but against the background of intellectual, cultural, religious, political, and economic dimensions. Critical historians are interested in how societies and individuals interpret the facts of socioeconomic and political life; they focus on the interaction between the ideas of key intellectual figures and their social and cultural contexts.

Critical historians also make space for voices and ideas that historians traditionally have marginalized. In the history of Psychology, marginalized issues include the contributions of women and cultural groups other than White US Americans, and the historical role of qualitative methods in Psychology. Moreover, critical historians exercise their social-ethical responsibility as authors to identify those social conditions and interpersonal dynamics that oppress people and limit their freedom to enjoy justice and community. At the same time, they identify alternative forms of human action that might facilitate people's emancipation from oppression and lead to social conditions of compassion and justice (see Chapter 12).

Focus Topics of psychology and Psychology as an institution can only be understood in the context of other disciplines. Thus, critical historians take a transdisciplinary (or interdisciplinary) perspective by studying relevant developments in philosophy, religion, medicine, biology, statistics, anthropology, etc. For instance, to understand the changing role of the computer metaphor in Psychology, one should understand changes in computer technology.

Conception of reality Many critical historians are sympathetic to the intellectual position known as *social constructionism* in that they ask how historical figures have constructed events and objects differently at various times. They also believe that there is an external reality and that there is a psychological world independent of scientific observers. However, this reality is represented differently at different times and in different contexts. Applying this orientation to Psychology, critical historians regard theories of psychological phenomena as human constructions that occur in historically changing cultural contexts. This approach to Psychology and its topics includes a critical stance towards the individuals involved in theorizing.

The interpretive frame of social constructionism implies that there are different pathways to history and that historical "truth" is constructed through a psychological process of interpretation. For example, people's understanding of the past has been shaped by different, often unconscious or implicit, philosophies of history. Thus, more than one academically legitimate version of the history of Psychology exists.

Even if we authors suggest that reality is socially constructed or embedded, with time and social context changing the meaning of social realities, we do not mean that we support the position that all judgments are relative (Bhaskar, 1998). We believe that certain approaches are better than others, certain ideas are false or wrong, and some theories do harm. But we are epistemological relativists in the sense that different times and places produce theories that make sense in a particular context, which might not make sense in another one. Thus, "the proper measure of a [scientific] system is not the degree to which it anticipated modern thought, but its degree of success in treating the [scientific] problems of its own day" (Lindberg, 1992, p. 67).

Linearity Regarding the continuity versus discontinuity debate, we take an empirical stance. Skeptical of the *a priori* assumption that the history of Psychology is a continuous evolution, we strive to be open-minded to evidence pointing in either direction of continuity or discontinuity. Indeed, many historical studies show discontinuous developments in Psychology.

Concrete steps of reflexivity

Many students taking a history of Psychology course are unprepared for dealing with the scholarly problems entailed in historiography. Here we provide practical answers to philosophical and historical questions students of Psychology might have.

"Where does my knowledge of Psychology come from?"

Most of your knowledge comes from secondary historical sources and from authorities (e.g., instructors, publications). But secondary sources might be problematic. Don't reproduce the first assessment of someone or something that you read or hear. Rather, consider multiple sources and if possible, although this might be very difficult to do, read primary sources in the original language. It is very important to distinguish among primary, secondary, and tertiary sources, as described above.

Avoid making quick assessments. Students often interpret something they do not understand as "incomprehensible." Find out whether a specific statement is typical for a time or indeed is unusual. Don't assume that, because you do not understand a published work, the author is arrogant. Your difficulty in understanding it might reflect your lack of knowledge.

Avoid "forward" comparisons. For example, it does not make sense to suggest that Plato (who lived 2,400 years ago in Athens, Greece) was like Wundt (who lived more than 100 years ago in Leipzig, Germany).

If you have time and financial resources, visit archives to develop a comprehensive picture of an individual. The Archives of the History of American Psychology at the University of Akron, Ohio, were established in 1965 to foster research in the discipline's history. Archivists there collect, catalogue, and preserve the record of mainly US Psychology.

"Am I presentist?"

The spontaneous methodological attitude of most students is *naïve presentism*. It is our goal, and we hope your own aspiration, to move away from naïve presentism towards *critical presentism* and even *critical historical objectivism*. A major difficulty with regard to naïve presentism occurs in the domain of language and translation.

For instance, as an exercise try reading an original work by Aristotle in English translation. His language (with the caveat that it is a translation) should give you a first insight on how different his thoughts and terms are from current usage. Check the etymology or origin of a translated word before you make confident interpretations. Ideally, you would verify a term or quote in the original language and check the translation.

Current psychologists often present sexism and racism in a naïve-presentist way. To say that Aristotle or the eighteenth-century philosophers **David Hume** (1711–1776) and **Immanuel Kant** (1724–1804) (see Chapter 3), were racist and sexist does not explain much, because these views were rampant then. It is more interesting historically to compare Aristotle's ideas, which were less favourable to women, to the views of his contemporary, Plato. In his discussion of women and men Plato argued that they should be treated equally and receive the same education and training, including military training. Even more interesting is to discuss the fact that two thinkers from the same era and society developed different positions on gender. It is important that you represent such nuances in your historical research.

Jean Piaget (1896–1980), the Swiss developmental psychologist (see Chapter 6), believed that humans adapt through the processes of assimilation and accommodation. When investigating the history and philosophy of Psychology we recommend that you accommodate but not assimilate. "Assimilation" in this context means that you include historical material in your thought structure, even though current concerns largely shape one's thought structure. "Accommodation" means that you change your cognitive structure based on the historical material that you are reviewing. Although accommodation is more desirable for doing history, it is intellectually challenging, like learning a new language.

"How do I develop good interpretations?"

Gadamer provided some important concepts that might help to improve your interpretation of historical material: horizon, fusion of horizons, tradition, prejudice, and dialogue.

Be aware of your own horizon. Each of us has a different horizon regarding issues of interest. One might be an expert on computers (large horizon) but know little about politics (small horizon). The same applies to historical material. You should also understand that each horizon of understanding is historically determined. For instance, individuals today understand air pollution differently than people at the time of the Industrial Revolution.

You can transcend horizons through exposure to other horizons that convey views and values that place your original horizons in context. But when you read and attempt to understand a historical text you have to merge your current horizon with the past horizon of the text in a fusion of horizons.

Be aware that you approach texts from a particular tradition. Everyone is embedded in a particular tradition, which influences one's horizon. Yet being situated within a tradition does not limit knowledge; rather, it makes it possible.

Traditions operate with prejudices. History produces prejudices in understanding. There is no prejudice-less objectivity in interpretation (and in the sciences). For example, historian Benjamin Harris (2011) disclosed his own journey and his own subjectivity in exposing problems with the "Little Albert" experiment. We cannot escape our pre-understanding, which is situated in the present horizon. Critical understanding might allow correcting prejudices, because we become reflexive about our own biases. But often one's knowledge and experiences are limits to understanding.

Understanding is not fixed, but changes over time. Yet the meaning and validity of understanding are interconnected with our historical situation. Understanding is like a dialogue between the interpreter and the text. Dialogue involves questioning from within our horizon. For instance, what is the meaning of a particular passage in Skinner's work? The questions posed will constrain the dialogue and a professor will ask different questions than a student. But you can transcend your own interpretive horizons in a constant process of synthesis of the past within the present, while you study primary and secondary sources.

Part 3 conclusion

In this part we discussed reasons and disciplinary support for studying the history and philosophy of psychological topics and Psychology. Then we described important issues in doing history and the historiographical challenges that present themselves to critical historians. In doing the history of Psychology critically, historians should use primary sources, be careful when interpreting the past in terms of the present, and develop research that goes beyond individuals by including a network of factors that influence any science. Moreover, understanding Psychology involves understanding developments in other disciplines from philosophy to biology.

We also suggested that in critical history, if one wants to present a complete picture of achievements, critique should accompany any celebration. We argued that there is evidence for discontinuity *and* continuity in Psychology's history and that reflexivity should be understood as a method for overcoming one's own historical prejudices.

Part 4   Issues in the philosophy and practice of science

In this part we discuss diverse definitions of science and its divisions; cognitive interests and types of sciences; definitions of "knowledge" and "truth"; different ways of thinking about science; the philosophical assumptions of the predominant approach, known as positivist science; how science changes; the game of science; common beliefs about doing science; and a "realistic" view of science as socially embedded.

Definitions and the division of science

Definitions of science and its divisions into disciplines have changed over time. Crucial for understanding the history and philosophy of Psychology is the distinction between natural science and human science.

Diverse definitions

The root of the term "science" is in the Latin word *scientia*, primarily meaning "systematic knowledge of the true causes of particular things" (R. Smith, 1997, p. 16) and refined in later centuries to mean "learning as a theoretical discipline" (p. 17). In the medieval era, for example, theology was considered a science, because it was a discipline demanding systematic thought. Scholars in the Renaissance began distinguishing "scientific" knowledge, believed to be revealed by nature, from Christian knowledge, believed to be revealed by the grace of God.

However, neither meaning of science was equivalent to the more modern term "natural science." This term did not become common in the English language until the nineteenth century. Thus, "science" originally referred to any type of knowledge, whether related to the natural world or not, that was shaped by standards of rigour and certainty.

By the seventeenth century, German-language scholars used the term *Wissenschaft*, typically translated in English as "science," to describe academic endeavours involving the development of systematic, theoretical knowledge. In recent English, "science" applies mostly to the natural sciences, but not to the humanities. However, in German-speaking societies one still can study *Religionswissenschaft*, which means studying the science of religion.

In the nineteenth century, German scholar **Wilhelm Dilthey** (1833–1911) divided the sciences into natural-scientific and human-scientific disciplines (*Naturwissenschaften* vs. *Geisteswissenschaften*). For him, *natural sciences* dealt with natural objects and they involved *explanations* rooted in causal laws, whereas the *human sciences* were concerned with describing and interpreting the meaning of human action (see Chapter 10). Another German scholar, **Wilhelm Windelband** (1848–1915), supported this dualism, based on a methodological opposition between *nomothetic* (sciences based on general laws) and *idiographic* (sciences based on the description of single events) programmes of scientific inquiry.

By contrast, Anglo-American scholars emphasized the *empiricist* basis of knowledge, thus they privileged the natural sciences, which became the standard anglophone meaning of "science" (R. Smith, 1997). Consequently, for some scholars, the discipline of history is a science, whereas for others, only the natural sciences qualify as scientific.

Natural-science and human-science Psychology

This history of the term "science" is relevant to any story of the origins, present, and future of scientific and professional Psychology, because tensions between the two poles, natural science and human science, have pervaded the discipline. Dilthey (1976) provided a systematic foundation for two different types of Psychology: *descriptive* (human-scientific) and *analytical* (explanatory, natural-scientific). He acknowledged the importance of a natural-scientific psychology, but he promoted the human-scientific approach, arguing that, because psychology's subject matter was human experience, its method must be *understanding*.

Early psychologists **Hermann Ebbinghaus** (1850–1909) and **Hugo Münsterberg** (1863–1916) rejected Dilthey's dualism. They endorsed Psychology as a natural science that did not require the method of understanding (Ebbinghaus, 1896; Münsterberg, 1899). Rather, they argued, Psychology should rely only on natural-scientific explanation and experimental methods. Münsterberg also rejected Windelband's nomothetic-idiographic distinction for Psychology.

Wundt, however, divided his Psychology into an experimental branch that focused on the precise analysis of the basic processes of consciousness and a non-experimental *Völkerpsychologie* (roughly, psychology of a culture). This latter branch covered psychological processes that accompany the development of human communities and mental products in the context of values, customs, and language (see Chapter 5) or what many psychologists today term "complex psychological processes."

This chiasm between natural-scientific and human-scientific Psychology generally is recapitulated in contemporary Anglo-American and European academic departments. They usually are located in faculties of arts or faculties of science, which grant either a Bachelor of Arts or a Bachelor of Science degree (or both).

Relevance to Psychology

Given the diverse definitions of science, one can study the history and philosophy of Psychology and its subject matter from a natural-scientific, human-scientific, or even critical point of view. Philosophically, as we explain in Part 5 below, the two perspectives promote different ontologies, epistemologies, and methodologies for their particular approach to addressing psychological topics.

Consider the study of memory. Natural-science psychologists investigate memory's physiological basis, its functions, principles, "laws," and divisions; typically, they are not interested in individually developed memory and its content. By contrast, human-science psychologists study a person's unique memory of past experiences that gives meaning to her or his identity and is part of a cultural-historical trajectory. From a natural-scientific perspective examining the meaning of memory is problematic, whereas from a human-scientific perspective the physiological basis of memory is important but not particularly significant for psychology.

Cognitive interests and types of sciences

In order to elucidate the meaning of different types of sciences, German philosopher **Jürgen Habermas** (b. 1929) argues that different sciences are based on different anthropological, cognitive interests. Emphasizing how human interests guide the scientific enterprise, he rejects the claim that the sciences are value-free. On the contrary, the sciences are always inspired by some kind of motivation. Habermas ([1968] 1972) distinguishes among **three types of sciences**:

(1) Practitioners of **empirical-analytic sciences** (e.g., physics, chemistry, and biology) are motivated by technical cognitive interests to gain instrumental knowledge that allows for prediction and manipulation of phenomena. These scientists might not be interested, for instance, in optical phenomena for the sake of pure knowledge, but because this understanding allows for prediction and control. In Psychology, fields such as cognitive psychology and neuropsychology that endorse the measurement of observable phenomena are empirical-analytic.

Habermas suggests that an empirical-analytic worldview promotes an *objectivist illusion*, meaning that the search for natural laws hides the fact that the natural sciences exist against the background of anthropological as well as sociohistorical interests. Consider, for example, how the debate about global warming follows not just scientific but also political interests.

Another problem of the empirical-analytic approach, due to its accumulated successes over the last 200 years, is its tendency to colonize other scientific approaches. Representatives of this approach often convey that their standpoint is the only way towards truth and is the only source of valid knowledge. But from a critical perspective, investigators from all types of science should reflect on the limitations of their interpretive statements.

(2) Practitioners of **historical-hermeneutical sciences** (interpretive sciences) are motivated by the cognitive interest to gain practical knowledge in providing an interpretive understanding of phenomena. This intellectual domain tends to be associated with the humanities disciplines (e.g., literature, languages, and history). As human beings we are interested in the meaning of our existence. For instance, histories and biographies give us examples of how to live or not to live. Examples of historical-hermeneutical approaches in Psychology are phenomenological, existentialist, and humanistic and transpersonal psychologies (see Chapter 10) and to some degree psychoanalysis (see Chapter 9).

Advocates of historical-hermeneutic sciences contend that practitioners of empirical-analytical sciences are reductionistic in their knowledge-claims and lack an understanding of the complex interrelationship between human beings and their cultures. Proponents of empirical-analytical sciences reply that historical-hermeneutic sciences are incapable of producing certain, authoritative knowledge and universal laws, although this is not the goal of historical-hermeneutic scientists.

(3) Practitioners of **critical sciences** are motivated by the cognitive interest to accomplish emancipation from ideological constraints and oppressive social systems through critical self-reflection and practice. The objective is not to establish technical control over phenomena or to produce meaning, but to identify and overcome power that is dogmatic, irrational, and unjust. Examples in Psychology are certain types of feminist psychology and of psychoanalysis, critical psychology, and postcolonial psychology. Of course, it is necessary to exercise critical reflection on these approaches as well. In Chapter 12 we consider Habermas's discussion of cognitive interests and types of sciences in relation to Psychology.

Definitions of knowledge and truth

Before the nineteenth century people believed that knowledge was produced by human activities. For example, the farmer who knows when and how to plow the fields and the midwife who knows when and how to deliver a baby operate on a foundation of knowledge specific to their practices. However, in the nineteenth century with the rise of the empirical-analytic sciences and the philosophy of *positivism* (see Chapter 4), many academics held that only controlled observation and experimentation could provide genuine knowledge. While scholars in philosophy and other disciplines discuss issues related to "knowledge" and "truth," our purpose is to raise these issues in connection with basic questions in Psychology.

If we define *knowledge* as *what is true*, then, from a historical perspective, the following paradox presents itself: what was true in the past often is not true anymore. If we apply this notion to the present, then the problem arises how we can be sure that what we consider true now will be true in the future. Thus, a better definition of knowledge would be: *that which is understood as true at a particular point in time and in a specific location*.

The next problem emerges when we have to define *truth*. Some philosophers have developed a *correspondence theory of truth* that suggests that we can speak of truth when there is a correspondence between an object/event and a statement about this object/event. The statement "this metal table is brown" is true, if it corresponds to the object (a brown metal table).

This traditional theory of truth seems self-evident. But what if someone argues that "this metal table is red but appears brown because the metal rusted"? We need someone else (or many others) to decide whether a statement corresponds to an object/event. Even such an obvious statement as "the earth is round" can be challenged: the earth is not flat but it is also not perfectly spherical.

But who decides whether a statement corresponds to an object/event when we consider complex psychological or social phenomena? Let's say psychologists investigate the psychological consequences for children of maternal employment. One hypothetical set of studies shows that there is a negative developmental outcome, another set that there is a positive developmental consequence, and a third set that the outcome depends on a variety of other factors (such as age, gender, socioeconomic status, family coherence, social support, social policy, employer attitude, maternal satisfaction with chosen role, etc.). Which statement corresponds with the event – all of them? Or are there only particular truths that apply to specific samples that cannot be generalized?

Very often the consensus of experts determines correspondence. In this sense, we speak of a *consensus theory of truth*. The assumption is that truth is based on the consensus of all who speak the same language with regard to the object/event. Consensus theory means that researchers who share the same worldview might determine what is considered true. But it might be unsatisfactory to suggest that consensus determines truth. From history we know that consensus was often wrong, for instance, the belief that the earth is flat. This situation means that the consensus of a given time and place constructs truth.

One could argue that implicitly psychologists have adopted a methodological theory of truth in the sense that something is considered knowledge/truth, if investigators follow all the latest methodological requirements of the discipline. But, we would argue, merely following methodological rules does not constitute knowledge.

Different ways of thinking about science

One can understand science as a systematic human activity oriented to the goal of under-standing and changing nature, society, or humans. However, debates about whether scien-tific knowledge is empirically or rationally derived and whether induction or deduction is the better method have occurred for centuries. As discussed below, these debates are related. Then we address common misconceptions about science.

Empiricism–rationalism debate

Important in the history of science is the tension between *empiricism* (i.e., reliance on sensory observations) and *rationalism* (i.e., reliance on systems of logical thought), which are different but potentially complementary ways of gaining knowledge. Individual philos-ophers from the seventeenth and eighteenth centuries, who influenced contemporary scien-tists, took different positions on this debate, although some adopted syntheses of empiricism and rationalism (see Chapter 3). Scientific controversy arises from the problem of whether to rely on sensory observations or thinking when attempting to understand nature and human beings. In current terms, the debate concerns the varied roles of observation and theory.

Nineteenth-century philosophers, scientists, and twentieth-century philosophers of sci-ence polarized the debate between empiricist and rationalist approaches. Today, some scientists assert that they practise their respective fields empirically not rationally. They trust their direct empirical observations and after reflecting on them, they theorize.

Other scientists argue that theory and data are interrelated in that theory guides research-ers' investigations. According to this rationalist perspective, scientists do not merely gather data. Rather, they ask theoretically driven questions about objects/events, and on the basis of hypotheses derived from their theory, they apply conceptual models to their observations. That is why psychoanalysts never observe schedules of reinforcement and behaviourists do not observe unconscious motives.

Induction–deduction debate

The empiricism–rationalism debate is closely related to the methodological debate of induction versus deduction. Philosophically speaking, the method commonly associated with empiricism is *induction* through which we derive the general from the particular. Based on several experiments we make a generalization.

The method related to rationalism is *deduction*, by which we derive the particular from the general. According to this option, knowledge-building should proceed deductively. For example, logical syllogisms operate deductively: based on the general premise that *all humans are mortal* and the specific premise that *Maria is a human*, we conclude that *Maria is mortal*.

Induction According to philosopher of science **Rudolf Carnap** (1891–1970), the natural sciences are *inductive*, because scientists collect observations from which they develop a general theory. The more an empirical hypothesis is verified, the higher its value.

One critic of induction was **Karl Popper** (1902–1994), who argued that the sciences could not be based on induction. If you observe white swans a thousand times, then you might want to draw the inductive conclusion that "all swans are white." But this is logically incorrect and empirically doubtful, because black swans exist; observing just one black swan disproves the induction "all swans are white."

For Carnap (1936), the more probable a theory is, the better it is. But for Popper (1959) one cannot decide probability statements; therefore, they are metaphysical. You can never observe all instances, and one counter-instance proves your generalization wrong. Popper proposed instead that theories should be subject to *falsification*; instead of looking for another white swan one should look for non-white swans.

Theories that survive these falsification attempts are not true but "corroborated." A theory that has withstood the most rigorous testing has not been verified but has received a high degree of corroboration. It may be retained as the best available theory until it is finally falsified or superseded by a better theory.

But critics have pointed out that actual scientists do not attempt to falsify the theories in which they have invested time, money, reputation, and emotion; rather, they strive to *confirm* them. Besides, Popper's own theory of falsification cannot be falsified and, thus, would be a metaphysical (non-scientific) theory itself – according to his own definition.

Deduction Deduction is another general method of the natural sciences. According to the deductive-nomological model of natural-scientific explanation (Hempel & Oppenheim, 1948), one can deduce what needs to be explained, based on presumed universal laws (hence the term "nomological") and based on certain antecedent conditions. For example, to explain why the part of an oar which is under water appears bent upward to an observer in a rowboat, we need to begin with general laws (the law of refraction and the law that water is optically denser than air) and with certain antecedent conditions (that indeed part of the oar is in the water).

However, it is questionable whether there are universal *psychological* laws that have the same intellectual weight as natural-science laws pertaining to natural objects and events. Rather, in Psychology, contradictory but empirically supported explanations for behaviour and mental processes often co-exist.

Common misconceptions

Here we evaluate common misconceptions about the meaning of science in the form of **three problematic statements**. These misconceptions abound among those who do not exercise critical thinking about what the practice of science involves.

(1) **The scientific method is equivalent to science**. Actually, science is more than a method and the scientific method appears in various forms across widely diverse scientific disciplines. Methodological criteria for the scientific method also are based on social customs, conventions, and norms created by scientists within given historical circumstances. This reality means that scientific norms are impermanent human creations.

Furthermore, scientific work consists not only of empirical testing but also of thinking and theorizing about observations. Such thinking does not follow the precise steps of the scientific method, as empirical studies of the thinking of twentieth-century scientists have shown. Scientists have made discoveries through flashes of insight and intuition, as well as through the laborious process of gathering facts through rigorous procedures, and sometimes accidentally.

(2) **Science is not art**. We can define "art" as the effort to masterfully create something. Artists, we could argue, produce something out of the chaos of sense perceptions. But how is this definition different from what we mean by "science"? Some say that artists strive for permanent contributions; engage in private, subjective expression; and do not submit their ideas to the challenge of reality.

Yet scientists also seek permanent recognition; as a human enterprise, scientific work is partially subjective; and many artists, such as actors, writers, and filmmakers, *do* submit their ideas to the challenge of reality to preserve authenticity and communicate a plausible facsimile of reality. Moreover, historically, science and art were integrated not segregated activities, as the Italian artist and inventor **Leonardo da Vinci** (1452–1519) exemplified. His fine art was integrated with his scientific work on anatomy, as depicted in Figure 1.2.

(3) **Scientists prove things correct**. Arguably, the main message derived from science courses in elementary and secondary education is that the function of science is to "prove" things and scientists' job is to find the "right" answers. In addition, the public has a tendency to use legal language when discussing science. For example, some political defenders of the status quo argue that environmental contaminants are "innocent until proven guilty by scientists." However, scientists cannot provide "proof," only data and interpretive explanations, all of which are bounded by more or less complexity, probability, and uncertainty.

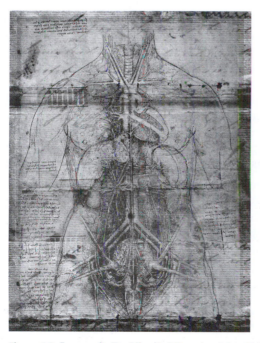

Figure 1.2 Leonardo Da Vinci's Vitruvian Man (1492) integrates fine art with scientific anatomy

Assumptions of positivist science

A particular approach to natural-scientific thinking, positivism, has dominated Psychology since the discipline's inception. Positivism originated in the writings of **Auguste Comte** (1798–1857), a French philosopher (see Chapter 4). His model is called positivism, because for him, "positive knowledge" was the highest stage of knowing. He confined such knowledge to the data of experience and excluded all theological or metaphysical speculations.

Ernst Mach (1838–1916), an Austrian scientist and philosopher (also Chapter 4), refined positivism by focusing on well-defined facts of reality and the functional relationship between variables. The Vienna Circle, a group of twentieth-century philosophers of science, refined positivism by introducing the term *logical positivism*, meaning that rigorous logical analysis can resolve all valid philosophical problems.

Although psychologists tended to interpret positivist science in a particular way, **three positivist assumptions** serve as the core *epistemology* (i.e., assumptions about knowledge) of natural-science Psychology: *naïve realism*, *determinism*, and *reductionism*.

(1) According to **naïve realism**, the sensed properties of objects are inherent in the objects themselves and the mind mirrors objects as they are. However, as we know from the psychological phenomenon of optical illusions, the mind adds to the sensation of external reality, that is, perception generates reality. Yet adherents to the assumption of naïve realism hold the following **four beliefs**:
   - Nature is the origin of knowledge, and scientists can capture knowledge of natural objects by strictly adhering to the rules of the pure scientific method.
   - Trained observers can mirror the world objectively as it actually exists, relying on empirical data and mathematical calculations.
   - Observers are independent of their observations, not merely separate from, but superior to natural objects; hence, trained observers, not the participating social actors in a human situation, are the best judges of reality.
   - Psychologists can reveal the realities of the psychological universe by representing the external environment as accurately as possible, if they minimize the potential distortions caused by observer bias.

(2) According to **determinism**, if scientists know the present state of any matter and apply Newton's laws of physics, they can identify linear cause-and-effect relations and can determine or predict the exact state or future of that matter. Insofar as scientists can know matter objectively and predict the physical dynamics of matter, they can manipulate the natural world. But developments in Einsteinian physics and beyond question the assumption of determinism (see Chapter 12).

(3) According to **reductionism**, scientists best understand the structure of psychological matter by learning about the most basic elements that form it. That is, they assume that the whole is the sum of its parts. If scientists know how the individual parts operate, they can determine the functioning of the whole. Yet, Gestalt psychologists' studies showed that in human perception the whole is more than the sum of its parts (also Chapter 6).

Proponents of reductionism contend that systematic examination of the underlying nature of the basic things that constitute all natural objects, including human action and consciousness, best explains change in the natural world. Furthermore, they believe that the elementary laws of pre-Einsteinian physics are the foundation for the theories and laws of all other sciences, including Psychology. This doctrine that everything can be explained through physical concepts and methods is termed *physicalism*.

Relevance to Psychology

Although in the drive to ensure their discipline's scientific credibility natural-science psychologists adopted the tenets of positivism and logical positivism, they have not always understood the sophisticated philosophical underpinnings of these doctrines. For example, many leaders of philosophical positivism (e.g., Mach) were not realists, let alone naïve empiricists. Furthermore, one can challenge current positivist-psychological attempts to produce objective knowledge on two grounds: facts themselves are dependent on theoretical perspectives and data are meaningless without interpretation.

Nevertheless, for most of the discipline's history, many natural-science psychologists have insisted that if they refine quantitative methods to make their measurements ever more precise and reliable, they will uncover scientifically legitimate truths. For example, behaviourists' goals were to predict and control behaviour. These goals, expanded somewhat, remain central to natural-science Psychology's main schools of thought: behavioural and cognitive neuroscience, evolutionary psychology, and cognitive behaviourism (see Chapter 7).

Critical thinkers about Psychology, however, might ask how suitable it is for psychologists to retain the assumptions of pre-twentieth-century physics. Physicists, after all, study presumably *inanimate* objects, not animal or human behaviour and mental processes. In fact, the assumptions of naïve realism, determinism, and reductionism underwent transformation in twentieth-century physics (see Chapter 12). Many contemporary physicists associated with such developments as relativity theory and quantum mechanics posited the counter-assumptions of mutual influence between observer and observed, indeterminacy, uncertainty, and even unpredictability and lack of control.

Perhaps these newer assumptions are better suited to the content of Psychology. But for the most part psychologists have not adopted and operated on the newer assumptions. Studying the history of our discipline critically might help you to understand why. Moreover, it is quite likely that the more interesting psychological questions defy precise experimental investigations, particularly if one believes that psychological events emanate from the personal agency of human goals, motives, and actions (D. N. Robinson, 1985), all embedded in changing social-historical situations.

Psychological events might not be reducible to the general laws of the natural sciences, hence might not be explicable sufficiently by a natural-science orientation. One could even argue that science is a form of history that proceeds in non-linear, often unexpected patterns. Similarly, Psychology might be a form of history, proceeding unpredictably but not randomly.

How science changes

One way to envision how scientists do their work is to regard them as architects and builders. Scientists are like architects in that builders of knowledge construct an edifice according to an architect's agreed-upon blueprint. The blueprint, or basic set of assumptions in scientific work, is termed a *paradigm*. Accordingly, science changes or proceeds according to changes to the blueprint, known as paradigm-shifts.

A paradigm consists of **two dimensions**:

- The often unstated but organized structure of theoretical, methodological, and social assumptions in any scientific discipline constitutes a *disciplinary matrix* (Kuhn, 1962). It consists of a set of essentially untestable concepts, such as *atomism* (i.e., reducing complex phenomena in the natural world to their most elemental parts).
- Models of "good" research that provide consensually approved methods for the investigation of new areas are termed *shared exemplars*. For example, the Skinner box was a shared exemplar for psychologists who espoused operant-conditioning theory (see Chapter 7).

Practically, paradigms represent a worldview that is shared by a group of researchers. Accordingly, one can say that devotees of different paradigms psychologically live in different worlds. From a critical perspective, paradigms present an inherent intellectual danger in that scientists learn to perceive phenomena of interest in certain ways, based on their acquired paradigms, while screening out other phenomena.

Evolutionary or revolutionary change?

The paradigm concept also has implications for understanding how science changes. The traditional view suggests that scientists accumulate knowledge incrementally. But in Psychology, for example, few know about Wundt's studies anymore, not because his research was scientifically incorrect, but because it was based on a passé paradigm.

Within an "evolutionary" perspective on how science changes (Toulmin, 1972), scientific concepts evolve over time in scientists' environment: the initial concepts vary, get selected and retained, or they are abandoned. The scientific community discards weak concepts, promoting the "survival of the fittest."

By contrast, Kuhn proposed a "revolutionary" perspective on how science proceeds. He showed that within a paradigm concepts change in a cycle of radical upheaval in which scientists overthrow the whole paradigm. For example, when **Albert Einstein's** (1879–1955) theory of relativity emerged in the early twentieth century, physicists did not adopt it immediately, but eventually it became the new paradigm, because it could solve problems that the old paradigm of Newton could not.

Kuhn's notion of scientific revolution consists of **five stages**:

- In a "pre-paradigmatic phase" many incompatible theories based on different worldviews, concepts, and methods exist. Scientists in diverse schools of thought gather facts randomly.
- During a "normal-science phase" scientists accept one prevailing paradigm, refine theories, and solve puzzles. Because a paradigm congeals, diversity dissolves and scientists solve the problems in their disciplines.
- The normal-science phase is followed by a "crisis phase" in which insoluble theoretical problems or experimental anomalies destabilize a given paradigm.

- The crisis is overcome by a "revolution" that replaces an old paradigm with a new one. Younger and some more established scientists switch to the new paradigm.
- The revolution ends in a new normal-science phase during which scientists accept the new paradigm, refine theories, and solve puzzles again. And the process repeats.

Kuhn, who reflected on the development of physics, emphasized non-rational elements in the development of science, incorporating sociological, psychological, and political motives. For example, he suggested that students' preference for a paradigm depends on their teacher's preference. Kuhn also directly applied Piaget's conception of how children develop the ability to think like scientists to his own explanation of how historical change occurs in a natural science. Critics, however, have pointed out that Kuhn's definition of paradigm is imprecise. In addition, whether Kuhn's analysis is applicable to Psychology's development is questionable.

The game of science

One way to conceive of the social nature of scientific processes that Kuhn's analysis partly illuminated is to employ the metaphor of a game (Pyke & Agnew, 1991). Traditionally teachers of science have focused only on the *rules* of the game of science, stressing the logic of the scientific method and its procedures. This emphasis, however, ignores the *social* dimensions of the game, namely, the team-owners, coaches, players, playing fields, fans, sponsors, awards, historical shrines, reporters, referees, schedules, recruitment, etc.

The game of science has counterparts to all these features. Thus, it includes scientific work that proceeds according to formal rules of inquiry *and* individual, small-group, organizational, institutional, corporate, and governmental structures, dynamics, and politics. Some of these processes are expressed in stereotypical masculine terms, such as adversarial competition and conquests.

Social and interpersonal dimensions pervade workaday scientific practice in Psychology as well (e.g., Walsh-Bowers, 2002). The social nature of conducting psychological research is most apparent in the immediate investigative situation of researchers and participants in which psychologists' institutionalized expectations about how to conduct rigorous research shape its content and processes. These expectations include methodological norms, ethical principles and guidelines, and report-writing standards (see Chapter 11).

Although less obvious, the structures, mores, and ideologies of Psychology as a social institution also mould workaday investigative practice. These more systemic, but typically covert features of the research landscape include **five aspects**:

- epistemological assumptions about making scientific knowledge;
- the enculturation of students in research norms, mediated by course instructors and research supervisors;
- methodological criteria promoted by funding sources, journal editors, and grant and journal reviewers;
- the socioeconomic function of research productivity within the academic reward-system;
- psychologists' beliefs, feelings, and wishes about what constitutes rigorous methodology.

Common beliefs about practising science

An informed approach to scientists' actual conduct includes a skeptical perspective on common beliefs that scientists themselves perpetuate about their work. In a sense, these beliefs operate like myths. Here we contrast **six beliefs** with social-psychological realities that underlie ordinary scientific practice:

(1) Many believe that scientists cooperate harmoniously in their pursuit of scientific discovery. However, although within groups scientists might or might not cooperate, between groups they compete aggressively. The race for first place in making a scientific discovery remains very common. Competition takes the form of racing for priority of discovery, expressed in rapid publication in scientific journals.

Competition among scientists has characterized the social reality of modern science since its inception in the seventeenth century. French scientist Louis Pasteur (1822–1895), for instance, was not only very skilled at rhetoric (i.e., the art of persuasion), and at public relations concerning his scientific activities, but he was also very competitive (Geison, 1995). Apparently, during the race to develop the anthrax vaccine he appropriated techniques from a rival scientist. In a notorious twentieth-century example, experimental data were taken from the lab of Rosalind Franklin, the geneticist noted above, without her knowledge; evidently, her model of DNA had preceded James Watson and Francis Crick's model (Sayre, 1975).

(2) The social climate of research institutes can also be competitive. The belief is that scientists form a cooperative community in pursuing truth. But the reality is that careers depend on the ability to get along with the powerful "in-group" that controls the rewards for employees within a research organization.

(3) Another common belief is that scientists write objectively, that is, their use of language in their formal journal articles suggests dispassionate detachment. But the reality is that scientists try to *appear* rational; meanwhile, they rely heavily on rhetorical devices in their writing, consciously or not, to persuade their readers that their work is better than their competitors'. Moreover, many scientists will admit privately that they experience strong social pressure to be on top in their field and to create this illusion in their writing.

(4) The common belief is that scientists' job security does not affect their objectivity. The reality is that there are extreme pressures on scientists employed by universities and colleges to publish a lot or not be tenured, receive research grants, or merit-pay or promotions. These pressures are very strong particularly for faculty without tenure. Scientists cope by tending to produce piecemeal studies, separately published, to boost the total number of their publications, because this quantity is a primary criterion on which their job-performance is based.

But there might be negative consequences of this reality for the ethical quality of relationships between researchers and participants in Psychology. The climate of "publish or perish" seems to have led to the mass production of studies in which investigators "run" passive participants (often university students) through experiments.

(5) Another typical belief is that scientists are honest and do not cheat, because they value truth. The reality is that some scientists lie, cheat, fabricate results, and make false claims, under pressure to claim a scientific discovery and secure grants in an increasingly competitive market. One systematic review showed that 14 per cent of scientists

had observed fabrication, falsification, and modification by colleagues (Fanelli, 2009). A more recent review suggests that in biomedical research most retracted journal articles, which are sharply increasing, are due to some type of investigator misconduct, including actual or suspected fraud, duplicate publication, or plagiarism (Fang, Steen, & Casadevall, 2012).

In Psychology, **Cyril Burt** (1883–1971) seemingly fabricated data to promote the idea of the heritability of intelligence. This claim had adverse consequences for children in the British educational system. In fact, the latest historical scholarship indicates that **Stanley Milgram** (1933–1984) (see Chapter 7) and a large proportion of current US psychologists reportedly engaged in some type of scientific dishonesty (John, Loewenstein, & Prelec, 2012).

(6) Many insist that scientists are apolitical and neutral about society. The reality is that for centuries war and science have served each other, and scientists are indirectly and increasingly directly dependent on societal and corporate support. During peacetime, scientists claim their work is value-free, but during wartime many scientists work for their nation's victory due to strong connections with the military and other government agencies.

Furthermore, corporations increasingly underwrite and fund scientists' research on psychotropic medication, electroconvulsive treatment, drugs for diseases, and other marketable topics. Such arrangements produce serious ethical conflicts of interest, when corporations

Box 1.2 Corporate–hospital–university interference

The players in this highly publicized situation were Dr. Nancy Olivieri, a blood researcher at a hospital and university in Toronto, Canada; a research institute of this hospital; and a pharmaceutical corporation. Olivieri found herself in a dispute with the hospital and the corporation, when she decided to publish her findings in the *New England Journal of Medicine* that showed potentially harmful effects concerning a drug produced by the corporation. She believed that she had an ethical responsibility to inform her patients, the scientific community, and regulatory agencies about her discovery.

But Olivieri had signed a confidentiality agreement in 1995 with the firm, so it threatened to take legal action against her. In addition, contrary to what the hospital's ethics board had recommended, the research institute urged her to discuss the possible harmful effects of this drug with the corporation, rather than involving regulatory agencies,. Furthermore, the hospital denied her request for legal counsel. In effect, the hospital's administrators failed to support her, even though during the dispute the senior vice-president of the pharmaceutical firm maintained research facilities in the hospital.

When a major newspaper published this story in August 1998 and Olivieri's colleagues expressed their displeasure with the hospital's decisions, hospital administrators quickly decided to conduct an external review of how it monitored clinical trials (J. Thompson, Baird, & Downie, 2001). Eventually, the university and hospital publicly apologized to Olivieri for their misconduct.

and their hospital and university allies attempt to prevent researchers from publishing negative findings about the corporation's product. This situation occurred in the case of a Canadian medical researcher, as described in Box 1.2.

Small-group discussion. Various societal and psychological influences evidently operate in scientists' work. These influences include the motivation to claim a discovery, opportunities for fraud, and the political and economic agendas of governmental and corporate funders of research. In your opinion, how influential are these phenomena in Psychology today and for the foreseeable future?

A "realistic" view of science as socially embedded

In light of the above social realities saturating ordinary scientific work we agree with US psychologist **Kenneth Gergen's** (b. 1935) claim in 1982 that scientists and psychologists do not merely respond to nature; rather, they construct it. A more "realistic" view, therefore, is that scientific knowledge is embedded in specific sociohistorical contexts and in the values of scientists whose theories shape their understanding of reality.

A critical goal of science – and Psychology – could be to try to provide understanding of existing conditions at a certain point in time and place, and not to strive for "universal truths" about human beings. Interpretations of existing conditions and their theories could generate debates and transform reality. Historically in fact, the sciences have thrived when there were competing theories and diverse methods.

Furthermore, the conduct of psychological research is saturated with psychological and social factors. Thus, psychologists' behaviour can be studied like anyone else's behaviour. One can examine the relation between specific aspects of academic and professional psychologists' culture, on the one hand, and individual psychologists' behaviour, on the other hand. One also could study psychologists' formal organizations; the political economy of academic psychology; the professional education and employment characteristics of psychologists; and the effect of psychologists' personalities on what they study, how they are influenced by what they study, including group dynamics and how research is used to enhance social power.

From a critical perspective, scholars must practise critical thinking about any claim by psychologists to have produced purely objective knowledge. Skepticism is warranted, because psychologists' scientific work, which is more socially and culturally complex than natural scientists' study of inanimate objects, is saturated with influences from multiple sources.

Part 4 conclusion

The modern term "science" is as contestable as the terms "psychology" and "history." Each has multiple legitimate meanings, interests, and functions. Some scholars in the discipline of Psychology emphasize the set of technologies associated with the applications of scientific methodology, whereby individuals define science solely in terms of particular procedures, preferably the laboratory experiment. From this perspective, science by definition is the use of the experimental method.

While we discuss the history of psychologists' research traditions in Chapter 11, here we focused on the evolution of scientific theory and practice. In addition, we use "science" to mean the systematic study of the natural and human world, mindful that the goals and methods of science have changed considerably across centuries. We do not assume that past figures adopted the approach to science that today's scientists take. To understand the history of science, scholars must transcend its modern definitions and connotations.

At this point in our journey to understand how the discipline of history and the sciences operate and intersect, and how these operations and intersections manifest in Psychology, we made explicit our assumption that the social and human side of science is at least implicit in any attempt to chart the history of Psychology and its subject matter. Specifically, we examined some interpersonal, organizational, and societal aspects of the conduct of any science.

It is wise to be realistic about the social and interpersonal processes that affect what scientists do, as opposed to scientists' idealized picture of what they do. We contrasted the common beliefs about science with what actually occurs. These realities show that scientific activity is subjective and objective, private and public, individual and societal.

Part 5   Philosophical questions in psychology

Psychology began to separate from philosophy only in the late nineteenth century; before then psychology was a branch of philosophy, and even by the 1920s in many prestigious institutions in Europe, Russia, the US, and Canada, it remained housed within departments of philosophy. When students explore the history of our discipline and its topics, they inevitably experience how Psychology has always been bound up with philosophical questions and still is. Accordingly, we need to discuss what these fundamental philosophical questions are before we can proceed to narrate Psychology's history.

Following US philosophical-psychologist Daniel Robinson's (1995) perspective on Psychology's intellectual heritage, *philosophy* (literally, the love of wisdom) is the systematic form of critical inquiry in which individuals subject their experience to scrutiny. Philosophy is distinct from folk wisdom because of philosophy's systematic nature. The ancient Greeks apparently were the first in Western society to engage in this reflective practice and to pose penetrating questions about their experience in the world. By adopting a skeptical, questioning attitude, individuals who practise philosophy challenge basic beliefs and values.

Philosophical links to Psychology

Many branches of philosophy are potentially germane to Psychology. In this textbook we connect historical issues in the discipline to **four philosophical branches**:

(1) *Ontology* studies the nature of being (i.e., existence) and inquires about the nature of the world, the universe, and the cosmos. These questions are relevant to scientific psychology, when we inquire about the nature of human nature, psychological categories, the

mind, and the relationship between mind and body. For instance, do psychological concepts, such as intelligence, mirror reality or are they inventions that become a social reality once they have been established? Another ontological question refers to whether Psychology can be a unified discipline (see Chapter 7).

(2) *Epistemology*, the branch of philosophy concerned with the nature of knowledge, deals with questions such as "how do we know that we know?", "how certain can we be of our knowledge?", "what are the methods for gaining knowledge?", and "what are the limits of knowledge?" One can apply these questions to the problem of how confident we can be of our academic and professional knowledge in Psychology. We can also question how compatible our discipline is with other paths to knowledge, such as the humanities and social sciences.

(3) *Ethics* is the branch of philosophy that tries to elucidate the nature of morality and its social applications, including questions of how we humans should conduct ourselves. In Psychology, reflections on the morality of conduct take the form of *ethical principles and guidelines* (i.e., general moral values and specific ethical responsibilities of scientific and professional psychologists) (see Chapter 8). For instance, ethical discussions have concerned the role of psychologists in developing techniques for interviewing prisoners or terror-suspects. Some psychologists have characterized these techniques as forms of torture.

(4) But ethics encompasses social responsibility as well. Thus, using *social and political philosophy*, one can question the role of Psychology in making a better world. Social and political philosophy also raises questions about how members of society deal with the problems of distribution of economic and social resources and of governance. Although some psychologists have claimed that our discipline is relevant to resolving social and political problems, notably absent in Psychology is discourse informed by social and political thought.

Critical thinking

Many concerns of modern psychologists about theory, research, and professional practice have their intellectual roots in the above philosophical questions with which humanity has struggled from time immemorial. After all, psychologists' predecessors, namely philosophers, sought meaningful answers to questions about human nature and psychological processes.

Clearly, prior philosophers' understanding of what is "psychological" differs from current conceptions of Psychology. Nevertheless, as a sophisticated form of systematic critical inquiry, philosophy is an indispensable tool for psychologists as we attempt to make empirical sense of and reflect meaningfully upon the natural world and human nature. Philosophy is invaluable, because, overtly or covertly, the empirical questions that psychologists pursue are often philosophical issues. In short, psychologists cannot escape philosophy.

As a philosophical tool, critical thinking about the assumptions behind given beliefs, values, and practices, which is pivotal in philosophical analysis, is also essential for Psychology (Slife, Reber, & Richardson, 2005). By *critical thinking* we mean sets of intellectual and moral resources that include the logical skill of analyzing the nature of claims in terms of the quality of the evidence and of the interpretation of that evidence used to support the claims. Critical thinking also encompasses the philosophical perspective of understanding psychological theories, investigations, and practices in social-historical context, shaped by such social categories as culture, gender, and social class.

Practically, critical thinking entails developing satisfactory questions and answers to **four basic questions**:

- *Internalist* (concerning the logic of research itself): the meaningfulness of theories, methods, and analyses. For instance, what's the claim that the psychologist is making?
- *Externalist* (concerning the embeddedness of research): why is the researcher pursuing this claim? How does the claim relate to external interests (corporations, government, other institutions, ideologies, worldviews, etc.)?
- *Hermeneutic* (concerning the interpretation of research): what's the evidence the researcher has used to interpret the claim? How well do the interpretations fit the evidence provided?
- *Ethical-practical* (concerning the social consequences of research): how might this study affect individuals and society? What does it mean for social action?

As a thought-experiment, consider answering these four basic questions in relation to the article entitled, "The weirdest people in the world?" which shows that mainstream psychological research is practised using very selected, often student populations (Henrich, Heine, & Norazeyan, 2010). The article title suggests the acronym WEIRD, referring to research participants from Western, Educated, Industrial, Rich, and Democratic societies.

Common critical terms

Before ending this chapter we offer some definitions of key terms employed throughout the text. In the preceding material on history, science, and philosophy we "problematized" (i.e., described the problems with conventional ideas about) and "contextualized" (i.e., described the social contextual features of) these disciplines. This critical framework has opened up space for scrutinizing the history and philosophy of Psychology.

A *critical history and philosophy* of Psychology includes tools developed by *modernist theory* (e.g., critical theory, feminism, and hermeneutics) and *postmodern theory* (e.g., discourse theory and social constructionism). Modernist theory or *modernism* refers to the traditional Western belief in inevitable human progress, a doctrine held since the Age of Enlightenment in the eighteenth century (see Chapter 3). Postmodern theory or *postmodernism* means the various sets of criticisms of *modernism* advanced in the late twentieth century (see Chapter 12). One term associated with postmodernism that we employ is *discourse*, which refers to "the system of language, objects, and practices that constitutes a particular domain of knowledge" (Marecek & Hare-Mustin, 1990, p. 1).

Social constructionism, applied to Psychology, means that psychologists interpretively "construct" so-called truths about behaviour and mental processes from their own discourse, which is always embedded in a particular sociohistorical context. Thus, psychological formulations of theory, method, and applications are historically relative to the time and place of the psychologists creating these formulations. For instance, the term "identity" should not be studied as representing a natural object but as having different meanings in different cultures.

Deconstruction involves critically analyzing an accepted discourse by describing what might have been hidden, ignored, or repressed in the traditional perspective. The critical thinker attempts to discern what has been marginalized and silenced and also attempts to uncover power relations. For instance, one could uncover the social context of academic psychologists' resistance to qualitative research methods (see Chapter 11).

Part 5 conclusion

We see our responsibility as authors and instructors to be uncovering the historically and socially embedded nature of Psychology. Above all, our intention is to encourage you to exercise your capacity for critical thinking about our science and its professions rather than to receive the standard views and lore of Psychology uncritically. This textbook does not encourage memorization of psychologists' beliefs about theoretical, empirical, and professional triumphs in preparation for writing examinations. Yet exercising critical thinking also means that you should be critical of this textbook.

Another responsibility of ours is to present the contested story of psychological topics and Psychology fairly. In that educational light, we hope that our approach becomes a tool for emancipating your own ideas concerning what is valuable or not in the science and profession of Psychology. To paraphrase the ancient Athenian philosopher **Socrates** (c. 469–399 BCE) (see Chapter 2), "*The unexamined discipline is not worth practising.*"

Your choice of how to understand psychological topics and Psychology should be as fully informed as possible. Our hope is that this textbook will facilitate your intellectual and moral growth in achieving that understanding. In large measure, the process of developing your own approach to psychological topics and Psychology entails clarifying for yourself your personal preferences for various types of Psychology, once you become acquainted with the range of possibilities and their historical and philosophical roots. We urge you to develop your own framework of understanding, because, consciously or not, your assumptions about the discipline influence your studies in Psychology, your choices of a vocation, and perhaps even your role as a citizen in society.

Now consider this last question: what are your own personal values and beliefs about what should be important in scientific and professional Psychology?

Part 6   Thematic review

From our perspective, understanding the history and philosophy of Psychology involves addressing the fact that the discipline is situated in complex layers of contested meanings that have shifted across time and place and that require philosophical thought to disentangle. Thus, appreciating both the philosophical issues and the social-historical context in which psychological theory, research, and practical applications have been embedded is necessary. Four interrelated themes discernible in Chapter 1 might capture these complexities: **multiple psychologies**, **reflexive historiography**, **intersubjective science**, and **critical thinking**.

Multiple psychologies

The diversity of meanings of the term "psychology" has been reflected in diverse perspectives on psychological thought and the discipline itself. Although many psychologists have regarded their work as a *natural* science, now akin to neuroscience, others have regarded Psychology as a *human* science, akin to history or philosophy. This lack of unanimity can be attributed to Psychology's "peculiar place among the sciences, suspended between methodological orientations derived from the physical and biological sciences and a subject matter that extends into the social and human sciences" (Ash, 2003, p. 251). Moreover, Psychology includes dozens of branches from community psychology to neuropsychology. Thus, multiple types and subdisciplines have prevailed historically.

Yet there are some common intellectual ties that bind diverse psychological scientific and professional practices (Ash, 2003). First, the discipline has had permeable, not firm, boundaries with other disciplines (e.g., philosophy, biology) and professions (e.g., medicine). Secondly, the dual aspects of scientific and professional Psychology are linked historically and presently with applications of Psychology influencing basic research and vice versa. Thirdly, from an international perspective, particular cultural traditions and circumstances have shaped psychologists' attempts to institutionalize their science and profession, so that Psychology in Japan, for example, has had a different trajectory than Psychology in the USA (Brock, 2006a).

Reflexive historiography

Any history of Psychology requires defining "history" and how to practise historiography. Rather than a simple chronological survey of famous names, dates, theories, and experiments, history, especially of a variegated discipline like Psychology, is immersed in philosophical issues, such as the place of interpretation in historicizing human phenomena and one's assumptions about how historical change occurs. Moreover, rather than pursuing an illusory historical objectivism, as if one can eliminate present biases entirely, or a presentist standpoint by which one judges the past primarily in terms of the present, the standpoint of sophisticated presentism enables scholars to do justice to the past and yet to consider the significance of past and current discourses.

Central in historiography is the concept of reflexivity, which implies that scholars acknowledge how objective and subjective aspects are simultaneously present in their interpretations of the past. In this way historians exercise their capacity for critical thinking about the meaning of past events. We authors attempt to do the same in this critical history and philosophy of Psychology.

Intersubjective science

Just as one can exercise critical judgment concerning history, so one can with science. But how do psychologists understand the term "science"? Not only have there been different conceptions of science over the centuries, but also empirical studies of how modern scientists conduct their work shows that science is socially embedded and saturated with societal and personal sources of bias or even fraudulent scientific claims. Science, then, comprises objective and subjective human dimensions.

In the case of Psychology, our desires as psychologists to accumulate facts and theorize objectively about often ambiguous phenomena that we might share with other creatures reflect subjective individual preferences and interpretations. In a sense, we study ourselves. Accordingly, the discipline's scientific and philosophical aspects are intertwined in theorizing, researching, and applying psychological knowledge. Rather than an objective enterprise, psychologists' work perhaps is better characterized by the principle of intersubjectivity by which attempts to be objective are always relative to subjective choices and social influences.

Critical thinking

These themes of multiple psychologies, reflexive historiography, and intersubjective science find their union in the philosophical orientation and set of resources known as critical thinking. If philosophy refers to systematic analysis of individuals' experience often with a skeptical orientation, critical thinking encompasses intellectual and moral resources for logical analysis of the nature of claims, including scientific ones, in relation to the evidence provided for the claims and of the interpretation of that evidence. Critical thinking also includes the philosophical capacities for understanding psychological theory, research, and practice in social historical context. In this spirit we have composed this text to encourage your thinking critically about psychological topics and Psychology.

Summary

In Part 1 we addressed what people mean when they use the term "psychology," because there have been different definitions, such as "psychology is the study of the soul," "psychology is the study of the mind," or "psychology is the study of behaviour," depending on a given historical era. Crucially for the rest of this text, we distinguish between natural-science and human-science Psychology. Psychologists holding a natural-science orientation stress the prediction and control of behaviour and cognitive processes, whereas psychologists holding a human-science orientation stress understanding the meaning of psychological experience.

In Part 2 we discussed what the term "history" means from different angles. First we considered different definitions of history and emphasized the role of interpretation in the practice of history. We described diverse philosophies on interpreting one's past. Next we discussed various types of history and addressed the question of how historical change proceeds. We concluded that interpretation is crucial in historiography and individuals' achievements are best understood when situated in their intellectual and social contexts.

Part 3 addressed the crucial question, why and how should we study the history and philosophy of psychological topics and Psychology? We discussed various reasons for and certain inhibitions against studying its history and noted the key scholarly issues in studying any history. In addition, we described the foundations and development of a critical history and introduced the term *critical historiography*. Most importantly, we suggested some concrete steps of reflexivity for scholars when practising the history and philosophy of Psychology.

Because psychologists since the nineteenth century have claimed that our discipline is a science, it is important to address what is meant by the term "science" and how it is distinct from other forms of knowledge. Thus, in Part 4 we discussed various types of science and its relationship to Psychology. We also introduced reflections on the concepts of knowledge and truth and how we can think about science, providing some conceptual tools in order to think about the development of Psychology. In addition, we uncovered the assumptions of positivist epistemology that undergird the conduct of natural-science Psychology: naïve realism, determinism, and reductionism. Next we discussed different ways of comprehending how science proceeds and whether change in science is evolutionary or revolutionary.

In Part 5 we discussed the relevance of philosophy and philosophical questions for our discipline. Practically speaking, philosophy's greatest gift to psychologists is the indispensable tool of critical thinking. Then we defined important terms that we use throughout this textbook. We concluded by making explicit our critical framework and our educational intentions for your engaging in critical thinking about the history, present, and future of Psychology as a science and professions.

Throughout the chapter we pointed out that a critical stance, meaning examining psychological topics and Psychology from an insider and outsider perspective, provides opportunities to understand the development of the subject matter, discipline, and profession. As well, we stressed that a critical look at the history and philosophy of Psychology should apply to this text. Just as psychological knowledge is provisional, so is any critique of that knowledge.

In Part 6 we discussed four interrelated themes that seem to summarize the main issues we addressed in Chapter 1: multiple psychologies, reflexive historiography, intersubjective science, and critical thinking. These themes will recur throughout the text as we attempt to foster the development of a critical history and philosophy of Psychology.

Sample essay questions

1. In your own words define what you mean by the terms: psychology, history, history of psychology, science, philosophy, critical history and philosophy of psychology.

2. What role does interpretation play in the history of any science? What might be some personal and social influences that affect historians' interpretations? Give an example of how interpretation plays a role in histories of Psychology.

3. The authors stress employing "critical thinking" when studying the history and philosophy of Psychology. Describe the components of critical thinking.

4. Studying the history of any science depends on drawing interpretations of certain terms, concepts, and theories as well as certain accepted practices of research; that is, making sense of the history of Psychology depends on philosophical content. Conversely, philosophizing about any science's content and practices depends on situating them in a particular time and place. Practically, what does this argument mean, if you wanted to investigate, for example, who "founded" cognitive psychology?

RECOMMENDED READING

Jenkins's (1991) *Re-thinking history* is a brief introduction to historiography that provides an overview of the complex issues involved in writing history. Jordanova (2000) *History in practice* reviews various approaches and methods in historiography.

R. Smith's (1997) *The Norton history of the human sciences* comprehensively and artfully places Psychology in the context of other human sciences. We also recommend competing texts: Pickren and Rutherford (2010) in *A history of modern psychology in context* focus on the discipline of Psychology but not its pre-disciplinary subject matter, while G. Richards (2010) in *Putting psychology in its place: An introduction from a critical historical perspective*, addresses many of the historical and philosophical issues, from a British critical perspective on psychology.

For an appreciation of the philosophical roots of scientific and professional psychology, read D. N. Robinson's book, *An intellectual history of psychology* (1995). For a biographical view on the history of Psychology we recommend Fancher and Rutherford's (2012) *Pioneers of psychology*.

For an introduction to many of the contentious issues and feminist debates in writing on the history of women in science read Whaley's (2003) *Women's history as scientists: A guide to the debates*.

Finally, we recommend Ward's (2002) *Modernizing the mind: Psychological knowledge and the remaking of society*, which, from a sociological perspective, asks why Psychology was such a successful discipline in the twentieth century, not in the sense of providing general truths or laws but in the "psychologization" of society, which means understanding and explaining many areas of social life, rightly or wrongly, using psychological categories.

ONLINE RESOURCES

History & Philosophy of Psychology Web Resource provides a large number of resources and is maintained by Christopher Green: www.psych.yorku.ca/orgs/resource.htm

Classics in the History of Psychology is also developed and maintained by Green: http://psychclassics.yorku.ca/

Consult "Psychology's feminist voices," developed and maintained by Alexandra Rutherford: www.feministvoices.com/

2 Ancient and premodern psychological thought

Chapter outline

Introduction

In Chapter 1 we discussed diverse meanings of "history," "psychology," and "science," and we explained our critical-historical orientation to the history and philosophy of psychology.

Now we can begin the first stage of our historical journey and consider how psychological questions were addressed in ancient, medieval, and Renaissance thought. New scholarship in these areas has generated controversy and new insights especially regarding interpretations of ancient thought (Rossetti, 2004). By addressing this research we clear up some long-standing misinterpretations, however, for the most part we present conventional ideas on the history of philosophy relevant to psychological inquiry.

We start with the ancient Greek philosophers: abstract descriptions of nature introduced by the presocratics, the Socratic method of inquiry, the psychological views of Plato, along with a differing orientation espoused by the Sophists. Then we discuss the psychological ideas of Aristotle. Next we consider developments in science and philosophical psychology during the Roman Empire. We discuss the practical views of therapeutic philosophies and religious reinterpretations of Plato in late antiquity important to medieval ways of thinking. Concerning the Middle Ages, we describe the influential ideas of Augustine and Aquinas on psychological subjects. Regarding the Renaissance, we note the cultural, scientific, and philosophical developments from which a *modern* scientific and a more intensely psychological focus began to emerge in the seventeenth century. That stage of our journey continues in Chapter 3.

Studying the treatment of psychological ideas in ancient, medieval, and Renaissance times can foster different ways of understanding present concerns in Psychology. Of course, historical understandings of psychological concepts are not completely continuous with current understandings. Interpretations always belong to an era. For example, ancient Greek philosophers discussed concepts such as memory and reason, but did not have terms such as "psychology," "consciousness," or "insanity" (Abma, 2004).

Nevertheless, current understandings of historical conceptions can provide new perspectives on both past and present. A modern reading of ancient ideas, for example, can generate fresh insights into current understanding. Accordingly, the primary value of the material in this chapter, apart from its intrinsic historical interest, rests in suggesting new ways of thinking about psychological subject matter and in appreciating how each particular understanding belongs to a social-historical context.

The **aims** of this chapter are to describe:

- Ancient understandings of nature and human psyche.
- The views of the presocratic Greek philosophers.
- The Socratic method of inquiry, some of the psychological ideas of Plato, and the dissimilar view of the Sophists.
- The scientific views and psychological ideas of Aristotle.
- Ideas of the Roman philosophers, derived from the Greek therapeutic philosophies of Epicureanism, Stoicism, Skepticism, and Cynicism.

- The psychological ideas of key medieval thinkers: Augustine, Bonaventure, Aquinas, John Duns Scotus, and William of Ockham.
- The psychological views of Renaissance thinkers.
- The central themes that link the ancient, medieval, and Renaissance eras: conflicting metaphysical positions, critical thinking, and a conscious psychological interior.

Part 1   Ancient Greek views on nature and the human psyche

In twenty-first-century scholarship in Europe, the US, Canada, Australia, Japan, China, and throughout South America, interpretations of ancient Greek philosophy continue to be made. Scholars generally believe that Greek views on nature and human nature will remain significant, because they form the conceptual infrastructure of Western ideology, spreading worldwide through globalization (Rossetti, 2004).

In early nineteenth-century China, for example, philosophy texts were translated and studied in order to improve economic and political organization (Yu, 2004). Studying Greek logic and rationalism was considered important to broaden Chinese ways of thinking. However, after the founding of the People's Republic of China in 1949, the study of Greek philosophy became marginal. Nevertheless, fifty years later, the Chinese translation of the complete works of Aristotle was completed.

Before we can comprehend the Greeks' monumental contributions we need to appreciate their many perspectives on the natural world. First, we will see how philosophy worked to free itself from poetry just as later science strived to become free from philosophy (Deely, 2001).

Homeric thought

Prior to the emergence of philosophy based on observation of the natural world, philosophy and poetry were more intertwined and mythology shaped Greek views of nature and human nature. The influence of the Homeric epic poems, the *Iliad* and the *Odyssey*, composed around the eighth century BCE, persisted in Greek education and culture even after the emergence of philosophy (Lindberg, 1992).

In these poems gods and goddesses directly, but unpredictably, intervene in human affairs. The focus is on one's relation to the gods, the order of things, and public life, *not* on the individual's capacities for realizing one's full potential (Danziger, 1997a). In later Greek thought, "knowing thyself" became a matter of rightly positioning oneself in the natural intelligent order of the cosmos (C. Taylor, 1989).

Although there is nothing resembling a philosophical theory of mind in the Homeric works, there is a tendency to account for mental states in terms of processes and agencies outside of oneself. Madness, for example, tends to be attributed to things outside of the person. Situations of internal conflict are portrayed as a personified interchange, the result of not knowing whether to act now or later, not knowing which of two actions to take, or as excessive forgetting (Simon, 1972; Simon & Weiner, 1966).

In these epics there is no word for "self" or "oneself." Rather, Homer's psyche (*psuche*) is the "breath of life" and very much integrated with the body. "Soul" is associated with death; it distinguishes the living from the dead and can be risked and lost (Lorenz, 2009).

Plato, the classic Greek philosopher and student of Socrates, also used the term psyche, but with a significant change in meaning. Arguably, for Plato, psyche is more active and self-moving and not as passive and receptive as Homer's notion of psyche. In addition, for Plato, psyche seems to have had more of an "intellectual" connotation, with associations to the immortal part of one's reason, implying a spiritual essence.

Background on the presocratics

The original philosophers in the Greek city-states, collectively known as *presocratics* (i.e., before the era of Socrates, although some were his contemporaries), explored nature both empirically, in the sense of making systematic observations, and conceptually (Lindberg, 1992). Whereas the language of the Homeric epics was more descriptive, using verbs and not abstract terms, the presocratics introduced more abstract discourse. This effort continued in Plato's dialogues and, by the time of Aristotle, non-poetic abstractions became more fully developed (Simon, 1972).

In their rejection of poetic myth as the most useful way of communicating knowledge, the presocratics changed views on natural objects. Hence, they are regarded as "the first investigators of matters which became the special objects of astronomy, physics, chemistry, zoology, botany, psychology and so on" (Barnes, 1987, p. 13). The presocratics explained nature and the cosmos independent of divine intervention, depicting a natural order and objective reality that could be systematically known. The presocratics defended their ideas with reasons and arguments instead of poetry, mythology, or opinions (Tell, 2007).

The presocratics wrote hundreds of "books," yet none has survived today. In ancient times, writing was preserved on scrolls wherein, for example, seventy pages of modern text would require a 22-foot long scroll (Deely, 2001). The scrolls were fragile and used more to support spoken discourse than as an independent form of communication. Yet many texts endured for at least a thousand years, and numerous authors preserved fragments of the presocratic writings as quotations in their own works (Barnes, 1987).

The early philosophers wondered at the mystery of life. Philosophical thinking, some argue, begins with this attitude of amazement and marvel towards existence (Curd, 2011). Although they were not scientists in the current sense, generalizing from controlled observation and experiment, the presocratics posed questions about reality, nature, change, and knowledge. Instead of contributing to poetic myth or religious faith, they formed naturalistic answers to their questions, grounded in natural causes, and they conceived of the natural world and human nature as orderly and predictable. For the presocratics, instead of gods there are material and mechanical explanations (Cavendish, 1964).

Diverse perspectives on nature

The presocratics had diverse ways of understanding existence, the natural world, and the origin of change. Here we discuss naturalistic, mathematical, and biological perspectives (Deely, 2001).

Perspectives on change

Although **Heraclitus** (c. 540–c. 480/470 BCE) and **Parmenides** (c. 515–c. 449/440 BCE) have more in common than usually is recognized (Graham, 2011), they tend to be portrayed as taking opposing positions on what kind of reality to trust (Deely, 2001).

Parmenides In his metaphysical and cosmological poem *On Nature* Parmenides considered the logic of existence and change. Change is impossible for something that exists. We can use a single account to describe something but, when we perceive it, there is change and plurality. As such, Aristotle regarded Parmenides as having understood that the "apprehension of what is unchanging is of a different order epistemologically than apprehension of things subject to change" (Palmer, 2012, p. 29).

According to many recent interpretations, Parmenides did not deny the existence or importance of the changing world we experience, nor did he espouse *monism*, the belief that there exists only one thing that is unchanging. Rather, Parmenides understood that which exists as absolute and that which changes as having different modalities of being. According to Parmenides, true change is only possible, if something can come from nothing. But because something from nothing is impossible, change must be illusory. Thus, we can trust only what is unchanging. For him, genuine conviction cannot be found by focusing on that which changes but, rather, on what is unchanging, deathless, whole, uniform, and perfect. This unchanging thing, Parmenides contended, need not be divine or a god. Thus, he argued for a non-theological understanding of the absolute (Palmer, 2012).

Heraclitus Communicating in puzzles that tended to support two or more understandings (Graham, 2011), Heraclitus held that life is possible and the world continues by virtue of conflict and change. Thus, the process of change is more substantial than the thing that changes. If basic material is always changing, then it does not matter what substance is primary. What is more important is to understand the process of change. Heraclitus's position on change poses an epistemological paradox: how can something truly be known, if it is constantly changing?

In comparing Parmenides and Heraclitus we might consider whether existence is dependent ultimately on a thing's ability to be sensed or on its ability to be known as true (Deely, 2001).

Perspectives on material elements

Many presocratic philosophers explained the cosmos without referring to gods or extra-natural forces. They proposed different unchanging elements or principles that persist and rearrange to generate the changing world of appearances (Berryman, 2010). Wondering how the physical world came into existence, some argued for a single material element or principle from which all things come and through which things persist despite changes (Cavendish, 1964; Curd, 2011). Heraclitus, for example, proposed that this fundamental principle is fire-like.

Thales The first ancient Greek credited with explaining material elements naturalistically, Thales (c. 624–545 BCE), was interested in what lay behind the diversity of nature's appearance. He worked out the distinction between the plural and changeable nature of the world using notions of origin and immutability (Finkelberg, 1993). He initiated a tradition of inquiry that identified unchanging root elements and first principles of nature (*archai*). For Thales, "the first principle, original form, and final destiny" of all natural objects is water (Deely, 2001, p. 22). This one primary cause, water, underlying the diversity of changing existence, is not susceptible to change.

Following Thales, different schools of thought developed different ideas about what principles underpin the diversity of the world and bring it into existence.

Anaximander A student of Thales, Anaximander (c. 610–546 BCE) proposed that an element called "apeiron" was the fundamental principle undergirding the change of the natural world. This substance was deathless and imperishable while also being unlimited, unbounded, and undefined. Apeiron is considered the origin from which everything arises and returns.

Anaximenes Arguing that the basic element of nature is air, Anaximenes (c. 580–500 BCE) claimed that things form from air through condensation and rarefaction. He considered the soul as air holding us together just as air surrounds the whole cosmos.

Anaxagoras According to Anaxagoras (c. 500–428 BCE), the world comes into being by way of a seed that contains a bit of everything (e.g., metal, flesh, the bright and the dark), thus potentially becoming anything. The seed is eternal and always a mixture (Curd, 2008). Things are not created or destroyed; rather, basic ingredients in the mixture shift and separate in different proportions to form the diversity of things in the world.

However, Anaxagoras set apart *nous* (mind) from everything else. Mind sets things in motion, actively controlling and organizing. Anaxagoras stated:

All other things have a portion of everything, but Mind is infinite and self-ruled, and is mixed with nothing but is all alone by itself . . . For it is the finest of all things and the purest, it has all knowledge about everything and the greatest power; and mind controls all things, both the greater and the smaller, that have life. (DK 503, Kirk & Raven, 1957, pp. 372–373)

Thus, mind is separate from matter; although it is a cosmic force, it is not identified as a divine principle or god (Curd, 2008).

Empedocles In contrast to those presocratics who proposed one element at the origin of things that exist, Empedocles (c. 495/492–c. 432 BCE) contended that existence originates from four: earth, air, fire, and water. These basic elements blend by way of Love while being driven apart by Strife. The alternating forces of Strife and Love precipitate not creation or destruction but change and motion in the natural world. Empedocles was interested not only in the physical nature of existence but also in the human soul, including human behaviour in religious contexts, the care of the soul, and appropriate behaviour with respect to the gods (Curd, 2011).

Democritus Also trying to account for change and the essential stability of existence, Democritus (c. 460–c. 385/362 BCE) argued that there are unchanging indivisible particles (Cavendish, 1964). An infinite number of perfectly solid atoms (from the

Greek word *atomos* meaning indivisible) of different shapes and sizes move about in infinite void, combining and repelling one another in a whirling motion that forms *kosmoi* or worlds (Berryman, 2010). For Democritus, everything that we experience in the world, including thought, is caused by the physical movement of these atoms; this belief is known as *atomism*. He did not explain change itself, but instead recast the problem as change of place.

Mathematical perspective

The presocratic philosopher associated with the mathematical perspective is **Pythagoras** (c. 570–c. 495/490 BCE). But the popular notion of Pythagoras as a master mathematician is considered a distortion and his contributions to mathematical knowledge and the Pythagorean Theorem are dubious (Huffman, 2011). The current consensus is that in his society he was regarded as an expert on the fate of the soul after death, a wonder-worker thought to have journeyed to the underworld, and a charismatic figure who gathered together a community with a disciplined way of life. Women joined this community as equal partners to men in reasoning. One female Pythagorean, Theano (n.d.), apparently not only studied mathematics but contributed to medicine and physics (Waithe, 1987).

The Pythagoreans proposed an immortal yet material soul able to move into different bodies across lifetimes. Although there is continued debate about it, some scholars regard the Pythagoreans as asserting that the soul is the seat of emotions and perception but not intellect (Curd, 2011; Huffman, 2011). The soul is the part of us that feels pleasure and pain and forms desires based on those feelings. The intellect is distinguished by its capacity to govern the desires of the soul.

Uniting cosmological, religious, and mathematical views, the Pythagoreans made personal salvation a philosophical matter (Cavendish, 1964). In a cosmos where everything is interrelated, harmony, balance, and reason become the aims of life. The human soul was considered a harmony that copied that of the cosmos.

A more traditional interpretation of the Pythagoreans deals with how they understood the universe, including human nature, health, and religion, as governed by mathematical principles and numbers. Number "was a guide to self-inquiry and the transformed experience of being, rather than a principle for organizing the data of experience and articulating the analytic and combinatory functions of the intellect" (Needleman, 1982, p. 51). In this way the Pythagoreans regarded everything, even concepts and opinions, as numbers that have position in the universe and owe their reality to the way they imitate numbers.

Mathematics allows for a definite explanation, one that is not open to further interpretation. This quest for mathematical precision and rational intelligibility motivated the work of early modern scientists such as **Johannes Kepler** (1571–1630) and Galileo. But unlike them, for the Pythagoreans, the development of one's whole way of being in the world, including mental, moral, and physical being, was necessary to know the cosmos.

Knowledge through numbers is a modern concept, but for the Pythagoreans, we cannot know something unless we become similar to it (Needleman, 1982). The Pythagoreans, who were oriented toward symbolic understanding, came to be known in the modern era as rationalists, insisting on intelligibility and closure in explanation.

Biological perspective

Within the biological perspective are physician-scholars from the fifth and fourth centuries BCE, known as the Hippocratics, after **Hippocrates** (c. 460–370 BCE). He sometimes is included with the presocratics because of his naturalistic explanations. The Hippocratics relied on naturalistic thought to develop their treatises, such as the *Hippocratic Oath*, which is a set of ethical principles for the conduct of medicine. The Oath's primary principle is that healers should "do no harm."

The Hippocratics held that all illness has natural not supernatural or spiritual causes. Illness is the result of an imbalance of the basic elements, identified by Empedocles, that comprise everything in nature – earth, air, fire, and water. For the Hippocratics, health results from a proper balance of these elements. As described below, the Roman physician and philosopher **Galen** (c. 130–210) developed the theory of the four elements, which resurfaces in the Renaissance as the theory of *humours*, bodily fluids believed to determine human functioning.

Part 1 conclusion

The naturalistic, mathematical, and biological perspectives of the presocratics began a rationalist and empiricist discourse on being and becoming in contrast to earlier mythopoetic discourses that anthropomorphized physical processes. The presocratics began with questions about nature, the nature of "being," and how things change and what remains immutable. This intellectual development eventually led to questions about the nature of knowledge, how we know what we claim to know, and on what basis we can make knowledge-claims (Deely, 2001).

The key point is not that the presocratics identified one or four natural elements from which all things are formed, but that they identified natural elements at all instead of mythopoetic forces. Contrary to the explanations in the Homeric epics, the presocratics' approach was "a new kind of discourse, analytic, logical, abstract ..." (Simon, 1972, p. 391). They considered the abstract superior to the poetic, although there was not yet a wide separation between poetic and philosophical or scientific thinking (Betegh, 2006). From this point on, philosophers had to consider how humans could think in such different ways: poetically and philosophically (Simon, 1972).

Part 2 Socrates, Plato, and the Sophists

Socrates, Plato, and Aristotle are major figures in the history of Western thought. However, Socrates's and Plato's views did not go unchallenged by their contemporaries, especially by the Sophists and, as we will see in Part 3, by Aristotle. Before delving into the psychological ideas of Socrates, Plato, and the Sophists, we consider their social context.

Social context

During Plato's lifetime, wars between Athens and Sparta, another Greek city-state, resulted in the Spartans imposing governance on the Athenians. The Greeks admired warrior virtues such as courage, skill in warfare, and loyalty to the state. The "good" citizen was one who served the state and contributed to democratic debate. Issues of social concern included morality and containment of impulsivity (Simon, 1972).

As the leading city-state in this era, Athens tolerated relatively open discussion among citizens and attracted natural philosophers from other Mediterranean societies (Tell, 2007). Rather than relying on unquestioned acceptance of cultural beliefs, Athenian intellectuals were strongly inclined to actively pursue knowledge in a critical and investigative fashion. In this atmosphere of critical reflection, philosophers further developed abstract language as well as vigorous argument for moral values that could guide Athens towards political stability. The abstract and the rational came to be equated with the good and self-restraint.

Status of women

In fifth and fourth century Athens, women focused on serving their children and husbands and managing the minutiae of domestic work. Although women could occasionally hold great power within the household, usually men and women worked together in this sphere. In the public world, however, with a hierarchical system of gender roles, only men could operate effectively (Foxhall, 1989). Women could not even deal in their own property and they were excluded from civic activities discussed and taught in public places.

Scholars disagree as to the nature and extent of Plato's views on women's capacities, but overall his proposals for women's participation in society were radical for their time and ours (Agonito, 1977; Tuana, 1994). Plato held that it would benefit society for women to fully participate in social and political affairs. He pointed out that such participation could occur if women were not burdened by household chores and the care of the family. As a solution, Plato called for the dissolution of the traditional family, promoting instead a community of families, common property, and common children.

By contrast, Aristotle proposed that women are incomplete men, deficient in physical ability, sentience, and rational soul, making them necessarily subordinate to male authority. Aristotle's views on women persisted through the Middle Ages such that when Aquinas's interpretation of Aristotle was accepted by church authorities, these patriarchal views of women became part of church tradition (Agonito, 1977).

Socrates

A highly influential and controversial teacher, Socrates and his teachings are known through the writings of his pupils, the most famous being Plato. In the earliest Platonic dialogues, considered most Socratic, there is little theorizing about the nature of existence, soul, or knowledge; instead, Socrates appears most concerned with how to live life in a state of inquiry.

Unlike the presocratics, Socrates was not concerned with the nature of the physical world. Rather, his aim seems to have been to encourage people to think for themselves (Deely, 2001). He questioned taken-for-granted meaning and contemporary intellectual foundations, promoting freedom of thought. For him, the process of searching for truth was the key to virtue and happiness.

Socrates struggled with the questions of what is the good, how do we know it, and why do we wish to pursue it (Simon, 1972). He did not seek to establish the basic material of the world or fundamental principles of being nor did he aim at organizing a community of thinkers or decide on moral doctrine. Rather, he wondered at the world. For Socrates, there is a special kind of attention that brings the philosopher face-to-face with unrecognized parts of oneself. As Needleman (1982) expressed it, "beyond the appearance, lies the Question . . . the power of real philosophy lies somehow in this special power of self-interrogation" (p. 24).

Socrates was both "the Gadfly," whose persistent questioning undermined pretensions and dogmatic thinking, and "the midwife," because he assisted in the birth of new knowledge. Arguably, the *Socratic Method* (see below) began a tradition of critical inquiry that came to be institutionalized in the practices of schools and universities. After centuries, this tradition made the establishment of modern science possible (Deely, 2001).

Some historians characterize Socrates as representing a humanistic perspective. Modern defenders of democracy recall the famous political trial and death of Socrates recounted in the Platonic dialogue: *Socrates's Defence* (c. 380 BCE). However, some evidence indicates that Socrates was neither a democrat nor a humanist in the sense that we mean those terms today. Rather, he seemed most focused on cultivating critical reflection.

The value of Socrates's thought

When considering the development of philosophical and scientific knowledge, at least **three points** about Socrates are noteworthy:

- Socrates developed what is known as the *Socratic Method* or Socratic dialogue. This method of inquiry is a conversational process of examining fundamental puzzles, contradictions, and absurdities obscured by common understanding (Juhasz, 1971).
- For Socrates, inquiry is a way of being in the world that makes life valuable. Plato represents Socrates as saying:

  I tell you that to let no day pass without discussing goodness and all the other subjects about which you hear me talking and examining both myself and others is really the very best thing that [one] can do, and that life without this sort of examination is not worth living. (*Socrates's Defence*, 38a, Hamilton & Cairns, 1961, p. 23)

- Like the Sophists, Socrates was skeptical about ultimate claims to knowledge. Instead, he emphasized inquiry, wisdom as skill, the uniqueness of each individual's immortal soul, and personal moral capacity.

Plato

Because Socrates encouraged questioning the most fundamental beliefs, he was seen as a threat to society. In 399 BCE he was given a choice to either leave Athens or drink poisonous hemlock; he chose to remain and die. Subsequently Plato left disgusted with Athens.

Travelling throughout the Mediterranean, he pursued his interests in mathematics and philosophy. Twelve years later Plato returned to Athens and established the Academy where he gave lectures. This school prospered for over 900 years, when it was shut down by a

Roman emperor in the interest of promoting Christianity. The transition from antiquity to the Middle Ages is often marked by this event.

After describing Plato's concept of dialogue and theory of ideas, including his famous allegory of the cave, we discuss his notions about psychological phenomena and ethical and social relations.

Dialogue and the forms

Although Plato was a writer, he distrusted the written word's ability to convey truth. Along with Socrates and the presocratics, he believed that "philosophy can be entrusted to the spoken word alone, and cannot be written down" (Deely, 2001, p. 55). Within Plato's Academy, teachings were communicated through dialogues, which were written down only to be conveyed to the extramural community.

Central to dialogue is dialectic, which is "a method of questioning and answering – dividing, defining, categorizing, and abstracting . . ." (Simon, 1972, p. 6). Plato contributed to developing the notion of dialectic in dialogue. This pursuit of definitions facilitated making abstractions. These idealizations are referred to as forms or ideas (sometimes capitalized as "Forms" and "Ideas" to convey their exalted status).

Not to be confused with the modern notion of ideas that are cognitive states, the forms stimulate philosophical inquiry and understanding, but they are more than language. Like Heraclitus and Parmenides, Plato thought that what we are certain of is that which is stable and perfect. Thus, there must be a realm of stable perfect forms beyond the fleeting sensory world (Deely, 2001).

The body belongs to the world of imperfection and change, but the soul has an affinity for the perfect world of forms. The forms exist apart from the world in that they only can be known through the mind. They are considered more real than the objects of the ordinary world, because they are unchanging universals and are a source for the existence of things sensed in the ordinary world.

Plato believed the distinctive work of the philosopher was to know the realm of forms (Kraut, 2008). Yet Plato did not present a system of doctrines. Rather, his readers are inspired to think and contribute to defining the forms. Sometimes the forms are described simply as hypotheses in need of exploration.

There are a number of lingering questions stimulated by Plato's theory of forms: are there forms of everything? How are forms and ordinary objects related? Are forms thoughts? Plato seems to have been aware of these problems, although he did not provide solutions.

The allegory of the cave The allegory or analogy of the cave, from Plato's work *The Republic* (c. 380 BCE), gives a narrative version of the theory of forms. He suggests picturing people living in a cave open to the light outside, but their legs and necks have been bound since childhood, so they are unable to move or turn towards this light. Also, there is light from a fire that burns at a distance behind them.

Between these people and the fire there is a road with a low wall. Other people living in the cave travel along this road. Like a puppet show, shadows of the people and the objects they carry are cast onto the wall that the bound people see. The prisoners name the shadows as if they were the objects themselves and come to see the shadows as reality.

Plato then suggests imagining the prisoners released from such fetters. When turning towards the road, they would be dazzled by the firelight. And if told that what they saw before was shadowy illusion and the objects and people on the road are more real, the prisoners might flee the blinding light and return to the shadows that are less painful to see and so seem clearer.

Moreover, if the prisoners went out of the cave and into the sunlight, they would find this experience even more painful. Blinded by the light, they would not be able to see what is real outside the cave. However, after a time, they would come to see this world and eventually the sun itself, understanding this reality as the cause of all the things they had seen before. Nevertheless, in returning to the cave, now unaccustomed to the dark, they would stumble and be ridiculed for being uninterested in the rewards and honours that the prisoners sought within the cave.

Plato explained:

The ascent and the contemplation of the things above is the soul's ascension to the intelligible region ... the last thing to be seen and hardly seen is the idea of good, and that when seen it must needs point us to the conclusion that this is indeed the cause for all things of all that is right and beautiful ... those who have attained to this height are not willing to occupy themselves with the affairs of men, but their souls ever feel the upward urge and the yearning for that sojourn above. (*Republic*, VII, 517 b–d, Hamilton & Cairns, 1961, pp. 749–750)

In sum, Plato believed that for most people mind and soul are imprisoned by the senses. Objects observed in the natural world are approximations of invisible perfect forms that endure eternally. Because individuals have encountered the forms in previous lives, they are innately capable of recognizing sensory information. Through dialogical inquiry into the definitions of things there is a remembering. But the least significant aspect of reality is one's perception of specific objects. Truer are the specific objects themselves, while the truest nature of reality is found outside the cave beyond the world of sensible objects in the intelligible realm.

For Plato, as for Parmenides, genuine knowledge derives from contemplation, not observation or practice. The form of the good is the dazzling sun outside the cave. Nevertheless, the usefulness of sensory knowledge is not excluded; for example, Plato made astronomical observations to theorize about the cosmos (Lindberg, 1992).

> **Small-group discussion.** Imagine how it might or might not be possible to leave Plato's cave. Plato emphasizes the importance of education for transcending observation of imperfect natural objects and rationally grasping the underlying principles of reality. What do you think of the claim that the allegory conveys an elitist view of education and society?

Psychological functions

In general, the notion of "soul" for Greeks of the fifth century is not only that which distinguishes the animate from the inanimate and the living from the dead. It is also responsible for mental and psychological functions including planning, perception, practical thinking, intense emotional states, and moral characteristics, including the capacity for courage, temperance, and justice (Lorenz, 2009). The soul acts and can be acted upon; it is subject to desire. Soul is distinct from body, allowing for the continued existence of the person after death but with something of one's personal identity associated with it.

Plato believed that just as the world soul governs the universe, the human soul should govern one's actions. One should be as intelligently ordered and balanced as the universe. Mind, for Plato, is a dimension of the soul (Kirk & Raven, 1957). Because of a love of beauty, the mind has an impulse to know, which moves the soul to contemplate truth. Through contemplating the natural world and the perfection and harmony in the cosmos one's soul is transformed (Hamilton & Cairns, 1961). Consequently, such reflection facilitates living an ethical life in human society.

For Plato, the psyche has **three parts** that sometimes conflict and sometimes cooperate (Simon, 1972):

- The rational psyche comes to know the abstract and timeless.
- The appetitive psyche apprehends ever-changing sensory objects and desires.
- Conflict develops between the rational and the appetitive, with each trying to gain the support of the affective psyche.

Plato also envisioned a relationship between the psyche and the organization of the city-state (*polis*).

For Plato, understandings of mind, madness, and remedy are interrelated. He regarded madness with a mixture of fear and awe (Simon, 1973). In the Platonic dialogue, *Phaedrus*, Socrates speaks of the blessings of madness, including prophesy, inspiration, mad love, and the importance of ritual madness. Nevertheless, irrationality and lack of virtue such as cowardice, intemperance, injustice, greed, and self-deception cause madness, and for Plato rationality is always superior (Simon, 1972).

In contrast to Homer's suggestions of eating, poetry, and music as remedies for madness, Plato advocated philosophy, that is, knowing oneself (Simon, 1972). Ignorance is a kind of evil of the soul that needs to be purified through education, advice, and reprove. Critical inquiry rids the soul of ignorance. Through cross-examination and demonstration of inconsistencies one is purged of conceit and prejudice.

Plato also argued that such dialectical inquiry promotes gentleness towards others. Thus, a society that allows philosophy to flourish brings balance and harmony to the psyche. However, philosophical inquiry, unlike the experiences of eating, poetry, and music, is a difficult and sometimes psychologically painful experience.

Ethics and social relations

Plato also is renowned for his notions of ethics and social relations. Many ancient Greek philosophers promoted a kind of warrior morality, valuing strength, courage, and action in the face of battle. However, the manic inspiration of a warrior is incompatible with rational contemplation of the forms. Plato posited that reason and reflection must dominate the aims of action and glory, just as the forms dominate the appearance of things.

In *The Republic*, Plato developed a proposal for an ideal state that eliminates excessive conflict and chaos. He allocated different capacities to different classes of people. These classes can be understood as metaphors for the structure of the psyche. The philosopher-kings correspond to the rational psyche, the guardians correspond to the affective, while the artisans and common citizens correspond to the appetitive. Harmony and balance require that each class does its job in society and that each part of the psyche does its job within the person.

Just as Plato proposed addressing madness by way of inquiry, he regarded social justice and political organization as achieved through critical reflection (Simon, 1973). As such, the health of the psyche and of the state are integrated. To access a higher moral condition we must reflect on the absolute (C. Taylor, 1989). Such reflection cultivates order, concord, and harmony in the cosmos. A good person, ruled by such contemplation, is calm, collected, self-possessed.

In modern conceptions the moral self is centred in reason. "To consider something rationally is to take a dispassionate stance towards it. It is both to see clearly what ought to be done and to be calm and self-collected and hence able to do it" (C. Taylor, 1989, p. 116).

However, in the ancient sense, to be ruled by reason is to allow one's life to be shaped by a pre-existent rational order. We come to know and love this order in contemplating the forms. This kind of reason is not the rationality of the modern age in that reason is found, not made, by thinking. Perhaps this is why, as we will see, for the Romantics (Chapter 3), psycho-analysts (Chapter 9), and postmodernists (Chapter 12), a moral take on reason is untenable.

Plato's ideal society was never realized, but he did establish the Academy. Moreover, he challenged generations of thinkers to consider practical but highly important issues, such as, what do we mean by reality and how should we construct a just society. Although Plato did not hold democratic views on education, he was one of the first Westerners to argue for its importance in the flourishing of the individual and the state (Deely, 2001).

The value of Plato's thought

Plato is considered a giant in Western intellectual history. Sometimes mistaken as an idealist, he struggled against the mythopoetic to discover the abstract and its place in understanding (Simon, 1972). As described below, **Plotinus** (204–270 CE) in late antiquity reinterpreted Plato's views, later known as Neoplatonism, which significantly influenced the formation of Christianity and Islam and the development of Judaism. Also, Plato's work was rediscovered during the Renaissance, becoming the basis for criticisms of medieval interpretations of Aristotle.

Arguably, Plato's writings are important for the history of science and psychological understanding in **three ways**:

- Plato advanced the presocratic way of thinking about the natural world in terms of what, how, and why the natural world exists; what and how we know about the natural world; and how to explain it (Melling, 1987).
- He continued to narrow the understanding of soul as cognitive and intellectual (Lorenz, 2009).
- Plato's theory of forms is significant for the history of science, because it emphasizes the importance of universal concepts and mathematical reasoning adopted from the Pythagoreans.

In addition, there are **three ways** in which Plato's notions about the natural world and the cosmos are important for the history and philosophy of psychology (D. N. Robinson, 1995):

- Plato agreed that knowledge begins with observation of imperfect natural objects, but this level of knowing is insufficient, because genuine knowledge entails rational understanding of the underlying principles of reality. Since Plato's day, natural philosophers and scientists have recognized the need to identify the causes and meanings behind mere observations.
- Plato argued that knowledge is innate, can be attained through introspection, and comes from remembering the experiences that the soul has had before entering the body. Accordingly, if you were inclined to find counterparts of Plato's notions in Psychology, you might perceive him as supporting *nativism* (i.e., innate to one's natural constitution) and search for contemporary theories in Psychology that are nativist (e.g., linguist **Noam Chomsky's** [b. 1928] account of language acquisition – see Chapter 7). But this would be a presentist historical interpretation.
- Plato's psychological thought is sometimes viewed as a precedent for a theory of internal conflict (Simon, 1973). But what ancient Greeks like Plato meant in their epoch about human action and what modern psychologists mean are not equivalent (Danziger, 1997a).

Counterpoint: the Sophists' relativism

While Plato championed faith in the ultimate reality of reason, the Sophists proposed a much more instrumental role for reason. Renowned for being able to make the weaker argument the stronger, the Sophists were a group of teachers who, for a price, taught rhetoric, grammar, and logic, including debating skills necessary for participation in Athenian democracy. They educated the rising middle class of traders and craftspeople to engage in public debate and, thereby, participate in political life. The Sophists emphasized how convincing discourse, not an idea's validity, determined whether or not the idea was publicly accepted. Thus, for them, persuasion, not knowledge, was the aim of argument.

Socrates and Plato rejected the Sophists' pursuit of worldly success, ridiculing them as "prostitutes of wisdom" (Deely, 2001, p. 43). On this view, the Sophists commercialized the pursuit of knowledge and degraded notions of virtue by failing to connect what was taught with how they lived their lives. Alternatively, the attainment of a successful life in the form of material goods, bodily and mental health, and political status is not inimical to communion with eternal forms (Cavendish, 1964).

In his dialogue, *Sophist*, Plato depicted a nocturnal hunt to snare and kill the Sophists, as if in pursuit of exterminating the Sophists' negation of eternal truths. However, the hunted Sophist was not simply the dark shadow of the "true" philosopher, but from a postmodern perspective, an almost allegorical figure for what Platonic philosophers found unthinkable, namely, non-being, paradox, difference, and multiple plausible interpretations of reality. The Sophists' interest in persuasion led to analysis of words and the confusions of common speech and to demonstrating what can and cannot be done with language (Cavendish, 1964).

Two implications for psychological thought seem to follow from the Sophists' views:

- There are no objective, universal truths, because there are no absolute first principles. Thus, truth is relative not absolute. Postmodern psychologists in the late twentieth century adopted a similar viewpoint (see Chapter 12).

- Sensory information is the only reliable source of knowledge, so we should study life as it is lived and focus on observable phenomena. Natural-science psychologists take a similar empiricist stance.

Part 2 conclusion

Socrates relentlessly practised freedom of thought and pursuit of the truth, which, for him, unlocked the doors of virtue. He interrogated taken-for-granted meanings and his society's intellectual foundations. The Socratic method of inquiry became highly influential not only in ancient Greece but also among later generations of scholars who studied philosophical and scientific matters.

Plato addressed complex matters of ontology, epistemology, and moral and social philosophy from a standpoint that privileged abstract discourse about knowledge. Moreover, Plato's standpoint that knowledge is innate, emanates from remembering the soul's prior experiences, and is attainable by practising introspection. These points became the basis for the philosophical position of rationalism, which profoundly affected Western thought for millennia.

Plato's psychological ideas were steeped in the language of abstraction. By contrast, his contemporaries, the Sophists, promoted the practical art of persuasion. In addition, the Sophists shared with Socrates skepticism about ultimate claims to knowledge.

Part 3   Aristotle

Aristotle's influence on Western culture also is very significant. Since the Middle Ages, there has been a long and intense tradition of reading and commenting on his work. As such, interpretations of even the most basic theses are controversial (Shields, 2011). With many linguistic translations of Aristotle, there also are many distinct Aristotelian influences. In some respects, current philosophy of mind and cognitive science look to Aristotle for affinities, although the similarity is debatable. There also has been renewed interest and much debate over Aristotle's meaning in Psychology (Green, 1998).

After providing a brief background, we introduce Aristotle's position on natural philosophy, the nature of change, causation, epistemology, and methodical inquiry. Then we discuss his views on ethics and politics, and psychological capacities.

Background

Aristotle's life can be divided into two periods (Shields, 2011). From age 17, for two decades, he was a member of Plato's Academy. Then, after Plato's death and a period of travel and study, Aristotle founded his own Athenian school, the Lyceum, in 334 BCE. There he developed his thought and his central psychological work *De Anima*. In this work Aristotle considers perception and thinking and in what ways psychological states might be considered material states.

Aristotle distinguished himself from the presocratics as well as from Socrates and Plato by developing a systematic method of observation and direct study of nature. In the idealized

Figure 2.1 In their contrasting gestures Plato and Aristotle at the School of Athens express their different orientations to inquiry into nature

depiction of the School of Athens in Figure 2.1, Plato, left centre, points up to the heavens, reflecting his theory of abstract forms, while Aristotle, right centre, gestures to earth, the sensory foundations of his theory of knowledge.

Throughout his career Aristotle was interested in the function of living things and made biology, instead of mathematics or physics, a fundamental framework of understanding. Thus, at the Lyceum, study of human and animal biological activities informed ways of making sense of human nature. But Aristotle also studied astronomy, geology, meteorology, and chemical substances (Lindberg, 1992).

Basic positions on nature, human nature, and inquiry

Consider again the opposing positions of Heraclites and Parmenides on the nature of reality and change. Aristotle agreed with Parmenides that the unchanging aspects of reality can be apprehended intellectually. But he also agreed with Heraclitus that change is real and reality is found in the sensible world, not beyond it (Deely, 2001).

Many commentators regard Aristotle as developing a *unitary* system of physical, psychological, and moral knowledge, being concerned with the *totality* of human knowledge from the perspective of its value to human life. As such, his goal was to understand essences or universal principles as they exist in nature. Aristotle criticized Plato for "putting mathematics in the place of philosophy" (Deely, 2001, p. 60).

Causation

Aristotle explained change in terms of growth and development as well as existence and ceasing to be. He discerned **four causes** upon which living beings depend:

- Matter: material cause refers to the concrete matter out of which a natural object is formed (e.g., clay vs. glass).
- Form: formal cause makes the object one thing and not another (e.g., a vase vs. a plate).
- Agent: efficient cause refers to that which generates an object and can produce transformation (e.g., a potter at her wheel vs. a glassblower with a pipe)
- Purpose: final cause refers to the ultimate *purpose* or function of the natural object. (In this context "final" does not mean "last.")

The definition of "cause" has changed historically. Modern scientists tend to concentrate on material and efficient causes, dismissing the purposive final cause as unscientific. But, by final cause, Aristotle did not mean there was a force external to the object that caused it to be; rather, final cause refers to a goal-oriented pattern of growth and development.

For example, the purpose of an acorn is to become an oak tree. Later, theological interpretations of *teleology* (i.e., an idealistic grand design or purpose attributed to nature) confused this notion of final cause with notions of divine intervention. Accordingly, modern scientists abandoned teleology when they studied natural objects (Deely, 2001).

Hylomorphism

Aristotle addressed not only issues of natural philosophy but also of *metaphysics*, meaning the study of ultimate reality existing beyond the appearances of the material world. He attempted to sidestep the two extreme positions: transcendent explanations (e.g., Plato's world of forms) and reductionistic explanations for natural phenomena (e.g., Democritus's atoms).

Accordingly, in answer to the question, "Of what are natural things made?" Aristotle argued that natural objects comprise the unity of matter (*hulê*) and form (*morphê*), hence *hylomorphism*. Everything that exists consists of a combination of what is potential (matter) and actual (form). In the case of a human being, the body is the matter of the soul, while the soul is the form of the body (Shields, 2011).

Aristotle used the popular ancient Greek comparison: matter is imprinted with form just as a seal makes an impression on a lump of wax. But he emphasized how the wax has the potential to actualize many forms. "It is what it is not only actually but at the same time potentially. Things are *both* what they are now *and* what they could be under other circumstances. And, since circumstances are always changing, so is being" (Deely, 2001, p. 72).

Aristotle rejected the Platonic notion of an intelligible world of forms that precedes and is independent of material reality. Instead, for Aristotle, there is "prime matter" or "pure potentiality," which is within material things insofar as those things can transform into other kinds of things. Again, matter (potential) and actuality are interrelated.

Nature of change

Aristotle argued that the natural philosophers did not really explain change. Parmenides flatly denied change, Heraclitus simply affirmed it, and Democritus described it as change of place or the rearrangement of atoms.

For Aristotle, matter is the subject of change and the character that matter gains is its form. Aristotle's response to the puzzle of how things come into being and change was to consider also why they change. Aristotle used hylomorphism and the four causes in most explanations of change. In addition, he described **three kinds of change**:

- Local, referring to change of location.
- Quantity, referring to change in size.
- Quality, meaning change in form, for example, from a green immature pear to a yellow ripe one.

Because of his biological orientation Aristotle tended to emphasize qualitative rather than quantitative change (Lindberg, 1992).

Epistemology

Some current commentators schematize Aristotle's understanding of knowing into **four steps**:

- Sensory experience – acquiring isolated experiences.
- Common sense – synthesizing experience from all the senses.
- Passive reason – using meaningful, synthesized experience in everyday life.
- Active reason – abstracting first principles from meaningful, synthesized experience.

The process of acquiring knowledge begins with sensory experience. Memory, which is the consequence of repeated sensory experience, activates the insight of the observer who then is able to discern universal principles underlying the objects observed. However, for knowledge to be considered true it needs to be expressed in such a way that it can be demonstrated deductively (Lindberg, 1992). But Aristotle's epistemology should be understood in the context of how he conceived causation, hylomorphism, and the nature of change.

Scientific method

Aristotle seems to have invented the study of logic. He "rightly boasted that no one before him had attempted to make explicit and systematic the rules and procedures which govern rational thought" (Barnes, 1987, p. 23). But he did not use the term "logic" to describe those "relatively context-independent principles . . . of organized investigation and presentation" that came to be known as "logic" (Deely, 2001, p. 87). Rather, he dealt with forms of reasoning and their relation to determining truth about the world.

For Aristotle, logic is not what *is* but what is *thought* to be; therefore, it is a tool for deriving truth. Later in the Aristotelian tradition these teachings were collected in the *Organon* or *Instrument of All Rational Discourse*. In the medieval era, the Latin version of this work was studied as an introduction to philosophy and considered important to all subjects including physics, mathematics, metaphysics, ethics, and art.

Psychological capacities

In *De Anima*, Aristotle treated psychology as a science of the soul. However, by "soul" he meant an animating principle of life. Dependent on the presence of physical parts but not itself material, soul is a principle of nature that accounts for change and rest in living bodies. Thus, the study of the soul comprises all living things, not just those things with an intellect.

Aristotle regarded the study of the soul as a science, because psychological states (e.g., anger or sadness) involve the body. Yet, insofar as the soul also involves mind or intellect and there is no mental substance to intellect, the soul is not entirely describable in physical terms (Green, 1998). Thus, psychological subjects are not completely within the purview of the natural philosopher or scientist. Aristotle puzzled about whether there can be one method for investigating psychological topics; if many methods are required, he foresaw there would be conflicts about how best to proceed (Shields, 2011).

Study of the soul, for Aristotle, involves the soul's capacities: nutrition, perception, and reasoning. The capacity for nutrition is shared with all living beings; animals have the capacity for nutrition and perception, while humans have all three capacities. Imagination is integrated with all of these capacities, but desire is a distinct capacity of soul that initiates movement and plays a role in purposive behaviour (Shields, 2011). However, Aristotle did not consider the soul a sum of different capacities but as an integrated unity.

What distinguishes human beings as animals is the capacity for "active reason" that enables abstract thinking, contemplation, and the development of universal principles. Active reason is distinct from mere passive reason insofar as a person organizes sensory impressions. Thus, to be a human animal is to be a rational animal. It is distinctly human to desire to know and understand.

Regarding social relations, for Aristotle, everything aims at the good or aims to flourish, and eudaemonia (i.e., the state of flourishing) is inextricably tied to ethical obligations. Being virtuous and wise makes it possible to live fully, to flourish, and be happy. Nevertheless, factors that contribute to the possibility of being virtuous are often outside of one's control. Thus, virtue and happiness depend on a kind of moral luck, making virtue more tenuous and fragile than commonly assumed (Nussbaum, 1986).

In his work *Nicomachean Ethics*, Aristotle inspired what is known today as "virtue ethics" (Hursthouse, 1999). According to this approach, the development of moral character, not consequences or duty, makes people well disposed towards others and able to contribute to the common good. The complex and changeable nature of human relationships requires neither calculation nor obedience to rules, but rather a civil discourse of negotiation and compromise among equals.

Part 3 conclusion

When considering the value of Aristotle's thought, his importance as a foundational figure in the history of Western philosophy, science, and Psychology cannot be exaggerated. Taking a rather different path to explaining knowledge of nature than Plato did, Aristotle described the acquisition of knowledge as proceeding from sensory impressions to the operation of active reason and discernment of principles that underlie reality.

He proposed a dialectical relationship between the matter and form of natural objects and explained how such objects change. Aristotle particularly was concerned with causes of natural objects, a standpoint that proved enduring in Western thought. Central to the history of science is his development of logic as a tool for studying nature, generating explanations, and determining knowledge.

Psychologically speaking, Aristotle did not address directly such modern questions as the nature of consciousness nor did he focus on the brain, which he regarded as a relatively useless organ. Rather, he concentrated on how the psyche activates bodily sensations, movement, growth, reproduction, and reasoning. In the medieval era Aristotle's hierarchy of capacities of the psyche was known as "the great chain of being" with levels of soul indicating closeness to God and abstraction from matter.

Some authors in Psychology in a presentist spirit have claimed that Aristotle greatly influenced not only the development of psychological ideas but also Psychology itself. However, Aristotle's notions and those of modern psychologists are quite different, because he studied psychological phenomena in terms of his own culture and language 2,400 years ago. Three dubious claims are:

- Aristotle believed that humans have the potential to become more actual through reason or contemplation. Some compare this position to the self-actualization concepts of **Carl Jung** (1875–1961), **Abraham Maslow** (1908–1970), and **Carl Rogers** (1902–1987). But Aristotle's notion of actuality and modern psychologists' notion of actualization are not equivalent.
- Aristotle studied many topics common in modern Psychology, including sensation, sleep, dreams, memory, emotions, and geriatrics. In fact, his *laws of association* (i.e., similarity, contiguity, and contingency) are regarded as the basis for twentieth-century learning theory; the assumption is that objects or ideas that are similar, contiguous in time or space, or contingently related as apparent cause and effect are learned more easily. However, Aristotle studied these topics as an ancient Greek not a modern psychologist.
- Aristotle's view of human behaviour motivated by desire and guided by reason seems to anticipate Freud's concept of unconscious drives tempered by the ego's *reality principle* (i.e., the ego function that regulates one's attempts to balance satisfying basic human drives with interpersonal and societal demands). But Aristotle's and Freud's concepts convey distinct meanings within different social-historical contexts.

On the other hand, the scientific method that we know today *indirectly* relies on two contributions from Aristotle: (1) the logical processes of induction and deduction; (2) the methodological procedures of observation, classification, and distinction of inanimate and animate nature.

Part 4   The Roman Empire and Hellenistic civilization

After Aristotle Hellenistic philosophy flourished. By 146 BCE, as the golden age of Greece and Hellenistic civilization faded, Greece came under the military and legal control of Rome. Nevertheless, natural philosophy did not become dormant. Rather, the Romans integrated Greek philosophy into their own Latin intellectual culture, with Greek becoming the language of learning. However, with the Roman influence, scientific activity shifted from theory to technical application. Therapeutic philosophies became popular as interest focused on practical considerations of life.

Besides assimilating Greek culture, beginning in the first century CE, the Roman Empire shifted gradually from paganism to Christianity. Plato's work was taken up, because it could readily address religious questions. In the centuries following the death of Christ, the writings of Plato were reinterpreted and later termed Neoplatonism. Study focused on ancient Greek works translated into Latin. This development meant the work of Plato dominated. Aristotle's work did not become known until much later in medieval Europe.

Social context

The Roman Empire's rise to political, economic, and cultural prominence from 27 BCE to 476 CE had profound effects on the Western world. By the end of the first century BCE the Romans had conquered Mediterranean civilizations, including the numerous Greek city-states. A historical map of the Roman Empire at the height of its power in the fourth century (see Figure 2.2) depicts the extent of its influence on and experience with culturally diverse territories as far from Rome as the Middle East, North Africa, and northwestern Europe.

Figure 2.2 This historical map shows the territory of the Roman Empire, which expanded as far as northwestern Europe, the Middle East, and North Africa

Around 334 CE the seat of the Roman Empire was moved to Byzantium, which came to be called Constantinople (now Istanbul, Turkey). In 395 the empire was divided into eastern and western parts. The eastern division was later called the Byzantine Empire, which lasted until 1453. With the centre of Roman culture in the East and a declining empire, the influence of Greek culture faded. Awareness of the contributions of the ancient Greeks to natural philosophy greatly diminished during the early Middle Ages in Europe.

Although Greece lost its prominence as a centre of scientific learning, studies of mathematics, astronomy, physics, and medicine flourished in Alexandria, Egypt. A hub of scientific activity, Alexandria was renowned for its huge library constructed in the third century BCE. A modern version of the Alexandrian library was opened in 2002.

Women were not completely absent from scientific activity during this era. As an astronomer, mathematician, philosopher, and the leader of a famous school in Alexandria, **Hypatia** (370–415 CE) contradicted Aristotle's doctrine about women's alleged inferiority and fundamental irrationality. However, her work tragically ended when she was executed by Christian monks (Dzielska, 1995).

Next we consider Roman applied science and education and the influence of therapeutic philosophies, originated by the ancient Greeks. The Romans adopted practical philosophies and technologies to deal with the social and political chaos of the early Roman era. The notion of soul during this period narrowed to mean specifically mental and psychological functions, minimizing the connection between the soul and being alive (Lorenz, 2009).

Roman applied science

The Romans specialized in technical areas rather than on the unity of knowledge or on questions of metaphysics, because technology advanced their goal of political and economic domination. The Romans developed elaborate hydraulic systems and aqueducts for transporting fresh water to their increasingly urbanized society; lead plumbing transported water for the indoor toilets of the wealthy and for public baths and fountains; they used concrete for construction; and they invented the more precise Julian calendar, which facilitated agricultural planning and production.

In this context, philosophers withdrew from abstract theorizing and from political discourse and took a stance of political neutrality towards the state. They concentrated on developing concrete, worldly philosophies about daily behaviour. Given that the Romans controlled most forms of communication, these therapeutic philosophies spread widely.

The Romans also popularized applied knowledge in the form of encyclopaedias. The most noteworthy of these was **Pliny the Elder's** (23–79 CE) *Historia Naturalis* (*Natural History*). This work comprised thirty-seven texts dealing with scientific and technological topics ranging from astronomy to zoology. Pliny mixed previous scientific contributions, such as Aristotle's, with personal suppositions, moralistic interpretations, and cultural myths. The specific points of his encyclopaedia were incorporated in the body of Western knowledge until the Renaissance.

Education

The Romans contributed to the popularization of natural philosophy in another influential way through the development of a standard educational curriculum that was intended to prepare aristocratic male youth for participation in civic life. Beginning in the sixth century, alongside the study of sacred doctrine students first studied three disciplines associated with the verbal arts – rhetoric, grammar, and logic – known as the *trivium*; next, students pursued the mathematical arts of arithmetic, geometry, astronomy, and music, known as the *quadrivium*.

These secular aspects of the standard curriculum continued until the twelfth century when new translations of Aristotle instigated the end of the liberal arts tradition (McInerny & O'Callaghan, 2010). Another innovation was the Roman introduction of "professional schools" beyond the core curriculum to prepare men for the professions of law and medicine (Lindberg, 1992).

Therapeutic philosophies: Epicurean, Cynic, Stoic, and Skeptic

The therapeutic philosophies circulating in Roman times were popularized through the work of **Marcus Tullius Cicero** (106–43 BCE), who translated and adapted Greek literature to the Roman environment (Grant, 1971). In these translations Cicero introduced new words into Latin, many of which had psychological significance; such words included (in English) "individual," "moral," "induction," "appetite," and "image."

Four Greek schools of thought flourished during the Roman era offering practical principles for governing one's life. Although each dealt with cosmological and metaphysical theory, they emphasized enhancing human conduct: *Epicureanism, Cynicism, Stoicism, and Skepticism*. These positions, originating in Greek antiquity, developed a body of knowledge that changed across time, especially in the case where original texts were lost. The dominant schools were Epicurean and Stoic.

Epicureanism

The founder of this philosophy, **Epicurus** (c. 341–270 BCE), integrated the aims of human life with a theory of knowledge and a description of the evolution of human societies, the formation of the world, and an atomistic view of existence similar to that of Democritus. Epicurus maintained a school that was open to all Athenians of both genders and all classes. The Epicureans avoided public life and politics, tending their own garden, literally and figuratively, and leaving the world to itself (Deely, 2001).

Epicurus held a materialist view of existence that did not allow for transcendent entities like Platonic forms. Thus, for him, the soul was material and, like everything else, made of atoms and void. Unlike for Plato and Aristotle, soul was a body, because soul and body affect one another and only bodies can have effects (Lorenz, 2009). Thus, all phenomena are embodied, including consciousness, thought, pleasure, and pain.

The Epicureans regarded that part of the human soul concentrated at the heart as the highest intellectual function. The heart experiences pain and pleasure directly; these sensations are not moral abstractions but an unfailing guide to what is good or bad. The goal of human life is to increase pleasure and minimize pain, leading to a healthy body and tranquil mind. Yet the rational part of the soul can have errors in judgment and lead us astray (Konstan, 2008).

Epicureanism should not be confused with *hedonism* (i.e., the pursuit of pleasure as the greatest good). The Epicureans viewed the goal of life as pleasure, which they thought could only be attained by avoiding extremes. But the greatest pleasure is found in simplicity and quiet contemplation, not through indulging the senses. The Epicurean position also should not be confused with individualism, because Epicureans placed the highest value on friendship.

For the Epicureans, although everything is composed of atoms moving according to definite laws, everything is not predetermined. Sometimes atoms move randomly and swerve, resulting in uncaused phenomena (Konstan, 2008). This notion of natural events having no causal connection with other natural events allows for human choice and free will (Deely, 2001).

With the disintegration of the Roman Empire, in the succeeding Latin Age, Epicurean philosophy waned, whereas Stoic teachings became central to Latin thought especially through the work of **Augustine** (354–430 CE) and Neoplatonic philosophers.

Cynicism

A less dominant school, the Cynics believed one should retreat from corrupt society and live close to nature. They held that by reducing the needs of the body to a bare minimum the mind gained maximum freedom. The Cynic philosophy of ancient times differs from the modern notion of "cynical" whereby a person is distrustful, scornful, and jaded.

Diogenes the Cynic

(c. 412–323 BCE) lived an ascetic life, giving up every possession and desire for wealth, power, health, and fame. Nevertheless, he became famous in his homelessness. When **Alexander the Great** (356–323 BCE) visited him, the story goes, Alexander offered him any favour. Diogenes simply asked Alexander to step aside, because he was blocking the sun. Diogenes promised that his philosophy would cure people of being foolish, wicked, and excessive (Tell, 2007). Later his thoughts were absorbed into Stoicism.

Stoicism

Both Epicureans and the Stoics adopted the idea that soul is corporeal. However, an early Stoic philosopher in Rome, Epictetus (60–120 CE), argued that it did not matter if things were made of atoms, fire, or water; all that was important was how to endure.

The Stoics separated the concept of soul from the general notion of animation (Lorenz, 2009). The soul does not animate things as much as it thinks and assents, positioning itself correctly in the cosmos so that one participates in the divine order and can justify the divinity within (Deely, 2001). The soul can think, plan, decide and command. In this way we become self-sufficient and free.

The Stoics upheld a philosophy of life, physical existence, causal determinism, logic, and ethics, but they are renowned for their valuing of emotional calm. They held that fear, envy, or passionate love is due to false judgment (Baltzly, 2010). A sage would not be swept away by excessive emotion. Happiness requires moderation but not elimination of desire.

Everyone seeks to be happy and flourish in life. The Stoics believed that we achieve these aspirations by following our original impulse toward what is appropriate. What is most appropriate or suitable is not what is pleasurable, but the perfection of our rational nature and association with things for which we feel affection. The pursuit of order, reason, and intelligibility leads to happiness. For the Stoics, ultimately, the way in which one strives for satisfaction is of greater value than the actual attainment of one's desires.

The Stoics held that all thought is subject to laws of logic. What makes an argument valid or invalid does not depend on the will, but is part of the natural order of the universe (Deely, 2001). Unlike Aristotle's notion of logic being a tool for arriving at truth, the Stoics believed that logic was worthy of study in itself. The argument over whether logic is a science per se or an instrument in the service of science continued throughout the Middle Ages.

To the call for simplicity of life echoed by all the therapeutic philosophies, the Stoics added that virtue consists of accepting one's station in life, performing one's duties loyally, and accepting nature's plan. Thus, they encouraged engagement in, not retreat from, society.

Skepticism

The skeptical way of thinking has been present from ancient Greece to the postmodern era (Vogt, 2010). In the Greco-Roman world, Pyrrho (c. 365–275 BCE) was one of the sources of skepticism. Other influences on skeptical thought originate in Plato's Academy, extending Socrates's realization that it is wise to question what one thinks one knows. Like the Sophists, the Skeptics realized it is possible to argue one way convincingly and, the next day, to argue against that proposition in an equally compelling way.

The Skeptics' basic argument is: because we cannot pin down the nature of things, nothing is known for certain, so assert nothing; in this way, without judgment, there is no anxiety. But, for the Skeptic, we cannot even be certain of uncertainty. If nothing is known, then any statement is self-refuting or self-contradictory (Vogt, 2010).

What is most central to Skepticism is suspension of judgment. We can act, the Skeptic explains, based on what seems convincing, but we cannot be sure it is true. Thus, non-assertion and an open attitude are best. In the end, "since certainty is unattainable, the wise man [sic] will seek not truth but tranquillity of life" (Deely, 2001, p. 99).

Skepticism influenced philosophers of the Middle Ages. Although Augustine, for example, did not become a Skeptic, he used skeptical thought in a way that resembles scientific thinking (Vogt, 2010). For example, he contended although we might not be able to find an objection to a current claim to knowledge, new arguments are continually being formed; therefore, it is best to keep an open mind.

Neoplatonism

Plotinus is a central figure in developing interpretations of Plato that were termed Neoplatonism by nineteenth-century historians. With cultural shifts and the prominence of religious concerns in the centuries before and after Christ, Plato's writings were taken up for their metaphysical teachings; thus, a new phase of understanding Plato seemed to develop (Gerson, 1996).

For Plotinus, the universe emanates from "the One" or "the Good" in diminishing degrees of perfection towards the physical or sensible realm, but then slowly can return by degrees to the One. The Good is called "the One," but ultimately it is indescribable and grasped indirectly. The One is self-caused and causes the being of everything, because everything depends on it for existence. It is the simplest basic principle, needing no explanation. As such, it can ground the explanation of everything else. Although it is not conceived as a material element, the explanatory power of the One is similar to the four basic elements posited in the presocratic tradition (Gerson, 1996).

Along with the One, Intellect and Soul are the basic principles of reality. Intellect provides intelligibility; thus, the Platonic forms find their home in the Intellect. Knowing the essence of things is considered the highest principle of life. The third principle, Soul, is the principle of desire.

In *Ennead IV*, Plotinus ([250] 1991) also described psychological phenomena. A person is a thinking agent distinct from the soul and body, who uses a body temporarily for embodied life. Because a person is subject to appetites and emotions, he or she might become conflicted. The person who chooses to act only on appetite and emotion is choosing a desire that can obstruct return to the One (Gerson, 1996). For Plotinus, it is best to identify with activity closer to the One (i.e., Intellect), because the beauty and delight we experience in forms and in the physical realm derives from the One.

Neoplatonic thinking surfaces across Western thought especially in the concepts of Augustine and **Thomas Aquinas** (1225–1274) and in the mystical writings of **Hildegard von Bingen** (1098–1179), and the work of scientist-philosopher **Blaise Pascal** (1623–1662). The idea of going forth from and then returning to God through the Saviour became central to Christianity. Moreover, in their formative periods Judaism, Christianity, and Islam looked to ancient Greek philosophy for language and arguments to express their theologies. Above all, they relied on Plato, for whom Plotinus was their main source of understanding (Gerson, 1996).

Augustine

A bishop in what is now Algeria, St. Augustine of Hippo facilitated the merging of Greek thought with its emphasis on rationality, empiricism, and natural processes with Judaeo-Christian traditions valuing faith, hope, and divine revelation. Augustine is considered by some commentators to be the last great classical philosopher and the first great Christian philosopher (Mendelson, 2010). His ideas and readings of the Neoplatonists had significant impact on medieval philosophy and into the early modern era.

Neoplatonic Christianity

Augustine's work *Confessions* is often hailed as the first autobiography with such developed language of inwardness, self-reflection, and first-person perspective (C. Taylor, 1989). The *Confessions* provides a concrete example of how a person can ascend from a state of isolation and alienation to the intelligible realm and then to an ultimate unity resting in God (Mendelson, 2010). Time is considered a psychological distension of eternity. The happiness we seek requires overcoming things in time, by way of the intelligible, to rest in the eternal.

Augustine described his psychological struggles and conversion to Christianity. Recalling the death of his friend, he wrote:

Within me I was carrying a tattered, bleeding soul that did not want me to carry it, yet I could find no place to lay it down. Not in pleasant countryside did it find rest, nor in shows and songs, nor in sweet-scented gardens, nor in elaborate feasts, nor in the pleasures of couch or bed, nor even in books or incantations. (Augustine, [397–401] 1997, *Confessions* IV, vii, 12)

This is a Neoplatonic notion, meaning we cannot overcome our sense of isolation by seeking unity in friendship or things we love. In the sensible realm we are separate physical bodies subject to dissolution. Unity only can be found in the One, the Good. For Augustine, God is the ultimate source of all things unfolding in stages of increasing plurality and fragmentation to the lowest realm of sensory impressions of material things.

For Augustine, as for Plotinus, it is best to focus on the intelligible order. The sensible is the external manifestation of God's ultimate rationality. What is external can absorb our attention, but the source of a good life and moral fortitude is love of the rational order of things.

Logical necessity and mathematical reasoning, for example, allow us to connect with immutable truths. Reason is distinctively human and gives us access to absolutely reliable truth (Mendelson, 2010). Thus, Augustine incites us to shift our focus from objects known to a way of knowing lit by our intellect, which allows us to see things as they truly are (Deely, 2001).

Augustine found Plato's forms intellectually satisfying, because the forms can be considered God's thoughts, eternal and essential to creation. Reading the Platonists gave Augustine rational grounds for believing in a non-physical being. Objects in the world are external realizations of an ultimate rationality. Thus, things we sense are "external expressions of God's thoughts" (C. Taylor, 1989, p. 128).

But Augustine was interested in the pursuit of wisdom, not logical analytic understanding. He sought wisdom and inquired into mysteries rather than espousing knowledge of what has been discovered (Spade, 2010). Like the Neoplatonists and therapeutic philosophers, he tried to make sense of life, which is fragile and rife with suffering, loss, and isolation.

Will

For Augustine, the sensible world is not evil, but it enables us to forget that it is only a small portion of what is real. When we forget about the larger unity of which the sensible world is a part, our will becomes attached to transitory things. This partial perspective leads to anxiety, misguided action, and moral evil. Appreciating the sensible as a sign of goodness within the context of an ultimate unity allows us to flourish and have a moral life.

In Augustine's early work he proposed that living a rational disciplined life brings about safety in an adverse and threatening world. However, in his later works he seemed to lose confidence in the power of reason to overcome attachment to the sensible world. Allegiance to community, traditions, authority, and conventional standards diverts one from the rational aspects of human will. As such, the will is powerless to overcome destiny. Only divine grace allows one to overcome the profound ignorance and difficulty that is typical of humankind.

Hence, in the end, Augustine relied on an article of Christian faith to ground his thinking on will and happiness.

The value of Augustine's thought

Augustine combined the ancient Greek notions of necessity and perfect form with scriptural notions of will, justice, and purpose. In this way he made unique contributions to ideas about belief, knowledge, psychology, the importance of will, and human history (Mendelson, 2010). One can find an emerging awareness of a psychological interior in Augustine's writing, as seen in Box 2.1.

Augustine adopted the ancient Greek notion that reason should dominate all other psychological capacities. Happiness, he proposed, is found by reorienting oneself away from the sensible world towards the intelligible, ultimately to rest in the unity of God. A hierarchy of reliable truth originates with God and works down through reason to inner sense and sense perception. Sensory awareness is furthest from the truth, being the most personal and private.

Augustine wed this standpoint with scriptural belief to form a Christian Neoplatonism that pervaded philosophy into modern times. Besides echoes of his work in the writings of Aquinas, Descartes, and Pascal, the twentieth-century philosopher **Ludwig Wittgenstein** (1889–1951) opened his *Philosophical Investigations* with a lengthy quote from Augustine. In 1999 an entire encyclopaedia devoted to Augustine was published (Fitzgerald, 1999).

Box 2.1 An emergent psychological interior

In contemporary times, one takes for granted the notion of an interior psychological space that is oneself and one's true being, but the experience of a psychological interior is specific to certain historical times and cultures (McMahon, 2008). Self-reflection and talk of private subjective experience, however, is central to psychology. To remove the notion of an inner self from psychology would strip it of most content.

It seems that Plotinus and Augustine were the first to begin developing this modern notion of identity (C. Taylor, 1989). In the *Enneads*, Plotinus suggested looking inward to know the Platonic forms and the One. Augustine demonstrated in the *Confessions* a self-reflective process of illumination. Where Plotinus turned inward to an intelligence and power that is non-local, Augustine seemed to turn inward to a place (McMahon, 2008). But there are even earlier developments of an inner dimension, when, for example, the Stoics move the source of all good from the gods to within human beings.

Also, changes in literary practices might have facilitated the development of an inner sense of self, generating more and more psychological language (Danziger, 1997b; McMahon, 2008). Instead of using awkward written scrolls, Augustine popularized the use of books in the form of bound pages (called codices) (Deely, 2001). A codex, compared to a scroll, enhances private reading, which may have facilitated the transition from oral to reading culture. With increasing use of codices, along with valuing of silent reading and private writing as spiritual exercise, reading performances in social gatherings declined.

Part 4 conclusion

In the social context of the Roman Empire where pragmatic considerations and technology were primary, Greek therapeutic philosophies flourished – Epicureanism, Cynicism, and Stoicism – that offered practical principles for governing a good life, based on simplicity and enhancing social conduct. A fourth contemporary philosophy, Skepticism, counselled suspending judgment about the certainty of knowledge.

During Roman times as Christianity emerged, Neoplatonists, principally Plotinus, reinterpreted the philosophy of Plato. Plotinus held that the basic principles of reality are the One (equivalent to Plato's the Good), Intellect, and Soul. As such, humans participate in a unity with the One.

An offspring of Neoplatonism was the philosophical psychology of Augustine who adopted the ancient Greek belief that reason should dominate all other psychological capacities. Happiness, he proposed, is found by orienting oneself away from the sensible world towards the intelligible world, ultimately to rest in the unity of the Christian God. A hierarchy of reliable truth begins with God at the apogee and descends through reason to personal sensory awareness, which is most distant from the truth. In addition, Augustine helped bring awareness of a psychological interior to the eventual forefront of Western thought.

Part 5 | Philosophy, science, and psychological thought in the Middle Ages

The notion of a "Middle Ages" in European history was introduced by fifteenth-century scholars to distinguish this era from their own time, the Renaissance, which they regarded as a rebirth of classical learning (Spade, 2010). The beginning and ending of the Middle Ages are subject to interpretation. Some historians assert that this era began with Augustine, the sack of Rome (410), or the collapse of the Roman Empire (476) and that it ended with the European invention of printing, the Lutheran Reformation (1517), or humanist scholars "discovering" ancient Greek philosophy. However, late ancient and early medieval periods overlap just as late medieval and Renaissance periods do.

As such, perhaps it is best to consider the Middle Ages as that period when "thinkers first started to measure their philosophical speculations against the requirements of Christian doctrine and as ending when this was no longer the predominant practice" (Spade, 2010, p. 3). In addition, the Middle Ages can be split into two periods: the early Middle Ages and the late or High Middle Ages, after 1000.

Early medieval thought characteristically was visionary, dominated by Neoplatonism, integrating theology and philosophy, and tending toward espousing wisdom rather than logical demonstration for a popular audience (Spade, 2010). The High Middle Ages were dominated by Aristotelianism and *Thomism* (i.e., the philosophy and theology of Thomas Aquinas) and tended towards distinguishing theology from philosophy and practising disciplined thinking and logical demonstration. As a result, philosophy became more technical and academic, less focused on the love of wisdom. During the High Middle Ages, rather than being a dark period of scientific dormancy, noteworthy scientific developments occurred (Lindberg, 1992).

Social and intellectual context

With the fall of the Roman Empire, violent invasions from non-Christian "barbarians" (i.e., foreigners) led to the destruction of large public libraries in major European cities. Europe became a collection of illiterate mini-societies organized feudally. Knowledge of the Greek language slowly disappeared and most ancient Greek texts were not available in Latin (Spade, 2010).

Nevertheless, in some monasteries, such as in Ireland, monks worked as scribes maintaining existing texts (Cahill, 1995). The rational discourse of abstract Greek philosophy was superseded by a focus on immediate sensory realities and natural mysteries, understood through elaborate myths and visual symbols, as expressed in Celtic legends and designs. Irish monasteries hosted thousands of foreign students who returned home to found institutions of learning and bookmaking throughout Europe, from Paris to Vienna and Naples.

Beginning in the eleventh century, the population and political organization increased, vernacular literature (e.g., Irish, Welsh, Anglo-Saxon, and Gothic) developed, and modern nation-states began to emerge in Western Europe. Societies also changed in response to the impact of the "Crusades." These violent expeditions to what Christians termed the "Holy Land" in and around Jerusalem indirectly generated a flow of commerce as well as transfer of scientific and philosophical knowledge from Arab civilizations to Europe.

The First Crusade in 1095 stimulated interest in translations of previously unavailable texts. By the twelfth and thirteenth centuries Latin translations of Aristotle from the Arabic became widely available in universities (Spade, 2010), and, by 1255, studying Aristotle's entire natural philosophy and metaphysics was required for graduation (Noone & Houser, 2010).

Subsequently, the travels of Marco Polo (c. 1254–c. 1324) and other international explorers enhanced trade with Asian societies. The towns and cities of Europe flourished with improved roads and abundant trade among many communities. A thriving business class, later known as the bourgeoisie, originated in this period (Barzun, 2000).

Universities and church-centred knowledge

Beginning in the sixth century, schools were associated with monasteries. Often these institutions consisted of a small group of self-governing teachers who provided curricula for boys who usually enrolled at age 13 or 14. Later, around 1050–1150, cathedral schools associated with the authority of a church bishop flourished (Spade, 2010). These were the original universities of Europe. An important cathedral school would draw students from across Europe, and the term "university" came to mean an international school that was self-governing. Women were excluded from attending universities, but later, especially in Italy, some women received university education and participated in science (Whaley, 2003).

Medieval scholars worked with the writings of Aristotle and considered Catholic doctrine in light of secular reason. Within this tradition, known as *scholasticism*, scholars practised speculative argumentation to achieve deeper understanding of Christian truths by defining, reasoning, and systematizing. Men such as **St. Bonaventure** (c. 1221–1274), **John Duns Scotus** (c. 1265–1308), **William of Ockham** (c. 1287–c. 1347), and Aquinas used logic, dialectical reasoning, and sensory experience to consider the problem of universals and whether they exist. Medieval universities from 1100 to 1500 set the stage for inquiry, but theologians dominated them.

Although the Middle Ages refer to a time and place dominated by Roman Catholicism, Islamic and Jewish scholarship also was influential.

Islamic contributions

From the eigth through the thirteenth century, Muslim scholars made significant advances in chemistry, astronomy, optics, and mathematics. Despite the Crusades, these scholars, impressed by Aristotle's notions of causality, reason, and logic, preserved his writings. When the Roman Empire disintegrated, virtually all of Aristotle's works were unknown in Western Europe, yet Muslim philosophers translated and wrote commentaries on them. Arabic thought came to be known through the Arabic–Latin translations made in the Middle Ages. These works transformed all philosophical disciplines but especially natural philosophy, psychology, metaphysics, logic, and ethics (Hasse, 2008).

In twelfth-century Spain, a translation movement occurred because of the availability of manuscripts in regions newly conquered by Christians, forwarding a hope of promoting Latin scientific culture. In addition, the philosophical culture of Italian universities resulted in Jewish scholars translating Hebrew versions of Arabic texts. Thus, Aristotle's writings emerged in Europe "through the prism of a thousand minds and at least four cultures" (Deely, 2001, p. 251).

Along with the emergence of Aristotle into the Latin world there were other ancient Greek thinkers (e.g., Hippocrates and Galen) and Arabic thinkers who had significant influence in the late Middle Ages. One important Islamic scholar known in the West, **Ibn Sina** (Latinized as **Avicenna**) (980–1037), made important contributions to mathematics, astronomy, linguistics, and politics. He also published *Canons of Medicine*, which remained the standard medical text for 800 years in European and Islamic societies.

Avicenna combined Aristotle's psychology with Galen's medical tradition. Avicenna adopted Aristotle's division of the person into three domains: rational, sensitive, and vegetative. But he proposed instinctive behaviour, seven interior senses (e.g., memory and common sense) as opposed to Aristotle's three, and a mind that can contemplate Allah.

The Persian scientist, philosopher, and physician, **Omar Khayyam** (1048–c. 1131), taught Avicenna's philosophy. Khayyam authored a poem, *The Rubaiyat*, which became famous in Victorian England. Besides poetry, he also wrote books on astronomy, mathematics, and medicine. Thus, Islamic scholarship has been prevalent in the West for centuries.

Jewish contributions

Anti-Semitic persecution saturated European society in the Middle Ages, through the Renaissance, and into the modern era. Nevertheless, Jewish scholars had a significant influence on Western thought. Preserving and translating the works of the ancient Greeks, as well as recommending Arabic texts for translation, Jewish scholars contributed to interest in Aristotle's ideas during the Middle Ages. Aquinas, for example, was influenced by interpretations of Aristotle made by **Moses Maimonides** (1135–1204), a notable Jewish philosopher writing in both Hebrew and Arabic.

The status of women

In the first two centuries of Christianity, women participated more fully in religion. Subsequently Christian women's experiences became systematically marginalized (Ruether, 1983). The misogyny of most Greek and Roman philosophies was perpetuated in Christianity throughout the Middle Ages and Renaissance. According to Aristotle, for example, female infants were undesirable, and a husband was to rule his wife and children as a king rules his subjects.

The standard Christian view was that women possessed a greater potential for evil and a lesser potential for spiritual growth. Augustine regarded only men, not women, as reflecting the image of God; women could attain this state only by being joined with a man. Thus, God created women only for the propagation of the species. Only men were viewed as complete creatures.

Nevertheless, in European societies, a few women exercised civil and religious authority. In the monastic tradition from the fourth to the twelfth century women could receive higher education, if they displayed sufficient masculine characteristics. Although contemporary Irish women, for example, generally did not possess equality with men, evidently some acted as clergy; this allowance deviated from European societal norms (Cahill, 1995). Further on, within the medieval tradition of "courtly love" (i.e., knightly admiration of a lady), upper-class women were regarded as worthy of respect and admiration (Barzun, 2000).

By the late Middle Ages, Aquinas defended patriarchal views with interpretations of Aristotle. Aquinas concluded that women are biologically and psychologically inferior; for example, the biblical character of Eve, the first woman, is responsible for "original sin" (i.e., the doctrine that all humans are born with sin). Consequently, Aquinas believed that men should rule women in the family and in society and women are incapable of holding priestly authority (Whaley, 2003). Furthermore, according to Aquinas, human sex is solely for the purpose of procreation. This viewpoint is the basis for the modern Vatican's opposition to homosexuality and sex for anything but procreation (Whaley, 2003).

Cultural fear of women escalated into a mania of social control and was expressed in the horrific violence of witch-hunting during the Renaissance and early modern era. Along with men and children, millions of European women were murdered. The famous treatise on witches, *Malleus Maleficarum*, originally written in German in 1486–1487 (Institoris & Sprenger, 2006), formalized the popular notion that women are more inclined towards witchcraft because of inferior mental and spiritual capacities, including susceptibility to demonic temptation.

Although masses of women were relegated to subordinate status, a few women became leaders, such as Hildegard von Bingen (see Box 2.2), while the figure of Joan of Arc (1412–1431) captured the imagination of generations upto the current era (Cantor, 1994).

Late medieval thought

The High Middle Ages are dominated by the figures Bonaventure, Aquinas, Scotus, and **William of Ockham** (c.1287–1347), whose influence persisted into the Renaissance. During this era metaphysics, natural philosophy, philosophy of science, theories of causality, and theories of mental representation flourished. Also, late medieval thought developed new understandings of logic as important as the development from mythopoetic to

Box 2.2 **Hildegard von Bingen**

Due to male domination, very few women rose to prominence in European societies. Hildegard was exceptional, living during a period when the church restricted women's participation in intellectual and social life even more than it had previously. She became head of a convent in Germany where she engaged in the work of natural philosophy, studying botany and psychology (Flanagan, 1998).

Being a woman, Hildegard was not formally educated. But she composed a two-volume encyclopaedia of herbal medicine alongside more mystical writings about human nature. Moreover, she is credited with being the first German woman to write about science and medicine and the first Christian writer to discuss the nature of women positively. Although she retained much of the early church's core ideology about women, Hildegard stressed the psychological interdependence of men and women (Newman, 1987).

Hildegard was also a musician, poet, and painter. As a composer of poetic religious music, she was unique in her use of surprising turns of phrase and soaring melodies. Her style of music composition had no direct antecedents or descendants.

philosophical thinking in ancient Greece. Arguably, these understandings contributed to nineteenth-century algebraic descriptions of logical thinking, facilitating the rise of computer technology (Spade, 2010).

Bonaventure

The University of Paris was considered the leading university in Europe in the thirteenth century (Spade, 2010). There Bonaventure, a Franciscan theologian, attempted to thoroughly integrate reason with faith (Noone & Houser, 2010). Arguing that God must be the source of our knowing the immutable truths of logic and mathematics, he viewed these truths as incommensurable with knowledge of ordinary objects.

Bonaventure was concerned with how to develop theology as an Aristotelian science, meaning "systematic knowledge of one limited subject developed through demonstrating necessary conclusions by making use of certain fundamental causal principles relevant to the subject at hand" (Noone & Houser, 2010, p. 9). Bonaventure proposed synthesizing Aristotle's notion of abstraction with the Christian notion of divine illumination. Although knowledge begins in faith for Bonaventure, it develops with rational understanding, leading to a divine mystical union.

In ethics, Bonaventure made a unique contribution, refocusing attention away from theoretical knowledge and practical wisdom towards the importance of love and affection at the centre of the good and moral life.

Thomas Aquinas

At first, because the new translations of Aristotle were unfamiliar and possibly heretical, contemporary Christian philosophers shunned his work in favour of Plato and

Neoplatonism. Eventually, however, a "'multicultural Aristotle' ... came to the Latins by way of the influence of Plotinus, Augustinian thinkers, and the 'gentile' Arabic thinkers of Islam" (Deely, 2001, p. 257).

One of the most influential scholars of the medieval era, Aquinas was indebted to previous Christian natural philosophers as well as Augustine and the Neoplatonists. As they did, Aquinas used logic and empirical knowledge of nature to support a notion of divinity. He reformed the Augustinian framework, which was based on Plato, by uniting it with the teachings of Aristotle and Avicenna.

Aquinas studied at a time when Latin translations of Aristotle provoked questions about the relation between faith and reason (McInerny & O'Callaghan, 2010). Aquinas adopted Aristotle's analysis of physical objects, place, time and motion, his argument for a prime mover, and his cosmology. However, Aquinas also made his own contributions, interpreting church doctrine in terms of Aristotelian principles and logic. He attempted to demonstrate that arguments for faith meet conditions of a science as described by Aristotle in the *Posterior Analytics*.

Aquinas distinguished reason from divine revelation but worked towards a unified truth. Although he made the study of nature respectable by emphasizing the reliability of sensory knowledge, he also made God, not nature, primary. Building on Aristotle, he defined natural law as a manifestation of divine law for the universe. For Aquinas, divine law enlightens human reason, which one is free to accept or reject but cannot avoid. Everyone has an innate orientation to submit to divine law through natural law and to behave morally by obeying it.

By the late nineteenth century the Roman Catholic Church with papal support used Thomistic thought to challenge the secular values of modernity and then in the late twentieth century, postmodernism. The church hierarchy has regarded Thomism as instrumental in reaffirming the search to reconcile faith and reason (McInerny & O'Callaghan, 2010).

The value of Thomistic thought Aquinas is important for the history of psychology for several reasons. First, he proposed reconciling two different kinds of knowledge: one based in faith and revealed truth, the other based in reason and rational truth. Different ways of knowing give us different sciences; hence, the science of theology is different from philosophy.

This was a common belief in his day, but Aquinas went further by insisting that anything that is held in faith must be subject to reason. If faith-based knowledge cannot withstand the rigours of reason then, according to Aquinas, it cannot be truth. There is only one truth. Thus, "There cannot be something true in revelation which truly contradicts what we know to be true in experience" (Deely, 2001, p. 304).

Secondly, Thomistic thought is related to "science" in the modern sense in **two ways**:

- Even though his standpoint presupposed Christian revelation, Aquinas demanded "respect for the 'rights of reason'" (Deely, 2001, p. 298).
- He distinguished between mind-dependent things and mind-independent beings. Mind-dependent abstraction is prominent in early modern philosophy, facilitating the development of hypotheses and instruments of science.

Thirdly, Aquinas argued that individuals should contain their passions through the exercise of reason. Individuals connect with the natural order of the universe by exercising their will to control their passions. Through reason, Aquinas asserted, the faculty of the will enables individuals to apprehend eternal truths.

The soul subordinates the intellect to the will, which is motivated to seek goodness. Thus, will is primary in Thomistic psychological thought as it was generally in the treatment of psychological subjects during the Latin Age. For example, in her written prayers, St. Catherine of Siena (1347–1380) referred to a hierarchy of capacities: memory, understanding (reason), and will (intentionality), the latter being the most influential capacity.

Some historians of psychology characterize Aquinas as a dualist. They argue that in medieval Christian psychology the Aristotelian capacity for appetites (desiring) was split from the soul, resulting in antipathy between body and soul. Others argue Aquinas taught that soul and body are interrelated in that the soul cannot fulfill itself without making use of the body's concrete, sensory reality. In this interpretation, flesh is different from, but not split from the soul.

From a Thomistic perspective, a human being's intellectual power is integrated with vegetative and sensitive powers of the soul. Nevertheless, understanding is independent of the objects of sense. Therefore, the rational soul survives the death of the body, because it participates in an activity that transcends the limits of matter. "And because it has a spiritual nature, it retains always a core of independence which transcends and eludes every external force, every probe from without of its innermost tendencies and secrets" (Deely, 2001, p. 303).

Morality, for Aquinas, requires a fullness of being as well as intelligibility (Flannery, 2003). If an action is compatible with reason, then it has the character of being good. However, Aquinas interpreted Aristotle as saying that a life in accord with reason leads only to imperfect happiness, whereas perfect happiness requires the divine (McInerny & O'Callaghan, 2010). Yet Aquinas followed Aristotle's view of eudaemonia, such that an ethical life leads to a good life. In sum, for Aquinas, there is an intellectual appetite for happiness and the will aims at this good.

John Duns Scotus

A Franciscan philosopher, Scotus focused on "the problem of universals, divine illumination, and the nature of human freedom" (Williams, 2010, p. 1). Like other medieval scholars, he was concerned to know the existence and nature of God without recourse to faith or revelation. As an Aristotelian, he assumed that all knowledge begins with experience of the sensible world. He differed from other medieval Aristotelians in his belief that matter and form can be independent of each other.

Scotus disagreed with Aristotle's ethical notion of eudaemonia. For Scotus, human happiness is not tied to morality for two reasons: moral norms are distinct from human nature. Secondly, morality requires freedom of will; but if freedom of will is tied to intellectual appetite, then will is bound by desire (Williams, 2010).

William of Ockham

"As Aquinas was the 'glory of the Latins,' so Ockham can perhaps be said to be the 'inspiration of the moderns'" (Deely, 2001, p. 386). He is regarded as one of the most important logicians of the Middle Ages (Spade & Panaccio, 2011) and contributed to refining an emergent scientific method.

Parsimony Like many medieval scholars (Spade & Panaccio, 2011), Ockham did not want to posit more entities than necessary for an explanation. He emphasized refraining from positing the existence of something when there is no compelling reason to do so. Mathematical entities, for instance, did not need to have a separate reality. For Ockham, rigorous thinkers should simplify explanations and shave away extraneous assumptions, hence the term, *Ockham's razor* (i.e., parsimony). Yet this principle does not allow us to deny entities, even presumed ones, which might be needed for an explanation.

Ockham's razor was an important advance in logic that eventually allowed late medieval scientists to apply mathematical analyses to non-mathematical objects of nature. This standpoint furthered an emergent scientific worldview that culminated several centuries later "in Galileo's famous statement that the 'book of nature' is written in the 'language of mathematics'" (Spade & Panaccio, 2011, p. 23).

> **Small-group discussion**. Some scholars question whether Ockham's razor should be applied to the human sciences. If we want to explain human psychology, is it best or not to demand an explanation with the least number of assumptions?

Nominalism Ockham placed human thought and language into categories such as noun, verb, as well as connotation, supposition, and signification. He rejected the idea that universals exist as a separate reality. Instead, for him, concepts exist in the mind, they are caused by objects, and universals are abstractions that signify individual things.

As noted above, Ockham also rejected the theory that the mind stores representations of external objects so that the intellect can produce an abstraction for use in cognition and thereby know the object. According to Ockham, not only is the notion of transmission of a species from object to mind unnecessary to explain cognition, but it is not supported by experience or introspection.

Instead, Ockham argued that we can explain cognition simply with reference to intuitive cognition (i.e., perception), imagination, and abstractive cognition (e.g., remembering). As such, abstractive cognitions are derived from intuitive cognitions, although they are not experienced directly (Spade & Panaccio, 2011). For Ockham, a habit instead of a species can account for cognition, learning, and imagining something previously seen (Kemp, 1998).

In short, the critical notion of *nominalism* means that individual things exist, but the names we give them, generalities, or universal statements are not subjects of existence. Simply naming a concept or experience does not make it exist. For Ockham, unlike Aquinas, and contrary to Plotinus, concepts are mere labels and cannot bring meaning into existence.

Mental representations

Due to the language that Arabic scholars used to translate Aristotle, the notion of representations in the soul took hold during this era (Lagerlund, 2011). For example, representations were considered material for such psychological activities as imagining and remembering. Representations in the soul could be abstracted into universal forms. Initially, representations were considered as images; it was Ockham who developed the notion of mental representations as signs.

Following Avicenna, Aquinas and others explained the nature of afterimages, imagination, and mental representations as follows: perceptions give rise to mental representations, which are the form of objects in the world without their matter. Thus, the form is extracted from matter and made more abstract. Aquinas termed mental representations "intelligible species" (Kemp, 1998; Lagerlund, 2011). The most abstract and complex cognitions do not rely on mental representations of external objects and bodily organs for intelligibility. For Aquinas, intelligible species hold a dual, somewhat contradictory position of being a universal that is common to all thought and also one's individual thought. Scotus understood representing as a mental act (Lagerlund, 2011).

But Ockham claimed the Thomistic notion of species was unnecessary, because the mind, he argued, can attend to an object directly without the need for an intervening representation. "A concept or a mental term on this view *represents* because it is caused efficiently by a thing in the world. It signifies that thing also because of the causal relation between them" (Lagerlund, 2011, p. 9, emphasis added). This medieval notion was revived by the phenomenological psychologist **Franz Brentano** (1838–1917), an expert on Aquinas and Aristotle (see Chapter 10), who insisted that mental states are always intentional (Lagerlund, 2011).

Medieval science

Medieval scholars understood nature in terms of constant conflict among the basic elements of earth, air, fire, and water (Lindberg, 1992). For them, the world is pulled between heaven and hell, just as the person is pulled between spirit and flesh. Whereas God is perfect, matter possesses imperfect qualities. Consequently, the most respected science during the medieval period, continuing into the Renaissance, was astronomy, because astronomers studied the perfect heavens, where a perfect God reigned over an imperfect earth.

The scholastic method of medieval scholars included use of *disputations* (i.e., making the most convincing logical arguments and guarding against indistinct or incorrect inferences). The chief model was the syllogism of Aristotelian logic. For example, given that the church authorizes faith in premise "A" and premise "B," therefore belief "C" follows logically.

Eventually, scholasticism became a dogmatic system of thought adhering to the church's authoritative interpretations of classic texts; accordingly, many scholars within this tradition refused to explore Aristotelian concepts empirically. The innovators of early modern science (see Chapter 3) rebelled against scholasticism, because it had distorted Aristotle's legacy of natural philosophy (Lindberg, 1992). On the other hand, the scholastic philosophers contributed to developing the method of scientific argument by insisting that natural philosophers determine what a statement implies as opposed to settling for mere plausibility (Barzun, 2000).

Furthermore, scientific inventions and investigations sometimes flourished during the medieval era (M. Hunt, 2007). Whether they were studying the stars or medicinal herbs, medieval scientists depended upon careful observation of nature. For example, a contemporary of Aquinas, **Roger Bacon** (c. 1214/1220–1294) resurrected Aristotle's emphasis on direct, careful, and controlled observation and conducted experiments in optics (Barzun, 2000). To understand and explain nature, Bacon also emphasized the roles of direct experience and mathematics in the validation of truths rather than church authority or logic alone. These emphases came to flourish during the next historical period, the Renaissance.

Part 5 conclusion

During the Middle Ages monastic study and then emergent church-centred universities advanced philosophy, science, and psychological thought. Aided by Jewish and Islamic translations and commentaries, scholars discovered Aristotelian thought about nature, human nature, and the soul's capacities. Moving beyond Aristotle, scholars debated whether abstractions really exist and whether Christian faith and divine revelation can be reconciled with secular reason and truths derived from empirical observation.

Aquinas accepted the Aristotelian tenet that sensory knowledge is reliable and posited that the body's concrete, sensory reality informs the soul. But it is human will, he asserted, that makes the grasping of rational truths possible. Moreover, for Aquinas, the Christian God is primary in the hierarchy of knowledge.

Ockham also insisted that all knowledge is tested by way of direct, infallible acquaintance with some object in the world. But Aquinas and Ockham debated the constituents of mental representations, the abstract products of perception. While Aquinas attributed "intelligible species" to mental representations, Ockham maintained that the mind perceives objects without depending on any intervening mental representation and that natural objects cause it. Also against Aquinas, Ockham claimed that God's existence cannot be proven by anything in nature; thus, belief in God depends only on faith.

In addition, Ockham proposed two concepts that have proved vital for critical thinking in philosophy and science: parsimony and nominalism. These concepts and medieval developments in systematic thinking and logical argument enabled the application of number to non-mathematical things, which eventually led to the modern scientific worldview.

Part 6 Philosophy, science, and psychological thought in the Renaissance

Social and intellectual developments emerged during the next epoch, the Renaissance, which ultimately shaped Western culture and influenced science and psychological thought.

Social and intellectual context

Renaissance society was organized in strict hierarchical form so that the masses of people of both genders were in subordinate social positions. Although patriarchy remained strong, a few women played major political roles, such as Queen Isabella (1451–1504) of Spain and Queen Elizabeth I (1533–1603) of England. Yet women remained subordinate economically and politically.

City-life, trade, and industry continued to expand, shaping social life, weakening the intellectual authority of the church and heightening a spirit of inquiry (M. Hunt, 2007). Rather than focusing on theology, society concentrated on the collection and handling of information required for business, military, and government taxation. These trends facilitated the birth of modern science in the sixteenth and seventeenth centuries.

Intellectually, socially, and politically, at least **six developments** distinguished the Renaissance from the medieval period to some extent (Barzun, 2000; R. Smith, 1997):

- Humanism
- Mechanically printed texts
- Global explorations
- Utopian visions
- Religious conflict within Christianity
- Individualism.

Humanism

During the Renaissance, *humanism*, that is, a system of thought stressing human rather than divine matters, rose to prominence and helped shape psychological thought (Park & Kessler, 1988). The Christian belief that God became human is perhaps the most radical form of humanism. But Renaissance humanism was fundamentally secular.

Whereas medieval scholars focused on God illuminating truth, Renaissance scholars returned to ancient Greek notions that exalted intelligibility and reason and recovered ancient-wisdom traditions as guides to living. In their translations of Aristotle and other ancient philosophers, humanists devised interpretations that attempted to answer the question of how to live a good life without recourse to notions of the divine. Essentially, humanists believed that reason and understanding nature are the best ways to improve society and achieve the good life. Although they were not interested in the technical philosophy of medieval scholastics, Renaissance scholars did not abandon the systematic logical thinking that scholasticism fostered.

A key Renaissance figure was **Desiderius Erasmus** (c. 1467–1536). Through his writings and publishing house, he criticized extant social hierarchies and stimulated social reform. He was a highly influential adviser to popes and princes and aided the early development of the upheaval in Christianity that soon was to consume European culture (Barzun, 2000).

Printing and texts

Chinese citizens had invented moveable-type printing perhaps as early as the eleventh century. In the Western world, however, Johann Gutenberg's (1398–1468) independent invention of this method of printing in 1454 facilitated the spread of literacy. The printing press gave easier access to and propagation of scholarship. The establishment of a set of technical inventions and formatting conventions in the late fifteenth and early sixteenth centuries, including punctuation, spacing between words, paragraphs, and uniform spelling, enhanced printing of books and pamphlets. The educated public now thirsted for knowledge from books.

When books were hand-printed there were very few in circulation and copies had to be chained to library walls to prevent theft. But during the Renaissance, even though it was the Bible that was made most available, printing enabled a wider range of people to read, making it easier to think independently. The increasing availability of Christian reading material for the laity enabled silent solitary reading and personal interpretation. This latter development contributed to a cultural shift embodied by the Protestant Revolution, which shook Westerners' faith in uniform church teachings (Barzun, 2000).

Innovations in printing also abetted scholarship. Cultivating a sense of history, humanists established the method of library research, critical reading of documents, and balanced writing. In their search for truth, scholars examined sources of knowledge in the original texts rather than relying on commentators. They compared sources, verified dates, weighed evidence, and only gave authority to oral traditions if they could be confirmed.

Global explorations

Medieval travel among capital cities in Europe contributed to the exchange of innovative ideas, increased multilingual fluency, and global explorations. The voyages of Christopher Columbus (c. 1451–1506) in the 1490s and Ferdinand Magellan's (1480–1521) expedition that led to the circumnavigation of the globe in 1522 shook the collective consciousness of Europeans. They became fascinated by an idealized vision of foreign civilizations, and many European states sought to acquire their wealth. By 1540 the Spanish empire became the dominant power in the Western world, including the Western hemisphere (Barzun, 2000).

Utopian visions of society

Influenced by increased awareness of diverse civilizations, Renaissance authors composed utopian visions of society: **Thomas More** (1477–1535), *Utopia*; **Tommaso Campanella** (1568–1639), *The City of the Sun*; and **Francis Bacon** (1561–1626), *The New Atlantis* (Barzun, 2000). Each advocated agrarian states of commonly shared wealth, liberated from poverty.

More's essay contains such a trenchant critique of wealth and power in English society that it was not published until fifteen years after he died. His alternative was democratic equality. Campanella advocated community well-being through moderate work, cooperation, and reason, and supported equal status for women. Bacon envisioned social progress achieved by scientific research. However, he promoted a life of celibacy for men, avoiding contact with women, because greatness of mind, he believed, is not compatible with sexuality and domestic concerns (Agonito, 1977).

The legacy of these utopias consists of **five concepts** that have affected Western thinking and practices for centuries (Barzun, 2000):

- Social equality is humane, hierarchies are not.
- All people must work and earn their rewards.
- The people should choose their leaders.
- The application of reason and will can change the social order.
- Marriage and divorce should correspond to actual marital experience rather than conform to one interpretation of divine law.

While economically Renaissance society was in transition from feudalism to early capitalism, theological ideas inspired economic and class revolution for some thinkers. **Thomas Müntzer** (c. 1489–1525), a German theologian and peasant leader, epitomized early class struggle. Some regard him as inspiring the French Revolution, twentieth-century liberation theology, and other critiques of class consciousness (Goertz, 1993). Müntzer understood how social institutions (e.g., church, government, feudalism) engender fear within people and survive by maintaining this fear. When the power of institutions to instil fear is broken, he reasoned, then the people can seize power for themselves and bring God's will and the kingdom of heaven to earth in the forms of freedom, justice, and solidarity.

Religious conflict

Beginning in the fifteenth century, complaints over abuses of church authority, ostentatious displays of wealth, and ruthless exercise of political power became more pronounced (Goertz, 1993). Conflict erupted during the Protestant Revolution of the sixteenth century.

Martin Luther and **John Calvin** (1509–1564) were among the primary reformers. They challenged Roman Catholic authority and sought a balance between service to the secular state and the exercise of individual Christian conscience. However, Lutheranism and Calvinism developed divergent positions, generating sectarian violence between their respective followers.

When Luther translated the Bible into the most common dialect of German, he provided the masses with the means to develop their own knowledge. The Bible became a resource for understanding human functioning in the psychological and historical senses, and generally was the only book in a home (Barzun, 2000). Luther also challenged societal traditions by opposing the complex system of paid indulgences (i.e., money paid to the local church in exchange for remission of time to be spent in Purgatory for one's sins) on which Catholicism had depended economically for centuries. Indirectly, Luther energized dissatisfaction with the monolithic belief system propagated by the Roman Church, thus encouraging diversity of thinking.

Within his strain of Protestantism Calvin reinforced belief in eternal salvation through faith alone and stressed the doctrine of predestination (i.e., God ordaining beforehand one's salvation). Calvin prescribed a strict regimen of religious practices that in later Protestant denominations was expressed in "puritanical" behaviour. Calvinism became associated with individuals' fear of sin and rejection of the earth as a place of exile.

In response to the Protestant Revolution, the Catholic Church instituted reforms to its institution at the Council of Trent (1545–1563). However, the Catholic hierarchy insisted on the primacy of their interpretive authority, which precipitated centuries of conflict between religion and scientific beliefs. Nevertheless, some Catholic religious orders (e.g., the Jesuits) specialized in education in the humanities and practised scientific inquiry for centuries thereafter.

The upheavals in Christianity did more than stimulate changes in theology and liturgical and institutional practices; they also led to fundamental changes in European society. Each Protestant denomination developed its own educational institutions, which made secular thinking more accessible. Arguably, Protestantism fostered diversity of opinion and aspirations for nationhood and promoted vernacular languages rather than universal Latin.

Individualism

Protestantism reinforced a growing sense of personal authority, thinking for oneself, and increased focus on difference and independence, along with belief in self-sufficiency. Consequently, a heightened focus on the subjective self occurred, and individualism began to spread and deepen in Western culture. Arguably, the history of the self is central to the story of psychology (C. Taylor, 1989). Educated Europeans became infatuated with the personal. They enjoyed portrait painting, mirrors, conduct-books on how to behave morally, and diaries for personal reflection. While consciousness of the private experience of autonomous individuals became culturally normative, a formal body of psychological thought began to emerge (Drunen & Jansz, 2004b).

Renaissance science

During this era increasing reliance on logic and mathematical reasoning in natural philosophy made way for the emergence of early modern science (Spade, 2010). As the number of universities expanded, commentaries on the works of Aristotle and Aristotelian logic proliferated, and philosophy of nature, metaphysics, and ethics were core subjects (H. Kuhn, 2009). In this sense, philosophy in the Renaissance is almost synonymous with Aristotelianism.

Yet Renaissance scholars also made new interpretations of Aristotle's thought and discovered Plato, Plotinus, the Stoics, and the Skeptics. Although works by Aquinas and Ockham continued to be printed, interest in the scholarship of the late Middle Ages significantly declined. Scholars now preferred secular humanist commentaries (Park & Kessler, 1988).

In addition to the revival of Aristotelianism, continuity of scientific activity occurred, facilitating the emergence of modern science (Lindberg, 1992). Medieval scholars had relied on careful observation of nature. But the Renaissance invention of "philosophical instruments" (i.e., measurement tools) aided empirical observations (Barzun, 2000) and advanced studies in astronomy, geography, surgery, anatomy, and mineralogy (M. Hunt, 2007).

Keeping time became central to the conduct of society and science (Landes, 1983). Prior to this era, citizens had been using sundials. But the clock and watch enabled more precise measurements. The Middle Ages and the Renaissance saw the invention of timepieces. In 1335, the first public clock that struck each hour appeared in Milan, followed by the personal watch two centuries later.

Renaissance psychology

Psychological inquiry during the Renaissance continued to be dominated by Aristotelian philosophy of nature along with Greek, Arabic, and Latin commentary (Park & Kessler, 1988). During this era, as in the late Middle Ages, the university curriculum began with studies of the nature and type of soul and then the specific capacities of reproduction, digestion, sensation, memory, imagination, appetite, will, and intellect.

With the soul understood as the animating principle of life, there was no clear distinction between the subject matter of biology and psychology. Psychological inquiry was considered the height of natural philosophy, investigating the principles of animate nature, unlike physics which concerned principles governing inanimate objects. Yet the soul was not considered entirely material, because its study included topics of ethics and metaphysics.

Renaissance writers tended to agree about the nature and functions of the organic soul, drawing from medieval scholars such as Aquinas and Ockham. Renaissance philosophers were interested particularly in "the principle responsible for those life functions inextricably tied to the bodies of living beings and immediately dependent on their organs" (Park, 1988, p. 464).

Of all biological and psychological functions, only intellect and will were considered to not require physical organs. Thus, the portions of the soul believed to be unique to humans were thought of as immortal. In this sense, then, Renaissance psychology was focused on *faculties* (i.e., abilities for particular activities). The common conception was that the soul was "composed of a large number of separate faculties or powers, each directed towards a different object and responsible for a distinct operation" (Park, 1988, p. 466).

Medieval scholars had stressed a "great chain of being" from the least animate objects to humans, estimated by increasing distance from the body to higher levels of the soul. By contrast, Renaissance scholars emphasized the close tie between body and soul. A crucial question for them was whether the intellect had immaterial functions independent of the body. Accordingly, Renaissance scholars tended to focus on sensory perception and intellect, paying relatively little attention to emotional, motor, and vegetative capacities. They posited five "wits" (i.e., powers of the mind): common-sense reason, imagination, fantasy, estimation, and memory (Barzun, 2000).

Although the idea that humans have an immortal intellective soul predominated, beginning around 1500 a gradual change distinguished Renaissance from medieval psychology. Explanations of everything except intellection tended to become simpler and more physiological. Understanding the organic functions of the soul came to require knowledge of anatomy and physiology rather than philosophical principles of nature and metaphysics (Park, 1988).

By 1520, a Serbo-Croatian author coined the word *psychologia* to capture increasing interest in psychological experience, while in 1590 a German encyclopaedist used it in a book title, *Psychologia Hoc Est, de Hominis Perfectione* [*This Is Psychology, On the Improvement of Man*] (M. Hunt, 2007). A distinct cultural shift towards psychological studies was emerging.

Psychology of humours Since the Middle Ages scholars held that astrological influences on four bodily humours, derived from the four basic elements, influenced an individual's "character" (personality). Hippocrates originally proposed the humours, Galen revised them, and Avicenna reinterpreted them medically. Renaissance scholars familiar with this tradition explained health, illness, and what we might call mental health according to the four humours.

Table 2.1 shows how each natural element was associated with a particular humour, which in turn was associated with a dominant temperament and personality disposition.

Character was understood in terms of one's "ruling passion," meaning that one of the four humours determined thoughts, feelings, and actions. For example, a person identified as melancholic, due to excessive black bile, generally would be sad. The characters in the dramas of **William Shakespeare** (1564–1616) exemplify this Renaissance conception of personality. The popular belief was that the four elements and their associated humours should remain in balance with each other to ensure good health, whereas lack of balance caused illness. The assumption was that love resides in the liver, feelings in the heart, and thoughts in the brain (Barzun, 2000).

On the other hand, Swiss natural philosopher **Paracelsus** (born Philippus von Hohenheim, 1493–1541) rejected the notion of bodily humours affected by astrological

Table 2.1 The psychology of humours

Element	Humour	Temperament	Personality disposition
Earth	Phlegm	Phlegmatic	Sluggish
Air	Blood	Sanguine	Optimistic
Fire	Yellow bile	Choleric	Hot-tempered
Water	Black bile	Melancholic	Sad

forces as well as notions of spirits and demons causing psychological imbalance. He posited psychological health strictly in terms of "the breath of life." Astrological configurations or bodily vapours, however, could upset it.

Michel de Montaigne Without resorting to the psychology of humours, French author **Michel de Montaigne** (1533–1592) attempted to make sense of behavioural inconsistencies. In his famous work, *Essays*, he distinguished between "type," which refers to the dominant humour with its consistent inclination, and "character," which refers to the well-rounded person who responds differently depending on different situations (Barzun, 2000). Furthermore, Montaigne, considered one of the most learned humanists of the sixteenth century, challenged many fundamental assumptions of contemporary Western thought (Foglia, 2010). He questioned the accepted beliefs that humans are superior to animals, European civilization is superior to other societies, and reason can be judged by a universal standard.

Taking into account the diversity of opinion across cultures, Montaigne developed a means of producing science founded on critique. He dismissed other forms of scientific inquiry as methods for justifying received opinion. In order to free our judgment one must begin, Montaigne argued, with questioning what we assume to be true. This foundation provides insight into the strengths and weaknesses of our knowledge-claims.

Montaigne understood beliefs as diverse and not always rational. The best judgment, for him, is dialogical and requires counterbalancing a single account with diversity of opinions. We then can compare and evaluate diverse viewpoints. Thus, epistemologically, Montaigne promoted entertaining multiple perspectives on phenomena. In advocating clear-mindedness and independence of thinking, Montaigne influenced the method of inquiry used by Descartes, the arguments of Pascal that challenged scholars' claims to knowing truth, and eighteenth-century French philosophers of the Enlightenment (see Chapter 3). Montaigne, then, marks the transition from the Renaissance to the early modern era, the subject of the next chapter.

Part 6 conclusion

During the Renaissance important intellectual, scientific, technical, and social developments in European societies influenced a cultural shift in conceptions of the soul, mind, and body. Secularism, expressed in humanistic rather than theological scholarship, became more prominent. Perhaps complemented by another revival of Aristotelianism, continuity of scientific activity occurred, which enabled modern science to emerge, as we explain in the next chapter. Renaissance inventions of measurement devices strengthened systematic observation of natural objects whether astronomical, geographical, or anatomical.

Possibly as a result of these developments, an individual's mind became an interior matter. In addition, preoccupations of individuals in the modern world with anxiety about life and death, the notion that human nature is fundamentally flawed, and the belief that our actions in the world are predetermined by larger forces seem to be rooted in Renaissance culture. Yet diverse rather than uniform philosophical discussions of psychological phenomena flourished.

Renaissance scholars tended to describe the soul's capacities and an individual's personality with physiological explanations that suggested consistent dispositions. But Montaigne challenged that view in observing that the actions of individuals quite often ought to be inconsistent across situations. He also stressed critical thinking about knowledge of the natural world and human action, a viewpoint that partially is reflected in the thought of many natural philosophers of the early modern era.

Part 7 | Thematic review

Reflecting on the broad span of psychological thought across the ancient Greek, medieval, and Renaissance eras, we discern three themes that, from a current perspective, might capture the core issues with which philosopher-scientists grappled: **conflicting metaphysical positions** concerning being and knowing, **critical thinking**, and **an emergent, conscious psychological interior**.

Conflicting metaphysical positions

In philosophy, *metaphysics* (i.e., study of ultimate reality existing beyond the appearances of the material world) includes an ontological aspect by which we ask what exists in the world and what the essence of existence is, and an epistemological aspect where we ask how we know what exists. Across the ancient, medieval, and Renaissance eras, different, often opposing, standpoints on these ontological and epistemological questions were at play and were expressed in at least two forms:

- Mythopoetic and religious vs. secular explanations of natural objects and humankind.
- Rationalist vs. empiricist–rationalist standpoints on how humans acquire knowledge.

Originally in ancient Greek culture mythopoetic explanations of natural objects prevailed, as evidenced by the Homeric epic poems. The significance of the presocratic philosophers' ontological speculations about nature and human nature is that they turned to naturalistic explanations, derived from impressions of their empirical observations, rather than mythological explanations. The work of Socrates, Plato, and Aristotle sustained this secular turn towards the conviction that reliable truth begins with humans' concrete perceptions of nature. But with the ascendance of Christianity as a state religion in European societies during the early and late Middle Ages a reversion to the position that reliable truth begins with the gods or the Christian God occurred. By the Renaissance with the rise of humanism and other cultural developments the pendulum swung back to secular naturalism.

As to how humans acquire knowledge, two epistemological positions were prominent: rationalism by which one distrusts sensory impressions and instead contemplates abstract ideas and pure forms of natural objects, and empiricist-rationalism by which one trusts sensory data and employs them as the foundation for drawing inferences about abstract principles. Plato, the Neoplatonist Plotinus, and Augustine represent the rationalist persuasion, while Aristotle, Aquinas, and Ockham represent empiricist-rationalism. An extreme empiricist position did not become prominent until the early modern era, which we discuss in the next chapter.

Critical thinking

Many ancient Greek scholars stressed critical thinking. For some, this orientation was grounded in empirical observations, while for others thinking critically required contemplation of abstract forms and eternal truths. Regardless of the metaphysical position, the art of systematic (logical) and critical thinking about nature and human nature came to the fore during the era of Socrates and Plato. Aristotle then developed formal logic, which facilitated this practice.

During the Middle Ages, an epoch of faith in the church's teachings, Ockham proposed that rigorous thinking entailed not positing more entities than necessary for explaining nature and refuted the notion that naming a concept or experience gives it actual existence. In addition, although scholastic argumentation became distorted, it emphasized determining the implications of any statement and preventing ambiguous or incorrect inferences. In this way scholasticism complemented critical thinking.

Yet skepticism about knowledge-making served as a counterpoint to the discourse of truth and definite knowledge. The Sophists challenged the certainty of knowledge, insisting, as Socrates did, that ultimate claims to knowledge were dubious. According to the Sophists, observers cannot step into the same river *once*, because each observer always perceives it somewhat differently. The Sophists' skepticism about objective, universal truths mirrored their belief that the aim of argument is not to establish laws of nature but to persuade others to adopt one's position.

In his approach to critical thinking the Renaissance scholar Montaigne questioned how one can know the truth about natural phenomena without entertaining multiple perspectives on one's observations. He advocated not simply clear, but independent thought, while challenging received wisdom. By the dawn of the early modern era a dialectical tension seemed to exist between the practice of observation and the practice of logic.

A conscious psychological interior

It is true that Plato and Aristotle wrote about psychological phenomena, but they relied on their own concepts that cannot be directly translated into modern languages. Centuries later Augustine disclosed intensely personal reflections on his emotions, desires, and thoughts, but his musings do not represent a "psychological sense of self" as we moderns living in psychologically minded societies would understand that term. The notion of a psychological interior did not become more culturally familiar in European thought until the Renaissance, when societies became more urban and mercantilistic, where a rising middle socioeconomic class and diminishing church authority enabled the emergence of secular humanism.

These cultural shifts culminated in a heightened focus on the individual, sensitivity to one's subjective experience, and speculation on the nature of human nature. In the sixteenth century the term *psychologia* was introduced, which captured this intellectual development. Although the intellect and will were still regarded as manifestations of the soul, biological bases for human action (e.g., bodily humours) were important in contemporary psychological conceptions.

Many characters in Shakespeare's dramas exemplify this enhanced awareness of one's psychological interior. Although Shakespeare's characters speak of bodily humours as determinants of human action, they are multifaceted individuals who behave differently in different situations rather than psychological types. Previously, Montaigne had expressed this understanding of behavioural inconsistencies. The cultural stage is now set to explore early modern conceptions of the self.

Summary

Psychology as a science and profession is indebted to a lengthy, complex intellectual and social history of the Western scientific worldview. This history is intertwined with philosophical concepts about psychological capacities advanced in ancient, medieval, and Renaissance thought. A central question was how reason and experience enable humans to make knowledge.

In Part 1 we focused on the diverse positions taken by the presocratic natural philosophers of ancient Greece. Of particular importance was the shift from mythopoetic language towards natural discourse and natural explanation. Operating from different perspectives, the presocratics identified immutable first principles and natural elements underlying the changeable nature of existence.

In Part 2 we described the highly influential method of Socratic inquiry in ancient Greece. Then we considered Plato's increasingly abstract discourse about knowledge against the Sophists' practical considerations. Whereas Plato furthered the language of objective abstraction, the Sophists practised the subjective art of persuasion.

Plato's student Aristotle pursued a rather different path to explaining knowledge of nature. As a foundational figure in the history of Western science and psychology, Aristotle's ideas about body and mind and his scientific contributions received extensive coverage in Part 3. Central to the history of psychology is Aristotle's development of logic as a tool for studying nature, generating explanations, and making knowledge.

In Part 4 we discussed the Roman Empire's emphasis on practical considerations and technology and reviewed four therapeutic philosophies – Epicureanism, Cynicism, Stoicism, and Skepticism – that offered practical principles for governing a good life. The spreading of these Greek therapeutic philosophies in the Roman Empire had a significant psychological influence. Then we described the development of Neoplatonic thought in Roman times and the related philosophical psychology of Augustine who described a psychological interior.

We addressed the Middle Ages in Part 5. First, we noted monastic study and church-centred universities; Irish, Jewish, and Islamic influences on medieval thought; and the status and influence of women. Then we addressed the contributions of Bonaventure, Thomas Aquinas, Jon Duns Scotus, and William of Ockham to the study of the nature and capacities of the soul. Medieval advances in logic, such as parsimony and nominalism, allowed for the application of number to non-mathematical things and furthered the scientific worldview. We discussed the medieval debate over whether abstractions really exist and whether faith and revelation can be reconciled with reason and truths derived from practical observation.

In Part 6 we considered Renaissance philosophical and scientific developments, when the mind became increasingly an interior matter. We described six important developments that influenced a cultural shift in conceptions of the soul, mind, and body: humanism, printing and distribution of texts, global explorations, utopian visions, Christian conflict, and individualism. After considering Renaissance science, we discussed how descriptions of the soul's capacities and an individual's character emphasized physiological explanations (e.g., humours). Adopting a more complex view, Michel de Montaigne not only addressed inconsistencies in individuals' behaviour but also advanced critical thinking about knowledge of the natural world. As such, he epitomizes the transition to the early modern era.

In Part 7 we presented three themes that summarize the main issues addressed across the ancient, medieval, and Renaissance epochs: conflicting metaphysical positions concerning being (ontological issues) and knowing (epistemological issues); critical thinking; and a conscious psychological interior.

Sample essay questions

1. Choose one person from among Plato, Aristotle, Augustine, and Aquinas who best represents and least represents your own philosophy of psychology. Then explain what it is about their views on human nature and human action that appeals to you or doesn't appeal to you in light of *your own* ideas about human nature and human action.

2. Aristotle, Ockham, and Montaigne each addressed how to conduct systematic investigations of nature and human nature. Compare and contrast their scientific approaches. Then discuss which approach or approaches fits best with your own views.

RECOMMENDED READING

Histories of women, such as Whaley (2003), Agonito (1977), and the two-volume work by B. Anderson and Zinsser (2000), *A history of their own: Women in Europe from prehistory to the present*, provide rich information and historical analysis.

A history of the different psychological conceptions of understanding across ancient, medieval, modern, and postmodern ages is provided in Deely's (2001) *Four ages of understanding*. C. Taylor's (1989) *Sources of the self: The making of the modern identity* is a seminal work charting the origin of modern notions of selfhood in the history of Western thought. Lindberg's (1992) *The beginnings of Western science* is extremely relevant for this chapter, as is Lawson's (2004) *Science in the ancient world: An encyclopedia*.

The Cambridge Companions to Philosophy is an internationally acclaimed series introducing major thinkers, topics, and periods in the history of Western thought. Each volume offers a variety of viewpoints provided by essays from leading scholars. Other good overviews include: Huizinga's (1956) *The waning of the Middle Ages* and Kristeller's (1979) *Renaissance thought and its sources*.

ONLINE RESOURCES

It is helpful to read encyclopaedia entries on individuals and concepts to grasp ideas succinctly. The online *Stanford Encyclopedia of Philosophy* is vetted through a scholarly process: http://plato.stanford.edu/contents.html

3

Early modern psychological thought

Chapter outline

Introduction

This chapter encompasses psychological thought during the "early modern" period of the seventeenth and eighteenth centuries, known as the Scientific Revolution and the Enlightenment respectively. These developments partially laid the foundation for

Psychology. However, early modern scholars were not interested in psychological questions as currently understood. Rather, their beliefs that mind was not material and humans were more than physical objects challenge current psychological assumptions. Furthermore, early modern scholars encountered a rather different cultural context than ours. Accordingly, some historiographical **cautions** are in order:

- Although the terms and concepts that early modern scholars used might appear the same as those in today's Psychology, their meaning has changed profoundly over centuries.
- Few early modern scholars conducted scientific inquiry about psychological phenomena. Rather, late eighteenth-century and nineteenth-century physiologists investigated human biological phenomena with psychological implications (see Chapter 4).
- Often contradictory historical accounts exist for those early modern scholars who described psychological phenomena philosophically.

Given these cautions, the **aims** of this chapter are to describe:

- Early modern natural philosophers' conceptions of psychological phenomena.
- The continuities and discontinuities between Psychology's philosophical heritage and current psychological ideas.
- The varieties of psychological discourse during the early modern period.
- Three themes that summarize this discourse: compatibility of scientific with theistic thought, objectivity–subjectivity of observation, and a self-contained vs. a relational self.

Part 1   The Scientific Revolution and the Enlightenment

When modern science and psychological thought began to emerge during the early modern period of the sixteenth and seventeenth centuries, Western culture was in a state of transition. Major societal changes were occurring, including the emergence of mercantile capitalism; expansion and consolidation of political power; colonization of the New World; European journeys to East Asia; violent conflicts over religion; and the use of the magnetic compass, gunpowder, and the printing press, all invented earlier by the Chinese. These developments aided the growth of science and technology, which in turn aided colonial and commercial expansion (R. Porter & Teich, 1992).

Two particular cultural developments – *social management*, meaning the increasing organization of economic, political, and social life, and *individualization*, meaning an increasing focus on the private experience of autonomous individuals – helped to shape philosophical discourse on psychological phenomena and facilitate Psychology's eventual emergence (Drunen & Jansz, 2004b).

Social management intensified with the establishment of formal social institutions to maintain control over society's members. Simultaneously, Western culture began to shift away from a collective mentality towards individualization. Individuals' differential character (today termed "personality") and abilities became important. By the seventeenth century, individualization entailed cultivating consciousness about one's subjective experience (i.e., personal feelings, wishes, and thoughts). During this period of cultural transition psychological sensibility emerged as a kind of interiority, reflecting a person's presumed inner nature (C. Taylor, 1989), and discourse about psychological subject matter increased.

The Scientific Revolution

The term "Scientific Revolution," referring to shifts in knowledge about nature and human nature that occurred during the period spanning the mid sixteenth to the early eighteenth century, was coined by twentieth-century historians. But during the early modern era the term "science" still meant different types of natural and religious knowledge. In fact, the designation "scientist" did not appear in an English-speaking context until 1834.

The Scientific Revolution partly denotes changing conceptions concerning Earth's place in the solar system and humankind's place on Earth, which contradicted the church's geocentric view of the universe. Astronomers Johannes Kepler and Galileo Galilei independently reported observations that confirmed the heliocentric hypothesis of their Renaissance predecessor, Nicolaus Copernicus, published posthumously in 1543.

Another hallmark of the Scientific Revolution is a discourse on systematic methodology for practising natural philosophy to which Galileo, Francis Bacon, René Descartes, and Isaac Newton contributed. Galileo, for example, avoided metaphysical and theological explanations of natural objects, stressing instead deductive science and mathematics. Yet early modern science did not proceed in a uniform direction. Natural philosophers also investigated astrology and the Bible; anatomy, botany, chemistry, physiology, and zoology emerged differently than astronomy, mathematics, and physics; and women played important roles in early modern science (Sarasohn, 2006).

Yet whether shifts in knowledge constituted a "revolution," that is, a discontinuous transformation, or simply a continuation of late-Renaissance practices, is debatable (Osler, 2000; Sarasohn, 2006). From a historical perspective of *continuity*, early modern scientific discoveries depended upon **three bodies** of Renaissance knowledge:

- Previous mathematical, astronomical, anatomical, and chemical traditions.
- Mechanical arts and inventors of tools and instruments who instructed natural philosophers in experimentation.
- The "Book of Secrets" tradition in which scholars who mixed magic rituals with extant science experimented to gain power and control over the mysterious forces of nature.

From a perspective of discontinuity, the Revolution originated in scientific discoveries in astronomy, mathematics, and physics that led to the rejection of Aristotelian and Scholastic thought. Early modern scholars who studied nature, known as "natural philosophers," mechanized, but did not totally despiritualize the religious picture of the natural world. They verified their observations for themselves rather than relying on church authority and religious argument. This cultural shift to empirically based knowledge transformed knowledge of nature and culminated in Newton's revelation of an infinite universe.

Nevertheless, most natural philosophers linked all natural objects with a creator God and believed in an immortal soul (Osler, 2000). They proposed "the idea of nature as another name for God," which they regarded as the most fundamental reality (Needleman, 1982, p. 157). In effect, they reframed the Platonic notion that there is a profound reality behind the veil of appearances. Descartes, for instance, distinguished knowing from believing and made scientific knowledge the foundation for contemplating the belief that an absolute God created and maintains a mathematically ordered universe. Consequently, natural philosophers' spiritual and theological concerns shaped how they interpreted their observations. Newton, for example, thought of himself as a natural philosopher investigating God's imprint on nature.

Scientific activity

Previously, scientific activity proceeded within parallel traditions of crafts and natural magic. Before there were formal laboratories in institutions, natural philosophers adopted the mechanical apparatus of craftspersons who experimented with biological, chemical, and physical materials. Laboratories typically were situated within scholars' homes, as depicted in Figure 3.1. Meanwhile, alchemists, healers, and witches secretly engaged in "natural magic," meaning quasi-experimentation to produce esoteric knowledge about natural substances (D. Clarke, 2006; Eamon, 1994).

The emergence of modern Western science is indebted not just to astronomy. Galileo developed a mathematical method describing the constituents and motions of matter, including acceleration and time (Machover, 1998). He called his influential innovation "the science of mechanics," meaning knowledge about matter and motion.

Figure 3.1 Scholars typically conducted their investigations in a laboratory situated in their home

Box 3.1 **Women in natural philosophy**

Ambivalent views about women's capacities as observers of nature prevailed among male natural philosophers (Sarasohn, 2006). The dominant doctrine was that women were mentally and morally inferior beings and intellectually ill-equipped for natural philosophy (Fara, 2004). Privileged women could pursue scientific activity for amusement as a "scientific lady" and some participated in learned discussion groups (Phillips, 1990). But women who were seriously curious about nature generally were isolated from one another and practised privately as complements to their male counterparts or disguised as men (Schiebinger, 1989).

  Prior to institutionalized laboratories, natural philosophers investigated in their residences, often in kitchens where the genders mingled. Supported by hired hands, natural philosophers typically employed sisters or spouses for unpaid and unrecognized work. These relatives organized a hierarchy of assistants and artisans, maintained supplies and equipment, operated apparatus, recorded and classified observations, and wrote and illustrated publications. Thus, the status of women in early modern science was marginalized, although vital, because science depended on women's subordinated and free labour behind the scenes (Fara, 2004).

Galileo also is important, because he promoted observation, experimentation, and mathematical explanation and argument (Drake, 1990). Avoiding metaphysical explanations, he measured natural objects precisely and analyzed his measurements mathematically. Furthermore, his mechanistic explanations for all natural objects inspired natural philosophers' speculations about human nature. In effect, he made comprehending matter central in Western culture.

But natural philosophy was not entirely a masculine enterprise, even though women were marginalized societally, as described in Box 3.1.

During this era the institutionalization of science began with the first scientific academies and journals, while reliance on measurement expanded from astronomy, optics, and technology to physics. But it took an effective communicator and a receptive society for natural philosophy to flourish culturally. That person was Francis Bacon, a lawyer, parliamentarian, and Chancellor of England. Later, France and Germany also embraced natural philosophy.

Francis Bacon

A contributor to the Renaissance tradition of rediscovering ancient Greek philosophy, Bacon was partial to the presocratics, particularly the atomist Democritus. Proposing a "new method" to replace Aristotelian logic, Bacon heralded a "new beginning" for understanding nature. He aimed to marry contemplative knowledge (philosophy) with the practical knowledge (applied science) of the mechanical arts. Captivated by natural philosophy, he believed that unifying knowledge and practice could transform society and provide power over nature; thus, he linked knowledge with power (Rossi, 1996).

Scientific method

Bacon sought to replace both Scholastic reasoning and natural magic with objective, methodical, and public accounts of natural phenomena (Gaukroger, 2001). He insisted that observers should concentrate on the empirical world. For him, observation was the authority for discovering the nature of natural objects, while experimentation was the authority for deriving correct causal explanations (D. N. Robinson, 1995).

Bacon argued that, just as honey-bees collect and digest raw material from which they make a new substance, honey, so understanding nature requires *both* inductive and deductive reasoning. Natural philosophers induce theoretical principles from factual experience *and* deduce new experiments from those principles (Garber, 2001). Bacon rejected only those hypotheses that were ill-supported by evidence or elevated to dogma (Urbach, 1987).

According to Bacon, knowledge and information gained through the senses must be corrected by way of experiments (Rossi, 1996). Inquiry, he argued, begins with observation, but must move through experimentation to reach laws of nature. To overcome biases and make correct inductive generalizations, observations must be put to the test. From laws of nature, new observations can be made and from them, new experiments.

Bacon prescribed **four methodological steps**:

- When investigating a problem, collect all the pertinent data but suspend any theoretical interpretation until you cross-check all possible solutions in a process of elimination.
- Be wary of "idols" (false gods), which are common, ineradicable faulty modes of thinking. Idols impair observer judgment and obscure accurate knowledge of nature. They are comparable to the current concept of observer bias. To counteract the influence of idols, search for negative instances.
- Observers should merely hold a mirror to nature so that she (*sic*) will reveal herself. Nature, not fallible observers, provides the appropriate interpretation (Whitney, 1986). This stance is comparable to the current expression, "let the data speak for themselves."
- Effective, useful findings depend on cooperation among investigators and clear communication of findings (Rossi, 1996).

From these steps Bacon's followers derived **four methodological principles**:

- Natural philosophers rely on objective observations, precisely record them, and generalize only from them, not from preconceived ideas.
- They accumulate knowledge incrementally.
- They achieve consensual validation by cooperating on solving a scientific problem.
- Their knowledge directly serves society.

Section conclusion

At the least, Bacon's natural philosophy contradicted established patterns of faith in religious authority and revelation and did the groundwork for Newton. Bacon's later supporters, including psychologists, claimed that he founded the Scientific Revolution, empiricism, and the scientific method. Yet, although he popularized the new natural philosophy, mathematical analysis played no role in his orientation (Perez-Ramos, 1996).

Bacon's critics concede that his ideas have had practical benefits. However, they contend that in promoting power and control over nature and reducing science to technology he launched centuries of exploitation of the environment and humanity to enrich the privileged and enhance colonial domination of other cultures (Merchant, 2008). Furthermore, critics assert that Bacon dehumanized women in that he subjected feminized nature to invasive examination of her secrets by masculinized natural philosophy, using metaphors of conquest, torture, and sexual assault (Barzun, 2000). Others contend that this criticism is exaggerated.

Isaac Newton

Bacon and Galileo's scientific activities signify a cultural shift in prosperous Western societies from private reflection towards publicly demonstrable claims about the natural world. Natural philosophers' successes, such as **Robert Boyle's** (1627–1691) explanation that chemical properties interact mechanically not spiritually, created a division in society between scholars and the masses, between presumably verifiable scientific "facts" and illusory human experience. This division was sustained by the growing importance of a mercantile economy, mechanized printing making secular readings available, and the diminished power of church authority.

A natural philosopher whose scholarly work accelerated the transition to publicly observable knowledge was Isaac Newton. At age 24, he theorized that gravity is a natural force that integrates the universe. Then in 1687 in his three-volume work, *Philosophiae Naturalis Principia Mathematica* [*Mathematical Principles of Natural Philosophy*], he stipulated laws of physics and methods for calculating their effects.

Newton explained how planetary and tidal motion occurs exactly as his principles predicted. He integrated astronomical observations with mathematics, concluding that a universal law of measurable and predictable gravity could explain all earthly or heavenly motion. Furthermore, he claimed, microscopic particles ("corpuscles") comprise all natural objects and their motion explains all physical events (Downing, 2005). Soon others extended Newtonian principles to psychological phenomena.

Newton's *Principia* had a monumental impact on Western scholars who believed that Newton had revealed the mind of God and made the human mind capable of comprehending a baffling universe. The later French scholar **Voltaire** (1694–1778) characterized him as the master of rationality, vanquishing traditional religious beliefs about nature. But for Newton, mathematical physics, religion, and *alchemy* were interdependent facets of his quest for truth (Westfall, 1980).

Rather than a pseudoscience, alchemy was the medieval, Renaissance, and early modern precursor of modern chemistry. Believing that metals are active but become inert when unearthed, alchemists such as Boyle and Newton tried to reanimate metals and convert them to the most precious metal, gold. In their attempts to imitate natural processes as they understood them, alchemists practised systematic experimentation and produced pigments, acids, and alloys (Westfall, 1980).

Scientific method

In a 1704 book on optics Newton presented his ideas on scientific inquiry and speculated about natural and social sciences. Like Galileo, he believed that the *only* suitable data for science are primary qualities, which are knowable precisely, according to God's laws. Newton's scientific approach consisted of **four principles**:

- There are no exceptions to the natural laws governing the universe. These laws are certain, perfect, and immutable.
- Accept Ockham's razor (i.e., posit no more entities than necessary for an explanation).
- Natural events occur only because of physical forces acting upon them, not because they possess any inherent properties.
- Because human understanding is imperfect, settle for probabilities.

Newton also advanced **four rules** for scientific conduct:

- Admit no more causes than are true and sufficiently explanatory.
- Assign the same causes to the natural effects of the same kind.
- Take as universal qualities what cannot be increased or decreased and what belong to all objects on which one can experiment.
- Consider propositions derived by induction from natural objects as precisely or very nearly true until more precise propositions or exceptions emerge.

Section conclusion

By proposing the laws of gravity and motion Newton explained naturalistically and mathematically with precision, which had an enormous impact on Western culture. Those educated individuals not intimidated by church dogma felt enlightened by his rational, empirically based explanations of Earth and the universe. Furthermore, Newton's scientific principles and rules proved extremely influential. Ever since, natural scientists have considered physics as the foundational science for **two reasons**:

- Physics is the study of the basic building blocks of the material world – the structure of matter and energy in particles and the processes by which they change. Everything that happens in nature depends upon the way that particles are arranged. Thus, to know any natural object one must know its material components and their arrangement.
- Physics was the first science to systematically employ quantitative experimentation as *the* method of inquiry.

These reasons largely formed the philosophical heritage of early natural-science Psychology, which emerged in the nineteenth century during an era of strong faith in Newtonian science. The new psychologists assumed that to know psychological objects one must know their material components. Moreover, for many psychologists Newton epitomized "mathematical deduction and experimental verification," which, taken together, constituted their ideal methodology (Boring, 1950, p. 11). But not all psychologists emulated Newton. Early German psychologists tended to follow Immanuel Kant's reconciliation of empiricism and rationalism.

Small-group discussion. According to the philosophical position of materialism, one can explain everything in nature, including humans, by the movement of atoms and mechanical principles. But if we are only machines, driven to pursue pleasure and avoid pain, what are the implications for morality and meaning in life?

The Enlightenment

The Newtonian framework evoked the next period in Western cultural history, the Enlightenment, which occurred in diverse locations and forms from the late seventeenth to the late eighteenth century. Historians dispute the meaning of the term and the content of Enlightenment thought (Outram, 2005). Some claim that it was a unitary, anti-religious movement, while others regard it as a mélange of tendencies among scholars who applied the principles of natural philosophy. The consensus seems to be that Enlightenment scholars perceived the natural world as knowable objectively through mathematical laws and committed themselves to using reason to solve human problems, based on systematic observation and experimentation (Crocker, 1991).

Enlightenment thought rapidly spread among contemporary natural philosophers. They reclaimed nature from theological interpretations and perceived the natural world as ordered by divine reason and knowable objectively through mathematical laws. Against church and state authority, Enlightenment scholars replaced religion with empirical science as the dominant ideology in Western culture. They felt that through naturalistic explanation and experimentation one could know with certainty everything about nature, human nature, and society, if not immediately, then in the future. Relatedly, Enlightenment scholars believed that progress is inevitable and the most progressive people embrace enlightened thinking, because, they thought, the latest scientific information affirms advances in knowledge.

Scientific advances, which are believed to be products of the scientific method, accelerated during the eighteenth century, stimulated in part by global expeditions, financially supported by royalty and private supporters, and facilitated by applied mathematics. Antecedents of botany, zoology, and physiology also came to prominence, strengthening the social influence of natural philosophy.

Although contemporary science was male-dominated, some wealthy, learned women in eighteenth-century Paris and London organized and administered *salons*. These were semi-formal discussions, with women as active participants, about the latest developments in science and the arts, at which natural philosophers discussed their work (Schiebinger, 1989). A few women were able to acquire education in natural philosophy and to make important scientific contributions.

Yet by the nineteenth century, the theory of *sexual complementarity* prevailed. According to this cultural belief, although women had their areas of expertise, they were essentially different from men biologically, were intellectually inferior, and should remain socially subordinate to men. Thus, middle- and upper-class society assigned the genders separate spheres: women must nurture their family at home, while men must earn income for the family.

Enlightenment psychology

The confidence generated by scientific discoveries inspired the application of natural laws not merely to natural objects and physiological functions but to human psychological phenomena and social relations. When natural philosophers explained human activity according to gravity that binds natural objects together, they extended to human nature a mechanistic conception of nature that operates according to cause-and-effect relations. Yet they did so from diverse perspectives and indebted to their predecessors (Hatfield, 1995).

"Psychology" still meant the study of the soul. Individuals did not yet use "psychology" to describe their reflections on their actions, feelings, and thoughts. In fact, many scholars used the term "anthropology" for the study of bodily aspects of human nature only, although Immanuel Kant used it to encompass all psychological phenomena. "Human nature" meant both understanding humans as natural objects and studying human action to improve moral conduct (R. Smith, 1997).

Christian Wolff's division of philosophical psychology into empirical and rational types bore fruit among some scholars, although Kant critiqued Wolff's polarities and devised his own resolution (Lapointe, 1970; Leary, 1982). Others ignored Wolff's distinction. By the nineteenth century, psychology in Britain generally meant natural philosophy applied to psychological phenomena, while in the US, psychology meant moral and mental philosophy, inspired by Scottish philosopher **Thomas Reid** (1710–1796). In sum, "psychology" had diverse meanings.

Part 1 conclusion

We began this chapter by sketching the cultural, philosophical, and scientific landscape of the early modern period. The spirit of empiricism was rejuvenated during the Scientific Revolution, when social management of societal institutions spread and individualism became more prominent. Astronomical discoveries inspired contemporary scientists, known as natural philosophers, to explore nature and human nature methodically. Bacon and Newton and their followers prescribed general principles and specific steps for practising natural philosophy. Women played important but subordinate roles in scientific activities during this period.

Newton's discoveries in particular stimulated the Enlightenment, an era in which scholars celebrated reason, empirical knowledge, and social progress, while challenging church and state authority. For the "enlightened," Newtonian physics became the standard by which all knowledge was assessed. However, psychological study as we know it did not yet emerge, even though a few natural philosophers investigated psychological processes empirically and many reflected on those processes and on social relations, as you will see in subsequent sections.

Part 2   Preview of early modern philosophical thought

During the early modern era, with the acceptance of Galileo's, Bacon's, and Newton's discourses on the logic of scientific investigation, natural philosophers enthusiastically expanded their explanations of the natural world, including psychological phenomena. In this chapter we examine some of these ideas. To aid your comprehending the diverse perspectives on psychological phenomena in early modern philosophy we review basic conceptions about nature and human nature. Then after defining four philosophical perspectives, we identify psychological questions that early modern natural philosophers addressed.

Basic conceptions

Early modern scholars construed psychological phenomena according to one or more of the following **five conceptions**: naturalism, materialism, mechanism, vitalism, and idealism.

Some natural philosophers proposed purely secular explanations, while for others their Christian beliefs influenced their scientific conceptions.

- *Naturalism* means understanding all reality in natural not religious or spiritual terms. Mental processes are explicable only by sensory processes and secular reason.
- Complementing naturalism is *materialism*, the belief that the only reality, including psychological phenomena, is matter. Many scholars adopted materialism and naturalism.
- According to *mechanism*, body and mind constitute one material substance that obeys mechanical, natural-scientific laws. In current terms, mechanism replaces mind and soul with brain and behaviour. Some early modern thinkers also took a mechanistic position.
- Other thinkers adopted *vitalism*, the belief that life processes cannot be reduced to material mechanisms but involve an immaterial life-force or soul and matter is capable of self-generation and motion.
- *Idealism* means that ultimate reality is not material but mental. Some early modern thinkers, commonly termed rationalists, were idealists.

Four philosophical perspectives on psychological phenomena

Traditionally, historians organize their narratives of the development of psychological thought according to an empiricist–rationalist distinction. But current scholarship suggests that most early modern philosophers who discussed psychological phenomena drew from both empirical and rational orientations. Consequently, our narrative includes **four perspectives**: empiricism/associationism, rationalism, reconciliation, and early romanticism:

- Empiricism in psychological thought was expressed in *associationism*. Inspired by Newtonian natural philosophy and **John Locke's** (1632–1704) philosophical psychology, associationists held that all psychological phenomena originate in atomistic, corpuscular sensations that laws of association combine into complex ideas.
- *Rationalism* stresses the complex operations of an active mind on sensory impressions. Yet many rationalists acknowledged the empirical foundation of knowledge.
- In their respective philosophical approaches of *reconciliation* Immanuel Kant and Thomas Reid balanced rationalism and associationism with moral agency.
- According to early *romanticism*, inspired by **Jean-Jacques Rousseau's** (1712–1778) writings, feelings and social relations are primary in human psychology.

Later in the nineteenth century, philosophical psychologists advanced these four perspectives.

Coupled with scientific and societal changes, these developments became the immediate context for Psychology's institutional emergence (see Chapter 4).

Part 2 conclusion

In this part we reviewed key philosophical terms and explained the main philosophical perspectives that we discuss in Parts 3 to 6. There we describe each scholar's philosophical orientation, scientific approach, and views on psychological processes including social relations, followed by the tenuous connections between each scholar's ideas and current Psychology. But before we proceed some cautions are in order.

The early modern philosophers addressed fundamental questions about body–mind relations, human nature, and social relations. However, the speculative answers they derived must be understood on their historical terms, not ours. Furthermore, although their speculations might help us to see what we presently take for granted, they do not "prefigure" the scientific answers of modern Psychology. From today's perspective, these basic questions might seem unanswerable, but the work of scientific psychologists depends on at least implicit engagement with and practical applications of these questions.

Six basic questions are:

- How are body and mind related? Are they one integrated entity, two aspects of one entity, or separate entities? How is mind related to soul?
- In what way is mind active? How necessary is the concept of mind to understand human psychology?
- How do ideas originate? Do we form ideas from sensory impressions only, from innate mental categories, or from both empirical and rational knowledge?
- Are human beings like all other animals, explicable purely by mechanical principles, or are we special creatures with a life-force unique to us?
- What determines our actions: free will (voluntarism) or other forces (determinism)?
- How can we produce social harmony? By conforming our behaviour to the natural order of the universe, which we can know through reasoned reflection, or by creating societal structures to contain our regressive nature to be selfish, or by exercising rational will and expressing our progressive nature to support one another?

Part 3   Associationist perspectives

Many historians have employed the term "empiricism" to describe various approaches to understanding psychological phenomena that depend on the concept of psychological association. The empiricists were responding to a social context of basic changes in socioeconomic organization and political power that promoted independent inquiry and deep skepticism about theological beliefs and metaphysical explanations. Central to this era of increased freedom of thought was the emergence of complex machines for early industries. Machines provided new metaphors for understanding nature and human nature.

Psychologically speaking, empiricists held that all ideas are derived from sensory experience. They explained the mind the way that Newton explained the universe by attributing thinking to a few laws. Yet their focus was on describing subjective mental experience and their research tool was introspection. Thus, their approach cannot be equated with that of behaviourist psychologists **John Watson** (1878–1958) and B. F. Skinner who banished the study of mental processes and the method of introspection.

Furthermore, diversity of views prevailed among the principal empiricists **Thomas Hobbes** (1588–1679), John Locke, **David Hume** (1711–1776), and **David Hartley** (1705–1757). Later, French scholars, also representing different positions, expanded associationist notions.

Thomas Hobbes

An English humanist, mathematician, and physicist, Thomas Hobbes struggled with developing philosophical principles about how people should live in the face of civil strife, given his distaste for abstract universal essences advanced by Scholastic philosophers and Descartes (Tuck, 1989). Hobbes found his answers in Galileo's materialistic and mechanistic study of natural objects, which, Hobbes believed, was transferable to human nature and society. Later he apparently shifted to dialectical thinking about nature and human nature (Herbert, 1989).

Psychological phenomena

The heart of Hobbes's natural, psychological, and social philosophy was his theory of the passions for which his integrative concept was *conatus* (Gert, 1996; Herbert, 1989). This term meant that motion, or "endeavour" (i.e., striving), characterized all natural objects, including humans' voluntary action. As such, specific psychological functions (e.g., sensing, imagining, desiring, and understanding) proceed from and mediate the passions.

Sensory processes and thinking For Hobbes, all natural objects, including humans, consist of matter interminably in motion. Atomistic particles, interacting restlessly with all other particles and naturally seeking self-preservation, comprise matter. Atomistic particles also constitute human mind and action, and society. Thus, atomistic particles stimulate the body's vital functions (e.g., the appetites), and activate the will.

Inspired by his vision research, Hobbes asserted that sensory impressions stimulate movements of atoms in the brain, resulting in complex mental processes. He denied that there is a central internal organ that synthesizes sensory perceptions, converting them to immaterial thoughts. Rather, he asserted, perceptions and thoughts activate the whole body. Perceptions leave a residue of decaying images, which initially constitute imagination and then with further decay, memory.

Modernizing Aristotle's concepts of contiguity and similarity of associations, Hobbes proposed that thinking results from imagining or remembering links among elements of experience. Directed by desire, associations of time and place evoke ideas and build knowledge from sensory impressions. Ordered thinking, he argued, results from a systematic biophysical process of arithmetically calculating consequences of actions. *deny*

Contending that the mind is wholly material and embodied in the brain, Hobbes repudiated Descartes' position that universal, innate ideas have real existence. He argued that a wholly material soul animates internal and external bodily action. For Hobbes, thinking is corporeal, because mind is matter (Martinich, 1999).

Hobbes ([1651] 1962) stressed that all knowledge comes through the senses: "[T]here is no conception in a man's mind, which hath not at first, totally, been begotten on the organs of sense. The rest are derived from that original" (p. 61). But Hobbes also claimed that whatever we perceive is illusory. He held that sensory qualities do not inhere in external objects but in the person experiencing them. Thus, ears do not hear, only humans do. Consequently, for Hobbes, sensory impressions are deceptive and our observations of the empirical world are biased.

Passions and motivation Hobbes's first law of human nature is that appetites are insatiable, while the second is that reason enables individuals to avoid death and seek peaceful living. From his apparently hedonistic standpoint, humans avoid painful experiences and seek pleasurable ones. Yet he also understood appetites as complexly caused partly by "familial, educational, cultural, or political" sources (Frost, 2008, p. 99).

Passions (affective states) are pivotal in Hobbesian psychology in that they motivate individuals to action. Passions result from two basic motions from the senses to the brain and from there to the heart: facilitative motion, experienced as pleasure, and inhibitory motion, experienced as pain (Martinich, 1999). During this era the term "passions" encompassed love, hate, desire, fear, joy, and sadness and implicated the will; thus, passions had moral and religious connotations. But during the nineteenth century the term "emotions," which came to supersede passions, morally neutralized and physicalized them (Dixon, 2003). Founding psychologists adopted the more scientific rhetoric of emotions rather than the moral rhetoric of passions.

According to Hobbes, two mutually influencing passions comprise conatus, which drives all human actions (Herbert, 1989): desire ("appetite"), which represents endeavour *towards* objects either present or absent, and fear ("aversion"), which represents endeavour *from*. Specific psychological functions (i.e., sensing, imagining, remembering, speaking, and understanding) proceed from and mediate these passions. But passions are distinct from *rational* desires that sustain individuals' well-being (Gert, 1996).

Hobbes asserted that imagination, not will or reason, enables human choice and action (Frost, 2008). Will is the ultimate passion immediately prior to bodily movement of enacted emotion. But he did not posit radically autonomous, rational individuals who author their own actions. Instead, he denied self-determination and understood individuals as embedded in social relations. Yet, for Hobbes, individuals are not mere passive recipients of stimuli, to use psychological language. Rather, he posited six sources of any particular action: one's body, experience, habit, luck, self-regard, and societal authorities (Gert, 1996).

Social relations In his infamous work *Leviathan* (1651), Hobbes discussed the complexities of human nature that a sovereign ruler or government must consider to rule effectively. A common interpretation of Hobbes's statement about a war of all against all, prompting submission to a sovereign to save ourselves, is that he justified an absolute monarchy.

A different interpretation is that Hobbes believed humans are not naturally sociable, yet we are social animals in that we satisfy our needs interdependently. Education works to contain radical individualism and resolve the tension between individuals and society, while actualizing justice and charity enables social harmony.

According to Hobbes, sociability is a product of a rational social order designed to neutralize **three motives** that cause social conflict (Herbert, 1989):

- "Competition," the desire for personal gain.
- "Diffidence," fear for safety.
- "Glory," the desire for reputation.

In this interpretation, Hobbes meant that individuals distrust everyone else's disposition yet we desire respect. Fear sustains hope for a social contract by which we, in rational pursuit of our self-interest, consent to a supreme authority governing a peaceful commonwealth.

For Hobbes, "the pursuit of peace" is humans' "primary commitment" (Frost, 2008, p. 122). Yet this pursuit stems from an interest in survival, not from a commitment to divine law, philosophy, innate virtue, or social mores. For Hobbes, what humans label "good" conduct is merely what gives one pleasure, while "evil" is what causes pain. Altruism is simply an expression of self-preservation. Consequently, free will and universal moral truths are illusions.

Section conclusion

Hobbes's writings have elicited widely divergent interpretations. Many believe his notions foreshadowed Locke's and Hume's. Some read him as a crude mechanist, pessimistic determinist, or radical individualist and associate him with a cynical view of human nature. Others claim he regarded humans as complex, interdependent thinking-bodies.

During his lifetime Hobbes expressed controversial social views, such as moral relativity, and he defended the English king against Parliament. Yet in a culture celebrating free will, his deterministic views antagonized the establishment and served to dissipate trust in the claims that church authorities made about nature and human nature. Consequently, English society regarded Hobbes as an atheist or heretic, which endangered his life.

Connection to Psychology Some historians of Psychology have depicted Hobbes, due to his focus on mechanical motion, as a "pre-behaviourist" who held that one can modify human nature just as one can manipulate natural objects. They claim that early Psychology is similar to his mental physics and that his notion of innate aggression is similar to Sigmund Freud's notion of the Id. But these presentist links to Psychology are rather tenuous.

From a critical perspective, Hobbes's conception of interdependent individuals situated in a constellation of relationships was central to his philosophy. For him, individuals are simultaneously active agents and objects of other agents' actions; accordingly, social relations and contexts shape an individual's passions and thinking. Furthermore, Hobbes valued introspection and subjective experience. Thinking and feeling, he argued, are interdependent, and embodied desire grounds and directs thinking. As we will see, his materialistic but subjectivist account of thinking, passions, and behaving differs radically from Descartes' belief in a dominant mind controlling a subordinate body.

John Locke

Another natural philosopher identified with British empiricism is John Locke, who was educated in medicine, practised chemistry with Boyle, and presented a political theory. Influenced by Newton, Locke turned to exploring the mental processes that produce knowledge and sought to uncover the atoms of human understanding. He tried to understand the nature of sensory experience and its relation to reflective thought.

Like Descartes, Locke made knowing what was conscious to oneself crucial for natural philosophy, thereby inserting psychological phenomena into philosophical understanding of the nature of knowledge (i.e., epistemology). In *An Essay Concerning Human Understanding* (1689) he addressed the origins, nature, and limits of knowledge. Arguably, his theory of knowledge provided an initial framework for natural philosophy.

Psychological phenomena

Although Locke did not present a comprehensive account of psychological phenomena (Jolley, 1999), his medical practice and research led him to apply a naturalistic and reductionistic perspective to some mental processes (McCann, 1993). He reasoned that mental matter consists of indivisible corpuscles or atoms, bonded by a psychological force, which is analogous to Newton's explanation of gravity.

For Locke, the mind's essence lay in its operations not its consciousness (Jolley, 1999). One can study mental operations that link personal existence to concrete relations with the empirical world, he reasoned. Thus, consciousness derives from direct experience and mental functions are located within individuals, not the cosmos or the soul.

Sensory impressions Locke believed that the content of consciousness consists of elements of sensation. Located in the body, sensory elements can be *primary* or *secondary*, he argued. Following Galileo's distinction, primary qualities refer to measurable mathematical properties of natural objects (e.g., the spatial dimensions and colour of yellow roses), while secondary qualities refer to subjective and uncertain impressions of those objects (e.g., seeing yellow roses), activated by a particular sensory mechanism (e.g., vision). Although scientists examine objects atomistically in terms of their primary qualities, ordinary perception deals with secondary qualities.

Locke proposed that human beings enter the world with a metaphorical *tabula rasa* (i.e., blank tablet) on which experience and education inscribe ideas (Wilson, 2007). Observing child development from infancy, he reasoned, shows that ideas originate from sensation or reflection. Locke ([1689] 1924) wrote:

In time the mind comes to reflect on its own operations about the ideas got by sensation, and thereby stores itself with a set of ideas, which I call ideas of reflection ...Thus the first capacity of human intellect is fitted to receive the impressions made on it, either through the senses by outward objects, or by its own operations when it reflects on them. (pp. 51–52)

To summarize Locke's views, the mind gives meaning to sensory impressions; all ideas result from connected sensations. Although the mind does not contain innate ideas, individuals have innate capacities to process the content of experience and instincts that require socialization. The mind operates the way in which natural philosophers function: verifying closely observed, lawful connections in the natural world.

Simple and complex ideas At the heart of Locke's framework is the notion of "ideas," which for him are generic mental objects, encompassing sensations, perceptions, and passions as well as thoughts, beliefs, or propositions (Billig, 2008).

There are **two sources** of *simple* ideas:

- Knowledge from sensation concerns the external world. Sensory experiences directly cause ideas, with simple sensations combining to form an idea from units of experience. Within this source of ideas the mind is passive.
- Knowledge from reflection pertains to consciousness of one's own mental processes. Within this source the mind is active.

Locke envisioned various mental operations on *complex* ideas, such as abstracting general principles from particular circumstances. In addition, he postulated three ways of deriving evidence: sensitive (factual) knowledge of the empirical world, intuition, and logical demonstration.

Will, motivation, and identity Locke also emphasized willing. Voluntary action, he asserted, is the result of a sense of uneasiness, which induces a desire for a positive or negative "absent good." Individuals' own pleasure and pain shapes their will (Chappell, 2007). In his explanation of "motives" Locke argued that individuals change their state when they are dissatisfied with it (Jolley, 1999). But he had little to say about emotions.

For Locke, experience in the empirical world forms the mind, the self, and personal identity. But he believed that, although mental content was learned, mental *operations* were innate. Locke also agreed with Descartes that every experience of consciousness implies the self's existence.

Memory serves a pivotal function in Locke's conception of personal identity. Memory enables us to construct a sense of self from experience. Thus, the sense of self is the consequence of a mental capacity for abstracting from particular individual actions (C. Taylor, 1989).

Social relations Because of his focus on self-interest, Locke philosophized about psychological functioning in autonomous individuals, abstracted from social-historical contexts. His underlying concept was that of individualistic detachment. This standpoint helped to birth modern psychological individualism and is one of the intellectual conditions that facilitated the birth of Psychology focused on individuals. Locke did not address interpersonal relations per se; rather, he championed the individualistic interests of the burgeoning middle class (Wood, 1983).

In discussing ethical conduct, which he claimed derives from experience, not from innate moral principles, Locke treated ethical conduct pragmatically (Wilson, 2007). He argued that "good" is simply that which causes well-being, while "evil" is that which causes misery and pain. To be ethical one does not have to know what the essence of good is, which is unknowable. One just needs to know, Locke claimed, what good persons *do*, which *is* knowable. Morality and ethical conduct depend on one's pragmatic experience with social mores.

Section conclusion

Locke's views influenced many contemporaries and successors who lionized him as much as Newton (Aarsleff, 1993). But despite his rejection of innate ideas, he assumed that natural law and natural rights were inborn phenomena. From a critical perspective, Locke, unusual for his time, recommended equivalent education for girls and boys, although he did not treat gender issues systematically (Schiebinger, 1989). In addition, he explained cultural differences in achievement as consequences of unequal opportunity (Aarsleff, 1993).

Locke's foster-son, Anthony Ashley Cooper (1671–1713), the third Earl of **Shaftesbury**, challenged his views. In *Characteristicks* [*sic*] *of Men, Manners, Opinions, Times* (1711),

Shaftesbury depicted human nature as intrinsically interpersonal rather than ignoring social-historical contexts as Locke had done (Billig, 2008). Whereas society's increasing individualism was expressed in Locke's privileging the sense of self and individual self-interest, Shaftesbury regarded it as impeding the sense of community. Instead, he proposed "common sense," an inborn disposition towards moral social relations. This notion influenced Reid and other Scottish Enlightenment philosophers (see below). Furthermore, whereas Locke sought clear truths, Shaftesbury rejected the certainty of knowledge. Locke reduced mental processes atomistically, but Shaftesbury understood mental processes as interrelated aspects of a total system.

Connection to Psychology Many psychologists have regarded Locke as a significant influence on the discipline. The **historical record**, however, tempers that assessment in **six ways**:

- Locke's empiricist belief that knowledge comes through sensory experience helped form the philosophical foundation of natural-science Psychology, but rational reflection, which behaviourists excluded, is central in his conception.
- Locke understood "association of ideas" to mean how humans *inhibit* rational thinking by trusting incorrect connections of ideas, which cause faulty thinking. But for Hobbes, David Hume, and David Hartley, association *enables* thinking. Later, many psychologists adopted the latter meaning but attributed it incorrectly to Locke (Aarsleff, 1993). In this sense, Locke was not an associationist.
- Locke has more in common with cognitive psychology than behaviourism, because he studied perceptual and thought processes empirically, atomistically, and individualistically, devoid of social-historical context. For instance, when he described infants, he excluded parental and generational influences (Billig, 2008).
- Locke connected objective knowledge with sensory impressions and subjective experience with passions. For him, sensation and perception are distinct from passions; what we sense and perceive differs from any feelings aroused by the perceived object. This distinction is one origin of the objectivity–subjectivity polarity in natural-science Psychology in which objectivity is celebrated and subjectivity denigrated.
- Locke's discourse on personal identity and the self was foundational in Western thought (Jolley, 1999). Afterwards, the traditional belief in personal identity stemming from an immortal soul waned.
- Locke's pragmatic approach to ethics is reflected in the APA's perspective on ethical principles and standards (see Chapter 8).

David Hume

A Scottish scholar of the eighteenth-century Enlightenment, David Hume aimed to situate a Newtonian atomistic philosophy of human nature in direct observable experience. For Hume, all thought and knowledge derive from the senses.

Philosophical approach

From Descartes, Hume absorbed the standpoint of radical doubt (Coventry, 2007) and insisted on separating verifiable knowledge from faith, knowing from believing. But Hume, regarded as a skeptic, rejected the Cartesian notion of innate ideas and the need to establish, *a priori*, first principles about the ultimate nature of reality. Instead, he adopted Locke's view that experience is the basis of all knowledge.

On the other hand, Hume challenged Locke's assumption that humans have access to an external world beyond perceptions and rejected Locke's distinction between primary and secondary qualities. Hume asserted that primary qualities are relative and as dependent on the observer as secondary qualities are.

Also, Hume cautioned that because humans are prone to cognitive errors, there are limits to understanding and to certainty of knowledge about nature. Like the Sophists, he asserted that there are no absolute truths. But he did not deny certainty about one's personal experience.

Psychological phenomena

Hume applied to human nature the same rigorous method as natural philosophers applied to nature (i.e., systematic empirical observation of human activity), because, he reasoned, humans are natural objects. In his major work, *An Enquiry Concerning Human Understanding* (1748), Hume contended that natural-science principles could explain mental processes just as gravity explains the dynamics of the universe (R. Smith, 1997). He then presented a mechanistic account of psychological phenomena as natural objects, examinable by experimental reasoning.

Hume envisioned a fully Newtonian mind in which impressions and ideas are the atoms of all psychological phenomena and social relations (Coventry, 2007). Although he acknowledged physiological mechanisms, he did not focus on the mind–body problem (Jolley, 1999). Rather, he explained psychological phenomena in terms of the association of ideas.

Hume began with perceptual processes, which for him were analogous to Newton's corpuscular elements that purportedly comprise all natural objects. Experience, mediated by perception, produces mental content, while the active mind is a heap of diverse perceptions. Hume posited two **types of perception** (Coventry, 2007):

- Simple or complex "impressions" are very powerful, foundational perceptions with associated feelings. Impressions include sensations, passions, emotions, and reflections on mental content.
- "Ideas," which include images, are persistent but frailer forms or copies of impressions.

Against Locke, Hume excluded sensations from his category of ideas. He held that ideas are the product of compounded impressions. Like impressions, ideas are simple or complex, but unlike impressions, they are expressed in imagination and memory, and manifest in processes of reasoning (or understanding). Reasoning pertains to relations of ideas or to matters of fact.

What binds ideas together is association. Hume argued that ideas possess a force of attraction to each other, comparable to gravity. When actualized by Aristotle's laws of association, the "gentle force" of mental gravity leads to the unconscious association of ideas. In sum, impressions are the foundation of ideas and ideas are the basis of thought. The mechanics of the mind, operating in predictable forms, produce human behaviour, there being no essential difference between physical and mental causality.

Although Hume posited that humans possess superior reasoning to animals (Coventry, 2007), he claimed that passions should rule reason. Passions motivate general conduct, while reason enables us to assess whether particular means will achieve what we want. In effect, Hume proposed "instrumental reason," meaning the mental capacity for calculating the optimum path for human action under the influence of passions (Danziger, 1997b). Thus, instrumental reason serves passions.

For Hume, patterns of passions, associated with particular impressions and ideas, differ across individuals and explain a person's characteristic behaviour. Rewards and punishments, he argued, not reasoning, shape the regulation of passions in animals, children, and adults. He said:

[A]nimals . . . , by the proper application of rewards and punishment, may be taught any course of action, [even] the most contrary to their natural instincts and propensities. Is it not experience, which makes [a dog] answer to his name, and infer from such an arbitrary sound, that you mean him rather than any of his fellows, and intend to call him, when you pronounce it in a certain manner, and with a certain tone and accent? . . . Animals, therefore, are not guided in these inferences by reasoning: Neither are children: Neither are the generality of mankind . . . (Hume, [1748] 1977, pp. 70–71)

Social relations Concerning personal identity, Hume rejected beliefs in an immortal soul connected to God and in a permanent, integrated self. Instead, selves are simply bundles of diverse perceptions and result from associated ideas. Memory unifies these ideas, he claimed, and is the source of our sense of identity. Self-image is the result of the social influence that humans exercise on one another (Penelhum, 2000).

By assuming that moral conduct is located in social relations (Hardin, 2007), Hume opposed the Scholastics' emphasis on virtues and Locke's emphasis on rational thinking. He contended that, although morality strongly influences human action, morality is neither objective nor derived from abstract reason. Rather, it consists of the useful consequences of individuals' actions; humans simply find utility pleasing.

In addition, Hume argued that besides self-interest, individuals possess innate capacities for moral conduct and public interest, which enhance survival. For him, the primary moral inclination is "sympathy" or "benevolence," that is, a natural feeling for humankind. Benevolence as a communicative act motivates individuals to perform acts of justice and bonds society together. For Hume, individuals' desire for social approval and recognition enables us to direct our social behaviour to benevolence. Thus, we are naturally inclined to conform to societal norms of expected social conduct, and personal motives mould individuals' moral character (Penelhum, 2000).

Section conclusion

The British establishment regarded Hume as a dangerous skeptic who questioned not only the existence of God but also empirical reality. However, what Hume repudiated was metaphysical speculation ungrounded in descriptive observation. Meanwhile, French scholars (see below) praised him for introducing a scientific approach to human nature and society. By emphasizing experience as the basis for all knowledge-claims Hume inspired the nineteenth-century positivist philosopher Auguste Comte (see Chapter 4) and twentieth-century logical-positivist philosophers (see Chapter 6).

Connection to Psychology For natural-science psychologists, the centrepiece of Humean thought is the association of ideas by which he stressed that associated empirical impressions are the foundation of ideas and ideas are the basis of thought. Although Hume's associationism contributed to behaviourism's implicit epistemological foundation, he based everything on subjective, first-person consciousness, which is antithetical to behaviourism. In addition, current psychological notions of a socially constructed self resemble Hume's notion of fluid and fragmented personal identity.

Historically, some modern scientists have celebrated Hume's admonition against value-judgments corroding analyses of everyday behaviour. One cannot derive an *ought* (what one should do based on values) from an *is* (facts that one has observed), he claimed. Some psychologists have invoked this position to argue against colleagues' involvement *as psychologists* in social and political change (see Chapter 12).

David Hartley

Although Hume and Locke ignored the body–mind problem, David Hartley, who was an English physician not a philosopher, did not. In *Observations on Man, His Frame, His Duty, and His Expectations* (1749), Hartley described human psychophysiology according to Newtonian mechanistic principles. In this work Hartley also speculated about human nature, theology, and moral philosophy.

Psychological phenomena

Indebted to Locke, Hartley assumed that just as mechanical laws govern natural objects, composed of atoms, so they govern the "component particles" of human bodies (Allen, 1999). But like Descartes, Hartley believed that natural objects and humans consist of both a material body and an immaterial mind/soul. He then united physiological and psychological phenomena, situating consciousness in neurological processes of the brain stem. Although this biological position contradicts his belief in an immaterial mind/soul, he held that God is the ultimate cause of all physical reality.

Hartley proposed two neurophysiological concepts, "vibrations" and "association," and applied them to all psychological processes. Thus, he explained perception, thought, and kinetic movement as the result of vibrations within nerve fibres that are transmitted to other fibres in interconnected webs of association. The conjunction of association and vibrations, he argued, is responsible for sensory processes, ideas, and human action.

Accepting Newton's hypothesis that physical impulses, such as nerve transmission, occur by vibrations, Hartley reasoned that the spinal cord, brain stem, and nerves govern sensation and movement, while the brain governs ideas. Sensory experience triggers vibrations of molecular particles of the nerves, which travel to the brain and produce sensations. If the vibrations are moderate, Hartley argued, pleasure results; if they are violent, pain results. Residues of weaker vibrations left behind by original vibrations cause ideas and memory.

Hartley proposed parallel, but not identical, laws for mental processes: cerebral vibrations parallel mental events in that they are correlated with the internal feelings of sensations and ideas, while association links sensations and ideas (Walls, 1982). For Hartley, like Hume, the association of ideas operates like the law of gravity (C. Smith, 1987).

Relying on association, Hartley explained perception (e.g., distance vision), language, and thinking as the consequences of neuronally associated, joint impressions. Through automatic successive or simultaneous association, simple sensations compound to form complex ones. Compounded sensations form a simple idea, while associated simple ideas assemble into a complex idea. Compounded complex ideas, in turn, can form "decomplex" ideas, such as sophisticated linguistic expressions.

According to Hartley, humans' involuntary reflexive activity, paradoxically, is the basis for voluntary actions. Stressing that voluntary control of physical activity occurs through association, he coined the term "automatic" to refer to involuntary, homeostatic physiological actions (e.g., heart rate). Moreover, he linked voluntary, skilled muscular movements, such as children learn to perform, to motoric vibration, physical sensation, and correlated ideas. Thus, he disposed of a will that directs the mind to execute a specific kinetic activity (Allen, 1999).

Social relations   For Hartley, complex associations also are the basis for the sense of self, which develops in a sociolinguistic context of relationships along with emotional memories of those relationships (Allen, 1999). His explanation of the origin of laughter in children illustrates how linguistic, interpersonal, and emotional development is intertwined:

As children learn the use of language, they learn also to laugh at sentences or stories, by which sudden alarming emotions and expectations are raised in them, and again dissipated instantaneously. And as they learnt before by degrees to laugh at sudden unexpected noises, or motions, where there was no fear, or no distinguishable one, so it is after time in respect of words. (Hartley, [1749] 1966, Part 1, pp. 438–439)

According to Hartley, in earlier developmental stages, individuals rely on imagination, ambition, and self-interest. But ideally in later stages, they develop social virtues. In Hartley's view, complete identification with divine purposes inclines humans towards moral conduct and happiness. Virtuous behaviour is associated with pleasure and the pleasurable effects of past behaviour guide future behaviour.

For Hartley, individual desire is related to the common good. Hence, for him, association has strong social connotations and serves as an adhesive for social relations (R. Smith, 1997). If one knows how association operates, one can identify and practise good associations, not evil ones. Central to cultivating this moral sense is nurturing relationships with others ("sympathy") and with God (for which Hartley coined the term "theopathy") (Allen, 1999). When the person fully expresses sympathy and theopathy, the self transforms from a lower to a higher state and eventually annihilates.

Section conclusion

Hartley took a mechanistic and naturalistic approach to many psychological phenomena by situating perception, emotion, thought, and kinetic activity in the brain. He also used the term psychology in a relatively modern sense (Allen, 1999). Although his peers criticized Hartley's doctrine of vibrations and his premise that neurological processes are the bases of consciousness, his speculations about localized brain functions and specific nerve energies emerged as important research findings in nineteenth-century physiology (Walls, 1982).

Connection to Psychology Hartley's psychology was a speculative amalgam of neurophysiology, human development, and religion. Yet he seems to have been closer than other early modern thinkers to establishing the intellectual framework for natural-science Psychology (Walls, 1982). Hartley's psychophysiological speculations proved influential thanks to founding US psychologist, **William James**, who discussed his work (Allen, 1999). In addition, founding French psychologist, **Theodule Ribot** (1839–1916) echoed Hartley's views on the relationship between thinking and voluntary and involuntary kinetic activity.

Furthermore, Hartley significantly advanced the concept of association, which became prominent in Anglo-American Psychology. Even Wilhelm Wundt based his mental-chemistry hypothesis on the concept. In addition, **Ivan Pavlov's** (1849–1936), neurophysiology and other physiologists' observations of "action potentials" in sensory nerves are similar to Hartley's concept of sensory vibrations irradiating the brain (C. Smith, 1987). As well, psychologist **Donald Hebb's** (1904–1985) "cell-assemblies" hypothesis resembles Hartley's explanation of compounded associations (see Chapter 6).

Some historians of Psychology claim that Hartley paved the way for behaviourism with his notion of passive mental processes. A different view is that behavioural psychologists ignored Hartley's broad metaphor of association to focus on stimulus–response connections and invoked the laws of contiguity and repetition to explain association literally and technically (Danziger, 1990). Furthermore, although Hartley believed that the formation of ideas was equivalent to physical processes involving natural elements, he and his contemporaries also used association to explain societal organization.

Early modern French psychologies

French intellectuals, representing diverse standpoints, were as inspired by the Enlightenment as British scholars. Some advocated developing knowledge and society on the basis of scientific reason, while others proposed explanations of body–mind relations.

The *philosophes*

One group of critical thinkers, the *philosophes* (philosophers), was enamoured of Newton's physics, French scientific discoveries, and Locke's psychological thought. The *philosophes* included François-Marie Arouet, known as Voltaire and renowned for his satirical writings, and the female natural philosopher Emilie du Chatelet (1706–1749).

The *philosophes* were committed to free debate guided by scientific knowledge so as to shape public opinion and improve society. They argued that reason enables progress through the accumulation of systematic knowledge about society just as scientists empirically observe nature. They urged rational social reform and scientific administration of society according to the laws of nature, free from church and state interference.

Underlying the vocation of the *philosophes* to contribute to society were three modernist concepts – reason, progress, and nature – and the conviction that scientifically derived knowledge could reform society. These notions prevailed among later natural scientists and formed the eventual rationale for applications of Psychology to society. But the privileged place assigned to scientific knowledge contributed to a distortion of that knowledge, known as *scientism*, meaning the exaggerated, almost religious faith in the powers of reason and natural science. Scientism became prominent in the nineteenth century (see Chapter 4).

French psychologies

The *philosophe* whose views seem most germane to extant psychological thought was **Denis Diderot**. Other French scholars who thought about psychological phenomena adopted the associationism of Hume and Hartley, but they did so differently from one another, as evidenced by the physicians **Julien de La Mettrie** and **Pierre-Jean-George Cabanis** and the philosopher **Etienne Bonnot de Condillac**.

Denis Diderot Addressing physiological and psychological phenomena, Denis Diderot (1713–1784) discussed the relationship between matter and consciousness of sensations, the sensory adaptation of individuals with compromised sensory functions, and the sensory origins of thought (Staum, 1980). Reflecting on the transitory nature of the self, Diderot argued, like Hume, that memory is the means by which individuals develop personal identity. Also, he understood organisms as composed of interdependent, unified systems. For him, the soul/mind is embodied, yet matter and nature are always in flux.

Later, Diderot argued that passions, impulses, and instincts are more powerful than reason (Barzun, 2000). He also asserted that, although human beings biologically are animals, we are not explicable mechanistically. Rather, reviving vitalism, Diderot insisted that matter possesses the capacity to sense, even to think. This vitalist position re-emerged as a major theme of romanticism.

Politically, Diderot promoted social benevolence and civic responsibility, and criticized contemporary sexual mores. Equating human nature with physical nature, he had a particular interest in the body–mind intimacy that sexual activity evokes (R. Smith, 1997). Although, like his contemporaries, he idealized Tahiti's "noble savages," unlike many contemporaries, he opposed colonialism and slavery (May, 1991).

Julien de La Mettrie Promoting a materialist conception of human nature and drawing from medical observations, Julien de La Mettrie (1709–1751) addressed a question that resonates today in behavioural neuroscience: how can we know human nature without comparing human and animal biology?

La Mettrie held that humans only differed from other animals quantitatively; all animals, he claimed, are made from the same metaphorical bread-dough. He also argued that, if apes learned human language, they would resemble us even more and learn to become little gentlemen (*sic*). Furthermore, if we accepted our commonality with other animals, we would treat each other more compassionately.

In *The Natural History of the Soul* (1745) La Mettrie criticized his predecessor Descartes for ignoring bodily effects on mental events. La Mettrie asserted that all natural objects, including humans, are composed solely of matter and motion and obey natural laws. Accepting the view that sensory impressions form ideas, he claimed that the interaction of sensory experience with brain functions, not the soul, is the source of knowledge (R. Smith, 1997).

In *Machine Man* (1748) La Mettrie argued that, if philosophers were physicians and understood the body, they would not be dualists and posit a separate soul. Instead, they would realize that humans are automata who automatically seek sensual pleasure (De Vos, 2011). Thus, bodily processes shape consciousness and thought. All mental events, such as thinking and doubting, La Mettrie contended, are as material as electricity and mental illness results from brain dysfunction.

For La Mettrie, the soul is "an enlightened machine," because its faculties are completely dependent upon the body. But he also held that matter is active, natural objects possess organizing capacities, and humans are symbol-making machines, analyzing the worldly objects we imagine with their names and symbols.

Etienne Bonnot de Condillac Superficially, the views of Etienne Condillac (1715–1780) reflect La Mettrie's dynamic mechanism. Against the Cartesian notion of innate ideas, he too argued that sensations were the basis for all ideas (R. Smith, 1997). Thus, he compared the person to an intelligent statue that learns about its environment through the awakening of one sense at a time. Sensory processes lead to feeling, seeking pleasure, avoiding pain, remembering, using words in place of sensations to speak and write, and generating complex ideas based on linguistic development.

However, although he dispensed with metaphysical explanations of mind, Condillac acknowledged the importance of reflection on mental processes. Moreover, humans, unlike statues, possess a soul. Evidently, he never claimed that sensations are only biological and the mind is passive (Staum, 1980). Condillac held instead that the human soul precedes sensations, language distinguishes humans from animals, and knowledge of human nature enables citizens to construct a rational society.

Pierre-Jean-George Cabanis Rejecting Condillac's and La Mettrie's materialism as well as Cartesian dualism, Pierre-Jean-George Cabanis (1757–1808) was involved in medical, educational, and social reform as a philosopher, professor of medicine, and senator (Staum, 1980). He envisioned human science as an integration of social ethics, philosophy, and medical physiology. Like many intellectual children of the Enlightenment, he believed that changing social-environmental conditions paternalistically would improve everyone's well-being and would perfect humankind.

Following Diderot's notions of an embodied soul/mind and of ever-changing matter and nature, Cabanis held that individuals are a physical and moral unity. Employing a term translated in English as "physical sensitivity," he developed a systematic psychophysiology. He argued that bodily sensations are interrelated and linked to the central nervous system and to cognitive and behavioural functions.

Cabanis was particularly interested in developmental, gender, and temperamental differences among individual cases. Based on clinical observations, he described the central nervous system in terms of three levels of functioning: mechanical reflexes, semi-conscious actions, and conscious thought and volition. He concluded that mental processes, such as consciousness, require active cortical functioning, yet the same mechanical principles control reflexes and full consciousness. On the other hand, he also held that subconscious physical sensitivity explains bodily and mental processes, for instance, empathy.

Because of his comprehensive, empirical account of unified body–mind relations Cabanis' views seem as important for understanding the origins of psychological ideas as Hartley's. Cabanis' emphasis on the central nervous system influenced the nineteenth-century physiologists François Magendie (1783–1855) and Marie-Jean-Pierre Flourens (1794–1867).

Section conclusion

During the Enlightenment, diverse French conceptions of human nature and society signified the secular turn in Western thought away from church doctrine about nature and human nature towards reason, supported by the natural philosophy of Newton and his followers. What the French Enlightenment scholars shared was a strong interest in understanding the relationship between bodily and mental processes. Diderot stressed the capacity of humans for reasoning while acknowledging that we also are passionate animals. La Mettrie viewed us as sensualist machines capable of making symbolic meaning. According to Cabanis, humans are statues, but intelligent ones animated by soul. Condillac also explained humans as psychophysiological beings endowed with soul/minds. Although in continental European societies, these distinct but related views of French Enlightenment scholars had some influence, in Anglo-American circles the discourse of associationism predominated.

Part 3 conclusion

The zeitgeist encouraged seventeenth and eighteenth-century philosophers during the Scientific Revolution and the Enlightenment to extend Galileo's and then Newton's materialistic and mechanistic studies of natural objects to human nature and psychological phenomena. Hobbes applied the ideology of the mechanization of nature to psychological processes and social relations, relying on the ancient concept of atoms. Later scholars, such as Locke, Hume, and Hartley, adopted Newtonian concepts to explain psychological processes.

According to the standard interpretation in natural-science Psychology of the origins of psychological thought, Locke's and Hume's associationism played the pivotal role conceptually in early Psychology and even in the psychoanalytic concept and practice of "free association" (e.g., Boring, 1950). A different interpretation is that, practically, Hartley's concept of association, which he linked with physiological functions, influenced emergent natural-science Psychology more than Hume's or Locke's (R. Smith, 1997).

Part 4 Rationalist perspectives

Although René Descartes, **Baruch Spinoza** (1632–1677), Gottfried Leibniz, and **George Berkeley** (1685–1753) typically are associated in Psychology with idealism and subjectivism, their respective rationalist positions were more subtle than the attributions of idealism and subjectivism suggest.

René Descartes

Employing a vision that was both empirical and rationalist, René Descartes (1596–1650) introduced psychological notions that disrupted extant thought. He explored body–mind relations, the certainty and reliability of knowledge, and the relation between subjective and objective knowledge. Descartes strove to balance reason and subjectivity with empiricism and mechanism when studying physiological and psychological processes (D. Clarke, 2006). He also contributed to the logic of scientific inquiry.

Congruent with his cultural-historical context, Descartes claimed that God was the ultimate criterion for creatures' mental activity (Sorrell, 1987). Like other natural philosophers, he sought a secular account of mind/soul/psyche that allowed room for theological beliefs. He was aware of the church's capacity to condemn new ideas and to place scholars, such as Galileo, under house arrest for defying church doctrine about nature and human nature.

Philosophical approach

Descartes believed that a God-given, comprehensive mathematical framework integrated with mechanical physics provided the most objective account of nature (D. Clarke, 2006). Like Locke, he affirmed Galileo's distinction between primary and secondary qualities of nature. Natural philosophy, these thinkers maintained, only pertains to knowledge of primary qualities. Accordingly, scientific knowledge of personal experience is impossible.

Descartes' basic philosophical approach was deduction from first principles. According to his "method of doubt," whatever one can doubt cannot be shown to be true. The method of doubt reveals only those things that are certain. Just as a house requires a firm foundation, he argued, only a complex, unified system of things established as certain can be the basis for true knowledge about natural objects.

Psychological phenomena

Descartes interpreted physiological functions and psychological phenomena largely from Scholastic and Galenic ideas. Thus, for him, mind existed as soul (Cottingham, 1998). Descartes described the nervous system as the mechanical movement of particles. He held that physical reality had cause-and-effect relations and was amenable to mathematical analysis. He applied this framework to psychological phenomena. But he never used the term "psychology" (Hatfield, 1992).

Sensory-motor processes Scholastic scholars adopted Aristotle's view that the human soul consists of vegetative, sensitive, and rational aspects. Following this system, Descartes applied a micro-mechanical explanation to vegetative functions (e.g., growth and reproduction) and sensitive functions (e.g., sensory processes and motion).

Automated, dancing musicians in the gardens of Saint-Germain, Paris, inspired the youthful Descartes to describe organic functions of the nervous system and behavioural tendencies (e.g., courage and tardiness) mechanistically (Gaukroger, 1995). Just as water powered these devices, he explained, so *animal spirits* (i.e., tiny material components of blood) are the dynamic force in animals' reflexive actions. Although animals are not literally machines, Descartes argued, they are like them in that they lack reason and will. For him, some animals have cognitive capacities but not judgment, reflective awareness of mental life, and language.

Descartes asserted that the soul's rational aspects do not derive from sensory experience. In addition, he rejected the naïve-realist view that perceptual images unerringly mirror the natural objects they represent. Instead, he argued that perceptual images differ from the actual objects perceived. He maintained that rather than having direct perceptual access to the real world, humans perceive natural objects indirectly and interpretively (D. Clarke, 2006).

Body–mind relation   Initially, Descartes argued that some experiences originate in the body and others in the soul. He equated superior mind with thought and the immaterial soul, and nature and the inferior body with measurable dimensions. He used the science of mechanics and physical cause-and-effect relations to understand living bodies and explain the passions. Thus, for Descartes, individuals ruled by their passions are "mechanical" persons. The term *Cartesian dualism* captures his distinction between voluntary (mind) and involuntary (body) action.

In his *Meditations on First Philosophy* Descartes ([1641] 1985) considered how a material body is connected with a bodiless mind/soul by describing awareness of bodily sensations:

Nature also teaches me, by these sensations of pain, hunger, thirst, and so on, that I am not merely present in my body as a sailor is present in a ship, but that I am very closely joined and, as it were, intermingled with it, so that I and the body form a unit. (p. 56)

Later Descartes integrated physiology and mental faculties. In 1642, his friend Princess Elisabeth of Bohemia (1618–1680) had challenged the contradiction in his supposition that an immaterial mind/soul could cause a material body to move (Fara, 2004). Subsequently, he proposed that the mind/soul has two interrelated functions: passions and actions. Any bodily action is also a passion of the mind/soul.

For Descartes, this interrelationship or substantial union of body and mind best explains emotions. Bodily appetites, sensory awareness, and passions are not reducible to either thought or physiology; rather, they are a blend of physiological and mental processes, and emotion is the link between bodily and mental processes. Specific passions, Descartes argued, are innate dispositions seeking what benefits the person and avoiding what is harmful (D. Clarke, 2006). To the basic passions, he added wonder. He also described how the will aids reason in moderating the passions (Gaukroger, 1995).

In his new synthesis, Descartes hypothesized learned connections among bodily actions, passions, and thoughts. He described such associations in terms of memory and imagination linking innate biological responses and emotional responses acquired from experience. Once the link is established, he argued, specific body movements and thoughts persist in their co-occurrence. In this sense, some claim that he partially laid the conceptual foundation for psychologists' conditioning theory (D. Clarke, 2006).

The thinking subject   Emphasizing self-examination and the subjective self, Descartes introduced radical doubt to the contemporary assumption of certain knowledge. He asserted that all that humans can know with certainty is that we are conscious that we are experiencing. By his famous statement (in Latin), "*cogito ergo sum*" (literally, "I think, therefore, I am"), Descartes meant, "My mind/soul makes me aware that I exist." He situated consciousness in point-like fashion within the human being, as depicted in Figure 3.2.

Descartes introduced this argument as fundamental to his philosophy – he cannot doubt that he thinks and if he thinks he must exist – which he linked to God. By his conception of "the thinking subject" he assumed that an immaterial mind/soul, dependent on God, originates the doubting and thinking (Gaukroger, 1995).

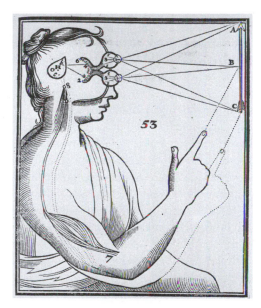

Figure 3.2 Descartes depicted consciousness as located in point-like fashion within the human being

Similarly, Descartes believed that only an immaterial mind/soul, independent of the body, can direct consciousness, thought, will, and language. When memory and inference are involved in thinking, we lose certainty, because they are faulty. But provided we draw from empirical demonstration, we can rely on memory and inference reasonably, although without certainty.

For Descartes, the immaterial mind/soul is distinct from and superior to matter just as men (*sic*) are superior to the rest of nature. He promoted the notion of a separate mental world, represented by reasoning, governed by innate ideas, and knowable by introspection. Subsequent natural philosophers (e.g., Locke) also would incorporate introspection.

Social relations In concert with his seventeenth-century Catholic milieu, Descartes made rational control of the passions the foundation of morality. He believed that understanding how body and mind interact in their substantial union to moderate the passions enables individuals to live morally (Gaukroger, 1995). By exercising the will, one controls the appetites and passions that environmental events arouse in the body. Thus, the will mediates reason, passions, and behaviour, harnessing desire to generate personal fulfillment and virtuous conduct.

However, the Cartesian view of the individual was not asocial. Descartes placed generosity to others, which requires mastery over one's desires and positive self-esteem, at the centre of his ethics. In his conception of ethical conduct he included the notion of the common good, arguing that public interest should have priority over individual interest (Sorrell, 1987). Descartes' primary ethical concern was the duty to foster the well-being of humankind.

Section conclusion

Descartes intended to overcome secular reliance on Galileo's mechanics to explain human nature, which threatened the Christian notion of free will, and aimed to assert freedom and dignity. He did so by proposing the dualistic position that physical mechanics did not apply to the non-physical world of mind. Until Newton's physics appeared a century later, Cartesian dualism was the dominant orientation in natural philosophy.

Descartes invoked mind to explain awareness of bodily processes (e.g., sensations, memory, and the passions), reasoning, and will (Hatfield, 1992) and stressed the independence of mental processes from the body. Nevertheless, he integrated body and mind when explaining all other functions. Many later scholars, however, exaggerated Descartes' rationalism and ignored his eventual synthesis of body–mind relations (e.g., Gaukroger, 1995).

Yet Descartes did not resolve fully the mystery of how the substantial union of body and mind works. If, as he insisted, mind is distinct from body, how does mind know matter? He also did not reconcile human thinking and language with the brain states shared with other animals (D. Clarke, 2006). How to explain the integrated experience of our lives as reflective biological creatures remained unanswered.

Connection to Psychology Some historians of Psychology claim that Cartesian thought made at least **five contributions** to our discipline's scientific foundations:

- Descartes' investigations of animal and human biology laid the groundwork for physiological psychology. Some also assert that his materialist approach to what we now term psychological processes and his notion of body–mind integration are represented at least indirectly in current behavioural and cognitive neuroscience formulations.
- His mechanistic explanations of learned connections among bodily actions, feelings, and thoughts allegedly provided the conceptual foundation for conditioning theories.
- Descartes' view that the mind has innate capacities and ideas, some historians of Psychology claim, influenced current psycholinguistics.
- His notion of internal conflicts between the passions and desires, and rational behaviour purportedly is part of the conceptual framework for psychoanalysis.
- His use of introspection to study whole, conscious, meaningful experience is one basis for *phenomenology*, the philosophical and psychological study of direct experience (see Chapter 10).

However, these presentist attributions presume a direct connection between Descartes' ideas and Psychology, which is historically incorrect. His psychological ideas are valuable in their own time and place. Most importantly, for him "psychology" concerned the soul.

Baruch Spinoza

Agreeing with Hobbes that an embodied mind integrates emotions and thinking in action, Baruch Spinoza stressed rational control of passions. Against Descartes' positioning superior spirit and mind against inferior matter and body, Spinoza integrated conceptions of mind, matter, and God. For him, scientific study was in harmony with religion, because the natural world was the deity. But because he rejected Judaeo-Christian belief in an anthropomorphic God, his society reviled him as an atheist (Yovel, 1989).

Spinoza was more interested in human nature and ethical conduct than in the material world (Gabbey, 1996). He explained passions, thought, and action as following natural laws and emphasized practical control of negative affect. Although some historians of Psychology see his thought as contributing to the discipline's foundations, there is no direct link.

Psychological phenomena

Spinoza held that because humans are embedded in nature, natural causes determine human action (Gabbey, 1996). Because, for him, all natural events are both mental and physical, a mental science is equivalent to a physical science. Passions, reason, and action, he argued, are as amenable to rational and geometrical analysis as are natural objects.

Spinoza did not regard body and mind as two aspects with separate but parallel sequences of events. Rather, he believed body and mind constitute a unified system, yet are conceived differently (Jarrett, 2007). Although his position entails parallelism of mental and physical processes, it is not Platonic, because he held that mental acts always are embodied and the body provides the experience of unity of mind.

Rejecting the scholastic assumption that humans are unique among creatures, Spinoza contended that natural laws regulate human desires and behaviour. He also argued that the body does not cause mental events nor does the mind activate bodily movement or rest. Rather, all natural objects are in motion and inclined to strive, while animate objects possess capacities for generation, growth, and passion. Internal or external motion determines activity for all objects, including humans.

Like Hobbes, Spinoza posited unconscious striving (conatus) towards self-preservation in all natural objects. This self-centred desire to persist in one's own being strengthens pleasure, but also produces pain, which weakens pleasure. Bodily and mental striving generates passions in the form of either appetites or desires. Appetites operate unconsciously as passions, producing confused thinking; appetites also are passive because the individual does not produce them. Desires, however, are conscious products of the individual's activity that yield clear thinking applicable to all human situations (Jarrett, 2007).

Passions, which Spinoza termed affects, are objective characteristics or properties, subject to scientific scrutiny. However, he excluded from his account the subjective feelings that accompany affects (Segal, 2000). The three basic affects – desire, joy, and sorrow – evoke different passions and are the foundation for human action. Joy (pleasure), which increases self-activity, and sorrow (pain), which decreases it, constantly challenge desire (the survival motive).

Only by clearly understanding the causes of human action, Spinoza argued, could one meet the challenge posed by affects, especially negative ones, such as anger, jealousy, and envy. By rationally controlling the causes of our desires, we enhance our freedom to take action and survive. By exercising clear reasoning and being conscious of bodily sensations and thoughts, we temper our passions and successfully mediate competing desires.

Although Spinoza attributed thinking to animals, he held that humans are unique in the potential for employing reason to control affects. The power of the embodied mind emancipates us from bondage to affects and leads to virtue and intellectual union with a naturalized God. But because, as natural objects, we are expressions of God and governed by natural laws, an autonomous self plays no substantive role in his conception of human nature.

Social relations Spinoza based the ethically sound life not on biblical teaching or morality but on conatus and the laws of nature (Della Rocca, 2008). For him, knowledge of psychological processes is essential for ethical conduct and the ethical ideal is the completely rational person (Jarrett, 2007; Yovel, 1989). Spinoza also believed that living virtuously in accord with reason includes a natural inclination to foster mutual aid and social harmony. Virtue resides in the self-realization that reasonable individuals recognize the value of treating others as they wish to be treated. He distinguished among three types of people: superior individuals guided by reason; ordinary people; and inhuman ones, dominated by passive affects, who lack empathy and behave cruelly.

For Spinoza, mental striving for power as a rational being constitutes human will. But because he believed that the mind and emotions are subject to natural law, he rejected free will. Everything has an inner necessity, he argued. Thus, one should be content with whatever occurs. The ethics of social conduct, according to Spinoza, follow the same cause-and-effect rules as the rest of nature. There is no objective good or evil; rather, individuals judge an object "good" when they desire it, but "evil" when they do not.

Section conclusion

There are sharp differences between Spinoza's psychological ideas and those of his associationist contemporary, Locke, who virtually ignored emotions. But Leibniz viewed Spinoza's ideas as innovative. The later Romantics found inspiration in his view of the oneness of nature, humankind, and God. In addition, the German idealists, principally **Georg Wilhelm Friedrich Hegel**, were attracted to his stress on reason and mental activity (see Chapter 4).

Karl Marx admired Spinoza's framework, but transformed it in terms of concrete economic conditions. **Friedrich Nietzsche's** concept of *will to power* as the single explanatory principle of nature and human nature (see Chapter 4) is comparable to Spinoza's conatus. Their individual notions of the superior person also are comparable (Yovel, 1989).

Connection to Psychology Some historians of Psychology claim that Spinoza held mechanistic ideas, such as the physiological nature of human emotions and their neutral properties, and mind and body as a unified system (e.g., Bernard, 1972). Allegedly, these notions influenced Psychology more directly than Descartes' ideas did. Other scholars contend that Spinoza rejected both mechanistic physiology that privileges bodily states and descriptive phenomenology that privileges mind and soul. Rather, in his unified body–mind–soul orientation, passions are integral to human action and an ethical life (Wartofsky, 1973).

Some psychologists regard Spinoza's denial of free will as laying the foundation for natural-science psychologists' epistemological assumption that all psychological phenomena are deterministically caused. Others claim that Spinoza's dialectical understanding of passions and reason, which transcended Descartes' revised view, and his emphasis on the need for self-control provided a basis for Freudian theory. However, Spinoza's concepts differ substantially from Freud's; for example, Spinoza did not propose a theory of unconscious processes (Yovel, 1989).

Spinoza's conception of an embodied mind in which passions and reason are integrated in action attracted Soviet psychologist **Lev Vygotsky** (1896–1934) (see Chapter 6)

(Wartofsky, 1973). Moreover, neuroscientist Antonio Damasio (2003) revived Spinoza's views in his own integration of embodied thoughts and emotions (see Chapter 7). There is also some similarity between Spinoza's ideas and cognitive therapy, given his emphasis on learning to think rationally to eliminate negative emotions ("passive affects"), such as anger. However, *direct* correspondence between Spinoza's ideas and scientific psychologists' ideas is dubious.

Gottfried Leibniz

Both attracted to and critical of Spinoza's ideas, Gottfried Leibniz (1646–1716) aimed to unite natural philosophy and Christianity within a comprehensive rationalist system. He rejected Cartesian mechanism, Hobbesian determinism, and Lockean materialism. Instead, Leibniz emphasized metaphysical principles and explored different levels of consciousness, using Anne Conway's (1631–1679) conception of an animated universe (Fara, 2004; Schiebinger, 1989).

A German courtier and virtual ambulatory encyclopaedia who might rank with Newton as a mathematical physicist (Jolley, 2005), Leibniz understood atomistic theory metaphysically. For him, the soul/mind is constantly active and is "the indivisible atom from which all things are created" (Stewart, 2006, p. 82). The basic elements of reality are immaterial, simple substances, termed *monads*, again borrowed from Conway. Monads are irreducible, conscious, microscopic points of energy that function harmoniously yet autonomously.

Because much of his writing remains unpublished, Leibniz's metaphysical interests are better known than his work on human nature. His ideas forwarded the cultural movement towards scientific understanding of the natural world, while leaving room for extant religious ideas.

Psychological phenomena

For Leibniz, monads are the psychic constituents of all matter; they have absolute reality and contain ideas. Monads also possess active powers or forces for action ("distinct perceptions") and passive powers or forces for reaction ("confused passions"). Leibniz held that appetite causes substances to move from perception to perception, while the soul/mind enables unity. Because matter has no soul, it cannot be a substance.

Natural phenomena are not themselves substances but are based on substances. You might regard an object as an oak tree, but for Leibniz, it is an aggregation of monads. Observable objects are mere appearances; thus, reality is basically mental (Jolley, 2005).

According to Leibniz, all matter, animate or not, varies in its capacities for consciousness. He theorized the mind as always engaged in some level of perceptual process on a continuum between totally unconscious processes and fully conscious, mental operations. Thus, he made a case for unconscious aspects of perceiving and thinking (Aiton, 1985).

Based on this understanding of consciousness, Leibniz advanced **two concepts** concerning perceptual experience:

- "Perception" refers to a monad's internal state of representing external objects. *"Petites perceptions"* (immediate sensory perception) of objects accumulate to produce *apperception*, which means reflective knowledge of the monad's internal state. Using current language, apperception is conscious awareness that one perceives.

- *Limen*, or sensory threshold, is the point at which a sensory experience became just strong enough to precipitate awareness.

For Leibniz, apprehension of the empirical world originates in **three levels**:

- Sensible concepts from sensory experience.
- An imaginative concept or "common sense" from the simultaneity of sense and intelligibility.
- Intelligible concepts from reflective understanding.

What enables humans to transcend empirical functioning and engage in reasoning is the capacity for reflection, which includes apperception or awareness of the self.

Rejecting the mechanistic view that brain processes explain mental processes, Leibniz agreed with Plato's notion of innate ideas. Humans, Leibniz argued, are disposed naturally to apprehend *a priori* truths and know the essence of objects. With Locke, he believed that the soul/mind gives meaning to sensory experience and that abstract thoughts require sensory perception and leave brain traces (Aiton, 1985; McRae, 1995). But, against Locke, he argued that the soul/mind exists prior to sensory experience.

Following Descartes, Leibniz believed that an immaterial self is central to reasoning. But, against Descartes, he denied the possibility that an immaterial substance (the mind/soul) can influence a material substance (the body). His solution to the mind–body problem was the concept of *pre-established harmony*. Leibniz contended that God, a supreme engineer, has established parallelism between the body and the mind/soul so that they operate in perfect harmony, functioning in synchrony but not causally related. Each entity presides over its own kingdom with its own laws.

Social relations Leibniz's views on social relations mirror Spinoza's. On the one hand, Leibniz assumed that morally good individuals "always choose what seems to them to be best," and they "always necessarily choose their own good" (Jolley, 2005, p. 199). On the other hand, he assumed that taking another person's perspective is the criterion for determining what is just. In addition, he proposed "disinterested love" (i.e., love of everyone), which in turn brought justice-seeking individuals pleasure. Thus, he balanced egoism and altruism, self-serving interests with sociability (G. Brown, 1995).

Section conclusion

In his synthesis of ancient and contemporary philosophy, Leibniz conserved traditional Christian conceptions, while adopting the extant notion of the individual's uniqueness and unity. He believed that he solved the mind–body problem by integrating Epicurean materialism and Platonic idealism (Aiton, 1985). Within his system, the individual was the centre of all creation and was isolated from the external influences that operated on a mechanistic world. However, most contemporary and subsequent natural philosophers thought that Leibniz's vitalist claims that all natural objects are full of life and every substance (monad) expresses the entire universe were irredeemably abstract and denied empirical reality.

Connection to Psychology Although his metaphysics had little influence on psychological thought, Leibniz's concepts of apperception and limen reappeared in the nineteenth-century

philosophical psychology of Johann Herbart and in the parallel German research programme, *psychophysics* (i.e., the scientific study of the subjective experience of sensory
stimuli – see Chapter 4). Furthermore, Leibniz's notion of a continuum of perceptual
awareness arguably contributed to the conceptual antecedents for a psychoanalytic psychology of unconscious processes.

George Berkeley

An Anglican bishop in colonized Ireland, George Berkeley presented a different philosophy
than Leibniz, interpreting nature, human nature, and society through Christian morality. He
also wrote about mathematics and the psychology of vision. Commentators have read him
variously as an idealist, an empiricist, or a theologian (Leary, 1977).

In Newton's account, if God created nature, He (*sic*) was peripheral, while nature
functioned mechanistically and material terms explained all natural objects, including
humans. Berkeley did not doubt natural philosophers' evidence. But he rejected their
materialistic interpretations, denied that they could uncover truths about the natural world,
and rejected their metaphysical premises concerning the causes of ideas. The logical outcomes of materialism, Berkeley argued, are atheism and denial of the soul, positions which
contradict Christian beliefs. Thus, for him, the most effective rebuttal to materialism was to
correct its erroneous conclusions.

In his *Principles of Human Knowledge* (1710), Berkeley agreed that external material
reality exists, but he claimed, against Newton and Locke, that there are no objects that are
independent of the perceiving mind. By his Latin dictum, "*esse est percipi*" (i.e., to be is to
be perceived), Berkeley meant every aspect of existence is mind-dependent. There *is* a
physical world, he insisted, but we cannot experience it directly. Our perceiving, our
subjective awareness, is our reality.

Thus, Berkeley was an empiricist, because he insisted that all knowledge comes from the
senses, *and* an idealist, because, for him, the perception of objects depends upon a perceiving mind. Moreover, he asserted that God caused the ideas that comprise natural objects and
the regularities of natural laws (Fogelin, 2001).

Psychological phenomena

Berkeley is important to early modern psychological thought, because he proposed a
different interpretation of perception than the norm. Although he emphasized subjective
perception, he did not claim that all natural objects and reality are imaginary. Rather, he
grounded the acquisition of knowledge in direct experience and focused his explanation of
psychological phenomena on sensory perception. He then applied this framework to thinking and willing.

Berkeley maintained, as Leibniz had, that a materialist account of perception is untenable.
He claimed that all that humans can know are secondary qualities (i.e., perceptual experiences). For him, primary qualities are as dependent on being perceived as secondary
qualities are.

Berkeley rejected Locke's theory of perception by which individuals indirectly perceive
and represent sensory characteristics of natural objects. He claimed that sensory qualities

pertain to what individuals *directly* perceive, which are immaterial "ideas," encompassing sensations, perceptions, images, and thoughts. For Berkeley, ideas are the only certainty. He also refuted the naïve-realist theory of immediately perceiving natural objects. Instead, he held that we perceive ideas, not immediate sensory qualities. Just as heat and other sensory qualities are mental so are pleasure and pain.

Furthermore, Berkeley argued, perception is relative to the perceiver; thus, what tastes sour to one person might taste sweet to another. Besides, a microscope reveals a different reality in an object than immediate sensory observation does. In Berkeley's view, an object's existence requires qualities of an object *and* individuals who perceive those qualities. If perceivers cease to perceive the object's qualities, it ceases to exist in that way. Thus, matter does not have absolute reality in and of itself.

Berkeley proposed that a conglomeration of contiguous, sensory experiences produces a complex perceptual event. For example, individuals acquire the cues for distance-vision by means of correlated ideas. Thus, distance is not a sensory process per se but the result of unified, visual ideas. Similarly, he explained the meaning of words by asserting that individuals acquire meaning through habitually connected ideas (i.e., sensations, perceptions, images, and thoughts) that accompany words. But he did not use the term "associations."

For Berkeley, humans construct the reality of material objects out of patterns of sensation. The perception of ideas entails apprehension of particular qualities not vague abstractions. All mental processes are particular, and a general idea results from a collection of similar, particular ideas. Thus, the existence of objects is mind-dependent. However, existence of objects is not subjective but objective, because God perceives material objects continually.

Berkeley believed that individual consciousness is primary, and the self animates the mental operations that evoke the unified experience of a phenomenon. An active, immaterial self, his synonym for mind/spirit/soul, permeates all psychological processes whether the function is perception, memory, imagination, or reason. But the self's central, organizing activity is intention (Lloyd, 1985). Thus, the primacy of human will is the principle by which he synthesized empiricism and rationalism (Ayers, 2005).

To paraphrase Berkeley, the objects of knowledge emanate from **three sources**:

- Ideas imprinted on the senses.
- Perceptions obtained by attending to the passions and mental operations.
- Ideas formed with the aid of memory and imagination.

Ideas as such are passive, while the mind/spirit/soul that generates ideas is active. The ultimate cause of sensory ideas is the greatest spirit, God.

Social relations Against individualism, Berkeley held that humans are naturally inclined to interdependence just as gravity binds natural objects together. But the source of this inherent inclination towards sociability and the common good is divine providence, not a mechanized universe. According to Berkeley, the human spirit's inherent freedom, which God bestowed, enables individuals of all social classes to choose morally correct, social behaviour (Darwall, 2005). Social inclinations, he argued, are essential for everyone's well-being, and social harmony requires order, virtue, and duty. He attributed individual differences in sociability to selfish interests (e.g., greed) that harm the public good (Leary, 1977).

Section conclusion

Many of Berkeley's contemporaries and successors dismissed him as an unrealistic idealist. But he did not deny that natural objects exist. In fact, Hume agreed with Berkeley that primary qualities are relative and as dependent on the observer as secondary qualities are. By presenting an immaterialist perspective on knowledge of nature and human nature, Berkeley made science and Christian theology compatible. Moreover, his approach to psychological phenomena bore fruit in later generations.

Connection to Psychology In addition to his general theory, Berkeley introduced unique empiricist theories of distance perception and language acquisition. He described visual phenomena that scientific psychologists later would term "convergence" and "accommodation." In effect, he laid the conceptual foundation for a contextual account of distance perception that appeared in **Edward Titchener's** (1867–1927) introspectionist psychology (see Chapter 5) and for a comparable account of language to emerge in **Frederic Bartlett's** (1886–1969) psychological research (see Chapter 6).

Furthermore, the position of Gestalt theorists and Jean Piaget that the mind projects a structure on the world that does not conform to physical reality (see Chapter 6) resembles Berkeley's notion of the structuring mind. Many cognitive psychologists share this theoretical assumption. Also, just as human will played a central role in Berkeley's psychology, so it did in Wundt's.

Part 4 conclusion

If current psychologists were to attribute rationalism to the psychological thought of Descartes, Spinoza, and Berkeley, implying that these philosophers ignored empirical reality and were antithetical to the associationists, such a presentist characterization would do an injustice to both associationists and so-called rationalists. Descartes, Spinoza, and Berkeley all noted the key role of sensory impressions while stressing the operations of a structuring reflective mind that exercises skepticism about the reliability of those impressions and that directs our actions. Thus, there are similarities as well as differences between rationalists and associationists.

Yet there are key differences within the rationalist group. For example, in Spinoza's account, in which echoes of Hobbes reverberate, mental acts always are embodied, whereas for Descartes they constitute a separate reality of a mental world. In this sense, Leibnizian thought extends Descartes' position on the mind to its roots in the Platonic idealism of pure forms, although in other ways Leibniz absorbed Spinoza's notions.

Taken together, the thought of Descartes, Spinoza, Berkeley, and Leibniz reveals the early modern origins of the notion proposed centuries later by European scientific psychologists that the mind structures psychological phenomena. Indebted to their philosophical heritage, Descartes, Berkeley, and Leibniz, like Aristotle and Aquinas, also gave pride of place to human will as the mediator of passions, reason, and human action. For Spinoza, however, will was superfluous, because passions and reason are governed by a natural law of inner necessity.

Part 5   Reconciliations of empiricism and rationalism

Two Enlightenment philosophers, Immanuel Kant and Thomas Reid, drew on the strengths of empiricist/associationist and rationalist positions while attempting to avoid their weaknesses, but from different standpoints and with different results.

Immanuel Kant

A German philosopher, Immanuel Kant (1724–1804) initially published works on physics, astronomy, and mathematics, and then explored metaphysics, epistemology, and moral and social philosophy (Kuehn, 2001). In his later work he discussed psychological issues, which facilitated the emergence of Psychology in Germany (Leary, 1982).

Kant's Latin motto was *aude sapere* (i.e., dare to practise wisdom), meaning, "exercise critical thinking rather than acquiesce to authority." He centralized the knower in any inquiry just as he centralized the human mind in the construction of objective experience; for Kant, mind shapes experience. In moral philosophy he centralized moral freedom and the categorical imperative for ethical conduct.

Philosophical approach

Kant's disagreement with Hume's philosophy was the catalyst for his attempt to reconcile empiricism and rationalism. Kant accepted the Enlightenment's emphasis on both sensory experience and reason, while examining the conditions for objective human knowledge in *Critique of Pure Reason* (1781), moral reasoning in *Critique of Practical Reason* (1788), and judgment of feelings in *Critique of Judgment* (1790). Table 3.1 depicts the subject, issues, and focus that Kant addressed in each of these works.

The three critiques correspond to theoretical understanding (knowing), moral reasoning (desiring and willing), and judgment (feeling). Just as judgment linked understanding and moral reasoning metaphysically, so feeling mediated knowing and desiring (Leary, 1982). For Kant, the three capacities were united by the presence of reason in thinking, willing, and feeling.

In the first critique, against the idealism of Leibniz and Wolff, Kant argued that reason should not be extended beyond the boundaries of experience. Rejecting speculative

Table 3.1 Kant's three critiques

Subject	Issues	Focus
Pure reason	Metaphysics and epistemology: the capacity for understanding	What we can know
Practical reason	Desire and human will enabling ethical conduct	How we should act
Reflective judgment	Feelings of pleasure, displeasure, beauty, and aesthetic taste	For what we may hope

metaphysics, he asserted that we cannot know the *noumenon*, the world as it is behind appearances, because we are limited to knowledge of phenomena, the world as it appears, which is derived from sensory impressions. That is, knowledge is limited to temporal and spatial dimensions and apparent causality.

In the second critique Kant asserted that when we exercise our capacity of will and enact our sense of moral duty, expressed in pursuing the ethical good, we are in relationship to the world behind appearances. In the realm of moral duty we are truly free, while in the phenomenal realm, explicable by matter and mechanisms, we are limited.

In the third critique Kant bridged the phenomenal and noumenal levels, connecting matter and spirit by positing *eros*, a generic life-force of psychic energy, in human nature. The mind enables us to experience wondrous beauty and feel pleasures and pains that transcend sensory impressions and emotions that we can neither know nor will (Needleman, 1982).

In sum, Kant synthesized empiricism and rationalism in his claim that knowledge of the natural world results from the union of *a posteriori* and *a priori* concepts; that is, experience and reason are reciprocally related. In his words:

There is no doubt whatever that all our cognition [knowledge] begins with experience; for how else should the cognitive faculty be awakened into exercise if not through objects that stimulate our senses ... [A]lthough all our cognition commences **with** experience, yet it does not on that account all arise **from** experience. (Kant [1781] 1998, p. 136; emphasis in the original)

When reason is disconnected from experience, it yields the illusion of objectivity, while experience disconnected from reason yields pure subjectivity. Paraphrasing Kant, thoughts without sensory content are empty; but sensory impressions without concepts are blind (Kuehn, 2001). Thus, knowledge of natural objects results from interdependent psychological processes.

> **Small-group discussion.** Discuss whether Kant's proposition – thoughts without content are empty; sensory impressions without concepts are blind – still holds true.

Epistemology Kant extended Hume's critique of Locke's empiricism and adopted Hume's claim that we can never observe causal relations directly; we merely attribute causality to events. Kant also agreed that Newtonian science was the acme of knowledge about nature. But the order of nature reflects the structure of human reason rather than concepts mirroring external reality; our minds project laws onto nature, Kant argued (Needleman, 1982).

However, Kant rejected Hume's skeptical standpoint that there are no truths and everything is subjective, because Kant perceived such skepticism as endangering the basis of true knowledge. He retorted that innate categories of thought, such as "cause and effect," "totality," and "negation" can produce true knowledge. Yet, against idealism, he claimed that humans know only the appearances of things not their essences.

Psychological phenomena

In Kant's view, the mind is composed of a complex set of processes, including perceptual and interpretive capacities, which operate synthetically and actively organize sensory impressions. Kant adopted Leibniz's concept of apperception to refer to the mind's capacity to organize and give meaning to perceptual experience.

Kant clearly distinguished sensory from mental processing, sensation ("sensibility") from intellect (Kuehn, 2001). Within the intellect he further distinguished between understanding, which pertains to apprehending and mastering natural objects instrumentally, and reason, which entails reflecting morally on the aims of instrumental mastery. Knowledge, then, depends on the three qualities of sensibility, understanding, and reason.

Sensibility consists of the senses and imagination (i.e., forming images of sensations), providing sensory impressions. Imagination links sensations and concepts, whereas understanding judges and categorizes them, producing objective knowledge. In sum, for Kant, sensory data and habits of association are important but insufficient; reason governs sensibility, imagination, and understanding.

Late in life Kant published in his *Anthropology* a framework for understanding humans as biological, psychological, and moral and social beings (Arens, 1989). In it he attempted to synthesize active mental processes, levels of consciousness, including unconscious ones, and social-historical contexts. By "anthropology" Kant meant a descriptive science concerning humans as moral agents in society (Leary, 1982). In speculating about diverse psychological processes, such as cognitive talents and deficiencies, he stressed the changing geographical and cultural contexts in which minds operate. He argued that anthropology should not be physiological because of the speculative state of contemporary physiology, not because he avoided biology.

Social relations Kant wanted to restore moral principles, which, in his view, are weakened by reducing morality to sentiments (e.g., Humean benevolence) or Hobbesian hedonism. As an Enlightenment philosopher, he sought to root morality in reason. Accordingly, Kant rejected the idea that nature dictates values and forms of moral behaviour. Instead, he claimed that humans create a moral life by transcending environmental conditions through reflection on objective, universal principles. Thus, the foundation of moral responsibility rests in individuals exercising their capacity for reason.

Kant's mission was to "transform us into autonomous moral agents" (Kuehn, 2001, p. 240). He held that "moral principles are necessary truths," the mind provides moral concepts, and morally good individuals discharge their duties in the belief that they are obliged to do so (W. Davis, 2006, p. 27). Kant believed that an innate moral principle, the *categorical imperative*, is universally present, which people are free to follow or not.

The categorical imperative comprises **three aspects**:

- Treat others as we wish to be treated. This principle, present in all religious and spiritual traditions, is known as "the golden rule."
- Regard everyone as "ends" rather than as "means" for our own ends. Actions are ethical when they reflect the principle of treating others as ends.
- Most importantly, act as if the motives for our actions could be general principles.

For Kant, human functioning at its highest level consists of the unity of morality, self-understanding, and artistic sensibility, and moral feeling plays a key role in the motivation of rational agents. This ethical approach, known as *deontology* (i.e., the study of ethical duties), stresses general principles that underlie codes of conduct. Kant's ethical theory is a foundation for the Canadian Psychological Association's (CPA's) ethical principles (see

Chapter 8). But feminist theorists who promote an ethic of caring relationships criticize Kant's principle-focused perspective, because it emphasizes autonomy of moral agents rather than their social interdependence (Simons, 2002).

Section conclusion

Kantian ideas have influenced generations of philosophers and scientists. The later physicist and physiologist **Hermann von Helmholtz** (1821–1894) (see Chapter 4) absorbed Kant's emphasis on the active mind. Kant also was a key influence on twentieth-century social philosophers Jürgen Habermas and Michel Foucault.

Even though Kant himself believed that knowledge of natural objects was partially the product of sensory experience, German idealist philosophers of the next generation polarized rationalism, insisting that the mind created reality, in their quest to know ideas with which they had no experience. But Kant opposed this idealist type of abstract thinking.

From a critical perspective, despite his position that wives and husbands should not treat each other as means to their ends (Kuehn, 2001), Kant subscribed to the cultural theory of women's complementarity to men. He held that because women should preserve the species and society, their education should be restricted (Kneller, 2006). He also held racist views concerning ethnocultural groups who differed from those of White European descent (Teo, 1999).

Kant's decades of lectures and treatises on psychological phenomena contributed to an intellectual climate of public interest in empirical knowledge about the mind. This climate enabled psychology to emerge as a subject distinct from philosophy (R. Smith, 1997). Moreover, his focus on the interface between mind and the cultural and natural environment was a new approach to psychology (Arens, 1989). Although Kant believed a scientific psychology was impossible (see Chapter 12), some nineteenth-century German philosophers argued the opposite (see Chapter 4); their vision helped birth Psychology.

Connection to Psychology Nineteenth-century German scholars took up Kant's reconciliation of empiricism and rationalism. Herbart applied mathematics to Kant's categories of sensory processes (see Chapter 4) and Wundt eventually shifted from experiments on consciousness to historical-cultural studies of societal influences on the mind. Active mental processes were central in the research programmes of other early German psychologists concerning sensory processes, perception, and cognition. Furthermore, Kant's insistence on will as fundamental to mind influenced early US psychologists, including William James and **John Dewey** (1859–1952).

Kant's framework also was evident in early human-science psychologies, such as phenomenology. Wilhelm Dilthey, who contrasted natural-science with human-science psychology, adopted Kant's recasting of Wolff's distinction between empirical and rational psychology. Current psychologists affiliated with social-constructionist or postmodernist persuasions are indebted to Kant, particularly his stress on subjective influences on observation.

Kant's emphasis on the unity of perceptual experience and the mind's organizational capacities, which contradicted empiricist philosophers' associationist account, indirectly influenced Gestalt psychologists' concepts, Piaget's developmental model, and Noam Chomsky's psycholinguistics. Lastly, similarly to Kant, natural-science psychologists stress the role of innate brain structures for perceptual and cognitive processes, such as the infrastructure of language (Brook, 1994).

Thomas Reid

In his "common-sense realism" Thomas Reid achieved a different reconciliation. He exemplifies the Scottish Enlightenment tradition of a mental science, rooted in empiricism and shorn of metaphysics. He and his peers viewed mental science as basic to all natural sciences, urging introspection on conscious experience as well as observational and experimental methods.

First a clergyperson, then an academic philosopher, biologist, and mathematician, Reid was a critical supporter of Baconian science and Newton's ideas. But his religious faith tempered his belief in the ultimate comprehensibility of nature and human nature (Wolterstorff, 2001). Alarmed by the popularity of Hume's skepticism among many contemporaries, Reid proposed a philosophical psychology of common sense and moral agency.

Reid discussed psychological and social phenomena in works on epistemology, *An Inquiry into the Human Mind on the Principles of Common Sense* (1764); philosophy of mind, *Essays on the Intellectual Powers of Man* (1785); and moral philosophy *Essays on the Active Powers of Man* (1788). His unifying assumption was that nature's creatures have a God-given constitution suited to their environments (D. N. Robinson, 1986).

Philosophical approach

Locke, Berkeley, and Hume had proposed that rather than seeing things directly, "we experience the world through ideas, cognitions, mental representations ..." (Billig, 2008, p. 188), and these mental states are actual physical objects. But Reid rejected these empiricist propositions.

Believing that perceptions of external objects are independent of mind, Reid advocated "direct realism" (naïve realism). We apprehend sensations directly, he claimed. Objects are physically present, but perception requires a mind that perceives the world directly in terms of meaningful wholes. Thus, Reid rejected the concept of association integrating atomistic sensations. Ideas only result from the mind imposing structure on perceived objects.

Partially influenced by Shaftesbury, Reid posited *common sense*, which encompasses a shared understanding of things that everyone takes for granted (Wolterstorff, 2001). For Reid, common sense is inherent in all languages, stems from intuitive judgments, and enables individuals to reason with each other. Thus, one can take sensory impressions at face value.

Psychological phenomena

Reid regarded purely biological explanations of psychological processes as degrading to human nature. Moreover, he warned against conflating perceptual apparatus with the perceiver. Yet he also investigated the anatomy and physiology of perceptual processes and explained depth perception (Nichols, 2007).

Reid's theory of sensation/perception, which was the psychological process to which he devoted the most attention, rested on empirical footing. In his view, **two processes**, sensations and conceptions, comprise all mental states:

- Sensations are the immediate feelings aroused by particular senses suggesting the qualities of real objects. Sensations are distinct from perceptions and unmediated by ideas. Perception, mediated by the senses, enables ideas about material reality.
- Conceptions are "apprehensions" (i.e., mental grips) of objects, expressed in beliefs about the objects' external existence. Conceptions are manifest in a range of God-given mental faculties and acquired capacities. Collectively, these "active powers" include perception, imagination, memory, reasoning, and judgment.
- For Reid, the mind/soul unifies the various faculties and performs all conscious mental operations. These operations consist of two general powers: "understanding" and "will." Understanding refers to one's capacities for reflection. Will refers to determining what is within one's power. Humans, he argued, can behave animalistically because of instincts, habits, and "appetites, passions, affections," which are basic to human survival (Lehrer, 1989). When we have conflicting motives, the faculty of will enables us to resolve to take appropriate action.

Contrary to Hume's associationist notion of the self as a procession of impressions, Reid contended that the mind, self, and personal identity are grounded in memory. That is, memory of past events supplies the means for a consistent sense of identity. The mind, which is immaterial, lends substance and permanence to the self.

Social relations Reid defended the classical view that the will gives active power or moral agency to human conduct (Haakonssen, 1990). For him, moral laws and the capacity of moral choice essentially differ from Newton's laws of nature. Postulating a "moral sense" (conscience), analogous to the judgments produced by sensory perception, Reid held that a moral reality exists and that judgments as well as motives determine actions. We can access our moral sense by making rational judgments systematically, just as Newton studied natural objects.

Reid assumed that God intended individuals as social beings and active agents in a moral community. He understood moral conduct in terms of virtues and corresponding duties. Prudence, temperance, and fortitude pertain to duties to oneself, whereas justice pertains to duties to others; we are obliged to honour others' rights as well as our own. Moral education, based on taking others' perspectives, would nurture this obligation (W. Davis, 2006).

According to Reid, two principles facilitate social intercourse: "credulity" and "veracity." By credulity Reid meant trusting what others tell us, which originates in infants' helplessness. By veracity he meant speaking truthfully and genuinely. (In the late twentieth century Habermas proposed an "ideal speech situation" – see Chapter 12.) For Reid, "social life and the practice of language depend upon principles of truth and trust" (Billig, 2008, p. 174). Moreover, because we have an innate moral capacity to make agreements, he asserted, we can keep commitments and contracts and form social institutions.

Section conclusion

Although he disagreed with Shaftesbury's notion of the sense of community specifically, Reid employed the notion of common sense to explain humankind as fundamentally social and opposed Locke's conception of self-contained individuals. Instead, Reid argued that many mental operations, such as answering questions, are social not solitary, because they require the interpersonal act of language (Billig, 2008).

Up to the twentieth century Reid's reputation among British, French, and US scholars was solid. During the nineteenth century, his concepts of active mental functions, moral agency, and common sense struck a responsive chord in the church-supported but pragmatic culture of the New World. In France, Comte adopted Reid's common sense for his positivist philosophy. But Reid's views had little influence on German thought, which Kant heavily influenced.

Politically, Reid was convinced that only moral reform could yield social justice. He actively opposed slavery and supported prison reform (Broadie, 2003). Although his stance on women's roles in society was conventional, he held that the genders were equal intellectually and morally, and he acknowledged **Mary Wollstonecraft's** (1759–1797) revolutionary 1792 treatise on women's rights (Haakonssen, 1990; Lehrer, 1989).

Connection to Psychology Early natural-science US psychologists regarded reductionism as a scientific necessity. Thus, they were averse to common-sense realism, because it rejected the reductionistic basis of associationism. Moreover, common-sense realism had dominated US philosophy, a discipline from which US psychologists sought distance.

In addition, early psychologists tended to denigrate the term, "faculty psychology," most likely because of its imprecise nature and Reid's assumption that mental faculties were innate and universal (Brooks, 1976). Some conflated faculty psychology with *phrenology* in which observers correlated mental faculties with brain locations and cranial shape (see Chapter 4), but Reid was never a devotee of phrenology.

On the other hand, Reid's position on perception of meaningful wholes resembles concepts in Gestalt psychology, Piagetian theory, and other twentieth-century psychological thought that emphasizes how individuals structure their experience. Although in his day Reid rivalled Kant and figured prominently in nineteenth-century accounts of psychological thought, he has been a neglected figure in modern Psychology (Billig, 2008; G. Richards, 2010).

Part 5 conclusion

Reid's and Kant's respective reconciliations of rationalism and empiricism were similar yet different. Kant posited a structuring mind, possessed of innate categories of thought, which reflects on concrete experience; for him, reasoning humans exercise moral agency. Reid also balanced empirical with rational knowledge, while proposing inherent mental faculties, and emphasized individuals' ethical conduct. But Kant envisioned autonomous, moral rational agents who integrate self-understanding with moral feeling and artistic sensibility. By contrast, in Reid's common-sense realism, perception played a central role, some mental operations are fundamentally social, and human will activates moral agency.

Part 6   Early Romantic perspectives

Associationism, rationalism, and reconciliation constituted the intellectual framework that the founding natural-science psychologists inherited, whereas Kant and the Romantic

Movement influenced human-science psychologists. The seeds of this fourth philosophical perspective began to germinate during the Scientific Revolution and the Enlightenment. One of the seminal thinkers was Blaise Pascal, whom we describe in Box 3.2. Another was Jean-Jacques Rousseau.

Box 3.2 Blaise Pascal

Rejecting Descartes' rationalism and notion of a mind/soul superior to body and nature, the early modern mathematician and philosopher Blaise Pascal viewed humankind as fundamentally connected to the physical order. He accepted a material universe governed by natural laws and the necessity for empirical knowledge produced by scientific investigations (Moriarty, 2006). But he also stressed the provisional subjective nature of knowledge.

Influenced by his compatriot Michel Montaigne, Pascal argued that the passions, such as love and ambition, represent an integration of thoughts, feelings, and bodily responses; the more one's mind develops, the stronger the passions one experiences (M. Bishop, 1968). For Pascal, embodied emotions, not reason, are primary (B. Rogers, 2003). Furthermore, he linked reason and emotion, saying, "One believes with the heart." He meant that the mind depends upon the wisdom of emotions. The heart is not only a literal organ but the "heart" of knowledge, charity, and connection to God as well as sinful desire (Davidson, 1983).

Pascal also advocated careful consideration of unconscious defensive processes, including projection, which motivate a desired action. In addition, he asserted that one's beliefs and desires are inherently unstable largely because of the influence of others' opinions about one's desired action.

Pascal believed that a basic component of human nature is self-love, which is moderated by relationships and social customs. Furthermore, enlightened self-love can direct individuals to behave morally. But he held that individuals' selfish desires precipitate interpersonal conflict. Indeed, any social relations, he argued, constitute a corrupt society, if they lack the ultimate foundation of love of God (Moriarty, 2006).

For Pascal, self-interest and personal vanity determine behaviour and unconscious strategies of self-deception. Defending against recognizing the truth about miserable personal conditions, people flee from their personal defects by creating illusory self-images of positive attributes. Beset by contradictions and inner conflicts, individuals can experience tranquillity, happiness, and justice only through reconciliation with God; otherwise, they become alienated and compelled to engage in self-deception. Thus, the self, for Pascal, is not a substance but a transitory set of socially perceived qualities, fluctuating across interpersonal situations.

In his own milieu Pascal was renowned. But, decades later, Enlightenment scholars celebrating scientific reason rejected his view of conflicted human nature and emphasis on subjectivity (Cole, 1995). Twentieth-century commentators sustained the image of Pascal as an irrational mystic. Although his reflections on his own unconscious processes, emotions, thoughts, wishes, and conduct resemble aspects of modern psychological thought, there is no direct link with Psychology.

Jean-Jacques Rousseau

The views of Rousseau directly inspired romanticism, which, with its stress on the wisdom of feelings and love of nature, was a kind of counter-Enlightenment during the nineteenth century that exerted noteworthy influence on Western culture (see Chapter 4). Rousseau introduced new ideas, but he spent most of his life in exile, because, although he was not an atheist, his ideas aroused hostile reactions from powerful political and religious figures.

Originally, Rousseau joined the *philosophes* but then repudiated their belief that civilization was progressive if it were rational. He proposed that humans are essentially good, but society's institutions corrupt human nature. When originally living in nature, people had been free and equal, but in so-called civilized societies people are neither free nor equal.

Psychological ideas

In Rousseau's writings four psychological ideas are apparent: the innate goodness of human nature, the primacy of passions, child-centred education, and contractual social relations.

Human nature Rousseau believed that the person is a naturally sociable being, capable of living in harmony with others. He also believed that perfection is possible by reforming society through proper education. He contrasted the innate goodness of humans with the corrosive effects of society.

Note that Rousseau neither invented the cliché of "the noble savage" nor deified "primitive" people (Barzun, 2000). In reflecting on the life of "savages," he rejected the notion of brutish human nature and denied "original sin." People only become evil, Rousseau argued, because of the institutions of civilized societies. For him, preserving a simple life prescribed by nature can prevent most of humanity's ills.

Primacy of passions Rousseau's faith in the fundamental goodness of humanity emanated from his belief in the wisdom of the heart where, he said, all virtue is written. He also is associated with another romanticist notion about human nature, namely, that passions are more reliable for guiding human conduct than reason. Just as Pascal critiqued Cartesian rationalism, so Rousseau critiqued Enlightenment rationalism (C. Taylor, 1989).

Yet, rather than rejecting reason, Rousseau acknowledged careful thinking as complementary to passions. Contemporary scholars questioned which mental function – thinking, feeling, or willing – should dominate the others. In Christian thought, the will held supremacy over intellect and emotions, whereas Enlightenment thinkers emphasized reason. Rousseau's response was to celebrate passions, declaring, *"Les grandes pensées viennent du coeur"* (literally, "Great thoughts come from the heart"). He argued that the specific quality of the mind is feeling. But, for him, the will mediates among passions, thinking, and actions.

Child-centred education Rousseau's 1762 treatise on education, *Emile*, was partly a response to Locke's views (G. Richards, 2010). Arguing for what today is known as child-centred education, Rousseau maintained that the best education aids actualization of innate human potential. But he focused exclusively on boys, because he regarded girls as inferior.

According to Rousseau, educators should respond to children's natural curiosity and desire to learn, which should be stimulated by a return to nature. Educators should create a learning situation that supports each child's natural curiosity rather than imposing a highly structured environment in which teachers deposit information into compliant children's minds. Nevertheless, Rousseau argued, behind the mask of permissiveness educators should be in firm control of children's development.

According to Rousseau, observation of and reflection upon direct experience in the natural world should be children's basis for acquiring rules to apply to other situations. Ideally, educators create situations in which children learn through discovery, proceeding from concrete sensory experience to concept formation and eventually abstract ideas. Furthermore, adept educators adjust the quality of educational stimulation as children proceed developmentally. Most importantly, educating emotions should take priority over educating reason.

Social relations Rousseau proposed that morality and politics should be integrated and that politics was a branch of social ethics. As a first principle, he regarded humans as equal to one another. He believed that when humans chose to live in society, competition and conflict associated with inequalities came to dominate their behaviour.

Furthermore, Rousseau regarded private property as the original cause of social corruption and evil. He maintained that the fruits of the earth belong to everyone. In the next century Marx developed this concept philosophically, economically, and politically (see Chapter 4). By contrast, Locke had argued that human beings have a natural right to private property.

Rousseau proposed a social contract in order for citizens to live in harmony. To realize social harmony, an individual's self-centred tendencies should be subordinated to community-centred intentions. This goal can be achieved by individuals surrendering their individual rights to what Rousseau termed the "general will" (in today's terms, "community well-being" or "the common good"). Consequently, individuals would identify with the collectivity of the state and would conform to government voluntarily.

Section conclusion

Rousseau influenced Western culture substantially, as evidenced by the concepts of other philosophers representing diverse perspectives. Kant emphasized the necessity of choosing the moral pathway for human action, and Marx recognized the interdependence of self-interest and general welfare. But Rousseau disagreed with those who supposed an immutable human essence. He assumed that human action is always acquired and that early experience shapes adult action. He understood society and individuals as contributing to each other's development and always in flux. This developmental perspective is evident in Hegel's and Marx's dialectical concepts.

Some commentators regard Rousseau as idealizing "primitive" societies. Although one could interpret his constructions of "savages" as benevolent, because he emphasized their superiority, positive evaluation of "racial" differences turned into its opposite in nineteenth- and twentieth-century science. Thus, some claim that he indirectly contributed to the Eurocentric concept of degeneration of putative racial purity. Furthermore, like most contemporary scholars, Rousseau explicitly attributed to girls and women such pejorative characteristics as cunning, regarded them as incapable of abstract thinking, and prescribed education that reinforced their "natural" inclination to serve men.

Connection to Psychology Some historians of Psychology link Rousseau's ideas on human potential to the concept of self-actualization of humanistic psychologists Abraham Maslow and Carl Rogers (see Chapter 10). However, Rousseau emphasized the well-being of the collective, whereas Maslow and Rogers emphasized the individual. Some also have characterized Rousseau as hostile to the Enlightenment's intentions, because he insisted on the wisdom of passions, but he did not reject reason.

Of the many psychological images that shaped educational theory and practices and ordinary child-rearing in European societies, the most influential has been the Romantic, originating in Rousseau's thought (G. Richards, 2010). According to the Romantic image, children have an innate potential for learning. They are like flower seeds, while educators are like careful gardeners, nurturing children's capacities and moderating their relative weaknesses. This is the origin of the German term *kindergarten*.

Rousseau's views on education were very influential. Johann Pestalozzi (1746–1827), a Swiss philosopher of education, emphasized that instructors should keep pace with children's natural development; John Dewey proposed progressive education (see Chapter 5); and the Italian physician Maria Montessori (1870–1952) prescribed child-centred early education. Piaget, who taught at the L'Institut de Rousseau in Geneva, also understood cognitive development as a natural progression.

Part 6 conclusion

Those Enlightenment scholars who privileged scientifically inspired reason were averse to the early Romantics' emphasis on the wisdom of passions. Nevertheless, romanticism exerted cultural and intellectual influence as the eighteenth century melded into the nineteenth. Pascal's reflective disclosures of his own experience eventually became an accepted public expression within some social circles of Western societies. Rousseau not only embraced the psychological interior, he socialized it by stressing environmental influences on human action, critiquing extant societal institutions, and proposing a natural inclination towards interdependence and collective well-being. These notions soon proved politically persuasive in Europe.

Part 7 Thematic review

Three themes summarize the varieties of early modern psychological ideas encountered in this chapter: **compatibility of scientific with theistic thought, objectivity–subjectivity of observation**, and **a self-contained vs. a socialized self**.

Compatibility of scientific with theistic thought

The early modern era is distinguished by the Scientific Revolution and the Enlightenment. Galileo and Bacon set the tone for a natural philosophy grounded in systematic observation of natural objects, while Newton made the natural world and the known universe plausibly explicable. Consequently, a new cultural ideology emerged, faith in science, which seriously challenged both Catholic and Protestant beliefs about nature and human nature.

Yet theistic, if not denominational, beliefs informed the views of many contemporary natural philosophers. From Descartes, Pascal, and Spinoza to Berkeley, and Reid, among others, many scholars took for granted fundamental compatibility of scientific with theistic thought. When Psychology formally emerged in the nineteenth century, many of its founders, particularly in the USA, reflected this scientific-theistic heritage. Meanwhile, as you will see in the next chapter, science began to take on exaggerated forms that distorted both science and religion.

Objectivity–subjectivity of observation

Central to the substance of early modern natural philosophy was the question of whether observations of natural phenomena were trustworthy or, in current terms, objective rather than subjective. Galileo, Bacon, Descartes, and Newton had prescribed specific concrete steps that observers should take to ensure trustworthiness. Clearly, they recognized that the human act of acquiring sensory impressions of natural objects entails accounting for sources of bias.

Although many in Psychology have portrayed Locke as an empiricist, as if he advocated pure objectivity, he held that human understanding largely depends on mental abstractions from sensory impressions and one's conscious knowledge. Another so-called empiricist, Hume held that perceiving primary qualities of natural objects is as dependent on observers as secondary qualities are, as did the so-called rationalist Berkeley, who studied perception scientifically. Kant also stressed subjective influences on observation, while Pascal understood the knowledge obtained from scientific observation as provisional. The objectivity–subjectivity theme resurfaces in subsequent chapters, because it is very relevant to modern psychologists' claims of producing legitimate scientific knowledge.

A self-contained vs. a relational self

During an era of increasing socioeconomic cultivation of individualism, natural philosophers discussed conceptions of the self as an expression of individuality or as embedded in relationships. But these two general orientations did not divide along associationist vs. rationalist, reconciliation, or early Romantic lines. Rather, the most fruitful distinction seems to be between one view that autonomous, self-contained individuals rationally direct their own actions and another view that interdependent selves are embedded in layers of influential social relations that shape any individual's actions simultaneously with individuals' active agency.

Among the British associationists, only Locke promoted the conception of autonomous selves, while La Mettrie took the individualistic position to its mechanistic extreme. Yet Hobbes situated individual motives and societal influences in dialectical tension. Hume rejected the notion of a permanent, integrated self, proposing instead interpersonal influences determining individual identity. Hartley considered complex associations as the human glue that bonds social relations and held that the sense of self emerges within a sociolinguistic web of relationships. Diderot also stressed the interdependence of selves, while Condillac regarded language, which is fundamentally interpersonal, as the hallmark of human nature.

Among the rationalists, although Descartes typically is described as focused on body–mind relations, his position was not asocial; rather, generosity to others took pride of place in his conception of social relations. Spinoza asserted that those who live virtuously according to reason are naturally inclined to practise empathy, mutual aid, and social harmony. Berkeley echoed the view that humans are naturally inclined towards sociability and the common good. Even the idealist Leibniz balanced interests of the self with sociability and altruism.

Among the reconciliationists, Kant privileged morality, which implicates social relations, in his emphasis on reason. Although, for him, individuals are autonomous moral agents and the concept of interdependence evidently is absent in Kant's philosophy, when acting morally we practise the categorical imperative, which again is fundamentally social. But Reid explicitly understood individuals as social beings and stressed mutual trust and truthfulness for harmonious social relations. Rousseau, of course, championed social selves within societies that fostered the common good.

It is curious that, although most early modern natural philosophers understood the self as inherently relational, Locke's standpoint of individualistic detachment apparently is the origin of modern individualism that has suffused psychological thought until recently (see Chapter 7). Perhaps the Lockean position prevailed, because it was most congruent with the advancing socioeconomic system of capitalism in which individual striving for material wealth rather than fostering the common good became the *raison d'être* of economically privileged Western nations. This system served as the societal foundation for a scientific psychology of individuals.

Summary

In this chapter we described diverse positions on psychological phenomena produced during the Scientific Revolution and the Enlightenment. Natural philosophers discussed diverse, often contradictory concepts, some secular, some religious. The first scientific psychologists of the nineteenth century inherited this legacy. But assuming direct connections between this heritage and current Psychology is dubious.

In Part 1 we described the new empiricism that emerged during the Scientific Revolution. Astronomical discoveries inspired Western societies, while Francis Bacon's prescriptions for the conduct of science, known then as natural philosophy, inspired others to explore nature and human nature methodically. Cultural developments, including increased social management and individualism, facilitated the Scientific Revolution. Isaac Newton's discoveries stimulated the eighteenth-century Enlightenment, an era in which scholars celebrated reason, progress, and empirical knowledge.

In Part 2 we presented a preview of early modern psychological thought by defining key conceptions and four philosophical perspectives: associationism, rationalism, reconciliation, and early romanticism. Then we posed basic questions about body and mind, human nature, and social relations that the scholars described in the following sections attempted to answer.

In Part 3 we described diverse associationist perspectives. Thomas Hobbes insisted on an empirical approach to nature and human nature. Although he emphasized the sensory foundations of knowledge, John Locke was more a rationalist than an empiricist. David Hume adopted a unique empirical and skeptical standpoint concerning mental processes. David Hartley emphasized body–mind relations and advanced the influential concept of association.

French Enlightenment perspectives ranged from the *philosophes* (e.g., Denis Diderot) to the different positions of Julien de La Mettrie, Pierre-Jean-George Cabanis, and Etienne Bonnot de Condillac. For Diderot, humans are reasoning but passionate animals. La Mettrie, a physician, regarded humans as symbol-making sensualist machines. For Cabanis, we are soulful, intelligent statues. Another physician, Condillac, viewed humans psychophysiologically as embodied soul/minds.

In Part 4 we described rationalist perspectives. René Descartes' dualism of mechanistic and rationalistic orientations is central to Western thought. Baruch Spinoza argued for an integration of the divine with natural objects and humans. Gottfried Leibniz contradicted him by championing an idealistic orientation in which pre-existing ideas produce human knowledge. George Berkeley stressed the operations of the mind on empirical reality.

In Part 5 we addressed the attempts by Immanuel Kant and Thomas Reid to reconcile rationalism and empiricism. Integrating reflection with concrete experience within a structuring mind, Kant promoted humans' capacity for moral agency. In his common-sense realism, Reid focused on balancing empirical with rational knowledge and emphasized inherent mental faculties and their ethical applications to everyday life.

Part 6 dealt with early Romantic thought. The seeds of the Romantic movement were sown in the seventeenth century by Pascal who argued that the mind is dependent on the wisdom of one's passions. In the eighteenth century the ideas of Jean-Jacques Rousseau about human nature, the primacy of passions, child-centred education, and social relations proved influential in both psychological and sociopolitical thought.

In Part 7 we presented three themes that summarize early modern psychological thought: compatibility of scientific with theistic thought, objectivity–subjectivity of observation, and a self-contained vs. a relational self.

Sample essay questions

1. If the human conditions of scientific observation include inevitable leakage from subjective sources, what are the implications for psychologists' claims to scientific truths?

2. How did the early modern philosophers envision the role of human will within psychological processes, if they did? What value for current Psychology is there, if any, in human will as a psychological construct?

3. What might Psychology look like, if a conception of the self as socialized and interdependent had prevailed, rather than Locke's individualistic notion of the self?

RECOMMENDED READING

Works cited in Chapter 1 also are germane to this chapter, especially Barzun's (2000) *From dawn to decadence: 1500 to the present*; G. Richards's (2010), *Putting psychology in its place: An introduction from a critical historical perspective*, D. N. Robinson's (1995) *An intellectual history of psychology* (3rd edition); R. Smith's (1997) *The Norton history of the human sciences*; and Whaley's (2003) *Women's history as scientists: A guide to the debates*.

Gribbin's (2002) *Science: A history, 1543–2001* covers the key figures, although he adopts a strict continuity position in historiography and concentrates on individual scientists. For scholarly assessments of the natural philosophers discussed see the References cited.

ONLINE RESOURCES

Stanford Encyclopedia of Philosophy: see entries for individuals and the entry Rationalism vs. Empiricism: http://plato.stanford.edu/entries/rationalism-empiricism/

4 The philosophical and scientific climate in the nineteenth century

Chapter outline

Introduction

In Chapters 2 and 3 we considered the philosophical and scientific ideas of previous centuries that laid the intellectual foundations for Psychology. Now we discuss the immediate roots of Psychology's inception in nineteenth-century philosophy and the natural sciences. But first we address the fractious state of society during this era. Due to the manifold developments occurring within and outside what are called Western nations (i.e., Europe, Russia, Canada, the US, Australia, and New Zealand), such a characterization remains fragmented itself.

Anglo-American and European culture was in turmoil economically, politically, and socially due to the Industrial Revolution, political strife, and social movements for the emancipation of workers, women, and slaves. Privileged nations cemented their roles as colonial and imperial powers during this time. Upheavals of thought, such as the Romantic movement, paralleled these developments. Yet the preponderant intellectual orientation remained the rule of reason and experience informed by scientific knowledge.

New expressions of Enlightenment thought appeared by mid-century: August Comte's positivism, John Stuart Mill's utilitarianism, and Karl Marx's dialectical materialism. In addition, philosophical psychologists discussed psychological processes, eventuating in a union between philosophy and natural science, called Psychology. Meanwhile, scientific developments in brain research and physiology gained momentum and social recognition. The most dramatic scientific development was the emergence of Charles Darwin's theory of evolution, which had major scientific, philosophical, and cultural ramifications.

To cope with the jolt to traditional conceptions of nature and human nature and with economic, political, and social turmoil, many turned towards the quasi-religious social movements of mesmerism, phrenology, and spiritualism. Literary authors and philosophers, such as Friedrich Nietzsche, addressed the psychological consequences of this cultural turbulence.

Given this context, the **aims** of this chapter are to describe:

- The turbulent social, economic, and political context in which Psychology emerged.
- The significance for Psychology of the Romantic Movement and of positivism, utilitarianism, and dialectical materialism.
- Philosophical and scientific developments, including evolutionary theory, which paved the way for a scientific psychology.
- Critics' and public responses to these developments.
- Three themes summarizing the main issues in nineteenth-century psychological thought: liberal individualism vs. socialist alternatives, scientific triumphalism vs. skepticism, and unresolved questions about body, mind, and human nature that underlay philosophers' conceptions of psychological phenomena.

| Part 1 | ## Change in Western culture |

During the late eighteenth century and for much of the nineteenth century, Western nations struggled with the effects of profound social changes that altered Western culture politically, economically, socially, intellectually, scientifically, and psychologically. On the one hand, the Industrial Revolution (see below), organized on the basis of capitalist economic theory, created structural forms of socioeconomic inequality, while on the other hand, the French Revolution of 1789 emphasized political equality. Simultaneously, colonialism contributed to the subjugation, exploitation, domination, and understanding of the "Other" (non-European cultures) as inferior.

The contradictory aims of the two revolutions precipitated social and intellectual conflict. Some of these conflicts escalated in 1848 when revolutions erupted in France, Austria, and Prussia and other countries, challenging monarchical rule. Consequently, societal tensions arose from political threats to social order and from erosion of the authority of the Catholic and Protestant Churches.

Philosophical psychologists at the time were ambivalent about how they should theorize or even participate in these struggles. German scholar Franz Theodor Waitz (1821–1864), for instance, did not allow political events to disturb his psychological studies, not because he was indifferent towards political reform, but because he never could decide whether to be active in matters that he felt he little understood. By contrast, his contemporary Friedrich Beneke discussed political, social, and religious conflicts as problems that could be overcome with the help of psychology. He criticized academics' tendency to restrict themselves to scholarship and refuse sociopolitical engagement (Teo, 2007).

Economic and political turmoil

Among the sources of societal upheaval were the Industrial Revolution, the emergence of capitalism, the status of science and technology, and urbanization and nationalism.

Industrial Revolution

Broadly speaking, the Industrial Revolution represented a major shift from a local agrarian, hand-based economy to a mainly urban, machine-based economy, enabled by the invention of technologies suited to mass production. Simultaneous with the development of large industries, wealthy landowners secured increasingly large tracts of agricultural land, resulting in a smaller number of people producing massive quantities of food. The surplus labour pool was then available for industrialists' use and exploitation.

Within this unregulated market system industrialists forced children, mothers, and fathers to work for extremely low wages, often for fourteen hours daily or longer. The consequences were huge profits and wealth for the industrialists, but poverty, exhaustion, and a very short lifespan for workers. Capitalist economic theories emerged in this economic context (Heilbroner, 1999). The most influential early theorists were Adam Smith (1723–1790), **Thomas Malthus** (1766–1834), and David Ricardo (1772–1823); they gave the Industrial Revolution a seemingly scientific rationale for the privileges of the capitalist class and its domination of the relatively impoverished masses.

Figure 4.1 The rising middle class was the subject of contemporary satirical drawings and literature

On the other hand, other social classes became prominent: an industrial working class and a burgeoning middle class, which had emerged during the Middle Ages, operating between landlord and peasant. The middle class included artisans, merchants, and early industrialists. They enjoyed relative freedom and appreciated the material benefits created by scientific discoveries and technological applications. Their aspirations to acquire the material comforts, learning, and prestige that the upper class enjoyed were the subject of contemporary satirical drawings and literature, as shown in Figure 4.1.

Previously only the nobility and church figures enjoyed political, economic, and social freedom and prosperity. By the twentieth century another class surfaced, professionals, to which the new psychologists would belong.

Science, technology, and tertiary education

Well into the nineteenth century, natural scientists tended to work autonomously and concentrated on their own projects that might or might not benefit society. Meanwhile, applications of mathematics to industry enabled the invention of more accurate and efficient machines. For example, automatic spinning and weaving machines created a massive textile industry in what is now Northern Ireland.

The Industrial Revolution had received huge boosts from previous inventions, such as the steam pump and steam engine. But in the nineteenth century, technology rapidly advanced such inventions as photography (1826), the telegraph (1837), the telephone and the four-stroke internal combustion engine (1876), the light bulb (1879), and the first gasoline-powered automobile 1885. Thus, in a practical sense, inventions rather science modernized society.

The character of universities changed as well. For example, Wilhelm von Humboldt's ideas significantly altered the Prussian educational system. At the university level he cemented the notion that teaching and research should be integrated instead of either researching or teaching; he promoted the notion of academic freedom where neither government nor industry should interfere in academic work; he fostered collegial, academic self-governance; and he identified philosophy as the location where specialized knowledge could be integrated.

In addition, Humboldt instituted changes in the education of grammar-school teachers. In 1824, Prussia established psychology as a required university course for teaching candidates, which some claim represents the birthday of Psychology as a discipline (Gundlach, 2004). In making psychology an examinable discipline, it became institutionalized, first in Prussia and then in other German states.

Urbanization and nationalism

A related societal change was the rise of nationalism, stimulated by the rapid growth of urban centres. London's population escalated from less than 1,000,000 in 1800 to approximately 6.5 million in 1900, while Paris expanded from 600,000 to 3.6 million. Urbanization complemented industrialization and the establishment of educational institutions in facilitating nation-building, aided by the development of newspapers for the middle class, popular novels, and cultural institutions (Barzun, 2000).

One type of ideological glue that bound the disparate elements of society together was the concept of "the brotherhood" of everyone in a society, which fostered the sense of national identity. State schooling often inculcated national identity in the population through the curriculum taught in a common language. The major urbanized nation-states each fostered *chauvinism*, the belief that it was unique, even superior to other nations.

Colonialism and imperialism

While internal domestic changes were occurring, overt colonial and imperial actions introduced rapid transformations in other countries and continents. The term *colonial project* refers to the establishment of a regime of subjugation by one group of people or nation over another, resulting in politically, economically, and socially dependent colonies (R. J. C. Young, 2001). Colonialism did not assume the same form and practice in all contexts: British colonialism against the Irish was not the same as Spanish colonialism in Latin America. Moreover, colonialist motives differed: sometimes political, economic, or religious motives took precedence, and sometimes settlement was more important than resource exploitation.

The dominant powers of Europe, beginning with Britain and including Belgium, Denmark, France, Germany, Italy, Netherlands, Portugal, Russia, and Spain, but also the USA, had colonies globally. For example, British Queen Victoria became Empress of India in 1876.

Shortly thereafter the Indian Famine, which resulted in approximately 10 million deaths, can be explained as a consequence of British imperialism (M. Davis, 2001).

The term *imperialism* refers to a process of political, military, economic, and cultural domination that several European powers and later the USA pursued globally. Sometimes used synonymously with colonialism, imperialism is the extension of nationalism on a larger geographical scale than colonialism. But whereas imperialism operated from the "centre" of power (e.g., London), colonialism operated in the colonies ("periphery"). Competitive imperial ambitions between various European nations were also the basis of World War I (1914–1918).

The dominant imperial powers have been Britain, France, and the USA, while Germany struggled unsuccessfully to compete. It is noteworthy that early Psychology flourished in these four nations (see Chapter 5). From a critical perspective, an important matter is whether the growth of the imperial powers influenced the social, human, and natural sciences that were developing during this era. For example, colonialism and imperialism evidently were the sources for constructing non-European peoples as inferior, for which extrapolations from Darwin's evolutionary theory provided an ideological tool (G. Richards, 2012).

Given this history, can the European sciences of the nineteenth century be characterized as colonial and does this characterization reverberate in current politics and science? Postcolonial (i.e., after colonial rule) thinkers who attempted to understand the human sciences against this colonial background answered affirmatively on both counts (e.g., Said, 1978). As we describe social movements for emancipation, keep the possible contributions of colonialism and imperialism to Psychology's outlook in mind.

Social movements for emancipation

While urban industrial development, nationalism, and imperialism escalated, agitation for equal rights progressed. The economic and social problems that the Industrial Revolution produced aroused many to press for economic, political, and social emancipation for workers, women, and slaves. These movements included socialists, feminists, and slavery abolitionists.

Socialism

According to early capitalist theory, poverty is a natural state, the masses should exist on subsistence-level wages, and private ownership of wealth benefits everyone. Early socialists rejected these principles. Some were inspired by Jean-Jacques Rousseau's notion that equality and cooperation are the natural bases of life.

The early socialists advocated a planned economy to stabilize the economic cycles inherent in a free-market economy. They developed plans to revolutionize industrialization and create a new society oriented to the common good that benefited everyone on the basis of economic, social, and political equality. For Karl Marx, *socialism* meant collective ownership of the means of economic production.

Prior to Marxist theory, a few individuals created various alternatives to capitalism. For example, Robert Owen (1771–1858), the owner of a cotton mill in Manchester, England, reconstructed a cotton factory in Scotland and organized it as a cooperative economic and social system, called New Lanark. He attempted unsuccessfully to replicate it in the USA.

Women's emancipation

During this time of extraordinary socioeconomic and political change, the movement towards women's emancipation gained momentum (Spender, 1983). Women gave birth to fewer children and had more independence in cities than they did in rural settlements. But they were far from being recognized legally as equal to men.

In 1791, **Olympe de Gouges** (1748–1793) of France wrote the *Declaration of the Rights of Woman and Citizen* in which she asserted that all the so-called "rights of man" were the rights of women as well: women should participate as fully as men in all aspects of society and should have the rights to vote, free speech, property, and divorce. However, the French revolutionaries executed her as a counter-revolutionary.

In 1792, **Mary Wollstonecraft** (1759–1797) of England published *A Vindication of the Rights of Woman*. Women should receive advanced education, she argued, so that they could take their rightful place in civil society, which would benefit everyone. Moreover, Wollstonecraft contended that just as kings should not have absolute power over their "subjects," which was the theme of the French Revolution, so husbands should not rule their wives. Yet her ideas held no social currency at the time.

After the French Revolution, conservative political groups still sought to confine political, economic, and social rights to upper-class men who could afford to hold property. Although liberals were ambivalent about equal legal rights for all classes, socialists agitated for extending legal rights to everyone including the working class. But women generally were excluded from these new movements.

Nevertheless, some women and a few male supporters continued to promote equality for women. Early feminist writers in Britain (e.g., Florence Nightingale, 1820–1910) and the USA emphasized equal voting rights and other legal reforms, such as the right to divorce. Some emphasized the similarities between female and male capacities, while others stressed gender differences, particularly the unique biological and social role of motherhood. In addition, African women in the USA (e.g., Harriet Tubman, c. 1820–1913) contributed to ending slavery, opposing racism, and promoting women's equality.

Abolition of slavery

The trade in African slaves connected the major European powers with their colonies in North, Central, and South America and the Caribbean. By 1776, the US colonials living in the southern states exploited the free labour of 200,000 Africans, while those in the north traded slaves and commodities to sustain their local economies (Barzun, 2000).

But a tide of indignation about slavery rose in Western culture. Britain abolished slavery in 1834, as did France in 1848, while US agitators for abolition became more prominent and many US states prohibited slavery. Yet after the US Civil War ended in 1865, governments only briefly enforced laws protecting the now emancipated Africans, resulting in over a century of racial segregation and denial of basic human rights for African Americans (Zinn, 2005).

Responses to these movements

The French Revolution and its aftermath threatened the powers of the ruling classes. Their response for decades afterwards was to create police-states. In this way, industrialists and royal heads of governments, buttressed by the military, contained political movements and violent revolts that threatened to replace the status quo with socialism.

Advocates for the emancipation of women and slaves also encountered negative reaction in the form of sociological, psychological, and biological arguments against equality. A popular claim was that women were inferior to men because of their unique reproductive functions that rendered them incapable of complete rational functioning. Many scientists contended that women's brains were smaller than men's; therefore, they were less rational, more emotional, hence suited to family life only (Shields, 1975). The biological argument against women's equality paralleled the popular view that Africans were biologically inferior to Whites.

Other writers insisted that the traditional patriarchal family of gender hierarchy served society well and that men should remain in their superior positions, because, the argument went, only the latter knew how to exercise leadership. Still other male objectors engaged in *ad hominem* rebuttals in which they dismissed early feminists' social criticisms by attributing them to the female authors' alleged personal problems.

Part 1 conclusion

The relevance of these emancipation movements and society's responses to them is that during the era when Psychology was emerging, many citizens were agitating for basic cultural and psychological change. However, many if not most contemporary scientists and the new psychologists pursued their activities relatively detached from extant social issues until the turn of the twentieth century (see Chapter 5). One exception was Friedrich Lange, one of the first formal critics of psychology, who was actively involved in the labour movement. Another exception was Wilhelm Wundt, who early in his career once ran for political office as a member of a left liberal party and engaged in workers' education (Rieber & D. K. Robinson, 2001).

Simultaneous with political, economic, and cultural developments during the nineteenth century were relatively new ways of thinking about nature and human nature. To cope with the realities of political repression and economic inequality, many thinkers turned to Romantic ideals.

Part 2 The Romantic movement

The Romantic movement in philosophy, philosophical psychology, literature, and the creative arts can be understood as a cultural response to the Newtonian mechanistic world-view, the rationalistic universe envisioned by Enlightenment thinkers, and the French Revolution. Although Rousseau is often credited with founding romanticism as a school of thought, the Romantic movement began in Germany with the writings of Friedrich Schlegel (1772–1829). Although the movement took diverse forms (Lovejoy, 1948), what Romantic devotees had in common was a desire for individual freedom and for creative expression while standing at the margins of society. By contrast, artists in the medieval, Renaissance, and Enlightenment eras were integrated with society and served individual patrons.

After describing the chief characteristics of the Romantic movement, we discuss the contributions of **Johann Wolfgang von Goethe** (1749–1832) and **Arthur Schopenhauer** (1788–1860) and the implications of their views for Psychology.

Chief characteristics

Plato had divided the human soul into three parts, later termed thinking, feeling, and willing. Whereas the Enlightenment project focused on thinking and reason, the Romantic movement underlined feeling, emotion, and volition.

> **Small-group discussion.** Which is more important in human life – thinking, feeling, or willing? Justify your argument. If you believe they are equally important, explain why and how, using examples from your own experience.

In literary works Romantic writers created psychological portraits of how contemporary (wealthy) young men struggled to find identity and a sense of self. The Romantic hero was highly conscious of his presumed unique capacities for expressing intense feelings in living a rebellious, alienated, or despairing life. Self-knowledge was a consequence of reflection on concrete experience with other cultures and societies, not of rational deliberation and controlled, predictable gentlemanly conduct. But women were excluded from these depictions of self-development except as objects of romantic and erotic fantasies.

The Romantic emphases on passion and intuition are evident, for example, in the English landscape paintings of J. M. W. Turner (1775–1851), as depicted in Figure 4.2.

Furthermore, the Romantics were infatuated with exotic non-European societies and extolled the presumed virtues of "noble savages." This construction of racialized groups might have had positive connotations by attributing nobility to "primitive" peoples, but it excluded the voices of the "Other" and how racialized groups saw themselves and Europeans. An overtly Eurocentric construction is exemplified by the views of German archaeologist Johann Winckelmann (1717–1768), who deplored the shape of Chinese eyes for aesthetic reasons and compared African facial features to those of monkeys (Bindman, 2002).

In brief, the Romantics departed from Enlightenment ideology in **four ways**:

- They contended that psychological phenomena, such as feelings and intuition, were valid pathways to truth, just as reason was to the Enlightenment. For the Romantics, reason by itself cannot account for the complexities of the human mind and the mysterious aspects of human life.
- The Romantics understood nature as fundamentally disordered and mystical, that is, not amenable to mechanistic explanations of lawful regularities. To the Romantics, industrialists were polluting the beauty of nature.
- The Romantics celebrated the unique powers of creative individuals who challenged and redefined cultural conventions.
- They understood nature, human life, and the creative process as always in flux.

Figure 4.2 This 1975 British stamp is dedicated to J. M. W. Turner, a Romantic landscape painter

Methodology

Romantic philosophy began with a universe that was a living being with a soul that pervaded and connected everything in it. For the Romantic, knowing something entailed drawing on one's individual connection with this greater whole by feeling one's way into nature. Consequently, Romantic methods of seeking knowledge characteristically were irrational, subjective, and mystical. The Romantics believed in spontaneous metamorphosis or sudden transformation. As such, they highly valued individual histories and descriptions of a person's emotional and intellectual development as unique developmental expressions of a universal soul (Ellenberger, 1970).

Spontaneous action and natural feelings were considered the best guide to knowledge and there was a strong belief in the power of inspiration and intuition. Improvisation and conversation were important methods of knowing along with the recognition of how dualities operate. Objects of study included folklore, myths, and symbols, which were taken up as expressions of the human soul and of nature's soul.

Hermeneutics was originally part of Romantic methodology, because intuitive and mystical expressions were considered veils hiding a deeper reality. Hermeneutic procedures were required to gain access to the forces and intentions underlying surface meanings. Using these procedures, one could discover primordial or universal principles in which all beings participate and that underlie surface changes.

Such Romantic themes are evident in the psychologies of Goethe and Schopenhauer.

Johann Wolfgang von Goethe

This literary author, philosopher, and scientist is Germany's national literary hero. In his 1774 sentimental novel, *The Sorrows of Young Werther*, Goethe depicted a love triangle in which the extremely intense, young hero fell hopelessly in love with his best friend's wife and out of despair of ever consummating his love for her committed suicide (Barzun, 2000). The novel, apparently the first literary "bestseller," depicted the struggles of living an unbalanced life.

Goethe also made **three contributions** relevant to the history of psychological thought:

- Colour, he claimed, is not just a physical phenomenon but also a sensory and perceptual one, that is, colour also is a subjective phenomenon. Hence, Goethe asserted, one should study colour from a psychological perspective (Treisman, 1996). Some have argued that his ideas became the foundation for phenomenology by examining sensory experiences as intact wholes not isolated sensations.
- Goethe believed that every living thing is in constant change and that all existing organic forms can be traced back to a primordial form. In doing so he proposed an early theory of evolution by which one species could be transformed into another.
- Goethe understood personal growth as enhanced by the conflicts and frustrations stemming from irrational instincts. For him, humans are torn by opposing forces of love and hate, life and death, good and evil. Thus, the goal of life is to embrace these opposing forces and find a balance, not to deny or suppress them, a standpoint that Nietzsche echoed and Carl Jung modified (P. Bishop, 2008).

Arthur Schopenhauer

A German philosopher, Schopenhauer promoted a Romantic psychology of the irrational and the will. As he put it (roughly translated in English), "In the heart of every person there lives a wild beast." The wildness of the beast within each individual implies conflict and pain, but also implies freedom, mediated by the will. Thus, for Schopenhauer, who was inspired by the French philosophical psychologist **Maine de Biran** (1766–1824) (see below), human will is the core of mental life. As the ultimate cause of everything that we say, think, or do, will is primary in human psychology, the intellect secondary.

Following Immanuel Kant's distinction between noumena and phenomena, Schopenhauer asserted that the external world that we believe we can both perceive and understand is really just a world of appearances, and the objects that we believe we perceive objectively are not separate from our way of perceiving them. The intellect deals with this world of appearances. On the other hand, genuine reality, the essence of the world behind those appearances, consists of the will. Taking a pessimistic view, Schopenhauer believed that desire never brings satisfaction, only life-long suffering (Janaway, 2010).

Schopenhauer's ideas influenced Sigmund Freud's conception of human psychology in that Freud regarded humans as capable only of minimizing irrational forces in our actions. He also credited Schopenhauer with the concepts of "repression" of undesirable thoughts and "resistance" to uncovering them. Yet Freud claimed that he too had discovered these processes.

Part 2 conclusion

The Romantics promoted the idea of a vitalistic, progressive "Nature"; they preferred "biology" to physics; and they emphasized human emotion and passion, freedom of choice, and the importance of viewing the world holistically. But from their privileged position, the Romantics idealized subjugated groups – women, pagans, natives, and peasants – whom they regarded as soulful bearers of un-alienated nature. Moreover, they failed to see that they inadvertently dominated these groups by idealizing them.

Politically, the Romantics were affiliated with the range of conservative, liberal, socialist, and nationalist views. In general, they believed that social institutions, science, and technology alienated human beings from their true state of nature; in other words, civilization was the antithesis of nature. Society was rational and mechanistic, whereas nature was irrational, intuitive, and organic. Thus, some have argued (e.g., Georg Lukács, 1885–1971) that romanticism paved the way for German fascism.

Psychologically speaking, the Romantics thought that the best way to understand individuals was to study the *whole* person, including fantasies, feelings, and aspirations, rather than just empirically determined ideas or rational capacities. But rather than an isolated individual, the Romantics explored the "Transcendent Self," that is, the person in union with "all Being," and they linked self-feeling with rootedness in nature.

Romanticism significantly influenced psychological thought and psychotherapy (Richardson, Fowers, & Guignon, 1999). Besides Freud's interest in conflicting drives, Jung's notion of the collective unconscious, his focus on dreams, myths, and symbols, and his belief in the healing power of nature, exemplify the Romantic spirit. Humanistic psychology (see Chapter 10) and transpersonal psychology also are considered products of the Romantic mentality.

The Romantic movement, however, was not the primary intellectual orientation in the nineteenth century. Three "rational" social philosophies that seemed scientific – positivism, utilitarianism, and dialectical materialism – rivalled each other for prominence and proved more influential in society and science than romanticism.

Part 3 The New Enlightenment

In different ways and on their own terms, positivism, utilitarianism, and dialectical materialism expressed the previous century's emphasis on reason informed by science. They recapitulated the values and beliefs of the Enlightenment, hence, the term, the New Enlightenment. Positivism, utilitarianism, and dialectical materialism had profound effects on society, science, and ultimately Psychology.

During this period many scholars believed that the purest, most reliable form of knowledge was scientific, the scientific method could and should be applied to society, and scientific findings could improve society. The most prestigious intellectual framework remained natural science. The emerging middle classes sought security and existential reassurance from faith in science and impressive scientific and technological achievements.

Despite the revolts of the Romantics and later social critics, most nineteenth-century philosophers and scientists upheld the doctrine of the steady march of rational, scientific progress (Brinton, 1963). The dominant beliefs were the perfectibility of human beings and

Table 4.1 New-Enlightenment perspectives

Founder	Philosophy	Political position
Auguste Comte	Positivism	Conservatism
John Stuart Mill	Utilitarianism	Liberalism
Karl Marx	Dialectical materialism	Democratic socialism

the realization of progress. Three "secular religions" (i.e., fervent belief systems without formal religious content) came to prominence: positivism, with its virtual worship of natural science; utilitarianism, which quantified happiness to create the greatest good for the greatest number of people; and dialectical materialism, with its biblical day of judgment, the socialist revolution.

Table 4.1 summarizes the founder of each perspective, his philosophy, and political position (Bailey & Eastman, 1994).

Although neither Mill nor Marx identified themselves as "positivists," Comte, Mill, and Marx shared **two assumptions** found in positivism:

- Social science is not fundamentally different from natural science and the latter can be adapted to inform the former.
- Social science should be used to improve human welfare.

During the twentieth century the second assumption took the form of the problem of whether the social sciences could be neutral regarding human values. Many philosophers of science, including Karl Popper, adopted David Hume's standpoint that "science in itself does not resolve questions of value" (Bailey & Eastman, 1994, p. 519) and should not. From this standpoint, Comte, Mill, and Marx conflated science with a moral imperative for societal betterment. Other scholars, however, believe science is infused with human interests and necessarily is laden with values (e.g., Habermas, 1988).

Positivism: Auguste Comte

Positivism as an ideology and social movement emerged in France. Its chief proponent was Comte (1798–1857). Rather than advocating a return to a monarchical regime, he placed faith in the capacity of science to produce truth, harmony, and order in society. For Comte, scientific knowledge was positive knowledge, hence the term *positivism*. Humankind proceeded, he asserted, from a primitive theological stage of development through a metaphysical phase inspired by René Descartes to the highest stage, a positive period of scientific development.

Although Comte was not a scientist, his notion of a positive science proved rather influential among nineteenth- and twentieth-century natural scientists, including the new psychologists. But over decades Comte's positivism took more philosophically sophisticated forms in Ernst Mach's positivism and logical positivism, which were incompatible with many of his ideas. Yet, regardless of the types of positivism, adherents to positivism demarcate science from non-science.

Epistemology

Comte's first mission was intellectual in that he aimed to reinforce the position that the only genuine form of knowledge was positive, scientific knowledge. He aligned his views with Francis Bacon, Descartes, and Galileo. Comte insisted that only publicly observable knowledge, limited to external descriptions of observable characteristics, met the criterion of truth. As such, his position was an extreme version of empiricism, which resurfaced in behaviourism. Indeed, variations of positivism have been very influential epistemological positions in Psychology.

Comte (1896) argued that all thought evolves through **three stages**:

- At the theological stage supernatural beings are thought to produce all natural phenomena. If we argue that lightning is the result of God's wrath, our thinking reflects this stage.
- At the metaphysical stage abstract forces are thought to produce phenomena. If we suggest that a life-force produces lightning, then our thinking is metaphysical.
- At the positive stage, the highest stage of development, all explanations are scientifically objective. Thus, lightning is an electrostatic discharge. In positive (scientific) thinking, humans study natural laws while using observation and reason within fields of specialization.

Society

Comte's second mission was to recreate society on the basis of sound science. For him, the scientific philosophy of positivism was the basis for a moral theory of administering society. Accordingly, he founded a new discipline, called "sociology," which he regarded as the apex of scientific knowledge and a tool for societal betterment. In Comte's social philosophy, "social physics" should be the foundation of society. Only scientifically educated experts who understand the "laws" of social development should advise government officials on appropriate legislation, policies, and practices to improve the status of the masses.

Psychology

Comte (1896) contended that philosophical psychology should be excluded from the positive sciences, because, for him, it was the latest stage of theology and merely a dream not a science. His critique of psychology targeted introspection, because this subjective method could not lead to a scientific consensus. Furthermore, he rejected mental operations as "private events" and therefore outside the realm of science. Instead, Comte proposed that mental phenomena should be studied within anatomy, physiology, and his own positive philosophy. He trusted sensory knowledge and the power of scientific methods, specifically experimentation, to show the operation of natural laws governing observable phenomena.

Section conclusion

From the perspective of modern Eurocentric knowledge, it is reasonable that humankind should shift its source of knowledge from myth to natural science (Horkheimer & Adorno, 1982).

However, positivism itself became a myth by Comte maintaining that it was the only approach to genuine knowledge; this commitment belied an exaggerated faith in science. In fact, Comte founded a "religion of humanity," which attracted women and blue-collar workers, and elected himself the virtual "pope" of this movement. He prescribed that on a daily basis people should utter the motto "Love, Order, Progress" in place of Catholic exclamations, such as, "Jesus, Mary, and Joseph, pray for us."

Politically, Comte and his conservative followers were averse to radical economic and political changes and revolutions. They favoured economic and political traditions instead. Comte's social and political mission was partially fulfilled in the mid-century regime of Napoleon III whose bureaucrats implemented rational planning (Barzun, 2000).

Liberalism and utilitarianism

Particularly in Britain but also France, liberalism not positivism was the more popular social philosophy. Liberals believed progress would occur naturally through the development of liberal social institutions, aided by science and technology. Given that nature operates lawfully, liberals argued, citizens should harness nature by using science and technology to create prosperity for all. Thus, the natural evolution of social reform eventually can eradicate injustice and achieve secular salvation. As the ideology of democracy, liberalism defended civic freedom.

Economically, liberals supported the free-market industrial economy and private property. Politically, they emphasized a secular state; rational, incremental social reform guided by legitimate institutions; and individual rights for legal equality, free speech, and a free press – for male property-owners. Initially, liberals held that men who did not hold property did not qualify as citizens and that all women were not legal persons. But in the twentieth century, liberals came to defend equal educational and professional opportunities for women, and extended citizenship to them and men who did not hold property.

Utilitarianism

Liberalism was closely related to *utilitarianism*. This term refers to the argument advanced by **Jeremy Bentham** (1748–1832), an English empiricist philosopher, that political leaders should calculate, literally, the greatest good for the most people by maximizing pleasure and minimizing pain. His aim was to quantify politics, morals, and ethics, calculating the difference between positive actions of pleasure ("benefits") and negative actions of pain ("costs"). Arguably, his conception of ethics as risk–benefit analysis undergirds customary conceptions of ethics in Psychology (see Chapter 8).

Bentham applied the ideas of the Enlightenment to organize society along rational lines and solve social problems scientifically (Dinwiddy, 1989). He invented a quasi-formula for social happiness, called "felicific calculus" and devised a "social biology" by which the state administers rewards and punishments, according to the principles of "political arithmetic." Moreover, he developed plans for reorganizing such social institutions as schools and prisons to maximize surveillance of students and prisoners.

John Stuart Mill

Profoundly affecting nineteenth-century thought and, to some extent, contemporary psychological thought, Mill (1806–1873) came to regard Bentham's type of utilitarianism as literally and figuratively calculating. Evidently influenced by his discussions with his companion **Harriet Taylor** (1807–1858), Mill revised empirical theory to incorporate emotions and artistic impulses (Capaldi, 2004). Yet, although he tried to balance empiricism with the Romantic vision of nature and human feelings, he distrusted mystical intuition and never abandoned empiricism.

A liberal positivist, Mill believed in scientifically guided social progress and the superiority of scientific knowledge. For example, he supported the notion that *all* phenomena are subject to natural law, comprehensible by science alone. However, he was less grandiose than Comte about the possibilities for social reform and was concerned about the potential for despotism and authoritarian control in positivism.

In his 1858 work *On Liberty* Mill argued that individual pursuit of personal development benefited an entire society. He objected to any restrictions on individuals' freedom and promoted political protection for civil liberties, including the free expression of even unpopular ideas and opinions. Mill formulated the *harm principle*, the idea that individual liberty should not be infringed by government, society, or individuals except when an individual's action might harm others. Yet, he was concerned that capitalist acquisition of wealth by individuals could threaten everyone's rights and came to regard socialism favourably (Capaldi, 2004).

Mill's last book, *The Subjection of Women* (1869), resulted from nearly three decades of discussions on gender equality between him and Taylor. In this work he described the subjugated status of women, argued for gender equality, and proposed social and political change to achieve equality. However, his proposal received little support from male scholars (Spender, 1983).

Psychology Earlier, Mill proposed in *A System of Logic* (1843) psychology as a descriptive science of human nature and character formation. This discipline, he believed, could explain the causes and effects of individuals' personal and social actions and provide the means for improving these actions. However, he held that this psychology could only be an inexact science, because its subject matter, like astronomy, was not amenable to experimentation, only to systematic observation. Again, Mill's belief received little peer support, although in the last decades of the twentieth century some critics of Psychology would echo this position (see Chapter 11).

Section conclusion

The utilitarianism of Bentham and Mill proved influential in contemporary Anglo-American circles of psychological thought. In the twentieth century B. F. Skinner's utopian speculations about reorganizing society along empiricist lines seem to echo Bentham's philosophy as well as Comte's (see below). Later, Michel Foucault ([1975] 1977) used Bentham's panopticon as representative of a new form of power in modern society that Foucault critiqued rather than celebrated. The knowledge and fear of constantly being under surveillance changed people's behaviour. For example, we have come to understand ourselves more as consistent, rational, and self-controlled, rather than as emotional and aesthetic beings.

In his version of utilitarianism, Mill contradicted John Locke's view that complex ideas are merely aggregates of simpler ideas. Instead, he proposed the concept of "mental chemistry," which is the process by which individual sensations can combine to form a new sensation that is different from any of the individual sensations that comprise it. This notion proved influential in twentieth-century Psychology among Gestalt theorists (see Chapter 6). Mill's conception of psychology was sustained by his successor Alexander Bain (see below).

Dialectical materialism: Karl Marx

The third, dominant intellectual perspective during the nineteenth century was dialectical materialism. A German scholar and political revolutionary, Marx neither corresponded with Comte nor used the term positivism. However, some of his writings, such as *Capital* (1867), show his reliance on contemporary scientific language. For example, he spoke of the "economic law of motion of modern society" and "natural laws" governing society.

Educated in the idealistic philosophy of Georg Wilhelm Friedrich Hegel, Marx believed that historical and social development proceeds deterministically. Like Comte and Mill, he saw the social scientist as no different from the biologist or physicist and agitated for scientifically planned social change. However, unlike them, Marx understood history and society in terms of dialectical conflict and struggle. Here we describe the evolution of Marx's theory, his concept of alienation, social philosophy, and psychological ideas.

Theoretical evolution

Marx's views are called *dialectical materialism*, because he turned Hegel's dialectical idealism – the primacy of ideas over matter – upside down. Marx asserted that concrete material conditions, chiefly those that pertain to economic and political power, shape ideas and are the basis for knowledge in any social-historical context. In today's psychological terms, he understood the person as acting upon yet changing in response to a constantly changing environment.

After Marx published *Economic and Philosophical Manuscripts* (1844), in which he analyzed the French and Industrial Revolutions, he declared that he had developed a *scientific* analysis of society that transcended the social analyses of his German predecessors. He wrote *The German Ideology* (1845) with his financial sponsor **Friedrich Engels** (1820–1895). In it they critically evaluated three sets of contemporary ideas: the philosophies of Hegel and Ludwig Feuerbach (1804–1872), French social and political analysis, and English economic theory. In 1848 Marx and Engels published their famous *Communist Manifesto*.

By this point, Marx believed that material realities and economic forces shaped society, ideas, and consciousness itself. Producing critical history, he argued that the French revolutionaries, despite their rhetoric of "the universal rights of man," only represented the interests of the bourgeoisie in maintaining economic, political, and social power in society, while ignoring workers' demands for justice. Moreover, Marx contended that Smith, Malthus, and

Ricardo had mistakenly assumed that the conditions of early English capitalism in which workers lived in gross poverty were universal expressions of natural laws. In his 1867 multi-volume, but unfinished, economic history, *Capital*, Marx railed against how industrial capitalists degraded workers as virtual commodities (Wheen, 2006). He concluded that capitalism is inherently dependent on the exploitation of alienated workers.

Alienation

Marx's worldview was built not just on political economic history and an implicit moral vision, but also on a particular view of human nature (Fromm, 1961). In his early writings he addressed the material conditions of *alienation*. Under capitalism, he asserted, workers are segregated from the planning of their work; they merely execute capitalists' plans for the objects that workers produce.

However, Marx believed that, if people do not have power over the planning ("conception") as well as the physical labour ("execution") of their lives, they are alienated from their true selves. Furthermore, he believed that *all* people have such power as their birthright; however, under capitalist economic conditions only the ruling class has the privilege to exercise this power. Marx viewed the split between conception and execution as the force motivating human development and political economic revolution. Under his ideal conditions of communism, alienation would end and the social essence of workers would be restored.

Social philosophy

Marx insisted that history proceeds according to the economic conditions of material life shaping social relations. Accordingly, he claimed that stages of historical development are essentially economic rather than expressions of a universal spirit that Hegel posited. The logical result of this historical progression would be socialism.

Marx understood the socialistic transformation of society as a consequence of historical dialectical conflict to which the socially engaged intellectual would contribute. He stated, as inscribed on his tombstone in London, "The philosophers have only interpreted the world in various ways; the point, however, is to change it." Marxism as an ideology and social movement strived for radical improvements to society by effecting economic, political, and social equality. Socialism was like liberalism in how it celebrated science and technology, but unlike it in how it promoted revolution through revolutionary class struggle, not evolutionary social reform.

Contrary to stereotypes about him, Marx's positions were implicitly moral. It is true that he envisioned socialism as a scientific project not a moral crusade; and he regarded traditional religion, just like traditional capitalist economics, as a fetish. However, his intention was to restore all people's rights to freedom. Like prophetic religion, Marx's views were a denunciation of oppression and an annunciation of justice.

Psychology

Identifying the cultural-historical essence of consciousness, Marx realized that an individual's mind always and necessarily was embedded in society and part of society.

In *The German Ideology*, he and Engels discussed the cultural-historical dimensions of the mind, suggesting that language development parallels the development of humanity's mind and unfolds historically from the need to interact with other humans (Teo, 2001). They wrote:

The production of ideas, of conceptions, of consciousness, is at first directly interwoven with the material activity and the material intercourse of men, the language of real life. Conceiving, thinking, the mental intercourse of men, appear at this stage as the direct efflux of their material behaviour . . . Men are the producers of their conceptions, ideas, etc. – real, active men, as they are conditioned by a definite development of their productive forces and of the intercourse corresponding to these, up to its furthest forms. Consciousness can never be anything else than conscious existence, and the existence of men is their actual life-process. (Marx & Engels, [originally written 1846–1847] 1983, p. 169)

Marx's cultural-historical conceptualization of the mind was part of his view on human nature in which the human essence is its societal quality. Thus, humans should be understood in the context of societal relations. The idea that the mind fundamentally is cultural-historical did not contradict the extant notion that the mind has a natural biological dimension. In fact, Marx understood Darwin's concept of natural selection as the foundation for his own position.

According to Marx, because of its cultural-historical quality, the mind is exposed to power in contexts and relations of production. The ideas of the ruling class, he asserted, are also the ruling ideas, which in turn are the cognitive expression of ruling material relations. Thus, morality, religion, and metaphysics cannot be independent of societal structures and processes.

For Marx, human beings as social actors produce their ideas, which are determined by a particular developmental stage of production. This conception of the mind led to the seminal idea for some psychologists (e.g., Lev Vygotsky) that *life is not determined by the mind, but the mind by life*. That is, it is not the mind of humans that determines our being; rather, it is our social nature as creatures in society that determines our mind.

Marx claimed that the history of industry (the production of goods) and its developing objective existence was the open book of human psychology. In the course of this argument, he expressed one of the first criticisms of the content of modern psychology in suggesting that psychology should study the history of production, the most tangible and accessible part of history. Marx urged philosophers to study actual individuals who live in concrete historical societies, but not to reflect upon the abstract individual beyond history, society, and culture.

Small-group discussion. What are your thoughts about Marx's psychological ideas and societal goals? What place have his ideas had in the Psychology that you have experienced? What place *should* they have in Psychology, in your opinion?

Section conclusion

Besides the work of Darwin and Freud, Marx's dialectical materialism had the greatest influence of any scientific philosophy on the twentieth century. But a significant problem with his worldview and its potential relevance for Psychology is that particularly in the

Soviet Union it became a doctrine with quasi-religious overtones. Marx himself, however, treated his theory as a critical dialectical process; as a skeptic, his favourite motto was "everything should be doubted" (Wheen, 2006).

Some psychologists, particularly in Central and Eastern Europe, based their theories on Marx's cultural-historical conception of the mind. His ideas inspired the Soviet philosophical psychologist Sergej Rubinstein (1889–1960), the cultural-historical school of Psychology initiated by Vygotsky, the French psychologist Georges Politzer (1903–1942), the German thinker **Klaus Holzkamp** (1927–1995) (see Chapter 12), and some varieties of current critical psychology. In addition, critical theorists of the Frankfurt School merged his theories with psychoanalysis, creating a Freudian–Marxist research approach (also Chapter 12).

But the impact of Marx's ideas on Psychology outside the former Soviet bloc and in North America has been repressed in the discipline (Harris, 1996). One explanation for this repression rests in the association of Marx's ideas with "dangerous" communist states and radical democracy. Another reason for the marginalization of Marx's ideas might be their complex nature and his unorthodox style of writing. Yet, the notion among some psychologists that basically we are societal and cultural–historical entities originates in Marx.

Part 3 conclusion

The principal social philosophies of the New Enlightenment were Comte's positivism, Mill's utilitarianism, and Marx's dialectical materialism. To summarize the **three positions**:

- A conservative testament to contemporary natural science, positivism exercised considerable influence intellectually and societally. In its original Comtean form positivism served as a philosophical justification for B. F. Skinner's operant behavioural theory (see Chapter 7), while in later incarnations, positivism was the epistemological justification for objectivistic methodology in Psychology (see Chapter 11).
- Utilitarianism and Mill's discourse of liberal individualism complemented John Locke's argument for autonomous human agents. This intellectual liaison partly enabled an individualistic psychology of the self to take precedence in European and Anglo-American thought (Taylor, 1989).
- Dialectical materialism represented not only a vision for overturning capitalist political-economic conditions, but also a radically different conception of humans as fundamentally social beings. Eventually, a Marxist psychology emerged that flourishes to this day in diverse forms (see Chapter 12).

The influence of positivism, utilitarianism, and dialectical materialism on the Psychology that you might recognize is evident. But four other, noteworthy philosophers discussed psychological phenomena during the same era that Comte, Mill, and Marx did. Although Maine de Biran, Johann Friedrich Herbart, Hermann Lotze, and Alexander Bain are relatively unknown in Psychology today, their ideas proved influential among founding psychologists.

Philosophical psychologies

Many psychologists sustain the view that Psychology originated as an experimental science *opposed* to philosophy. But this belief is historically inaccurate. Nineteenth-century philosophers explored the significance of developments in the natural sciences for the human mind, and natural scientists were educated in philosophy. Rather than polar opposites, contemporary philosophy and natural science were complementary, each producing valuable knowledge about nature, the body, and the mind/soul.

Maine de Biran, Johann Friedrich Herbart, Hermann Lotze, and Alexander Bain shared faith in the fundamental compatibility of philosophy with the natural sciences, but they explored psychological phenomena quite differently from one another. Their systems of thought served as transitional points for emergent natural-science and human-science psychologies.

Maine de Biran

A mathematician, Biran studied the nature of psychological experience philosophically. But he also investigated individuals who were hearing or visually impaired, the development of mental faculties in feral children, hypnotism, and subliminal perception (F. Moore, 1970). In a progression of thought from mechanistic to idealistic, Biran originally identified himself with Etienne Condillac, who limited mental processes to sensory impressions evoking brain associations that eventuated in human understanding. But later Biran rejected this mechanistic standpoint and developed a theory of dynamic mental activity.

Scientific approach

Biran opposed the application of mathematical formulas to exploring the mind. He took scientific classification and identification of causes seriously, but he held that "one can no more explain psychological phenomena by physics, than one can explain the facts of chemistry by the laws of astronomy" (F. Moore, 1970, p. 42). Biran recognized that "other sciences study what we can see or touch; but the central concern of psychology is in motives, intentions, mental faculties, emotions, dreams, ideas" (F. Moore, p. 43).

Positing that it is necessary to balance both inductive and deductive methods when studying psychological phenomena, Biran argued that the capacity for reflection and introspection is necessary as a "privileged source of knowledge" (F. Moore, 1970, p. 54). He also asserted that scientific study can be problematic, if one assumes that experimenters do not influence their research even unintentionally. Understanding scientific inquiry as a situation of mutual influence, he cautioned that a scientist "always has to fear that his [*sic*] imagination will alter the elements that he intends to define" (F. Moore, p. 43).

Central concepts

Asserting that human will is the heart of psychology, Biran proposed that the basic reality is the active self. Against Descartes' declaration, "I think, therefore I am," Biran offered,

"I will, therefore I am." Accordingly, the basic goal of a scientific psychology should be the study of the self's volition or the agentic character of the individual soul.

Biran posited that the self mediated *effort voulu* (in English, the spontaneous intention to act), which he believed was the primary experience, whereas sensory awareness was secondary. For example, "language originates in the self-activity of speech" (R. Smith, 1997, p. 366).

Biran believed that consciousness was the basic fact of psychology (Hallie, 1959). The central aspect of consciousness was the self, which was a form of energy instigated by willing, which could be intense, as in voluntary activity, or less intense, as in automatic activity. The self enabled recognizing an external object or remembering it. Subsequently, he expanded his view of psychology to incorporate spontaneous, creative activity.

Section conclusion

Biran emphasized that human will was the heart of human nature and a person's exercise of will evoked self-awareness. In this sense he followed Augustine and Thomas Aquinas. Biran's insistence on will reappeared in the works of Schopenhauer and human-science psychologist Franz Brentano (see Chapter 10).

In addition, founding US natural-science psychologist, William James (see Chapter 5), regarded Biran very highly because of his broad understanding of human psychological processes. On the other hand, Theodule Ribot, who helped to form early French Psychology, rejected Biran's *spiritualisme* (i.e., idealistic emphasis on inner awareness of an essentially spiritual self) and his later turn towards mystical metaphysical explanations.

Johann Friedrich Herbart

Immanuel Kant's successor in philosophy, Herbart developed a mathematical approach to psychological processes and applied his theory of consciousness to pedagogy (Dunkel, 1970). He proposed that psychology could be both a metaphysical and a mathematical science, although, agreeing with Kant, not an experimental one.

Central concepts

Herbart attempted to map the mind's mathematical laws to legitimize psychology as a science (Leary, 1978). He described psychological phenomena with numerical formulas based on calculus. He rejected popular categories of faculty psychology, such as Thomas Reid's, because they lacked scientific precision (Teo, 2007).

In addition, Herbart developed an abstract psychological theory, known as "mental mechanics," concerning the struggle of ideas coming to consciousness. He envisioned mental content derived from sensory information as "presentations" (ideas) in dynamic interaction with each other. Ideas, for Herbart, are measurable mental units, but are not mere objects of external forces; rather, they possess independent energy or force.

Borrowing from Gottfried Leibniz's conception of natural objects, Herbart argued that intensity is a dimension that lends itself to quantification (Leary, 1980). The intensity of all stimuli exists along a continuum, with those on the high end occupying attention, while those on the low end are pushed out of consciousness. Intensity is continuous and variable over time.

Herbart understood conscious awareness as a dynamic unity of elements in a presentation at its fullest strength and clarity. Employing Leibniz's concept of limen, he described the point at which an idea becomes clearly conscious. While some presentations of elements are conscious, others remain unconscious. Incompatible ideas are repressed but not eliminated, passing into a state of potential activity from which they can enter consciousness eventually.

Herbart substantially modified Leibniz's concept of apperception to emphasize the unity of the mind. He aimed to explain not only how new and old ideas attract and repel each other in consciousness, but also how they form a mass of compatible ideas. His concept of an "apperceptive mass" is similar to the current psychological notion of attention to ideas.

For Herbart, mental forces penetrate consciousness when they combine or compete with other ideas. However, he did not distinguish among thoughts, desires, and emotions. Rather, they were all ideas, subject to the same basic laws and processes of magnitude and inhibition (Boudewijnse, D. Murray, & Bandomir, 2001).

Philosophy of education

Herbart drew from his concept of apperceptive mass to propose that previous learning is the basis for new learning (Dunkel, 1970). Concretely, he recommended that teachers review previously learned material and then integrate new with familiar material to enhance students' capacities for attention and assimilation of the unfamiliar material. The underlying principle was compatibility with students' apperceptive mass. In addition, he proposed that teachers provide a vast array of stimulating objects, encouraging children to explore and develop multiple interests.

Herbart emphasized moral education. He assumed that under conditions of active, experiential learning children develop their moral will. For him, the development of moral beings requires that teachers form close relationships with individual children to monitor the structure of their developing morality.

Implementing his individual-centred teaching model was impractical in large classrooms. Nevertheless, Herbart's theory of education remained influential in Western societies into the twentieth century, leading to the formation of Herbartian societies.

Section conclusion

Arguably, Herbart was "the most influential writer on psychological topics for much of the 19th century" (Danziger, 2001, p. 52). He proposed a mathematical system of mental mechanics to distinguish the borders of conscious from unconscious awareness of sensory-based ideas. This proposal and his concept of apperceptive mass had significant applications to empirical psychology and pedagogy. But his abstract mathematical psychology was not easily converted into practical educational research (Boudewijnse *et al.*, 2001).

German scholar **Gustav Fechner** (1801–1887), an originator of *psychophysics* (i.e., the scientific study of the psychological experience of sensory stimulation), noted that Herbart had not addressed two basic problems: "(a) how mental phenomena depended on physio-logical phenomena and (b) how they could be measured" (Boudewijnse *et al.*, 2001, p. 114).

Furthermore, Herbart did not test his abstract system against observations of psychological phenomena. His mathematical psychology contained a significant epistemological problem, namely, finding "a language for mental content that did not simply transfer notions appropriate to the physical world to the mental sphere" (R. Smith, 1997, p. 360).

Lastly, although Herbart's framework incorporated levels of consciousness and the terms repression and resistance, it was not an early form of psychoanalysis, because it excluded unconscious motivational processes (R. Smith, 1997). In contrast, Freud's more accessible theory earned far greater eventual acceptance (Boudewijnse *et al.*, 2001).

Hermann Lotze

A German physician and philosopher, Lotze (1817–1881) linked a younger generation of scientists and philosophers who investigated psychological issues scientifically with an older generation who explored them philosophically. Trained in psychophysics, he attempted to unite body and mind philosophically and to encourage the development of a scientific psychology.

Lotze explicitly used the term "physiological psychology" and gave a physiological account of how physical phenomena become psychological (Boring, 1950). But he did not explain mental activity as primarily biological. Rather, he held that the soul mediates sensory experiences conducted through the nervous system, and the soul unifies mental processes with human activity.

According to Lotze, although mental processes are related to physiological ones, physical processes and mechanical laws cannot explain mental processes and the significance of personal experience (Murphy, 1949). Because, by definition, experiences are qualitative, quantitative methods cannot be used to study them. Brentano, one of Lotze's protégés, adopted these conceptual and methodological positions in his foundational human-science psychology.

Section conclusion

Lotze contributed to Psychology in **three ways**:

- He developed a conception of emotions that united feelings with bodily expressions, paving the way for the next generation, such as Ribot and **Alfred Binet** (1857–1911) (see Chapter 5), to empirically investigate emotions.
- Lotze introduced the influential concept of "local signs" on the retina and the skin. He argued that individuals learn that "to each point experienced in the visual world there is a corresponding point in objective external space" (D. Murray, 1988, p. 192).
- Lotze held that kinaesthetic sensations are important in space perception. For him, the mind "has an inherent capacity for arranging its content spatially" (Boring, 1950, p. 267).

In sum, Lotze's theorizing, steeped in physiology, helped to legitimize the terrain of a scientific psychology located between natural science and philosophy. He also introduced an enduring concept applicable to the new Psychology, local signs. Ultimately, Lotze influenced better-known contributors to Psychology as a natural science (e.g., Wundt) and as a human science (e.g., Brentano).

Alexander Bain

A British philosophical psychologist, Bain (1818–1903) took Mill's psychological ideas to their logical extension. He strongly influenced later Anglo-American and French natural-science psychologists through two books, *The Senses and the Intellect* (1855) and *Emotions and the Will* (1859). In them he systematized knowledge about sensing, thinking, feeling, willing, and consciousness. Bain connected German physiologists' findings with practical interpretations of psychological processes (Murphy, 1949), while relying on the rationalist explanations of mental processes by categories (D. Murray, 1988).

To the standard associationist proposition that sensory impressions were the foundation of all psychological phenomena, Bain introduced the concept of voluntary action, including spontaneity, which Biran and Mill previously had suggested. Replacing the older view of passive beings reacting sensorily to environmental conditions, Bain's notion implied self-initiating agency. Voluntary action was the connecting link among sensing, feeling, and thinking. He stated, "Thinking is restrained speaking or acting" (cited by Greenway, 1973, p. 49).

Bain diminished the importance of attention and consciousness, believing that an organism's actions determine what it experiences. His concept of voluntary action influenced Ribot and early developmental psychologists, such as Binet. But because of the impact of Darwinism, this concept was incompatible with the learning theories of US psychologists for whom simple laws of association were pivotal.

In an 1873 book, *Mind and Body*, Bain understood the mind as active not passive and activity as preceding not following sensation (R. Smith, 1997). He interpreted mental processes biologically as related to electro-cellular change in neurons, triggered by concrete experience. Moreover, in contrast to strict associationists, he inserted inherited dispositions or "instincts" into his explanation, although he never incorporated Darwinian theory.

In effect, Bain promoted a kind of body–mind parallelism, positing two aspects – physical and psychological – for any phenomenon (Boring, 1950). Although the body was subject to quantifiable causal relations, mental processes, which were qualitative in nature, were not. Thus, despite his physiological orientation, he regarded experimentation as limited in value. For him, conscious data and introspection are primary in psychological inquiry (R. Smith, 1997).

Section conclusion

Bain significantly contributed to the formal emergence of Anglo-American Psychology in **three ways**:

- He amplified associationist explanations of sensing, thinking, feeling, and willing, systematically integrating them with contemporary physiological evidence. He grounded what became natural-science Psychology conceptually and methodologically in experimental physiology.
- His books functioned as standard texts in Anglo-American Psychology for decades until William James's *Principles of Psychology* (1890). In fact, Bain's conception of human habit influenced James's position.
- In 1876 Bain founded *Mind*, the first journal intended for discussions about psychological phenomena (Green, 2009a).

Part 4 conclusion

Even though their influence on Psychology waned by the mid twentieth century, Biran, Herbart, Lotze, and Bain had a marked effect on psychological discourse in the nineteenth century. Biran's emphasis on human will appealed to those inclined to human-science psychology, while the concepts of Herbart, Lotze, and Bain appealed to natural-science psychologists.

During this era psychological inquiry was shaped largely by attempts to answer philosophical questions about body and mind by means of contemporary physiology and physics. In this context Herbart's mathematized but non-empirical account of apperception, limen, and consciousness of ideas held some cachet. He also promoted a systematic pedagogy that informed the theory and practice of public education at least in Germany.

Lotze straddled natural science and human science. His grounding of the psychological in the physiological and his concept of local signs in sensory perception influenced early natural-science psychologists. Yet his insistence that psychological experience was qualitative, hence was knowable only by qualitative methods, captured the interest of human-science psychologists.

Although Bain worked within the associationist tradition and incorporated physiological evidence, he significantly altered associationism by proposing voluntary action as the pivotal explanation of sensory and mental processes. Like Lotze, he understood mental processes as fundamentally qualitative, hence not very amenable to quantitative experimentation. In these ways Bain promoted a more complex theoretical approach than did many founding Anglo-American psychologists, for whom a simplified interpretation of psychological associations sufficed.

Part 5   Developments in the natural sciences

Psychology emerged as a formal discipline in a multifaceted societal and intellectual context. Competing philosophical positions about science, nature, and human nature swirled about Western culture: rationalism, idealism, romanticism, positivism, and empiricism/associationism. Meanwhile, experimental physiology and evolutionary biology became prominent, which set the stage for Psychology as a natural science and relegated philosophical psychology to a lesser role.

In this part we review the modern origins of brain research, physiology, and psychophysics. Practitioners of these disciplines, in conjunction with evolutionary biologists, laid the foundation on which other scholars constructed natural-science Psychology. But first we situate scientific developments in social context.

Science in nineteenth-century society

Although the term "scientist" did not appear in English until mid-century, science as a set of disciplines in European and Anglo-American societies already was established as the primary intellectual framework for understanding the natural world. Scientific foundation now was regarded as the true test of knowledge and human progress. Consequently, scientific thought overshadowed philosophical perspectives and challenged the Christian view of human nature.

Societal context

During this era science became an invaluable component of economically privileged societies. Viewing science and technology as vehicles for elevating their social standing the ascendant middle class rapidly absorbed scientific findings that they believed could facilitate their own contributions to society (Waller, 2001).

Originally, private patrons or a scientist's own resources financed scientific activity. But in German society, the state, industries, and public universities were interconnected, a social system that facilitated the development of science and its systematic applications to society. Other economically privileged nations followed suit. Soon science became a public pursuit.

When new US universities, financially supported by industrialists, were founded at this time, they trained students in applied science and technology, because industrialists now were using basic scientific knowledge much more directly for economic expansion and hired scientists to invent procedures to speed economic profit. Chemists, for example, produced lighter metals, alloys, and eventually synthetics such as plastics.

Some governments initiated national educational policies to promote economic self-reliance and foster national identity (R. Smith, 1997). For example, in 1880 the United Kingdom instituted universal, elementary education. Society also feared degenerate tendencies in the working class because of apparently high rates of crime, mental illness, and alcoholism. These societal developments made possible a new profession, Psychology, whose practitioners would specialize in developing human abilities and managing mental life and behaviour, all allegedly supported by scientific inquiry.

Women in science

When society was reorganized on the basis of a sharp division between public and professional life, on the one hand, and private domestic life, on the other hand, the production of science shifted to universities and industries. Science became professionalized as men's public activity, while family life became institutionalized as women's private domain. This division of labour was rationalized by the cultural doctrine of "separate spheres" for men and women (Kerber, 1988).

The first women's movement contributed to universities slowly admitting women students. Prior to 1890, only 25 US women compared to 974 men had attained a doctorate in any field, due to societal constraints on women (Bohan, 1990). Women's participation in graduate education remained restricted until the 1920s.

During the nineteenth century **three scientific doctrines** circulated, allegedly validated by evolutionary principles, regarding women's presumed biological and psychological inferiority:

- The inferior female brain
- Greater male variability
- Maternal instinct.

For instance, prominent biological and social scientists emphasized brain sizes, using a formula showing that women's brains were smaller than men's. They concluded that women had inferior brains. In this sense, then, science played handmaiden to social values (Shields, 1975).

Male scientists also speculated that women lacked the biological and intellectual capacities necessary for scientific pursuits. The dominant rationale was that mental activity, such as participation in science, could jeopardize a young woman's physical health and well-being by channelling the blood away from her most valued possession, her reproductive organs, and towards her less valued brain. Consequently, women generally were excluded from university education, while the culture of science remained male turf.

The few women who participated in natural science tended not to have family responsibilities or they practised science at home, supervised by their scientist-husbands who, by contrast, received ample institutional support (M. Rossiter, 1982). Yet, male scientists depended upon a division of household labour in which women members played significant, but unpaid, supportive roles (Lerner, 1993). For example, Ivan Pavlov's wife, Sara Pavlov, supported his workaholism by allowing no distractions from his scientific activities in return for his socializing on weekend evenings and abstaining from alcohol and card games (Boakes, 1984). Women's attempts to practise science in such a patriarchal social climate are described in Box 4.1.

Box 4.1 **Women in science**

Four scientists exemplified women's struggles for legitimacy during this era.

Mary Somerville (1780–1872) was an English mathematician, physicist, and astronomer. Even though she displayed considerable aptitude for mathematics during childhood and adolescence, her parents discouraged her from engaging in mathematics. After her first husband died, she became financially independent and pursued scientific interests, which her second husband strongly supported (Spender, 1983). In 1832 Somerville wrote a book on the mathematical astronomer Pierre-Simon Laplace (1749–1827). Although it became required reading at Cambridge University, as a woman she was excluded from enrolling there. Undaunted, she published an acclaimed book on Isaac Newton and at age 89 published a book reviewing contemporary discoveries in chemistry and physics.

Ada Lovelace (1815–1852), daughter of the English poet George Byron (1788–1824), also excelled in mathematics. With her friend Charles Babbage (1791–1871) she developed principles that a century later became the basis for computer programming and computer languages (Green, 2001).

During her youth Englishwoman **Beatrix Potter** (1866–1943) identified and classified fungi. When she attempted to interest eminent scientists in her discovery of lichens, she was rebuffed. She then enlisted the aid of her uncle, a noteworthy chemist, who urged her to write a paper for the 1897 meeting of the Linnean Society (a prominent scientific body), even though women were excluded from attending and presenting. Unlike male presenters' papers, hers was never published. Potter turned to composing and illustrating children's books, such as the *Tale of Jemima Puddle-Duck* and *Tale of Peter Rabbit*.

From 1898 to 1907 **Harriet Brooks** (1876–1933) studied radioactivity as a pioneer nuclear scientist in Canada. She joined the research group of Ernest Rutherford (1871–1937) at McGill University in Montreal and also worked with Marie Curie (1867–1934) in Paris. However, Brooks could not obtain academic employment in physics (Rayner-Canham, 1992). By 1907 she became Mrs. Frank Pitcher, left science, declared that only exceptional women could meet the demands of scientific work, and urged women to stay at home.

Brain research

Two individuals illustrate the innovations that occurred during this era in scientific understanding of the brain: Franz Gall and Paul Broca.

Franz Gall

A German–French scholar, Gall (1758–1828) investigated neuroanatomy and physiology. For him, the brain is the organ of all mental processes (e.g., memory), even sentiments and tendencies, and moral and intellectual capacities are innate and unmodifiable (R. M. Young, 1970). In addition, he tried to establish how the links that he perceived between human skulls and locations of brain functions were related to and explained human nature, twenty-seven mental faculties, and behaviour (R. Smith, 1997).

In relating behavioural functions to particular brain regions, Gall speculated that larger, better-developed cortices are associated with more intelligent behaviour. Then he charted the skull to map individual character. For example, he argued, a person with excellent memory has bulging eyes, allegedly caused by an enlarged brain site for memory. Gall proposed that the strength of specific mental faculties and functions is related causally to the physical size of specific areas and structures of the brain and skull (Krech, 1962). He termed the study of this relationship phrenology, which became a pseudoscience (see Part 7).

Paul Broca

A French physician, Broca (1824–1880) was the first to examine the link between brain lesions and speech areas in the brain's left hemisphere (Schiller, 1992). After assessing a male adult who could only utter the syllable "tan" but whose intelligence was intact, he proposed that a lesion to the left side of the frontal lobe would cause aphasia (i.e., loss of the ability to speak one's thoughts). This region became known as "Broca's area," which also is involved in "working memory, gesture recognition, mirror drawing, and aspects of musical analysis" (Aboitiz, Garcia, Brunnette, & Bosman, 2005, p. 4).

Prior to Broca's discovery, scholars assumed that, as Kant proposed, the brain operated as a *sensori commune*, one sensory mass where the external world meets the internal neural world. Broca's explanation of an anatomical and physiological basis for aphasia provided a researchable model for such disturbances, separating areas of the brain responsible for specific cognitive processes. Although he retained the *sensori commune* explanation, belief in this assumption began to wane after his discovery.

In addition, Broca contributed to the simplification and standardization of neural nomenclature, for example, "'fissures' to separate the five lobes of the brain 'sulci' for the grooves between the convolutions" (Schiller, 1992, p. 270). He also explained the neural basis for the production of human language. He concluded that the brain controls expressive language, each type of language corresponds to its own cortical region, and loss of language does not mean loss of intelligence.

Politically, impressed by evolutionary theory, Broca founded a society of physical anthropology to explore ethnocultural and gender differences. The method was "craniometry," the measurement of cranial capacities of human skulls. On this basis he inferred brain volume and assumed the larger the volume, the greater the intelligence (R. Smith,

1997). Broca argued that the brains of men in general, eminent men, and superior races were larger than the brains of women, mediocre men, and allegedly inferior races. His work bolstered contemporary cultural views promoting White male dominance (Gould, 1996).

Physiology and psychophysics

Initially, nineteenth-century physiologists were the only natural scientists, other than Gall, who addressed psychological issues. Physiologists believed that studies of perception could help resolve philosophical debates about consciousness and body–mind relations. They turned to experimental accounts of conscious sensory perception, such as the touch threshold. Consequently, new university laboratories in German-speaking nations became the site for experimentation on human functions (R. Smith, 1997). Here we describe the principal figures of this prehistorical stage of Psychology: Jan Purkyně, Ernst Weber, Johannes Müller, Gustav Fechner, Hermann von Helmholtz, and Ewald Hering.

Jan Purkyně

A Czech physiologist, also known by his Germanized name, Johannes Purkinje (1787–1869), he investigated sensory physiology, including such topics as peripheral vision and visual accommodation (Boring, 1950). He observed that the relationship between eye structure and its neural link to the brain determined afterimages and illusions.

Purkyně discovered the difference in the luminosity of colours between bright and partial light at dawn, known as the "Purkinje shift," by which "blue objects that appeared brighter than red ones before sunrise reverse thereafter" (Wade & Brozek, 2001, p. 1). To explain this phenomenon he speculated that the eye contains two different receptors. Subsequent investigators found that rods mediate vision in dim light, while cones mediate it in bright light (Coren, 2003). Practising neurophysiology, he identified cells in the cerebrum, since known as "Purkinje cells."

Methodologically, Purkyně studied his own responses to visual stimuli phenomenologically, that is, through careful self-observation and description, which strengthened phenomenology as a scientifically valid method. Psychophysicists, who were of the next generation, were indebted to this aspect of Purkyně's methodology, as were Gestalt psychologists in the twentieth century (Boring, 1950). But for Purkyně, physiological analysis of sensory processes was primary.

Ernst Weber

A German sensory physiologist, Weber (1795–1878) investigated the cutaneous and kinaesthetic senses, which previous researchers had ignored (Boring, 1950). In his research on touch Weber mapped tactile sensitivity in terms of temperature, acuity, and pressure. He demonstrated the phenomenon of "double touch" whereby simultaneous skin pressure at two points feels single on some body parts but feels double on other parts (e.g., finger tip), depending on the distance between points.

Applying the philosophical concept of threshold to experiments on touch, muscle, vision, and hearing, Weber introduced the term, *just noticeable difference* (jnd), meaning the least amount of difference between two stimuli needed to distinguish them. Observers' accurate discrimination depended not on the absolute difference between stimuli but on their relative difference. He demonstrated that the jnd usually is a constant mathematical fraction of this difference, but the specific fraction differs for each sense.

Weber concluded that physical stimuli and psychological sensations are not equivalent. He interpreted his findings according to Kant's concept of the *sensori commune* (D. Murray, 1988). Weber adopted this explanation based on *a priori* mental categories, because "psychological" explanations were unknown then.

In sum, Weber's principle of the jnd, arguably, is the first empirical "law" in Psychology, even though his interests were physiological not psychological. In 1860 Fechner formulated Weber's simple characterization of the jnd as a constant ratio, which he called "Weber's law" (see below). Fechner then revised it to demonstrate the relationship between body and mind.

Johannes Müller

The first professor of an independent German department of physiology, Müller (1801–1858) published a handbook of human physiology that became a highly influential resource for natural scientists. During his career he investigated optics, space perception, and reflex activity (Boring, 1950). Although his students disagreed with his interpretive framework for his experimental programme, they absorbed his systematic findings and commitment to empirical testing.

Müller is best known for his so-called *doctrine of specific nerve energies*: each nerve releases specific qualities or energy and no matter how it is stimulated, every sensory nerve responds uniquely. Moreover, he asserted that the mechanism of a specific nerve and its end-point in the brain, not the physical stimulus, determine a specific sensation.

Müller concluded that human beings are not aware of objects in the physical world, only of various sensory impulses. In other words, psychological experience is not the same as what is physically present to human awareness; the senses do not directly represent external reality. Rather, he agreed with both contemporary and classical thinkers (e.g., Aristotle) that the sense organs, the nerves, and the brain are the intermediaries between the physical object and the mind's interpretation of it.

Müller believed that he had found the physiological mechanisms to support Kant's claim that presumably *a priori* mental categories mediate sensory impressions through perceptual processes. He departed from the extant explanation of perception as the consequence of images or symbolic representations somehow conveyed along the nerves. Although he retained his support for vitalism as the chief agent of image-conveyance (Coren, 2003), his students adopted a thoroughly materialist explanation.

Gustav Fechner

A physicist and philosopher, Fechner endeavoured to know how the mind functioned. His orientation was neither idealism nor materialism but a monistic attempt to solve the mind–body problem (Woodward, 1972). He combined mathematical analysis of ideas held in consciousness and the notion of limen, both of which Herbart had proposed, with Weber's use of the experimental method.

Within his conceptual system of "inner psychophysics" Fechner believed that the physical and the mental were two conscious aspects of the same reality in which the sensory system connected the external world with mental processes (D. K. Robinson, 2010). As he was resting in bed one morning, Fechner had an insight: he could demonstrate a measurable relationship between bodily and mental experience, if an individual observer (i.e., research "subject") reported changes in sensations of pitch, volume, weight, and brightness, while an experimenter systematically varied a physical stimulus. This was Weber's method of quantifying thresholds and represented an "outer psychophysics" of the relation between stimulus magnitude and intensity of sensory responses.

Fechner then produced a mathematical formula showing the mind–body relation: $S = K \times \text{Log } R$. The formula means concretely that for the magnitude of a sensation to rise arithmetically, the magnitude of the physical stimulus must rise geometrically. In other words, as a stimulus gets larger, the size of the change must become larger and larger in order for the mind to detect it (Boring, 1942).

In his 1860 book, *Elements of Psychophysics*, Fechner defined and described three investigative methods: the jnd, average error, and right and wrong cases. He applied a testable law of correlation concerning mental processes and a research programme that inspired a generation of natural scientists. Mental measurement then became the norm. Fechner also was alert to observer variability due to individual differences in the nervous system.

All this work laid the foundation for Psychology's emergence as a natural science (R. Smith, 1997). In current perception research, investigators use Fechner's methods and signal detection theory, which is an extension of his work, to study discrimination tasks, such as perception of colours similar in luminance and saturation.

Fechner has been criticized for his pantheistic writings on religion and philosophy. Yet this latter work and his inner psychophysics of mind–body relations were equally, if not more, important to his scientific programme than his "outer psychophysics" of the relation between stimulus magnitude and intensity of sensory responses (D. K. Robinson, 2010). Fechner was keen to pursue applications of psychophysics to more complex psychological phenomena, which, in effect, is the path that many new psychologists began to follow.

Hermann von Helmholtz

A renowned German physiologist and physicist, Helmholtz (1821–1894) had studied with Müller and was influenced by Kant (D. Cahan, 1995). At age 26, Helmholtz formulated the *law of conservation of energy*. This physics principle states that energy is never created or lost in a system; it only changes from one form to another. The foundational formulation of libidinal energy in Freud's psychoanalytic theory was indebted to the law of conservation of energy. Helmholtz's later work in physics, such as thermodynamics and electromagnetics, proved very influential for science and society.

Like his physiological predecessors, Helmholtz's experimentation on sensation and perception had a direct influence on emergent natural-science psychology. Helmholtz gave **two answers** to the question of how humans obtain knowledge about the external world, given their sensory limitations (Turner, 1977):

- Each sense organ and its physiology have a function, but only those qualities that provide a certain function for the individual dominate perceptions.
- Innate physiological processes determine perception's limits, but learning enables interpretation of perceived sensory stimulation.

Helmholtz concluded that all one can know for certain are images and ideas of the world gathered by experience.

In vision research, he proposed the concept of accommodation, explained colour perception (see below), and investigated the optics of artistic painting. Helmholtz also conducted experiments in audition, including musical harmony, and proposed resonance theory. Overall, he believed that he had demonstrated that psychological categories, which Kant had asserted existed *a priori*, could be studied empirically.

Helmholtz did not find a good fit between physical events and psychological sensations (e.g., the experience of colour). He explained the mismatch as resulting from the properties of the body's receptor systems and the unconscious inferences that individuals make when interpreting sensory cues. In his "theory of signs" he assumed that the information obtained from the excitation of nerves and the subsequent impulses that inform conscious awareness of the world did not provide a true picture of reality. According to this explanation, which actually is neo-Kantian, images present in consciousness are the mind's interpretations of reality.

For Helmholtz, the mediating influence in interpretation was "unconscious inference," an automatic and passive, but learned process that filters every perception. However, for him, unconscious processes were rational, contrary to Schopenhauer's and Freud's emphasis on irrational processes. Helmholtz extended his notion of unconscious inferences to musicians' apprehension of harmony and painters' artistic interpretations of nature (Turner, 1977).

Helmholtz viewed the nervous system as analogous to telegraph wires connecting sensory organs to the brain electrically (Turner, 1977). But he did not believe that the mechanisms that determine perception lay within neural paths and structures. Rather, his explanations were psychological, while his assumptions enabled him to investigate the sense organs mathematically and explain them mechanically.

Methodologically, Helmholtz devised the reaction-time experiment to investigate nerve conduction. When he found that reaction time varied considerably among and within individuals, he abandoned it as unreliable. Helmholtz then relied on introspection to inform his theorizing, because it illuminated inferential judgments made consciously, while controlling the received stimuli. However, he "occasionally reported perceptions that consistently eluded other observers" (Turner, 1977, p. 55).

Ewald Hering

Another German physiologist, Hering (1834–1918) disagreed with Helmholtz regarding space perception. He believed that a strictly empirical account of space perception could not explain satisfactorily total perception of objects. He too rendered memory a fundamentally biological concept (Danziger, 2001).

Hering also is known for his rival theory of colour vision, which is described in Box 4.2.

Box 4.2 **The Helmholtz–Hering debate**

The questions that the physiologists of vision Helmholtz and Hering debated were: what explains depth perception, beyond the apparently two-dimensional image represented in the retina? Is depth or spatial perception innate or learned? What explains colour perception? Must there be a mind that perceives what humans understand through vision? How does the mind synthesize information received from vision and kinetic energies to produce conscious reality?

In his trichromatic model of colour vision Helmholtz posited three light frequencies (blue, green, and red). The subsequent Young–Helmholtz theory was applied to retinal processing. By contrast, Hering held that colour vision consisted of yellow, blue, red, and green. His opponent-process theory applied to the colour processing that occurs in the retina, the thalamus, and visual cortex.

Helmholtz the empiricist focused on the correspondence between visual images of objects with the reality of physical space and physical processes, while Hering the nativist focused on the phenomenology of perception. Helmholtz employed functional analysis, while Hering relied on a phenomenological method.

In the rhetoric of their research report-writing Hering accused Helmholtz of extending functional, mechanical explanations to *teleology*, an idealistic grand design or purpose of nature. For his part, Helmholtz contended that nativists were unempirical and ignored Ockham's razor (Turner, 1994). This debate over competing theories of colour vision also shows how clashes of opinion and their rhetorical expression shape scientific practice. It was psychologist **Christine Ladd-Franklin** (1847–1930) who resolved the polarized views of Helmholtz and Hering (see Chapter 5).

Ernst Mach

An Austrian mathematician and physicist, Mach (1838–1916) took the position that sensations were the data of natural science and that psychologists dealt with the same sensations that physical scientists explored. He believed that natural scientists should describe mathematically the relationships among sensations. His sensory emphasis planted Psychology firmly on the terrain of natural science, and most natural-science psychologists, but not Wundt, subsequently adopted a sensory emphasis (Danziger, 1979).

Mach investigated sensory processes using mobile stimuli. Sitting in a rotating chair, he found that the semicircular canals of his inner ear mediated the sensation of bodily rotation, not his brain, eyes, or skin. In researching the perception of brightness with rotated black-and-white disks, he found that at the transition-point between the black and white areas the dark and bright values intensified as rings, known as "Mach bands."

Furthermore, Mach observed that when listening to music people hear not just individual notes but their relationship to one another, so that a melody is recognizable regardless of the major or minor key in which it is played. Describing only the melodic elements would miss the whole form of the musical experience. Gestalt psychologists adopted this principle.

Mach also is noteworthy in the prehistory of Psychology for his version of positivist epistemology, known as *empiriocriticism*. According to this doctrine, all natural events consist of physical and psychological aspects of sensory observations. Thus, given Mach's premise that the essence of science is sensory data, Kant's putatively abstract categories of space and time are sensory processes.

Part 5 conclusion

During the nineteenth century the societal status of science and technology escalated. Physiology, which included brain research and psychophysics, was esteemed highly by many natural philosophers, known in this era as scientists, because they believed experimental physiology could answer basic philosophical questions about the relationship between body and mind. Female scholars, however, were relegated to the sidelines.

By maintaining that the brain is the seat of mental activity Gall made psychology the province of scientists not philosophers. His work ultimately led to the experimental study of the brain, mapping of the brain based on the localization of sensory modalities and motor abilities, and current investigations of brain–behaviour relations and neural modules. For his part, Broca paved the way for the association method of correlating cognitive functions and behaviour with specific cortical areas. Neuropsychologists today use the association method in lesion studies.

According to Purkyně, subjective sensory phenomena, investigated phenomenologically, were a legitimate pathway towards mapping their physiological basis. However, subjective experience could complement but not substitute for physiological analysis of sensory processes.

Assuming that they could measure human responses to the physical world, psychophysicists employed physiological methodology to answer questions about mental processes. In this way, they enabled the eventual emergence of natural-science psychology. For example, Müller, who understood the potential for a scientific psychology to illuminate body–mind relations, demonstrated the physiological complexity of sensory perception.

The foundations of experimental psychology's original methodology were located in the psychophysical experimentation of Weber and Fechner. Weber systematically varied different factors under controlled conditions to quantify the relationship of physical stimuli with corresponding psychological experiences or sensations. Fechner established how to quantify the mental processes of judging sensations with the jnd. Later, Wundt employed this same method in experimenting on consciousness: the experimenter controlled the stimulus conditions, while observers reported the resulting conscious content.

Two contemporaries, Helmholtz and Mach, also shaped the foundations of Psychology. In his physiological experimentation Helmholtz gave Psychology "a precise content and a rigorous method" (R. Smith, 1997, p. 502). He published influential works on the application of physiological concepts and methods to audition and vision. Methodologically, he turned from reaction-time experiments to reliance on introspective accounts of sensations, a shift that many of the new psychologists adopted.

Mach strongly emphasized the experimental acquisition of sensory data as the foundation for a natural-science psychology. Moreover, his revisions to positivism became more influential than Comte's version among many early psychologists (Winston, 2001).

Hermann Ebbinghaus and Edward Titchener, for example, sided with Mach's staunchly empiricist position against Wundt's rationalist orientation (Danziger, 1979).

Part 6   The Darwinian revolution

While advances in physiology proceeded, biology underwent a revolution at the hands of Darwin's evolutionary theory. In previous conceptions of evolution, Western thinkers employed variations of the concept of the great chain of being to explain biological phenomena. In Aristotle's scale of nature, natural objects were organized within a hierarchical system, ranging from the lowest forms of life to mammals and then humans. Later, the Christian view was that all of nature, from the least natural objects to the earthly beings considered closest to God, humans, existed in a perfect, stable universe.

Nevertheless, at least since the Scientific Revolution natural philosophers speculated about the evolution of animal species and proposed different explanations about matter (Barzun, 2000). The Newtonians believed that God set matter into mechanical motion like a clock fixed to the universal law of gravity and knowable mathematical laws. Vitalists, however, believed that matter was self-directing and progressed to perfection over time. French biologist **Jean-Baptiste de Lamarck** (1744–1829) argued not only that species naturally emerge when animals adapt to environmental conditions, but also that *acquired* characteristics are passed on to offspring. Darwin's paternal grandfather, Erasmus Darwin (1731–1802), even proposed that evolution resulted from the will of a given creature to adapt to environmental conditions.

In the nineteenth century Hegel, then Marx argued for the progressive nature of history, human societies, and the economy. But when Charles Darwin developed the notion of evolution of biological objects into a theory based on voluminous empirical observations, it proved revolutionary for science and society. The theory was radical culturally, because Darwin stressed nature as dynamic and changeable not fixed and permanent.

Evolutionary theory

Darwin's conception had great impact, because it flowed from both contemporary geological and economic theories that were accepted widely (Bowlby, 1990). **Charles Lyell** (1797–1875), one of his steadfast supporters, had argued that geological evidence, such as fossils, showed that Earth had been changing slowly but predictably over many thousands of years. This position challenged the standard view, based on a literal interpretation of the Bible, that God had created Earth exactly 6,000 years before. During Darwin's global expedition of 1831 to 1836 he absorbed Lyell's argument.

Darwin also was influenced deeply by Malthus's early capitalist argument that, given limited resources, including food supply, human beings engage in a struggle for survival, governed by natural laws. Darwin fit his data to the notion that population growth necessarily exceeds food supply. He concluded that it is the struggle for survival that motivates natural selection. According to this view, life is a struggle of too many creatures for too few resources.

Darwin reasoned that every species produces more offspring than its environment can sustain. He posited that *natural selection* is the mechanism in the struggle for existence by which nature selects changes in species that enable them to adapt to their environments over time and survive.

One could interpret this conclusion to mean that humans who are weak and unhealthy cannot support themselves and will die without reproducing. In this interpretation, only the strong or the best adapted are selected to survive the competition for resources. Social Darwinists (see below) followed this reasoning and applied the notion of the "survival of the fittest" to human society.

Later, Darwin addressed the relevance of his evolutionary theory for humankind. Comparing the mental powers of humans and animals, he stated:

Nevertheless the difference in mind between man and the higher animals, great as it is, certainly is one of degree and not of kind. We have seen that the senses and intuitions, the various emotions and faculties, such as love, memory, attention, curiosity, imitation, reason, etc. of which man boasts, may be found in an incipient, or even sometimes in a well-developed condition, in the lower animals. (Darwin, *Descent of Man*, 1871, p. 101)

In sum, Darwin's contribution lay in his providing a database for pre-existing ideas about evolution. His evidence showed that over many generations small, more adaptive variations in life-forms can be inherited, help life-forms survive, and prevail over less useful characteristics. But his evolutionary theory was based on the assumption that natural selection is a random, not purposeful, process. Current thinking is that this assumption is questionable (Fodor & Piatelli Palmarini, 2010). As noted in Chapter 7, biogenetic research is showing complexities and subtleties of evolutionary processes that were unforeseeable in Darwin's day.

Priority of discovery

In 1838 Darwin developed serious health problems that might have been related to his concerns about the ramifications of his discovery. Although he was extremely dedicated to his scientific work, he decided not to publish his theory and findings for a further twenty years. Perhaps he feared the theological implications of his revolutionary theory. Another explanation for the publication delay is that Darwin was meticulous about marshalling evidence to support his theory.

Then in 1858, another biologist, **Alfred R. Wallace** (1823–1913), sent Darwin a letter in which he described an identical theory with similar evidence, based on his observations in a region now known as Malaysia. Wallace's revelation caused Darwin considerable personal conflict: should he let Wallace claim the discovery or should he take the credit for over twenty years of his own hard work?

In 1859, Darwin shared his unpublished manuscripts on evolution with his friends, Lyell and Joseph Hooker (1817–1911), a prominent botanist. They presented Darwin's and Wallace's respective papers on evolution at a scientific meeting. Two months later, Darwin's brief version of his projected book went to publication. The 1,250 copies sold out on the first day.

Traditionally, historians credit Darwin with the discovery of evolutionary theory due to the mass of data he employed to support it, while Wallace's contributions tend to be overlooked. Yet Darwin's explanation for the transmission of variations in species was derived from a theory of heredity based on Lamarckian assumptions no longer credible. Darwin was unaware of Gregor Mendel's (1832–1884) work on heredity, which provided a plausible genetic account.

Cultural consequences

Shortly after the publication of *The Origin of Species*, considerable public controversy ensued. In 1860 a famous debate on the implications of evolutionary theory occurred at Oxford University in which an advocate, Thomas Huxley (1825–1895), according to popular consensus, triumphed over a Christian critic, Bishop Samuel Wilberforce (1805–1873). In fact, Darwin's evolutionary theory shook the foundations of **three beliefs** about the origins of nature and human beings that were cherished in European and Anglo-American societies:

- The biblical story of Creation that God fixed species should be taken literally.
- Humans are superior to all other life-forms.
- Any variation in species is part of God's plan.

But Darwin's evolutionary theory intimated that the biblical account was a fable. Although some Christians now reconceived the story of Creation as metaphorical rather than literal, many others adhered to the belief that God had directly intervened in the natural world. For them, evolutionary theory negated spirituality and offended human dignity.

In addition, evolutionary theory challenged religion by replacing the idea of a chain of being with the assumption that human beings essentially are the same as other animals, humans do not have superior souls, and instinctual behaviour is natural not inspired by God. Nor did Darwin attribute any divine purposefulness to evolutionary processes. In this way, evolutionary theory contradicted the Newtonian position that God was a wise watchmaker who set the Earth and human beings into fixed and permanent motion.

Evolutionary theory had sociopolitical consequences. To some thinkers, the poor, the "non-White races," and militarily weaker nations should be left to fend for themselves according to the "laws of nature." These views represent *social Darwinism* (see below), which Darwin opposed in his book *The Descent of Man* (1871). He contended that survival in nature was not equivalent to success in human society and that all animals, from single-celled to mammals, split off to reproduce but unite to survive. Therefore, a general principle *within* species might be cooperation not competition; cooperation is essential for survival in both nature and society.

Against racist interpretations of evolutionary theory, Darwin argued that all human beings, regardless of "race," share the same biological heritage: they are more alike than they are different. On the other hand, he promoted the view that women are biologically inferior to men (Shields & Bhatia, 2009).

Social Darwinism

Before Darwin published his theory English author **Herbert Spencer** (1820–1903) envisioned the applications of evolutionary thought to society. In fact, it was Spencer, not Darwin, who coined the phrase, "the survival of the fittest." Spencer used evolutionary theory to justify scientifically his argument for minimizing government intervention in society and for facilitating capitalist economic expansion through the "natural" principle of survival.

The basic assumption of social Darwinism is that the challenges that human societies face reflect the evolutionary struggle for survival in nature; that is, there is no essential difference between human society and nature (Hawkins, 1997). But Darwin (n.d.) himself wrote, "If the misery of our poor be caused not by the laws of nature, but by our institutions, great is our sin" (Darwin, *Voyage of the Beagle*, Chapter 21, p. 314). Thus, social Darwinism is distinct from and a distortion of evolutionary theory.

Inspired by Spencer, social Darwinists envisioned a scientific utopia. They believed that only the fittest humans would survive, just as occurs in nature. For social Darwinists, competition is "instinctual" and only superior people or groups deserve society's rewards. If governments allow evolution to operate freely, then those who survive through competition would approximate perfection. The elite merits its economic success; everyone else deserves to wither away without government aid.

As noted above, some social Darwinists argued that evolutionary theory justified belief in the racial superiority of White Europeans over other groups; Europeans were believed to be the fittest and they alone would survive. This ideology served to rationalize European domination of African, American, and Asian societies. Other social Darwinists claimed that the strongest, "fittest" nations would survive even warfare in the competition for scarce resources.

In the USA, social Darwinism became very popular with many in the public and with many academics, because it pointed to practical applications of the "American pioneer" spirit. Social Darwinism could rationalize enslavement of Africans, decimation of aboriginal peoples, quotas on non-White immigration, and advancing imperialism. In the evolutionary rationale for the view that the unregulated free-market produces inevitable progress, US industrialists now had a pseudoscientific justification for exploiting child labour and expanding capitalism.

Today, social Darwinism suffuses the economic and political assumptions undergirding neoliberalism and social Darwinism remains influential among some psychologists who espouse evolutionary psychology (see Chapter 7).

Part 6 conclusion

Darwin's influence on Psychology is evident in at least **four ways**:

- In his 1872 book, *The Expression of Emotions in Man and Animals*, Darwin asserted that human emotions are remnants of animal emotions that once were necessary for survival, but still are part of our biological makeup. Thus, he showed continuity between humans and animals, meaning that humans share an origin as well as psychological functions with other species and studying lower animals can produce knowledge about human behaviour (Dewsbury, 2003). This argument soon led to the establishment of animal and comparative psychology in which commonalities and differences between humans and animals are studied (see Chapter 11).
- Evolutionary theory included the notion that within any species individuals' biological characteristics differ and these differences can affect how well individuals adapt to their environment. Darwin's concept of individual differences encouraged many Anglo-American psychologists to focus on measuring them.
- With his work "A Biographical Sketch of an Infant" (1877) Darwin is credited with contributing to the origins of developmental psychology.

- Conceptually, the Darwinian notion of adaptive function spawned the school of thought known as the psychology of adaptation or *functionalism* in US Psychology (Green, 2009). Functionalists stressed adaptation to the environment and sought purpose and function in animals' and humans' behaviour (see Chapter 5). Behaviourism followed from the psychology of adaptation. Skinner, for example, based his theory of operant conditioning on evolutionary ideas, although ethologists, such as **Konrad Lorenz** (1903–1989), who considered themselves true followers of Darwinism, viewed behaviourism as opposed to Darwin's intentions.

Part 7   Responses to the pre-eminence of the natural sciences

Although the natural-science orientation of the New Enlightenment, boosted by evolutionary theory, pervaded Western culture, some devotees of natural science distorted the scientific worldview into a virtually religious system of thought in the name of science. The term that captures this distortion of both science and religion is *scientism*. After discussing scientism, we explore the relationship between science and nineteenth-century society in relation to pseudosciences that entrepreneurs invented to capitalize on the public's anxieties aroused by the scientific worldview. Then we describe some rebuttals of the scientific worldview and its societal effects offered by philosophical critics.

Scientism: false science and quasi-religion

The critical term "scientism" enables understanding how strongly held beliefs about the natural world and human nature can function like a secular religious-system. Some scholars assert that scientism has played a significant role in Psychology's history (Slife & Reber, 2009).

One definition of scientism is that it is the firm conviction that the only form of genuine knowledge is scientific. Thus, "truth" is defined only according to scientific achievements and scientific rules. In other words, scientism is science's belief in itself (Habermas, 1972). Another definition is "the fallacy of believing that the method of science must be used on all forms of experience and, given time, will settle every issue" (Barzun, 2000, p. 218).

This exaggerated faith in method aided by logic and measurement is motivated by a desire for certainty of knowledge and predictability of future events. However, scientists in thrall to scientism might behave like zealots, not like critical thinkers. Furthermore, a likely consequence of scientistic behaviour is *objectivism*, meaning an obsession with abstract ahistorical objectivity, accompanied by neglect of the social context and human interests saturating scientific activity. In an ideal Psychology, objectivity would include subjectivity not exclude it (see Chapter 12).

Ironically, members of the early Royal Society, such as **Joseph Glanville** (1636–1680) and Newton, fused natural science with religious studies. Glanville contended that scientists should investigate witches and the world of spirits sympathetically not hostilely (Barzun, 2000). Moreover, James actively explored psychic phenomena, much to the discomfort of his US Psychology peers (see Chapter 5).

Implications for Psychology

Scientism is germane to the history of Psychology for several reasons. When the early psychologists in the USA adopted the experimental model, they classified all other methods as inferior. In a sense, psychologists worshipped experimentation, engaging in "method-olatry" (Bakan, 1967) and focusing on "facts" acquired under strictly controlled conditions. In pursuing this path, psychologists failed to develop other objectives for science, such as exploring our existential conditions and our capacities for transcending them.

Some famous psychologists in the twentieth century illustrate scientism. John Watson and B. F. Skinner, among others before and since, believed that reform and stabilization of society were achievable through applications of experimental findings. They persuaded leaders in government and industry that they could provide the scientific knowledge necessary for administering society and modifying people's behaviour to suit society's purposes (Rutherford, 2009).

One explanation for the emergence of psychologists' scientism is sociopolitical. Early psychologists endeavoured to show how relevant their science was to economic and governmental interests (Danziger, 1979). To achieve this goal they needed to establish their natural-science credentials so that their claims to expertise would be persuasive. The means to this end was to adopt the laboratory experiment, which was the most credible investigative method in late nineteenth-century natural science.

Secular religions and quasi-sciences: mesmerism, phrenology, and spiritualism

Many Westerners were troubled by the successes of the natural sciences and by evolutionary theory and positivism. The Romantics represented one type of response to the dominant worldview. Another response was the rise of quasi-sciences. These "secular religions" were based on the idealistic belief that human beings are unique among all creatures. In the nineteenth century, three social movements flourished that had the hallmarks of secular religions: mesmerism, phrenology, and spiritualism. "Con artists" sold these pseudo-sciences to a gullible public hungry to fill a spiritual void.

Mesmerism

A German physician who settled in Paris, **Anton Mesmer** (1734–1815) proposed that an imponderable fluid that many contemporaries believed permeates the universe could be manipulated to cure certain illnesses through the process of "animal magnetism." But his proposal was not new. Alchemists also had believed in a universal fluid essential to health. Newton, who practised alchemy, had proposed "ether" as the central fluid in the universe carrying electromagnetic waves.

Mesmer tried to convince his medical colleagues that his approach was a science, but his use of trances, magic wands, and seances smacked of the occult. Consequently, his peers rejected his claims of cures. Mesmerism, however, became popular with the public eager for the security of plausible ideologies. In the USA, "mesmeric magnetism" flourished as a kind of self-help psychology to build a "magnetic mind" for business success. Many embraced the practice, while thousands attended lectures and supporters conducted studies and treated the sick (Schmit, 2005).

Sixteen years after Mesmer died, the French Royal Academy of Sciences accepted his trance state in the form known as hypnotism. It became a treatment for hysteria, and eventually Freud and others studied this clinical technique.

Phrenology

As noted earlier, Gall had claimed that well-developed mental faculties would produce corresponding well-developed bumps and depressions on the skull that suggested particular character traits were associated with specific cranial bumps. For example, a cranial prominence located just above the ear was said to be associated with "destructiveness." Gall's assistant, **J. G. Spurzheim** (1776–1832), widely promoted phrenology. But Gall and Spurzheim erred by concluding that their practice of correlating traits with cranial topography indicated causation and by attributing this spurious causation to all individuals. In effect, subjective impressions of individuals' personality were presumed scientifically legitimate.

Phrenology flourished in the US, arguably suiting the national temperament, where it became a social movement for reforming systems of education and prisons (Bakan, 1966). Entrepreneurs capitalized on the masses' hunger for "scientific" advice by marketing applications of phrenology to businesses for personnel selection and for men choosing "wives." Phrenology served as an amusement for some in society, because they could speculate about individuals' character and make behavioural predictions about them (Barzun, 2000).

Phrenologists, however, insisted their practice constituted legitimate applied science and they established a "scientific" journal in 1823 that lasted to 1911. However, the scientific community rejected phrenology as if it were astrology (R. M. Young, 1970), although Comte regarded phrenology as scientifically credible (Guillin, 2004).

Spiritualism and psychic research

The Society for Psychical Research was founded mid-century to search scientifically for immortality. Members of the society focused on conversion hysteria, by which body parts became immobile without any apparent biological cause, because this disorder seemed to show the power of purely mental activity over the body. One of the society's founders, Frederic Myers (1843–1901), a scholar of language, published an influential book, entitled, *Human Personality and Its Survival of Bodily Death* (E. Taylor, 2010).

James was impressed by the society's work and later became its president. Other scientists ridiculed psychic research. Early US psychologists particularly tried to debunk it to rescue their science from association in the public's mind with the bizarre, the subjective, and the unscientific (Coon, 1992). In the early twentieth century the US Congress and the editors of *Scientific American* respectively launched committees to debunk the claims of spiritualism.

Early existentialism

A very different response, at least among some European authors and philosophers, to the rise of an apparently atheistic science and the decline of organized religion was existentialism in its early form. We have seen that the classical thinkers, Socrates, Plato, Aristotle, Augustine, and Aquinas, had taught that people are free to decide their individual fates and must accept the consequences of their decisions. These are the same themes that nineteenth-century existentialists echoed in a kind of spiritual protest movement against the cultural values and beliefs that also had aroused the Romantics.

Nineteenth-century existentialists rebelled against the rise of mechanistic science and the philosophical positions of empiricism and rationalism. They promoted the uniqueness of each individual and freedom of choice, which demands personal responsibility for one's actions.

Fyodor Dostoevsky

The Russian novelist **Fyodor Dostoevsky** (1821–1881) expressed in his psychological novels, such as *Notes from Underground* (1864), the deep anxiety aroused by personal responsibility. Reacting negatively to the scientism of Western mass societies (Frank, 1986), he denied that the positivist approach to understanding human nature adequately accounted for individuals' internal experience. Irrational, spiritual, and mysterious processes, he believed, were the more important aspects of human life. Furthermore, Dostoevsky contended that, rather than attempting to reform society scientifically to exterminate human unhappiness, individuals should face the reality that life is inherently painful and disappointing.

Søren Kierkegaard

A Danish philosopher, **Kierkegaard** (1813–1855) claimed that society, dominated by an obsession with economic life, inhibited genuine ethical action and individuality. In his view, society induced slavish conformity. He promoted instead a radical spiritual shift in each individual towards acknowledging the absurdity of existence, confronting the anxiety evoked by this new awareness, and then connecting with the infinity of the divine by a leap of faith.

Kierkegaard rejected science and rationalism, because, for him, they prevented individuals from viewing themselves as emotional and choosing beings. Instead, he promoted the concept of the *authentic life*, meaning, taking responsibility for one's life, which enables full maturity. Complete transformation of the self occurs when the person accepts a personal relationship with God. An *inauthentic life*, by contrast, produces guilt, dread, and despair.

Kierkegaard celebrated spiritual renewal to transform the self, as opposed to reason, science, conventional logic, and materialistic values. He conceived of religious faith as a kind of divine madness into which the individual's capacity for reason is suspended. On the other hand, he argued against organized religion. Moreover, although he opposed oppressive European political regimes, he rejected both democracy and socialism. His psychological views resurfaced a century later in existential philosophy and psychology (see Chapter 10).

Friedrich Nietzsche

Another early existentialist thinker is the later German author Friedrich Nietzsche whose intellectual scope was broad and deep. His critique of the traditions and values of Western culture mark him as a key transitional figure in the shift from nineteenth- to twentieth-century psychological thought. Marx and Freud also are known as "masters of suspicion" about Western conceptions of morality, philosophy, and science. Nietzsche addressed major psychological issues that became important in the twentieth century, such as the role of language; the nature of power, morality, and ethics; and the relativity of knowledge and truth.

Intellectually, Nietzsche was influenced by Schopenhauer's distinction between appearances and reality behind appearances and his view that suffering was one's lot in life. But later Nietzsche emphasized joyful affirmation of the life-force, instead of Schopenhauer's pessimism and negation of life. Another influence was Goethe, who in his literary, philosophical, and scientific activities had embodied Nietzsche's notion of "the Superhuman" (in German, *der Übermensch*) or person who rises above the ordinary (Tanner, 2000).

Nietzsche was ambivalent about what he regarded as deeply flawed cultural values. On the one hand, he shared belief in unlimited human potential. On the other hand, he was highly skeptical of blind faith in reason; he depicted universal truths as culturally specific, that is, as creations of language and culture; and he advanced the *will to power* (i.e., the tendency to gain mastery over one's self and one's destiny) as the central human characteristic rather than the capacity for reason.

Nietzsche attacked the character not only of the masses but also of conformist intellectuals during this period of deep cultural change. He rejected academic discourse abstracted from concrete action in the world.

Theory of knowledge

Nietzsche stressed that there is no immaculate perception. Rather, objectivity is a painful illusion, limited by human reason and sensory perception. Moreover, philosophical or scientific rationality is infused with feelings, intuitions, desires, and moral values; that is, personal prejudices precede thinking. Nietzsche was concerned not with what human beings could know but what it was *good* to know in the material world of action.

Nietzsche opposed the modernist notion of a "grand narrative" of human existence, supposedly based on universal and eternal truths. He claimed that universal truths are culturally specific creations. Rather than expressing faith in the possibility of abstract eternal truths and values, he advocated provisional assumptions or probabilities that serve as guides to personal conduct and thought.

Rather than accepting the positivist position of empirically verifiable "facts," Nietzsche advanced the notion of multiple perspectives on reality (Tanner, 2000). For him, genuine objectivity is contingent upon multiple viewpoints and there are no facts without interpretations. Scientists only can interpret empirical phenomena filtered by their implicit value-judgments, which are driven by the individual's will to power.

Nietzsche was skeptical not only about religion but also science, which he perceived to be a new religion (i.e., scientism). In objecting to the pursuit of knowledge for its own sake he stressed clarifying the purpose of pursuing scientific knowledge. The phenomena that scientists believe they are explaining, in his view, are as mysterious as they appeared to primitive humans.

Psychological views

Nietzsche discussed many psychological issues. Here we address **four topics**: the balance between reason and passion, the self, the heroic person, and the will to power. His philosophical observations influenced later psychological theorists whom we describe in Chapters 9 and 10 on human-science psychologies.

(1) Nietzsche observed that the human experience of different art forms represented tension between rational functions (e.g., painting, epic poetry) and irrational functions (e.g., tragic drama, music). He believed that the rationalist tradition of ancient Greek society, practised by Socrates, repressed human beings' instinctual drives. Like Schopenhauer, he stressed the irrational side of human nature, but, unlike Schopenhauer, he believed that the "instincts," including aggression, should be fully expressed not repressed or sublimated.

In ancient Greek mythology reason was embodied in the god Apollo, whereas the god Dionysus embodied passion. According to Nietzsche, the opposing tendencies of Apollonian reason and Dionysian passion should be dialectically united in the person and society (Tanner, 2000). He argued for a return to the presocratic heroic tradition of autonomous, strong-willed men who balance reason and passion.

(2) Nietzsche argued that human beings cannot have a substantial self that operates independently of the person's environment. Rather, impulses, emotions, and memories shape perceptions, which in turn are moulded by social-historical conditions (Tanner, 2000). Suggesting that ordinary persons are doomed to mediocre conformity with corrupt society, he maintained that the rare independent, strong thinker would express his personal will to power. Human will emanates from biological instincts and is the only genuine force in life.

Nietzsche also argued that neither faith in the Christian god nor saturation in high culture can enable the heroic individual to transcend the vacuity of society. He opposed the traditional Christian virtues of humility and charity and the French Revolution's idea of equality among common people, because he believed that both the secular and religious traditions deny the individual's will to power.

(3) For Nietzsche, the greatest challenge is to be an *Übermensch*, a person who transcends desires and exercises creative powers to the fullest. Above all, the fully alive individual is a master of reality rather than its slave, who accepts whatever occurs, knowing that sorrow and joy are inseparable (Tanner, 2000). Conventional morality is anathema to the individual who transcends corrupt cultural beliefs of the herd. Heroic people create their own values, moved by the will to power to define truth for themselves.

Although some have associated Nietzsche with nihilism, what animated him was his strong sense that society was in danger of imminent decline to a value-less state. In his words:

What is to be feared and can work more calamitously than any other calamity is not great fear of, but great nausea at man; similarly, great compassion for man. Assuming that these might one day mate, then immediately and unavoidably something most uncanny would be produced, the "last will" of man, his will to nothingness, nihilism. And in fact: a great deal has been done to prepare for this ... The sickly are the greatest danger to man: not the wicked, not the "beasts of prey." Those who, from the start, are the unfortunate, the downtrodden, the broken – these are the ones, the weakest, who most undermine life amongst men, who introduce the deadliest poison and scepticism into our trust in life, in man, in ourselves. (Nietzsche, *On the Genealogy of Morality*, [1887] 2007, p. 89)

Furthermore, although he said, "God is dead," he was not a crude atheist (Barzun, 2000), rather, a fierce critic of conventional Christianity. Nor was he a materialist, rather, he regarded the creative spirit and human will as playing central roles in human life ideally.

(4) Nietzsche asserted that the fundamental reality of life and primary motive was the will to power. In opposition to Darwin's notion of the basic struggle for existence, Nietzsche posed the struggle for power and preservation of a great individual who rises above the tribe (Tanner, 2000). Human beings only can exercise their will to power individually, because one person cannot find another person's pathway to greatness.

Nietzsche objected to the Judaeo-Christian ethical system, because it favoured the weak over the strong and healthy. In addition, he characterized morality as the reproduction of the herd instinct in the individual, as always partisan, and as directed at keeping human action under the control of its natural instincts. Instead, he promoted the notions of self-mastery and the will to power of the strong and noble.

Section conclusion

Nietzsche has been considered a forerunner of postmodern social constructionism (Warren, 1988). He emphasized the centrality of interpretation and the fragmentation of the modernist belief in ethics and religion as eternal truths. By stressing interpretation and questioning the use of words to mask preconceived judgments Nietzsche paved the way for the late twentieth-century movement of deconstruction. For example, **Jacques Derrida** (1930–2004) practised an intellectual strategy of disrupting the illusion of foundational, universal truths and essences, and Foucault analyzed the intersections of knowledge and power in diverse institutional practices (see Chapter 12).

Regarding gender and race, although in some of his writing Nietzsche argued for women promoting their self-development, overall he exaggerated gender differences, depicting women as essentially passive and less rational than men. But he opposed anti-Semitism and argued against judging others on their ethnocultural origins rather than on their behaviour. Contrary to the claim that he was a prophet of Nazi racial and social ideology, he argued against populist points of view and contemporary ideals of European culture (Barzun, 2000). The Nazis, assisted by Nietzsche's sister, distorted his concept of the *Übermensch* and made him the favourite philosopher in the Third Reich.

On Psychology Historians of Psychology tend to depict Nietzsche as an early existentialist and a precursor to Freud. Some of his ideas were similar to Kierkegaard's (e.g., living an authentic life), but he apparently was unaware of the older man's work. Central to Nietzsche's understanding of psychology is that the certainty of death imposes the responsibility of free choices on every individual. For Nietzsche, each person should become the artist of his or her own life, a key existentialist emphasis (Tanner, 2000). In his view, all that humans have is the present moment; thus, we must make the best of this moment by exercising our will to power.

Connections are apparent between Nietzsche's thought and psychoanalysis as well. His notions of Dionysian impulses and Apollonian rationality are similar to Freud's notions of primary process (unconscious impulses) and secondary process (conscious reason) respectively. Nietzsche also frequently referred to the repression of painful memories, and he believed that greater self-knowledge could be obtained by understanding deviant persons.

Nietzsche apparently influenced the psychoanalyst **Alfred Adler** (1870–1937) concerning the notion of a will to power. For Nietzsche, transformation of the self occurs when the individual achieves his or her full potential. Adler absorbed this notion, theorizing about an "inferiority complex" and individuals' attempts to compensate by gaining power. Nietzsche's concept of will to power also is evident in Abraham Maslow's humanistic ideas of self-actualization and the self-actualized individual (see Chapter 10).

Part 7 conclusion

The zealous pursuit of objective natural science and its rise to prominence in society as a new ideology, trends which partly are captured by the critical term scientism, evoked varied cultural, intellectual, and moral responses. Three pseudosciences ascended – mesmerism, phrenology, and spiritualism – which contained quasi-religious elements. These pseudosciences appealed to many members of the public who felt threatened by the advances of the natural sciences generally and evolutionary theory specifically. Scientific knowledge seemed to contradict taken-for-granted cultural beliefs, shaped by Christian teachings and practices, about nature and human nature.

From moral and intellectual perspectives, Kierkegaard and Dostoevsky expressed early existentialist protests against nineteenth-century science and society. Nietzsche practised the principle of suspicion by which he refused to accept common cultural beliefs at first glance because of every individual's inclination to mask psychologically painful realities. Like Marx, Darwin, and Freud, he exposed society's false consciousness. In psychology, Nietzsche's views influenced the development of existential and psychoanalytic theories.

Part 8   Thematic review

Three themes summarize the principal issues in nineteenth-century psychological thought: **liberal individualism vs. socialist alternatives**, **scientific triumphalism vs. skepticism**, and **unresolved philosophical questions** about psychological phenomena.

Liberal individualism vs. socialism

During the nineteenth century, economic, social, and political upheavals deeply affected European and Anglo-American nations. Capitalism, colonialism, and imperialism became more entrenched globally, and authoritarian states, whether self-styled democracies or not, managed to defuse political revolutions. Meanwhile, movements towards workers' rights, socialist economies fostering the common good and socioeconomic equality, the emancipation of women and slaves erupted with only partial success.

Yet there was no diminution of the cultural mentality of liberal individualism fostered within Enlightenment discourse that promoted the autonomy of (male) human agents. On the contrary, personal acquisition of wealth became idealized in the nineteenth century, while individuals' sensitivity to their inner experience was heightened, at least among the privileged classes. Given such inclinations in European and Anglo-American societies, an individualistic orientation suited to economically advantaged White men predominated among emergent schools of psychological thought as distinct from a dialectical social-cultural orientation (see Chapters 5 and 6). Meanwhile, the Romantic strain connected consciousness of one's personal freedom with other beings and nature in a mystical union.

Scientific triumphalism vs. skepticism

Newer generations of natural philosophers, now known as scientists, were supported in their investigations of psychological phenomena by a cultural shift away from faith in religion to faith in natural science. A kind of triumphalism about natural science superseded the Enlightenment's celebration of reason derived from empirical evidence. The critical term, scientism, encapsulates this inordinate faith in scientific knowledge. Aided by institutional support, technical advances in experimentation, and the rise of evolutionary theory, physiologists took up the challenge of answering philosophical questions about psychological processes.

On the other hand, significant strains of skepticism about natural science permeated economically privileged European and Anglo-American societies. These skeptical strains were embodied by the Romantic movement and early existentialist protests that reached their peak in Nietzsche's comprehensive and trenchant critique of the cultural emphasis on scientifically based reason. In fact, the nineteenth century witnessed the emergence of three pseudoscientific yet quasi-religious expressions: mesmerism, phrenology, and spiritualism. Clearly, large segments of the population were ambivalent about the ascent of science and descent of religion.

Unresolved philosophical questions

In Chapters 2 and 3 we saw that ancient, medieval, Renaissance, and early modern natural philosophers were keen to answer basic questions about body and mind, the activity or passivity of mind, and the derivation of rational thinking. During the early modern era many natural philosophers centred on sensory-motor functions, and some spoke of the human being as "the brute machine." Discourse on higher-order functions tended to be abstract and detached from empirical observations. For example, some natural philosophers invoked the notion of invisible "animal spirits" that reputedly influenced animals and humans.

Nineteenth-century scientists sought the answers to inescapable philosophical questions about psychological phenomena through explorations of sensory-motor mechanisms and were less inclined than their predecessors to interpret their data through metaphysical lenses. Instead, many new scientists found empirically grounded explanations much more credible. On the other hand, others remained convinced that a Kantian explanation, drawing from a reconciliation of associationism with rationalism, was best. Overall, unresolved ontological and epistemological questions about psychological phenomena persisted and resisted tidy resolutions despite impressive advances in the natural sciences.

By the end of the nineteenth century four philosophical questions pertinent to psychological studies remained unresolved:

- How are mind and body related? A few natural philosophers and scientists subscribed to a monist explanation (i.e., a single principle), some posited dual aspects to body–mind relations, while others held a dualist position.
- How passive or active is the mind? For some thinkers, the mind was relatively passive, whereas for others it was active, even determinative.
- How do we derive knowledge and form ideas? Is knowledge a matter of our blank slates being filled by experience or do we inherit certain capacities for thought or even core values and ideas? Some scholars adhered to an empiricist/associationist explanation for the origins of knowledge. Others attempted to reconcile the latter explanation with the operation of reason, including moral judgment. Few adopted an idealistic explanation.
- What is the nature of human nature? This question subdivides into the following debates:
  - Are human beings in general rational or irrational?
  - Do people's actions generally show change or stability?
  - Is human nature a consequence of each person's unique experiences or of common dimensions?
  - What is our capacity to know the ultimate reality of the universe – the Good?
  - Are people's actions primarily due to nature or nurture? Is determinism or voluntarism a better explanation? Does "free will" exist?
  - Are human beings like all other animals, explicable purely by materialism, namely, the movement of atoms and mechanical principles? Or are we special creatures with a vital life-force unique to us? Or, to take an aboriginal perspective, are humans intimately related to all creatures, all of whom have spirits?

> **Small-group discussion.** What is your position on these debates concerning human nature? If we are only biological machines, destined to pursue pleasure and avoid pain, what are the implications for morality and meaning in life?

Summary

This chapter provided social historical context for the formal emergence of Psychology in the nineteenth century. In Part 1 we described the economic and political transformations (e.g., the Industrial Revolution) that deeply affected Western societies. We noted the rise of social movements for emancipation from the oppressive conditions that these transformations produced: socialism, feminism, and the abolition of slavery.

In Part 2 we addressed the concepts and methodology of what became the Romantic movement. Romantic thinkers approached the polarity of rationalism and empiricism by stressing feelings and communion with nature. Then we discussed the contributions of Johann Wolfgang von Goethe and Arthur Schopenhauer to psychological ideas.

Part 3 covered three principal ideologies of the New Enlightenment: positivism represented by Auguste Comte, liberalism and utilitarianism represented by John Stuart Mill, and dialectical materialism represented by Karl Marx. We identified the historical relevance to Psychology of these diverse positions.

In Part 4 we described influential philosophical psychologists. Maine de Biran stressed the role of human will. Johann Herbart mathematically expressed apperception, limen, and ideas coming to consciousness. Hermann Lotze united physiological with psychological processes and theorized space perception. Alexander Bain reconceived associationist concepts of sensory and mental processes.

In Part 5 we discussed the elevated status of science and described the challenges that the few women then in science faced. Next we identified new knowledge created in physiology and in what then was called brain research and psychophysics, all of which had import for psychological processes. Franz Gall and Paul Broca made significant contributions in brain research, while Jan Purkyně and Johannes Müller contributed to physiology and psychophysics.

Ernst Weber's physiological research inspired the psychophysicist Gustav Fechner to employ the just noticeable difference to show the relationship between physical properties and psychological experience of sensations. Weber's quantitative experimentation set the methodological stage for natural-science Psychology.

We highlighted the psychologically relevant accomplishments of the physicist and physiologist Hermann von Helmholtz and described his debate with Ewald Hering regarding colour vision. We concluded with coverage of Ernst Mach's emphasis on concrete experimental observations and empirically grounded explanations of data.

We devoted Part 6 to describing the background to Darwin's evolutionary theory, the theory itself, its cultural consequences, its implications for Psychology, and the social movement of social Darwinism led by Herbert Spencer.

In Part 7 we discussed the critical concept of scientism, meaning the overly zealous pursuit of objective science, which we contrasted with three quasi-sciences – mesmerism, phrenology, and spiritualism – that cloaked themselves in both science and religion. Critics of science and society, such as Fyodor Dostoevsky, became prominent, while philosopher Søren Kierkegaard expressed psychological views that earned the term early existentialism. Influential social critic Friedrich Nietzsche took radical positions on psychological topics; epistemology; gender, race, politics, and social class.

In Part 8 we discussed three themes that capture the core issues addressed in this chapter: liberal individualism vs. socialist alternatives, scientific triumphalism vs. skepticism, and unresolved philosophical questions about psychological phenomena. The unresolved questions divide into fundamental issues about body and mind and debates about human nature.

Sample essay questions

1. Compare and contrast the views of the natural philosopher whose positions you find most congenial with those of the natural philosopher whose positions you find least congenial.

2. As review and preparation for encountering the story of Psychology's formal emergence in Chapter 5, spatially locate where all the major figures described in Chapters 2 to 4

stood on these four issues: how mind and body are related, the activity-level of the mind, how we derive knowledge and form ideas, and the essence of human nature.

RECOMMENDED READING

In addition to the references cited, previously recommended authors provide valuable information: Barzun, Fancher & Rutherford, Gribbin, G. Richards, Russell, and R. Smith.

For the history of women in science see Alic's (1986) *Hypatia's heritage: A history of women in science from antiquity to the nineteenth century*; Schiebinger's (1989) *The mind has no sex? Women in the origins of modern science*.

The *Annual Review of Critical Psychology*, an online journal, devoted the 2011 issue to the relationship of Marxism and psychology.

For Darwin in Psychology see the *American Psychologist* February–March 2009 issue.

ONLINE RESOURCES

For entries on individuals and some topics covered in this chapter see the *Stanford Encyclopedia of Philosophy*: http://plato.stanford.edu/entries/

For dialectical materialism see: www.marxists.org/reference/archive/hegel/help/sampler.htm.

For the complete works of Charles Darwin see: http://darwin-online.org.uk/

On women in science and Psychology see: www.feministvoices.com

5 Early natural-science Psychology

Chapter outline

Introduction

Although early modern natural philosophers were interested in the relationship between biological and psychological processes, psychology remained a branch of philosophy or theology. Then nineteenth-century physiologists demonstrated experimentally that neuro-muscular functions, perceptual processes, and mental operations were interdependent, a consistent finding that created space for a natural-science psychology. Some German scholars, then British, French, US, and Russian scientists began to adopt physiologists' methodology to analyze conscious experience of sensory-motor functions and answer such philosophical **questions** as:

- What is a mind? Of what does it consist? How is it related to the brain?
- What roles do biology and evolution play in psychological processes?
- How do psychological capacities develop?
- How do humans gain knowledge of the empirical world? How do physical phenomena become sensations? How do emotions and thoughts originate?
- What is an action? How is action related to emotion, thought, and will?
- How do humans remember their experiences?
- What is a self? How is it related to other selves?
- What is the individual's relation to society?

In answering these questions many new psychologists used extant language concerning brain–behaviour relations and evolutionary adaptation. They adopted biological notions, expounded by Alexander Bain and Herbert Spencer, about cerebral localization, sensory-motor activity, and the association of ideas (R. M. Young, 1970). In addition, Gustav Fechner's psychophysics, "the institutionalization of laboratory instruction" (Ash, 2003, p. 253), and British innovations in statistical analyses of population data became the components of natural-science Psychology's methodology.

But early psychologists encountered a problem: they could only provide functional explanations according to physiological sensations and movements, not across all levels of brain and behavioural relations. Thus, while scholars struggled with the insufficiency of purely physiological, contemporary explanations for psychological phenomena, the discipline of Psychology took shape.

In this chapter, we trace how Psychology emerged from its societal, scientific, and philosophical context to develop organizational and institutional supports necessary to sustain a new discipline. Then we present developments up to World War I, concerning diverse schools of thought, basic psychological processes, interpersonal processes, and the relationship of Psychology to the social order.

The **aims** of this chapter are to describe:

- The social and intellectual context for Psychology's emergence.
- The diverse national origins of Psychology and the status of women in it.
- Diverse schools of early psychological thought.
- How early psychologists understood basic psychological and interpersonal processes.
- The relationship between the new Psychology and society.
- Conceptual themes underlying the new Psychology that set its direction for future decades: boundary maintenance, biological reductionism, ambiguity about mind and brain, and alliance with the political and socioeconomic status quo.

Origins of institutionalized Psychology

Social and intellectual conditions prevailing in Western culture enabled Psychology's birth as a distinct academic discipline. Contemporary novelists, such as the Russian Leo Tolstoy (1828–1910), were giving vivid accounts of their characters' motives, wishes, and feelings. Meanwhile, in 1867 a young William James proclaimed that psychology should become a science of the interface between the nervous system and consciousness (Roback & Kiernan, 1969). Psychological thought pervaded the cultural atmosphere. By 1889, scientific psychologists held their inaugural International Congress.

After sketching the societal and scientific terrain on which Psychology took its first steps, we describe German, British, French, Russian, and US Psychology, then the discipline's more modest beginnings in Canada, China, India, and Japan.

Societal and scientific context

During the nineteenth century in economically privileged societies, massive migration transpired from agrarian communities to cities where industries dependent on cheap labour were located. Children and youth from labouring families, as depicted in Figure 5.1, typically worked in urban factories from an early age.

Rapid urbanization and industrialization precipitated widespread health and mental health problems, because housing and working conditions for workers and their families were

Figure 5.1 Boys queue up for work, 1909, Rhode Island, USA

bleak. Conflicts between society's power-brokers, and citizens and emergent labour unions agitating for political and economic rights and healthier lives escalated (Zinn, 2005). These conditions impelled politicians and business leaders to ask scientists to help solve social crises. The general public desired explanations and practical applications of scientific discoveries and seemed to yearn for "a new relationship with mind" (Bjork, 1983, p. 9) beyond the elusive characteristics of phrenology, hypnotism, and spiritualism. The new Psychology suited this zeitgeist.

US context

Social conditions in the USA differed from those in Europe. After the US Civil War ended in 1865, while settlements expanded westward and eastern cities industrialized, science and systematic technological knowledge were in high demand. Scientific activity shifted from domestic locations to colleges and universities where scientists sought academic careers. Partly funded by industrialists, post-secondary institutions invested in science and technology programmes with university presidents demanding applications of research to society. By World War I, university research was intertwined with federal and private financial support (Bakan, 1998).

Within US tertiary education, administrators organized the sciences into specialized departments modelled on German precedents. Given the prestige associated with graduate education in Germany, many early US psychologists studied there to advance their career opportunities. They adopted German research practices but soon abandoned German interest in philosophical laws of the mind.

By World War I, US psychologists outnumbered German, British, and French psychologists combined (Joncich, 1968). Arguably, US Psychology thrived, because increasing bureaucratic organization of society and public demand dovetailed with psychologists' apparent scientific expertise. The establishment, capitalizing on expanding markets, recognized a new social class: scientifically trained professionals (Zinn, 2005). Government, business, and labour leaders joined with professionals to administer a complex society, believing that applied science was essential for economic development. Social reformers aiming to improve living and working conditions also sought to manage "progress" scientifically (Morawski, 1982).

Many academic US psychologists strove to fill the perceived need for administering society and aligned themselves with society's goals of economic expansion, efficiency, and progress. To win societal support psychologists promised applications of "knowledge of individual psychological capacities" (R. Smith, 1997, p. 523). They claimed that they could predict and control human nature just as natural scientists had organized the natural world. Cultural receptivity to Darwinian concepts and European scientific developments reinforced this claim (Cadwallader, 1992). Adopting the evolutionary term "survival," many psychologists focused on individual differences in adaptation to society and harnessed "knowledge of the faculties of the mind to the task of building the nation" (Rieber, 1998, pp. 212–213).

Society's administrators generally welcomed psychologists' applications, perhaps because they were impressed by scientific rhetoric. In effect, the US version of the discipline became an administrative science, designed to help manage people in society's institutions. Psychology flourished in what seemed to be an increasingly "psychologically minded" society seeking practical applications (Danziger, 1990).

Institutionalization of Psychology

Due to heightened interest and demand, Psychology required institutional and organizational structures beyond university laboratories for psychologists to practise their science. European institutionalization was the model (Joncich, 1968). Professional societies and scientific journals legitimized the new discipline and strengthened psychologists' identification with their new profession.

German Psychology

As we have seen, scientific study of psychological topics originated in nineteenth-century Germany as empirical philosophy. German scholars inspired and trained most early psychologists. However, Psychology was not an independent discipline in Germany until 1941, and the early psychologists there held academic appointments as philosophers not as psychologists.

Indebted to Johann Herbart and Hermann Helmholtz, Wilhelm Wundt institutionalized Psychology and supported a distinct scientific identity for the new discipline. His classic book, (in English) *Principles of Physiological Psychology*, helped to legitimize natural-science Psychology. He was innovative in using two experimental procedures – Helmholtz's reaction-time and Weber's and Fechner's psychophysics – to investigate sensory experience. Later, his *Völkerpsychologie*, meaning "shared psychology of a people," affirmed Psychology as a *human* science.

Wundt influenced Psychology substantially. He "provided a social organization for scientific pursuits: a laboratory, a journal, a research agenda, and an experimental ideology" (O'Donnell, 1985, p. 24). Furthermore, many psychologists responded to his concepts and methods by accepting, modifying, or rejecting them. However, Wundt did not found Psychology as distinct from philosophy (Blumenthal, 1998). Rather, he practised experimentation to improve philosophy through empirical evidence, not in order to escape philosophy.

In 1879, Wundt initiated the first European laboratory practicum in Psychology. His famous institute at the University of Leipzig was established in 1897, significantly expanded in 1914, and was emulated internationally. He supervised at least 200 doctoral dissertations and trained most of the first generation of psychologists, including sixteen US citizens and one Canadian.

But other German psychologists also directed influential laboratories into the twentieth century. Georg Müller's (1850–1934) laboratory at Göttingen was second only to Wundt's in its capacity for training the next generation of natural-science psychologists. Müller contributed to the fields of psychophysics, colour vision, perception, and memory (Haupt, 1998). He epitomized the methodical experimentalist, while supporting applied psychology (Kusch, 1999).

Furthermore, in 1893, Carl Stumpf (1848–1936) founded an Institute of Psychology at Berlin where he emphasized holistic thinking, influencing the Gestalt psychologists and **Kurt Lewin** (1890–1945) (see Chapter 6). Also at Berlin, Hermann Ebbinghaus helped develop German Psychology through popular textbooks, journal editing, and support for the German Society of Experimental Psychology. Then in 1896, **Oswald Külpe** (1862–1915), who promoted the applicability of experimental physiology to all psychological phenomena, founded a laboratory at Würzburg.

British Psychology

Conceptually, evolutionary theory largely shaped early Psychology in the UK. British scientists established comparative psychology (see Chapter 11) on the foundation of Darwinian thought, while **Francis Galton** (1822–1911) explored how it explained human nature and individual psychological differences.

Also influential were the medical authorities who introduced physiological psychology to the UK (Danziger, 1982). **Hughlings Jackson** (1835–1911) and **Henry Maudsley** (1835–1918) worked empirically to establish body–mind connections, discussed psychological processes medically and biologically, and recommended practical applications to social problems. **Charles Sherrington** (1857–1952) laid the foundations for neurophysiology, practised psychological experimentation before Britain had Psychology labs, and supported industrial applications of psychology (Hearnshaw, 1964). However, natural sciences in the UK, particularly experimental physiology, were weakly developed. Consequently, early British psychologists struggled for institutional support and lacked lab infrastructure for decades (Hearnshaw, 1964), and psychological applications played a more prominent role than basic research until World War II (N. Rose, 1985).

Formally, British Psychology emerged in 1897 when **James Sully** (1842–1923) and James Ward (1843–1925) instituted the first laboratories: Sully at University College London and Ward at Cambridge University (Hearnshaw, 1964; Thomson, 1968). Furthermore, the first British female professor of Psychology, Beatrice Edgell (1871–1948), introduced experimentation to Bedford College, London (Valentine, 2005).

But neither Sully nor Ward was an experimentalist. Britain's first "experimental psychologist" was a physician, **W. H. Rivers** (1864–1922), who had introduced an experimental psychology course to Cambridge in 1893. In 1909, C. S. Myers (1873–1946) succeeded Rivers and subsequently expanded the facilities and its training function. Cambridge remained the centre of British experimental psychology for decades.

Meanwhile, Oxford did not permit an institute of experimental psychology until 1936 (Donald & Canter, 1987). Psychologist **William McDougall** (1871–1938) had lectured on psychology at Oxford in 1904, but the university forbade him from conducting experiments. Qualified as a neurologist, he published an influential book in 1905 on physiological psychology in which he discussed the significance of Sherrington's neurological investigations (Innis, 2003).

French Psychology

The origins of Psychology in France partly lay in philosophical, spiritual, and theological perspectives on psychological experience known collectively as *spiritualisme*. Yet although this movement and Jean-Jacques Rousseau's sensibility of feelings and emotions remained influential, so did Julien de La Mettrie's and Pierre Cabanis' emphasis on unifying body and mind.

Two physicians paved the way for a physiological orientation to French natural-science Psychology: **Claude Bernard** (1813–1878) and **Jean-Martin Charcot** (1825–1893) (Reuchlin, 1965). They conducted clinical case studies, often investigating a phenomenon coined "neurosis." Although a unique blend of physiological, philosophical, psychiatric, and eventually psychoanalytic interests prevailed, the measurement of mental phenomena flourished as well.

The catalyst for the emergence of French Psychology per se was philosopher **Theodule Ribot**. He committed himself to a physiological psychology in opposition to Maine de Biran's human-science psychology of dynamic mental activity. Instead, Ribot introduced both Spencer's interpretation of evolutionary psychology and German physiological psychology to France (Guillin, 2004). Ribot theorized about memory, will, personality, and the relationship between ideas and bodily movement. He also promoted the field of psychopathology, uniting medical and empirical psychology.

Ribot became the new chair of Psychology at the Collège de France (Nicolas & D. Murray, 1999). Then in 1889 he established a laboratory at the Sorbonne, teaching France's first experimental psychology course. **Pierre Janet** (1859–1947), whose research on psychopathology influenced Sigmund Freud (see Chapter 9), sustained the Ribot tradition and co-founded the French Psychological Society in 1901.

Renowned for assessing intelligence, Alfred Binet furthered French Psychology's institutionalization by administering the Sorbonne lab and mentoring future psychologists (Wolf, 1973). His successor, **Henri Pieron** (1881–1964), expanded the lab into an institute that became France's first Psychology graduate programme (R. Smith, 1997). He too adopted a strong psychophysiological standpoint.

Russian Psychology

Three physiologists, **Ivan Sechenov** (1829–1905), Ivan Pavlov, and **Vladimir Bekhterev** (1857–1927), known as "reflexologists," played formative roles in early Psychology nationally and internationally. Stressing empirically knowable properties of the brain, they contended that physiology completely explained psychological phenomena.

Sechenov insisted that scientists should employ objective, hypothesis-testing physiological experiments to study subjective psychology (Yaroschevskii, 1982). His proposal for a physiological science of mind greatly influenced his students, Pavlov and Bekhterev, who systematically experimented on reflexes. Sechenov's orientation became the template for "reflexology" (a term that Bekhterev coined), which included complex mental processes.

In 1885 Bekhterev established Russia's first Psychology laboratory and the Moscow Psychological Society was founded, while the first Russian Psychology journal appeared in 1889 (Kozulin, 1985). But **Georgy Chelpanov** (1862–1936) initiated academic Psychology in pre-Soviet Russia. He founded a Psychology curriculum at Moscow University in 1906, produced two textbooks on experimental psychology, and opened the era's largest Institute of Psychology in Europe.

Thus, by the Russian Revolution of 1917, **three centres** of psychological inquiry thrived. In effect, the concepts of reflex, mind, and soul co-existed in the same cultural-historical space (Barabanschikov, 2006).

- In Moscow, Chelpanov's institute represented an eclectic experimental-philosophical disposition to studying psychological processes.
- Pavlov pursued physiological research at the Military-Medical Academy in St. Petersburg.
- In the same city, Bekhterev attempted to integrate physiological, clinical, and philosophical interests at his Psychoneurological Institute (Kozulin, 1984).

US Psychology

During its founding decades Psychology grew most rapidly in US academic institutions, laboratories and journals, and professional organizations.

Academia Originally in US academia, psychology meant studying the soul through the mental and moral philosophy of Scottish common-sense realism, primarily Thomas Reid's, which legitimized natural science. For instance, US philosopher **Thomas Upham** (1799–1872) addressed psychological subject matter with practical applications in mind (Fuchs, 2000). He sought "a means of applying knowledge of the faculties of the mind to the task of building the nation" (Rieber, 1998, pp. 212–213). US psychologists came to serve this same function.

Nineteenth-century US philosophy mediated between science and religion in that philosophers invoked spiritual explanations of the nature that scientists investigated. Although many philosophers welcomed the new Psychology, some US psychologists retained philosophical interests, while many others spurned them.

When many institutions began to include doctoral education and research institutes, Psychology quickly took root. At Harvard, William James offered the first graduate course in Psychology in 1875–1876 and initiated an introductory course the next year. In 1878, Harvard awarded the first PhD in Psychology to **G. Stanley Hall** (1844–1924). Then in 1890, James published *Principles of Psychology* in which he reviewed extant international knowledge of psychological phenomena and advanced his seminal views. This work placed US Psychology on the discipline's world map.

Initially, US Psychology was a Germanic experimental science aimed at deriving general laws of mental organization by means of introspection of consciousness. Yet by 1898, only 2 per cent of experimental papers in US journals reported introspection, while 25 per cent were focused on practical applications (Bruner & Allport, 1940). By World War I, US Psychology was mainly an applied experimental science of the prediction and control of behaviour (O'Donnell, 1985).

However, heterogeneity of thought among US psychologists was the norm. The discipline struggled with debate about its status as a natural science and its purpose as a theoretical or practical science. The founding of the American Psychological Association (APA) in 1892 fashioned a public face of organizational unification, masking personal rivalries. Intensifying psychologists' debate over their ambiguous boundaries was the fact that academic biologists, representing an established discipline, and some psychologists regarded Psychology as either physiology or philosophy.

US psychologists' solution to this foundational identity crisis was to adopt applications of evolutionary biology to psychological phenomena, manifest as "genetic [developmental] psychology" or "functionalist psychology" (see below). Some hoped to unite the developmental standpoint with laboratory experimentation (O'Donnell, 1985). For example, **Edward Thorndike** (1874–1949) formed educational psychology from his animal experiments.

Labs and instruments The new psychologists required labs to establish their credibility. Initially these were housed within philosophy departments, because Psychology was not yet separate from its academic parent. But soon the development of a decentralized system of departments in many universities facilitated the discipline's institutionalization, and labs and their instruments became the heart of US Psychology.

At Harvard, James initiated a very modest demonstration lab in 1875, although it was not in continuous operation. By 1890, nine US Psychology labs existed, rivalling the sum of European labs (Capshew, 1992). Within two decades approximately seventy US universities and institutions for individuals with disabilities had labs (Sokal, 1992). Arguably, the most influential was at Cornell headed by **Edward Titchener** (1867–1927) who laid an experimental foundation for the discipline (Tweney, 1987).

The standard Psychology lab included a technician and a shop. This was the era of "brass-instrument Psychology" – brass, because it was prevalent in the composition of research instruments. Although labs and their research instruments enabled professors to do research, labs also served to indoctrinate students in experimentation and demonstrate known, rather than unknown, phenomena to them. However, research instruments are not essential for experimentation and not all research reliant on instruments is experimental (Sturm & Ash, 2009).

Whatever concepts early psychologists had in common, lab practices united their heterogeneous interests and experimentation gave their investigative activity scientific authority (Ash, 2003). Moreover, society influenced what psychologists did in their labs and they increasingly concentrated on producing practical knowledge for governmental institutions, commerce, and industry.

Journals Research journals enable psychologists to publish manuscripts that editors and reviewers, who are the authors' peers, believe are worthy of archival preservation. In the US, Hall founded the *American Journal of Psychology* in 1887, the first English-language journal in Psychology, while **James Cattell** (1860–1944) and **Mark Baldwin** (1861–1934) instituted *Psychological Review* in 1894. Ten years later *Psychological Bulletin* appeared.

However, the first scientific-psychological papers appeared in two European philosophical journals, founded in 1876, *Mind* and *Revue Philosophique* (Carpintero, 1997). In 1881, Wundt initiated *Philosophische Studien* (later *Psychologische Studien*), which published empirical reports on philosophical questions.

Initially, Psychology journals, like the discipline, were generalist. The first specialty journals were in abnormal, educational, and industrial-organizational psychology. But the *Journal of Experimental Psychology* did not begin until 1916, and specialty journals did not proliferate until after World War I.

Professionalization The formation of the APA in 1892 also aided the discipline's institutionalization and facilitated Psychology's influence on US society (Cadwallader, 1992). Hall along with twenty-six other men from the US, as well as Hugo Münsterberg from Germany, Titchener from England, and two Canadian men founded the association (Sokal, 1992). Disagreement surfaced during the APA's annual meetings concerning what constituted Psychology and what types of papers – experimental or philosophical – were permissible at the conference. These tensions persisted for decades.

Like many experimentalists, Titchener felt he did not fit in the APA, so in 1904 he formed a group for the exclusively male directors of US Psychology labs (Goodwin, 2005). Known later as the Society for Experimental Psychologists, its mainly male membership includes eminent natural-science psychologists.

International Psychology

During the discipline's founding decades it developed a modest presence in Canada and in China, India, and Japan. More recently Psychology has expanded significantly in these nations, achieving some prominence globally.

Canadian Psychology

Ostensibly, Canadian Psychology emerged in 1889 when the University of Toronto invited Baldwin to initiate a lab and curriculum (Hoff, 1992). But he departed in 1893 because of a delay in receiving the equipment required. The lab and Psychology courses materialized and expanded under the direction of Baldwin's German successor, **August Kirschmann** (1860–1932), who presided until 1908.

Edward Bott (1887–1974), who led a rehabilitation unit on campus for Canadian soldiers injured in World War I, headed the Toronto department from 1926 to 1956. He practised John Dewey's approach to child study, working with school administrators, teachers, and parents to foster healthy development. Bott's colleague **William Blatz** (1895–1964) established a child study centre in 1926. He investigated parenting practices that fostered children's sense of security, a concept that he believed was integral to mental health (Wright, 1996).

Overall, prior to World War II, Psychology at Toronto was distinguished by a strong sense of social purpose (Line, 1951). In facing the problem of wide variations in the intellectual functioning of public-school students, psychologists not only tested them, they also intervened to improve classroom climate and develop more psychologically appropriate curricula and educational policies. Rather than adopting a psychology of individual adjustment, they focused on the relationship between development and social environmental factors, such as families, neighbourhoods, and schools. Rather than adopting behaviourism, they regarded individuals as creators of their environments.

The second leading centre of early Canadian Psychology was at McGill University in Montreal, where the second lab was established in 1910 and an independent department in 1924 (Wright & Myers, 1982). Perhaps because of its historical ties to its US counterpart after World War II, Canadian Psychology expanded in anglophone and francophone institutions and exercised some international influence.

Asian Psychologies

During the imperialist era Westerners and some indigenous scholars imported Psychology to Asian societies. The responses to this alien legacy varied across China, India, and Japan. But subsequently most Western psychologists ignored these developments.

China In nineteenth-century Chinese culture there were no terms for psychological discourse (Blowers, 2006). When contemporary scholars translated the few available texts into Chinese, they used the term *xinlixue*, which meant "science of laws of the heart," for psychology (Petzold, 1987, p. 217). This term connoted a commitment to ethical conduct, because in Chinese culture, knowledge and practical action were linked (H. Zhang, 1987). Categories for the soul, consciousness, or unconscious processes did not exist.

Some early Chinese scholars had studied Psychology in the West, primarily the US. But they retained their traditional concepts while selectively adopting Japanese versions of Western concepts for practical applications. Thus, Psychology became a staple of teacher-training institutes. During the 1920s, the Chinese Psychological Society, autonomous departments, a few journals, and a laboratory were established. Nevertheless, Psychology in China developed slowly and then halted when Japanese invaded in 1937.

India Psychology was formed within a colonial British educational system that prepared Indians for subordinate occupations in administering the colony (Joshi, 1992). British administrators transplanted Western concepts in India and denigrated ancient, indigenous psychological thought (Paranjpe, 2006). Consequently, Indian academics adopted Anglo-American Psychology rather than develop a Psychology grounded in their own complex culture.

Institutionally, early psychologists obtained their training in the US or the UK. When they returned to India, some founded a Psychology lab at Calcutta University in 1905, replicated Anglo-American experiments, and reproduced Anglo-American tests (Sinha, 1987). Although the Indian Psychological Association and the *Indian Journal of Psychology* were established in the 1920s, an academically independent Psychology did not yet exist. It remained embedded in philosophy or education curricula until India's independence in 1947.

Japan Nineteenth-century Japanese industrialization encouraged educational development and the emergence of Psychology suited to the administration of social institutions, particularly education. Two scholars, who studied in the US and Germany respectively, returned to develop Psychology with an indigenous orientation (Iwahara, 1976; Kaneko, 1987).

Japan's first professor of Psychology, Yujiro Motora (1858–1912), initiated psychophysics at Tokyo in 1888. Matataro Matsumoto (1865–1943) founded experimental labs at two Tokyo institutions in 1903, established the discipline at Kyoto, and introduced applied psychology. As a result, practical psychological applications flourished in Japan even before World War II.

Women in early Psychology

During Psychology's founding decades, economically privileged societies witnessed the emergence of the New Woman who confronted patriarchal gender-roles; rejected the belief that women were inferior to men; and demanded economic, civil, intellectual, and sexual autonomy. Noteworthy Anglo-American women envisioned how gender relations could be different in the twentieth century, if society restructured its social and economic relations (Rowbotham, 2010). The US writer Charlotte Perkins Gillman (1860–1935) repudiated the subordinate position of women and promoted a positive women's psychology (Spender, 1983), while the British sexologist Havelock Ellis (1859–1939) expressed male support for feminism (G. Richards, 2010). Nevertheless, the societal and scientific consensus was that women were biologically, and therefore psychologically, inferior to men.

Meanwhile, societal resistance to gender equality impinged upon women's career opportunities (Bohan, 1990). Married women were ineligible for employment outside the home. Thus, women had to choose either marriage or a professional career that excluded marriage but demanded caring for aging parents (Furumoto & Scarborough, 1986). This fact limited women's career opportunities, such as taking a position in a different geographical area.

Furthermore, women's participation in post-secondary education was very constrained. In 1900, although 80 per cent of tertiary institutions accepted women, very few attended (Solomon, 1985). If women reached graduate school, they were excluded from important networks of male academics who assessed their scholarly potential with sexist bias.

In research universities, where male professors enjoyed a steady stream of graduate students, administrators tended to bar women from professorial positions, while administrators excluded female professors from all-male institutions, reasoning that women were incapable of instructing male students. When female researchers were permitted to join the professoriate, administrators typically assigned them a heavier teaching load than male colleagues (Joncich, 1968). At women's colleges and "normal schools" (teachers colleges) where most female academics worked, Psychology labs were meagre or non-existent. Yet US female psychologists contributed to many subdisciplines in publications and conference papers.

The APA was the first professional society open to women, such as **Mary Calkins** (1863–1930), Christine Ladd-Franklin, and **Margaret Washburn** (1871–1939). By contrast, the American Medical Association excluded female physicians until 1915. However, although the APA elected seventy-nine women (15 per cent of the total membership) during its first thirty years, women rarely participated in governing it (Scarborough, 1992). Calkins was president in 1905 and Washburn in 1921, but the association did not elect another female president for fifty years.

Part 1 conclusion

Natural-science psychology became institutionalized in the late nineteenth century primarily in economically privileged nations. In Germany, France, the UK, Russia, and the USA sensitivity to psychological interiority already was a norm. But now rapid urbanization and industrialization precipitated a need for the social management of masses of urbanized workers and their families. Taken together, scientific and educational conditions, medical advances, and industrial and commercial interests were conducive to the emergence of the new discipline. While some early psychologists devoted themselves to investigating philosophical problems empirically, others promised practical applications of knowledge about mental processes.

Labs and research instruments necessary for experimentation, undergraduate and graduate programmes, journals, professional associations, and conferences enabled diverse fledgling psychologies to flourish. Psychologists also were active in several nations with less developed economies but robust social institutions (e.g., Canada, China, India, Japan). Although generally women were discouraged from pursuing advanced education and careers, some women found an intellectual home in early Psychology despite overt and covert opposition from many male colleagues.

Part 2 Schools of thought

Founding psychologists proposed broad explanations encompassing the gamut of psychological processes rather than theories specific to particular phenomena. The principal schools of thought in early Psychology were voluntarism, structuralism, reflexology, functionalism, social practice, self theory, and hormic theory. Gestalt theory (see Chapter 6) and psychoanalysis (see Chapter 9) did not become prominent until after World War I.

Voluntarism

Wilhelm Wundt used experimental methods to address philosophical questions related to sensory functioning and body–mind relations and establish universal truths about the mind. He extended physiological understanding to psychological functions, based on the philosophical concept of apperception. Wundt's focus for investigating psychological causality was the individual's active response. Hence, his school of thought qualified as a form of voluntarism because, for him, thinking constituted an internal choice (Kusch, 1999).

Nineteenth-century psychologists often presented their attempts at explaining action, as distinct from passive responding, in terms of the concept of volition. This concept covered a great deal of what would later be discussed in terms of the psychology of drives and motives ... Wundt played a significant role in preparing for this change. (Danziger, 2001b, p. 97)

Basic concepts

During the 1880s with tests of muscular reaction and reaction time, Wundt observed "automatization," meaning automatic reactions to sensory stimuli. By varying the required response in testing conditions he mapped simple (lower) to complex (higher) voluntary activity. He concluded that aspects of complex mental processes function together, with higher functions (e.g., attention) evolving from lower ones (e.g., reflexes). Therefore, studying mere elements of consciousness (i.e., awareness of simple sensations), he believed, can provide partial insight only.

Wundt distinguished between the mind's inferior functions (e.g., sensory processes), which the laws of association govern, and its superior functions (e.g., thinking), which the laws of apperception govern (Kusch, 1999). He held that apperception as an active, central-control process plays a central role in higher functions. He defined apperception as the psychophysiological process of assimilating and transforming new information in relation to existing information. Individuals also can apply existing constructs to new information.

According to Wundt, apperception consists of **three components**:

- "Psychological causality," based on purpose, value, and anticipation of the future.
- "Creative synthesis," meaning dynamic selective attention organizing experiences into coherent units.
- "Psychic relations," meaning mental events depend on their context.

Philosophically, Wundt espoused *psychophysical parallelism*, distinguishing between physical and psychic (mental) causality. For him, the physical and mental are on parallel tracks; immediate experience is physical and mediate experience is mental. In an introductory text, translated into English as *Outlines of Psychology*, Wundt (1897) stated:

[T]here must be a relation between all the facts that belong at the same time to both experiences of the natural sciences and to the immediate experiences of psychology, for they are nothing but components of a single experience which is merely regarded in the two cases from different points of view. Since these facts belong to both spheres, there must be an elementary process on the physical side, corresponding to every such process on the psychical side. (pp. 317–318)

According to Wundt, physiological experimentation is suitable only for simple psychological functions. But complex psychological functions are reflections of personal experience, influenced by the cultural products of language, myth, and custom. Only mental events, he insisted, can cause other mental events. Consequently, their investigation requires the cultural and philosophical analysis of the human sciences. In Wundt's schema of Psychology, experimentation serves as a kind of nursery school with more advanced work taking place in the theoretical human science of *Völkerpsychologie* (described below).

Section conclusion

By World War I, many US psychologists regarded Wundt as an old-fashioned dualist who clung to idealist philosophy and overemphasized mental processes. Others rejected Wundt's introspective evidence as worthless, but they confused his approach to consciousness with Titchener's structured elements of mental content (Blumenthal, 1998). Wundt himself rejected such elementism; he was not a structuralist and never used the term.

Meanwhile, other psychologists, including his German contemporaries, investigated higher-order processes that Wundt viewed as untestable experimentally. Unlike Wundt, they created flexible boundaries with lay terms and concepts, because they realized that applicability and everyday usage were important for formulating psychological categories (Danziger, 2001a). Furthermore, given that he ignored individual differences, Wundt had little influence on British Psychology. Yet by the 1970s, cognitive psychologists were exploring similar topics to his, such as selective volitional attention and automatic processing (Blumenthal, 1975).

Structuralism

Edward Titchener learned from Wundt how to investigate basic processes and administer a productive laboratory. His interest, like Wundt's, was in general laws about the abstract, adult mind, not in individual psychological differences. But he abandoned Wundt's notions of apperception and psychic causality in favour of *structuralism*, by which Titchener meant the core elements in the structure of consciousness.

Basic concepts

Titchener's investigations were atheoretical in that he concentrated on observable data. He believed that only hypotheses derived from experimentation are legitimate. In addition, he considered the attribution of meaning to elements of sensation irrelevant and rejected conceptual explanations because, for him, science is incompatible with philosophy (Bjork, 1983).

Instead, Titchener explained complex mental processes according to the structural arrangement of elements of sensations or attributes of sensations (Tweney, 1987). For him, Psychology should consist of the rigorous examination of strictly observable elements of consciousness. Titchener contended that functionalism's evolutionary premise that consciousness facilitates environmental adaptation is suited to biology but not Psychology. Understanding the structures of basic psychological processes should precede studying their functions. Thus, mind is the sum total of a person's experience rather than an organism's functional activity.

For Titchener (1909), psychologists attempt to answer the what, how, and why of mental experience, that is, they analyze, synthesize, and explain it:

The psychologist answers the question "what" by analyzing mental experience into its elements. He answers the question "how" by formulating the laws of connection of these elements. And he answers the question "why" by explaining mental processes in terms of their parallel processes in the nervous system. (p. 41)

In Titchener's lab, members of the research team were trained to be "introspectors" (Tweney, 1987). They observed conscious elements, reporting sensations only, not perceptions (Bjork, 1983). Introspectors described the spatial and colour aspects of an object, but did not call it by its name. To name the stimulus was to commit the "stimulus error" of confounding the experience of observed elements with interpretation of their meaning. Titchener also proscribed data from animals, children, and disordered adults, because he believed that these organisms could not distinguish reliably between admissible data (i.e., sensations, images, and feelings) and inadmissible data (i.e., attributed meanings).

Section conclusion

Seeking to legitimize Psychology, Titchener agreed with Ernst Mach that Psychology could be as exact a science as physics purportedly was. For Titchener, lab experimentation was the hub of Psychology conceptually and institutionally. Despite his introspection studies, which bordered on subjective consciousness, his doctrine of experimentally derived observables attracted the behaviourist John Watson and, later, B. F. Skinner, and this doctrine remains the bedrock of methodology in natural-science Psychology.

Titchener spurned practical applications of Psychology as premature, claiming its scientific foundation was insecure. Thus, he regarded the emergence of behaviourism as Psychology's conversion to a biological technology. Given that he banned evolutionary instincts, basic habits, and social applications, Titchener's structuralism held little appeal for many US psychologists who were devoted to evolutionary theory and viewed structuralism as abstract scholasticism (Bjork, 1983). By the 1920s Titchener's school of thought expired, triggered by the "imageless-thought" debate over mental content and meaning (see below).

Reflexology

A rather different school of psychological thought prevailed among the Russian reflexologists Ivan Sechenov, Ivan Pavlov, and Vladimir Bekhterev. They concentrated on biological mechanisms involved in connecting particular senses, organs, sensory nerves, the spine, and motor nerves. Sechenov, Pavlov, and Bekhterev posited that reflexes proceed in a linear, mechanical relation: a stimulus leads to a response, mediated by a sensation.

Sechenov's perspective

According to Sechenov, the elements of all behaviour are: "a sensory nerve, a central connection [involving brain processes], and a motor nerve" (Kimble, 1996, p. 37). In applying the notion of reflex both to learned and inborn behaviour, he held that motor activity is the basis of mental processes. As a Darwinian, he assumed that animal behaviour is foundational to human behaviour (Boakes, 1984).

Sechenov distinguished between involuntary reflexes and voluntary activity, arguing that learned behaviour can be reflexive or involuntary. He postulated that the cerebral cortex can inhibit reflexes because of previous experience or strengthen reflexes in situations of pain or pleasure. Jettisoning the concept of volition or will (Kimble, 1996), he argued that humans acquire increasingly inhibitory control over their reflexes as they develop (Yaroshevski, 1968).

For Sechenov, reflexes and inhibition partially characterize mental processes. Thinking originates in empirical experience, not in innate ideas, he claimed, and is impossible without sensory stimulation. Reflexes aid the brain's capacity for producing "a subjective reflection of the objective world" (Lomov, 1987, p. 420), while thinking consists of inhibited inner speech. Thus, sensing and thinking are aspects of reflection, which is the central concept of his model.

Pavlov's perspective

During his digestive research Pavlov observed by chance that experienced dogs salivate simply when harnessed, prior to the presence of food. Initially he interpreted the dogs' secretions as "anticipatory" responses to "psychical processes" (Todes, 2001). To provide an "objective" explanation, he adopted Sechenov's reflex concept. Pavlov reasoned that excitation and inhibition of reflexes are intertwined; excitation evokes reflexes, while inhibition curbs them.

To convey the notion that "the reflex was contingent upon the presentation of the originally neutral stimulus" Pavlov introduced the term "conditional reflex" (Kimble, 1991b, p. 31). After a translator used the less accurate "conditioned" instead of "conditional," this terminological error became the norm in Psychology.

"Unconditional reflexes" are inborn, automatic, and mediated by connections between sensory and motor nerves in the spinal cord and the lower brain cortex. They are composed of an unconditional stimulus and response. "Conditional reflexes" result from learned connections between unconditional and associated, but biologically neutral, stimuli. The connection is temporary, because conditional stimuli can lose their capacity to evoke a response once primary reinforcement is removed.

Pavlov also created the category of "acquired reflexes" (Lowry, 1970). Observing that extinguished responses spontaneously recover with time, he concluded that extinction represents new learning and does not erase the memory for conditioning. For Pavlov, specific types of inhibition control the probability of conditional responses and organisms adapt to changing stimulus conditions (Kimble, 1991b).

Clearly, Pavlov's (1926/1928) concept of adaptable conditional reflexes encroached upon psychological territory. Eventually he did turn to Psychology, aiming to experimentally control human behaviour; he applied his concept of conditional reflexes to "higher nervous activity" (i.e., mental processes), including language, personality, and the diagnosis and treatment of mental health disorders (see Chapter 6).

Bekhterev's perspective

Following Sechenov's vision, Bekhterev identified physiological laws that substantiated reflexes. He considered these laws the most objective account of animal and human biological, psychological, and social processes.

Bekhterev criticized Pavlov's methods and focus on salivary secretions as already known (Logan, 2002). According to Bekhterev, an unconditional stimulus evokes a conditional response of *motoric* behaviour, such as a dog withdrawing a paw to a tone. He believed that conscious and unconscious phenomena express themselves in external motoric action.

Furthermore, Bekhterev regarded all psychological processes as either simple, innate "associative reflexes" or complex, learned "aim reflexes." He held that complex reflexes constitute higher mental processes. For example, language and thought result from inhibited speech, while unique "personal reflexes" constitute one's personality.

Complex reflexes, Bekhterev asserted, also explained consciousness of experience and the ability to interpret information from the outside world. But he viewed self-observation as an untrustworthy estimate of one's inner world. Thus, he rejected introspection, because he denied that mental activity is different from physiological activity.

Yet Bekhterev maintained that mind and body are twin aspects of "energy, which manifests itself sometimes in matter, sometimes in mind" (Joravsky, 1989, p. 151). Moreover, he used the notion of reflex metaphorically "to explain action as the consequence of organic connections between a person and surrounding conditions" (R. Smith, 1997, p. 786).

Initially, Bekhterev's perspective was popular in post-revolutionary Russia. Unlike Pavlov, he embraced subjective psychological concepts and abstractions like Marxism (Joravsky, 1989). But by the late 1920s Soviet critics claimed that Bekhterev's assumption that physical laws explain psychological and social phenomena contradicted dialectical thinking about the complexity of psychological phenomena and the centrality of human social relationships. Thus, his reflexology was discredited.

Dewey's critique

Earlier, John Dewey (1896) argued for a *psychological* interpretation of reflex. He agreed that the reflex, not the neuron, was the fundamental psychological unit and acknowledged that stimulus–response connections form habits. But he asserted that stimulus and response are interrelated aspects of a goal-oriented sequence of activity that enhances adaptation to the environment.

Dewey inserted perception, consciousness, and activity in reflexes. Psychologists, he argued, should understand the perceived meaning of the stimulus in the particular situation. Rather than mere sensory experience, the way individuals act on this perceived meaning "determines the character of the stimuli that appear to us" (Brinkmann, 2011a, p. 306). Thus, mind-in-action is crucial to reflex.

With this integrative conception of psychological processes, Dewey's interpretation greatly differed from those of reflexologists and behaviourists. Consequently, his transactional perspective on reflexes was not persuasive during his lifetime.

Functionalism

The original school of thought in US Psychology was functionalism. It reflected two major influences: the adaptive principle of evolution, and US cultural conditions of economic expansion and social unrest.

Like Charles Darwin, functionalists assumed strong psychological continuity between humans and other mammals (Greenwood, 2009). They held that mind is an organism's functional activity, while consciousness guides adaptation to the environment. Functionalists were interested in the functional utility of behaviour, body–mind interaction, and practical mental operations, not the content or structure of consciousness. For them, Psychology should be "a practical science of conduct and character [personality]" (O'Donnell, 1985, p. 174).

James Angell (1867–1949) presented the functionalist programme as follows:

Our adaptation of the biological point of view . . . will mean not only that we shall study consciousness in connection with physiological processes, whenever possible, but it will also mean that we shall regard all operations of consciousness – all our sensations, all our emotions, and all our acts of will – as so many expressions of organic adaptations to our environment which we must remember is social as well as physical. (Angell, 1904, p. 7)

Functionalists' evolutionary premise inspired interests in biological and mental development and in improving the species through social reform, such as education and child study (R. Richards, 1987). For functionalists, everyone has a duty to adapt to society to benefit the nation. Functionalists transformed mental processes into habits of mind, manifest in external behaviour and subject to experts' manipulation, to ensure an efficient social order (Hale, 1980).

In addition, functionalists encouraged marketing Psychology's utility to society. They studied psychological phenomena in animals, children, and adults with practical consequences for education, criminal justice, commerce, and industry. Functionalists converted the difficulties that educators, judges, industrialists, and business owners encountered with their subordinates to problems of administration that required "psychological" solutions. In effect, adaptation to society meant deference to social hierarchies.

Pragmatism, neorealism, and radical empiricism

Subjecting all psychological phenomena to scrutiny by evolutionary biology (R. Smith, 1997), William James proposed a functional Psychology, focused on the mind's practical role of facilitating adaptation to their environment (Bjork, 1983). His philosophical development of pragmatism, neorealism, and radical empiricism gave theoretical depth to functionalism.

Pragmatism was not a set of beliefs but an umbrella term for a relativist approach to metaphysical, epistemological, and ethical questions. For pragmatists, ideas are true to the extent that they work in their environments. Pragmatists emphasized multiple pathways to knowledge and the actions that individuals take to balance reason and desires as they adapt to ever-changing situations.

Pragmatism reflected US cultural concern with practicality, envisioning the mandate of scientific knowledge as directly enhancing wealth and progress. James obliged by uniting observable action with introspection of mental processes. In stressing the fluidity and totality of consciousness he prefigured Gestalt theorists' concern with conscious states and the knowledge they contain.

Then James shifted emphasis from pragmatism to *neorealism*, claiming that the empirical world is that which is perceived. For him, experience is ordered *and* chaotic, predictable *and* novel. He emphasized the value of "each individual's distinctive interests and point of view" (Leary, 1990b, p. 106) and held that the truth of psychologists' claims depends on all human experience not just sensory knowledge.

In the end James adopted *radical empiricism*, which subsumed pragmatism and neo-realism (E. Taylor, 1998). (Skinnerians will use the term radical empiricism quite differently – see Chapter 7.) Attempting to clarify the metaphysical foundation of his Psychology, James made direct experience primary (Farrell, 2011), stressing how matter and mind are only concepts generated by interpretations of experience. Thus, he focused on "the reality of experience" rather than, as most empiricists did, "the experience of reality" (D. Crosby & Viney, 1993, p. 103).

In rejecting absolutes, James understood the subjective self and the objective world as interconnected aspects of direct experience. Hence, radical empiricism placed him at odds with the naïve-realist assumption of objectivity undergirding natural-science Psychology. Yet during the 1990s, postmodernist psychologists adopted a standpoint similar to James's (see Chapter 12).

In sum, James transcended lab-based psychological inquiry and delved into all aspects of human life (Bjork, 1983). As a nineteenth-century scholar, he promoted consciousness of the self and moral individualism and advocated the rapprochement of science with art, religion, and spirituality. These inclinations endeared him to European psychologists, novelists, and philosophers. Furthermore, as an advocate of applied psychology, he "served as midwife to the birth of the new . . . therapeutic society" (Karier, 1986, p. 28).

Because James studied topics that stretched the boundaries of US natural-science Psychology, such as spiritualism, many peers dismissed him as once a psychologist and then a philosopher. Consequently, his durable impact on US Psychology was mixed (Croce, 2010). To some commentators James was inconsistent and contradictory in his views, while others regard him as dancing between rationalist (following Kant) and evolutionary (following Spencer) positions (E. Taylor, 1998). After *Principles*, James did recast his views on such phenomena as spatial perception, emotion, consciousness, and the self, informed by his philosophical reflections (D. Crosby & Viney, 1993; Farrell, 2011).

Section conclusion

Influenced by James's concepts, functionalists asked not what the mind contains, but how the mind works practically to enable the individual to adapt. Functional psychologists "addressed not only adaptation of individuals to environments but also differential adaptation [given that] some people seemed to adapt better than others to particular environments" (Landy, 1992, p. 788). Hugo Münsterberg exemplified this practical application of evolutionary theory's emphasis on individual differences (see Chapter 8).

Although there were precedents in European Psychology and in US philosophical and theological psychology, functionalism as a school of thought was quintessentially "American" in its basic notions. Moreover, it was considerably more popular among US psychologists than Titchener's structuralism.

Social practice

John Dewey was a functionalist and pragmatist who found the term "behaviour" problematic, because it excluded human agency; he preferred "conduct" (Barone, 1996). Accordingly, he termed his school of thought "social practice," meaning individuals' transactions with their social world. For him, Psychology consists of five facets: theory, laboratory science, applied science, social applications, and public policy.

Central to Dewey's epistemological standpoint is the dialectical unity of theory and practice and the importance of subjecting psychological investigation to what today is known as ecological validation. He stated, "While the psychological theory would guide and illuminate the practice, acting upon the theory would immediately test it, and thus criticize it, bringing about its revision and growth" (Dewey, 1900, p. 146).

Dewey strongly believed that Psychology should be problem-focused. He produced a major theory in educational psychology (see below) and advocated applying Psychology to society. Research in real-world settings was central in Dewey's vision. Furthermore, he stressed that psychologists should only use observations of consciousness as their data.

Development of artistic capacities has received short shrift from psychologists historically, although some early psychologists studied aesthetics empirically and Binet investigated the psychology of theatre acting. But Dewey specifically addressed ordinary people's abilities in varieties of artistic expression. In *Art as Experience*, Dewey (1933) asserted that society mistakenly regards art as the domain of special, talented people. Consequently, society has segregated artists into a minority of creators and so-called ordinary citizens or social actors into a majority of spectators. He advocated integrating the activities of the artist and the non-artist, postulating that everyone has the capacity to develop artistic capacities in some medium at least to some degree.

Section conclusion

Dewey understood mind in terms of consciousness and human agency, emphasizing the transactional nature of human experience. Mind consists of a personal system of beliefs, motives, and intentions that are the product of biological predispositions interacting with one's social environment. However, Dewey's psychological concepts and social applications were incongruent with his contemporaries. Thus, his approach did not inspire a theoretical system or a large following in Psychology despite his considerable influence on educational theory.

Self theory

A philosopher as well as psychologist, Mary Calkins (1910) attempted to reconcile functionalism with structuralism. She defined Psychology as "*the science of the self as conscious*" (p. 1) rather than merely the science of consciousness. For Calkins, the discipline's central fact was the conscious self in relationship to others. Therefore, the mere elements of consciousness, sensations, or behaviours cannot explain the self. She believed that lived experience of the self is not reducible to measurement of natural phenomena, such as the physical conditions of perception (Heidbreder, 1972).

After behaviourism supplanted functionalism (see Chapter 6), Calkins (1915) countered behaviourists' denial of the self by coining the term "psychological behaviorism" to integrate consciousness and behaviour within a theory of the self. She assumed that the self is the soul as a conscious being, which deserves scientific study. Therefore, investigators should focus, she argued, on studying individuals in relation to their social and physical environment.

Section conclusion

Swimming against the theoretical tide of contemporary US Psychology, Calkins intended to change the discipline's subject matter (Furumoto, 1991). She believed that experimental psychologists were out of touch with mundane experience that confirms the self's centrality. Thus, according to her, self psychology could accommodate any psychological meta-theory, including Gestalt theory and psychoanalysis (Heidbreder, 1972). But Calkins's school of thought had little impact in natural-science Psychology until feminist psychologists revived it as self-in-relation theory in the late twentieth century (see Chapter 12).

Hormic psychology

In *An Introduction to Social Psychology* (1908), which went through twenty-three editions, William McDougall addressed the broad spectrum of psychological processes. Intrigued by body–mind relations, his mission was to integrate physiological and comparative observations with introspective accounts and even life-after-death experiences within a total system of human nature (Innis, 2003). McDougall dubbed his orientation "hormic psychology," by which he meant purposeful striving.

McDougall proposed a new orientation of intelligent, goal-seeking behaviour for which he invoked the evolutionary principle of natural selection. He described all behaviour and experience in terms of the perceptual and behavioural components of numerous instincts, their associated emotions, and the learned sentiments (e.g., self-regard) that constitute an individual's personality. He stressed the important role of mental events, attributed intelligent purposiveness to animal behaviour, and championed goal-seeking as biologically energized by instincts.

Later, McDougall rejected reflex explanations of human behaviour. In his revised conception, the interaction of body and mind evokes behaviour, with human will and freedom of choice distinguishing the mind. Moreover, he explained the unity of conscious experience spiritually, and he believed that empirical data substantiated his defence of the soul as the ultimate source of behaviour and justified studying animism.

Section conclusion

In the UK, hormic psychology, along "with mental testing and psychoanalysis ... constituted the working capital for a generation of psychologists between the wars" (Hearnshaw, 1964, p. 195). McDougall's opposition to mechanism reflected the reservations that British psychologists had about behaviourism. Furthermore, he facilitated a positive reception for Freud's more enduring dynamic psychology of irrational processes. Yet to many, McDougall's metaphysical interpretations and study of extrasensory processes seemed scientifically regressive.

In addition, McDougall's defence of *eugenics* (i.e., belief in selective breeding and preventing parentage by the intellectually and morally unfit) evoked controversy in the USA to which he immigrated in 1920 (Innis, 2003). His insistence on the category of instincts after US psychologists had abandoned them also proved controversial. When he pursued his career-long interest in clairvoyance and telepathy with US psychologist **J. B. Rhine** (1895–1980), McDougall was far out of step with behaviourists (Asprem, 2010), who rejected the instinct concept and parapsychology, and with those psychologists who stressed the influence of culture on individuals (Joncich, 1968).

> **Small-group discussion.** Considering the above schools of thought (voluntarism, structuralism, reflexology, functionalism, social practice, self theory, and hormic psychology) explain which one or ones appeal to you and which do not.

Part 2 conclusion

When natural-science Psychology emerged as a formal scholarly discipline, it not only took diverse conceptual forms internationally and within nations, but it also gave birth to at least seven distinct schools of thought.

Since the twentieth century many psychologists have associated Wundt with studies of consciousness. Yet he conducted experimentation on sensory processes not for their own sake, but to answer philosophical questions about body–mind relations. It was Titchener's structuralism that concentrated on studies of the basic elements of consciousness. In Wundt's theoretical approach, known as voluntarism, the concept of voluntary activity explained higher-order mental processes.

The reflexology theorized by Sechenov and practised by Bekhterev and Pavlov also was diverse. Sechenov and Pavlov adhered to a basic reflexive explanation, while Bekhterev moved well beyond a simple reflex account of human thought, emotion, and action towards a metaphorical perspective on reflexes manifest in social and clinical applications. But later, Pavlov extended his notion of conditional reflexes to explain complex psychological phenomena.

Inspired by evolutionary theory, functionalist psychologists assumed that organisms emit mental processes and the function of consciousness is to guide their adaptation to the environment. Consequently, functionalists focused on the practical mental operations entailed in biological and mental development and on social reforms to enhance personal adjustment to society and ensure an efficient social order. Although originally involved with functionalism, James explored a wide range of human phenomena and infused US Psychology with philosophical depth in his turn toward pragmatism, neorealism, and then radical empiricism.

Another nonconforming functionalist, Dewey advanced Psychology as social practice, meaning human experience is transactional in nature. Thus, mental processes result from an individual's biological inclinations interacting with her or his social environment, and the relevant research data are observations of her or his consciousness. Dewey envisioned theory, laboratory and applied research, and applications to social settings and public policy as a totality.

In her approach to Psychology, self theory, Calkins centralized the conscious self in relationship to other individuals. Like Dewey, she advocated understanding individuals in relation to their social and physical environments. Calkins also endeavoured to integrate competing schools of thought, namely, consciousness with functionalism and then behaviourism.

Yet another grand theory was McDougall's hormic psychology in which he integrated evolutionary theory, physiology, and introspection of consciousness. He asserted that a wide range of instincts energized organisms' intelligent goal-seeking. But later, while retaining the notion of body–mind interaction, McDougall emphasized human will, freedom of choice, and the spiritual foundation of conscious experience, and investigated parapsychology.

Part 3 Basic psychological processes

Many early psychologists concentrated on sensory processes and consciousness, although a few also studied extrasensory perception and paranormal phenomena. Early psychologists also explored emotion, instincts, habits, learning, memory, thinking and problem-solving, mind in relation to physical movement and human will, and psychological development.

Sensory processes, consciousness, and extrasensory processes

German psychologists were committed to investigating the operations of sensory functions, within the context of the advanced state of German experimental physiology and physics. For them, the key to answering philosophical questions about body–mind relations lay in understanding sensory processes. Drawing from their philosophical heritage and experimental practice, some early psychologists attempted to describe consciousness. At that time, consciousness generally meant the mental processes associated with attention to and awareness of sensory stimuli, the first stage of perception; consciousness did not include thought processes per se. Thus, "consciousness" in this sense is not equivalent to the current term, "cognition."

Sensory processes

In psychophysics Georg Müller extended Gustav Fechner's research on threshold sensitivity and made adjustments to the normal curve representing psychophysical judgments (Haupt, 1998). Furthermore, Müller advanced an empirically based theory in a major work on colour vision to reconcile the theoretical debate between Hermann Helmholtz and Ewald Hering. Christine Ladd-Franklin (1929), who had studied with Müller, also synthesized the Helmholtz–Hering polarities. She proposed in 1892 that animals initially are colour-blind but develop colour vision over time as an evolutionary adaptation to enhance survival. Her theory explained colour-blindness and afterimages (Cadwallader & Cadwallader, 1990).

Some early psychologists studied auditory phenomena and other sensory modalities. For example, Carl Stumpf investigated tones and melody, the psychology of music, and musicology (Sprung & Sprung, 2000a). In works on acoustic perception, phonetics, and auditory pathology, he stressed theoretical foundations and proposed a theory of sensory discrimination.

Consciousness

For Wilhelm Wundt, consciousness included emotion and motivation. As noted above, he studied apperception, the psychophysiological process of assimilating and transforming new information in relation to existing information. Consciousness, Wundt reasoned, consists of the mind engaging in purposive activities. It is "governed by lower and higher principles of association and apperception" with "association as the principle underlying the reaction to one stimulus, and apperception as the principle underlying the reaction to two or more stimuli" (Woodward, 1982, p. 183).

For James, consciousness is explicable in terms of the evolutionary concepts of variation, selection, and function. Personal interest "directs attention, attention directs selection, and selection confers coherence on each level of psychological functioning," including a motoric component (Leary, 1992, pp. 156–157). Consciousness is inclined towards comparing and selecting simultaneous possibilities and solving problems. Human minds are biological tools of survival, enhancing adaptation to the environment. Thus, individuals' central reality is learning to adapt to constant change.

According to James, consciousness is personal, continuous, indivisible, selective, and purposeful. Extending the concept of consciousness, he held that the basis of mental life is consciousness of thinking and feeling, akin to René Descartes' *cogito*. Any speculations about psychological functions have to arise from this experiential foundation (Leary, 2003). Moreover, consciousness and thinking processes constitute a metaphorical stream of thoughts, images, and feelings, constantly refreshing themselves; consciousness encompasses all of one's subjective experience, not just thoughts. Thus, James argued, biology is a necessary but insufficient explanation of consciousness.

By contrast, as described earlier, Edward Titchener viewed the mind as comprising conscious sensory elements only and assumed that a combination of elementary units constitutes mental content. An associationist, he reduced sensations to distinct, enumerable elements, supplemented by neurophysiological explanations. What he called "content processes" (i.e., sensations, images, and feelings) convey meaning. For Titchener, consciousness is the sum total of a person's experiences at one point in time, whereas mind is the sum of conscious moments across the individual's life-span.

Extrasensory processes

During Psychology's founding decades the public remained infatuated with extrasensory perception, including hypnotic states, telepathy, and communication with "spirits" of deceased individuals. Most natural-science psychologists, however, refused to study extrasensory processes for fear of compromising their new science (Coon, 1992). Undaunted, William James incorporated findings from investigations of psychic phenomena in his theorizing about consciousness (B. Ross, 1991; E. Taylor, 1998). He also supported studying unconscious processes in artistic creativity and religious and mystical experience (Bjork, 1983). In the 1890s he and James Cattell argued over the scientific validity of psychic phenomena.

Meanwhile, Julian Ochorowicz (1850–1917), who initiated Polish Psychology, studied spiritualism, telepathy, and hypnosis (Chlewinski, 1976). In addition, Dutch psychologist **Gerardus Heymans** (1857–1930) experimented on visual illusions and telepathy (Strien, 1997). As noted above, William McDougall and J. B. Rhine investigated clairvoyance and telepathy. But the findings from these inquiries did not change extant natural-science explanations of sensory processes and consciousness fundamentally.

Emotion

Stressing the important role of behaviour in emotion, James held that in the face of perceived emotionally arousing situations an individual acts first and then feels afraid. Awareness of bodily responses evokes the associated emotion not the reverse; emotion consists of the feeling of bodily changes. Thus, the experience of emotion includes motoric, physiological, and psychological aspects. Accordingly, James advised people to act the way they want to feel. His notion that action precedes emotion aroused in a perceived situation became a key principle of behaviourism and cognitive behaviour therapy.

A Danish physiologist, Carl Lange (1834–1900), proposed a very similar explanation, hence the two proposals became known as the James–Lange theory. This theory is important, because it relied on neurophysiological evidence to explain a psychological phenomenon and led to decades of investigations on the physiology of emotion (D. N. Robinson, 1995).

In later modifications James clarified that the total stimulus situation arouses motoric responses. Different contextual circumstances will give rise to different responses. Secondly, individuals can exercise intentional ("cognitive") control over their emotions. Current psychologists similarly stress the relationship among emotion, cortical processes, the limbic system (i.e., emotional centre) in the brain, and cognitive appraisal.

Instincts, habits, and learning

McDougall gave "instincts" a prominent role in Psychology. But his peers favoured the categories of "habit" and "learning," although they agreed with him that evolution established biological boundaries around behaviour. For instance, James acknowledged that human functioning originates in animal ancestry and that humans have the greatest number of instincts of all creatures. But, James argued, habits derive from experience and modulate instincts' expression. Thus, he treated evolution metaphorically as suggestive of natural and experiential processes rather than as definitive statements about fixed biological realities (Leary, 2003).

In addition, James believed that the brain acquires habits, which are the consequence of repeated transmission over neural pathways. Habits serve adaptive functions and contribute to learning. Thus, "proper" habit formation is conducive to character formation and essential for education, and by exercising human will individuals establish good habits of thought and work.

Dewey's social perspective on habits included their functional nature. But he added the notion that habits were transactions between individuals and their social contexts. For him, habits were actions in the material world (Brinkmann, 2011a). Soon, however, Edward Thorndike's concept of learning supplanted instincts and habits.

Thorndike's learning theory

Thorndike began his lengthy career in the 1890s conducting quantitative experiments on animal learning. Using a replicable and controlled experimental procedure developed in his PhD research, he enclosed hungry cats, dogs, and chicks in puzzle boxes that required two consecutive responses for their escape and food-reward. Observing trial-and-error attempts to escape, Thorndike interpreted his data (e.g., learning speed) as evidence for associationist learning and against animal intelligence, insight, or imitation. According to his "connectionism," intelligence is the ability to form connections in the brain.

Thorndike's **assumptions** about how all species learn were:

- Human cognitive capacities extend from animal capacities.
- Increasing the quantity and "complexity of associations between sense impressions and impulses" (Joncich, 1968, p. 267) produces complex intellectual processes.

Thorndike's laws of learning explain the learned behaviour and purposeful activity of any species (Tomlinson, 1997). According to his *law of effect*, responses leading to pleasure are "stamped in" incrementally, strengthening connections; he termed this observation "reinforcement." He proposed but later abandoned the view that responses leading to annoyance or pain, what others termed "punishment," weaken connections.

With his *law of exercise* Thorndike proposed that repeating a response (i.e., habit) strengthens associations; the greater the repetition, the greater the learning. Conversely, decreased responding weakens connections. He abandoned this law too, because he found that repetition alone was insufficient and lack of exercise did not weaken associations.

Concerning human learning, Thorndike (1931) stated, "Higher animals, including man, manifest no behavior beyond exception from the laws of instinct, exercise, and effect" (p. 122). For him, the association of stimulus–response habits in lower mammals explains human thinking. Nevertheless, Thorndike held that more sophisticated intelligence requires a greater number of connections, just as brighter people possess a greater number of connections than other people (Sternberg, 2003).

Thorndike's position that simple learning explained complex learning was the foundation for John Watson's stimulus–response behaviourism, while his theory of connectionism was the basis for B. F. Skinner's operant-conditioning model and concept of "reinforcement" modifying behaviour. But, unlike Watson and Skinner, Thorndike never rejected introspective methods for studying the role of consciousness in human learning. Moreover, he shifted to investigating human individual differences, intelligence, and learning and to developing tests of intelligence, achievement, and vocational ability (Joncich, 1968; R. Thorndike, 1991).

Many US psychologists adopted Thorndike's experimental exemplar of maze learning, because it requires motor activity, which reduces learning to an identical operation for animals and humans. But later psychologists questioned whether reward and punishment are necessary for learning, what the components of reward and punishment are that affect learning, and whether associations are formed immediately or gradually (Leahey, 2003).

Animal mind

Thorndike regarded animals as essentially mindless. But Margaret Washburn explored how animals' behaviour affects their conscious states. In her 1908 book, *The Animal Mind*, she contributed to the field of *comparative psychology* (i.e., behavioural and animal-cognition experimentation from an evolutionary perspective) in an era when few psychologists, other than Thorndike and Watson, conducted animal research. In later editions, Washburn (1936) integrated studies of animal behaviour, perception, emotion, and cognitive processes. She studied lower-order and higher-order animals' ability to discriminate various senses and to create associations and remember (M. Martin, 1940).

Adopting a colleague's notion of "ejective consciousness," similar to the current concept of *theory of mind*, Washburn recommended combining naturalistic observation with experimentation to best understand how animals attain awareness of other animals' thinking. But because behaviourism and most forms of neobehaviourism, which excluded mental processes, dominated US psychology, animal cognition did not emerge as an accepted domain of interest until the 1980s (Baenninger, 1990).

In the clash between structuralism (i.e., the science of consciousness) and behaviourism (i.e., the science of behaviour), Washburn developed a theoretical integration that she believed could advance Psychology beyond the polarized positions of Titchener and Watson. Washburn introduced the notion of kinaesthetic processes and consciousness in relationship to animals' higher-order mental processes.

She viewed introspection as an objective method that provides invaluable information about kinaesthetic processes of interest to behaviourists. For Washburn, psychologists employing diverse methods of introspection could accurately access individuals' descriptions of inner experience (Viney & Burlingame-Lee, 2003). But given most contemporary US psychologists' concentration on stimulus–response connections, her theoretical integration was ignored.

Memory

According to Wundt, memory is a relatively insignificant phenomenon and unsuited to experimentation (Danziger, 2008). Moreover, he opposed compartmentalizing particular psychological functions (e.g., memory) that one experiences in their totality (e.g., remembering). For him, the concepts that psychologists attributed to specific human psychological processes did not capture the quality of experience.

Hermann Ebbinghaus, Georg Müller, and Mary Calkins experimented on memory functions, although differently. The prototype of the modern natural-science psychologist minimizing theory and maximizing facts, Ebbinghaus emulated Gustav Fechner's quantitative self-experimentation. He invented nonsense syllables, which he presumed were meaningless, to control precise variations of stimuli and measured the time to recall them. He also studied relearning, practice styles, list length, primacy and recency effects, and fatigue effects.

Ebbinghaus is credited with discovering the usefulness of "over-learning" (i.e., repeated practice of correct recall beyond a single instance) and the effects of sensible versus nonsensical memory and graphed the first curve of memory-retention (Postman, 1969). Some cognitive psychologists perceive continuity between his work and theirs in that he measured the systematic effects of independent variables on behaviour, supported by statistics, and claimed discovery of laws governing memory.

The Ebbinghaus exemplar of memory experimentation rested on **five assumptions**:

- Memory is "a transaction between a single individual and an objective reality outside the individual" (Danziger, 2008, p. 214).
- Memory is separate from perceptual processes.
- It consists solely of memorizing, which operates as a more or less reliable copying tool and entails mental search of stored memory-traces for recovery.
- One measures memory in terms of accurately reproducing bits of impersonal information.
- Experimental lab results explain universal laws of memory in everyday life.

For Ebbinghaus, memory consisted of the formation of associations and meant simple retention of objectively performed tasks. Thus, he studied memory by exposing socially isolated individuals to "objective" stimuli and then assessing accuracy of recall. In effect, he removed meaning from the retention processes of everyday life; memory of language, for instance, is culturally embedded (Danziger, 2008).

Methodologically, Ebbinghaus's research participants apparently "privately turned nonsense into meaning by various strategies" (Leahey, 2003, p. 118). Furthermore, investigators employing his exemplar seem to ignore how individuals interpret the stimuli and consciously experience remembering, and how investigators' construction of an artificial experimental situation constrains interpretations of memory (Danziger, 2008).

By contrast, Müller observed that memory entailed complex processes. When he incorporated introspective accounts of participants' experimental experiences, he found they engaged in a wide variety of conscious strategies, such as rhythmical grouping, to make the memory task meaningful and improve their retention. Müller also proposed an early interference theory by which psychologists explain forgetting as a result of interference from other memories, and he explored retrieval processes that later psychologists called retroactive inhibition, proactive inhibition, and consolidation (Haupt, 1998).

Methodologically, Müller standardized nonsense syllables of relatively equivalent difficulty. Furthermore, he mechanized the Ebbinghaus method by co-inventing the revolving memory drum to uniformly present syllables successively rather than simultaneously (Sprung & Sprung, 2000b). Eventually computerization replaced this widely adopted machine.

Taking a different tack, Calkins experimented on the conditions of association in consciousness (S. Madigan & O'Hara, 1992). Addressing short-term memory functions, she researched the effects of primacy, recency, frequency, and vividness, finding that frequency had the most influence on associations. She also invented a prototype for the technique of paired associates, long used in memory research, and described the influence of distracting activities on recency, currently known as serial-position effects.

Thinking and problem-solving

For many early psychologists, research on cognitive operations had social applications useful for teachers, physicians, and judges. To understand thinking processes practically, Alfred Binet studied "typical children and adults; children and adults with varying degrees of mental retardation; residents in mental hospitals; experts at chess and mental calculation; and professional actors, directors, authors and artists" (Siegler, 1992, p. 179). Emphasizing individual differences and mental testing in studies of children, he took a clinical approach to intellectual processes. He understood intelligence as a process of reconstructing one's world through perceptions.

Other Europeans also studied higher mental processes. In Germany, at Oswald Külpe's Würzburg School, investigators conducted research on "mental set" (i.e., readiness to respond to certain stimuli in a particular way), on the motive to persevere until a solution is found, and on imageless hesitation in thinking and judgment. The Würzburg School focused on how the mind works rather than its contents (Mack, 1997). A debate ensued with Titchener and others over the possibility of imageless thought, as recounted in Box 5.1.

Box 5.1 **The imageless-thought debate**

The Würzburg School believed that lower and higher mental processes differed quantitatively not qualitatively. Focusing on meaning, they introduced a new methodology,
documenting an observer's immediate, retrospective self-observation (i.e., describing
experiences of thinking after their occurrence) in the presence of an experimenter. The
Würzburg School concluded that thoughts that are not complex can occur without
sensory, affective, or imagery content; hence, they established the notion of "imageless
thought" (Lindenfield, 1978).

The ensuing intercontinental debate over imageless thought contained important questions for natural-science psychologists: what is the nature of thought? Is it accessible to
observation through introspection or retrospection? Might thinking occur outside awareness? What is the role of experimentation in psychology? What are the differences
between the natural and the social sciences (Kusch, 1999)?

The debate hastened the demise of Titchener's structuralism, because many peers
concluded that experimenter expectations biased his introspective method. In response,
Titchener asserted that imageless thought is reducible to observable sensory elements,
whereas, he asserted, the Würzburg School conflated meaning with images.

Wundt and Müller also opposed the Würzburg School's position. For Wundt, imageless
content of consciousness does not exist and the Würzburg School's method of retrospection is unreliable and susceptible to bias. For Müller, laws of association, which explain
the strength of connections between objects in consciousness, and the law of persevera-
tion, which explains the tendency of objects to remain in consciousness, explain the
Würzburg School's findings.

The debate also encompassed social-institutional matters, such as how leadership of
psychological research should be organized, hierarchically (Müller, Titchener, and Wundt)
or collectively (the Würzburg School). Moreover, Wundt insisted that Psychology was a
theoretical, *human* science, far from ready for social applications. But the Würzburg School
held that Psychology was a *natural* science; aspects of it were reducible to physiology; and
Psychology should be applied to mental health, forensics, and education.

In US Psychology, Dewey understood thinking as problem-solving that encompassed
habitual perceptions of the world and bodily action as well as reflection. Accordingly, for
him, thinking is "what the organism does when it reflects intelligently" (Brinkmann, 2011a,
p. 308). The human mind is inextricably connected with one's transactions with social
contexts.

Mind and movement, and human will

Eighteenth-century philosophers had divided psychological capacities into three dimensions: feeling, thinking, and *conation* (i.e., expressing an intention, leading to motoric
activity). Dewey's understanding of thinking as embodied, for example, reflected this
conceptual tradition. When some contemporaries studied mind–body relations, they also

perceived links between mental processes and motoric activity in humans and other animals.

Expressing an intention is a behavioural manifestation of human will. But by World War I, terms used in US Psychology that connoted scientific validity and moral neutrality (e.g., motive) soon replaced terms that carried strong moral connotations (e.g., human will) (Danziger, 1997b).

Mind and movement

Theodule Ribot's conception of body–mind relations included consciousness, thinking, and memory (Guillin, 2004). He stressed the intimate complementarity between the physical and the psychological. Thus, for him, thinking always tends towards muscular activity, and motoric action evokes feelings.

Echoing Ribot, James (1892) insisted that "*All mental states . . . are followed by bodily activity of some sort . . . all* states of mind, even mere thoughts and feelings, are *motor* in their consequences . . ." (p. 5, emphasis in original). Whether the motoric activity is conspicuous or not, it occurs bodily. Thinking correlates with brain processes.

Charles Sherrington explored the behavioural significance of posture and muscle-tone. He claimed that "attitude is as significant as action, psychologically as well as neurologically" (Hearnshaw, 1964, p. 80). He described muscular feedback mechanisms, introducing the term "proprioceptive" concerning muscular regulation. For him, all behaviour, including cognitive processes, is rooted in integrated motor activity and occurs neurologically. Frederic Bartlett built his influential psychological account of thinking on Sherrington's foundation (Thomson, 1968).

Initially, Hugo Münsterberg explored the connection between mind and movement. Assuming that measurable physiological events accompany and explain mental events (Hale, 1980), he investigated individual differences in the physiology of consciousness. In his "action theory" he stressed that muscular stimulation and activity produce perception and consciousness, while subsequent motoric responses modify consciousness (Landy, 1992). For Münsterberg, individuals perceive what they are prepared to enact. This principle was the basis for his applied psychology (see Chapter 8).

In response to Titchener and Münsterberg debating mind–body relations, Margaret Washburn (1916) also used bodily movement as a central concept. She held that all animals are fundamentally locomotor beings that respond to perceptions through movement. Thinking entails muscle movement, she argued, and somatic postures and mental processes are evidenced by animals' movements.

Washburn examined the relationship of motor responses to stimuli by way of consciousness and imagery. She postulated that bodily movement links consciousness, including mental imagery, with behaviour, while images are conscious mental events, originating in movement. Thus, external behaviour and complex mental processes are interrelated.

For Washburn, only a unified theory incorporating motoric responses can account for perception, emotion, learning, and thinking. Thus, she integrated overt behaviour and covert perception, emotion, imagery, and thought, prefiguring cognitive behaviourism. Like Mary Calkins, she stressed conceptual complexity and inclusiveness. Washburn's standpoint also prefigures "psychology of action" in current cognitive neuroscience.

Human will

According to Wundt's school of thought, thinking and feeling are synthesized in willing, which is the main impetus of behaviour. His notion of volitional control refers not to "free will" philosophically or theologically but to one's general system of emotions, motives, and automatic processes (Blumenthal, 1998). Wundt assumed that central processes of selective volitional attention control psychological functions (Blumenthal, 1975).

James offered a different explanation of will, proposing that it is the crucial link between body and mind. He argued that, given a particular object in consciousness, first reflexive brain action occurs, followed by emphasizing and selecting certain content over other content, then thinking and intending. Out of one's stream of consciousness an individual compares possibilities and chooses an action, mediated by selection and inhibition (Rychlak, 1993).

For James, will is related to the selective functions of consciousness (Leary, 2003). Intentionally selecting what one thinks by engaging in deliberate attention, he argued, can change one's behaviour and counteract powerful habits. Furthermore, choosing and willing are connected to the view that individuals who express their "free will" behave as if they believe in it. But James's vague attempts to explain the relationship among impulses, emotion, and will were difficult to investigate experimentally. Consequently, his experimental peers dismissed his approach as untestable, hence unscientific (Danziger, 1980).

Developmental processes

The current term "developmental psychology" refers not just to a subdiscipline of Psychology but to a broad orientation to the subject matter. Arguably, developmental psychology serves as a scientific intersection for Psychology's many subdisciplines. Inherited disposition and environmental conditions converge in the development of psychological processes. Although originally children were the focus, developmentalists study all psychological phenomena across the life-span and from the biological to the interpersonal. Moreover, developmentalists' findings are applicable to education, child welfare, and other social institutions, thereby enhancing Psychology's societal value. Initially, however, developmental psychology played a minor role in the discipline's growth.

European origins

Discussion about the characteristics of children and how to treat them was prominent in early modern Europe. By the late nineteenth century, treatises on education and childcare were common. In addition, formal biographical accounts of individual infants and children, typically the authors' own children, were popular. Early developmental research focused on educational and social relations of children. Although some European researchers experimented with children, investigators favoured naturalistic case-study research and theorizing, which US psychologists viewed skeptically.

Wundt did not engage in child study, but he theorized that drive was the "'fundamental psychic phenomenon from which all mental development originates'" (Blumenthal, 1985, p. 25). Furthermore, he argued, children are born with innate abilities of expression that become more differentiated with experience, resulting in volitional action. Activity is constantly goal-directed, necessary for achieving a certain affective outcome. Wundt also held that "automatized processes (complex unconscious controls) are the result of a progressive development that occurs as organisms become more complex" (Blumenthal, 1985, p. 82).

By conceptual contrast, a British scholar in Germany, **William Preyer** (1841–1897), applied social Darwinist interpretations to detailed observations of young children's sensory and cognitive processes, including language (Jaeger, 1982). He searched for patterns of reflexes in human infants. Preyer's 1882 book on children was so popular that it received nine German editions and was translated into English, French, and Russian. His line of research also influenced Watson's initial behavioural research on infants (O'Donnell, 1985).

Meanwhile, Binet emphasized the role of individual differences in children's capacities to express their intellectual potential (Sternberg & Jarvin, 2003). He first employed a physical-anthropological, hereditarian explanation of that potential. But eventually he regarded sociocultural considerations and educational programmes as more influential in shaping intellectual development (Staum, 2007).

US origins

The European discourse on education and childcare influenced thinkers in the US (e.g., German-style kindergartens). The US child-study and childcare movements of the late nineteenth and twentieth centuries also strengthened public concern about child welfare and sensitized US scientists and professionals to developmental issues. In 1917, the Iowa Child Welfare Research Station became the foundational centre for child study.

Two individuals made noteworthy contributions to early developmental psychology in the US: Stanley Hall and Mark Baldwin.

Stanley Hall As a "genetic" (i.e., developmental) psychologist, Hall advocated the concept of *recapitulation*. This is the idea that individuals across their life-span repeat the evolutionary stages of development of the entire human race. As expressed in the German zoologist Ernst Haeckel's (1834–1919) statement, "ontogeny recapitulates phylogeny," human development proceeds from fish to amphibians to birds to mammals. However, the recapitulation concept lost credibility after World War I (Youniss, 2006).

As children proceed from primitive to civilized functioning, Hall asserted, "older areas of the brain mature before evolutionary newer areas" (White, 1992, p. 28). In his child-study research he aimed to catalogue the development of behavioural traits and explain individual differences by appealing to heredity. For him, instinct links biological endowment with psychological processes.

Hall and his colleagues at Clark University substantially contributed to developmental psychology. With educational collaborators (e.g., principals, teachers, and mothers) Hall observed everyday behaviour to study children's thinking, emotions, dreams, and religious experience. He also relied on questionnaire data. Most of his peers, however, did not consider this programme genuinely scientific. The more "objective" quantitative approach of the mental-testing movement in the 1920s eventually replaced it.

Hall also initiated the category of "adolescence," viewing it as a unique stage of strong psychological polarities, determined by evolution, in which depression, delinquency, and cravings for new sensations are common (D. Ross, 1972). Moreover, he introduced the developmental psychology of aging.

Mark Baldwin The second instigator of developmental inquiry in the USA, Mark Baldwin also applied Darwin's ideas to mental processes (Cairns, 1992; Wozniak, 1998). Rejecting introspective psychology as asocial, Baldwin studied individual differences in the developing mind, the structure of intelligence, and general developmental mechanisms. He emphasized the origins of mental functions in children's interactions with their interpersonal environments.

Baldwin authored books describing children's intellectual and social development, supported by observational data. He postulated four stages of cognitive and interpersonal development whereby fundamental reorganization of children's intellectual abilities occurs.

According to Baldwin, the evolutionary concepts of variation and selection provide the platform on which the development of knowledge unfolds. Infant survival and development are contingent upon **two mechanisms**:

• Imitating others, primarily parents, in habitual patterns.
• Accommodating their actions to environmental changes.

Baldwin extended his biosocial theory of mind to childhood socialization mediated by imitation and to social adaptation. After he immigrated to France, his work influenced Jean Piaget's conceptions of cognitive development. Furthermore, Lev Vygotsky acknowledged Baldwin's influence on his own theorizing (see Chapter 6).

Educational applications

In Europe, James Sully founded the British Child Study Association in 1893 to investigate children's mental characteristics and published the first scientific book in England on child development. Sully's approach included practical applications for schools and teachers (N. Rose, 1985). In France, Binet was similarly involved, experimenting on effective classroom instruction (Sternberg & Jarvin, 2003).

Although German psychologist **Ernst Meumann** (1862–1915) investigated memory, attention, embodied emotion, intelligence, and will in relation to personality, and aesthetics (Stoerring, 1923), he also contributed to experimental education and school reform. His publications, integrating experimental psychology, human learning, and educational applications, were well received internationally. His educational interests encompassed intelligence testing, memory practice, instruction in reading and writing, and the mental health of students and teachers (Probst, 1997).

A Polish psychologist, **Jan Władysław Dawid** (1859–1914) systematically observed children's development with an elaborate questionnaire and created a measure of children's intelligence in 1911 that Polish practitioners employed for fifty years. He pursued educational psychology, contributed to Polish educational reform, and emphasized teachers' spiritual sensitivity to pupils' feelings as well as to their thinking (Kupisiewicz, 1993).

In the US child-study movement school principals, teachers, and mothers collaborated with social scientists in studying child development. Hall was a central figure in this movement, investigating curriculum development, pedagogical methods, and the professionalization of teachers (Brooks-Gunn & Johnson, 2006). During the 1890s his reliance on data from questionnaires and contributions to the child-study movement proved very popular with school administrators and teachers. Despite questionable research (D. Ross, 1972), Hall influenced US education and policies on child and adolescent development. Dewey and Thorndike did as well, although they disagreed with one another in theory and practice, as explained in Box 5.2.

Box 5.2 Different approaches to education

At Chicago, Dewey founded an experimental grade school to test his beliefs about child development and education (E. Cahan, 1992). This "lab" was the basis for his educational theory and practice, while he focused on transforming schools into a system of democracy in action. Dewey advocated *progressive education*, that is, learning through active participation rather than rote learning in which students regurgitate what their teachers "feed" them. For him, conventional schools inhibit actualizing human potential, whereas "experiential learning" in progressive education prepares students to adapt.

Dewey (1909) argued that teachers should foster the integration of intellectual and emotional interests in their students. Students, in turn, need moral values for cooperative social relations to adapt well in their community. But without group-centred, interpersonal education, moral judgment will not develop fully. Thus, educators should nurture social intelligence. The current notion of "emotional intelligence" is indebted to Dewey (Goleman, 1995).

His student-centred approach proved very influential in educational theory. Like Hall, Dewey promoted respect for children's natural development by encouraging free activity in the classroom, learning by doing, and practical training. Unlike Hall, he believed that children's intellectual capacities were malleable (D. Ross, 1972). Dewey's theory proved quite influential.

But in educational *practice* Thorndike's administrative-centred model of directive education based on rote acquisition of habits prevailed. For him, educational psychology was as inclusive as general psychology in researching learning, motivation, and intelligence. Thorndike measured achievement and intelligence and produced seminal educational-psychology textbooks (Joncich, 1968). He applied his learning theory to education by combining the study of sensation with the study of motoric responses into a single quantifiable unit.

In 1901, Thorndike and **Robert Woodworth** (1869–1962) experimentally showed that "transfer of training" (learned information) depended on the degree of similarity in elements between one task and another. As a result, they debunked educators' belief in the value of classical disciplines for "exercising the mind" and developing critical thinking. Thereafter, public educators shifted to practical tasks transferable to job situations, and classical education declined (Karier, 1986).

Moreover, Thorndike promoted "educational tracking" (segregated schooling on the basis of ability). Following Francis Galton, he believed that intelligence was primarily inherited. He argued that elementary and secondary schools should teach practical knowledge and skills useful to occupations. As an advocate of "measurable behavioral objectives" (Karier, 1986 p. 97), his textbooks, tests, manuals, research, and consulting helped to shape an educational model of preparing a malleable workforce to serve bureaucratic efficiency.

Thorndike's mission was to demonstrate that Psychology could operationalize the goals of public education. He was more cautious about the scientific foundations of his applications and enjoyed a stronger reputation in educational circles than Hall (D. Ross, 1972). Furthermore, he had a more direct impact on mainstream teachers and administrators than Dewey (Karier, 1986). Thorndike's model came to dominate policy and practice in US public education.

Part 3 conclusion

Early psychologists studied a range of simple and complex phenomena. Many research programmes involved experimentation on consciousness of sensory functions. Müller examined psychophysical judgments, while he and Ladd-Franklin independently proposed solutions to theorizing colour vision. Stumpf investigated sensory discrimination and auditory perception.

Consciousness for many simply meant awareness of sensory stimuli. For Titchener, consciousness included sensory elements only and was the total of one's experiences. But Wundt relied on association and apperception to explain how we assimilate and transform new information. For James, consciousness enables the comparison and selection of simultaneous possibilities and problem-solving. Like James, Heymans and McDougall studied extrasensory perception, but their inquiries did not alter the dominant materialist view of sensory processes.

The primary perspective on emotions originally was the James–Lange theory. In this view, emotions consist of the sensations of bodily changes and follow actions. Later, James inserted what today we term "cognitive appraisal" of situations that arouse emotions. He also added the potential for intentional control of emotions, a position Baruch Spinoza had taken.

Impressed by evolution, many early psychologists, such as McDougall, invoked instincts to explain behaviour. James accepted instincts, but favoured habits formed from experience, while Dewey understood habits as social transactions. But Thorndike, developing learning theory, insisted that the reinforcement of learned connections explained even the most complex phenomena. By contrast, Washburn held that many species possessed higher-order mental processes; however, her US peers did not embrace the now accepted notion of animal cognition.

Ebbinghaus established the tradition of studying memory as mechanical acquisition of isolated functions, abstracted from complex mental processes and social context. Within this tradition Calkins studied various aspects of short-term memory. Müller, however, accounted for how research participants used conscious strategies to make experimental tasks meaningful and facilitate recall. But investigating memory as contextualized meaning embedded in everyday retention did not occur until Frederic Bartlett's experiments in the 1930s.

Early psychologists adopted different standpoints on thinking and problem-solving. For Wundt, mental content was primary, accessible only by qualitative methods, and insufficiently understood for social applications. But Külpe and Müller were interested in mental operations, employed quantitative experimentation to study them, and advocated practical applications from their research programmes. Binet had a similar practical orientation but employed a clinical research method. For Dewey, thinking and problem-solving represented an embodied transaction with one's social world, such as in educational situations.

Indebted to Ribot, James emphasized how thinking leads to motoric activity. This popular notion received physiological support from Sherrington and psychological support from both Bartlett and Washburn, who observed how bodily movement is linked to animals' consciousness. Münsterberg showed how human motoric responses modify consciousness. Although central in philosophy, human will soon petered out in Psychology. Wundt regarded will as selective volitional attention, which for him is the control centre for psychological processes. James understood will as a process of intentional selection, animated by conscious attention.

Concerning development, Preyer observed young children's sensory and cognitive processes, Binet examined individual differences in children's abilities to realize their intellectual potential, Hall proposed the category of adolescence, and Baldwin explained cognitive development in terms of imitation and accommodation. Many psychologists applied developmental concepts to education, while Dewey and Thorndike debated styles of pedagogy.

Part 4 | Interpersonal processes

We turn now to describing how early psychologists understood interpersonal processes. These phenomena include individual differences in character (or "personality," as we say today), the nature of the self, and the individual's relation to others and society. In explaining interpersonal phenomena, many psychologists drew from extant ideas in the emergent social sciences and in the humanities rather than from physiology and evolutionary biology. But the formal subdisciplines of personality and social psychology did not emerge until after World War I.

Personality perspectives

Some historians claim that personality theory originates in Franz Gall's phrenology. But among Psychology's founders Theodule Ribot also took a strong biomedical approach to personality differences, characterizing them in terms of psychological pathology and deviance from the norm (i.e., disordered individuals, "primitive" people, and children). Furthermore, Ribot adopted neurological ideas from Hughlings Jackson to support his focus on pathological processes in memory (e.g., amnesia), will, and personality (Danziger, 2008).

The personalist orientation of German philosopher and human-science psychologist **William Stern** (1871–1938) strongly influenced later US psychologist **Gordon Allport** (1897–1967). In 1900, Stern introduced a differential psychology encompassing the individual's total personality. Although he initiated systematic quantitative research on personality, he qualitatively studied how a person's psychological characteristics are organized in a totality unique to that person. For Stern, psychometric study of individual differences was an unsatisfactory solution to the problem of individuality (Lamiell, 1996).

Stern approached personality as a dialectical relationship between individuals and their environment, aiming to understand human nature in real-life situations. He also promoted the concepts of a unified personality and human will and emphasized higher motives towards spiritual transcendence. Stern theorized that individuals' self-focused goals of personal maintenance and development should be moderated by spiritual goals. These higher goals link individuals' personal goals to their family relations, ethnocultural niche, humankind, and a divine being.

By contrast, Gerardus Heymans studied inherited personality quantitatively (Strien, 1997). To depict the characteristics of individuality he designed a personality typology and questionnaire measuring three dimensions of personality: emotionality, activity, and secondary cerebral functions. Each dimension had positive and negative poles, resulting in eight different types. Known as "Heymans's Cube," the typology popularized Psychology in the Netherlands (Dehue, 1995) and later influenced the personality model of German–British psychologist **Hans Eysenck** (1916–1997).

The self

Among the early psychologists who explored the psychological category of the self, William James and Mary Calkins are noteworthy.

James discussed the self in relation to psychic phenomena and religion as well as psychological categories (Leary, 1990b). In his *Principles*, he viewed the self in terms of "me" and "I." The "I" or pure ego is the self as thinker that directs knowing the "me" or the empirical self. The "me" consists of **three dimensions**:

- The material self includes one's body, family, and possessions.
- The social self is the dimension that others observe but that varies with each observer.
- The spiritual self includes the individual's subjective experience of reality and consciousness of oneself as a thinker yet is rooted in the individual's physical experience.

James (1892) formulated self-esteem as "determined by the ratio of our actualities to our potentialities" (p. 187): self-esteem equals successes divided by pretensions. He also described mutations and multiplications of the self, discussing abnormal states, altered personalities, and possession by spirits. Furthermore, he understood the self as embedded in a network of relationships. When he characterized the self as transcendentally linked to others' consciousness, this notion went beyond the pale of legitimacy for natural-science psychologists.

Like James, Calkins argued that the self was unique to the individual, inherent in every experience, and subject to contextual influences. For her, the self only exists within relationships; in effect, if there is no relatedness, there is no self (Bohan, 2002). Her theory paved the way for current self-in-relation theory and resembles postmodern ideas on the self.

Calkins also invested her self theory with spiritual and moral themes (Wentworth, 1999). Awareness of oneself in relation to others evokes not just social but moral consciousness without which relationships are problematic. Thus, awareness of one's relationships implies ethical consciousness. In this way, Calkins echoed Enlightenment philosophers.

Social perspectives

Early psychologists' conceptions of social behaviour stemmed from diverse eighteenth- and nineteenth-century social philosophies (G. Jahoda, 2007). In a famous 1896 book, *The Crowd*, French author Gustave Le Bon (1841–1931) speculated about mob effects (G. Richards, 2010). In addition, William McDougall claimed that social behaviour was rooted in instincts, while Sigmund Freud ([1921] 1955) described group psychology, including horde effects, in terms of individual unconscious processes.

Adopting a biosocial orientation, Vladimir Bekhterev conducted experiments on group behaviour, termed "collective reflexology" (Budilova, 1984). He studied the influence of communication patterns on the collective action and decision-making of military groups. Stressing the notion of a collective mind, he concluded that group processes can have facilitative or inhibiting effects on individuals.

In Britain, **Graham Wallas** (1858–1932) helped to establish social psychology with a 1908 book in which he used stimulus–response terminology to systematically describe individuals in society. But he also was concerned with individuals' perceived meaning of social situations, thinking and feeling, and the influence of societal organizations on individuals (Hearnshaw, 1964).

The founders of US psychology addressed social phenomena in similar ways to each other. James stressed the plurality of the social self, Mark Baldwin insisted that the individual is fundamentally a social product (Morawski & Bayer, 2003), and John Dewey regarded social psychology as a domain straddling sociology and Psychology (R. Smith, 1997). Similarly, sociologist George Herbert Mead (1863–1931) viewed all psychological categories, including biologically based activity, as socially rooted; for him, society precedes individuals.

Cultural psychology

Since the 1860s Wilhelm Wundt had discussed how to scientifically study the developmental laws of language, myth, and custom (G. Jahoda, 2007). In fact, some contemporaries (e.g., Johann Herbart) focused on the intersection between mind and culture. At the end of his career Wundt systematically addressed this intersection in his ten-volume opus *Völkerpsychologie*. This title often is translated as "cultural psychology," but the term "communal spirit" might better reflect Wundt's attempt to understand how the collective identity of a people shapes the consciousness of the individuals within it (Arens, 1989).

Wundt argued that the developmental capacity for selective volitional attention generates culture. Thus, as humans develop, so does culture (Blumenthal, 1975). He focused on higher-order mental processes shaped by society and value-judgments. For him, the essentially cultural processes of feeling, thinking, and willing can be studied only through what today is known as naturalistic observation and through historical analysis, not experimentation.

Wundt was particularly interested in the interpersonal aspects of language, because how people relate gives cultural form to ideas and feelings. While thinking, feeling, and willing express individual souls, for Wundt, language, religion, and customs transcend individual consciousness and constitute a collective soul that expresses group psychical life (G. Jahoda, 2007).

Although he proposed that individual minds create a shared culture through gestural communication, Wundt viewed individual and group development as separate. In *Völkerpsychologie* he concentrated more on language and thought than on the mutual influence among individuals, their relationships, and culture (Arens, 1989). Accordingly, anthropologists and sociologists criticized him for "psychologism," that is, basing social phenomena on individual psychology (Danziger, 1983).

Part 4 conclusion

Compared to the present status of personality and social psychology, the interests expressed by early psychologists in these fields seem overshadowed by investigations of basic processes. But by the 1930s personality and social psychology became prominent.

During Psychology's founding decades many investigators explored personality differences. Some took a quantitative, even biomedical approach (e.g., Ribot, Heymans) to studies of personality, others a qualitative personalistic approach (e.g., Stern). James and Calkins theorized the self, stressing its uniqueness to each person and its fundamentally relational nature. They also attributed transcendental qualities to the self – for James, spiritual connectedness with others; for Calkins, moral consciousness. Presently, as subsequent chapters show, many psychologists are retrieving these interests in personality phenomena.

Originally, psychologists (e.g., McDougall) tended to explain social behaviour in terms of instincts. Bekhterev even characterized individuals' behaviour in small groups as collective reflexology. Eschewing instinct theory, James, Baldwin, and Dewey construed humans as essentially social. In his cultural psychology Wundt investigated how the shared identity of a cultural group moulds the higher-order psychological processes of the individual members of the particular cultural group. But with the exception of Wallas's attempts to formulate an empirical model, the subdiscipline of social psychology did not emerge until the 1920s (see Chapter 6).

Part 5   Psychology and the social order

The political and socioeconomic implications of early psychologists' investments in social applications of Psychology also deserve historical review. Central to psychologists' standpoints concerning society were their gender and ethnocultural biases.

Political and socioeconomic standpoints

Some early natural-science psychologists promoted explicit political and socioeconomic standpoints. But many did not consider the implications of their theorizing about psychological processes in relation to societal structures, leaving this task to social scientists.

Taking a social Darwinist position, William Preyer criticized nineteenth-century socialist movements and equated unfettered economic and social competition with scientific and psychological progress. He claimed that nature necessitated social inequality, including the division of labour between managers and workers, and that as a culture became more advanced inequality would and should deepen (Jaeger, 1982). Working conditions under industrialization in the nineteenth century were difficult and even dangerous, as illustrated in Figure 5.2.

In the UK, the British psychophysiologists, Hughlings Jackson and Henry Maudsley, claimed scientific validity for the health-policy issues that they promoted to contain societal discontent and preserve the hierarchical social order (Danziger, 1982). For their part, Francis Galton and Charles Spearman (1863–1945) scientifically rationalized eugenics, meritocracy, and the class structure.

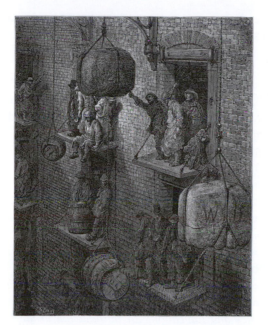

Figure 5.2 These men are loading goods in and out of a warehouse in nineteenth-century London

Striving to unify pure and applied psychology, Hugo Münsterberg argued that experimental investigations of causal relations only had value if they ultimately contributed to practical purposes. For him, Psychology should include the study of the values and ideals of everyday life. In his view, the inherent inequality of individuals required differential social functions and societal rewards. On the other hand, he advocated integrating politics, natural science, and idealist philosophy in service to a pacifist, utopian global community founded on Western values (Morawski, 1982). He envisioned experimental psychology, converted to "psychotechnics," as the primary facilitator of his ideal social order.

Similarly, Edward Thorndike advocated employing Psychology to create a more efficient, rationally organized, and moral social order in which all adapt to their place in the capitalist system. Moreover, he promoted meritocracy, arguing that social power belongs in the hands of economically privileged White men whom he believed to be superior intellectually and ethically (Karier, 1986). For him, a scientifically trained elite should plan how others adapt to their fixed station in life (Tomlinson, 1997).

William James also supported the social Darwinist notion of an autonomous individual who competes in a free-market society of capitalist institutions led by intellectually superior men. Moreover, he advocated *noblesse oblige*, the duty of aristocrats to dole out charitable donations to the allegedly inferior classes. Some claim that James held that the desire for accumulating wealth and private property is biologically driven (Karier, 1986). But others claim that he was a social activist (E. Taylor, 1998), even a radical communitarian.

Few early psychologists aligned themselves with anarchist or socialist ideas and movements. Instead, most tended to adopt politically conservative or reformist standpoints. One exception was Edward Abramowski (1868–1918), a Polish socialist theorist, political activist, and promoter of workers' cooperatives, who reformulated Marxism as an integration of the psychological with socioeconomic conditions (Chlewinski, 1976).

Social reform

John Dewey adopted James's pragmatist position that ideas become truths when they make a difference to individuals and society. He espoused "progressivism" to respond to the social challenges precipitated by a rapidly changing society. Progressives aimed to improve the status of the urban masses and to counter society's exploitation of marginalized people (E. Cahan, 1992; Manicas, 2002).

For Dewey, social reform also depended upon individuals being educated for full participation as citizens. The goal of the ideal society, he argued, is to enable individuals to express their capacities for community well-being (Tomlinson, 1997). But unlike Münsterberg's and Thorndike's approaches to social reform, according to Dewey's rethinking of individualism (Karier, 1986), the goal of an ideal democratic society is to enable the expression of each individual's capacities to contribute to society's well-being (Tomlinson, 1997).

A principal means to achieve this goal is educational reform, energized by a consciously developed set of values promoting community life and expressed in the practice of progressive education. In *Democracy and Education: An Introduction to the Philosophy of Education* (1916), Dewey asserted that schools should educate students about contributing to a true democracy. When individuals are educated for full participation in democratic citizenship, then genuine social reform is possible.

From a critical perspective, some contradictions about democracy are evident in Dewey's standpoint. In his 1899 APA presidential address he argued that facts and values, and theory and practice are intertwined. But he also argued that the "rank and file" (e.g., teachers) must understand, support, and comply with the interventions and programmes instituted by the "officers" of institutions (e.g., administrators) (Sarason, 1981). Like other progressives, Dewey believed that social reform should spring from the scientific laws of human behaviour, rationally administered by a scientifically trained core of planners in bureaucracies. His "top-down" administrative model seems paternalistic, militating against "bottom-up" democratic change.

> **Small-group discussion.** Since the founding of Psychology as a natural science, psychologists have promoted political and socioeconomic positions, usually supporting the societal status quo. How would you explain the contradiction between psychologists' commitment to certain social values, on the one hand, and their espousal of scientific objectivity, on the other?

Scientific racism

Early psychologists practised their new discipline during an imperialist epoch in which an ideology of White male supremacy and political-economic elitism prevailed in Western culture and science. Extant notions in evolutionary theory and physical anthropology provided "scientific" support for this ideology. W. H. Rivers and William McDougall, for example, were members of the Cambridge University anthropological team that investigated mental processes in the "primitive" inhabitants of the Torres Strait and Borneo in 1898–1899.

In addition, Theodule Ribot derived from social Darwinism a physical-anthropology perspective on psychological capacities and a racial hierarchy of abilities. He believed that Africans and Jews were biologically and psychologically inferior to Europeans. Initially, Ribot adopted perspectives that assumed that personality, intellect, and psychopathology are inherited (Staum, 2007). Later he held a Lamarckian view that acquired characteristics, such as memory, intelligence, and personality, can be inherited.

For his part, Francis Galton introduced ranking "races" in terms of alleged natural ability and characterized Anglo-Saxons as psychologically superior to all ethnocultural groups. He aimed to accelerate evolution to encourage these "superior" individuals to mate and produce more intelligent Englishmen (*sic*). Coining the term eugenics, Galton promoted the concept as a social policy "positively," whereby individuals of the best family "stock" increase their productivity, and "negatively," whereby society prevents the lower classes, believed to be mentally deficient, from breeding (Gillham, 2001).

Eugenics proliferated in the early twentieth century, supported by scientific research, journals, and societies. For instance, psychologists Charles Spearman and Cyril Burt studied the hereditary transmission of individual differences and abilities, which led to their concentration on identification and institutional programmes for mental deficiency.

In US Psychology, James and Münsterberg believed that ethnoracial differences derived from "instincts" and Stanley Hall attributed different levels of evolutionary maturity to the "races" (D. Ross, 1972). Not only should the superior Anglo-Saxons improve their racial stock, according to Hall, but he considered all Africans, North and South American "Indians," indigenous Hawaiians, and the Irish permanent adolescents because of alleged diminished evolutionary inheritance.

According to Edward Thorndike, the most significant individual differences are inherent inequalities in learning potential (Joncich, 1968). For him, not just intelligence but strength of character and wealth are primarily innate qualities rather than attributes (Karier, 1986). Accordingly, superior individuals should receive elite education. He too advocated eugenics to breed the fittest people for governance and maintained that White people are genetically superior to African Americans.

Scientific sexism

Intersecting with psychologists' notions of the social order and ethnocultural status are their assumptions about gender. Although a few male psychologists supported women's aspirations to a PhD, patriarchal ideology suffused early Psychology, academia, and society. Thus, psychologists, such as Galton, believed that because psychological differences between the genders are innate, different social roles are appropriate to uphold: women should be homemakers and mothers, while men work in the world. By contrast with Psychology, female psychoanalysts played a prominent role in their discipline (see Chapter 9).

Although changes eventually occurred in national educational policies towards women, German universities excluded them, in part, because girls and young women received little preparatory education. Wilhelm Wundt had only one female student, **Anna Meyer Berliner** (1888–1977), who enrolled in 1910 and received her PhD in 1914 when Wundt was 82. Evidently, he was opposed to women seeking doctorates. In order to gain admission, Berliner approached him in her best white dress.

Georg Müller, however, "was unusual in his openness to women as scientists and colleagues" (Sprung & Sprung, 2000b, p. 86), who included Christine Ladd-Franklin. August Kirschmann also supported women's equal place in psychological research. His Toronto student Emma Baker (n.d.) was the first female PhD graduate (1903) in any Canadian discipline.

In Russia, Vladimir Bekhterev admitted female and Jewish students to his institute (Joravsky, 1989; Kozulin, 1984). Although originally Ivan Pavlov opposed women working in his lab, in 1905 he began to admit them and approximately twenty were among the Pavlovians (Windholz, 1997). N. R. Shenger-Krestovnikova (n.d.), for example, produced experimental neurosis in a dog conditioned to salivate to a circle but not an ellipse (R. Smith, 1997).

At a time when Harvard and Columbia did not admit women for graduate study, Edward Titchener admitted them to Cornell (Evans, 1991). The first woman to earn a PhD in Psychology (1894), Margaret Washburn, was a Titchener graduate. In fact, 19 of his 56 PhD graduates were women, which distinguished him from his peers. On the other hand, he banned women from attending his Society for Experimental Psychologists, which had negative consequences for their careers; even after his death women were only marginally included (Furumoto, 1988).

Also in the US, James Cattell introduced in his *Biographical Directory of American Men of Science* (1906) the method of order of merit by which he ranked scientists' characteristics. After assigning 18 women to his list of the 1,000 most eminent scientists, he concluded that women were genetically inferior. Similarly, Thorndike claimed that men had greater biological variability than women and were biologically destined for doing science, philosophizing, and governing, while women were destined for helping, teaching, and caring (Joncich, 1968).

Agreeing with James that gender differences are heritable instincts, Münsterberg held that male philosopher-academics should head society's social hierarchy; husbands should head their families; and women, even if educated, should devote themselves to matrimony and motherhood (Hale, 1980). Nevertheless, James and Münsterberg encouraged Mary Calkins in her quest for a PhD. Although Dewey supported women's suffrage, he and Hall believed women's biological imperative is to reproduce the species. Yet later, Hall supported women as graduate students and described the 1920s cultural symbol of "flapper girls" (fashionable young women) as heralding a new era of womanhood (D. Ross, 1972).

During this era societal prejudices about gender influenced scientists' work. Most early psychologists were men and believed that psychological differences between genders are innate. Because women have a "maternal instinct," they claimed, different social roles are appropriate, that is, women should stay at home, while men work outside the home. Furthermore, in early British and US psychological thought, authors asserted a natural gender difference concerning emotion whereby men, but not women, were capable of harnessing their passions in service to reason (Shields, 2007).

An early critique

In her PhD dissertation, completed in 1900, **Helen Thompson Woolley** (1874–1947) subjected the claim of gender differences and male superiority to critical analysis (Morse, 2002). First, using her family name, Thompson reviewed the existing literature on gender differences and similarities and found contradictory results. Then she systematically compared the sensory-motor skills, intellectual faculties, and affective processes of 25 undergraduate men and 25 women on lab tasks.

Thompson found that the distribution of scores on the same test overlapped almost completely for men and women. She concluded that experience and society, not biology, account for any psychological gender differences. Without a scientific basis for psychological sex differences, she contended, societal conventions about gender concerning home, school, workplace, and social organizations were unjustified.

Thompson Woolley's findings and conclusions on gender differences and similarities were controversial, because they challenged societal norms alleging that women are biologically inferior. Her demystification of the patriarchal belief in women's natural inferiority threatened society and psychologists' belief systems and practices. Consequently, some male psychologists claimed that "feminist bias" contaminated her research (Scarborough & Furumoto, 1987).

Part 5 conclusion

During an era of political and socioeconomic inequalities some psychologists directly expressed professional opinions about these conditions. Some also were candid about their views on the equality of "races" and gender. Generally, few psychologists deviated in their views from extant cultural norms.

Appealing to the doctrine of social Darwinism, Preyer explicitly argued for economic and social inequality. Galton, Jackson, Maudsley, and Spearman each invoked science to justify maintaining the societal status quo. Although Münsterberg also advocated allocating differential social functions and societal rewards to inherently unequal social groups, he envisioned a pacifist utopia, founded on applied natural-science principles. Thorndike envisioned a stable capitalist hierarchy in which all accepted their place. Some evidence suggests James supported meritocracy, other evidence suggests an inclination towards social reform. Arguably, Dewey epitomizes the "progressive" standpoint of social reform for the purpose of enhancing everyone's adaptation to a democratic capitalist social order. Abramowski appears to be one of the few early psychologists explicitly aligned with a socialist alternative to the status quo.

Psychology emerged in a social context in which scientists rationalized a hierarchy of psychological functions and abilities with wealthy Anglo-Saxon White men at the apex of society. Thus, it was normative for psychologists, such as Burt, Galton, Hall, James, McDougall, Münsterberg, Ribot, Rivers, Spearman, and Thorndike to posit inherited White superiority. Paralleling scientific racism in early Psychology was scientific sexism, which reflected society's patriarchal belief in women's natural inferiority. Although some male psychologists (e.g., Bekhterev, Müller) supported women pursuing academic careers as psychologists, others opposed women's participation in the discipline entirely (e.g., Cattell) or in part (e.g., Dewey, Hall, James, Münsterberg, Pavlov, Titchener). As we will see, these racist and sexist inclinations persisted through most of Psychology's history.

Part 6

Thematic review

Four themes are common to the diverse types of early natural-science Psychology and their primary concepts that we have reviewed (cf. Ash, 2003): **boundary maintenance**, **biological reductionism**, **ambiguity about mind and brain**, and **alliance with the societal status quo**.

Boundary maintenance

The early psychologists pursued philosophical questions, such as mind–body relations, but primarily with physiological methods. Thus, they were ambivalent about their heritage and the boundaries between their new discipline and the established disciplines of philosophy and physiology.

Some, like Wilhelm Wundt, wanted to render mental philosophy scientific and he contributed to philosophical subdisciplines. Others, like William James, joined philosophy and physiology in a way that diverged significantly from Wundt's psychology of consciousness and cultural psychology. Still others, like Edward Thorndike, regarded Psychology as a natural science exclusively and ignored or rejected its philosophical parentage.

Psychology's boundaries with the natural sciences were also ambiguous. Many natural-science psychologists adopted experimental physiologists' framework for investigating animal activity and human bodily movement. Also, Russian reflexologists advanced a physiological interpretation of psychological phenomena. But for other psychologists, like John Dewey, more than mechanical principles explained psychological phenomena. Whether *physiological* concepts and methods could produce knowledge about *psychological* processes remained a contested point (Danziger, 1997b).

Many natural-science psychologists vigorously protected the boundaries of their discipline in the face of curiosity among some colleagues, such as James, about psychic phenomena. The majority sharply distinguished Psychology from anything that seemed "unscientific" (Coon, 1992). Moreover, few founders studied humans' subjective experiences such as contemporary novelists artfully described. The subjective domain appealed mainly to psychoanalysts (see Chapter 9) and human-science psychologists (see Chapter 10).

Excepting James, the early psychologists also erected firm boundaries around their own schools of thought, precipitating intense theoretical rivalries. The structuralist Edward Titchener contended with functionalists, then with behaviourists, while Mary Calkins and Margaret Washburn tried to reconcile the polarities between studies of consciousness and behaviour. Overall, conceptual diversity and disunity characterized Psychology's founding decades.

Biological reductionism

The new psychologists struggled to find language and conceptual categories that would do justice to their discipline. While the physiologists clearly distinguished between the physical and the mental, psychologists developed categories to explain the relationship between them (Danziger, 1997b). Early natural-science psychologists adopted physiological terms, based on biological and mechanical metaphors, to characterize *psychological* functions (e.g., "inhibition," "psychic energy," and "stimulation"). One popular term was *organism*, which for psychologists encompassed the characteristics that human and nonhuman animals shared.

Meanwhile, functionalist psychologists drew a sharp distinction between behaviour and consciousness, denoting the former as objectively knowable and the latter as fundamentally subjective, hence non-scientific. Influenced by Darwinian theory, functionalists aimed to make the study of animal behaviour and the human mind objective by regarding their discipline as a branch of biology. The term behaviour implied no essential difference of meaning across animal and human activity. This assumption became the conceptual basis of behaviourism.

Ambiguity about mind and brain

Notions about the mind and brain remained ambiguous among early psychologists, leaving complex content-areas, such as consciousness and intentions, problematic. Contemporary physiologists concentrated on sensory-motor action directly affecting the brain, which they believed evoked consciousness. The new psychologists emulated physiologists, but they were vague about the relationship between mind and body (and brain). Although some, like James, regarded body and mind as a unity, most early psychologists were dualists, at least implicitly. They seemed to take consciousness and body–mind relations for granted, focusing instead on concrete problems in their respective research areas.

The new psychologists disagreed concerning the role of will. For Wundt and James, will was central, but most peers considered this notion a vestige of discredited philosophical psychology. Most natural-science psychologists distanced themselves from previously accepted but somewhat nebulous concepts to concentrate on specific material factors that they could subject easily to experimental manipulation. To counter the ambiguity inherent in their discipline, psychologists studied psychological processes (e.g., memory), as separate, almost autonomous functions rather than embedded in interpersonal phenomena and social contexts.

Alliance with the societal status quo

Scientific and societal purposes were intertwined from Psychology's inception. Early psychologists' chief aim was to develop a body of plausible knowledge readily applicable to social problems. Despite Wundt's and Titchener's opposition to this agenda, most psychologists energetically sought to apply their findings to society.

Many assumed that Psychology's techniques were essential to realizing societal reforms, managing individuals' behaviour, and ensuring people's adjustment to industrial urban society (G. Richards, 2010). While every aspect of daily life became grist for the mill, some psychologists even designed utopias (Morawski, 1982). Thus, arguably, Psychology was founded more as an *administrative science* (Danziger, 1997b) or a managerial technology of the masses, in keeping with the modern Western trend of social management, than as a strictly academic discipline based on the nineteenth-century experimental method.

Apparently, Psychology originated in psychologists' attempt to secure societal legitimacy as expert specialists of a socially valuable commodity, namely, centuries-old psychological ideas, now marketable for business, industry, and government. To exercise societal influence, many psychologists persuaded authorities that psychologists' expertise lay in Psychology's scientific objectivity.

Psychologists' claims to natural-science credentials seemed to function as persuasive rhetoric in their campaign to secure a prominent societal role. The new Psychology met a receptive audience in society's movers and shakers who were anxious to contain "irrational" elements in society, such as labour unions and socialists, which threatened the economic and political establishment. Psychologists' alliance with the establishment helped to legitimize their new science and profession.

Consequently, while many early psychologists supported extant political regimes and the capitalist social order, many others simply ignored the political implications of their work. Most did not labour with citizens to challenge society's injustices. Rather, they implemented planned change to improve the masses' adjustment to the existing social environment, reinforcing bureaucratic control of industrializing societies.

Moreover, most early psychologists were economically privileged White men of European descent who regarded other humans as intellectually and morally inferior. Thus, early psychologists' discourse and practices were deeply racialized and gendered, and many promoted eugenics and White supremacy. These views reflected the contemporary imperialist ideology of Western superiority and the corresponding inferiority of diverse cultures. Indigenous psychologies were ignored and the contributions of "non-White" psychologists minimized. Furthermore, psychologists tended to view women as inherently inferior, employed androcentric scientific language, and obstructed women's participation in Psychology.

Summary

In this chapter we introduced the social and intellectual contexts for natural-science Psychology's emergence. After noting the philosophical questions with which founding psychologists grappled, we described various schools of psychological thought, psychologists' diverse interests in basic and interpersonal processes, and their conceptions of the social order, gender, and ethnocultural biases.

In Part 1 we described the societal and intellectual contexts for Psychology's formal emergence as a natural science in late nineteenth-century Europe, principally, Germany, France, the UK, Russia, and in the US. Our emphasis was on Psychology's institutionalization up to World War I, including the status of women in early Psychology. The new discipline also had modest beginnings in Canada, China, India, and Japan. Within the description of each national psychology we identified noteworthy founders.

In Part 2 we discussed diverse schools of thought that gained prominence in natural-science Psychology: Wundt's voluntarism; Titchener's structuralism; the reflexology of Sechenov, Bekhterev, and Pavlov; US functionalism; Dewey's social practice; Calkins's self theory; and McDougall's hormic psychology. Evolutionary theory was influential particularly in British and US Psychology. Reflexology prevailed in Russia, while variations of voluntarism persisted in German Psychology.

In Part 3 we described early psychologists' different conceptions of basic psychological processes pertaining to sensory processes, consciousness, and extrasensory perception; emotion; instincts, habits, and learning, including animal mind; memory; thinking and problem-solving; mind and movement, and human will; and early conceptions of developmental processes, including education. Rather than narrow purviews, broad domains of scientific interest prevailed among the first generations of natural-science psychologists.

In Part 4 we reviewed early notions of personality, conceptions of the self, and social processes, including Wundt's cultural psychology. These notions drew less from fledgling Psychology, which was focused on basic processes, than from the social sciences and humanities. With some exceptions, psychologists were eager to apply their knowledge of interpersonal processes socially. But the subdisciplines of personality and social psychology and categories familiar today (e.g., attitudes) did not emerge formally until after World War I.

Then in Part 5 we addressed how the founding natural-science psychologists, most of whom were citizens of economically privileged nations, understood the relationship between their new discipline and the social order. Most natural-science psychologists aspired to make their research findings directly applicable to the established, political and socioeconomic order of their respective societies. Early psychologists also absorbed common cultural beliefs about ethnocultural status and gender. Many overtly expressed views that reflected scientific racism and sexism.

In Part 6 we presented a thematic summary of Parts 2 to 5. The four themes that connect the disparate standpoints and conceptions of the original natural-science psychologists are: boundary maintenance, biological reductionism, ambiguity about mind and brain, and alliance with the political and socioeconomic status quo. Psychologists struggled to establish their field's legitimacy vis-à-vis the parent disciplines of philosophy and physiology, many reduced psychological phenomena to physiological concepts, clarity and consensus about the relationship between mind and brain eluded early psychologists, and most aligned themselves with the accepted social order. Taken together, these themes represent the philosophical and scientific legacy that future generations of psychologists inherited.

Sample essay questions

Evaluate the following claims and support your position with evidence from the text:

1. Regarding the status of women, Psychology played handmaiden to social values.

2. William James and John Dewey had interesting ideas, but Edward Thorndike made more enduring contributions to Psychology.

RECOMMENDED READING

R. Smith's (1997) *Norton history of the human sciences* places the emergence of Psychology in societal, scientific, and philosophical context. His bibliography is extremely helpful. G. Richards's (2010) *Putting psychology in its place* is briefer but a more critical examination of Psychology's history. Danziger's (1997) *Naming the mind: How psychology found its language* aids understanding the history of psychological concepts, while his 2008 book, *Marking the mind: A history of memory*, does the same for memory.

If you prefer a biographical approach, then Fancher and Rutherford's (2012) *Pioneers of psychology*, the APA series Portraits of Pioneers in Psychology, and Scarborough and Furumoto's (1987) *Untold lives: The first generation of American women psychologists* are useful resources. See also the journal articles and books that we cited and referenced.

ONLINE RESOURCES

For primary sources consult: "Classics in the History of Psychology": http://psychclassics.yorku.ca/ and "Psychology's Feminist Voices": www.feministvoices.com/

To inspect early psychological laboratories and instruments consult two sites: University of Toronto http://home.psych.utoronto.ca/resources/museum.htm and University of Akron www.uakron.edu/chp/archives/instruments.dot.

6

Natural-science Psychology between the world wars

Chapter outline

Introduction

From the 1910s to World War II natural-science Psychology expanded its scope internationally, while in the USA it also became a prominent social force in its practical applications. In this chapter, we discuss the discipline's social context and institutional development during this period. Then we review the major schools of thought and scientific developments in basic psychological, developmental, and interpersonal processes. Next we consider psychologists' relationship to the social order. We conclude with themes that capture the intellectual development of natural-science Psychology in the post-World War I era.

The **aims** of Chapter 6 are to describe:

- The social context, including socioeconomic conditions and scientific developments, which facilitated Psychology's expansion after World War I.
- Developments in Psychology internationally during this period.
- The principal schools of thought between the wars: Gestalt theory, field theory, higher nervous activity, and neobehaviourism.
- The major contributions in basic psychological processes, including brain mechanisms and learning, memory, and language.
- The emergence of developmental psychology internationally.
- The major developments in the interpersonal areas of Psychology.
- Psychologists' relationship to the social order, including collaboration with the state and responses to the Depression, sexism, and racism.
- The central themes that summarize Psychology's development between the wars: narrow purview, biological reductionism, disciplinary fragmentation, and alliance with the political and socioeconomic status quo.

Part 1 | Social and intellectual context

During and after World War I, economically privileged Western societies linked science more closely to industrial, commercial, and military interests. Meanwhile, although most psychologists continued to identify with the older assumptions of the established natural sciences, natural scientists themselves challenged these assumptions and contributed new explanations of nature. Technological innovations proliferated in society and impacted on psychological theory and research. But despite some gains, women remained marginalized in society and science.

Societal developments

In economically privileged Western nations, wealth expanded for some citizens after World War I, while many others struggled for basic amenities, particularly in the war-ravaged nations of Europe. Society in the 1920s was beset by conflicting trends of prosperity and enhanced professional influence as well as intense labour strife and abject poverty (Dumenil, 1995).

When governmental controls on the US economy imposed during wartime were dropped, industry and commerce ran unbridled, corporations dominated society, and urbanization intensified, necessitating effective means of controlling urban dwellers. Academic and human-service professionals came to serve efficient management of society's economic, social, and educational institutions (Alchon, 1985).

Yet, unemployment escalated with the cessation of a war-economy. Workers were agitated because of low wages, oppressive working conditions, and the authorities' violent suppression of labour strikes. Social paranoia (known in the US as the "Red Scare") about communists, socialists, and anarchists gripped society (Zinn, 2005).

Meanwhile, capitalists created new conditions that established a consumer society: assembly-line technology, marketing and advertising, and the easy flow of instalment credit. Advertising on the new medium of radio served to mediate citizens' perception of reality and create a mass culture of standardized expectations for the consumption of disposable commodities. Psychologists advised advertisers how to market products, projected as essential for consumers' well-being.

But the bubble of prosperity burst in 1929 with stock-market crashes, the collapse of banks, and millions of people unemployed or relegated to temporary, low-wage jobs. Hunger and famine were rampant during the Depression, particularly among numerous migrant families, who were agricultural labourers if they could find work. A 32-year-old mother and children from a migrant family with no food are shown in Figure 6.1.

Society's principal challenge was to maintain economic structures and political institutions while alleviating the pressures of massive unemployment and avoiding rebellion and the radical change that socialism posed. Preserving society's core economic and social institutions required a conforming public. Governments aimed to induce conformity by increasing economic and social planning, and moulding public opinion through mass communication and propaganda. Some academic psychologists contributed to this latter

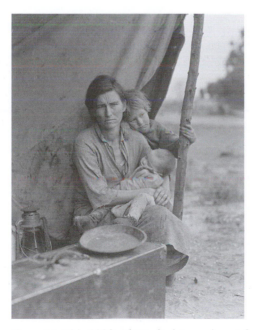

Figure 6.1 This 1930s photo depicts a migrant family in the USA during the Depression

purpose, while many, indirectly or directly, promoted personal adjustment to society (Napoli, 1981).

By 1939, socioeconomic conditions remained very problematic, even for graduating psychologists seeking academic employment. The Depression did not end until nations concentrated on producing war materials and weaponry for World War II; increased production yielded greater employment and a strong sense of social purpose in support of the war effort. Yet nearly 50 million people perished during World War II, many more suffered debilitating injuries, major portions of Europe and Japan were obliterated, and nuclear warfare was unleashed. Overall, the period covered in this chapter can be characterized as an age of extremes (Hobsbawm, 1996).

Status of women

Systemic disadvantages militating against equality for women persisted throughout the twentieth century, although many women continued to agitate for greater public participation and equality in society. This activism eventuated in many economically privileged societies granting women the right to vote. In undergraduate and graduate education, during the 1920s and 1930s, US universities increasingly admitted women. But in Europe the pace of admissions was slower.

The general expectation was that women choose between marriage and homemaking or a career, whereas men could enjoy both marriage and a career. During World War II women "kept the home fires burning." After the war most women who had taken men's jobs were required to return to homemaking to ensure that men discharged from military service were employed.

Scientific developments

During this era, previous scientific conceptions of nature, largely based on Isaac Newton's notions, changed dramatically (Goldman, 1989) (see Table 6.1 below). For instance, in 1900,

Table 6.1 Scientific conceptions

Former scientific conceptions	Revised scientific conceptions
Separate natural objects.	Natural objects embedded in networks, structures, processes, and relationships.
Independent objects, acting as basic building blocks.	Systems comprising parts that support the whole (e.g., sodium and chlorine together comprising salt).
Immutable objects in equilibrium.	Systems in perpetual states of imbalance.
Simple and predictable objects.	Complex and unpredictable systems.
Theory generating technology.	Reciprocity between theory and technology.
Binary thinking (e.g., matter *or* energy).	Dialectical thinking (e.g., matter and energy in reciprocal interaction).

geologists considered Earth to be relatively stable, but within decades they held that Earth is a dynamic turbulent system embedded within an influential solar system and universe.

Meanwhile, nineteenth-century physicists had recognized but could not explain anomalies, such as radioactivity. Some began to doubt the accepted explanations for the nature of atoms, matter, and energy. Then Scottish physicist **James Clerk Maxwell** (1831–1879) showed that light travels in electromagnetic waves at 186,000 miles per second. He also introduced the notion of fields of forces acting upon particles.

Drawing from Maxwell, German physicist **Max Planck** (1858–1947) proposed *field theory* by which natural phenomena are caused by a network of intersecting forces that take a particular form or structure. Observers attend to the field or pattern of elements that form the new structure. Planck also proposed that when light and matter interact, radiated energy exists in multiples of a unit (a "quantum") and that energy transfers occur only in discrete chunks. The theory of quantum mechanics then emerged (see Chapter 12).

In Newtonian physics, space is a purely objective property of an object, which appears the same independent of persons observing it, and time passes at the same uniform speed for every observer. But Albert Einstein showed that the perception of time is related to the location of the observer (Stachel, 2005).

According to relativity theory, time and the three dimensions of space (height, width, and length) are interrelated, not separate phenomena. Measurement of natural events is relative to the observer's position in time and space. The perceived temporal order of natural events depends on an observer's spatial position, and measurement can shrink or expand depending on the speed at which it moves. Thus, measurement is the result of a relationship between observers and objects.

These advances in physics had differential effects on Psychology. Generally, natural-science psychologists remained committed to the Newtonian model of science, searching for precise cause-and-effect relations through presumed objective measurement, whereas Gestalt theorists and Kurt Lewin adapted the new physics to psychological phenomena.

Meanwhile, the pace of technical invention accelerated. The Wright brothers accomplished flight in 1903. Ten years later Henry Ford developed the mass-production assembly line to build cheap cars. In 1926 the original television was developed in London. By 1939 the first electronic digital computer was produced in the US.

With industrialists seeking practical benefits, corporate funding of natural-science research escalated. Research institutes supported by government and industry were flourishing in Germany since the nineteenth century, yielding industrial and military applications of science. Japan also became technologically advanced.

Part 1 conclusion

After World War I, economically privileged societies struggled with competing social demands for expanding capitalist production and protecting industrial workers' rights. Movers and shakers working in industry, business, and government welcomed technological applications of the natural sciences. Some founding psychologists and their successors maintained an arm's-length distance between their scientific work and society. But many if not most contemporary psychologists responded enthusiastically to society's expectations for producing psychological knowledge conducive to economic growth.

Although an emergent social class of professionals became more influential in society and many individuals enjoyed the hedonism of the 1920s, the exploitation of labour, poverty, and the denial of civil liberties for women were entrenched. When the ballooning global economy burst in 1929 and failed to recover during the 1930s, massive unemployment posed a threat of socialist revolution. Social scientists contributed to the containment of radical change by refining techniques of encouraging citizens' conformity and adjustment to the status quo.

While these socioeconomic trends and events unfolded, discoveries in the natural sciences prompted many scientists to propose an alternative epistemological position that was expressed initially as relativity theory and systems theory and later as quantum mechanics. However, with few exceptions psychologists retained a conception of natural science that relied on the now questionable Newtonian assumptions of realism, reductionism, and determinism.

Part 2   Expansion of Psychology internationally

Although the discipline began to develop in Argentina, Holland, Poland, Spain, and other nations after World War I, Germany, Britain, France, the Soviet Union, and the USA remained predominant in Psychology.

European Psychology

German, British, and French Psychologies consolidated their earlier advances and developed their institutional structures.

Germany

Participation in World War I marked a watershed for German psychologists. They placed their laboratory expertise in service to military technology to strengthen the "human factor" in the German military. In return, institutions enhanced their support for academic psychologists' research (Ash, 1995).

The primary natural-science schools of thought in Germany were the Würzburg School, Gestalt theory (see below), and a revitalized Wundtian approach known as *Ganzheitpsychologie* (roughly, "psychological processes in their total development"). German psychologists studied complex processes, applied psychology to industry and personnel-selection, and exercised international influence (Pongratz, 1976). But they still taught in philosophy departments, because Psychology in German-speaking regions did not become an independent discipline until 1941, when the professionalization of Psychology, including licensing for practice, also began.

When the Nazis took political power in 1933, some psychologists expressed sympathies for National Socialist ideology (Mandler, 2002). Of those who dissented, some were expelled and others emigrated from Germany. During World War II the Nazis converted Psychology into a policy-tool for military and industrial applications (Geuter, 1992). Thus, psychologists had to negotiate a difficult terrain between total accommodation and complete resistance to the regime. Many provided diagnostic assessments for selecting military officers. Others adapted basic concepts (e.g., *Gestalt*) to Nazi ideology.

United Kingdom

Strong social-class divisions and weak institutional support for Psychology inclined British psychologists to specialize in applied psychology and psychometrics. During World War I, psychologists provided psychotherapy to military patients and studied the environmental conditions affecting the productivity of munitions workers. After the war, practical applications persisted (N. Rose, 1985). For example, Cyril Burt used Charles Spearman's concept of general and specific intelligence to assess educational performance in developmentally delayed and delinquent children. Consciousness and cognitive functions were central for British psychologists, yet academic Psychology remained diminutive, with only two research centres in England.

France

French Psychology began its second phase in 1912 when Henri Pieron, who maintained the Sorbonne lab previously led by Alfred Binet, took Psychology in a physiological direction (Reuchlin, 1965). In the cultural spirit of generating rational solutions to social problems, Pieron developed an experimentally based approach to vocational guidance and investigated the psychological characteristics of geniuses.

During the 1920s Pieron facilitated the institutionalization of French psychology, founding institutes for advanced training in psychological applications. However, a degree in Psychology was not available until 1947 in France (Ash, 2003), and until World War II many psychologists continued to pursue philosophical or medical concerns.

Soviet Psychology

During the Soviet era the discipline took a rather different form and content than in European psychologies. After the Revolution of 1917, civil war and martial law halted academic activity and the Moscow Psychological Society was disbanded. Many whose views did not adhere to the regime's interpretation of dialectical materialism, including psychologists, were exiled. The remaining psychologists laboured to create a rationally planned socialist utopia under authoritarian rule (Kozulin, 1984).

Russian psychologists initially relied on behaviourist concepts and on testing to apply Psychology to industry, mental health, and education. Finding these tools inadequate for building socialism, they developed a Marxist dialectical-materialist approach (London, 1949). By the 1930s, Soviet authorities insisted that Marxist–Leninist categories were the only legitimate ones for Psychology (Joravsky, 1989). Hence, they banned personality and social psychology as manifestations of "bourgeois ideology." Soviet psychologists then implemented a state programme to re-educate society.

The conceptual leader for a dialectical-materialist orientation to Psychology was Lev Vygotsky. He argued that human nature cannot be reduced to psychophysiology; rather, the social relations in which individuals develop form human nature (Barabanschikov, 2006).

Thus, for him, to understand psychological processes one must investigate individuals' relations with their social worlds.

US Psychology

The discipline expanded most dramatically in the USA. Psychologists numbered roughly 300 in 1919 but 3,000 in 1939 (Capshew, 1999). Although behaviourism provided many psychologists with a common creed, no single school of thought dominated. Meanwhile, success in classifying nearly 2 million army recruits in World War I boosted psychologists' societal status. In 1929, for the first time US psychologists hosted the International Congress of Psychology. "American" Psychology now led the world.

Organizationally, despite relatively standardized curricula, academic autonomy, and proliferating laboratories, US Psychology showed considerable disunity rather than uniformity. During the 1930s conflicting views about the nature of the American Psychological Association (APA) and of the discipline's identity abounded. For the most powerful but diminishing group, academic psychologists, the discipline was an experimental science, whereas for less powerful but expanding groups whose members did not hold academic positions, Psychology was an agent of social reform or a clinical profession. The result was that professional psychologists formed their own organization in 1937 only to reunite with the APA in 1945 (Napoli, 1981).

Women in US Psychology

For most of the twentieth century, female psychologists were expected to work with children and families, domains that men thought suited women's "natural" capacities (Bohan, 1990). Women predominated in clinical and school psychology, administering psychological testing as lower-rank employees, because male academic psychologists regarded these occupations as inferior to their own (Scarborough, 1992). Overall, a two-tiered labour-market in Psychology existed: high-paid academic positions for men, lower-paid applied positions for women (Capshew, 1999).

After Margaret Washburn was APA president (1921), no woman attained this position until 1972. Sexist practices institutionalized in US tertiary education militated against women's success in academic Psychology. Nevertheless, by the 1930s, women represented an increasing proportion of APA members and increasingly were making scholarly contributions (Johnston & Johnson, 2008).

Part 2 conclusion

Between the wars natural-science Psychology flourished institutionally in those nations where it had its origins, namely, Germany, the UK, France, the Soviet Union, and the USA. Whereas psychological applications rather than academic research were prominent in the UK, in the other four nations psychologists were active in both academic and professional domains. However, in the USA, tensions between these domains persisted and multiple theoretical orientations rather than uniformity prevailed. Psychology as a discipline did not significantly expand in other European nations, Canada, and some nations in Asia and Latin

America until after World War II. The academic climate for female psychologists remained chilly, although women increasingly pursued vocations in professional psychology.

Part 3 | Schools of thought

The chief schools of thought in natural-science Psychology after World War I were Gestalt theory, field theory, higher nervous activity, behaviourism, and neobehaviourism.

Gestalt theory

In English the German word *Gestalt* roughly means overall form, shape, or configuration. It connotes a structured whole system, comprised of interdependent parts subordinate to the whole such that change in "one part inevitably also produces changes in other parts and in the whole itself" (Michael Wertheimer, 1991, p. 195). In German, *Gestalt* signifies a dynamic unity of subjective experience and natural objects and implies "higher" philosophical values.

In Psychology, "Gestalt" applies to all psychological processes not just perception. Moreover, Gestalt theorists viewed their programme as "Gestalt theory," not as "Gestalt Psychology," because their priority was theorizing, not simply investigating, psychological processes. Lastly, "Gestalt therapy" bears little resemblance to Gestalt theory (Henle, 1978).

The instigator of the Gestalt movement was **Max Wertheimer** (1880–1943), who served at Frankfurt in 1910–1912. However, the hub of Gestalt theorists' activities occurred at Berlin during the 1920s. **Kurt Koffka** (1886–1941) introduced Gestalt theory to US psychologists in 1922. Of the three founders, **Wolfgang Köhler** (1887–1967) received the most US recognition, becoming APA president. By 1935, all had emigrated and joined US institutions.

Antecedents

Like their German Psychology predecessors who investigated problems in epistemology and logic, the Gestalt founders began with studies of perception and cognition, but sought a new solution to the problems of knowledge (Ash, 1995). They aimed to reconcile nature with mind at a time when idealists among the German intelligentsia viewed positivist natural science as encroaching on philosophy's traditional territory, threatening mind and culture. Similar to William James and John Dewey, the Gestalt theorists in a Kantian spirit intended to bridge the gap between idealism and positivism.

The Gestalt theorists sought to re-establish Psychology as a natural science capable of resolving philosophical issues by renewing its foundations in ontology, epistemology, and values and ethics. Accordingly, the Gestalt founders aimed to unify philosophy and phenomenological experience within an experimental framework, reliant on holistic thinking.

They did so by reformulating the concepts and modifying the methods of their common teacher, Carl Stumpf. The Gestalt theorists learned from Stumpf how to experiment and theorize their findings within a phenomenological framework of discovering structural laws inherent in psychological processes. Another influence was Oswald Külpe and the

Würzburg School whose phenomenological method integrated associationism and idealism experimentally.

Adopting Einstein's and Planck's field theory as the scientific basis for Psychology rather than Newtonian mechanics, Wertheimer, Koffka, and Köhler sought to determine the relations of force-fields affecting psychological phenomena. They assumed that just as force-fields operate on inanimate physical objects, all events are interrelated in human environments. In addition, they agreed with Ernst Mach that investigators should incorporate the spatial and temporal configurations of the total relationship of elements rather than analyze individual elements. The Gestalt theorists held that the structure of consciousness is the result of biological, perceptual, cognitive, and environmental fields of interacting forces.

Research programme

For Wertheimer, Koffka, and Köhler, Wilhelm Wundt's and Edward Titchener's rational dissection of experience into atomistic elements produced artificial abstractions. They also regarded behaviourists' reduction of psychological processes to stimulus–response connections as devoid of meaning, incompatible with the richness of human experience, and disconnected from fundamental human values (R. Smith, 1997).

Instead, the Gestalt theorists argued that the mind organizes elements into a meaningful form. For example, when listening to music we experience individual musical elements as a totality. When the musical key changes to one with different notes, we still recognize the melody, because we perceive the relationships among the elements, not the elements themselves. The whole determines the individual dimensions. Thus, the Gestalt founders explained consciousness in terms of organized forms and structures comprising ideas.

The mission of Wertheimer, Koffka, and Köhler was to explain all psychological processes by a unitary principle of organization rather than by separate hypotheses. They began with perceptual phenomena because of their accessibility. Köhler (1959) explained, "It was the hope of everybody that, once some major functional principles had been revealed in this part of psychology, similar principles would prove to be relevant to other parts, such as memory, learning, thinking, and motivation" (p. 729). Then they extended their concept of a perceptual field to all natural objects, convinced that adopting their functional principles would centralize meaning in Psychology.

Although their individual research programmes differed, Gestalt theorists studied whole mental phenomena and employed phenomenological introspection: by focusing on ongoing, conscious, meaningful experience, one presumably can observe phenomena just as they occur, unanalyzed, and without preconceptions. This phenomenology of direct experience was the Gestalt founders' "first step . . . to a science of functional relations that transcends phenomenology" (Henle, 1978, p. 30).

The career of Gestalt theory took **three stages** (Ash, 1995):

- From 1910 to 1920, Wertheimer devised the basic conceptual framework, applied it to experiments on perception of motion, and theorized about human problem-solving. He studied the *phi phenomenon*, which is the perception of apparent, continuous movement from stationary flashing lights, as occurs when viewing a film. This phenomenon shows that perceptual experience as a whole is essentially different from the sum of unrelated elements. Koffka and Köhler linked Wertheimer's framework to studies of perception and animal problem-solving.

- From 1920 to 1933, the founders elaborated their concepts; initiated their own journal; and studied emotion, human development, and social relations. They inspired related conceptual orientations, hosted international scholars, and visited US institutions, finding receptive audiences (Sokal, 1984).
- In 1933 the Nazi regime impeded Gestalt psychologists' activities. The coerced immigration of Wertheimer and Köhler to the US resulted in some colleagues leaving for Nordic nations or the Soviet Union. Those who remained in Germany made compromises with the Nazis. After the war Gestalt theory withered away. By the 1960s, with the founders and several key students deceased and an information-processing metaphor of mind ascendant in a hegemonic US Psychology, Gestalt theory expired.

Basic concepts

The gist of Gestalt theory is as follows: because organisms structure situations and because phenomena are qualitatively different than the sum of their parts, psychologists should take a molar or holistic approach and concentrate on investigating large segments of goal-directed behaviour.

Across their careers Wertheimer, Koffka, and Köhler proposed original concepts – *Praegnanz, isomorphism,* "insight learning," "productive thinking," and the behavioural environment – and addressed developmental issues.

Praegnanz The Gestalt theorists believed that all psychological experiences are pregnant with the potential to be as organized, symmetrical, meaningful, and regular as they can be, given the pattern of brain activity at any given moment. Based on this notion of *Praegnanz,* the founders devised **four principles** of perceiving and construing the environment:

- In "figure–ground" relationships, which occur in all sensory modalities, one aspect of stimuli stands out against its background. "Figure" means what individuals attend to, while "ground" means what we use as background or context.
- In "contrast" relationships, individuals amplify perceived differences in stimuli, while in "closure" we are motivated to complete unfinished activities.
- In relationships of "constancy" individuals perceive the same form despite its presentation in different perspectives.
- In "transposition" individuals recognize new forms of familiar stimuli, as in caricatures of political figures.

Isomorphism This concept means "identical form," that is, forms are isomorphic when they "share a common structure" (G. Richards, 2010, p. 84). Applying mathematical topology (i.e., the non-quantitative study of properties of different forms) to the relationship between conscious experience and the field activities of neurophysiological processes, Köhler posited structural correspondence between experience and underlying neural events. Sensations interact with the brain's pre-existing structures to cause mental activity, although ideas themselves are not innate.

Isomorphism helps to resolve the mind–body problem by the supposition of a functional relationship of structural similarity between perceptual experience and neural processes, particularly cortical events. But, for the Gestalt theorists, isomorphism does not mean a relationship between sensory events and neural processes, and no mental images correspond to experienced sensory events.

Problem-solving Wertheimer, Koffka, and Köhler investigated problem-solving in relation to a situation's field-structure. They believed that organisms come to see solutions to problems with insight. Thus, a problem is either unsolved or solved. Insight learning, therefore, is a result of a dynamic sequence of comprehending the nature of the unsolved problem, then resolving the tension with a solution. Although they acknowledged that trial-and-error, incremental learning, promoted by behaviourists, plays a role in problem-solving, the Gestaltists claimed that it is inferior to insight learning, because incremental learning is not remembered long and is not easily generalizable.

After placing apes in situations demanding complex responses, Köhler understood their problem-solving as "recognizing the interrelationships among objects in their perceptual field," then restructuring it (Sokal, 1984, p. 1242). In a famous study he set a banana out of reach of caged chimpanzees but included boxes and sticks that they could use to retrieve it. Initially, the chimpanzees engaged in trial-and-error, as if they were testing hypotheses about how to solve the problem. Suddenly they achieved insight into the solution, which Köhler interpreted as the chimpanzees mentally restructuring the situation, then adapting accordingly.

In a 1945 book, *Productive Thinking*, published posthumously, Wertheimer argued for creative or "productive" thinking in science and the arts. He interviewed excellent problem-solvers, including Einstein, about their thought-processes. Wertheimer observed that productive thinking proceeds from perception of the total problem in its complexity to examination of the relationships of its parts. He concluded that finding a solution to a problem is governed by intrinsic not extrinsic motivation. Productive thinking involves emotions, attitudes, and perceptions; it occurs unconsciously; and rigid dependence on linear reasoning can stifle creative problem-solving (Weisberg, 2006).

The behavioural environment The Gestalt theorists held that one's actions are more a consequence of brain activity than of environmental stimuli. Based on this proposition, Koffka argued that objective reality is not the physical or geographical environment but the behavioural environment, that is, one's *interpretation* of the geographical. Thus, from the Gestalt perspective, one's subjective experience of the geographical environment shapes behaviour, and residents of the same community do not live in the same community *behaviourally.*

Development Applying Gestalt concepts to human development, Koffka (1935) argued that infants' experience is both perceptual and affective. Even the sensory-motor learning upon which infants and very young children depend, he claimed, entails learning configurations of relations between objects in their world. Also, his interest in social development had relevance for pedagogy and partly inspired Vygotsky's explorations of societal determinants of development.

Section conclusion

Gestalt theory thrived in continental Europe for decades. However, it played a secondary role in US Psychology where its concepts and methods were contested.

German reception Many contemporary German scholars perceived a crisis in their culture over the place of the new physics of relativity and quantum mechanics within traditional German cultural values of order, transcendent unity, and the refined individual. Some physicists wished to retain a causal worldview, while others promoted uncertainty of judgments about natural objects. Some interpreted the crisis in physics as a metaphor for fragmentation in their economically and politically unstable society (Ash, 1995). In this cultural climate, a holistic worldview that synthesizes competing positions and overcomes dualisms held considerable appeal. The Gestalt theorists seized the moment to promote a holistic, natural-science school of thought.

Nevertheless, some German psychologists critiqued Gestalt theory. **Karl Bühler** (1879–1963) contended that it neglected how human language structures phenomenal experience. For William Stern, Gestalt theorists ignored psychological applications and underestimated the person as the origin of perceptual and cognitive processes. Stern asserted that in their attribution of objective structure to perceived situations between organisms and their environments, Gestalt theorists abandoned subjectivity and human agency (Ash, 1995).

US reception Gestalt concepts received mixed reviews from US psychologists. Initially, some accepted these concepts. US neuropsychologist **Karl Lashley** (1890–1958), for instance, incorporated field theory in his descriptions of basic neural mechanisms underlying behaviour. However, because the Gestalt theorists lacked the institutional resources to educate doctoral students in the USA, they could not establish an intellectual presence comparable to that which their US contemporaries enjoyed.

The Gestalt founders' rejection of behaviourism irritated some US psychologists who in turn claimed that Gestalt research lacked rigour and Gestalt concepts were vague; Köhler (1959) later acknowledged these problems. US psychologists distrusted Gestalt theorists' privileging scientific philosophy and psychological theory over experimental data. They regarded the Gestalt founders as proselytizers for their own Psychology, which to the critics resembled a movement with religious undercurrents (Sokal, 1984).

But their US critics ignored the fact that Gestalt psychologists operated from a different epistemological standpoint and employed a more fluid methodology. While the Gestalt theorists embraced the new physics of relativity theory and field theory, US behaviourists and neobehaviourists clung to Newtonian mechanistic physics (R. Smith, 1997). Underlying these negative responses to Gestalt theory was the cultural-linguistic difficulty of transferring Gestalt concepts from Germany to the US (G. Richards, 2010). Nevertheless, eventually the reception became more positive and some US psychologists incorporated Gestalt concepts (Sokal, 1984).

Many historians of Psychology conclude that the net effect of Gestalt theory on US Psychology was to redirect it towards mental processes, influencing the concepts that cognitive psychologists employ (e.g., Gardner, 1985). Others contend that the resemblance between Gestalt theory and cognitive psychology is superficial (e.g., Michael Wertheimer, 1991). They assert that Gestalt theorists were not proto-cognitive scientists, because an information-processing model of psychological processes is incompatible with Gestalt concepts of insight, meaning, and understanding.

From a critical perspective, although the Gestalt theorists claimed to study lived experience of perceptual and cognitive phenomena, they were *natural*-science psychologists, not *human*-science psychologists who stressed subjective experience. Like behaviourists, the Gestalt theorists accepted the environment as it appears to ordinary observation and held that only scientific observers have an objective perception of phenomena. Moreover, despite their holism, they assumed organisms were relatively passive. For instance, according to Wertheimer, Koffka, and Köhler, an interaction between forces in stimulus-objects and in an individual's cortex determines perception.

Field theory

Interacting with the Gestalt theorists at the Psychological Institute in Berlin, Kurt Lewin accepted their tradition of viewing phenomena holistically, also from a natural-science standpoint. He explored motivational, developmental, personality, and social phenomena. For instance, he "studied the mental development of children as the gradual differentiation and integration of perceived interrelationships among stimuli within the overall social field in which they live" (Sokal, 1984, p. 1244). Most influentially, he aimed "to make psychological theory practical" through research and apply it to humanize work, school, and community conditions (Ash, 1995, p. 264).

Yet, for Lewin, Gestalt concepts, such as "field" and "isomorphism," were only analogies to explain human activity, needs, fears, motives, and aspirations. Moreover, he incorporated intrapsychic processes into his psychology of action and emotion and employed terms that the Gestalt founders considered imprecise (Sherrill, 1991).

Lewin elaborated Koffka's notion of person–environment relations before he emigrated from Germany in 1933. He called his conceptual framework "field theory" after he landed in the US. In field theory, which united his diverse interests, he rejected instincts, stimulus–response connections, personality types, and stage theories. Instead, he stressed how individuals perceive their physical settings and how the ways in which they attempt to satisfy their needs affect how they interact with their perceived environments.

In the US, Lewin sustained his deep interest in personality development broadly conceived, including conditions of frustration, although US psychologists initially regarded him only as a child-development specialist. Lewin then broadened his scope to encompass psychological issues concerning minority groups. In the late 1930s his team's work on group-leadership styles established his US reputation, while he accelerated his social research, designed to enhance adaptation to democratic capitalism (Ash, 1992).

In their famous paper on leadership styles Lewin, Ronald Lippitt, and Ralph White (1939) claimed real-world generalizability for their experimentation:

The field theoretical approach also provides implications for the circumstances under which one might generalize the results of such experimental group studies. One must be careful of making too hasty generalization ... The varieties of democracies, autocracies, or "**laissez-faire**" atmospheres are, of course, numerous. Besides, there are always individual differences of character and background to consider. On the other hand, it would be wrong to minimize the possibility of generalization. The answer in social psychology ... has to be the same as in an experiment in any science. The essence of an experiment is to create a situation which shows a certain pattern. What happens depends by and large upon this pattern and is largely although not completely independent of the absolute size of the field ... The generalization from an experimental situation should, therefore, go always to those life situations which show the same or sufficiently similar general patterns. (p. 297, emphasis in the original)

Basic concepts

In Lewin's field theory goal-directed activity is pivotal and **seven concepts** are fundamental.

- Behaviour is a function of the interaction between persons and their perceived environments. The equation, $B = f(P, E)$, depicts this relationship. Interactions constitute a "field of forces" effecting action. The person is always engaged with fields of energy within her or his psychological environment.
- According to "universal causation," only the total environment, as the individual or group experiences it subjectively at the time, explains behaviour.
- Person and perceived environment are indivisible. This unity constitutes *life-space*, Lewin's central concept. Life-space incorporates all perceived physiological, sensory, motivational, cognitive, interpersonal, and cultural influences operating on an individual presently. Some influences have physical existence, others cognitive or even imaginary existence. Life-space shifts when individuals shift their attention, and it expands and becomes more differentiated developmentally.
- Originally, Lewin focused on immediate environmental influences within life-space. Later he added "social space" to the concept of life-space, expanding the environmental component to include social relations and sociocultural, economic, and organizational influences (Cartwright, 1978).
- Psychological structures (i.e., cognitive "regions" connected by pathways) and motivational dynamics (i.e., goals and conflicts) link the individual to her or his perceived environment.
- A person's goals and endless striving for equilibrium are integral aspects of life-space. Goals vary in their importance ("valence") for individuals and are activated in the present.
- Lewin understood motivation as tension systems; when we satisfy our needs, we reduce tension. He postulated motivational conflicts involving desirable and aversive objects in individuals' life-space. These conflicts became known as approach-approach, approach-avoidance, and avoidance-avoidance.

Section conclusion

Lewin's theoretical and methodological innovations embrace the relational dynamics of human nature. Furthermore, community psychologists' notions of "person-environment fit" and "participatory action research" are indebted to him. But his school of thought, which included intrapersonal phenomena, interpersonal relations, and social forces, did not survive his premature death, because it was at variance with neobehaviourist specialty-areas that proliferated in US Psychology (Ash, 1992). The common criticisms of his work were that he employed unclear terms (e.g., life-space) and weak experimental methodology.

Lewin's blended methods and critique of experimental elementism became extinct after most of his many US students abandoned them for manipulation of independent variables in social psychology experiments. Furthermore, his research on group dynamics, which resulted in workshops on training group leaders, and industrial relations proved less influential in social psychology than in professional schools of business. Nevertheless, some commentators believe that "it is hard to overstate his influence on American psychology" (Sokal, 1984, p. 1250) and his integration of theory, research, and practice remains neglected in Psychology.

Theory of higher nervous activity

For some psychologists, Ivan Pavlov was the true founder of Psychology, because, they believe, he laid the conceptual foundation for behaviourism and for experiments on learning. According to this argument, one can investigate psychological phenomena objectively by adopting his methodology as opposed to introspection and speculation about subjective states of organisms. Pavlov insisted that his exemplar of physiological conditioning, known later as the theory of higher nervous activity, was the *only* means of investigating *all* types of behaviour. Furthermore, he frequently challenged psychologists' claims and scientific status. On the other hand, from early in his career Pavlov was curious about mind and behaviour and frequently relied on contemporary psychological interpretations of his physiological data (Todes, 1997).

Theory and research

Pavlov accepted neither early European psychologists' conceptions nor behaviourists' notion that behaviour is a collection of reflexes. Rather, he integrated psychological concepts, such as association, with neurophysiological, biochemical, and clinical dimensions.

Pavlov held **four assumptions**:

- Associationist principles of contiguity and frequency best explain conditional reflexes.
- Associations between organisms and their environment produce "higher nervous activity."
- The discovery of the physiological foundation of associationism was his.
- His conditioning model supplanted mentalistic explanations and introspection.

In response to the contention by Lashley that reflex theory obstructed the study of cerebral functions, Pavlov (1932) asserted that reflex activity was based on principles of exact scientific investigation that psychologists failed to employ: "Every effort should be made to interpret phenomena in a purely physiological way, on the basis of established physiological processes" (p. 448). Nevertheless, invoking associationism, he insisted that the neural mechanisms of conditional reflexes were temporary connections in the cortex.

During the 1930s Pavlov intensified his longstanding commitment to *psychological* inquiry, applying reflex theory to complex cognition, even freedom of will. He proposed the notions of the "lower" central nervous system in internal processing and the "higher" central nervous system in scrutinizing the environment. Pavlov also postulated a "goal-reflex" that others investigated in terms of motivation and satisfaction (Sudokov, 2001).

Pavlov then extended his conditioning model to **three areas**:

- Conditional stimuli, he argued, function as warning signals about important biological events, which he called a "first signalling system." Humans also acquire conditional responses to symbols of biological events in the form of language. Thus, speech constitutes a "second signalling system."
- Pavlov posited individual differences in personality, drawing from his typology of canine temperaments and from Ivan Sechenov's excitatory, equilibrated, and inhibitory processes. He distinguished between individuals dominated by primary signals (e.g., visual artists) and secondary signals (e.g., scientists). Hans Eysenck adapted Pavlov's concepts of excitation and inhibition to personality theory in the form of extraversion and introversion as the dominant personality patterns (see Chapter 7).
- Pavlov applied his notions of excessive or deficient inhibition and excitation associated with experimental neurosis to mental health disorders. He even recommended treatments to correct inhibitory or excitatory imbalances in mental health patients (Windholz, 1997). These applications inspired the founding of behaviour therapy in the 1950s and its subsequent revisions (Wolpe & Plaude, 1997).

Section conclusion

Pavlov's work had a substantial impact on Psychology globally. But, although he *claimed* that he reduced mental to neural processes, he did not discover neurological foundations for conditional reflexes and did not demonstrate how combinations of reflexes produce higher nervous activity. His extrapolation of conditional reflexes to higher mental processes was based on speculation, not experimentation (Kozulin, 1984).

Furthermore, Pavlov explained language and thought as the consequence of established nerve associations, which he termed a second-signal system. Instead of language being a symbolic system of meaning, it was as if "higher nervous activity" were a nineteenth-century telephone-switchboard of stimulus–response connections. In short, his notion of primary and secondary signal-systems exemplified biological reductionism.

In the 1930s Soviet psychologist **Nikolai Bernstein** (1896–1966) challenged Pavlov's reactive model of conditional reflexes with an antimechanistic standpoint of active psychophysiology. Bernstein investigated "feedback mechanisms in the physiology of [human] body movements" and individual capacities for sensory self-corrections of movements (Kozulin, 1984, p. 62). But Bernstein's position did not gain traction until the 1960s. Rather, Soviet society, eager for national heroes, celebrated Pavlov's extrapolations to human behaviour.

Although Pavlov intended to supplant Psychology with his model of higher nervous activity, initially it thrived only in the Soviet Union and its satellites. For example, a Polish reflexologist, Jerzy Konorski (1903–1973), who had worked in Pavlov's lab, discovered the distinction between classical and instrumental conditioning. By the 1950s new concepts evolved, such as *second-order conditioning* (i.e., a previously neutral stimulus [e.g., a light] paired with a conditional stimulus [e.g., a tone] that elicits the same response as the conditional stimulus).

Relation to behaviourism What distinguished Pavlov's conceptual orientation from behaviourists' was that his was more holistic and his experimental methodology more rigorous than theirs. He rejected behaviourists' tendencies to explain all human behaviour by rudimentary laws of learning. Moreover, Pavlov contended that behaviourists could not account adequately for higher cerebral functions. According to him, conditioning created new reflexive pathways in the cerebral cortex that differed from the cortical area responsible for unconditional reflexes. Yet, he too used one principle – conditional *reflexes* – to account for all acquired behaviour including *cognitive* functions (Danziger, 1997b).

Generally, although some US psychologists adopted Pavlov's methodology, they failed to comprehend the significance of his conceptual orientation. They overlooked the subtleties of his model, particularly his neurophysiology, in their quest to establish a purely objective and autonomous Psychology that excluded mental events. Yet, despite the impression he projected to his scientific peers, Pavlov always had psychologized in his theorizing (Todes, 1997), just as behaviourists did. Still, not all contemporary US psychologists embraced narrow behavioural interpretations of Russian reflexology and Pavlov's work. In fact, some animal-learning investigators (e.g., Robert Yerkes) retained subjective aspects in their explanations, while others (e.g., Margaret Washburn) studied animal consciousness tied to observable behaviour.

Interest in Pavlovian conditioning declined in mid-century US Psychology for at least two reasons. First, the tenets of neobehaviourism militated against examining the biological aspects of behaviour. Secondly, simplistic textbook definitions led to misconceptions about Pavlovian conditioning (Rescorla, 1988).

In recent decades, however, a resurgence of interest in higher nervous activity has occurred with the turn to neuroscientific psychologies (Domjan, 2005). Pavlovian revisions incorporate a broader range of techniques in diverse species, for example, in studying drug-tolerance and addiction. Revisionists view organisms as information-seekers relying on preconceptions and perceived logical relations among events to represent their environment and the elements involved in complex mental processes and learning (Rescorla, 1988).

Although Pavlov was unable to specify the mechanism of conditional reflexes, neuro-physiologists today build on his foundational work and he enjoys iconic status as the forerunner of behavioural neuroscience. Research in avoidance-learning and taste-aversion shows applications of the Pavlovian model to the treatment of substance-abuse disorders (Domjan, 2005). In addition, the "reinforcement sensitivity theory" (RST) of personality includes neurophysiological explanations of positive and negative emotions (Corr & Perkins, 2006).

Behaviourism

By World War I, behaviourism was the dominant school of thought in US Psychology and its dominance persisted for decades. However, many US functionalists were behaviourists *before* John Watson published his behaviourist manifesto in 1913. In addition, behaviourism's influence was not total, and it played a negligible role in international Psychology (O'Donnell, 1985). Furthermore, behaviourism and its successor, neobehaviourism, included various types (Leahey, 2003): the stimulus–response (S–R) theories of Edward Thorndike and Watson; the purposive theory of **Edward Tolman** (1886–1959); the drive-reduction S–R theory of **Clark Hull** (1884–1952); and B. F. Skinner's operant behaviourism (see Chapter 7).

Antecedents

Franz Gall's phrenology, Alexander Bain's associationism, and Herbert Spencer's evolutionary concepts paved the way for functionalism and behaviourism (O'Donnell, 1985). They all stressed practical applications to personal and social reform, which functionalist and behaviourist psychologists adopted.

Phrenologists aimed to determine physiological functions first, then mental structures, through objective analysis of biological functions and behaviour. Attempting to predict and control human behaviour, they focused on individual differences in abilities and character. When early US psychologists pursued human engineering through eugenics, intelligence testing, and child study to effect social control, their aims converged with phrenologists' in that both phrenologists and psychologists endeavoured to induce others to behave predictably. As we have seen, however, psychologists distanced themselves from the pseudoscience of phrenology.

Bain's associationism and Spencer's evolutionary theory, both partly influenced by phrenology, were more scientifically respectable schools of thought. For Bain, Psychology's task is to explain human character and learning through trial and error, and habit. For Spencer, natural selection operates on human mental processes in ways that differ only quantitatively from the processes of "lower" animals. Intelligence, language, and even morality, in his view, aid survival and adaptation to the environment.

Like his Psychology peers, Watson absorbed the concepts of individual variation, practicality, and adaptation. Thorndike's experiments in animal learning encouraged him to explain all behaviour as stimulus–response connections. But whereas functionalists and other behaviourists retained mental constructs and consciousness, Watson ostensibly expelled them as unnecessary for predicting and controlling organisms' adaptation. Instead, he adopted Auguste Comte's positivist rejection of consciousness.

Watson's research programme

At the University of Chicago, Watson followed the practices of biologist Jacques Loeb (1859–1924) who emulated Ernst Mach's insistence on functional relations and who emphasized experimental manipulation of variables rather than naturalistic observation. By 1902 Watson developed his behaviourist principles after studying learning in lab rats. However, he delayed disclosing his theory publicly apparently due to negative responses from contemporaries, including Titchener.

In his famous manifesto, "Psychology as the Behaviorist Views It," Watson (1913) defined Psychology as:

a purely objective experimental branch of natural science. Its theoretical goal is the prediction and control of behavior. Introspection forms no essential part of its methods, nor is the scientific value of its data dependent upon the readiness with which they lend themselves to interpretation in terms of consciousness. The behaviorist, in his efforts to get a unitary scheme of animal response, recognizes no dividing line between man and brute. (p. 158)

Like Titchener, Watson stressed observable elements and reductionistic laws. But whereas Titchener focused exclusively on conscious experience, Watson repudiated any explanation of behaviour based on consciousness, language, ideas, and philosophical speculation, or even physiology. For him, a simple stimulus–response explanation sufficed.

By 1915 Watson shifted to studying humans to expand his behaviourism. He now introduced a modification of introspection into his method, calling it "verbal report," when he found that the experimental procedure he employed with animals was insufficient for humans. Other US psychologists had already been collecting participants' reports of their experimental experiences (Woodworth, 1924). Although participants' reports obviously depend on language and mind and the inclusion of these reports contradicts Watson's behaviourist principles, he never revised his S–R model.

In the US and Canada, many Psychology instructors acquaint students with the "Little Albert" study (1920) that Watson and **Rosalie Rayner** (1899–1935) conducted. In Box 6.1 we provide a critical historical perspective on this infamous study.

> **Small-group discussion.** How have your instructors or authors of Psychology text-books described the Watson and Rayner "Little Albert" experiment? What scientific value do they attribute to it?

Box 6.1 The "Little Albert" study

Examining the assumptions, method, and ethics that Watson and Rayner (1920) used reveals major conceptual, methodological, and ethical problems.

Assumptions. The authors stated that complex human emotions stem from original conditioned responses of fear, rage, and love and these emotions are equivalent to reflexes. They intended, they said, to give a conditioned-response account of both normal defences and pathology. The authors interpreted phobias, emotional disturbance, and Freudian theory in stimulus–response terms. They claimed that infants and children have erogenous zones, including lips, nipples, and genitalia, like those of adults.

Method. Watson and Rayner assessed the acquisition of fear with N = 1, which can be legitimate experimentally, as Skinner later showed. The authors paired the presence of a rat with noxious stimuli (e.g., extremely loud noise) to induce fear. However, reading their report shows that the authors mixed the procedures of classical conditioning and instrumental conditioning, which is illegitimate methodologically. Thus, contrary to the authors' claim, this study was an uncontrolled experiment that only yielded speculative and inconclusive findings (Harris, 1979).

Ethics. By declaring, "We felt we could do him relatively little harm" (p. 1), the authors dismissed the potential harm to this infant, treating him as a means to their ends. Yet they also claimed that conditioned emotional reactions "persist and modify personality throughout life" (p. 12). If conditioned responses have such enduring effects and Watson and Rayner believed they conditioned Albert, how could they not have done harm to Albert? They also knew when he would leave the hospital, but did not report whether they attempted to desensitize him. Apparently, Albert was a developmentally challenged infant. Although psychologists had no ethical standards of research until 1953, the Hippocratic Oath of "do no harm" was known for millennia.

Box 6.1 (cont.) The "Little Albert" study

A historical perspective. Afterwards, Watson distorted the study in different, popularized versions, always claiming generalization effects (Harris, 1979). Subsequent psychologists mythologized the study. Some invented a fur coat as a conditional stimulus, others a happy ending; for still others, Albert was "Peter" and the rat was a rabbit. For decades psychologists ignored the problems of the "Little Albert" study and celebrated it as an example of the scientific power to predict and control human behaviour and of Psychology's social utility (e.g., Beck, Levinson, & Irons, 2009). But historical inquiry shows that this iconic study was compromised conceptually, methodologically, and ethically.

A behaviourist revolution?

Many psychologists cast Watson as the leader of the behaviourist revolution, but this depiction deserves historical scrutiny. When he began directing the animal lab at Johns Hopkins University in 1908, only 4 per cent of US Psychology experiments published that year used animals (O'Donnell, 1985). To elevate the status of animal psychology Watson resolved to redefine all Psychology as the study of behaviour. But first he had to surmount formidable barriers.

To most peers, animal research reduced Psychology to physiology. Animal psychology also lacked obvious social applicability, when compared, for example, to Alfred Binet's popular intelligence testing. Moreover, administrators and colleagues regarded the costs of animal research and odiferous labs as liabilities. These considerations explain why, years before Watson's manifesto, Thorndike abandoned animal research for "experimental pedagogy," a practical science of educational behaviour.

By 1910, the APA recommended teaching the discipline as the science of behaviour rather than the introspective study of consciousness. US psychologists were converting to behavioural technology because of strong societal demand for practical applications. Consensus was that the "applied psychology of individuals could be rigorously experimental" (O'Donnell, 1985, p. 209).

This was the disciplinary, institutional, and societal context in which behaviourism became equated with applied psychology and in which Watson (1913) rebranded animal psychology as behaviourism. But his manifesto was anti-climactic, because most US peers already were generic behaviourists. Although Watson claimed that behaviourism was an innovation, it was functionalist in emphasizing self-improvement, active coping with life's challenges, and practical advice. Thus, rather than starting a revolution (Leahey, 1992), he transformed extant functionalist and behaviourist trends into individualistic self-focused activity useful for maintaining social institutions.

Section conclusion

For Watson, rewards and punishments shape all organisms according to stimulus–response connections drawn from animal experimentation, which became an investigative exemplar for US natural-science psychologists (Danziger, 1997b). Many believed that they could develop invariant, universal laws of human behaviour, only if they studied it in its purest form, without human communication and mind, by experimenting on animals in isolated lab situations. Although covertly Watson did not banish mental processes, his overt expulsion of them substantially impacted US psychologists experimenting on basic processes in that it took nearly fifty years before many of them restored human communication and mind to Psychology's ambit.

As a group, then, behaviourists reduced the term "behaviour" to biologically directed physical movements to make practical applications of external control of organisms (Danziger, 1997b). Yet simple physical movement was insufficient to account for apparently purposeful, human activities. Thus, indirectly they inferred mental processes. In effect, behaviourism was fundamentally flawed, which neobehaviourists recognized.

Neobehaviourism

Focusing on elementary cognitive capacities that lay in the gap between stimuli and responses, functionalist psychologists created intellectual space for revisions to behaviourism. This revision became known as neobehaviourism. By the 1930s, neobehaviourists expanded the original Watsonian model to more adequately account for animal and human behaviour. In US Psychology they predominated for roughly thirty years.

Although their theoretical positions differed substantially from one another, neobehaviourists were committed to experimentation with lab animals to study basic human processes, stressing learning and motivation. They converted perception to studies of sensory discrimination, memory to learning, and intelligence to scores on a test (G. Miller, 2003).

Neobehaviourists (e.g., Tolman and Hull) retained behaviourism's S–R framework but inserted an "O," standing for "organism" variables, in between stimulus and response. These variables encompassed internal psychological processes (e.g., hunger or expectancies) that affect learning. The result was an S–O–R behavioural model. Thus, what made behaviourism "neo" was the introduction of organismic (i.e., motivational or cognitive) variables that mediate between environmental stimuli and overt responses. But Skinner followed a rather different behaviourist path than neobehaviourists did (see Chapter 7).

Tolman's approach

As a student, Tolman participated in some of Koffka's research and learned Gestalt concepts, yet he appreciated Watson's behaviourism (Gleitman, 1991). As an academic, he amalgamated behaviourism with Gestalt ideas, inserting cognitive and motivational variables, yet abandoning consciousness and complex mental processes.

For Tolman, learning was not simply the result of a stimulus–response chain of conditional responses. Rather, explanations of learning entailed inferred cognitive structures. Moreover, he distinguished learning from performance: he showed how simply by manoeuvring in their environment, organisms acquire "latent learning" without reward; then, they perform when a reward is present.

Although the particulars of his theorizing changed over time, Tolman held **five assumptions**, addressing them experimentally:

- Data obtained from maze-learning can be made reliable.
- Learned behaviour is purposive, goal-oriented. But purpose is not a mental entity.
- Organisms learn by acquiring a molar understanding of their environments rather than by accumulating molecular motoric behaviours.
- Different laws govern various types of learning. Acquiring motor skills and solving problems are different processes.
- Operationally defined variables that intervene between stimuli and responses explain learning. These *intervening variables* link unobservable processes (e.g., expectancies) to observable independent and dependent variables.

Conceptually, Tolman described learning as a consequence of a goal-oriented cognitive process, termed "purposive behaviourism." Learning was the result of rats acquiring "cognitive maps" that resemble Gestalt perceptual fields. When attempting to master mazes, rats learn the relationship between cues in the experimental situation and their "expectancies" about the choice-points in mazes. Tolman termed this relationship a "sign Gestalt." The pattern of sign Gestalts constitutes the rats' acquired map of the maze.

Tolman (1948) explicitly employed field theory to explain maze-learning:

in the course of learning something like a field map of the environment gets established in the rat's brain . . . the rat in running a maze is exposed to stimuli and is finally led as a result of these stimuli to the responses which actually occur. We feel, however, that the intervening brain processes are more complicated, more patterned and more often, pragmatically speaking, more autonomous than do the stimulus-response psychologists . . . the incoming impulses are usually worked over and elaborated in the central control room into a tentative cognitive-like map of the environment. And it is this tentative map, indicating routes and paths and environmental relationships, which finally determines what responses, if any, the animal will finally release. (pp. 192–193)

For Tolman, human learning proceeds similarly. Expectancies develop when reinforcement follows successful responses. Thus, purposefulness and cognition were explicit assumptions in a framework that he riveted on observation of behaviour.

In sum, the use of lab rats in maze-learning experiments for understanding basic psychological processes was central to Tolman's approach. He claimed that one could draw purely objective inferences from observations of organisms' behaviour. In effect, this position strengthened US psychologists' commitment to animal models of human behaviour. Tolman also is noteworthy for pioneering the use of selective breeding in experiments on rats' ability to learn mazes, which led to behaviour genetics (Innis, 1992).

Hull's approach

Inspired by Pavlovian conditioning and Newtonian physics, Hull formalized a systematic theory of functional behaviour. For him, all organisms are machines that automatically adapt to their environments (Kimble, 1991a). Hull believed that the general laws of learning established with animal models explain human functioning. He assumed that interspecies differences in outcomes are secondary. Adapting what he dubbed a "Skinner box" to a non-Skinnerian system of mental processes as stimuli and responses, he created a mathematically precise account of behaviour with theorems and proofs (Hilgard, 1987).

Central to Hull's mechanistic model were intervening variables: *habit strength*, drive, stimulus intensity, and incentive. Habit strength is the quality of stimulus–response connections; the greater the number of reinforcements, the stronger the habit. Learning is incremental and requires reinforcement. Primary reinforcement occurs when a primary drive is reduced.

Primary drives refer to generic biological needs essential for survival. Secondary drives are learned from situations in which primary drives occur. Other intervening variables are the intensity and incentive value of given stimulus conditions.

For Hull, potential behaviour is a multiplicative function of habit strength × drive × the intensity of stimulus conditions × incentive. Thus, learning results from an interaction of generic biological and specific environmental variables.

Fascinated with formulas, Hull developed a kind of psychological algebra, reminiscent of Johann Herbart's mathematical psychology, to account for the components of his model. Yet he also attempted to accommodate differences between species and individuals and within the same individual organism. Most importantly, he insisted that "all behavior, individual and social, moral and immoral, normal and psychopathic, is generated from the same primary laws" (Hull, 1943, p. v), solely derived from his mechanistic principles of behaviour.

Hull's version of neobehaviourism, strengthened by **Kenneth Spence's** (1907–1967) research programme, surpassed Watson's simplistic model. During the 1940s and 1950s the Hull–Spence theory of learning was very influential in US Psychology. Hull's numerous followers extended his concepts to the experimental study of verbal learning, frustration and aggression, and social learning. John Dollard (1900–1980) and Neal Miller (1909–2002) even integrated Hullian with psychoanalytic concepts, reducing the latter to testable hypotheses. Yet despite its operationally defined terms and mathematical formulations, Hull's school of thought did not survive, because his abstract theorizing was derived from narrow experiments on one species.

Section conclusion

With Tolman's retrieval of "mentalistic" terms and his and Hull's insertion of motivation into the behaviourist equation, Watson's S–R theory crumbled. Beyond its scientific merits, as a US cultural product (Bakan, 1998), behaviourism also might have been successful for socioeconomic and religious reasons. Behaviourists persuaded society's power-brokers that prediction and control were essential for society's progress. Behaviourists' implicitly moral message of reward and punishment echoed the extant Methodist Christian belief in original sin by which humans are no better than beasts.

Nevertheless, neobehaviourism expired for at least **four reasons**:

- Neobehaviourists could not explain adequately more complex psychological phenomena either cognitively or biologically. Canadian physiological psychologist Donald Hebb effectively accounted for how organisms organize their behaviour biologically (see Chapter 7).

- Neobehaviourism heavily depended on animal models of learning and innate characteristics of species. But comparative psychologists observed that "A similarity of behavioural outcomes [between species] does not prove that the processes underlying those outcomes [are] similar" (Baenninger, 1990, p. 256). Species differ in the complexity of their processing, a principle that eluded neobehaviourists.
- Focused on isolated organisms devoid of mind and language, neobehaviourists claimed their terms and concepts were universally valid. By contrast, contemporary European and Soviet psychologists did not subscribe to the US view of learning; Gestalt theorists, Pavlov, Karl Bühler, Jean Piaget, and Lev Vygotsky pursued rather different schools of thought than behaviourism.
- Even though neobehaviourists inserted the "organism" into their conception of human functioning, their model of learning abstracted organisms from natural environments and social-historical conditions.

Part 3 conclusion

Five schools of thought prevailed in natural-science Psychology after World War I: Gestalt theory, field theory, higher nervous activity, behaviourism, and neobehaviourism.

The Gestalt theorists aimed to discover structural laws inherent in perceptual and cognitive processes from a phenomenological perspective. For Wertheimer, Koffka, and Köhler, the mind organizes elements of sensory stimuli into meaningful totalities and consciousness exists in terms of organized forms. Thus, they argued, psychologists should study large units of goal-directed behaviour. Although congruent with a continental-European approach, Gestalt theory was less successful in the USA where behaviourism and neobehaviourism reigned. Yet some claim Gestalt theory contributed to the cognitive turn in US Psychology.

Influenced by the Gestalt theorists, Lewin adopted field theory in his experimentation on motivational, developmental, personality, and social processes in children and adults. He promoted the centrality of person–environment interactions and individuals' perceptions of their lived environments. Lewin also had a particular interest in fostering the reciprocal relation between theory and practical application. Although influential in the middle decades of the twentieth century, field theory eventually was overshadowed by the cognitive turn in Psychology.

Pavlov proposed conditional reflexes as the basic explanation for human behaviour, even for what he later termed higher nervous activity, including cognitive processes. But although his proposal and his methodology appealed to many natural-science psychologists internationally, his conception lacked neurophysiological substance, hence was speculative. In the recent past, however, some behavioural neuroscientists have refined the Pavlovian model.

Watson was inspired by Thorndike to explain all human behaviour solely in terms of stimulus–response associations. But then without changing his theory Watson added introspection of consciousness to interpret his experimentation with human behaviour. His "Little Albert" study illustrates the conceptual leaps he made from trial-and-error study. Moreover, the claim that he initiated a behaviourist revolution is dubious historically. Within a few decades Watson's simplistic behavioural model yielded to neobehaviourist models.

In his version of neobehaviourism Tolman inferred cognitive processes from his animal-learning programme, which arguably facilitated the emergence of cognitive psychology and legitimized animal cognition (Olton, 1992). But he never explained the origins of purposive behaviour and cognitive maps. Hull relied on mathematical models and formal logic in presenting an experimentally verifiable, drive-reduction theory of behaviour. Although it resembles Thorndike's law of effect, Hull's theory postulated intervening variables, but not cognitive processes, to account for the complexity of psychological phenomena.

Beyond their pronounced but short-lived scientific effects, behaviourism and neobehaviourism had ideological effects in US Psychology. The discipline had been branching out to many academic and applied domains. But a term and a rationale for whatever it was that united these subdisciplines was lacking. "Behaviour" became that identity label. Consequently, "behaviourism" and a rationale based on learning theory served as the semantic glue that seemed to bond the disparate aspects of US Psychology together. Yet by the 1970s, behaviourism broadly defined was eclipsed on both sides by the emergence of cognitivism and by Skinner's more conceptually elegant operant behaviourism (see Chapter 7).

Part 4   Basic psychological processes

Many psychologists between the wars experimented on basic psychological processes, such as learning, memory, and language, but there were pronounced international differences in content and methodology. A few psychologists investigated neurological dimensions of learning and memory, while others explored memory and language from diverse perspectives.

Brain mechanisms and learning

Still a small minority in the discipline, biological and physiological psychologists relied on experimental studies of animal models of human functioning. In the USA, behaviourism and neobehaviourism overshadowed biological and physiological psychology until after World War II, when it became more influential. A chief exponent of this content-area was Karl Lashley. Arguably, experimental physiological psychology, as presently conceived in Psychology, originated with his 1929 book, *Brain Mechanisms and Intelligence*.

Educated in genetics, Lashley sought physiological explanations of basic psychological processes (Bruce, 1991). After working with Watson on comparative psychology and conditioning, he studied cerebral mechanisms of the conditional reflex, learning, and intelligence. From 1942 to 1958 Lashley directed the Yerkes Laboratories of Primate Biology in Florida, while a Harvard professor.

After Lashley trained rats to perform specific tasks, he found that systematically administered lesions on cortical areas had specific effects on learning acquisition and retention. The amount of cortex removed was critical to the rats' learning ability. He concluded that Franz Gall's assumption of localized functions and Pavlovian reflex theory were incorrect; rather, the cortex functions as an integrated whole, he argued, which better explains the maze-learning of brain-lesioned rats than reflexes can.

Even though he seemed pessimistic about the potential for a valid biological explanation of behaviour (Glickman, 1996), Lashley advanced a set of principles that contradicted Pavlovian theory and eventually weakened behaviourism. The **three principles** are:

- *Mass action*. The rate of learning depends on the mass of cortical tissue, not on individual cells. Thus, the greater the extent of a cerebral injury, the more restricted and inhibited performance becomes.
- *Equipotentiality*. No cortical area is more important to learning than any other area and many parts of the brain are used at one time to complete a task. Yet, although Lashley supported the notion of an equipotential brain, he observed localized neural functions.
- *Neural plasticity*. If injured, nerves and neurons, which are inherently adaptive and malleable, reorganize to restore basic behaviour.

Lashley confirmed that the cortex works as a unified whole, as Gestalt theorists had maintained, even after severe structural changes. He claimed:

The units of cerebral function are not simple reactions ... but are modes of organization. The cortex seems to provide a sort of generalized framework to which simple reactions conform spontaneously, as the words [of a speaker] fall into the grammatical form of a language. (Lashley, 1930, p. 17)

During his career Lashley maintained that all behaviour, including intelligence, has a strong genetic component. However, he also held that the number of connections and size of cerebral "storage" is genetically determined, a position which contradicts equipotentiality. In fact, he adhered to racist views about African Americans and supported racialized studies of the heritability of intelligence (Weidman, 1999).

Memory

Between the wars two different programmes on memory ultimately proved significant – Lashley's and Frederic Bartlett's.

Lashley studied the effects of cortical lesions on the recollection of trained rats. Overall, his results showed that the size of the lesions mattered but the cortical location did not. His behaviourist and neobehaviourist colleagues, who understood Psychology as the connection between stimuli and responses, concluded that the brain location of memory was best left to physiologists. As a result, little memory research occurred in US Psychology between the wars.

Perhaps the UK's most important twentieth-century psychologist (Roediger, 2000), Bartlett promoted the notion of memory as a process of active reconstruction. He studied memory of detailed, meaningful material from ordinary life with two primary methods: serial and repeated reproduction. Employing a story from an unfamiliar cultural background that research participants related serially in successive renditions, he examined qualitative differences in individuals' reproductions of the story. Observing that participants "reduced [their recollections] to an orderly narration" (p. 86), Bartlett (1932) concluded that remembering is an act of perceptual-cognitive reconstruction that is culturally grounded.

Bartlett borrowed the neurological term *schema* (i.e., mental representations) to express his conception of remembering as active organization of past responses into an adaptive mental framework that inaccurately captures memory of actual personal experiences. Influenced by Gestalt theorists, he argued that schemata organize perceptions, but we modify them because we reflect on what we learn (Billig, 2008).

Bartlett's "cognitive" explanation contradicted the standard views of memory as stimulus–response associations, neural memory traces, and, after World War II, information-processing.

Besides these contradictions, which, from a behavioural perspective, were liabilities, his methodology allegedly lacked rigour. Not until **Ulric Neisser** (b. 1928), a founding cognitive psychologist, acknowledged Bartlett's contributions did US psychologists accept his notion of active mental reconstruction (Neisser, 1967).

Bartlett proposed the concepts of conservation and constructiveness operating in active mental processes that are influenced but not determined by social-cultural conditions (Collins, 2006). In this view, our flexible mind imposes order on stimuli while accommodating to them; for Bartlett, humans are inclined biologically to balance stability and change. Yet, although his experiments were unusual relative to contemporary Psychology, his theorizing became less sociocultural and more individualistic and he did not address how ordinary interpersonal situations frequently shape remembering (Danziger, 2008).

Language

Behaviourists' aversion to *mentalism* (i.e., the belief that mental processes constitute the ultimate reality) included rejecting the psychological aspects of language and communication. By contrast, international psychologists freely investigated language and communication.

A prominent example is Karl Bühler, who studied the relationship of language, mind, and behaviour. In 1934 he published *Sprachtheorie* (*Theory of Language*), which had a profound effect on European psychologists, linguists, and philosophers (Brock, 1994). In 1922 Bühler became director of the Vienna Psychological Institute, while **Charlotte Bühler** (1893–1974), his psychologist life-partner, headed its division of child and youth research. Together, they studied children's cognitive development until 1938, when the Nazis removed them from their positions.

Taking an interpersonal approach, Karl Bühler understood language as "an utterance in a 'performance field' consisting of the speaker, the hearer, and the meanings that they share" (Woodward, 1982, p. 190). For Bühler, language not only has structure, representation, and expression, but also meaning and value (Ash, 1995). Furthermore, he studied the language of bees, reasoning that animals` communicative behaviour closely parallels human behaviour. According to Bühler's *sign theory*, words serve as signs or representations, not as unambiguous reflections, of objects, events, and experiences. Thinking is similarly psychologically complex, consisting of consciousness of rules, awareness of social relationships, and intentions.

In European circles, Karl Bühler's research and theorizing were influential for decades. Although he visited the US in the 1920s and declined an offer of a Harvard professorship in 1930, his work was not translated into English. Consequently, many US psychologists have been unaware of his theory of language; his developmental research with Charlotte Bühler; and his integration of Gestalt theory, behaviourism, and psychoanalysis (Brock, 1994).

Part 4 conclusion

Psychologists between the wars investigated basic psychological processes, such as physiological substrates of conditioning, memory, and language, but from diverse perspectives. Using animal models, Lashley studied the organizing capacities of brain functions. By successfully linking neurology and Psychology, he paved the way for biological and physiological psychology and eventually neuroscientific psychology. Rather differently than how Lashley and Hermann Ebbinghaus each investigated memory, Bartlett showed how recollection of detailed, meaningful material from ordinary life is an act of culturally grounded, active mental reconstruction. His work initially was unknown in US Psychology, but it proved seminal in the formation of cognitive psychology. Another European psychologist, Karl Bühler, demonstrated how social relationships affect cognitive processes at a time when behaviourists and neobehaviourists ignored both sets of psychological phenomena. His interpersonal approach to understanding the constellation of language, mind, and behaviour was highly influential in European circles.

| Part 5 | Developmental psychology |

To paraphrase Lev Vygotsky, understanding any psychological phenomenon requires understanding how it develops. Thus, developmental psychology spans the two fields of basic and interpersonal processes. Furthermore, it has direct application to education and parenting, while reflecting Western culture's anxiety about how to raise children (G. Richards, 2010).

During the interwar period developmental psychology emerged differently in Europe than in the USA. Generally European psychologists lacked institutional support for their scholarly work. Consequently, those who investigated developmental processes and their applications tended to operate in isolation from one another.

By contrast, US institutions, coupled with a national "Decade of the Child" during the 1920s, facilitated the subdiscipline's emergence as a research programme on normative development. University nursery-schools served as labs for researchers, while private benefactors funded the establishment of institutes of child study in the USA and Canada. Then in 1933 the Society for Research in Child Development was founded and the journal *Child Development* began publication in 1935.

Child-development research attracted female psychologists' involvement in both Europe and the USA. Although women played prominent roles in the field, they encountered personal and organizational obstacles to gain academic recognition because of women's marginalized status in Psychology (Cameron & Hagen, 2005).

After describing the chief developmental perspectives, we discuss the conceptual issues they faced.

Developmental perspectives

At least **four orientations** have informed psychologists' interests in developmental issues and their social applications (G. Richards, 2010):

- The Romantic perspective, inspired by Jean-Jacques Rousseau, was prominent in European developmental psychology. Its premise is that, just as gardeners cultivate gardens so that seeds transform into flowers, so educators should cultivate children's natural potential. The German noun *kindergarten* expresses this view, which Piaget's stage theory reflects.

- Environmentalist perspectives include US behaviourism and Marxist psychology. According to behaviourism, development mainly results from adults applying principles of learning theory to mould children's behaviour. According to Marxist psychology, development reflects societal norms and children's social relationships shape language, thinking, the sense of self, and behaviour.
- According to early psychodynamic perspectives, unconscious biological drives of libido and aggression impel children to behave according to the demands of developmental stages, and early family experiences determine children's defence mechanisms and subsequent inner conflicts. Later types of psychoanalysis were more optimistic regarding the potential for self-development.
- Within evolutionary or ethological perspectives, inspired by Charles Darwin's developmental studies, children's relations with their mothers (e.g., "maternal bonding") have survival value.

Developmental concepts

Between the wars developmental concepts unfolded quite differently in Europe than in the USA, whereas afterwards national differences subsided. The prominent European developmental theorists were Charlotte Bühler and Karl Bühler, Jean Piaget, and Vygotsky.

The Bühlers' conception

The Bühlers held that biological and psychological development was interdependent and they posited **three developmental stages**:

- Control of instincts.
- Training of sensory-motor skills.
- Adaptive learning mediated by language.

In *Die geistige Entwicklung des Kindes* (*The Mental Development of Children*), published in 1918, Karl described the Bühlers' theory and research. The book was widely used in teacher-training institutes (Brock, 1994) and strongly influenced Vygotsky's perspective on thinking and language. Charlotte's own theoretical perspective integrated cognitive with personality development and incorporated a stage theory of development parallel to Piaget's: Individuals proceed through phases of self-determination, motivated to fulfill personal life-goals.

Piaget's conception

In his *genetic epistemology* Piaget investigated how children develop the capacity to think scientifically. His heritage was zoology, philosophy, and the history and philosophy of science, not Psychology (Inhelder, 1998), although he absorbed the developmental concepts of Mark Baldwin. Using an individualized, descriptive approach to answer his research questions, Piaget described children's language, thinking about the natural world, and moral judgment. Later he studied emotion, memory, and intelligence.

Like Binet, Piaget observed how individual children, including his own, solved problems that he presented to them. Evolving over time, his method synthesized the methods of psychiatric examination with naturalistic observation and psychometrics (Mayer, 2005). He posed open-ended questions to elicit children's perspectives on the experimental situation through which he discerned their processes of reasoning.

Piaget (1952) described how he studied children's reasoning in contrast to standardized questioning about their thought processes:

it was much more interesting to try to find the reasons for the failures [in the children's reasoning]. Thus I engaged my subjects in conversations patterned after psychiatric questioning, with the aim of discovering something about the reasoning process underlying their right, but especially their wrong answers. I noticed with amazement that the simplest reasoning task . . . presented for normal children up to the age of eleven or twelve difficulties unsuspected by the adult. (p. 244)

Basic concepts Piaget (1971) investigated how children proceed from subjective egocentric thought to objective logical thought. He assumed that organized cognitive structures shape experience as individuals develop. He held that an invariant process of discontinuous stages determines cognitive development; just as children cannot dance until they are sufficiently mature physically, so they cannot think logically until they are ready cognitively.

Piaget's basic concepts fall into **three domains**:

- Children employ *schemes* and *operations* as they organize and construct reality from physical and social experience. Schemes are organized patterns, generalized from specific motoric actions; operations refer to schemes implemented mentally.
- Repetitions of the twin processes of *assimilation* (i.e., using available concepts to perceive and interpret one's environment) and *accommodation* (i.e., altering these schemes to suit particular environmental demands) enable adaptation.
- Children's construction of reality differs across developmental stages due to maturation of inherited biological structures that shape intellectual development. But the age-range assigned to each stage is merely an approximation.

After World War II, Piaget deepened his theory in concert with his female colleague, **Bärbel Inhelder** (1913–1997). They argued that infants cannot begin genuine thinking until aided by sensory-motor intelligence, they develop *object permanence* (i.e., objects retain their existence even when invisible). Infants, Piaget and Inhelder argued, construct the basic forms of knowledge before language appears.

Educational applications During the 1960s and 1970s Piagetian theory soared in popularity in the USA because of the perceived inferiority of education in science and technology relative to that of the Soviet Union, which in 1957 began launching satellites orbiting Earth. Some US psychologists attempted to find ways to accelerate the Piagetian stages of development by "programming" cognitive development. But this goal contradicted Piaget's, namely, to understand how children construct reality.

Piagetian theory remains influential in education, because it illuminates children's intellectual development for curriculum planners and teachers. **Three Piagetian principles** are relevant for primary education (Brainerd, 2003):

- Based on the premise that cognitive operations develop through concrete experiences, "discovery learning" refers to teachers encouraging students to concretely explore their immediate environments.
- Derived from Piaget's belief that cognitive operations are founded on social transmission, "children's readiness to learn" refers to teachers guiding students through the steps of learning.
- Although children proceed through the same stages of intellectual development they mature at different rates. Thus, the principle of "acceptance of individual differences" refers to teachers tailoring activities to individuals and small groups and assessing progress in relation to each child's rate of skills development.

Section conclusion By Piaget's estimation, his most significant contributions were *constructivism* and *structuralism*. In this context, constructivism means that children construct meaning from their experience, a capacity which mediates between inherited and environmental influences. Structuralism, in Piagetian discourse, means that children's constructions of knowledge produce knowledge-structures as children develop in stages (Brainerd, 1996).

From its inception Piaget's view of children as constructing agents in dialectical relation to their environments influenced psychologists internationally and stimulated decades of critical discussion. But after World War II, many US psychologists with experimental and behavioural inclinations rejected Piaget's qualitatively derived data and cognitive framework. When his theory became more widely known in the USA and Canada, others generalized his conclusions universally. Ever since, "Piaget bashers," devotees, and critical thinkers have debated his work.

Four bodies of research challenge Piaget's principles (H. Keller, 2000):

- Infants' and preschoolers' capacities (e.g., for object permanence and empathy) that exceeded Piagetian expectation.
- Learning mechanisms specific to particular domains rather than a general-purpose conception of learning.
- Interpersonal experience that demands that children restructure their schemes.
- Cultural influences on cognitive functions.

Some also claim that Piaget assumed that individual differences in social class and gender do not influence the origins of cognitive structures. Others, however, argue that common criticisms of Piaget's voluminous work are based on misconceptions and ignore the modifications he made to his concepts (Lourenco & Machado, 1996).

Vygotsky's conception

Although influenced by Piaget, Vygotsky situated the developing self in the context of cultural-historical conditions and social relations, and attributed psychological activity and consciousness to the minds of social actors (Joravsky, 1989). He held that development is interpersonal and societal as well as biological and cognitive. Thus, his broad research programme encompassed the historical development of human mental life (Yasnitsky & Ferrari, 2008).

Basic concepts In his cultural-historical theory Vygotsky aimed to explain how bodily functions and material objects transform into immaterial knowledge. For him, language is the psychological tool of mental organization that distinguishes human from nonhuman development. Inspired by Karl Bühler, Vygotsky argued that language occurs in culturally mediated contexts, shapes the development of higher mental processes, and enables control of one's actions.

Yet Vygotsky's theory was not merely cognitive. Rather, in the tradition of Baruch Spinoza whose philosophy he admired, thinking, feeling, and willing are intertwined, although culturally and historically constituted. Lower mental processes (e.g., attention) and higher ones (e.g., willing) comprise the mind. Social intercourse mediates mental processes while individuals master biological development, aided by symbols and speech.

In recasting Piaget's concept of egocentric speech, Vygotsky distinguished external from internal speech or tacit self-talk. As children develop, he asserted, they respond to adult requests or directions, they repeat them aloud as self-directions, and they internalize the requests or directions and tacitly direct themselves. Thus, inner speech increasingly serves a social-control function, directing thoughts, feelings, wishes, and actions. Moreover, children internalize external actions, symbolic tools, and interpersonal relationships.

For Vygotsky, communication in systems of symbolic interaction and social activity in systems of material production in work or study mediate development. In effect, society and the person intersect in symbolic interaction.

In sum, Vygotsky's **four developmental principles** are:

- Biological development is intertwined with social context.
- Human development proceeds continuously, not by stages.
- Children construct their knowledge and learning can instigate development.
- Verbal and nonverbal language, socially shaped but biologically dependent, is central in development.

A popular Vygotskian concept is the *zone of proximal development*, which is: "the distance between the actual developmental level as determined by independent problem solving and the level of potential development as determined through problem solving under adult guidance or in collaboration with more capable peers" (Vygotsky, [1935] 1978, p. 86). The related concept, "scaffolding," refers to adults assisting children to solve a problem beyond their present autonomous capacities. Practically, these concepts mean teaching to children's potential levels to enable them to actualize their potential and exceed their developmental levels (Langford, 2005).

Section conclusion In the 1930s students employing Vygotskian concepts circulated among institutes in Moscow, Leningrad (St. Petersburg), and Kharkov in Ukraine (Yasnitsky & Ferrari, 2008). But in 1936, Soviet authorities declared Vygotsky's cultural-historical theory heretical and its pedagogical applications perverse. In the 1950s his former student, Alexei N. Leontiev (1903–1979), proposed a theory of psychological activity whereby "material activity mediates between the subject and the external world" (Kozulin, 1984, p. 111). Then in the 1960s Soviet psychologists rediscovered Vygotsky's cultural-historical theory, which became the basis for current cultural-historical activity theory (Vassilieva, 2010).

Many psychologists tend to downplay the theory's Marxian roots and ignore the fact that Vygotsky envisioned intervening scientifically in social practices in everyday settings

(Sannino & Sutter, 2011). Instead, they view him as a specialist in children's cognitive development. In this reading, his signature concept is the social-control function of language, which links symbolic thought, speech that eventually becomes internalized ("self-statements" in cognitive–behavioural therapy), and overt behaviour.

US developmental thought

Between the wars US developmental theory included three perspectives: behaviourist, biological, and social. The prominent theorists were John Watson, **Arnold Gesell** (1880–1961), and **Lois Barclay Murphy** (1902–2003).

Watson's conception Behaviourists held that infants were "blank slates," and parents and teachers held the power to train children. They acknowledged that biological states played a role, but they emphasized environmental contingencies of learning processes. Although Watson accepted that structural changes affect motoric behaviour, for him, conditioning is the sole explanation for child development. But by the 1960s, investigations showed that newborns already have well-developed abilities, contradicting behaviourist assumptions (Horowitz, 1992).

Yet Watson's influence was profound. In his popular book *Psychological Care of Infant and Child*, he urged mothers to withhold expressing affection and to treat children "as though they were young adults" (Watson, 1928, p. 81). He insisted that parents and educators inculcate rigorous habit-formation in children. These admonitions both echoed and strengthened extant cultural beliefs about parenting. They stood in stark contrast to psychoanalytically inspired permissiveness and encouragement of self-regulation (Joncich, 1968).

Gesell's conception Focusing on biological maturation, Gesell, a psychologist and paediatrician, studied physical development in infants and children (Thelen & Adolph, 1992). For him, behavioural development was the consequence of inherited capacities, and children's inherent growth processes show uniformity and continuity. Due to his influence on US society, for decades health professionals and parents relied on Gesell's tables of developmental milestones of children's behaviour. However, he did not deny environmental effects on learning. In fact, socialist, progressivist, and eugenics positions co-existed in his thinking, and Gesell remained a leading advocate for child, school, and mental hygiene (Harris, 2011).

Murphy's conception Influenced by Lewin's field theory, Murphy integrated developmental, personality, and social-psychological concepts in studying children's interpersonal behaviour (Pandora, 1997). Engaging in intensive field observation and composing case studies of children, she used triangulating sources of evidence to account for cultural and situational phenomena.

For instance, during the 1930s Murphy investigated social-personality development (e.g., the experience of empathy) in preschool and elementary school contexts partly by employing play materials and projective testing. She interpreted her findings in relation to the school context and competitive individualism of US culture. In addition, she contributed to the progressive education movement in the 1930s and to the Head Start programme in the 1960s.

Part 5 conclusion

The interwar era saw the advent of developmental psychology as a subdiscipline that bridges research on basic processes and interpersonal phenomena with societal applications of theory and research. But multiple rather than uniform perspectives on development prevailed.

In Europe, Charlotte Bühler and Karl Bühler proposed a stage theory of human development and integrated cognitive with personality processes. Piaget studied how objective logical thought develops in children and elaborated the influential developmental concepts of schemes, operations, assimilation, accommodation, and object permanence. Particularly in the USA, these concepts proved valuable for educational applications, but they also provoked much debate. In Vygotsky's sociocultural perspective on development, language mediates between biological and cultural-historical demands. Whereas in a Marxist context Vygotsky is renowned for his conception of the social actor as dialectically related to material social conditions, in mainstream Psychology he primarily is associated with the social-control function of language and its practical applications to education and cognitive–behavioural therapy.

Although Watson's behavioural notion of development was sketchy conceptually, it influenced interwar parenting practices in the USA. Gesell's strong emphasis on children's biological development and milestones also had practical impact as did Murphy's interest in children's socioemotional development. But fuller investigative expressions of the range of developmental phenomena occurred after World War II (see Chapter 7).

Part 6   Interpersonal processes

. . . .

Personality and social psychology are the subdisciplines of Psychology that pertain to the study of interpersonal processes, but their historical trajectories differ.

Personality psychology

Personality psychologists investigate individuals' presumed internal characteristics that explain their behaviour (Hogan, Harkness, & Lubinski, 2000). Personality psychologists ask two basic questions: how are people alike? How do they differ? The answers to these questions have practical consequences. From ancient times medical practitioners also have studied the relationship between personality and health to explain differential adjustment, as do modern professionals responsible for managing individual differences in pupils, employees, clients, patients, and inmates (N. Rose, 1996).

Institutional recognition of personality as a psychological category emerged in the 1920s when psychologists increasingly were preoccupied with practical problems. During this era US society cultivated a marketable "personality," characterized by assertiveness, social efficacy, and extraverted adaptability. Citizens sought advice on self-improvement and psychological adjustment (Barenbaum & Winter, 2003), while social workers and psychiatrists assessed the personality functioning of their clients and patients.

The development of personality psychology received impetus from natural-science psychologists' response to the conceptual and practical threat to their scientific status posed by the growing popularity of psychoanalysis in Western culture. Although psychologists reduced psychoanalytic concepts to testable propositions, a fundamental problem remained: by definition, psychoanalysis deals with phenomena present underneath the surface of observable reality, for which ordinary language frequently is a disguise (Danziger, 1997b).

Another contextual factor at this time was the societal demand for applications of personality measurement, which gave impetus to psychologists studying individual differences. Psychologists assumed that teachers and social workers could do their jobs better, if these professionals scientifically understood the personalities of their service-recipients. Psychologists began to attribute the causes of individual and social problems to personality and marketed personality tests as necessary for understanding how to aid people to adapt to society.

Concepts and terms

Prior to William James adopting the term personality from Theodule Ribot, it was used in theological, legal, and ethical contexts, but it was not yet a psychological category (Danziger, 1997b). For twentieth-century natural-science psychologists, previously common terms like character, will, wish, motive, desire, and soul were rooted in subjectivity, hence were unacceptable scientifically. This is why personality came to replace character, formerly associated with human will.

Personality now connoted objective measurement of presumed constant inclinations of the total person. The general supposition was that "human conduct was directly governed by universal biological principles, irrespective of its context" (Danziger, 1997, p. 117). Personality was becoming a scientifically legitimate category.

During the 1930s, neobehaviourists employed drive to explain human motives, because drive had its roots in mechanistic biology and lab experiments in animal learning. By contrast, William McDougall had proposed instinct to denote purposeful human inclinations. Although instinct remained popular in British Psychology for decades, US psychologists favoured drive. The term "motivation" also was invented during this period.

However, **Henry Murray** (1893–1988), a US psychoanalytic investigator, proposed a different psychological term, need, which was not rooted in biology. After World War II, this term was expressed in the "need for achievement" and Abraham Maslow's familiar "hierarchy of needs" (see Chapter 10). By using need, psychologists assumed that human activity is much more a result of internal motives than of social-historical contexts.

Although US psychologist Gordon Allport evidently invented the category of personality, he did not establish its status as an object of scientific inquiry. Rather, his notions about personality stemmed from a web of contemporary academic and clinical discourse (Nicholson, 2003). Seeking to integrate his humanitarian inclinations with natural-science Psychology, he introduced the quantification of traits and values in two personality scales and posited a biological basis for personality.

Allport's mission was to preserve psychologists' scientific authority over the subjectivity of personality and to guard against common-sense knowledge and quackery. He accepted psychoanalytic belief in unconscious libidinal and aggressive drives, but he rejected psychoanalytic belief in biological determinism. Allport accepted behavioural belief in conditional reflexes, but he rejected behavioural belief in environmental determinism. Instead, his interest was in personality structure and motivation.

Idiographic and nomothetic approaches

During the interwar years some psychologists (e.g., William Stern) described personality as a conjunction of individuals and their environments. They studied individuals qualitatively, employing case-studies or life-histories, centring on each person's uniqueness and the meaning attributed to personal experience. Other psychologists relied on psychometric or experimental studies of personality inferred from quantitative group comparisons. Allport termed these two approaches *idiographic* (referring to qualitative case studies of individuals) and *nomothetic* (referring to quantitative group comparisons) respectively.

But after the subdiscipline of personality was established in US Psychology in 1937, nomothetic studies came to predominate. Many academic psychologists regarded the study of individual lives as clinical territory and of dubious scientific value. In addition, although Allport taught the idiographic study of individual lives as a method of understanding personality, he rarely published idiographic research (Barenbaum & Winter, 2003).

Within the nomothetic orientation, which is associated with natural-science Psychology, scholars explain personality according to particular *types* or *traits*. Types comprise traits organized into conceptual categories, whereas traits are descriptions of individual differences in biologically based dispositions or *temperaments* that emerge early in life and are expressed in behavioural attributes. Hans Eysenck's theory of basic temperaments exemplifies a nomothetic, natural-science approach to personality type.

During the interwar period two human-science approaches to personality type were prominent. Carl Jung (see Chapter 9) and his followers elaborated a popular but complex explanation of type based on core psychological "attitudes" and "functions." **Eduard Spranger** (1882–1963) (see Chapter 10) described personality type in relation to different value-orientations. Yet for some theorists the heart of personality is neither types nor traits but the self.

The self

In previous centuries Anglo-American and European scholars held that an immortal soul guides an individual's actions. But Enlightenment, romanticist, and early existentialist thinkers conceived of an independent private self responsible for its own fate (N. Rose, 1996). A common belief was that self-made agents determine their own fate by exercising, in Friedrich Nietzsche's term, the will to power.

According to Allport, the self, always in a process of becoming, represents expressions of goals and intentions for present and future action. Intentions, in turn, unify the self. As individuals develop selfhood, they generate new motives (e.g., service to others and spiritual/religious commitments) that operate independently of their instinctual origins. This transcendent self represents the mature personality.

In his concept of *functional autonomy* of motives Allport claimed that libidinal urges and basic childhood experiences do not primarily determine an adult's behaviour. Rather, an individual's actions stem from present traits and values that function independently of their early origins. Motives that are adaptive in one situation can take a different form in another situation (Pettigrew, 1999). Allport acknowledged that culture influenced personality, but he promoted the ideal of an autonomous, individual agent, detached from socioeconomic realities, who searches for personal fulfillment while adjusting to the environment.

Allport (1937) explained the importance of adjustment to the environment thus:

This [concept] has a functional and evolutionary significance. Personality is a mode of survival. "Adjustment," however, must be interpreted broadly enough to include maladjustments, and "environmental" to include the behavioral environment (meaningful to the individual) as well as the surrounding geographical environment. (p. 50)

In sum, Allport's key contribution was to convert the unscientific concept of "character" to the scientific concept of "personality," which in his social-historical milieu implied measurable assertiveness, social efficacy, and extraverted adaptability (Nicholson, 2003). Thus, as a natural-science psychologist, he regarded personality as an actual natural object rather than a social construction of the self. Nevertheless, his personal inclinations towards spiritual development, moral integrity, and active citizenship, which the term character had connoted, invariably seeped into his natural-science orientation.

In the category "personality," Allport fashioned a concept about the self that bridged scientific and spiritual notions of the soul. Thus, he advocated a blend of quantitative and intuitive methods to encompass both causal explanation and interpretation of meaning attributed to the self. But, given the cultural value of quantification in US society and Psychology, psychometric methods enjoyed much more credibility than qualitative ones, which resulted in most US psychologists studying personality quantitatively.

Needs

Another important category in personality psychology during this era was the needs of the self. A physician, biochemist, and trained psychoanalyst, Murray directed Harvard's psychological clinic where he also conducted personality research to understand the depths of human nature. He postulated twenty psychological needs with associated traits and regarded needs as potentially combining in numerous interactions with environmental influences ("press") operating on a person (Barenbaum & Winter, 2003). Press comprises situations, including cultural and societal influences, and the person's perception of them.

For Murray, Psychology is a descriptive and explanatory science of human perceiving, feeling, thinking, and acting. His investigative focus was whole individuals rather than aggregated characteristics of individuals. Accordingly, composing a biography was the best test of his personological approach. Because he believed that multiple internal and external processes cogently explain individual personality, he regarded experimental manipulations of single variables as inadequate for personality research (Triplet, 1992).

Murray's orientation to personality assessment, known as the "multiform method," featured multiple sources of data, interpreted from multiple perspectives. In a "diagnostic council" investigators from diverse disciplines rated an individual's personality and reached a convergent diagnostic formulation through group discussion. This method influenced clinical research and practice and the selection of managerial personnel.

The personality instrument associated with Murray, the Thematic Apperception Test (TAT), was co-created with **Christiana Morgan** (1897–1967), a psychological associate and his paramour (F. Robinson, 1992). Morgan and Murray (1935) developed a method for therapists to uncover patients' projections. By "projection" the authors meant unconscious verbal or symbolic processes rather than a defence mechanism (J. Anderson, 1999). Murray subsequently used the TAT in his personality investigations concerning needs and environmental press.

Murray's (1938) personality research established him as a leading theorist. He also introduced abnormal psychology and psychotherapy, which originally were medical fields, to US Psychology (Barenbaum, 2006). Although some peers admired the scope and depth of his work, others regarded it as methodologically deficient. Yet as the founder of "personology," the study of individual life histories, his standpoint remains influential.

Section conclusion

Conceptually, **two propositions** underlay the new personality psychology:

- Personality is consistent across time and place. "Human conduct is the expression of some essence within the individual . . . irrespective of the conditions under which the conduct occurs and is observed" (Danziger, 1997, p. 128). That is, personality and motivation are natural objects that exist independently of psychologists' observations.
- Personality is as universal and objectively measurable as intelligence reputedly is.

Despite these propositions, personality investigators had to employ subjective human language to describe what they observed, thus contradicting their claim to purely objective measurement of natural objects.

Social psychology

Although experimentation on social phenomena was rare during Psychology's founding decades, accounts of social psychology's history typically celebrate famous experiments, "American" contributions, and social psychologists' alleged progressive values (Cherry, 1995). Our focus is on the origins of social psychologists' conceptual and methodological approaches, the popular category of attitudes, and conceptions of small-group behaviour.

Origins

Gordon Allport's eldest brother, **Floyd Allport** (1890–1978), developed experimental social psychology in the 1920s and introduced concepts and methodology that moulded the subdiscipline's future (Katz, Johnson, & Nichols, 1998). Conceptually, by simplifying complex social relations, he converted social psychology into a natural science (Greenwood, 2004). Although he believed that individuals interact with other individuals and environments and relationships shape behaviour, Allport admitted only facts about individuals to explain social phenomena.

Allport advocated defining concepts in measurable behavioural terms and spurned the metaphorical language of sociologists and European notions of the collective, the crowd, or group mind. Thus, he shifted social psychology away from its original social orientation to an individual-centred approach, yet generalized to all social phenomena.

The US socioeconomic context shaped these intellectual practices. Invoking a social Darwinist notion, Allport emphasized rivalry in groups, attributing it to a natural tendency towards individualistic competitiveness. This personality disposition is characteristic of unregulated free-market societies. In later developing the category of attitudes with his brother, Floyd was responding, at least indirectly, to public calls for social scientists to aid policy-makers in manipulating public opinion and making "individuals more predictable, calculable, and manageable" (Danziger, 1997, p. 147).

By World War II, social psychology remained a small branch of US Psychology, and its practitioners, who followed different approaches, struggled for scientific legitimacy (Capshew, 1999). What seemed to unite social psychologists were **three assumptions** about their domain (Morawski & Bayer, 2003):

- Human nature was irrational, amoral, multi-determined, and socially embedded.
- Only the scientific method, understood as quantitative experimentation, could yield trustworthy, rational knowledge about humans as social beings.
- Social psychologists should contribute to improving human welfare.

Attitudes

When US social psychologists developed techniques for measuring attitudes in the 1920s comparable to intelligence tests, attitudes became their metaphorical signature. They studied intra-individual phenomena in contrast to sociologists' focus on the influence of institutional and cultural factors on individuals. As noted above, there was a ready US market for attitudes in that assessing them was useful commercially for advertising products and politically for tapping into public sentiments.

The specific technique employed in attitude measurement was *scaling*, adopted from the judgment-paradigm in nineteenth-century psychophysics. This is the origin of the familiar research term, "scale." Psychologists assumed that measuring an opinion or an attitude is just like comparing physical objects; in other words, measuring attitudes is reputedly just as objective as interpreting physical stimuli (Danziger, 1997b).

But what do attitudes actually measure, how permanent are they, and how enduring is the meaning of the concept to which they refer? Social psychologists long have had difficulties addressing these questions (G. Richards, 2010). Meanwhile, they held that attitudes actually exist as the mental property of individuals, not groups. The result was a kind of dualism: psychologists claimed that their focus was on external, observable behaviour; yet attitudes clearly are concerned with internal characteristics. This contradiction precipitated years of debate about the link between attitudes and behaviour.

A different approach to investigating attitudes was exemplified by social scientists in the early 1930s at the Frankfurt Institute for Social Research in Germany. These scholars, known as critical theorists (see Chapter 12), studied the relationship between socioeconomic conditions and attitudes in relation to social consciousness.

After relocating to the USA, one critical theorist, **Theodor Adorno** (1903–1969), led a famous study, *The Authoritarian Personality*, co-authored by Else Frenkel-Brunswick, Daniel Levinson, and Nevitt Sanford (1950), on attitude formation and change. The authors blended the socially engaged approach of psychoanalytically inspired ideological analysis with the allegedly neutral approach of measuring anti-Semitic attitudes as if they were physical objects. Using case histories and scales, the authors concluded that personality dispositions (e.g., rigid thinking) were associated with authoritarianism.

Small-group behaviour

Social psychologists approached the study of small-group behaviour either individually, as Floyd Allport did, or as a group entity, as Kurt Lewin and his associates did.

Originally, Allport asserted that the extant concepts of "crowd," "collective," or "group" mind only could be understood as manifestations of individual consciousness. Moreover, for him, groups do not have their own "identity," because only individuals can have an identity. Accordingly, he insisted that psychologists should only investigate individuals in a group; the group itself was sociologists' domain.

Later, reiterating that Psychology only apples to the individual, Allport (1962) acknowledged the operation of "frames of reference," "social norms," or "reference groups" on an individual's judgments or perceptions, but he contended that these concepts "lack motivational dynamics" (p. 11). Although he acknowledged the value of Lewinian small-group processes, Allport insisted that they did not explain the connection and distinction between the individual and group.

By contrast, Lewin compared *group* processes rather than the individuals within them. He studied patterns of group interaction in complex social situations, based on the Gestalt concept of whole situations. He argued that a small group of any type has a characteristic Gestalt influencing each of its members. If membership changes in the group the entire configuration will rearrange itself, because the members are dynamically interdependent. He coined the term *group dynamics* to refer to group processes.

Lewin earned a reputation as a founding social psychologist because of his famous study (1939) on leadership styles. This investigation was not a conventional statistical experiment but a blend of methods tailored to a complex comparison of group climates. The authors compared democratic, authoritarian, and laissez-faire styles of leadership to show that democracy works best in the face of fascism in Europe.

However, the participants in this study were US boys not adults, and even in the democratic condition the researchers restricted them to discussing the researchers' stipulated options; the boys could not determine the plan or the eventual outcome directly (Franks, 1975). Thus, the investigation only reflected a veneer of democratic participation, contrary to the universalized claims for superior democratic leadership that many psychologists attribute to it.

Section conclusion

Some commentators credit Floyd Allport with transforming social psychology from philosophical speculation to a virtual cognitive behavioural science of individuals (e.g., Katz *et al.*, 1998). He gave US social psychology enduring investigative direction and situated it in the undergraduate curriculum (R. Smith, 1997). He also secured social psychology's natural-science status by adopting a behavioural explanation and using the power of experimentation to study social psychological questions.

Other commentators argue that Allport reduced social phenomena to internal processes such as attitudes (Parkovnick, 2000). Furthermore, not all contemporaries emulated Allport's conceptual and methodological approach. Lewin studied small-group behaviour as a group, whereas Allport focused on individuals. Methodologically, before lab experiments became standard in social psychology after World War II, diverse methods were the norm and experimentation was more broadly conceived by US social psychologists (Greenwood, 2004).

Part 6 conclusion

The interpersonal areas of personality and social psychology came into their own between the wars during a time when Psychology served the function of modernizing the mind.

Personality psychologists investigate the similarities and differences between individuals, which during the 1920s became a preoccupation with administrators in industry and commerce. Business seemed to demand a scientific approach to categorizing employees. Although the language of character, will, motive, and desire existed for centuries, personality itself did not emerge as a subdiscipline until the 1930s, when Gordon Allport introduced the distinction between idiographic and nomothetic approaches to understanding personality. Natural-science and human-science psychologists differed in their investigations of personality type, a psychological category with ancient roots; Allport, for instance, practised objective measurement of traits and subjective values.

For many psychologists (e.g., William James, Mary Calkins), the notion of a self is central to the discipline's content. So it was in early personality psychology. Allport promoted the common view of the self as an autonomous, individual agent. In his personological theory of personality Murray imputed the now familiar psychological term "needs" to human motivation and showed how needs are intertwined with the various environmental factors influencing an individual. Ever since, needs became part of Psychology's discourse.

During Psychology's founding decades those psychologists who considered social phenomena tended to emulate the contemporary sociological approach of describing cultural and institutional influences on collective mentality. But in the 1920s, appealing to the social Darwinist notion of natural inclinations towards individualistic competitiveness, Floyd Allport established an individual-centred social psychology and defined his concepts in measurable behavioural terms. The category of "attitudes" that he and Gordon Allport introduced epitomized psychologists' preference for studying presumed mental properties of individuals. Floyd Allport's conception of the behaviour of individuals interacting in small groups also reflected his individualistic orientation, whereas Kurt Lewin studied small-group behaviour in terms of group dynamics. After World War II the individualistic orientation in social psychology prevailed, enhanced by the emergence of social cognition (see Chapter 7).

Part 7 Psychology and the social order

Between the wars while natural-science Psychology was still a young science, its knowledge-base came to serve the functions of modernizing the mind and reforming society

Figure 6.2 A shopping catalogue for games and toys, London, 1920

(Ward, 2002). Here we address the relationship between Psychology and the state in European and US contexts, including psychologists' responses to the Depression, and psychologists' responses to ethnocultural and gender issues in society and their own discipline. Although there was much social turmoil in Anglo-American and European nations between the wars largely due to severe economic disparities, which escalated during the Depression, ignoring economic and social inequalities was common within privileged classes, as the 1920 advertisement reproduced in Figure 6.2 illustrates.

Psychology and the state

In effect, the discipline became integrated with the social order, which took different forms in diverse nations.

The European context

European psychologists' responses to political conditions during the interwar period are exemplified by the Vienna Psychological Institute, Gestalt psychology under the Nazi regime, and the Stalinization of Soviet Psychology.

After World War I, a social democratic party promoting an equal-opportunity political agenda governed Vienna, which became an autonomous province in 1920. Reorienting public education towards child-centred, active learning was a key government policy. Psychology suited this aim, because the discipline had been a cornerstone of curricula in pedagogical institutes since the nineteenth century.

With government support Karl Bühler and Charlotte Bühler founded a Psychological Institute in 1922 (Ash, 1987). Karl investigated topics in perception, cognition, and language, while Charlotte with primarily female investigators directed child and youth research. Shortly after the Nazis occupied Vienna in 1938, Karl was incarcerated briefly for his political views. The Bühlers then immigrated to the US and the Institute expired in 1942.

Escaping Nazi persecution in Vienna, **Marie Jahoda** (1907–2001) immigrated to England, the USA, and England again. From the 1930s to the 1970s, she researched social issues (e.g., unemployment, ethnoracial prejudice, and positive mental health) with psychoanalytic and social concepts and non-experimental methods. In 1953 she became the first female president of the Society for the Psychological Study of Social Issues (SPSSI) in recognition of her advancing the Lewinian integration of theory, research, and action (Unger, 2001).

When the Nazi regime in Germany began in 1933, a diaspora ensued with the Gestalt founders relocating to the USA and other nations. For instance, Wolfgang Köhler, who was not Jewish, refused to conform to the Nazis' anti-Semitism.

But **Wolfgang Metzger** (1899–1979), a leading member of the second generation of Gestalt psychologists, joined the Nazi party while trying to preserve Psychology (Götzl, 2003). He rendered Gestalt concepts ideologically acceptable by claiming they were compatible with Nazism. After the war he rejected Nazism and applied Gestalt theory to public education.

In the Soviet Union after World War I, government authorities excoriated one school of psychological thought and championed another then reversed themselves. Yet coerced accommodation with changing Soviet ideology influenced, but did not determine Psychology totally. Some psychologists appeared to conform ideologically but maintained their scientific positions covertly or in disguised form (Kozulin, 1984).

Nevertheless, during the 1930s, responding to the Stalinization of Psychology, Lev Vygotsky distorted Piagetian theory by accusing it of metaphysical idealism. Furthermore, he permitted the concealment of his own concepts lest the state declare him a "bourgeois" psychologist (Joravsky, 1989). This circumstance explains why much of his work was not published until decades after he died.

Meanwhile, Soviet authorities championed Ivan Pavlov despite his deriding dialectical materialism as unscientific and avoiding public Soviet events (Joravsky, 1989). Then in 1934 he reversed himself, praising the regime for funding his work and for rejuvenating society with a bold social experiment. Thus, Pavlovian theory – conditional reflexes are the foundation for higher nervous activity – and Soviet ideology – the brain enables knowledge that reflects objective, external reality – converged.

The US context

Due to psychologists' contributions to World War I, US society regarded them as capable of providing scientifically sound advice on social behaviour. Keen to maintain their societal utility, psychologists tailored their discipline to society's economic expansion and progress, which required a compliant populace. Psychologists' scientific goals mirrored society's aims of adaptation to the environment, social control, and management of external behaviour. By the 1920s, US Psychology resembled "an administrative science, a technology to be wielded by society's managers to direct the actions of those in their charge into desired channels" (Danziger, 1979, p. 38).

Implicit in psychologists' commitments *as scientists* to the social order was a tacit moral framework of **four assumptions** about their societal role (Morawski, 1986):

- Reason inhered in nature, which only scientific expertise could reveal.
- Scientists were objective, value-neutral, and rational.
- Human nature was irrational, and the laity, unlike scientists, relied on backward thinking.
- Accordingly, the best guide for preserving a rational, stable social order was efficient application of social-scientific knowledge.

The Depression

During the 1930s social psychologists contributed to social reform while refining techniques for experimenting on social processes and studying aggression, racial prejudice, and authoritarianism (Morawski & Bayer, 2003). As scientists, they believed that they should manipulate the masses for their own good. They perceived no contradiction between their claims to be independent of political biases and their belief that the highest criterion of scientific validity was the practical control of behaviour to ensure adjustment to the social order (e.g., G. Allport, 1940).

Although some psychologists engaged in social-reform activities and social research between the wars, others ignored social and national problems, as evidenced by journal content (Bruner & G. Allport, 1940). From 1929 to 1937 the ratio of learning experiments to studies on unemployment was approximately 16:1 (Reiff, 1970). Moreover, some psychologists (e.g., Edward Thorndike) promoted societal remedies to strengthen US capitalism (R. Thorndike, 1991).

Organizational responses Despite the Depression's societal impact, the APA resisted impulses for social change (Nicholson, 2003). Initially, the APA insisted that the fittest PhD Psychology graduates would survive and find employment independently. Meanwhile, some psychologists formed alternative organizations (e.g., the Psychologists League) partly to agitate for expanding the number of psychologists in public service to alleviate psychologists' unemployment (Finison, 1976).

But the APA received considerable pressure to change direction regarding employment prospects for psychologists and social and economic conditions in society. In 1935 and 1936 under the successive presidencies of Clark Hull and Edward Tolman, who advocated social reform directed by scientific research, the APA supported the founding of the SPSSI in 1936.

Originally, SPSSI members, who represented diverse subdisciplines, aspired to make research politically relevant (Finison, 1986). Their audience was the public, labour groups, and activist professionals. They took explicitly partisan positions as scientist-supporters of the elected government in the Spanish civil war and as scientific workers in solidarity with industrial workers.

By 1940 the SPSSI's critical edge was dulled. During World War II, SPSSI members received government funding for applied research. Their wartime participation resulted in

Box 6.2 **Social reformers**

Rather than rebelling against Psychology and society (Pandora, 1997), US psychologists were ambivalent about participation in social reform. Initially, Gordon Allport opposed psychologists' direct involvement in social reform, contending that societal applications would contaminate the discipline's scientific core. Then in the 1930s he reversed his position. But many Psychology peers regarded his new reformist inclinations as contaminating science with politics (Nicholson, 2003).

Allport, Lois Barclay Murphy, and her life-partner Gardner Murphy (1895–1979) participated in debates over the place of science in a democratic society that was compromised by the Depression (Pandora, 1997). Their mission was to reconstruct psychological science and society jointly. Although to some extent they deviated from conventional scientific and psychological positions, they remained members of the psychological establishment and defenders of US society.

Another social reformer was Kurt Lewin, who advocated rational management of society. Although in action research he incorporated participants' involvement throughout the process of planning and evaluation, the effect was to serve managers' or administrators' purposes, who might or might not use the research findings to serve subordinates' interests (Sanford, 1970). Similarly, Lewin tried to improve assembly-line conditions for workers by improving managers' paternalistic relations with workers, but not by changing the nature of work (Ash, 1992).

changing their audience from the public to corporations and government. Their political stance became public education and research on social issues to strengthen US society.

The SPSSI never became a radical organization, because the larger discipline's value-neutrality restrained the aspirations of some SPSSI members for a politically engaged Psychology of direct action (Harris, 1986). Compared to APA, SPSSI members appeared anti-establishment. But they were social reformers, as the examples in Box 6.2 show. Moreover, SPSSI members promoted Psychology as a scientific defence of the status quo in the tradition of Thorndike and Watson. Meanwhile, SPSSI members ignored issues of power and gender in society and in the SPSSI itself (Morawski, 1986).

Section conclusion

Arguably, Psychology between the wars became a form of moral technology (G. Richards, 1995), intertwined with its administrative function in society (Danziger, 1979; N. Rose, 1996). Psychologists took on the task of shaping human nature to fit the demands of capitalist democracy. Their mission was to provide the psychological expertise to maintain an efficient socioeconomic system and extant cultural mores.

Facilitating personal adjustment to one's given environment became psychologists' applied focus. The means to their end was to employ an implicit moral framework, reputedly grounded in objective science. Psychologists regarded those who criticized social institutions or agitated for political and economic revolution as "maladjusted"; only scientifically trained experts should plan social change (Napoli, 1981).

Psychological discourse provided a plausible rationale for and enhanced the capacities of administrators of social institutions (i.e., educators, employers, government officials) to steer the public, overtly or covertly, to adapt to the social order. The discourse consisted of concepts, terms (e.g., "behaviour" and "motivation"), and techniques for measuring them (Nicholson, 2003). In effect, applications of Psychology functioned as social engineering, institutionalizing corporate profit-making and reinforcing citizens' adjustment to the status quo.

While their ranks and societal influence expanded, US psychologists confronted **four social requirements** (Harris & Nicholson, 1998, p. 1):

- Their concepts and methods had to be "new and superior to common sense."
- Psychologists' expertise had to seem "both relevant and objective."
- Alliances with the power-brokers in their intended social settings were necessary.
- Psychologists had "to balance the roles of social critic and social engineer."

But psychologists' investment in responding to sociopolitical interests overshadowed questions about their discipline's relationship to the social order. For example, Tolman objected to the USA entering World War I, and during World War II he published a book explaining motivation for war and advocating its containment. In the 1950s during the national fear of communist infiltration he defended academic freedom by refusing to sign a loyalty oath imposed by the University of California, an oath that subsequently was ruled unconstitutional. But Tolman's personal actions ignited a discipline that tended to regard itself as value-free.

In addition, psychologists' implicit political interests eclipsed discourse on the discipline's scientific underpinnings. Whereas in previous centuries the language and logic of scientific inquiry became increasingly abstract and sophisticated, psychologists largely avoided their epistemological foundations until their peculiar perspective on positivism emerged in the mid 1930s (see Chapter 11).

> **Small-group discussion.** In your opinion, should psychologists respond as psychologists or private citizens to pressing social issues such as war, economic inequalities, and environmental threats to human survival?

Ethnocultural and gender issues

Beyond psychologists' contributions to their respective nations' military and economic efforts, they struggled with issues of ethnocultural status and gender among psychologists themselves and in their respective nations. Internationally, racism and sexism remained significant strains in the discipline.

Race and racism in Psychology

Discussion of race and racism in the history of Psychology mainly has concerned African Americans, although there is some literature on scientific racism in Germany, South Africa, and Britain (Winston, 2004b). Originally, psychologists, who were White and enculturated in nineteenth-century notions of superiority over "darker races," aimed to identify racial differences with psychological and physical-anthropological instruments (Guthrie, 1998). In segregated "America," psychologists concentrated on testing the alleged intellectual deficiencies of children of African, Native, and Mexican descent during much of the twentieth century.

Some White psychologists, Lewin for instance, responded assertively to racism. Organizationally, the SPSSI issued a public statement in 1938, criticizing the alleged scientific basis for "racial psychology" in response to the anti-Semitism and racial purity doctrines of the fascist governments in Nazi Germany, Spain, and Italy. Among the twelve authors of this statement were Tolman and the Allports.

During this era education in Psychology for African American students was quite limited, even though by 1899 eighty-two Black colleges existed. The first African American to earn a Psychology PhD was **Francis Sumner** (1895–1954) in 1920. He headed the Psychology department at Howard University, but scholarly opportunities for African American professors were also limited.

Gender and sexism in Psychology

Critiques of gender in the discipline and in society were rare during Psychology's founding decades. For much of the discipline's history, many psychologists regarded gender differences, which they emphasized over gender similarities, as a function of inherited biology. Furthermore, they took men as the basis for generalizing about both men and women. On the other hand, other psychologists and social scientists between the wars debated the notion of gender differences and rejected the sexist standpoints that some psychologists explicitly adopted (R. Rosenberg, 1982).

One example was an early clinical psychologist, **Leta Stetter Hollingworth** (1886–1939). Building on Helen Thompson Woolley's research, Hollingworth challenged the scientific doctrine of biological determinism and explored gender differences (A. Klein, 2002). She found that gender similarities occur on most psychological variables and gender differences are related to age and context.

As a citizen, Hollingworth publicly supported contemporary feminism. For example, the title of her 1927 article in the periodical *Current History* was "The new woman in the making." An advocate for gifted children, Hollingworth believed that children of all levels of intelligence should receive educational stimulation suited to maximizing their potential, but she also maintained that mental ability was fixed at birth and advocated eugenics.

Part 7 conclusion

Social applications of natural-science Psychology in Europe and then in the USA before and during the Depression reflected a relationship of social reform between Psychology and the social order. Although many psychologists engaged in various types of social reform, others took explicit positions in support of authoritarian governments, racism, or sexism.

Between the wars Vienna was a site for psychological expertise contributing to social democracy. When the Nazis increasingly seized power, many psychologists, including the

Bühlers, who opposed Nazi policies were persecuted. Other psychologists, such as Metzger, collaborated with the regime. In the Soviet Union psychologists, including Vygotsky and Pavlov, capitulated to the Stalinization of Psychology.

In the US context psychologists in the name of value-free science committed themselves to the practical control of behaviour to ensure the populace's adaptation to the social order. During the Depression, although many psychologists ignored societal conditions, others as individuals and through the SPSSI attempted to shore up democratic capitalism threatened by protracted economic collapse. Rather than serving as anti-establishment activists, psychologists promoted the discipline as a scientific contributor to conserving the social order.

Since Psychology's inception, racism and sexism operated within the discipline itself in terms of systemic obstacles militating against equal opportunities for visible minorities and women as well as in the racist and sexist views of individual psychologists. These oppressive trends continued during the interwar years, when African American and Jewish psychologists were the recipients of racist practices and women were subjected to sexist practices. With some exceptions psychologists did not exercise leadership in challenging racism and sexism in society.

Part 8   Thematic review

In retrospect, **four themes** characterize the development of natural-science Psychology between the wars:

- Narrow purview
- Biological ambivalence
- Disciplinary fragmentation
- Alliance with the societal status quo

Narrow purview

Natural-science psychologists concentrated on individual functioning abstracted from social structures and historical contexts (Sarason, 1981) and disconnected from relevant collateral disciplines, such as biology and political science (Rozin, 2007). Moreover, they did not study the meaning of individuals' experience. Rather, psychologists investigated isolated segments of psychological processes. One dissenting voice in this disciplinary consensus was Gordon Allport (1940), who argued that only by including meaning and social-historical contexts could psychologists understand the uniqueness of individuals and effectively influence human behaviour.

Internationally, psychologists investigated the range of basic processes, including mental phenomena. By contrast, US psychologists had to invent cognitive behaviourism to catch up with their international peers who had never abandoned mental processes.

Methodologically, theoretical discourse, case studies, societal applications, and non-statistical studies of memory, thinking, and language that incorporated private experience had been common during the discipline's founding decades, even in US Psychology journals (Bruner & G. Allport, 1940). But by World War II, US natural-science psychologists were heavily engaged in statistical experiments on animal learning or motivation.

Biological ambivalence

Although William James had regarded body and mind as a unity, Watson and other behaviourists ignored physiology and psychophysiology as much as they rejected introspection and philosophical speculation. Academic psychologists between the wars generally held a dualist position on body–mind relations. Similarly, professional psychologists pursued clinical practice as if their clients and patients were disembodied. Although Gestalt and Pavlovian psychologies obviously were biologically oriented, biological and physiological psychology remained a relatively rare practice until the post-World War II era, when it re-emerged in more sophisticated versions as behavioural and cognitive neuroscience during the late twentieth century (see Chapter 7).

Disciplinary fragmentation

Rather than a unified entity, Psychology between the wars was as fragmented as it was from its inception conceptually, organizationally, and institutionally (Capshew, 1999). From a global perspective, Psychology lacked unity, partly because US psychologists seemed unaware of international developments in the discipline.

Conceptually, US psychologists, in particular, explored psychological processes in compartmentalized ways, yielding a segmented picture of psychological functioning; they did not investigate how sensory, perceptual, motoric, emotive, unconscious, and cognitive phenomena were coordinated in actual experience.

In addition, organizationally and institutionally, US Psychology, at least, was disunited. Tensions between primarily applied and primarily academic psychologists resulted in the APA splitting in 1937, then reuniting in 1944.

Alliance with the societal status quo

Historically, Psychology has been primarily a product of economically privileged societies. Thus, its theory and research have reflected capitalist ideology of competitive, individualistic, hedonistic motivation (Sarason, 1981). Yet mainstream psychologists have not examined how conflicting socioeconomic classes and power-disparities in society might affect psychological development.

In every nation where Psychology enjoyed a significant institutional presence, psychologists encountered new societal demands on their science and profession, largely fuelled by participation in or preparation for war, which influenced the development of all aspects of the discipline (G. Richards, 2010). The evolution of the SPSSI exemplifies this alliance. Although some psychologists studied the origins of war and speculated about preventing it, many others, when their own national interests were at stake, directly contributed to improving the efficacy of war-making (Napoli, 1981). Moreover, few studies in the 1930s pertained to social issues despite the Depression and rise of fascism in Europe.

Summary

In Part 1 we observed that significant socioeconomic changes occurred that affected Psychology's development. Societal conditions were conducive to natural-science psychologists persuading society's movers and shakers that they had scientific knowledge that would benefit industry, business, and government. Psychologists, particularly in the USA, rode the crest of a wave of public enthusiasm for science and its technological applications. Stimulated by scientific discoveries, major epistemological change occurred in the natural sciences, but by and large natural-science psychologists persisted in their adherence to Newtonian assumptions.

In Part 2 we noted the expansion of Psychology as a natural science in those nations in which the discipline had a significant presence – Germany, the UK, France, Russia / the Soviet Union, and the USA. Although academic and professional Psychology existed in Canada and in some other European nations and in some Asian and Latin American nations, the discipline flourished more in these societies after World War II. Female psychologists, however, struggled to gain societal and professional acceptance.

In Part 3 we discussed prominent schools of thought in natural-science Psychology between the wars: Gestalt theory; Kurt Lewin's field theory; Ivan Pavlov's theory of higher nervous activity; behaviourism as manifest in John Watson's version; and neobehaviourism as exemplified by Edward Tolman and Clark Hull. Although in US Psychology behaviourism and neobehaviourism prevailed, in European circles Gestalt and Pavlovian psychology were prominent.

In Part 4 we described influential programmes in basic psychological processes. We noted Kurt Lashley's studies of the organizing capacities of brain functions; Frederic Bartlett's demonstrations of memory as active reconstruction; and Karl Bühler's interpersonal conception of language, mind, and behaviour.

We described developmental psychology in Part 5. We noted the comprehensive orientations and influential concepts that European psychologists Charlotte and Karl Bühler, Jean Piaget, and Lev Vygotsky promoted. Piaget's and Vygotsky's work was particularly influential in US Psychology. There John Watson, Arnold Gesell, and Lois Barclay Murphy also explored developmental issues and their applications from quite different perspectives: behavioural, biological, and socioemotional respectively.

In Part 6 we discussed the formal emergence of the interpersonal subdisciplines of personality and social psychology. Gordon Allport instigated personality psychology, while Henry Murray focused on complex case studies. In social psychology, Floyd Allport and Kurt Lewin energized the experimental turn in their subdiscipline. In addition, the content areas of attitudes and small-group behaviour became prominent in social psychology.

In reflecting on the relationship between Psychology and the social order we described in Part 7 social applications of natural-science Psychology in Europe and then in the US before and during the Depression. In the latter period many psychologists engaged in various types of social reform in society for the ultimate purpose of encouraging individuals' adaptation to the status quo, while others supported fascistic regimes, racism, or sexism.

In Part 8 we summarized the principal conceptual and methodological developments in natural-science Psychology between the wars. We identified four themes: the discipline's narrow purview, ambivalence about biological processes, disciplinary fragmentation, and psychologists' explicit or implicit alliance with the political and socioeconomic status quo. To some extent these developments persisted during the next phase of natural-science Psychology's development, the post-World War II era, which we address in the next chapter.

Sample essay questions

Evaluate the following claims, which are not necessarily "true" statements. Take a position and support it with specific historical evidence.

1. Although the Watson and Rayner "Little Albert" experiment is questionable ethically, it remains a powerful demonstration of behavioural theory with useful practical implications.

2. Ivan Pavlov was a better "psychologist" than the behaviourists and neobehaviourists were.

3. Gestalt theory had little impact on US Psychology.

RECOMMENDED READING

The key critical, background works for the interwar period are G. Richards's (2010) *Putting psychology in its place* and R. Smith's (1997) *Norton history of the human sciences*.

Resources on Psychology in various nations include: Brock's (2006a) *Internationalizing the history of psychology*, Gilgen & Gilgen's (1987) *International handbook of Psychology*, and Sexton & Hogan's (1992). *International psychology: Views from around the world*.

A general source for exploring the history of African American psychologists is Robert V. Guthrie's (1998) work *Even the rat was white*.

ONLINE RESOURCES

Web sources on women in science include:

Association for Women in Science (AWIS): www.awis.org and "4000 years of Women in Science": www.astr.ua.edu/4000WS/4000WS.html.

For women in Psychology: www.feministvoices.com/.

7

Natural-science Psychology after World War II

Chapter outline

Introduction

In this chapter we address the major changes that natural-science Psychology underwent after World War II. First we describe cultural and scientific developments that affected the discipline. Then we note the ways in which Psychology took shape internationally but in diverse forms. Next we describe developments in basic processes, developmental psychology, interpersonal processes, and psychologists' relationship to the social order. We conclude by discussing thematic issues that link Psychology's disparate domains.

Throughout this chapter we refer to **four domains** of natural-science Psychology:

- *Behavioural neuroscience* focuses on *animal* models of basic psychological processes of sensation, perception, learning, cognition, emotion, and motivation. Behavioural neuroscience encompasses the subdisciplines of biological and comparative psychology, which previously were known as biopsychology or physiological psychology.
- *Cognitive neuroscience* focuses on the same basic psychological processes in *humans*. Cognitive neuroscience encompasses cognitive psychology and overlaps with neuroscience and philosophy.
- *Developmental psychology* focuses on animal and human development and links biological and cognitive domains with interpersonal processes.
- *Interpersonal psychology* encompasses the subdisciplines of cultural, gender, personality, and social psychology.
- Another domain of current natural-science Psychology is *applied and professional psychology*, which we describe in Chapter 8.

The **aims** of this chapter are to describe:

- Cultural conditions and scientific developments, including the status of women, which were the context for Psychology's development after World War II.
- The discipline's growth internationally in relation to globalized US Psychology.
- The principal schools of thought after World War II: operant behaviourism, biological organization of behaviour, and cognitivism.
- Developments in psychological neuroscience, neurogenetics, and evolutionary psychology.
- The expansion of developmental psychology since World War II.
- Developments in personality and social psychology and the psychological issues they have in common.
- Psychologists' relationship to the social order, including responses to racism and sexism.
- Central themes that summarize Psychology's development after World War II: neuroscience of the evolutionary brain and consciousness, self and identity in context, disciplinary fragmentation, and alliance with the status quo.

Part 1 Social and intellectual context

Since World War II, economic and political conditions in economically privileged nations altered previously established patterns of research funding, institutional control, and academic freedom and responsibility. Current social conditions similarly affect the status of the sciences in academic institutions where most science and psychological research are done.

Societal and scientific developments

The development and deployment of nuclear weapons and the extraordinary economic and social changes that transpired in economically privileged societies after the war shaped scientific practices. Societal influences included technological inventions, such as computers and electronic-recording devices; proliferation of institutions of post-secondary education; generous public research-funding; rapid population growth; and movements for equal rights expressed by ethnocultural minorities, colonized peoples, and women. Then in the 1970s a new economic order, termed neoliberalism, was instituted globally, which ultimately led to deteriorating socioeconomic conditions for most people relative to a small minority (Hobsbawm, 1996).

A third Industrial Revolution – computerization – initiated a new era of relationships among transnational corporations and global capital, government, the military, technology, and science. *Cybernetics* (i.e., massive digital, automatized communication systems) created and sustains reciprocal relations among these sectors. The internet has evolved to three dimensions in creating online, virtual worlds of avatars (i.e., three-dimensional representations of actual selves) for recreational games, entertainment, business transactions, conferencing, and shopping in virtual malls.

One consequence of these institutional entanglements is increased governmental and corporate control of science. In addition, the social organization of science shifted from "little" to "big" science (Ravetz, 2005). Previously, a loose collection of practitioners of "little science" worked independently, supported by women in their households and often by wealthy patrons or the state. Scientists saw themselves as working for the public interest, although applications of their discoveries contributed to the development of capitalism and war-making. But World War II changed the nature of scientific activity with the deployment of nuclear weapons.

Big science entailed the massive expansion of scientific disciplines and research with direct government and business aid (Galison & Hevly, 1992). Cold-War struggles for scientific supremacy led to huge increases in government-funded scientific research, including Psychology, in both the West and the Soviet Union. At this point, big science became integrated with the state, the military, and corporate power. Large-scale projects with numerous staff and expensive equipment proliferated. Although many academic scientists toiled on their individual projects, they were subjected to state, military, or corporate funders.

Given this massive expansion of science, its organization, practice, and content changed substantially. In the postwar era physics, chemistry, and biology increasingly were linked to technological innovation for societal application. The most celebrated big science was physics, because physicists, as the inventors of nuclear weapons, had the most political influence.

Current climate

"Mega science," as exemplified by the synchrotron particle accelerator shown in Figure 7.1, has superseded big science. Mega science requires vast budgets; for instance, the

Figure 7.1 The Synchrotron Light Source II at the US Department of Energy's Brookhaven National Laboratory is expected to be operational in 2015

synchrotron light source depicted will cost nearly a billion dollars when completed in 2015. Mega science also is an engine of economic development and is absorbed into governmental, military, and global corporate agendas associated with "the knowledge economy."

Science now must show direct applications to enhancing "the new economy." A major function of mega science is to support **four fields**, known collectively as "GRAIN" (Ravetz, 2005), which dominate current science and technology:

- *Genomics* refers to manipulating life at the genetic level.
- *Robotics* is the technology of designing, constructing, operating, and applying robots.
- *Artificial intelligence* (AI) refers to computer systems programmed to implement applications of human intelligence that can exceed it in certain domains; AI can meld the operations of genomics and robotics.
- *Nanotechnology* is a form of biotechnology and bioengineering operating on an extremely microscopic scale.

In this social climate technology based on biology (e.g., genetic engineering) predominates, and developments in nanotechnology are likely to surpass the transformative impact that computerization based on physics had (Lipsey, Carlaw, & Bekar, 2005). Some authors even claim that non-biological systems, deeply integrated into individuals' bodies, brains, and the environment, greatly will exceed the biological limits of human intelligence and that the union of nanotechnology with artificial intelligence will produce "nanobots" (i.e., robots the size of blood cells) that will traverse the body to improve an individual's genetic coding, repair all the body's systems, and obliterate disease and overcome aging.

In this new context technology and science are two sides of the same coin. Governments enable technology, supported by science, to flourish in society. Governments, corporations, and the military exercise control over GRAIN and employ these instruments of technical knowledge and social power to safeguard corporate profits. Consequently, many scientific activities have become commercialized, requiring huge financial investments that big business can afford, which makes scientists subservient to economic purposes.

Academic climate

Late nineteenth-century science resided primarily in academia. But the early twenty-first century saw a distinct shift away from the mission of scientific research advancing knowledge towards a new mission of financially linking university research with the expansion of corporate wealth and profit (J. Washburn, 2005). University administrators, business executives, and politicians assert that the role of tertiary education is to "partner" with corporations to produce technical knowledge, create wealth, and make national economies more competitive globally (G. Jones, McCarney, & Skolnik, 2005). Politicians restructure public universities along corporate lines, while decreasing public funding for the social sciences, humanities, and the arts.

The corporate mentality in academia privileges applied science, technology, and business programmes. In this climate, scholarly research must be relevant to economic expansion and provide service for industry through applied science. Thus, basic research mingles with technology and venture capital for commercial purposes. Some universities have established "research parks" in which technology-transfer to corporate interests occurs on campus (J. Washburn, 2005).

Two consequences for universities ensue from this societal climate:

- Administrators seek support from corporations, trading financial resources for direct corporate influence on the education and research practised in the academy.
- Administrators phase out academic programmes that are not amenable to corporate manipulation or seriously weaken them by absorbing them into more malleable programmes. This restructuring thwarts the development of the social sciences, humanities, and arts despite student interest in them.

In a university climate of weakened government funding that demands direct economic benefits of scholarly research, granting agencies and university administrators encourage academics to contract with commercial interests. In the UK, national policy dictates that universities' *raison d'être* is the economic impact of scholarship, which necessitates a virtually exclusive focus on innovation of local and immediate commercial benefit. Academic staff is expected to commercialize intellectual property by applying for patents on products invented and creating spin-off businesses. Meanwhile, commercial interests are welcomed to shape curricula to suit business requirements.

The danger of this conception of university research and practical arrangements is that it can compromise scholars' academic freedom and ethical integrity of independent thought. The adage "Whoever pays the piper calls the tune" aptly describes a situation in which corporate funders prescribe what should be researched. In effect, universities become corporations' research-and-development branches but supported by public not corporate funds.

Section conclusion

Scientific objectivity and integrity might become casualties, when researchers and institutions are compromised by corporations' controlling interests in scientific endeavours. Besides the inclinations of researchers and their institutions, corporations are motivated to publish positive findings and suppress negative ones. Science now operates less in the public interest and more as technology in the private interest of corporations and their government backers. This situation raises **two questions** about the governance of any science:

- Who decides scientific priorities and what kind of scientific research gets done or not?
- How should scientific discoveries be applied in society?

As we have seen, scientists speaking out against such corporate and institutional influence take professional risks. Ethically, a model of research in which granting agencies and university administrators encourage academics to contract with commercial interests can compromise scholars' academic freedom and integrity of independent thought, while co-opting scientists as tools for commercial and institutional profit.

Gender and cultural diversity in science

Historically, in Anglo-American and European nations women and ethnocultural minorities have been relatively absent as academics in the natural sciences, technology, engineering, and mathematics (the "STEM" fields) and in Psychology. Science faculties remain predominantly male, while women tend to be clustered in lower-status positions and discriminated against in hiring, laboratory space, and salary negotiations.

Although tertiary education and academic science in Europe significantly expanded after the war, opportunities for women in science were very limited (Stolte-Heiskanen, 1991). In 1998 the European Union (EU) established a Women and Science Unit to increase women's inclusion in science (Schiebinger, 2002). But EU nations still trail the USA concerning women in science.

During the 1960s, US women promoted institutional reform to achieve parity with men in STEM fields. By the 1990s, the proportion of women with science PhDs had increased substantially, but it remained quite unequal to men, particularly in physics and mathematics (Schiebinger, 1999). In 2006, the US National Academies identified gender bias as the source of barriers to women's representation and advancement in science professorships, despite increased female enrolment in undergraduate science.

Insufficient numbers of female applicants and the slow rate of faculty turnover partly explain continuing gender inequity in faculty positions. Furthermore, universities impede women's success by requiring full-time employment and productivity early in one's career. If they are parents, female scientists provide more caregiving and face greater domestic pressures on their academic careers than male scientists (Xie & Shauman, 2003).

Advocates identify **three types of institutional change** to effect gender equity:

- Achieving a critical mass by systematically exposing more female students to science, pushing them through the "pipeline" from primary school to university.
- Reforming science education to enhance women's participation in science.
- Creating a supportive working environment for female scientists in academic institutions.

The participation of individuals in cultural minority positions in STEM fields also has been problematic. In 2004, less than 4 per cent of professors in the physical sciences and engineering in the fifty top US universities were African American or Hispanic (Rimer, 2005). Moreover, women from ethnocultural groups can be subjected to the double oppression of sexism and racism.

Psychologists' perspective

Some psychologists have attempted to explain the fact that, although women increasingly are earning PhDs in STEM fields, their proportion among the professoriate in Canada and the USA has not increased correspondingly (e.g., Ceci & W. Williams, 2007a). Some believe that only those who are extraordinarily talented in underlying aptitude (historically, men) will attain success in STEM fields, while others believe that superior aptitude is sufficient when supported by environmental conditions.

The main point of contention concerns the influence of biologically based psychological capacities. The least contentious conclusion is that "a biological or genetic factor may create the possibility for some behaviour, but whether the possibility will materialize depends critically on the environment" (Ceci & W. Williams, 2007a, p. 222). In addition, many key questions, including measurement ones, remain unanswered.

But regardless of viewpoint, psychologists conclude, popularized characterizations of gender differences (e.g., male left brain – female right brain) are simplistic and misleading. Many variables affect gender differences in cognitive functions. Although girls and women score lower than boys and men on spatial-rotation tasks that might be related to certain STEM fields in which women are underrepresented, no direct evidence connects these skills to those fields (Ceci & W. Williams, 2007a). Furthermore, when cultural differences are introduced to the mix, these differences often evaporate or show that the female gender is superior. The male gender is not superior in performance in all cultures across all times of sampling.

Psychologists shed less light on key contextual issues, namely, family and workplace. Female professors face domestic pressures on their academic careers that have been less influential on male professors due to society's gender-role expectations. Interpersonal responses to biologically based abilities also can shape career aspirations. Furthermore, the tenure system in academia militates against women's success, because the system requires full-time employment and scholarly productivity early in one's career. Yet psychologists caution that more research is needed before concluding that family-friendly changes, for example, adjusting the tenure-clock, will improve women's success in STEM fields.

Equity in Psychology

Despite women constituting the large majority of undergraduate and graduate students in Canadian and US Psychology, they remain the minority of faculty especially in the higher ranks (American Psychological Association, 2005). Furthermore, in US departments with a PhD programme, the proportion of ethnic-minority faculty has been less than half the proportion of ethnic-minority students. As Kite *et al.* (2001) noted, "[the culture of academe] must change and those in positions of power must implement [institutional] changes" (p. 1092).

Part 1 conclusion

Current societal conditions have had mixed effects on Psychology. Although applied science and technology are thriving, which benefits natural-science Psychology, particularly behavioural and cognitive neuroscience, the social sciences and humanities are diminishing, which weakens human-science Psychology. In Canada and the USA far more government funding is available for technological innovation, practical applications stemming from investigations of basic psychological processes, and psychological aspects of health and mental health than for other areas.

Furthermore, gender equality and cultural diversity in academic Psychology remain deficient. The fact that White male faculty continue to predominate in Psychology does not reflect the diversity of the discipline's undergraduate and graduate students and society. In addition, publicly accessible information on the status of women, ethnic minorities, and lesbian, gay, bisexual, transgendered, or disability status in Psychology internationally is scarce. These situations suggest that globally psychologists lack commitment to achieving equity.

Part 2 | Expansion of Psychology internationally

After World War II a hierarchy of power to influence Psychology's development existed. Because of the magnitude of its academic and professional infrastructure the US discipline dominated globally (Brock, 2006). Moderately influential were Psychologies in other economically privileged nations (e.g., Canada, the UK), followed by developing nations (e.g., China and India) (Moghaddam, 1987).

European Psychology

Psychology in Germany, the UK, and France gained momentum into the twenty-first century.

Germany

Overall, German psychologists retained their labs, journals, and scientific association during and after the war. However, they were in a weak institutional position relative to US psychologists. Consequently, under the Allies' occupation when German society was rebuilding, US Psychology was very influential. Many younger Germans adopted US psychologists' passion for quantitative laboratory experimentation and emulated their research specialties and societal applications of Psychology.

In 1949 when Germany split into two nations, West Germans maintained their US-style Psychology, which prospered in dozens of universities, and training in clinical psychology expanded to meet societal demand. East German psychologists adopted the concepts of

Soviet Psychology, stressing the unity of biological and sociocultural influences on psychological processes (Schmidt, 1987). They established their own journals, textbooks, and organization, and expanded societal applications.

But after national reunification in 1990, the differences between East and West German Psychologies began to dissolve. The discipline developed generally within a US conceptual and methodological framework. As the century ended, German psychologists exercised international influence by taking academic positions in the USA and the UK (Plath & Eckensberger, 2004).

United Kingdom

After the war, British psychologists shifted away from their psychometric tradition towards experimentation on memory, thinking, and cognitive development. Frederic Bartlett's investigations of memory and motor skills and Hans Eysenck's personality and behaviour-therapy studies were esteemed, while Charles Sherrington's heritage prevailed in physiological psychology.

Yet British psychologists remained strongly inclined to practical applications. When the National Health Service was established in 1948 and psychologists were accepted on health-care teams, clinical psychology received a boost. Educational psychology received state support in 1968. Occupational, counselling, and forensic psychologies flourished as well.

By 2000, the British Psychological Society was publishing ten journals and had nearly 36,000 members. But many academics were members of the Experimental Psychology Society instead. As in the USA and Canada, the discipline was much more popular among female than male students (Lunt, 2004).

France

Many French psychologists adopted Anglo-American approaches to natural-science Psychology, and some, eager to distance themselves from philosophy, sustained the French psychophysiological tradition. Yet others remained committed to psychoanalysis, phenomenology, and existentialism.

Developmental psychology thrived in France with Jean Piaget's work exerting considerable influence. Meanwhile, industrial applications escalated, clinical psychology became quite popular, and even a "clinical social psychology" emerged in Parisian universities (Trognon, 1987). By the 1990s, Psychology was a major discipline in at least thirty universities, dozens of journals existed, academic and professional organizations were thriving, and applied psychologists were a significant presence in French society (Sanches, 1992).

Soviet and Russian Psychology

When Soviet psychologists turned from military applications to academic research, many specialized in child development and applications to education. Others expanded Pavlovian psychophysiology, while Psychology remained in bondage to Soviet ideology. When Josef Stalin died in 1953, Pavlovian psychology weakened, previously suppressed notions of higher mental processes were rehabilitated, and Western concepts were reintroduced (Kozulin, 1984).

The Soviet-approved school of thought then was Alexei Leontiev's activity theory. Its premise was that goal-directed activities of work, study, and play, including communication, shape internal mental processes, which in turn enable individuals to regulate their activity (Barabanschikov, 2006). By the 1970s, Soviet psychologists studied thinking, problem-solving, language, as well as consciousness, motivation, and creativity, and expanded to child development. Because clinical psychology remained weakly developed, social psychologists intervened in work, community, and family problems (Kozulin, 1992).

Institutionally, although the Soviet Psychological Society was formed in 1957, autonomous departments did not exist until the 1960s. In 1971 the Academy of Sciences formed an Institute of Psychology. Still, research equipment was sparse, only one journal existed between 1955 and 1979, and the proportion of psychologists to the general population was low.

When the Soviet regime expired in 1989 and Russia converted to market capitalism in 1991, the educational sector was deregulated, Psychology programmes proliferated, and psychologists gained access to previously censored Russian and Western sources (Vassilieva, 2010). Conceptually, Lev Vygotsky's cultural-historical theory supplanted activity theory. Many psychologists turned to cognition and personality; some recuperated metaphysical, spiritual, and transpersonal phenomena; and many practised psychological applications in an increasingly "psychological" culture (Barabanschikov, 2006). Currently, the discipline is represented in approximately seventy tertiary-education institutions.

US Psychology

After the war US federal agencies massively funded psychological research and graduate training. In the quintessential "psychological society" psychologists received high levels of research funding from public and private sources, providing opportunities for researchers in basic processes, developmental and interpersonal psychologists, and professional psychologists. Educational capacities mushroomed. Most undergraduate students took at least one Psychology course and psychological popularizations in print and broadcast media and professional applications proliferated. By 1995 US Psychology was a virtual industry with over 250,000 psychologists, mainly non-academic, while the proportion of psychologists to the general population was 1 to 1,000 (Capshew, 1999).

Significant intra-disciplinary tensions, however, remained. First, while clinicians increasingly outnumbered specialists in basic processes, the APA became an organization mainly of professional psychologists. Secondly, although male psychologists benefited from Psychology's expansion, female and African American psychologists were marginalized (Capshew, 1999). During the postwar era Psychology maintained a chilly social climate for female academics, as the case of Eleanor Gibson illustrates (see Box 7.1).

In 1969, riding the second wave of feminism, female psychologists organized to address sexism in the discipline and society (Tiefer, 1991). APA then recognized a psychology of women division in 1973. Thereafter, division members established individual task forces concerning Black, Hispanic, Asian American, and American Indian Women (Comas-Diaz, 1991). By the twenty-first century, 48 per cent of Association members were women. Yet

Box 7.1 Eleanor Gibson

Female psychologists faced systemic gender discrimination in academia. Eleanor Gibson (1910–2002) was an experimental psychologist who studied perceptual learning developmentally and was known for her "visual cliff" experiments (Caudle, 2003). After receiving a master's degree in Psychology in 1933, supervised by her husband, James Gibson (1904–1979), at Smith College, she hoped to pursue a PhD in comparative psychology with Robert Yerkes at Yale. But because Yerkes banned women from his lab, Clark Hull supervised her. She became an instructor and then a professor at Smith College, while bearing and raising two children.

When James Gibson took a faculty position at Cornell in 1949, the institution's anti-nepotism policy prohibited Eleanor Gibson from also taking one. She was forced to conduct her research as an unpaid associate with no laboratory and no research funds. Despite her distinguished record, Cornell only gave her a half-time professor position in 1966 and her own lab in 1972. Nevertheless, during her seventy-year career, Gibson contributed to the literature through her ecological perspective on infants' prelinguistic perceptual learning, verbal learning and memory, psycholinguistics, and motivation and emotion.

female psychologists remained underrepresented in academia, still facing systemic barriers to equity (Kite *et al.*, 2001).

International Psychology

Since the end of World War II, Psychology has become an international enterprise. As before, our focus is on Canada, China, India, and Japan.

Canada

In the 1950s, Psychology at Toronto shifted to the study of basic processes exclusive of societal applications. Other anglophone departments, such as McGill's under the leadership of Donald Hebb, took similar measures. Many departments relegated professional psychology to a faculty of education.

In the 1960s and 1970s, anglophone universities hired scores of US-trained psychologists to fill faculty vacancies and introduced clinical psychology programmes. Academics specialized in "physiological psychology, animal models, cognitive processes, developmental psychology (primarily cognitive and language), and perception" (Adair, Paivio, & Ritchie, 1996, p. 349). Others explored personality, social, and cross-cultural phenomena, or mental health and general health.

After World War II, francophone departments of Psychology integrated experimental and professional orientations. Although initially francophone psychologists followed continental-European developments, subsequent generations relied heavily on US Psychology while expanding undergraduate and graduate programmes. By the 1970s the Canadian Psychological Association (CPA) was publishing three bilingual journals.

Although by 1970 one-quarter of CPA members were women, they had to struggle for recognition (Pyke, 2001). During International Women's Year (1975) a task force on the status of women in Psychology confirmed that female psychologists and female students were marginalized. One result was the still-thriving CPA section on Women and Psychology. But when feminist and professional psychologists became more prominent in the CPA, academics studying basic processes established a separate organization, the Canadian Society for Brain, Behaviour, and Cognitive Science, in 1989.

China

In 1949 when the People's Republic was founded, the discipline revived, but psychologists were compelled to adopt Marxist–Leninist and Maoist thought and Soviet Psychology. Journals and research resumed, but practical applications to the state prevailed.

After the Cultural Revolution (1966–1976) when the authorities dismantled Psychology's infrastructure, the discipline was restored and expanded in universities and teacher-education institutes. Conceptually, psychologists understood human nature as a dialectical relation of social and biological forces. They studied child development and basic processes; many applied Psychology to pedagogy, medicine, industry, sport, and law. Some turned from revising US psychological tests to constructing ones adapted to China.

By 1984 the Chinese Psychological Society had 2,000 members (Petzold, 1987). Numerous books were published, over two dozen universities offered the discipline, and societal applications predominated. In 2004, Chinese psychologists hosted the International Congress of Psychology. Recently, some have focused on the interplay between their cultural traditions and psychological thought (Wang, 1993).

India

Autonomous departments of Psychology were established after India's independence in 1947. Although the Indian discipline's imitative bent persisted, an indigenous Psychology emerged in the 1980s (Paranjpe, 2006). By then, eighty-one institutions awarded doctoral degrees in Psychology. Many psychologists were employed in the military, other governmental branches, and clinical service, yet Psychology remained largely academic. Textbooks were almost completely Anglo-American and research-infrastructure was rudimentary (Sinha, 1987).

Japan

After World War II when the US imposed its educational system on Japan, Psychology was fixed in the US orbit. The discipline expanded rapidly regarding textbooks, journals, and graduate programmes; research funding; and several professional associations. By the 1980s, psychologists investigated basic processes, developmental issues, and interpersonal phenomena, while others practised societal applications (Misumi & Peterson, 1990). By 1992 the Japanese Psychological Association had approximately 4,400 members. In more recent decades, some psychologists have been investigating local and national, indigenous cultural interests.

Part 2 conclusion

At first glance, Psychology today appears to be a virtually universal, scientific and applied phenomenon. Upon further examination, however, fundamental problems are apparent.

The ambiguous term "international psychology" can mean involvement in multicultural applications of Psychology, psychological applications to public policy internationally, or participation in international congresses of psychological organizations (David & Buchanan, 2003). The critical question, however, is can Psychology be international or is international Psychology a euphemism for US Psychology's dominion over other psychologies (Brock, 2006)?

Some have criticized the term and practices associated with international Psychology as representing exportation of Western Psychology (Gergen, Gulerce, Lock, & Misra, 1996), even a form of cultural imperialism (Danziger, 1994). They claim that US Psychology is virtually hegemonic because of the APA's sophisticated network and resources; the global distribution of Psychology textbooks published by multinational, primarily US corporations; and the political, economic, military, and cultural dominion that the USA exercises globally. Seen in this light, when US psychologists seek to expand international cooperation, they do so, consciously or not, on their terms. Thus, the tendency to extrapolate US data to all humankind can seem ethnocentric (Arnett, 2008).

Scholars who espouse *polycentrism* for Psychology, meaning culturally diverse centres of disciplinary activity, reject the view that psychological processes and mechanisms are universal; instead, they contend that psychological phenomena are relative to individual cultural environments (Staeuble, 2004). Polycentrists hold that psychological concepts are based in language from particular cultural communities and that the terms used to express these concepts derive their meaning from that language (Danziger, 1994). This argument is an application of Karl Marx's view that cultural conditions shape consciousness.

Polycentrists urge decentring Western perspectives, developing multicultural psychology, and promoting indigenous psychologies (Moghaddam, 1987). But they caution that a multilateral, international psychology can flourish, only if "the West has gained sufficient self-reflexivity to prevent further patronizing and the rest of the world has gained sufficient self-assertion for emancipation" (Gergen *et al.*, 1996, p. 501). Merely adding international samples to research projects does not address the culturally laden nature of psychological concepts.

Part 3 Schools of thought

The chief schools of thought in natural-science Psychology after World War II, other than neobehaviourism, were operant behaviourism, the biological organization of behaviour, cognitivism, behavioural and cognitive neuroscience, and evolutionary psychology.

Operant behaviourism

Perhaps no psychologist has earned as much disciplinary and societal popularity in the USA as B. F. Skinner (1904–1990) because of the appeal of operant behaviourism to mainstream psychologists, his inventions, and his popular writing. His school of thought fundamentally differed from Edward Tolman's and Clark Hull's neobehaviourist attributions of internal processes. Operant behaviourism, or as some termed it, "radical behaviorism," is an inductive, functional analysis of environmental contingencies (independent variables) of behaviour (dependent variables).

Skinner distinguished his operant conditioning of emitted behaviour from Pavlov's respondent conditioning of elicited reflexes (Bjork, 1998). In his 1938 book, *The Behavior of Organisms*, he reported the effects of different schedules of reinforcement, after studying the lever-pressing of lab rats. Then he switched to pigeons. Beginning in the 1950s his followers extended operant principles to humans and introduced social applications (Rutherford, 2009).

Basic concepts

Founded on the premise that environmental contingencies determine everything we do, operant behaviourism encompasses all aspects of organisms' behaviour (Delprato & Midgely, 1992). It excludes psychophysiological and internal psychological phenomena (e.g., emotion) to concentrate solely on their behavioural manifestations. Skinner (1957) claimed that humans even acquire language through reinforcing interactions with caregivers and private mental events can be observed in behaviour.

The core principle of operant behaviourism, which is derived from Edward Thorndike's instrumental conditioning, is that any behaviour evokes consequences and is reinforced by them, depending upon the type of schedule of reinforcement. The goal is to control behaviour by modifying responses. One increases the probability of an organism's responses by manipulating the consequences of its behaviour ("contingencies of reinforcement"). The basic dictum is: behaviour is controlled by its consequences.

Skinner emphasized the power of immediate vs. delayed reinforcement. He described how "reinforcing stimuli" can be positive or negative, and "discriminative stimuli" signal the occasion for responding. Accordingly, because responding is primary in operant behaviourism, it is an R–S–R model rather than an S–R one.

Crucial for facilitating new behaviour is the concept and methodical procedure of shaping. In Skinner's (1953) words:

Operant conditioning shapes behavior as a sculptor shapes a lump of clay. Although at some point the sculptor seems to have produced an entirely novel object, we can always follow the process back to the original undifferentiated lump, and we can make the successive stages by which we return to this condition as small as we wish. At no point does anything emerge which is very different from what preceded it. The final product seems to have a special unity or integrity of design, but we cannot find a point at which this suddenly appears. In the same sense, an operant is not something which appears full grown in the behavior of the organism. It is the result of a continuous shaping process. (p. 91)

Applied behavioural analysis

Skinner also is renowned for his applications of operant-behaviourist technology and his speculations about reforming society along behaviourist lines. During the war, concerned about minimizing deaths from enemy bombing, he conditioned pigeons to guide missiles to intercept bombs, but the US military did not employ his invention. In 1944 he invented a "baby tender" (a comfortable crib with sensory stimuli) for his second daughter, who contrary to rumours has lived a healthy life (Rutherford, 2009).

In 1953, concerned about the quality of his daughter's education, Skinner invented a "teaching machine." The principle of this technology is that systematically presenting questions in a programmed order for correct responding at students' own pace reinforces learning. However, programmed learning and the baby tender emerged when US society regarded these technologies as dehumanizing; consequently, they were mass-market failures. Computer-assisted instruction, founded on cognitive not operant principles, eclipsed programmed learning.

Skinner also gained public notoriety for his social philosophy, expressed in quasi-philosophical works and in his 1948 utopian novel, *Walden Two*. In his imagined commune, contingencies of positive reinforcement controlled all behaviour, gender discrimination and competitiveness were discouraged, and private property was banned.

In *Beyond Freedom and Dignity* (1971) Skinner claimed that humanistic concepts of freedom and dignity obstructed solutions to the global problems of potential nuclear war, overpopulation, and pollution. For him, experimental demonstrations of cause-and-effect relations render the values of "freedom" and "dignity" useless for structuring and maintaining positive social relations. Behavioural engineers, he said, should restructure the environment to reinforce prosocial and extinguish dysfunctional behaviour.

Section conclusion

The heir to John Watson's science of the prediction and control of behaviour, Skinner regarded his comprehensive research on schedules of reinforcement as his signature scientific accomplishment. His school of thought rests on a voluminous set of validating data, produced by a powerful single-subject methodology. But his esteemed status in US Psychology and society arguably rests more on his symbolizing impressive psychological applications in a psychologically inclined culture than on his science (Rutherford, 2009). Unlike other behaviourists, he created a simple technology for reliably producing behavioural baselines in real-life situations.

Operant behaviourism offers many applications for modifying behaviour, including self-control. This technology has led to more humane treatment of institutionalized individuals, but its effectiveness is limited to situations in which authority-figures (e.g., hospital staff) exercise control over situational variables. Politically, some have argued operant behaviourism takes paternalistic social control to a technocratic, authoritarian extreme. Others interpret Skinner's prescriptions for social engineering as a commitment to social justice (Rakos, 1992).

Biological organization of behaviour

Meanwhile, other natural-science psychologists worked to restore the discipline's physiological roots. Although biopsychology, neuropsychology, behavioural neuroscience, and cognitive neuroscience are the rubrics employed today, the common term in mid-century was physiological psychology. Its adherents practised a heterogeneous school of thought, the biological organization of behaviour. Among the proponents were Donald Hebb, Roger Sperry, Alexander Luria, and Magda Arnold.

Donald Hebb

Rather than clinging to variants of behaviourism, postwar physiological psychologists observed that "the brain as a whole is involved in every psychological event" (Gilgen, 1982, p. 138). Canadian Donald Hebb investigated his mentor Karl Lashley's propositions about brain–behaviour relations during the behaviourist era, when few psychologists deviated from a reflex-based explanation of behaviour (Glickman, 1996). Hebb's contributions facilitated the eventual emergence of behavioural and cognitive neuroscience.

While working with famed neurosurgeon Wilder Penfield (1891–1976) in the Montreal Neurological Institute at McGill, Hebb observed that large lesions of the frontal lobes minimally affected general intelligence. In addition, he found that "the effects of brain damage on the development of intelligence depended on the age when the damage occurred" (Brown & Milner, 2003, p.1015).

Subsequently, Hebb studied the effects of early experience on problem-solving. His lab rats exposed to an "enriched" environment showed greater problem-solving skills and neurological development than control subjects. This research programme provided the basis for a biological theory of the enduring neural effects of early experience. Developmental psychologists absorbed the theory, which became the rationale for preschool enrichment programmes (e.g., Head Start).

In 1942 Hebb rejoined Lashley at Robert Yerkes's primate centre where Hebb composed his 1949 seminal work, *The Organization of Behavior* and investigated emotions, fears, and temperamental differences. In 1947, he returned to McGill to conduct research on attention, perception, learning, and memory and continue his neuropsychological theorizing. Later Hebb became the second Canadian president of the APA.

Basic concepts Hebb's central premise was that understanding behaviour and the totality of the central nervous system were interrelated problems. His mission was to legitimize "physiologizing" behaviour among behaviourists who studied basic psychological processes but who had abandoned both mind and brain. From studying the neural circuitry involved in perception, he proposed that, when neurons are simultaneously active, an association is distributed over its synaptic connection and synaptic activity induces greater neural development.

Through experience, Hebb (1958) argued, neurons group themselves into a *cell assembly*, which "corresponds to a particular sensory event or a common aspect of a number of sensory effects" (p. 628). An assembly represents an image or thought. Individuals construct neural-cell assemblies that prime perceptual sensitivity to particular stimuli. Hebb termed the activity of cell assemblies before permanent connections are set "reverberatory circuits."

The term *Hebb's rule* refers to interacting neurons becoming permanently associated and is expressed in a quasi-equation predicting the rate of learning, given the nature of neural connections. "Hebb synapses" refers to synapses that follow Hebb's rule and change with experience. Presently, behavioural and cognitive neuroscientists employ the Hebb synapse rule for neural-network models of learning and memory.

Cell assemblies, in turn, organize into "phase sequences," which is how the brain represents connected thoughts stimulated by particular events. Activity patterns within phase sequences represent the psychological function of attention and, when acquired during infancy, explain the Gestalt principle of holistic perception of objects (Glickman, 1996).

Against behaviourism, Hebb (1949) proposed that brain function and neuronal structure, shown in their central organizing capacity, explain behaviour. Furthermore, as Lashley had argued, no distinct brain regions control any specific behaviour, although different processes occur in different brain regions. For Hebb, learning by association characterizes infancy and childhood, but insight-learning characterizes adulthood.

Hebb (1958) later asserted that because Psychology is a biological science, psychologists should expand their awareness of biological foundations by investigating psychological entities physiologically. Furthermore, psychologists' dependence on lower mammals' simple neurological systems, he claimed, produced inconsistencies among theories of learning. Because brain function is inherently complex, psychologists can enrich their research by employing both psychological and biological perspectives. Congruent with this biopsychological orientation, Hebb understood behaviour as the interactive product of heredity and environment.

In retrospect, although neuroimaging and simulating attention-networks provide support for Hebb's concepts, given the limitations of knowledge about the brain available to him, the particulars of his theory have not stood the test of time (Posner & Rothbart, 2007). Nevertheless, his approach influenced at least **four areas** of Psychology (Brown & Milner, 2003):

- The effects of early environmental stimulation on emotional, perceptual, and intellectual development.
- The study of attention, perception, motivation, learning, and memory.
- In cognitive neuroscience, connectionist theories, artificial intelligence, and the concept of synaptic plasticity.
- The treatment and rehabilitation of neurological patients.

From a critical perspective, when researching at Yerkes's primate centre, Hebb felt he was observing pure psychological processes. Glickman (1996) reports, "He once told me that watching the chimpanzees was like seeing humans with the veneer of culture stripped away" (p. 231). Hebb evidently regarded extrapolating from animal models, while excluding human culture saturated with language and history, as Psychology's lodestar, not as inherently problematic.

Roger Sperry

US psychologist Roger Sperry (1913–1994) also studied with Lashley at the Yerkes Labs. He spent the bulk of his career exploring the biological origins of behaviour and the nature of consciousness (Puente, 2000). Initially he investigated nerve-regeneration and plasticity and refined Lashley's explanation for equipotentiality through experimentation on visual discrimination. His research programme on the visual cortex merited a shared Nobel Prize.

Intrigued by the central nervous system's plasticity, Sperry studied the neurological and behavioural effects of severing the optic chiasm and corpus callosum. He investigated how information is conveyed and psychological functions in human patients are integrated between cerebral hemispheres, which he characterized as separate brains with different functions.

Subsequently, popularizers drew simplistic conclusions about brain–behaviour relations from Sperry's "split-brain" research. They claimed that some ethnocultural groups (e.g.,

White Westerners) and men were more left-brain dominated, hence analytical, while other groups (e.g., aboriginal individuals) and women were more right-brain dominated, hence intuitive.

Sperry (1988) was fascinated by the nature of consciousness, which for him was the result of a functionally unified brain. He argued that higher-order consciousness subsumed cognitive functions and was the foundation for a scientifically grounded framework of human values that could ensure humankind's survival. His metaphysical speculations appealed to some psychologists who regarded him as pivotal in restoring consciousness to cognitive neuroscience (Thompson & Zola, 2003). Others viewed Sperry's interests in consciousness and in scientized morality as unscientific and disregarded his contributions to behaviour's physiological roots.

Alexander Luria

Soviet psychologist Alexander Luria (1902–1977) emphasized the holistic nature of the physiological and psychological dimensions of personal experience, while his research integrated laboratory and clinical data. Initially, employing his mentor Lev Vygotsky's cultural-historical school of thought, he investigated language as the mediating function between thought and external action. Speech-production, he concluded, proceeds through four developmental stages: initiating activity, inhibiting it, externally regulating activity, and internally regulating it.

Luria then departed from Vygotsky's model to concentrate on correlating types of neurological damage (e.g., aphasia) with specific behavioural deficits. After medical training, Luria pursued neuropsychological investigations. Aided by his assessing the behaviour of individuals with brain trauma during World War II, he identified behavioural patterns localized in cortical functions, language areas in the left cerebral hemisphere, and the retrieval processes entailed in remembering.

Luria's (1980) neuropsychology proved influential theoretically. He explained cortical functions in terms of three increasingly complex components that collectively evoke psychological processes. This model explains the biological foundations of intelligence (Sternberg, 2003). The **three components** proceed serially:

- Basic arousal, aided by the brain stem and mid-brain.
- Sensory-motor processing for which posterior cortical sections are responsible.
- The unifying organizational function of the frontal cortex, which formulates behavioural intentions.

Clinically, Luria's qualitative assessment procedures with brain-injured patients led to US psychologists creating a standardized quantitative test, the Luria-Nebraska Neuropsychological Battery. Thus, he is regarded as a founder of clinical neuropsychology.

Magda Arnold

Emigrating from a former region of Austria to Canada in 1928 as a homemaker with three children, Magda Arnold (1903–2002) obtained a PhD at Toronto in 1942. Because she was not offered a professorship there, she took academic positions in the USA.

Situating emotion and memory in the unity of bodily and mental processes, Arnold challenged **two predominant conceptions** about emotion:

- US physiologist Walter Cannon (1871–1945) had explained emotion as the by-product of biological processes mediated by the thalamus. But Arnold showed how responses from cortical areas and the autonomic nervous system are linked and how perceptual–cognitive appraisal mediates bodily arousal.
- Behaviourists explained emotions as mere learned associations and regarded experienced emotions as mired in subjectivity and immeasurable, as if they existed in an unknowable "black box." But Arnold argued that the unity of biological and psychological processes better explains emotion.

In the midst of neobehaviourism, Arnold investigated emotion from the standpoint of human agency, unifying biological and psychological processes. She aimed "to develop a theory that would integrate the psychological, neurological, and physiological aspects of affective phenomena to explain the place of emotion in personality organization" (Shields, 2006, p. 223).

According to Arnold, there are **three steps** in the pathway of emotions:

- When individuals automatically perceive a given situation, first they unreflectively appraise it as positive or negative, evoking an embodied emotional response.
- Then they reflectively judge the situation, connecting their direct emotional experience with intention, personal values, and action in the situation.
- Their action, in turn, can evoke secondary appraisals of bodily responses.

In the 1960s, Arnold began to explore the neural pathways of memory functions in relation to perception, emotion, and action. Employing her notion of appraisal, she reframed the popular, information-processing explanation of memory as "interconnected dynamic processes," an interpretation that some cognitive psychologists also employ (Shields, 2006, p. 234). Because appraisal is pivotal in her conception, some cognitive psychologists claim her as a pioneer.

Section conclusion

During the heyday of neobehaviourism Hebb, Sperry, Luria, and Arnold contributed to psychologists' understanding of brain–behaviour relations. Their lines of research ultimately proved influential in Psychology.

Hebb addressed human and animal behaviour and cognition in terms of the brain. Thus, he equated understanding the total activity of the nervous system with understanding psychology, which is why some claim that Hebb transcended both behaviourism and Gestalt theory. However, until the 1950s, neobehaviourism overshadowed neural explanations of behaviour. Consequently, his school of thought, the biological organization of behaviour, was overshadowed initially. When cognitivism replaced neobehaviourism, psychologists studying basic processes became more receptive to Hebb's concepts.

Sperry studied how information is conveyed and psychological functions are integrated between cerebral hemispheres in human patients. Luria investigated behavioural deficits associated with specific types of neurological damage; he is credited with founding clinical neuropsychology. Stressing the role of cognitive appraisal, Arnold researched the psycho-physiology of emotion and memory, two topics that now bear her conceptual imprint.

Cognitivism

The term "cognitivism" refers to the school of thought focused on identifying the brain–behaviour relations inherent in mental phenomena and processes, while *cognitive psychology* is the subdiscipline focused on symbolic representations of those phenomena and processes. Cognitive psychologists investigate "the psychological mechanisms by which people acquire, store, and evaluate beliefs about the world" (Leahey, 2003, p. 109).

Cognitive psychologists assert that Psychology's subject matter should consist of cognitive objects. Many hold that we are biologically disposed to structure sensory experience and to receive and express language. Cognitive psychologists answer the problem of how we obtain knowledge of the empirical world by positing that an individual mind/brain contains a neuropsychological apparatus for receiving, computing, and organizing sensory information into cognitive representations.

Cognitive psychology began to emerge from neobehaviourism during the 1950s, when some US psychologists demonstrated the operation of various cognitive phenomena. One catalyst for the advent of cognitivism was the Center for Cognitive Studies at Harvard founded in 1960 by **Jerome Bruner** (b. 1915) and **George Miller** (b. 1920). Another catalyst was Ulric Neisser's (b. 1928) *Cognitive Psychology* (1967), which served as a definitive text for what he envisioned as the true alternative to behaviourism and psycho-analysis. But the conversion from neobehaviourism to cognitivism primarily involved those US psychologists who specialized in basic processes. Neither contemporary clinical and social psychologists nor international psychologists had abandoned mental processes.

By the 1960s cognitivism was institutionalized as the experimental study of visual and auditory processing and psychological aspects of language, memory, and thinking. Cognitivists believed that such categories as images, memories, and decision-making are as measurable and subject to experimentation as overt behaviour is. By the 1990s, linked with neuroscience, cognitivism permeated the theories, research, and professional practice of Psychology's major subdisciplines to such an extent that some psychologists in the US and the UK renamed their departments "cognitive science."

Yet theoretical heterogeneity characterized cognitivism. For instance, Neisser (1967) originally adopted the dominant information-processing model of cognitive processes by which discrete psychological functions interact and internal processing accounts for perception and cognition. But within a decade, drawing from James Gibson's theory of direct perception and Frederic Bartlett's concept of schema, Neisser proposed a perceptual cycle by which individuals actively derive sensory information and alter their schemas, which shape action and then in turn shape schemas.

Research domains

Perception, information-processing, memory, emotion, thinking, and language have been popular research topics among cognitive psychologists.

Perception During the wars US investigators of perceptual processes focused on stimuli. But after World War II, they introduced new approaches to studying perception. Theoretically, researchers were divided between those who held that perception occurs indirectly through internal information-processing and those who held that we directly perceive phenomena.

Wartime research on military personnel's ability to detect radar and sonar signals spawned postwar investigations of the human–machine interface. British psychologist **Donald Broadbent** (1926–1993) experimented on competing attentional demands. Relying on the information-processing metaphor, he proposed a selective-filtering process that facilitates paying attention to one of multiple sources of information (the "cocktail party" phenomenon). Broadbent re-established attention as a central process of perception, while assuming that individuals perceive stimuli indirectly.

By contrast, James Gibson, held that, rather than imposing meaning on stimuli, as both Gestalt theory and the information-processing model (see below) claimed, individuals perceive stimuli directly. The debate between direct and indirect positions on perception led one historian of Psychology to conclude that "The perception of objects and the perception of meanings have proved impossible to separate, as have the meanings of objects and how we perceive them" (G. Richards, 2010, p. 115).

Bringing a "new look" to visual perception, Bruner demonstrated how personality factors, including motives and emotions, and social background affect perception of stimuli. He posited "perceptual readiness," an automatic tendency to perceive certain aspects of a situation. Bruner concluded that perception is an active, not passive, unconscious and conscious process.

Information-processing The postwar arrival of computers, cybernetics, and artificial intelligence generated a computer metaphor of mind/brain and information theory (Gardner, 1985). New terms derived from computing emerged to describe mental processes: feedback mechanisms, information-processing, and computation, as metaphorically depicted in Figure 7.2. Many psychologists came to believe that during cognitive activity, individuals process information serially and perform computations on symbolic representations just as a computer motherboard does. "Information" replaced physical stimuli in psychologists' discourse.

Norbert Wiener (1894–1964), a US mathematician, had proposed a theory of control systems and feedback mechanisms. Termed cybernetics, the theory refers to the central role of feedback in navigating between partially known agents and unpredictable events. Relying on this explanation, information theory, and computational methods to simulate mental processes, Miller, Galanter, and Pribram (1960) linked thinking with behaving. They hypothesized a feedback loop, known as TOTE (test–operate–test–exit), by which organisms operate on environmental stimuli and assess the fit between their current and planned states.

The basic information-processing analogy is as follows: mind/brain is to body as program is to computer. According to this explanation, the mind/brain executes computational functions on internal representations of external stimuli and sequentially manipulates symbolic systems, human memory is like computers' storage capacity, and language is like computers' programming codes.

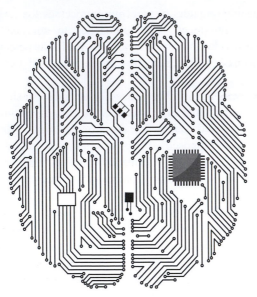

Figure 7.2 According to the information-processing model, the brain is like a computer motherboard

By the 1980s, however, some psychologists abandoned mechanistic information-processing and adopted the notion of the mind as an active organizer (Miller, 2003). Other cognitivists forsook the computer analogy for a neural model. Inspired by Hebb's rule, they revised Thorndike's premise that stimuli and responses are connected neurally. These cognitivists held that behavioural and cognitive activities are represented by temporal neural patterns. An alliance with neuroscientists evolved, which generated the field of cognitive neuroscience in which investigators analyze cognitive concepts with neuroscientific methods.

Memory Little memory research had occurred in US Psychology between the wars (Danziger, 2008). Considering Lashley's work on the effects of cortical lesions on rats' recollection, US psychologists concluded that the brain location of memory was best left to physiologists.

However, during World War II, military technology required that human operators be closely integrated with complex machines in "man–machine systems" to detect and interpret signals correctly and swiftly. Psychologists used the term "short-term memory" to describe the tasks associated with immediate recollection that signal-detection operations entailed. By the 1980s with the language of information-processing, short-term memory became "working memory."

Subsequently, some investigators redesigned experiments to incorporate memory as an active organizing process, akin to computer functions. They distinguished a sequence of cognitive operations – recording ("encoding"), storing, and retrieving – that hypothetically occur within an individual's mind/brain independently of sensory-motor processes and perception. As the "cognitive revolution" unfolded in the 1980s, its followers described memory as an internal process of retrieval of stored items (Gardner, 1985).

Most investigators, however, persisted in reaffirming and expanding Hermann Ebbinghaus's laws of memory, based on mechanized memorizing (e.g., Erdelyi, 2010). Yet in the 1970s some prominent investigators regarded it as a dead-end and urged a shift to investigating cognitive, perceptual, and contextual phenomena affecting memory (Danziger, 2008).

By the 1990s, some investigators realized that the notion of information-processing restricted their field of research to internal symbol-manipulation. They sought to study remembering as human bodily activity in social situations. Other investigators, such as Endel Tulving (b. 1927), distinguished types of memory – procedural, semantic, and episodic – that they linked to different types of consciousness. Still others pursued cerebral localization studies, seeking evolutionary and neurophysiological explanations for memory processes that Lashley had abandoned.

Experimentation on memory now included studies of traumatic memory, frequently on whether recollections of childhood abuse were truthful (Erdelyi, 2010). This research lent itself to clinical and forensic applications (e.g., eyewitness testimony), which enhanced Psychology's social relevance. But conceptually, investigators employed the same individual-centred, acultural explanation of traumatic-memory processes as they did concerning "objective" memory processes routinely tested in labs (Danziger, 2008).

Emotion In current psychological thought, the four external signs of an emotion are brain states, awareness of a sensory feeling, personal semantic description of that feeling, and motoric action or preparation. For some scholars, the third sign represents an emotion (Kagan, 2007). But these four components arguably are distinct phenomena; for example, changed brain activity does not necessarily trigger an emotion or a motoric action.

Furthermore, individuals' conceptions of the social situations in which emotions occur, which are historically based, influence their interpretation of that emotion. In turn, individuals' locations in social categories (e.g., ethnocultural status, gender, social class, age, etc.) shape their appraisals of emotions. But the neuroscientific trend is to rely heavily on patterns of brain activity as the functional equivalent of a given emotion, exclusive of conscious awareness or personal appraisals of feelings. However, explaining how a neurophysiological event evokes a *psychological* process remains unresolved.

Thinking During the heyday of US behaviourism and beyond, Bartlett investigated thinking as a form of skilled activity. The few US psychologists in the 1950s who studied thinking understood it as "verbal learning," meaning that they applied behavioural concepts and associationism to thinking, remembering, and communicating. For them, such processes constituted "verbal behaviour," which mediated between stimuli and responses.

In their influential work *A Study of Thinking*, Bruner, Goodnow, and Austin (1956) transcended the verbal-learning approach. Employing experimentation on rudimentary strategies for forming artificial categories, they explained concepts as comprised of groups of attributes and thinking as active hypothesis-testing. But psychologists did not investigate concepts employed in everyday life nor complex thinking until cognitivism was more established partly because of peer prejudice against the cognitive turn in Psychology (Baars, 1986).

Language Another marker in the story of cognitivism is the work of Noam Chomsky, a US linguist, who in the 1950s introduced the notion of innate mental operations to psycholinguistics. Behaviourists had insisted that individuals acquire language through association with particular experiences; for them, language is learned behaviour. But Chomsky claimed that psychologists ignored the biological predispositions that enable humans from infancy, regardless of culture, to communicate in increasingly complex ways and generate statements or questions that they never had expressed previously.

Terming his programme a Cartesian theory of language, Chomsky posited that all humans possess an innate capacity for employing grammatical structures, produced by a "Language Acquisition Device" that unfolds developmentally but requires experience to trigger it. Language acquisition, he argued, is partly a result of specific forms of innate linguistic knowledge; that is, we are biologically prepared to understand the rules for language.

Chomsky's standpoint, modified over his career (S. Rosenberg, 1993), strengthened the emergent positions that mental representations are symbolic and that just as grammar has structure so do mental processes. His famous critique of Skinner's explanation of language acquisition also endeared Chomsky's ideas to those psychologists who found Skinnerian insistence on stimulus control and reinforcement contingencies fundamentally inadequate.

Section conclusion

By the 1970s cognitive explanations became the dominant school of thought in theory, research, and practice of US Psychology, including developmental, personality, and social psychology. Concomitant with the expanded influence of the US discipline globally, psychologists internationally also adopted cognitivism.

The cognitive turn was not without conceptual problems, however. The metaphor of information-processing compares the brain to computer hardware and the mind to software. Thus, the mind is a machine, abstracted from biology, including sex and aggression; in this sense, the computer metaphor is a form of dualism. From a critical perspective, however, thinking is a dialogical activity of external and internalized conversation, expressed in social relations, and reflective thinking consists of debating multiple viewpoints (Billig, 2008).

Critics identified other problems. In its founding decades cognitivism excluded embodied emotion, wishing, fantasizing, and subconscious processes (e.g., intuiting), and interpersonal and historical contexts (Norman, 1980). Study of contextualized, everyday cognitive processes that ordinary people employ in real life is needed, if cognitive psychologists' research is to have any ecological validity. Thus, cognitivism can be subjectivistic, ignoring concrete environmental conditions, and individualistic, ignoring personal relationships (Sampson, 1981). Presently, some scholars use "embodied, active, situated cognition" to denote a socially situated phenomenology of cognitive operations employed in real-world activities (Larkin, Eatough, & Osborn, 2011).

From a different perspective, discursive psychology, some psychologists assert that the very notion of subjective cognitive processes, whether thoughts, memories, emotions, and fantasies, as the instigators of action and interaction is flawed. Instead, discursive psychologists regard so-called inner states as produced within instances of talk-in-interaction between people, that is, as the *result* of human interaction (Hepburn & Wiggins, 2007). Discursive psychologists do not deny that internal experiences exist; rather, they claim that such experiences are inaccessible by conventional quantitative or even qualitative methods. They advocate analyzing the discourse, the conversation, of interacting parties. Although discursive psychology has its adherents, particularly in the UK, it remains on the margins of mainstream Psychology.

A cognitive revolution? Psychologists debate whether cognitivism emerged continuously as reform or represented a revolution (Greenwood, 1999; Leahey, 1992). On one account, US psychologists found neobehaviourism incapable of explaining complex behaviour, so a replacement was inevitable. Gestalt theory, European research on perceptual and thought processes, and Tolman's studies of animal learning served as catalysts for reform.

Another reform account is that psychologists retrieved "mentalistic" concepts (e.g., mind and consciousness) from the discipline's founders to explain behavioural data adequately (Miller, 2003). Because "mentalistic" had been a behaviourist epithet, the cognitivist founders chose the adjective "cognitive" to attain legitimacy in their peers' eyes.

Other commentators contend that reintroducing mental processes to US Psychology constituted a genuine cognitive revolution (Gardner, 1985). The allegedly radical break from behaviourism resulted from psychologists adopting computer technology and psycholinguistics. But cognitive psychologists' interests were broader and deeper than artificial intelligence, computer simulation, and psycholinguistics. Moreover, most international psychologists, who had never abandoned cognitive processes, did not need a revolution.

On balance, cognitivists did return to the subject matter, but not the methods, that interested Wundt, Titchener, some functionalist psychologists, and mid-century European psychologists. Yet despite their different terms and concepts, cognitivists shared behaviourists' goals of predicting and controlling behaviour. Cognitivists' innovation largely consisted of inserting mental processes into the behavioural equation (Greenwood, 1999).

Psychological neuroscience

Since the 1990s, specialty areas pertaining to brain and cognition have secured the highest prestige in natural-science Psychology under the rubric of neuroscience. In their quest to understand mind/brain relations involved in the gamut of basic psychological processes, many psychologists assume that "virtually all psychological functioning can ultimately be traced to underlying origins in the brain" (Gergen, 2010, p. 796) and their electrochemical pathways. After defining terms and concepts, we discuss current issues in psychological neuroscience.

Terms and concepts

Behavioural neuroscience encompasses laboratory experimentation on the biological basis of the behaviour of small animals to extrapolate to basic, animal and human psychological processes. Behavioural neuroscientists focus on the interaction among animal neurobiology, learning, motivation, and cognition. Some study medical and mental health issues (e.g., addictions, eating disorders, and Parkinson's disease). Others investigate neural plasticity, the neurobiology of learning and memory, time and number processing, and the interface between learning and motivation. Thus, behavioural neuroscience integrates genetics, physiology, and neurology with Psychology, based on animal models.

Meanwhile, as a newer generation of cognitive psychologists became comfortable with a biological emphasis, they linked cognitive psychology with multidisciplinary studies of mind, brain, and behaviour. Cognitive psychologists and biological psychologists joined forces with neuroscientists, physicians, behaviour geneticists, computer scientists, and philosophers to create a multidisciplinary field, known as cognitive neuroscience, to study the intersections of mental phenomena and processes with brain structures and electro-chemical functions.

Thus, cognitive neuroscientists investigate human behavioural and neurological processes underlying perceptual processes in various sensory modalities; cognition, including memory and language; and motor control and human action. They assume that brain processes (e.g., ever-changing networks of neuronal connections) are the foundation for cognitive processes, but they believe that cognitive approaches can guide testable hypotheses for brain-imaging research. Collectively, behavioural and cognitive neuroscientists assume that animals and humans process information, hold it in memory, and then recall it to guide their behaviour.

Although no common definition of mind has emerged, psychological neuroscientists have integrated previously competing views of mind-design: the older, *functionalist* view of serial symbol systems with the newer, *connectionist* view of parallel processing occurring both intuitively and consciously. In the neuroscientific context, functionalism refers to a model of cognition based on the functions of serial information-processing; functionalists employ the analogy of computer hardware to the brain and computer software to the mind.

Connectionism in neuroscience refers to a model of cognition, based on brain organization, by which mathematized neural activity undergirds complex cognitive functions. Neuroscientists hold that complex cognitive functions operate within a system of "parallel distributed processing" (simultaneous multiple sequences of neural networks). This concept is an analogue to the new architecture in computer science of linked multiple processors, working in parallel, which supplanted the older architecture of single serial processing.

Basic issues

Observations of brain structures and neuronal functioning have confirmed previous suppositions about the functions of neural networks and their relation to higher cognitive processes, such as pattern recognition. Research on split-brains, for instance, revealed not only the importance of the connecting function of the corpus callosum but also communication between the hemispheres and their respective specializations (Gazzaniga, 2011).

The present conceptual integration in psychological neuroscience includes **two principles**:

- When the mind functions automatically or "unconsciously," which is most often, it proceeds in a non-linear, intuitive way.
- But when thought is conscious, which is not very often, thinkers process symbolic representations serially.

Put differently, in accounting for social-cognitive phenomena and the so-called, adaptive "social brain" (Adolphs, 2009), neuroscientists distinguish between two basic processes: automatic and controlled. The former is fast, involving stimulus-driven, unintentional and emotional responses, while the latter is slow, involving reflective thinking. These processes and principles evoke **five important questions** (Horgan, 1999; Leahey, 2003; Gazzaniga, 2011):

(1) *How apt is the metaphor of the mind as an information-processing computer?* According to the "strong AI" position, computer simulation is functionally equivalent to human intelligence and, scientifically speaking, humans are complex machines. The opposing view, "weak AI," is that computers function without understanding their programmed operations, but we *do* understand our functioning, more or less (Searle, 1992). We solve problems, make knowledge, and develop understanding by accessing our emotions, feelings, and intuition, not simply by following a formal procedure of mechanized rules (Damasio, 1999).

> **Small-group discussion.** Is there such an entity as a "thinking computer?" Is an AI artifact of consciousness equivalent to human consciousness? Does an AI machine have "rights," such as the right not to be turned off or the "right to life"?

(2) *How is the immaterial mind related to the body and brain?* Although the philosophical term "mind" encompasses sensory perceptions, emotion, beliefs, and intentions, in neuroscientific discourse it refers to intellectual functions that generate intelligent behaviour. Until recently, neuroscientists regarded the role of non-rational functions as inconsequential, but now some investigate the affective and intentional aspects of mental life. However, findings about the neural correlates of cognitive processes do not address the matter of the psychological experience (*qualia*) of those processes.

Many psychological neuroscientists rely on an information-processing explanation. But for US Nobelist Gerald Edelman (1991), a neuro-immunologist, what or whom you perceive is a result of your brain's creative activity, rather than a fixed representation of an object or person, and memory is the generation of a new act of imagination, rather than a retrieval process of coded information. Consequently, some question whether neuroscience can encompass individuals' subjective experiences and talents (Kagan, 2009).

(3) *What exactly is consciousness?* Investigations of consciousness resurfaced with the emergence of neuroscience. Investigators debate explanations of consciousness and its neural location (Seth, Baars, & Edelman, 2005). Neuroscientists' unsolved problem is to understand the relationship between brain activity and the experience of consciousness (Gazzaniga, 2011).

For some neuroscientists, brain creates mind, objective neuronal processes cause subjective feelings, and consciousness has no material influence over neural events. Thus, neurophysiology provides a complete explanation for consciousness. For other investigators, consciousness refers to immaterial, subjective phenomena, produced by neural functions but distinct from them; mind and brain are separate; and only aspects of consciousness are measurable (Revonsuo, 2001).

There are **philosophical arguments** concerning consciousness as well:

- Physical entities per se are meaningless until we construe and impute meaning to them.
- Because we live in social contexts, human life is intersubjective, transcending individualistic experience. To live civilly we are obliged to become empathic, which "is a form of co-consciousness" (Robinson, 2010, p. 792).
- Although brain mechanisms, subject to physical laws, shape consciousness, mental processes and social interaction constrain the brain and determine human action (Gazzaniga, 2011). The ancient concepts of responsibility and free will remain relevant.

(4) *How is cognition related to emotions, feelings, and intuition?* Natural-science psychologists used to segregate emotion from cognition. Now in integrating them, some claim that emotion and cognition function in a unified way, while others assert that although they interact, emotion is linked with motivation and cognition with knowledge (Izard, 2009).

Three lines of research on this question are instructive:

- Psychologist Candace Pert (1997) has demonstrated that the biological components of emotions connect body and mind. She focuses on peptides, which are the proteins that direct cell activities throughout the body and are the chemical basis for emotions.
- Neurologist Antonio Damasio (1999) contends that biologically emotions are necessary to make sound social and personal decisions. He reverses René Descartes' famous statement to read: "I am, therefore, I think with invaluable help from my feelings."
- From studies of the human amygdala, which is instrumental in processing emotion and interacts with brain systems responsible for cognition, psychologist Elizabeth Phelps (2006) concludes that "the mechanisms of emotion and cognition are intertwined from early perception to reasoning" (p. 27).

(5) *Do nonhuman animals have mental life and consciousness? What forms does animal "theory of mind" take in which species?* Specialists in animal cognition study how aquatic and land mammals, birds, and some insects process and remember information in visual and auditory forms (Emery & Clayton, 2009). Some neuroscientists investigate more complex cognitive functions, such as language and intelligence (Wynne, 2001). But which animal species have mental life and consciousness? Given that the number of neurons necessary for consciousness is unknown, perhaps even fruit flies are conscious.

Section conclusion

Natural-science psychologists' greater openness to what their behavioural predecessors rejected as mentalistic research topics eventuated in cognitivism, which morphed into behavioural and cognitive neuroscience. These twin schools of thought, along with evolutionary psychology (see below), dominate current Psychology's landscape, yet represent a return to the discipline's conceptual roots in neurophysiology (Gergen, 2010).

In addition, there has been a marked increase in specific issues guiding research as opposed to building grand theories of behaviour. In previous decades, investigators attempted to create universal laws of behaviour and develop broad theoretical concepts.

Psychologists today specialize in developing micro theories in a particular field, for instance, visual recognition in infant development, although their claims to generalizability persist.

Another current hallmark is greater fertilization across subdisciplines. Some neuroscientific psychologists who study basic psychological processes also explore the physiological foundations of learning, memory, and motivation. Many also are more interested than previous generations in multidisciplinary cooperation with both biologists and philosophers.

With the advent of cognitivism, psychologists appeared to treat the brain independently of other biological functions as if it had no body. Ironically, many neuroscientists whose original disciplines are biological and/or medical seem to have been more psychological than many cognitive psychologists, because they address the psychological content of the interrelationship of brain, mind, and body. For example, Damasio (1999) promotes biopsychological interpretations of consciousness in relation to the self. The widely accepted notion of the brain's plasticity and its capacities to undo damage seems to unite investigators from medical, biological, and psychological disciplines.

Some current neuroscientific investigations connect the territories of cognitive psychology and biopsychology with developmental, personality, and social psychology. In addition, "neurophenomenology," for example, entails correlating neurological and phenomenological data on a given, experienced psychological process (van de Laar & de Regt, 2008). However, from a critical perspective, "when closely examined, most brain research is irrelevant to understanding human action" (Gergen, 2010, p. 806), because the embodied human brain always is embedded in cultural-historical situations. Thus,

[T]he brain in itself proves of limited significance in either determining or providing a basis for understanding human action. On the contrary, it is far more promising, both scientifically and in terms of societal value, to view the brain primarily as an instrument for achieving culturally constructed ends ... [Consequently] the brain [is] but one participant in a bodily system in motion. Thus, there is no essential distinction between brain and behavior; instead, there is simply bodily behavior within which brain functioning may play an important role. (Gergen, 2010, pp. 798–799, 812–813)

Evolutionary psychology

Behavioural neuroscientists typically attribute the results of their animal experimentation to evolutionary processes, cognitive neuroscientists study adaptive inclinations in cognitive processes, and social psychologists find them in social relations. Psychological neuroscientists assume that natural selection designed the adaptive mind. Thus, evolutionary psychology complements neuroscience in that, advocates argue, the mind works on the basis of adaptations for survival and reproduction. The mind purportedly contains specialized modules, adapted by evolution for different psychological functions. Not only physical characteristics but also behavioural and mental ones produce evolved design of species on the basis of the relationship between genetic and environmental determinants (Tooby & Cosmides, 2005).

Several decades ago evolutionary psychologists adopted *sociobiology*, which deals with the biology of social behaviour, particularly racial, intellectual, and gender differences (Dagg, 2005). Because of academic and public conflicts over some sociobiologists' politically conservative views, such as eugenics and rationalizations of sexual assault of women, a new term, "behavioural ecology" or "behavioural biology," emerged (Hagen, 2005). Originally, behavioural ecologists focused on the function and evolution of behaviour. In the 1980s some shifted to applying the methods of comparative evolutionary biology to "questions about the role of learning, memory, and cognition in adaptive behavior" (Sherry, 2006, p. 168).

Current evolutionary psychologists stress the ultimate causes of all animal and human behaviour and mental life according to the concepts of evolutionary biology. They ask what the adaptiveness is of any psychological capacity and how it boosted the reproductive fortunes of organisms in their ancestral environment. Although evolutionary psychologists offer different explanations for the adaptiveness of certain behaviours, they agree that understanding why "the evolved function of a psychological mechanism" exists and "how the mechanism works" is essential "for a mature psychological science" (Confer *et al.*, 2010, p. 111). Moreover, they claim that their school of thought has "no social agenda" (Confer *et al.*, 2010, p. 121).

Principles

Evolutionary psychologists adhere to **four principles**:

- Evolutionary biology explains all human behaviour, which allegedly is inherited from primate ancestors 6 million years ago (Buss, 2009). Today's descendants of human ancestors are genetically shaped to struggle successfully for existence.
- The purposes of life are survival and reproduction and every aspect of life has a genetic component. Natural selection proceeds "primarily at the level of individual or gene, not the group or species" (Dewsbury, 2003, p. 77). Organisms' reproductive capacity is enhanced by evolutionary adaptations.
- Future gene pools are a consequence of *inclusive fitness*, meaning genes transmitted to the next generation through direct reproduction or by "the reproduction of close relatives" (Dewsbury, 2003, p. 78). Inclusive fitness explains the paradox of altruistic, even self-sacrificial behaviour as biologically adaptive over time. The drive to maximize "reproductive fitness" determines the longevity of any behaviour.
- Instincts and culture shape human behaviour: genes selected through evolution determine biological structures and mechanisms, while cultural conditions enable the internalization of ideas that guide choices of behaviour (Smits, 2011).

Section conclusion

Evolutionary psychologists hold that, although species differences exist, humans and other animals only differ in degree. Vertebrate and some invertebrate animals show continuity across various species anatomically and physiologically. Furthermore, behaviour patterns previously thought to be exclusively human, such as culture, empathy, and personality, are observed in a wide range of species.

Evolutionary psychologists believe that natural selection is the most credible scientific explanation of human nature. For example, in response to the counter-intuitive fact that some mothers murder their children, evolutionary psychologists argue that they do so because they feel incapable of parenting them and it is in the mothers' survival interests to murder them. Moreover, evolutionary psychologists claim that advances in genetics and neuroscience confirm that the "central theorem of biology" – evolution – has a central place in understanding psychological functions (e.g., H. Plotkin, 2004, p. 159).

A different standpoint is that humans are the same *and* different from other animals (Dagg, 2005). We are like our closest relatives, primates, in basic behaviours, such as sociability and the incest taboo. But we differ from them in more complex, but still universal characteristics that apparently have an evolutionary component, such as cooperation within groups and speech.

Other behaviours seem to be the result of cultural development and individual tendencies rather than biological evolution, such as male dominance and territoriality; although some primates have these characteristics, others do not. According to critics of evolutionary psychology, biology is not destiny regarding gender differences, for instance, because of the developing brain's plasticity and responsiveness to sociocultural conditions (Eliot, 2009).

From another critical biological perspective, evolutionary psychologists' heavy reliance on a Darwinian explanation of random natural selection is problematic. Evolutionary developmental biologists investigate genes within developing organisms situated in particular ecological locations (Carroll, 2006). They argue that the dynamic interaction of genes, development, and environmental context shapes any organism's life-span.

Neurogeneticists who take a "weak" neurogenetics position support this argument. They believe that genetic predispositions are subject to environmental modification from pregnancy onwards (Cacioppo, 2002). They conclude that the relationship of genes, organisms, and their environments better represents natural conditions than the "strong" position of unidirectional neurogenetic determinism (Lewontin, 2000; Linden, 2009), namely, the view that specific genes cause particular brain and behaviour relationships (Joseph, 2004).

Part 3 conclusion

Since World War II, neobehaviourism yielded to more powerful schools of thought: operant behaviourism, the biological organization of behaviour, cognitivism, behavioural and cognitive neuroscience, and evolutionary psychology.

Skinner specialized in demonstrations of a powerful technology for modifying behaviour. He always spurned hypothetical mental processes and literally to his death critiqued cognitive psychology. Yet arguably his school of thought is problematic for **two reasons**:

- Operant behaviourists cannot explain innate behaviour, psychophysiology, and complex activity (e.g., perception, memory, and creativity). They dismiss experiential phenomena, including unconscious ones, as scientifically inadmissible. They construe emotions and cognitive processes merely as embodied private events, and they regard the person simply as a conjunction of genetic endowment and reinforcement-history.
- Operant behaviourism relies on circular definitions of its key terms and is limited theoretically to describing correlated observable variables.

Some psychologists investigated the biological organization of behaviour, demonstrating how biological processes shape behaviour. Hebb, Sperry, Luria, and Arnold introduced concepts explaining brain–behaviour relations that eventually became very influential in the discipline as it turned towards cognitivism and neuroscience. Currently, behavioural neuro-scientists, employing animal models, exemplify this development.

By the twenty-first century, cognitivism and neuroscience became psychologists' most common identity-label for studies of basic processes as well as for developmental, person-ality, and social processes (Robins, Gosling, & Craik, 1999). From a critical perspective, however, psychologists employ cognition as an umbrella term for hypothetical and unob-servable mental structures and processes that they assume exist as physical objects. But "[t]he individual mind/brain does not invent its own language, social rituals and structures of interaction. It always exists within, and is determined by, patterns of social life that have their own history" (Billig, 2008, p. 185).

Cognitive neuroscience represents a return to Psychology's foundations in physiology but expressed now with considerable neuro-anatomical sophistication. Yet core questions with which ancient philosophers struggled, such as the nature of body–mind relations, underlie the topics that psychologists pursue under the rubric of cognitive neuroscience. Furthermore, current conceptual approaches do not seem to provide a satisfactory account of individuals' subjective experiences.

Evolutionary psychologists infer causal relationships between ancestral genetic endow-ment and present behavioural attributes. They emphasize "adaptiveness at the time that mechanisms of behaviour evolved in the ancestors of humans . . . [yet they recognize that] many behavior patterns and tendencies . . . might not be as adaptive under present con-ditions" (Dewsbury, 2003, p. 78). In fact, the concept of adaptation and the nature vs. nurture debate have lengthy histories, particularly in Anglo-American Psychology.

According to critics, however, evolutionary psychologists commit **two errors in reason-ing** (Dagg, 2005; Rose & Rose, 2001):

- They have no fossil records of putative ancestral behaviour and dubious evidence about how dominant and recessive genes operate in the behaviour and mental life studied. Thus, they do not define concretely the genetic bases of behaviours and mental capacities.
- Evolutionary psychologists' hypotheses about the adaptive value of specific behaviours, particularly complex phenomena, are untestable, hence speculative. For example, what might be an evolutionary explanation for mental conflicts (Smits, 2011)?

Part 4   Developmental psychology

Developmental psychology, which has grown remarkably since World War II, directly deals with the problem of nature and nurture.

After the war, behaviourists continued to minimize developmental differences and max-imize environmental contingencies, while social learning theorists presented new ways of explaining social development. Stage-theorists assumed the operation of genetically pro-grammed psychological capacities. Infant specialists showed that infants enter the world equipped to structure their sensory-motor experience.

In the 1960s under Piagetian influence, many US developmentalists shifted to a cognitive orientation, which they adapted to lab experimentation. Others studied the influence of early experience on development or included middle-adulthood and aging.

During this era enduring concepts emerged: "the competent infant," referring to the sensory information that neonates and infants actively acquire; and "temperament," referring to individual differences in physiological dispositions towards emotional reactivity (Keller, 2000). Many developmentalists studied how children develop a sense of competency and sense of self. Child development and social cognition intersected in research on theory of mind, how children learn the inner psychological states of others (Wellman, 2006).

By the 1970s, some German psychologists revived Charlotte Bühler's vision of lifespan development (Baltes, Staudinger, & Lindenberger, 1999). This perspective encouraged developmentalists to investigate, for example, the ways in which psychological processes, particularly intellectual abilities, decline with age. Contextual factors, including family, work, education, and extant sociocultural conditions, also affect lifespan development.

Two key questions that developmentalists investigated include (Keller, 2000):

- How do biology and culture, heredity and the environment affect development and what are the limits of nature and nurture?
- What is the sequence of developmental tasks?

Developmental theories

Major postwar theories include social learning, perceptual learning, attachment, contact comfort, and social ecology.

Social learning theory

Two influential US psychologists applied learning principles to understand human social development. **Robert Sears** (1908–1989) relied on stimulus–response theory to explain socialization processes and parenting, while **Albert Bandura** (b. 1925) stressed "modelling" (learning by imitation) and cognitive concepts.

Sears borrowed from psychoanalytic theory but ignored its attention to developmental stages. Focusing on aggression, dependency, and identification, he investigated how parental behaviour affected the process of children internalizing societal values. He emphasized **two interpersonal notions**:

- Individuals affect and are affected by their environments.
- A dyadic, not an individualistic analysis enables understanding social relationships.

For his part, Bandura initially asserted that observational learning was the principal social-learning mechanism. According to his "Bobo doll" experiment, neither behaviourism nor psychoanalytic theory can explain the effect of exposure to aggressive models on levels of expressed aggression (Bandura, Ross, & Ross, 1963). Rather, he concluded, behaviour, environment, and the person interact in a given situation, and modelling accounts for the acquisition of novel responses.

Then Bandura proposed that children employ cognitive processes (e.g., memory) that change with maturation and experience but not in stages. Forming mental representations of social situations, children create response-expectancies of certain outcomes concerning how effective they might be in particular situations, thereby developing standards for evaluating their behaviour. Central to these processes are parents' and teachers' guided instruction and modelling.

Because Bandura and Sears did not focus "primarily on age-related changes in behavior and thinking" (Grusec, 1992, p. 776), their influence on cognitive developmentalists waned.

Perceptual learning

In the 1950s, Eleanor Gibson explored how infants learn to perceive their environment, which she believed was essential for understanding cognitive development (Pick, 1992). She concluded that perceptual learning is not an associative process of past experience enriching immediate experience through generalization. Rather, perceptual learning occurs through a process of differentiation by which infants distinguish between stimuli in their environments to guide their behaviour.

Subsequently, Gibson investigated how depth perception occurs in infants, inventing the technique of the "visual cliff." She focused on meaningful objects (e.g., faces) in infants' environment. In addition, she studied reading as the conjunction of perceptual discrimination, speaking, and thinking, and interpreted the process of learning to read as a search for meaning.

Towards her career's end Eleanor Gibson used James Gibson's concept of "affordance" (i.e., organisms' perceived meaning and value of objects that they encounter) to investigate how infants develop the capacity to distinguish properties of their environments. For her, perceptual activity, which is exploratory not executive, mediates between cognition and action.

Attachment

Attachment theorists, who unify evolutionary, ethological, cognitive, and psychoanalytic perspectives, stress that "[e]stablishing a secure base is the most important developmental milestone of early childhood" (Cortina, 2004, p. 133). They argue that our early sense of security, defined as attachment, creates within children cognitive representations of all future relationships. From this theory stem the popular concepts of separation anxiety, the value of natural childbirth and breastfeeding, and loss of a parent during childhood as a precursor of adult depression.

Attachment theory is associated with **Mary Salter Ainsworth** (1913–1999) and **John Bowlby** (1907–1990), who studied mother–infant relations (Ainsworth & Bowlby, 1991). Devising the lab technique of the "strange situation," Ainsworth tested attachment-security by measuring infant adaptation to separation from the mother. She identified secure, avoidant, and ambivalent patterns of attachment that resulted from interactions with primary caregivers. This research supported psychodynamic hypotheses about the importance of mother–infant relations (see Chapter 9).

Attachment research has influenced ideas about how to socially accommodate the needs of children. However, the theory rests on the individualistic-cultural assumption that separation and independence are developmental achievements, which might be alien to cultures stressing interdependence. Furthermore, attachment theory mirrored postwar emphasis on a family structure of women serving as mothers and homemakers primarily.

Although some aspects of the theory remain supported, others (e.g., the link between attachment and psychopathology) are questioned (Mercer, 2011).

Contact comfort

Converging with attachment theory is the concept of contact comfort. US psychologist **Harry Harlow** (1905–1981) strengthened the popular proposition that the quality of mother–infant relations, or "bonding," affects the child's capacities for attachment for life. To investigate human maternal love he subjected rhesus monkeys to experimental-lab conditions, believing that the two species are biologically very similar (Blum, 2002). Although Harlow (1958) excluded basic species differences concerning culture and language, his research showed that infant monkeys' drives to satisfy thirst and hunger are secondary to their drive for "contact comfort" (i.e., comfortable physical attachment) received from a cloth "mother."

Harlow's finding contradicted the behavioural position that "nursing comfort" (i.e., suckling at a mother's breast) was sufficiently reinforcing. Instead, he promoted the view that contact comfort produced healthy attachment and "togetherness" between mother and child. Although he equated contact comfort with human love and the needs of rhesus monkeys with humans, Harlow did not posit that infants' need for maternal love was instinctive. Upon further research he "rejected the necessity of mother love in the development of rhesus infants, while emphasizing the important role of peers and social stimulation" (Vicedo, 2009, p. 214).

Social ecology

US psychologist **Urie Bronfenbrenner** (1917–2005) argued that a person's development is shaped by social forces – cultural, economic, and political – as well as psychological ones. Ecologically, human development spans the life-cycle and changes in relation to immediate and more remote environmental influences and social systems. Reflecting Kurt Lewin's thought, Bronfenbrenner (1977) proposed the concept of "person–environment fit" and a topological model of influences on individuals. He identified **four ecological systems**:

- The microsystem is the relation between the developing person and the immediate home, school, and work settings that prescribe particular social roles.
- The mesosystem refers to the hierarchy of interacting microsystems, such as school and religious-congregation interactions.
- The exosystem consists of the societal institutions of work, neighbourhood, government, media, and the person's social networks.
- The macrosystem encompasses socioeconomic and political structures and ideologies of a society, which prescribe "blueprints" for individuals in society.

Bronfenbrenner believed that the quality of family relations enables children's learning in school and that awareness of social forces, primarily strong family ties, should underpin social policy for children and families. To these ends he conducted comparative studies of child-rearing in other cultures, including the Soviet Union, showing how social-contextual variations facilitate and inhibit individuals' lives.

Nature and nurture

Psychologists have differentially emphasized biological and environmental determinants of development. After the war, psychologists stressed the role of parents in terms of risk factors in families, social influences on parenting practices, critical periods in development, and parenting behaviours as moderators of societal risk factors for children's development. A durable assumption is that experiences in infancy mould psychological structures with great impact on later childhood, adolescence, and even adulthood (E. Maccoby, 2000). But substantial empirical support for this assumption is lacking (Kagan, 2010).

Proponents of the "nature" view claim that children's genetic legacy powerfully influences the psychological characteristics that children develop. Nativists believe that effective parenting that balances responsiveness with firmness likely represents parents' responses to their children's genetic dispositions towards competency and cooperation. That is, parenting behaviours probably are the effect, not the cause, of children's behavioural dispositions.

An integrative view is that parenting and children's genetic predispositions are interwoven phenomena and jointly shape children's development. Improved research on parenting influences, using multiple sources of data, confirms these effects, although peer relations also are important influences. Overall, twin and adoption studies have tended to underestimate environmental influences, such as parenting practices (E. Maccoby, 2000). Strong heritability of a characteristic can be compatible with strong environmental influence.

In sum, life experience in cultural context, biologically based temperaments, and chance constitute the whole cloth of developing individuals (Kagan, 2010).

Part 4 conclusion

After the war developmentalists became preoccupied with learning theories, while ignoring biological influences, cognitive processes, and sociocultural factors. Later, they shifted towards close examination of interrelated biological and psychological processes. In addition, they constructed specific rather than stage theories of development and encompassed the stages of emerging adulthood, middle adulthood, and aging.

Presently, many developmentalists are studying "which aspects of behavior are likely to be altered by environmental events at specific points in development and which aspects remain more plastic and open to influence across wide spans of development" (Parke & Clarke-Stewart, 2003, p. 216). Some explore the potential for conceptual integration of biological, cognitive, and social systems to understand the developing individual as a complete person rather than as a biological organism or a cognitive or social entity exclusively.

From a critical perspective, however, there are at least **four problems** with psychologists' constructions of developmental phenomena (Burman, 1997):

- Until recently, the theoretical and investigative unit of analysis in developmental psychology primarily consisted of individuals living out a presumed natural and universal developmental process, as if they were self-contained organisms abstracted from social-historical contexts. Rather than study specific individuals living in specific situations, developmental psychologists treated "development" as an abstract entity and focused on the generalized child.

- Generally, psychologists did not study developmental issues in diverse cultures. Concentration on mother–child interactions in White middle-class families led developmentalists to interpret the psychological phenomena of those who differed from these norms as deficient or deviant. Eventually developmentalists rendered fathers visible and extended the notion of family relations to siblings and grandparents.
- Developmentalists used masculine activities and attributes as normative. Psychologists' common term "mastery" (derived from "master") implies a presumed natural progression from feminized, attached dependence, ruled by emotion, to masculinized, detached independence, achieved by rational problem-solving.
- The concept of development itself is dubious. Rather than a natural object proceeding organically and universally, development is an attribution to some phenomena of interest.

Part 5 | Interpersonal processes

Like developmental psychology, personality and social psychology also significantly expanded after World War II.

Personality psychology

After identifying five prominent perspectives on personality, we describe the historical debate between traits and situational influences on personality. Then we review discourse on the self, which is the lay interpretation of personality.

Perspectives

Since the postwar era **five personality perspectives** have prevailed in Psychology (Wiggins, 2003):

- The psychodynamic perspective, substantially modified since Freudian theory, is focused on how individuals cope with basic erotic and aggressive impulses in relation to societal constraints and inhibitions.
- The interpersonal perspective is concerned with how individuals relate with others in reality, their memory, or their imagination.
- In the personological perspective, indebted to Henry Murray's theory, the focus is on psychological individuality across the life-span (McAdams & Olson, 2010).
- Within the empirical-clinical perspective, psychologists diagnose an individual in terms of psychiatric classifications, relying, for instance, on the Minnesota Multiphasic Personality Inventory (MMPI).
- The multivariate perspective entails assessment of traits presumed to be partially genetically based and relatively stable. Trait theorists have shown that five factors reliably constitute the common features of personality description. The "Big Five" factors are extraversion, agreeableness, conscientiousness, emotional stability, and openness.

Societal demands for practical applications of personality-measurement, coupled with psychologists' commitment to quantitative methods, led to a strong postwar inclination towards studying individual differences (Barenbaum & Winter, 2003). Thus, the multi-variate and empirical-clinical perspectives ascended in popularity, while the psychodynamic waned.

Hans Eysenck, for example, emulated the Galtonian tradition of measuring biologically based individual differences in intelligence and personality (Jensen, 2000). Based on his wartime experience assessing and treating soldiers, he developed a theory composed of two factors and their associated traits – Extraversion (e.g., sociability) and Neuroticism (e.g., emotional stability). Eysenck used his Maudsley Personality Inventory to distinguish abnormal from normal personality and connect personality factors to diagnostic categories. His later version, the Eysenck Personality Inventory, included a third factor: Psychoticism (e.g., egocentricity).

Some postwar investigators conducted correlational research on personality factors. Others tended to test micro theories in single-session experiments with aggregated undergraduate samples rather than study individual lives. By the 1970s, psychologists debated whether traits or situations are more influential on personality. The structural approach of traits emphasizes stability of data, whereas the process approach of situations emphasizes variability.

Traits or situations

Proponents of the Big Five perspective claim that the environment does not influence personality structures and psychometric differences between individuals explain personality architecture on the basis of inherited characteristics. Because Big Five traits show high levels of stability *and* variability in everyday behaviour, advocates conclude that structural and process approaches to personality are complementary not antagonistic (Fleeson, 2001).

By the 1990s, some recommended that, rather than pitting traits against situational influences, investigators should study person-by-situation interactions and the attributions of meaning that individuals give to their responses to changing situations over time. For instance, US psychologist Walter Mischel (2004) proposes observing persons in multiple contexts and then inferring a behavioural or personality "signature" that can explain the person's relatively stable actions across contexts. Others perceive "patterns of coherence . . . in terms of functional relations among underlying personality structures and processes" across situations (Cervone, 2005, p. 443). Traditionally, the notion of the self has provided personality coherence.

The self

Cultural discourse on the self resonated with individuals seeking personal fulfillment in postwar, economically privileged societies (Herman, 1995). For many psychologists, the self meant a stable sense of personal identity or self-image. During the 1970s feminist scholars introduced gendered constructions of the self.

Generally, when personality psychologists used the term "the self," they meant operationalized and quantifiable categories of self-concept and self-esteem. Their primary interests were in trait or factor theories, whether moderated or not by situational influences.

More recently, some psychologists have advanced the notion of a "dialogical self." Rather than autonomous, the self intrinsically engages in dialogue with others in reality or in imagination, thereby bridging self and society (Hermans & Hermans-Konopka, 2010). In this sense, psychologists are responding to the challenge of integrating psychological systems.

Section conclusion

Many psychologists understand personality as a set of relatively durable internal character-istics that distinguish one individual from another. Others analyze personality processes by examining the content and dynamic organization of an individual's personality structures. Critical psychologists argued that, although cognitive contributions are valuable reminders of personality's inescapable connections to brain and body, they do not address the socio-cultural context of personality, including oppressive social conditions (T. Sloan, 1997).

Currently, personality theorists typically attempt to explain human nature totally by reduc-ing individuals' subjectivity to basic traits. However, the abstract framework of the Big Five model does not describe the personality structure of actual individuals and is devoid of cultural context (Kagan, 2007). All conceptions of personality reflect social-historical constructions of individuality in a given society and are neither invariant nor universal.

Another challenge for interpersonal psychologists is to conceptually integrate biological, cognitive, emotional, and cultural-historical systems to understand the individual as a complete person rather than as a biological, cognitive, or interpersonal entity exclusively. According to "a critical theory of personality in social context" (T. Sloan, 1997, p. 98), **three points** are crucial:

- The term "personality structure" can connote rigid dispositions and problematic commu-nication. Accordingly, psychologists could study personality dimensions that inhibit capacities for nurturing others' psychological growth through open communication.
- "Personality" can include societal categories of ethnocultural heritage, gender, sexual orientation, class, ability, and religious preference. Thus, psychologists could investigate how these fluid social realities affect personality throughout life.
- Studying personality critically enables identifying ideological systems that adversely affect the well-being of all people and proposing alternative social systems that can enhance well-being.

Social psychology

After the war, US social psychologists expanded their terrain from social influences on individuals (e.g., attitudes) to group behaviour (e.g., group leadership) and interpersonal relations (e.g., couples' communication). By the 1960s they pursued a subdiscipline mod-elled on experiments on basic processes. While claiming that they recreated external reality with this methodology (Nisbett, 2000), they reduced social realities to artificially controlled laboratory conditions, studying aggregated strangers, usually university students.

Social psychologists assumed that their theories, such as the motive for consistent attitudes, were universally applicable historically and culturally. Critics assert, however, that given that social behaviour is historically and culturally shaped, social-psychology experiments conducted in one cultural-historical context cannot be universally valid. Thus, for example, US psychologist Stanley Milgram's studies (see Box 7.2) only revealed psychological processes of his era (Billig, 2008).

Box 7.2 The Milgram studies

A celebrated line of social-personality research is the Milgram studies. Animated by the Holocaust, Stanley Milgram studied the conditions of obedience to authority. His mission was to examine the conditions of compliance with explicit commands from an authority figure to inflict harm (Blass, 2004). He conducted eighteen such experiments.

In his basic procedure a male experimenter directs a male participant ("teacher") to give graduated shocks when a male confederate ("learner") gives incorrect responses to a test. Although the learner reacts realistically to the increased shock-levels, no actual shock occurs. Milgram published a brief paper in 1963, which elicited ethical controversy, more details in 1965, and a 1974 book describing and justifying his work.

Milgram (1974) asserted that, because the experimenter as authority figure explicitly took responsibility for the outcome, participants believed that they were not personally responsible for shocking the learner. He concluded that people will violate the moral principle of hurting another person, because of innate potential for, and a learned sense of, obedience to authority figures.

Ethical debate arose from Milgram's procedure of refusing individuals' desire to leave the experimental situation due to their distress. Some psychologists argued that such a restriction is patently unethical, while others retorted that without it he could not have achieved high-impact results and the participants' stress was transitory. This debate led to changes in APA ethical guidelines for research (see Chapter 11).

Partially replicating Milgram's studies but screening out potentially vulnerable participants, Burger (2009) tested 29 men and 41 women, averaging 43 years old, to the point when they heard verbal protest from the "learner" (at 150 volts). Burger obtained obedience-rates comparable to Milgram's; although slight personality differences were obtained, there were no differences due to age, ethnicity, gender, or education.

Burger concluded that in a somewhat ambiguous situation of incremental demands people will obey legitimate authority, even when they believe they are harming others. His conclusion converges with that of previous replications of Milgram's procedures (Blass, 2004). Milgram's advocates claim universal applicability of the effects of destructive obedience, with psychologists in Australia, Jordan, and Spain, for example, producing similar results. Many celebrate Milgram's paradigm of high realism and high impact as reaffirming Psychology's social utility.

However, fundamental problems remain. There is no satisfactory explanation for the behaviour of those participants who disobeyed the experimenter's orders. Secondly, whether the Milgram paradigm is equivalent to Nazi soldiers' following their superiors' orders to exterminate Jews or whether the participants in this elaborately staged experiment believed that they were in a real situation is unknown.

Moreover, recent archival examination showed that Milgram misrepresented the risks and harm to his participants and the nature of his ethical safeguards (Nicholson, 2011). Yet, although he himself doubted the scientific value of his experiments, he justified his extreme treatment of his participants. This evidence suggests that disciplinary celebrations of the Milgram studies are misplaced. From a critical perspective, they appear to rival the "Little Albert" experiment as an ethical and interpretive failure.

Not all social psychologists practised lab experimentation. Moreover, a formal European specialty in social psychology did not emerge until after World War II. Eventually, however, it was closely, but not totally, aligned in content and method with US developments (G. Richards, 2010).

During the 1970s some authors charged that experimental social psychologists were in a "crisis" of social relevance. The more social psychologists strove to implement the natural-science model of individual psychology, the critics contended, the less they succeeded at accounting for the impact of social conditions on individuals (e.g., Pepitone, 1981). Furthermore, social psychologists ignored individuals' social relations in the ordinary contexts of living and working, weakening their claims to generalizability.

Two responses to the problem of social relevance ensued. A minority of social psychologists, many in Europe and the UK particularly, turned towards a social-constructionist, even postmodernist perspective (see Chapter 12), and some challenged mainstream Psychology. But the majority identified with the cognitive turn in Psychology, which became social psychologists' chief school of thought.

The cognitive turn

When US psychologist **Leon Festinger** (1919–1989) proposed a "cognitive dissonance" explanation of attitudes, he persuaded his peers that an experimental cognitive approach not only could transcend the limitations of reinforcement theory in explaining behaviour, but it also could explain the psychoanalytic defence mechanism of rationalization (Brehm, 1998). Incorporating motivation and attitudes within the Lewinian framework, Festinger (1957) defined dissonance as the inconsistency between an individual's ideas and behaviour. He assumed that the amount of dissonance varies with the importance of the person's decision, individuals are inclined to reduce and avoid further dissonance, and cognitive dissonance is applicable to biological needs as well as social situations. Thus, social cognition emerged.

Social cognition signified cognitivist concepts employed to study the structure and change-processes of attitudes and the mechanisms of causal attributions and self-deceptions. Aided by Susan Fiske and Shelley Taylor's (1982) eponymous text, social cognition swept over social psychology. Social psychologists then defined their mission broadly as understanding "the impact of the social environment on the individual and how the individual constructs meanings from social situations" (Taylor, 1998, p. 86). Some even have practised "social neuroscience" to study automatic processes involved in social phenomena out of awareness, such as attitudes and goals (Cacioppo, 2002).

A common view is that the brain is essentially social in that, the argument goes, the brain is equipped to identify, interpret, and respond to interpersonal contexts. Because of many decades of separation between biological and social systems in natural-science Psychology, a biological approach to social phenomena might seem strange. But to its advocates the integration of the biological and the social potentially enriches the field and can produce valuable social applications, such as coping with stress.

Presently, in theory, social psychologists study social processes at one or more levels of analysis: intrapersonal (e.g., attitudes), interpersonal (e.g., altruistic volunteering), intra-group (e.g., decision-making), and intergroup (e.g., negotiation). Historically, however, they concentrated on attitudes and persuasion, largely because they assumed that attitudes predict behaviour and they perceived applications of attitudes research to marketing and opinion-polling.

Section conclusion

Postwar social psychologists adopted contemporary natural-science psychologists' emergent belief that intra-individual physiological processes provide the most legitimate explanation of psychological phenomena. Although they aimed to study social life, social psychologists generally excluded culture and language. Their orientation reflected the mainstream view that the psychological core of the biological person, namely, perceiving, feeling, and thinking, is asocial (Greenwood, 2004).

The assumption that biologically based, social-psychological processes function autonomously, abstracted from cultural phenomena that affect only the content of those processes, prevails today. Social psychologists view themselves as studying biological and evolutionary processes in social phenomena (e.g., human mating patterns); social neuroscience; the self, self-attributions, and self-enhancement; social perception (e.g., stereotypes); and the influence of gender and ethnocultural phenomena.

Critics, however, argued that social psychologists study presumably universal internal processes of individuals, devoid of social-historical context, rather than individuals in relation to actual social relationships and social issues. Adopting social neuroscience and studying automatic processes in individuals' responses to social stimuli reinforce this orientation. Although physiology is relevant, the more important influences on human *social* behaviour reside in social ecological and sociocultural contexts (Pepitone, 1981).

Given these concerns, **two critical questions** for social psychology are (Pancer, 1997):

- Is it an *applied* subdiscipline of Psychology focused on the intersection of individuals and societies or a *basic* subdiscipline focused on internal processes?
- Is social psychology an integration of science and social action oriented to progressive social change or primarily an academic pursuit of experimentally verifiable universal laws of behaviour?
- According to its critics, the subdiscipline is out of touch with its subject matter: the relationship between individual and society

Others, however, assert that social psychology has been more varied in its content, methods, and social values throughout its history than its critics suggest (Morawski & Bayer, 2003). Furthermore, the subdiscipline includes diverse perspectives, such as feminist and cultural; diverse topics, such as the boundaries between humans and technologies; and diverse social values, such as critical responses to globalization. In addition, the SPSSI, composed mainly of social psychologists, continues to thrive. Nevertheless, some social psychologists hold a different epistemology than their mainstream peers and conceive of social phenomena, including attitudes and attributions, in relation to language, culture, and social power (Cherry, 2009).

Part 5 conclusion

Consensus among late twentieth-century personality and social psychologists was that three sources of influence determine interpersonal behaviour: personal variables, situational variables, and their interaction. More recently, some psychologists have investigated these determinants more complexly by examining how different individuals respond to the same situation and to several situations over time. One conclusion is that individuals do not respond merely to a situation; rather, an "event is multifaceted just as a person is" (Moskowitz, 2008, p. 39).

By the twenty-first century, interpersonal psychologists were studying person–environment interactions and situations of dyadic interdependence, integrating situational factors and cognitive processes. Notions of identity and intersectionality, cultural influences, and interdependence are current common issues in personality and social psychology. The narrative theoretical and methodological approach also has gained currency in the interpersonal areas as well as in developmental psychology, and clinical, community, and health psychology.

Identity and intersectionality

The psychological concept that connects individual and social influences on personality development is identity, which becomes salient during adolescence with sexual maturation and gender identity. But identity and self-concept are affected by gender and complex social contexts (Stewart & McDermott, 2004). Personal identity includes identification with different social groups and with one's ethnocultural heritage.

Individuals can develop multiple identities (e.g., Chinese Canadian, female, Christian, clinical-psychology graduate student), depending on where they locate themselves socially. The concept of *intersectionality* of social categories explains this phenomenon. Intersectionality refers to the "meaning and consequences of multiple categories of social group membership," typically, ethnocultural status, class, and gender, particularly concerning multiply disadvantaged groups (Cole, 2009, p. 170). Thus, some psychologists study "the interaction between one's many social identities ... and the influences of different social structures on the construction of these identities and relations between members of diverse social groups" (Stewart & McDermott, 2004, p. 531).

Cultural influences

Historically, culture has played a weak role in interpersonal psychology, and Western psychologists assumed that the individualistic pathway is universal. In recent decades, psychologists have become more cognizant of cultural influences on interpersonal phenomena and accept that autonomy and relatedness vary across ethnocultural groups within the same society. Rather than polar opposites, individualism and collectivism are independent dimensions and are present, to some degree, globally (Moghaddam, 1987).

Consensus is that culturally based social structures, institutions, and ideologies shape psychological phenomena, such as parenting, family structure and processes, and self and identity. Characterizations of the self differ across cultures and aspects of the self need to be understood relative to the culture from which psychologists extract their observations (Triandis & Suh, 2002). Moreover, Western notions of identity and self have been used historically to project stability and coherence of the (male) person. But in the contemporary

world of mass migration, the social norms are instability, incoherence, and multiple identities (Berry, 2002).

Interdependence

Influenced by social learning theory and social cognition, some social and personality
psychologists share a vision of person–situation interactions and situations of dyadic
interdependence. Proponents of "interdependence theory" investigate the interplay of "cognition, motivation, and behavior in long-term relationships" in particular situations
(Rusbult & Van Lange, 2003, p. 370). They study interactions between two parties, focused
on their needs, thoughts, and motives in relation to one another. Thus, interdependence
theorists research how interpersonal realities are a consequence of the structure of situations
and social cognitive phenomena, including expectations, motives, needs, and affect.
Interdependence theory is a concrete application of Mischel's (2004) notion of "personal
signatures," and extends Kurt Lewin's formulation of person–environment interaction.

Narrative psychology

This orientation to psychological inquiry, also known as "storied lives," has deep roots in
both natural-science and human-science Psychology (Bruner, 1990; Polkinghorne, 1988).
The term "narrative" refers to a person's or group's story incorporating interpretations of
life-events that are filled with meaning. The narrative approach not only is suited to
personality and social psychology but also to developmental, clinical, community, and
health psychology and connects Psychology with other social and humanities disciplines.

In the narrative approach individuals give a temporal form to their stories, which is called
"emplotment" (Polkinghorne, 1988). They often configure their stories into episodes with a
plot line with a beginning, middle, and ending in which they emphasize meaningful points
and ignore other points. Individuals shape their emplotments according to cultural influences, such as influential myths in society, popular literature, and cinema, as well as personal
beliefs and values. The stories become co-creations of narrators and their listeners (e.g., an
interviewer).

The cognitive process of categorizing can explain individuals' inclination to interpret
their life-events as a story (Bruner, 1990). In categorizing, individuals retain examples of
situations or cases with which they have had some direct or vicarious experience in order to
make sense of that experience. For example, formal diagnostic classifications serve as a
categorizing system for clinical psychologists formulating a diagnosis of a client or patient.

Part 6   Psychology and the social order

Whether interpersonal, developmental, cognitive, or biological in orientation, most natural-
science psychologists, particularly in the USA, endeavoured to actualize their belief that
progress in quantitative laboratory science would rebuild society shaken by World War II
(Sarason, 1981). But they needed private and public financial support to sustain their
investigative programmes (Morawski, 1986). Consequently, the political agenda of

psychologists studying basic processes became as pro-establishment as that of applied and professional psychologists.

US psychologists conveyed to the public a strong commitment to social applications. The theme of the 1969 APA meeting was psychological solutions to contemporary social issues, including racism and poverty. Then-president George Miller (1969) advocated giving Psychology away to promote human welfare. Ever since, psychologists have echoed this exhortation. When feminist, postcolonial, and liberatory approaches emerged in Psychology (see Chapter 12), some psychologists explicitly adopted a critical stance towards society.

The relationship between the subdiscipline of developmental psychology and society illustrates the larger issue of Psychology in society.

Developmental psychology and society

Developmental psychologists' scientific interests reflected unexamined societal agendas, which had considerable influence on lay psychology and on the discourse of health-service and social-service professions (Burman, 1997). For example, in postwar Britain, child welfare workers began to speak of "attachment disorders" and teachers referred to "critical periods of learning." When women were required to surrender their wartime jobs and return to homemaking, developmentalists and other professionals invoked the notion of "maternal deprivation" (i.e., mothers failing to meet their children's needs) in popular media to justify keeping mothers out of the workforce.

In US society, psychologists focused on mother–son relations, because they believed mothers had the capacity to inculcate in their sons the skills necessary to achieve economic growth and national superiority. Harry Harlow's (1958) research, for instance, conducted when some women were beginning to work outside the home, legitimized professional and societal concerns about potential maternal deprivation. However, developmentalists' expertise was saturated with cultural assumptions about gender, family status, and social class.

Psychology and race

Psychology's social history is also noteworthy for its contradictory stance on racism.

Overcoming racism

Psychologists contributed to social engineering and government policy concerning racism. They treated racial prejudice like mental disorder, devising means of social engineering to eradicate suffering caused by racism (Herman, 1995). Psychologists became involved in uncovering racial prejudice and improving the morale of minority groups, in the hope that addressing individual and social problems would prevent future conflict.

In Britain, this inclination took the form of group relations training at the Tavistock Institute. In the USA, a community programme known as "human relations training" emerged. Using Kurt Lewin's group dynamics, training groups ("T groups") reputedly helped participants gain perspective on how they related to others. Such groups were promoted as a way of combating racial and religious prejudice.

With explosive urban riots in the 1960s, the US government commissioned an investigation of racism against African Americans. The resultant Kerner Commission Report concluded that the USA was a nation of unequal societies: one white and one black. Psychological expertise was used to explain "race riots" and develop federal policy to address racism. Proposed solutions included the need for increased employment opportunities, minimum wage, and welfare benefits, and increased funding for education and housing.

In promoting awareness of the effects of racism and segregation and in their personal commitment to effecting racial equality African American psychologists **Kenneth Clark** (1914–2005) and **Mamie Phipps Clark** (1917–1983) epitomized scientific psychologists as social activists. They investigated the racial identity of US children, comparing segregated and integrated schools. Their studies illustrated the cruelty and degrading effects of exclusion and subjugation on African American children's intellectual development and personal identity (Jackson, 2006). The Clarks' research was instrumental in the US Supreme Court decision to outlaw school segregation in 1954.

Manifesting racism

Yet African American psychologists had been marginalized in the discipline for most of its history (Guthrie, 1998). In response to APA ambivalence about their training and employment needs, African American psychologists formed an association in 1968. Many challenged the applicability of standard psychological concepts to African Americans, stimulating a "Black Psychology" movement. These developments facilitated the emergence of other ethnocultural, lesbian-gay-bisexual-transsexual groups, and women's movements within US Psychology demanding more inclusive affiliation with the discipline. Collectively, these movements "led to changes in training, practice, and theory" (Pickren, 2007, p. 293).

Nevertheless, vestiges of White superiority persisted in Psychology. In their 1994 book, *The Bell Curve: Intelligence and Class Structure in American Life*, **Charles Murray** (b. 1943), a political scientist, and **Richard Herrnstein** (1930–1994), a psychologist, argued that African Americans as a group are genetically less intelligent than Whites. In promoting the "objectivity" of their scientific data the authors held **three assumptions**:

- 60 per cent of intelligence is inherited, therefore is immutable.
- Scores on IQ tests are accurate indicators of intelligence.
- One's IQ score predicts social destiny as student, worker, and citizen.

The authors' logic was that IQ is largely inherited, African Americans have lower IQ scores, and low IQs are statistically related to poverty, welfare dependency, and crime. Therefore, African Americans, they argued, are intractably linked to social pathologies and compensatory programmes, like affirmative action in employment, waste tax dollars.

To strengthen their case Murray and Herrnstein cited Canadian psychologist **J. Philippe Rushton's** (1943–2012) evolutionary analysis. Rushton (1994) classifies human intelligence in terms of three racial groups – Negroid, Caucasoid, and Mongoloid – and argues that Asians are most intelligent with Whites a close second and Blacks a distant third, because "the races" have evolved away from one another. But from a critical perspective, rather than relying on behaviour-genetics research, these authors employed a questionable methodology using statistical analyses of population data, in which they assigned certain amounts of genetic influence to behaviour and to IQ scores using culturally biased tests. An alternative view is that environmental conditions, including ethnocultural status, social class, and education, are more influential than heredity is in shaping intelligence and IQ scores (Nisbett, 2009).

> **Small-group discussion.** What should ethical psychologists and students do in response to colleagues who promote racist views as scientifically legitimate?

Psychology and gender

Arguably, women's unequal status in society has affected psychological thought just as racism has. While feminism resurfaced in the 1960s, many scholars began to reject psychologists' historical use of theory, research, and professional practice that supported indirectly or directly traditional gender roles and relationships of independent males and dependent females. Moreover, clinical psychologists had attributed the origins of mental health disorders and developmental problems to mothers (O'Connell & Russo, 1991).

Since the institutionalization of the psychology of women as a subdiscipline in 1973, US feminist psychologists studied gender differences and similarities, sexuality, relationships, health and mental health, life-span development, and violence and harassment against women. Some even questioned Psychology's methodological assumptions and conception of scientific objectivity (Riger, 1992).

However, instead of investigating gender in specific social, economic, and political contexts, some feminist psychologists ignored contexts and employed individualistic explanations of sexism in society (Marecek, 2001). Their concepts and research methods reflected natural-science psychologists' quest for universal truths about behaviour rather than making emancipation from sexism the priority. Furthermore, until recently psychologists primarily studied economically privileged White women, neglecting girls and women from minority positions concerning ethnocultural status, sexual orientation, or disability.

Part 6 conclusion

After World War II particularly in the USA (Herman, 1995), psychologists made applications of academic psychological knowledge a priority such that Psychology became integral to the aims of economic advancement and a stable social order of individuals, families, and groups adapting to society. One example of the reciprocal relationship between the discipline and the state is the social agenda of developmental psychologists during this period. In effect, they reinforced gendered parental roles and child-rearing. Rather than universal truths, developmentalists fostered culturally laden perspectives on developmental phenomena with regressive societal effects.

On two burning issues of the day in Anglo-American and European societies – race and racism, and equality for women – psychologists evinced contradictory positions. Some psychologists diligently applied their scientific expertise to support the societal construct of racial equality, while others asserted scientific evidence for a Galtonian construct of a hierarchy of inherited racialized abilities. Furthermore, although the second wave of feminism inspired many women to demand gender equality and some female psychologists to organize for change in Psychology, the discipline itself continued to drag its heels concerning the gender composition of the professoriate; academic Psychology remains male-dominated, despite the predominance of female students in undergraduate and graduate programmes.

Part 7   Thematic review

Four themes appear to characterize natural-science Psychology after World War II. These themes represent issues with which current psychologists continue to struggle implicitly or explicitly: **neuroscience of the evolutionary brain and consciousness, self and identity in context**, **disciplinary fragmentation**, and **alliance with the societal status quo**.

Neuroscience of the evolutionary brain and consciousness

With the advent of Donald Hebb's thesis on the biological organization of behaviour, natural-science psychologists regained their original inclination towards biological reductionism. Their avid pursuit of tracking brain–behaviour relations culminated in the emergence of new identity-labels for content-areas related to basic psychological processes: behavioural and cognitive neuroscience.

Central to this discursive shift are two highly influential schools of thought: cognitivism and evolutionary psychology. Across all psychological functions, investigators seek to identify not only specific brain–behaviour relations and neurological correlates but also presumed evolutionary and genetic roots. The core assumption is that evolutionary pressures genetically endow all animals with specific behaviours.

However, behavioural and cognitive neuroscientists continue to have difficulty explaining the relationships among mind, brain, body, and consciousness in human and nonhuman animals. Furthermore, biologically and experientially, the aspects of cognition operate as one accord, but natural scientists generally study these aspects individually. Psychology's textbooks, curricula, journals, and organizations reflect these artificial divisions of biological, psychological, and social dimensions. Compartmentalized biopsychosocial phenomena, of course, do not correspond to individuals' experience of themselves. In this respect, the challenge of integrating psychological systems remains unmet.

Meanwhile, scholars affiliated with "experimental philosophy" have returned to the fundamental philosophical questions that many founders of Psychology investigated (Knobe, Buckwalter, Nichols, Robbins, Sarkissian, & Sommers, 2012). Furthermore, applications of brain imaging and brain enhancement to business, the military, and criminal justice raise ethical, legal, and societal concerns (Farah, 2012). For example, an ethical question is, given the potency of neuroscientific procedures, should psychologists implement them?

Self and identity in context

Developmental, personality, and social psychology converge on the problem of self and identity. For most of the discipline's history, psychologists have posited an authentic self that represents personal identity. Implicit in this conception are **two psychological "truths"** that insinuated themselves into lay psychology:

- Well-adjusted individuals proceed from attachment to separation to individuation to autonomy.
- This process culminates in a core self and personal identity.

However, a new consensus has emerged in Psychology: the self develops in and through interpersonal relations. Some scholars assert that the self is as variegated as an individual's relationships; others promote a dialogical self intrinsically related with real and imagined others. If self and identity develop in context, then one's social location in terms of ethnocultural status, class, gender, family relationships, historical time and place, and dominant discourses produces multiple selves in diverse social relations and gives meaning to private experience.

Disciplinary fragmentation

Psychology always has struggled with disunity. Generations of psychologists have been concerned that the focus on developing professional applications neglects the discipline's scientific foundations. When US clinical psychology programmes were instituted after World War II, federal support legitimized professional psychology, which attracted aspirants to careers, including African Americans and other visible minorities (Pickren, 2007). But academic subcultures of experimentalists and clinicians competed over resources (Chein, 1966).

These persistent institutional tensions led to disaffected experimentalists establishing the Psychonomic Society in 1959. By the late 1980s, many psychologists attempted to reorganize the APA to centralize science in the discipline. When this attempt failed, they formed a new organization, now known as the Association for Psychological Science. Currently, natural-science psychologists have rallied around the view that, even if the discipline has been fragmented, which not all concede, it is unifiable under the rubric of psychological neuroscience or evolutionary psychology.

However, significant problems with the unification movement exist (Walsh-Bowers, 2010). Conceptions of unification exclude the varieties of *human-science* Psychology, which belies unity. Secondly, unification presumes a rational process of dialogue among different schools of thought. But natural-science psychologists' traditions, vested interests, subdisciplinary specialization, and fragmented organization have evoked distrust and even hostility among colleagues representing different fields. Unifying Psychology, therefore, requires mitigating these non-rational and irrational elements entrenched in the discipline's intellectual and cultural history.

Alliance with the societal status quo

The international record since World War II indicates that when they have given the discipline away, natural-science psychologists generally have taken extant societal conditions for granted. In this regard, psychologists have strengthened individuals' and groups' adaptation to the status quo of hierarchies of economic and social relations. Historically, psychologists' interests in sustaining society's institutions and its ideology of adaptation to existing socioeconomic conditions were reflected in the social applications of their research and in professional practice (see next chapter). Furthermore, mainstream psychologists regard themselves as politically neutral, but when their nation calls them to war they become partisans for their national interests.

In addition, evolutionary psychologists tend to focus on behaviours with negative social-policy implications for marginalized groups in society, providing scientifically plausible rationales for neoliberal economic and social policies that have predominated in the last three decades. Strong neurogenetic positions on social issues confirm popular prejudices among those who strive to conserve White male privilege.

On the other hand, the evidence also shows psychologists overcoming sources of resistance in society and in the discipline to ethnocultural and gender equality. In US Psychology, African American psychologists have made their intellectual presence felt and a psychology of women and gender thrives. Yet, regardless of psychologists' personal stances for or against racial and gender equality, there is little evidence of psychologists challenging the socioeconomic and political foundations of their respective societies. Rather, the discipline, arguably, is best characterized as an instrument of state ideology, whether democratic capitalist as in Anglo-American nations or state capitalist as in the Soviet Union / Russia and China.

Summary

In Part 1 we described societal and scientific developments that have affected natural-science Psychology's development since World War II. Corporate power, government and academic compliance, and societal emphasis on technology have shaped recent scientific research. We also discussed systemic disadvantages in the sciences that militate against equality for women and individuals in cultural minority positions in society while identifying institutional remedies.

In Part 2 we described the development of the discipline internationally, concentrating on the founding European nations; the Soviet Union and Russia; the USA; and Canada, China, India, and Japan. Then we discussed whether Psychology can be genuinely international, given the dominant influence of US Psychology, or whether a polycentric approach, based on indigenous knowledge within multiple national Psychologies, is preferable.

In Part 3 we addressed the diverse schools of psychological thought that emerged since the war. Operant behaviourism, associated with B. F. Skinner, was behaviourism's sole survivor, neobehaviourism having outlived its usefulness. The biological organization of behaviour, led by Donald Hebb, Roger Sperry, Alexander Luria, and Magda Arnold, rose to prominence. The emergence of cognitivism in the 1960s, expressed in the fields of sensory-perceptual processes, information-processing, memory, emotion, thinking, psycholinguistics, and social cognition marked a new period of development in US Psychology. But no "cognitive revolution" was necessary internationally, because most international psychologists never emulated US psychologists' temporary abandonment of complex psychological phenomena.

During the late twentieth century newer subdisciplines dealing with the brain and cognitive processes, behavioural and cognitive neuroscience, emerged. We discussed the main conceptual and methodological issues, including the relation of mind, brain, and behaviour, and identified unsolved problems, such as explaining consciousness. Then we reviewed two closely related and increasingly prominent perspectives, evolutionary psychology and neurogenetics.

In Part 4 we described the current status of developmental psychology, which has greatly expanded since World War II. We discussed the prominent theories – social learning, perceptual learning, attachment, contact comfort, and social ecology – and the nature–nurture debate.

In Part 5 we noted postwar developments in personality psychology, focusing on the traits vs. situations debate. We also discussed how social psychologists' concentration on artificial experiments precipitated a crisis of social relevance that was suspended by the turn to social cognition and social neuroscience. Then we described four current notions that are common to the interpersonal areas as well as developmental and professional psychology: the intersection of social categories, cultural influences, interdependence in dyadic relationships, and the narrative theoretical and methodological approach.

In Part 6 we addressed Psychology's relationship to the social order after the war, using the example of developmental psychology's societal influence. Then we considered psychologists' historically ambivalent stance towards race and racism, with evidence for overcoming racism and manifesting racism. This was the context that noteworthy African American psychologists encountered. In addition, we discussed psychologists' ambivalence regarding gender equality in society and the discipline.

In Part 7 we addressed four themes that capture Psychology's most recent history: the celebration of the evolutionary brain but the unsolved puzzle of consciousness despite neuroscience; self and identity in context as the ties that bind developmental, personality, and social psychology; disciplinary disunity and fragmentation; and Psychology's alliance with the societal status quo. Psychologists' conformity with society's aims will be evident even more in the applications of psychological research and practices described in the next chapter.

Sample essay questions

1. Some psychologists insist that subjective consciousness cannot be reduced to matter, while others assert that only a material explanation of consciousness can be scientific. What's your position?

2. Enthusiasts believe that robots working in partnership with scientists in laboratories render scientific activity more efficient and scientific problem-solving more effective. What's your view on the potential for robot scientists to conduct psychological research?

3. Based on your understanding of this chapter, describe what you think natural-science Psychology will be like ten years from now. Identify the trends and issues that you think will be important and justify your choices. Give relatively equal coverage to cognitive and behavioural neuroscience, developmental psychology, and the interpersonal areas.

RECOMMENDED READING

Concerning the societal context for science, read Ravetz's (2005) brief *The no-nonsense guide to science*. For psychological perspectives on equity in science see Ceci & W. Williams's (2007b) *Why aren't more women in science? Top researchers debate the evidence*.

The *Annual Review of Psychology* contains systematic reviews of specific content-areas across mainstream Psychology's subdisciplines.

See the third issue of the *Journal of Social Issues* 2010 volume regarding social neuroscience.

Buss's (2005) *The handbook of evolutionary psychology* includes chapters by prominent EP devotees, H. Plotkin's (2004) *Evolutionary thought in psychology* represents an enthusiast's brief but informative history, while Dagg's (2005) *"Love of shopping" is not a gene* serves a critical function concerning evolutionary psychology.

ONLINE RESOURCES

For cognitive neuroscience consult www.cogneurosociety.org.

For evolutionary psychology consult www.plato.stanford.edu/entries/evolutionary-psychology and www.cep.ucsb.edu/primer.html.

8

Applied and professional psychology

Chapter outline

Introduction

While a field of study that is "applied" aims to have a practical purpose, a "profession" is generally understood as an occupation practised not only for societal gain but also as a source of personal livelihood. The first and oldest professions recognized were theology, medicine, and law. In the nineteenth century, other learned studies were accepted as professions, such as architecture and engineering. In the twentieth century, professionalization of labour became more pervasive, and accounting, teaching, and nursing as well as Psychology developed professional associations. Professionals were an expanding class of people given the authority to govern and shape the conduct of others (Miller & Rose, 1994). Applied psychology was the first occupational group to emerge entirely from academia (Napoli, 1981).

In this chapter we consider the historical development of applied and professional psychology as it emerged in response to problems of war, education, business, medicine, mental disturbance, crime, sports, community, and environmental concerns as well as the ethical codes and standards of professional conduct developed for clinical and counselling psychology.

The **aims** of this chapter are to describe:

- The escalation of psychologists' societal influence as related to sociopolitical issues, including changes in the nature of capitalism, war, racism, and social conflict.
- The history and issues in the principal specializations of applied and professional psychology: industrial/organizational, school, counselling, and clinical psychology.
- The scope and issues in new areas of specialization: forensic, sport, environmental, health, and community psychology and psychopharmacology.
- The capacity for harm in and ethical nature of applied and professional psychology and challenges to conventional conceptions of ethical practice.
- Two themes that seem to capture the central issues underlying psychologists' historical practices of applications of their science: unreflective faith in the scientific basis of social and professional applications, and alliance with the societal status quo.

Part 1   The emergence of applied and professional psychology

Psychology is self-consciously concerned with applications and relevancies to everyday life (Rose, 1979). It has promised to be the scientific discipline that would address the practical needs and problems of contemporary society: education, war, crime, insanity, and business. Allegedly unburdened by metaphysical speculation and the philosophy of human nature, this new discipline would use the discourse and practices of science and medicine to take on the problems of maintaining and promoting social order.

In early twentieth-century US society, psychologists did not distinguish distinct specialties. Only later did the application of Psychology to contemporary problems result in psychologists claiming specialization in areas of industrial/organizational psychology, school psychology, counselling psychology, and clinical psychology.

Furthermore, the distinction between applied and basic psychology, often made in the period before World War II in US Psychology, is misleading, because there was very little basic Psychology to apply to societal problems. Psychologists found applications as they went along, searching for areas to apply principles and techniques. Responding to market forces meant Psychology became intertwined with socioeconomic and political developments in the culture at large (Danziger, 1990).

Psychology as a science that measures and classifies individuals came to be of primary importance for managing people and upholding institutions such as commerce, industry, prisons, hospitals, schools, and the military. By responding to problems of living in society at the level of the individual, much of the work in Psychology, as we have seen in Chapters 5 to 7, came to uphold the status quo and support existing institutions with little critical reflection on society.

Global events and the rise of psychological expertise

Before World War I, although some psychologists in European and US communities were employed in hospitals, schools, courts and businesses, most worked as teachers and researchers in academic settings. Thus, much of applied and professional psychology resulted from wartime demands. The need to test military recruits and deal with shell shock, displacement, and separation as a result of war that military personnel experienced stimulated the development of professional organizations, therapy, and assessment tools.

The mobilization of millions of military personnel for World War I required massive organizational efforts by the major powers. After the war as society shifted from the original capitalism of individual entrepreneurs to large corporations and monopoly capitalism, adaptation to group situations became more important for economic growth than individual characteristics. In the postwar economy effective management of work-groups to ensure their adjustment to the new forces of production was central.

Psychologists' conceptions of their vocation shifted accordingly. Previously many attempted to establish their societal usefulness as objective experts. But during the postwar era the social role of presumed "neutral and professional psychological expertise became increasingly institutionalized" (Hale, 1980, p. 162).

Psychologists not only placed their problem-solving technology at the service of administrators managing society's economic, educational, health, and criminal-justice institutions. But also, unlike their prewar predecessors' concern with social reform, postwar psychologists focused on producing research that directly or indirectly supported corporate growth and encouraged the public's adaptation to the new socioeconomic conditions. While economically privileged nations became bureaucratically controlled societies of consumption of disposable commodities, psychologists applied their scientifically derived principles to industrial and commercial management aiming to strengthen workers' adaptation to group situations, to the assessment of personality and intellectual characteristics suited to the economic climate, and to advertising to encourage consumption.

Therapeutic management

Psychology, or more generally the "psy" disciplines, recast the management of social problems and difficulties of daily life broadly as therapeutic issues. Thus, Psychology became the new authority, deemed to have expert knowledge and techniques needed to address difficulties in industry and commerce, schooling, the criminal-justice system, the military, medical practice, and marriage. Assessing problems as psychological entailed intervening at the level of psychological processes and interpersonal relations (N. Rose, 1979).

A new species of authority emerged, legitimizing a unique way of exercising significant and extensive power over others and oneself. Difficulties now would be considered mental health issues. Thus, professional authority became tied to psychological development, which was measured by psychological testing.

In the USA, for example, by the end of World War I, *Army Alpha General Intelligence Examinations* had been used to assess nearly 2 million army recruits and military personnel. Eventually, more than 100 selection tests were developed and approximately 3.5 million soldiers were assessed (Benjamin & Baker, 2004). Having successfully contributed to the war effort, psychological study and research became firmly wedded to social demands.

The credibility and prestige of Psychology rose in the public eye and a culture of testing developed in the USA and Canada that continues to this day. Clinical psychologists use tests of personality, intelligence, and psychopathology to generate diagnoses, case formulations, and treatment plans; school and counselling psychologists use tests to assess student abilities and vocational interests and to place students in education programmes; industrial/organizational (I/O) psychologists use tests to measure aptitudes, job satisfaction, and potential job placement, and to improve the efficiency of business and industry.

In 1921 James Cattell founded the Psychology Corporation to develop, copyright, and market a battery of "mental tests." To bolster flagging sales, in 1924, Cattell hired a female psychologist to revise the *Army Alpha* test so that businesses and educational institutions could use it (Koppes, 1997). During this era, psychological service typically involved the arduous and often grinding work of psychometric testing. Much of this work was done by the women who comprised more than 60 per cent of all applied psychologists in the USA (Napoli, 1981).

Tavistock Clinic and Institute

The example of the Tavistock Clinic and Institute in London shows the expansion of professional expertise to which psychologists contributed. During World War I, physician **Hugh Crichton-Miller** (1877–1959) and colleagues treated soldiers with shell shock or "battle neurosis" (Dicks, 1970). Extending what he had learned to civilians, he established the Tavistock Clinic ("the Tavi") in 1920 to provide psychotherapy to outpatients who could not afford private fees.

During World War II, Tavistock professionals focused on helping those who were traumatized or displaced to adapt to their new situation. Staff also worked on building morale and managing problems between military ranks, selecting and placing individuals in the military according to skills, and analyzing the mentality of enemy nations. By 1948 the Clinic was incorporated into the National Health Service in Britain.

The Tavi integrated traditional medical psychology, social psychiatry, and psychoanalysis, including not only psychiatrists and psychologists, but also anthropologists and sociologists (Dicks, 1970). It became a leading clinic globally, influencing the rethinking societally of social problems in terms of psychological processes and inter-personal relations.

After the war the Tavistock Institute for Human Relations ("the Institute") was founded. It publishes the journal *Human Relations*, which was conceived jointly by the Institute, Kurt Lewin, and his co-workers. Professionals reasoned that their work had implications not only for individual mental health but also for the efficiency of organizations. The Tavi trained not only physicians, psychiatrists, social workers, and psychologists but also teachers, ministers, probation officers, and industrialists. Training did not entail traditional lectures, seminars, reading, and essay writing, but engaged students through group processes and experiential learning (Miller & Rose, 1994).

The history of the Tavi Clinic and Institute shows how Psychology, among other professions and disciplines, arose as a field of expertise willing to assess and intervene in everyday problems of life and work. Other organizations emerged in clinics and academic departments in Anglo-American and European nations following World War II in an effort to understand the causes of social conflict. Scholars communicated across nations and across disciplines on these matters.

Professionalizing psychology

Although during the 1920s professional psychologists were increasingly popular, they were too few and insufficiently professionalized to meet public demand for services for the maladjusted. The emerging profession of clinical psychology had to find a respectable niche in mental health clinics in which male-dominated psychiatry and female-dominated social work were complementary but clinical psychology was relegated to psychological assessments (Napoli, 1981).

With the possibility of another world war looming on the horizon in the 1930s, the US federal government urged psychologists, psychiatrists, counsellors, and social workers to organize their efforts and further professionalize their disciplines for the national good. Professional standards became an issue also because of the Depression when academic jobs became scarce and Europeans, including psychologists, were immigrating to Canada and the USA (Benjamin & Baker, 2004). After World War II, pressure from the US Veterans' Administration and other agencies for more mental health services, along with the threat of professional competition, moved psychologists towards standardized training programmes, credentialling bodies, professional organizations, and stronger alliances with the natural sciences.

Physicians had been addressing psychological issues with their patients for more than 100 years before the advent of Psychology. Now psychologists were vying for the right to assess mental functioning, while in subsequent years they would fight for the right to practise psychotherapy, be reimbursed through health insurance, and receive prescription privileges. Consequently, tension between psychiatrists and psychologists transpired in the USA and other nations. Italy, for example, addressed the problem by allowing both professions to become mental health practitioners (Gemignani & Giliberto, 2005). Yet even by the twenty-first century, Russian psychologists were not permitted to conduct psychotherapy, because it was deemed a medical practice (Balachova, Levy, Isurina & Wasserman, 2001).

The Boulder model

In the USA, to define the activities of clinical psychologists and determine what constituted standardized training, David Shakow (1901–1981) initiated a conference in 1949 to set standards for training and practice. At the Boulder Conference, representatives of academic and applied psychology, medicine, nursing, and education agreed to establish the identity and training of the professional psychologist in a "scientist-practitioner" model (Baker & Benjamin, 2000). In 1951 and 1954 respectively, the specialties of counselling psychology and school psychology identified distinct training expectations (Benjamin, 2001).

The original intent of the Boulder Conference was to provide a model of training that would foster diversity, provide innovative training, and promote values that typify a good scientist (i.e., skepticism, curiosity, and open inquiry). But by 1966, a series of conferences questioned this model and proposed alternative training standards. This process resulted in the emergence of US professional schools of Psychology offering PsyD (doctoral) degrees in clinical psychology (Stricker, 2000). These strictly professional programmes focus on practice and do not require original research.

Critics of the Boulder model have argued that it has promoted medical explanations for psychological issues, thereby forfeiting Psychology's presumed, unique interdisciplinary and social perspective (Albee, 2000; Joseph, 2007; Newnes, 2002). Some have recommended replacing the scientist-practitioner model with a scholar-practitioner model that includes cultural, spiritual, emotional, physical, and discursive aspects of psychological life as well as qualitative, collaborative, meaning-focused, and person-sensitive methods of inquiry (Larner, 2001).

International status

Currently, most clinical psychology training programmes in the USA and Canada follow the Boulder model and advocate strict adherence to empirically validated therapies, rigorous administration of assessment tools, and critical reading of research methodology. Although this critical awareness includes methodology, the standard model does not include critique of theoretical assumptions, epistemology, or sociopolitical factors that impinge upon clients' lives. Moreover, it promotes clients' adaptation to the status quo as a legitimate outcome of therapy.

Nevertheless, the Boulder model has had international impact. Even though psychologists might be trained locally without having overseas experience, the US model of clinical training, practice, and regulation ideologically prevails globally (Manganyi & Louw, 1986). Furthermore, international scholars and practitioners rely on US publications, while literature that is produced and published in languages other than English has little or no impact on US psychologists (Gemignani & Giliberto, 2005). When English textbooks are translated, the problem arises of finding appropriate terms for concepts generated in Anglo-American contexts. To address this problem, for example, Egyptian psychologists have been attempting to standardize the way English psychological terms are translated into Arabic (Soueif & Ahmed, 2001).

Although the Boulder model has promoted uniform clinical training throughout much of the world, a significant movement towards deregulation has developed. In the UK, advocates of deregulation argue that regulation entails unnecessary bureaucracy, excessive training, false notions of protecting the public, increased costs for clients, and self-aggrandizement by boosting image and status, while having a deadening effect on innovations in practice and training (Bates & House, 2003; Mowbray, 1995). Critics see regulation as driven by commercial competition, professional self-interest, and an anxious need for control. Some Australian psychologists question the Boulder model's stress on empirically supported treatments while ignoring the uniqueness of psychological relationships in clinical work (Hambridge & Baker, 2001).

Across Europe, although most nations have some form of certification, there is no common system of regulation (Lunt, 1999). The European Association for Counselling, the European Association for Psychotherapy, and the European Union have been slow to agree on minimum professional requirements (Gemignani & Giliberto, 2005). In the UK, the British Psychological Society (BPS) controls education and training of psychologists but, unlike in Canada and the USA, it is voluntary for psychologists to register with a regulatory body.

Over the last sixty years, in nations that provide psychological training, legislation has been or is beginning to be developed, requiring mandatory certification for psychologists and accreditation requirements for training. "Chartered" or "registered" are titles used in different geographical areas, protected by law, regulated by local professional bodies, restricting certain activities to those having the required training. The belief is that regulation of a profession increases its prestige and privileges.

Worldwide, the professionalization of Psychology has seen significant growth and has had a similar course of development across nations, although it has followed different timelines (Gemignani & Giliberto, 2005; Manganyi & Louw, 1986). In 1938, Calcutta University was the first Indian university to establish an applied section of Psychology (Prasadarao & Matam Sudhir, 2001). In Egypt, the legal status of psychotherapy was defined in 1956, with applied psychology established in 1959 at Cairo University (Soueif & Ahmed, 2001). Apparently, Brazil is the only South American nation that regulates Psychology, giving it professional status in 1962 (Andrade & Bueno, 2001).

In Iran no system of credentialling psychologists exists (Ghobari & Bolhari, 2001). Iranian psychologists provide psychological assessment and psychotherapeutic interventions always under the supervision of psychiatrists or neurologists. Consequently, establishing licensure for psychologists is a priority for the Iranian Psychological Association.

The professionalization of Psychology, however, has significantly increased the length of training. For example, in the UK prior to the 1970s, a bachelor's degree was required to practise clinical psychology; then a master's degree was compulsory; and by the 1990s, a doctorate became required to qualify as a "chartered" or "registered" psychologist (Lunt, 1999). In some instances, postdoctoral training is now expected, pushing the level of qualification even higher. When counselling, I/O, educational, and school psychology became professions, educational requirements also increased.

Section conclusion

Overall, political and economic pressures professionalized many areas of Psychology, resulting in credentialling and standardized training. Practices emerged from national and military needs by which psychological knowledge has been allied with political power

(N. Rose, 2008). Consequently, Psychology has provided effective means of social control and administration of societal institutions. Managing human subjectivity was a military priority but also regarded as essential for civilian competence, social organization, psychological health, schools, commerce, industries, and life in general.

The Cold War era

Political ideology and behavioural science research were mutually influential during the Cold War era. Researchers were devoted to developing "automatic mechanisms and instruments that could generate data, or model social process, or take care of difficult administrative decisions about the allocation of important economic resources" (Isaac, 2011, p. 229). The prominence and power of Psychology rose during the Cold War era with the capitalist need for marketing, quest for self-discovery, decline of religion, fear of nuclear annihilation, suburban isolation, and general feelings of panic and helplessness. Psychology researchers found a welcome home in the military–industrial complex.

In the USA, psychologists explained to government and business leaders how the Cold War could be won on the battlefield of the psychological mind. They also provided plausible rationales about how citizens of "Third World" nations become susceptible to underdevelopment. To ensure a continuing wealth of research funding from US agencies, psychologists promised that "psychological science and technology would help manage political change in a dangerous world in exchange for continued state support and a part in determining the direction of US foreign and military policy" (Herman, 1995, p. 239).

Psychologists received massive financial support for research from various government sources, including the National Science Foundation, the US Navy, and the National Institute of Mental Health. This research included the ethically and politically dubious practice of investigating "brainwashing" techniques. Three different psychologists in Canada – Donald Hebb, Peter Suedfeld, and John Zubek – with government funding investigated the psychological effects of modifying sensory-perceptual environments.

During the Cold War, US psychologists helped the government and military to ensure that political revolutions in the Third World were contained. Psychology enabled the state to "maintain ideological control over a potentially unruly population, shield a murderous foreign policy from public view, and 'manufacture consent' by insisting that US motives were always pure and US power always legitimate" (Herman, 1995, p. 173).

Psychologists, for example, were actively involved in the infamous "Project Camelot," intended as a form of controlling Third-World revolution. Initiated in 1963 by the US Department of Defense and directed by psychologist Theodore Vallance, the project was initially formed with the intention of using social science research to understand and preclude the causes of war. With a budget of $8 million, researchers went to Latin American countries to poll attitudes on politics. However, the information was used to develop an advertising campaign that dissuaded voters from voting for communist candidates (Horowitz, [1967] 1974).

Project Camelot is an example of sponsored research in which psychologists conceive of their involvement as neutral. In this case, psychologists assumed that US national interests were congruent with other nations' views and that contributions to the US military would further universal goals of democracy and capitalism. The climate within the social sciences was such that many regarded Project Camelot "as an example of socially engaged research," and the US psychologists involved evidently were not concerned that contractual research can compromise scientific integrity significantly (Herman, 1995, p. 159). During this era, psychologists in general did not advocate halting military-funded research; on the contrary, they sought its expansion.

The global war on terror

From the Cold War to the so-called global war on terror, some US psychologists have advised military interrogators how to improve extracting information from detainees and enemy combatants. Based on US Army and university psychological research, the CIA also has used psychological research to investigate the deliberate, systematic use of torture techniques, such as isolation, disorientation, and the destruction of personal identity for intelligence-gathering during the Vietnam War, in Latin America during the 1970s and 1980s, and during the global war on terror following 9/11 (McCoy, 2006).

For example, since 2002 in Guantánamo Bay, Cuba, US behavioural scientists from Psychology and psychiatry helped to design a total institutional environment to extract information from detainees (Soldz, 2006). "Behavioral Science Consultant Teams" identify psychological vulnerabilities using such psychological manipulations as extremes of temperature, sleep deprivation, strobe lights, loud music, and intimidation by military dogs to coerce detainees to cooperate with the military (Okie, 2005).

The organization Physicians for Human Rights reviewed the techniques used by US forces on detainees and concluded that the consequences of psychological torture were devastating (Borchelt & Pross, 2005). When it became public knowledge that psychologists were advising US military facilities on the use of techniques tantamount to torture, the American Psychological Association (APA) initially directed members to follow its ethical guidelines but did not state a position on these intelligence-gathering operations. Instead, it initially responded to abuses of psychological knowledge with silence. Possibly psychologists did not want to alienate as powerful an institution as the US military, but, for "ethical" reasons, they could not endorse outright the potential contributions of Psychology to military intelligence-gathering (Soldz, 2006). Acceptance of the status quo permitted psychologists continued access to power.

Subsequently, the APA came under increasing pressure to adopt a decisive position on interrogations taking place at US military detention centres. Then the American Medical Association and the American Psychiatric Association declared that any involvement with such interrogations, even in an advisory role, was a professional transgression and would be punished. Because Psychology was without a similar policy, the Pentagon stated that it would replace psychiatrists with psychologists.

Publicity on the abuses at Guantánamo, the positions taken by medicine and psychiatry, and internal pressure from APA members, prompted discussions to change APA policy on aiding military interrogations. The APA's council of representatives initially adopted a resolution against torture and other cruel, inhuman, and degrading treatment or punishment (American Psychological Association Governance, 2008). However, the resolution made no mention of interrogations and did not specifically state which methods were unethical. The terms "cruel and inhumane" were left open to interpretation.

Then at the APA's annual meeting in 2007, members voted to reaffirm the position against torture. The list of specific treatments now proscribed includes hooding, using dogs to threaten and intimidate suspects, sleep deprivation, and mock executions. However, the APA rejected a measure that would ban its members from participating in US government interrogations of terror suspects.

> **Small-group discussion.** When, if ever, should psychological knowledge be used to extract information forcibly from persons considered a threat to national security? What are the alternatives?

Part 1 conclusion

Psychology partly developed in response to government needs for social organization and control of society. Emerging primarily in the cultures of Europe and the USA, Psychology has been exported globally and has contributed to an increasingly individualized and psychologized global culture. Psychology has become indispensable for policy-making, redefining the political by extending the reach of government to include emotional and subjective realities (Herman, 1995). Perhaps the motivation for much of this work was to find technical and rational ways to manage what the powers-that-be hoped was a productive, well-functioning society. As mentioned in earlier chapters, one of the hallmarks of early modern cultural mentality in Western societies was the notion of social management. This concept captured the twentieth-century imagination and continues to do so, while Psychology has provided a new form of authority that people, particularly those wielding power in society, have found legitimate and persuasive.

Part 2 Specializations in applied and professional psychology

By the latter part of the twentieth century, Psychology continued to serve applied needs with increasingly demarcated professional specialties and subspecialties. Originally, business psychology or I/O psychology, clinical, counselling, and school psychology were distinct areas. Later, forensic psychology, sport psychology, environmental psychology, health psychology, community psychology, and psychopharmacology developed, among others. Formally, the American Board of Professional Psychology recognizes clinical, counselling, I/O, school, psychopharmacology, forensic, family, health, behavioural, psychoanalysis, and rehabilitation psychology (Bent, Packard, & Goldberg, 1999).

These specialized areas of applied psychology emerged in response to a rapidly changing social order, industry demands, and society's desire for continual improvement. Eventually, schools, government, hospitals, businesses, the military, and nearly every individual felt Psychology was needed in some way, often in the form of specialized testing, administered by credentialled psychologists. Critical historians observe that "psychological knowledge became a cultural commodity that was easily manufactured and widely distributed by a self-sustaining community of technoscientific professionals" (Capshew, 1999, p. 264).

Industrial/organizational psychology

As the twentieth century advanced, commercial and industrial firms were interested in employing Psychology to develop persuasive advertising, determine the best person for a particular job (personnel selection), provide guidance to best utilize talent (vocational guidance), develop effective management techniques, and identify the most efficient way to complete a job. As new forms of media such as radio and magazines expanded their social influence, businesses became increasingly interested in manipulating consumer needs through advertising.

With empirical methods and instruments, scientific psychologists offered the owners of business and industry the promise of harmonious work environments, cost-cutting, increased market share, and better worker-productivity. In the USA there were publications on what was called business psychology as early as 1901. As noted earlier, the Tavistock Clinic began work in human relations in the 1920s.

Origins

At first, industrial/organizational psychology was known as "business psychology" or "industrial psychology" in Canada and the USA. "Organizational" was not added to the subdiscipline's title until 1973.

Hugo Münsterberg sometimes is cited as the founder of industrial psychology. However, **Walter Dill Scott** (1869–1955) was the first to publish a book on the topic of advertising psychology in 1903 (Benjamin & Baker, 2004). Scott's work investigated the hypnotic influence that advertising can have. He observed how humans can be very prone to suggestion and argued that most people cannot help but be persuaded by advertising.

For his part, Münsterberg published over twenty books on applied topics from 1906 to his death in 1916. He hoped that applied psychology would mean the application of experimental psychology to practical problems in the fields of business, law, education, and medicine (Benjamin, 2006). However, a bias against applied psychology as scientifically inferior to experimental psychology initially made Münsterberg reticent to endorse it. In 1898, he stated that laboratory work is not of direct use to educators and that measuring states of consciousness is not scientifically possible. He eventually reversed his position, claiming what he meant was that basic research needed to be more developed.

John Watson also was a central player in advertising psychology. After he was dismissed from his academic position at Johns Hopkins University in Baltimore because of a scandalous sexual affair with his research assistant, Rosalie Rayner, Watson found work at a prominent advertising agency in New York City. There he promoted testimonial advertising. Celebrities and scientists were hired to endorse certain products and manipulate what Watson identified as basic emotions such as fear, love, and rage in order to produce persuasive advertisements.

Scientific management

Assembly-line factory work entails a particular type of organization of labour that arose in the late nineteenth and early twentieth centuries. At this time, a sharp division in the workplace between workers and managers, conflict between employers and employees, and powerful labour unions emerged. Industrial engineer **Frederick Winslow Taylor**

(1856–1915) introduced the idea of *scientific management*, known as "Taylorism," which generated a niche for industrial psychologists (Braverman, 1974). Scientific management refers to the assessment and control of segmented aspects of the process of labour for a particular job to increase efficiency and reduce the costs of production.

Taylor argued that wages and production could be increased by assessing the workplace and designing it for maximum efficiency. For example, managers would determine the most efficient way to do a job by observing workers and timing their movements. Managers would use the results to develop expectations and set wages based on productivity. Instead of consulting experienced workers about the best way to do a job, managers assessed workers' movements as if they were machine-parts. These conditions of assembly-line work exemplified the alienation that Karl Marx described in the nineteenth century.

Scientific management might have boosted productivity and industry profits, but it mechanized and seemed to dehumanize the workplace and did not result in increased wages for workers. Control of production passed from the shop floor where the workers had knowledge and power to production engineers and personnel managers who made all labour-related decisions according to presumed scientific principles (Gillespie, 1988). Such expertise entered "the workplace not as the representative of science, but as the representative of management masquerading in the trappings of science" (Braverman, 1974, p. 86). But at least one industrial psychologist contributed to moderating efficiency-management, as we note in Box 8.1.

Box 8.1 **Contrasting management approaches**

Those psychologists following Taylorism, such as Hugo Münsterberg and Elton Mayo (1880–1949), an Australian psychologist at Harvard, saw their role as helping the worker to cooperate with management and adjust to an engineered work-environment. Management called upon psychologists to deal with employee resistance to the prescribed work pace, worker indifference, neglect, absenteeism, turnover, and overt hostility to management (Braverman, 1974).

In his two books on industrial psychology Münsterberg advocated efficiency. In keeping with extant social values of progress and productivity, he argued that Psychology could contribute to notions of success, because it could provide a science of human efficiency.

By contrast, US psychologist Lillian Moller Gilbreth (1878–1972) observed psychological needs in factories and assembly-line work and advocated consideration of workers' interests and needs. Actually, a number of early women I/O psychologists blended practical field research, application of research, and service (Koppes, 1997).

Gilbreth wrote what has been considered one of the most influential textbooks on industrial relations, *The Psychology of Management* (1914). She championed the significance of the human being as the most important element in industry. Regarding productivity and increased efficiency, she modified Taylor's ideas to include the worker's perspective. She promoted the idea that people need to be treated as unique human beings who value the process of their work instead of analyzing work only in terms of economic incentives and possibilities for greater efficiency.

Maximizing capital from a day's labour was at first limited to Britain and the USA, but this modus operandi quickly spread to all industrial countries. With the accelerating use of technology, each person's work became simplified, stripped of its potential creativity, and monotonous, which impoverished the nature of work. As such, the financial interests of a capitalist workplace superseded workers' interests and human-centred values.

Vocational psychology

During the early twentieth century vocational guidance was introduced as a professionalized means of matching employers' requirements with the interests of those seeking work and meeting commercial and industrial demands for systematic personnel selection. Encouraged by their partial success in classifying recruits during World War I, US psychologists turned their testing efforts to personnel work for corporations. The joint aim of business, government, and psychologists was the need to induce citizens, primarily White men, to adapt to the demands of large organizations (Napoli, 1981).

Prior to industrial psychology, phrenologists read bumps on people's skulls and physiognomists read the shape of people's faces to guide them in making decisions about what job they should pursue. When phrenology reached the USA in the nineteenth century, automatic devices were invented such as the electric phrenometer, which assessed character by measuring the shape of one's head. The new psychologists strongly dismissed these practices and set up vocational guidance clinics, using questionnaires and "scientific tests."

Historically, tests of vocational fitness are indebted to concepts and procedures developed in laboratory psychology. These tests were based on scientific psychologists' belief that they could measure basic mental functions, thereby securing both the esteem of academic colleagues and public respectability (Strien, 1998). Although measurement with lab instruments continued in Europe and especially in Germany, the more pragmatic orientation of paper-and-pencil tests predominated in the USA after the war.

Vocational guidance per se became systematized in 1927 with the *Strong Vocational Interest Blank*. Its successor, the widely known *Strong–Campbell Interest Inventory* (1974), compares one's interests to those of people in different occupations. Other popular questionnaires used in vocational guidance include the *Kuder DD Occupational Interest Survey* (1964), which assesses broad areas of interest along different vocational categories, and the *Campbell Interest and Skill Survey* (1992), which estimates one's interests and confidence in different occupational areas.

Following the successful psychological assessment of the emotional stability of US military personnel during World War I, personality testing also was used in I/O psychology for vocational counselling, employee selection, and evaluation of emotional adjustment (Gibby & Zickar, 2008). Psychologists initially promoted intelligence testing across all levels of education. But administrators in industry and government aimed to ensure that subordinates adjusted to bureaucracies. In addition, personnel officers needed efficient devices to match individual personalities to particular occupations.

In a culture that craved psychological information, personality tests proliferated. Psychologists used them to serve the interests of society's administrators in industry, commerce, education, and government to reinforce management of their subordinates (Barenbaum & Winter, 2003). Psychologists constructed tests that showed individuals' scores on personality characteristics that they believed were associated with sound adjustment to practical demands (Nicholson, 2003). The most desired attributes were instrumental reasoning, expressed in pragmatic intelligence and manipulating the environment, and a "winning personality."

I/O research

Research into human relations and work productivity occurred in the Hawthorne Works of the Bell System Western Electric Company in Illinois. Results of the Hawthorne experiments (1924–1933), which Mayo supervised, suggested that managers could raise productivity simply by observing workers or by attempting to increase interpersonal harmony between workers and managers, without changing the job itself. Under these conditions of harmonious cooperation, researchers concluded that workers would enthusiastically accept changes in work conditions imposed by supervisors.

Many reports of the Hawthorne studies portray workers as irrationally hostile towards management and the company and as easily pacified by expertise, while downplaying the potential exploitation of workers. Closer examination of the Hawthorne research reports found that when worker productivity declined, researchers pressured workers to increase their productivity or risk being demoted or fired (Bramel & Friend, 1981). The original researchers downplayed the effects of physical work conditions, such as the impact of regular rest periods on productivity.

Thus, the Hawthorne effect was most likely due to the researchers accepting views conducive to industrial managers' interests, manufacturing "scientific" knowledge according to management values, while ignoring the perspective of workers (Gillespie, 1988). The researchers explained worker dissatisfaction as psychological resistance manageable with human-relations techniques promoting harmony. Yet, such techniques occlude awareness of social oppression and exploitation in the actual work situation (Bramel & Friend, 1981).

After World War II, partly with impetus from Kurt Lewin's applied research, motivation, satisfaction, and leadership became important areas of study and practice for I/O psychologists along with the more traditional areas of job analysis, selection, and performance. In the 1950s, when psychologist Morris Viteles (1898–1996) revised his influential textbook, *Industrial Psychology* (1932), he renamed it *Motivation and Morale in Industry* (Benjamin & Baker, 2004). More recently, I/O psychologists have moved from the assessment of individuals to considering groups and social interaction, analyzing and intervening at the level of the organization itself. For example, psychologists might assess organizational climate to determine if workers experience the work environment as pleasant rather than stressful.

Personnel counselling

In the USA at least, as unions became stronger, management handled increasing complaints from workers by way of personnel counselling. The Hawthorne studies also assisted the birth of personnel counselling. In the Hawthorne Interviewing Program employees reported problematic working conditions during interviews so as to have their comments brought to management for consideration.

Overall, "The typical personnel counselling program employed a large number of counsellors who circulated among the workforce and conducted 'interviews' with employees volunteering to discuss personal and work-related problems" (Highhouse, 1999, p. 318). As part of the initial interview, personnel counselling was suggested to diffuse worker grievances and address such management issues as absenteeism, recruitment, and turnover problems.

But this type of personnel counselling appears to strengthen the power of management instead of improving factory conditions for workers. In the Hawthorne context, focusing on individual complaints prevented awareness of workers' common experience. Management understood worker complaints as symptoms of individual psychology and not as problems in the work environment (Gillespie, 1988). Thus, solutions focused on the adjustment of workers to management's demands.

Personnel counselling declined in importance in I/O psychology for several possible reasons: counselling is an inefficient way of communicating worker concerns to management; counsellors were in conflicting roles as both employee advocate and adviser to management; counsellors did not address tangible problems, so did not provide concrete solutions; there was little empirical evidence for the effectiveness of personnel counselling; after World War II with the increased pool of job applicants, management increasingly viewed workers as a disposable commodity (Benjamin & Baker, 2004).

Section conclusion

Historically, I/O psychology has been constructed according to administrators' and managers' usually implicit assumptions about the nature of work and organizations within capitalist societies. Presently, there are changing demographics in many industrialized nations with significant periods of low unemployment rates and worker shortages. Especially in businesses with "highly skilled" intellectual workers (e.g., information-technology developers), companies seek to improve productivity by addressing psychological well-being, offering free food, massage, beds for napping, recreational games, and other amenities in the workplace, and campus-like settings for their facilities. In such environments, attention to employee mental and social health seems to be increasingly important.

With the advance of economic globalization, I/O psychology might play a more international role, requiring greater cultural awareness. Some psychologists argue that "to comprehend unique cultural characteristics, one has to engage in an in-depth study of the historical, social, political, economical, and institutional systems of cultures" (Aycan, 2000, p. 117). For example, selection criteria for employees might vary by culture, given that what counts as good performance is culturally specific. Businesses in cultures that value individualism might select personnel according to intelligence, education, skills, and personality. However, selection criteria in communities with more collectivist values might focus on interpersonal competencies such as agreeableness, trustworthiness, belonging, and positive attitudes towards family life.

Concerning I/O research, multidisciplinary and interpretive approaches seem appropriate for the advancement of cross-cultural I/O psychology, because such approaches are more likely to respect distinctive cultural meanings and particular social interactions. However, I/O psychology has tended to rely on quantitative experimentation. Although this methodology has predominated in Psychology, it might not be suited to current or future I/O needs.

As an applied science, I/O psychology is particularly vulnerable to the power of large organizations offering significant amounts of money for research to support business interests. An early example of dubious contract-research occurred in 1911, when Coca-Cola arranged with psychologists Harry Hollingworth (1880–1956) and Leta Hollingworth to conduct a series of double-blind experiments on the effects of caffeine, which was an ingredient in the beverage. This study served as a model for future I/O research and bridged academic and applied concerns (Benjamin & Baker, 2004). However, when a business with vested interests contracts for research, investigators who offer their expertise for hire risk representing their data selectively in favour of the company's interests, a practice which is both an ethical and a scientific problem.

School psychology

Before World War I there were opportunities in Europe and the USA for psychologists to apply their concepts to improvements in pedagogy (Drunen & Jansz, 2004a). For example, Arnold Gesell called himself a "school psychologist." But a distinct specialty of school psychology did not develop in the USA and Canada until the 1960s and 1970s. Then professional journals, curricula, and a master's level of entry into the profession emerged.

Social origins

Like counselling psychology, school psychology developed within economically privileged societies that believed in education and the potential of democratic capitalist society to realize progress, efficiency, and a new and more perfected social order. Supporters of the progressive movement in early twentieth-century US society were sensitive to the discrepancy between the rich and the poor. They believed that applying scientific principles of human management to school-aged children was a form of Christian charity that would achieve better social organization.

In 1900, Swedish feminist Ellen Key (1849–1926) published *The Century of the Child*, proclaiming that the new century would liberate children and reform education (Ellenberger, 1970). But children did not have a distinct social identity until the late eighteenth century; beforehand, they were part of the regular labour force and adult social world (Drunen & Jansz, 2004a).

Gradually, society came to believe that child development should not be disturbed by labour and that schooling should be central to a child's life. Children became a symbol of hope for the future and many social reforms were focused on them. Governments initiated child-labour laws, juvenile courts, compulsory schooling, and other institutions to serve children.

Within increasingly multicultural societies of European and Anglo-American nations, the public school system promised that education would be a unifying force contributing to the maturity and happiness of its members. In theory this promise made sense, but in practice urban schools became overcrowded, health problems spread, and students from the working classes tended to drop out to work in factories. Rural schools were understaffed and accommodated all students in one room, regardless of age and ability. In North America, schools for First Nation, African American and Hispanic American students were segregated, and their psychological and physical security was seriously threatened.

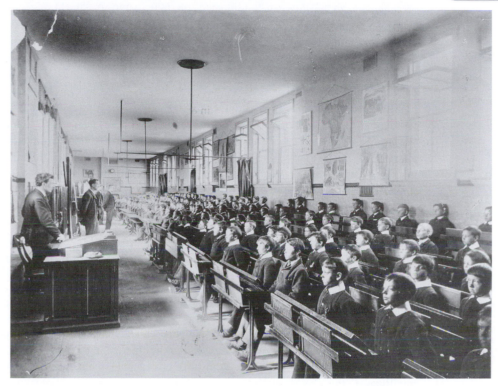

Figure 8.1 In this early twentieth-century residential school in London, a teacher conducts a lesson

Intending to help people adjust to the new industrial society, governments made education mandatory for school-aged children. For First Nations peoples, this regime meant being separated from family and community, being forced to speak English, and abandoning their cultural traditions in residential schools. Such cultural dispossession severely impaired the psychological and spiritual health of the First Peoples for many generations (York, 1989). In effect, mandatory education interfered with existing cultural forms of education and naturally occurring child guidance.

From a critical perspective, the best intentions of school psychologists met the reality of mandatory educational systems. In a societal atmosphere of valuing industrial efficiency and scientific prediction and control, school administrators promoted student adaptation to a regimented curriculum that was implemented with quasi-military discipline (see Figure 8.1).

In this social context psychologists attempted to measure educational abilities with the same exactness as natural scientists exercised in chemistry or physics. Intervention and control took precedence over understanding in an effort to attain exactness and efficiency. As testing became indispensable for sorting children in compulsory schools, some commentators viewed school psychologists as inmates of a "testing prison" for much of the twentieth century (Fagan, 1992). But, given their expertise in testing, school psychologists became increasingly influential in the educational system.

Much of the impetus for focusing psychological guidance on children originated in the USA. The "mental hygiene movement" of the early twentieth century promoted social arrangements to improve psychological health. In the 1920s this development resulted in the opening of child guidance clinics intended to serve disturbed and delinquent youth. As these clinics proliferated, they came to serve all of society by addressing problems of adaptation at home and school and by providing child-rearing advice to parents. The clinics were interdisciplinary, with physicians directing treatment and psychologists testing children's capacities (Drunen & Jansz, 2004a).

After World War I the mental hygiene movement became known as the "mental health movement," which refocused attention on children in schools instead of in clinics. "Whereas the Child Guidance Clinics had limited reach, education provided an avenue for making every child subject to psycho-hygienic interference" (Drunen & Jansz, 2004a, p. 79). School psychologists aligned themselves with the mental health movement and became established throughout the nations of North America and Europe.

The Tavistock Clinic provided services for children with criminal records and for those suffering anxiety or maladjustment in school. In the late 1920s, the model of child-guidance clinics was adopted in Europe with the first clinics opening in London and shortly thereafter in Amsterdam. This model expanded throughout Germany after World War II.

Section conclusion

Currently, school psychologists work in schools with students to assess and manage issues related to intelligence, placement, learning environments, and development. School psychologists promote education, the study of child development, systematic estimation of intelligence, the classification of extremes of intelligence (i.e., mental retardation and giftedness), and managing and sorting students by working to develop more productive educational settings. It seems, however, that these systems increase the capacity for control, order, and efficiency, while ignoring distinct cultural traditions and the unique needs of individual students.

Intelligence testing

The most popular applied psychology, historically, has been intelligence testing for educational and business purposes. Psychologists always have claimed intellectual functioning as their unique territory and the career of school psychologists depended on employing them. Applied research on intelligence intersected with early psychologists' service to society's administrative requirements and their desires for professional and societal legitimacy (R. Smith, 1997). Newly formed institutions of elementary education gave psychologists opportunities to test their concepts and practical applications.

Psychologists served an administrative function in the new, elementary-education system in industrialized societies, assessing and intervening with "defective" children. The predominant view during this era was that heredity determined social degeneracy, and "feeblemindedness" and mental pathology were physiologically based (N. Rose, 1985). Thus, psychologists' development of intelligence testing took a social-hygienic focus.

However, what constitutes intelligence and how to assess it have been bones of contention in Psychology. The assessment of intelligence also was bound up with psychologists' assumptions about the intelligence of "non-White" populations.

Terms and definitions

Charles Darwin had prepared the way for the category of intelligence by his claim that animals, including humans, differ only in degrees of intelligence. He believed that there were inherited gradations of intelligence between what society termed "savages" and the brightest men (*sic*) of the most advanced "races." Because the term "reason" connoted philosophical rationalism and natural scientists were keen to distinguish their work from speculation, biologists preferred "intelligence" when addressing the question of whether animals reasoned (Danziger, 1997).

Originally, however, "intelligence" was not part of psychologists' language; they preferred "intellect." But early psychologists adopted the biologists' term, which coincided with Herbert Spencer's evolutionary definition of intelligence as the capacity of the mind to adapt to its environment. Subsequently, intelligence became cultural baggage in that psychologists and the public understood it as a concrete natural object that determined individuals' behaviour. In contemporary public education, intelligence "characterized a child's performance relative to other children and to a set educational standard" (R. Smith, 1997, p. 590).

But there were different foundational approaches to theorizing and assessing intelligence: the individualized approach, epitomized by Alfred Binet, and the psychometric approach of Francis Galton, represented by Anglo-American psychologists.

Individualized approach

Parisian educators endeavoured to select mildly retarded children for special education to enable them to achieve their potential. This administrative purpose was the context for Binet's innovative applied research (Sternberg & Jarvin, 2003). Contracting with the French government and working with Theodore Simon (1872–1961), Binet's mission was to develop a practical scale of intelligence that could inform educational decisions about children lagging behind their peers academically. Accordingly, Binet and Simon created an individually administered test that was sensitive enough to assess the extremes of poor performance and estimate at what age children could be expected to perform certain tasks.

Binet published the *Metric Intelligence Scale* in 1905 and revised it in 1908 and 1911. However, he cautioned that scores on his test only had practical value for identifying and classifying children slow to develop; it could not substantiate claims about intellectual capacity (Carroy & Plas, 1996). In fact, he "insisted that his scale did not really measure an entity called 'intelligence'" (Danziger, 1997, p. 77).

Binet's society considered low academic achievement as a moral weakness deserving punishment. But he showed that psychologists can assess children with intellectual challenges and recommend effective remediation that protects them from prejudicial treatment (Sternberg, 2003). He denied the notion that "retardation" was simply an arrest of development, because, for him, individuals differed in their specific capacities of intelligence (Wolf, 1973).

In Binet's testing approach an examiner administered items verbally to a single child. He held that the artificial testing situation and environmental influences on a child's development usually understated ability; thus, test performance did not yield an accurate account of individual's mental operations (Siegler, 1992). Eventually, Binet shifted to a normative focus of assessing all children's adaptation to classroom requirements for which the criterion was the average level of performance (N. Rose, 1985).

Remaining committed to the individual approach, William Stern introduced the term, "intelligence quotient" in 1912. For him, the ratio of mental age divided by chronological age was a more meaningful index for comparison purposes than Binet's concept of mental age. However, Stern's quotient was not equivalent to a "quantifiable entity in human nature," although in subsequent decades psychologists used IQ scores that way (R. Smith, 1997, p. 595). Rather, as a human-science psychologist, Stern sought to understand how individual children deal with their environment.

Psychometric approach

Two traditions emerged within the Anglo-American psychometric approach to intelligence: British and US.

British tradition Darwin had shown that natural selection operated according to variation of biological characteristics. Rooting mental processes in evolutionary concepts, Galton proposed that human psychological characteristics are functionally equivalent and constitute inherited traits (Gillham, 2001). For him, psychological variability is as inherited as biological variability, and heredity overshadows environmental influence on intelligence (R. Smith, 1997).

Although Galton could not measure directly what he termed "natural ability," he devised the first questionnaire to investigate hereditary and environmental influences (e.g., birth order) on contemporary English male scientists. Keen to enhance differential selection, he investigated how individual variation in abilities is distributed in the population. This focus on individual differences is also known as *differential psychology*. Then he proposed the concept of correlation and a means to measure it.

Galton's mission was to advance practical applications of psychological categories. To fulfill his goal of improving the human race scientifically he began "anthropometric" testing (i.e., mental measurement of individual differences) at the 1884 International Health Exhibition in London and maintained his testing programme for six years thereafter at South Kensington Museum. He obtained data on 9,337 individuals from which he derived a distribution of the population's characteristics.

British proponents of intelligence testing and individual differences and developers of the US intelligence-testing movement recapitulated Galton's hereditarian position (Sweeney, 2001). Aided by new statistical techniques, British psychologists developed assessment tools of presumed innate intelligence suited to mass-testing. They aggregated individuals' test scores to generalize about populations.

Inventing factor analysis, Charles Spearman proposed a two-factor theory of intelligence: a general ability ("g") shared by all specific factors ("s") (Hearnshaw, 1964). Rather than following Galton's assumption that individual differences in intelligence were highly correlated with differences in sensory discrimination, he explained intellectual functions in terms of hypothesized cognitive structures. Spearman constructed paper-and-pencil intelligence tests, which he organized into test batteries and investigated the statistical relationships among the batteries' components. In addition, he invented the techniques of rank-correlation method and estimation of reliability gained by increasing test items (Danziger, 1997). With a more sophisticated rationale than Galton's, he too claimed that general intelligence constituted natural ability, was primarily heritable, and was evident in social rank (Rose, 1985).

Spearman and his student Cyril Burt criticized Binet's approach as atheoretical, disconnected from biological functions, and unreliable. But the school system employed the Binet–Simon scale, so Burt sought to reform the scale. His research provided the foundation for a group, paper-and-pencil test of intelligence before US psychologists constructed one during World War I.

In 1920 Burt published a popular revision that he thought measured innate intelligence. His testing boosted the British psychometric model (Hearnshaw, 1964), while his view that intellectual differences between social classes were inherited informed educational policy until after World War II (Tucker, 2007). He effectively established Psychology's function as an administrative technology in the UK.

US tradition Adopting the British emphasis on assessing individual differences, US psychologists soon converted the Binet–Simon test into a group-administered IQ test with standardized scores. Test items assessed speed and obedience, which suited regimented school and work environments. A virtual industry of intelligence testing then emerged, boosted by its service in screening recruits for the US Army in World War I.

Former students of Stanley Hall, **Henry Goddard** (1866–1957), who adapted the Binet–Simon tests, and **Lewis Terman** (1877–1956), who developed the Stanford–Binet tests, advanced the British tradition in the USA. They aimed to distinguish the feebleminded from those who were allegedly lazy.

While working at the New Jersey School for Feebleminded Boys and Girls, Goddard decided to abandon using tests designed for adults with normal intelligence (Fancher, 1985). He travelled to France where conceptions of developmental challenges were more advanced and in 1911 translated the Binet–Simon test into English. To this day, Goddard's adaptation defines psychologists' conception of intelligence pragmatically as abilities required to succeed in school.

Responding to the demands of US public education for assessment tools, US psychologist Terman also translated but expanded the Binet–Simon test in 1912. Then he converted Stern's intelligence quotient to the familiar IQ score. Because Terman was working at Stanford University, he named his revised test the Stanford–Binet, which was published in 1916 and was standardized on approximately 2,300 California children.

This test was the breakthrough to societal utility that US psychologists sought (T. Rogers, 1995). However, Terman and other Anglo-American psychologists, influenced more by Galton than by Binet, held that intelligence was hereditary and impervious to educational programmes. Their assessment tool became the means for psychologists to segregate children with special needs rather than integrate them in classrooms with extra support. The assumption was that "special classes" provided a benign environment for children for whom there was no hope.

In 1917 Terman and Goddard developed the *Army Alpha* test to assess the intelligence of military personnel and army recruits. With the success of mass intelligence testing US psychologists now possessed a marketable product and a supportive rationale, evolutionary adaptation, that could persuade the public of the discipline's social utility (Danziger, 1997).

In the 1920s, Terman also studied giftedness by looking at retrospective reports of people considered to be eminent or geniuses. He believed that intelligence did not develop with experience but was inherited and fixed. He aimed to help gifted students who were disadvantaged by social and economic conditions. Thinking it would better the human community, Terman argued for sterilizing people assessed to be mentally retarded. Besides fuelling the eugenics movement, intelligence research also was used as evidence for racial and cultural discrimination.

Lightner Witmer (1867–1956), considered the founding clinical psychologist in the USA, also concentrated on individual differences. He aimed to change the circumstances of the individual child and employed a team approach with psychologist and physician working together along with teachers and parents. He developed special-education classes and studied the way that emotional and behavioural problems are related to learning. He also pioneered the practice of "diagnostic teaching" where a child's learning is assessed in the process of the teacher providing instruction (Benjamin & Baker, 2004).

Unlike Terman, Witmer believed that environmental factors could lead to retardation. He agreed, however, that some forms of developmental challenge were intractable, due to heredity, and these individuals should be segregated for fear of contaminating the environment of normal children. But he was not a eugenicist. He is quoted by Benjamin and Baker (2004) as claiming, "The more mongrel a people, the more intelligent; the purer the blood, the more stupid" (p. 92).

Section conclusion

Historically, diverse notions of intelligence prevailed in Psychology. In Europe, Binet and others understood intelligence as ability across a range of activities. Studying the problem-solving of apes, Gestalt psychologist Wolfgang Köhler distinguished between mechanical cognitive functions and insightful ones. Later, Max Wertheimer investigated scientists' insightful problem-solving. In addition, developmental psychologists Jean Piaget and Lev Vygotsky conceived of intelligence as a process rather than as a product. By contrast, Anglo-American psychologists stressed general intelligence as Spearman conceived it.

Defining intelligence in terms of a single reliable entity was useful for practitioners, but conceptually questionable (Mayhauser, 1992). The concept of intelligence was shaped by the social need for an intelligence test that could measure students' and employees' individual performance, which could be compared to the performance of large numbers of individuals and yield an estimate of mental age based on what the majority of respondents were able to do. This conception is problematic, if general intelligence is viewed as located within an individual and not as an interaction of potential abilities, opportunities, and resources. A person cannot be deemed "generally intelligent" or "unintelligent" *absolutely*, because what is intelligent in one situation might be unintelligent in another.

Some scholars, such as Howard Gardner in *Multiple Intelligences* (1993) and Stephen Jay Gould in *The Mismeasure of Man* (1996), argued that "intelligence" is not a unified object that can be measured. More recent work in emotional intelligence attempts to redress the idea of a single form of intelligence (Goleman, 1995). But even if psychologists can measure different kinds of intelligence, they still might ignore situational influences on any kind of intelligence. Meanwhile, evidence from the "Flynn effect" suggested that IQ levels had been increasing by three percentage points per decade in economically privileged societies at least since the turn of the twentieth century to the 1980s (Flynn, 2012). Although the causes and implications of these increases are unclear, intelligence and its measurement seem like less stable phenomena than many psychologists might prefer.

Another criticism is that scientific racism lay just beneath the surface of the intelligence-testing movement. Many early psychologists believed that the test scores could further the mission of eugenics, because the concept of intelligence provided a plausible scientific rationale for differences in school success (Danziger, 1997). This ideology was part of the hostile social context that early African American psychologists encountered (Guthrie, 1998) and is related to the argument advanced by some psychologists for a racial hierarchy of intelligence.

Counselling psychology

Practically, counselling psychology has its roots in educational, religious, and pastoral settings (Dryden, Mearns, & Thorne, 2000). Counselling was not a profession so much as an extension of service in professions such as teaching, religious ministry, and nursing. Many counsellors volunteered their services. At present, counselling psychologists are a distinct class of professionals with a different programme of education than clinical psychologists that stresses the psychology of adjustment. Yet like clinical psychologists, counselling psychologists provide psychotherapy, administer psychological tests, and work in private practice and hospitals.

In the UK, beginning in the 1940s, counselling became an organized activity in response to wartime crisis, mental health demands of returning war veterans, immigration, and changing social situations. With so many men away from home for military service, marital breakdown was perceived as a threat to the social order. Guidance and counselling developed as responses to this emergent social problem.

In the USA, the rise of counselling also coincided with the increasing move from rural to urban culture, modern conveniences, consumerism, mass production, and an influx of immigrants to the USA from overseas pursuing a better life in a land of opportunity. In this new societal context the pioneering spirit of rugged individualism had to be subordinated to greater social organization. For counselling psychologists, facilitating personal adjustment became a primary focus. The belief was that psychologists could help people "fit in" and curtail the experience of loss of freedom (Napoli, 1981).

With the expanding provision of counselling services, there followed a demand for greater organization, scientific evidence, ethical codes of practice, accreditation of training programmes, and registration of practitioners. Standards were raised, training improved, and the subdiscipline was held to greater accountability. Regulating counselling psychology, however, threatened innovation in practice. With increasing professionalization, "a pioneering and creative activity pursued by the talented few [becomes] an institutionalised, rule-bound and essentially stultifying pursuit which loses the vitality and the imaginative élan on which it depends for its effectiveness and healing power" (Dryden et al., 2000, p. 471). Furthermore, support for the assumption that regulating training and practice through accreditation and registration results in more effective and reliable services seems to be lacking (House & Totten, 1997).

Section conclusion

Originally, counselling psychologists worked in educational settings providing guidance and counselling to prevent serious disturbance, whereas clinicians worked in hospitals or private practice providing services for the more seriously mentally disordered. Currently, clinical and counselling psychologies have similar standards for registration and their domains of practice overlap, although their education and training programmes are distinct.

Academically, counselling psychology typically is housed in a faculty of education and clinical psychology in a faculty of science or arts. In English-speaking Canada and in the USA, a degree in counselling psychology is typically considered to be less rigorous and less prestigious than a degree in clinical psychology, whereas in French-speaking countries, schools of education and counselling psychology tend to be more highly regarded.

Part 2 conclusion

At first, the focus of industrial/organizational psychology was commercial and industrial applications of psychological research; applications to organizations were recognized formally in the 1970s. Applied psychologists provided vocational guidance to employers, aiding them in matching their job requirements with potential employees' skills and occupational interests. Although psychologists did not develop the principles of scientific management, they supported them and did not question the industrial goals of productivity and increased efficiency nor advocate reorganizing the actual conditions of work and of industries themselves. Rather, they counselled managers on how to humanize the alienating conditions of labour that factory workers experienced and instituted personnel counselling programmes at job sites for workers. After World War II, psychologists studied and consulted with businesses concerning worker motivation, satisfaction, and leadership, and attended to the efficacy of work-groups and the effects of organizational climate on productivity.

As noted in Chapter 5, applications to education have characterized Psychology since its inception. School psychology emerged as a specialty in response to educational administrators' needs for managing and sorting students to ensure that they adapted to the conditions of mandatory education. Initially school psychologists offered expertise in assessing children's abilities. Thus, the work of school psychologists largely has entailed intelligence testing, which is an expertise that distinguishes Psychology from all other professions. While Binet's individualized and Galton's psychometric approaches to intelligence were very influential for decades, more recently psychologists entertain diverse conceptions of intelligence.

Counselling psychology also originated in school settings, but over the twentieth century expanded its scope to encompass working with all age groups primarily on matters of personal adjustment. Although in North America it enjoys less professional prestige than clinical psychology, counselling psychology serves as yet another professional specialty that offers psychological solutions to the problems encountered in psychologically minded societies stressing adaptation to the status quo.

Part 3 Clinical psychology

As noted above, counselling, school, and clinical psychologists have had overlapping concerns. But the domain of clinical psychology became so vast and clinical psychologists so numerous, at least in the USA and Canada, that it deserves separate historical examination.

Witmer initiated the first psychological clinic in 1896 at the University of Pennsylvania and the journal *The Psychological Clinic*. However, his model of clinical psychology had more in common with current school psychology and community psychology than with the Boulder and PsyD models of clinical psychology (Benjamin & Baker, 2004). For Witmer, clinical psychology meant formulating social interventions to address circumstances affecting the welfare of children, but not assessing medical concerns and providing consultation to the medical community. In fact, during the early twentieth century, "clinical psychology" was used generically in US Psychology to refer to all the various activities of applied psychology.

Presently, clinical psychologists work in general hospitals, physiotherapy clinics, community mental health centres, schools, university counselling centres, hospices, aftercare homes, rehabilitation centres, addiction centres, juvenile homes, and in private practice. The current understanding of clinical psychology has its own history of concepts, research, diagnostic methods, and treatment practices.

Early modern history of mental health practices

The psychotherapeutic practices of clinical psychology can be traced to early nineteenth-century hypnotic and suggestive techniques used in medicine alongside the more biophysical treatments of mental illness. In France, at the La Bicêtre and the La Salpêtrière, which were insane asylums for men and women respectively, Philippe Pinel (1745–1826) introduced non-physical treatments and became renowned for liberating "the insane" from their chains, as shown in Figure 8.2.

Figure 8.2 This 1795 Romantic painting by Tony Robert-Fleury (1837–1912) depicts Philippe Pinel at the Salpêtrière releasing "lunatics" from their chains

Later, in 1882, also working at La Salpêtrière, Jean-Martin Charcot established a neurology clinic. Much of his work involved anatomical pathology, but he became famous for his studies of hypnosis and hysteria. He managed, somewhat, to redeem hypnosis from the damaging reputation it had gained through its association with the work of Franz Mesmer (Ellenberger, 1970).

There was a great deal of public interest in trance and other altered states of consciousness. By the late nineteenth century, investigators of *psychotherapeutics* (i.e., psychotherapy in the form of rational persuasion, hypnosis, and suggestion) began to adhere to the controlled experimental conditions established in German physiology laboratories and the French medical standard of *La Clinique*. This standard required that experimental findings be verified by way of clinical case-examples (i.e., in actual living situations) (Taylor, 2000). The conjunction of experimental laboratory studies of physiological psychology with the clinical case study of unusual states of consciousness laid the ground for investigating the unconscious. Subsequently, the field of psychotherapeutics blossomed (Ellenberger, 1970).

Psychotherapeutics and altered states of consciousness were also of interest in the USA. The American Society for Psychical Research was established in 1885 by a small group of Harvard professors who studied hypnosis as well as clairvoyance, thought-transfer, mediumship, telepathy, and spirit-visions. These studies followed the experimental tradition of natural science and thereby influenced medical psychology practices. For example, although the legitimacy of hypnosis remains debatable, beginning in the 1880s experimental reports provided support for the use of hypnosis as a psychotherapeutic technique (Taylor, 2000).

In the mid 1890s, a new graduate specialty in experimental psychopathology was taught by William James at Harvard and Adolf Meyer at Clark University (Taylor, 2000). Clark University was also a major centre for developments in psychotherapy between 1880 and 1890 with studies of therapy, abnormal psychology, and psychopathology.

Psychotherapy as psychological practice

Academic psychologists endeavoured to develop graduate training and research programmes that distinguished Psychology and the practice of psychotherapy from the work of psychic healers and spiritualists (Benjamin & Baker, 2004). Medicine and experimental verification were considered the legitimate frameworks for addressing psychological disorder and treatment. Thus, psychical research and psychotherapy became distinct lines of inquiry.

With Sigmund Freud and Carl Jung visiting America in 1909, some embraced psychoanalysis as *the* science of clinical psychology, stressing psychological, not biological or genetic, causes of mental illness (Abma, 2004; Benjamin & Baker, 2004). Freud had stipulated that a doctoral degree, not a medical degree, should be the foundation for training in psychoanalysis. But **Abraham Arden Brill** (1874–1948), an Austrian pioneer of psychoanalysis in the USA, persuaded him that an MD should be required to practise psychoanalysis to prevent charlatans from taking over. Brill was the first to translate many of Freud's major works into English, and Freud conceded to his recommendation.

Thereafter, for the first half of the twentieth century, the medical community controlled the training and accreditation of psychoanalysts in the USA and Canada. However, with psychologists responding to government pressures to attend to the needs of demobilized veterans in the late 1940s, and Psychology becoming a professional organization with its own standards of training and codes of conduct, psychologists made a formidable claim to the right to practise psychotherapeutics; regardless, psychoanalysis tended to remain a distinctly psychiatric practice.

With the emergence of the twentieth-century disciplines of neurology, neurophysiology, and psychopharmacology, physicians regained physically based treatments as distinctly their own. Brain surgery, insulin shock therapy, major tranquilizers, and electroconvulsive therapy were techniques available only through psychiatrists. Those with severe and long-term mental health problems tended to be treated by psychiatrists with invasive treatments that assumed the brain was the problem. With mental illness perceived to be an extreme burden on society, frontal lobotomy came to be enthusiastically promoted. However, it was used indiscriminately by physicians without surgical training, resulting in seizure disorders and death by infection (Mashoura, Walker, & Martuza, 2005).

Then in 1963 the Community Mental Health Act took effect in the USA, which eventually moved hundreds of thousands of patients out of custodial care in psychiatric hospitals (Benjamin & Baker, 2004). Subsequently, many community mental health centres (CMHCs) were established across the country with the hope of generating greater social stability. At least in theory, emphasis shifted from mental illness to mental health and prevention. Accordingly, some psychologists broadened their purview from clinical activities to administering psychological interventions for all individuals and life issues (Herman, 1995).

Deinstitutionalization

In the USA and Canada, during the early nineteenth century, asylums for the mad spread with physical treatments existing alongside psychotherapeutics. In the USA, physician **Benjamin Rush** (1745–1813) at Pennsylvania Hospital tried to introduce a humanitarian approach to asylums, embodying the hope for cure, respectful sympathetic care, and no physical restraints (Benjamin & Baker, 2004). He encouraged staff to go for regular walks with patients, read and talk with them, and even offer small gifts. Dorothea Dix (1802–1887) also helped establish humane treatment in hospitals throughout the USA. During the early twentieth century a mental hygiene movement also advocated humane care.

But sociopolitical developments in the 1960s as well as the reported effectiveness of psychotropic medication changed asylum psychiatry and paved the way for a community approach to mental health and deinstitutionalization. The deinstitutionalization movement aimed to release patients with severe and long-term psychiatric disorders to their local community where their families primarily would care for them rather than being warehoused in asylums. The vision included CMHCs attending to crises or acute needs of discharged individuals. As a result, some provincial and state psychiatric hospitals in Anglo-American nations closed.

However, the rise of social and community psychiatry was short-lived for several reasons. The CMHCs were too few and severely understaffed. Hospitals and local communities received insufficient funding to sustain a strong fabric of community supports, and many discharged individuals did not have family members to support them. In effect, the lack of adequate funding and the absence of preventative mental health services produced a "revolving door" syndrome with patients with severe and long-term psychiatric disorders being treated as outpatients or repeatedly being admitted for short-term care.

The trend towards closing large psychiatric hospitals and developing community services occurred worldwide in slightly different time-frames and frequently for reasons of government budgets. For example, in Australia during the 1980s there was a push to fund community services by closing psychiatric hospitals; attempts continue to coordinate hospital and community efforts (Hambridge & Baker, 2001). In Brazil during the 1990s, psychologists fought for deinstitutionalization of patients (Andrade & Bueno, 2001). At the turn of the twenty-first century, Russia began decreasing the number of patients admitted to psychiatric hospitals, creating a situation similar to the USA in the 1970s, with massive release of patients and associated problems of community adjustment (Balachova, Levy, Isurina, & Wasserman, 2001).

Theories of psychotherapy

Alongside the community mental health movement of the 1960s, to which some academic and many professional psychologists contributed, Psychology continued to delineate its practice of psychotherapy and new ways of thinking about therapy emerged.

Client-centred treatment

Humanistic psychologies and the client-centred work of Carl Rogers (see Chapter 10) provide a form of therapy that psychologists offer to the general public (Abma, 2004). This non-directive supportive approach to psychotherapy trusts in clients' ability to explore problems and come to their own solutions. The client-centred approach is achieved through active listening and reflection.

Humanistic therapies focus on human goodness and a natural orientation to self-actualization. Therapists encourage conditions under which clients can discover their potential and live out their wishes. Rogers laid out the principles of this work in his ground-breaking book *Counseling and Psychotherapy* (1942). But his approach tends to be associated with counselling rather than clinical psychology.

Three criticisms of client-centred psychotherapy continue to be debated:

- It has not developed cumulative empirical evidence (Seligman & Csikszentmihalyi, 2000).
- It is preoccupied with a glorified view of self that diverts attention from socioeconomic realities and inequality of political power (Prilleltensky, 1992).
- Client-centred psychotherapy ignores the self-destructive tendencies of human nature that sustain the need for questioning notions of "self" and "humanity."

Behavioural therapies

Behavioural treatments flourished from the 1950s to the 1970s, vindicating the widely accepted belief among many Anglo-American psychologists that their experiments would lead to practical ends. Different forms of behavioural treatments were offered by some clinical psychologists in the burgeoning mental health clinics, in university clinics, and in private practice.

Based on animal-lab studies of Pavlovian conditioning, behaviour therapy became a popular psychotherapy intervention. Joseph Wolpe (1915–1997) coined the term "systematic desensitization," which describes the pairing of incompatible states (e.g. fear with pleasure) to condition new associations. Although much less popular today, largely because of the rise of cognitive–behavioural treatments, some clinicians still employ this technique.

Beginning in the 1950s, followers of B. F. Skinner's operant behaviourism used behaviour modification in hospitals and other institutions to shape the behaviour of patients, inmates, or residents by positive reinforcement. Mental disorders were considered strictly in terms of problematic behaviours that could be modified in more functional directions. But as noted previously, the effectiveness of the technology of behaviour modification is limited to situations of institutional control.

From a critical perspective, there are other limitations of behavioural treatments. At the root, it is very difficult to identify "a behaviour" per se without either making reference to the unobservable intention of the movement or else reducing the behaviour to purely observable movement. Because behavioural therapists hope to determine the universal tendencies of organisms, they discount the social and cultural intentions that define the meaning of an individual's behaviour. Thereby, behavioural therapists risk dealing in meaningless abstractions.

Cognitive therapies

The emergence of cognitive psychology in the USA, which supplanted behaviourism, led to a popular integration with behaviour therapy in the 1970s, termed "cognitive–behavioral therapy" (CBT), which takes multiple forms.

Clinical psychologist **Albert Ellis** (1913–2007), who coined rational-emotive therapy, and psychiatrist **Aaron Beck** (b. 1921), who developed cognitive therapy, focused on problematic thinking, not problematic behaviour, as central to mental disorder. Ellis used rational persuasion to restructure irrational beliefs – the "shoulds," "oughts," and "musts" of one's thinking. Beck's therapy restructured problematic thought-patterns by considering evidence as to their unrealistic nature and the effect that negative thinking has on one's mood. Ellis and Beck assumed that altering clients' thought-patterns leads to behaviour change and improved feelings.

A third founder of CBT is psychologist **Donald Meichenbaum** (b. 1940). Originally, he emphasized the importance of aiding clients in modifying negative self-statements about their situation to positive statements of coping, based on appreciation of Lev Vygotsky's developmental research on the control function of speech. More recently, Meichenbaum includes a narrative approach, encouraging clients to alter the narratives or stories they tell about themselves and their situations.

Clinical trials of CBT indicate that it can be as effective as medication, while also providing a form of prevention. As such, the US Veterans' Administration has provided more than $250 million a year to train therapists in CBT in hopes of addressing the suffering of traumatized veterans returning from military campaigns in Afghanistan and Iraq. Furthermore, the US military committed to training more than one million active-duty soldiers, reservists, members of the National Guard, civilian employees, and military-family members in the principles of CBT to promote resiliency. In the UK, the government in 2007 pledged to spend US$300 million to train and hire primarily cognitive–behavioural therapists (D. Smith, 2009).

Psychologists have been very successful in accumulating empirical evidence within the natural-science tradition to support the manualized treatment of psychological disorders using CBT. This research secures publicly funded services that depend on medical understandings of Psychology (Baydala, 2001; House, 1996; Mowbray, 1995). Critics argue that psychologists working in a medical disease model of disorder and treatment betray the particular strength of Psychology to focus on the individual (Aspinwall & Staudinger, 2003), potentially ignoring the unique therapeutic relationship between client and therapist (Bergin & Garfield, 1994).

Currently, academic clinical researchers debate the most appropriate methods for conducting research on therapy. Some psychologists argue that qualitative methods, such as narrative histories, ethnography, discourse analysis, and intensive case studies, should be incorporated into research on psychotherapy (e.g., McLeod & Balamoutsou, 2001).

Positive psychology

More recently, "positive psychology" has developed as an extension of humanistic psychologists' concern with strengths and human potential (see Chapter 10). Like humanistic psychologies, positive psychology offers an alternative to clinical approaches that focus on disorder, distress, disease, and repair. It addresses the importance of optimism, positive thinking, prevention, health, and wellness, and constructs "personal control strategies" for developing a "maximal self" (Seligman, 1991). The goal of positive psychology is to aid individuals, communities, and societies to flourish.

Positive psychologists conduct empirical research on such topics as positive emotions, healthy institutions, character strength, and the pursuit of happiness, and they work to amalgamate the wisdom of religious traditions into a psychogenic theory of happiness with self-control techniques (Haidt, 2006; Layard, 2005; Wallace & Shapiro, 2006). Advocates promote a "science of happiness" that draws on neuroscience, sociology, economics, philosophy, and psychology, while incorporating cognitive–behavioural therapeutic strategies.

Recently, using the principles of positive psychology, a preventative programme was initiated to enhance psychological resilience in the US Army (Casey Jr., 2011). The programme aims to assess psychosocial strengths and assets while providing training to facilitate emotional, social, family, and spiritual resilience (Algoe & Fredrickson, 2011) and promote "posttraumatic growth" (Tedeschi & McNally, 2011).

Critics of positive psychology, however, are concerned with who gets to define what is "positive." Under the auspices of a positive psychological science, what counts as the "good life" comes to rest on the authority of empirical findings. Moral claims are hidden in reputedly neutral empirical facts without recognizing the cultural and historical context of research (Sundararajan, 2005). Research, then, is used to promote particular cultural ideals and values.

Moreover, for some commentators, positive psychology is "American" in its values, reflecting a dedication to an ethos of achievement and self-improvement that avoids recognizing and accepting tragedy, loss, and suffering as inherent in meaningful existence (Aspinwall & Staudinger, 2003; Wilson, 2008; Woolfolk, 2002). As such, positive psychology seems to promote a simplistic version of happiness that has more to do with personal comfort than compassion and justice.

Commonalities

Most psychotherapists assume that mental problems are predominately psychological, not biological, that these problems can be solved through verbal communication, and that psychotherapy should be based on science and not morality (Abma, 2004). There are, however, many versions of psychotherapy that tend to be marginalized in the conservative training programmes of North American clinical psychology; for example, narrative therapy pioneered by Michael White (1948–2008) in Australia and David Epston (b. 1944) in New Zealand; and psychosynthesis developed by Roberto Assagioli (1888–1974) in Italy. Also in Italy, there is a strong phenomenological approach to therapy, originating in the work of psychiatrist Franco Basaglia (1924–1980).

Beginning in the 1970s, some academic clinical psychologists discerned the commonalities between psychodynamic models of therapy and behavioural techniques (e.g., Wachtel, 1977). Common factors included processes of exploration, understanding and action; therapeutic dynamics of resistance, transference, and counter-transference; and the non-specific relational qualities of faith, hope, and caring. These conceptual and practical developments led to the emergence of a movement towards psychotherapy integration, uniting psychodynamic, client-centred, and cognitive–behavioural perspectives.

An integration of the various treatment perspectives potentially meets the clinical and community needs of individuals more effectively. Although there are critics of integration, some academics continue to promote the clinical value of psychotherapy integration (Stricker, 2010). In 1991, the *Journal of Psychotherapy Integration* was established by the Society for the Exploration of Psychotherapy Integration.

Part 3 conclusion

Historically, clinical psychology was understood as addressing applied and practical concerns that overlapped with school and counselling psychology. However, at least since the end of World War II, clinical psychology distinguishes itself by focusing on mental disorders. Yet its history is linked with early psychotherapeutic medical practices such as hypnosis, rational persuasion, and suggestion, as well as the pursuit of happiness (Caplan, 1998). With the postwar emergence of clinical psychology defined within medical frameworks of research and practice, physicians and psychologists have overlapping professional territory. In recent decades clinical psychologists have focused on developing and promoting evidence-based psychological therapies (McHugh & Barlow, 2010), usually cognitive–behavioural. Nevertheless, there is some sustained interest in the concept and practice of psychotherapy integration.

Yet from a critical perspective, clinical psychologists tend to take for granted workaday practices of psychodiagnosis and treatment, which results in excluding analysis of sociopolitical oppression of individuals, families, and groups and consideration of community mental health and psychosocial interventions from their practice. In addition, they seem to ignore the ways in which the specialty of clinical psychology functions as a virtual industry, at least in North America, which encourages adaptation to the societal status quo. Moreover, "[a]s clinical psychology comes under the sway of corporate interests such as insurance companies, managed care organizations, and pharmaceutical companies, the challenges to professional integrity and progressive ideals will multiply" (Marecek & Hare-Mustin, 2009, p. 91).

Part 4   New areas of applied and professional psychology

By the late twentieth century, Psychology helped maintain social institutions as diverse as policing, sport, medicine, and the drug industry. In "the psychological society" virtually everyone came to describe everyday experience in psychological terms. Culturally, as historian Roger Smith (1997) observed, there developed an "internalization of belief in psychological knowledge, so that it acquired a taken-for-granted quality, altered every-one's subjective world and recreated experience and expectations about what it is to be a person" (p. 575).

Although some psychologists lamented the demise of a unified discipline, for others, specialized pursuits in Psychology were signs of creativity and innovation, offering work for everyone (Benjamin, 2001). Besides business people, educators, and healers, police officers, athletes, chemists, economists, environmentalists, anthropologists, sociologists, political scientists, and even historians were concerned with the psychological.

As new areas of interest developed in society, psychologists responded by claiming new forms of expertise and new specializations. These areas include forensic psychology, sport psychology, environmental psychology, health psychology, community psychology, and psychopharmacology.

Forensic psychology

Psychologists specializing in forensics offer psychological expertise about aspects of civil-law cases and the criminal-justice system. This work supports such social institutions as police departments, court rooms, detention centres, and prisons. The scope of forensic psychology is wide and includes at least **seven areas of research and practice** (Bartol & Bartol, 1999; Lösel, Bender, & Bliesener, 1992):

- Studies of criminal behaviour, deception, intelligence, and crime.
- The preventative role of psychology; mental status and criminal responsibility.
- The psychology of testimony.
- Child custody evaluations.
- Clinical services to officers, staff in correctional facilities and offenders.
- Inmate classification.
- Selection of police officers.

Historical roots

Forensic psychology has its roots in early European experimental and psychoanalytic research. Carl Jung and Max Wertheimer independently explained how the "association experiment" could help identify criminals. This model explored how emotionally charged words tend to be more difficult to remember. Other European psychologists studied guilt and deception, which evolved into the practice of lie detection. Beginning in the early 1900s, German psychologists became expert witnesses in criminal cases (Lösel *et al.*, 1992). Some claim that Münsterberg launched the field of psychology and the law in 1906 (Hale, 1980).

Criminology was of intense interest to psychoanalysts. In 1929, Theodore Reik (1888–1969), a Viennese student of Freud who settled in the USA, theorized the compulsion to confess. Hungarian-American analyst Franz Alexander (1891–1964) published work on judges and criminals also in 1929. In 1931, **Erich Fromm** (1900–1980) wrote on the psychology of the criminal and proposed the concept of a corrective society.

Psychologists also became involved in issues of eyewitness testimony. Alfred Binet replicated studies by James Cattell that demonstrate how emotions interfere with the accuracy of recall. William Stern conducted research on the psychology of testimony. Hugo Münsterberg (1908/1925) published his controversial book *On the Witness Stand*, highlighting the fallibility of human testimony because of conscious and unconscious suggestion.

Although Binet and others thought that errors in recollection in court were due to leading questions, experimental findings on the inaccuracy of recall were used by many psychologists to challenge the credibility of witnesses, especially child witnesses and victims of sexual abuse. Initially in Germany, Psychology was regarded as an unwelcome interference in the judicial process. Contrary to the inclinations of the court, psychologists tended to be biased against the truthfulness of claims made by victims (Undeutsche, 1992).

For his part, Münsterberg believed that only genuine scientists, like experimental psychologists, had the power to tell the truth and that scientifically objective psychologists alone understood the natural laws of mental processes (Hale, 1980). As such, the best judges of others' behaviour were psychologists, not individuals themselves or other professionals, because the judgment of the latter groups was intrinsically unreliable. Thus, Münsterberg reasoned, society required expert scientific evidence for determining matters of fact. That is, psychologists, not juries and judges, were best able to determine the reliability of testimony and confessions. The experimental "facts" upon which Münsterberg relied were that people's perceptions did not correspond to external reality and their memory distorted previous perceptions.

By 1954, the German parliament, when revising the Criminal Code, sought guidelines from psychiatrists and psychologists on issues of criminal responsibility. Psychiatrists argued that only states of mental disease should release a person from criminal responsibility. Psychologists, however, argued that very high emotional arousal, without necessarily being pathological, also should be grounds for claiming absence of criminal responsibility.

US and Canadian psychologists in the early twentieth century were relatively less involved in law-related matters. Following World War I, forensic psychology in the USA became more prominent. Psychologists did not regularly testify in US courts until the 1940s, which coincides with psychologists' rise in status as mental health professionals.

Law enforcement

In Germany, as early as 1919, police departments used the services of psychologists, and by 1922 in the USA, testing was used to screen police candidates (Bartol & Bartol, 1999). In the 1960s, US federal concern over police handling of public demonstrations and riots led government to consult psychologists to suggest more publicly acceptable ways of pacifying crowds. However, many recommendations had disappointing and sometimes counter-productive results (Bermant, Charlan, & Vidmar, 1976).

Within the prison system psychologists struggled to establish their work, vying with social workers, physicians, and psychiatrists for professional territory (Lösel *et al.*, 1992). During the 1970s Canadian and US mental health services were integrated into prison systems. However, limited financial resources, increasing crime rates, and social pressure hampered the therapeutic dimension of corrections. Neither the majority of police nor community members considered psychological rehabilitation an important part of law enforcement. Some prominent scholars even contended that inmates were not redeemable and deserved a life of isolation and punishment (Bermant *et al.*, 1976).

Although originally the US penitentiary system was based on the idea of rehabilitation and not incarceration or revenge, early theories of criminal behaviour were strongly influenced by social Darwinism, lending support to "lengthy incarcerations of the disadvan-taged, confused, and powerless" (Bartol & Bartol, 1999, p. 17). Contrary to this tendency, Stanley Brodsky during his tenure as APA president in the 1960s made rehabilitation the focus of incarceration.

Section conclusion

In terms of credentialling, many forensic psychologists are educated as clinical and coun-selling psychologists, but they also might be trained as experimental psychologists or social psychologists (Bermant *et al.*, 1976). Currently, forensic psychology draws on work in clinical and counselling psychology and research in developmental and social psychology, perception, memory, and suggestibility.

Practically, forensic psychologists might conduct assessments of individuals accused of a crime, which can serve an important function during the pretrial stage in legal proceedings. Forensic psychologists also might offer consultation to police officers, attorneys, and judges concerning individual cases. However, psychological treatment for prisoners is complicated by such issues as the right to refuse treatment and the potential lack of confidentiality for certain disclosures by prisoners or accused individuals in treatment. From a critical per-spective, the ambit of forensic psychology typically excludes reflective discourse on both the concrete practice of Psychology in relation to the law and legal policy and on concepts of and assumptions about what constitutes justice itself (Arrigo & Fox, 2009).

Sport psychology

Historically, sport psychology has been associated with physical education, kinesiology, leisure studies, and Psychology. Tests of movement, studies of reaction times, and analysis of kinaesthetic judgment have been part of the discipline dating back to Wundt and Ribot. Unlike present efforts, these investigations were not concerned with enhancing perform-ance, but intended to illuminate coordination of mind and body.

For example, in the 1890s, **Norman Triplett** (1861–1931) investigated the phenomenon of "social facilitation" wherein runners demonstrate faster times when they are with people. Some label this the first study of sport psychology, but Triplett was more interested in the phenomenon of social facilitation than improved running performance (Cratty, 1989).

Throughout the early decades of the twentieth century, there were sporadic articles in Psychology dealing with the expression of emotion in sport spectators, sport as an aesthetic expression, or sport as a test of will and power. Of particular interest in China and the Soviet Union was the link between political philosophy and strivings in athletics (Cratty, 1989).

In the USA, **Coleman Roberts Griffith** (1893–1966) is considered the father of sport psychology. In the late 1920s and early 1930s his textbooks spawned many college courses. However, it was not until the late twentieth century that sport psychologists rediscovered Griffith and used his work to secure a historical legacy for the field (Green, 2003).

Internationally, the first congress in sport psychology was held in Rome in 1965, followed by national organizations of sport and exercise psychology worldwide. In 1970, the *International Journal of Sport Psychology* was founded; it was the first journal dedicated to sport psychology.

Presently, researchers tend to investigate the effect psychology has on sport behaviour or the physiological effect of sport on psychological factors; in addition, some study exercise in terms of health, well-being, and mental health (Drapeau, 2012). Sport psychologists utilize relaxation techniques, visualization, and biofeedback to adjust habits of mind and body. Cognitive–behavioural techniques also are used to manage unhelpful thoughts, improve powers of concentration, and maintain optimal levels of emotion to enhance performance.

In the USA, most sport psychologists focus on teaching and research. But in Japan, Russia, and China many more psychologists work exclusively with athletes and teams, advising on psychological methods for enhancing performance. They also provide individual consultation on issues such as depression associated with athletic injury, relationship problems, career goals, academic issues, or athletic identity (Petrie & Diehl, 1995).

Section conclusion

Like other specialty areas in Psychology, a professionalization for sport psychology was envisioned and publicly condoned before the subdiscipline had actually formed a course of education. Public interest in using experts in the area of sport pressured disciplines to determine what counted as expertise. Psychological understandings of sport developed in other disciplines besides Psychology, such as education, kinesiology, and medicine. Furthermore, sport psychology now encompasses exercise psychology (Drapeau, 2012).

Currently, sport psychologists can be educated in counselling, clinical, or social psychology. General training in these areas is thought to be suited to many of the needs of athletes and sports teams. However, sport psychologists also might be trained in the disciplines of kinesiology or physical education, and many specialize in the effects of exercise on health, well-being, and mental health across the life-span.

The term "psychologist" is legally restricted in many countries, such as Canada, the USA, and South Africa. Thus, anyone stating he or she is a "sport psychologist" must be trained in Psychology and be licensed as a psychologist by a state or provincial college of psychologists, or be working on faculty at a university. Besides being trained in Psychology, it is recommended that sport psychologists seek experience with sports organizations, sport-psychology practica, and sport-science coursework (motor learning or kinesiology) to prepare for working with athletes and sports teams (Petrie & Diehl, 1995).

Environmental psychology

Also known as ecopsychology and psycho-ecology, environmental psychology is a loosely defined subspecialty. It deals with the way that the natural and social environment is related to human behaviour, cognition, and mental health. Issues addressed include resource management, common property, conservation behaviour, and sustainability. Environmental psychology is an interdisciplinary domain that draws from anthropology, sociology, history, political science, geography, architecture, urban design, ergonomics, and human factors psychology.

Beginning in the 1960s, environmental psychology has considered how people are affected psychologically by their situations in environments (Barker, 1968). Not only intrapsychic and interpersonal relationships but also the nature of human relationships with other species and with ecosystems are seen as affecting mental health. Some environmental psychologists focus on understanding irrational environmental behaviour (Roszak, Gomes, & Kanner, 1995). Others investigate environmental sensitivity, documenting images of human/nature relationships, the psychological effects of pollution, overcrowding, habitat loss, environmental toxins, and the possibilities of modifying human behaviour to promote environmental responsibility (Bell, Greene, Fisher, & Baum, 1996). Some psychologists have been addressing individual, group, and societal responses to climate change (Swim *et al.*, 2011).

Section conclusion

Environmental psychology is another example of how Psychology has insinuated itself in far-ranging fields of study and practice. Current international concern for environmental issues, sustainable development, understanding climate change, and environmental protection includes the psychological impact of these problems as well as ways of changing people's behaviour using transdisciplinary cooperation (e.g., Swim *et al.*, 2011) and psychological principles (e.g., Kazdin, 2009).

Environmental psychologists seek to influence urban planners, designers, architects, and politicians to support more hospitable environments. One layperson with similar interests was **Jane Jacobs** (1916–2006) who fought to preserve neighbourhoods in large developing cities. An American who became Canadian in protest against the Vietnam War, she worked to build liveable and living cities. As a writer and activist, she worked in the spirit of environmental psychology at the intersection of multiple disciplines.

Health psychology

Health psychology is another relatively new, applied and professional subdiscipline of natural-science Psychology. Generally, health psychologists conceive of health as a dynamic relationship between individuals' biological functioning and behaviour on the one hand, and their social and physical environments on the other. This is known as the "biopsychosocial" model (Engel, 1977).

In theory, health psychologists address **four areas** (Chamberlain & Murray, 2009):

- the treatment and prevention of physical illness,
- the promotion and maintenance of health,
- the role of psychological factors in illness and health,
- the development of health policy and improvement of health-care services.

Efforts at preventing illness through promotion of health have a history of more than 100 years. The possibility of mental states causing physical symptoms inspired the work of Jean-Martin Charcot and Sigmund Freud (Ellenberger, 1970). In the late nineteenth century there was a prevention group in the USA called the National Association for the Protection of the Insane and the Prevention of Insanity (Spaulding & Balch, 1983). In the late twentieth century, deinstitutionalization brought to light the environmental and social forces that contribute to mental illness.

During the 1970s, the intersection of biomedical and behavioural science led researchers to use biofeedback machines to demonstrate how people can learn to control autonomic responses, such as body temperature and heart rate, thereby potentially mediating the impact of stressors on the development of illness and disease. By 1981, health psychology was recognized as a specialty area in US Psychology (Prokop, Bradley, Burish, Anderson, & Fox, 1991). Then in 2001, the APA adopted a by-law change to its mission statement acknowledging the role of Psychology in health and illness (Johnson, 2003).

Currently, many specialize in health psychology, and some clinical, community, and social psychologists have concentrated on the specialty. Increasing numbers of psychologists are finding employment in hospitals, supporting the administration of medical care by providing psychological services in cardiology, paediatric, and obstetric units. Services include pre-operation preparation, reducing patient stress, facilitating adherence to drug regimes, and reducing length of hospital stay and patient complaints. Cognitive–behavioural techniques generally are used for health promotion, health maintenance, illness prevention, behavioural treatment of illness, and for understanding the psychological implications of the health-care system (Arnett, 2006; Prokop *et al.*, 1991).

Section conclusion

Some proponents of health psychology, in Canada and Israel for example, argue that psychologists have not promoted their usefulness and cost-effectiveness adequately in medical contexts (Arnett, 2006; Jacoby, 2001). Health psychologists are anxious to persuade government (i.e., politicians, bureaucrats, and policy-makers) that psychological services are evidenced-based and have a broad scope of application. They argue that Psychology as a natural science of human behaviour should be at the centre of health and health care in Canada – as accessible as medical services presumably are for lower and middle-income Canadians (Dobson, 2002).

Other critiques are more foundational. Despite having a biopsychosocial philosophy of health, the approach many health psychologists take is focused on the behavioural without involving social or cultural determinants of health (Chamberlain & Murray, 2009). Most health psychologists are trained in clinical psychology graduate programmes. What students learn in these programmes about mental health is not necessarily tied to family, culture, and environment.

For example, stress-management programmes teach "at risk" groups how to change their behaviour to avoid diseases. However, conditions most closely linked with common mental disorders are "unemployment or economic inactivity, poorer material circumstances, and less education" (Melzer, Fryers, & Jenkins, 2004, p. S14). Stress as a social, political, and economic condition, involving, for example, abusive bosses, poor working conditions, racism, sexism, or poverty, generally is not systemically addressed in Psychology.

Some psychologists recognize the significance of health disparities across social classes (Adler, 2009). Yet it seems that many health psychologists inadvertently support the status quo by helping people adjust to existing social economic conditions. Health psychologists have tended to neglect family, culture, and the environment as important determinants of health. Perhaps, to integrate Psychology throughout hospitals as health psychologists envision, training in the specialty of health psychology would need to address the social determinants of health, such as income inequalities and their impact on health and treatment.

However, many health professionals oppose a preventative model, because it takes away from a clinical focus on treatment. Furthermore, it is difficult to justify spending health-care time trying to detect problems before they arise; it is also difficult to measure success when it entails maintenance of health; and preventative health care is philosophically at odds with a service-delivery setting suited to treatment.

Moreover, historically, prevention programmes have flourished with enthusiasm and then faltered (Prokop *et al.*, 1991). Some critics argue that refocusing health psychology on fostering positive growth, instead of trying to prevent pathology, could better distinguish Psychology from medicine. New criteria then could be used to judge the effectiveness of a psychology of prevention (Spaulding & Balch, 1983). From a different perspective, "a critical psychology of health focuses on research seeking [social] transformation and . . . insight into the sociocultural processes and power relations that sustain disadvantage" (Chamberlain & Murray, 2009, p. 156).

Community psychology

In theory, community psychologists aim to study individuals in their social contexts, focusing on strengths instead of deficits, while striving to prevent illness and disease by means of social change instead of adjustment to existing institutions. Community psychologists understand psychological disorder as resistance to a society that is dysfunctional. They include the importance of social power and wealth for well-being and advocate redistributing power and wealth by mobilizing community resources to aid individuals, groups, and organizations. As a newer specialty area, community psychology emerged differently in Canada and the USA.

Canada

Although the term "community psychology" was used at the Swampscott Conference for Community Mental Health, held near Boston in 1965, and is sometimes thought to have originated there (Revenson & Seidman, 2002), **William Line** (1897–1964) introduced the term "community psychology" in 1951 to capture the way that Canadian Psychology, as he conceived it, had developed into a science of social policy (Babarik, 1979). In the 1940s and 1950s, Line and some colleagues at the University of Toronto promoted community research and action.

Even earlier, the psychologists who gathered in 1939 to form the Canadian Psychological Association (CPA) stated a commitment to studying people in the context of their communities. From the early twentieth century, public mental health education and social interventions were integral to some segments of Canadian Psychology. After World War II, the

Canadian Mental Health Association, supported by Line, provided the World Health Organization with a definition of mental health as involving social, physical, mental, and economic well-being. In addition, UNESCO commissioned Line to create the International Institute for Child Study, which developed the model for the Head Start programme that was instituted in several nations.

Although Canadian community psychology originally had international impact, psychologists at Toronto turned to experimental and biological studies in the mid 1950s. Graduate training in community psychology has remained available in a few Canadian programmes, but today few psychologists are aware of the subdiscipline and community psychologists constitute a small minority in Canadian Psychology (Walsh-Bowers, 1998).

USA

Along with the community mental health movement, the war on poverty, and the civil rights movement, US community psychology emerged within the political and cultural climate of the 1960s. Psychologists recognized that service delivery was uneven with the poor receiving no treatment or only custodial care in mental hospitals, and the middle and upper classes receiving private therapy. In 1955, the National Institute of Mental Health in the USA funded a postdoctoral programme in community mental health under the leadership of German-American psychiatrist Erich Lindemann (1900–1974) to promote mental health for all of society.

George Albee (1921–2006) was another US pioneer and champion of preventative mental health in the community psychology tradition. He showed that there would always be a shortage of mental health personnel for individuals needing individual psychotherapy, but he argued that addressing housing, nutrition, education, and drug use could alleviate psychological disorder effectively.

By 1977, two seminal texts were published which consolidated the theory and practice of the field. Julian Rappaport's *Community Psychology: Values, Research, and Action* and Kenneth Heller and John Monahan's *Psychology and Community Change* presented basic principles and values. The authors viewed people as inextricably linked with social systems and acknowledged that Psychology is a belief system that has implicit social values.

In the 1980s, in the USA, with a decade of "Reaganomics" and government retreating from its role in solving social problems, activism and visions of grand social change became unpopular in the public eye. During that time, there was a move in community psychology away from prevention towards empowering people to develop community resources. In collaboration with schools, neighbourhoods, hospitals, and community agencies, some community psychologists developed projects to empower people, marginalized by poverty and physical and mental disabilities, to find their own solutions.

Section conclusion

Rather than function as "architects of adjustment" (Napoli, 1981), community psychologists see themselves as architects of social change or social justice. However, critics argue that typically community psychologists do not define clearly what they mean by these terms nor do they challenge the socioeconomic foundations of society directly. Like other applied and professional psychologists, community psychologists have adopted values of mastery,

Box 8.2 **Cultural deprivation**

The concept of deprivation is the basis for Head Start and similar programmes in the USA and Canada. Targeting low-income families, these programmes aim to increase children's readiness for school.

During the 1960s and 1970s, when racial prejudice and racism remained a major societal concern for psychologists, a debate surfaced in Psychology over the role of "nature vs. nurture." Advocates of the nurture side argued that minorities, aboriginal peoples in Canada, or Native Americans in the USA, for instance, are not genetically inferior in intelligence, but are living in "culturally deprived" environments. Those who supported an explanation weighted towards nature refuted the environmental position.

The term "cultural deprivation," however, deserves attention. First, the term can imply a cultural environment stripped of everything valuable. "Deprived" refers to not having privileges, usually the privileges of White middle-class life. Yet, every cultural group has its own sources of cultural enrichment.

Researchers and educators made assessments based on values of the dominant culture. Confronted with a different culture, they concluded that First Nations peoples and African Americans were culturally deprived and deficient. Historically, some clinical, community, developmental, educational, school, and social psychologists supported this covertly prejudiced ideology.

control, power, and progress (Revenson & Seidman, 2002), aligning themselves with contemporary public interests and forging an identity of expertise around those concerns. For example, some studies exclusively focus on lower-income communities when investigating teen-pregnancy or promote ideas of "cultural deprivation" in programmes such as Head Start (see Box 8.2).

During the 1990s community psychologists became more self-critical. They began discussing issues of feminism and cultural diversity, attempting to make them central to their community research and action. Others raised awareness of diverse notions of empowerment, strength, prevention, and what counts as context. The methodology and research focus of community psychology moved from an "androcentric, heterosexist, European-American worldview to a more social-constructionist perspective," including more qualitative and context-sensitive research approaches (Revenson & Seidman, 2002, p. 16).

Currently, community psychologists remain focused on primary prevention, cultural contexts, strengths, and community resources. Some adherents advocate adopting the language and practice of social justice to ensure that community psychologists fulfill their promise of social change (e.g., Prilleltensky & Nelson, 2009). But whether community psychologists actually can engage in social justice, given Psychology's and their own specialty's history of avoidance of challenging the socioeconomic status quo, remains questionable.

Psychopharmacology

Psychopharmacology involves the use of drugs to treat mental disorders. It is the result of a collaboration of biochemists, psychiatrists, pharmacologists, neurophysiologists, neurochemists, and pharmaceutical companies (Jacobsen, 1986). The strong tendency towards understanding mental disorder as neurochemical means there are power and wealth in the production and distribution of psychopharmacological treatments (Cosgrove, Krimsky, Vijayaraghavan, & Schneider, 2006).

Applied research on brain, behaviour, and neurochemistry has been and continues to be heavily funded by pharmaceutical companies with vested interests (Cosgrove *et al.*, 2006). In the USA, pharmaceutical companies were reported to fund 70 per cent of all clinical drug trials. Thus, pharmaceutical companies wield substantial power over the conceptualization and treatment of mental disorders.

Prescription privileges for psychologists

Many clinical psychologists work with clients who are taking medications, regularly addressing medication issues and making referrals for prescriptions in concert with family physicians and psychiatrists. Some argue that this practice would be more efficient if psychologists were permitted to prescribe medications directly.

Since the 1980s, US clinical psychologists have pressed for prescription privileges and for training in the administration of pharmaceuticals for treatment of mental disorder. Other non-physicians, they argue, such as dentists, podiatrists, and optometrists, have the legal authority to prescribe a limited class of drugs. In New Mexico, Louisiana, and the US territory of Guam, doctoral psychologists now have the same prescription rights as psychiatrists – provided that psychologists take 450 hours of course work, pass an exam, and have their prescriptions approved by a psychiatrist for two years before they prescribe independently.

Critiques

Medication has been the primary treatment for persons with severe and long-term psychiatric disorders. However, arguably, these individuals need adequate income, suitable housing, and social support to address psychological disorder. Critics, such as those involved in the anti-psychiatry movement of the 1960s and feminists in the 1970s, have pointed to the history of physicians using psychotropic drugs to socially control segments of the population, many of whom live under conditions of social oppression, financial dependence, or abject poverty (Abma, 2004). Some claim that physicians narrowly focus on the physical and prescribe drugs while interpersonal and social health concerns are ignored (Szasz, 1970).

A further concern of psychologists is the ease with which medication can be prescribed compared to the difficult work of psychotherapy. The quickness of writing a prescription could lead to over-prescribing. A nation-wide study in the USA showed that, although the percentage of the population being treated for depression tripled between 1987 and 1997, nearly three-quarters of patients in 1997 received only medication for depression, whereas about one-third did in 1987 (Olfson *et al.*, 2002).

Some psychologists argue that drugs, such as Prozac, do not deal with the underlying causes of mental health disorders, as symptoms return when medications are discontinued. Other psychologists believe that a combination of medications and psychological treatment, rather than either medication or therapy alone, is best in managing pain, attention deficits, and thought disorders.

However, for many conditions, like depression and anxiety, psychotherapy alone has been shown to be more cost-effective and to provide better resistance to relapse than pharmacological approaches (Arnett, 2006) and is not complicated by side-effects. Serious side-effects of psychotropic medications can include incidents of deeper depression, cardiovascular disease, suicide, and even homicide. For instance, a US federal court jury in 2001 found that the producer of Paxil, a common antidepressant, was responsible for a man killing himself and three family members; family survivors were awarded $8 million in damages.

A prominent English psychiatrist, David Healy (2002), has long contended that pharmaceutical corporations have a duty to warn about the risks of suicidal ideation and or violent behaviour from the use of Paxil, Prozac, and other SSRIs (selective serotonin reuptake inhibitors). But when Healy presented data linking SSRIs to increased risk for suicide for certain patients, he temporarily lost his job contract at the University of Toronto, because the university received funding and donations from a pharmaceutical corporation.

Section conclusion

If psychologists do acquire prescription privileges, then their research and clinical decision-making are likely to become affected significantly by the influence of pharmaceutical companies. For example, the *Diagnostic and Statistical Manual of Mental Disorders* (DSM) is used by psychiatrists and psychologists to group experiences into diagnostic categories. However, the panel members who advise on diagnostic criteria have extensive ties with the pharmaceutical industry (Cosgrove *et al.*, 2006). In the DSM-IV-TR (2000), *all* professionals who determined criteria for psychological disorders had professional-corporate connections to drug companies by way of accepting research funding or honoraria, having equity holdings in drug companies, being patent or copyright holders of drugs, or receiving gifts such as travel grants and research materials.

Considering how psychiatric research and education have deteriorated and lost credibility through association with the pharmaceutical industry, policies and procedures have been suggested for psychologists to preserve academic and clinical integrity (Antonuccio, Danton & McClanahan, 2003) Policies to support integrity when conducting research funded by a pharmaceutical company include: maintaining availability of raw data, independence in research design, the right to publish the results, limits on purchasing advertising space in academic journals, and no sponsorship of continuing education. Other scholars suggest that journals introduce conflict-of-interest disclosure requirements, which now has become quite common (Cosgrove *et al.*, 2006).

> **Small-group discussion.** What is your position on whether psychologists should have the legal right to prescribe medication?

Part 4 conclusion

The second half of the twentieth century has been a time of further professional specialization in multiple areas of applied psychology: forensic, sport, environmental, health, community, and psychopharmacological. Specialized training has developed in each of these areas with some of them moving towards credentialling and regulation. Many communities throughout the world have accepted these new areas of psychological expertise. Nevertheless, practitioners in each subdiscipline face conceptual, ethical, and political problems related to their specialty. Although there are some exceptions, psychologists affiliated with these newer specialty areas tend to ignore the larger socioeconomic context within which they work and the ways in which they directly or indirectly encourage the recipients of their services to adjust to society's expectations.

Part 5 | # Ethics in professional psychology

The expansion of Psychology into professional realms eventually led to statements of ethical values and codes of conduct. Among the many taken-for-granted notions in professional psychology is that psychologists know how to, and do, behave ethically in their relationships with clients and patients. Professionals wield considerable social influence and have appealed to scientific principles to establish their legitimacy. Laypeople also tend to believe that professionals who claim scientifically supported foundations for their expertise are better equipped to solve physical health, mental health, and social problems than the laity (Lenrow & Cowden, 1980). But experts' privileged position vis-à-vis laypeople opens the possibility for unethical practices.

Psychologists' conceptions of human behaviour are played out in the relationships that they establish and maintain with patients, clients, consultees, community groups, and research participants. Although the overarching values of the profession include respecting human dignity and protecting human rights, psychologists have been trained to function from a supposedly value-free position of objective detachment (Hobbs, 1965). When striving for neutrality in professional relationships, psychologists sometimes avoid the inherently value-laden and emotionally involving nature of such relations. Ethical misconduct might result.

Capacity for harm

Although one might assume that all professional psychologists engage in ethical relations with their clientele, ethical malpractice does occur. It can take either gross or subtle forms. Currently, there is a lack of consensus regarding how to detect harm and what to do about it when it occurs (Dimidjian & Hollon, 2010).

Gross harm

An obvious instance of grossly unethical behaviour occurs when therapists act on their sexual attraction to their clients by engaging in sexual activity with them (Seto, 1995). Surveys of practising psychologists in the USA have shown that, although only a small percentage of respondents reported sexual intimacies with clients, sexual relations with clients remain a serious social problem for the profession. The suffering that clients endure as a consequence of these exploitive relationships can resemble post-traumatic stress disorder.

Gross harm also can take the form of unintended negative outcomes (Mays & Franks, 1985). For example, depressed clients might deteriorate in treatment, or improvements in clients might precipitate dissolution of marriages or intimate relationships. Negative outcomes are termed *iatrogenic effects*, meaning negative effects from psychotherapy or psychological treatments (Barlow, 2010; Illich, 1976; Morgan, 1983).

Subtle harm

Subtle types of harm perhaps occur with greater frequency than gross misconduct. For example, at the start of assessment or treatment, psychologists can fail to adequately inform recipients of their rights regarding services provided. Psychologists can neglect to maintain confidentiality about client disclosures or test scores. In therapy sessions, psychologists can go beyond the limits of their understanding of the client's state by making untimely interpretations that the client might experience as hurtful, by rigid adherence to the application of psychotherapy techniques, or by encouraging inordinate dependency on the therapist (Castonguay, Boswell, Constantino, Goldfried, & Hill, 2010).

Psychologists' ethics codes

Codes of ethics for psychologists are not only relatively recent developments in the evolution of the profession but initially were created to reassure the public of professional psychologists' competency (Hobbs, 1965). Hence, the purpose of developing a professional code of ethics might have as much to do with ensuring the longevity of a given professional group as with the safety of recipients of professionals' services (Pettifor, 1996).

Ethical values and codes of conduct have been set out to guide psychological activities. But general "ethical values," such as compassion and justice, are distinct from specific "codes of conduct" that provide guidelines for professional behaviour (Pettifor, 1996). "Ethical dilemmas" pertain to situations where ethical values conflict, such as when client confidentiality needs to be tempered by the duty to warn others of the client's intentions to harm.

The ethical guidelines of professional psychology are constructed to demonstrate professionalism, aptitude, and expertise. For example, psychologists do not provide a service, if it is inappropriate or unnecessary. In addition, many professional psychologists provide some services *pro bono* – free for the good of society – out of a sense of social responsibility.

The APA code

In 1948, the APA formed the Committee on Ethical Standards for Psychology to create the first set of ethical standards for psychologists. The committee surveyed a representative sample of its members concerning actual professional activities and critical incidents concerning ethics. The belief was that an empirically derived set of standards would render a statement of ethics relevant and applicable and promote ethical behaviour better than ethical imperatives developed by a committee (Pope & Vetter, 1992). The APA code based on this research appeared in 1953.

The original code prescribed conduct in specific domains, such as consent and confidentiality. In subsequent years refinements of the code appeared, expanding coverage of clinical

Table 8.1 CPA approach to clinical ethics

I. Respect for the dignity of persons	Informed consent, confidentiality, considerations for vulnerable persons
II. Responsible caring	Psychologists' competency, minimal harm to clients
III. Integrity in relationships	Psychologists' honesty, avoidance of conflict of interests
IV. Responsibility to society	Professional conduct, collegial relationships, responsibilities to local community and society

areas of conduct as well as research. Currently, the APA code includes a statement of ethical principles along with specific and elaborate standards and rules. In the 1970s and later, psychology associations in other nations also developed codes of ethics (Lunt, 1999).

The CPA code

For decades, Canadian psychologists relied on the APA code until they developed their own in 1986, which they revised in 1991 (Sinclair & Pettifor, 2001). Although similar to the APA model, the CPA code is distinct in that it rests on four foundational principles of ethics, indebted to Immanuel Kant's ethical theory, which are ordered hierarchically beginning with the most basic.

The intention of the CPA code is for psychologists to rely upon an understanding of the relevant principles and their respective values. In turn, the principles and values are used as the basis for ethical decision-making in relation to specific standards. Thus, each principle subsumes common ethical values from which particular issues and standards flow, as shown in Table 8.1.

According to the CPA code, when ethical principles are in conflict, psychologists are to depend on the ordering of the principles. For example, respect for the dignity of persons, which stresses moral rights, is the first principle invoked when considering applications to particular instances. Furthermore, clinicians employ **three steps** analogous to cognitive problem-solving:

- Identify the relevant issues and practices.
- Assess risks and benefits associated with possible courses of action.
- Evaluate the action taken.

Clinical ethics in critical perspective

The APA and CPA codes of ethics deal with important issues in clinical services, but their codified approaches to clinical ethics present several problems.

There are **two questionable assumptions** in the APA code (Hobbs, 1965):

- The criteria for judgments about what is ethical depends on consensus derived from professional traditions, not from public notions of morality and virtue.

- Implicit belief in the ethical neutrality of science and in the purely objective vision of scientifically trained psychologists contradicts the view that psychological science never can be free of human interests, values, and ideologies.

The APA and CPA codes share **four additional problems**:

- They are reactive in nature, directed at transgressions, instead of being proactive and directed at improvement and prevention (Prilleltensky, Rossiter, & Walsh-Bowers, 1996).
- They focus on professionals' perspectives and privileges rather than include clients' rights. Ethical norms advise practitioners to "do no harm" and "protect confidentiality" (Pope, Keith-Spiegel, & Tabachnik, 1986). But emphasizing the ethical rights of *clients*, such as the right to the least intrusive, least restrictive intervention and the right to refuse treatment (Tutty, 1990), would balance professionals' power.
- The APA and CPA codes fail to address the social context in which ethical issues and dilemmas are played out. Feminist psychologists, for example, note that oppressive social realities, such as sexism and racism, are inadequately addressed (e.g., Lerman & Porter, 1990). Professional psychologists operate from positions of privilege, but do not seem to respond to the full diversity of humankind, most of whom are in vulnerable social-political positions (Pettifor, 1996).
- The trend in the USA and Canada is for professional psychologists to work in private practice, making a profit, which can affect ethical practice. Moreover, when working for "managed care" businesses, psychologists are likely to encounter conflicts between their ethical principles and the employer's demands (Pettifor, 1996).

Yet the ethics literature in Psychology contains very little discussion about the social context of ethical decision-making for clinical situations, including professionals' places of work. Some investigators have argued that sound ethical decision-making does not consist of a lone clinician making a choice. Rather, it is a social process of understanding ethical dilemmas and relevant principles, values, and standards of practice in relationship with other professionals (e.g., Rossiter, Walsh-Bowers, & Prilleltensky, 2002).

However, the reality is that even when professionals have time in which to discuss ethical questions, they typically are anxious about being judged as professionally inadequate if they acknowledge ethical misgivings. Particularly in organizational settings, the tacit belief of mental health workers seems to be that a competent therapist is one who already knows the answers to ethical questions (Rossiter *et al.*, 2002). Yet professionals desire a safe space in which to discuss their ethical concerns without fear of judgment and surveillance by supervisors. By a safe space, clinicians mean small-group discussion with trustworthy peers, but that would require managers fostering an organizational climate conducive to the safe discussion of professional ethics.

In 1999, the British Association for Counselling halted developing a code of ethics out of concern that increasing professionalization brings with it the institutionalization of practices. Professionalization could pressure practitioners to look to their institution to determine how to behave (Dryden *et al.*, 2000). Instead of practitioners reasoning out the best course of action for a specific situation, interpreting moral principles, and taking personal responsibility, they might follow an imposed professional code of conduct reflexively. However, such unreflective obedience to authority could promote dependency, increase demand for more detailed guidelines, and result in negative responses to innovation and perceived professional deviancy.

Part 5 conclusion

Although ethical issues seem most obvious in the work of applied and professional psychologists, all branches of Psychology encounter ethical problems and dilemmas. However, disciplinary ethical codes might not provide sufficient intellectual and moral preparation for psychologists to engage in sound ethical decision-making. Some literature on psychologists' experiences with practising ethics indicates that the social context in which psychologists are called upon to reflect ethically on their actions and behave accordingly requires as much consideration as individual practitioners' deliberations.

Furthermore, a major deficiency of current ethical conceptions in Psychology, arguably, is the relatively marginalized position of the ethical principle of responsibility to society. This deficiency will need to be rectified, if the increasingly popular call for psychologists to practise social justice is to be actualized. In short, it appears that more reflective inquiry is necessary concerning the moral foundations and societal ramifications of applied and professional psychologists' ethical principles and their practical applications.

Part 6 Thematic review

Two themes appear to summarize the various applications of Psychology to society historically: **unreflective faith in the scientific basis of social and professional applications of Psychology expertise** and **alliance with the societal status quo**.

Unreflective faith in the scientific basis of social and professional applications

Social applications of psychological knowledge are fraught with the potential for ethically and politically dubious practices. One root of applied and professional psychologists' questionable ethical conceptions and practice might be the assumption that psychological expertise resides only with scientifically trained and credentialled psychologists. Historically, psychologists have adhered to the belief that adoption of empirical methods, principally quantitative experimentation, which distinguishes them from the laity, provides psychologists with sufficient knowledge for making claims to professional expertise. But laypeople have their own base of knowledge and perspectives that ought to be respected, and psychologists' faith in their presumed scientific expertise can border on scientism.

Relatedly, generations of psychologists have shown considerable confidence in their capacities to advise individuals, community groups, businesses, and governments. Simultaneously, this confidence has enhanced the authority and legitimacy of Psychology across diverse cultural contexts and has situated psychologists at the centre of "the psychological society." Indeed, psychologists engage in professional applications, because they believe that their presumed scientific knowledge about individuals' subjective experience can benefit human welfare and society's purposes. In this sense the discipline can contribute to emancipation.

Alliance with the societal status quo

Since the inception of applied and professional psychology and the emergence of a "psychological society" (Hale, 1980), practitioners evidently believed that they occupied a valued niche as purveyors of a technology that could enhance prosperity and well-being. They expressed their commitment to human welfare paternalistically through social control by shaping individuals' adjustment to society and extant social mores. Invoking their scientific expertise and projecting an aura of political neutrality, psychologists have employed an administrative technology of social management (Drunen & Jansz, 2004b).

In the US context the mechanical metaphor that was central to behaviourism facilitated external manipulation of personal adjustment to the social order. Psychologists believed that the most expedient route to citizen adjustment was to focus on behavioural control and to abandon introspection and the life of the mind. For example, the primary value of the Hawthorne experiments, within the dominant perspective, was the alleged positive adjustment of workers to their jobs when they received special attention. Individuals who failed to adapt to society then required psychological intervention. Nearly a century later the discipline's applied orientation has expanded, now under the aegis of cognitive behaviourism and positive psychology.

Yet psychological applications can be lucrative for practitioners and are laden with ethical and sociopolitical ramifications. Intentionally or not, psychologists encourage adaptation to socioeconomic conditions of individualistic consumption of disposable commodities. In effect, psychological applications reinforce individuals' adjustment to the societal status quo. Thus, if psychologists' faith in scientific expertise is not tempered by critical and ethical reflection, professional applications of Psychology might contribute to exploitation and oppression rather than emancipation.

Summary

In Part 1 we discussed how social-historical influences, such as war, industry, and commerce, influenced the global rise of psychologists' presumed expertise and their agenda of applying Psychology to society. We also noted the history of psychological applications in the context of industrial and commercial interests and the two world wars, the Cold War, and the global war on terror. Rather than a completely objective enterprise, applied and professional psychology cannot but help reflect society's interests.

In Part 2 we addressed the historical professionalization of Psychology, concentrating on four of the oldest specializations: industrial/organizational (I/O), school psychology, intelligence testing, and counselling psychology. I/O psychologists played roles in the scientific management of assembly-line industries, vocational guidance, research on work productivity and human relations, and personnel counselling. School psychologists used testing to classify children, but testing rests on different definitions of intelligence and different approaches to assessing it. Counselling psychologists, who deal with problems of adjustment and originally were employed in educational institutions, now are affiliated with diverse settings.

In Part 3 we considered the largest and most influential branch of applied and professional psychology, clinical psychology. We described the early modern history of mental health practices and the role of psychiatry in them. Then we noted how the new profession of psychology gained a foothold in psychotherapy practice, the problems associated with deinstitutionalization of the mentally ill, various theories of treatment to which psychologists made contributions, and the commonalities across treatment models that has led some clinical psychologists to pursue integration of psychotherapies.

In Part 4 we discussed the history of relatively new specialty areas. Forensic psychologists have contributed to law enforcement and the criminal-justice system. Sport psychologists have investigated sport behaviour and its physiological effects on psychological factors. Environmental psychologists have shifted from studying how individuals situate themselves in environments to how individuals and groups practise environmental sustainability. In the spirit of health promotion health psychologists have focused on strengthening individuals' health behaviours. Inspired by prevention, empowerment, and the desire for progressive social change, community psychologists have practised research and action with individuals, groups, and communities. Some clinical psychologists have sought prescription privileges for psychotropic medication, but this expansion of clinical psychologists' expertise has advantages and disadvantages and threatens the domain of medicine and its branch of psychiatry.

In Part 5 we examined professional ethics in Psychology. We considered psychologists' capacity for gross and subtle forms of harm or ethical malpractice. Then we described traditional ways of understanding clinical ethics, comparing the APA and CPA approaches to general ethical principles and specific ethical standards. We discussed the social contextual realities, such as organizational climate, that can affect psychologists' ethical decision-making. Lastly, we noted that the ethical principle of responsibility to society has received short shrift in psychologists' discourse on ethics.

In Part 6 we present two summary themes concerning the social function of applied and professional psychology: unreflective faith in the scientific basis of social and professional applications, and alliance with the societal status quo. Application of psychological knowledge became an instrument for strengthening individual adjustment to the social order. Social and professional applications of Psychology can lead to emancipation or exploitation, partly because psychologists have insisted that their expertise distinguishes them from ordinary citizens.

Sample essay questions

1. Imagine that you are a clinical psychologist and you are about to treat a member of an ethnocultural group that is in a minority position in your nation. What considerations would you keep in mind when formulating and administering your treatment approach?

2. In your opinion, what do you believe should be applied and professional psychologists' responses to the clinical and social significance of the relationship between health and its social determinants (e.g., inequitable income distribution)?

3. Imagine that the jurisdiction in which you live permits trained and certified clinical psychologists to prescribe psychotropic medication. Describe what your position would be on the matter of such psychologists prescribing drugs that purportedly enhance cognitive performance.

RECOMMENDED READING

The various encyclopaedias and handbooks of Psychology contain ample material on applied psychology, professional psychology, and professional ethics. A value-based, critical assessment of the various fields of applied and professional psychology, such as clinical, community, counselling, educational, and health psychology, is Prilleltensky and Nelson's (2002) book, *Doing psychology critically: Making a difference in diverse settings*. For interested readers, Bryden (1992) addresses the underlying assumptions of the professional psychology enterprise. A special issue of *Canadian Psychology* (Berwald, 1998) was devoted to anticipated issues of the Canadian workplace for industrial/organizational psychologists.

ONLINE RESOURCES

Both the APA and CPA websites contain links to matters of professional and research ethics: www.apa.org/topics/ethics/index.aspx and www.cpa.ca/aboutcpa/committees/ethics/.

9

Human-science psychologies: psychoanalysis

Chapter outline

Introduction

Alongside developments in natural-science Psychology there emerged a rather different trend in psychological thought and practice known as psychoanalysis. Nineteenth-century philosophy, medicine, and physiology formed the context in which Sigmund Freud developed a theory of unconscious psychological dynamics. Many previous thinkers promoted the idea of unconscious psychic processes, but Freud creatively integrated these ideas into a complex theoretical system. Although he intended it as a natural science, with various practitioners understanding and interpreting it, psychoanalysis evolved into a human science of subjectivity. Many natural-science psychologists have been dismissive of much of psychoanalysis, but some claim that its diverse theories continue to have an enduring influence on psychological thought.

In this chapter, we begin by considering pre-psychoanalytic constructions of unconscious phenomena, emphasizing how Freud was not the first to theorize unconscious processes. Then we review the social, cultural, and political context of Freud's life to situate the emergence of his ideas. Next you will encounter different threads of psychoanalytic thought and a range of key thinkers. We consider the analytical psychology of Carl Jung, followed by analysts who stressed the sociopolitical, the ego, object relations, postmodern thinking, and gender. Lastly, we examine how psychoanalysis has been received and uniquely developed in different cultural contexts and discuss the possibilities for psychoanalysis in scientific and professional Psychology.

The **aims** of this chapter are to describe:

- Some of the historical context of the psychoanalytic movement.
- The historical and continuing struggle of psychoanalysts of diverse theoretical perspectives.
- Complementary and competing notions such as: drive theory, father-centred psychology, ego psychology, object relations, intersubjectivity, pre-Oedipal child psychology, mother-centred psychology, and the feminization of psychoanalysis.
- The scholarly work and the clinical applications of different theories of psychoanalysis.
- The international scope, scientific nature, and feminist perspectives on psychoanalysis, and its relationship to natural-science and human-science Psychology.
- Themes that summarize the cultural, intellectual, and practical import of the story of psychoanalysis: illumination of the psychological interior, and Psychology's ambivalent relationship with psychoanalysis.

Historical conceptions of unconscious phenomena

Often, psychoanalysis is considered the product of Freud's self-analysis and clinical work. However, psychoanalysis arose in the context of nineteenth-century developments in biology, neurology, anthropology, psychology, psychotherapy, psychiatry, and philosophy (Ellenberger, 1970; Shamdasani, 2003). Here we consider pre-psychoanalytic investigations into unconscious phenomena driven by interests in the fields of philosophy, science, and medicine.

Philosophical and scientific context

From the seventeenth to the nineteenth century there was considerable interest in private mental states and unconscious processes. For example, the philosopher Gottfried Leibniz, the psychophysicist Gustav Fechner, and the psychologists Wilhelm Wundt and William James studied these phenomena. Previous scholars proposed many concepts that Freud systematized in his theory, but the precise sources for his synthesis cannot be determined.

Investigating how ideas move from unconsciousness to consciousness, Johann Herbart proposed that an idea weakened by inhibition could sink below the threshold of consciousness. He provided a mechanical description of ideas having energy independent of external forces and coming to consciousness when they combine or compete with other ideas. Also, Friedrich Beneke explained how stimuli can leave a trace in unconsciousness and resurface into consciousness in the presence of another stimulus.

Although interested in the unconscious, Freud's predecessors did not tend to consider personal motivation. Herbart used the terms *repression* and *resistance* in his theory (R. Smith, 1997), but repression, in Freudian theory, refers to the policing and keeping away of unacceptable unconscious impulses. In language and through censorship the ego flees from itself to remove itself from dangerous instinctual demands (Habermas, 1972). Resistance, on the other hand, is more specific to the psychoanalytic situation and can take the form of patients' ambivalence about their progress in therapy (Frosh, 2002).

Romantic philosophers Johann Wolfgang von Goethe and Arthur Schopenhauer and the existential philosopher Friedrich Nietzsche also were interested in unconscious dynamics. Schopenhauer emphasized the importance of human sexuality and how it tricks the will in service of procreation (Ellenberger, 1970). Schopenhauer and especially Nietzsche used the notion of *sublimation* wherein sexual impulses are transformed into socially acceptable actions.

Significantly, **Eduard von Hartmann** (1842–1906), a German philosopher, interpreted Schopenhauer's concept of the autonomous, blind, dark will as "unconscious mind." Von Hartmann postulated unconscious forces that govern the universe and human action through physiological and psychological processes. Along with Schopenhauer and Goethe, he noted slips of the tongue as unconscious manifestations.

Some consider Freud as having linked Schopenhauer's and Hartmann's impersonal notions of the unconscious with personal history. In this view, Freud linked the unconscious with individual motives, personal meanings, and idiosyncratic desires rooted in one's life-history. Instead of providing explanations that transcend the ego, Freud conceived of the ego as the result of a specific local history with intentions that can be understood only in the context of that personal world. From philosophers' diverse but abstract and universal conceptions of mind, Freud forwarded a cultural shift towards a focus on subjectivity and deeply personal experience (Zaretsky, 2004).

Medical context

Towards the end of the ninteenth century, prominent medical and scientific interests also formed the intellectual context in which psychoanalysis developed. There was significant professional interest in hypnosis, the interface of conscious and unconscious mind, fragments of personality, mental energy, and *hysteria*. Historically, "hysteria" refers to a condition where physical symptoms are present that do not correspond to underlying physiology but are attributed to a psychic cause. Contemporaries explained hysteria in terms of sexual pathology, meaningful dreams, self-deception, repression, and hidden desires (Ellenberger, 1970; D. Murray, Kilgour, & Wasylkiw, 2000).

By the end of the nineteenth century throughout France, Germany, and later in England and the USA, there were many conceptions of dynamic unconscious psychology that developed outside formal psychiatry (Ellenberger, 1970). These conceptions emerged in explanations of possession, animal magnetism, hypnosis, somnambulism, hysteria, and multiple personality.

Models of the mind explaining these phenomena differed. Some proposed that the unconscious is open to an "extra-individual and mysterious realm" or "World Soul," past-life memories, spirits, or universal symbols (Ellenberger, 1970, p. 146). Some theorists conceived of a duality of mind, others a cluster of personalities. Methods used by mediums became of interest, such as trance-speech, automatic writing, and crystal-gazing. Of interest was the way these experiences reveal subliminal ideas, hidden memories, and general human psychology (Shamdasani, 2009).

By 1880 investigations of the unconscious mind received academic acknowledgment and were accepted by official medicine in the work of Jean-Martin Charcot and Pierre Janet. Charcot sought to understand hypnosis and hysteria. He gave spectacular demonstrations of hysteria; however, these are now considered to have little scientific value, because participants were so suggestible.

Janet explained how traumatic memories can form fixed ideas that are dissociated from consciousness. Treatment, for Janet, involved having the patient retrace a chain of unconscious fixed ideas through recognizing forgotten memories as they arise in dreams, hypnotic states, automatic writing, and automatic talking (D. Murray *et al.*, 2000). He coined the word "subconscious" and called his practice "psychological analysis."

Late nineteenth-century medicine also involved moral psychological treatment wherein madness was understood as moral degeneracy and clinicians appealed to the capacity for reason in treating psychologically disturbed individuals. By contrast, Freud, along with other late nineteenth-century physicians, was influenced by both the rise of neurology and romanticism. They understood madness in terms of unconscious desire wherein "the unconscious" refers to primitive parts of the brain that automatically govern reflexes, sleep, impulsivity, hypnotic states, crime, and drunkenness.

Interest in neurology and the influence of romanticism continued in the new world. In the USA, around 1900, Freud was mostly known as a junior collaborator of Breuer on work initiated by Janet (Fancher, 2000). Freud's work attracted independent attention when a group of Boston-area doctors led by **Morton Prince** (1854–1929) and James Jackson Putnam began to use psychotherapeutic techniques for hysteria. Prince, a US physician who specialized in neurology and abnormal psychology, was a friend and colleague of Janet (Ellenberger, 1970). Prince took up the work of understanding dissociation, trauma, multiple personality, and hypnotic states. He founded the *Journal of Abnormal Psychology* in 1906 and helped establish Psychology as an academic and clinical discipline.

However, Freud uniquely stressed the importance of retrospective meaning and the way a desirous mind shapes, and not merely records, experience. Lechte (2008) explains,

The psyche is thus a meaning structure before it is a physical entity. It has to do with symbolic processes, and so calls for interpretation. Once the element of interpretation is seen to be crucial to psychical life, a quantitative – and more latterly, a behaviourist – model of the psyche becomes inadequate. (p. 390)

Part 1 conclusion

Psychoanalysis arose within a context of Romantic and early existentialist philosophers reflecting on unconscious behaviour, on the one hand, and scholars conducting empirical investigations of unconscious phenomena, on the other hand. These investigations led to explanations of human thought in terms of associations, without positing *a priori* a faculty of reason. Rational conduct, served by the mechanism of association, was considered a matter of biological adaptation.

For Freud, as for many of his generation working in a medical context, biological explanations, including the inheritance of acquired characteristics, were fundamental. However, Freud uniquely emphasized unconscious psychology. Many credit him with initiating a cultural shift in individual subjectivity towards recognizing the power of deeply personal experiences that form motivation out of awareness.

Part 2   Sigmund Freud and the personal unconscious

Here we describe the social context of Freud's revolutionary work; some of the scientific investigations that led to his clarification of personal unconscious dynamics, including his theory of dreams and sexuality; aspects of psychoanalytic treatment; and the changing relationship between psychoanalysis and medicine, mental health, and society.

Social–intellectual context

Freud's understanding of human psychology is compatible with the intensely self-reflective tendencies of twentieth-century European societies (Zaretsky, 2004). Psychoanalysis tends to emphasize personal history, to deconstruct the identities that we are given, while inviting us to question authority and unconscious patterns of living. Freud's notion of the unconscious makes it impossible for the individual to be reduced to environmental contingencies, because in his framework early childhood and personal social conditions shape motives, generating a private world of symbolic meaning dynamically interacting with the observable.

As we have seen, Freud was influenced by both the natural-science and the human-science traditions. He took philosophy courses from Franz Brentano at the University of Vienna, studied neuroanatomy, and worked as a physician. In 1885, Freud won a fellowship to study with Charcot in Paris, where he investigated the origin of hysteria and the therapeutic potential of hypnosis. Later, Freud collaborated with physician **Joseph Breuer** (1842–1925) and, in *Studies on Hysteria* (1893–1895), they theorized how hysterics suffer from reminiscences.

Breuer had a patient, Bertha Pappenheim, known in the literature as "Anna O.," who seemed to improve when she entered a meditative state and spoke about her memories. Pappenheim called such talk "chimney-sweeping" (R. Smith, 1997, p. 710). She offered ideas about her condition that formed the basis of Breuer's understanding of catharsis and the importance of releasing psychic energy. However, Pappenheim's conceptual contribution went unacknowledged for many years.

Studies in Hysteria exemplified a prevailing notion in dynamic psychiatry that an idea split off from consciousness becomes repeated over and over in various ways (Zaretsky, 2004). In 1886 Freud developed a technique very similar to Pierre Janet's practice of psychological analysis, wherein the patient recalls an original traumatic event under hypnosis and then suggests that the symptom disappear (Ellenberger, 1970). Convinced that psychoanalysis developed from his own ideas, Janet was hurt and irritated when Freud did not acknowledge his work. Many have claimed that the theory and practice of psychoanalysis were modelled after the work of Janet. Nevertheless, Freud's work differs from nineteenth-century French psychiatric thought in stating that not only unconscious traumatic memories are at the root of neurosis but so too are unconscious wishes (D. Murray *et al.*, 2000).

Hysteria as a substitute for painful memories and the notion of a talking cure were not original ideas for dynamic psychiatry, but the notion of defence rooted in personal history was new. Breuer argued that if an idea was not conscious, it was because the individual was in a hypnotic state when the event occurred. But Freud postulated that hysteria was a defence against trauma rooted in a personal history of sexual experience (Zaretsky, 2004).

Freud's perspective was that the need and effort to repudiate wishes, not wishes or experiences per se, lead to neurosis. Departing from the influence of Charcot and Breuer, he began to develop a unique notion of defence as a way of keeping painful ideas unconscious in an attempt to protect oneself (Frosh, 2002). Thus, he came to see hysteria as originating in defence, not in trauma per se. Freud's interpretation, known as seduction theory, elicited some controversy in psychoanalytic circles since its inception (see Box 9.1).

> **Small-group discussion.** The seduction theory remains controversial even as it illuminates the problem of who is the best judge of what really happened to the patient. How can the analyst and patient work out the difficulty of judging the veracity of a patient's reports?

Theory

In his 1895 work, *Project for a Scientific Psychology*, Freud presented his first general theory of psychology. He proposed a correlation between psychological processes and

Box 9.1 **Seduction theory**

In two papers published in 1896 Freud claimed that hysteria and obsessional neurosis are the result of repressed memories of childhood sexual abuse (Esterson, 2002). But he abandoned this seduction theory in 1897, claiming that what is repressed is not the memory of a traumatic event but a taboo fantasy and impulse (S. Mitchell & Black, 1995). He meant that children typically do not experience sexual abuse, but all experience sexual fantasies that they defend against in healthy or unhealthy ways.

However, writer Jeffrey Masson (1984, 1988) charged that Freud abandoned the seduction theory because of fierce professional opposition to the notion of extensive child sexual abuse among his female patients, perpetrated by their relatives and family friends. Masson argued that Freud succumbed to peer pressure in claiming that his patients' allegations were fantasies. Furthermore, Masson alleged, subsequent genera-tions of psychoanalysts and psychotherapists adopted the belief that the best judge of what really happened to the patient is the analyst or therapist, not the patient. This position of power and influence, Masson claimed, is intrusive and potentially abusive.

Critics rejected Masson's assertions (Esterson, 2002). First, they argue, Freud did not deny the presence of childhood sexual abuse; rather, "what Freud repudiated was the seduction theory as a general explanation of how all neuroses originate" (Gay, 1988, p. 95). Second, concern about how seduction theory would be received was not a factor in Freud changing his sexual theory of neurosis to focus on forbidden fantasies rather than actual events (Ellenberger, 1970). Arguably, Freud's peers rejected his initial focus on child sexual abuse, not because of the social implications, but because the seduction theory contradicted the widespread belief that nervous disorders are predominately constitutional. They also objected to his basing his theory on the unreliable testimonies of people with neurotic disturbances under various levels of hypnosis (Esterson, 2002).

quantities of energy present in hypothetical brain structures (Ellenberger, 1970). Many concepts that emerged later in psychoanalytic theory first appeared in the *Project*. In this work Freud first wrote "on the drives, on repression and defense, on the mental economy with its contending forces of energies, and on the human animal as the wishing animal" (Gay, 1988, p. 78). He offered mechanistic explanations that developed into emotional and psychical understandings.

Dreams

By 1896 Freud began calling his practice psychoanalysis and, after his father died, he developed neurotic symptoms that he analyzed in terms of his unconscious wishes. Freud's symptoms ended when he completed an explanation of the principles of psychoanalysis in his famous 1900 work, *The Interpretation of Dreams* (Zaretsky, 2004). The psychoanalytic movement began when, after reading this work, several physicians expressed interest in working with Freud. A secret group of six invitees began weekly meetings in 1902, devoted to furthering the cause of psychoanalysis.

Freud understood dreams in terms of unacceptable fantasies. "The restricting agency that controls speech and action by day slackens its domination during sleep because it can rely on the suspension of motor activity" (Habermas, 1972, p. 223). But dreams are also guardians of sleep such that they disguise wishes in ways that will not disturb and awaken the dreamer. Freud did not propose that dreams literally represent wishes. Although dreams may be based on actual experiences, they are *symbolic* fantasies, the meaning of which is concealed in dreams and revealed through free association.

Sexuality

Freud then concentrated on theorizing unconscious processes of sexuality. He did not explain gender and sexual attraction as biologically fundamental but as the outcome of an individual psychical process in which the individual works out ambivalence and contradiction (Zaretsky, 2004). From Freud's perspective, "The coexistence in the same person of love and hate for the same object, is the most natural and most common of conditions" (Gay, 1988, p. 364). Neurosis, therefore, involves extremes of positive and negative feelings as well as the tendency to mistake fantasy as doing.

Freud's perspective on the role of memory and sexuality in neurosis received many favourable reviews. But before he published *Three Essays on the Theory of Sexuality* (1905), other scholars had presented similar ideas in the literature on sexology (Ellenberger, 1970). Freud contributed by explaining the repression of fantasies and memories, theorizing how the unconscious is socialized, describing psychotherapy as analysis of psychic resistance, and elaborating the meaning of libido (Frosh, 2002).

Practice

Prior to the development of Freudian psychoanalysis, hypnotism was a popular form of psychological treatment (Gay, 1988). The gradual modification of hypnosis into conscious association led to the practice of psychoanalysis (Ellenberger, 1970). Ultimately, Freud rejected hypnosis as a therapeutic technique, because patients are not entrusted with remembering and insight; "the hypnotic release of the unconscious only manipulates processes of consciousness" (Habermas, 1972, p. 251).

In classical Freudian analysis, patients free-associate while the analyst maintains a state of alert passivity or what Freud called "evenly hovering attention." As sessions develop, the analyst becomes a screen onto which patients project fears and desires. In a process known as *transference*, patients come to behave as if the analyst were someone from their past. Often, patients experience irrational expectations and feelings of love or hostility towards the analyst. Many hypnotists before Freud were aware of this phenomenon and the importance of rapport, but Freud seems to have been the first to make analyzing the transference a basic therapeutic technique (Ellenberger, 1970).

Analysis can be understood as self-reflection and moral insight (Habermas, 1972). The analyst offers an interpretation and insofar as patients recognize this interpretation in their interactions with the analyst, they can see their symptoms as the consequence of their own actions. The analytic situation removes the pressure of everyday life so patients can remember instead of enact psychological conflict. Lost portions of one's life are retrieved in this way.

"The analyst instructs the patient in reading his [*sic*] own texts, which he himself has mutilated and distorted, and in translating symbols from a mode of expression deformed as a private language into the mode of expression of public communication" (Habermas, 1972, p. 228). As such, psychoanalytic therapy can produce "reconciliation with excommunicated language" and potentially release us from dependence on existing power structures and set ways of thinking (Habermas, 1972, p. 245). In this way, ideology can be personally transformed.

Some forms of psychoanalysis that arose since Freud seek to foster adjustment and control; other forms try to cultivate a non-judgmental, reflective attitude towards the self, giving patients vocabularies and practices to counter social control, exposing illusions that serve forces of repression (J. Smith, 1990; R. Smith, 1997; Zaretsky, 2004). Arguably, Freud continues to be relevant to this day because, through self-reflection, psychoanalysis provides a unique way of disrupting assumptions and revising discourses.

Part 2 conclusion

Although many physicians and scholars considered unconscious phenomena before Freud, some claim that he was the first to systematically focus on personal history and the impact of desire on interpretation, working at the intersection of the biological and the symbolic (Zaretsky, 2004). Moreover, he openly broke with medicine, founding an independent school of thought with its own organization, journals, and training requirements. As the founder of psychoanalysis, Freud's thought had an enormous influence not only on generations of psychoanalysts but also on psychiatrists, psychologists, and Western culture in general. Many scholars consider him as one of the most important thinkers of the twentieth century, stimulating a major shift in thinking comparable to the thought of Karl Marx, Charles Darwin, and Friedrich Nietzsche (Ellenberger, 1970; R. Smith, 1997).

Part 3   Carl Jung and analytical psychology

Whereas Freud initiated a new science of the individual unconscious, Carl Jung, a Swiss psychiatrist, focused on collective dimensions of unconscious psychology. Many Jungians insist that Jungian "analytical psychology" is distinct from the lineage of psychoanalytic thinkers and should be considered on its own terms (Shamdasani, 2003; E. Taylor, 1996). However, more recently, Jungians in the USA are exploring overlapping interests across analytical and psychoanalytic theory and practice (Eisold, 2002).

After describing the social and intellectual context for Jung's perspective we outline two aspects of his general theory: archetypes and psychological types; describe his therapeutic analysis; and discuss the current significance of his work.

Social–intellectual context

Much of the information on Jung's life is coloured by a famous 1963 biography, *Memories, Dreams and Reflections* edited by Aniela Jaffé. This work was allegedly autobiographical; however, Jung never saw or approved it before publication (Shamdasani, 2003). Consequently, more professional biographies and documentary studies need to be considered (Elms, 2005).

There has been some controversy regarding Jung's role during German fascism. As President of the International Psychoanalytic Association (IPA) in 1933, Jung upheld the IPA's mandate to maintain international contacts. The German section of the IPA was pressured by the Third Reich to be sympathetic to Nazism and, during Jung's term as president, the IPA published explicitly anti-Semitic material. However, others believe that Jung mediated the situation as best he could, because the IPA was able to "shield not a few colleagues, Jews and others, who would otherwise have fallen foul of the Gestapo" (Ellwood, 1999, p. 62).

At first, Jung was admittedly naïve about National Socialism and believed it had positive potential. He was apt to make racial and national interpretations at the level of the collective unconscious, believing that bringing to consciousness the archetypal symbolism inherent in the movement signalled the potential for greater wholeness. However, before the war broke out, he warned against and outright condemned events developing in Germany as an apocalyptic and shameful tragedy (e.g., Jung, [1945] 1970). The Gestapo subsequently banned Jung's publications and listed him for extermination (Ellwood, 1999).

In his academic and clinical work, Jung emphasized how psychology is a science of subjective phenomena, such as the contents of consciousness, not objective realities (J. Clarke, 1992). Jung focused on the "symbol-making character of human psychology" establishing links among psychoanalysis, religion, ritual, myth, alchemy, astrology, and indigenous psychologies (Zaretsky, 2004, p. 99). Arguably, because he tried to bring together science and religion through psychology (Shamdasani, 2003), many academic psychologists and psychoanalysts marginalized his concepts and practices.

Originally, when Freud envisioned Jung as his successor, he believed that Jung's experiments with the Word Association Test would provide scientific evidence for psychoanalytic concepts, earning societal legitimacy for psychoanalysis (S. Mitchell & Black, 1995). However, Jung did not believe that experimentation was appropriate for investigating psychological experience. He argued that the world is the appropriate lab, and validity depends on value for living, not on scientific correctness (Shamdasani, 2003).

Whereas Freudian psychoanalysis includes elements of positivism, scientism, and Darwinism, Jungian analytical psychology is more aligned with romanticism and philosophy than natural science and medicine. Jung's way of thinking, influenced by the works of Immanuel Kant, Goethe, Schopenhauer, and Nietzsche, seems to have been well established before he met Freud (Ellenberger, 1970). Furthermore, although Jung worked closely with Freud for several formative years, Jung's most important ideas (e.g., the collective unconscious and archetypes) were formulated following his break with Freud.

Theory

Two important aspects of analytical psychology are archetypes and psychological types.

Archetypes

While working with patients with severe psychosis, Jung was struck by the frequent occurrence of patterns of symbolic expression in their delusions and hallucinations. He later understood these in terms of *archetypes* and the collective unconscious that all humans

Figure 9.1 In Jungian theory, a mandala, such as this Tibetan one, symbolizes the Self in its totality

share (Ellenberger, 1970). The archetype in itself is considered to be something fundamentally unknown that only comes to expression in the symbolism of certain emotions, images, and inherited cultural forms. Archetypal symbols are understood as having a transpersonal quality with meanings that do not arise directly from personal experience (Eisold, 2002).

Archetypal symbols are considered foundational for consciousness, limiting meaning but also making understanding possible. These symbols occupy a paradoxical position in that they manifest and are experienced in different ways by different cultures, yet they form a common ground of human experience. Jungians argue that this universal psychic heritage makes it possible to understand others despite radical differences of cultural and historical interpretation. The mandala, for example, is considered to be an archetypal symbol for the Self in its totality, as depicted in Figure 9.1.

Personality types

When Jung's *Psychological Types* was translated into English in 1923, many scholars received it with great acclaim as a new system of dynamic psychiatry. But behaviourists viewed it as the work of religious mysticism, a criticism that has prevailed in Psychology.

According to Jung, personality consists of a dominant type, introvert or extravert, which has **two pairs of functions**:

- Ways of perceiving: sensing (conscious attention) vs. intuiting (unconscious attention).
- Ways of evaluating: thinking (objectively) vs. feeling (subjectively).

For Jung, mental health depends on the balanced development of all the functions. Rigid reliance on dominant functions and repression of the others are thought to create mental health disorders.

Like archetypes, Jung's theory of psychological type limits yet allows for variation (Shamdasani, 2003). Types are abstractions meant to facilitate understanding of individuals; they are not meant to initiate a search for empirical instances. As such, Jung's theory is more about subjectivities than personalities.

General application of Jungian personality types to human relationships, including parenting and teaching, are popular. A widely used personality test in Anglo-American circles is the Myers-Briggs Type Indicator, derived from Jung's work on psychological types. In the test respondents identify their dominant and subordinate personality functions, including a third pair of functions that represent lifestyle: judging (orderly) vs. perceiving (spontaneously).

As helpful practically as the test might be, Jung did not intend that people's personality be typed in this way (Shamdasani, 2003). Evidently, he took a different approach with each one of his clients, depending on their personality and their needs (Ellenberger, 1970).

Practice

Jung compared psychotherapy to Christian confession in which the sinner reveals secrets in a presumably safe context. Also, he compared psychotherapy to alchemy with the mixing of conscious and unconscious material. He transformed free association into a method of active imagination that involves representing and integrating figures and insights from dreams through forming moral and ethical responses in daily life. Jung believed that dreams were not only unconsciously determined but also purposeful. He amplified the meaning of symbols with the help of comparative mythology and translated images into the language of consciousness to determine actions that could be taken in everyday life.

Although many Jungian analysts work to bring patients back to the present situation, some critics contend that Jung's therapy is overly preoccupied with spiritual development to the neglect of patients' histories, which frequently include trauma, abuse, and family violence (e.g., Masson, 1984). Nevertheless, some commentators believe Jung's work has contributed to social theory, providing psychological perspective on such themes as distribution of wealth, Third World development, and nationalism (e.g., Samuels, 1993). Jung elevated the psychological over the social and the political, and insisted that all transformation begins with the individual.

Part 3 conclusion

Jung can be seen as having integrated science with faith during a cultural crisis of meaning precipitated by the dominance of the scientific worldview (R. Smith, 1997). He advanced his concepts not as definitive truths, but as working models that are not discovered so much as projected onto nature. Archetypes and personality types illuminate and reflect ways of understanding human psychology. In this sense Jungian analysis is a hermeneutic science, interpreting the world and analyzing concepts that are products of the mind (J. Clarke, 1992).

Although Jung's experiments in word association gained notoriety a century ago, analytical psychology has played a marginal role in Psychology, most likely because of its commitment to exploring mythical and spiritual phenomena that natural-science psychologists find speculative if not hopelessly mysterious. In undergraduate curricula Jungian psychology is relegated to personality textbooks. But in other disciplines, such as religious studies and at Jungian institutes worldwide, scholars vigorously pursue ideas and applications of analytical psychology (Shamdasani, 2009).

Part 4 | Social theorists

In his social-political writing, Freud considered the relationship between psychology and civilization, questioning the pathology of society in works such as *Totem and Taboo*, *Group Psychology and the Analysis of the Ego*, *The Future of an Illusion*, *Civilization and its Discontents*, and *Why War?* Some psychoanalytic thinkers made central to their theorizing the connection among unconscious experience, internal conflict, societal influences, and politics. Most of the second-generation psychoanalysts in Vienna, Berlin, Budapest, and London were socialists (Young-Bruehl & Dunbar, 2009). In this part we concentrate on five social theorists in psychoanalysis: Alfred Adler, Karen Horney, Erich Fromm, Erik Erikson, and Wilhelm Reich.

Alfred Adler – individual psychology

A Viennese psychiatrist and founding member of Freud's original group, Adler was attracted to the biological aspects of Freudian theory. But he was Freud's first public critic and the first to leave the inner circle. Some scholars now consider Adler's "individual psychology" not as a version of psychoanalysis but as a psychology in its own right (e.g., Eisold, 2002).

In 1911, Adler initiated his own group, which had the character of a political movement focused on social problems. When Nazism became increasingly ominous in Austria in the early 1930s, he decided to move the centre of individual psychology to the USA where he and his family eventually settled (Ellenberger, 1970). Because his ideas were practical and concrete, US culture easily absorbed them.

Theory

Adler, like Jung, had ideas that were significantly developed prior to his being swept up by the psychoanalytic movement (Ellenberger, 1970). Since his youth Adler was attracted to Marxism. Primarily concerned with practical applications of theory, he linked psychoanalysis with social democracy and feminism, promoting the idea that physical illness and psychological neuroses have social and economic causes (Zaretsky, 2004).

Adler made important contributions to the theory of social medicine and argued that medicine's most important challenge is to be available to the poor. He developed ideas about organ inferiorities, masculine protest, social medicine, and the role of educational errors in the development of emotional disturbance. Physicians should be educators, he asserted, and education should instil a sense of confidence and courage in a child.

Adler called his psychoanalytic approach "individual psychology," because he viewed each human being as a unified whole with all parts striving together towards a common goal. He introduced the notion that aggression and striving for respect are primary drives, equally important to the drives for pleasure and for preservation of the species. Each person has a sense of self-respect, he claimed; when it is violated, sensitivity or neurosis develops. Poverty and discrimination are social examples of insults to a person's dignity. Thus, social conditions can evoke feelings of inferiority and the process of compensation.

However, Adler did not argue that striving for personal power was a primary drive, unless a person was neurotic and had no sense of community. Part of being an individual involves what he called "community feeling" whereby we sense the interdependence of everything and empathize with others. Sometimes community feeling is restricted to one's family or nation, but it can extend to all of humankind, natural objects, and the entire universe (Ellenberger, 1970). As such, the striving for superiority is not necessarily antagonistic to community feeling.

Interestingly, Freud agreed with Adler's formulation of inferiority and compensatory striving. However, he disagreed with Adler's proposition that guarding against feelings of inferiority and avoiding a passive, subordinate position are the only or even most important motives. In addition, the Freudian circle questioned sharp gender dichotomies and argued that the pleasure of submitting or being "under" can be as powerful as the desire to "be on top" (Zaretsky, 2004, p. 95).

Section conclusion

Although Freudians shunned Adler's professional practices of face-to-face conversation and direct interventions concerning the patient's style of life, later generations of psychoanalysts adopted some of his practices. Adler influenced European and US practices in psychotherapy, counselling, parent education, and teacher education. He and his colleagues applied their version of psychoanalysis in child-guidance clinics and schools, providing public education on mentally healthy living. In addition, community psychologists' concepts of the "psychological sense of community" and "empowerment" are indebted to individual psychology.

Although not a political activist per se, Adler was very much associated with the social-democratic (socialist) movement in Austria. He was very influential and accepted in Red Vienna and taught at People's Colleges there. He connected Marx's concept of alienation to his own concept of community feeling by recommending that each person's compensatory struggle to overcome the feeling of inferiority and to experience creative power should be integrated with that of all other people. He argued that only workers' full participation with one another in the conceiving and administering of the processes of production will overcome alienation (Murphy, 1949).

Adler's emphasis on social and political factors affecting an individual's development prefigured the social psychoanalytic focus of Karen Horney and Erich Fromm.

Karen Horney – female psychology

One of the first women of her generation admitted to medical school, Horney (1885–1952) received psychoanalytic training in Berlin from an associate of Freud. In 1920 she became a founding member of the Berlin Psychoanalytic Institute (Eckardt, 2005). After her immigration to the USA in 1932, due to Hitler's rise to prominence, Horney's attempts to challenge Freud became successful. The publication of her book, *New Ways in Psychoanalysis* (1939), stirred professional uproar (Eckardt, 2005).

Horney believed in the potential for personal development and adaptation throughout life and worked to include cultural and social forces in understanding human psychology. She emphasized the importance of specific causes of current anxieties rather than defences linked to childhood memories or fantasies. Because she positioned her views as incompatible with classical psychoanalysis, in 1941 she was expelled from the New York Psychoanalytic Society and founded her own association, emphasizing the impact of different cultural influences on psychological processes (Westkott, 1986).

Theory

Initially, Horney incorporated many of Freud's concepts into her work, but she was critical of his devaluation of women (Kurzweil, 1995). She also rejected Freud's assumption that there is an intrapsychic realm that can be understood independently of interpersonal relations and culture.

In 1922, Horney presented a paper in which she questioned the notion that penis envy was a fixed and universal characteristic of women. She did not dispute its existence but observed that penis envy could be due to social and cultural factors that make being a man preferable (Raphael-Leff, 2001). She argued that gender differences are due to patriarchal domination; consequently, women show a lack of confidence in their competencies and overemphasize the importance of "having a man." As such, she proposed the concept of "masculine complex" to encompass all the feelings women have because of sexism.

Contrary to the Freudian focus on genital differences between the sexes, Horney focused on the different roles that men and women play in reproduction (Zaretsky, 2004). She argued that men's awareness of this difference generates "womb envy" and an unconscious wish to give birth. She questioned whether men overcompensated in their achievements because of the relatively small role that they play in procreation.

Women's problems, Horney argued, arise not in childhood, but in adulthood when women become part of a cultural double-bind. Conflict occurs not between instinct and culture, but between expectations that women be affectionate, cooperative, nurturing, and supportive in order to achieve security in a capitalist culture that requires competition and shrewdness to become financially successful. As such, according to Horney, women's primary problem is dependency, not penis envy (Zaretsky, 2004).

Horney refused to call herself a feminist; rather, she insisted on promoting personal autonomy not gender loyalty. Nevertheless, her work on women's psychology had a significant influence on feminist psychological theory in the 1970s and beyond. For example, Jane Ussher (1997), a British psychologist, studied the phallocentric nature of representations and constructions of the feminine in pop culture. In line with Horney's thinking, Ussher explains how these representations are constructions of the "male gaze," created by men and women who have internalized patriarchal values of male dominance.

In a second phase of her work, Horney developed a clinically influential theory of anxiety. In her 1937 book, *The Neurotic Personality of Our Time*, Horney addressed the socially constructed nature of anxiety, theorizing that internal conflicts arise not because of instincts but because of social conditions. Societal structures and cultural values, especially those affecting the course of early development, precipitate internal conflicts.

Section conclusion

Horney contributed to the development of social psychoanalysis initially by stressing the psychological status of women in an androcentric culture and later by advancing a social explanation of anxiety. Like her colleague Fromm, Horney believed that mind, culture, politics, and economics are intertwined. She argued that aspects of patriarchal, industrial society potentially shatter young children's sense of security, potentially creating a variety of neurotic disorders. However, in other respects Fromm's psychoanalytic perspective on social–political psychodynamics is quite different from Horney's perspective.

Erich Fromm – social–political psychology

A psychoanalytic psychologist in Berlin whose work can be seen as a conceptual union of Freud and Marx (Burston, 1991), Fromm associated with social theorists at the University of Frankfurt who developed critical theory (see Chapter 12). This standpoint was of interest to many leftist-thinking psychoanalysts who investigated relationships between specific socio-economic conditions and conscious and unconscious dimensions of personality.

Many émigré psychoanalysts, such as Fromm, were not physicians. In 1934, when Fromm immigrated to the USA, a medical degree was required to practise psychoanalysis. Consequently, Horney expelled him from her training institute (Zaretsky, 2004). Nevertheless, he became a fixture at the New School for Social Research in New York and produced influential works for a general audience.

Theory

In *Escape from Freedom* (1941), Fromm situated psychoanalysis within a Marxian conception of history and an existentialist view of human nature (S. Mitchell & Black, 1995). He argued that different types of character develop at different points in history, depending on what is needed to perform under specific socioeconomic conditions. Fromm coined the term *social character* wherein personality characteristics are shaped by particular socio-economic systems. For example, in capitalist societies of the late nineteenth and up to the mid twentieth century, thrift and saving money were highly valued. This structural reality rendered the personality traits of hoarding and stinginess, associated with obsessive–compulsive tendencies, culturally adaptive.

In addition, individuals most suited to fascism would have a submissive attitude to authority, while those most resistant to fascism would be individuals raised in an environment of optimistic trust in unconditional love (Zaretsky, 2004). In the 1970s Fromm's notion of social character was updated to account for the more recent effects of monopoly capitalism on personality development (M. Maccoby, 1976).

Fromm also took an ethical–political stance with his patients (Burston, 1991). He observed that a central problem in society is that people live with profound dishonesty, lying to themselves and others to conform to social expectations. Psychoanalysis, he maintained, could offer more honest responses and a space in which to become more authentic. However, this development required analysts to be honest, aware of *counter-transference* (i.e., analysts' unconscious positive and negative attachments to patients), and open about how they feel about their patients.

Section conclusion

Fromm's blend of ethical–political, Freudian, and Marxian approaches was unique. In addition, he emphasized the need for relatedness, which aligned with later feminist notions of relationality and interconnectedness. However, mainstream US psychoanalysts and psychologists tended to ignore his concepts and neglect his qualitative studies on conformity and obedience to irrational authority, arguably because few US psychologists in his era regarded qualitative methods as scientific (Burston, 1991). Nevertheless, Fromm had some influence on the public through his several books.

Wilhelm Reich – political–economic psychology

An Austrian psychiatrist, Wilhelm Reich (1897–1957) made significant contributions to the theory of defences and argued that the individual could be a point of social transformation.

Theory

Whereas many Freudians described the sublimation of instinct as necessary for civilization, Reich proposed the socially radical idea that sublimation is a political pressure that reproduces existing power structures. Liberation of pleasure, then, is a path towards political freedom and happiness. By promoting more sensuous and humane relations, psychoanalysis, he believed, could radically transform social institutions.

In addition, Reich ([1942] 1973) developed the notion of *character armour*, observing that patterns of bodily movement result in psychological character embodied in muscular tension. He asserted that the embodied character of the ego was basically a conflict that had become solidified in the person, making one immune to pleasurable bodily sensations and defensive against full experience. In his therapeutic conception of "character analysis" Reich introduced what some ego psychologists later called "defence analysis." But unlike them, he explained that being out of touch with natural bodily sensations and impulses serves the existing social and economic order.

According to Reich, we learn to give up our pleasure to a leader, a religion, or an institution and do not take responsibility for our own sensuous experience. We become dead to pleasurable bodily sensations to sustain the responsibilities demanded of us. Dissociated from our bodies, we work hard, live in our minds, and plan for a better future, but are unable to enjoy the present moment. From an early age we learn to conform to society and obey authority other than our own. By internalizing the social order in our character we preserve the status quo.

Like Fromm and Horney, Reich claimed that society, not the individual, is problematic. A non-repressive society, not analysis of the ego, is necessary for personal liberation.

Dismantling the defensive character-armour that keeps natural expression repressed requires institutional reform.

Reich had a utopian vision that Freudian psychoanalysis in the appropriate political–economic climate, namely Marxism, could liberate people from sexual and psychological oppression, eliminating neurosis. Accordingly, Reich worked to liberate sexuality, challenged traditional family forms, and strived to make the private public in the name of greater authenticity and free expression. Instead of being driven to acquire power and wealth, with Marxist reforms, Reich argued that the body could become an instrument of pleasure, even in work. However, critics argue how economic scarcity limits potential for psychological emancipation. Reich did not seem to consider fully the tension between psychosexual liberation and political–economic organization (Baydala & Stam, 2004).

Furthermore, Reich understood the ego only as a locus of resistance, the instincts as benign, and analysis as a matter of interpreting the ego's resistance in order for the individual to be released from conflict and tension. By contrast, Freud argued that the ego is a source not only of resistance but also of "reason, self-knowledge, and instinctual modification" (Zaretsky, 2004, p. 172).

Section conclusion

During the 1930s psychoanalysts became increasingly conservative politically. Many believed the survival of their movement was endangered by linking psychoanalysis with political activity (Reich Rubin, 2003). At the 1934 meeting of the IPA, members repudiated any such link. Yet, with the rise of German fascism, other analysts asserted that a social and political perspective should be included. Nevertheless, the association expelled Reich for his radical ideas and political activities.

In sum, Reich expanded the Freudian idea that neurosis was caused by societal oppression and argued that politics is really about sexuality, sex education, family, and child-rearing (Zaretsky, 2004). Although Reich and Anna Freud (see below) agreed that defence mechanisms are important for understanding psychoanalysis, Reich's work was much more focused on the role of the family, sexuality, and political economy than on the ego.

Erik Erikson – cultural psychology

Another German psychoanalytic psychologist who had some public influence, Erik Erikson (1902–1994), always claimed he was a Freudian. Yet his work differed significantly from Freudian psychoanalysis. He was a pioneer in understanding the cultural dimensions of psychology but also strived to belong to the Freudian establishment (Sharma, 2000).

Theory

Freud viewed culture as an extension of the ego, helping to channel and control the powerful impulses of the id, so, to live in society one had to sacrifice instincts. Erikson (1963) provided a different, non-conflictual view of the relationship between the individual and culture, highlighting what society gives to the individual and the ways society and the individual are interrelated (S. Mitchell & Black, 1995). He regarded biological givens as shaped by culture and history. Society not only gratifies or frustrates the drives, he asserted, but specifically forms them. Thus, by shifting the centre of the mind from the individual to society he introduced a strikingly different psychoanalytic viewpoint with major implications for practice and research.

Working with the Sioux of South Dakota and the Yurok of the coastal northwest USA and studying child development at Berkeley, California, Erikson, in one of his most influential books *Childhood and Society* (1950), argued that development depends not only on sexuality but on society. According to his theory of ego development, there are eight stages of dialectical tension in relationship with significant others: basic trust/mistrust; autonomy/ shame and doubt; initiative/guilt; industry/inferiority; identity/role confusion; intimacy/ isolation; generativity/stagnation; ego integrity/despair. Although the sequence unfolds in time, the individual actively negotiates all these tensions across the lifespan and within particular societal conditions that moderate the expression of the eight stages.

With greater awareness of the damage that misrecognition can cause, Erikson made important contributions to the study of identity and coined the phrase "identity crisis" (Zaretsky, 2004). He observed that ego identity is formed as the individual proceeds from childhood to adulthood, and individual and society interweave (S. Mitchell & Black, 1995). In this way Erikson was part of a larger psychoanalytic trend shifting from intrapsychic to interpersonal dynamics, recognition, and intersubjectivity.

Erikson observed that the family, as a unit, was no longer as important as a source of production. As such, adolescence gained new importance as a stage of life and identity became a matter of recognition, not only by the family, but by communities, religions, economic institutions, and the state (Zaretsky, 2004).

Section conclusion

Some consider Erikson an ego psychologist because of his emphasis on individual identity. However, instead of reducing the psychological to individual dynamics, Erikson focused on the dialectics of culture and the individual, and the social and biological. Similar to Fromm, he observed how "geography and economics, mediated through child-rearing practices, shape personality to create the sort of individuals the culture requires" (S. Mitchell & Black, 1995, p. 143).

Erikson was perhaps the first cultural psychologist. He had personal experience with cultures other than his own and was familiar with the work of famous cultural anthropologists. Although Erikson had little influence on mainstream psychoanalysis, he pushed psychoanalysis past a colonial attitude and universalistic claims to respect the relativity of psychological processes and the mutual influence of individual and culture.

Part 4 conclusion

Socioeconomic conditions at the turn of the twentieth century helped transform the original psychoanalytic notion that desire is unconscious and insatiable to complement capitalist society's manipulation of desire encouraging personal acquisition of wealth, hedonism, and mass consumption (Ellenberger, 1970). The careers of Adler, Horney, Fromm, Reich, and Erikson show how each in her or his own way used psychoanalysis to understand human psychology as formed through social–political and cultural contexts. For these social theorists, individuals, families, cultures, and societies are engaged in a complex set of mutual influences, both consciously and unconsciously. They strived to advance progressive ideas about social reforms, even transformations, that they believed were conducive to fostering healthier human relations.

Yet much of the psychoanalytic movement tended not to focus on social–political or cultural context but, instead, on intrapsychic and interpersonal psychology.

Part 5   One-person, two-person, and no-person dynamics

Prior to World War II and subsequently, psychoanalysis took multiple, enduring forms such as *ego psychology*, which considers one-person psychodynamics; *object relations theory* and *self psychology*, which consider two-person psychodynamics; and Lacanian postmodern theory, which could be seen as theorizing a no-person psychodynamics.

Analyzing unconscious resistance to treatment became foundational in various forms of psychoanalytic psychotherapy. Classical (i.e., Freudian) psychoanalysis, object relations, and ego psychology diverge on many points both within these groupings and between them, but all can be seen as agreeing on the importance of analyzing resistance. By contrast, in non-analytic therapies, such as cognitive–behavioural therapy, which promote rational thinking, working with resistance is not central to understanding the patient's psychology.

Ego psychology arguably was instigated by **Anna Freud** (1895–1982). Later this term would come to describe the dominant forms of psychoanalysis in the USA. The object relations model, now seen as instigated by both **Sándor Ferenczi** (1873–1933) and **Melanie Klein** (1882–1960), and the so-called middle group, led by **Donald Winnicott** (1896–1971) among others, also emerged at this time. After World War II, John Bowlby's attachment theory and self psychology, which **Heinz Kohut** (1913–1981) and **Otto Kernberg** (b. 1928) developed, also became prominent. Although originating prior to the war, postmodern versions of **Jacques Lacan**'s (1901–1981) psychoanalysis were popular in the 1990s.

Ego psychology

Ego psychology was a major emphasis in psychoanalysis from the 1920s to the 1960s first in Europe and then in the USA. Although ego psychology was not a distinct organization and separate institution, Anna Freud, who explored one-person intrapsychic dynamics, ego functions, and defence mechanisms in terms of her father's drive theory, evidently initiated a discernible emphasis commonly termed ego psychology. Its US version is linked to the work of **Heinz Hartmann** (1894–1970) who focused on individuality, adaptation, and a sphere of the ego that purportedly operates without conflict.

With the rise of Nazism, psychoanalysis was virtually eliminated from central Europe while analysts fled to England, Australia, North and South America. The IPA became a predominately English-speaking organization, as analysts adapted to new social environments. There was pressure for psychoanalytic institutes to provide medical service through systematic training and certification of analysts. Ego psychology had a technical focus that lent itself well to standardized teaching and clinical practice.

Anna Freud

Martha and Sigmund Freud's last child, Anna began training as a "lay psychoanalyst" with the highly irregular experience of having her father as her analyst. Later, she began a practice with children and published a book on child analysis. She recalled that this work was a response to her father's request in 1918 to extend psychoanalysis into new fields (Viner, 1996).

Anna was a member of her father's "Secret Committee" and served as his secretary and "public relations officer." She also headed the IPA for seven years and directed the Vienna Psychoanalytic Training Institute. Because she enjoyed privileged status in the psychoanalytic community, she could promote her ideas on ego functioning and child and adolescent development, which diverged from her father's focus on instinctual drives, without fear of expulsion from the inner circle.

In 1937, responding to bleak economic conditions, Anna and a female colleague opened a nursery where they studied infant and child attachment, until the Nazis occupied Austria in 1938. The psychoanalytic community then helped thirty-eight analysts, including the Freuds, move to London, which became the only major psychoanalytic centre in Europe. There she established her practice, stressing the importance of attachments, and initiated another nursery to provide foster care for children displaced by the war.

Theory In *Ego Psychology and the Mechanisms of Defense* (1936), Anna explored ego functions more fully than her father, describing how the ego disguises the impulses of the id. She illuminated a wide range of defence mechanisms. By emphasizing ego functions, Anna developed a theory that was oriented to clinical practice, helping to make consciousness and "real-world" issues valid domains of inquiry in psychoanalysis (S. Mitchell & Black, 1995).

Although her advocacy for the mental health issues of children and youth was profound (Donaldson, 1996), Anna encouraged the emphasis in classical psychoanalysis on father–son relations rather than the emerging emphasis on mother–child relations, taking an anti-feminist position that supported traditional gender and sexual norms. Anna and Melanie Klein engaged in fierce debate (see below) over the classical emphasis on gratifying or repressing drives compared with Klein's stress on interpersonal relations.

Americanized ego psychology Whereas many European analysts tended to emphasize "self-reflective exploration of internal limitations," most US analysts were focused on "personal empowerment, self-regulation, and individual charisma" (Zaretsky, 2004, p. 76). Ego psychology flourished in the USA perhaps because of the culture's belief in the power of the mind to surmount external obstacles.

A prime catalyst for the Americanization of psychoanalysis was the Viennese émigré psychiatrist Heinz Hartmann, who explored the strength of the ego and its ability to adapt and master the external world. Working towards a general psychology of perception, memory, and thinking, he downplayed the importance of drives and the death instinct. Ultimately, Hartmann held an optimistic view of human nature, believing that the intelligent and knowledgeable ego is suited to its environment and capable of addressing the world's ills. Some commentators view his variation of ego psychology as an attempt to domesticate psychoanalysis to extant social conditions (Frosh, 1999).

Section conclusion

In classical psychoanalysis the ego is not only rational and self-reflective but also resistant to being rational and self-reflective. In the USA, however, this two-sided sense of the ego was lost; rather, the ego was seen increasingly as an agent of reason and control. With increased focus on the ego and its functional adaptation, analysts emphasized cultivating ways of tolerating anxiety and fostering adjustment and control. This form of psychoanalysis is particularly compatible with US ideals of self-management and personal empowerment (Zaretsky, 2004).

However, critics argue that there is a psychological cost to an emphasis on adjustment. Strengthening the ego by bolstering defences might increase self-control, make difficult feelings more tolerable, and allow us to get on with life, but it also can alienate us from our unconscious desires. Interpreting defences and strengthening the ego "give it practical utility, but reduce its critical force" (Frosh, 1999, p. 90). A psychoanalysis focused on adaptation ceases to uncover how we are at odds with parts of ourselves and with the world. Therapy in this case is not subversive or evolutionary but encourages conformity that supports the status quo. Mental health then becomes a matter of adjusting to one's culture, which assumes that the culture is legitimate.

Ego psychologists seem to have refocused psychoanalysis on resistance and adjustment to the societal status quo (Parker, 2008). Many of these analysts are considered socially conservative because of their rejection of non-traditional family forms and of homosexuality. Some supported the Vietnam War and viewed those who thought mental disorder was due to social inequalities as Marxist dreamers. When US analysts who emphasized ego psychology aligned themselves with medicine, psychoanalysis began to slip into decline, unable to defend concepts within the medical model of research.

Object relations

In contrast to classical Freudian theory and ego psychology, the collection of diverse object-relations theories tends to stress two-person dynamics, meaning how human behaviour is fuelled by the desire for interpersonal connection. These theories also focus on how libido is object-seeking instead of pleasure-seeking. Object-relations theories include Kleinian theory, the middle group, attachment theory, and self psychology,

Object-relations theorists are critical of the classical Freudian conception of the person as a closed system. Most argue that Freud diminished the importance of the external world and the human objects that are always linked with drives. Object-relations theorists replace Freud's concentration on instinctual sexual or aggressive drives with the overarching impulse to establish and maintain human relationships. All object-relations theories have a pre-Oedipal focus on early infant–mother relations. This early relationship is thought to form a template for all further object relations.

Two figures are considered central to the beginning of object-relations theories: Sándor Ferenczi and Melanie Klein. After receiving analysis from and studying with Ferenczi, Klein evidently provided the link between Freudian theory and later object-relations theories by redefining drives as including relations with objects. For her, these objects are internal, but, for the middle group and later object-relations theorists concerned with interpersonal or intersubjective relations, objects are primarily external.

Sándor Ferenczi

A Hungarian psychiatrist, Ferenczi was a young member of Freud's original inner circle. Since the 1990s, Ferenczi's work has received new-found interest (Erös, 2003). Some now consider him to be a pioneer of object-relations theory and one of the earliest forerunners of relational or interpersonal psychoanalysis.

At first, Ferenczi refused to take Freud's work seriously, but Jung convinced him it was worthwhile (Zaretsky, 2004). He then became one of the most influential analysts in Freud's original circle. Although his ideas helped to shape Freud's (Aron & Harris, 1993), ultimately Freud rejected them. Thereafter, for sixteen years the *International Journal of Psycho-Analysis* refused to publish Ferenczi's work (Berman, 1999).

Conceptually, Ferenczi attended more to the importance of family and environment in shaping personality, whereas Freud was more concerned with inner fantasy (Zaretsky, 2004). Ferenczi focused on early traumatic experiences that actually occurred (S. Mitchell & Black, 1995), whereas, as we saw, Freud argued that fantasies about sexual experiences, not actual events, were the basis of neurosis.

Concerning practice, Ferenczi departed from the Freudian model of a strictly hierarchical relationship wherein the analyst makes interpretations and the patient receives them. He understood analysis as a mutual intersubjective process and advocated openness, equality, and sharing of knowledge within the doctor–patient relationship (Berman, 1999). Instead of Freud's focus on transference and view of counter-transference as undesirable, Ferenczi was an early proponent of exploring counter-transference with his patients in empathic but frank discussion about the therapeutic relationship.

Freud sometimes is understood as having prescribed emotional detachment with patients for the purpose of enabling analysts' observation of intrapsychic dynamics. By contrast, Ferenczi believed that a nurturing therapeutic relationship, not insight, is the healing factor in analysis and that an analyst who is emotionally distant could reproduce in patients a childhood experience of deprivation and trauma (Zaretsky, 2004). For a patient to overcome traumatic experience, Ferenczi argued, a democratic and humanistic experience with a warm, giving, and empathic analyst nurturing patient autonomy and responsibility is vital (Rachman, 1988). Hence, the analyst should be flexible and emotionally available, meeting the patient's needs and wishes as best as possible.

Melanie Klein

Born in Vienna, Klein settled in Budapest and studied with Ferenczi before moving to Berlin to work with an associate of Freud. She then settled in London in 1926. Klein aimed to extend Freud's ideas through direct observation of and clinical work with children (S. Mitchell & Black, 1995). Although her theorizing was controversial and clashed with Freudian theory, Klein had a significant following in England, where her work flourished. She saw herself, not Anna Freud, as Sigmund Freud's true successor.

A common understanding of Klein is that she led the historical shift in psychoanalysis from a father-centred to a mother-centred psychology (Alford, 1989). Freud had explained female sexuality in terms of the male-centred concepts of the phallic stage, castration anxiety, and the Oedipus complex. But beginning in the 1920s, female analysts studied mother–daughter relations, conducted the first child analyses, and drew from their personal experiences as mothers to provide a different explanation of female psychology.

Until the female analysts began to write on the subject, female sexuality had been defined in terms of deficiencies: penis envy, ignorance of the vagina, the need to subordinate the clitoris, the need to turn away from the mother, the centrality of envy to female development. But women analysts reconceived the womb as teeming with resources, being the source of children, milk, the father, and love. Thus, mother supplanted father as the most important figure for the development of all later relationships. Arguably, this was the most important paradigm shift in the history of psychoanalysis (Zaretsky, 2004)

Theory Klein agreed with Freud's position that libidinal and aggressive instincts drive psychology and that gratifying these drives or defending against gratification is the drama of human existence, but not without an object (S. Mitchell & Black, 1995). Drives do not exist, she argued, without something or someone as their aim. In the first instance, infants do not discover the breast because of hunger; rather, they are born with awareness of this object, the breast.

Instead of a developmental passage from nonhuman animal to human, as Freud implied, Klein (1959) asserted that "the ego exists and operates from birth" and object relations begin almost from birth (p. 293). She observed children experiencing conflicts, guilt, aggression, and responsibility during infancy. For her, "the superego originated in early representations of the mother, long before the Oedipus complex came into being" (Zaretsky, 2004, p. 256).

An infant's feeling of being loved and understood by the mother forms a fundamental experience for all further relations in life. Klein (1959) claimed that, "however good are the child's feelings toward both parents, aggressiveness and hate also remain operative" (p. 295). Aggressive impulses, then, become a source of psychic instability and point of growth in early development along with guilt and reparation becoming important as ethical relations with the maternal object develop (Alford, 1989).

In 1934 Klein proposed the idea of the paranoid and depressive positions. She termed these positions, not conflicts, to portray the sense of a general attitude that is pervasive. We shift between these positions throughout life.

For Klein, we experience aggression as overwhelmingly strong and capable of annihilating the other to the point that our own existence feels endangered. The terror of one's constitutional aggression can be soothed and ameliorated with good parenting; nevertheless, the environment is secondary to the personal experience of one's constitution. This problem of aggression is resolved in the paranoid position through projecting the aggression outside oneself onto an object from which one can escape. If the aggression is within oneself, then there is no escape. Aggression is safely distanced and contained in a hateful relationship with a bad object. However, this results in a sense of persecution and of others being dangerous.

Throughout life, we struggle to protect the loving from the hateful, yet we must also knit together the traumatic difference between love and hate to feel whole, healthy, and balanced (S. Mitchell & Black, 1995). The depressive position involves experiencing a mixture of love and hate, loss and guilt (Frosh, 1999). In this position one learns that "one's love can survive one's destructiveness" (S. Mitchell & Black, 1995, p. 97).

To relate with both love and hate towards objects requires belief in the capacity for reparation. Instead of the search for an original state of goodness there is the urge

Box 9.2 The object relations – ego psychology conflict

Melanie Klein and Anna Freud were alternative authorities on child psychoanalysis who engaged in a protracted conflict over their conceptions (Viner, 1996). Sigmund Freud's death in 1939 brought their conflict to a head. The end result was a major enduring schism between what many have characterized as two camps: Kleinians and ego psychologists (Zaretsky, 2004).

Anna Freud concentrated on ways that internally generated ideas are accommodated to external reality. She maintained the classical view of drive theory wherein aims and ideas battle with drives while trying to keep the individual functional in a civilized community. Klein recast this insight in terms of interpersonal relations and the longing for unity with the mother (Zaretsky, 2004). For Klein, we do not struggle with desires and defences against our desires but with the paranoia of persecution: the devastating sadness of abandonment and the terror of annihilation (S. Mitchell & Black, 1995).

Klein maintained that one could analyze children's play in the same way as adult's free associations. She saw the child's ego, like the adult ego, as fluid, dynamic, and responsive to deep interpretations. In fact, she believed that the child is more capable of deep insight than the adult, because the connection between conscious and unconscious processes is much stronger in children (Donaldson, 1996).

By contrast, Anna argued that a child's ego is undeveloped; accordingly, deep interpretations of instinctual conflict are dangerous. Many ego psychologists believed Kleinians were wildly interpretive and that they overwhelmed patients, arguing that an educational approach is more appropriate to strengthen the ego. Most Kleinians believed this involved surface interpretations that were ineffective.

---

towards conditions that allow for the most complete expression and experience of reparation. According to Kleinian theory, we have an unending need for reparation, as long as we experience our instinctual aggression in terms of others causing our frustration and psychic pain.

All told, Klein's views on object relations set her apart from Anna Freud and her ego-psychology followers, and the two figures engaged in intense debate over their respective positions (see Box 9.2).

Section conclusion

Common understanding of object-relations theory is that Klein conceived of human development as a struggle to integrate love and hate and shifted psychoanalysts' focus from impulses to relationships. The Freudian position was that therapeutic analysis should strengthen the ego, making it more independent from the demands of the id, the superego, and society.

But Klein contended that the ego could never be free and self-governing because of the relations we have with others. Instead of emphasizing psychological autonomy, Klein focused on how we make and maintain personal relationships. She emphasized that, as humans, we are inseparably connected to others (Zaretsky, 2004). Thus, a sense of self develops from caring relationships (Frosh, 1999).

According to Klein, instead of an initial wholeness that becomes split because of experience, infants experience an initial split that can become whole with experience. Thus, psychological healing is accomplished through relationships and not through withdrawal. Analysis can be seen as helping to temper the punitive nature of the superego to facilitate connections with others by building an internal world of whole objects that are not split into good and bad parts. Yet, because Klein's focus on fantasy ignores actual object-relations, some commentators do not consider her an object-relations theorist. For example, a Kleinian focus on an infant's aggression overlooks the quality of parenting the infant receives (S. Mitchell & Black, 1995).

Overall, Klein is said to have "had more impact on contemporary psychoanalysis than any other psychoanalytic writer since Freud" (S. Mitchell & Black, 1995, p. 85). Although some ego psychologists absorbed many of her ideas, this appropriation was not acknowledged as such (Zaretsky, 2004). The controversy surrounding her ideas seems to have resolved into three groups of psychoanalysts: Kleinians, ego psychologists, and the middle group who made a compromise between the two.

Independent or middle group

Klein apparently influenced the principal members of what tends to be referred to as the independent or "middle group." The members included British psychiatrists **W. R. D. Fairbairn** (1889–1964), Donald Winnicott, and John Bowlby. They were object-relations theorists in the sense that they focused on personal relationships and the intrapsychic drama of connection and rupture instead of instinctual desires and the production of gratification or repression. Their theories tend to be concerned with responsibility instead of autonomy and with the mother instead of the father.

But unlike Klein, the middle-group theorists did not see the human being as naturally at odds with the world. Winnicott and Bowlby emphasized how we are suited to the world in which we are born and believed that development is not traumatic unless there is inadequate parenting. In contrast to Klein, the middle-group theorists concentrated on actual mother–infant relations.

W. R. D. Fairbairn

William Ronald Dodds Fairbairn, a Scottish psychiatrist, was trained in psychoanalysis at the time when Klein's ideas predominated (S. Mitchell & Black, 1995).

Often considered a typical object-relations theorist, Fairbairn observed that pleasure is one form of connection with others but pain is another way in which we connect. For example, a child who experiences her or his parents as depressed, detached, bullying, or narcissistic might become depressed, detached, bullying, or narcissistic to feel a connection with his or her parents. Depending on predominant childhood experience, we learn that either pain or pleasure is the usual way to connect. To overcome this typical way of connecting with others threatens that original relationship, at least until other less painful ways of relating are experienced.

Fairbairn also developed a theory of internal object relations. If a child's needs are not adequately met, he or she will turn inward, away from reality, to fantasize connections in lieu of actual interactions with others. What is repressed is not a traumatic memory or a forbidden impulse but a relationship that does not make sense in terms of other relationships.

Analysis offers the possibility of forging new ways of relating, according to Fairbairn, not through interpretation or uncovering unconscious dynamics, but primarily through internalizing a new way of relating that is experienced in the analytic relationship. As Stephen Mitchell and Margaret Black (1995) explained, "no one can give up powerful, addictive ties to old objects unless she believes that new objects are possible" (p. 122).

Donald Winnicott

Following World War II, health professionals in England worked with children who had been traumatized by their separation from their family of origin. The separations occurred in massive evacuations from cities to escape the Nazi bombings. Many children were placed in safe havens in rural areas with strange families, while difficult children were sent to hostels. The importance of mothers in young children's lives and the impact of separation and loss were evident. During and after the war, Donald Winnicott, an English paediatrician, gave radio broadcasts to parents on children's mental health. Donald and his future wife Clare, a social worker, met while working with displaced children.

The Winnicotts developed **four enduring concepts**: the false self, the good-enough mother, the holding environment, and the transitional object (Kanter, 2000).

(1) Mothers' personal responsiveness to their infants' experience affects the way that infants experience themselves as adults. Infant experiences of unresponsive mothering are linked, for the Winnicotts, to adult experiences of a "false self" (S. Mitchell & Black, 1995). The false self is heavily oriented to the expectations of others, resulting in the person feeling unreal, not one's own person.

(2) The idea of the "good-enough mother" is that, if mothers are free to be themselves and respond spontaneously to their infant's needs, the mothering is good enough to satisfy the infant's psychological development. This concept represents a significant shift in analytic thinking towards trusting mothers' untutored practices of care rather than promoting expertise and calculated behaviour. The frustration that children experience with imperfect, good-enough mothering is considered optimal for development. When a good-enough mother is not only physically but psychologically present for the child, she reflects the child's self back to him or her, fostering the development of a true self (Zaretsky, 2004).

(3) Equally important as being psychologically present for children is for mothers to recede when not needed. This maternal action, according to the Winnicotts, provides a reliable "holding environment" in which children are protected without knowing it. As children develop, mothers no longer sacrifice themselves so entirely for their child's needs. Children begin to realize their dependence on others and that others have desires and needs of their own. Consequently, children discover that having their needs met is not just a matter of expression but of negotiation (S. Mitchell & Black, 1995).

Donald and Clare applied the concept of a holding environment to the therapeutic relationship. They construed therapy as providing a nurturing context in which patients can find uncertain parts of themselves. Analysts are able to tolerate difficulties that their patients might not be able to accept, the Winnicott argument goes. When patients emulate accepting painful experiences without turning away, they gain the courage to feel the full impact of their life. Having a good-enough experience of "holding" gives a person a healthy sense of self.

(4) In their work with traumatized children, Donald and Clare observed that many children would cling to their old clothes, a filthy teddy bear, or a torn blanket to an extreme degree. The Winnicotts began to see that these possessions represented a transitional space between what the child had in the past and now refused to lose (Kanter, 2000). Clare referred to such objects as the child's first treasured possession.

"Transitional objects" are separate from children and have a life of their own, but they are also partly within children's control. They represent for children creative ambiguity and fantasy play. A "good-enough" parent does not challenge this play as unreal. A transitional space or object does not belong to one person, but is the meeting point between the child's inner world and the outer world shared with significant others.

John Bowlby

An English psychiatrist, Bowlby developed his ideas within a community of social reformers aware of the needs of young children for love and security and the irreparable effects of abandonment and neglect (van der Horst & van der Veer, 2010). He too argued against Freudian and Kleinian insistence on innate aggression derived from the death instinct. Instead, Bowlby asserted that we tend towards harmonious interactions and non-traumatic development unless there is inadequate parenting (S. Mitchell & Black, 1995). Natural selection, he claimed, has provided us with useful instincts so that we come into the world prepared to adapt to our environment. As such, he maintained traditional views on gender roles, believing in an evolutionary fit between our nature and our environment.

Bowlby developed attachment theory in conjunction with psychologist Mary Salter Ainsworth. This theory is concerned with relations, not with drives. Experiences of attachment, separation, and loss explain motivation and how we regulate our emotions and arousal levels, using cognitive appraisals and memory to support attachment ties. Attachment theory also explains how we tend to cope when those who are significant to us are neglectful or rejecting or when there is trauma or loss.

Originally, Sigmund Freud argued that anxiety is due to a build-up of libido, but later he developed his signal theory of anxiety, which is central to attachment theory. In this explanation, when a person experiences a situation similar to a previous experience where one felt helpless and in danger, anxiety ensues. For his part, Bowlby described the main anxiety of childhood as the threat of losing an attachment figure: "In early childhood, the most common situation leading to a sense of danger and helplessness is an unexpected separation or loss of an attachment figure" (Cortina, 2004, p. 137).

Section conclusion

The middle group of Fairbairn, Winnicott, and Bowlby concentrated on mother–child relations and the psychodynamics of attachment and loss. The concepts of the false self, the good-enough mother, the holding environment, and the transitional object not only exemplify the middle group's interpersonal perspective on psychological dynamics but also are directly applicable to parenting, childcare, and psychotherapy.

But a significant criticism of Winnicott's theory is that he identifies women with mothering, instead of emphasizing the nurturing that both parents can provide. Arguably, Winnicott's standpoint idealizes the role of women as full-time stay-at-home mothers. In addition, the theory apparently is not fully intersubjective. "In the image presented by Fairbairn and Winnicott, the external world functions only as interference: in a perfect mothering environment, there would be but mother and babe, and nothing else" (Frosh, 1999, p. 117).

Many psychoanalysts largely ignored attachment theory, viewing it as a behavioural approach, overly focused on external realities. Attachment theorists, however, criticized those psychoanalysts who ignored the reality of abuse and neglect that many children suffer. Although Bowlby did not disregard the importance of the fantasy of persecution, for him, it was subordinate to the realities of separation and loss.

Meanwhile, self psychologists Heinz Kohut and Otto Kernberg concentrated on object relations in terms of relations with oneself. Although indebted to object-relations theory, these self psychologists dealt with the needs for self-esteem and self-cohesiveness. For them, issues of narcissism, not instincts, ego, or object relations, primarily motivate behaviour.

> **Small-group discussion.** Consider the debate over individual vs. interpersonal dynamics. What is the difference between object-seeking and pleasure-seeking?

Self psychology

Traditional psychoanalysis, with its ideas of unconscious conflict between id and ego and a personality dominated by forbidden desire, dealt with neurotic conditions that predominated in the first half of the twentieth century. However, arguably, a more common group of patients in the second half of the century presented with problems of narcissism. Individuals with a narcissistic personality relate to others as parts of themselves. They tend to have an exaggerated sense of self-importance and exhibit grandiosity and an intense personal focus. Two noteworthy psychoanalysts who developed theoretical approaches and clinical practices that addressed these issues are Heinz Kohut and Otto Kernberg.

Heinz Kohut

A Vienna-born, Chicago-based psychiatrist, Kohut observed that many of his patients had narcissistic tendencies. People were not struggling with inner conflicts or conflicts between self and society, he concluded; rather, they were experiencing isolation, alienation, and life without meaning. Difficulties arise, according to Kohut, not because of intrapsychic conflict, but because of experiences of emptiness and meaninglessness and the unfulfilled need for nurturance in the form of recognition, admiration, and approval. Kohut's insights led to innovative concepts and treatment.

According to Kohut, a "core self" develops in **two ways**:

- Parents recognizing and reflecting the infant's and toddler's sense of grandiosity, enabling the child to assert him or herself.
- Parents allowing themselves to be idealized, which enables the child to develop central values in her or his superego.

Infants' libidinal energy tends to be so self-directed that they come to feel omnipotent while their needs and desires are effortlessly met. When experiences of frustration disrupt children's primary narcissism, they direct their energy outward in search of satisfaction from others. In this way children form attachments to their caregivers, giving up early narcissism.

In psychoanalytic circles narcissism had been understood as an immature stage of development since Freud's essay on the topic in 1914 (Zaretsky, 2004). Reformulating this conception, Kohut argued that the need to be mirrored and the desire for recognition and validation by others, making one feel whole and important, were legitimate (S. Mitchell & Black, 1995). Instead of denying the validity of narcissistic needs or interpreting them as immature defences, Kohut took seriously those striving to be different by rejecting family, following a unique path, and pursuing activities that had no social purpose. Arguably, his positive attitude towards narcissism generated a version of psychoanalysis more in line with the popular culture of the 1960s focused on recognition and identity.

Kohut seems to have redefined the purpose of therapeutic analysis. In classical psychoanalysis the goal is to cultivate the patient's ability to love and work. But Kohut insisted that analysis should result primarily in joy and pride in one's life. He wanted to make room for healthy narcissism, childlike exuberance, and a personal sense of vigour in adulthood. Therapy, he believed, should provide not only insight into one's condition but also a corrective emotional experience that fulfills the patient's need for approval, affiliation with a powerful figure, and identification with the therapist.

Analysts, including Freud, did not always refrain from satisfying their patients' desires, acting as a blank screen in an attempt to bring about awareness of these needs and desires. In Kohut's system the analyst becomes an extension of the patient's self and a resource to meet her or his narcissistic needs. In this way, a stalled developmental process is resumed. Empathy is central, in Kohut's mind, to all psychoanalytic psychotherapy. Thus, he encouraged empathic exploration of childhood experiences to sustain a sense of self on the basis of self-evaluation, not others' evaluation.

Otto Kernberg

While Kohut seemed to be transforming psychoanalysis into a self psychology of "do your own thing," Kernberg, a Viennese-born Chilean psychiatrist who settled in the USA, reasserted the pathology of narcissism. Since the nineteenth century, scholars have recognized the problem of normalizing narcissism. Kernberg considered perspectives within ego psychology in order to better understand contemporary narcissistic culture.

According to Kernberg, narcissistic patients are deeply disturbed, driven by oral greed and the pain of ruptured connection. They are very insecure and protect themselves through contempt of others. Superficial charm masks explosive rage that is unleashed whenever their sense of grandiosity is not mirrored (Zaretsky, 2004). This condition might include a cavalier attitude, for example, resulting in a lack of responsibility or high-risk behaviour such as substance abuse and unprotected sex.

Kernberg identified children's first developmental task as clarifying what is self and what is other. Without clear boundaries between self and other, psychosis is thought to result. In the next task, children need to relinquish splitting of good and bad for whole objects that are both good and bad. By integrating good and bad, children temper the intensity of their feelings. When good and bad are split, a "borderline personality" develops whereby the person can distinguish self from object but cannot tolerate good and bad in one object.

Narcissistic patients, according to Kernberg, need steady objective distance in therapy and not gratification. Rather than relying on empathic reflection, analysts should interpret narcissistic patients' hostility as a defence so that they can develop more integrated object relations and a healthy sense of self (S. Mitchell & Black, 1995).

Section conclusion

As psychoanalytic theorists and practitioners, Kohut and Kernberg responded to a distinct cultural shift, at least in the USA, towards narcissistic personalities. Each in his way produced a "self psychology."

Kohut evidently had a significant impact on psychoanalytic discourse. The concepts of narcissistic transference, narcissistic disorders, and the maturation of narcissism are now part of common psychoanalytic understanding (Goldberg, 1998). His work highlights the shift in psychoanalysis from valuing rational objectivism to greater respect for subjectivity and personal meaning (S. Mitchell & Black, 1995).

Some commentators claim that Kernberg integrated divergent psychoanalytic traditions including instinct theory, object relations, a developmental perspective, the importance of interpretation, and the significance of the analyst's personality for meaningful change in therapy (S. Mitchell & Black, 1995). He provided an important counterpoint to Kohut's views on narcissism in an era that some authors characterize as narcissistic.

Lacanian psychoanalysis

In France, Jacques Lacan, a psychiatrist, developed a postmodern, intersubjective psycho-analytic theory that impacted humanities departments in universities worldwide as well as medical psychology and popular culture in Latin America (Young-Bruehl & Dunbar, 2009). Trained in psychiatry in the 1920s, Lacan was influenced by the contemporary movements of *structuralism* and *surrealism*.

Modern European humanists tended to emphasize individual consciousness and existential freedom (see Chapter 10). By contrast, scholars who subscribed to structuralism held that language, ritual, and myth shape social customs and generate subjectivity. These structuralist notions became central to the intellectual movement known as postmodernism (see Chapter 12), which emerged after World War II.

Lacanian theory also can be understood within the social–intellectual context of surreal-ism. After World War I, anti-intellectualism and contempt for the older generation and

Figure 9.2 *Salvador Dalí A* (1948): this artwork depicts Dalí's dream-like surrealism

traditional values arose (Ellenberger, 1970). Those who subscribed to surrealism rejected traditional values of honouring country, religion, and work. Instead, they valued exploring hidden dimensions of mind such as the unconscious, dreams, mental illness, the uncanny, coincidences, and fantasy.

The surrealists used the practice of automatic writing to promote full psychic energy, creativity, and access to points of consciousness where the waking mind and dream-states meet. This is exemplified by the paintings of Salvador Dalí (1904–1989), as depicted in Figure 9.2. Although Freud was baffled by their interest in his work, the surrealists counted Freud among their forefathers, and Freud's papers appeared in surrealist journals.

The most important figure to catalyze this cultural transformation is Jacques Lacan. During the 1960s and 1970s, at a time of declining interest in psychoanalysis, Lacan's work provided a fresh interpretation, resuscitating it in certain non-English speaking countries (Zaretsky, 2004). Traditional psychoanalytic theory seemed to misunderstand the alternative lifestyles and non-traditional family forms that developed in those decades. Consequently, psychoanalysis appeared old-fashioned and overly conservative. Lacanian theory resonated with contemporary generations, inspiring new centres of psychoanalysis in Latin America and Europe. Lacan's public lectures drew an international audience and were considered major events (S. Mitchell & Black, 1995).

Theory

Lacanian theory is quite different from general trends in classical psychoanalysis, social psychoanalytic theory, ego psychology, object-relations theory, and self psychology. Lacan disagreed with Freud that instincts are basic to psychology. Moreover, he argued, neither ego nor object relations are central to human experience, because experience is always inter-subjective and is linguistically embedded in cultural trends. Here we address three aspects of Lacanian theory: language, ego development, and desire.

Language For Lacan, Freud's most important ideas occurred prior to 1905 when he linked dreams, neurotic symptoms, and slips of the tongue to the language of the unconscious mind. Like many critics and revisionists of Freud's work, Lacan contended that Freud's attempt to position psychoanalysis as a natural science obscured his most significant contribution, namely, the significance of language for experience and subjectivity (S. Mitchell & Black, 1995).

Lacan rejected basic assumptions about the ego. For him, the ego is an imaginary wholeness constructed to conceal fragmentation, conflict, and internal deficiency. Similarly, Lacan considered object relations as a psychology of interpersonal fictions. He was skeptical about the possibility of mature relationships and genuine knowledge of others, because "all inter-personal relationships, and indeed the structure of the individual human subject as well, are penetrated by cultural and social forces with distorting and obscuring effects" (Frosh, 2006, pp. 19–20).

Both object-relations theory and ego psychology, Lacan claimed, missed Freud's most important point that unconscious processes operate beneath all of our experience. In Lacan's interpretation, however, the unconscious is strictly linguistic, not instinctual. We do not create the language we speak, he claimed. Rather, we are born into language, and chains of associated meanings shape all of our experience, including our sense of self (S. Mitchell & Black, 1995). Social and personal worlds interpenetrate, while symbolic representations of society form deeply felt identity-positions in each of us (Frosh, 1999).

Lacanian theory is appreciated as an attempt to account for what is impossible to say (Malone, 2008). Affect is included in a most respectful way by recognizing that emotions and moods cannot be put into language in ways that are entirely truthful. Thus, Lacanian theory insists on a psychological subject that cannot be referred to wholly. Affect is not absence; rather, it is included where speech stops, because words block the appearance of the thing in itself.

Ego development Freud emphasized the importance of narcissism for the development of the ego, but Lacan puzzled about the fact that narcissism is not present from birth. In this case, how does ego development begin? Lacan explained that humans take on the character-istics of their environments. We include others in our existence and identify with others to attain a sense of completeness that we cannot experience in our individual limited selves.

As newborns, we cannot move or eat without another. Instead of being overwhelmed by a sense of lack or absence, we identify with the image of the other and organize an imaginary sense of self that extends beyond our own limitations. What are reflected back in the mirror of others are not parts of self but a whole, integrated, and coordinated image. The ego is built around such images (S. Mitchell & Black, 1995).

This extension of the ego brings with it a sense of alienation, because the ego, at least in part, is "other." No longer simply a whole being, the self symbolized as "I" or "ego" is a loss of the capacity to simply be oneself. Lacan understood the individual as a "split subject" who will always struggle with a kind of self-alienating narcissism. In this way he talked about the ego as imaginary.

The self we take ourselves to be is constructed out of images and reflections of others. Not only do our identifications with the image of others form our ego, we also identify with how people describe us. Our sense of self is elaborated in the stories that others tell about us. But these stories do not have single meanings. They are symbolic, because we make associations to the words they use.

Desire   Another important feature of Lacanian theory is his explanation of desire as desire of the other. Lacan observed that desire can be all-encompassing and ultimately insatiable. The child wishes to be everything the mother desires, he argued, but desire is an unending passion that no object can complete. We can only desire that which we perceive to be separate from ourselves; thus, in the experience of desire there is a loss that never can be recovered. Desire cannot be overcome entirely and the search for the (m)other is a search for existential reparation (S. Mitchell & Black, 1995).

Practice

Lacan challenged traditional beliefs about analytic practice (Grossman & Silverman, 2002). He rejected the notion that the patient's ego needed to be strengthened in relation to drives (Fink, 2007). He contended that analysts who became overly enthusiastic about helping their patients better adapt to reality were suffering counter-transference issues.

According to Lacan, psychoanalytic therapy is meant to relax the ego, not to strengthen it. Analysis, for him, should wear down defences and promote a detached attitude towards one's narcissism (Zaretsky, 2004). Lacanian analysis is not meant to reveal the meaning of what is said; rather, it allows us to see the images of the ego that capture the imagination. We begin to relate to these images, not as solid and stable parts of ourselves, but as parts of language with symbolic associations and constantly evolving meanings.

The intention of a Lacanian analytic relationship is to "subvert" and "disperse" the self we take ourselves to be, thereby realizing a "transindividual" unconscious, a revitalized life, and a more authentic voice (S. Mitchell & Black, 1995). The end results are not necessarily decreased symptoms, improved interpersonal relations, or a more coherent sense of self. Rather, Lacanian analysis may result in a more transparent ego, less self-consciousness, and the experience of being part of a network of relevant associations, spontaneously enacting unconscious meanings.

Furthermore, desire does not become more rational. Rather, the patient names and accepts the imaginary, the symbolic, and the real that jointly constrain and form the reality that he or she experiences.

Section conclusion

Lacan is heralded by some adherents as the most important French thinker since Descartes. But some critics argue that he is deliberately obscure, his theory without substance, and his followers "la-conned" (S. Mitchell & Black, 1995). He refused to make psychoanalysis a mother-centred theory (Zaretsky, 2004). Instead, he emphasized sexual difference and the father's importance in an era that was very mother-and-child focused.

Lacan's unconventional clinical practices led to his expulsion from the IPA. He termed the decision an excommunication, but it bolstered his reputation as an important representative of the new psychoanalysis. His ideas continue to be influential internationally, especially in European and South American universities.

In US psychoanalytic circles, the Lacanian approach temporarily flourished. However, many have rejected Lacanian theory and analysis, because in his emphasis on language he seems to avoid emotions and moods (Malone, 2008). Some perceive his theory as overly intellectual; toying with concepts; overplaying the role of language in psychological development; neglecting the importance of power, ideology, and social institutions; and reducing the individual to a social construction devoid of fundamental human rights (Frosh, 1999).

Nevertheless, Lacanian theory had a major impact on the twentieth-century disciplines of cultural studies, feminism, and social criticism and is still considered important. For example, Lacan's influence is evident in the works of the French social philosophers Roland Barthes (1915–1980), Michel Foucault, and Jacques Derrida; and many important French feminists (see below). Some psychologists perceive Lacanian psychoanalysis as valuable for critical theory, research, and practice in Psychology (Owens, 2009). Arguably, Lacanian theory provides an important way of disrupting what psychologists are and what they think they do as theorists and practitioners (Parker, 2003).

Part 5 conclusion

The shift in much of the psychoanalytic movement towards stressing maternal rather than paternal influence on intrapsychic development and the emphasis on one-person, two-person, and even no-person subjectivities took multiple forms that often, but not always, overlapped. Anna Freud emphasized ego psychology and the range of defence mechanisms, which were advances, but otherwise she adhered to her father's standpoint. Within US culture Hartmann promoted the adaptive capacities of the ego that became a popular rationale for social adjustment to the status quo of postwar society.

Meanwhile, Ferenczi proposed concepts and clinical practices that laid the foundation for object-relations theory, which Klein fully developed theoretically and clinically. Kleinian psychoanalysis emphasized the ambivalent motives and feelings that infants have about their mothers, which purportedly are determinative of later development. Although the middle group also focused on mother–infant relations, Fairbairn, Winnicott, and Bowlby addressed the psychodynamics of attachment and loss. They emphasized practical applications of their theorizing to parenting, childcare, and psychotherapy.

For the self psychologists, Kohut and Kernberg, narcissism, not object relations, ego, or instincts, motivates human action, given a cultural context of strong desires for personal recognition and identity. To Kohut and Kernberg, object relations meant relations with oneself, expressed in the needs for self-esteem and self-cohesiveness. But Kernberg countered Kohut's acceptance of healthy narcissism by viewing narcissism as problematic and insisting on objective distance in therapy rather than indulging clients' narcissistic tendencies.

Rejecting other psychoanalysts' emphases on basic drives, ego, object relations, or the self, Lacan stressed the relationship among language, cultural meaning, and unconscious processes. Thus, for him, personal subjectivity is embedded in the interpersonal contexts of cultural trends and language. In Lacanian analysis patients come to embrace fluid conjunctions of what is real with the imaginary and symbolic and to accept the interpersonally constructed nature of their experiential realities. Lacan's approach has proved influential internationally.

Part 6

Psychoanalysis and gender

Since its inception, there has been much debate about the gendered nature of psychoanalysis in its Freudian and subsequent forms. In Sigmund Freud's time, European culture prided itself on rationality, realism, and the freedom from illusion. But women continued to suffer oppressive social restrictions that prevented economic and political equality. Overt discussion about gendered differentials in employment and income, domestic violence, and sexual abuse was rare.

All forms of Psychology, including psychoanalysis, emerged from this gendered context. The term *patriarchy* captures this cultural reality, depicting men's domination and control of social institutions and the psyche through, often unconscious, male-centred values and practices (J. Smith, 1990). Patriarchy, therefore, is the underlying ideology that infuses the structures and dynamics of all aspects of the social order, including psychological concepts.

Although initially male psychoanalysts debated whether to allow women entry into their profession, eventually women were more welcome than was typical of other professions. By the late 1920s the majority of new adherents to psychoanalysis were women and in the 1930s women became dominant figures in the field (Zaretsky, 2004).

Women analysts investigated female identity, sexuality, eating disorders, abortion, menstruation, and developmental issues, as well as psychoanalytic understandings of children (Viner, 1996). Women also helped develop psychoanalysis in Latin America (Raphael-Leff, 2001). During the 1960s, the questioning of patriarchal authority and the emergence of the second wave of feminism further influenced psychoanalytic theory, especially in the USA (Buhle, 1999). Below we describe women's challenges to patriarchal ideology within psychoanalysis and the use of psychoanalysis to challenge this ideology.

Psychoanalysis and patriarchy

Originally, many psychoanalytic theorists pinned women to gender difference, while at other times they covertly made gender difference invisible, assimilating women to a male norm in conformity with patriarchal society (Moi, 2004). Freud, for instance, explained female sexuality in terms of deficiency, making little mention of what women have. From his perspective, a girl notices that she lacks a penis. The mother is experienced as responsible for cheating her daughter and the girl seeks compensation in a fantasy of having a child of her own, by and for the father, with the mother becoming her rival.

Yet psychoanalysis has proven to be very helpful for feminism by elaborating concepts of desire, the unconscious, defence, fantasy, projection, alienation, and narcissism.

Psychoanalysis dispelled the idea of absolute gender difference, redefined gender as sexual-object choice, and made conscious the depth of human dependence, the dynamics of female development, and the significance of women's mothering (Zaretsky, 2004). Significant work also has been done regarding the nature of women's sexual desires. No longer seen as lack, female analysts have provided representations of female sexuality in terms of presence.

After World War II, focus on the mother–infant relationship intensified. But with the rise of ego psychology and the medicalization of psychoanalysis, the number of female analysts dropped steeply and psychoanalysis became male-centred once again, particularly in the USA. This male-dominated version of psychoanalysis had far-reaching impact internationally and "the analytic theory of the mother–infant relationship became a medical theory directed against women" (Zaretsky, 2004, p. 297). Some psychoanalysts regarded maternal power in families as all important such that they alleged that bad mothering was the primary cause of autism, schizophrenia, and homosexuality.

In the 1980s and 1990s, feminists who found psychoanalysis useful had to justify their interest against claims that it contributed to women's oppression (Flax, 2004). In her influential work, *Psychoanalysis and Feminism,* British psychoanalyst Juliet Mitchell (1974) explained how psychoanalysis could provide an analysis of patriarchal sexist culture. Although psychoanalysis itself was patriarchal, its practitioners took seriously the personal, the private, and the family, finding words to describe what had seemed invisible (Eichenbaum & Orbach, 2003).

In recent decades, feminist psychoanalytic reflection has contributed concepts and methods to object relations, Kleinian thought, self psychology, and Lacanian thought. For example, US psychoanalyst **Jessica Benjamin** (b. 1946) expanded object-relations theory to include the possibility of intersecting subjectivities, mutual recognition, the tolerance of difference, and the awareness of a shared world wherein there is a tension between accepting another's reality and asserting one's own. She stated, "A relational psychoanalysis should leave room for the messy, intrapsychic side of creativity and aggression; it is the contribution of the intersubjective view that may give these elements a more hopeful cast, showing destruction to be the other [*sic*] of recognition" (J. Benjamin, 1990, p. 45).

Feminists employ psychoanalysis to stress the instability of meaning, fact, and what counts as valid (Code, 2003). For example, **Judith Butler** (b. 1956), a US post-structuralist (see Chapter 12), argues that gender is a performance that stabilizes sexual difference and the compulsory nature of this performance makes gender seem like a natural fact. She employs a unique writing style to challenge normative discursive forms that maintain traditional structures of meaning. US scholar **Nancy Chodorow** (b. 1944) uses object-relations theory to deconstruct gender identity and the choice to be a mother, challenging the commonplace notion that women are naturally predisposed to nurture infants.

Applying psychoanalytic thought to critique itself, **Luce Irigaray** (b. 1932), a Belgian-French scholar, focuses on pre-Oedipal forms of knowledge and communication that are based in early body contact, and foresees as yet unrealized representations of the feminine. **Julia Kristeva** (b. 1941), a Bulgarian-French psychoanalyst, is a linguist and cultural theorist whose work on semiotics is important for psychologists interested in hermeneutics, symbolism, and prelinguistic significance. **Hélène Cixous** (b. 1937), a French psycho-analytic literary theorist, studies the impact of phallocentric language and how social and linguistic structures are inseparable. Using poetic language to highlight how words are ambiguous in meaning, much of her work is more poetic than theoretical as she explores language for new forms of representation.

Irigaray, Kristeva, and Cixous are among the leading figures in French psychoanalytic feminist thought. Although they flourished from the 1970s to the 1990s, psychologists interested in how discourse produces the subject continue to study their work (Walkerdine, 2008; Wetherell, 2008).

Part 6 conclusion

The debate on psychoanalysis and feminism continues. Some commentators assert that despite careful theorizing of female sexuality, gender stereotypes persist in mainstream psychoanalytic practice (e.g., Raphael-Leff, 2001). Others believe that psychoanalysis has proven very helpful for feminism by illuminating the depth of patriarchal concepts. It seems that psychoanalysis can be employed as an instrument of critical social theory for understanding patriarchal domination in society and for envisioning emancipatory relations between women and men in society and intimate relationships (J. Smith, 1990).

Part 7   Cultures of psychoanalysis

As we have seen, psychoanalysis has flourished in association with medicine and played a significant role in psychological theory and clinical practice. Yet psychoanalysis has found different receptions in various countries. In order to understand how lines of psychoanalytic inquiry have opened and closed in distinct social–cultural regions, we review the state of the discipline in selected nations. Then we consider psychoanalysis and postcolonial perspectives. This is followed by examining how psychoanalysis is taken up within cultures of psychological science, both natural science and human science. In conclusion, we consider reasons for the popularity of psychoanalysis in modern Western cultures.

Diverse national approaches

Psychoanalysis has taken different forms in Argentina, Australia, Brazil, Canada, China, India, Japan, Russia, and the USA.

Argentina

Throughout Latin America, psychoanalysis has been widely received, although not uncritically (Grossman & Silverman, 2002). In Argentina, with intense immigration and the welcoming of European culture, the personal and social applications of psychoanalysis have been prominent since the 1950s.

Beginning in 1922, the complete works of Freud were translated into Spanish. In the 1930s and 1940s, psychoanalysis provided a means for some Argentinians to disrupt the discourse of fascism by deconstructing it in psychoanalytic terms. A psychoanalytic association was formed in 1942 (Arbiser, 2003), and by the late 1950s a diffusion of psychoanalytic ideas occurred in society as psychoanalytically oriented psychiatric care was offered in public hospitals.

During the 1970s Argentina experienced a great deal of political and ideological tension. The role of psychoanalysis, its power and authority, and its social and political implications were intensely debated. Some saw psychoanalysis as a potentially liberating force associated with modernity and personal freedom, providing a private non-repressive space to understand social modernization and political instability in a highly repressive political environment (M. Plotkin, 2003). Yet psychoanalysts also were accused of "helping" their patients adapt to the injustices of the state (Arbiser, 2003).

Today, many Argentinians have undergone psychoanalysis, and the concepts of psychoanalysis are part of everyday speech. "From taxi drivers to soap opera stars, from politicians to generals, all speak in 'psy-dialect'" (M. Plotkin, 2003, p. 2). Currently, Argentina has one of the largest communities of psychoanalysts worldwide.

Australia

Another important centre of psychoanalytic activity has been Australia (Damousi, 2005). Initially, psychoanalysis gained acceptance during the world wars when psychiatrists found it useful to understand and treat "shell shock." After World War II, with European psychoanalysts immigrating to Australia, psychoanalysis became more institutionalized and predominantly Kleinian. In the 1970s, Argentinean exiles who immigrated to Australia introduced Lacanian theory.

Brazil

Psychology was established in Brazil in 1962 as a distinct discipline in universities, with psychoanalysis being the most important theoretical orientation (Dunker, 2008). During the military regime of 1964–1974, government policy imposed replacing social science and philosophy courses with Psychology and pedagogy courses. The intention was that Psychology would bring stability to Brazilian society. As a result, psychoanalysis now is integrated throughout Brazil's schools, places of business, general and psychiatric hospitals, and legal settings.

Psychoanalysis, arguably, has thrived in Brazil, because it is a society based on distrust of authority (Dunker, 2008). As such, psychoanalysis can exist alongside many different belief systems within Brazilian institutions, because inherent problems with authority call for reflection and elaboration of meaning, which psychoanalysis can offer. Some psychoanalytic processes emerged in unique ways in the Brazilian context. For instance, psychoanalysis is understood more as a way of intensifying pleasure than as an expansion of confessional practices (Dunker, 2008).

Canada

It was not until the 1940s that a Montreal psychoanalytic group was formed to discuss clinical cases according to Freudian doctrine; they did not, however, provide training.

Interested candidates travelled to the USA for training and rarely returned. By the 1950s some analysts began immigrating to Montreal.

In order to become recognized by the IPA, Canadians requested affiliation with the American Psychoanalytic Association. However, the Canadian Psychoanalytic Society intended to admit lay analysts and had a member who was not a physician. The American Psychoanalytic Association had a ban on most non-physicians becoming members and declined their request. Upon appeal, a training institute was established at the Alan Memorial Institute of McGill University identical to the British Training Institute and by 1957 the Canadian Psychoanalytic Society became officially recognized by the IPA. Members of the American Psychoanalytic Association protested, citing a 1936 agreement with the IPA giving them exclusive control over North America. Canadian psychoanalysts maintained their independence; nevertheless, most psychoanalysts in Canada have a medical degree.

China

The first translations of Freud's work into Chinese date back to the 1920s (Zaretsky, 2004). Some Chinese scholars adopted psychoanalytic theory before the 1949 revolution and used it to promote ideas of social reform (Yuan, 2002). But afterwards the authorities viewed psychoanalysis as a product of bourgeois culture. By the time of the Cultural Revolution, psychoanalysis was forbidden in 1966.

Since 1978 with political and economic change in China, increasing interest in psychoanalytic ideas and their application to psychotherapy has occurred. Psychoanalytic theory is taking hold within those elements of Chinese society more focused on the individual. Some universities and medical schools now offer courses in psychoanalysis taught by Westerners (J. Zhang, 2003). But practising psychoanalysts are few.

India

With a theory that differed from Freud's and reflected Indian family life, **Girindrasekhar Bose** (1887–1953) introduced psychoanalysis to India. Sometimes received with hostility as a form of colonialism, more recently Bose's approach has been appropriated by some European, Canadian, and US psychologists in the form of "cultural psychology" (Kakar, 1990). Such cultural psychology examines how values and attitudes affect the way family life and bodily experiences are represented.

Currently, Indian psychology seems most concerned with representing local communities, histories, and social institutions. Because much of psychoanalysis, like Psychology in general, is focused on the individual, it tends not to be considered as important in India as sociology. No matter how psychoanalysis is transformed, some believe it will always be, fundamentally, about the individual and not the group (Parker, 2008; Sharma, 2000).

Japan

Psychiatrist **Kiyoyasu Marui** (1886–1953) received approval from Freud to establish the first branch of the IPA in Japan in 1933 (Alvis, 2003). A student of Marui, **Kosawa Heisaku**

(1897–1958), studied at the Vienna Psychoanalytic Institute; upon his return he established the Kosawa School, which forms the core of the association's Japanese branch. It tends to accept only those with a classical Freudian orientation and a medical degree.

However, when psychoanalysis came to Japan, it had to contend with longstanding Buddhist healing practices deeply embedded in Japanese culture (Shingu & Funaki, 2008). Many Japanese scholars believe that psychoanalysis is a Western theory inappropriate for Japan. Nevertheless, there are points of convergence between the two traditions. Freud's notions of the pleasure principle and the death drive are similar to the Buddhist notion of extinguishing desire and being truly settled in the world. Drawing on traditional cultural forms, Japanese psychoanalysts have made original contributions to psychoanalytic theory.

Russia

In pre-revolutionary times, Freud's works were translated into Russian and influenced psychiatry and psychotherapy. The development of psychoanalysis in Russia persisted through the revolution (Zaretsky, 2004). In 1922, the second analytic institute in the world was established, but three years later the Soviet state dismantled it, because the authorities regarded a focus on intrapersonal dynamics as contrary to state interests.

By the 19030s, psychoanalysis was prohibited (Balachova, Levy, Isurina, & Wasserman, 2001). Anyone who requested access to psychoanalytic literature was put on a list of suspected persons (Vasilyeva, 2000). This period lasted until the 1960s, when during the Khrushchev period far-reaching changes occurred. Psychoanalytic theory regained footing after officially approved critiques enabled people to read about it.

Presently in Russia, distinct groups of psychoanalytic professionals exist, for example, the Association of Jungian Therapy and the East-European Institute of Psychoanalysis. In 1996, the Russian government authorized funds to revive psychoanalysis, produce translations of psychoanalytic works, and become better integrated with international developments. Nevertheless, by the twenty-first century there were no training institutes and few if any trained psychoanalysts in Russia (Vasilyeva, 2000).

USA

Psychoanalysis thrived in the USA with a strong cultural alliance with medicine forged during the 1930s. But a conflict ensued between those who wished to maintain psychoanalysis as distinct from psychiatry and those who sought to adapt psychoanalysis to contemporary expectations of medicine. Freud had predicted a gloomy future for psychoanalysis, if it could not establish a place for itself outside medicine. Despite his opposition, by the mid 1930s all candidates for psychoanalytic training in the US required a medical degree and a psychiatric residency (Zaretsky, 2004). Later, insofar as US analysts were linked with psychiatry they gained prestige and financial reward. However, they also tended to become authoritarian, conformist, repressive, scientistic, and grandiose.

Meanwhile, US psychiatry was split into two feuding camps, with the psychoanalysts at one extreme and the physicalists at the other. Medicine encouraged the simplified notion of mental disorder as disease with a biological cause and a physical cure (i.e., drugs or electroshock therapy). This view won in the end, because it had the support of the increasingly powerful pharmaceutical industry.

Currently, there is a crisis in US recruitment for psychoanalysis and mostly elderly analysts teach new psychoanalysts (Malone, 2008). Numbers of trainees, patients, and training cases are declining. Most analysts have only one or two cases, if any, with the bulk of their practice focused on other forms of psychotherapy. Fewer and fewer psychiatrists seek training in psychoanalysis (Eisold, 2005).

Postcolonial perspective

Postcolonial studies consider the cultural legacy of colonialism and imperialism. Postcolonial critics of psychoanalysis can be grouped into three categories (Jonte-Pace, 2006). One camp focuses on how psychoanalysts have disregarded the effects of culture and ethnicity on psychological experience and ignored the psychology of racism. A second group emphasizes how psychoanalytic discourse has marginalized culturally diverse voices; these scholars make space for and highlight ethnocultural diversity. A third approach reads psychoanalytic theory as offering a fertile explanation and way of analyzing racism and colonialism.

Currently, some psychologists argue that psychoanalysis can contribute to postcolonial critique (see Chapter 12), analyzing colonialism and racism and the ambivalence, uncertainty, and ambiguity of personal desire as it manifests in colonial relationships (e.g., Hook, 2008). In this line of thought, there is a risk of reducing sociohistorical events to the level of individual psychology. Yet, some argue, social-historical analysis also can be reductive, if it ignores the dynamics of desire at the individual level. Personal desires and social relations – intrasubjective and intersubjective experience – need to be respected as mutually informing.

Psychoanalysis and psychology

Freud recognized that poets had understood the human mind well before psychologists (Ellenberger, 1970; Gay, 1988). He was painfully aware that his theory was based on a small number of case studies and that the themes he articulated were present in ancient myths and folktales. Freud intended for psychoanalysis to describe natural laws, causation and the limits of reason, believing that we must find guidance in how to live without religious direction or the centuries-held belief that the mind is transparent to itself, the centre of initiative and the origin of meaning (S. Mitchell & Black, 1995).

However, since the inception of psychoanalysis, critics have questioned its scientific legitimacy. In what follows, we review the historical debate on this issue in terms of how psychoanalysis has been taken up within the distinct cultures of natural-science and human-science psychology. We conclude that psychoanalysis can be considered a critical hermeneutic science.

Historical relationship

Psychologists have held ambivalent views on psychoanalysis historically. For many early US scientific psychologists, psychoanalysis threatened their new field. The core problem was that psychoanalysts dealt with subjective human experience, while natural-science psychologists used presumably objective methods to study behaviour (Hornstein, 1992).

During the 1920s when psychologists offered diplomatic, constructive criticisms and psychoanalysts responded by claiming that only those who had been analyzed could legitimately criticize psychoanalysis, psychologists launched a campaign of negative criticism. Psychologists became more defensive about what constitutes science. In addition, most Psychology textbooks in this era contain no mention of psychoanalysis.

Before long, two significant anomalies appeared in US psychologists' opposition to psychoanalysis. First, in 1940 Edwin Boring, an experimentalist critic of psychoanalysis, and other psychologists disclosed their experiences as psychoanalytic patients in a prominent Psychology journal. Despite their scientific skepticism about it, they made public their personal choice of psychoanalytic treatment.

Secondly, psychoanalysis was quite popular in US society, but popular culture conflated psychoanalysis and Psychology, which made natural-science psychologists uncomfortable. Accordingly, after World War II, many psychologists initiated experimental tests of psychoanalytic concepts to demonstrate their lack of validity. Although some findings confirmed invalidity, others did not; yet mainstream psychologists interpreted them as mostly negative. Thus psychoanalysis lost credibility and did not achieve the scientific status to which Freud aspired. Eventually, when psychologists recognized that the public remained fascinated with psychoanalysis, they accommodated by incorporating into their science what they found useful.

Presently, the newly coined field "neuropsychoanalysis" indicates a rapprochement of cognitive neuroscientists and psychoanalysts. The International Neuropsychoanalysis Society, founded in London in 2000, promotes interdisciplinary work between the fields of psychoanalysis and neuroscience on such topics of mutual interest as emotion, sexuality and gender, dreams and psychosis, depression, the self in conflict, and play.

Without the integration of psychoanalysis with neuroscience, some argue, psychoanalysis will be obsolete; others foresee the disappearance of psychoanalysis as a separate field of study. Objective investigation of material correlates of psychoanalytic concepts might make room for psychoanalysis within mainstream Psychology, introducing analytic metaphors and ways of understanding to audiences typically hostile to psychoanalysis (Fonagy, 2003). On the other hand, researching the biophysical correlates of psychoanalytic dynamics shifts emphasis to the biomedical and could ignore ontological inquiry and political implications of the phenomena that psychoanalysis can reveal.

Although psychoanalysis has a contemporary presence in Psychology in psychosocial studies of subjectivity, cultural resources, and discursive practices, its place remains contentious and openly debated (Frosh & Baraitser, 2008). For its part, psychoanalysis makes room for reflexivity in some psychological research. Outside Psychology, psychoanalysis is contributing to important studies in postcolonial theory and post-structural feminist theory.

A natural science?

Historically, the meaning of the term "science" is ambiguous. Freud described psychoanalysis with the German word, *Wissenschaft*, meaning a disciplined process of gaining systematic and consistent knowledge (i.e., a human science). Yet he also hoped psychoanalysis would prove to be a natural science. As a child of the Enlightenment, Freud intended psychoanalysis to describe natural laws, causation, and the limits of reason. However, he did not promote formal psychoanalytic research. Rather, he argued that the thousands of hours he and his colleagues spent with patients in analysis provided evidence for his ideas.

With a dismissive stance towards research, the number of empirical outcome studies of psychoanalysis did not keep pace with studies of other treatments. As a result, psychoanalysis garnered a reputation for lack of empirical support. Nonetheless, some claim, "Effect sizes for psychodynamic therapy are as large as those reported for other therapies that have been actively promoted as 'empirically supported' and 'evidence based'" (Shedler, 2010, p. 98).

To this day, opinion is divided sharply about the aim of psychoanalysis: to make sense of subjective experience or to determine objective, scientifically valid knowledge. Moreover, Freud has been the object of vitriolic criticism. He has been labelled an intellectual coward (Masson, 1984, 1988), a faulty logician (Grünbaum, 1984), and a scientific fraud (Crews, 1975, 1998; Eysenck, 1953; Gellner, 1985; Popper, 1959).

The critics of psychoanalysis have rejected it on at least **five grounds**:

- They repudiate psychoanalysts' attitude of interpreting skepticism about psychoanalysis as "being resistant" unconsciously to its truth (Zaretsky, 2004). Critics also attribute the popularity of psychoanalysis to public gullibility, intellectual fashion, and analysts' persuasive writing.
- Psychoanalysis fails as a natural science. Karl Popper (1959) famously claimed that psychoanalysis could not be empirically validated by the standards of natural science. For him, a scientific theory had to be falsifiable, which psychoanalysis is not.
- Psychoanalysis cannot be a science, because the analyst's suggestions and presence bias its outcomes (e.g., Grünbaum, 1984). Furthermore, although psychoanalysis might work as a placebo, it cannot produce testable hypotheses (Grünbaum, 1993).
- Subjectivity and unconscious processes cannot be investigated scientifically, and the untestable concepts of psychoanalysis and its unsubstantiated claims about therapeutic efficacy make it more like religion than science (Gellner, 1985).
- Psychoanalysis relies on "reified" concepts and misused analogies. Using metaphors can deceive the theorist into mistaking the metaphor itself for reality. This is the problem of nominalism that William of Ockham identified in the fourteenth century.

Overall, natural-science psychologists have concluded that psychoanalysis is not scientific. In addition, "The accumulated weight of anecdotal evidence [in support of psychoanalysis] is formidable. But the kind of statistical evidence that carries weight in hospitals and academic settings, that impresses insurance companies and government agencies, is still sadly lacking" (Eisold, 2005, p. 1191). Critical review of psychoanalysis raises deeper questions concerning the meaning of science, the nature and intent of claims to knowledge, and whether knowledge of human subjectivity and unconscious processes must conform to natural-scientific standards (Zaretsky, 2004).

A human science?

For some scholars, natural-science criticisms of psychoanalysis are expressions of scientism and inapplicable to psychoanalysis. Natural-science psychologists tend to define science as based only on testable hypotheses, observable data, and the ability to predict and control. In 1976, bowing to this natural science tradition, the American Psychoanalytic Association began funding psychoanalytic research that adopted testable research questions with measurable variables (Wallerstein & Fonagy, 1999). The association did not challenge the relevance of conventional scientific standards to psychoanalysis as a science of subjectivity and unconscious processes (Parker, 2008).

Psychoanalytic theory was maligned as speculation without critics recognizing how speculation is an inseparable part of empirical research and essential for data-interpretation (Teo, 2008). By contrast, many mainstream psychologists assume they can transcend speculation by methodological means. As such, they dismiss psychoanalysis as an archaic and unscientific approach and force it to prove itself by the very scientific paradigm that it questions.

Many other scholars understand psychoanalysis, not as a natural science, but as a human science of reflection and interpretation (Ricoeur, 1970). Psychoanalysis offers a different language for human experience, situated in historical and cultural context (Parker, 2008). It fosters a radical notion of subjectivity that violates the possibility of objectivity. Although not Freud's own intention, some psychologists have come to value psychoanalysis as a science of subjectivity and provider of knowledge inaccessible to quantitative inquiry. They argue that it is not valid to assess psychoanalysis using natural-science standards, because they are inappropriate for understanding interpretive sciences (Frosh, 2006).

Moreover, in practice, the psychoanalytic therapist or researcher studies herself or himself to raise awareness of her or his influence on the patient or the interview participant. As such, psychoanalysis can be considered more scientific than non-reflective mainstream Psychology. Willingness to consider transference and counter-transference issues fits with the principle in modern physics that observer and observed reciprocally influence each other (see Chapter 12). For example, Evelyn Fox Keller (1985) has used object-relations psychoanalysis and feminist theory to deconstruct scientific practices and knowledge-claims and to demonstrate how any understanding of nature occurs within a socially constructed context of historically bound values, meanings, and conventions.

Part 7 conclusion

The diverse national expressions that psychoanalysis has taken suggest versatility as well as diversity in that in some contexts psychoanalytic theory and social critique, such as an intellectual tool in postcolonial studies, are as prominent as psychoanalytic treatment is. Yet in other nations in which psychoanalysis formerly played a significant role, such as the USA, this type of human science appears to be losing its influence. The historical relationship between psychoanalysis and US Psychology suggests considerable ambivalence on psychologists' part, arguably because of conflicting conceptions of what constitutes legitimate science. For many natural-science psychologists, psychoanalysts' claims seem mired in personal subjectivity; as such, these claims are incapable of contributing to making objective scientific knowledge about mental processes and behaviour. Clearly, a clash of scientific worldviews has been occurring.

On the other hand, others argue that psychoanalysis as a hermeneutic human science enriches personal and cultural understandings, but the practice of psychoanalysis also is considered to be a critical science that can emancipate diverse forms of unnecessary domination (Billig, 1997). Jürgen Habermas (1972) sees the potential for psychoanalysis as emancipation through the experience of self-reflection. According to him, psychoanalysis can elicit communication that is less distorted by ideology than most conversation such that "the subject frees itself from a state in which it had become an object for itself" (p. 247). This possibility requires, however, a situation where equality, sincerity, honesty, and morality define the analytic relationship, a situation which seems to be of most concern for feminist and intersubjective forms of psychoanalysis.

Part 8   Thematic review

Two themes appear to capture the story of psychoanalysis: **illumination of the psychological interior** in diverse and versatile ways and **Psychology's ambivalent relationship with psychoanalysis**.

Illumination of the psychological interior

Instead of representing the creative striving of one isolated genius, psychoanalysis is best understood as the consequence of a particular social-historical moment that blossomed into diverse perspectives that illuminate the psychological interior (Plotkin, 2003). Repeated criticisms of psychoanalysis have helped clarify what it is (Frosh, 2006). Psychoanalysts include unconscious dynamics, fantasy, and desire in the construction of knowledge without denying that distress is rooted in such oppressive realities as war, sexual and physical abuse, poverty, racism, and sexism. Psychoanalysts deal with the personal histories through which individuals relate to the world.

Diversity in psychoanalysis is evident as in any other psychological school of thought, because theory and practice arise in social-historical contexts based on theorists' self-reflection in response to their times. Arguably, the subjective basis of any psychological theory is intrinsic to a discipline in which its scholars and practitioners reflect as humans on what it means to be human. Thus the variety of psychoanalytic conceptions corresponds to different modes of life. As historian Roger Smith (1997) observed, "Unity in the human sciences would become possible only if people were to lead a uniform life" (p. 22).

Furthermore, psychoanalysts accept irrationality, fantasy, and desire as well as history, culture, politics, economics, and society as conditions under which meaningful facts are known. As such, psychoanalysis provides a critical framework for making and questioning empirical observations (Parker, 2008) (see Chapters 11 and 12).

Forged in the midst of industrial revolutions, two world wars, major geographical shifts and emigration, modernization, the suffragist movement and waves of feminism, along with intense self-reflexivity and the postmodern dispersion of subjectivity, psychoanalysis has communicated meaningful psychological ideas that masses of ordinary people have adopted to guide their lives. Many contemporary psychoanalytic writings as well as the classic writings of Freud, Jung, Klein, and Lacan continue to be read and used in the fields of art history, literature, cultural studies, feminist theory, and critical psychology. Many also have found psychoanalysis a valuable critique of societal structures and ideologies.

Throughout its history, then, psychoanalysis has generated various forms of social critique, theories of unconscious and conscious subjectivity, diverse therapeutic practices, and a type of hermeneutic inquiry. In short, diversity and versatility have characterized a discipline aimed at illuminating the psychological interior.

Psychology's ambivalent relationship with psychoanalysis

Historically, psychoanalysis has had a lengthy ambivalent relationship with mainstream Psychology, and psychoanalytic influence in Psychology, particularly clinical psychology, seems to have waned considerably. Natural-science psychologists employ psychoanalytic contributions in courses that introduce Psychology and that cover abnormal, clinical, and personality psychology and the history of Psychology, but do so typically with dismissive discourse. Moreover, undergraduate and graduate courses in psychoanalysis are rare in Psychology.

Nevertheless, the American Psychological Association maintains a division on psychoanalysis, which publishes a journal, *Psychoanalytic Psychology*. Some graduate Psychology programmes teach psychoanalytic theory, and some students identify with a psychoanalytic orientation, finding it intellectually challenging, compared to other forms of psychotherapy (Eisold, 2005). Outside mainstream Psychology, scholars and practitioners affiliated with human-science Psychology generally hold in high esteem the knowledge about the vast terrain of human subjectivity that psychoanalytic perspectives can produce.

Summary

In Part 1 of our history of the psychoanalytic movement we described pre-psychoanalytic conceptions of unconscious phenomena in terms of philosophical antecedents in the context of nineteenth-century medicine and science. This was the intellectual climate within which Sigmund Freud introduced the scientific study of the significance of unconscious processes and the therapeutic practice of psychoanalysis.

In Part 2 we discussed Freud's development of psychoanalytic theory and practice. We began by describing the social and intellectual context of his work. Then we summarized his investigations, concentrating on his dream theory, sexual theory, and therapeutic practice, ending with considerations of why Freudian thought remains very important for Psychology.

In Part 3 we presented a quite different form of early psychoanalysis, Carl Jung's analytical psychology. We discussed its social–intellectual context and described his concepts of archetypes and personality types and the focal points of his approach to psychoanalytic practice.

In Part 4 we explored diverse forms of psychoanalysis in which theorists stressed social and political influences on unconscious processes. First we described the theory and clinical practice of Alfred Adler, whose individual psychology had many social applications. We discussed Karen Horney's appreciation of women's psychology that challenged Freudian beliefs and her conception of the varieties of anxiety. Erich Fromm integrated psychoanalysis with Marxian concepts, expressed in his notion of social character. Wilhelm Reich emphasized the embodied nature of personality and the importance of challenging repressive social norms. Rather than linking Freud and Marx, Erik Erikson explored cultural and social developmental phenomena and contributed notions of "identity crisis" and stages of personality development.

Psychoanalysis took many other forms that also significantly altered psychoanalytic theory and practice. In Part 5 we discussed how the psychoanalytic movement subsequently shifted its focus to maternal influence and addressed both intrapsychic and interpersonal subjectivities. We described the emphasis on ego psychology in Anna Freud's work and in the work of Heinz Hartmann within US culture; object-relations theory prefigured by Sándor Ferenczi and developed by Melanie Klein; the mother–infant emphasis of the middle group, exemplified by W. R. D. Fairbairn, Donald Winnicott, and John Bowlby; self psychology, promoted by Heinz Kohut and countered by Otto Kernberg; and the work of Jacques Lacan, who stressed the relationship of language, cultural meaning, and unconscious processes.

Scholars and practitioners inspired by both feminism and psychoanalysis have explored the gendered nature of existence and the influence of patriarchal ideology on unconscious processes. We addressed these issues in Part 6, discussing challenges to patriarchal psychoanalysis from feminist thought and the emergence of new psychoanalytic ideas.

In Part 7 we placed the story of psychoanalysis in cultural perspective in three ways. First, we examined how psychoanalysis has been received in different nations in the past and more recently among postcolonial scholars. Secondly, we considered the status of psychoanalysis as a science, that is, a body of knowledge, way of understanding, and method of research, and, third, we discussed the underlying issues regarding many modern psychologists' ambivalence about psychoanalysis.

In Part 8 we reflected on two themes that summarize the successful and considerable impact that psychoanalysis has had on Western culture: illumination of the psychological interior in diverse and versatile ways, and natural-science Psychology's ambivalent relationship with the various forms of psychoanalysis as theory, social critique, psychotherapeutic practice, and scientific inquiry.

Sample essay questions

1. Psychoanalysis is distinguished by its considerable diversity of positions and of their respective emphases in theory and practice. Give a rationale for selecting the psychoanalytic perspective that you find most congenial and which perspective you find least congenial.

2. Explain how psychoanalysis can be reconciled with feminism.

3. Many natural-science psychologists assert that psychoanalysis has not been and cannot be a science. Critically reflect on this statement.

RECOMMENDED READING

There is a vast literature on all aspects of psychoanalysis and the historiography of psychoanalysis is a discipline unto itself. We have not been able to include all of the important theorists and developments in the history of psychoanalysis.

A visual timeline of 100 years of psychoanalytic history and an excellent study tool is found in the work of Young-Bruehl and Dunbar (2009). Excellent social-historical treatments of psychoanalysis are made in Ellenberger's (1970) *The discovery of the unconscious*, Zaretsky's (2004) *Secrets of the soul*, and Gay's (1988) *Freud: A life for our time*. The seventh issue of the *Annual Review of Critical Psychology* explores the value of Lacanian psychoanalysis for critical psychology, research, theory, and practice.

The critique of psychoanalysis is also an intellectual tradition; see Crews's (1975) *Out of my system: Psychoanalysis, ideology, and critical method*, Gellner's (1985) *The psychoanalytic movement: The cunning of unreason*, and Grünbaum's (1984) *The foundations of psychoanalysis: A philosophical critique*. These works criticize psychoanalysis, because it does not generate hypotheses testable by way of experiment or standardized measurable outcomes. A more contemporary perspective is Frosh's (1999) *The politics of psychoanalysis: An introduction to Freudian and post-Freudian theory*, which critiques psychoanalysis in terms of its limited power to effect social change.

ONLINE RESOURCES

The Stanford Encyclopedia of Philosophy contains entries on multiple aspects of psychoanalysis.

For Jacques Lacan, see www.lacan.com/ and http://lacansociety.com/

For psychoanalysis and feminism, see: http://plato.stanford.edu/archives/sum2011/entries/feminism-psychoanalysis/

On narcissism, see www.narcissismepidemic.com/

Chapter outline

Introduction

In this, the second chapter on human-science Psychology, we trace its origins to the interpretive discipline known as hermeneutics. Then we describe the multiple facets of human-science Psychology as expressed in phenomenological, existentialist, humanistic, and transpersonal psychologies. Although these alternatives to natural-science Psychology initially emerged in continental Europe, they have proved influential elsewhere, including in Anglo-American nations.

The **aims** of this chapter are to describe:

- The pivotal problem of interpretation in Psychology and how the discipline of hermeneutics is a viable solution.
- Wilhelm Dilthey's foundational distinction between the natural sciences and the human sciences and his approach to studying human mental life.
- The contributions to Psychology of Eduard Spranger and Karl Jaspers, who extended, modified, and applied Dilthey's concepts and methods.
- The concerns of phenomenological and existential psychologies and one particular application, Viktor Frankl's logotherapy.
- The development of "American" adaptations of these European psychologies in the diverse forms expressed by Rollo May, George Kelly, and the humanistic psychologists: Abraham Maslow and Carl Rogers.
- Transpersonal psychologies and the historically contested place of spirituality and religion in Psychology, including the implications of psychologists' incorporating spirituality and religion for the discipline and for individuals' physical and mental health.
- Two themes that summarize the issues addressed in this chapter: the centrality of understanding and interpretation, and the disputed border between body and mind, soul, and spirit.

Part 1   The hermeneutic problem

In Figure 10.1 you can see a reproduction of **Pablo Picasso's** mural, *Guernica*. Try describing and interpreting it. When you do, you realize that in order to understand this painting you have to find answers to a variety of questions. You might ask: "What do I see depicted in this mural? What meaning does it have? What is it about myself and my historical circumstances that makes me have these interpretations and not others? What do the various figures and symbols in the mural mean for Picasso? Who is Picasso? What is *Guernica* and why did he paint it?"

Picasso (1881–1973), a Spanish painter, was one of the most important visual artists of the twentieth century. Guernica is a town in the Basque region of northern Spain that was bombed by German military airplanes in 1937. This event took place during the Spanish

Figure 10.1 A Spanish postage stamp shows Pablo Picasso's painting *Guernica*

Civil War (1936–1939) between politically left and right factions. Adolf Hitler's military supported the Spanish Nationalists under General Francisco Franco (1892–1975) and was responsible for the bombing and killing of thousands of civilians in Guernica, a town that had no military-strategic significance. Thus, Guernica stands as a symbol for systematically exterminating civilians in modern, technology-driven warfare.

The painting shows a distressed horse in the middle; desperate, fleeing humans who cannot escape; a bull on the left side and apparently a "pietà" (traditionally, a painting or sculpture of Mary, the mother of Jesus Christ, holding his lifeless body in her arms). The painting also portrays a lamp with beams pointing towards the dismembered humans, while under the horse lies a warrior with a broken sword and a flower (or something else) in the hand. It seems Picasso depicted the victims but not the perpetrators of this crime. Note that in this description we already have used words, such as "desperate" or "pietà," that belie interpretations. This fact shows that an interpretation without any knowledge of preconceived notions is impossible.

Now, what could the symbols and objects in the painting *mean*? The light bulb at the top might symbolize destruction from exploding bombs. Picasso might have used the light bulb to contrast with traditional Christian paintings in which light and illumination were intended to convey salvation through Christ. But in *Guernica*, he depicts light produced by human technology as producing helplessness. In this case, then, light might be a symbol of death.

What about the bull in the mural? It has been interpreted in at least two ways. The bull might represent the Spanish people who are aware of the atrocities of the Nationalists and their allies. In this interpretation Picasso might have expressed hope that General Franco would be held accountable. The bull also might represent fascism in general or even Franco: while his own people are slaughtered by anonymous machines of death, he stands impassively at the sideline, but is ultimately responsible for what is happening to innocent civilians.

How is this discussion about Picasso's *Guernica* relevant to the history and philosophy of Psychology? We did not offer the interpretations above to provide a lesson in art; perhaps art historians would consider our interpretations simplistic. Our point simply is that a painting as a human act needs to be *interpreted* and *understood*. Despite the fact that different interpretations are possible, not all possible interpretations will be equal. It is clear that an expert on art and Picasso will produce different interpretations than a novice who sees this painting for the very first time or than professors of Psychology who are familiar with it.

The notions of *understanding* and *interpretation* are very relevant to Psychology, because some psychologists have argued that mental life should be *understood* and *interpreted* rather than (causally) *explained*. This orientation means that psychologists should work with the methods of the humanities and social sciences (sometimes known collectively as "human sciences") rather than exclusively emulate the natural sciences.

Speaking in a generalized way without referring to a specific author or a specific reader, if "I" want to understand "you," I have to understand the meaning of your mental life, which might include your personal history, memories, and activities that form your identity. In order to understand your interpretations of Picasso's painting, the most important part is not the chemical composition of Picasso's colours, the painting's physical dimensions, or quantifiable attitudes about it, which is a natural-scientific approach, but the meaning the painting expresses and invokes, which is a human-scientific approach.

Similarly, for psychologists, according to a human-science approach, the most important subject matter is not the brain's neuroscientific qualities but the content of the mind and the situation of the person. What makes you "you" are your lived experiences and your interpretations of these experiences. In order to understand "you" one must try to recapture what you have experienced and how you have *interpreted* these experiences. This is the starting point for the human-science psychologies discussed in this chapter.

Meanings of hermeneutics

Hermeneutics is the discipline of understanding and interpreting meaning or the art and science of interpretation. The term is derived from Hermes, the messenger of the gods in ancient Greek mythology, who conveyed to humans the meaning of divine messages. Thus, hermeneutics has a long history and was discussed by Aristotle (2001) for whom interpretation was part of logical thinking.

Judaeo-Christian context

Later, hermeneutics involved the Judaeo-Christian practice of biblical interpretation. In contrast to the Greek philosophers who emphasized gaining knowledge through experience and reason, Christian philosophers such as Augustine emphasized that one should gain knowledge through revelation by way of contemplating the Bible. Based on the assumption that it expresses God's ideas, words, and will, understanding and interpreting the Bible became a central feature of study and learning. Within Christianity, for a variety of cultural-historical reasons, it became important to understand the differences between the Old Testament (the Hebrew Bible) and the New Testament (the Christian Bible).

Biblical hermeneutics distinguishes among **four types of interpretation**:

- *Literal*: understanding the actual message. For example, the biblical book Genesis mentions that pairs of animals entered Noah's ark. According to a literal interpretation, this event occurred just as described.
- *Moral*: understanding the moral message of stories. One can interpret the story of Noah's ark as teaching humans that they should be righteous and obey God's rules in order to be saved.
- *Allegorical*: understanding the hidden meaning of biblical stories. Noah's ark, then, could refer to the Christian church and how it should be organized. The story of the ark could be an allegory for the way living beings should be saved.
- *Mystical*: understanding the divine message, for instance, of the mystical significance of numbers in the Bible, such as entering the ark two-by-two.

During the Renaissance the question arose about who has the authority to provide the best biblical interpretation. In the Roman Catholic Church this competence was assigned to church authorities. In the Protestant tradition it was Martin Luther who insisted that all humans have the ability to understand the Bible for themselves. His stance required translating the Bible into a language that ordinary people could understand, in his case, sixteenth-century German.

Yet, translation is an act of interpretation itself, because the translator must interpret the text when choosing words from the second language to express the original language. Furthermore, interpretations can have real consequences. In several cases, Jehovah's Witnesses, a Christian sect originating in the nineteenth century, have insisted that blood transfusions are not allowed according to their interpretation of the Scriptures. When a religious group believes that it is God's will not to have blood transfusions, then there might be serious health consequences for its members.

Secular context

Hermeneutics was secularized when used to understand law, philosophy, history, and medicine. For example, when questions arise about how to interpret legal texts, a judgment must be made by higher courts of law. Beginning in the eighteenth century, hermeneutics became important for understanding not only texts but human action (e.g., to understand a specific behaviour), or the products of human action (e.g., to interpret music), and human mental life (e.g., to understand emotions). These developments provided a new context for hermeneutics.

German scholar Johann Gottfried von Herder (1744–1803) suggested that understanding is the ability to empathize with the thoughts of other people and other times. Similarly, one of the key figures of German hermeneutics, Friedrich Schleiermacher, argued that understanding refers to empathizing with the thoughts and intentions of an author.

Recognizing the possibility for empathic awareness led Johann Droysen (1868) to make the famous distinction between a natural-scientific methodology, which he identified as "explanation," and a historical methodology, which he identified as "understanding" the unique meaning of events and objects. Similarly, Wilhelm Windelband distinguished nomothetic sciences, searching for general laws, and idiographic sciences, attempting to describe and understand individual events, objects, and persons. Hermeneutics was developed further in the nineteenth century by Wilhelm Dilthey (see below) and by Hans-Georg Gadamer in the twentieth century.

Gadamer's approach

Gadamer took from philosopher **Martin Heidegger** (1889–1976) the idea that the nature of being is interpretive. In other words, as Aristotle asserted, the defining feature of humans is their interpretive nature. Thus, interpretations play a significant role in all human activities.

One of the central features of interpretation, according to Gadamer, is the notion that interpretation is influenced by pre-understandings. We cannot present an interpretation from nowhere, he argued; rather, an interpretation is based on what we have learned and accepted before. This principle applies to mundane *and* scientific experiences. Consequently, Gadamer is critical of natural-scientific approaches in which scholars assume that they are completely objective. For him, they are not aware of the assumptions that precede research and influence its outcome.

Gadamer also suggests that *ontology precedes epistemology*, which means that in Psychology the nature of the subject matter (i.e., what is mental life?) precedes the methodology employed to study the subject matter. Thus, for Gadamer, method does not necessarily lead to knowledge. This stance is in opposition to the unexamined assumption held by many natural scientists, including psychologists, that method leads to knowledge, as in the statement, "If you get your method right, you will make a scientific discovery."

"Philosophical hermeneutics" is the term that describes Gadamer's ([1960] 1997) approach to the art of understanding and interpretation. For him, hermeneutics should correct an important falsehood of modern consciousness: idolatry of the scientific method (see Chapter 11) and the presumed anonymous authority of the sciences. Instead of conceding one's responsibility for decision-making to the expert, Gadamer assigns this task to every citizen.

Gadamer is critical of those human sciences that attempt to emulate the natural sciences. Just as the natural sciences are not designed to provide an understanding of human experiences, the human sciences do not exist in order to discover natural laws. In Gadamer's words:

The individual case does not serve only to confirm a law from which practical predictions can be made. Its ideal is rather to understand the phenomenon itself in its unique and historical concreteness ... the aim is not to confirm and extend these universalized experiences in order to attain knowledge of a law ... but to understand how this man, this people, or this state is what it has become, or more generally, how it happened that it is so (*Truth and Method*, Gadamer, [1960] 1997, pp. 4–5)

Instead of expecting the natural sciences to be the source of all knowledge, Gadamer suggests exploring the arts, which reveal truths that cannot be captured via natural-scientific methodology. What kind of truth can be revealed by the arts? If we want to understand the psychological meaning of Picasso's *Guernica*, we might explore the interpretation that waging war against a civilian population is unacceptable and heartbreaking.

Gadamer's belief that art can produce truth is based on a concept of aesthetic experience, a form of knowledge that has moral but not conceptual dimensions. He labels this form of knowledge as moral knowledge (*phronesis*), and he contrasts it with conceptual knowledge (*episteme*). Furthermore, he suggests that the human sciences are based on *phronesis* and not on *episteme*. Thus, the subject–object dualism ("I vs. my object of research") is inappropriate in the human sciences, because the so-called "objects" of the human sciences are interwoven with the subject.

In Psychology, both the investigators and the object of their investigations are human, whereas in chemistry, investigators are human but their object is a chemical substance. In historiography, history is not just an object but also a part of the researcher's identity and practices. Thus, the concept of *experience* has a different meaning in the different sciences: whereas the natural sciences depend on the notion that experiences (e.g., observations) are only valid if they are repeatable, a similar concept of experience does not apply to history or Psychology, because historical and personal experiences are not repeatable (for instance, "my" experiences of wartime).

To elucidate the problem of understanding and interpretation, Gadamer elaborated a set of **six concepts** that are integral to hermeneutics. Here we translate these ideas in terms of Psychology.

(1) Hermeneutic circle: understanding is always framed by something that is already understood. For instance, if you want to understand a text, you must consider the whole in order to understand the meaning of its particular parts. Yet you must also understand the parts of the text in order to understand the whole meaning of the book.

Likewise, if you want to understand another person, you must understand the particular actions and statements that the person makes, yet you must also consider the person as a whole in order to understand her or his actions. Thus, interpreting a few personal statements out of context can lead to misinterpretation of the whole person.

Conversely, understanding the general worldview of a person does not ensure understanding the specificities of particular statements. This circle of interpretation need not lead to desperation, with the ultimate truth always out of grasp. Rather, it can be an opportunity to develop one's understanding of another person.

(2) Horizon: one's personal knowledge and experiences are the ground and limit of understanding. On a larger scale each horizon of understanding is historically determined and culturally embedded. The way men thought about women 150 years ago is somewhat different from today.

Gadamer suggests that we cannot escape our pre-understanding, situated in the present horizon, and that our current understanding determines how we interpret gender. Thus, my own current understanding of men or women, my own horizon, is influenced by such developments. In the process of understanding, my immediate horizon is mediated by the historically emerging horizon of understanding.

(3) Fusion of horizons: one's horizon can be transcended through exposure to another horizon, which conveys a view and values that place one's own horizons in a new context. When we understand someone, we merge our horizon with their horizons.

Gadamer compares the ability to transcend one's own interpretive horizon to Georg Wilhelm Friedrich Hegel's dialectical reasoning, invoking the notion of a synthesis: when one understands a person, one approaches the person with a certain horizon. But the person also expresses a certain horizon, and understanding occurs in the process of putting these two horizons together. In short, I might understand another human being's experience by merging my horizon with that person's horizon.

(4) Tradition and prejudice: everyone is embedded in a particular tradition. This determines one's horizon. Yet realizing that one is situated within a specific tradition does not limit freedom of knowledge; it makes it possible. I produce knowledge out of something, not out of nothing.

At the same time history constitutes prejudices in understanding. There is no prejudice-less objectivity. Gadamer even suggests that modern science displays a prejudice against prejudice – meaning that science pretends that it is possible to proceed without any assumptions. It is important to underline that Gadamer does not use the term prejudice in a pejorative manner but in a descriptive way.

Consider this example: if I want to understand someone from another culture, I enter the process with certain assumptions. Instead of denying that I have these assumptions it would be better to admit and reflect upon them. Thus, critical reflection and dialogue provide the opportunity to adjust prejudice, but I never can eradicate it.

(5) Dialogue: hermeneutic experience is a dialogue between the interpreter and the object of interpretation, whether text, event, action, or a person. Gadamer emphasizes the importance of questioning from within our horizon. Understanding, then, can be described as a form of dialogue or a conversation between, for example, two lovers.

Understanding is constrained and made possible by the questions posed. Thus, as my questions change, my understanding of my partner changes over time. Gadamer ([1960] 1997) even suggests that "the logic of the human sciences is a logic of the question" (p. 370). This claim emphasizes that the meaning and validity of knowledge is interconnected with a scholars' historical situation.

(6) Language: the universal medium for understanding is language and interpretation takes place in a linguistic medium. Language determines who we are and how we understand the world as much as history does.

Section conclusion

For Gadamer, conflicting possibilities of understanding in the human sciences must be, and should be, settled on moral grounds. Interpretation is part of all human knowing, and understanding is not merely a mode of knowing, but a mode of being. However, Gadamer's philosophical hermeneutics did not deal with the issue of how one distinguishes good and bad interpretations and how one can establish guidelines for producing critical interpretations.

Critical hermeneutics

Jürgen Habermas (1972) promoted the idea of critical hermeneutics in the social sciences. In his view, critical hermeneutics should challenge the notion of objectivity in the human sciences (e.g., most psychologists assume that Psychology is an objective science) and allow reflection on the historical relationship between subject and object (e.g., when is a psychological object considered the same as a natural-scientific object?).

Habermas points out that choosing a theoretical framework prejudges a field of investigation. For example, if one chooses a behavioural framework for analyzing the attachment of children to parents, then one accepts certain pre-judgments about the situation (including the idea that behavioural concepts are appropriate for addressing attachment). In addition, Habermas emphasized looking at the consensus-making processes of a scientific community regarding theories, research strategies, and methods. The consensus might be rational but it is never entirely convincing, because perfectly rational systems do not exist.

It is possible to blend hermeneutics and critical theory, that is, to temper hermeneutics with a critical reflection on power relations in society. In his book *The Power of Dialogue: Critical Hermeneutics after Gadamer and Foucault* Kögler (1999) amalgamated Gadamerian philosophical hermeneutics with Foucauldian post-structuralism. Central to this amalgamation is integration of the concepts of pre-understanding and dialogue with an analysis of power.

Critical hermeneutics for Psychology

Recently, Thomas Teo (2008, 2011) claimed that hermeneutics plays an important role in empirical research, especially when it comes to the interpretation of empirical data ("results" or "findings") in published work. Data alone do not determine interpretations; otherwise psychologists would not need to include discussions in their works, and the data would be sufficient by themselves. Interpretations of data necessarily and always contain a hermeneutic moment, because discussions are *under-determined* by empirical data.

Philosophers of science have discussed a similar problem, the under-determination of theory by data (Quine, 1969). The thesis is that radically different theories can be supported equally on empirical grounds. This thesis was developed by the physicist Pierre-Maurice-Marie Duhem (1861–1916), who asserted that experiments in physics contain observations of phenomena *and* theoretical interpretations (Duhem ([1905] 1954).

> **Small-group discussion.** Imagine that you select a Psychology article on a critically challenged topic in which interpretations are under-determined by the data. After you remove the authors' discussion you distribute it to a group of peers for their responses. Would different individuals come to the same conclusions as the authors did?

In Psychology, as in other disciplines of study, the data are not identical with the interpretation of the data. Discussions are not just descriptions of data; rather, they impart meaning to data and make results understandable. Data require interpretations to make them comprehensible for the authors, peers, and an audience or a readership.

We term this phenomenon the *hermeneutic surplus* of interpretation: through interpretive speculation data are understood better than they would be if presented by themselves. An analysis of the rhetoric of facts in academic discourse reveals that often what are presented as "facts" are indeed data *and* interpretive speculations.

The same argument applies to the concept of empirical knowledge. The knowledge that is produced in psychological studies and published in research articles and books contains data *and* interpretations. This hermeneutic surplus is often the most important part of a study, as authors convey meaning to peers in presentations, to students in the form of textbooks, and to the general public via the mass media. Yet, according to mainstream methodological

Box 10.1 Interpretation in composing a psychology article

From the perspective of publication manuals on how to develop a research article, only the following parts of a research article would be needed in Psychology if interpretive speculations were determined by data alone: title, abstract, introduction, method, and results. No discussion would be required. Yet the *Publication Manual of the American Psychological Association* (2009) specifically assigns interpretation to the discussion part of an article. Indeed, it even promotes speculation.

Instead of criteria to determine what constitutes valid discussions, interpretations, or speculations, the *Manual* recommends: "You are *free* [our emphasis] to examine, interpret, and qualify the results, as well as to draw inferences from them" (p. 26). However, examinations, interpretations, qualifications, and certainly all inferences are not determined by results and contain degrees of speculation.

Although separating the results from the discussion is a step that underlines the qualitative difference between data and interpretations, this distinction does not solve the problem of the speculative character of interpretation itself. This problem might be resolved by providing rules, guidelines, and criteria for valid discussions. For example, a basic guideline would be that an interpretation must simultaneously do justice to the data obtained and to the data that exist in the literature.

standards, it would be incorrect to present data *and* interpretations as facts or knowledge, as explained in Box 10.1.

Methodological and epistemological problems surround the issue of interpretive speculations, but these tend to be neglected in Psychology. This *hermeneutic deficit* poses a threat to any concept of objectivity, because it opens the door to ideological interpretations or to speculations that are meaningful within a *zeitgeist*, a subgroup, or a consensus that discourages psychologists from reflecting upon the limitations of their research (Gadamer, [1960] 1997).

The lack of awareness about hermeneutics is an enormous problem from an educational point of view. Despite the huge amount of didactic tools pertaining to methods and methodology, psychologists have not developed textbooks, courses, or training manuals for distinguishing "good" from "bad" interpretations of data. Nor have psychologists provided students and academics with clear criteria to evaluate their own interpretive speculations. Rather, it merely is assumed that in the course of a career the *discussion* part will improve with the author's experience.

Another implicit assumption is that an expert's discussion is more valuable than a novice's interpretation of data. Yet perhaps experts use reason *intuitively* (Dreyfus, 2004) and might even have difficulty providing explicit criteria for their interpretations. However, it remains a task for hermeneutic-critical psychologists to identify those implicit rules and to evolve guidelines for more adequate interpretations.

To summarize, we have argued that psychological research contains a hermeneutic dimension; that is, investigators want to *understand* empirical findings. Although interpretations of findings are presented as facts, they contain speculative elements. Interpretations are not determined solely by data and thus involve a hermeneutic process.

We do not suggest that there is no relationship between data and interpretation. Even in the worst developed interpretations there is a relationship in the sense that interpretations draw upon some kind of data. Yet, typically in Psychology, investigators do not articulate this "drawing upon" and do not reflect on the context and values that make their interpretations seem valid.

Epistemological violence

Opponents of the idea that interpretations should be subject to scrutiny equivalent to other parts of a research article could argue that for the majority of psychological research it does not matter what kind of hermeneutics one is using. But we would contend that as soon as an interpretation has practical, behavioural, or existential consequences, the choice of interpretive framework and awareness of tradition and prejudice become relevant.

This argument is even more significant for interpretations that involve groups of human beings such as women, visible minorities, gays and lesbians, persons with disabilities, and so on, who have been marginalized in society. Members of privileged, dominant traditions can produce interpretations that construct the "Other" as problematic or inferior, with possible negative consequences for the "Other." As such, "objective knowledge" (data and interpretations) can produce violence, which is termed *epistemological violence* (Teo, 2008).

Epistemological violence can occur when interpretations are taken as pure facts, even though in practice this knowledge is the outcome of interpretation of data. The noun "violence" denotes that this "knowledge" has a negative impact on the "Other" and that the interpretations are detrimental to the "Other." The negative impact can range from misrepresentations and distortions, to a neglect of the voices of the "Other," to statements of inferiority, and to recommendations for adverse practices concerning the "Other." Epistemological violence does not refer to the misuse of research in general but to a hermeneutic process (interpretation of data) that is critically unaware and has negative consequences for the "Other."

Some of the most significant cases of epistemological violence emerge from research on gender differences and "race" differences, discussed in previous chapters (G. Richards, 2012; Tucker, 1994). If one finds gender differences, for instance, in terms of numbers of full professors in science programmes, and concludes, based on these data, that women are by nature less able to perform science than men, then one has entered the realm of hermeneutic deficit and epistemological violence. Interpretations that construct women as inferior and present these interpretations as expertise, knowledge, or fact, while the data allow for equally valid alternative interpretations, are examples of epistemological violence. Alternative interpretations also might be under-determined by data, but they might not be considered epistemologically violent.

Part 1 conclusion

Hermeneutics provides insights into the process and skills of understanding and interpreting, which are central to human-science Psychology. Originally applied to the study of texts, hermeneutics can be extended to the study of human mental life and scientific practice.

Although there is not much attention paid to interpretation in our discipline, psychologists always operate within a hermeneutic dimension.

But hermeneutics needs to be accompanied by a critical dimension, because reliance on authority and tradition as the sources for a correct interpretation is problematic. Authority alone can never be the final source for supporting an interpretation. Instead, understanding requires stepping outside a proposed interpretation to examine it from an outsider's perspective.

We also argued that interpretations that bring harm to other people and that at the same time are framed as knowledge – although alternative interpretations are possible and equally probable – should be labelled as epistemological violence. In short, psychologists can do harmful things with unreflective interpretations.

Part 2 | Dilthey's *Geisteswissenschaftliche* psychology

One of the originators of hermeneutic psychology was Wilhelm Dilthey who had a significant impact on alternative conceptions of the human mind (Teo, 2001). However, most psychologists do not know about hermeneutic concepts and methods, because hermeneutics was not given the same institutional support as natural-science Psychology. Consequently, hermeneutic concepts never became part of mainstream Psychology and these ideas survive only at the margins of the discipline.

But the dominance of psychological experimentation by the end of the nineteenth century did not solve the problematic subject matter of Psychology or the hermeneutic nature of mind. Instead, this dominance merely excluded methodological ambiguity. Not surprisingly, this exclusion has led to recurring dissatisfactions with the status of Psychology as expressed historically in various crisis-of-psychology discourses (Goertzen, 2008).

Limitations to an individualistic conception of mind

Current psychologists study concepts such as memory, perception, consciousness, belief, intention, reasoning, and language in order to understand the mind. They assume that these domains belong to an individual and that they can assess certain central tendencies within or between populations of individuals in descriptive and inferential ways. Seldom do psychologists realize that they base their theories and research practices regarding mental processes on an *individualistic* conception (Teo, 2001).

The assumption of an individualistic mind has historical-philosophical roots. When René Descartes ([1637–1641] 1996) used his widely known *cogito* (I think) argument on which to base knowledge, *cogitamus* (*we* think) apparently never entered his foundational framework. On the contrary, he was skeptical of the *cogitamus*, viewing it as a source of bias, while not seeing the dependence of the *cogito* on the *cogitamus*, of the individual on the cultural-historical. Similarly, Immanuel Kant ([1781] 1998) advanced the individual ego as the thinking being and subject matter of rational psychology. Although he used concepts such as community in his epistemological writings, they were not essential to his theoretical reflections.

In our own (Western) identity it seems self-evident that the mind is individual. But consider the following issue: the fact that you speak a particular language is part of your identity, your tradition, your prejudice, and your hermeneutic framework of understanding. You are able to produce unique sentences in English, sentences that might have never been expressed before, while at the same time these sentences are embedded in a sociohistorical reality.

Yet your sentences might have been incomprehensible to persons who lived 500 years ago (the vocabulary, meaning, and purpose of language change over time), even if these hypothetical individuals spoke the same language as you. A person who speaks English but lives in another historical time or in a significantly different cultural milieu might not understand the statement, "I am taking a history of psychology course at a university and I am challenging the problematic nature of psychological concepts."

Although language can be unique to an individual, it only makes sense within a larger community in which one has been socialized, a community that shares the linguistic conventions of your communication. It also would be insufficient to understand sociohistorical reality as a stimulus environment to which one responds, because the environment is not independent of the individual. Thus, this relationship requires a different conception.

Because of the individualistic focus of the Western philosophical tradition, it is not surprising that philosophy and Psychology have accumulated a vast literature on the mind–body problem, yet there is only marginal reflection on the mind–culture or mind–history question. Although philosophers have reflected upon external influences on the individual's thinking processes, these external influences often were defined as negative or extraneous. Thus, they did not result in a cultural-historical or sociohistorical conception of the mind.

Hegel's distinction

The first Western philosopher who systematically elaborated a sociohistorical understanding of the mind was Hegel (1966) who distinguished among the **subjective, objective, and absolute mind:**

- *Subjective*: an individual mind, encompassing sensation, habit, consciousness, perception, reason, desire, memory, imagination, etc.
- *Objective*: the mind of a social community or era, expressed in law, morality and ethics.
- *Absolute*: an infinite entity, expressed in art, religion, and philosophy.

Hegel connected the subjective and objective mind by arguing that no individual can leap beyond his time and that the mind of the time is also the individual's mind. Critics have argued that Hegel's idealism, according to which the mind is the self-becoming of the Absolute, and his lack of interest in the detailed mechanisms of the relationship between the subjective and objective mind are not helpful to Psychology.

However, Hegel challenged the assumption that the individual is at the core of the philosophy of mind, which stimulated the rethinking of mind as sociohistorical in nineteenth-century German philosophical psychology. More recently, some cognitive scientists also have acknowledged the idea of an "extended mind" where the separation of mind, body, and an external environment is seen as a problematic (Osbeck, 2009).

From the Hegelian challenge emerged two historically significant, often considered opposing orientations, one founded by Karl Marx and the other by Dilthey. Although both rejected the idea of an absolute mind, the concept of an objective mind has played an important role in both of their conceptions.

Mental life

Dilthey (1976), who wrote a biography of the young Hegel, emphasized the social and historical character of the mind. He pointed out that the human being as a history-preceding and society-preceding idea was a fiction. He meant that thinking about a concrete individual without thinking about her or his historical and cultural context would be completely deceptive.

Dilthey accepted the Hegelian view that individual mental life is influenced by the objective mind. Dilthey suggested that language, myth, religious customs, ethos, law, and external organizations are products of a whole mind in which human consciousness has become objective. He maintained that the objective mind can be found in all expressions and effects that humanity has left for succeeding generations. These external objects are connected with the human mind.

Psychologists, he argued, could use technical and artistic creations as the material for an analysis of mental life. Dilthey believed that one should look at the creations of humankind in order to gain a deeper and more complete understanding of mental life. For example, examining the development of motor vehicles or homes can reveal something about the human mind.

Dilthey emphasized the sociohistorical character of psychological subject matter. For him, the object of Psychology was the individual as part of society and the individual developing in concert with society. But Dilthey did not suggest that history and culture *determine* the individual. He acknowledged individual contributions as much as sociohistorical reality; both fashion the mental world.

Furthermore, Dilthey's sociohistorical understanding of the mind did not contradict the idea that human beings are natural beings. He acknowledged that humans are influenced by nature, but they also influence it. His focus, however, was not on biology but on the integration of Psychology with history and the objective with the subjective mind. Dilthey was aware of the scope and originality of this attempt and called it a demanding task for psychologists to build a bridge between Psychology and history. He believed that such a goal would involve the study of human products (such as a painting) in psychological research.

Dilthey's psychologies

Instead of experiments or self-observation, Dilthey believed that psychologists could learn much about the human mind through the study of history (Teo, 2001). He argued that the nature of humans only can be told by their history; humans understand themselves not through introspection but through history. Thus, he suggested that all human sciences are based on study of the past.

For the field of Psychology, Dilthey promoted three approaches: content psychology, descriptive (or analytical) psychology, and structural psychology.

Content psychology

The distinction between form and content is significant philosophically. But Dilthey asserted that focusing on forms and processes of mental life prevents an examination of the content of mind. Content is not essential for natural-science psychologists who focus on the behaviour of mental life. For example, one can plot the statistical curve of forgetting nonsense syllables, as did Dilthey's contemporary Hermann Ebbinghaus.

However, for Dilthey, focusing on the behaviour of mental life is unsatisfactory, because it does not address the content of mind ("the content of my memory"). In studying psychological processes and their presumed regularities, natural-science psychologists do not explain psychological contents. Yet every human experience contains content. The meaning of life, Dilthey claimed, is not captured by determining psychological tendencies, but through describing the meaningful content of our mental lives.

Descriptive psychology

In order to do justice to the content of human life, Dilthey promoted the concept of a descriptive psychology as an alternative to explanatory experimental psychology. This descriptive psychology focuses on the parts and connections of mental life as they are experienced in their totality.

For example, for Dilthey, cognition was only one part of mental life. The other parts were emotion, which he considered at the centre of mental life, and acts of volition or desiring (known today as motivation). Thinking, feeling, and desiring – based on traditional philosophical–psychological distinctions – always are interconnected. Only in a process of scientific abstraction is it possible to distinguish them. Thinking, feeling, and desiring are not opposed as three separate domains; rather, feeling and desiring contain thinking and vice versa.

Structural psychology

For Dilthey, the task of descriptive psychology is to study the structure of mental life and the knots that bind the psychological strings to the totality of mental life. The concept of structure has theoretical implications: in contrast to British associationists, Dilthey argued that mental life does not grow from its parts; it is not built from elements; it is not a composite, not a result of interacting atoms of sensation or emotion. Rather, it is originally and at all times an overarching unit.

Challenging contemporary natural-science Psychology, which focuses on elements, Dilthey put forth the alternative notion of the Gestalt of mental life. He asserted that, in our experiences, mental life is connected and we experience a connection of experiences through which we live our life. This unity and totality of mental life in a person distinguishes the human sciences from the natural sciences. For Dilthey, literature is one way to gain an intuitive understanding of the Gestalt of mental life. However, a descriptive psychology would have to clarify these experiences in a general way.

Dilthey also pointed out that action or behaviour would only be one dimension of human mental life. The problem with behaviour as a potential core category of Psychology is that it does not allow the complete portrayal of our inner life. Psychologists can achieve a complete portrayal by including the concept of *experience* – in the sense of a person's meaningful encounters with the natural, cultural, historical, and human world.

Methodologies for studying mental life

Dilthey's psychological writings challenge attempts to capture psychological phenomena of the mind through natural-scientific experimentation. He invoked Wilhelm Wundt as a witness, who also realized that experimental psychology would be limited to basic psychological processes and that the study of mental life requires more than causal explanations. Dilthey proposed a hermeneutic alternative rather than a non-experimental one. Here we situate his proposal in the context of his attempt to establish an epistemological foundation for a human science of Psychology.

Dilthey put forward a dualistic view of sciences, encompassing the natural sciences (*Naturwissenschaften*) and human sciences (*Geisteswissenschaften*). The latter include history, political science, law, political economy, theology, literature, and art. More generally, *Geisteswissenschaften* refer to sciences encompassing historical-social reality as far as this reality has been conserved historically in the consciousness of humankind (the humanities).

Dilthey himself was not completely content with the term *Geisteswissenschaften*. He was concerned that a focus on the mental (*Geist*) would draw attention away from the emotional and the motivational, whereas in his descriptive and structural psychology he contended that one should account for the totality of human nature. In addition, he was wary about constructing an absolute dualism. Ultimately, however, he stressed that experience of the mental world is unique and justifies the concept of *Geisteswissenschaften,* which cannot be executed in accord with the natural sciences.

Epistemological foundation

Dilthey sought to develop a critique of historical reason in the same manner as Kant developed a critique of pure reason for the natural sciences. It became clear that the epistemological positions of Auguste Comte and John Stuart Mill were unsatisfactory, because they assimilated history into the concepts and methods of the natural sciences. By contrast, Dilthey argued that the anchor for the *Geisteswissenschaften* was the analysis of human experience, the facts of consciousness, and the mind.

Originally, Dilthey suggested that Psychology would be one of the most important disciplines for understanding the mind. Psychology and anthropology study humans and include history and life-experiences in their research material. Early on he thought that both disciplines would be the foundation for knowledge of historical life and provide rules for the development of society. In his later (hermeneutic) writings, Dilthey became skeptical of Psychology as a fundamental human science, contending that all *Geisteswissenschaften* are important for understanding and interpretation.

Based on the distinction between natural and human sciences, Dilthey composed his *Ideas on a Descriptive and Analytical Psychology.* He argued that natural-scientific psychology was not able to study mind sufficiently, as causal explanations used in the natural sciences cannot be applied to the mental world. While explanatory (natural-scientific) psychology builds on basic processes such as association, descriptive psychology separates description and analysis from the explanatory hypothesis.

In descriptive psychology the complete reality of mental life must be used for description and preferably analysis, which must have the highest achievable degree of certainty. In order to achieve this goal, descriptive psychology must begin with the developed mental life and not with elementary processes.

Dilthey on methods

Dilthey considered understanding (*Verstehen*) to be the most appropriate "method" for Psychology, aptly captured by his basic dictum: "We explain nature, but we understand mental life." Thus, he promoted understanding as a core method but also acknowledged a variety of other approaches to Psychology, including introspection, comparative methods, experimentation, and the study of abnormal psychology.

Based on his view of the human mind, according to which the objective mind (expressed in the lifestyle, interaction, customs, laws, state, religion, art, and science of a culture) and subjective mind are interconnected, Dilthey emphasized the study of the products of mental life as a very important complement in the canon of psychological methods. He suggested that understanding is only possible because of the objective mind. Each word, sentence, gesture, act of politeness, work of art, and historical act can be understood because a commonality connects expression with understanding.

Understanding is important because the nexus of the psychological cannot be expressed simply in concepts. The totality of mental life and its nexus exist only in experience and in immediate consciousness. Human beings experience the totality of their being and this totality should be reproduced in understanding.

Dilthey (1958) distinguished **four forms of understanding**:

- *Elementary*: forms ubiquitous in everyday life as immediate processes.
- *Higher*: forms starting with examination of the problem and the context of the problem, finally reaching understanding of a person modelled on an understanding of poetry or an interpretation of literature or art.
- *Highest*: forms arising from empathy whereby the totality of mental life is effected by re-experiencing other people's experiences. This re-experiencing of the psychological world distinguishes all mental operations from the knowledge of nature.
- *Scientific*: forms of understanding and interpretation leading to hermeneutics. The final goal is to understand a human being better than she or he has understood herself or himself.

Dilthey believed that an objective knowledge of the processes that constitute the mental life of humankind is possible and would lead to an objective science of the mental world. He tried to analyze and understand the particular while aiming for general principles. For him, the relationship between generality (uniformity) and particularity (singularity) was crucial for any understanding of mental life, because the particular arises on the basis of uniformities.

Dilthey's desire for generality is also evident in his suggestion to develop *types*. Particular and individual expressions are not random but can be subsumed under a type, because certain basic forms recur in the play of variations. Humankind contains a system of order just as the objective mind contains an order, organized according to types. This system of order leads from the regularity and the structure of the generalized human to types, through which understanding construes individuals.

The focus on types was an essential dimension in Dilthey's psychology and philosophy. One of his students, Eduard Spranger (1928), developed types of personality. In his personality measure, the *Study of Values*, Gordon Allport adopted Spranger's orientation.

Part 2 conclusion

Dilthey laid out a systematic critique of the limitations of a solely natural-science Psychology and provided a wealth of ideas for why and how an alternative should be construed. He emphasized the content of mental life and how aspects of a psychological totality (the human mind) interact in a meaningful Gestalt. Although he did not leave behind a concrete system of Psychology, he can be credited with initiating various forms of hermeneutic psychology.

Dilthey's psychological ideas had a significant influence on twentieth-century Psychology (Harrington, 2000; Rickman, 1988), including Spranger. Dilthey also influenced the philosophers Karl Jaspers and Edmund Husserl (see below), and Gadamer's hermeneutics. In the USA, Canada, and Australia his spirit infused existential and humanistic psychologies. The Americanization of West German Psychology after World War II led to the significant decline of hermeneutic psychology, but presently some Canadian psychologists and philosophers subscribe to a hermeneutic approach (e.g., J. Martin & Sugarman, 2001; Mos, 1998; Rennic, 2007; Taylor, 1985).

Part 3 | Hermeneutic psychologies

Dilthey's ideas remained philosophical and did not seem relevant to concrete research. But the German philosopher, pedagogue, and psychologist Eduard Spranger, who sustained Dilthey's vision, applied it to psychological studies of personality and adolescence. **Karl Jaspers** (1883–1969) also applied it to psychopathology.

Spranger on understanding, personality, and adolescence

The individual closest to Dilthey's intention was Spranger. He was a prolific and respected writer, not only in Psychology, philosophy, and education, but also in political and cultural studies. Spranger ([1914] 1928) published an influential monograph on personality psychology and its relationship to ethics. Later at Berlin, Spranger (1929) published a widely read developmental treatise on the phase of youth, which was never translated into English.

Dilthey and Spranger differed significantly on the concept of understanding. For Dilthey, it was important to reproduce the totality of experience in the process of understanding, the highest form of which is a kind of empathy. Although Spranger called his psychology hermeneutic, he did not share Dilthey's commitment to understanding as the essential method.

For Spranger, understanding is not just empathy and re-experiencing the other's experiences. Understanding must also capture the mental connections not given to an individual. This is easier to achieve from an outsider perspective. Thus, in Spranger's view, an understanding of the other is less limited than an understanding of oneself. Moreover, we might understand people of the past better than they have understood themselves. This process of understanding must be represented in the form of objectively valid knowledge.

Spranger's methodology

According to Spranger, **two methodological statements** are important:

(1) True understanding requires knowledge of the objective-mental connections that transcend immediate life-consciousness. We can understand a person of the past better, because we can see the historical context. We can understand a child better than she or he can understand herself or himself, because we know the developmental background. We can understand adolescence better, if we understand its historical and societal constructions. Thus, the totality from which the human being must be understood is much larger than the totality of her or his individual world of experiences.

(2) Spranger (1929) asserted that understanding is not identical with empathy for another's experiences or behaviour. Indeed, empathic re-experiencing cannot be accomplished without cognitive concepts. Even if we understand someone of the same generation, age, or class, this understanding does not allow us to grasp the complex connections of subjective meaning that are involved and that are significant for a psychology of understanding. Spranger's hermeneutic psychology intends to grasp connections that are not consciously given to individual subjectivity.

For example, why does a child play? A simple answer would be that she plays, because it is fun. Even if you ask a child, she might say because she likes to play. But if somebody answers that the child plays in order to practise future activities relevant to cultural interests and life, then we have a theory of understanding that goes beyond the subjective experience of the child.

The questions "why do we think as we think, why do we evaluate as we evaluate, why do we act as we act" cannot be answered by examining the individual. To answer these questions we must understand the cultural connections of meaning and mental objects; these connections transcend individuals. Similarly, a hermeneutic psychology must grasp the larger connections of meaning.

Personality type

In his personality psychology Spranger ([1914] 1928) theorized **six ideal types** of individuality. Each type fulfills the quality of a Gestalt and corresponds to an ethical system.

- *Theoretic*. Accords with the ethics of general legality and the value of objectivity. Such individuals – objective, logical, and scientific – are interested in finding intellectual truth and might make a career in science or philosophy.
- *Economic*. Reflects a utilitarian ethic and is focused on the value of what is useful. This person is interested in what aids self-preservation and material success. Her or his goal is to surpass others economically, and she or he might choose a career in business.

- *Aesthetic*. Expresses an ethics of inner form. Aesthetic persons hold form and harmony at the highest value and might equate truth with beauty. They find direction in life through participation in the creative arts, and they value feelings and sensations as worthwhile experiences.
- *Social*. Represented within an ethics of helpful love and loyalty. Social individuals value love of others, and might be unselfish and kind. They are interested in friendly, romantic, and philanthropic relationships. They also might find the theoretical and the economic types cold.
- *Political*. Operates within an ethics of a will to power. This type is concerned with gaining power over others, can be found as leaders of their fields, and can be competitive and ambitious.
- *Religious*. Expressed within the ethics of blessedness in God. For these individuals, unity with the divine is of highest value. Some religious persons might express their religious stance though active participation, while others might become mystics who withdraw from mundane life.

Spranger argued that his system of types has implications for both research and practical life. He cautioned that individuals might not belong exclusively to one type, because mixed and historically determined types exist. Indeed, no individual belongs solely to one type without expressing some characteristics of another type.

Adolescence

In his developmental psychology, Spranger (1929) offered a holistic characterization of adolescence (from age 13 to 19 for girls, and 14 to 22 for boys). His goal was a deeper understanding of youth through a complete portrayal of the psychological organization of adolescence. This portrayal was not targeted at concrete individuals as performed in autobiography and literature; psychologists would never be able to exhaust concrete individuality. Instead, Spranger's aim was a picture of typical adolescence. In a general manner, adolescence is characterized by the discovery of a self, the emergence of a life-plan, and ventures into different domains of life.

Nevertheless, Spranger was aware that this typical picture is limited to a certain cultural stage and cannot transcend time and space. Any typology is part of historical-societal reality, based on a concrete culture and society. Therefore, a psychology of adolescence in general was impossible.

Spranger acknowledged that he provided a psychology of the German adolescent of his cultural time, focused on boys. He added that some psychological features that he found might or might not be valid for English, French, and US adolescents and that issues of gender, social class, and education should be considered.

According to Spranger (1929), a purely biological explanation of adolescence cannot address the psychological problems of development. Thus, although the activity of hormones can explain something of the transition from childhood to adolescence, they cannot explain adolescents' feelings of isolation or loneliness, radicalism, or tendencies to idealization. For Spranger, biological facts are interesting and valuable, but by themselves they do not contribute to an understanding of adolescence. He concluded that anatomical–physiological changes of structure represent one realm of facts and psychological–mental changes of structure another realm.

Section conclusion

Historically, psychologists have criticized reliance on typologies, because they simplify realities and can produce stereotypes that do not do justice to the complexity of mental life. Spranger admitted that his typologies do not transcend time and space and that his theory is not valid for all adolescents. He even admitted that his approach was limited to a certain group of adolescents.

Nevertheless, Spranger claimed that nature was more powerful than society in female adolescents' development and attributed inherent biological and metaphysical differences to female adolescents but not to males. This interpretation, problematic from a current perspective, shows that in human-science as well as natural-scientific psychologies, not only is the object of research historical, but the mind of the researcher is as well. Understanding and interpretation are limited by the researcher's social context.

In this case, Spranger, a well-known conservative but anti-Nazi intellectual, was trapped in his own political orientation and the German zeitgeist that included patriarchal views of the female gender. On the other hand, Spranger's interpretations are not more biased than the ideas of Stanley Hall, who also wrote a book on adolescence and who contended, based on empirical research, that so-called lower races are in an arrested state of adolescence; Hall even provided a rationale for segregation and separate education for Whites, Blacks, and Native Indians (Tucker, 1994).

Despite these entanglements, Spranger's hermeneutic psychology offers relevant, but neglected insights into human psychology. His notions suggest that current developmental psychology, which seems to be a patchwork of disparate ideas, theories, research programmes, and results, has accumulated a vast amount of information on detailed problems, but has lost its understanding of the Gestalt of development.

Karl Jaspers on understanding psychopathology

A German philosopher, Karl Jaspers nowadays is best known as a significant representative of existentialism. He is relevant to the history and philosophy of Psychology, because he addressed psychopathology. Influenced by Dilthey and Husserl and realizing that the natural-science approach in psychiatry was well established, Jaspers ([1913] 1997) promoted the idea that psychiatry requires an integration of natural-science and hermeneutics to understand mental illness.

For Jaspers, psychiatrists should causally *explain* mental illness but also *understand* the patient's disorder. Understanding is based on the notion that the person and her or his psychological life should be understood as a whole, not only in its elements. Any psychiatric study, therefore, should include "nosology" (study of the disease from a medical point of view), "eidology" (study of patients in their physical, psychological, and cultural aspects), and biography (study of a person's life as a whole).

However, like Spranger, Jaspers argued that a completely individualistic description, which grasps the individual as a unique irreplaceable totality, would make the practice of psychiatry impossible. Thus, he rejected an idiographic approach that focuses solely on the description of the individual, often with a moralistic attitude. What he strongly preferred was a phenomenological tradition, fostering an understanding of the facts of psychological life without any specific attitude.

Clinical understanding

Jaspers distinguished **five hermeneutic forms** that are germane to clinical applications:

- *Phenomenological understanding* represents patients' experiences based on their self-description.
- *Understanding of expression* is the direct perception of a patient's movements, gestures, and physical expressions.
- *Static understanding* captures a particular psychological quality (e.g., anger).
- *Genetic (developmental) understanding* grasps the emergence of one psychological event from another (e.g., from anger to violence).
- *Rational understanding* is the cognitive understanding of rational content.

These types of understanding contradict the notion that it is sufficient for mental health professionals to just observe and interpret the physical expressions of mental life.

Jaspers asserted that neurosis can stem from a failure in *marginal situations*. Arguably, this is his best-known existential idea. It expresses the notion that human existence sooner or later entails confronting situations that stretch the limits of a person's thinking, feeling, and willing. These situations include dying, suffering, and feelings of deep guilt. For Jaspers, successful coping with these situations might allow the individual to experience a more authentic existence.

Concerned with finding solutions to genuine clinical problems, Jaspers was critical of psychiatrists and psychologists making methodology primary and conceptual understanding secondary. Instead, he defended hermeneutic thinking against the primacy of method and advocated *methodological pluralism*. By this term he meant appreciating the limits of any method in psychopathological research and the need to combine a variety of methods in order to understand a disorder. Other critics have advanced similar arguments throughout Psychology's history.

The distinction between natural and human kinds

More recently, Dilthey's distinction between the natural and human sciences has found its reflection in discussions surrounding the distinction between natural and human kinds in Psychology. The core question is what is the nature of psychological concepts or categories, such as cognition, learning, motivation, personality, attitude, or intelligence? Danziger (1997) has argued that categories are based on the language of the community of which psychologists are a part and that they are historically and culturally constituted. That is, psychological observations cannot be made without psychological categories.

Arguably, **three criteria** distinguish psychological kinds from natural kinds (J. Martin & Sugarman, 2009):

- Psychological categories are *socially constituted* (see Chapter 11). History and culture play an important role in the development of psychological categories in that such categories do not exist in a separate form before they are introduced in social life. For instance, no one spoke of "IQ" in the nineteenth century, and it was not relevant in many parts of the world until the term was introduced.

- Psychological categories produce a looping effect (Hacking, 1994) or *reactivity* in that they affect psychological processes. That is, there is an interaction between people and the classifications to which they have been assigned. If we say to you that you have a low IQ, your self-understanding and behaviour might change based on this attribution.
- Psychological concepts are also *value-laden*. To say to someone that he or she has a low IQ might imply less worth in our culture.

Compare these characteristics with those of water: it does not care about its characterization as liquid in ambient conditions; water is not value-laden, but independent of humans who attribute value not to its concept but to its existence; and water exists independent of our interventions and separate from us (Brinkmann, 2005).

Based on such distinctions, J. Martin and Sugarman (2001) proposed the development of a hermeneutically informed interpretive psychology. At the core of such endeavours is the concept of a person (J. Martin, Sugarman, & Hickinbottom, 2010). (For a critique of the interpretive turn in philosophical psychology see Held, 2007.) Finally, one can argue that many qualitative methods are based on arguments developed in hermeneutic psychology.

Part 3 conclusion

Although Dilthey pioneered hermeneutic psychology, Spranger and Jaspers developed it and applied it in different subdisciplines of Psychology. By contrast with Dilthey, Spranger's concept of understanding does not denote the act of empathizing with another person. Rather, it refers to the individual transcending immediate consciousness by grasping mental structures such as meaningful cultural objects and events. Spranger's goal was to provide objective and valid knowledge.

From the perspective of current natural-science Psychology, Spranger's approach and concepts are not scientific, because they mainly derive from psychologists' philosophical–intellectual capacities and expertise in understanding. Yet, from a critical perspective, Spranger raised questions that psychologists should address. For example, do we acknowledge differences in human groups to understand the specific needs of individuals or to justify the *Other* as problematic?

For his part, Jaspers introduced hermeneutic thinking to psychopathology and provided important ideas about reconciling human-scientific and natural-scientific approaches. He showed that the conventional medical approach should be complemented by a hermeneutic approach that takes the lived experiences of patients into account.

Spranger's and Jaspers's ideas on hermeneutic methods in Psychology are considered classical and still draw scholarly attention. Recently, there have been calls to rediscover Jaspers's concepts of marginal situations and methodological pluralism (e.g., Ghaemi, 2007), and Dilthey's distinctions have resurfaced in debates about natural and human kinds in Psychology. The notion of Psychology as an interpretive, phenomenological human science also has its defenders in North America (e.g., Giorgi, 1970).

Phenomenological and existential psychologies

Dilthey emphasized that "experience" is central to human mental life. But what is essential in experience? You could reply that what is essential is the search for meaning or that the essence of experience is *intentionality* (i.e., being intentional or conscious about conducting one's life). As shown above, human-scientific approaches differ quite substantially from one another.

In the USA and Canada, humanistic and existential psychologies became known during the 1960s as "The Third Force," in contrast to the two forces in extant North American Psychology – behaviourism and psychoanalysis. In this part, we describe phenomenological and existential psychologies and their relationship to natural-science Psychology.

Intentionality

Psychologists who focus on intentionality start with the idea that our experience is always an experience *of* something, or to be more precise, our consciousness is always consciousness *of* something. The concept of intentionality can be traced at least to Roman antiquity and a millennium later to Avicenna and Thomistic philosophy.

In 1874, Franz Brentano, who was a philosophical psychologist at Vienna and an expert in Thomistic and Aristotelian philosophy, reintroduced intentionality. He inaugurated his own school of thought that influenced a variety of important philosophers, including Husserl (see below), who is considered the most important figure in phenomenological philosophy, and experimental psychologist Carl Stumpf.

Brentano is best known for redeveloping the concept of intentional object or intentional relation (intentionality) in psychology. These terms express the idea that every mental act refers (is intended) towards an object or event. When we hear, something is heard; when we think, we think of something; when we judge, we agree or disagree on something; when we love, somebody or something is loved. Every mental act refers to something outside the mind, even if the something in consciousness is immanent (inherently operating within).

Section conclusion

Brentano's singular contribution was to emphasize that psychological processes should be characterized through their intentionality for which there is no equivalent in the physical world. For example, a stone is a stone and does not inherently relate to something else.

In the same year that Brentano ([1874] 1995) published *Psychology from an Empirical Standpoint*, Wundt ([1874] 1910) published *Principles of Physiological Psychology*. The latter work was central to natural-science Psychology initially, whereas Brentano's work was central to human-science Psychology. The term "empirical" in his title emphasizes that Brentano attempted to exclude metaphysical speculations from Psychology (e.g., "is the soul a substance or not?") and to keep his approach empirical, although not in the current methodological sense.

For Brentano, Psychology should be an exact but not an experimental science. A description of phenomena was more important to him than their causal explanation. He argued that investigating the physiological mechanisms underlying mental events diverted psychologists from describing mental operations, which should be their first task. This standpoint meant that psychological processes should be studied without including causal physiological processes ascertained by experimentation.

Phenomenology

A student of Brentano, **Edmund Husserl** (1859–1938) traditionally is considered the founder of phenomenology, the study of experiences as they appear. Although intentionality was one of the core ideas of Husserl's philosophy, his philosophy went far beyond what his teacher taught him. He developed phenomenology as an accurate way of reporting what appears in consciousness without preconceived theories or models.

The dictum "*to the things themselves*" expresses the goal of Husserl's phenomenology. He insisted that phenomenologists report exactly what appears in consciousness, and he believed that the observation of the mind independent of the physical world would allow discovering the essence of conscious experience. Thus, the goal of phenomenology was the discovery of the essential structures of psychological acts and entities through pure intuition.

This orientation allowed phenomenologists to move beyond the analysis of intentionality to explore the essence of conscious experience. The description of concretely experienced phenomena, free from conceptual and theoretical presuppositions, would make psychology *objective*; it would identify what is in consciousness, not what should be there (Husserl, [1925] 1977).

Husserl ([1936] 1996) also criticized the failures of natural-science psychologists to address issues of human subjectivity. He recommended **three forms of *reduction*** as methodological tools that would allow arriving at the phenomena:

- *Phenomenological* reduction moves from objects towards consciousness and is used to find out what is known in and by consciousness. One grasps something immediately in this process.
- During *eidetic* reduction consciousness intuitively grasps the essences and essential structures. For instance, attention towards unchanging features allows identifying the essence of phenomena.
- During *transcendental* reduction the ego is the source for the foundation and constitution of all meaning.

Hand in hand with his methodological recommendations, Husserl criticized the "naturalism" of the sciences. He used this term to identify a process by which the methods of the natural sciences are exported to all other types of knowledge. Instead, he believed that philosophy could be a rigorous science and that it was possible to arrive at understanding the phenomena themselves. His phenomenology involved the knowledge of essences.

Section conclusion

Husserl rejected historicism (i.e., all knowledge is embedded in history) as relativistic. Instead, he promoted the idea of *historicity*, meaning that the concrete life-world of a researcher would be the immediate context for the foundation of all scientific meaning.

Because Husserl also suggested that humans should live according to the demands of reason and that they can discover themselves through phenomenology, he deserves consideration as someone who laid out important elements for a systematic, human-science psychology of experience.

Later Gadamer ([1960] 1997) criticized the assumption that we can approach phenomena without traditions. He held that traditions actually make knowledge possible.

French contributions

In France, **Maurice Merleau-Ponty** (1908–1961) contributed to a phenomenology of perception and **Emmanuel Levinas** (1906–1995) to a phenomenological psychology of alterity ("Otherness").

Merleau-Ponty (1962) argued that the basic feature of human existence is not intentionality but embodiment. Perception is always connected with a sense that depends on the relationship of one's body with the world. Spatial perception is not a geometrical experience but rather influenced by one's own body. Our bodies are always engaged with the world, not as objects but as necessary conditions of our existence. The notion that the mind takes place in a body challenges the Cartesian idea that the mind is opposed to the body and the late twentieth-century idea that the mind is like a computer.

Levinas (1996), influenced by both Husserl and Martin Heidegger, suggested that the subject, the "I," which is central in much of Western philosophy, is problematic. Rather than understanding the "I" as the source of moral judgments, our focus should turn to the "Other." Yet we never can do justice to the "Other." Thus, any dialogue with the "Other" will be limited and asymmetrical. Levinas believed that our preoccupation with reason, immanence (here and now), and the "egological" individual became a problem in Western thinking (Goodman, 2012).

Human existence

Phenomenology and hermeneutics helped give birth to existential and humanistic psychologies. All these approaches agree with the idea that traditional Psychology is unable to describe, understand, or explain the specificity of human mental life and human nature. Specific to human existence are experiences such as existential anxiety, despair, death, but also freedom, hope, and openness. We focus in this part on these existential experiences and how scholars have accounted for them.

Søren Kierkegaard provided much of the inspiration for twentieth-century existentialists. He emphasized the uniqueness of the individual who is basically inexplicable either by speculative, rational philosophy or by mechanistic science. He argued that truth resides with each person; thus, human subjectivity is truth.

Friedrich Nietzsche also is considered a precursor of existential thinking with his famous dictum that, because "God is dead," humans must rely on themselves. Instead of submitting to conventional morality, they should develop their own truths and morality.

The twentieth-century figures central to understanding the origins and concepts of European existentialism are Martin Heidegger, **Jean-Paul Sartre** (1905–1980), **Simone de Beauvoir** (1908–1986), **Albert Camus** (1913–1960), and **Ludwig Binswanger** (1881–1966).

Martin Heidegger

A student of Husserl, Heidegger used phenomenology to investigate the totality of human existence, meaning all those general experiences that humans have in their lives. His work, *Being and Time* ([1927] 1962), often considered one of the most important philosophical statements of the twentieth century, can be read as providing a bridge between existential philosophy and existential psychology. In the following description we focus on how psychologists can incorporate his ideas.

Heidegger attempted a comprehensive analysis of *Dasein*, a German word for existence ("being-in-the-world"). *Dasein* suggests that existence is a holistic phenomenon as opposed to a dualistic separation (e.g., me *against* the world) and emphasizes the nexus of human existence and the world: a person's existence occurs in the world. The concept of *world* includes the totality of things and events around us, including the localized environment.

For Heidegger, a fundamental fact of existence is that every person must face non-being, that is, one's death. Whereas animals perish, humans have a different relationship to dying: Individuals can make choices about how they live and deal with their knowledge about mortality. Heidegger claimed that death is a non-relational possibility ("it is *my* death") and is characterized through "mineness" ("*I* must die"); thus, we all have our own individual deaths.

As Kierkegaard had argued, individuals can choose to live an authentic or an inauthentic life. According to Heidegger, living an authentic life requires understanding, realizing, and accepting the possibility of the impossibility of life. However, "I" can exercise freedom and responsibility to create a meaningful existence, for instance, by exploring life's possibilities and attempting to become all that "I" can become. Death shows us that we are unfree and subject to external circumstances and forces, a realization that allows us to embrace change.

An inauthentic attitude towards life refuses to acknowledge mortality. In an inauthentic mode of existence life means that external forces make all the decisions in my life and "I" have given up my freedom. Failing to take responsibility for one's life and to exercise personal freedom produces (existential) guilt.

Existential anxiety (anxiety about death or one's existence) is pivotal in human life, because death ends our hopes and worries. One who lives an authentic existence realizes the finitude of life, which gives meaning and purpose to her or his activities, frees the person from conformity and compliance with social norms, and entails the fullest possible consciousness. The assumption is that the individual is responsible for the consequences of personal choices; that is, freedom and responsibility work together.

However, Heidegger noted that there are limits to personal freedom in that individuals are *thrown* into *Dasein* by circumstances beyond their control because of gender, ethnocultural status, social class, and other social categories. The term "thrownness" refers to the conditions under which we exercise freedom.

In conclusion, despite his profound ideas, Heidegger has been controversial because of his support for and lack of reflection on German fascism. He reframed his notion of "authentic being" in terms of the "spiritual renewal of the German people through fascism ... Spirit power followed material power," flowing from fidelity to Hitler (Kovel, 1991, p. 90). That is, one could be an "authentic" fascist.

One could say that there is a social–ethical dimension lacking in Heidegger, who was forbidden after the war to teach at German universities. He exemplifies how a very thoughtful thinker can be trapped in destructive ideas, if they are not combined with a critical attitude that challenges relentlessly one's assumptions and notions of power. Heidegger provided no moral framework for choosing radical democracy over fascism in the individual's quest for authenticity (Roderick, 1986). Moreover, his work lacked a critique of political, social, and economic conditions of Western societies.

Nevertheless, Heidegger's ideas had a significant influence on mid-twentieth-century European theorists, for instance, Sartre, **Herbert Marcuse** (1898–1979) (see Chapter 12), and Jacques Derrida. Heidegger's contribution to Psychology rests in his highly influential attempt to focus attention on the immediate psychological roots of human existence. (For applications in psychotherapy, see Hersch, 2003.)

Jean-Paul Sartre

Taking a radically different stance than Heidegger, Sartre personified philosophy as a life worth living by putting into concrete practice his philosophical discourse: he fought in the Resistance against the Nazi occupation of France and developed his views from his political experience with fascism.

Sartre came to balance the notion of the solitary self, seeking authentic existence, with the need for collectivity. He forwarded, as some psychologists say today, a psychological sense and reality of community. He envisioned liberation in terms of the virtues of solidarity, peace, love, and respect.

Originally, Sartre emphasized the aloneness of the individual and his first principle is that "existence precedes essence." These tenets mean that the truth that we are alive and will die confronts us with the responsibility to determine our identity or being. We cannot escape the burden of making choices about how to live our life.

In his drama *No Exit*, Sartre ([1949] 1956) depicted a second existential principle beyond the fact that "I must die," namely, "there are others in this world besides myself." In the play the primary male character states, "Hell is just other people." This famous statement does not mean that Sartre supported "rugged individualism." On the contrary, in the context of the play and his later philosophy the statement means, "When others reject my social image that I project to them, when they see through the metaphorical mask I wear and scrutinize the real me, it's hell for me." In other words, Sartre's position became *social* existentialism. He believed that other people are crucially important for our knowledge about ourselves.

To conclude, for Sartre, pursuing personal freedom and free choices requires us to promote the full freedom of others. Thus, he modified his earlier emphasis on the solitary individual. He came to understand from his own political experience the nature of groups seeking to change their political, social, and economic conditions. But many psychologists, if they show awareness of Sartre's psychological thought at all, tend to celebrate his earlier position rather than his later social existentialism.

Simone de Beauvoir

The long-term partner of Sartre and key figure in feminist theory, Beauvoir introduced the notion that existence is gendered in a patriarchal society. Even our description is gender-biased. In saying that Beauvoir was the partner of Sartre we define her through a man. But

Sartre usually is not defined through her. This important distinction is taken up philosophically in her book *The Second Sex* ([1949] 1972).

In this highly influential book Beauvoir asserted that men consider themselves as subjects, as essential, as the first sex, whereas women are constructed as objects and as secondary. In addition, she contended, no female essence exists; rather, women are made into women (sex versus gender). Instead of relying on a natural science of women, which in her view cannot do justice to women, Beauvoir preferred a phenomenologically based description of women's experiences.

Albert Camus

A French author and philosopher who was awarded the Nobel Prize for literature in 1957, Camus was influential in existential reflection, although he rejected this label for his philosophy. He began his philosophy with the concept of the *absurd*. The absurd consists in the discrepancy between human beings' search for meaning and a world devoid of meaning. Consequently, his philosophy is sometimes labelled "absurdism."

Camus, however, was not a nihilist. He valued solidarity, friendship, and love as important in human existence. Although he suggested that the most important philosophical problem is suicide, he argued that suicide is not the solution to absurdity. Rather, rebellion is. In *The Rebel* Camus ([1956] 1991) stated:

What is a rebel? A man who says no, but whose refusal does not imply a renunciation. He is also a man who says yes, from the moment he makes his first gesture of rebellion. A slave who has taken orders all his life suddenly decides that he cannot obey some new command. (p. 13)

To conclude, Camus' writing had some influence on existentialism and on postcolonial psychological and sociopolitical thought.

Ludwig Binswanger

An important clinical figure influenced by Heidegger was Binswanger, a Swiss psychiatrist who applied existentialism and phenomenology to psychiatry. In effect, he blended the ideas of Heidegger and Husserl with psychoanalytic theory in an approach to psychotherapy known as *Daseinsanalyse* (existential analysis). Binswanger's theory of psychotherapy is based on the notion that effective helping requires understanding how a person views his or her life at a particular moment in time. This orientation includes understanding the person's interpretations of life-events, anxieties, fears, personal values, etc.

To systematize and understand a person's experiences Binswanger (1968) postulated **three modes of personal existence**:

- *Umwelt*, the natural world of things and events.
- *Mitwelt*, shared interactions with fellow human beings.
- *Eigenwelt*, the person's subjective experiences.

For Binswanger, an individual lives life through a particular *Weltentwurf* (world-design). It is the therapist's task to point out that there are other ways of understanding the world (*Umwelt*), other humans (*Mitwelt*), and oneself (*Eigenwelt*). Binswanger accepted

Heidegger's notion that thrownness limits personal freedom, but he also believed that humans try to transform their circumstances by exercising their free will.

Overall, Binswanger's orientation had some influence on subsequent existential psychology and on the theory and practice of existential psychoanalysis in Europe and North America (Frie, 1997).

Logotherapy

A Viennese psychiatrist, Viktor Frankl developed *logotherapy* to emphasize the importance of meaning in life. Logotherapy focuses on human beings' search for meaning and can be described as a form of existential psychology. Based on his personal survival of Nazi concentration camps, including Auschwitz, Frankl argued that even horrific circumstances allow growth and meaning-making, if one is able to recognize possibilities for turning misery into human achievement.

Theory

Frankl, who started with existentialism's insight into the finitude of human life, disclosed that he himself was startled by the idea that one day he would have to die. Yet he was less concerned with the fear of dying than with the question of whether the limited nature of individual life might destroy its meaning. His experiences in concentration camps helped him to answer the problem: death itself makes life meaningful. For Frankl, everything is irrevocably stored, and there is no one and nothing that can undo whatever one has done, created, learned, and experienced.

In his book *Man's Search for Meaning* ([1946] 1992), Frankl described how some internees found meaning, even when every object was taken away from them and they chose their own way within these circumstances. Others, he observed, could find no meaning in their lives and were giving up. He concluded that as soon as meaning vanishes from a person he or she begins to stop living.

In this context Frankl realized for himself that love would be the ultimate and the highest goal to which one can aspire. He grasped the idea that the salvation of humans is through love and in love:

> For the first time in my life I saw the truth as it is set into song by so many poets, proclaimed as the final wisdom by so many thinkers. The truth – that love is the ultimate and the highest goal to which man can aspire. Then I grasped the meaning of the greatest secret that human poetry and human thought and belief have to impart: *the salvation of man is through love and in love.* I understood how a man who has nothing left in this world still may know bliss, be it only for a brief moment, in the contemplation of his beloved. In a position of utter desolation, when man cannot express himself in positive action, when his only achievement may consist in enduring his sufferings in the right way – an honorable way – in such a position man can, through loving contemplation of the image he carries of his beloved, achieve fulfillment. (Frankl, 1992, p. 57)

Frankl also argued that it did not matter what humans expected from life, but rather what life expected from humans. Accordingly we should stop asking about the meaning of life and not focus on talk and meditation, but rather focus on right action and right conduct. Based on his own experiences, Frankl suggested that life means assuming the responsibility to find the right answers to life's problems.

Practice

One therapeutic technique in logotherapy is "dereflection," which Frankl intended to counteract a compulsive tendency for self-observation. For example, an insomniac patient might be acutely aware of the problem of falling asleep at bedtime, yet this awareness inhibits sleeping and perpetuates the waking state. The patient must be dereflected *from* the disturbance *to* the task at hand or the partner involved. However, patients only can achieve dereflection to the degree that they are focused on positive aspects.

Another technique is *paradoxical intention*, which Frankl used for the short-term treatment of obsessive–compulsive and phobic patients. Paradoxical intention means that the therapist encourages patients to do or desire the very things that they fear. Many individuals develop "anticipatory anxiety," which means reacting to an event with a fearful expectation of its occurrence. For instance, if a student is anxious about giving class presentations and is afraid of being ridiculed, this anticipation can produce precisely what the student fears, in a vicious circle of anxiety.

Logotherapy is based on the idea that no negative aspects in life exist that cannot be changed into positive accomplishments. Logotherapy operates on the notions of freedom of the will, the will to meaning, and the meaning of life. These principles mean that humans are capable of choosing their attitude towards themselves. Thus, individuals are free to shape their own character.

Section conclusion

Frankl's concepts contributed to the late twentieth-century discourse on existentialist psychology, while his clinical techniques had some influence on therapeutic practice including the use of paradoxical intention. But his impact on Psychology has been limited.

Frankl was critical of humanistic psychologists' goal of self-actualization (see below), which cannot be the ultimate destination of human beings, he contended, because self-actualization is the *effect* of meaning-fulfillment. Only if one fulfills a meaning in the world does one fulfill oneself. Moreover, excessive concern with self-actualization might be based on an individual's problems with her or his will to meaning.

For Frankl, meaning is what is meant by a person or by a situation. Both imply questions that call for answers. Each person is responsible for giving the right answer to a question and for finding the true meaning of a situation. Meaning is found rather than given, discovered rather than invented.

Part 4 conclusion

Beginning with Brentano, various forms of phenomenological and existential psychologies developed in the nineteenth and twentieth centuries. Brentano, who intended psychology as a human, but completely exact, science, emphasized the specificity of the psychological versus the physical. This notion was further developed by Husserl, who had an impact on Heidegger and other important figures in existential psychology.

Phenomenologists try to describe phenomena as they appear without invoking traditions and preconceived notions. Rather than a system of thought, phenomenology is a practice. Heidegger, who provided a comprehensive analysis of *Dasein* and emphasized the knowledge of death as central in human life, influenced thinkers such as Sartre who stressed a form of social existentialism. Beauvoir argued that in a patriarchal culture existence is gendered. For Camus, the contradiction between the individual's search for meaning and a culture stripped of meaning is absurd. Frankl, who developed logotherapy from his own oppressive experiences, converted existential thought into therapeutic strategies for making meaning in one's life.

These European approaches to understanding the psychology of human existence, often directly connected with miserable societal conditions, stand in some contrast to the approaches taken by US psychologists in what is known as humanistic psychology.

Part 5   Humanistic psychologies

In English-speaking contexts, existentialism and phenomenology have had a pronounced but not determinative effect on the emergence of several types of humanistic psychology. Existentialist psychologies, which are mainly European, and humanistic psychologies, which are quintessentially "American," converge on the notions of free will, the individual's uniqueness, the search for meaning, and studying whole experiences. Thus, both schools of thought concentrate on uncovering the *meaning* of behaviour, which distinguishes them from natural-science Psychology.

The two schools of thought diverge, however, on at least **two points**:

- Existentialists viewed human nature as open. They asserted that we are born with the freedom to choose and making choices is our major motive. By contrast, humanistic psychologists assumed human nature is fundamentally good, or, for example, that individuals have a natural tendency towards self-actualization.
- Humanistic psychologists tended to be more traditional in their research methods, whereas the existentialists relied on qualitative methods.

Four individuals are noteworthy in the formation of humanistic psychologies: **Rollo May** (1909–1994), **George Kelly** (1905–1967), Abraham Maslow, and Carl Rogers. The concepts of Maslow and Rogers are likely to be as well known to Psychology students as those of Ivan Pavlov and B. F. Skinner. But the ideas of May, Kelly, Maslow, and Rogers converge on the proposition that a self-purposive and active person exercises autonomous judgment in giving meaning to life.

Humanistic psychologies had their heyday in the 1960s and 1970s in the USA and Canada when they challenged the shortcomings of behaviourism and of psychoanalysis. For Maslow in particular, it was important to develop a third force in Psychology that provided, in contrast to psychoanalysis, a model of humans that stressed their uniqueness and positive attributes, and in contrast to behaviourism, a model that understands that the cause of human behaviour often is one's subjective reality. Rogers, Kelly, and May shared these inclinations as well.

Rollo May

With two books, *Existence: A New Dimension in Psychiatry and Psychology* (1958) and *Existential Psychology* (1961), May introduced Heidegger's existentialism to US Psychology. He emphasized that human beings are both objects and subjects. As physical objects we are exposed to physical influences, for instance, when we catch a cold, while as subjects we interpret our experiences of the cold and make choices about how to cope with it. For May, this subjective dimension of producing meaning makes us unique as a species. Again, we could say that humans are interpretive by nature.

In addition, May distinguished between normal and neurotic anxiety: normal anxiety is produced by our psychological freedom that involves responsibility as well as uncertainty. Authentic individuals live their freedom and thus experience anxiety, but this anxiety is normal in the course of life. On the other hand, a fear of freedom that involves conformity to tradition can lead to neurotic anxiety.

Furthermore, individuals who accept values and ideas imposed by society rather than those they have personally constructed might experience self-alienation. In this context, May stressed the importance of myths, because they provide meaning in life in a meaningless world. For him, the greatest myths are those that encourage a sense of nexus among humans. Individualistic myths, however, encourage people to live isolated and lonely lives, emphasizing violence as means for the solution of problems.

Section conclusion

May introduced the idea of a human science specifically developed to study humans scientifically while understanding them as a whole. In this regard, May served as a transitional figure between the European tradition of multiple human-science psychologies and the emerging US tradition of what became known as "humanistic psychology."

George Kelly

Another transitional figure who was not a humanistic psychologist was George Kelly. Rather than being directly influenced by existential philosophers, he drew eclectically on various ideas from the natural and human sciences to create a conceptual synthesis with personality and clinical applications that complemented the phenomenological concerns of humanistic psychology. Against the dominant behaviourist perspective, Kelly observed in the 1950s that change in one's worldview can evoke change in one's life. Thus for Kelly, it is important to understand and alter how individuals construe themselves and their issues. He systematized his ideas in his work *The Psychology of Personal Constructs* (1955).

According to Kelly's framework of *constructive alternativism*, humans want to reduce uncertainty and construct worldviews to predict what will happen next, because they have the freedom to choose how to construct their psychological reality. For example, although you share the same cultural heritage as someone else, you experience yourself as very different from that person in your outlook on the world. But with another person who has a different cultural background but the same worldview as you, you are likely to experience that person as similar. This example shows that understanding a person depends on appreciating how that person construes her or his world.

Based on his constructive-alternativist framework, Kelly devised a therapeutic intervention, "fixed-role therapy," designed to enable clients to view their world and themselves differently. He would create a role for the client that was different from the client's original self-characterization. The client in a sense becomes an actor trying out new ways of perceiving, thinking, and behaving. In the process the client realizes that other ways for understanding life are possible, and the therapist corroborates the client's new construct system.

For Kelly, what counts is not what a human being is but what the person decides to make of him- or herself. Accordingly, when individuals understand that a different kind of life exists, their next challenge is to find ways of overcoming moments of threat and doubt and to envision what they are about to be.

Section conclusion

Kelly's conceptual synthesis and therapeutic approach complemented what humanistic psychologists promoted, although Maslow and Rogers each offered unique concepts. In addition, Kelly's central notion of changing a person's worldview contributed to the mix of concepts that led US psychologists to abandon behaviourism, neobehaviourism, and behavioural therapies and to reintroduce mental processes under the rubric of cognitive psychology in the research domain and cognitive–behavioural therapy in the clinical domain.

Abraham Maslow

Like most US psychologists of his generation, Maslow originally was interested in behaviourism. After his PhD with Harry Harlow, he worked with Edward Thorndike, yet he also affiliated with famous Gestalt psychologists and psychoanalysts.

The basic **principles** of Maslow's version of humanistic psychology were:

- One's subjective reality is the source of human action.
- Psychology should encompass what makes human beings particular.
- Psychology should provide solutions to human problems.

Maslow is famous for his theory of motivation, *hierarchy of needs*, which are essential for an individual's health. In Maslow's scheme, lower needs in the hierarchy are similar to the needs of animals, while the higher the needs, the more human they are. Only when a lower need is satisfied can one deal with the next higher need. At the base of the hierarchy are physiological needs, followed by safety needs, belonging and love needs, and esteem needs, while at the peak is self-actualization.

By self-actualization, Maslow meant reaching one's full human potential. His concept was indebted to Nietzsche's notion of the superior person who transcends ordinary life. Maslow considered self-actualized people as rarities, because self-actualization required complete honesty about oneself, spontaneity, a strong ethical sense, and creativity. For him, Albert Einstein, Albert Schweitzer, Sigmund Freud, Jane Addams, William James, and Abraham Lincoln exemplified self-actualization.

Maslow also introduced a useful **pair of categories** for understanding motivation:

- "Deficiency motivation" means that one is motivated to possess things that one does not have, for instance, if you want to have a larger car, a larger house, or a nicer holiday.
- "Being-motivation" refers to the realm of self-actualized persons who cherish higher values such as beauty, truth, and justice.

For Maslow, those who are being-motivated embrace Being-love, which unlike Deficiency-love is non-possessive.

Section conclusion

Towards the end of his life, Maslow (1969) began to focus on the mystical and spiritual aspects of human nature, which he envisioned as best incorporated within a new subdiscipline of Psychology, *transpersonal psychology*. However, although humanistic psychology conceptually is human-focused, it does not mean that individuals involved in promoting its concepts and values actually practise them or are more virtuous and politically progressive than the hoi polloi.

Maslow, for instance, viewed knowledge in sexualized, gender-specific terms (Nicholson, 2001, 2007). He combined intellectual ability and scholarly power with masculinity and male sexual potency; he vowed not to compromise his intellectual virility, which he feared would be compromised in doing psychological research; and he believed that women desire to be dominated. Furthermore, on numerous occasions Maslow promoted a form of social and political elitism and vigorously supported the US war against Vietnam (Herman, 1995). These contradictions do not mean that Maslow's ideas about human motivation were not inspiring to emancipatory movements in the USA and Canada. Rather, the contradictions reveal the complex interplay of psychological theorists, their theories, and social contexts.

Carl Rogers

Most famous for developing client-centred therapy in his 1951 book, *Client-Centered Therapy: Its Current Practice, Implications, and Theory*, Rogers replaced the concept of patient with the concept of client. For Rogers, the therapist's goal must be to understand and accept a client's subjective reality. This standpoint stood in some contrast to that of the dominant form of contemporary psychotherapy, psychoanalysis, in which analysts privileged their own perspective over patients'.

Rogers also broke new ground by actually investigating the effectiveness of psychotherapy. He proposed assessing effectiveness by examining the correlation between the clients' self-described real selves and their ideal selves (i.e., who they would like to become). In effective therapy, the correlation should become larger, meaning that the real self becomes more similar to the ideal self. Rogers, in fact, devoted quite a bit of his writing to exploring personality implications for the notion of self-concept.

In the Rogerian model of psychotherapy and counselling, therapists attempt to foster a climate of psychological growth for their clients. Growth requires **three "core conditions"** in the therapeutic relationship:

- As infants and children, we have a need for *unconditional positive regard* (love, warmth, and acceptance). However, parents often give children positive regard only if they act or think in certain ways. Rogers recommended that parents give their children unconditional positive regard, to love them for who they truly are.
- Rogers emphasized the importance of emotional genuineness, authenticity, or *congruence*. An incongruent person is one who has not experienced unconditional positive regard in her or his upbringing and is not true to her or his real feelings. Rogers posited that lack of congruence can be the cause of mental disorders.
- *Empathic understanding* means sensitive, active listening and understanding clients' feelings at the level at which they express them. Empathic listening facilitates psychological growth. This principle applies to relationships between therapist and client, parent and child, leader and group, teacher and student, or administrator and staff.

In addition, Rogers postulated an innate human drive towards self-actualization. Using this tendency, humans will live fulfilling lives and reach their potential. These persons are motivated by their own true feelings rather than by conventions imposed by others. Yet, he argued, most persons do not live according to their inner feelings.

Section conclusion

In his approach to humanistic psychology, Rogers advanced fertile therapeutic concepts, such as shifting therapists' attention to the client's perspective and expressing unconditional positive regard through acceptance and caring. He explored the psychological importance of a person's self-concept and the motive towards self-actualization. Lastly, he initiated psychological research on psychotherapy outcome and processes. These are all enduring contributions to Psychology.

Part 5 conclusion

Another key player in the humanistic-psychology movement was Charlotte Bühler, who with Karl Bühler had immigrated to the USA in 1938. She characterized the core concepts of humanistic psychologies as their holistic approach to psychological processes, stress on an individual's developmental history, and focus on the motive of each person to actualize her or his potential (Bühler, 1971).

In response to the concepts and practices of the various humanistic psychologies that challenged contemporary natural-science Psychology **four mainstream criticisms** of humanistic psychologies emerged:

- Third Force psychologists offered an outdated critique of Psychology, because behaviourism and neobehaviourism were on the wane.
- By rejecting the experimental method – but Carl Rogers did not – humanistic psychologists doomed Psychology to its "prescientific" past.
- By rejecting the relevance of animal research for human psychology, humanistic psychologists ignored valuable knowledge gained from an evolutionary perspective.
- The terms and concepts that humanistic and existential psychologists used defied clear, operational definitions.

Partly as a consequence of these criticisms, the durable impact of humanistic psychologies on mainstream Psychology in Canada and the USA is questionable except for certain subdisciplines, such as personality, counselling psychology, and clinical psychology. Nevertheless, Third Force psychologists nudged some natural-science psychologists to study higher human attributes such as creativity and humour and to study the whole person and the meaning of experiences. Yet, arguably, the greatest influence of the Third Force has occurred in popularizations of Psychology in the form of personal-growth workshops, self-help books, and the New Age movement.

Politically, Maslow and Rogers were instrumental in promoting the notion that Psychology was compatible with democratic ideals, although each did so from his unique vantage point. Rogers, for example, advocated the congruence between realizing an individual's human potential with democracy, pointing out that one was necessary for the other. In other words, humanistic psychologists had a clear political agenda and a political project to expand their understanding of democracy on a scientific basis (Herman, 1995). Humanistic psychologists' active involvement in promoting democracy stood in some contrast to Skinner's view that could be interpreted as suggesting that modern science renders democracy obsolete.

More recently, positive psychologists have converted the ideas of humanistic psychologists into the discourse of current natural-scientific psychology. Similarly to humanistic psychologists, Seligman and Csikszentmihalyi (2000) argue that a focus on pathology in applied and professional subdisciplines has prevented a focus on the positive features of human life such as hope, wisdom, creativity, courage, spirituality, and responsibility. Some hermeneutic psychologists, for instance, have provided a systematic critique of the assumptions of positive psychology (e.g., Slife & Richardson, 2008).

Part 6   Transpersonal psychologies

Transpersonal psychologists believe that the spiritual dimensions of human experience are central to an understanding of mental life and that there is something that transcends the person (Maslow, 1969). In the past, philosophers focused on the transcendental concept of the soul, often considered immortal. Indeed, for many centuries the soul was the subject matter of psychological thinking. Plato and Aristotle, Augustine and Aquinas, Descartes and Leibniz, and many others took the soul for granted.

Many psychologists would agree that religion and spirituality are domains of human activity that are extremely important in many people's lives and that historically a tangled web of science, psychology, soul, spirituality, and religion has existed in Western culture (G. Richards, 2011). Moreover, discussing the soul means recognizing the influence of spirituality on history within changing cultural contexts. But it was only in the 1860s that Friedrich Lange proposed an objective psychology *without* a soul (see Chapter 12). Since then, the soul has more or less disappeared from academic discourses, including most Psychology, but not from theological, religious, spiritual, and transpersonal-psychology discourses. In addition, scholars in other disciplines such as biblical studies employ psychological concepts as hermeneutic aids (e.g., Rollins, 1999).

In our account we use the term "transpersonal psychologies" to mean multiple perspectives on psychological thought and practice in relation to soul, spirituality, and religion. We use the singular form "transpersonal psychology" to denote a particular branch of human-science Psychology that addresses these matters as well as holistic and personally trans-formative experiences that can occur with or without alternative states of consciousness (Hartelius, Caplan, & Rardin, 2007). But before discussing this subdiscipline we define what we mean by religion, spirituality, spirit, and soul.

Definitions

From a critical perspective, a *religion* is:

an ideological and organizational system of belief, ritual, and ethics centred on some notion of transcendence; hence, Christianity is but one form of organized religion. To be "religious" is not necessarily to be spiritual or soulful, as one could simply participate in a religious congregation for materialistic and egotistical motives. (Walsh-Bowers, 2000, p. 223)

Spirituality can refer to both subjective individual practices, some of which involve per-forming rituals, and to socially based activities, including social movements, that are oriented to developing sensitivity to spirit and soul. These activities challenge notions of spirituality as exclusively internal to the person. Thus, when people unite to engage in social action, for example, for protection of the biosphere or global-justice initiatives, their collective effort can foster spirituality. The term spirituality also encompasses sexuality in its mystical as well as orgasmic forms in the sense that one's body with all its imperfections is the grounding for one's soul, spirit, and spirituality.

Spirituality can entail a process of moral courage, involving denunciation of social relations of domination and annunciation of relations of equality (Kovel, 1991). Spirituality in this sense is motivated by radical egalitarianism, as exemplified by the historical Jesus (Crossan, 1994), and connects directly with environmental, economic, and social justice. For psychologists who are social activists, this orientation to spirituality can be emancipating personally, because spirituality is connected with working for societal conditions of justice and peace.

Regarding the relationship between religion and spirituality, a formal religion can repre-sent the institutional form of spirituality but also the denial of spirituality. Those who participate in activities associated with "New Age" spirituality (i.e., an alternative move-ment in Western culture emerging in the late twentieth century, stressing spiritual develop-ment) might decline to join a religious congregation, because they regard organized religion as ignorant of, or hostile to, spiritual development.

For critical scholar-activist and former psychoanalyst **Joel Kovel** (b. 1936), *spirit* is as an eternal life-force that abides in one's flesh yet exists beyond immediate sensory perception (Kovel, 1991). Spirit unifies body with mind, bestows purpose and guidance to the individ-ual, and connects one's self to the universe.

In this context, *soul* refers to the particular spiritual form that an individual self takes, but "soul" is not synonymous with the psychological and non-spiritual concept of "ego" and its functions. Ian Hacking (1995), a philosopher of science, limits soul to an individual's psychological capacities, such as for reflection, choice, and love. Jungian psychologist Thomas Moore (1992) defines soul as "the infinite depth of a person and of a society, comprising all the many mysterious aspects that go together to make up our identity" (p. 267). Here soulfulness means apprehending the biological and spiritual ties that bind all things and creatures together.

Psychological perspectives on the soul

In the ancient Greek comedy *The Frogs* by Aristophanes (448–380 BCE) the central characters are frogs. As amphibians, they thrive both above and below the surface of water. Frogs personify the richness of human beings who can fully explore the depths of meaning in life and actively participate in ordinary material realities (Moore, 1992). From a spiritual perspective, amphibian exploration of personal depths of meaning by cultivating the soul and spirituality develops human wisdom. For this development to occur, psychologists would have to centralize soul in the discipline, which would transform natural-science Psychology.

In recent decades some scholars have been cultivating intermingled strains among Psychology, ecopsychology, spirituality, religion, and theology. The relationship among Psychology, the soul, and spirituality incorporates biological and global ecology, "because care of the world is attending to the soul that resides in nature as well as in human beings" (Moore, 1992, p. 270). This view is indebted to the medieval concept of *anima mundi* (the spirit of the world that enlivens all nature) in which there is no separation between individual souls and the world soul.

Accordingly, attending to nature's soul requires realizing that fostering one's spiritual development is incomplete until one is fostering a sense of respect for the integrity of biological creation. Furthermore, it would seem that attention to the therapeutic benefits of cleansing oneself of one's internal pollution needs to be coupled with the benefits to the world's soul, and the individuals within it, of cleansing the world of its pollutants and containing global warming. From outer space, as the NASA photo in Figure 10.2 shows,

Figure 10.2 NASA image of Earth

Earth appears strikingly beautiful and pure. Yet we know how imperilled the biosphere is unless we effect radical change in our relationship with it.

Others have been recuperating subjectivity for Psychology, while incorporating socio-political considerations. For example, in addressing the contested place of spirituality in Psychology, Walsh-Bowers (2000) critiqued scientism and what in critical theory is known as *instrumental rationality*. This modernist inclination refers to society's administrators using reason for instrumental and authoritarian purposes. Reliance on instrumental rationality includes a seeming devotion to technological efficiency and scientific progress, domination over nature, cognitive control of emotions, and mechanistic and rationalist orientations to the soul and subjectivity.

Historical perspective on spirituality and religion in psychology

In answering the question of the compatibility of psychological science with spirituality it is useful to consider the sometimes harmonious, often conflictual relationship between science and spirituality within the history of science in general and Psychology in particular (G. Richards, 2011).

> **Small-group discussion.** How compatible is science with spirituality? What should be the relationship between soul and spirit on the one hand and scientific psychology on the other hand, if any?

Science

During ancient times there was no sharp distinction between objectively and subjectively derived systematic knowledge (Lindberg, 1992). In ancient Egypt and in Babylon scientist-priest-healers recorded case studies of different, carefully observed disorders. They developed medicinal remedies, based on herbs, created forms of surgery, and integrated healing with spirituality and the importance of magic rituals.

What connected such practices across disparate cultural-historical contexts was a shared belief in a spirit or spirits that reside in every person, object, and place. In medieval and Renaissance Europe the cultural belief was that the *anima mundi* breathed into and gave life to individual soul-bodies (Moore, 1992). Even in the premodern era the practice of religion, spirituality, healing, and science constituted an integral whole. Consequently, when modern science emerged, it was suffused with religious beliefs.

For example, Johannes Kepler and Galileo Galilei regarded their astronomical observations as revealing the wisdom of a creator God who had authored the book of nature (Kors & Korshin, 1987). Physicists as well as theologians flocked to Descartes' vision of a perfect world that operates according to God's laws and to Isaac Newton's conviction that he revealed the mind of God through the laws of motion.

Yet since Cartesian dualism, Westerners have tended to separate body from mind and nature from spirit. As a consequence, we have had to solve the problems of how presumably immaterial mind knows matter and how humans are reflective and biological creatures simultaneously (Ruether, 1983). By contrast to Western dualism, many other cultures understand the psyche as "complex, dynamic, and composed of indwelling spirit beings, separated from objective reality by a kind of shell" (Kovel, 1991, p. 44). Moreover, aboriginal cultures in Australia, Canada, New Zealand, and the USA understand all beings, things, and locations as interconnected.

An example of how the conventional disconnection between Psychology and spirituality might limit our understanding of human phenomena can be found in the domain of theatre acting and spirituality (see Box 10.2).

Psychology

Rather than being antagonistic towards religion, many founders of US Psychology, such as John Dewey and Stanley Hall, were firmly planted in religion, because during the nineteenth century, religion, science, and philosophical psychology were co-constructed disciplines in

Box 10.2 Theatre acting and spirituality

Brian Bates (1987) argued for the retrieval of soul in Psychology by drawing from theatre actors' reports of spiritual connectedness, out-of-body, and other paranormal experiences. He observed that in exercising their craft, theatre actors test the limits of ordinary human communication. They stretch themselves psychically in that they come to rely on access to unconscious resources that enliven both the development of their roles and their everyday functioning as social actors. Whether they employ a technical or psychological performance-style, all theatre actors explore the same territory: the union of conscious and unconscious psychological functions.

Access to unconscious processes enables theatre actors to give authentic, believable performances. In fact, without this resource actors' performances would be flat and unconvincing for audiences and themselves (Walsh-Bowers, 2006). Whereas many psychologists seek to predict and control behaviour and mental life, theatre actors seek self-understanding, rendering them less predictable.

Based on the assumption that everyone is a social actor in ordinary life, Bates (1987) asserted that we could emulate theatre actors to live life more fully. Thus, developing an emotionally rich life, sharpening powers of observation, and taking physical as well as emotional risks "in character," all deepen personal knowledge, contribute to a balanced life, and enable social actors to live each moment more flexibly.

Bates also explored the spiritual dimension of the psychology of acting. In traditional societies shamans are like actors who are guardians of wisdom and direct communicators with the spirit world, while bringing healing and wholeness to their communities. In taking on a spirit's identity, in becoming "possessed," so to speak, shaman-actors gain access to deep cultural truths.

Similarly, consciously or not, theatre actors nurture their capacity to explore themselves emotionally and spiritually, while loosening intellectual control. They breathe life into their on-stage character by connecting with their personal emotional, intuitive, and spiritual history. Theatre actors' experience shows the limitations of a Psychology that dismisses some psychological phenomena as irrational.

the US context and relied on Scottish common-sense realism (Spilka, 1987). Like the natural philosophers of the seventeenth and eighteenth centuries, the new psychologists held that science shows the hand of God operating in the world (Davis, 1936). Similar developments occurred in British Psychology circles (G. Richards, 2011).

But in the USA psychologists needed support from a public that apparently identified Psychology with a godless materialism (Pickren, 2000). Hence, some early psychologists incorporated religious ideas into their publications designed for the popular press. In these writings they showed the public that religious faith and the new discourse of Psychology were complementary.

Later generations of psychologists, however, were committed staunchly to materialist explanations of natural objects within a knowable universe; consequently, they were skeptical about contemporary spirituality and organized religion. In fact, many responded with alarm to widespread public interest in psychic phenomena and spiritualism, even though the esteemed William James studied and described them (Coon, 1992). These popular practices offered some solace to individuals anxious about the impending demise of religion's influence on popular consciousness.

But the popularity of psychic phenomena and spiritualism threatened the new psychologists' quest for scientific status. After initially dismissing psychic research and spiritualism to preserve their scientific reputation, some psychologists studied "mediums" and "ESP sensitives" in the hope of uncovering fraudulence or of explaining these phenomena naturalistically. They then shifted to explaining spiritualism and psychic experiences as the results of deception and suggestibility. At this time, Psychology seemed to operate along a disputed border between the natural and the supernatural (Coon, 1992). Thus, early psychologists were keen to legitimize their claim that their investigations of spiritualism and psychic experiences were just as objective as any natural-scientific inquiry.

By the 1920s US psychologists were challenged by the emerging varieties of psychoanalysis (Hornstein, 1992). Although Freud viewed religion as an illusion and denigrated spirituality, the content of psychoanalysis, namely, unconscious irrational impulses and potentially disruptive desires and emotions, is patently subjective, which was unscientific territory for natural-science psychologists in the USA. Carl Jung's explorations of paranormal experiences and of spiritual development in older adults was even more antithetical to mainstream psychologists' interests.

During the 1980s after the cognitivist school of thought attained conceptual dominance in US Psychology, the historical ambivalence between Psychology and spirituality seemed fruitless to some cognitive neuroscientists. Roger Sperry (1988), for instance, "argued that the cognitive paradigm significantly modifies materialist science by attributing a pivotal, causal function for subjectivity, consciousness, and spiritual qualities within embodied corticate beings. Like Baruch Spinoza's, Sperry's metatheoretical project is to unify mind, body, and spirit" (Walsh-Bowers, 2000, p. 228).

From a philosophy of science perspective, the mission of natural-science Psychology since its inception has been to secularize the soul. Psychologists "learned how to replace the soul . . . with science . . . on the terrain of memory" (Hacking, 1995, p. 5). According to this argument, cognitive psychologists assume that memory is the marker of personal identity; thus, what humans remember and forget constitutes one's soul. The corollary is that when psychologists discover the empirical facts about memory, in effect they have obtained objective knowledge about "the soul."

Viewed against the history of science and the persistent tensions between objectivity and subjectivity, the roots of natural-science psychologists' antipathy towards, or at least skepticism about, spirituality becomes clear. Indeed, the American Psychological Association (2011) explicitly encourages authors of Psychology textbooks to persuade their readers that belief in subjective phenomena, such as paranormal experiences, which are common for many aboriginal individuals, is out of bounds for a genuine science and simply reflects superstitious behaviour.

Spirituality and religion in relation to physical and mental health

Some scientists are becoming more vocal about the interplay among faith, spirituality, health, and healing. In recent decades researchers from a wide range of disciplines and professions have been exploring numerous topics that bear relationship, indirectly or directly, to religious practices and spirituality. Biological psychologist Candace Pert (1997) has advocated restoring spirituality to medicine, based on her conclusion that health is affected by the soul, mind, and emotions as well as the body.

Mind–body medicine is a growing orientation in Western nations and complements alternative ancient practices from other cultures. The current revival of scientists' interest in transpersonal phenomena includes investigations of the effect of prayerful meditation on reducing stress and the impact of prayer on patients' healing. **Herbert Benson** (b. 1935), a cardiologist from Harvard, has been researching the healing benefits of what he terms "the relaxation response," by which he means the body's positive responses to meditative practices (Benson & Proctor, 2011). He promotes the notion that human beings are "wired" for God and claims that religious beliefs have tangible health benefits and even genetic effects.

However, other scholars challenge such claims and question the viability of any alliance between medicine and religious and spiritual matters (e.g., R. Sloan, 2006). Scientific issues include methodological and interpretive biases on the part of investigators who assert they have found healing effects from religious or spiritual practices. Health issues include the possibility of iatrogenic effects from such research. Issues of spirituality and religion include the possibility of medical scientists trivializing religious or spiritual practices in their research.

Assuming that research can demonstrate that spiritual and religious practices, such as prayer, have a positive effect on people's physical and mental health, at least **three important questions** come to mind:

- How does prayer work? Does it release a psychological or biochemical curative agent within the patients? Or, are faith-filled scientists suggesting that prayer actually induces God to intervene and heal?
- What are the implications for psychologists of scientific studies of the impact spirituality on physical and mental health?
- What is the relationship between this emerging body of research and neuro-immunology?

Transpersonal psychology

Despite the differences in scientific worldviews between human-science psychologies and natural-science Psychology, concepts from transpersonal psychologies have seeped into the mainstream, particularly clinical and health psychologies. One of the more popular concepts is that of "mindfulness," which has a Buddhist root (Kabat-Zinn, 1990).

Some psychologists investigate the role of mindfulness training on health or on depression. In one study investigators examined how teaching hatha yoga, meditation, and qigong to graduate students reduced stress (Schure, Christopher, & Christopher, 2008). The students reported positive physical, emotional, mental, spiritual, and interpersonal changes from practising these regimens.

Arguably, the best-known thinker in the subdiscipline of transpersonal psychology is **Ken Wilber** (b. 1949). In what he calls "the revolutionary integral approach to life, God, the universe, and everything" Wilber (2007) divides reality into **four quadrants**:

- The upper-left one refers to the interior-individual, labelled as "I." It includes a person's sensations, perceptions, experiences, emotions, symbols, concepts, etc.
- The upper-right quadrant refers to the exterior-individual (behavioural) dimension and includes molecules, neural cord, limbic system, and the neocortex, etc. Wilber calls it "IT."
- The lower-left quadrant refers to the "WE" and includes our interior-collective and cultural dimensions and aspects such as the locomotive, archaic, magic, mythic, and rational.
- The lower-right quadrant is called "ITS," meaning the exterior-collective, such as galaxies, planets, tribes, nation/state, etc.

Wilber challenges medicine, business, and ecology for focusing on certain aspects of this system without integrating them into a whole. Based on his system, which is more sophisticated than our brief description, Wilber provides concrete practical suggestions for health and well-being. He has published a number of books, developed a variety of programmes, and established institutes where one can study his integral vision.

Part 6 conclusion

Perhaps many psychologists have struggled to reconcile their professional life as academic or professional psychologists with their personal practices of spirituality and religion (G. Richards, 2011). Psychologists' enculturation in Psychology, which is rooted in a materialist science, was alienated from transpersonal experiences. But some psychologists, uncomfortable with this disjointed experience, conclude that only a holistic psychology that integrates spirit with matter can enable scientific psychologists to effectively understand human action. As such, some have attempted to retrieve religion and spirituality for their science and profession (e.g., Walsh-Bowers, 2000), while others acknowledge, as James (1902) did in *The Varieties of Religious Experience: A Study in Human Nature*, that potentially Psychology is "interposed between religion and the physical sciences" (G. Richards, 2011, p. 36).

Arguably, broadening the discipline to incorporate religion and spirituality consciously can benefit some psychologists personally and professionally. Our hope is that you might discern how your personal experiences with religion and spirituality might affect your life-journey and a possible career in Psychology. Transpersonal psychologies provide pathways for such explorations.

Nevertheless, the cultural revival of spirituality and religion, and Psychology's role in this revival, deserve critical thinking (G. Richards, 2011). Spirituality, for instance, has become a commodity in advanced capitalist countries, while thriving outside academic Psychology. The wise scholar would evaluate carefully the alleged merits and be alert to possible dangers in the many transpersonal approaches and particularly their claims to healing.

Part 7   Thematic review

Two themes seem to capture the main issues discussed in this chapter on human-science psychologies: **the centrality of understanding and interpretation** and **the disputed border between body and mind, soul, and spirit**.

The centrality of understanding and interpretation

Understanding and interpreting the complex phenomena of individuals' mental life are essential aspects of psychologists' work as theorists, investigators, and professional practitioners. But as we have seen, natural-science psychologists have been disinclined to describe, understand, or interpret the specificity of human mental life and human nature. Rather, human-science psychologists (and diverse psychoanalysts) have pursued these goals, taking one of three routes historically.

First, the discipline of hermeneutics provides insights into the process and skills of understanding and interpreting; accordingly, hermeneutics is germane to all psychological theory, research, and practice. As Dilthey argued on behalf of a descriptive human-science psychology, trying to understand individuals without understanding their meaningful experiences in historical and cultural contexts yields deceptive knowledge. However, instead of relying on authority and tradition, scholars who practise critical thinking should scrutinize a proposed interpretation from an outsider's perspective to guard against harming other people. Unreflective interpretations, framed as definitive knowledge, might constitute epistemological violence.

A second route to understanding psychological phenomena is phenomenology, which Husserl intended as the discovery of the objective essence of conscious experience. Although he identified the elements for a systematic psychology of experience, he assumed that we can approach phenomena without traditions. But in Gadamer's revision, traditions are the enabling conditions for knowledge.

A third route to understanding is the study of intentionality, which seems to be at the heart of positive and negative existential experiences. Existential philosophers and psychologists, led by Heidegger's interests in the immediate psychological roots of existence, have pursued these concerns. Existence, of course, is fundamentally interpersonal and cultural, being shaped by social categories such as ethnocultural status and gender. But as Frankl showed, even extraordinarily adverse social conditions can be occasions for making meaning and avoiding existential despair.

What understanding the psychology of human existence meant was quite different in the eyes of European existentialist than of US humanistic psychologists. Although both groups focused on the individual's perceived meaning of her or his actions, humanistic psychologists extolled the virtues of self-actualization and individual human potential. This self-development programme has been sustained and subsumed by "pop psychology" and by positive psychologists for whom understanding and interpretation seem subordinate to pragmatic applications of natural-science Psychology.

The disputed border between body and mind, soul, and spirit

In science and Psychology there has been a great deal of tension between objectivity and subjectivity, science and spirituality, natural-science and transpersonal psychologies. We have seen natural-science psychologists' adverse reactions to psychoanalysis and to humanistic and existential psychologies. In fact, transpersonal discourses on the soul and spirituality have haunted natural-science Psychology from its inception, persistently threatening its claim to scientific objectivity.

As the new millennium approached, however, psychologists' interest in spirituality and religion seemed to increase. The more psychologists have resisted subjectivity, the more irrepressible subjectivity and spirituality have become. Arguably, to defend against a spectre of transpersonal psychologies haunting Psychology, to paraphrase Karl Marx and Friedrich Engels ([1848] 1968) in *The Communist Manifesto*, psychologists have erected scientistic structures of hyper-objectivity that replace organized religion's hold on early modern society (Walsh-Bowers, 2000).

One major implication of natural-science psychologists' scientism is that they cannot appreciate spirituality and religion without redefining, expanding, and deepening Psychology. US psychologist Seymour Sarason (1981) argued that the discipline has been "misdirected" historically, but some advocates of transpersonal psychologies retort that Psychology has been misconceived (e.g., Walsh-Bowers, 2000). In this view, by their adoption of a natural-sciences model that excludes spirituality, psychologists reproduce alienated rationality.

Since the dawn of the discipline, many natural-science psychologists have investigated nearly disembodied and soulless processes of behaviour, emotion, and cognition. This dualism splits body from mind and spirit, thereby compartmentalizing human experience and valorizing instrumental reason. "What psychologists need instead is dialectical integration of all human systems: body, mind, heart, soul, contextualized in changing human relationships, which, in turn, are embedded in historically changing social structures and ideologies" (Walsh-Bowers, 2000, pp. 232–233).

For psychologists to create a new science that overcomes splitting the subjective from the objective, accepting the union of spirituality with the created world, and allowing for expressions of the sacred in science, they would have to accept the belief that Earth has spirit and scientists' responsibility is not to dominate nature but to cooperate with it. Moreover, if psychologists are serious about restoring soul to Psychology, then they cannot reduce subjectivity to cognitive neuroscientific processes.

From a transpersonal perspective, an epistemological, ethical, and aesthetic vision is required, comparable to Kant's project, which would encompass every facet of human life. Such an integrative framework for Psychology "would be centred on the primacy of soulful, interdependent relationships with all creatures and all creation within egalitarian relationships" (Walsh-Bowers, 2000, p. 233).

Erich Fromm (1955) considered the needs for community and transcendence as fundamental to healthy living. As Buddhists and other spiritually experienced thinkers claim, the emancipatory practice of spirituality facilitates the fulfillment of these deeply human needs. The challenge for psychologists is whether we can "overcome the discipline's historically rooted antipathy to subjectivity and . . . actualize the significance of spirituality and religion for our materialist discipline" (Walsh-Bowers, 2000, p. 234).

Summary

In Part 1 we discussed the meaning of hermeneutics, arguing that it is a central part of human activity as well as of any empirical Psychology. We introduced the idea of critical hermeneutics to underscore that empirical data do not fully determine the interpretations that we choose as psychologists and that interpretations can have a negative impact on certain groups of people.

In Part 2 we described opposing perspectives in nineteenth-century Psychology. Wilhelm Dilthey intended to align psychology with the humanities rather than the natural sciences, particularly history. In the tradition of German historiography, he distinguished natural-science psychology from human-science psychology. In doing so, Dilthey critiqued the limitations of psychology as a natural science and laid the foundation for a hermeneutic psychology, with its core method of understanding. We also showed that the discipline of Psychology did not follow Dilthey's direction but Wundt's instead.

In Part 3 we explained how hermeneutic psychology's method of understanding was applied to personality, developmental, and clinical psychology. Unlike Dilthey, Eduard Spranger did not believe that personal empathy should be central in understanding; rather, he suggested that understanding includes trans-subjective meaning-constellations that might not be given to the individual. Karl Jaspers applied a method of understanding to lay the foundation for a theory of psychopathology combining hermeneutic with natural-scientific principles in Psychology.

In Part 4 we described phenomenological and existential psychology, which are associated with mainly European psychological concepts and practices. We described Franz Brentano's concept of intentionality and noted his role in the emergence of hermeneutic and phenomenological psychology. Phenomenology itself was fostered by Edmund Husserl. The key figures in European existentialism are Martin Heidegger, Jean-Paul Sartre, Simone de Beauvoir, Albert Camus, and Ludwig Binswanger. We also discussed Viktor Frankl's existential logotherapy.

In Part 5 we suggested that phenomenological ideas and existentialism had an impact in the English-speaking world in the works of Rollo May and to a lesser extent George Kelly. We also described the basic ideas of humanistic psychology, represented by Abraham Maslow and Carl Rogers. Humanistic psychology as an "American" phenomenon had some durable effect on Psychology in the USA and Canada.

In Part 6 we described transpersonal psychologies. First we defined religion, spirituality, soul, and spirit. Then we reviewed diverse psychological perspectives on the soul, spirituality, and religion, and described the field of transpersonal psychology. We showed how the contested field of psychoneuroimmunology exemplifies the intersections among science, medicine, Psychology, spirituality, and religion as does research on the impact of spirituality and religion on physical and mental health.

In Part 7 we discussed two themes that capture the contested relationship between science and Psychology, on the one hand, and transpersonal psychologies: the centrality of understanding and interpretation for the various transpersonal psychologies, and the disputed border between body and mind, soul, and spirit.

Sample essay questions

1. Discuss how you might employ a hermeneutic approach in studying a psychological phenomenon that captures your interest.

2. A common statement about existentialism is that existentialists believe "Hell is other people." Under what circumstances, in your experience, is hell other people? What about the reverse: under what circumstances is heaven other people?

3. Explain which school of thought you prefer, humanistic or existential/phenomenological psychology or neither.

RECOMMENDED READING

For a history of paintings, see the latest edition of Gombrich's (2006) very successful *The story of art*.

Good texts on hermeneutics can be found in Mueller-Vollmer (1985) and Ormiston & Schrift (1990). Good introductions and expert explanations of phenomenology are provided by Moran (2000) and, with a focus on Husserl's psychological phenomenology, by James (2007).

Due to the importance of Heidegger and existentialism in the twentieth century there are many introductory books. Interested readers are best advised to seek out specialized literature for existential psychology, phenomenological psychology, and humanistic psychology respectively.

The conflictual relationship between Psychology and spirituality can be approached from several angles, including the subdiscipline known as the psychology of religion. See Paloutzian and Park's (2005) *Handbook of the psychology of religion and spirituality*. For a critical-historical perspective see G. Richards's (2011) *Psychology, religion, and the nature of the soul*. Also see the fourth issue of the 2005 volume of the *Journal of Social Issues*, which is devoted to psychological perspectives on religion.

ONLINE RESOURCES

On existentialism, see *Stanford Encyclopedia of Philosophy* http://plato.stanford.edu/entries/existentialism/

On existential therapy, see www.existential-therapy.com/

On phenomenological psychology, see http://phenomenologicalpsychology.com/

On the phenomenological psychology centre at Duquesne University, see www.duq.edu/phenomenology/

On transpersonal psychology, see Association for Transpersonal Psychology www.atpweb.org/ and International Transpersonal Association www.transpersonalassociation.org/

Introduction

After the Scientific Revolution natural science came to overshadow religious knowledge about nature and human nature. Many natural philosophers became disenchanted with divine and mysterious explanations. They regarded nature as mechanistic, manipulable for human ends, even conquerable. Emergent empirical methods and quantification techniques enhanced scientists' confidence about their work.

Societally, economically privileged Western nations became increasingly rationalized and bureaucratic. Efficient administration of industry, commerce, and government depended on applications of systematic knowledge; consequently, social management of individuals escalated. In addition, cultivating individual experience became culturally desirable.

This scientific and societal context was early psychologists' legacy. Their new science blended the study of individuals with practical applications for managing them. To legitimize Psychology, natural-science psychologists adopted the methodology of the natural sciences. They assumed that rigorous application of empirical methods and precise and reliable measurement would reveal socially useful truths.

Empirical methods, then, typically supported by quantification, have been the basis for natural-science psychologists' claims to scientific knowledge. However, it seems that, rather than being purely objective and universal, these claims depend on modes of conducting research and writing about it that have a social history. In short, societal and scientific contexts guided Psychology's research traditions.

Epistemologically, many natural-science psychologists assume that their investigations reveal independent truths about animal and human nature. They believe that rigorously following methodological procedures yields results that are natural objects existing independently of social-historical contexts. Similarly, their concepts and terms, such as "learned helplessness," are believed to reflect natural objects.

A different perspective is that psychologists *construct* psychological objects that are artifacts of an investigative situation shaped by investigators and participants. Rather than "methodology," which means a general orientation to specific methods, here we use the term *investigative practice* as proposed by Kurt Danziger (Brock, 2006b). This concept encompasses the social aspects of conducting research as well as the logical procedures that scientists follow. Investigative practice implies that scientific work is partially subjective and that social-historical conditions shape notions of "objectivity, measurability, repeatability, and cumulative knowledge acquisition" (Ash, 2003, p. 251).

With these contextual points in mind, the **aims** of this chapter are to describe:

- The scientific and social consequences of psychologists' research language.
- How investigative practices with humans and animals, including ethical principles and standards, have changed.
- How psychologists have adopted investigative methods, including qualitative ones, and the various sources of bias to which all methods are prone.
- The problems in measuring and quantifying psychological data and using statistical techniques, and the issues involved in analyzing qualitative data.

- The story of standards for writing psychological research reports and the disciplinary significance of "APA style."
- Two themes – science, pseudoscience, or interpretive science, and intersubjectivity – that capture the issues discussed in this chapter.

Part 1   The language of research

In this part, we consider how psychologists developed a scientific language that is now taken for granted. Since the 1930s, two epistemological propositions, "operationism" and "logical positivism," along with the term "variables," have been have been central to that language, particularly in US Psychology.

Psychologists' scientific language

Arguably, scientific categories, including psychological terms, "are always embedded in a network of semantic relationships from which they derive their meaning and significance" (Danziger, 1997b, p. 13). This semantic network is known as a *discursive formation*. Every generation of psychologists constructs a particular discourse or language of research in relation to their particular historical circumstances.

The early psychologists' terms were diverse, reflecting contemporary heterogeneity of concepts and methods. Although the first generation of human-science psychologists relied on philosophical discourse, their natural-science peers shared a strong preference for the language of nineteenth-century physiology (e.g., "stimulus" and "response"). By also emulating physiologists' experimental methods, natural-science psychologists aimed to achieve objectivity and produce causal explanations of their psychological observations. In the USA, physiological discourse soon permeated natural-science Psychology and led to heavy reliance on the language of "behaviour" rather than the philosophical discourse of "mind."

There are **two perspectives** on what constitutes scientific language (Danziger, 1997a):

- Within *language as representation*, scientific words mirror an independent non-linguistic reality. Thus, the term "hyperactivity" represents a natural object.
- Within *language as a formative practice*, scientific language shapes discursive practice. Thus, "hyperactivity" affects who uses and who is labelled by this term.

Natural-science psychologists adopted the first perspective. They assumed that their conceptual categories represented natural realities invariant across humankind. Yet certain concepts in Western culture did not exist until psychologists invented them (e.g., "attitudes"), psychologists altered other concepts (e.g. "personality"), and some previously salient concepts (e.g., "will") nearly disappeared. For instance, "socialization" originally meant transforming economic conditions to achieve socialism. After World War II, socialization in Psychology came to mean social aspects of individuals' development leading to autonomous agency (Morawski & St. Martin, 2011).

During the neobehaviourist era psychologists developed concepts such as "operational definitions" and "variables" that became routine in the discipline. This discourse enhanced the scientific legitimacy of the description of mental processes.

Operational definitions

Ernst Mach had advocated defining scientific categories only in relation to the methodological procedures employed to measure them. He aimed to eradicate any speculation on implicit underlying essences or ultimate metaphysical causes by substituting "functions" for "causes." Emphasizing economy of scientific discourse and practice, he believed that only mathematical descriptions of the functional relations of phenomena constituted scientific explanation (Winston, 2001).

Then in 1927 a US physicist, **Percy Bridgman** (1882–1961), proposed that every abstract concept in physics be defined only in terms of the procedures used to measure the concept. This is the origin of the term *operational definition*. By 1954 Bridgman regretted that he had made his proposition so narrow. Natural-science psychologists, however, adhered to his original position.

Edwin Boring had asserted in the 1920s that intelligence was whatever capacity a given test measured. But *operationism* as a formal methodological doctrine did not emerge in US Psychology until the 1930s (Feest, 2005), when **S. S. Stevens** (1906–1973), a sensory psychologist, asserted that psychologists could measure any mentalistic concept as objectively as physicists could measure natural objects (Stevens, 1935). Neobehaviourist Edward Tolman publicly adopted this position. By World War II, many psychologists embraced operationism, applying it to all psychological concepts. Operational definitions then became descriptions of the observable behaviour that could be used to quantify an abstract concept.

As a methodological system, operationism provided psychologists with a scientifically plausible rationale for discarding mentalistic meanings from psychological theory. Psychologists defined learning, for instance, as X number of successive correct turns in a rat maze or intelligence as a score on an IQ test.

From a critical perspective, **three assumptions** undergird operationism:

- Measurement of psychologists' phenomena is equivalent to measurement of physicists' phenomena.
- The meaning of concepts is identical to the operations employed in measuring them.
- Psychologists have vanquished the vestiges of subjective psychologies and have secured the same prestigious scientific status as physicists.

Variables

Historically, Mach reinterpreted the metaphysical concept of causality, which Aristotle, David Hume, and Immanuel Kant discussed in depth, as a functional mathematical–physical relationship between *variables*. This term, which denotes a variable quantity, was not a working concept in Psychology until neobehaviourism, when "variable" came to imply linear cause-and-effect relations (Winston, 2004a).

In 1932, Tolman used variables to refer to psychological constructs and to provide a rigorous explanation of behaviour. Soon natural-science psychologists substituted "independent variable" for stimulus and "dependent variable" for response and characterized any psychological dimension as a variable. What then defined the meaning of psychological concepts was research conducted only with variables (Danziger, 1997b).

Independent and dependent variables began to serve key functions in Psychology. In his popular 1934 introductory textbook Robert Woodworth defined experimentation as the manipulation of an independent variable to evoke changes in a dependent variable (Winston, 2004a). (Boring and B. F. Skinner previously had characterized the experiment similarly.) The subsequent shift to the language of variables that reputedly reveal cause-and-effect relations took several decades to solidify but was central to the eventual reign of experimentation in natural-science Psychology (Danziger, 1997b).

However, the simple term variable was inadequate to the task of addressing the complexities of psychological phenomena. So Tolman invented the term *intervening variable*, which is a construct mediating between independent and dependent variables. Psychologists' new reliance on operational definitions facilitated using this new term and led to swelling confidence that operationism linked with variables enabled psychologists to attain physicists' vaunted objectivity.

Overall, "variables" served to connect many subdisciplines of Psychology that had divergent concepts and categories. In experimental papers many psychologists identified the influences or the effects of particular variables on particular behaviours, as in the statement "X is a function of Y." Yet this language resembling physics allowed researchers to sidestep problems of the meaning of the particular behaviour investigated as well to neglect theoretical assumptions and cultural contexts for that behaviour.

Variables and operational definitions are associated with a philosophical system justifying scientific knowledge known as *logical positivism*, which has played a key role in natural-science Psychology since the 1930s.

Logical positivism

Building on Auguste Comte's doctrine of positivism, Mach proposed that one obtains objective knowledge only through the natural sciences, chiefly physics. He asserted in his "doctrine of elements" that progressively and methodically acquired facts are the constituents of knowledge.

However, when Albert Einstein showed that matter and time, two fundamentals of nature, are relative and not absolute, the mechanistic and materialist assumptions of positivism required reassessment. The problem was how to retain the power of scientific method to determine facts in a relativistic universe yet avoid the extremes of faith in absolute reality and idealistic theorizing. In 1923, Rudolf Carnap introduced a solution, logical positivism, to systematically meld empirical knowledge with scientifically respectable explanations.

Three assumptions constitute a logical-positivist analysis (T. Rogers, 1995):

- Theoretical terms can be expressed mathematically (e.g., Clark Hull's formulae involving habit strength, drive, and organisms' readiness to respond).
- Correspondence-rules can translate theoretical terms into observational statements (e.g., prior experience in the experimental situation, duration of hunger, and response-speed).

- Observational statements can describe particular natural objects (e.g., hungry subjects run faster in a maze than satiated subjects under the same conditions).

In the strong version of logical positivism, only correspondence-rules can contain conceptual meaning. All other theoretical terms (e.g., "expectancy") are considered subjectivist. Carnap and colleagues, collectively known as the Vienna Circle, asserted that scientists can use theoretical terms only if they are tied to "observables," in other words, if scientists operationally define their concepts.

In sum, logical positivism provided support for a neobehaviourist approach to psychological inquiry and justified repudiating metaphysical claims about psychological knowledge. Neobehaviourists now believed that psychological *theory* could be just as empirically grounded and objective as they believed the experimental method is. This development partially explains why many neobehaviourists rejected Gestalt theory in which perceived subjective experience is pivotal. But unlike neobehaviourists, the logical-positivist philosophers understood objectivity, method, and knowledge as relative, not absolute concepts (Mitchell, 2002).

Part 1 conclusion

The logical-positivist framework of justification complemented both the scientific language of operational definitions and variables and natural-science psychologists' preference for experimentation. After Clark Hull introduced the *hypothetico-deductive method* in the 1940s (Kimble, 1991a), testing hypotheses became natural-science psychologists' methodological "gold standard." According to the hypothetico-deductive doctrine, investigators propose theoretical postulates about behaviour, then deduce from them operationally defined hypotheses testable in quantitative experiments. If the results do not support the hypotheses, investigators revise the postulates; if the results provide support, investigators accept the postulates as a scientific contribution.

The strong connection between Psychology's scientific language and preference for lab experimentation had **six epistemological, scientific, and social consequences**:

- By adopting the positivist language of objective observation and assuming stable and permanent behaviour, natural-science psychologists believed their mechanistic explanations accurately reflected reality. They held that rigorously controlled experimentation of operationally defined variables permitted generalizations to real-world behaviour.
- In contrast to early psychologists, many natural-science psychologists narrowed their theorizing and concepts to use language relatively devoid of metaphorical expression (Gentner & Grudin, 1985). Until cognitivism rose to prominence, many US psychologists avoided such terms as "thoughts," "intentions," "experience," and "feelings," which they regarded as mentalistic, hence subjective.
- Psychologists relied on the discourse of operational definitions and variables to claim the scientific high ground relative to the social sciences, because they maintained that using lab experiments could determine causal explanations of interpersonal phenomena (e.g., aggression).

- US psychologists' postwar scientific language and emphasis on experimentation became the discipline's modus operandi internationally. Yet at least in the USA, the public might be skeptical of the discipline's scientific status, despite decades of effort to legitimize Psychology as a science, perhaps because citizens intuit that psychological concepts depend upon social-historical contexts (Lilienfeld, 2012).
- Rather than being a socially and politically neutral technology, psychologists' scientific language and experimental methodology enabled them to convince the movers and shakers of US society that psychologists were authentic experts with socially useful scientific knowledge (Danziger, 1997b). Their limited theorizing about the meaning of their variables, despite Hull's hypothetico-deductive model, complemented psychologists' aims of contributing to society's administrative control of the population in response to pressing social issues. For this societal purpose no theoretical reflections were necessary.
- The language of experimental variables obscured the influence of the relationship between the investigator and the human or animal source of data. This language also allowed experimenters to rationalize their reliance on nonhuman animals and captive "subjects" (e.g., mental patients and undergraduate students).

Part 2   Investigative practice with humans

Psychologists not only employ the scientific language of their discipline, but also they construct the investigative situation in particular ways. Of course, the objects of their psychological investigations are animals and humans, which are qualitatively different from the natural objects of other sciences. Because psychologists investigate phenomena that they themselves might have experienced, they are intimately connected with their subject matter. This connection between animate objects and the psychologists who observe them is the focus of this and the next section.

In reflecting on the relationship between observers and the humans who are observed we rely on the concept of a *research relationship* (i.e., the professional relationship in which researchers engage with the individuals – "participants" or "subjects" – who provide data). In reviewing this history we include ethical matters affecting research. But unless one examines it, the research relationship is not self-evident, given Psychology's history of taking it for granted (Danziger, 1990).

Research relationships

Small-group discussion. What research roles have you played? How would you describe the quality of the relationship between yourself as participant and the research assistant or between yourself as research assistant and your participants? As a participant, what feedback on the study's findings did you receive from the research team? As a research assistant, what feedback do you provide for your participants?

Histories of psychologists' investigative practice span over a century of journal reports and include behavioural, interpersonal, and applied subdisciplines (Danziger, 1990; Walsh-Bowers, 1995). These histories show that distinct models of investigative practice flourished in Psychology's founding decades.

But after World War II, most natural-science psychologists adopted a formulaic investigative practice. The disciplinary expectation was – and remains – that in collecting data and reporting their findings, researchers should be as objective as possible and emotionally detached in a hierarchical relationship with research participants. In reporting their investigations, psychologists depersonalized them. This set of practices became institutionalized and an unquestioned norm in the discipline.

Paralleling this investigative standard were two significant developments. First, psychologists' failed to address ethical considerations in human research until the 1950s. Until that point few seemed to care about the fact that, above all, the research relationship was a social process of persons who shared a common humanity (Danziger, 1990). Since the emergence of formal ethical guidelines for research (see below), psychologists espoused respect for the dignity of participants. However, they continued to practise a relationship of dominant investigators – subordinate participants.

The second development in psychologists' culture that minimized attention to research relationships was the institutionalization of the American Psychological Association's (APA) *Publication Manual* in 1952. This widely used tool has indoctrinated researchers in formal standards for the composition of research papers, in which many Psychology instructors in Canada and the US drill their students.

In sum, the research relationship consists of **three interrelated dimensions**:

- Investigative roles
- Standards for ethical conduct of research
- Expectations for research report-writing.

History of research roles

Few mainstream psychologists have paid attention to the social origins of investigative practice. The assumption seems to be that Psychology originated as an experimental natural science in which the individuals serving as data sources serve no other function in an investigation (e.g., Chastain, 1999). But this version is historically incorrect.

Exploring how investigators construct their relationships with human data sources in studies published in Psychology journals from 1879 to 1939, Danziger (1990) identified **five functions or roles** in research:

- Designer of the study
- Data collector/administrator of the study
- Human source of data (previously known as "subject" and known today as "participant")
- Data analyst
- Author of the research report.

Theoretically, these functions can be shared between the members of the investigative team and the participants in any particular study. Generally, however, only team members play the roles of designer, administrator ("experimenter"), data analyst, and author, whereas participants serve only as data sources.

Historically, there were **four early models** of conducting human research with different social arrangements between experimenters and participants, depending on the aims of each approach (Danziger, 1990; Kusch, 1995):

(1) In Wilhelm Wundt's studies of consciousness, an individual man serving as data source (women were excluded from laboratory science in nineteenth-century Germany) held pride of place in that his experiential awareness of experimentally varied, sensory stimuli was the investigative team's point of interest. Accordingly, Wundt occasionally served as data source in his team's experimentation. In this model of shared roles among team members, the least desired role was data administrator.

(2) In nineteenth-century French clinical research, the standard research relationship was a dominant medical experimenter and a subordinate *sujet* ("subject"), often a medical patient, as exemplified by Jean-Martin Charcot's studies of hypnosis. By the twentieth century, French experimental psychology consisted of two orientations (Carroy & Plas, 1996): case studies of pathological states, hypnosis, and paranormal phenomena (known as *La Clinique*), and content and methods modelled on German psychophysiology.

(3) Oswald Külpe and his associates constructed a research relationship in which the data collector representing the investigative team jointly produced the experimental findings with the person serving as data source. Within this relatively egalitarian relationship both roles were esteemed (Kusch, 1995).

(4) The model of experimenters testing anonymous masses of "subjects" evolved in Anglo-American Psychology with Francis Galton's focus on testing individual differences. In this model, researchers hold hierarchical power throughout the investigative situation. Participants' only job is to provide data as researchers see fit. Researchers and their assistants design, administer, analyze, and author.

Given the common assumption that psychological knowledge rests in the content of individual minds, early research reports typically contained personalized findings in terms of individual participants (Danziger, 1990). However, those psychologists (e.g., John Watson) who regarded experimental studies of animal behaviour as functionally equivalent to human behaviour dealt with human participants in as detached a way as they dealt with animals. Their research reports reflected this depersonalized approach.

By the 1920s there was little evidence in US Psychology journals of the Wundtian model of shared research roles (Danziger, 1990). From this point on, generally speaking, psychologists produced empirical papers in a formulaic way, using rhetoric that kept the social characteristics of the data collectors invisible and gave only the barest information about the social characteristics of the human sources of data (Morawski, 2007).

When neobehaviourist research came to dominate US Psychology, research participants mattered even less. Investigators focused on observing natural objects and deriving universal laws of behaviour. Their methodological and reporting standard, therefore, was to reduce participants to anonymous aggregates from whose data investigators could make universalizable generalizations.

In US and Canadian Psychology after World War II, abnormal, developmental, and personality and social psychology and the numerous applied subdisciplines (e.g., educational, industrial/organizational, and clinical psychology) rapidly expanded. Investigators had ample opportunities to conduct research in community settings with heterogeneous individuals providing data and to attend to the quality of research relationships. However, journal reports published from 1939 to 1989 showed that, with rare exceptions, researchers employed participants as data sources only and displayed impersonal rhetoric when referring to them (Walsh-Bowers, 1995). Alternative investigative models involving citizens' active participation in research roles other than data source became virtually extinct in psychologists' realm until recently.

Similar trends are evident in five English-language European journals of Psychology published from 1966 to 2006 (Walsh-Bowers, 2007). Authors followed the standard US practice of producing generalizable findings to demonstrate laws of human behaviour that presumably transcend both social location and the human relationship that produced the findings.

Are the above disciplinary norms for investigative practice still prevalent among today's psychologists? The findings from an interview-study conducted in 1999–2000 suggest that they are (Walsh-Bowers, 2002), as summarized in Box 11.1.

Box 11.1 Current investigative practices

Thirty-six researchers (professors, postdoctoral fellows, and graduate students), representing a range of subdisciplines from eight Canadian Psychology departments, individually discussed their views on the past, present, and future of the research relationship (Walsh-Bowers, 2002). If the findings can be applied to similar scientific psychologists, the following conclusions are warranted:

(1) When carefully preparing participants for controlled participation in natural-science investigations, researchers take for granted conventional research roles and functions, ethical guidelines, and report-writing. The notion of a research relationship is foreign to them and they see no reason to use precious journal space for reporting standard practice with participants. This finding corroborates the historical pattern of psychologists excluding "the social aspects of scientific practice" from their reportage about methodology (Danziger, 1990, p. 13).

(2) Hierarchical data extraction and depersonalized reporting are intertwined not only with the production of research papers, but also with undergraduate and graduate curricula in Psychology, including supervision of student research. The premise is that students must be trained to do research like a psychological scientist. This is an explicit purpose of the *Publication Manual* (Madigan, Johnson, & Linton, 1995).

(3) Intersubjectivity (i.e., acknowledging the mutual influence of researchers and participants on the psychological phenomena of interest) and investigator reflexivity (i.e., discussing this mutual influence in research reports), with possibilities for explicitly shared research roles, only surface among a minority of faculty and graduate students who identify with research positions such as qualitative methods or participatory action research.

Section conclusion

Histories of investigative practice suggest that natural-science psychologists have taken for granted the standard construction of research roles in which the investigative team performs all functions except data source. The research relationship becomes even more distant than bureaucratically administered face-to-face investigations, when psychologists use the internet in experiments as well as web-based survey research (Skitka & Sargis, 2006).

However, from a critical perspective, there is nothing intrinsically "scientific" about researchers having total control over the investigative situation and nothing "unscientific" about investigators sharing research functions and control with participants. Many qualitative researchers, feminist psychologists, and community psychologists have shifted to a more participatory model of investigative practice with participants contributing to study-design, data analysis, and interpretation. Just as psychologists have constructed the research relationship in particular ways historically, so they can reconstruct it.

Ethical relationships with humans

Since the 1950s, psychologists have believed that ethical standards or rules, if not ethical principles based in moral values, should direct the conduct of members of the investigative team. In this section we review psychologists' traditions and current practices of research ethics.

Historical development of ethical standards

The impetus for creating psychologists' ethical standards came from the Nuremberg Military Tribunal, which investigated Nazi atrocities, including those committed by scientists and physicians, such as torturous experimentation on captive-twin children. The Tribunal's inquiry led to a 1949 code of ethics. Subsequently, US medical and social scientists produced ethical guidelines for their respective professions. US psychologists followed suit.

The first version of the APA's ethics code, published in 1953, consisted of a brief statement of general standards concerning scientific practice; specific guidelines for research conduct were rudimentary. Underlying the development of this code were concerns with protecting investigators against possible litigation. Furthermore, in a context of advancing professional regulation, psychologists were anxious to ensure that the public had confidence in Psychology's compliance with ethical regulations (Berg, 1954). Previously, psychologists had demonstrated in journal reports very little awareness of research ethics (Walsh-Bowers, 1995).

By the 1970s, US psychologists had to become more vigilant about research ethics, again due to external pressures, although the infamous experiments by Stanley Milgram on obedience aroused some internal controversy. In 1974 the federal government issued regulations for the ethical conduct of research. Five years later the National Commission for the Protection of Human Subjects in Biomedical and Behavioral Research established institutional review boards to enforce investigators' compliance.

Ethical regulations now include special protection for vulnerable groups, such as children, institutionalized persons, and prisoners. These populations, historically, served as captive research subjects of convenience. Investigators, including psychologists, have to weigh the costs and risks to all types of participants against the expected benefits to them and the importance of the anticipated knowledge (Ceci, Peters, & Plotkin, 1985).

Current practices

To expedite the management of research participants and ensure that the public views researchers as treating participants with dignity, the standard ethical guidelines consist of: voluntary, informed consent; freedom to withdraw at any time; anonymity and confidentiality; debriefing if deception is used; and information ("feedback") on an investigation's general findings. Institutional ethics-review boards monitor researchers' adherence to these guidelines.

Since the 1980s, at least **three ethical practices** are now expected in mainstream Psychology, although the extent to which editors and authors have complied with them is questionable (Walsh-Bowers, 1995):

- Ethics guidebooks (e.g., Sieber, 1992) and casebooks (e.g., Bersoff, 1995) stipulate that investigators should ensure that their team members correctly and efficiently administer ethical standards. Increased knowledge of risk–benefit ratios, guided by reliance on ethics casebooks, reputedly constitutes sound ethical decision-making (Rosnow, Rotheram-Borus, Ceci, Blanck, & Koocher, 1993).
- When authors submit research manuscripts to APA journals, they are required to indicate how they met ethical standards.
- Editors are to encourage authors to designate individuals who provide data as "participants" instead of "subjects."

In addition, some psychologists identify "rewards" for investigators gained by complying with ethical requirements (Blanck, Bellack, Rosnow, Rotheram-Borus, & Schooler, 1992). The rewards envisioned include better recruitment, more representative samples, and insights into the meaning of one's data. This argument makes it seem as if psychologists require inducements to take ethical standards seriously.

Internationally, researchers might follow APA ethics guidelines, although some national associations have developed their own. The Canadian Psychological Association code, for example, includes investigative practice. But in 1998 the three Canadian research funding councils established the "Tri-Council Guidelines," which are a unified policy for ethical conduct that psychologists in Canada formally follow. Informally, however, most psychologists adhere to the APA code.

Some US and Canadian psychologists also engage in ethically questionable activities that seem peculiar to the discipline: deception and departmental "subject pools."

Deception

This investigative practice of researchers misleading participants about an experiment's purpose dates back to Alfred Binet, who arguably "originated the concern with objectivity in observer-observed relations" (Carroy & Plas, 1996, p. 82). He emphasized rigorous experimental control, including deception, to neutralize any contaminating influences on the research situation. Binet also argued that the schoolchildren to whom he administered forerunners of his intelligence test should be kept ignorant of his testing purposes.

After World War II, some social-personality psychologists adopted deception as standard procedure, hoping to achieve experimental control over the interpersonal phenomena they studied. Beginning in 1966, an APA committee reviewed the ethics of investigative practice, surveying the opinions of thousands of APA members (Stark, 2010).

Initially, the committee characterized deception as unacceptable, because it violated the concept of informed consent. But this standpoint aroused negative reactions from defenders of deception who objected to the recommended ethical restraints. Consequently, the committee decided that participants are sufficiently resilient to recover from any stress that deception induces; it recommended that psychologists employ deception correctly to sustain extant investigative practice. Yet subsequently, Leon Festinger abandoned social psychology, while other social-personality psychologists turned to experimental investigation of "social cognition," partly to avoid ethically disputable methodology (Aronson, 1980).

Presently, many psychologists do not employ deception in their studies, but others, such as social-personality psychologists, defend its use. Focused on the pragmatics of investigative practice and convinced of deception's methodological advantages, the latter psychologists argue that deception can be used ethically under certain circumstances (Pascual-Leone, Singh, & Scoboria, 2010). They claim the right to deceive participants when it is necessary, in their view, to pursue knowledge that benefits society as a whole (e.g., Adair, 2000; Stanley, Sieber, & Melton, 1996).

From this perspective, deception is justifiable when no other method permits studying certain interpersonal phenomena (Sieber, 1999). Advocates of deception also justify the procedure on the basis of some participants reporting positive perceptions of deception's risks and benefits (Fisher & Fryberg, 1994). Advocates assert that because exploitation of others is normative in real life, deception cannot be seriously harmful. Besides, they argue, the benefits to knowledge outweigh the minor costs to participants.

Positively sanctioned by ethics review boards, some investigators now distinguish between "deception," deliberately misleading participants, and "concealment," keeping information from participants without deception. They rationalize either procedure as necessitated by a study's design. They claim that disclosing a study's actual purpose would alter participants' responding and invalidate it. Such investigators then inform participants in a debriefing session of the true purpose of the study.

From a critical perspective, psychologists could use methods other than deception-experiments, such as observation and qualitative inquiry, to address their research questions. But this choice would require abandoning strict experimental control and would compromise mainstream psychologists' scientific assumptions. A second criticism is that the cost–benefit rationale for deception and concealment constitutes a fallacious ethical argument of ends justifying means.

Departmental subject pools

According to mainstream psychologists, "subject pools" give undergraduates experience with research and facilitate the efficient administration of psychologists' mission to conduct publishable research (e.g., Chastain & Landrum, 1999). From a critical perspective, this widespread practice consists of employing the free labour of Psychology students as participants. Arguably, subject pools are a source of convenient labour for psychologists and their assistants, enabling them to conduct research conveniently on institutional premises. Because a publishable research programme is essential for psychologists' career advancement, their chief concern is to efficiently operate subject pools to maintain research productivity.

But how well do subject pools serve students? Findings from the few surveys in Canada (Lindsay & Holden, 1987) and the USA (Landrum & Chastain, 1999; A. Miller, 1981; Sieber & Saks, 1989) contradict the public image of ethically responsible scientists. Apparently, many departments do not have ethical guidelines for subject pools, yet require student participation or a substitute activity as a component of the course grade (Stanley *et al.*, 1996). Moreover, viable alternatives to subject-pool participation have been lacking, which has been characterized as coercive (Sieber, 1999).

The **following three conditions** rarely prevail in subject pools:

- Students participate of their own choice.
- No grades are given for research participation or identified alternatives.
- Penalties for non-participation are non-existent.

How do psychologists justify subject pools? Primarily, they claim that coerced participation has educational value if properly done (e.g., Landrum & Chastain, 1999), but the evidence for this claim is dubious. The database is meagre, definitions of "done properly" and "educational value" are absent, and most departments do not evaluate students' perception of the subject-pool experience. In this light, the standard practice of subject pools appears to manipulate relatively disempowered students, contravene the ethical standard of free and informed consent, and abrogate students' rights.

Participants' rights

To recast ethical requirements in terms of what students are entitled to expect from their participation, some psychologists have advocated for student-participants' rights. These authors encourage investigators to treat the investigative situation with students as an exchange with each party having valuable resources (Korn, 1988; Prentice, Reitemeier, Antonson, Kelso, & Jameton, 1993; T. Rogers, 1997). Relatedly, fostering participants' ethical rights in Psychology requires treating informed consent as a communicative process between researchers and participants. Investigators also could incorporate into their investigations systematic assessment of participants' understanding of their ethical rights and responsibilities (Stanley *et al.*, 1996).

Yet recommended changes, such as improved quality of the information that investigators provide on their findings, only reform, not transform, standard investigative practice. The recommendations do *not* include participants sharing power with the investigative team across the five research functions of designing, administering, responding, analyzing and interpreting, and writing.

Section conclusion

From a critical perspective, a substantial gap apparently exists between psychologists' ethical responsibilities to their research participants, on the one hand, and their commitment to the use of deception and subject pools, on the other hand. This gap suggests a more systemic problem of lack of reflection on the ethical principles and standards guiding investigative conduct. There seems to be a historical contradiction between psychologists' espoused ethical principles and psychologists' dependence on a hierarchical model of research relationships.

Typically, psychologists follow the ethical rules that enable them to conduct a methodologically sound investigation (e.g., Rosenthal, 1994; Rosnow, 1997). Thus, the conventional mentality concerning research ethics appears rule-bound and utilitarian. Many investigators appear motivated more by pragmatic interests and compliance with "cookbook" directions than by appreciation for the underlying ethical principles of respect and dignity for participants.

For example, some psychologists argue that participants' compliance facilitates cooperation with research protocols, which produces quality research, which in turn enhances researchers' career-development (e.g., Stanley *et al.*, 1996). Others observe that resolving threats to participants' privacy enhances investigators' administrative efficiency (e.g., Blanck *et al.*, 1992).

According to this reasoning, the primary ethical criterion is the investigator's benefit, not participants' welfare. The pragmatic orientation to ethics suggests that psychologists use participants as means to their ends to "get better data." Although the practice of using others for one's own purposes may be normative in many societies, it is questionable ethically.

Part 2 conclusion

The history and philosophy of psychologists' investigative practice with humans encompass **two interdependent, social dimensions**:

- historically constituted constructions of investigative roles within the relationship between members of the investigative team and the individuals who provide data;
- ethical principles and their corresponding guidelines for investigative conduct.

These two social dimensions have been embedded in psychologists' underlying social context, including the political economy of psychological research (i.e., the "publish or perish" ethic), the power imbalance inherent in the conventional research relationship, and the fact that the conduct of psychological inquiry has a social history.

Mainstream discourse on research ethics consists of a rationale for methodological traditions that preserve the most esteemed investigative practice – the laboratory experiment – and the objectifying research relationship of dominant investigators and subordinate "subjects" that has been Psychology's norm for a century. In our view, psychologists cannot actualize their expressed concerns about ethical investigative conduct without addressing their beliefs about what constitutes sound investigative practice, whether qualitative or statistical, and objective research report-writing. To repeat, psychologists' research relationships are played out in their practices of investigative roles, ethics, and report-writing.

Part 3 | Investigative practice with animals

Psychologists' relationships with animal subjects have their own history. Although Westerners have interpreted animal behaviour as a guide to moral conduct for millennia (e.g., Aesop's *Fables* of ancient Greece), we tend to distinguish ourselves as superior to animals. By contrast, aboriginal societies have viewed themselves as interdependent with the natural world and its creatures.

Animal research accelerated in the nineteenth century, when Western biologists and psychologists studied animals both for their own sake and for the purpose of generalizing to human conduct. In fact, German philosopher Friedrich Lange asserted that scholars could learn more about psychological phenomena from animal experiments than from philosophical inquiries (Teo, 2002).

But the terms for categorizing animal investigations have changed over time. Currently, *animal psychology* refers generally to any research with nonhuman animals or specifically to **four domains** with different conceptual and methodological focuses:

- *Behavioural neuroscience*: psychophysiological experimentation.
- *Animal behaviour*: learning, motivation, memory, and social processes experimentation.
- *Comparative psychology*: behavioural and animal-cognition experimentation from an evolutionary perspective.
- *Ethology*: field research, using observation or experimentation, on animal behaviour.

Historically, methods have varied. Charles Darwin's legacy of observing animals in their natural habitats is profound in ethology and comparative psychology (Burghardt, 2009). Yet twentieth-century ethologists Konrad Lorenz and Niko Tinbergen (1907–1988) conducted experiments as well as observation. In addition, although animal behaviour is associated with US scientists and ethology with Europeans, comparative psychologists and ethologists have influenced each other, British scientists have shaped comparative psychology, and some comparative research entails studying single species rather than comparing at least two.

Although a few early psychologists studied animal behaviour and Margaret Washburn found evidence for and theorized animal awareness, arguably it was Donald Griffin's (1976) book on this subject that legitimized the scientific study of animal cognitive processes. Currently, evolutionary scientists perceive continuity between humans and nature and classify humans with other animals, as Darwin did (R. Smith, 1997). Behavioural biologists (or "behavioural ecologists") also study animals from an evolutionary perspective, while "neuro-ecologists" employ this orientation to research the neural mechanisms of cognition (Sherry, 2006). Behavioural neuroscientists use animal models to experiment on basic psychological processes (Shapiro, 1998).

Orientations towards animal psychology

Psychological research on animals has rested on **three assumptions** about the meaning of animal conduct for humans. These assumptions share the belief that animal behaviour is simpler than human behaviour, but they have different consequences for psychological evidence and theory construction (G. Richards, 2010; Shapiro, 1998).

Psychologists have:

- Minimized the differences between animals and humans by animalizing humans.
- Achieved the same aim by humanizing animals.
- Denied that humans and animals have any inborn essence, only overt behaviour.

Historically, the first two – animalizing humans and humanizing animals – have been complementary orientations in humans' attempts to understand ourselves by studying the boundary between us and nonhuman animals (G. Richards, 2010).

One also can understand the historical place of animal psychology by comparing evolutionary, experimental, and humanizing orientations, as follows.

Evolutionary orientation

Some scientists, including psychologists, have traced human behaviour to its pre-ancestral roots. These include Darwin and his British successors, ethologists, sociobiologists, and most recently evolutionary psychologists. In this orientation investigators "animalize" humans by minimizing differences between humans and other animals.

For the Darwinians, instinct was the central concept, but this broad notion yielded to ethologists' more specific concepts of "fixed action patterns," "innate releasing mechanisms," and "imprinting." Ethologists held that much human behaviour (e.g., mother–infant attachment) closely paralleled other animals' behaviour. Using animal–human parallels and drawing on social Darwinism, sociobiologists concluded that much human behaviour (e.g., gender differences) is innate, therefore impervious to environmental intervention (G. Richards, 2010).

Having demonstrated kinship between humans and other animals, Darwin studied the evolution of mind (Hearnshaw, 1964). He used comparative evidence from his extensive observations of humans and animals to substantiate his theory of evolutionary change through natural selection (Sherry, 2006). In his seminal 1872 work, *The Expression of the Emotions in Man and Animals*, Darwin argued for the animal origins of the motoric expression of simple and complex human emotions. He also stressed individual differences in biological and psychological characteristics within species.

Compatriot **George Romanes** (1838–1894) sustained Darwin's evolutionary interest with anthropomorphized descriptions of fish, birds, and dogs. Apparently "the first systematic comparative psychologist" (Hearnshaw, 1964, p. 94), Romanes speculated about animal intelligence, based on anecdotal evidence presented in a popular book. But he also conducted field observations and experiments on a range of species and proposed empirically based comparative concepts.

British scientist **Lloyd Morgan** (1852–1936) distinguished between innate and acquired behaviour and detailed processes of animal learning, including the role of imitation. In addition, he coined the influential terms "behaviour," "trial-and-error," "reinforcement," and "inhibition." Morgan proposed that mental qualities were continuous in evolution and that animals' consciousness enhanced the process of natural selection (Hearnshaw, 1964).

According to *Morgan's Canon*, scientists should not interpret animal behaviour in terms of higher faculties associated with humans when lower ones suffice. However, Morgan did not favour simplistic, mechanistic explanations (R. Smith, 1997). Rather, he aimed to prevent anthropomorphized interpretations of anecdotal animal behaviour without support-ing evidence from controlled experiments. Thus, he did not reject the notion of animal consciousness, although behaviourist psychologists interpreted the canon that way, thereby avoiding studying complex psychological processes.

Experimental orientation

Historically, many psychologists also have "animalized" humans and minimized differences between humans and other animals. In recent decades, behavioural neuroscientists have experimented on specific aspects of animal behaviour to generalize to humans with some regard for differences between humans and other animals (Shapiro, 1998). Their focus is not zoological interest in particular species' adaptations to natural habitats but psychological categories (e.g., learning or addiction).

Experimental animal psychology most likely began with Edward Thorndike's 1898 paper on animal intelligence (Stam & Kalmanovitch, 1998). He initiated **two conventions** that significantly shaped subsequent Psychology:

- Using mechanistic principles to explain animal behaviour.
- Generalizing this explanation to humans.

Emulating British comparative psychologists, Thorndike accounted for human mental functions in terms of conceptual hierarchies of intelligence in animals. Under his leadership, the methodological norm in animal psychology became experimental manipulations with repeated observations under controlled lab conditions.

Behaviourists and neobehaviourists, such as John Watson, Clark Hull, Edward Tolman, and B. F. Skinner, experimented on rodents, cats, dogs, or pigeons to generalize to human functioning (Boakes, 1984). Later, Stanley Schachter and Jerome Singer's (1962) influential experiments on emotional states and human cognition had their basis in animal research.

Meanwhile, physiologist Ivan Pavlov and his team contained all extraneous stimuli to concentrate on the specific experimental stimulus tested in measuring conditional reflexes in harnessed dogs (Gray, 1979). They studied differences in individual dogs trained over years. Pavlov chose dogs rather than other animals because of their historical association with humans. The team prepared the dogs to ensure that they obtained their desired experimental effects (Kimble, 1991b). This practice reveals that another layer of investigative reality lies beneath authors' objectified descriptions in journal articles of their actual investigative procedures.

Taken together, these investigative practices legitimized the study of basic processes with just a few species rather than studying a range of species for a more comprehensive picture of behaviour (Dewsbury, 1992). Following the reductionist assumption of natural science, early animal-psychologists believed that using simpler organisms than humans enabled them to explore complex human phenomena under controlled lab conditions and to explain these phenomena with mechanistic principles.

An exception to this trend is the fact that some early psychologists in the USA regarded raccoons as inhabiting the territory between animal instinct and human reason (Pettit, 2010). They inferred raccoons' keen sense of touch and intelligence from field experiments. At this time raccoons were partially domesticated and US society attributed curiosity, mischief, even deception to them.

Most psychologists, however, who had interest in animals, which was a small minority, adhered to Thorndike's view that animals merely learn by rote mechanics. Following the reductionist assumption of natural science, they believed animals to be simpler organisms that enabled the exploration of human problems in controlled lab experiments, explicable by mechanistic principles. Moreover, maintaining colonies of rodents and managing their compliance with lab protocols were much easier than maintaining and managing unpredictable raccoons. For practical and conceptual reasons, then, rodents prevailed.

Yet other psychologists experimented on primates to extrapolate to the prediction and control of human behaviour, exemplified by the Yerkes Laboratories of Primate Biology during the 1930s and 1940s (G. Richards, 2010). In addition, Harry Harlow (1958) studied infant–mother attachment in rhesus monkeys. Rather than adopting evolutionary behaviourism, the Gestalt psychologist Wolfgang Köhler experimented with chimpanzees' problem-solving and found evidence for insight learning (Boakes, 1984).

Another mode of animalizing humans through lab experimentation was to derive knowledge about environmental influences on social behaviour, such as crowding. Some psychologists linked the behaviour of lab rats with societal problems, such as increased violence, which the investigators attributed to "natural" responses to extreme conditions.

Humanizing orientation

Other scientists have used animals to study the presence of human attributes in mammals. In this orientation investigators "humanize" animals, again minimizing differences between humans and other animals.

In 1908, Margaret Washburn published a book describing her research on consciousness in animals. Yet for decades behaviourist psychologists refused to study this topic. Nevertheless, recent researchers with a more biological orientation have investigated emotional, sociolinguistic, and cognitive functions in primates, aquatic mammals, and elephants (Wise, 2000).

Investigators representing the humanizing orientation believe they demonstrate phenomena that resemble human behaviour and that there is more continuity between humans and other animals than the Enlightenment doctrine of human superiority can acknowledge. An international movement recognizing the similarity of great apes (bonobos, chimpanzees, gorillas, and orangutans) to humans gained such prominence that in 2006 the Spanish parliament declared the latter legal persons. Although most ape research occurs in the USA and Japan, the UK banned it in 1998.

In addition, the field research of primatologists **Jane Goodall** (b. 1934) and **Dian Fossey** (1932–1985) captured the popular imagination and raised ethical misgivings about psychologists' experimentation on animals. Goodall and Fossey named the apes that they observed rather than enumerating their subjects as lab experimenters tend to do. Living with her subjects in their habitats, Goodall described five cases of young chimpanzees' death from grief after their mothers died. For example, referring to Flint's sense of loss at Flo, his mother who died of old age, Goodall (1990) observed, "His whole world had revolved around Flo, and with her gone life was hollow and meaningless" (p. 89).

In theorizing about the wisdom of emotions and drawing from comparative psychological and ethological literature, philosopher Martha Nussbaum (2001) concludes that the emotions of nonhuman animals "like ours, are appraisals of the world, as it relates to their well-being" (p. 119). Domestic dogs, for example, appear to be capable of empathic responding to their human partners and to have cognitive capacities for selective attention, appraisal, and intentions (Coren, 2004).

Section conclusion

Inspired by Darwinian theory, some early psychologists initiated animal research, which took diverse forms. In US Psychology particularly, investigators subjected live lab animals to psychological and physical constraints and surgical procedures to isolate specific functions for experimental manipulation; this practice was known as *vivisection*, as illustrated in Figure 11.1. In treating animals as objects of convenience researchers severed the tie between lab and natural environments and formulated mechanical explanations concerning behaviour and mind (Stam & Kalmanovitch, 1998).

This tradition of conceptually mechanizing laboratory animals is the context for current animal research. Advocates of animal research believe that major advancements in human health and psychological welfare follow from their programmes. But the mechanized understanding and the objectified experimentation on animals led to debate about the ethicality of animal research. Some psychologists reject the notion that findings from animal studies are relevant to human psychology, because they regard the differences between animals and humans as essential rather than accidental. The advent of the animal rights movement during the 1980s intensified this dispute.

Figure 11.1 Nineteenth-century scientists demonstrate vivisection to onlookers

Ethical relationships with animals

Just as psychologists have ethical responsibilities with humans, so they have them with animals. Historically, William James criticized scientists for their disdainful treatment of laboratory animals, a position that alienated some peers (Taylor, 1990). Psychologists' ethical sensitivity to animal rights and welfare evidently took an even longer time to materialize than their concern for human participants, and sociopolitical events prompted psychologists to action.

The 1975 publication of Peter Singer's *Animal Liberation* heralded the emergence of animal-rights advocacy and of social tensions between animal researchers and their opponents. During the 1980s, US organizations advocating for animals became more prominent and a debate ensued between advocates of *animal welfare* and *animal rights* (Finsen & Finsen, 1994). This debate, which contains important ethical questions, had an impact on Psychology.

Animal welfare refers to the tradition, associated with "humane societies," of treating nonhuman animals with respect and preventing cruelty to them. Animal-welfare advocates stress regulated standards of care when animals are necessary for research (Baldwin, 1993). Animal-welfare advocates assume that humans are superior to animals and thus must shepherd them.

In contrast, animal-rights proponents reject the assumption of human superiority, which they term "speciesism." Promoting the notion of equal rights for animals, they engage in social action to abolish exploitation of animals including lab research. Activists connect animal rights with environmentalists' appreciation for the interconnectedness of all living things.

Debating animal research

Some psychologists argue against using animals in lab research (Bowd & Shapiro, 1993), while others support animal experiments conducted with care (Baldwin, 1993). Behavioural neuroscientists, for instance, cooperate with institutional animal-care committees to ensure humane treatment and project a public image of scientific responsibility. Furthermore, the APA maintains a Committee on Animal Research and Ethics. Meanwhile, the organization Psychologists for the Ethical Treatment of Animals continues to promote animal rights. Thus, lack of consensus about the value of animal research persists in Psychology.

There are **two arguments** *for* animal experimentation:

- Animals' physiology is very similar to humans'; therefore, their responses enable us to learn about ourselves.
- The human benefits outweigh the costs of animals' suffering and death. Martin Seligman (1975) used this rationale to defend his "learned helplessness" experiments with shocked dogs strapped into a hammock: "Is it likely that the pain and deprivation that this animal is about to endure will be greatly outweighed by the resulting alleviation of human pain and deprivation? If the answer is yes, the experiment is justified" (p. xi). In part, this modernist justification is rooted in René Descartes' view that humans are essentially different from other animals (Masson & McCarthy, 1995).

There are **two arguments** *against* animal experimentation:

- According to the principle of equality, all beings with the capacity to suffer deserve equal moral treatment. Therefore, scientists should not use animals for experimentation unless they also would use human beings for the same purpose.
- Animals have fundamental rights and inherent value. Therefore, causing animals to suffer in experimentation is not acceptable, even if thousands of humans would benefit from the research. Scientists should treat them with respect rather than as commodities or renewable resources.

Animal-rights advocates also raise **three practical points**:

- The appropriateness of animal models for human functioning is questionable, given the substantial differences between humans and animals at the cellular and molecular levels, which are the locations of pathology. This concern is particularly relevant for drug research, where viable alternative methods exist.
- Most animal experiments are tests of the effects of chemical substances rather than single experiments that ultimately save human lives. Besides, animal research does not necessarily "discover" so much as validate advances discovered without animal research.
- In Canada and the USA, animal researchers dominate animal care committees. (Information on other nations' practices is lacking.) Their advocacy is not only for animal welfare but also for the viability of their research programmes. When animal researchers depict animal-rights advocates as "extremists," they divert attention from their own treatment of animals.

Part 3 conclusion

What are psychologists' current practices with animals? By the 1990s, some US Psychology departments closed their animal labs due to the high costs of purchasing, maintaining, and collecting data from animals. Meanwhile, surveys suggested that fewer US Psychology students (Plous, 1996b) and APA members (Plous, 1996a), particularly younger and non-academic psychologists, are interested in animal research. Furthermore, women might be less supportive than men of animal research (Eldridge & Gluck, 1996).

Despite these trends, behavioural neuroscientists maintain that they are concerned not with human or animal subjects per se, but with psychological concepts, and their primary interest is in understanding the evolution of brain–behaviour relations in a variety of species. Although they extrapolate from animal experimentation to complex human behaviour, other psychologists consider these generalizations inappropriate and some contend that the enterprise of animal models of human psychology also is flawed ethically (e.g., Shapiro, 1998).

It is likely that, given government and corporate support for behavioural neuroscience, some psychologists will continue to use animal experiments exclusively. Nevertheless, the objects of their investigations generally remain lab rodents. As a prominent US animal-experimenter noted over sixty years ago, heavy reliance on simple organisms might inhibit the advancement of psychological knowledge (Beach, 1950).

Just as psychologists' research relationships with humans and animals have a social history, so do research methods, which is our next focus.

Part 4   Methods for gathering data

According to the APA's principles for education in the discipline, "Research methods are at the heart of psychological science. They distinguish psychology as a science from psychology as a pseudoscience" (American Psychological Association, 2011, p. 852). In this part, we examine the history of psychological methods, whereas in Part 5 we review the history of measurement and quantification and methods of analyzing data.

To gain legitimacy as an authentic science, early natural-science psychologists relied heavily on extant, scientific instruments of measurement. They proceeded in **two methodological directions**:

- Experimental investigators compared the performance of individuals, increasingly favouring group-administration of measures.
- Within the psychometric tradition, correlational investigators compared individuals on population traits.

The new psychologists did not copy a well-established, pre-existing laboratory tradition, because none existed. Rather, nineteenth-century German experimental physiology, Psychology's predecessor, was in flux, while its practitioners worked out problems in the reliability of their instruments for observation (G. Richards, 2010). Moreover, psychologists shared the term "experimental" with contemporary psychic and spiritualist investigators who used it in their studies of paranormal phenomena.

Some early natural-science psychologists confined their inquiries to responses to external stimuli measurable in labs. Others avidly investigated practical problems in society. However, the administrative demands of social institutions, commerce, and industry shaped their evolving rules about particular investigative methods and their scientific beliefs about managing the specifics of investigative practice (Danziger, 1990).

Non-experimental methods

Experimentation was not early natural-science psychologists' only research method. Rather, some employed systematic observation, while others employed qualitative methods and still others correlational methods.

Observing and describing behaviour in its environmental context, Darwin classified and compared species when investigating nonverbal movements (e.g., posture) and paralinguistic characteristics (e.g., vocal pitch) associated with emotional expression (Thomson, 1968). He also photographed individuals enacting emotions and conducted observational study of his preschool children. In addition, psychologist William Preyer established rigorous observational and experimental methods in child research and stipulated procedures for observers' biographical diaries of infants (Jaeger, 1982).

For their part, correlational researchers have studied individual differences in personality and intelligence and tested for "variations and relationships among variables *within* treatment conditions" (Cowles, 2001, p. 35, emphasis added) rather than regarding individual differences as error. By contrast, experimentalists minimized individual differences and searched for differences *between* treatments. Thus, correlational research and experimentation functioned as two solitudes (Cronbach, 1957), even though their respective statistical techniques stem from the same mathematical model. Given natural-science psychologists' commitment to generating universal, *causal* laws of behaviour, which correlational research cannot provide despite its merits and value for societal applications, experimentation became and remains the preferred method in Psychology.

Experimentation

After describing the origins of psychological experimentation, we discuss two general types: *controlled experiments* with grouped data and *experimental control* of individual performance.

Origins of experimentation

When investigating the interaction of mental processes and psychological causality, Wundt's team systematically presented variations in physical stimuli to experienced researchers. Through introspection these "observers" reported changes in their sensory experience of the stimuli (Woodward, 1982). Rather than an incorrigibly subjective method, introspection enabled the Wundt team to explain differences in quantitative data and to check experimental manipulations using measures of time and quantities (Danziger, 1980).

In Külpe's model of "systematic experimental introspection" experimenters gave trained observers word-problems or puzzles to solve; then observers reported the mental operations they used before, during, and after the problem-solving (Mack, 1997). Karl Bühler, an assistant to Külpe, developed this *Ausfragemethode* by which experimenter and observer engage in dialogue to interpret thinking processes.

By contrast, Edward Titchener concentrated only on observable elements of mental content (Tweney, 1997). An esteemed methodologist, he published instructor and student manuals for *qualitative* experiments to describe the "what" and "how" of conscious experiences, and parallel volumes for quantitative experiments to account for the "how much" of previously examined experiences. Qualitative experiments played the primary role, because Titchener "sought to describe experience, not measure it" (Evans, 1990a, p. 27).

Hermann Ebbinghaus employed a different approach to experimentation. He formulated its practical foundation, stressing uniform testing conditions, replication, and statistical analysis. Although he used himself as data source in his memory studies and his nonsense syllables proved to be limited, later psychologists regarded him as methodologically meticulous and concerned about experimenter bias (Hoffman *et al.*, 1987; Postman, 1969).

For early French investigators, abnormal cases constituted natural experiments. Theodule Ribot's preferred objects of inquiry were disordered adults, "primitives," and children (R. Smith, 1997). Alfred Binet, following the tradition of *La Clinique*, valued case studies and individual testing to examine the unique qualities of intelligence (Fancher & Rutherford, 2012). Although he understood the value of statistical comparison of individuals and employed averages to discuss general trends, he viewed experimentation as limited in describing individuals. Binet also criticized as artificial and simplistic US psychologists' laboratory model of attempting to erase individual differences (Wolf, 1973).

In US Psychology, James Cattell established the tradition of quantifying mental processes. He asserted that establishing Psychology as quantitative experimentation would achieve "the certainty and exactness of the physical sciences" (Cattell, 1890, p. 373). But Mark Baldwin objected to Cattell's measurement of sensory-motor capacities. Baldwin preferred that psychologists employ psychological rather than exclusively physiological indices of complex mental processes, such as memory (Sokal, 1982).

For William James, the boundaries between rational and irrational psychological processes, such as consciousness, are permeable (Leary, 2003). Consequently, introspection, which he defined as phenomenological description of personal experience, is the primary method. Although skeptical about laboratory experimentation (E. Taylor, 1990), he perceived potential for a science of mental processes (Evans, 1990b).

According to James, comparison of animal, child, and "savage" behaviour with "civilized" adults, what he termed the "comparative method," supplemented introspection. Moreover, he argued that replication led to consistency and countered introspective bias. Yet James appreciated that investigators can mistakenly attribute universalizable objectivity to their specific findings. He termed this misattribution "the psychologist's fallacy." Consequently, he held that hypothesis-testing was not appropriate for all psychological questions.

Also a critic of US psychologists' emergent experimental practices and a supporter of introspection, Mary Calkins (1915) contended that psychic facts were not amenable to the same sort of manipulation whereby investigators measure, repeat, and vary natural objects. Moreover, description and explanation are the same in Psychology as in all sciences, she argued, but introspection should be Psychology's signature method (Calkins, 1910). She advocated studying the self introspectively with trained participants who would report on the sensations of thinking and experiences of their environment. For her, the role of the self should be included in any experimental report.

Two experimental strategies

The early forms of experimental practice faded away by World War II, replaced by controlled experimentation based on grouped data. By the 1950s the familiar hierarchy of research methods from the least valued (observational research) to the most valued (statistical experiments) was the norm, even in the interpersonal and applied areas, where non-experimental methods had prevailed originally. But there is more than one way to experiment in Psychology.

Controlled experimentation Some early psychologists (e.g., Galton) aggregated groups of individual scores on questionnaires to generalize to populations. Others (e.g., Wundt) emulated physiologists' controlled experimentation and focused on the performance of individuals. Subsequently, lab experiments administered to individuals and questionnaires administered to large samples coalesced to form the foundation for the now-familiar experimental strategy of grouped data (Danziger, 1990).

During the pre-World War I era, educational researchers in British and US school systems tested students to study their adaptation to classroom interventions. For instance, Thorndike conducted group experiments on learning fatigue. But in 1907, **John Coover** (n.d.) was the first to advocate control-group experiments as a necessity (Dehue, 2000). In 1917, he published a book about thousands of randomized control-trial experiments on telepathy with "blind" experimenters (Hacking, 1988). Previously, US philosopher Charles S. Peirce (1839–1914) had introduced "blind," randomized-control trials (Stigler, 1999) in 1884.

During the interwar period, psychologists increasingly based their scientific claims on aggregated scores from individuals in artificially constructed groups. At least one of these groups received an "experimental treatment." Researchers then statistically compared group averages on experimental tasks and generalized to populations.

The next step was to integrate aggregated questionnaire data with manipulating an independent variable to register its impact on a dependent variable. Randomized control-trial experiments became popular in the 1930s, originating in **Ronald Fisher's** (1890–1962) agricultural research (Hacking, 1988). Thus *controlled experimentation* was born.

Ideally, this method has **three characteristics**:

- An independent variable is administered to a treatment group whose performance is compared to a group that does not receive the treatment.
- The treatment and comparison groups are equivalent in all other respects.
- Uncontrolled factors reputedly operate randomly and statistical techniques separate experimental effects from error variance.

Experimental control A minority of psychologists have employed the second strategy, *experimental control* (also known as experimental analysis) (Cowles, 2001). Originating in Watson's behaviourism, experimental control perhaps is best known as the methodological heart of Skinner's operant conditioning. In the "experimental analysis of behaviour," investigators aim to control as much variability as possible, while repeatedly observing the antecedents and consequences of manipulated variables in individual organisms.

Investigators employing experimental control practise single-case, rather than comparison-group, experimentation. They trigger and terminate specified behaviours consistently, recording their observations descriptively not inferentially. Inferential statistical analysis plays a minor role in this strategy.

The distinction between the two types of experimentation – the less familiar experimental control and the more common controlled experimentation – remains relevant for applications of psychological knowledge, as explained in Box 11.2.

Section conclusion

Regardless of the type of experimentation that psychologists employed, by World War II, individuals' performance on research tasks disappeared from most psychologists' view. During the postwar era, a preference for large samples yielding quantifiable data replaced earlier commitments to experimentation with a small number of individual participants (Danziger, 1990). Natural-science Psychology became depopulated in the sense of ignoring individuals' performance.

In pursuit of laws of behaviour that transcended time, place, and person, investigators discounted the social-historical situations of their research participants, which contradicted psychologists' claim to understanding individuals (Billig, 1994). All that psychologists could claim legitimately was knowledge of abstracted, *average* performance of population samples. To use Gordon Allport's (1962) classic terms, mainstream Psychology shifted to an almost exclusively nomothetic orientation, focused on aggregated information, rather

Box 11.2 **Group vs. case studies**

The debate in Psychology over group studies with aggregated data versus single-case studies continues, as evidenced by neuropsychology and developmental psychology. The issue is whether reliance on aggregated data on task-performance by experimental and comparison groups obscures differences among individuals.

In neuropsychology some assert that obscuring individual differences compromises investigators' ability to understand the clinical significance of differences in symptoms among patients who share the same diagnosis (D. Jones & Elcock, 2001). An averaged pattern of symptoms does not capture the reality of individual patients whose individual patterns could differ quite markedly. Exceptions to mean scores might be the more interesting findings.

In research with children, developmental psychologists tend to rely on group means and infer trends that "lead to an idealized, universal child" (Mishler, 1996, p. 78). But findings from population-based methods do not fit well with findings from individual cases. Consequently, combining case studies with longitudinal analysis of temporally ordered sequences can provide more contextualized information about actual individuals.

In sum, advocates of aggregated group-data believe that case studies cannot permit generalizations because of idiosyncratic responses of individuals. Case-study proponents retort that, beyond the in-depth knowledge that case studies provide, relative generalization is possible by showing the similarities across individuals, which is more meaningful and applicable than group data in which individual differences are obscured (Damasio, 1999).

The debate over group studies with aggregated data versus single-case studies also is relevant to research in applied and professional psychology and to evaluation of clinical and community services.

than an idiographic orientation, focused on unique individuals, or even a mixed-methods approach. The typical study was an experiment on lab rodents or an experiment on university students using self-report questionnaires.

But by the twenty-first century some diversity of quantitative methods seemed evident. A random sample of 200 Psychology articles from a population of 36,000 research papers published in English during 1999 and covering applied-professional (e.g., clinical/health psychology), behavioural–cognitive neuroscience, developmental, and interpersonal fields, revealed **three major findings** (Bodner, 2006):

- Only 41% of articles reported experiments; behavioural–cognitive neuroscientists used them the most (79%) and applied-professional psychologists the least (15%).
- Overall, 45% of studies employed self-report questionnaires; interpersonal psychologists relied on them the most (88%), behavioural–cognitive neuroscientists the least (13%).
- Of 169 studies using participants, only 25% overall employed university students; interpersonal psychologists relied on university students the most (50%), clinical/health psychologists the least (5%).

Despite this apparent recent shift in methods, psychologists' tradition of a hierarchical relationship between "experimenters" and "subjects," which was established prior to World War II (Danziger, 1990), has endured (Walsh-Bowers, 1995). However as described next, this type of research relationship evokes unanticipated reactions from participants, which led to some investigators discussing how to tighten procedures to maintain control over the investigative situation.

The social psychology of psychological research

To obtain empirical knowledge about humans, psychologists must engage in a professional relationship with them. But this relationship poses problems of interpersonal biases or methodological artifacts that US psychologist Saul Rosenzweig (1933) discussed long ago. Binet also was sensitive to controlling for unintended influences that transpire between investigators and participants (Carroy & Plas, 1996).

In the 1960s and 1970s, a literature in Psychology called "the social psychology of the experiment" flourished. Its premise was that human research is a social interaction like any other. Within this interaction those individuals who collect data (e.g., research assistants) can influence the participants who provide the data, contrary to investigators' intentions, while participants can respond to investigative situations in unintentional or deceptive ways that invalidate investigators' claim to valid data.

Researcher effects

Traditionally, psychologists believe that they have no unintended influence on research tasks with participants, as long as they remain objectively detached. But four types of researcher effects potentially operate in any investigative situation: biopsychosocial attributes, expectancy effects, errors in investigative procedures, and social-contextual influences.

Biopsychosocial attributes The biopsychosocial characteristics of data collectors can affect participants' responses and bias results. Depending on what is being studied, the experimenters' gender, age, ethnocultural background, physical attractiveness, attire, social status, and interpersonal style (e.g., warm, task-oriented, anxious, etc.) might affect participants' responses significantly. Influences can be communicated by data collectors' facial expressions, body movements, and vocal qualities (Rosenthal, 1969). These influences can affect investigations conducted with one participant, small groups, or large groups, because data collectors inadvertently can serve as a behavioural model for the topic under investigation.

The recommended antidote to the possibility of such confounding effects is the use of multiple data collectors. This procedure is thought to cancel out influences on participants (Rosenthal, 1969). But what might enhance this counter-measure is systematic classification of sources of experimenter influence in relation to particular investigative conditions and topics of inquiry.

Currently, some psychologists plan their experiments and informally manipulate biopsychosocial characteristics of their data collectors to produce significant effects. But these "tricks of the trade" go unreported in research presentations and publications. Consequently, the significant effects that are reported publicly could be artifacts of methodological procedures. In these cases a covert methodological norm operates. Typically researchers exclude two aspects from formal reports: their *informal* manipulation of data collectors' biopsychosocial characteristics, and participants' views of the research task, which might not match investigators' intentions (see below).

Expectancy effects   *Experimenter bias* or the "self-fulfilling prophecy" refers to data collectors unwittingly communicating expectations to participants regarding the investigators' experimental hypotheses (Rosenthal, 1969). The story of "Clever Hans," the horse that seemingly could count, shows the operation of nonverbal cues – visual and auditory – that communicate the expectations of trainers, researchers, or teachers.

During the opening minutes of the instruction period, data collectors' vocal intonation, gesture, and body movement, and the content of the instructions unintentionally can convey the investigators' expectations. Unconsciously data collectors can encourage and obtain good performance from the participants in the experimental condition, while data collectors subtly can discourage participants in the control condition.

The standard control for these expectancy effects is to use a "double-blind procedure" in which both data administrators and participants are ignorant of the hypotheses. Yet "[d]espite the long-established findings of the effects of experimenter bias … many published studies appear to ignore or discount these problems … there are no valid excuses, financial or otherwise, for avoiding an opportunity to double-blind" (Wilkinson & the Task Force on Statistical Inference, 1999, p. 596).

Procedural errors   Researcher errors, judging by the lack of discourse on them, might be more common in Psychology than psychologists are prepared to admit. Nearly 200 years ago, a German astronomer, Friedrich Bessel (1784–1846), observed errors in astronomical observations, quantified individual differences in observers, and attributed them to physiological variability. This work led to a corrective observational procedure in astronomy, the "personal equation" (Boring, 1950).

Errors in Psychology can occur during applications of methodological and statistical procedures. Furthermore, scientific dishonesty also occurs (e.g., in Watson's and Stanley Milgram's infamous experiments). A recent survey of more than 2,000 US psychologists reveals how widespread dishonest research practices might be. About 70 per cent of respondents acknowledged some type of data-fudging, about a third disclosed they had reported an unexpected finding as predicted from the start, and about 1 per cent admitted they falsified data (John *et al.*, 2012).

Social-contextual influences   Researchers also can convey unintended social, economic, and political influences on psychological research. Any psychological inquiry is partly shaped by institutionalized expectations about how to conduct rigorous research. Not only do psychologists' methodological, ethical, and reporting standards mould workaday investigative practices, so do the structures, mores, and ideologies of Psychology as a social institution (Walsh-Bowers, 2002).

These more systemic but **covert features** of the research landscape are **sevenfold**:

- Epistemological assumptions about making scientific knowledge.
- The enculturation of students in investigative customs, mediated by course instructors and research supervisors.
- The role of research productivity ("publish or perish") within the academic reward system.
- Methodological criteria promoted by funders, journal editors, and grant and journal reviewers.
- The corporate funding of research and pressure from industry for positive results.
- Psychologists' beliefs and feelings about what constitutes rigorous methodology. (E.g., at times psychologists rely on samples such as White middle-class university students, schoolchildren, psychiatric patients, and prison inmates for their data, but then generalize the findings to all persons.)
- Researchers producing findings that benefit the bearers of power and promote the status quo in society. (E.g., it is a rarity in Psychology for an oppressed ethnocultural group to contract with researchers to study White supremacy.)

Participant effects

Regardless of the research method, participants react and think about the topic of research and the investigative situation to which they are contributing (Schultz, 1969). In an alienating research relationship, participants can respond, unconsciously or not, to *demand characteristics*, *evaluation apprehension*, and *negativism* and respond less than truthfully to the situation. Psychologists do not know the extent of these sources of bias, because typically we do not inquire about them.

> **Small-group discussion.** Imagine that some undergraduate students organize an oppositional strategy regarding participation in Psychology experiments. They urge every student-participant to do the opposite of what they think the experimenters are expecting them to do. The experimenters, however, are unaware of this strategy; they conduct their research as usual. So, are the experimental results caused by manipulation of independent variables or by something else? What are the consequences of either conclusion for the authenticity of psychological knowledge?

Demand characteristics In a classic experiment participants performed a series of highly repetitive activities, but no matter how tedious the task, they persisted (Orne, 1962). The study showed that participants are inclined to cooperate subtly with what they perceive to be investigators' intentions. Participants discern what they think is the hypothesis from the verbal, nonverbal, and environmental cues embedded in the situation (i.e., the characteristics of the setting and the behaviour of the data collector). Then, aiming to please, participants strive to produce data that will support their perception of the hypothesis.

These cues are known as demand characteristics, while the term, "the good subject," refers to participants' inclinations to give experimenters the results that the participants think are expected. In the above study participants apparently believed that the researchers were responsible scientists who had some larger, but concealed, purpose underlying the apparently boring tasks. Yet the crucial point is that if participants are responding to demand characteristics instead of the independent variable, then the study is confounded by these characteristics and is invalid.

Evaluation apprehension A second strategy that affects responses to research situations is participant anxiety about presenting themselves to data administrators in the most favourable way possible. This phenomenon is known as *evaluation apprehension* (M. J. Rosenberg, 1969). When participants are anxious about what the researcher, usually seen as an expert on human behaviour, thinks of them, some participants cope by altering their research performance to make themselves look good.

Negativism Sometimes called the "screw-you effect," *negativism* refers to another form of participant response to the investigative situation. In this case, participants deliberately falsify their performance, either covertly or overtly, due to feelings of resentment directed at data collectors (Masling, 1966). Negativism is common in research done in business, industry, institutions, and aboriginal communities and can occur in research dependent on university "subject pools." Again, the extent of the problem is unknown, but might be related to an alienating situation in which participants lack personal investment in research that appears foreign to their interests but seems imposed upon them.

Section conclusion

The fact that sources of bias vitally affect investigative situations indicates that psychological research cannot be purely objective, despite, or even because of, investigators' rigorous procedures, no matter which research methods are employed. Rather, data collectors and data sources bring their biological, psychological, and social characteristics into the professional relationship of researchers and participants, however briefly it is maintained. Thus, the investigative situation is intersubjective, that is, each party's subjectivity affects the research relationship and the quality of the data obtained.

When the literature on the social psychology of the experiment emerged, some psychologists regarded it as signifying fundamental problems with standard methodology and its underlying epistemological assumptions (e.g., Argyris, 1975, 1980; Giorgi, 1970). They concluded that with psychological research embedded in the interpersonal processes of everyday life and in social-historical contexts, investigators cannot control the investigative situation totally.

Mainstream psychologists, however, have attempted to prevent methodological artifacts from contaminating the investigative situation either by denying the significance of interpersonal threats to the validity of psychologists' data collection (e.g., A. G. Miller, 1972) or by instituting procedures thought to minimize or eradicate sources of bias (e.g., Adair, 1973; Rosenthal, 1969). Apparently, they have tried to keep their conventional procedures intact so as to preserve their conceptions of what constitutes sound scientific inquiry. By instituting tighter investigative controls, for which the double-blind, control-group experiment is the ideal (Wilkinson & the Task Force on Statistical Inference, 1999), psychologists perpetuate hope for unbiased, rigorous research that will yield objective universal truths.

Qualitative methods

Qualitative methods are congruent with human-science psychologists' goal of understanding human experience and have a long history in Psychology, for example, in hermeneutics. Wundt and Titchener partially relied on qualitative methods, while in mid-century, Allport, Lois Barclay Murphy, and Gardner Murphy used them. But by the 1930s most natural-science psychologists only employed quantitative experimental research. Then during the 1980s qualitative methods began to re-emerge in such areas as feminist psychology and counselling psychology (Rennie, Watson, & Monteiro, 2002).

However, considerable skepticism about the value of qualitative methods remains prominent among natural-science psychologists who aim to predict and control mental life and behaviour (Kidd, 2002; Walsh-Bowers, 2002). Although in one survey editors of prominent Psychology journals indicated openness to qualitative research, publication rates in their journals were very low (Marchel & Owens, 2007). Furthermore, a sample of Psychology journal articles published in 1999 showed that the frequency of qualitative research was 8 per cent across all fields of the discipline (Bodner, 2006); applied/professional psychologists used qualitative methods the most (36 per cent of studies sampled), while behavioural–cognitive and interpersonal psychologists not at all.

Basic principles

There are many types of qualitative methods, such as grounded theory, narrative analysis, and discourse analysis. (See Madill & Gough, 2008, for an overview.) In addition, some primarily quantitative researchers prefer to perform content analysis of participant interviews by counting the frequency with which participants use certain words. Thus, it is useful to distinguish between "Big Q" and "little q" versions of qualitative methods (Kidder & Fine, 1997).

Emanating from the mainstream tradition, "little q" methods are adjuncts to quantitative, hypothesis-testing investigations. By contrast, "Big Q" methods are characterized by **four principles**:

- Inductive, flexible exploration of the phenomena of interest by which the investigator seeks to understand rather than predict and control these phenomena.
- Careful attention to the quality of research relationships.
- Reflexivity concerning the intersubjective nature of investigative processes; that is, authors formally report how they think their social characteristics and values affected their dialogues with their participants.
- Cultivation of multiple and partial interpretations.

As is evident in these principles, Big Q methods have their own epistemic roots, which flow from a social-constructionist standpoint. For example, the principle of reflexivity stands in some contrast to the natural-science assumption of naïve realism and its corollary, pure objectivity. Another feature of Big Q methods is that one can employ various rather than uniform interpretations, whereby, for example, researchers report multiple perspectives on interview data; the assumption is that there is no single correct interpretation of data.

Barriers to legitimacy

The investigative norms of natural-science psychologists have not been conducive to practising qualitative methods for much of Psychology's history, particularly its recent past, as independent studies on the recent status of qualitative methods in Psychology conducted in the USA and Canada have shown (Kidd, 2002; Marchel & Owens, 2007; Walsh-Bowers, 2002). Evidently, **three social-contextual phenomena** impinge upon psychologists' capacity to practise qualitative methods. These phenomena include the historical place of qualitative methods, the paucity of education in them, and a socioeconomic reward system for faculty that is oriented to quantitative experimentation (Walsh-Bowers, 2002):

(1) Positioning oneself as a qualitative researcher has been difficult, given the view in natural-science Psychology that quantitative experiments are the pinnacle of scientific method. Since World War II until recently, mainstream Psychology journals typically did not publish qualitative research. Furthermore, legitimate status for qualitative methods varies dramatically across Psychology programmes. Although tenured faculty and their students might pursue qualitative methods freely in some departments, evidently the social climate has been chilly elsewhere.

(2) Relatedly, few precedents of qualitative research have appeared in undergraduate and graduate curricula. In fact, although a few departments have an undergraduate or graduate course (or both) in qualitative methods, apparently most do not. This situation is arguably the most formidable obstacle to enculturating students in the range of these methods and the principle of investigative pluralism. When faculty and students do learn about qualitative methods, they tend to impose quantitative language on qualitative alternatives, describing them, for example, by using the oxymoron, "qualitative measures." Changes to educational practices in Psychology would enhance the status of QR "immeasurably."

(3) Receiving tenure, promotion, and research grants partly depends upon publishing conventional research in conventional journals. Although some journals are now more receptive to publishing qualitative methods, a hierarchy prevails – the most prestigious journals privilege sophisticated quantitative techniques. Disciplinary segregation exists in that specialty journals now exist for qualitative methods, but they do not have the same legitimacy as the top-rank journals. Thus, psychologists less securely established in academia take a career-risk publishing in lower-ranked outlets. Relatedly, the academic reward system is linked to conformity with the *Publication Manual*'s prescriptions for quantitative experimental report-writing, which do not suit qualitative methods (see below).

Section conclusion

Resistance to publishing qualitative studies among natural-science psychologists seems to be related to disagreements with qualitative investigators about philosophical and practical issues concerning methodology. Big Q methods do contradict basic epistemological assumptions undergirding psychological science, including the possibility of objective observation of phenomena. Although it might not be possible to resolve the disagreements, some believe that quantitative and qualitative traditions can be complementary without compromising the integrity of either tradition (Madill & Gough, 2008). Thus, many psychologists advocate "mixed methods," employing both types of method, when appropriate for certain research questions.

To some observers, cautious optimism for disciplinary acceptance of even Big Q methods is warranted. Guidelines for authors to prepare qualitative research for publication exist (Elliott, Fischer, & Rennie, 1999), and more journal space and institutional support for it is occurring. For example, in 2005, British psychologists initiated the first section on qualitative methods in a psychological association.

Yet US historian Jill Morawski (2011) cautioned that qualitative methods remain in a relatively marginalized position in Psychology. In fact, qualitative researchers typically operate from ontological, epistemological, ethical, and political standpoints that differ substantially from quantitative traditions; for example, the principles of researcher reflexivity and intersubjectivity that are at play in qualitative inquiry clearly distinguish it from positivist and postpositivist epistemological assumptions held by mainstream psychologists. Thus, the future of qualitative research in Psychology is uncertain.

Moreover, to legitimize qualitative methods in Psychology, **systemic changes** are necessary in journal policies and practices, and curricula and research mentoring:

- Academic psychologists in general should become more open to the value of qualitative methods, changing journal policies and practices regarding report-writing so as to accommodate journal space for them.
- More institutional funding should be made available for qualitative projects and for supporting graduate students interested in qualitative methods. External funding has been limited, because funding evaluators from Psychology have tended to evaluate qualitative proposals according to quantitative criteria.
- Students should receive positive exposure to qualitative methods in their undergraduate courses. When students learn alternative ways of doing research, this exposure influences their vocational choice and their identity in Psychology.

Part 4 conclusion

For natural-science psychologists, quantitative methods are essential tools for producing scientific knowledge. Non-experimental methods, such as correlational research, have played important parts in the discipline historically (e.g., in intelligence testing) and still do. However, mainstream psychologists generally regard lab experimentation as the acme of methodological perfection. Yet there are two general types of psychological experimentation: the familiar type of controlled experiments with grouped data and the unfamiliar type of experimental control of individual performance. Controlled experimentation lends itself to group studies with aggregated data, whereas experimental control is ideal for studies of individual organisms or humans. Thus, diverse quantitative methods have been the historical norm in natural-science Psychology.

Nevertheless, as the literature on the social psychology of psychological research showed, any investigative situation in our discipline is rife with unintended sources of influence that contaminate psychologists' ideal of unambiguous objectivity. These sources of bias stem from researchers and their assistants and from participants. Psychologists do not know the extent of these subjective influences, because either we do not inquire about them systematically, but conduct investigative business as usual instead, or we strive to contain the biases.

From a critical perspective, however, it is futile to treat investigators' biopsychosocial influences, investigator expectancies, and participant effects as technical problems to solve so as to keep psychological research "unbiased." Using a double-blind procedure cannot eradicate all uncertainties from psychologists' investigations; rather, every investigative method is limited and provides only partial knowledge of psychological phenomena, because psychological inquiry is always an intersubjective situation. Reflexively attending to the inherently interpersonal nature of psychological investigations could yield more honest, but less certain, knowledge-claims rather than perpetuating a myth of unsullied scientific objectivity that presumably sustains psychological inquiry.

Qualitative methods in their purer incarnation, although virtually ignored after World War II, directly address the inevitable subjectivities that saturate the investigative situation in Psychology. Of course, all methods of inquiry, qualitative or quantitative, have their limitations. Furthermore, discursive psychologists would argue that the search for internal psychological phenomena by means of interpretive qualitative methods is illusory; instead, psychologists should study what people say and do in their interactions with each other (Hepburn & Wiggins, 2007).

Yet natural-science psychologists have erected formidable social and institutional barriers to acceptance of qualitative research that only slowly are coming down. Instead, methodolatry and methodologism have prevailed in mainstream Psychology rather than investigative pluralism. Welcoming diversity of methods still might be difficult for many natural-science psychologists, because the traditional approach to methodology is deeply ingrained in a discipline apparently dominated by a scientistic conception of science.

Part 5   Measurement and quantitative analysis

Counting, ordering, and expressing the relationship between events numerically according to prescribed rules are "*the essence of measurement*" (Cowles, 2001, p. 40). For natural-science psychologists, measurement and quantitative analysis are basic components of genuine psychological research, such that "studying something scientifically means measuring it" (Mitchell, 2002, p. 6). Adherents to this belief, known as the *quantitative imperative*, assume that psychological attributes are, like natural objects, measurable and statistically analyzable. Such analyses are thought to be essential for producing psychological knowledge.

The term "quantification" refers to psychological tests and scales ("measures") used to quantify observations or data. But rather than being neutral, psychologists' measurement tools and statistical techniques for analyzing data are products of social history and laden with certain assumptions (Hornstein, 1988). In this part we provide a brief history of quantification and identify the disciplinary consequences of this tradition. Next we describe the roots of statistical techniques and discuss critiques of psychologists' use of statistics. Then we review data analysis employed in qualitative methodology.

History of quantification and measurement

Quantification and measurement were central to the investigative practice of the founders of the Scientific Revolution, Galileo, René Descartes, and Isaac Newton (Mitchell, 2002). Quantification of traded objects apparently became normative during the High Middle Ages in Europe (A. Crosby, 1997). Measurement as we know it today dates back to seventeenth-century attempts to gauge visual acuity and eighteenth-century measurement of human "passions" (e.g., voluptuousness).

Thereafter measurement conveyed both to scientists and the public an aura of objective certainty, rendered the phenomena measured socially important, and served as a reassuring remedy for individuals anxious about the ambiguities and uncertainties that beset rapidly urbanizing societies. The at least implicit assumption was that societal upheavals could be managed numerically and, ultimately, predicted and controlled. Since Psychology's inception, when economically privileged societies increasingly demanded methods for assessing individuals' abilities and socially ordering their behaviour (Danziger, 1990), most psychologists have measured psychological phenomena.

Quantification in Psychology

Swept up in the cultural wave of quantification, many early psychologists sought to generate empirically validated applications to address societal problems. Quantification enabled psychologists to respond to societal needs and to make research more efficient (Hornstein, 1988). Early psychologists rendered some phenomena, previously studied philosophically (e.g., perception), quantifiable, but excluded other phenomena not easily measured (e.g., will) (Danziger, 1997).

Insofar as measurement connected Psychology with mathematics, the discipline gained a desirable aura of order, precision, economy, clarity, and rationality. Lange, for example, promoted the value of statistics for psychological inquiry. Psychologists' association with the precision of mathematics reinforced the quest for objectivity while strengthening the discipline's scientific credibility.

When psychological measurement and increasingly sophisticated statistical techniques became routine, the discipline's identity as a natural science became more solidified. By World War II, psychologists' social identity was associated with expertise in statistical analysis, and fluency in methodology and statistics became psychologists' preoccupation rather than the research relationship that produces data.

Two research areas in nineteenth-century Psychology facilitated the quantification of psychological phenomena: psychophysics (i.e., the study of sensory processes) and mental testing (i.e., intelligence and personality testing). Initially, these areas relied on different approaches to quantification, but the invention of psychological scaling in the 1930s united them (Hornstein, 1988).

Psychophysics In 1860, Gustav Fechner developed statistical methods of quantifying just-noticeable-differences in sensations (Cowles, 2001). When he adapted contemporary astronomers' statistical methods to psychophysics, he set the stage for what became experimental studies of such psychological processes as sensory responsiveness and memory (Stigler, 1999).

Some early psychologists objected to Fechner's assumption that sensations could be quantified meaningfully. They argued that he conflated the psychological sensation with the physical stimulus presented in experiments (Hornstein, 1988). But psychophysicists disregarded the objections in their quest to establish themselves as legitimate natural scientists. Meanwhile, Galton quantitatively examined the distribution of individual differences in populations and developed tests of perceptual-motor skills.

Mental testing The mental-testing movement, which initially concentrated on intelligence but later encompassed a range of abilities and personality characteristics, gave momentum to quantification in Psychology (Hornstein, 1988). Overcrowded, public-education systems in industrialized, urbanized nations required the identification and placement of children with special needs, and psychologists' new tools for testing filled the bill. The social purpose of Binet's intelligence testing was clear: "The psychological test, in origin, was first and foremost a technology to order the child's development in mass society" (R. Smith, 1997, p. 588).

In US society the introduction of the IQ index of intelligence gave psychologists considerable professional prestige. By the end of World War I, intelligence testing in groups became a useful tool in society's administration of masses of people.

Psychological scaling In the 1920s US psychologist Leon Thurstone (1887–1955) pioneered psychological scaling, advocating the quantification of all psychological phenomena. Next, S. S. Stevens proposed four types of measurement scales: nominal, ordinal, interval, and ratio. The two types of quantification – psychophysics and mental testing – then united as scaling methodology.

However, psychologists assumed that in the most popular scale employed, the interval scale, "the psychological distances between the numbers are equal across the entire scale" (T. Rogers, 1995, p. 60). Actually, the typical measure functions like an ordinal scale, that is, it only permits inferences about the relative positions of test-takers.

Section conclusion

The union of psychophysics and mental testing as scaling arguably had **four profound consequences** for Psychology (Hornstein, 1988):

(1) Psychologists took for granted that psychological objects are measurable. They assumed that, because they used the same tools as natural scientists, there was no essential difference in measuring *psychological* phenomena and the natural objects of the natural sciences (Danziger, 1990, 1997). But *are* they measurable?

Psychologists make publicly observable in numerical form their phenomena of interest (e.g., memory or the self), which are largely experiential, and then subject them to testing. Psychologists take for granted that when raters select a particular numerical integer on a scale, their selections are objective quantities representing natural objects comparable to natural scientists' measurements. But, from a critical perspective, rating entails the psychological process of introspection, which is a subjective process and is not reducible to a natural object (Rosenbaum & Valsiner,

2011). Moreover, some claim that intangible psychological phenomena cannot be manipulated or controlled sufficiently to meet measurement requirements (Trendler, 2009); one only can practise introspection on psychological phenomena and interpret them, which are inherently subjective acts.

(2) Psychologists' phenomena of interest are impermanent, shifting across social-historical conditions. Consequently, they require modifications to the original measuring instruments, a process which results in changing the meaning of the concept under study. For example, personality traits might be merely artifacts of the procedures that psychologists use to "discover" them. When a Nazi psychologist studied authoritarianism, he considered it a laudable disposition, whereas postwar psychologists investigated authoritarianism as a liability associated with Nazi atrocities.

(3) Scaling methodology facilitated communication and cooperation among psychologists working independently on the same problem (e.g., educational measures). Psychological testing itself became an industry in the sense that psychologist-entrepreneurs standardized the technical features of tests and copyrighted them, making them available to others only on condition of purchase rather than freely sharing their contribution to knowledge in a scholarly outlet.

(4) Psychologists began to produce textbooks in research methods and mental testing that prescribed objective techniques for specific investigative situations in a "cookbook" fashion. The result of this pragmatic manoeuvre was to suggest that scaling methodology was devoid of social history or epistemology.

In conclusion, psychologists measure phenomena by asking concrete and specific questions of their respondents. Whether psychometric testing or survey research, psychologists aim to elicit the true value of responses as distinct from random error (Strack & Schwarz, 2007). Within the psychometric tradition the assumptions are that an answer to any given question is merely a response (a dependent variable) to a stimulus (an independent variable) and respondents' interpretation of the questions is not crucial to the response. Within the survey tradition of attitudes and beliefs respondents' interpretation of the questions *is* crucial to the response, because of the introspective nature of the procedure, which is dependent on respondents' motivation to participate. This is why practitioners of survey measurement historically have studied the permissible format of responses, the wording of questions, and the social context and relationship between data collectors and respondents, particularly as perceived by the latter.

History of statistics

Statistical thinking took root in economically privileged, nineteenth-century societies (Porter, 1995). The Belgian mathematician **Lambert-Adolphe-Jacques Quetelet** (1796–1874) influentially applied statistics to human biological measures, such as the height of army recruits (Stigler, 1999). He proposed that the normal curve of distributed scores indicates an ideal natural observation, the statistical mean (*l'homme moyen*). The mean became the normative standard, literally and figuratively.

By the late nineteenth century, professional statistical associations were formed to collect actuarial data to influence public policy and enhance administration of society (Gigerenzer,

1989). Statistical thinking and probability theory subsequently had a marked and durable influence on science; on the economic, political, social, and psychological aspects of increasingly urbanized societies; and on the functions of bureaucratic administration in centralized governments (Dehue, 2000). As a result, numeracy became as socially desirable for individuals' social advancement as literacy (Barzun, 2000).

Technically, mathematicians developed statistical procedures for analyzing complex data to identify regularities in human life, moving from descriptive to inferential statistics. Statisticians believed that the perceived order "beneath the surface complexity and apparent randomness of social life" reflected orderliness in nature (R. Smith, 1997, p. 539). This belief was the origin of the scientific inclination to the dictum, "let the facts speak for themselves," as if data have purely objective standing.

Statistics in Psychology

While attempting to scientifically justify eugenics on the basis of a selective interpretation of Darwinian theory, Galton encountered the problem of how to measure variation in individuals' psychological traits (Cowles, 2001). Based on Quetelet's mathematical foundation, Galton's solution was to introduce the concepts of regression, standard deviation, and "co-relation."

In the twentieth century, the statistical procedures developed by **Karl Pearson** (1857–1936) for correlational research and Fisher for experimental research arguably revolutionized science (Cowles, 2001). A eugenicist like Galton, Pearson developed a theory and formulation for a measure of relatedness between two variables ("correlation"). He then could justify with large samples the argument for inherited biological and psychological characteristics (R. Smith, 1997).

Generally, early psychologists used descriptive statistics, within-subject designs, replications, tables, graphs, and curve-fitting techniques (L. Smith, Best, Cylke, & Stubbs, 2000). After World War I, Charles Spearman's factor analysis strengthened psychologists' confidence in statistical manipulations of data measuring intelligence or personality structure.

But inferential statistics and null-hypothesis significance-testing did not take root in natural-science Psychology until the 1930s, when Fisher's t and z tests and analysis of variance became quite influential (Cowles, 2001). By 1940, psychologists began to adopt analysis of variance, which they soon employed routinely for experiments.

Thereafter, null-hypothesis significance testing became psychologists' new norm, supported by the language of operational definitions and variables (Mitchell, 2002). The disciplinary consensus now was that scientific rigour consisted of inferential and correlational methods. The social context for this development was that US government funding for psychological research was contingent on grant applicants employing them.

Meta-analysis By the 1980s, the new technique of meta-analysis augmented the disciplinary preference for aggregated experimental data. This procedure entails researchers combining entire sets of data from dozens of individual experiments for the purposes of estimating the size of an experimental effect within a particular population and then making a claim about the "true" nature of the relationships between variables (Schmidt, 1992). Proponents claim that meta-analysis controls for statistical artifacts by focusing on the strength of statistically significant effects. Therefore, it reputedly yields a more objective interpretation of a body of quantitative studies than authors can produce in a narrative assessment.

However, a review of meta-analyses published during 1993 to 2003 in *Psychological Bulletin*, an APA journal specializing in literature reviews, revealed numerous violations of meta-analysis methodology (Shercliffe, Stahl, & Tuttle, 2009). Practitioners of meta-analysis evidently assume that the individual experimental reports that are its foundation reflect actual relationships in nature, whereas published studies represent journals' bias towards reporting positive results only (Sohn, 1996). Moreover, even if conducted correctly, meta-analyses cannot substitute for theoretical analysis of psychological phenomena.

To promote a cumulative approach to psychological investigations, touted as the discipline's goal, some psychologists now advocate "integrative data analysis" that integrates results from multiple studies (e.g., Curran, 2009). This innovation apparently bridges the gap between single-study analysis and meta-analysis. According to its proponents, integrative data analysis is a promising solution to Psychology's historical lack of accumulated generalizable findings that distinguish other natural sciences.

Section conclusion

Psychologists have maintained two quantitative orientations: Pearson's correlational approach, emphasizing individual differences, and Fisher's statistically supported experiments, emphasizing treatment differences between groups (Cronbach, 1957). Both orientations hold the promise of making complex psychological phenomena comprehensible and enhance the plausibility of psychologists' claims to scientific knowledge (Cowles, 2001). However, quantifying psychological phenomena is more problematic than psychologists generally convey in their curricula and discourse.

An axiom in natural-science Psychology, attributed to Edward Thorndike, is that every object exists in some quantity, thus is measurable. However, "everything that can be measured does not necessarily exist" (G. Richards, 2010, p. 280). This latter statement means that psychologists' interpretations of what they measure are partially subjective and are not determined only by the data themselves. Thus, psychological test-scores and statistical results cannot represent "objective" reality.

Issues in psychological statistics

Here we discuss the assumptions underlying psychologists' use of statistics, problems with statistical inference, and contextual issues underlying psychologists' misuse of statistics.

Statistical assumptions

The traditional statistical procedures in Psychology (e.g., t, F, or z tests, analysis of variance, and multiple regression) are based on the general linear model in statistics. The **mathematical assumptions** underlying these techniques are:

- The observations come from a normal, bell-shaped distribution (which is just one kind of distribution).
- They are independently and identically distributed; that is, each datum is a random variable, unrelated to the other variables with independent probabilities.

Concerning the first assumption, in reality, it is doubtful that strict normality of observations occurs, especially in applied settings but also in university-lab sampling. Nevertheless, psychologists adhere to the belief that observed variations among people are distributed normally.

Regarding the second assumption, independence occurs when research participants are randomly assigned or randomly sampled. But many Psychology studies, including animal lab studies, use convenience samples that are neither randomly sampled nor assigned.

Four additional problems with quantification in Psychology exist:

- Research topics in the interpersonal, applied, and professional areas are difficult to subject to statistical control (Meehl, 1978).
- Drawing inferences about human phenomena based on Fisher's statistical techniques is questionable, because he devised them originally to measure production in *agricultural* plots.
- The routine practice of using significance tests as primary evidence of research findings also is dubious. Many physicists and biologists, for example, do not do significance testing; instead, they employ consistency testing and use two or more non-redundant estimates of the same theoretical quantity.
- If psychologists do not account for the influence of intervening or moderating variables on the given theoretical variable tested, their experimentation does not qualify as scientific (Meehl, 1978).

Problems with statistical inference

For decades, experts in psychological statistics questioned the quality of inferential statistics reported in Psychology journals and challenged psychologists' dependence on null-hypothesis significance testing (e.g., Cohen, 1994). Common criticisms concerned the logic, capacities, limits, and applications of statistical inference (Finch, Thomason, & Cumming, 2002). For example, "the method [of null-hypothesis significance testing] discourages replication and encourages one-shot research" (Cowles, 2001, p. 83). Consensus was that, if investigators attended to sample sizes, the power of statistical tests, and statistical-effect sizes, they could resolve problems with statistical inference.

Psychologists' apparent misuse of statistics was embarrassing for a discipline that prided itself on its quantitative credentials. Consequently, in 1996, the APA established a Task Force on Statistical Inference that published guidelines to effect change in statistical practices (Wilkinson & the Task Force on Statistical Inference, 1999). The recommendations pertained to selecting suitable methods, presenting results, and drawing conclusions correctly.

Crucially, the Task Force recommended that the next edition of the *Publication Manual* incorporate its prescriptions, because the *Manual* helps to set standards of preparing statistical evidence. Historically, however, the *Manual*'s authors missed opportunities to respond to criticisms of "seriously flawed statistical practices" (Finch *et al.*, 2002, p. 832).

The Task Force prescribed that authors incorporate visual depictions of data in graphs and tables, measures of effect-sizes, and confidence intervals. The *Manual*'s sixth edition now incorporates these prescriptions.

Section conclusion

One could reasonably expect that, when psychologists use quantification to answer their research questions, they follow "best practices" in statistics. But the APA Task Force was necessary, because for the past seventy years since statistics became the norm in Psychology, an unknown number of authors of research reports, reviewers, and editors neglected basic statistical principles. Thus, for decades, at least some psychologists have made claims to authentic scientific knowledge on the basis of flawed applications of statistics. This historical disposition prompts **two questions**:

- If in their investigative enterprise psychologists linked their scientific identity to expertise in statistical analysis, but that expertise has been dubious, how credible has natural-science Psychology been?
- If the assumptions for statistics were not met in actual practice, why did psychologists behave otherwise and what is the social function of this tradition?

Furthermore, even though natural-science psychologists generally are staunchly committed to quantification and statistical techniques despite the fact that many engage in questionable statistical practices, **five metaphysical–ontological, epistemological, and sociopolitical problems** with psychologists' reliance on statistics remain:

(1) Since the Scientific Revolution, natural scientists and their Psychology cohorts have tended to believe in the ordered, numerical nature of an objective mathematical and mechanistic entity that exists independently of the scientists who investigate it. Figure 11.2, which is a 1794 painting by William Blake (1757–1827), conveys this underlying cultural, metaphysical–ontological belief in a metaphorical wise man who can define natural objects precisely with instruments of measurement.

(2) Epistemologically, naming measured phenomena does not mean that they have objective existence other than their discursive label; this is the logical error of *reification* (Gould, 1996). Statistical manipulations of test scores cannot convert quantities into concrete objects purportedly existing in reality, even though psychologists might treat them that way. Consider whether a statistical mean represents a concrete object. For example, if one finds that couples in country x have an average of 1.43 children, does this literally mean that each couple has 1.43 children?

In short, numbers can tell only part of the story of phenomena, because numbers represent an *abstracted* aspect of psychologists' understanding of phenomena. Measurement and statistics per se are meaningless, because they cannot reveal causes. Knowledge-making requires *interpretation* of data.

(3) Absolute accuracy in psychological measurement is impossible. All psychologists can do is *estimate* accuracy "in terms of the inherent variation within and between individuals" (Cowles, 2001, p. 46). Compounding the relative accuracy of measurement is the fact that data administrators and participants can contribute unintended variation to measurement in the investigative situation.

Figure 11.2 In William Blake's painting *The Ancient of Days* a patriarchal incarnation of reason defines the world with a compass

(4) The contradiction between natural-science psychologists' devotion to quantification and their historical misapplications of statistical inference reflects their historical struggle against subjectivity (Gigerenzer, 1987). For them, psychological science is objective and independent of social history, because they employ quantitative methodology, whereas human-science Psychology (e.g., psychoanalysis and phenomenology) is inescapably subjective. In pursuing objectivity, natural-science psychologists assume that quantification is an absolute requirement for scientific activity, but it is not (Mitchell, 2002; Porter, 1995).

(5) Western cultural trust in quantified knowledge inclined scientists and the public to believe that numerical data would provide objective knowledge suited to managing a complex society. Founding psychologists created and later generations perpetuated an illusion of science, when they promised to deliver quantified findings useful to society for administrative purposes (Danziger, 1990). Thus, quantification in Psychology, with all of its difficulties, has served a larger sociopolitical purpose.

Qualitative methodology

Generally speaking, qualitative procedures are somewhat different for each method but many include interviews of participants (Madill & Gough, 2008). In qualitative interviewing, investigators attempt to build and maintain rapport with their participants and seek feedback at the conclusion of the interview on the content and climate of the conversation. Because of the idiosyncratic demands of interviews, researchers do not necessarily ask every participant questions on every intended topic. Nor do they ask every respondent the same questions in the same order; rather, they adapt to what the individual responds to and desires to discuss. In addition, when relevant, investigators share their own views with their participants. After the interviews are transcribed, investigators share with participants their transcript and potential quotes, then delete material and make changes at participants' request.

When composing a journal article based on interviewing, qualitative researchers typically describe the participants' circumstances, use illustrative quotes, account for the credibility of the data, and provide information about the specificity and transferability of the findings (Elliott, Fischer, & Rennie, 1999). In addition, authors include their contributions to the dialogue in quoted material to account for their interests constraining the participants' responses and shaping the discourse. Some authors weave their own experiences into the narrative when describing the participants' experiences.

Part 5 conclusion

The history of psychologists' methods for measuring and analyzing quantitative data suggests **three problems** both in past and in present investigative practice in Psychology.

(1) Historically, psychologists' adoption of measurement by scaling established a methodological consensus for assessing any knowledge-claim in the discipline. Subsequently, testable propositions and quantifiable phenomena had greater rhetorical value than claims that lacked them. Convinced that they had rendered subjective phenomena objective, natural-science psychologists differentiated themselves from philosophers as well as pop psychologists and charlatans. The belief was that psychologists practised authentic science, whereas the latter practised pseudoscience.

(2) Yet critics assert that psychologists cannot measure their phenomena in the same way as natural scientists measure physical objects, because psychologists' quantified observations encompass not only tangible objects but also intangible phenomena that they only can access indirectly and interpretively. Although psychologists infer some underlying hypothetical construct for these phenomena, the construct per se is not equivalent to an actual natural object. Natural scientists, even geophysicists and biochemists, have held for decades that their objects of inquiry are contingent upon context and interpretation, whereas natural-science psychologists have tended to deny or ignore these contingencies (see Chapter 12).

(3) Although natural-science psychologists have been devoted to the use of statistical techniques, their adherence to the mathematical assumptions underlying these techniques is questionable. Moreover, an implicit culture of using inferential statistics incorrectly evidently pervaded investigative practice in the second half of the twentieth century. This tradition, which compromised the integrity of the discipline and its claim to legitimacy as a science rather than status as a pseudoscience, led an APA-appointed committee in 1999 to prescribe explicit instructions on appropriate employment of inferential statistics.

Furthermore, statistical procedures seem to have "wagged the dog of research" instead of serving as its tail. That is, psychologists' heavy reliance on statistics apparently has shaped how they design investigations and interpret their results, rather than their investigative questions prompting choices of methods, data analysis, and interpretation.

But even if psychologists have misused statistics and violated assumptions of statistical theory in journal reports, are statistics essential for producing durable and genuine scientific findings, even discoveries? Although it is likely that some research questions cannot be answered without them, inferential statistics frequently are not relevant and in any case cannot replace good ideas (Meehl, 1978). Some research questions demand correlational methods or words as the most appropriate data.

Part 6   Research report-writing

The primary outcome of psychologists' investigations is publication in a reputable journal. Hence, we turn now to the history and philosophy of writing journal reports. Like the other aspects of their investigative practice, psychologists' ideas about how to describe the research they have conducted has a social history. We begin by examining the assumptions underlying scientific writing in general.

Scientific rhetoric and report-writing

Making scientific knowledge includes presenting persuasive arguments to an intended audience. Because all writing is dependent on authors' choices of words in a given text, writing like a psychological scientist is as partially subjective as is writing in the humanities and arts. Scientists, however, typically do not associate rhetoric with scientific activity. But historically what has constituted scientific rhetoric?

Definitions

According to scholars of scientific writing (e.g., Bazerman, 1988; Gross, 1990; C. A. Taylor, 1996), creating scientific knowledge begins and ends with the art of persuasion, which is one meaning of the term *rhetoric*. Technically, rhetoric means "discursive structures and strategies used to render arguments persuasive in given situations" (Schuster & Yeo, 1986, p. xii). Rhetoric as a social practice entails literary construction, while rhetoric as a discipline refers to the study of argumentation.

Arguably, rhetoric is as intrinsic to scientific activity as rationally connected propositions, methods, procedures, and analysis are, because data are always subject to interpretation and description, which entail linguistic choices. Scientists persuade themselves of a particular position privately; they empirically investigate this position with private and public language; and then they publicly attempt to persuade their peers that their claim to knowledge is legitimate and valuable. Thus, scientific communication is both social and rhetorical.

Within the study of argumentation, attempts to pit rhetoric (presumed to be subjective) against scientific discourse (presumed to be objective) are misguided. Although the extent of rhetorical influence on the logical construction of scientific facts is debatable, scientists' choice of words expresses their discursive constructions of their observations (Simons, 1993). As one psychologist noted, "all scholarship, including science, uses argument, and argument uses rhetoric" (Bevan, 1991, p. 478).

Rhetoric in science

Any particular discipline's rhetoric is historically constituted within the expectations of a given social institution, which shape any text in a particular discourse (Latour & Woolgar, 1979; C. A. Taylor, 1996). In the natural sciences, explicit standardization of the format of research reports began in the early twentieth century with specific sections for introduction, method, results, and discussion (Bazerman, 1988). This format has an implicit structure of "problem-cause-solution" (Simons, 1993, p. 155); that is, ideally, authors narrate a specific problem that they solve in a psychologically and aesthetically satisfying conclusion.

As for writing-style, at least since the eighteenth century, authors have valued precision, logic, order, and clarity. By the twentieth century English supplanted German as the international language of science. Yet scientific writing can be poor from the point of view of good English. For example, the common objectified phrase, "It was found that," illustrates four problems: needless words, pomposity, vagueness, and passive voice, which obscures the person(s) who made the finding.

The history of scientific report-writing reveals rhetoric at work. For example, in a 1672 paper on optics, Isaac Newton sharply criticized René Descartes' explanation of optics (Gross, 1990). Yet Newton did not show the continuity between his work and earlier studies, he failed to describe his experimental procedures, and his explanation of his findings was weak. Consequently, he was not persuasive and his peers criticized his paper. Then thirty-two years later in book form he presented his findings from detailed experiments, emphasizing the fit between his innovations and previous research. This time his claim secured legitimacy, because he adapted his claim to his scientific culture.

Newton's case shows that scientific report-writing is a carefully constructed, partially subjective exercise in presenting a rhetorical argument to a scientific community. In the twentieth century, some natural scientists admitted that they experience strong social pressure to be on top in their field and to create the impression in their writing that they are (Gilbert & Mulkay, 1981). Historically, however, many natural scientists have opposed recognizing rhetoric and incorporating metaphorical expressions intentionally in their reports. Instead, rooted in the epistemological assumption of naïve realism, they promoted objective writing, as if words merely held up a mirror to nature and reflected an unblemished natural world back to readers (Leary, 1990a).

Furthermore, manuals of scientific writing ignore the realities of rhetoric and counsel scientific writers to be completely objective. Consequently, authors of research reports typically dance between advocating for a particular position and striving to be scientifically neutral (Gusfield, 1976). They cope by adopting the rhetorical style of "non-style," that is, by attempting to convey the written impression that they are objectively detached. But the fact that a scientific paper *seems* to be free from emotional appeal does not mean that the paper *is* neutral (Schuster & Yeo, 1986). Apparent neutrality represents authors' pose of scientific detachment to enhance their scientific credibility among their peers.

In sum, consciously or not, scientists depend on rhetorical devices in their writing to convince readers that their work represents a contribution worthy of archival preservation. In contrast to the rational image that many scientists project to their audiences, their presumed dispassionate activity is saturated with the desire for career-advancement, competitiveness, and strong belief in an objective mathematical and mechanistic reality.

APA style

Rhetoric also has played a pivotal role in Psychology (Bazerman, 1988). Watson, for instance, was a master of rhetoric who changed the US discipline through his rhetorical choices. William James understood the foundation of psychological knowledge metaphorically (e.g., "stream of consciousness") and employed Darwinian metaphors (e.g., "function") (Leary, 1987). Mental testers in the 1920s adopted the rhetoric of medicine (e.g., "mental disease") and engineering (e.g., "mental stress"). Other early psychologists employed metaphors of efficiency, productivity, and exchange, to secure societal legitimacy for their enterprise (Leary, 1990a), although they interpreted such terms literally when explaining psychological phenomena.

Nevertheless, founding natural-science psychologists adopted natural scientists' assumption that their terms, concepts, and categories directly reflected natural objects as they existed in the real world (Danziger, 1997). Early psychologists – and their successors – also believed that the scientific language that they employed in their conference presentations and journal articles was purely objective.

But from a critical perspective, psychological language does not reflect psychological phenomena unambiguously; rather, it mediates them subjectively. Language, of course, is the basis for scientific argument and any argument is a rhetorical act. Generally, however, natural-science psychologists do not acknowledge the rhetorical aspect of constructing psychological knowledge.

Rationale for APA style

Although there was a prehistory of rhetorical codes for the construction of research reports in US Psychology (Bazerman, 1988), its rhetoric, known as APA style, was not standardized until the emergence of the *Publication Manual* in 1952 (American Psychological Association, 2009). The term "APA style" refers to explicit directions for composing journal reports and includes both format and style. These prescriptions have been systematized and increasingly specified in five subsequent editions of the *Manual*. The APA committee responsible for the *Manual* has accommodated contemporary concerns, such as changing the previously acceptable terms "Ss" and "subjects" to "participants" and requiring authors to employ gender-inclusive rhetoric. In response to criticisms of psychologists' use of inferential statistics, the latest edition contains substantial change in regard to reporting statistical information.

Over recent decades many international English-language journals have followed the *Manual*'s prescriptions. Thus, the formative social institution for the scientific rhetoric in postwar Psychology is APA style. Many psychologists and students seem to assume that APA style is the only way to compose research reports.

The *Manual*'s prescriptions match natural-science psychologists' explicit intentions to establish laws of behaviour that transcend specific persons and social-historical contexts (Madigan *et al.*, 1995). **Two epistemological assumptions** underlie these prescriptions (Walsh-Bowers, 1999):

- Participants are sources of objective data.
- As long as researchers follow rigorous procedures, they will be scientific in collecting, analyzing, interpreting, and reporting data.

Also apparent is a **metaphysical–ontological assumption** about the nature of reality as inherently mathematical in structure and mechanistic in operation, independent of the researcher's relationship to it. Thus, when authors construct an empirical paper, they take great pains to characterize their inquiry as a totally objective product of preferably exper-imental manipulations.

Practice of APA style

Psychologists' standardized rhetoric is intended to convey scientific detachment. Proponents assert that APA style is a means for psychologists to communicate the "facts" about psychological objects in a universal language as transparently and authoritatively as they believe natural scientists do (Madigan *et al.*, 1995). But behind this public image there are **two unreported sources of data** that investigators typically exclude from professional presentations:

- The actual procedures that the investigators employed to obtain their significant effects, mediated by the data administrators' biopsychosocial influences.
- The participants' views of the investigative situation.

In effect, then, researchers conduct three studies in any single investigation. However, authors exclude the subjectivity of the two parties in the research relationship to construct what they project as a purely detached account of the phenomena under observation.

Scrutiny of the *Publication Manual*'s requirements uncovers **four aspects** of psychologists' explicit and implicit rhetorical conventions of APA style.

- There is only one research model for emulation – the quantitative laboratory experiment. Correlational, observational, and qualitative studies are invisible.
- The required format of introduction, method, results, and discussion reproduces the standardized lab reports of the natural sciences. However, how suitable is this format that suits experimentation for other research methods?
- The writing style should be detached, objective, and rational. Personal information, feelings, and metaphors are forbidden, because subjective writing is inappropriate for science.
- Authors receive no encouragement to acknowledge the interpersonal nature of human research (i.e., the research relationship). Thus, by design, research papers usually contain only sketchy information about the participants and their context. Authors typically do not provide information about the conditions of informed consent for participation or any feedback on the findings, or information about the researchers' characteristics, as if automatons had conducted the research.

Part 6 conclusion

Clearly, guidelines for composing research reports serve a very important practical function for authors, reviewers, editors, and readers. But in Psychology's case, the hegemony of rules intended for only one research method suggests that a kind of scientistic fundamentalism is at work. Many psychologists drill their undergraduate and graduate students in mastering APA style, as if the *Manual* were a bible for the faithful.

But must we psychologists write research reports with minimal information about our research relationships and with a rigid format and style? From a critical perspective, no, because this practice, enforced by instructors, journal editors, and reviewers, represents human conventions that change over time as disciplinary preferences change. Psychologists need flexibility in both format and style so that our writing corresponds to the complexity and ambiguity of our subject matter and the intersubjectivity of our methods (Walsh-Bowers, 1999). In fact, intentional modifications of APA style have emerged in at least one subdiscipline; community psychology journals recommend that authors describe the research relationship in their articles.

Adherence to APA style is particularly problematic for authors of qualitative research, because their investigations typically lend themselves to innovative compositional forms and writing styles. But these authors encounter the dilemma of creating discursive space for their research in the context of the discipline's deeply rooted commitment to quantitative laboratory experimentation and APA style (Walsh-Bowers, 2002). This commitment is epitomized by the exclusion of qualitative methods from every edition of the *Manual*, even though its expressed purpose is to set standards for all scientific discourse in Psychology.

Part 7   Thematic review

In stipulating its principles for what reputedly constitutes high-quality content for undergraduate education in Psychology, the methods and statistical procedures employed in positively sanctioned psychological science are vital components for US Psychology's gatekeepers, because they are believed to confer scientific legitimacy for the discipline (American Psychological Association, 2011). In this chapter we addressed this claim by examining **six metaphysical–ontological, epistemological, and methodological issues** in Psychology traditions of investigative practice, including:

- The objectivistic nature of the scientific language upon which psychologists' rely.
- The hierarchical structure and function of investigators' professional relationships with humans and other animals.
- Psychologists' conformity with a quantitative imperative in methodology, especially lab experimentation, over against qualitative methods.
- Psychologists' failure to acknowledge the inescapably transactional nature of psychological research.
- Psychologists' dubious assumptions about measurement and history of flawed practice of statistical inference.
- Their staunch commitment to objectivistic APA style for writing about all types of psychological research.

Natural-science psychologists' responses to these problems typically have consisted of denial and avoidance or justifications for standard practice.

Considering the history and philosophy of investigative practice in Psychology, two themes appear to be central: **science, pseudoscience, or interpretive science**, and **intersubjectivity**.

Science, pseudoscience, or interpretive science

Psychologists' problems with measurement exemplify how historically many psychologists in their quest to project a natural-science persona might have neglected to account for inevitable tension between objectivity and subjectivity, given the nature of psychological subject matter. Consider these **two critical-historical points**:

- Although modern physicists recognized that the act of measuring inanimate objects changes those objects (see Chapter 12), natural-science psychologists have believed that when they measure an animate object, they do not affect it. But drawing from the perspective of modern physics, the two parties in the research relationship each contribute unintended variation to the investigative situation.
- Psychologists have assumed that their phenomena of interest are permanent. But from a critical perspective, these objects shift across social-historical conditions, requiring modifications of measurement and interpretation. As such, different psychologists investigate and interpret a phenomenon differently because of different social contexts.

Moreover, investigative practices change over time. What once was regarded as legitimate scientific conduct (e.g., self-experimentation or shared experimental roles) now is illegitimate. Quite likely, what will be regarded as legitimate in the future will be different than today's standards. Consequently, adherence to current methodology alone cannot advance Psychology, because making psychological knowledge requires critical reflection and ethical conduct (Danziger, 1994). Moreover, responding to the quantitative imperative and fulfilling the agenda of methodologism suggest unreflective practice, which is characteristic of pseudoscience.

From a critical perspective, psychologists' compliance with the quantitative imperative is also known as *methodolatry* or the virtual worship of quantitative methods to the exclusion of other paths to knowledge (Bakan, 1967). Arguably, methodolatry is psychologists' particular expression of the hoary problem of scientism, the strong belief in the explanatory powers of a putatively objective scientific method. It seems that when we psychologists invest inordinate faith in an objectivistic conception of investigative practice, paradoxically we distance ourselves from science and approximate pseudoscience.

Furthermore, we might delude ourselves if we think we can eradicate ambiguity from our investigations and can discover indubitable universal laws concerning behaviour and mental processes. We also might perpetrate epistemological violence by taking psychological knowledge as pure fact rather than as the outcome of interpretation of data (Teo, 2008). Instead of upholding psychological truths and claiming intellectual certainty, we could recognize that psychological events are culturally and historically bound. Moreover, we could recognize that they are subject to multiple transitory interpretations, as a critical hermeneutics for Psychology suggests.

In short, there are human limits to scientific psychological knowledge (Koch, 1981). Furthermore, *methodological pluralism*, the principle of appreciating the limits of any research method and combining methods to better understand observed phenomena, would be better suited to our discipline than methodological fundamentalism. Although natural-science psychologists have always aspired to attain a scientific ideal, we conclude that, given its enduring fundamental metaphysical–ontological, epistemological, and methodological problems, scientism and pseudoscience seem to have played significant roles in the history of natural-science Psychology.

For some psychologists, a turn towards Psychology as an interpretive science, as demonstrated by the various human-science psychologies, constitutes a constructive alternative. At the heart of an interpretive scientific approach is the epistemological principle of intersubjectivity.

Intersubjectivity

Regardless of the particular research questions pursued and the accompanying methods selected, making psychological knowledge ultimately is informed by acknowledging that we psychologists study ourselves and cannot avoid influencing how we proceed methodologically and how we interpret our findings. That is, intersubjectivity, the mutual influence of researchers and participants on the psychological phenomena of interest, prevails. Accordingly, investigator reflexivity (i.e., discussing this mutual influence in research reports), nurtures the development of a more realistic approach to what actually occurs in the conduct of psychological inquiry. Perhaps practising the principles of reflexivity and intersubjectivity can counteract Psychology's regression towards the scientistic and pseudoscientific mean.

Summary

In this chapter we dealt with Psychology's *raison d'être*, namely, its research traditions, which stem from societal, philosophical, and scientific foundations.

In Part 1 we described the origins of natural-science psychologists' scientific language of operational definitions and variables. This objectified language, which complemented psychologists' swelling preference for quantitative laboratory experimentation, shaped the psychological concepts that psychologists produced and conveyed an aura of scientific expertise to society and themselves.

In Part 2 we introduced the concept of the research relationship and examined psychologists' historical construction of research roles and functions in their investigative practice with humans. We described precedents for sharing research roles and concluded that there is nothing intrinsically "scientific" about psychologists controlling all aspects of investigative practice. Then we described the historical place of ethical issues in psychological research with humans, including deception and "subject pools."

In Part 3 we reviewed Psychology's long history of using animals for experimentation. We analyzed psychologists' orientations towards the value of animal research for understanding psychological phenomena. Discussing issues voiced by animal welfare advocates and animal rights activists, we placed psychologists' relationship with animals in ethical context.

In Part 4 we addressed the history of psychological methods for gathering data, focusing on psychologists' preferred method, statistical experimentation. We noted two types of experimentation: controlled experiments with grouped data and experimental control of individual performance. Then we discussed methodological artifacts or sources of bias in research, discussing research as a transaction between two parties who can affect research findings in unintended ways. These effects stem from researchers' attributes or their expectations and from participants who can play biasing roles. We described the principles and procedures of qualitative methods, favoured by human-science psychologists, and the challenges that qualitative researchers face.

In Part 5 we discussed the history of measurement and quantitative analysis in Psychology. Natural-science psychologists generally have employed numbers rather than words for their data. Accordingly, we addressed the philosophical, scientific, and societal roots of psychological measurement. Then we discussed psychologists' historical use of statistics, including the assumptions underlying statistical tests and psychologists' misuse of statistics. Lastly, we reviewed the issues involved in analyzing qualitative data.

Investigative practice includes composing articles for research publication. In Part 6 we defined the term scientific rhetoric and described the history of conventions of report-writing in the sciences. Then we described the traditions of writing research reports in Psychology and analyzed the assumptions behind, and prescriptions of, "APA style." We also discussed the problems of composing research reports of qualitative investigations, given that Psychology's standards for report-writing are not congruent with the nature of qualitative inquiry.

In Part 7 we discussed two themes – science, pseudoscience, or interpretive science, and intersubjectivity – that capture the history of psychologists' investigative practice. Fundamental philosophical and practical problems suggest natural-science psychologists have practised a pseudoscience rather than the equivalent of a natural science. An alternative is to turn towards Psychology as an interpretive science and practise the principle of intersubjectivity in psychological research.

Sample essay questions

1. Explain what your position is on the claim that even though animals have emotions, it is ethical for scientists to harm them in experiments for the good of humanity.

2. What is your view: can one practise legitimate psychological research without operationally defining one's terms and specifying one's variables?

3. Evaluate the claim that the investigative practice in Psychology is inherently intersubjective.

RECOMMENDED READING

Danziger's (1997) *Naming the mind* aids understanding the development of psychologists' concepts and terms in relation to the quantitative experiment. T. Rogers's (1995) *The psychological testing enterprise* provides a history of the assumptions and pragmatic applications of tests and measurement.

Danziger's (1995) *Constructing the subject* analyzes psychologists' constructions of the investigative situation and the literature on the social psychology of the experiment. Morawski's (1988) edited book, *The rise of experimentation in American psychology*, contains analyses of diverse aspects of investigative practice.

Walsh-Bowers's (2004) chapter in Brock *et al.* (eds.), *Rediscovering the history of psychology: Essays inspired by the work of Kurt Danziger* summarizes his studies of the research relationship in terms of research functions, ethics, and reporting.

G. Richards's (2010) *Putting psychology in its place* and Stam and Kalmanovitch's (1998) article summarize the core issues of psychologists' use of nonhuman animals. Wise's (2000) *Rattling the cage: Toward legal rights for animals* details research on animals' capacities. The third issue of the 2009 volume of the *Journal of Social Issues* is devoted to animal psychology and ethics.

Gould's (1996) *The mismeasure of man* is a critique of biological and social scientists' measurement assumptions and practices. Hornstein's (1988) chapter and Danziger (1995) address the origins of psychologists' use of statistics and measurement.

Kidder and Fine (1997) introduce qualitative methods in Fox and Prilleltensky (eds.), *Critical psychology*. W. Rogers (2009) describes so-called critical research methods in Fox *et al.*'s second edition of *Critical psychology*.

ONLINE RESOURCES

Individuals and topics are available in the *Stanford Encyclopedia of Philosophy* at http://plato.stanford.edu/contents.html, while topics from a critical perspective (e.g., publication manuals) are available in the *Encyclopedia of Critical Psychology* at http://SpringerReference.com.

Many of Kurt Danziger's works are available at www.kurtdanziger.com.

The American Psychological Association provides information on APA style at www. apastyle.org, on research ethics at www.apa.org/ethics/code/index.aspx, and on "Guidelines for ethical conduct in the care and use of nonhuman animals in research" at www.apa.org/science/leadership/care/guidelines.aspx.

The British Psychological Society provides its "Code of human research ethics" at www. bps.org.uk/sites/default/files/documents/code_of_human_research_ethics.pdf and a link to the BPS section on qualitative research at http://qmip.bps.org.uk/

12

Critical philosophical and historical reflections

Chapter outline

Introduction

In this closing chapter we synthesize our account of Psychology's history and philosophy by presenting multiple critical frameworks for appreciating the past, present, and anticipated future of the discipline. The central theme is that many individuals and groups have described Psychology throughout its history as a problematic science due to its disputed concepts, methodology, and practices, yet they also proposed alternative approaches. We trace these critiques back to Immanuel Kant, Auguste Comte, and nineteenth-century German scholars Friedrich Lange and **Rudolf Willy** (1855–1918).

Turning to the twentieth century, we review developments in physics, biology, and fuzzy logic, which have implications for Psychology's scientific and epistemological foundations. Then we describe critiques by social philosophers, Herbert Marcuse and Jürgen Habermas, known as critical theorists, and discuss modern critical approaches in Psychology, including the work of Klaus Holzkamp and current critical psychology.

Next we review more recent critiques of mainstream Psychology from feminist and postmodern perspectives. Then we trace the inclination to critique Psychology to advocates of postcolonial perspectives who assert that psychologists have tended to ignore the discipline's cultural embeddedness and who propose respect for culturally diverse psychologies. We conclude our review of critiques with a philosophical analysis of the ontology, epistemology, and ethics of Psychology.

As authors we have an ethical responsibility not just to criticize but to propose constructive alternatives. Accordingly, we conclude with an outline of what a socially responsible, politically engaged Psychology might look like. Lastly, we encourage you to formulate your own position on the central questions raised by a social-historical assessment of Psychology's foundations.

The **aims** of this chapter are to describe:

- The history of critiques of extant psychology from eighteenth- and nineteenth-century philosophers concerned about psychology's compatibility with natural science.
- The significance of twentieth-century developments in the natural sciences for Psychology.
- The main points of critical theory and of past and present critical psychologies.
- Feminist critiques of science, Psychology, and research methods.
- The relevance of postmodernism for Psychology.
- Postcolonial perspectives on Psychology, focusing on the liberation psychology of Ignacio Martín-Baró.
- The themes that summarized the preceding chapters; the core theme of this chapter: the problematic nature of Psychology from the philosophical perspectives of ontology, epistemology, and ethics and politics; and the keys issues that might foster the development of an alternative vision of Psychology's future.

| Part 1 | ## History of the critiques of psychology |

In the late eighteenth century Immanuel Kant argued that the study of the soul, which was the contemporary meaning of the term psychology, could not be natural-scientific, because it could not be developed into a true experimental discipline like physics. Instead, he recommended that psychology should limit itself to describing the soul and focus on moral agency, meaning the person's ability to act intentionally according to moral principles.

But in the nineteenth century, psychology was transformed from a philosophical discipline into a natural-scientific discipline (Green, Shore, & Teo, 2001). This shift meant that the new psychologists, who were educated in both philosophy and science, marginalized the study of the soul and subjectivity, because they adopted the principles and methods of the natural sciences to study psychological processes.

The transformation of psychology to a natural science had both intellectual and social-historical origins. When Psychology emerged, its practitioners had to struggle for respect in academia. They reasoned that it was more promising to align themselves with the highly successful natural sciences, which enjoyed academic recognition and social power, than with seemingly ambiguous human sciences such as history (Ward, 2002).

Later psychologists hoped that natural scientists, principally physiologists and physicists, would appreciate Psychology, if its practitioners committed themselves to ostensibly objective topics such as behaviour rather than notions of the soul or human experience. This inclination to establish Psychology as a rigorous discipline was so strong that even a young Sigmund Freud intended psychoanalysis as a natural science.

Meanwhile, a parallel movement to establish Psychology as a human science flourished. Beginning in the 1860s, Wilhelm Dilthey divided the sciences into natural-scientific analytical disciplines and human-scientific descriptive disciplines. He argued that if scientists' experience was human, then their method must entail understanding. Dilthey's critique inspired others to pursue a human-science approach.

European Psychology evolved into natural-science and human-science branches, a division that persisted for decades. Human-science Psychology eventually expressed itself as phenomenological, existential, and psychoanalytic branches. What bound these human-science perspectives together was their collective emphasis on the meaning of conscious and unconscious human action.

Against Dilthey, Hermann Ebbinghaus and Hugo Münsterberg asserted that Psychology should rely only on natural-scientific explanation and experimental methods. This and similar debates over the decades led to diverse critiques and "crisis discussions" concerning Psychology's scientific status. Indeed, Rudolf Willy published the first systematic book on the crisis in Psychology in 1899. The most influential early critique, however, was Kant's.

Immanuel Kant's critique of psychology

Since the time of Aristotle's challenge to Plato's conception of the psyche, philosophers over the millennia disagreed with one another on various points regarding psychological processes. Despite the importance of these controversies they did not systematically challenge a whole field of research. But Kant did. In his *Metaphysical Foundations of Natural Science* (1786), Kant argued that empirical psychology, as Wolff understood it, could not be an experimental natural science for **three reasons**:

- Because psychology was not composed of *a priori* principles discoverable by reason, it could not be mathematical, which was his key criterion for a genuine natural science. For Kant, quantification was essential.

- Because mental content did not stand still, it did not permit experimental analysis, which requires holding constant the object of observational interest, in current language, the independent variable.
- The very act of introspective observation affects the observed object, thereby introducing, in current terms, observer bias.

The common interpretation of Kant's argument is that he claimed quantification of psychological phenomena was impossible. But another perspective is that he was cautious about, yet not entirely dismissive of, quantification (Sturm, 2006). Although in his revised formulation he regarded introspection as incompatible with scientifically studying the mind, he accepted quantitative investigations of mental processes, gave examples of quantitative studies of sensory and perceptual processes, and suggested methodological directions for such inquiries. Furthermore, in his *Anthropology from a Pragmatic Point of View* (1798) Kant prescribed an outline for empirical investigations of *external* human nature, that is, of individuals in their culturally situated interpersonal relations, to enable them to live more consciously and ethically (Leary, 1982).

Kant's critique of psychology had implications for the status of psychology as a natural science. His original argument fuelled important controversies and encouraged natural-science psychologists to prove him wrong. They refuted what they interpreted as his totalizing claim for the impossibility of a scientific psychology by treating mental content as if it were a static object amenable to quantitative experimentation.

Others have sought to prove Kant correct. In a current debate Charles Tolman (2001) appealed to his original argument: "Only a psychology that is at once moral and natural has the capacity to rise above the merely empirical" (p. 182).

Kant's critique also has implications for current beliefs about the historical origins of Psychology as a distinct discipline. The standard view is that before Wilhelm Wundt's "founding" of Psychology in 1879, only speculative psychology (e.g., Herbart's) existed. However, definitive discontinuity between 1879 and previous centuries of empirical psychological inquiries is questionable (Sturm, 2006).

Natural-science critiques of psychology

While biological investigations of animal and human functioning expanded in the nineteenth century, giving natural scientists increasing confidence in their studies of human nature, Christian leaders and theologians, and philosophical psychologists persisted in their religious and metaphysical explanations of psychological phenomena. Three individuals deeply committed to a natural-science orientation – Auguste Comte, Friedrich Lange, and Rudolf Willy – criticized this type of psychological thought from distinct angles.

Auguste Comte

From 1830 to 1842, Auguste Comte formulated a stage theory of the ideal development of human thought. In the "positive" state of human development, unfolding since Francis Bacon's era, humans studied the positive sciences: they employed the scientific method to investigate natural objects and observed empirical facts, accompanied by some reasoning and academic specialization.

But Comte ([1853] 1896) argued that psychology should be excluded from the positive sciences; he believed that philosophical psychology represented the last phase of theology, which was the least form of development; he suggested that mental phenomena should be studied within the disciplines of anatomy, physiology and his own programme of positive philosophy; and he repudiated introspection.

Comte's perspective on psychological phenomena was realized partially in John Watson's behaviourism and more fully in B. F. Skinner's operant behaviourism. Although initially Watson insisted on proscribing introspection, eventually he admitted verbal reports from his research participants. Skinner, however, adhered to a strict operant-conditioning account of psychological phenomena to his death.

Friedrich Lange

The first systematic critique of psychology formulated from a natural-science perspective combined with an extensive alternative programme was expressed by Friedrich Lange, who criticized the subject matter and methodology of philosophical psychology (Teo, 2002). But he also presented an alternative framework for an objective psychology half a century before Watson and others expressed similar ideas.

Against his contemporaries, Lange ([1866] 1950) denied the common notion that one can determine the subject matter of psychology *a priori*. For him, it was not reasonable to start with metaphysical principles of the soul, because this approach would not permit scientific treatment. Moreover, he claimed the concept of a soul was empty. Instead of defining psychology's *a priori*, he asserted, one should define it *a posteriori* as a psychology *without a soul*.

Lange's vision for a natural-science psychology entailed systematic experiments on sensation, perception, human action, language, and all mental life. Instead of self-observation (introspection) and subjective accounts, psychologists would employ the objective, controlled observation of others. Lange reasoned that it would be easy to experiment on animals and human infants. If investigators focused on animals' and infants' movements and repeated experimental procedures, they could successfully guard against the influence of personal preconceptions, he thought. He even recommended statistical manipulation of observations.

Rudolf Willy

A Swiss philosopher, Willy argued that Wilhelm Wundt's approach, then the most important type in the German language, was saturated with speculation. Willy (1899) began his essay on the crisis in Psychology with the statement that contemporary Psychology, already flourishing for several decades in Germany, was still caught in the bonds of speculation. He identified two aspects of the crisis: metaphysical and methodological.

The metaphysical crisis lay in Willy's belief that Psychology remained bound by speculation, largely due to the influence of metaphysical spiritualism. According to him, psychologists like Wundt, in the name of exact empirical science, returned to the lap of speculation. If psychologists wanted to succeed as scientists, then they should abandon metaphysics.

Willy understood the methodological crisis as psychologists' inability to resolve basic methodological questions. The unresolved issues included the possibility of transferring natural-scientific methods to Psychology, the correct method for Psychology (experimentation or introspection), the role of psychological causality, and the roles of intuition and abstraction in acquiring scientific knowledge.

Part 1 conclusion

Critiques of Psychology have a long tradition and date back at least to Kant's assessment of psychology as a subject matter suitable for natural-scientific inquiry. Comte rejected the possibility of psychology as a natural science. However, just as Psychology was about to emerge, Lange argued that one could study appearances and events with rigorous natural-science concepts and methods, including laboratory animal research, and could formulate natural laws based on those appearances. Although the new psychologists ignored his critique and alternative programme, Lange's viewpoint was sympathetic to their natural-scientific orientation.

Several decades later when Willy reflected on the new Psychology, he regarded it as afflicted by fundamental metaphysical and methodological problems in its claims to be a legitimate natural science. But early Anglo-American psychologists ignored his critique too. Furthermore, subsequent generations of natural-science psychologists did not seem to be aware of developments in the natural sciences, particularly in their most admired science, physics. These developments had major implications for the new Psychology's metaphysical and methodological foundations.

Part 2   Critique from developments in the natural sciences

While psychologists were formally establishing and developing their new science, natural scientists, particularly physicists, were pushing the conceptual boundaries of their disciplines. Here we review philosophical challenges to what constitutes sound psychological research originating in developments that occurred in the natural sciences since Psychology's emergence. Developments in physics, biology, and fuzzy logic present important implications for psychologists' epistemological assumptions and investigative practice. Natural scientists themselves have not drawn out these implications for Psychology; rather, some psychologists and other scholars have.

Physics

Since the Scientific Revolution, Western culture has considered the science of physics as the foundation for all natural sciences. It would make sense, then, for the founding generations of natural-science psychologists to attempt to emulate the worldview and methodology of Newtonian classical physics, quantitative laboratory experimentation, to establish Psychology as a legitimate natural science.

However, even while early psychologists were endeavouring to secure scientific acceptance, physicists were changing their concepts. In classical physics, scientists studied the large objects of the everyday world. But in twentieth-century physics, scientists study the "behaviour" of minute objects, like tiny particles of light, where what physicists of the old paradigm regarded as impossible arguably occurs (Atkins, 2003).

By the early twentieth century, classical physicists had applied Isaac Newton's laws of mechanics and gravity to a wide range of earthly and cosmic natural events. Despite these successes, doubts emerged concerning the nature of atoms, matter, and energy. This was the intellectual context in which Albert Einstein, a clerk in a Swiss patent office, published five papers in 1905 that radically changed both physics and the modern world, meriting the Nobel Prize (Stachel, 2005).

In classical physics, space was a purely objective property of an object, which would appear the same regardless of the person observing it, and time passed at the same uniform speed for every observer. But Einstein showed in his theory of relativity that the perception of time is related to the observer's location. Later he showed that gravity actually bends space and time, and established the equivalency of mass and energy. Relativity theory permits treating space and time as unitary or "spacetime." As physicist Lisa Randall (2005) puts it, "Mass and energy make spacetime curve" (p. 114).

Subsequently, profound changes occurred in physicists' conceptions of the universe and of methodology. In Newton's model, everything about an object was predictable. In contrast, according to Werner Heisenberg's (1901–1976) *uncertainty principle*, the more accurately one wishes to measure an object's position, the less accurately one is able to measure the object's velocity, and vice versa.

Although Newtonian physics pertains to objects of the natural world, quantum physics pertains to human *observations* of those objects. The twentieth-century paradigm of *quantum mechanics* is a theory of matter and energy investigating objects ranging from the invisible and subatomic to the cosmic. Quantum physicists contend that objects of observation materialize when and where the observer finds them, multiple interpretations of natural phenomena are scientifically plausible, and the future determines the past, not the reverse (Rosenblum & Kuttner, 2006). Quantum mechanics goes well beyond what Einstein envisioned, and it has presented theoretical dilemmas that he flatly rejected as impossible. Instead of a single, certain result, several outcomes, each with its own probability of occurrence, are possible.

Broadly, the concepts and investigative practice of twentieth-century and current physics call into question the traditional epistemological assumptions of natural science: naïve realism, determinism, and reductionism. Moreover, physicists use psychological language to describe particle "communication." In the field of particle physics, investigators' primary aim is to test a prediction about the action of particles. They are not focused on how manipulated variables function as causes (Franklin, 1990).

Implications for Psychology

Generally, natural-science psychologists remained strongly committed to a pre-Einsteinian model of science in search of precise cause-and-effect relations, but Gestalt theorists and Kurt Lewin adopted aspects of the new physics, such as field theory. Although much of what physicists propose about mass, energy, spacetime, and cosmology is very theoretical and difficult to relate to Psychology, **three implications** for psychologists' epistemology and methodology are apparent:

(1) Instead of the assumptions of naïve realism and pure objectivity in scientific observation, the new assumption is that the observer and the observed influence each other. Making scientific knowledge, therefore, entails a fundamentally trans-subjective process. This principle means that the observer is a key part of observing and of interpreting the observation. The practical implication is that in doing research, psychologists should account for how the relationship between researchers and participants affects any particular investigation.

(2) Instead of the assumptions of determinism and precisely determined cause-and-effect relations, scientists can only estimate ranges of probabilities for events. In addition, time becomes not a predictable series of predetermined events but basically unpredictable. The practical implication is that psychologists cannot predict and control human action, which is much more complex and multiply influenced than the inanimate objects that physicists study.

(3) Instead of the assumption of reductionism, some physicists attempt to observe holistic patterns of movement, rather than reducible, individual elements. The practical implication is that psychologists need to focus on the totality of specific human activities, as the Gestalt psychologists demonstrated.

Chaos theory

The study of chaos, which should not be equated with anarchy, is another important development in physics with ramifications for all sciences (Gleick, 1988). The premise of *chaos theory* is that the universe functions in terms of sensitive dependence on initial conditions such that small changes in them can alter the ultimate state of a system dramatically.

A system manifesting chaos will not repeat the same pattern twice. Although the final outcome might be unpredictable, it is not random. The process by which an initial orderly pattern disintegrates into turbulent behaviour appears to have a certain form. In tracking chaos, the complexities that scientists observe rarely fit a linear description.

The practical implication for Psychology is that what might seem like insignificant actions of individuals can have substantial consequences. An innovative idea for combating global warming, for example, can be the spark that brings many people to awareness and action. Furthermore, psychologists can apply chaos theory to basic cognitive processes and interpersonal phenomena (Abraham & A. Gilgen, 1995).

Biology

Since the Darwinian era, biologists have believed that humans are a part of nature, having evolved from simpler forms. Evolution occurred according to the impersonal processes of variation and natural selection to promote adaptation for survival (Atkins, 2003). The emergence of genetics, then DNA research, and the first mapping of the human genome in 2001 provided an explanation for these evolutionary processes.

Microbiologists study cellular structure and processes. Traditionally, they described the functions of an individual cell as autonomous and disconnected from its environment of other cells. A different interpretation is that all cells are in continuously interconnected relations with other cells and can serve multiple functions among multiple systems, such as the immune and nervous systems (Weasel, 1996).

Research on the structure and functioning of DNA molecules shows that "information" flows from the genes to the developing organism, affecting its structure and sustainability. As the organism experiences its environment, "messages" flow back to the genes that might alter their structure. Thus, another way of characterizing cellular activity is that cells "communicate" structurally and functionally with other cells, mediated by the biochemical composition of cell membranes. In addition, some microbial evolutionary biologists have argued that Darwinian evolutionary theory does not apply, for example, to bacteria and that the metaphor of a Darwinian tree of life requires rethinking (Sapp, 2009).

In reductionistic biology scientists assume that they can understand biological processes by investigating elementary particles, molecules, and genes. But according to "synthetic biology," emergent patterns of organization better characterize biological processes in living creatures and the inanimate universe (Goldenfeld & Woese, 2007). Advocates of synthetic biology assume that a different scientific paradigm is necessary to make sense of current scientific problems, such as the origin of life and the evolution of the universe and Earth's climate.

In sum, developments in biology imply strong support for psychologists to adopt a person–environment or transactional perspective across their scientific and professional domains. The principle in synthetic biology of diverse and dynamic patterns of organization might best aid, for example, psychologists' quest to understand the nature of human consciousness. At a macro-level of analysis, the "Gaia hypothesis" about the interdependent, active relationship between the Earth and its surrounding atmosphere (Lovelock, 2006) also underscores the importance of focusing on the context of relationships in psychological theory, research, practice, and education.

Fuzzy logic

In ordinary language individuals describe aspects of nature and concepts with the use of adverbs on a sliding scale. When speaking of weapons, for example, a sword is a weapon to a "very great" degree, but a fountain pen "scarcely" qualifies. Humans employ linguistic devices, termed "hedges," to handle complexity. Hedges include adverbs like "very," probabilities such as "likely," quantifiers like "most," and possibilities like "that's impossible."

On the other hand, humans seem to have a tendency towards relying on precision as a means of smoothly handling complex information. Traditionally, scientists, mathematicians, logicians, and philosophers have encouraged human beings to create sharp distinctions between two or more natural objects or concepts. In Aristotelian logic a thing cannot both be and not be; it must be either one thing or another. Thus, formal logical thinking demands that things are true or false, logical or illogical.

In contrast, fuzzy logic "reflects how people actually think" by assigning gradations of meaning (McNeill & Freiberger, 1993, p. 12). Ordinary human life, especially those aspects mediated by language, requires a conceptual explanatory system that accounts for complexity, variability, and absence of precision. Fuzzy logic is all about gradations in the meaning of the descriptive and inferential language that scientists use in reference to observations.

Fuzzy rather than crisp and precise measurement more accurately estimates reality, because uncertainty and imprecision are the norm in nature, even though humans seem to crave certainty.

In sum, the implication of fuzzy logic for Psychology is that it exposes the dubious nature of strong faith in measurement and statistical analyses. Both the act of measurement and the use of statistical techniques to make sense of numerical observations with absolute certainty are questionable. Fuzzy logic adds another critical dimension to the historical problems of psychologists' investigative language and uncritical reliance on quantification.

Part 2 conclusion

Developments in contemporary natural science suggest **three principles** that bear implications for psychological theory, research, and practice:

- Understanding the connectedness of all natural phenomena is a central theme in the Gaia hypothesis and in relativity theory, while diverse and dynamic patterns of organization represent synthetic biology.
- Any kind of scientific inquiry is an inherently transactional process between knower and known (Manicas & Secord, 1983).
- Measurement of natural objects present limits to certainty and precision, because the observer and observed influence each other.

These principles prompt concern about psychologists' faith in literal applications of outmoded scientific principles and suggest alternative epistemological principles and investigative practice.

From the perspective of critical history, the objects of investigation in any science have a history of human observation that has not remained static across time and cultural settings. Moreover, psychological objects obviously are more socially and historically embedded than the inanimate objects of the natural sciences and more susceptible to the mutual influence between the material and the personal, the known and the knower. Psychologists' subjectivity affects their scientific activity, because they are intimately connected with the animate objects of their inquiry. Figure 12.1, *Earth*, a painting by Giuseppe Arcimboldo (c. 1570), suggests the connectedness between human beings and nature.

Developments in the natural sciences imply that a more scientifically credible position for psychologists would be to adopt the principle of intersubjectivity in their methodology. Thus, a relational understanding of investigation and interpretation that takes subjectivity into account is more appropriate for Psychology. This recommendation echoes what critical theorists and critical psychologists, whom we discuss next, have proposed concerning studying psychological phenomena.

Part 3 Critical theory and critical psychologies

In this section, we review twentieth-century and current critical approaches to mainstream Psychology, beginning with the social philosophy known as critical theory. We focus on three critical theorists: **Max Horkheimer** (1895–1973), Herbert Marcuse, and Jürgen

Figure 12.1 Giuseppe Arcimboldo's painting *Earth* suggests the connectedness between human beings and nature

Habermas. Next we discuss diverse critical approaches that psychologists have advanced. We include US psychologists Gordon Allport and Amedeo Giorgi, German psychologist Klaus Holzkamp, and current critical psychology of which there are many varieties.

Although some psychologists use the term "critical psychology" for their own position (e.g., Fox, Prilleltensky, & Austin, 2009; Hook, 2004; Sloan, 2000; Walkerdine, 2002), others are critical of the mainstream but do not use the label (e.g., Bradley, 2005; Danziger, 1990, 1997, 2008; Watkins & Shulman, 2008). Or they frame their critical stance as applying critical thinking to Psychology without claiming to propose a radical alternative (e.g., Slife, Reber, & Richardson, 2005). Very prominent in, but not limited to, critical psychology are cultural-historical (Marxist), feminist, social-constructionist, and more recently, postcolonial critiques. All these positions have fuelled the literature on the limitations of mainstream Psychology.

Critical theory

The forerunners of critical theory were Charles Darwin, Karl Marx, Friedrich Nietzsche, and Sigmund Freud, all of whom had an impact on Psychology. As masters of suspicion, they elaborately uncovered how individuals create false consciousness, generally produced by personal or social motives that remain hidden.

Critical theory was a research programme on the relation between individuals and society, which German philosophers and social scientists developed in the 1930s at the Institute for

Social Research in Frankfurt. The principal first-generation figures were Max Horkheimer, Erich Fromm, Theodor Adorno, and Herbert Marcuse. Jürgen Habermas belongs to the second generation.

Employing Marxian ideas, Horkheimer ([1937] 1992) distinguished traditional from critical theory. For him, traditional theory applied logic, mathematics, and deduction for the assessment of its ideas. Rejecting the standard separation between values and research and between knowledge and action, he argued that the narrow focus of traditional theory hid the social formation of scientific facts and the historical character of research objects.

Horkheimer proposed an alternative theory to critically assess the separation of individual and society. He grounded "critical theory" on a moral foundation by recommending that critical theorists engage in the struggle for the abolition of social injustice and for the reorganization of society to meet everyone's needs. Marcuse and Habermas in different ways extended critical theory's basic orientation.

Herbert Marcuse

Kant had urged his readers to rely on their own capacity for reason by which he celebrated reliance on rational thought as opposed to authority. This challenge greatly appealed to followers of the Enlightenment. Critical theorists conceded that reason could facilitate meaningful dialogue among humans to address, discuss, and solve problems. But reason also can be used as an instrument to solve technical and social problems under a given state authority. Critical theorists invented the term *instrumental rationality* to capture this phenomenon.

An example of instrumental rationality is the Nazi regime's programmes of the Holocaust and Nazi death-camps. Some critical theorists made the argument that Nazi authorities engaged in a type of rationality that became irrational, because they did not examine the meaning of their actions, but instead concentrated on the most efficient administration, organization, and application of mass death.

Marcuse's particular contribution to critical theory was to identify the impact of instrumental rationality on individuals. He asserted that instrumental reason is the product of a one-dimensional society that produces one-dimensional human beings, riveted on consuming disposable commodities.

Marcuse (1964) identified the consequences of living a one-dimensional life. Individuals struggle with a world of alienating bureaucracies and popular culture that tends to banalize human suffering, turning it into media entertainment. As a result, a one-dimensional culture that trivializes human desires and pain desensitizes individuals to one another's psychological and social circumstances. The impact is that individuals in societies dominated by instrumental rationality desire to retreat from complexity, are deeply skeptical and cynical about "society" in general, and have difficulty finding meaning and purpose in life. Marcuse's interest was in emancipating people from this kind of needless suffering.

The method that Marcuse employed is known as *immanent critique*, that is, criticism of a particular system or ideology by the terms of the systems or ideology itself. His intention was to identify the gap between the espoused principles and actual social practices and to encourage corrective action. He had strong faith in the capacities of human beings to reconstruct themselves.

In sum, Marcuse explored the question, how did the modernist Enlightenment with its celebration of the power of reason itself evolve into undemocratic, alienating, and irrational systems? He exposed a central contradiction in modernity, namely, the deification of reason, rationality, and technology, which produced hyper-specialization, infatuation with rational control, and subservience to authoritarian influences. Psychologists who profess concern for individual and communal well-being would do well to absorb Marcuse's societal analysis, which can expose the social forces that impinge upon actualization of Psychology's ideal of promoting human welfare.

Jürgen Habermas

Like Marcuse, Habermas is concerned about the status of individuals in a world of inequities. He argues that each self is composed of three aspects: a natural world, a social world, and an inner reflective world. But all three aspects are under siege because of the difficulties in trying to understand one another that human beings encounter in everyday life. Individuals' difficulties primarily pertain to problems of communication and interpretation, hence his concern with "ideal speech situations" (see below). Habermas's concerns clearly can be connected with scientific and professional psychologists' interests and espoused social values.

In the 1960s and 1970s, Habermas published important works on epistemology and influenced critical discussions in Germany on social-sciences methodology. In his attempt to develop an epistemological foundation for critical theory Habermas ([1968] 1972) incorporated Anglo-American philosophy of language into his thought. This linguistic turn of critical theory indicated a shift away from its Marxian roots and was central for his communicative foundation for social theory. In his later writings he embraced psychologists such as Jean Piaget and **Lawrence Kohlberg** (1927–1987) in his social philosophy and integrated traditional sociological theory into his concept of society.

Initially Habermas ([1968] 1972) analyzed the relationship between knowledge and interests. Based on this conception, he delineated three qualitatively different categories of science, each guided by a different interest: empirical-analytic (i.e., the natural sciences), historical-hermeneutical (i.e., the interpretive sciences), and critical sciences (e.g., psycho-analysis). One can apply Habermas's conception of different knowledge-functions to **three types of Psychology** – natural-science, human-science, and critical (Teo, 1999) – as described in Box 12.1.

Habermas (1984) argues that, ideally, individuals form themselves in relation to other people through dialogue. He proposes an intrinsic survival-inclination in human beings, which is the capacity for "critical emancipation," meaning the inclination to free oneself from oppressive circumstances through critical thought. He asserts that individuals have an interest in demystifying distortions of reality. These distortions (e.g., fighting a "war on terrorism" to make one's nation peaceful) are expressed in the ideology of ruling groups in systematic ways and serve to maintain economic or political oppression.

Habermas claims that humans have a built-in desire to be understood in their communicative acts. He identifies **four conditions** that must be met for undistorted communication to occur:

- There must be symmetry, that is, equal power in human relationships such that each party has an equal chance to talk and listen.

Box 12.1 Applying Habermas to Psychology

(1) Natural-science psychologists investigate well-defined and specific research problems. They reduce their subject matter to components to produce detailed facts about psychological objects or events. They intend to provide knowledge of psychological laws, using analytic methodology (dividing the whole). Since the twentieth century, with some exceptions, adherents have considered only quantitative methods, preferably laboratory experiments, appropriate.

Natural-scientific Psychology also is associated with the traditional philosophies of science, often labelled as positivist epistemologies. Accordingly, its adherents operate on the premise that they can attain the truth of an object through more sophisticated, future research. They believe in the continuous progress of knowledge regarding psychological functioning.

Over the decades, functionalism, behaviourism, neobehaviourism, structuralism, cognitivism, and neuroscience have served as natural-science psychologists' schools of thought or meta-theoretical frameworks.

(2) Human-science psychologists produce knowledge primarily about a subject for a subject, which may be an individual, group, community, or a whole culture. Their basic methodology is synthetic, putting together psychological parts into a larger whole. The scope of human-science Psychology is the human psyche in its totality. Hermeneutic epistemologies represent corresponding philosophies of knowledge, while qualitative methods traditionally have been appropriate for this knowledge-function.

The premise in this psychological tradition is that the provision of meaning allows individuals, groups, communities, and cultures to achieve their potential. The notion that humans can transform the status quo into something more compassionate and just motivates psychological intervention. Hermeneutic, some phenomenological, existential, humanistic, and dialogical psychologies as well as psychoanalysis fall into this perspective.

(3) Critical psychologists produce critical knowledge about Psychology as a field. The status of this knowledge-function differs from the others, because its level of inquiry is often meta-psychological and it operates from a distance regarding the other perspectives. Critical psychologists assume that critical reflection can change and improve theories, concepts, methods, and practices of the psychological community.

Critical perspectives on Psychology are not a new phenomenon. In more than a century of discussions about crises in Psychology, some type of critical psychology has been integral to the discipline's history.

- Sincerity is essential, in that each person should mean what he or she has to say.
- There is a truth condition, that is, that everyone should disclose what he or she believes to be true.
- Everyone should attempt to say what is right morally.

If these four conditions are met, then an "ideal speech situation" of equality and free speech exists, enabling individuals to change their minds, if they hear a better argument.

Critics of Habermas's proposal for undistorted communication, however, claim that as an abstracted dialogue it ignores power and the structures of domination produced by class, gender, and ethnocultural status.

Critics and critical psychology

Human-science critiques of Psychology as a natural science surfaced across the twentieth century, although they tended to fall on deaf ears. William Stern had questioned his contemporaries' natural-science concepts and methodology. After World War II, Gordon Allport, whom Stern influenced, criticized the natural-science approach. Several decades later another US psychologist, **Amedeo Giorgi** (b. 1931), advanced a critique from a phenomenological perspective, while German psychologist Klaus Holzkamp promoted a critical psychology beginning in 1970. Other contemporary critiques were termed "dialectical" (e.g., Riegel, 1978) and "critical emancipatory" psychology (Sullivan, 1984).

Gordon Allport

When he launched personality psychology in the 1930s, Allport adopted Wilhelm Windelband's conversion of Dilthey's natural-science/human-science distinction into nomothetic and idiographic methodological programmes (R. Smith, 1997). Struggling to reconcile natural-science and human-science psychology in his own career, Allport was troubled by contemporary natural-science psychologists' admiration of physics. He considered psychological subject matter to be more complex than the natural sciences and criticized the exclusion of the individual from Psychology (Nicholson, 2003).

Reflecting on US society's postwar problems, Allport (1947) asked what Psychology could contribute to their solution and to the improvement of human relationships, but in his view academic psychology's concepts and research findings were rather inadequate. He proposed that, instead of pursuing the mechanistic models of behaviourism, neobehaviourism, and even psychoanalysis with its developmental determinism, Psychology should follow a human-scientific programme. To be a meaningful discipline, he argued, Psychology should actualize the intentions of moral science, which recognized morality as a central feature of mental life.

Allport's critique facilitated the eventual but partial rehabilitation of human-scientific reflections in North American Psychology in the form of humanistic psychology. Humanistic psychologists, as Allport did, straddled the two traditions, with one foot in human-science concepts and the other foot in natural-science methodology. Inevitably, the latter co-opted the former so that mainstream Psychology eventually diluted or absorbed humanistic psychologists' criticisms of natural-science Psychology.

Amedeo Giorgi

Reviving interest in Dilthey's critique for a US audience, Giorgi (1970) contended that Psychology should not be part of the natural sciences. At the same time he argued that a human-science Psychology could retain its genuinely scientific character. A relatively small group of psychologists has practised Giorgi's orientation in a few US institutions.

The major points of Giorgi's (1970) critique of natural-scientific Psychology were that it lacked unity by growing through proliferation rather than internal progress; it lacked direction because of unformulated goals; it pursued an unwarranted emulation of the natural sciences; it was unable to investigate significant phenomena in a meaningful way; it lacked holistic methods; it was insensitive to and failed to do justice to the human person; and it failed to be relevant to the life-world. Giorgi believed that the root of these deficiencies was psychologists' adoption of a natural-scientific viewpoint.

Klaus Holzkamp

The most comprehensive critical psychology was advanced by German psychologist, Klaus Holzkamp, whose international influence continues, even though there are no English translations yet of his books (Painter, Marvakis, & Mos, 2009). Initially Holzkamp identified basic differences between physics and Psychology and rejected mainstream psychologists' physicalism. Physicists study inanimate objects, he argued; they engage in a subject–object relationship with their subject matter. By contrast, psychologists study animate objects; they engage in a subject–subject relationship with their subject matter.

Holzkamp argued that the problems of Psychology constituted ideological influences that reflected the sociohistorical context in which Psychology exists. According to his Marxian, anti-capitalist analysis, traditional psychologists view the individual as concrete and society as abstract, but they abstract individuals from their social-historical contexts, a practice that stems from the cultural ideology of individualism.

Distinguishing between psychologists' artificial world of laboratory investigations and real-life settings, Holzkamp (1972) contended that the sophistication of experimental methodology and inferential statistics led to the reduction of reality in psychological research. In real-life settings, psychologists investigate human problems in social contexts where all variables, which laboratory researchers control or exclude, show effects. Thus, he argued, Psychology cannot achieve technical relevance.

Moreover, even if it could, technical relevance alone would imply working for the powerful in society, unless psychologists were committed to "emancipatory relevance." Psychologists accomplish emancipatory relevance when their research helps individuals become more aware of their societal and social dependencies. Holzkamp advocated binding theory to practice, fostering a free and symmetric dialogue within research purged of power, and developing a socially responsible Psychology.

Later, building on prior work by Alexei Leontiev, Holzkamp (1983) attempted to develop basic categories for Psychology in order to understand the specificities of human subjectivity, which for him, was the only viable Psychology. Yet viewing the person as part of a larger historical and socioeconomic context did not contradict taking the agency of individual subjects or social actors and their societies seriously.

Holzkamp termed his Psychology *Subjektwissenschaft*, meaning science from the subject's (social actor's) standpoint. Investigators should be able to capture this standpoint. For example, in psychotherapy research it is more important to learn how a person contributes to her or his own change than how therapy itself shapes a person (Dreier, 2007). Given his orientation to the subject's standpoint, Holzkamp transformed psychological research into a dialogical relationship of exchange between investigators and individuals on problems that subjects, not investigators, pose. Investigators exchange knowledge for individuals' experience, then jointly develop a conceptual understanding sensible and beneficial to the individuals (C. Tolman, 2009).

Present critical psychology

Because many varieties of critical psychology have emerged (Dafermos, Marvakis, & Triliva, 2006), it is difficult to identify a common ground beyond the dissatisfaction with the mainstream and the need to make Psychology ethically, politically relevant. Besides, many who systematically assess the discipline's fundamentals choose not to adopt the term. But generally, critical psychology is an international movement of psychologists who apply critiques of power, domination, and oppression to Psychology and who promote empowering dialogue and emancipation concerning all aspects of psychological theory, research, practice, and education in the discipline.

Turning away from a mechanistic and individualistic approach to human mental life, critical psychologists advocate understanding its nature as active and social. Some critics assert that psychologists should focus on describing how the personal and social are intertwined in intersubjective experience and become meaningful in present contexts of human action and should reorient their theories, methods, education, and, most of all, their ethical-political standpoint to oppose oppression and foster social justice (e.g., Bradley, 2005). Kurt Lewin, for instance, considered the human social contexts that gave behaviour its meaning and he engaged in social reform projects and practised action research, although some regard his work as reformist.

Those critical psychologists who promote cultural-historical approaches have argued that the environment, culture, and history are not just extraneous variables, as many mainstream psychologists have dealt with them. Rather, context is interwoven with the very fabric of personal identity. For example, Lev Vygotsky's ([1935] 1978) concept of the zone of proximal development challenged the individualistic nature of Psychology (Roth & Lee, 2007).

In terms of methodologies for critical psychology, no consistent one exists. Many critical psychologists aspire to use methods that strive to do justice to the subject matter and that capture the active, meaning-oriented, intentional nature of human mental life embedded in sociohistorical contexts. Some critical psychologists have incorporated psychoanalysis, often Lacanian psychoanalysis, an approach that privileges subjectivity in research (Parker, 2003). Other critical psychologists emphasize the transformative potential of research (Fine, 2006). This term means that critical inquiry not only addresses the status quo but also provides knowledge on how to change it.

Some critical psychologists contend that qualitative methods are more appropriate for understanding human subjectivity than quantitative ones. However, it is evident that certain issues should be addressed quantitatively. In fact, quantitative methods can be critical and can challenge the status quo (Martín-Baró, 1994).

For example, to investigate whether men interrupt women more often than vice versa, one can begin with a quantitative method in order to measure the frequency of interruptions by men and by women. Thus, quantitative methods are not inherently problematic, because the choice of methods depends on the subject matter, the specific question, or the particular issue. The problem is not quantitative methods per se; the problem is giving primacy to natural-scientific methodology without considering the object of the investigation.

Part 3 conclusion

Critical theory, past critiques of Psychology, and the diverse forms of current critical psychology have provided important insights into the relationship of society, science, and the individual. These approaches can illuminate the emancipatory potential of the dialectical unity of theory and practice, known as *praxis*, which connotes a clear moral intention. However, although the critical psychology movement might be stirring the intellectual pot, this approach is still marginal and has barely registered on mainstream Psychology's radar screen.

On the other hand, what's "critical" about critical psychology? In our view, advancement of critical psychology requires both self-reflection on critical psychologists' assumptions and an understanding of the history of various critical movements in Psychology (Teo, 2005, 2009). Following are **four problems** in critical psychology:

(1) Some critical psychologists fail to acknowledge the history of human-science approaches to the discipline. But since Psychology's formal emergence, phenomenological, existential, hermeneutic, and psychoanalytic psychologists have taken the road less travelled by natural-science psychologists, placing the meaning of human experience from the individual's standpoint at the heart of their concerns. In fact, various forms of psychoanalysis (e.g., Fromm's social psychoanalysis) have featured a critical orientation to society.

(2) Critical psychologists do not consider how their movement, which is an intellectual one not a political or social movement, will resist the capacity that mainstream Psychology historically has possessed to co-opt impulses for fundamental change in the discipline, just as capitalist society does to social movements (Parker, 2009).

For example, after its so-called "radical" founding in 1936 the Society for the Psychological Study of Social Issues soon became a mainstream organization shoring up the disciplinary status quo (Harris, 1986). Presently, some critical psychologists claim that US community psychology was originally a quasi-radical branch of Psychology, then became reformist. But the historical evidence clearly shows that US community psychology emerged from the reformist community mental health movement and always has avoided links to radical politics (Walsh, 1987).

(3) Although some critical psychologists use the language of radical change to describe Psychology and society, as if they advocated actual political engagement, they do not address how concretely they might implement their proposals for "social transformation." A few critical psychologists, following Holzkamp, are specifically anti-capitalist in that they analyze monopoly capitalism, including its ideologies and conformist academic disciplines (e.g., Psychology), and they aim to revolutionize society (e.g., Parker, 2009). But some apparently accept capitalist socioeconomic structures and ideologies despite their rhetoric of social transformation and do not analyze how these structures and ideologies neutralize and co-opt impulses for social change.

(4) Critical psychologists do not address how natural-science Psychology colleagues, who represent the vast majority, would respond to the changes that critical psychologists envision for Psychology. Critical psychologists ignore the interpersonal and organizational processes and institutional structures within which academic psychologists work. Until critical psychologists address these processes and structures and the political conflict that their desired changes would evoke in Psychology, their ideas are unlikely to have any transformative disciplinary impact (Walsh-Bowers, 2010).

One major social conflict in Psychology's history with major implications for theory, research, and applications is the status of women and feminism in the discipline.

Part 4   Feminist critiques

Gender is another aspect of Western culture that has shaped Psychology's theories, research, and professional practices. The term *feminism* designates theory and action committed to political, economic, and social equality, although there are politically conservative feminists. As a social practice, feminism typically means direct action promoting women's rights and interests.

The common feminist notion that "the personal is the political" evolved during the Vietnam War era as "women's liberation" became more socially prominent. This new social consciousness entailed two positions: "emotional experience and social organization could not ultimately be separated," and "oppression and liberation alike took internal as well as external forms" (Herman, 1995, p. 277). In a sense, the feminist movement contributed to public questioning of the boundaries between the private and the public and between the individual and society.

Adopting this social consciousness, feminist psychologists, whose movement emerged in the 1970s, examined mainstream Psychology, found it deficient, and began to propose alternatives (Rutherford, Vaughn-Blount, & Ball, 2010). But rather than a single point of view, multiple feminist perspectives have prevailed in Psychology. Before we describe the diverse forms of feminist psychology and research orientations, we identify different types of feminism.

Types of feminism

In feminism **four types** can be identified – liberal, socialist, and romantic, all of which are indebted to early movements for women's equality, and "third-wave" feminism, which is a response to the second wave (Rebick, 2005).

- Liberal feminists aim to achieve gender equality. They focus on ensuring that women are equal to men in all aspects of public and private life, including science. Liberal feminists stress equal legal, property, employment, educational, health, and safety rights and duties. But until recent decades they have tended to neglect class structures and ethnocultural differences and disadvantages that benefit economically privileged White women.
- Socialist feminists emphasize fundamentally restructuring the organization of labour at work and home, and they strive to change the cultural ideology that socializes girls and

women into subordinate roles in society and relationships. But socialist feminists tend to neglect psychological factors (e.g., internalized patriarchal values) that serve to perpetuate male domination.

- The varieties of romantic feminists – traditional, reform, and radical – share belief in essential differences between the genders and the view that women are more psychologically pure than men, whom the male-dominated world allegedly corrupts. Reform-romantic feminists, for example, hold that women have superior inherent capacities for empathy and social relations. Adherents overlook the possibility that women are as capable as men of violence, competitiveness, and oppression of others.

- Some women are discontented with the three forms of second-wave feminism, which they perceive as ineffective (Rebick, 2005). Calling themselves third-wave feminists, they are not committed to any particular ideology. Rather, aspiring to effect societal and institutional change that will benefit women of all colours, creeds, and sexual orientations, they resist the glacial pace of social change for women.

Feminist critique of science

Since the second women's movement, feminist scholars have evaluated the gendered nature of natural science and its epistemology. Some concluded that natural scientists' preference for variables, devotion to quantification, reliance on abstract concepts, focus on separation and compartmentalization as opposed to studying interaction and interdependence, and rigid objectivity reflected a masculine worldview and practice. A feminist recasting of objectivity and subjectivity suggests that scientific knowledge is a process of creating intersubjective, humanly situated knowledge that is only ever partial and is always contestable. That is, investigators' social locations influence particular research questions, the investigative tools adopted, and the interpretations of findings. Thus, some feminists have redefined science to become located, partial knowledge (Harding, 1986).

Feminist standpoint theorists claim that women (or feminists), but not men, are the ideal creators of scientific knowledge. Proponents consider women less partial and more objective in understanding the social world, because it is in their interest to disclose the truth (e.g., Hartsock, 1985). These theorists suggest that women possess a unique standpoint from which they approach knowledge and scientific inquiry. Standpoint theorists emphasize beginning with women's lives in order to explore repressed aspects of social reality and develop a politically engaged theory that operates from the social experience of subjugated women.

Rethinking objectivity

Exploring the association between scientific objectivity and gender, Evelyn Fox Keller (1985) contended that conventional scientific thought is based on masculine ideals, metaphors, and practices. She argued that the emphasis on power and control, widespread in the rhetoric of Western science historically, represents the projection of male consciousness and expresses a preoccupation with a dominant and adversarial relationship with nature. Moreover, male-centred science divides reality into two parts, the knower (the subjects of study) and the known (the objects of study), with an autonomous knower purportedly in control and separated from the known.

According to Keller, the separation of scientist and subject matter opposes the female-centred notion of connectedness and at the same time reinforces cultural beliefs about the "naturally" masculine character of science. Historically, objectivity, science, and masculinity have been linked so that science and masculinity are valued and women's capacities denigrated. Because men have had more power in society and dominated science, the masculine way of relating to the world has had a higher social value. However, for Keller, the association of objectivity with masculinity does not reflect intrinsic biological differences between men and women, but rather cultural beliefs.

Keller argued that many female scientists found it valuable to establish a relationship between themselves and what they were investigating, that is, between the knower and the known. In opposition to the traditional, static concept of objectivity, which separates subject (knower) and object (known), Keller proposed *dynamic objectivity*, a term that embraces subjectivity, connectedness, and empathy towards the subject matter.

To show dynamic objectivity, Keller (1983, 1985) analyzed the work of Barbara McClintock (1902–1992) recipient of a Nobel Prize in medicine for her discovery of mobile genetic elements. McClintock described her methodological approach as empathetic towards the maize plants she studied. Thus, she rejected subject–object dualism. Keller concluded that McClintock adopted a more feminine approach towards the object of her study. Although aware that this approach was not typical of all female scientists, Keller characterized McClintock's interactive, non-hierarchical model as more reflective of feminine values.

Feminist critique of psychology

Since Psychology's inception there has been a substantial lack of research on women's concerns and an emphasis on gender differences rather than similarities. Within dominant discourses, psychologists regard gender differences, and women's behaviour, in particular, as a function of biology or nature. Mainstream psychologists have emphasized individualistic explanations for behaviour, while ignoring social, economic, and political contexts and their influences on psychological functions.

From different perspectives, feminist psychologists have criticized mainstream Psychology on several grounds. Feminists challenged psychologists for the ways in which they used research and knowledge to support, directly or indirectly, traditional gender-roles and existing gender/power relationships. For example, they have raised consciousness regarding male-centred theories of personality that assumed that the personality development of girls and women is identical to boys' and men's. Personality theorists have believed that the goal of healthy personality development is psychological autonomy, rather than relatedness or interdependence.

Current feminist psychologists are committed to overcoming stereotypes regarding gender and eliminating the biases that oppress women. However, the identification of problems and programmes for the solution of these problems varies significantly. Three feminist critiques of Psychology have been prominent: feminist empiricism, which is the most prominent perspective in the field of women's psychology; feminist standpoint theory; and feminist postmodernism (S. Wilkinson, 2001).

Feminist empiricism

Advocates of "non-sexist" (or "gender-fair") research, who are also known as "feminist empiricists," criticize Psychology as lacking relevance to women because of empirical deficiencies. They view sexist claims, biases, and errors regarding women (and men) as the result of inadequate science. Their solution is the rigorous and systematic application of the highest standards of science.

Feminist empiricists believe that research methods, including laboratory experiments and statistical analyses, are basically sound, but they must be followed more objectively. In other words, feminist empiricists assert that androcentric science is not objective, because it is biased against women; therefore, it is "bad science." They aim to eliminate sexist bias at each stage of the research process; they study topics relevant to women and reject male psychology as standard; they include more women as participants or researchers; and they avoid biased measures and research designs.

Feminist empiricists criticize some feminist scholars for alleged lack of scientific objectivity and essentialism in their work. They argue that feminism can be assimilated into traditional methodology and that all methods can be feminist. They oppose sexist bias not mainstream science itself.

The research of some early psychologists (e.g., Helen Thompson Woolley) qualifies as feminist empiricism, because they used accepted laboratory techniques for challenging contemporary, sexist beliefs about women. In addition, a huge literature on gender differences and similarities exists, supported by sophisticated statistical techniques (Hyde, 2005). Consequently, gender has become less relevant as an explanatory variable, and over time many investigators have had difficulty finding statistically significant gender differences.

Feminist standpoint theory

An example of feminist standpoint theory is **Carol Gilligan's** (b. 1936) influential deconstruction of Kohlberg's theory of moral development. Basing his ideas on Piaget's studies of morality in early and middle childhood, Kohlberg investigated the moral development of US boys over twenty years. To assess moral judgment, he used moral dilemmas in which one value was in conflict with another (e.g., the right to live vs. the right to property). Based on his findings, he proposed a theory of moral development that included invariant universal stages.

Gilligan (1982), of course, observed that Kohlberg used only male participants in his original study. But she argued more cogently that his and other psychologists' theories do not capture the experiences of girls and women, which are based on a morality of care, not just a morality of abstract justice. Gilligan raised an important question: do traditional theories of Psychology misrepresent female experiences and voices? Although one cannot answer this question *a priori* in either direction, psychologists who propose a theory should ensure its gender validity (see also Harding, 2008).

Postmodern feminist psychology

Postmodern feminist psychologists share some premises with feminist empiricists, but they replace androcentric values with feminist ones (Bohan, 2002). **Three premises** of postmodern feminist psychologists are:

- Human behaviour is shaped complexly by biology and social, historical, and political forces.
- Science is not purely objective or value-free but is informed by subjectivity, personal experience is an important source for scientific theory, and scientific knowledge is always socially and politically constructed.
- Psychology is a social and political institution, not an abstract intellectual exercise isolated from social history.

Postmodern feminists regard scientific research and social-political activism as complementary, for feminist research can facilitate social change by documenting inequities. Moreover, they consider values to be ever-present in the research process and to be an important source of ideas for theory, research, and practice. Because their research commitment diverges quite markedly from traditional methodology, postmodern feminists have not made a significant impression on mainstream Psychology.

Feminist research alternatives

In proposing alternatives to androcentric Psychology and traditional feminist empiricism, feminist-standpoint and postmodern feminist investigators contend that Psychology needs a unique feminist methodology (Febbraro, 1997; Campbell & Wasco, 2000). Instead of experiments, questionnaires, and tests, feminist researchers mainly should use qualitative methods, such as interviews and personal documents, and employ mostly female instead of male participants. Feminist-standpoint and postmodern feminist psychologists recommend establishing trust between researchers and participants, recognizing sociocultural influences on mental life, and reflecting on the relevance of values in research practices.

Postmodern feminist research methods, ideally, are relational, participatory, and non-hierarchical. They feature an intersubjective research relationship and collaboration with research participants. Instead of "data" (i.e., from the Latin root, things freely given), which really are "capta" (i.e., from the Latin, things seized from subordinates), they evoke "communicata" (i.e., from the Latin, things shared in dialogue) (Walsh, 1989). Postmodern feminist psychologists devote special attention to incorporating the voices of marginalized groups, and they strive to produce research with a social-action component to achieve equality.

In sum, much of the research debate among feminist perspectives concerns quantitative and qualitative methods. Some claim that conventional implementation of quantitative methods creates a hierarchical research relationship, removes behaviour from its natural context, and converts women's experiences into masculine categories. These critics favour qualitative methods, because they perceive them as correcting biases in quantitative methods, as useful in identifying and representing women's experiences, and as legitimating women's lives as the basis for making knowledge. Other feminists claim that qualitative methods offer no inherent protection against sexist bias and beliefs.

> **Small-group discussion.** What exposure have you had to feminist research in Psychology? What social conditions are necessary to engage in feminist research?

Part 4 conclusion

Theoretically speaking, liberal feminism has informed feminist empiricism in Psychology. Like liberal feminists who seek reform in legal, institutional, and private inequalities but not radical change of society's foundations, feminist empiricists seek reform but not radical change in research, because they support the conventions of psychological science. Feminist empiricism appeals to many academics, because it does not challenge mainstream epistemology and standard methods. Furthermore, feminist empiricists can rely on institutional and disciplinary acceptance, because their research identifies problems of inadequate science not of science itself.

Reform-romantic feminism, which holds that women are superior to men in interpersonal capacities, has informed feminist-standpoint theory in Psychology. Like romantic feminists who claim an essential gender difference, feminist-standpoint psychologists identify domains in which women are inherently superior or different to men. The influence of this approach on feminist psychology seems to be waning.

Socialist feminism with its emphasis on the socially constructed nature of society and the function of science in patriarchal society has informed postmodern feminist psychology. Like socialist feminists who press for fundamental changes in hierarchical social structures and in a cultural ideology of women's subordination, postmodern feminist psychologists seek to restructure the very nature of making knowledge in Psychology, particularly about girls and women, in theory, investigative practice, and social applications. Although postmodernism in Psychology appears to be less influential than it was previously (see next section), postmodern feminist psychologists remain active in promoting a different orientation to Psychology than other feminists.

Part 5 Postmodern perspectives

Postmodern psychologists also have challenged the theory, research, and practice of mainstream Psychology. They are skeptical about psychologists' capacities to generate objective, universal laws of behaviour on the basis of laboratory experiments and empirical–statistical research. Instead, postmodern thinkers emphasize multiple perspectives on (as the multiple faces of Buddha show in Figure 12.2) and provisional explanations for psychological phenomena and believe that scientists can only ever produce localized, partial knowledge. This position has led to various critiques of mainstream Psychology and its positivist conception of knowledge.

However, the term "postmodernism" itself is ambiguous and is used differently across disciplines, which render understanding its discourses in a precise way difficult (Rosenau, 1992). We use "postmodern" to mean the era that follows the "modern" period that spanned the sixteenth to the twentieth century and coincided with the Scientific Revolution, the

Figure 12.2 This statue depicts the multi-perspectival capacity of Buddhahood

Enlightenment, and the emergence of the sciences and professions. Aiming to liberate humanity from ignorance, modernist scholars emphasized reason and progress.

Postmodernists challenged modernists' track record. Instead of reason and progress they see slavery, colonialism and imperialism, subjugation of women, world wars, genocides, the Holocaust, and the atomic bombing of Hiroshima and Nagasaki. To them, modernity was oppressive not liberatory.

Based on French philosopher **Jean-François Lyotard's** (1924–1998) rejection of meta-narratives, postmodernists challenge all totalizing thought systems, such as Christianity, Marxism, fascism, capitalism, liberal democracy, liberal feminism, rationalism, empiricism, and science. They argue that these worldviews predetermine questions and answers. Philosopher Paul Feyerabend (1975), for example, contended that science resembles astrology or primitive cults and scientists use rhetoric to support their position on empirical facts. Because in his view any strict method hinders the course of science, Feyerabend pleaded for a single methodological rule: *Anything goes.*

Although one can locate the origin of postmodern reflections in Friedrich Nietzsche's writings, more recent antecedents are the works of philosophers Jean-François Lyotard and Michel Foucault. In Psychology, postmodernism found its expression in the writings of Kenneth Gergen and others.

Jean-François Lyotard

A leader of postmodernism, Lyotard established the critical standpoint of ending meta-narratives or grand thought-systems. He focused on the epistemological dimension of postmodernity and defined the postmodern attitude as incredulity towards meta-narratives, including science. Postmodernism seemed to render grand narratives vacuous.

Lyotard (1984) identified **two grand narratives of modernity** that secured societal legitimation:

- The *political* meta-narrative suggested that humanity became the agent of its own liberation by making systematic knowledge. According to this narrative, science emancipated humanity from superstition, ignorance, and oppression to achieve freedom and dignity.
- The *philosophical* meta-narrative referred to the progressive unfolding of knowledge and ultimate truth.

For Lyotard, since World War II both meta-narratives had lost their credibility, and the notion of science as a liberating and progressive instrument appeared meaningless. He argued that scientific knowledge was no more or less necessary than general narrative knowledge. Although scientific knowledge was intolerant of narrative knowledge, the former relied on the latter, because science could not legitimize its own activity.

In mainstream Psychology, the political meta-narrative has not played an explicit role historically. Natural-scientific psychologists have rejected political goals and social-ethical ideals, even though many pioneers of Psychology had utopian ambitions (Morawski, 1982) and psychologists have made direct contributions to war-making (Herman, 1995, Soldz, 2008). The philosophical meta-narrative of progressively unfolding knowledge and ultimate truth, however, has played a determinative role in Psychology, as the preceding chapters have shown.

Michel Foucault

Although often cited as a postmodern philosopher, in his later works Foucault rehabilitated subjectivity and enlightenment, which have been core targets of postmodern reflection. In his early studies he demonstrated that the history of mental illness, the definition of normality, the division between reason and unreason, and the identification of social and medical practices did not follow a rational process of knowledge accumulation, as traditional disciplinary historians have suggested, but rather a practice of exclusion.

Foucault ([1965] 1988), who was trained as a psychologist, demonstrated that during the Middle Ages and the Renaissance, madness was an accepted fact of daily life and did not elicit scholarly interest. He understood society's exclusion of madness and the subsequent rise of psychiatry in the context of seventeenth-century rationalist philosophy, whereby reason needed madness for its own definition.

Knowledge and power

Foucault is noted for his analysis of power, which, as a structural phenomenon, has been widely neglected in traditional discourses of Psychology. Drawing on Nietzsche, Foucault analyzed power's positive function in the administration of life and power's connection to the production of knowledge in the human sciences. For Foucault, power was an all-encompassing reality in which everyone was caught and participated (Hook, 2007).

When Foucault ([1975] 1977) analyzed the exercise of power in the context of criminal behaviour, its connection with punitive practices, and the modification of practices of power over time, he found that physical space was significant. A new form of punishment – centralized surveillance of totally visible prisoners and their self-surveillance in a panopticon – superseded corporal punishment. By similar means, he asserted, society administers efficient and effective systems of discipline and punishment.

Some feminist authors have welcomed Foucault's perspective because of the connection and transformation of power and the body. For instance, beauty standards might work as Foucault has described self-surveillance. If women can be conditioned to scrutinize their weight, beauty, health, and social behaviour perpetually, then there is no need for patriarchy to impose demands on them. Corporeal power and control of femininity can be reframed as individual choices and marketed.

Foucault ([1976] 1978) also tracked the development of professions' intrusions into highly personal domains of life and disguised forms of power over others. In previous centuries in Western societies, Christian pastors looked after each individual and knew their congregants' thoughts, feelings, wishes, and actions. With the rise to power of health and mental health professionals in the twentieth century, clinical psychologists and social workers adopted the pastoral mantle of authority and similarly engaged in surveillance of the population's intrapersonal and interpersonal problems in living. In this context, professional systems of clinical ethics become forms of power and control whereby supervisors in health-care institutions exercise surveillance over their supervisees to ensure adherence to ethical guidelines (A. Rossiter *et al.*, 2002).

One also can apply Foucauldian thought to the making of academic psychologists, as explained in Box 12.2. Foucault's studies open many critical points for reflection on Psychology's own disciplinary power in its institutions and techniques by which

Box 12.2 Applying Foucault to the making of academic psychologists

Canadian and US undergraduate students require high grades to enter university and four years for an honours bachelor's degree. The bachelor's curriculum in Psychology is heavily structured and requires many specific Psychology courses and the writing of a thesis, which itself follows specific structured criteria.

Students are carefully selected for graduate programmes, then directed by their supervisors. Each student has a place in a specific specialty-area, which calls for specific training and evaluation mechanisms. Students must adhere to allocated times for finishing the required courses and independent research in their programme. Faculty committees decide, based on disciplinary and university standards, when a student deserves the title of master or doctor.

Psychology faculty proceed through the ranks from assistant to associate to full professor in their institutions and from being a student member to full member, and to the highest rank, "fellow," in psychological organizations. Professors progress by ensuring that they meet peer standards for scholarly productivity. Assessment of productivity is a carefully structured and controlled system of faculty performance that rewards piecemeal production of marketable research papers in acceptable journals. The consistent acquisition of external grants has become a further requirement for faculty progress. In all these processes academics submit to and embrace power.

the fledgling psychologist is manipulated, trained, and formed to become an academic. The subject's moves from undergraduate and graduate student status to professor status are controlled and monitored, and power can intervene at each stage.

Methodology

Foucault developed a unique critical method. He avoided the use of the term "history," because it is linked with a kind of progressivism and a rational narrative. Instead, he used the terms archaeology and genealogy, adopting an anti-narrative so as to account for all the human contingencies involved.

Foucault's method entailed **five procedures**:

- Reversal, or taking into perspective a standard history and then reversing it.
- Marginality, examining the aspects of cultural history that have been excluded, thereby taking the focus away from what has traditionally been central.
- Discontinuity, searching for catastrophes, gaps, and breaks, as opposed to focusing on what is assumed to be necessary human linear progress.
- Materiality, looking at actual, concrete practices rather than at belief systems and ideologies.
- Specificity, focusing on single instances to illuminate larger points and claims.

Foucault initiated various methods of *discourse analysis*. In this critical approach scholars analyze written or spoken language as a social practice that is infused with human interests and biases. Discourse analysis is based on the premise that language is embedded in ideological, oppressive, or exploitative practices, which is an insight that some critical psychologists have taken up (Parker, 2002).

Postmodernism in psychology

The most prominent spokesperson for a postmodern approach to Psychology has been Kenneth Gergen, a personality and social psychologist. Initially he argued that psychological knowledge is not an objective reflection or a veridical map of the world but an artifact of human interaction. This notion of the socially constructed nature of psychological knowledge became the foundational premise of postmodern psychology.

Gergen (1985) also asserted that psychological theory and research should shift from the presumed ahistorical character of psychological objects and events to an appreciation of their social-historical dimensions. As described in previous chapters, psychological objects and events have undergone significant changes over time as well as across cultures. Thus, knowledge was not something that people possessed somewhere in their minds but something that they produced together.

Gergen (1990) did not believe in an independent subject matter of Psychology, because its objects are not real; rather, psychologists construct psychological objects according to changing conventions and rhetorical rules. For example, emotions are not real objects or mental states but socially constructed in the context of language-use and social roles. Individual experiences are not at all unique, but are embedded within sociolinguistic constructions that depend on culture and history.

Instead of psychologists' traditional focus on methods, which Gergen (1985) critiqued for separating subject and object and producing alienated relationships between investigators and participants, he advocated a focus on language. The dominance or acceptance of an existing form of understanding did not depend primarily on empirical evidence, he argued, but on social processes, particularly language.

Rejecting the standard belief that scientists attain truth through method, Gergen (1985) embraced the notion that moral criteria should play an important role in psychological research. This embrace is noteworthy, because it suggests that an ethical standpoint inspires his postmodern epistemology. Gergen stressed that psychologists should participate in conversations on values, although he rejected abstract moral principles and universal human rights. More recently, Gergen (2009) argued that knowledge and language have their roots in social relationships, which challenges Western individualism. Because psychological phenomena, such as thinking and feeling, are always embedded in relational processes, psychotherapies also require remodelling.

In addition, based on postmodernism's idea that disciplinary boundaries are arbitrary, there have been attempts to transform academic styles of presentation and to develop new forms of delivery, research, and practice, such as dramatized enactments. Mary Gergen (2001) has termed these innovations "performative psychology." Assuming that psychologists should exploit the potential to perform more fully, performative psychology can contribute to education and human development (Holzman, 2000).

Social constructionism

Some psychologists have incorporated postmodernism in the form of a social constructionism by which they examine how scholars have constructed psychological theories, concepts, methods, and practices socially and historically. Arguably the most noteworthy practitioner of social constructionism in the field of the history of Psychology is Kurt Danziger (1990a, 1997b, 2008). Partly influenced by the critical and methodological spirit of Foucault, he first demonstrated that the concept of an experimental research "subject" was not all natural but has undergone significant historical and cultural role changes.

Danziger (1997a) then studied the historical formation of psychological concepts and language such as "the self." He rejected the representational theory of language that suggests words mirror and represent a non-linguistic reality. Representational theorists assume that the self is a natural object that remains the same independent of how one describes it. But the way one conceptualizes the self cannot be separated from what the self is. Most recently, Danziger (2008) examined the history of memory, dating from the ancient Greeks to recent cognitive-neuroscience experiments.

Part 5 conclusion

Lyotard's principal contribution to critical discourse in Psychology is his notion of the end of meta-narratives. Based on this notion, one can argue that natural-scientific psychologists developed a singular meta-narrative that was and is central to their self-understanding. The terms methodologism, methodolatry, and scientism capture this social-historical phenomenon.

Foucault's viewpoint stands in stark contrast to the Enlightenment belief that knowledge is abstract, a position that both human-science and natural-science proponents took. Foucault paid particular attention to the implicit and explicit rules and the discourses of communication by which people are excluded, disciplined, and punished in various human institutions. He conceived of society as a prison but on a more subtle and internalized level. For example, eating disorders represent his principles of discipline and punishment by which women administer to themselves forms of sexist oppression.

Postmodernism in Psychology has taken the form of social constructionism, which generated a productive perspective on psychological concepts, theories, and practices. But overt affiliation with postmodernism has not occurred in mainstream Psychology for philosophical and practical reasons. The principles and practices of postmodernism and social constructionism challenge the epistemological foundations of natural-science psychologists. Practically, the latter fail to see the relevance of postmodernism for their particular research programmes.

Some commentators sympathetic to postmodern Psychology have suggested that its star already has passed (e.g., Teo & Febbraro, 2002). In addition, Kenneth Gergen earlier seemed to conflate positivism and modernism by suggesting that modernism was incompetent on questions of value. However, modern philosophers from Kant to Habermas have made moral philosophy a central topic. It was positivist philosophers and their followers in natural-science Psychology who excluded questions of value and morality from science. More recently, Gergen (2001) has concentrated on the positive consequences of postmodern reflections rather than deconstructing Psychology.

To some extent postmodern, feminist, and critical psychology critiques are congruent with postcolonial critiques of Psychology, which we consider next.

Part 6   Postcolonial perspectives

The critical term *postcolonial* has descriptive and normative meanings. It refers to the period when overt colonialism faded, which occurred after World War II at different rates in diverse locations. "Postcolonial" also suggests that colonial ideas and practices should not play a role in science and Psychology. That is, postcolonial scholars take an ethical-political stance against colonialism, identify the problems it created, and consider the life-conditions of marginalized peoples (Harding, 1998, 2008; Hook, 2005).

The postcolonial critique begins with the argument that not only is psychological subject matter part of a wider historical and cultural context, but also the theories that try to capture that subject matter reflect Western theorizing. Thus, these theories must be understood as Western models of human mental life (Teo & Febbraro, 2003). The question is how concepts developed in European and Anglo-American nations can be applied meaningfully to different cultural contexts.

From a postcolonial perspective, the task for psychologists from "the rest of the world" is to find psychological concepts that work in their life-worlds rather than importing or exporting Western notions. For instance, Ignacio Martín-Baró (1994) developed concepts and practices that specifically address psychological issues in Latin America. He applied to Psychology the belief of Brazilian educator **Paolo Freire** (1921–1997) that learners should be treated as subjects and not as objects (Freire, 1997).

Below we discuss the relevance of a postcolonial critique for Psychology by addressing Western ethnocentrism; we propose broadening Psychology's horizon of knowledge and discuss the concepts of hidden neocolonial thinking and problematization. Next we describe different perspectives on cultural diversity in Psychology, including Asian, African, and Canadian and US aboriginal perspectives. We conclude by describing Martín-Baró's liberation psychology.

Western ethnocentrism

Postcolonial critiques of Psychology focus on Western ethnocentrism. One way to understand how culture shapes knowledge is to consider **two types** of intellectual limitations – "time-centrism" and "culture-centrism" (Teo & Febbraro, 2003):

- Time-centrism means that a given time (e.g., our time) is the criterion from which members of a given culture develop and understand knowledge. A time-centric culture assumes that current knowledge is superior to earlier knowledge. A time-centric culture generally does not compare present to previous knowledge except for its historians.
- Culture-centrism means that one's own culture is the criterion by which knowledge is produced and understood. Epistemologically, culture-centrism is a precondition for the production of knowledge in that all knowledge is inescapably culture-bound. A culture-centric culture also assumes that knowledge from outside its psycho-geographical boundaries is inferior.

These cultural forms of knowledge are not limited to everyday life but play a significant role in psychological inquiry. Psychologists usually perceive, understand, and interpret psychological phenomena in the way that they have learned in their particular cultural contexts, including their educational institutions, to perceive, understand, and interpret their phenomena of interest. In this sense, culture-centrism is a principle before empirical research is conducted. Yet culture-centrism also means that empirical research and methodology inevitably represent one particular cultural perspective.

Historically, culture-centrism developed into an explicit programme of scientific racism in the context of colonialism. As an important academic orientation that legitimized colonialism, slavery, and racial segregation, culture-centrism continues to influence the spirit of Western society. Practitioners of scientific racism, for example, construe certain ethnocultural groups as inferior, while depicting those of European descent as the guardians of evolution.

Psychology's history shows abundant evidence for scientific racism, and many of the discipline's pioneers and American Psychological Association presidents were among the leaders of scientific racism (Gould, 1996; Guthrie, 1998; G. Richards, 2012; Tucker, 1994; Winston, 2004b). Although scientific racism has been on the decline, it persists, as does the problematic concept of "race" (Tattersall & Desalle, 2011).

Hidden neocolonial thinking

Culture-centrism developed, perhaps without malevolent intentions, into a hidden form by which a given Western culture holds that Western knowledge is superior to non-Western cultures. Hidden culture-centrism is expressed in the belief that Western knowledge-claims are superior and Western approaches to the social and human sciences are the only reasonable ones, while other cultures' forms of knowledge are neglected, minimized, or rejected. Hidden neocolonial thinking often occurs in a process of unintentional exclusion or when psychologists attempt to assimilate non-Western perspectives into Western psychology.

Consider basic psychological concepts such as memory, intelligence, emotion, motivation, and personal identity. Euro-American researchers tend to teach, write, and act as if these concepts are inclusive. In fact, these concepts tell a psychological story only from the perspective of Euro-American history, culture, and science (Spivak, 1999). This historical inclination constitutes "psychological colonialism." To overcome it, psychologists should study and describe concepts from diverse cultures to develop an inclusive understanding of mental life.

Problematization

A second historically rooted manifestation of culture-centrism is *problematization*, which in the postcolonial context refers to making into problems groups of people who differ from one's own cultural standpoint (Teo, 2004). A classic example is how Western culture constructed "the Orient" (i.e., the Middle East and Asia), which made colonization appear as necessary (Said, 1978). Problematization also was evident in rationales for the slave trade and the various European empires. Some contend that when Psychology emerged, it contributed to the problematization of Eastern cultures and perpetuated Western notions of superiority (e.g., Bhatia, 2002).

In the USA, problematization of African Americans played a prominent role in psychologists' conceptual and empirical tools (Guthrie, 1998). For centuries, US society's basic assumption was that African Americans were morally, aesthetically, and psychologically inferior and required direction, control, and surveillance. Escaped slaves were labelled as mentally ill and their "disease" was termed drapetomania (Gould, 1996).

Many early and some recent psychologists interpreted empirical differences in African Americans' psychological abilities, such as intelligence, as biological differences. This type of problematization received widespread attention even within the last decade (e.g., Rushton & Jensen, 2005). Reflections that challenge the dubious concept of IQ and the many unknowns that surround it must always catch up with questionable findings and, we would add, race-based speculations (Jackson & Weidman, 2004).

Different perspectives on cultural diversity

In recent decades some psychologists have come to appreciate how ethnocultural status in particular societies shapes psychological topics (Moghaddam & D. Taylor, 1986). They reject the traditional assumption that Psychology's generalizations about human functioning are valid for all people under all circumstances in all historical epochs. They also are skeptical about *cross-cultural psychology* by which investigators, typically from privileged nations, compare psychological phenomena endemic in their own ethnocultural domain to other ethnocultural domains, often formerly colonized.

By contrast, some psychologists seek to develop a culturally appropriate Psychology through culturally sensitive investigative practice (e.g., Zebian, Alamuddin, Maalouf, & Chatila, 2007). Others propose indigenous and cultural psychology to recognize and study unique and common psychological aspects of individual cultures (e.g., Kim, Yang, & Hwang, 2006).

The term *cultural diversity*, meaning respect for the inherent value of all cultures, has gained currency in Psychology. Diversity theorists value human localism, meaning that they appreciate the many different solutions that the globe's peoples have devised for the problems of human existence. They also hold the view that "it is unjust for any one population to impose its standards or will on other populations" (Watts, 1992, p. 117). In other words, diversity theorists typically are sensitive to the oppressive experience of minority groups as marginalized peoples.

When psychologists adopt a diversity viewpoint, they understand the cultural limitations of all psychological concepts such as memory, self, coping, and empowerment. In addition, they show respect for every population's strengths, competencies, and distinctive solutions to problems of living.

The term "cultural diversity," reflects this conceptual and value framework. It can facilitate overcoming the conventional tendency to privilege Western over indigenous knowledge. Diversity theory challenges psychologists to move beyond a cross-cultural approach towards celebrating cultural diversity in the form of equally valid, diverse psychologies. On the other hand, recognizing other cultures' contributions to Psychology, as important as this task is, should not obscure the economic inequalities that exist globally (Arfken, 2012). From a critical perspective, acknowledging other cultures should be accompanied by a focus on international social justice.

Historically and presently, diverse cultures have produced psychological knowledge. In the following sections we discuss Asian, African, and aboriginal psychological concepts.

Asian psychologies

In the 1970s some experimental psychologists in Canada and the US became infatuated with the reality that Yoga experts can exert remarkable mental control over their bodily functions, such as their heart rate. This phenomenon is contrary to what Western science taught about the autonomic nervous system. Other psychologists began to experiment with meditation and altered states of consciousness. These developments opened the door to the Western "discovery" of Asian indigenous psychologies.

Kurt Danziger (1997b) related his story of teaching Psychology at an Indonesian university early in his career. There he encountered a colleague who had been teaching a Psychology course that was rooted in Hindu philosophy with Indonesian concepts and interpretations. Danziger quickly discovered that the concepts and categories his colleague employed bore no resemblance to those of mainstream Psychology. For example, motivation was not a topic that his colleague included.

Danziger recognized that he had been taking for granted distinctions among various psychological categories that Westerners have regarded as universal and intrinsic to human nature. He was facing the ethnocentric nature of Western psychology. He came to see that diverse cultures have produced ways of understanding psychological phenomena quite differently from Western notions, for example, of intelligence, cognition, and identity.

Local Asian psychologies exist, but knowledge of them in Canada, the USA, or Europe depends on translations or visits to or from the local culture. One indigenous psychology is **Virgilio Enriquez's** (1942–1994) liberation psychology. He argued that in order to understand Filipino thought and experiences it is necessary to take a Filipino orientation (Enriquez, 1992). In his view, Western psychology, which had dominated the research, teaching, and practices of Filipino psychologists, was significantly limited when one attempted to understand local experiences and activities. Indigenous approaches also have emerged in China (Hwang, 2012) and India.

Indian psychology Ancient Indian psychology illustrates cultural differences in psychological conceptions. An oral tradition of transmitting scientific knowledge about human psychology dates back to at least 2000 BCE in India (Kuppuswamy, 1990; Paranjpe, 1998). Five methods of investigation were used: observation, introspection, personal experience, reasoning, and the "guru–shishya" (educator–learner) relationship.

Ancient Indians specified standards of correct observation and inference. They even discussed several human factors that contributed to faulty observations, such as defects in one's vision or environmental conditions like poor lighting, and they were aware of predispositions and prejudices affecting judgment. Concerning sensory perception, they concluded that we perceive distance through visual light waves or auditory sound vibrations, and they distinguished between illusion and delusion.

Ancient Indian scientists also studied the meanings of words in sentences and children's acquisition of language. They described two general types of abnormal states: severe, meaning psychoses, epilepsy, and alcoholism; and mild, meaning fears and anxiety. At the same time they believed consciousness pervaded all forms of existence, such that plants and animals had souls.

Three perspectives concerning the relationships among body, mind, and self have pervaded Indian psychological thought: Hindu, Yogic, and Buddhist:

- In the *Hindu* system, there are two selves: "lower," which is transitory and driven by biological and social needs, and "higher," which is permanent and seeks understanding and transcendence. Thus, the lower self is an empirical ego and the higher self is ultimate reality. The *Upanishads*, which are commentaries on the ancient Hindu scriptures, the *Vedas*, contain an analogy that describes body–mind–self relationships: two birds are perched in a tree: one enjoys the fruits of the tree, while the other, perched above it, observes.
- In *Yoga* the individual gradually develops awareness of unconscious processes, bodily predispositions, and emotions for the purposes of health, enlightenment, and inner peace. The methods employed are bodily postures, regulated breathing, and meditation.
- In *Buddhism* there are no ego and self, because ultimately individuals originate interdependently with all reality; to be oneself is to be part of others. Thus, Buddhists valorize relationship over individualism, which, they hold, obstructs the development of community. Buddhists also assert that the world's suffering is addressed best through human consciousness not social structures. The ultimate goal is experiencing the relatedness of all things through prayer and detachment from

mundane objects and activities. Contemplation and spiritual practice are essential for genuine liberation.

However, for the past several decades Western psychology has prevailed in Asian societies with little deference to the traditional psychologies within Hindu, Yogic, and Buddhist thought. US psychological theory, research, and professional practice are the norms, although they might be modified to account for cultural differences.

African psychologies

Afrocentrism is a pluralistic collection of worldviews from the diverse cultures of Africa. Afrocentric scholars investigate psychological phenomena from African-centred values, "critique the continued exclusion and marginalization of African knowledge systems," and validate African peoples' experiences (Dei, 1996, p. 4).

Afrocentric **values** include these **five**:

- The primacy of relationships with others and harmony with nature.
- The unity of spirit with matter.
- Collective rather than individual responsibility.
- Communal interdependence rather than individualistic independence.
- Preference for dynamic, flexible, and fluid processes rather than a static, fixed goal-orientation.

Afrocentric epistemology deals with the commonalities of shared experiences, that is, it honours collective subjectivity. Knowledge and its expression are reflections of the subjective perspectives of those who have constructed "facts" and their forms of communication. Afrocentric epistemology is also characterized by a preference for dialectical logic, that is, for the unity of opposites rather than dichotomies.

Ideally, African psychologies would reflect this worldview in theory, research, professional practice, and education in the discipline (Holdstock, 2000). But the effects of colonialism in African university education remain pronounced in that standard Western psychology prevails. However, some scholars are developing indigenous psychologies based, for example, on **Frantz Fanon's** (1925–1961) concept of "psychopolitics" and Steve Biko's concept of "Black consciousness." In South Africa a critical psychology is emerging that incorporates the role of ancestors, the hierarchy of beings, an organic view of the universe, and the key role of community and its relation to personhood (Hook, 2004).

Fanon ([1952] 1967), a Black psychiatrist who trained in France and engaged in the Algerian independence struggle, challenged the applicability of certain psychiatric and psychoanalytic concepts to Africans. For example, the Oedipus complex does not make sense in the African context because of a matriarchal culture. He also challenged professionals' pathologization of the behaviour of many North Africans, which construed them as primitive creatures.

Fanon understood that biological, medical, and neuroscientific explanations can be used to perpetuate racism and paternalism. Instead, he provided a political and economic explanation that can support an African liberation psychology. Moreover, his standpoint incorporated the necessity for both mental and political revolution, that is, a radical change in consciousness as well as oppressive social structures (Fanon, 1963).

First Nations' psychologies

In Canada and the US, First Nations psychologies operate from different assumptions and values than Psychology does and are relative to each aboriginal nation (Walsh-Bowers & Johnson, 2002). First and foremost, spirit is central to aboriginal persons. Spirit is an eternal life-force, giving meaning and direction; and spirit is a personal guide and guardian in a parallel reality of dreams, visions, and extrasensory experiences. For example, dreams provide access to another path to reality, which is concurrent with and parallel to observable, everyday reality. In dreams the person actually experiences the events, no matter how fantastical they might appear to the linear thinker. "It is the soul of the person that moves about in the non-ordinary reality, and dreams provide contact with the spirit-world" (Walsh-Bowers & Johnson, 2002, p. 89).

Secondly, relationships *are* the aboriginal person who lives psychologically with an extended family and clan connected to the land, even if the person is geographically removed from her or his tribe or nation. Like other creatures, human beings are dependent on each other for survival and on all creation. Humans are part of the network of life. Consequently, one's responsibility is to be respectful, cooperate, and share the bounty of the land.

Thirdly, the circle is the primary pattern by which all things begin, change, end, and begin again. Circular thinking, in the aboriginal worldview, is culturally appropriate, not a sign of faulty linear logic. History, for example, is regarded as the union of the past, present, and future generations at this particular moment of suspended time. A circular perspective connects with the entire created world, which nurtures the interrelatedness of all beings, and respects the experiences of all people.

As is evident in these principles, spirituality is the foundation of aboriginal knowledge. Consequently, the goals of "native science" are to understand why things happen the way they do and to experience balance, harmony, and peace with the created world. In First Nations' aboriginal science, knowers honour their own subjectivity, that is, their feelings and intuition, rather than prediction and control.

In sum, traditional European and Anglo-American thinking and practices have been dangerous for Native peoples, because they have contributed to cultural domination. European and Anglo-American nations and scientists have regarded the values and assumptions of aboriginal or native peoples as "primitive." But one can question how it is "backward" to understand the vital need to care for all natural objects and the ecological systems on which life depends.

Ignacio Martín-Baró's liberation psychology

Martín-Baró (1942–1989) was a Western-educated priest and psychologist who served as a professor at the University of Central America in El Salvador. He devoted his professional life to the mental health and social justice of the Salvadoran people. Defending the poor and describing and explaining their oppression made him a subversive individual in the eyes of the Salvadoran elite and their supporters. In 1989 he was murdered on campus by the military with five other priests and their housekeepers.

Martín-Baró (1994) argued that Psychology should make a contribution to the social development of Latin America from the standpoint of suffering people. Drawing from the principles of *liberation theology*, he termed his orientation "a liberation psychology," which he intended primarily as a practical not a theoretical programme.

Liberation theology originated in the 1960s as a Latin American Christian movement integrating Marxian interpretation of the Hebrew and Christian bibles with political action. Liberation theology's premise is that, inspired by the biblical call to practise justice, citizens should transform the societal structures that cause poverty, inequality, and distress through collective, non-violent action.

According to Martín-Baró, liberation psychology should emancipate itself from Western perspectives. He rejected mainstream psychologists' idea of value-neutral science and the primacy of research and theory in academia. Latin American psychology should not be concerned about whether it would be recognized in the rich countries, he claimed, but rather whether it served the marginalized majority.

Citing Freire's literacy programmes, Martín-Baró promoted "social liberation" in place of Psychology's traditional goal of personal liberation, because for him, personal and social existence were intertwined. He also rejected psychological concepts such as learned helplessness, because, from a liberation psychology perspective, they fail to provide an analysis of objectively based social structures that oppress people.

Martín-Baró urged a transformation of psychological knowledge from a focus on the powerful to the liberation needs of the oppressed Latin American people. He intended that a "psychology from the oppressed" (rather than for the oppressed) would replace studying psychological issues from the professional perspectives of government, managers, scientists, and health and mental-health experts.

Martín-Baró assumed that psychological truths about the oppressed only can be attained from their perspective. Thus, examining psychosocial processes from the viewpoint of the dominated requires developing educational psychology from the standpoint of illiterate persons, studying industrial psychology with the eyes of the unemployed, focusing on mental health from the perspective of tenant farmers on haciendas, theorizing personal maturity from the standpoint of those who live in town dumps, and defining motivation from the perspective of women selling wares in street markets.

In Martín-Baró's approach of critical praxis, epistemology is intertwined with direct action and ethics. The methodology that he prescribed was participatory action research whereby research participants contribute to all phases of the research process. Some feminist, postmodern, and postcolonial approaches have actualized Martín-Baró's vision as a "methodology of the oppressed" (e.g., Sandoval, 2000). In Martín-Baró's (1994) words:

> Thus, to acquire new psychological knowledge it is not enough to place ourselves in the perspective of the people; it is necessary to involve ourselves in a new praxis, an activity of transforming reality that will let us know not only about what is but also about what is not, and by which we may try to orient ourselves toward what ought to be. (pp. 28–29)

Along these lines, Mary Watkins and Helene Shulman (2008) propose a multidisciplinary approach to psychological and social emancipation incorporating the arts and spirituality. Based on their extensive engagement with Latin American practitioners of liberationist theory, the authors revised Martín-Baró's critical praxis for a postcolonial world seeking environmental, economic, and social justice. They situate psychological health and illness in social-historical context and describe numerous community-based interventions, grounded in dialogues that evoke critical consciousness. The methodology they advocate is participatory action research, maximizing citizen involvement in all roles of an investigation.

Part 6   conclusion

During the ascent of colonialism, which facilitated Western culture's rise to global economic and political domination, an interest in understanding non-Western groups of people scientifically emerged and produced the concept of race. This notion allowed for the justification of colonialism, domination, and slavery, because Western scholars and their followers constructed non-European groups (and certain European populations) not just as different but as essentially inferior. Scientific interest in human ethnocultural variety was not a value-neutral endeavour.

Postcolonial approaches begin with the assumption that this type of thinking must be overcome in academia. In response, postcolonial psychologies have been developed in many countries. Unfortunately, neocolonial ideas persist in the social sciences and Psychology. For some critics, cross-cultural psychology has served this function. Yet the principles of cultural diversity and social justice enable psychologists to transcend the limitations of a cross-cultural approach.

Rooted in ancient traditions, psychologies indigenous to Asian, African, and aboriginal societies deviate quite substantially from natural-science Psychology's concepts, particularly concerning perspectives on the relationship of body, mind, and self. They have produced their own approaches to psychological phenomena. Furthermore, these indigenous psychologies have implications for theory, research, professional practice, and education in natural-science Psychology.

In his liberation psychology Martín-Baró argued for praxis that transforms social reality. In his view, psychologists should serve less as traditional researchers or clinicians than as resources for communities to effect economic justice, hence psychological well-being. Current postcolonial revisioning of Martín-Baró's programme is gaining traction in critical psychology circles, but like other critical approaches it has not yet reached the consciousness of mainstream psychologists.

Part 7   Thematic review

As we approach the end of this, the final chapter, we show the interrelationships among the themes reviewed in previous chapters. Then we discuss the core theme of our book – **Psychology as a problematic science** – from the philosophical perspectives of ontology, epistemology, and ethics and politics. In our last words we consider issues that, in our view, should be central in attempts to transform Psychology, and we invite you to envision your own alternative conception of the discipline.

Review of previous themes

Previously we discussed themes within each chapter that seemed to summarize the history and philosophy of Psychology and earlier psychological thought. Here we show how these themes are connected and converge on the conclusion that Psychology is a problematic science ontologically, epistemologically, and ethically and politically.

In Chapter 1 we advocated **critical thinking** about Psychology's subject matter, investigative practice, and professional applications to individuals, groups, organizations, and institutions. We practised critical thinking by underscoring the reality of **multiple psychologies** and the historical facts of diverse definitions of Psychology and the important distinction between natural-science and human-science Psychology. Yet practising the history of our discipline requires **reflexive historiography** and relies on the disposition of critical presentism. Similarly, practising critical thinking about science leads to practising an **intersubjective science**, which is particularly valuable for Psychology, because we study ourselves when we study humans and other animals.

Animated by this critical spirit, we observed in Chapter 2 "Ancient and premodern psychological thought" **conflicting metaphysical positions** with ontological and epistemological aspects and the emergence of two enduring cultural trends: a **conscious psychological interior** and the mentality and skills of **critical thinking**.

In Chapter 3 "Early modern psychological thought," in which we discussed the Scientific Revolution and the Enlightenment, three themes were apparent. First, the **compatibility of scientific with theistic thought** suggested that scientific advances and ideas frequently were embedded in religious, even theological views rather than cast as polar opposites. Secondly, the theme of **objectivity–subjectivity of observation** intimated that while early modern natural philosophers stressed the objectivity of scientific observation, many identified sources of bias and the subjective human limits of observation. Thirdly, the theme of **a self-contained vs. a relational self** revealed that natural philosophers disagreed about the social nature of the psychological self within a social context of social management and individualism.

In Chapter 4 "The philosophical and scientific climate in the nineteenth century," the theme of **liberal individualism vs. socialist alternatives** showed the clash of contemporary ideas about the nature of society and social relations. We identified a second theme of dualities: on the one hand, **scientific triumphalism** about advances in physiology, physics, and evolutionary theory prevailed among many natural scientists and their citizen-advocates, often expressed in scientistic beliefs and practices; on the other hand, a minority expressed **skepticism** about surging cultural faith in the certainty of scientific knowledge. As Psychology dawned, numerous inescapable and **unresolved philosophical questions concerning psychological phenomena** remained that encompassed profound ontological, epistemological, and ethical-political issues.

In Chapter 5 "Early natural-science Psychology," at the point of Psychology's formal emergence, we observed that psychologists engaged in **boundary maintenance** over against philosophy, human-science psychologies, and public fascination with spiritualism and extrasensory phenomena to secure, in their eyes, the new discipline's scientific legitimacy. A significant dimension of this endeavour was to engage in **biological reductionism**, typically manifest in identification with evolutionary concepts. Yet early natural-science psychologists, with some exceptions, adopted **ambiguous positions concerning the mind and brain**, as if they were avoiding underlying philosophical issues. Meanwhile, most psychologists endeavoured to demonstrate the practical utility of their investigations to society's power-brokers and, consciously or not, formed an **alliance with the societal status quo**.

As described in Chapter 6 "Natural-science Psychology between the world wars," natural-science Psychology as practised in the USA became the dominant form of the discipline. Within this context many psychologists, particularly behaviourists and neo-behaviourists, appeared to adopt a **narrow purview of** what they considered to be genuine **Psychology** yet were **ambivalent about the biological basis of behaviour and mental processes**. Perhaps as a result, **disciplinary fragmentation** ensued for several reasons. Other US psychologists studied developmental, personality, and social phenomena, most international psychologists never abandoned the study of mental processes, and subdisciplines representing various societal applications proliferated. All told, psychologists enhanced their **alliance with the societal status quo** as World War II loomed on the horizon.

In Chapter 7 "Natural-science Psychology after World War II," we observed a recent shift towards a **neuroscience of the evolutionary brain and consciousness**. Perhaps natural-science psychologists' former inclination towards biological reductionism remains operational, although with more sophisticated technology and substantial government and corporate support at their disposal. We also noted a trend of studying **self and identity in context** rather than developmental, personality, and social psychologists by tradition assuming an autonomous individual. Yet **disciplinary fragmentation** and an **alliance with the societal status quo** have remained hallmarks of Psychology to the present.

As described in Chapter 8 "Applied and professional psychology," most psychologists have aimed to apply their science to society either directly or indirectly, generally within a context of social management and individualism. Early psychologists and their successors have absorbed the spirit of scientific triumphalism that natural scientists and their natural-philosophy predecessors have displayed. Consequently, it seems that psychologists have held **unreflective faith in the scientific basis of their social and professional applications**, which they have presumed to be socially beneficial. At the same time, they have conveyed the public impression to the powers-that-be that they can aid individuals' adaptation to the social order. Thus, applied and professional psychologists have also been **allied with the societal status quo**.

In Chapter 9 "Human-science psychologies: psychoanalysis," we showed how diverse and versatile manifestations of psychoanalysis as theories and practices of unconscious processes have **illuminated the psychological interior** in fundamentally different ways than natural-science psychologies have. It is no wonder, then, that for nearly a century natural-science psychologies have had an **ambivalent relationship** with the varieties of psychoanalysis, alternately welcoming and rejecting it.

As described in Chapter 10 "Human-science psychologies: hermeneutic to transpersonal," natural-science Psychology also has had an ambivalent relationship with these human-science alternatives, while attempting to mould human-science psychologies into its own image. Relying on the **centrality of understanding and interpretation** of human experience, phenomenology, existentialism, and postmodern forms of human-science psychologies have illuminated the psychological interior in fundamentally different ways than natural-science psychologies have. Like certain forms of psychoanalysis, phenomenology, existentialism, and postmodern forms of human-science psychologies have traversed the disputed border between the body and mind, soul, and spirit that natural philosophers and their predecessors dating back to the ancient Greeks explored. In this way many varieties of human-science psychology assume compatibility of scientific with religious and theological thought.

In Chapter 11 "Constructing psychological research," we applied critical thinking to Psychology's scientific foundations. A strain of skepticism has persisted in Western thought and scientific practice since Socrates and the Sophists such that the early modern natural philosophers took diverse positions on the objectivity or subjectivity of empirical observation. Human-science psychologists in particular opted for an intersubjective science in which reflexivity and reflexive historiography are central. Arguably, however, many natural philosophers and subsequent natural scientists displayed a spirit of scientific triumphalism that they expressed in unreflective faith in scientific expertise. The new scientific psychologists and their successors absorbed this mentality.

Although natural-science psychologists forged ahead with an objectivistic scientific disposition in their scientific language and methods, historical examination of their investigative practice has revealed the presence of systemic biases in methodology, measurement, and inferential statistics. This dubious state of scientific affairs evokes the question of whether natural-science Psychology has been a **science, pseudoscience, or interpretive science**. Moreover, it suggests the pervasive presence of **intersubjectivity** in psychologists' presumed objective investigative practice. From a scientific perspective, therefore, Psychology seems to have been and remains problematic.

Psychology as a problematic science

When considering the panoply of perspectives always present in Psychology and the historical debates about the nature of its subject matter, its scientific status, and its ethical and political relationship to the social order, we conclude that the discipline has struggled with significant ontological, epistemological, and ethical-political problems.

Ontological problems

Ontology refers to the study of being (i.e., the fundamental characteristics of reality). Applying ontology to Psychology, one would ask what is the nature of the psychological "object," what should psychologists study, and what are the specific and defining characteristics of psychological subject matter? Ontological discussions can encompass a wide range of topics, such as the proper definition of Psychology, metaphors for understanding psychological phenomena, theories of human nature, and models of mind including the body–mind relationship.

The most prominent ontological models in Psychology have been technological ones. Indeed, the history of Psychology often parallels the development of technology. For instance, cognitive psychology's model and metaphors of human mental life are based on the computer, whereas in earlier eras, psychologists borrowed simpler mechanical devices to express their concepts (e.g., clocks, steam engines, and radios). Like any intellectual construction, machine models are embedded within a network of ontological assumptions. One assumption is that a person responds to an external stimulus like a mechanism, not like a human agent; that is, a machine model excludes notions of subjectivity and agency (i.e., the person's ability to reflect, choose, and act).

Mainstream Psychology has operated according to a *mechanistic*, hence an *atomistic* and *reductionistic* model of human mental life. An obvious example of a mechanistic concept of human action is the assumption that an individual animal or human organism responds to stimuli. Dividing psychological phenomena into stimuli and responses, as behaviourists did, or into independent and dependent variables, as natural-science psychologists have done since the 1930s, is problematic, because these mechanistic terms neglect subjectivity and agency.

When psychologists select variables to study isolated aspects of human mental life, which is a form of atomism, they do not do justice to the ordinary integration of psychological processes in the mental life of individuals in concrete social-historical contexts. Instead of investigating the complexity of human mental life, mainstream psychologists assume that it is sufficient to study manipulable bits of behaviour. But it is reductionistic to assume that the parts sufficiently explain the complexity of subjectivity and agency.

From the perspective of the subject, thinking, feeling, and willing are usually experienced in their connection in concrete life-situations and not in isolation. The notion that studying the parts of a whole is sufficient and that the parts will fit together into a meaningful whole by adding them up is limited, as Gestalt psychologists demonstrated. Parts do not just add up when it comes to mental life. To do justice to their subject matter psychologists should begin with the nexus of human experiences in order to understand the parts and not vice versa.

The machine-model of mental life has another consequence: regarding a person's society as an external variable separates individuals from their cultural niches (Parker & Spears, 1996). It is inaccurate to conceive of social-historical reality as only a stimulus environment to which one responds, because individuals are not independent of their environments and vice versa. Psychology's credibility as a science would be enhanced, if it studied human subjectivity as embedded in specific historical and social conditions.

Such an ontological shift with its epistemological ramifications might be facilitated by psychologists adopting a reflexive standpoint whereby we consciously become the objects and subjects of our own study. Although generally not discussed per se, reflexivity has a long history in Psychology with such figures as Gordon Allport, Edwin Boring, George Kelly, Carl Kurt Lewin, Carl Rogers, and B. F. Skinner actively reflecting on their own psychology-making. As historian of psychology James Capshew (2007) put it:

> Understanding the role of reflexive practices in psychological investigations, in the evolution of professional identities in psychology, and in the social surroundings of the field could provide a crucial element in explaining psychology's ascendancy and ubiquity in the 20th century. (p. 353)

Epistemological problems

Epistemology refers to the study of knowledge. Psychologists, of course, must deal with the nature of knowledge, ways of achieving it, and the meaning of knowledge and truth. Yet in practice epistemology and ontology are intertwined. Certain ontological assumptions and decisions have epistemological and methodological consequences. A commitment to a specific conception of Psychology's subject matter implies specific methodological commitments and vice versa. For example, a machine-model of human mental life implies a mechanistic methodology, and the results based on this methodology seemingly support and are implied in such a model.

From a critical perspective, the specificities of an object or event of mental life in context require appropriate methodologies. If researchers are interested in the biological basis of memory, then using a biological, natural-scientific methodology makes sense. But if they are interested in studying the subjective meaningful content of memory, then they need a methodology that can do justice to it, such as hermeneutic approaches that emphasize the understanding of meaning.

However, natural-science psychologists tend to insist that their methodology must be applied to all research questions. This position is rooted in physicalism by which twentieth-century scientists believed that everything in the empirical world could be studied with the concepts and methods of physics.

As taught at most universities and expressed in most textbooks, natural-science Psychology has been committed to an empirical–statistical methodology in emulation of the natural sciences. Investigators operationalize psychological concepts as independent, dependent, moderating, or mediating variables to examine the functional relationship among them (C. Tolman, 1994). Within the logic of this methodology, psychologists take **three investigative steps**:

- Formulate hypotheses within theoretical arguments and express their hypotheses as law-like statements.
- Test their hypotheses using objective, valid, and reliable observations and measurements.
- Based on the results of hypothesis-testing, provide deductive–nomological (law-providing) or statistical models of explanation and prediction.

But any given study, whether experimental or correlational, only can capture what investigators insert into their theoretical and methodological frameworks, which typically excludes the experience of research participants in that study. For instance, if you as a participant suggest to investigators or their assistants that the task expected of you does not make sense, they will exclude your responses to the investigative task. Even though your action is based on a legitimate concern, they treat your data as error.

Natural-science psychologists' investigations depend upon compliant and well-behaved participants. But investigators' analysis and interpretations of their findings exclude the social realities in the investigative situation. Furthermore, although psychologists typically examine the functional relationship of isolated variables, in the real world all the factors that they exclude from their investigations play a role in human action (Holzkamp, 1972). Thus, psychological studies often do not have practical relevance, let alone *emancipatory* relevance, which is a core deficiency for critical psychologists. Emancipatory relevance means that research should contribute to overturning oppressive social conditions.

Consider the problem of unemployment. Mainstream psychologists examine the functional relationship between unemployment and other variables such as well-being, depression, self-esteem, and personality. Depending on the nature of the research design, they understand this relationship as causal or correlational. But psychologists could study the *why* of unemployment in a person's life, which would necessitate analyzing the problem as a social-historical, political-economic issue.

Since Thomas Kuhn (1962), historians of science have emphasized the difference between what scientists espouse and what they actually do. In Psychology, critics have questioned whether psychologists actually generate psychological laws equivalent to the laws of natural science. Sigmund Koch (1981), for instance, contended that despite over a century of a natural-scientific orientation, despite the thousands of empirical studies and accumulation of research-reports, one is hard-pressed to find statements that qualify as a universally valid natural law. The fact that Psychology has been failing as a law-providing science should give pause for reflection on whether the prevailing methodology does justice to the discipline's subject matter.

Psychology initially struggled with acceptance in academia and society. Psychologists employed physiologists' and physicists' mechanically sophisticated brass and steel instruments and literally cloaked themselves in the white coats of laboratory scientists. In addition, early psychologists and subsequent generations have claimed that psychological measures possess the same status as physical measures. Recently psychologists have relied on complex machines such as computers and fMRI apparatus. Critics, however, suggest that the adoption of natural-scientific regalia and terminology cannot itself confer scientific legitimacy (Politzer, 1928/1994).

Methodologism   Natural-science psychologists' longstanding focus on methodology rather than on subject matter led to a general epistemological orientation known as methodologism (Teo, 2005). This term refers to an investigative standpoint in which the subject matter is secondary but the method is primary. Methodologism means that quantitative methodology is applied to all research questions. Comparable terms are methodolatry (Bakan, 1967), the cult of empiricism (Toulmin & Leary, 1985), and the methodological imperative (Danziger, 1985).

Mainstream psychologists' methodologism leads to a methodological theory of knowledge that inhibits critical questions about the purpose of research, such as, what are the personal, social, and political-economic interests involved in executing a certain study and who benefits from which results? Just as critical psychologists do not accept that methodology is independent of subject matter, so they reject the notion that methodology is independent of the social-historical context from which it emerged. Psychologists' ontological and methodological commitments cannot be resolved by only examining the discipline's scholarly shortcomings. Any science also operates as a social enterprise in an institutional context of power, money, and prestige.

Ethics and politics

Psychological practice, whether consisting of theory, research, clinical and community interventions, or applications to social institutions, is interconnected with epistemology and ontology. If psychologists assume that humans act like machines, then psychologists' scientific and professional practice will emphasize control, manipulation, technologies, and adaptation to the environment and will neglect the emancipatory potential of Psychology. If one conceptualizes humans as meaning-making agents embedded in sociopolitical contexts, then practice will call attention to human agency and will foster emancipation.

Psychology has been an extremely successful discipline in European and Anglo-American nations as evidenced by its academic and professional expansion since World War II. However, success does not certify the ethical-political quality of its practice. Psychological practice often has involved abuses perpetrated by the powerful, from using intelligence testing as a means to control immigration into the USA to applying psychological techniques to extract information from suspected terrorists.

Linking "is" with "ought." Mainstream psychologists' reliance on David Hume's admonition concerning value-judgments biasing the interpretation of everyday behaviour does not solve the issue. Like Hume, psychologists have insisted that facts (what *is*) and values (what *ought* to be) should remain distinct. However, mainstream Psychology is as guided by certain values, beginning with the value of value-neutrality, as any other social institution. Furthermore, a lack of reflection on the values that guide research maintains the disciplinary and societal status quo.

In any science that claims social relevance, such as Psychology, the domains of *is* and *ought* are intertwined, a symbiosis that evokes ethical-political responses. Even in natural sciences, *is* and *ought* are intertwined. For example, that human activity has produced global warming is not just an ecological fact but has implications for human action.

Critical psychologists have challenged the assumption that one cannot derive *ought* from *is* and that as scientists they should remain neutral on political issues. In fact, they contend that psychologists *should* derive *ought* from *is*. For instance, they claim that, if research shows the negative effects of poverty on mental life, then society should target poverty and ultimately abolish it, and psychologists should participate in its abolition.

Ideally, critical psychologists make issues of inequality and environmental, economic, and social injustice an explicit, practical research-concern. They also have analyzed the role of Psychology in maintaining capitalism, patriarchy, colonialism, and Western ideology. Martín-Baró (1994) pointed out that such an ethical-political stance and objectivity are not in conflict with each other. For example, when it comes to torture it is possible to be ethical and reject torture, while simultaneously maintaining objectivity to understand the consequences of torture on mental life.

Small-group discussion. Compare how a traditional psychologist would research homelessness and how a critical psychologist would study it.

One even could argue that natural-science psychologists have been ambivalent about ethical-political issues, because in reality they do not maintain separation of *is* and *ought* in their professional organizations and when the public demands an ethical position on certain issues. The American Psychological Association, the Canadian Psychological Association, and other national psychological organizations have adopted codes of ethics to which members subscribe when joining. Obviously, values come into play in all aspects of doing Psychology (Brinkmann, 2011b).

Critical praxis By not challenging basic societal structures and ideologies, psychologists reinforce the status quo, which also means performing Psychology in the interest of the powerful and in service to individuals' adaptation to society. The embeddedness of Psychology in market economies, however, has made it difficult to promote the discipline as an emancipatory science.

Consider an example from psychotherapy. Clinical psychologists could work with gay and lesbian clients to make their homosexuality (seemingly) disappear. In the 1970s psychologists regarded this practice as scientifically and professionally sound, although under political pressure they abandoned it later. Yet clinical psychologists could work with gay and lesbian clients on transforming personal attitudes *and* societal perspectives, praxis that could include social action. Rather than making homosexuality into a problem, psychotherapy should be about working on problems that homosexuals encounter in a homophobic society.

An overtly ethical–political, emancipatory praxis for Psychology does not silence the needs and concerns of people suffering from societal pathologies. Rather, it enables them to confront their oppression and work collectively to overcome it. Current examples of critical psychological praxis include HIV/AIDS interventions in South Africa (Hook, 2004) and liberation psychology in Latin America (Montero, 2003).

A vision of Psychology's future

The themes from Chapters 1 to 11 that appeared to represent key historical and philosophical issues and the history of psychological thought, research, and practical applications are interrelated and point to a general conclusion: Psychology has been a problematic discipline from ontological, epistemological, and ethical–political perspectives (Teo, 2009). Yet, as we conclude this text we sound a cautionary note. Critical awareness that Psychology has been a problematic science should not be understood as a call to abandon it. Rather, critical awareness and reflexivity might enable us to transform Psychology in a direction that does justice to the complexity of its subject matter conceptually, with methodologies for the particularities of mental life embedded in cultural-historical context and ethically responsible concepts and practices that challenge the societal and disciplinary status quo and foster emancipation. On the other hand, we also must keep in mind the institutional and ideological forces within Psychology that have the potential to resist or thwart proposed changes to the discipline's fundamentals (Walsh-Bowers, 2010).

Our vision

Imagining a Psychology that fulfills the above challenging promise requires naming the concepts and practices that we believe are central and sharing our vision in a way that elicits your own reflections on Psychology's future. **The internationalization of Psychology** and **key issues of praxis** are central in our vision:

(1) The future of Psychology, including critical psychology, depends first on understanding that the world has become more interconnected. Despite the problems of economic globalization with all its negative consequences for many nations, groups, and individuals, opportunities present themselves for emancipatory theory, research, and professional practice in the discipline. This opportunity is captured partly by the term *internationalization* (Brock, 2006a). But the term connotes opposing strategies.

Since the post-World War II era, internationalization has meant the distribution and propagation of US Psychology to the rest of the world or at best, cross-cultural Psychology based on a Western worldview. But the term can also mean a shift to an international postcolonial Psychology. Such a shift involves a process of assimilation by which mainstream psychologists incorporate non-Western concepts into the discipline; but more importantly, a process of accommodation, by which the very nature of Psychology changes based on concepts and practices from around the world. If one assumes that any local Psychology can learn from other local perspectives, then an international postcolonial Psychology requires more than assimilation.

The notion of internationalization that we espouse is based on the idea that Western psychological concepts are neither universally applicable nor superior to concepts from other cultural contexts. Indeed, we all have limited horizons, and all psychologists have restricted psychological perspectives within which they develop concepts, research, and social applications. Exposure to historically and culturally significant horizons that transcend one's own point of view will allow the development of broader, deeper, and more sophisticated perspectives that might address the discipline's core problems. One consequence of centralizing internationalization might be the emergence of a polycentric Psychology rather than a primarily US perspective.

(2) Earlier in this chapter we implied that developing a keen eye for justice is essential to the creation of a full range of possibilities for basic and applied psychology to contribute to human welfare and emancipation. Essentially we were presenting a moral argument with ethical-political implications for the discipline. On this critical foundation, we identify **key issues** of praxis for imagining the future of Psychology:

- A critical image of Psychology's past and present, especially in relation to the social realities of oppression and the imperilled status of the biosphere.
- Human diversity concerning ethnoracial group, gender and sexual orientation, socioeconomic and educational status, physical and mental ability, and religious preference.
- Ethical–political values of relationality (i.e., the centrality of relationships), fully democratic participation, and environmental, economic, and social justice.

What might instigate a conscious shift among psychologists towards an emancipatory orientation of justice-seeking is fostering a disciplinary climate of social-ethical responsibility in three areas of critical praxis. Thus, in democratizing Psychology (Sampson, 1991) psychologists would engage in **three practices**:

- Produce relevant empirical knowledge that is partial, reflexive, and represents localized findings laden with contextualized meanings rather than universalizable and value-free truths and facts.
- Practise as radical egalitarians not as elite, paternalistic professionals when conducting research, engaging in professional practice, and educating students, which means learning about others' worlds as they experience them, through open dialogue, mutual learning, and co-authorship.
- Develop a practicable political vision for societal transformation in concert with social-movement activists, not avoid the moral responsibility of articulating an agenda for creative maladjustment to the societal status and for engaging in non-violent social transformation.

Your vision

Whatever your engagement with Psychology will entail from this point on, develop your own answers to the critical questions that pervade the history and philosophy of the discipline. Then, whether you become a psychologist or not, engage in the work of transforming Psychology. We urge you to rely on your idealism to promote compassion and justice in all your relationships, in science, and in society.

To aid your reflection and contributions to Psychology's transformation we raise **four key questions** implicit in the conclusion of Chapter 1:

- Can Psychology be a unified science?
- How certain can psychologists be of their research and professional knowledge?
- How compatible is Psychology with other paths to knowledge?
- What are the social responsibilities of scientific and professional psychologists?

Summary

In Part 1 we reviewed historical critiques of Psychology. Criticizing extant psychology, Immanuel Kant proposed an ethically relevant psychology. Auguste Comte thought a natural-scientific psychology was impossible, but Friedrich Lange contradicted him. For Rudolf Willy, Psychology was philosophically and scientifically weak.

In Part 2 we argued that twentieth-century developments in physics, determinism, and reductionism have important implications for Psychology. However, natural-science psychologists generally have not recognized and incorporated the new scientific assumptions – mutual influence between observer and observed, and multiple realities; uncertainty, indeterminacy, and multiple causation; and interconnected phenomena.

In Part 3 we noted how critical theory endorsed the unity of the individual and society, values and research, and knowledge and action, and critiqued instrumental rationality. Herbert Marcuse showed how a capitalist consumer-society produces one-dimensional individuals. Jürgen Habermas justified the pursuit of critical knowledge and showed how to identify distorted communications with an ideal speech situation.

Gordon Allport and Amedeo Giorgi critiqued natural-science Psychology. Klaus Holzkamp, however, centralized praxis and advocated a Psychology from the standpoint of the subject (the social actor) not the psychologist. Current critical psychologists critique Psychology yet propose alternatives in theory, research, and practice.

In Part 4 we reviewed the principles and different types of feminism. In describing feminist critiques of science, we introduced dynamic objectivity, which recasts the observer–observed relationship as scientists' embrace of intersubjectivity and empathy towards their subject matter. Feminist psychologists take different positions on promoting equality for women and on epistemology and methodology in Psychology.

In Part 5 we reviewed postmodern perspectives. After describing Jean-François Lyotard's argument for abandoning grand narratives of universal truths, we explained how Michel Foucault applied critical analyses of the intersections of knowledge and power in societal institutions. In Psychology, Kurt Danziger expressed this social-constructionist orientation and Kenneth Gergen has promoted postmodernism.

Postcolonial critiques target the lack of recognition of current Psychology's cultural embeddedness. In Part 6 we discussed Western ethnocentrism in terms of time-centrism and culture-centrism and noted Psychology's epistemological problems of hidden neo-colonial thinking and problematization. Then we discussed the concept of respect for cultural diversity; reviewed Asian, African, and aboriginal viewpoints on psychological phenomena; and described Ignacio Martín-Baró's liberation psychology.

In Part 7 we described in the philosophical spirit of critical thinking how the themes that summarized the preceding chapters are interrelated and converge on the core theme of our book and this chapter: the problematic nature of current Psychology from the philosophical perspectives of ontology, epistemology, and ethics and politics. Yet we asserted that Psychology should not abandon its emancipatory potential; facts and values inherently are intertwined in all sciences. Hence, we proposed turning Psychology towards justice-seeking. In envisioning a transformation of Psychology in which international perspectives are central, we identified key issues and areas of critical praxis for theory, research, and social applications of Psychology.

Sample essay questions

1. In 1956 an infamous nuclear physicist, Robert Oppenheimer, advised psychologists that the worst mistake for them would be to emulate an outmoded physics; he was referring to contemporary natural-science psychologists' uncritical adoption of positivist epistemology with its objectivistic assumptions of realism, reductionism, and determinism. Explain why many psychologists continue to adhere to this standpoint.

2. What's critical about critical psychology in its current incarnation (e.g., the contributions to Fox *et al.*, 2009)? Compare this version to Holzkamp's critical psychology or Martín-Baró's liberation psychology.

3. In your opinion, should psychologists respond as psychologists or as private citizens to current sociopolitical issues, such as income inequity, threats to ecological survival, war, racism, sexism, homophobia, and ablism?

RECOMMENDED READING

On modern developments in the natural sciences Atkins (2003) discusses the major contributions, although with a presentist bias. Bryson (2003) summarizes the main achievements, debates, and controversies in physics, astronomy, biology, chemistry, and geology to the start of the twenty-first century. Manicas and Secord (1983) summarize clearly the implications for Psychology of developments in philosophy of science, which were stimulated by innovations in the natural sciences. Hallman (1992) describes the implications of scientific developments for ecologically sound living and global survival.

For an introductory overview of the various forms of critical psychology, see Hook's (2004) textbook, which provides critical psychological theory and praxis from a South African perspective. C. Tolman (1994) provides reviews the history and theory of Holzkamp's critical psychology. Sloan (2000) includes the personal voices as well as the ideas of critical psychologists. Teo (2005) provides a historical and systematic reconstruction of the various critiques of psychology. Slife *et al.* (2005) address critical thinking in Psychology and its areas. Prilleltensky and Nelson (2002) explore critical praxis. The chapters in Fox *et al.* (2009) provide an overview of recent developments.

There are many sources on feminism in Psychology. Rutherford *et al.* (2011) provide a current overview from an international perspective.

For overviews of postmodern perspectives on Psychology see Kvale (2003) and K. Gergen (1994).

Watts (1992) presents cultural diversity theory for psychologists. Two sources for postcolonial perspectives are Martín-Baró (1994) and Watkins and Shulman (2008).

ONLINE RESOURCES

Many of the individuals and concepts discussed in this chapter are addressed in the *Stanford Encyclopedia of Philosophy*: http://plato.stanford.edu/contents.html.

History & Philosophy of Psychology Web Resource provides a large number of resources and is maintained by Christopher Green: www.psych.yorku.ca/orgs/resource.htm.

The *Encyclopedia of Critical Psychology* has an online version available at: www.Springer Reference.com.

Timeline for the history and philosophy of psychology
c. 600 BCE – 2000 CE

Timeline for the history and philosophy of psychology c. 600 BCE – 2000 CE

600 BCE	0 CE	500	1000	1600

Ancient Greece (600–300)

Presocratic views of nature and human nature (600–385)

Socrates (469–399): critical thinking

Plato (429–347): idealism

Sophists (460–380): relativism

Aristotle (384–322): balance of empiricism and rationalism

Hellenistic civilization (c. 300 BCE–c. 0)

Therapeutic philosophies: Epicureanism (c. 300 BCE),
Stoicism (c. 300 BCE–c. 180 CE), Skepticism (c. 300 BCE–200 CE),
Cynicism (c. 400 BCE–c. 400 CE)

The Roman Empire (c. 44 BCE–c. 410 CE)

Galen (130–210): personality typology

Plotinus (204–270): Neoplatonism

Augustine (354–430): the psychological interior

The Middle Ages (c. 400–c. 1300)

Avicenna (980–1037): psychological ideas and treatments

Aquinas (c. 1225–1274): union of Platonic, Aristotelian, and
Avicennan thought

Emergent universities (1088–1600)

Scholasticism (c. 1100–1400): critical thinking

Ockham (c.1287–1347): nominalism and parsimony

The Renaissance (c. 1300–1600)

Humanism (c. 1300–1600)

Printing of texts (c. 1454),

Protestant Reformation (c. 1517–1600)

Emergent individualism (c. 1300–1600)

Global explorations (1490s–1600)

Copernicus (1473–1543):
heliocentric worldview

Montaigne (1533–1592):
critical thinking

Timeline for the history and philosophy of psychology 1600–1900

1600	1700	1800	1900

Modern era (c. 1550–1900s)

Colonialism and imperialism (c. 1500–1900s), industrial capitalism (c. 1760–1900s), socialist alternatives (1830s–1900s), urbanization (c. 1600–1900s), social management and individualization (c. 1500–1900s)
Abolition of slavery (1772–1865), women's movements (1848–1900s)

The Scientific Revolution (c. 1543–c. 1800)

Kepler (1571–1630) and Galileo (1564–1642): research confirmations of heliocentric worldview

Bacon (1561–1626): epistemology and methodology

Newton (1642–1727): ordered universe, laws of gravity and motion

Scientific developments (c. 1800–1900)

Gall (1758–1828): brain–behaviour
Broca (1824–1880): neuropsychology

Purkyně (1787–1869), Weber (1795–1878), J. Müller (1801–1858), Fechner (1891–1887): physiology and psychophysics

Helmholtz (1821–1894): law of energy conservation

Mach (1838–1916): positivism

Darwin (1809–1882): law of natural selection

Mendel (1822–1884): laws of heredity

New Enlightenment (1843–1880)

Comte: (1798–1857): positivism
Mill (1806–1873): utilitarianism
Marx (1818–1883): dialectical materialism

Psychological thought (c. 1600–1900)

Associationist philosophers:
Hobbes (1588–1679), Locke (1632–1704), Hartley (1705–1757), Hume (1711–1746)

French Enlightenment philosophers:
La Mettrie (1709–1751), Diderot (1713–1784), Condillac (1715–1780), Cabanis (1757–1808)

Rationalist philosophers:
Descartes (1596–1650), Spinoza (1632–1677), Leibniz (1646–1716), Berkeley (1685–1753)

Reconciliationist philosophers:
Reid (1710–1796), Kant (1724–1804)

Romantic philosophers:
Pascal (1623–1662),   Rousseau (1712–1778),   Goethe (1749–1832),   Schopenhauer (1788–1860)

Existentialist philosophers:
Kierkegaard (1813–1855),   Nietzsche (1844–1900)

Philosophical psychologists:
Biran (1766–1824), Herbart (1766–1841), Lotze (1817–1881), Bain (1818–1903)

Timeline for the history and philosophy of psychology 1875–1925

1875	1900	1925

Societal context (1875–1925)

Capitalist expansion and labour strife (1875–1925)   World War I (1914–1918)

Women's suffrage movement (1875–1925)

Expansion of tertiary (post-secondary) education and science programmes (1875–1925)

Scientific developments (1875–1925)

Sechenov (1829–1905), Pavlov (1849–1936), Bekhterev (1857–1927): Russian reflexology

Einstein (1879–1955): relativity theory

Planck (1858–1947): field/systems theory

Heisenberg (1901–1976): quantum mechanics

Natural-science psychology (1875–1925)

Wundt (1832–1920): voluntarism   Pavlov and Bekhterev: reflexology

James (1842–1910): functionalism   Titchener (1867–1927): structuralism

Dewey (1859–1952): social practice

Calkins (1863–1930): self theory

McDougall (1871–1938): hormic psychology

Watson (1878–1959): behaviourism

Wertheimer (1880–1943), Koffka (1886–1941),
Köhler (1887–1967): Gestalt theory

Human-science psychology (1875–1925)

S. Freud (1856–1939): psychoanalysis

Jung (1875–1961): analytical psychology

Adler (1870–1937): individual psychology

Dilthey (1833–1911), Spranger (1882–1963), and Jaspers (1883–1969): hermeneutic psychologies

Brentano (1838–1917) and Husserl (1859–1938): phenomenological psychologies

Wundt (1910–1920): cultural psychology   Stern (1871–1938): personalism

Societal applications of psychology

Galton (1822–1911): measurement of individual differences

Binet (1857–1911), Terman (1877–1956): intelligence testing

Thorndike (1874–1949): educational psychology

Münsterberg (1863–1916): industrial/organizational and forensic psychology

Personality testing (1920s)

Timeline for the history and philosophy of psychology 1925–2000

1925	1950	1975	2000

Societal context (1925–2000)

The Depression (1929–1930s), World War II (1939–1945), Cold War (1950s–1980s), neoliberal globalization (1980s–2000)
Anti-colonial and civil-rights movements (1950s–2000)　　Feminist movements (1960s–2000)

Scientific developments (1925–2000)

Molecular genetics (1925–1950s)　　Artificial intelligence (1940s–2000)　　Human genome project (1990s–2000)

Natural-science psychology (1925–2000)

Lewin (1890–1945): field theory　　　　　　Bruner (b. 1915), Miller (b. 1920), and Neisser (b. 1928): cognitivism

Piaget (1896–1980): genetic epistemology　　　　Behavioural and cognitive neuroscience (1980s–2000)

Vygotsky (1896–1934): cultural–historical theory　　　　Evolutionary psychology (1980s–2000)

Hull (1884–1952) and Tolman (1886–1959): neobehaviourism

Skinner (1904–1990): operant behaviourism

Pavlov: higher nervous activity (1920s–1938)
Lashley (1890–1958), Luria (1902–1977), Hebb (1904–1985), Sperry (1913–1994): biological psychology

Human-science psychology (1925–2000)

Freudian, Jungian, and Adlerian Psychoanalysis (1925–2000)　　Lacan (1901–1981): postmodern psychoanalysis
　　Horney (1885–1952), Fromm (1900–1980),　　　　Feminist psychoanalysis (1980s–2000)
　　Reich (1897–1957), Erikson (1902–1994): social psychoanalysis
　　A. Freud (1895–1982), Hartmann (1894–1970): ego psychology
　　　　　　　　　　　Kohut (1913–1981), Kernberg (b. 1928): self psychology
　　Klein (1882–1960): object relations　　Winnicott (1896–1971), Bowlby (1907–1990): middle group

Gadamer (1900–2002): hermeneutic psychology　　　　Giorgi (b. 1931): phenomenological psychology
Heidegger (1989–1976), Sartre (1905–1980), Binswanger (1881–1966): existentialism
　　　　Frankl (1905–1997), May (1909–1994): existential psychology
　　　　Maslow (1908–1970), Rogers (1902–1987): humanistic psychologies
　　　　　　　　Transpersonal psychologies (1969–2000)

Societal applications of psychology (1925–2000)

Industrial/organizational, educational, school, clinical, counselling, and sport psychology (1925–2000)
Intelligence and personality testing (1925–2000)
　　　　　　　Environmental and community psychology (1960s–2000)

Critiques of psychology

Marcuse (1898–1979): critical theory　　　　　　Habermas (b. 1929): emancipatory critique
　　　　　　　　　　　　Holzkamp (1927–1995): critical psychology
　　　　　　　Foucault (1926–1984): postmodern critique
　　　　　　　　　　Gergen (b. 1935): postmodern psychology
　　　　　　Postcolonial and indigenous psychologies (1960s–2000)
　　　　　　　　Feminist psychologies (1970s–2000)
　　　　　　　　Critical psychologies (1970s–2000)

GLOSSARY

absurd   In Camus' existentialism, the discrepancy between human beings' search for meaning and a world devoid of meaning.

accommodation   In Piaget's theory, altering *schemes* to suit particular environmental demands.

administrative science   Technology for administering mass groups in social institutions (e.g., workers, pupils, patients) in concert with the societal aim of social management.

affects   Early modern term for objectively knowable properties of emotions.

alchemy   The medieval, Renaissance, and early modern precursor of modern experimental chemistry by which practitioners believed that metals are active but become inert when unearthed; if reactivated, alchemists can convert them to the most precious metal, gold.

alienation   According to Marx, the concrete material conditions by which workers have no power over the planning and physical labour in contrast to capitalists. This segregation of conception from execution motivates human development and revolution.

anima mundi   A medieval Latin term, meaning the spirit of the world that enlivens all nature and individual soul-bodies; the world soul and individual souls are united.

animal behaviour   The scientific field of study focused on experimentation with animals concerning learning, motivation, memory, and social processes.

animal psychology   Generally, any research with nonhuman animals; specifically, any one or more of four domains: *animal behaviour*, *behavioural neuroscience*, *comparative psychology*, and *ethology*.

animal rights   A social movement promoting equal rights for animals by engaging in social action to abolish exploitation of animals including laboratory research.

animal spirits   The early modern view that tiny material components of blood are the dynamic force in animals' reflexive actions.

animal welfare   The social orientation to treating nonhuman animals with respect and preventing cruelty to them.

animism   Belief in a spirit or spirits present in all natural objects, including humans.

apperception   Reflective knowledge of the internal state of monads; using current language, apperception is conscious awareness that one perceives.

archetypes   In Jungian psychology, universal, unconscious symbolic expressions of certain emotions, images, and inherited cultural forms, manifest and experienced in different ways by different cultures, yet forming a common ground of human experience.

artificial intelligence   Computer systems programmed to implement applications of human intelligence that can exceed it in certain domains.

assimilation   In Piaget's theory, the process of using available concepts to perceive and interpret one's environment.

associationism   The belief that all psychological phenomena originate in atomistic, corpuscular sensations that mechanistic *laws of association* combine into complex ideas.

atomism   The belief that everything experienced in the world, including thoughts, is caused by the physical movement of atoms.

attachment theory   In Bowlby and Ainsworth's psychoanalytic approach, the proposition that infants' relations with their mothers have survival value; experiences of attachment, separation, and loss explain motivation and how we regulate our emotions and arousal levels, using cognitive appraisals and memory to support attachment ties.

authentic/inauthentic life   According to Kierkegaard's existential philosophy, in an authentic life, accepting the fact of inevitable death; in an inauthentic life, denying one's mortality.

behavioural neuroscience   Laboratory experimentation on the biological basis of the behaviour of small animals to extrapolate to basic, animal and human psychological processes.

behaviourism   A school of psychological thought focused on predicting and controlling the external behaviour of animals and humans.

"Book of Secrets"   Renaissance tradition in which scholars mixed magic rituals with extant science to gain power and control over the mysterious forces of nature.

Cartesian dualism   The belief in a sharp distinction between a superior voluntary mind and inferior, involuntary bodily action.

categorical imperative   An innate moral principle, universally present, which people are free to follow or not and which includes treating others as one wishes to be treated.

cell assembly   In Hebb's biopsychology, a representation of an image or thought, corresponding to a particular sensory event or a common aspect of a number of sensory events.

chaos theory   In current physics, the view that the universe functions in terms of sensitive dependence on initial conditions such that small changes in them can alter the ultimate state of a system dramatically.

character armour   In Reich's psychology, an unconscious psychic conflict solidified in an individual's personality, embodied in muscular tension, making one immune to pleasurable bodily sensations and defensive against full experience.

chauvinism   The belief that one's nation is unique, thus superior to other nations.

cognitive neuroscience   The study of the intersections of mental phenomena and processes with brain structures and functions.

cognitive psychology   The subdiscipline of Psychology focused on symbolic representations of mental phenomena and processes.

cognitivism   A school of psychological thought focused on predicting, controlling, and understanding mental processes.

colonial project (colonialism)   The establishment of a regime of subjugation by one group of people or nation over another.

common sense   The Enlightenment belief in an innate disposition towards moral social relations and towards a shared understanding of things that everyone takes for granted.

community feeling   In Adler's psychology, sensing the interdependence and empathizing with people in one's family and community, extending to all humankind, natural objects, and the universe; in community psychology, the psychological sense of community.

comparative psychology   The field of study focused on behavioural and animal-cognition experimentation from an evolutionary perspective.

compensation   In Adler's psychology, struggling for respect to overcome feelings of inferiority.

conation   Early modern term meaning expression of an intention that evokes motoric activity.

conatus   an early modern term meaning that motion or "endeavour" (i.e., striving) characterized all natural objects, including humans' voluntary action.

congruence   In Rogerian theory, emotional genuineness or authenticity; being true to one's emotions evokes mental health, while lack of congruence can evoke mental disorders.

connectionism   A model of cognition based on brain organization by which mathematized neural activity undergirds complex cognitive functions.

constructive alternativism   In Kelly's form of psychotherapy, motivation to reduce uncertainty and construct worldviews to predict what will happen next, because individuals have the freedom to choose how to construct their psychological reality.

constructivism   In Piaget's theory, the belief that children construct meaning from their experience, a capacity that mediates between inherited and environmental influences.

contextualize   To describe the social-historical features of a body of knowledge or social practice.

controlled experimentation   The method of administering an independent variable to a treatment group whose performance is compared to a group that does not receive the treatment but is otherwise equivalent to the treatment group.

corpuscles   Microscopic particles believed to comprise all natural objects.

counter-factualism   A method of history that considers alternative possibilities to actual events, speculating on what might have happened, while mindful of plausible dimensions of character, time, and place.

counter-transference   Psychotherapists' unconscious positive and negative attachments to their patients.

critical historical objectivism   The scholarly practice of doing full justice to historical perspectives while mindful that present horizons infiltrate historical studies.

critical (sophisticated) presentism   The scholarly practice of using historical material for the intention of elucidating current perspectives theoretically.

critical science   Any discipline motivated to accomplish emancipation from ideological constraints and oppressive social systems through critical self-reflection and practice.

critical thinking   Sets of intellectual and moral resources that include the logical skill of analyzing the nature of claims in terms of the quality of the evidence and of the interpretation of that evidence used to support the claims and the analytic and synthetic skills of understanding theories and practices in cultural-historical context, shaped by social categories.

cross-cultural psychology   The standpoint by which investigators, typically from privileged nations, compare psychological phenomena endemic in their own ethnocultural domain to other ethnocultural domains, often formerly colonized.

cultural diversity   In Psychology, understanding the cultural limitations of all psychological concepts and showing respect for every population's strengths, competencies, and distinctive solutions to problems of living.

cybernetics   Massive digital, automatized communication systems. Also, in Wiener's model, a theory of control systems and feedback mechanisms navigating between partially known agents and unpredictable events.

Dasein   German noun for existence ("being-in-the-world"); the person's existence occurring in the totality of things and events around her or him, including the localized environment.

Daseinsanalyse   German term for existential analysis, Binswanger's approach to psychotherapy.

deconstruction   A strategy of disrupting the illusion of foundational, universal truths and essences by means of critical analysis of an accepted discourse by describing what might have been hidden, ignored, or repressed in that discourse, particularly in relation to conditions of power and authority, including what might have been marginalized and silenced.

deduction   The act of deriving knowledge of particular instances from general logical principles.

demand characteristics   An artifact of experimentation whereby participants subtly produce data that will support their perception of the investigators' hypothesis.

deontology   An approach to ethics emphasizing the study of ethical duties.

determinism   The belief that external forces induce the actions of all natural objects, including humans; also, the positivist principle that with knowledge of the present state of any matter and with Newton's laws of physics, one can identify linear cause-and-effect relations and can determine or predict the exact state or future of that matter.

dialectical argument   Historical or philosophical argument by which a given *thesis* and its opposite, an *antithesis*, produce a *synthesis* that sooner or later divides into new clashes, and so forth.

dialectical materialism   The belief, associated with Marx, that concrete material conditions, principally who holds economic and political power, shape ideas and are the basis for knowledge in a given social-historical context.

differential psychology   The study of how individual variation in psychological characteristics is distributed in a population.

disciplinary matrix   The often unstated but organized structure of theoretical, methodological, and social assumptions in any scientific discipline.

discourse   The system of language, objects, and practices embodying a particular domain of knowledge, which is embedded in a particular cultural-historical context.

discourse analysis   In Foucault's approach, scholars analyze written or spoken language as a social practice infused with human interests and biases; the premise is that language is embedded in ideological, oppressive, or exploitative practices.

discursive formation   In social constructionism, a semantic network from which psychological terms and concepts derive their meaning and significance.

disputations   In medieval scholasticism, the method of making the most convincing, logical arguments and guarding against indistinct or incorrect inferences.

doctrine of specific nerve energies   According to Müller, the belief that each nerve releases specific qualities or energy and no matter how it is stimulated, every sensory nerve responds uniquely.

dynamic objectivity   A feminist term that embraces subjectivity, connectedness, and empathy towards the subject matter.

ego psychology   A form of psychoanalysis, associated with Anna Freud and Heinz Hartmann, stressing ego functions, defence mechanisms, and adaptation to one's environment.

empathic understanding   Active listening in any helping relationship and understanding the other's emotions at the level at which he or she expresses them. For Rogers, empathic understanding facilitates psychological growth.

empirical–analytic sciences   Natural sciences (e.g., physics, chemistry, and biology) motivated by technical interests to gain instrumental knowledge that permits prediction and manipulation of natural phenomena according to universal laws.

empiricism   The belief that sensory observations are primary in gaining natural knowledge and that all ideas are derived from sensory experience.

empiriocriticism   Mach's epistemological standpoint that all natural events consist of physical and psychological aspects of sensory observations.

the Enlightenment   A stage of intellectual history in the eighteenth century of regarding the natural world as proceeding progressively and as knowable objectively, involving the use of reason based on natural knowledge alone, rather than religious faith and dogma.

Epicureanism   Founded by Epicurus, a materialist philosophy of nature, stressing the goal of life as pleasure, only attainable by avoiding extremes.

episteme   Ancient Greek term for causal knowledge; in Gadamer's hermeneutics, conceptual knowledge.

epistemological violence   A hermeneutic process of interpreting data that is critically unaware and has negative consequences for historically marginalized social groups.

epistemology   The branch of philosophy concerned with the nature of knowledge and how one acquires knowledge.

equipotentiality   Lashley's principle that no cortical area is more important to learning than any other area and many parts of the brain are used at one time to complete a task.

eros   A generic life-force of psychic energy in human nature.

ethics   The branch of philosophy that tries to elucidate the nature of morality and its social applications, including how we should conduct ourselves.

ethnocentrism   The tendency to use one's own culture or ethnicity as the criterion to judge all others.

ethology   A field of study focused on field research, using observation or experimentation, on animal behaviour.

eudaemonia   In Aristotle's thought, the state of flourishing (happiness), which is inextricably tied to ethical obligations; everything aims at the good or aims to flourish.

eugenics   Victorian belief in selective breeding and preventing parentage by the intellectually and morally unfit.

evaluation apprehension   An artifact of experimentation whereby participants are anxious to present themselves to data administrators in the most favourable way possible.

existential anxiety   Anxiety about mortality, avoidance of which leads to inauthentic living.

experience   A person's meaningful subjective encounters with the natural, cultural, historical, and human world.

experimental control   Also known as "experimental analysis," the method of repeatedly observing antecedents and consequences of manipulated variables in single cases.

experimenter bias   Artifact of experimentation whereby data collectors unwittingly communicate expectations to participants regarding the investigators' experimental hypotheses.

faculty psychology   The Enlightenment belief that mental faculties (capacities) are innate and universal.

falsification   The logical process by which one establishes truth by searching for negative empirical instances of one's hypothesis.

feminism   Theory and action committed to political, economic, and social equality for women and men.

field theory   In physics, a network of intersecting forces that take a particular form or structure by which natural phenomena are caused; observers attend to the field or pattern of elements that form the new structure. In Lewin's psychological theory, how individuals perceive their environments and how their attempts to satisfy their needs affect their social interactions.

functional autonomy   In G. Allport's explanation of motivation, actions stemming from present traits and values that function independently of their early origins.

functionalism   A school of US psychological thought, based on Darwinian theory, stressing purpose and function in animals' and humans' behaviour and how the mind works practically to enable individuals to adapt to their environments. In the neuroscientific context, a model of cognition based on the functions of serial information-processing and reliant on the analogy of computer hardware to the brain and computer software to the mind.

fusion of horizons   According to Gadamer's hermeneutics, in the process of understanding phenomena, the act of merging the interpreter's (current) horizon with the (past) horizon of the interpreted.

Geisteswissenschaften   German term, introduced by Dilthey, meaning generally the disciplines encompassing historical-social reality as far as this reality has been conserved historically in the consciousness of humankind; specifically, "the humanities," e.g., history, political science, law, political economy, theology, literature, and art.

genetic epistemology   In Piaget's theory, the study of how children develop the capacity to think scientifically.

genomics   Technology for manipulating life at the genetic level.

Gestalt   German noun roughly meaning in English overall form, shape, or configuration and connoting a structured whole system of interdependent parts subordinate to the whole.

group dynamics   Term coined by Lewin to refer to small-group processes (e.g., patterns of group interaction).

habit strength   In neobehaviourism, the quality of stimulus–response connections; the greater the number of reinforcements, the stronger the habit.

harm principle   In Mill's social philosophy, the idea that individual liberty cannot be infringed by government, society, or individuals except when an individual's action might harm others.

Hebb synapse rule   Hebb's principle of biological psychology referring to interacting neurons becoming permanently associated and a quasi-equation predicting the rate of learning, given the nature of neural connections; presently employed by behavioural and cognitive neuroscientists for neural-network models of learning and memory.

hedonism   The belief in the pursuit of pleasure as the greatest good.

hermeneutic circle   According to Gadamer's hermeneutics, understanding the meaning of a fact in history by understanding its context, but also understanding the whole context as the totality of the parts that comprise the whole.

hermeneutic deficit   A hermeneutic principle referring to methodological and epistemological problems surrounding the issue of interpretive speculations.

hermeneutic surplus   A hermeneutic principle that one always and inevitably understands any set of data by interpretive speculation; thus, there are no "facts," only data and interpretations.

hermeneutics   The discipline of and procedures for understanding and interpreting the meaning of particular human practices.

hierarchy of needs   In Maslow's theory of motivation, hierarchical organization of needs according to how human they are with self-actualization at the peak.

historical-hermeneutical sciences   Interpretive sciences (e.g., literature, languages, and history) that are intended to derive practical knowledge in providing an interpretive understanding of human phenomena.

historical objectivism   Cautious, methodical interpretation that measures the past according to its own standards.

historicism   The act of interpreting the past from the perspective of the past.

historicity   In Husserl's phenomenology, the concrete life-world of a researcher as the immediate context for the foundation of all scientific meaning.

historiography   The philosophy, history, and methods of history as a scholarly pursuit.

history   The discipline of interpreting past events and objects from multiple perspectives in order to understand their meaning.

horizon   According to Gadamer's hermeneutics, the extent of one's perspective.

human nature   The subject matter of the nature of human beings; the view that humans are natural objects and studying human action can improve moral conduct.

human sciences   Various disciplines concerned with describing and interpreting the meaning of human action.

humanism   A system of Renaissance thought stressing human rather than divine matters.

humours   In Renaissance thought, bodily fluids determining human behaviour and personality.

hylomorphism   In Aristotle's thought, the belief that natural objects are composed of the unity of matter and form.

hypothetico-deductive method   According to Hull, the experimental method of proposing theoretical postulates about behaviour, then deducing from them operationally defined testable hypotheses.

hysteria   A psychological disorder whereby physical symptoms are present that do not correspond to underlying physiology but are attributed to a psychic cause; in Freudian theory, an unconsciously motivated defence against traumatic sexual experience during childhood.

iatrogenic effects   Healer-caused harm; in mental health, negative effects from psychotherapy or psychological treatments.

idealism   The belief that ultimate reality is mental or spiritual and consists of ideas in one's consciousness; conversely, material phenomena are illusory.

idiographic   Methodology oriented to describing single human events to facilitate understanding them; compatible with a human-science approach; contrasted with *nomothetic*.

immanent critique   In Marcuse's framework, criticism of a particular system or ideology by the terms of the systems or ideology itself.

imperialism   A process of political, military, economic, and cultural domination that several European powers and later the USA pursued globally. Sometimes used synonymously with colonialism, imperialism is the extension of nationalism on a larger geographical scale.

inclusive fitness   An evolutionary term, meaning genes transmitted to the next generation through direct reproduction or by the reproduction of close relatives.

individualization   Cultural emphasis, emerging during the Renaissance and predominating in modern Western thought, on the subjective experience of each individual.

induction   The act of deriving generalizations from particular instances.

instrumental rationality   In critical theory, the modernist practice of using reason as an authoritarian administrative instrument to solve technical and social problems efficiently.

intentionality   In human-science psychologies, the act of being intentional or conscious about conducting one's life.

internationalization   Originally, the distribution and propagation of US Psychology to the rest of the world or at best, cross-cultural psychology based on a Western worldview; presently, the term also means a shift to an international postcolonial Psychology.

intersectionality   In interpersonal psychology, a concept referring to the meaning and consequences of one's multiple social identities, such as ethnocultural status, class, and gender.

intersubjectivity   Belief in the mutual influence of researchers and participants on particular psychological phenomena of interest.

intervening variables   In neobehaviourism, operationally defined variables that link unobservable processes (e.g., expectancies) to observable independent and dependent variables.

investigative practice   Danziger's social-constructionist term referring to the logical procedures and social aspects of conducting research.

isomorphism   A Gestalt concept meaning identical forms, that is, forms that share a common structure.

just-noticeable difference (jnd)   In psychophysics, the least amount of difference between two stimuli needed to distinguish them.

Lacanian theory   A form of psychoanalysis positing that unconscious processes are fundamentally linguistic not instinctual; neither ego nor object relations are central to human experience, because experience is always intersubjective, linguistically embedded in cultural trends.

law of conservation of energy   Helmholtz's principle of physics, stating that energy is never created or lost in a system; it is only changed from one form to another.

law of effect   According to Thorndike, responses leading to pleasure are "stamped in," reinforcing stimulus–response connections.

laws of association   As originally proposed by Aristotle, the laws are similarity, contiguity, and contingency. To wit, if objects or ideas are similar, contiguous in time or space, or contingently related as apparent cause and effect, they will be learned more easily than objects or ideas that lack such association.

liberation theology   A Latin American movement integrating Marxian interpretation of the Hebrew and Christian bibles with political action. The premise is that, inspired by the biblical call to practise justice, citizens should transform the societal structures that cause inequality and distress through collective, non-violent action.

life-space   A Lewinian concept, meaning the indivisible unity of a person and all perceived physiological, sensory, motivational, cognitive, interpersonal, and cultural influences operating on the person.

limen   Sensory threshold, the point at which a sensory experience becomes just strong enough to penetrate awareness.

logical positivism   A system of philosophical justification of scientific knowledge stipulating three conditions: theoretical terms expressed mathematically, correspondence between theoretical terms and observational statements, and observational statements describing particular natural objects.

logotherapy   Frankl's form of existential psychotherapy, based on the notions of freedom of the will, the will to meaning in the social world, and the meaning of life.

mass action   Lashley's principle that the rate of learning depends on the mass of cortical tissue, not on individual cells.

materialism   The belief that all natural objects, including psychological phenomena, and the only reality are composed of matter, not spirit, and are explicable completely by the movement of atoms and mechanical principles.

mechanism   The belief that mechanistic natural-scientific laws explain all natural objects and their motion; when extended to explaining human nature, body and mind are believed to constitute one material substance that obeys mechanistic principles.

mentalism   The belief that mental processes constitute the ultimate reality.

metaphysics   The philosophical study of ultimate reality existing beyond the appearances of the material world.

methodolatry   Psychologists' virtual worship of quantitative methods, particularly lab experimentation, exclusive of other paths to scientific knowledge.

methodological pluralism   The principle of appreciating the limits of any research method and combining methods to better understand observed phenomena.

methodologism   An epistemological orientation focusing on methodology rather than on subject matter and an investigative standpoint in which the subject matter is secondary but quantitative methodology is applied to all research questions.

middle group   Forms of psychoanalysis, associated with Bowlby, Fairbairn, and Winnicott, focusing on the intrapsychic drama of attachment and loss within actual mother–infant relations.

modernism   The belief since the eighteenth-century Age of Enlightenment in inevitable human progress, facilitated by science and technology.

monads   Irreducible, conscious, microscopic points of energy that function harmoniously yet autonomously.

monism   The belief that ultimately there exists only one unchanging substance in nature.

naïve presentism   The act of describing and evaluating the past in terms of present perspectives, oblivious to the problem of presentism.

naïve realism   The positivist principle that the sensed properties of objects are inherent in the objects themselves and the mind mirrors objects as they are.

nanotechnology   A form of biotechnology and bioengineering operating on an extremely microscopic scale.

natural magic   Quasi-experimentation to produce esoteric knowledge about natural substances.

natural philosophy   Premodern and early modern term for systematic study of nature and natural objects, including humans.

natural sciences   Various disciplines concerned with investigating natural objects and involving explanations rooted in causal laws.

natural selection   The Darwinian principle that nature selects changes in species that enable them to adapt to their environment over time and survive.

naturalism   The belief that all reality is explicable in strictly natural, not religious, terms and that mental processes are explicable completely by sensory mechanisms and secular reason.

negativism   An artifact of experimentation whereby participants deliberately falsify their performance, either covertly or overtly, due to feelings of resentment directed at data collectors.

Neoplatonism   A philosophical movement during the Hellenistic era, associated with Plotinus, reviving Plato's metaphysics and psychological thought.

neorealism   The belief that the empirical world is that which is perceived.

neural plasticity   Lashley's principle that if injured, inherently adaptive and malleable nerves and neurons reorganize to restore basic behaviour.

neuroscience   A school of psychological thought focused on predicting, controlling, and understanding the relationship between neural processes and structures with behaviour.

nominalism   The belief that individual things exist, but the names we give things, generalities, or universal statements are not subjects of existence.

nomothetic   Methodology oriented to producing universal laws of explanation; compatible with a natural-science approach; contrasted with *idiographic*.

noumenon   The world behind appearances.

object permanence   In Piaget's theory, belief that infants learn that objects retain their existence even when invisible.

object relations theory   A general theory of psychoanalysis with specific variants, stressing the drive for connection with internalized or external human objects (interpersonal relationships) and focusing on pre-Oedipal infant–mother relations that are thought to form a template for all further object relations.

objectivism   A critical term, meaning obsession with abstract ahistorical objectivity, accompanied by neglect of the social context and human interests saturating scientific activity.

objectivist illusion   An epistemological consequence of the avid search for universal laws to explain empirically observed natural objects that obscure cultural and sociopolitical interests.

Ockham's razor   The belief, advanced by William of Ockham, in simplifying explanations of natural phenomena by using the least number of assumptions necessary; also known as the law of parsimony.

ontology   The branch of philosophy that studies the nature of being (i.e., existence) and inquires about the essential properties of the world, the universe, and the cosmos.

operational definition   Bridgman's proposal for physics, which US psychologists adopted in the 1930s, that every abstract concept be defined only in terms of the procedures used to measure it.

operationism   The methodological doctrine stipulating that psychologists can measure any mentalistic concept as objectively as physicists can measure natural objects.

operations   In Piaget's theory, referring to how the mind implements *schemes*.

panopticon   An architectural design for an ideal prison where the guard tower located in the middle always allows guards to observe prisoners in their cells.

paradigm   The basic set of assumptions, or cognitive blueprint, that scientists employ in their work; a paradigm comprises a *disciplinary matrix* and a *shared exemplar*.

paradoxical intention   Frankl's therapeutic technique of encouraging a client or patient to do or desire the very things that he or she fears.

paranoid and depressive positions   In Klein's form of psychoanalysis, inborn dispositions through which infants develop as they attempt to integrate hate and love; first in the paranoid position, organizing discomfort and pain into fantasies of bad, hateful, persecuting human objects; then in the depressive position, organizing comfort and pleasure into fantasies of good, loving, rescuing human objects.

patriarchy   Men's historical domination and control of social institutions and the psyche through, often unconscious, male-centred values and practices that devalue the female gender; an ideology that infuses the structures and dynamics of all aspects of the social order, including psychological concepts.

phenomenology   The study, without preconceptions, of individuals' direct experience of phenomena as they appear and the meaning individuals attribute to that experience.

phi phenomenon   The perception of apparent, continuous movement from stationary flashing lights, showing that perceptual experience as a whole essentially differs from the sum of unrelated elements.

philosophes   French term for a group of eighteenth-century French scholars who embraced natural philosophy, celebrated reason, and rejected church and state control of knowledge.

philosophy   Literally, the love of wisdom; the systematic form of critical inquiry with many branches in which individuals subject their experience to scrutiny.

phrenology Gall's belief that brain locations and cranial shape cause mental faculties. Later popularized by Spurzheim, the practice of linking particular personality traits with presumed causal, specific cranial bumps and brain locations.

phronesis An ancient Greek term for rationally exercising "good sense" in one's sociopolitical context; in Gadamer's hermeneutics, moral knowledge.

physicalism The positivist belief that everything can be explained by means of the concepts and methods of physics.

polycentrism A critical standpoint advocating culturally diverse centres of disciplinary activity, based on the view that, rather than universal, psychological processes and mechanisms are relative to given cultural environments.

positive psychology An approach to natural-science Psychology in which adherents study human happiness with the goal of aiding individuals, communities, and societies to flourish.

positivism The epistemological doctrine that science pertains only to the acquisition of empirical facts by controlled observation and that all concepts and conclusions are deduced exclusively from those facts. Also, Comte's ideology and social movement, according to which scientific knowledge is, by definition, positive knowledge that yields truth, harmony, and order in society.

postcolonial Referring to the period when overt colonialism faded, this critical term implies that colonial ideas and practices should not play a role in science and Psychology.

postmodernism Various sets of criticisms, advanced in the late twentieth century, of modernism.

Praegnanz The Gestalt principle that all psychological experiences are pregnant with the potential to be as organized, symmetrical, meaningful, and regular as they can be, given the pattern of brain activity at any given moment.

pragmatism A relativist philosophical approach to metaphysical, epistemological, and ethical questions; true ideas are those that work in their environments.

praxis In critical psychology, the dialectical unity of theory and practice.

pre-established harmony The belief that God established parallelism between body and mind/soul so that they operate in perfect harmony, but are not causally related.

presentism A bias in historiography by which one interprets the past from a current perspective or interprets the past primarily in terms of its value for the present.

presocratics Ancient Greek philosophers before the era of Socrates and Plato.

primary vs. secondary vs. tertiary sources Original writings vs. commentaries on those writings vs. third parties' interpretations of commentaries on the original writings.

problematization In the postcolonial context, making into problems groups of people who differ from one's own ethnocultural standpoint.

problematize To describe the problems with conventional ideas about a body of knowledge or social practice.

progressive education Dewey's theory of adaptive learning based on active participation rather than rote acquisition of habits.

psychoanalysis Various theories of unconscious psychological dynamics, various forms of psychotherapeutic practice derived from psychoanalysis, and an investigative method.

Psychology or psychology   *Psychology* (with an upper-case *P*) means the modern discipline as a science and profession, whereas *psychology* (with a lower-case *p*) refers to psychological subject matter with ancient roots, practised in diverse cultures through philosophical inquiry or self-reflection.

Psychology – modern   See *Psychology as a human science* and *Psychology as a natural science*.

psychology – premodern   The study of the human soul.

Psychology as a human science   The modern science of the subjective experience of thinking, feeling, and willing, and making one's intentions known to oneself or others in a social context of meaningful action and reflection.

Psychology as a natural science   The modern science of the prediction, control, and understanding of behaviour and mental processes.

psychophysical parallelism   The belief that physical and psychic (mental) causality are distinct and on parallel tracks; immediate experience is physical, while mediated experience is mental.

psychophysics   The scientific study of the psychological experience of sensory stimulation.

psychotherapeutics   Psychotherapy in the form of rational persuasion, hypnosis, or suggestion.

qualia   The psychological experience of cognitive processes and their neural correlates.

quantitative imperative   The belief and practice in natural-science Psychology that measurement and statistical analysis are essential components of genuine psychological research.

quantum mechanics   In physics, a theory of matter and energy stipulating that when light and matter interact, radiated energy exists in multiples of a unit (a "quantum") and energy transfers only in discrete chunks. The theory pertains to objects ranging from the invisible and subatomic to the cosmic.

radical empiricism   The belief that direct experience is primary such that matter and mind are only concepts generated by interpretations of experience.

rationalism   Belief that the exercise of reason, expressed in logical thought, is the ultimate source of truth rather than empirical observation or intuition; in psychological thought, the belief that higher mental processes, rather than emotion and unconscious motives, are primary and that an active mind engages in complex operations on sensory impressions.

reality principle   The ego function that regulates one's attempts to balance satisfying basic human drives with interpersonal and societal demands.

recapitulation   The concept that individuals across their lifespan repeat the evolutionary stages of development of the entire human race; evolutionary older functions mature before newer ones.

reconciliation   A philosophical orientation to psychological thought balancing empiricism/association with rationalism and moral agency.

reduction   According to Husserl's phenomenology, a methodological tool taking three forms – phenomenological, eidetic, and transcendental – that enables understanding phenomena as experienced subjectively.

reductionism   The positivist principle that systematic examination of the underlying nature of the basic elements that constitute all natural objects best explains natural objects.

reflexivity   The act of acknowledging openly how personal biases might have shaped one's interpretations.

reflexology   The study of reflex mechanisms involved in connecting particular senses, organs, sensory nerves, the spine, and motor nerves, and their application to psychological functions.

reification   The logical error of assuming that naming an examined phenomenon gives it objective existence.

relativity theory   In physics, the theory that time and the three dimensions of space (height, width, and length) are interrelated, not separate phenomena, and measurement of natural events is relative to the observer's position in time and space.

repression   In psychodynamic thought, unconscious self-policing and avoidance of unacceptable erotic and aggressive impulses.

research relationship   Professional relationship in which researchers engage with individuals who provide data; the term includes research roles or functions, ethics, and reporting standards.

resistance   In psychoanalysis and other psychotherapies, a client's or patient's unconscious avoidance of confronting psychologically threatening material evoked during treatment.

rhetoric   The literary art of persuasion; as a social practice, discursive structures and strategies used to make arguments persuasive; as a discipline, the study of argumentation.

robotics   The technology of designing, constructing, operating, and applying robots.

romanticism   The philosophical, artistic, and social movement stressing love of nature, the wisdom of feelings, and beneficent social relations.

salons   Semi-formal discussions, emerging in the early modern era, among privileged Europeans, including women, about the latest developments in natural philosophy and the arts.

scaffolding   A Vygotskian concept referring to adults assisting children to solve a problem beyond their present autonomous capacities.

scaling   A quantitative technique employed in attitude measurement, adopted from the judgment-paradigm of nineteenth-century psychophysicists.

schema   A neurological term meaning mental representations, adopted by Bartlett to express remembering as active organization of past responses into an adaptive mental framework.

schemes   In Piaget's theory, organized patterns of constructing reality, generalized from specific motoric actions.

scholasticism   The medieval tradition of speculative argument to achieve deeper understanding of Christian truths by defining, reasoning, and systematizing.

science   Originally, any type of systematic knowledge, whether related to the natural world or not, shaped by standards of rigour and certainty; in modern German-speaking societies, any type of theoretical knowledge, but in modern Anglo-American societies, any of the *natural sciences*.

scientific management   In industrial/organizational psychology, the assessment and control of segmented aspects of the process of labour for a particular job to increase efficiency and reduce the costs of production; also known as "Taylorism."

scientific racism   Scientific rationales for and practices of marginalizing an ethnocultural group or people.

Scientific Revolution   Modern term for changed conceptions concerning Earth's place in the solar system and humankind's place on Earth and for discourse on a systematic methodology for practising natural philosophy.

scientism   Emergent during the Enlightenment, a distortion of science, the exaggerated, almost religious belief in the powers of scientific knowledge and research methods.

second-order conditioning   In the Pavlovian model, a previously neutral stimulus (e.g., a light) paired with a conditional stimulus (e.g., a tone) that elicits the same conditional response as the conditional stimulus.

self psychology   A form of psychoanalysis, associated with Kohut and Kernberg but indebted to object-relations theory, concentrating on relations with oneself and emphasizing basic narcissistic motives and the needs for self-esteem and self-cohesiveness.

sensori commune   Latin term for common sensibility, which according to Kant and early modern scientists is a unified sensory mass where the external world meets the internal neural world.

sexual complementarity   The Enlightenment belief that, although women had their areas of expertise, they were essentially different from men biologically, were intellectually inferior, and should remain socially subordinate to men.

shared exemplars   Consensually approved methods for a given science that serve as models of "good" research to guide the investigation of new areas.

sign theory   In K. Bühler's approach, the notion that words serve as signs or representations, not as unambiguous reflections, of objects, events, and experiences.

social character   In Fromm's psychology, personality characteristics shaped by particular socioeconomic systems.

social constructionism   The practice of studying how historical figures have constructed events and objects from their own discourse at different times and in different cultural-historical contexts.

social Darwinism   The belief that all societies reflect the struggle for survival in nature; the poor, the "non-White races," and militarily weaker nations should be left to fend for themselves according to the "laws of nature."

social management   The increasing organization of economic, political, and cultural life, escalating since the early modern period, to maintain control over society's members and achieved by the establishment of formal social institutions.

social and political philosophy   The branches of philosophy that raise questions about how members of society deal with the problems of distribution of resources and of governance.

socialism   In Marxist terms, collective ownership of the means of economic production.

sociobiology   The biological study of social behaviour, particularly racial, intellectual, and gender differences.

Socratic method (dialogue)   A method of inquiry, associated with Socrates, taking the dialectical form of a conversational process of examining fundamental puzzles, contradictions, and absurdities obscured by common understanding.

solipsism   The notion that nothing beyond "me" exists and that everything else in the world is "my" invention; a product of complete subjectivity.

spiritualisme   French term for a nineteenth-century idealistic emphasis on inner awareness of an essentially spiritual self.

structuralism   According to Titchener, the core elements in the structure of consciousness. In Piaget's theory, the belief that children's constructions of knowledge produce knowledge-structures. In twentieth-century European thought (e.g., Lacan's form of psychoanalysis), emphasis on language, ritual, and myth shaping social customs and generating subjectivity.

subjectivism   The belief in the primacy of personal subjective experience over against "objective," directly observable empirical reality.

subjectivity   Personal experiences of thinking, feeling, and willing and the meanings that individuals attribute to these experiences.

sublimation   An unconscious process of transforming sexual impulses into socially acceptable actions.

surrealism   An interwar cultural movement that rejected traditional values of honouring country, religion, and work, and stressed exploring unconscious mental phenomena such as dreams, mental illness, the uncanny, coincidences, and fantasy.

tabula rasa   Empiricist metaphor of a blank tablet on which experience and education inscribe ideas in opposition to the idealist position that children express innate ideas.

teleology   An idealistic grand design or purpose attributed to nature, a modern criticism of Aristotelian theory.

temperaments   In personality theory, individual differences in biologically based dispositions that emerge early in life and are expressed in behavioural attributes.

theory of mind   Notions about how humans and other animals attain awareness of other creatures' emotions and thinking.

Thomism   The philosophy and theology of Thomas Aquinas.

time-centrism   A presentist bias in historiography by which our own time is the criterion for all other times, based on current standards.

traits   Descriptions of temperaments.

transference   Unconscious process in psychotherapies whereby clients come to behave as if the therapist were someone from their past, generating feelings of love or hostility towards the analyst; in Freudian psychoanalysis, a therapeutic technique of making the unconscious positive or negative transference available for analysis.

transpersonal psychology   A body of psychological knowledge that focuses on mystical and spiritual aspects of life that are believed to be central to human nature.

truth   According to *correspondence theory*, truth is correspondence between an object/event and a statement about this object/event; according to *consensus theory*, truth derives from the consensus of all who speak the same language with regard to the object/event.

types   Conceptual categories that organize traits.

uncertainty principle, the   In physics, the notion that the more accurately one wishes to measure an object's position, the less accurately one is able to measure the object's velocity, and vice versa.

unconditional positive regard   In Rogerian theory, showing others in one's care (e.g., children, counselling or psychotherapy clients) acceptance without conditions for who they truly are.

utilitarianism   In Bentham's social philosophy, calculating the greatest good for the most people by maximizing pleasure and minimizing pain.

variable   In physics and mathematics, a variable quantity; in Psychology, implying actual or intended linear cause-and-effect relations between two or more psychological quantities.

vitalism   Renaissance and early modern beliefs that life-processes involve an immaterial life-force or soul, present in all natural objects, which cannot be reduced to material mechanisms, and that matter is capable of self-generation and self-motion.

vivisection   The practice of subjecting live lab animals to physical constraints and surgical procedures to isolate specific functions for experimental manipulation.

Völkerpsychologie   A German noun, meaning, roughly, psychology of a people or culture; for Wundt, how the collective identity of a people shapes individual consciousness.

voluntarism   The belief that exercising free will is the primary human capacity and instigates action.

Whig history   The inclination of historians to characterize British history as a steady march of progress leading inevitably to constitutional monarchy; by extension, an interpretive bias by which scholars wrench historical actions from their context and evaluate them in terms of how they illustrate progress.

will to power   In Nietzsche's psychological thought, the single explanatory principle of nature and human nature by which individuals exert their capacities to gain mastery over one's self and one's destiny.

zeitgeist   A German noun meaning literally "the spirit of the time," referring to the intellectual and cultural climate of an era.

zone of proximal development   In Vygotskian theory, a term denoting the gap between a child's actual and potential developmental levels.

REFERENCES

Aarsleff, Hans (1993). Locke's influence. In Vere Chappell (ed.), *The Cambridge companion to Locke* (pp. 252–289). Cambridge University Press.

Abir-Am, Pnina G., & Outram, Dorinda (eds.) (1987). *Uneasy careers and intimate lives: Women in science 1789–1979*. New Brunswick, NJ: Rutgers University Press.

Abma, Ruud (2004). Madness and mental health. In Jeroen Jansz & Peter van Drunen (eds.), *A social history of psychology* (pp. 93–128). Oxford: Blackwell.

Aboitiz, Francisco, Garcia, Ricardo, Brunnette, Enzo, & Bosman, Conrado (2005). The origin of Broca's area and its connections from an ancestral working memory network. In Yosef Grodzinsky & Katrin Amunst (eds.), *Broca's region* (pp. 3–16). New York: Oxford University Press.

Abraham, Frederick David, & Gilgen, Albert R. (1995). *Chaos theory in psychology*. Westport, CT: Praeger.

Adair, John G. (1973). *The human subject*. Boston, MA: Little, Brown.
  (2000). Ethics of psychological research: New policies; continuing issues; new concerns. *Canadian Psychology*, 42, 25–37.

Adair, J. G., Paivio, A., & Ritchie, P. (1996). Psychology in Canada. *Annual Review of Psychology*, 47, 341–370.

Adler, Nancy E. (2009). Health disparities through a psychological lens. *American Psychologist*, 64, 663–673.

Adolphs, Ralph (2009). The social brain: Neural basis of social knowledge. *Annual Review of Psychology*, 60, 693–716.

Adorno, Theodor, Frenkel-Brunswick, Else, Levinson, Daniel, & Sanford, R. Nevitt (1950). *The authoritarian personality*. New York: Harper & Row.

Agonito, Rosemary (1977). *History of ideas on women*. New York: Pedigree Books.

Ainsworth, Mary D. Salter, & Bowlby, John (1991). An ethological approach to personality development. *American Psychologist*, 46, 333–341.

Aiton, E. J. (1985). *Leibniz: A biography*. Bristol: Adam Hilger.

Albee, George (2000). The Boulder model's fatal flaw. *American Psychologist*, 55, 247–248.

Alchon, Guy (1985). *The invisible hand of planning: Capitalism, social science, and the state in the 1920's*. Princeton University Press.

Alford, C. Fred (1989). *Melanie Klein and critical social theory: An account of politics, art, and reason based on her psychoanalytic theory*. New Haven, CT: Yale University Press.

Algoe, Sara B., & Fredrickson, Barbara L. (2011). Emotional fitness and the movement of affective science from lab to field. *American Psychologist*, 66, 35–42.

Alic, Margaret (1986). *Hypatia's heritage: A history of women in science from antiquity to the nineteenth century*. Boston, MA: Beacon Press.

Allen, Richard C. (1999). *David Hartley on human nature*. Albany, NY: SUNY Press.

Allport, Floyd D. (1962). A structuronomic conception of behaviour: Individual and collective. I. Structural theory and the master problem of social psychology. *Journal of Abnormal and Social Psychology*, 64, 3–30.

Allport, Gordon W. (1937). *Personality: A psychological interpretation*. New York: Holt.
(1940). The psychologist's frame of reference. *Psychological Bulletin*, 37, 1–28.
(1947). Scientific models and human morals. *Psychological Review*, 54, 182–192.
(1962). The general and the unique in psychological science. *Journal of Personality*, 30, 405–422.

Alvis, Andr (2003). Psychoanalysis in Japan. *International Institute for Asian Studies*, 30, 9.

American Psychological Association (2005). *Graduate study in psychology*. Washington, DC: Author.
(2008, February 22). Reaffirmation of the American Psychological Association Position against Torture and Other Cruel, Inhuman, or Degrading Treatment or Punishment and Its Application to Individuals Defined in the United States Code as "Enemy Combatants." Retrieved from www.apa.org/about/governance/council/policy/torture.aspx
(2009). *Publication manual of the American Psychological Association*, 6th edn. Washington, DC: American Psychological Association.
(2011). Principles for quality undergraduate education in psychology. *American Psychologist*, 66, 850–856.

Anderson, Bonnie S., & Zinsser, Judith P. (2000). *A history of their own: Women in Europe from prehistory to the present*. 2 vols. New York: Oxford University Press.

Anderson, James W. (1999). Henry Murray and the creation of the Thematic Apperception Test. In Lon Gieser & Morris I. Stein (eds.), *Evocative images: The Thematic Apperception Test and the art of projection* (pp. 23–38). Washington, DC: American Psychological Association.

Andrade, Vivian M., & Bueno, Orlando F. A. (2001). Medical psychology in Brazil. *Journal of Clinical Psychology in Medical Settings*, 8, 9–13.

Angell, James R. (1904). *Psychology: An introductory study of the structure and function of human consciousness*. New York: Henry Holt and Co.

Antonuccio, David, Danton, William, & McClanahan, Terry (2003). Psychology in the prescription era: Building a firewall between marketing and science. *American Psychologist*, 58, 1028–1043.

Arbiser, Samuel (2003). A brief history of psychoanalysis in Argentina. *Journal of the American Psychoanalytic Association*, 51, 323–335.

Arens, Katherine (1989). *Structures of knowing: Psychologies of the nineteenth century*. Dordrecht: Kluwer Academic.

Arfken, Michael (2012). Scratching the surface: Internationalization, cultural diversity and the politics of recognition. *Social and Personality Psychology Compass*, 6, 428–437.

Argyris, Chris (1975). Dangers in applying results from experimental social psychology. *American Psychologist*, 30, 469–485.
(1980). *Inner contradictions of rigorous research*. New York: Academic Press.

Aristotle (2001). *The basic works of Aristotle*, ed. R. McKeon. New York: Random House.

Arnett, Jeffrey J. (2008). The neglected 95%: Why American psychology needs to become less American. *American Psychologist*, 63, 602–614.

Arnett, John (2006). Psychology and health. *Canadian Psychology*, 47, 19–32.

Aron, Lewis, & Harris, Adrienne (eds.) (1993). *The legacy of Sandor Ferenczi*. Hillsdale, NJ: Analytic Press.

Aronson, Eliot (1980). Persuasion via self-justification. In Leon Festinger (ed.), *Retrospections on social psychology* (pp. 3–21). New York: Oxford University Press.

Arrigo, Bruce, & Fox, Dennis (2009). Psychology and the law: The crime of policy and the search for justice. In Dennis Fox, Isaac Prilleltensky, & Stephanie Austin (eds.), *Critical psychology: An introduction*, 2nd edn. (pp. 159–175). Thousand Oaks, CA: Sage Publications.

Ash, Mitchell G. (1987). Psychology and politics in interwar Vienna: The Vienna Psychological Institute, 1922–1942. In Mitchell G. Ash & William R. Woodward (eds.), *Psychology in twentieth-century thought and society* (pp. 143–164). Cambridge University Press.

(1992). Cultural contexts and scientific change in psychology: Kurt Lewin in Iowa. *American Psychologist*, 47, 198–207.

(1995). *Gestalt psychology in German culture 1890–1967: Holism and the quest for objectivity*. Cambridge University Press.

(2003). Psychology. In Theodore M. Porter & Dorothy Ross (eds.), *The Cambridge history of science*, vol. VII (pp. 252–274). Cambridge University Press.

Aspinwall, Lisa G., & Staudinger, Ursula M. (2003). *A psychology of human strengths: Fundamental questions and future directions for a positive psychology*. Washington, DC: American Psychological Association.

Asprem, Egril (2010). A nice arrangement of heterodoxies: William McDougall and the professionalization of psychical research. *Journal of the History of the Behavioral Sciences*, 46, 123–143.

Atkins, Peter (2003). *Galileo's finger: The ten great ideas of science*. Oxford University Press.

Augustine, Aurelius (1997). *The Confessions*, trans. Maria Boulding. Hyde Park, NY: New City Press. (Original work published 397–401 BCE)

Aycan, Zeynep (2000). Cross-cultural industrial and organizational psychology: Contributions, past developments, and future directions. *Journal of Cross-Cultural Psychology*, 31, 110–128.

Ayers, Michael (2005). Was Berkeley an empiricist or a rationalist? In Kenneth P. Winkler (ed.), *The Cambridge companion to Berkeley* (pp. 34–62). Cambridge University Press.

Baars, Bernard J. (1986). *The cognitive revolution in psychology*. New York: Guilford Press.

Babarik, Paul (1979). The buried Canadian roots of community psychology. *Journal of Community Psychology*, 7, 362–367.

Baenninger, Ronald (1990). Consciousness and comparative psychology. In Michael G. Johnson & Tracy B. Henley (eds.), *Reflections on* The principles of psychology: *William James after a century* (pp. 249–269). Hillsdale, NJ: Lawrence Erlbaum Associates.

Bailey, James R., & Eastman, Wayne N. (1994). Positivism and the promise of the social sciences. *Theory & Psychology*, 4(4), 505–524.

Bakan, David (1966). The influence of phrenology on American psychology. *Journal of the History of the Behavioral Sciences*, 2, 200–220.

(1967). *On method: Toward a reconstruction of psychological investigation*. San Francisco: Jossey-Bass.

(1998). American culture and psychology. In Robert W. Rieber & Kurt Salzinger (eds.), *Psychology: Theoretical-historical perspectives*, 2nd edn. (pp. 217–225). Washington, DC: American Psychological Association.

Baker, David B., & Benjamin, Ludy T. (2000). The affirmation of the scientist-practitioner: A look back at Boulder. *American Psychologist*, 55, 241–247.

Baker, Rodney, & Pickren, Wade (2007). *Psychology and the Department of Veterans Affairs: A historical analysis of training, research, practice, and advocacy.* Washington, DC: American Psychological Association.

Balachova, Tatiana, Levy, Sheldon, Isurina, Galina, & Wasserman, Ludvig (2001). Medical psychology in Russia. *Journal of Clinical Psychology in Medical Settings*, 8, 61–68.

Baldwin, Elizabeth (1993). The case for animal research in psychology. *Journal of Social Issues*, 49, 121–131.

Baltes, Paul B., Staudinger, Ursula M., & Lindenberger, Ulman (1999). Lifespan psychology: Theory and application to intellectual functioning. *Annual Review of Psychology*, 50, 471–507.

Baltzly, Dirk (2010). Stoicism. In E. N. Zalta (ed.), *The Stanford encyclopedia of philosophy.* Retrieved from http://plato.stanford.edu/archives/win2010/entries/stoicism/

Bandura, Albert, Ross, Dorothea, & Ross, Sheila (1963). Imitation of film-mediated aggressive models. *Journal of Abnormal and Social Psychology*, 66, 3–11.

Barabanschikov, Vladimir A. (2006). Russian psychology at the crossroads. In Qicheng Jing, Mark R. Rosenzweig, Gery d'Ydewalle, Houcan Zhang, Hisuan-Chi Chen, & Kan Zhang (eds.), *Progress in psychological science around the world*, vol. II (pp. 417–431). New York: Psychology Press.

Barenbaum, Nicole B. (2006). Henry A. Murray: Personology as biography, science, and art. In Donald A. Dewsbury, Ludy T. Benjamin Jr., & Michael Wertheimer (eds.), *Portraits of pioneers in psychology*, vol. VI (pp. 169–187). Washington, DC: American Psychological Association.

Barenbaum, Nicole B., & Winter, David G. (2003). Personality. In Irving B. Weiner (series ed.) & Donald K. Freedheim (vol. ed.), *Handbook of psychology*, vol. I: *History of psychology* (pp. 177–303). Hoboken, NJ: Wiley.

Barker, Roger G. (1968). *Ecological psychology: Concepts and methods for studying the environment of human behavior.* Stanford University Press.

Barlow, David H. (2010). Negative effects from psychological treatments: A perspective. *American Psychologist* 65, 13–20.

Barnes, Jonathan (1987). *Early Greek philosophy.* London: Penguin.

Barone, David F. (1996). John Dewey: Psychologist, philosopher, and reformer. In Gregory A. Kimble, C. Alan Boneau, & Michael Wertheimer (eds.), *Portraits of pioneers in psychology*, vol. II (pp. 47–61). Washington, DC: American Psychological Association.

Bartlett, Frederic C. (1932). *Remembering: A study in experimental and social psychology.* Cambridge University Press.

Bartol, Curt R., & Bartol, Anne M. (1999). History of forensic psychology. In C. R. Bartol (ed.), *The handbook of forensic psychology*, 2nd edn. (pp. 3–23). Hoboken, NJ: Wiley.

Barzun, Jacques (2000). *From dawn to decadence: 1500 to the present.* New York: HarperCollins.

Bates, Brian C. (1987). *The way of the actor.* Boston, MA: Shambhala Publications.

Bates, Yvonne, & House, Richard (eds.) (2003). *Ethically challenged professions: Enabling innovation and diversity in psychotherapy and counselling.* Ross-on-Wye: PCCS Books.

Baydala, Angelina (2001). The soliloquy of empirical validation in cognitive psychology. *Australian Psychologist*, 36, 44–50.

Baydala, Angelina, & Stam, Henderikus (2004). The polis, emancipation and subjectivity: On the social uses of psychoanalysis. In W. E. Smythe & A. Baydala (eds.), *Studies of how the mind publicly enfolds into Being.* Lewiston, NY: Mellen Press.

Bazerman, Charles (1988). *Shaping written knowledge: The genre and activity of the experimental article in science*. Madison, WI: University of Wisconsin Press.

Beach, Frank A. (1950). The snark was a boojum. *American Psychologist*, 5, 115–124.

Beauvoir, Simone de (1972). *The second sex*, trans. H. M. Parshley. Harmondsworth: Penguin. (Original work published in French 1949)

Beck, Hall P., Levinson, Sharman, & Irons, Gary (2009). Finding Little Albert: A journey to John B. Watson's infant laboratory. *American Psychologist*, 64, 605–614.

Bell, Paul, Greene, Thomas, Fisher, Jeffrey, & Baum, Andrew (1996). *Environmental psychology*. Fort Worth, TX: Harcourt Brace.

Beneke, Eduard (1845). *Lehrbuch der Psychologie als Naturwissenschaft*, zweite, vermehrte und verbesserte Auflage [Textbook of psychology as a natural science, 2nd edn.]. Berlin: Mittler. (Original work published 1833)

Benjamin, Jessica (1990). An outline of intersubjectivity: The development of recognition. *Psychoanalytic Psychology*, 7, 33–46.

Benjamin, Ludy T. (2001). American psychology's struggles with its curriculum. Should a thousand flowers bloom? *American Psychologist*, 56, 735–742.

(2006). Hugo Münsterberg's attack on the application of scientific psychology. *Journal of Applied Psychology*, 91, 414–425.

Benjamin, Ludy T., & Baker, David B. (2004). *From séance to science: A history of the profession of psychology in America*. Belmont, CA: Wadsworth/Thomson.

Benson, Herbert, & Proctor, William (2011). *Relaxation revolution: The science and genetics of mind body healing*. New York: Quill.

Bent, Russell, Packard, Ralph, & Goldberg, Robert (1999). The American Board of Professional Psychology, 1947 to 1997: A historical perspective. *Professional Psychology: Research and Practice*, 30, 65–73.

Berg, Irwin A. (1954). The use of human subjects in psychological research. *American Psychologist*, 9, 108–111.

Bergin, Allen, & Garfield, Sol (eds.) (1994). *Handbook of psychotherapy and behavior change*. New York: Wiley.

Berman, Emanuel (1999). Sándor Ferenczi today: Reviving the broken dialectic. *The American Journal of Psychoanalysis*, 59, 303–313.

Bermant, Gordon, Charlan, Nemeth, & Vidmar, Neil (eds.) (1976). *Psychology and the law*. Toronto: Lexington Books.

Bernard, Walter (1972). Spinoza's influence on the rise of scientific psychology: A neglected chapter in the history of psychology. *Journal of the History of the Behavioral Sciences*, 8, 208–215.

Berry, John W. (2002). *Cross-cultural psychology: Research and applications*. New York: Cambridge University Press.

Berryman, Sylvia (2010). Democritus. In E. N. Zalta (ed.), *The Stanford encyclopedia of philosophy*. Retrieved from http://plato.stanford.edu/archives/fall2010/entries/democritus/

Bersoff, Donald N. (ed.) (1995). *Ethical conflicts in psychology*. Washington, DC: American Psychological Association.

Berwald, Marc C. A. (1998). The challenge of profound transformation for industrial and organizational psychologists: Are we meeting the challenge? *Canadian Psychology*, 39, 158–163.

Betegh, Gabor (2006). Greek philosophy and religion. In Mary Louise Gill & Pierre Pellegrin (eds.), *A companion to ancient philosophy* (pp. 625–639). Oxford: Blackwell.

Bevan, William (1991). Contemporary psychology: A tour inside the onion. *American Psychologist*, 46, 475–483.

Bhaskar, Roy (1998). *The possibility of naturalism: A philosophical critique of the contemporary human sciences*, 3rd edn. London: Routledge.

Bhatia, Sunil (2002). Orientalism in Euro-American and Indian psychology: Historical representations of "natives" in colonial and post-colonial contexts. *History of Psychology*, 5, 376–398.

Billig, Michael (1994). Repopulating the depopulated pages of social psychology. *Theory & Psychology*, 3, 307–335.

(1997). The dialogic unconscious: Psychoanalysis, discursive psychology and the nature of repression. *British Journal of Social Psychology* 36, 139–159.

(2008). *The hidden roots of critical psychology*. London: Sage.

Bindman, David (2002). *Ape to Apollo: Aesthetics and the idea of race in the 18th century*. Ithaca, NY: Cornell University Press.

Binswanger, Ludwig (1968). *Being-in-the-world: Selected papers of Ludwig Binswanger*. New York: Harper.

Bishop, Morris (1968). *Pascal, the life of genius*. New York: Greenwood Press.

Bishop, Paul (2008). *Analytical psychology and German classical aesthetics: Goethe, Schiller and Jung*. London: Routledge.

Bjork, Daniel W. (1983). *The compromised scientist*. New York: Columbia University Press.

(1998). Burrhus Frederick Skinner: The contingencies of a life. In Gregory A. Kimble & Michael Wertheimer (eds.), *Portraits of pioneers in psychology*, vol. III (pp. 261–275). Washington, DC: American Psychological Association.

Blanck, Peter David, Bellack, Alan S., Rosnow, Ralph L., Rotheram-Borus, Mary Jane, & Schooler, Nina R. (1992). Scientific rewards and conflicts of ethical choices in human subjects research. *American Psychologist*, 47, 959–965.

Blass, Thomas (2004). *The man who shocked the world: The life and legacy of Stanley Milgram*. New York: Basic Books.

Blowers, Geoffrey (2006). Origins of scientific psychology in China, 1899–1949. In Adrian Brock (ed.), *Internationalizing the history of psychology* (pp. 94–111). New York University Press.

Blum, Deborah (2002). *Love at Goon Park: Harry Harlow and the science of affection*. New York: Perseus.

Blumenthal, Arthur L. (1975). A reappraisal of Wilhelm Wundt. *American Psychologist*, 30, 1081–1088.

(1985). Wilhelm Wundt: Psychology as the propaedeutic science. In Claude E. Buxton (ed.), *Points of view in the modern history of psychology* (pp. 19–50). Orlando, FL: Academic Press.

(1998). Why study Wundtian psychology? In Robert W. Rieber & Kurt Salzinger (eds.), *Psychology: Theoretical-historical perspectives*, 2nd edn. (pp. 77–87). Washington, DC: American Psychological Association.

Boakes, Robert (1984). *From Darwin to behaviourism*. Cambridge University Press.

Bodner, Todd E. (2006). Design, participants, and measurement methods in psychological research. *Canadian Psychology*, 47, 263–272.

Bohan, Janis S. (1990). Contextual history: A framework for re-placing women in the history of psychology. *Psychology of Women Quarterly*, 14, 213–227.

(1992). *Seldom seen, rarely heard: Women's place in psychology*. Boulder, CO: Westview Press.

(2002). Sex differences and/in the self: Classic themes, feminist variations, postmodern challenges. *Psychology of Women Quarterly*, 26, 74–88.

Borchelt, Gretchen, & Pross, Christian (2005). *"Break them down": Systematic use of psychological torture by US Forces*. Cambridge, MA: Physicians for Human Rights.

Boring, Edwin G. (1942). *Sensation and perception in the history of experimental psychology*. New York: D. Appleton-Century.

(1950). *A history of experimental psychology*, 2nd edn. New York: Appleton-Century-Crofts.

Boudewijnse, Greet-Jan A., Murray, David J., & Bandomir, Christina A. (2001). The fate of Herbart's mathematical psychology. *History of Psychology*, 4, 107–132.

Bowd, Alan D., & Shapiro, Kenneth J. (1993). The case against animal laboratory research in psychology. *Journal of Social Issues*, 49, 133–142.

Bowlby, John (1990). *Charles Darwin: A new life*. New York: Norton.

Bradley, Benjamin (2005). *Psychology and experience*. Cambridge University Press.

Brainerd, C. J. (1996). Piaget: A centennial celebration. *Psychological Science*, 7, 191–195.

(2003). *Jean Piaget, learning, research, and American education*. New York: Academic Press.

Bramel, Dana, & Friend, Ronald (1981). Hawthorne, the myth of the docile worker, and class bias in psychology. *American Psychologist*, 36, 867–878.

Braverman, Harry (1974). *Labour and monopoly capital: The degradation of work in the twentieth century*. New York and London: Monthly Review Press.

Brehm, Jack W. (1998). Leon Festinger: Beyond the obvious. In Gregory A. Kimble & Michael Wertheimer (eds.), *Portraits of pioneers in psychology*, vol. III (pp. 329–344). Washington, DC: American Psychological Association.

Brentano, Franz (1995). *Psychology from an empirical standpoint*. New York: Routledge. (Original work published 1874)

Brett, George (1962). *Brett's history of psychology*, 2nd edn., ed. R. S. Peters. London: Allen & Unwin.

Brinkmann, Svend (2005). Human kinds and looping effects in psychology: Foucauldian and hermeneutic perspectives. *Theory & Psychology*, 15, 769–791.

Brinkmann, Svend (2011a). Dewey's neglected psychology: Rediscovering his transactional approach. *Theory & Psychology*, 21, 298–317.

(2011b). *Psychology as a moral science: Perspectives on normativity*. New York: Springer.

Brinton, Crane (1963). *The shaping of modern thought*. Englewood Cliffs, NJ: Prentice Hall.

Broadie, Alexander (ed.) (2003). *The Cambridge companion to the Scottish Enlightenment*. Cambridge University Press.

Brock, Adrian C. (1994). Whatever happened to Karl Buehler? *Canadian Psychology*, 35, 319–329.

(2006a). Introduction. In Adrian C. Brock (ed.), *Internationalizing the history of psychology* (pp. 1–15). New York University Press.

(2006b). Rediscovering the history of psychology: Kurt Danziger interviewed by Adrian C. Brock. *History of Psychology*, 9, 1–16.

Bronfenbrenner, Urie (1977). Toward an experimental ecology of human development. *American Psychologist*, 32, 513–531.

Brook, Andrew (1994). *Kant and the mind*. Cambridge University Press.

Brooks, G. P. (1976). The faculty psychology of Thomas Reid. *Journal of the History of the Behavioral Sciences*, 12, 65–77.

Brooks-Gunn, Jeanne, & Johnson, Anna Duncan (2006). G. Stanley Hall's contribution to science, practice and policy: The Child Study, Parent Education, and Child Welfare movements. *History of Psychology*, 9, 247–258.

Brown, Gregory (1995). Leibniz's moral philosophy. In Nicholas Jolley (ed.), *The Cambridge companion to Leibniz* (pp. 411–441). Cambridge University Press.

Brown, Richard E., & Milner, Peter M. (2003). The legacy of Donald O. Hebb: More than the Hebb synapse. *Nature Reviews Neuroscience*, 4, 1013–1019.

Bruce, Darryl (1991). Integrations of Lashley. In Gregory A. Kimble, Michael Wertheimer, & Charlotte L. White (eds.), *Portraits of pioneers in psychology* (pp. 307–323). Washington, DC: American Psychological Association.

Bruner, Jerome S. (1990). *Acts of meaning*. Cambridge, MA: Harvard University Press.

Bruner, Jerome S., & Allport, Gordon W. (1940). Fifty years of change in American psychology. *Psychological Bulletin*, 37, 757–776.

Bruner, Jerome S., Goodnow, Jacqueline, & Austin, George (1956). *A study of thinking*. New York: Wiley.

Bryden, Ronald B. (ed.) (1992). *The restoration of dialogue: Readings in the philosophy of clinical psychology*. Washington, DC: American Psychological Association.

Bryson, Bill (2003). *A short history of nearly everything*. New York: Broadway Books.

Budilova, Ekaterina A. (1984). On the history of social psychology in Russia. In Lloyd H. Strickland (ed.), *Directions in Soviet social psychology* (pp. 11–28). New York: Springer.

Buhle, Mari Jo (1999). *Feminism and its discontents: A century of struggle with psychoanalysis*. Cambridge, MA: Harvard University Press.

Bühler, Charlotte (1971). Basic theoretical concepts of humanistic psychology. *American Psychologist*, 26, 378–386.

Burger, Jerry M. (2009). Replicating Milgram: Would people still obey today? *American Psychologist*, 64, 1–11.

Burghardt, Gordon M. (2009). Darwin's legacy to comparative psychology and ethology. *American Psychologist*, 64, 102–110.

Burman, Erica (1997). Developmental psychology and its discontents. In Dennis Fox & Isaac Prilleltensky (eds.), *Critical psychology: An introduction* (pp. 134–149). Thousand Oaks, CA: Sage.

Burston, Daniel (1991). *The legacy of Erich Fromm*. Cambridge, MA: Harvard University Press.

Buss, David M. (ed.) (2005). *The handbook of evolutionary psychology*. New York: Wiley.
   (2009). The great struggles of life: Darwin and the emergence of evolutionary psychology. *American Psychologist*, 64, 140–148.

Butterfield, Herbert (1931). *The Whig interpretation of history*. London: Bell & Sons.

Cacioppo, John T. (2002). Social neuroscience: Understanding the pieces fosters understanding the whole and vice versa. *American Psychologist*, 57, 819–831.

Cadwallader, Thomas C. (1992). The historical roots of the American Psychological Association. In Rand B. Evans, Virginia Staudt Sexton, & Thomas C. Cadwallader (eds.), *The American Psychological Association: A historical perspective* (pp. 3–37). Washington, DC: American Psychological Association.

Cadwallader, Thomas C., & Cadwallader, Joyce V. (1990). Christine Ladd-Franklin (1847–1930). In Agnes N. O'Connell and Nancy F. Russo (eds.), *Women in psychology: A bio-bibliographic sourcebook* (pp. 220–229). New York: Greenwood Press.

Cahan, David (1995). Introduction. In David Cahan (ed.), Hermann von Helmholtz, *Science and culture: Popular and philosophical essays* (pp. 1–16). University of Chicago Press.

Cahan, Emily D. (1992). John Dewey and human development. *Developmental Psychology*, 28, 205–214.

Cahill, Thomas (1995). *How the Irish saved civilization*. New York: Nan A. Talese/Doubleday.

Cairns, Robert B. (1992). The making of a developmental science: The contributions and intellectual heritage of James Mark Baldwin. *Developmental Psychology*, 28, 17–24.

Calkins, Mary (1910). *A first book in psychology*. New York: Macmillan.

(1915). The self in scientific psychology. *American Journal of Psychology*, 26, 495–524.

Cameron, Claire E., & Hagen, John W. (2005). Women in child development: Themes from the SRCD Oral History Project. *History of Psychology*, 8, 289–316.

Campbell, Rebecca, & Wasco, Sharon M. (2000). Feminist approaches to social science: Epistemological and methodological tenets. *American Journal of Community Psychology*, 28, 773–791.

Camus, Albert (1991). *The rebel: An essay on man in revolt*. New York: Vintage Books. (Original work published in French 1956)

Cantor, Norman F. (1994). *Medieval lives: Eight charismatic men and women of the Middle Ages*. New York: HarperCollins.

Capaldi, Nicholas (2004). *John Stuart Mill: A biography*. Cambridge University Press.

Caplan, Eric (1998). Popularizing American psychotherapy: The Emmanuel Movement, 1906–1910. *History of Psychology*, 1, 289–314.

Capshew, James H. (1992). Psychologists on site: A reconnaissance of the historiography of the laboratory. *American Psychologist*, 47, 132–142.

(1999). *Psychologists on the march: Science, practice, and professional identity in America, 1929–1969*. Cambridge University Press.

(2007). Reflexivity revisited: Changing psychology's frame of reference. In Mitchell G. Ash & Thomas Sturm (eds.), *Psychology's territories: Historical and contemporary perspectives from different disciplines* (pp. 343–356). Mahwah, NJ: Erlbaum.

Carnap, Rudolf (1936). Testability and meaning. *Philosophy of Science*, 3, 419–471.

Carpintero, Helio (1997). Psychological journals. In Wolfgang G. Bringmann, Helmut E. Lück, Rudolf Miller, & Charles E. Early (eds.), *A pictorial history of psychology* (pp. 529–535). Chicago, IL: Quintessence Publishing.

Carroll, Sean B. (2006). *Endless forms most beautiful: The new science of Evo Devo and the making of the animal kingdom*. London: Weidenfeld.

Carroy, Jacqueline, & Plas, Regine (1996). The origins of French experimental psychology: Experiment and experimentalism. *History of the Human Sciences*, 9, 73–84.

Cartwright, Dorwin (1978). Theory and practice. *Journal of Social Issues*, 34(4), 168–180.

Carus, Friedrich A. (1808). *Geschichte der Psychologie* [History of psychology]. Leipzig: Barth & Kummer.

Casey, George W., Jr. (2011). Comprehensive soldier fitness: A vision for psychological resilience in the US army. *American Psychologist*, 66, 1–3.

Castonguay, Louis G., Boswell, James F., Constantino, Michael J., Goldfried, Marvin R., & Hill, Clara E. (2010). Training implications of harmful effects of psychological treatments. *American Psychologist*, 65, 34–49.

Cattell, J. McKeen (1890). Mental tests and measurements. *Mind*, 15, 373–381.

Caudle, Fairfid M. (2003). Eleanor Jack Gibson (1910–2002). *American Psychologist*, 58, 1090–1091.

Cavendish, A. P. (1964). Early Greek philosophy. In D. J. O'Connorm (ed.), *A critical history of Western philosophy* (pp. 1–13). New York: The Free Press of Glencoe.

Ceci, Stephen J., Peters, Douglas, & Plotkin, Jonathan (1985). Human subjects review, personal values, and the regulation of social science research. *American Psychologist*, 40, 994–1002.

Ceci, Stephen J., & Williams, Wendy M. (2007a). Are we moving closer and closer apart? Shared evidence leads to conflicting views. In Stephen J. Ceci & Wendy M. Williams (eds.), *Why aren't more women in science? Top researchers debate the evidence* (pp. 213–236). Washington, DC: American Psychological Association.

Ceci, Stephen J., & Williams, Wendy M. (eds.) (2007b). *Why aren't more women in science? Top researchers debate the evidence*. Washington, DC: American Psychological Association.

Cervone, Daniel (2005). Personality architecture: Within-person structures and processes. *Annual Review of Psychology*, 56, 423–452.

Chamberlin, Kerry, & Murray, Michael (2009). Critical health psychology. In Dennis Fox, Issac Prilleltensky, & Stephanie Austin (eds.), *Critical psychology: An introduction*, 2nd edn. (pp. 144–158). Thousand Oaks, CA: Sage.

Chappell, Vere (2007). Power in Locke's Essay. In Lex Newman (ed.), *The Cambridge companion to Locke's "Essay concerning Human Understanding"* (pp. 130–156). Cambridge University Press.

Chastain, Garvin (1999). Introduction. In Garvin Chastain & R. Eric Landrum (eds.), *Protecting human subjects: Departmental subject pools and institutional review boards* (pp. 3–19). Washington, DC: American Psychological Association.

Chastain, Garvin, & Landrum, R. Eric (eds.) (1999). *Protecting human subjects: Departmental subject pools and institutional review boards*. Washington, DC: American Psychological Association.

Chein, Isadore (1966). Some sources of divisiveness among psychologists. *American Psychologist*, 21, 333–342.

Cherry, Frances (1995). *The stubborn particulars of social psychology*. London: Routledge.
  (2009). Social psychology and social change. In Dennis Fox, Issac Prilleltensky, & Stephanie Austin (eds.), *Critical psychology: An introduction*, 2nd edn. (pp. 93–109). Thousand Oaks, CA: Sage.

Chlewinski, Zdzislaw (1976). Poland. In Virginia S. Sexton & Henryk Misiak (eds.), *Psychology around the world* (pp. 341–356). Monterey, CA: Brooks/Cole.

Clarke, Desmond E. (2006). *Descartes: A biography*. Cambridge University Press.

Clarke, John James (1992). *In search of Jung*. New York: Routledge.

Code, Lorraine (2003). *Encyclopaedia of feminist theories*. New York: Routledge.

Cohen, Jacob (1994). The earth is round (p <.05). *American Psychologist*, 49, 997–1003.

Cole, Elizabeth R. (2009). Intersectionality and research in psychology. *American Psychologist*, 64, 170–180.

Cole, John R. (1995). *Pascal: The man and his two loves*. New York University Press.

Collins, Alan (2006). The embodiment of reconciliation: Order and change in the work of Frederic Bartlett. *History of Psychology*, 9, 290–312.

Comte, Auguste (1896). *The positive philosophy of Auguste Comte*, freely translated and condensed by Harriet Martineau. With an introduction by Frederic Harrison. London: George Bell.

Comas-Diaz, Lillian (1991). Feminism and diversity in psychology. *Psychology of Women Quarterly*, 15, 597–609.

Confer, Jamie C., Easton, Judith A., Fleischman, Diana S., Goetz, Cari D., Lewis, David M. G., Perilloux, Carin, & Buss, David M. (2010). Evolutionary psychology: Controversies, questions, prospects, and limitations. *American Psychologist*, 65, 110–126.

Coon, Deborah J. (1992). Testing the limits of sense and science: American experimental psychologists combat spiritualism, 1880–1920. *American Psychologist*, 47, 143–151.

Coren, Stanley (2003). Sensation and perception. In Donald K. Freedheim (ed.), *History of psychology*, vol. I: *Handbook of psychology*, ed. Irving B. Weiner. Hoboken, NJ: Wiley.

Coren, Stanley (2004). *How dogs think*. New York: Free Press.

Corr, Philip J., & Perkins, Adam M. (2006). The role of theory in the psychophysiology of personality: From Ivan Pavlov to Jeffrey Gray. *International Journal of Psychophysiology*, 62, 367–376.

Cortina, Mauricio (2004). Reclaiming Bowlby's contribution to psychoanalysis. *International Forum of Psychoanalysis*, 13, 133–146.

Cosgrove, Lisa, Krimsky, Sheldon, Vijayaraghavan, Manisha, & Schneider, Lisa (2006). Financial ties between DSM-IV panel members and the pharmaceutical industry. *Psychotherapy and Psychosomatics*, 75, 154–160.

Cottingham, John (1998). Introduction. In John Cottingham (ed.), *Descartes: Oxford readings in philosophy* (pp. 1–27). New York: Oxford University Press.

Coventry, Angela M. (2007). *Hume: A guide for the perplexed*. London: Continuum.

Cowles, Michael (2001). *Statistics in psychology: An historical perspective*, 2nd edn. Mahwah, NJ: Erlbaum.

Cratty, Bryant, J. (1989). *Psychology in contemporary sport*. Englewood Cliffs, NJ: Prentice Hall.

Crews, Frederick (1975). *Out of my system: Psychoanalysis, ideology, and critical method*. New York: Oxford University Press.

(1998). *Unauthorized Freud: Doubters confront a legend*. New York: Viking.

Croce, Paul J. (2010). Beyond Uncle William: A century of William James in theory and in life. *History of Psychology*, 13, 351–377.

Crocker, Lester G. (1991). Introduction. In John W. Yolton, Roy Porter, Pat Rogers, & Maria Stafford (eds.), *The Blackwell companion to the Enlightenment* (pp. 1–10). Oxford: Blackwell.

Cronbach, Lee J. (1957). The two disciplines of scientific psychology. *American Psychologist*, 12, 671–684.

Crosby, Alfred W. (1997). *The measure of reality: Quantification and Western society, 1250–1600*. New York: Cambridge University Press.

Crosby, Donald A., & Viney, Wayne (1993). Toward a psychology that is radically empirical: Recapturing the vision of William James. In Margaret E. Donnelly (ed.), *Reinterpreting the legacy of William James* (pp. 102–117). Washington, DC: American Psychological Association.

Crossan, John Dominic (1994). *Jesus: A revolutionary biography*. New York: HarperCollins.

Curd, Patricia (2011). New work on the presocratics. *Journal of the History of Philosophy*, 49, 1–57.

(2008). Anaxagoras and the theory of everything. In P. Curd & D. W. Graham (eds.), *The Oxford handbook of presocratic philosophy* (pp. 230–249). New York: Oxford University Press.

Curran, Patrick J. (2009). The seemingly quixotic pursuit of a cumulative psychological science: Introduction to the special issue. *Psychological Methods*, 14, 77–80.

Dafermos, Manolis, Marvakis, Athanasios, & Triliva, Sofia (eds.) (2006). *Critical psychology in a changing world: Contributions from different geo-political regions* [special issue]. *Annual Review of Critical Psychology*, 5. http://www.discourseunit.com/annual-review/arcp-5-crtical-psychology-in-a-changing-world-contributions-from-different-geo-political-regions

Dagg, Anne Innis (2005). *"Love of shopping" is not a gene: Problems with Darwinian psychology*. Montreal: Black Rose Books.

Damasio, Antonio (1999). *The feeling of what happens: Body and emotion in the making of consciousness*. San Diego, CA: Harcourt.

(2003). *Looking for Spinoza: Joy, sorrow, and the feeling brain*. Orlando, FL: Harcourt.

Damousi, Joy (2005). *Freud in the Antipodes: A cultural history of psychoanalysis in Australia*. Sydney: UNSW.

Danziger, Kurt (1979). The social origins of modern psychology. In Allan R. Buss (ed.), *Psychology in social context* (pp. 29–45). New York: Irvington.

(1980). Wundt's psychological experiment in the light of his philosophy of science. *Psychological Research*, 42, 1–2, 109–122.

(1982). Mid-nineteenth-century British psycho-physiology: A neglected chapter in the history of psychology. In William R. Woodward & Mitchell G. Ash (eds.), *The problematic science: Psychology in nineteenth-century thought* (pp. 119–146). New York: Praeger.

(1983). Origins and basic principles of Wundt's Voelkerpsychologie. *British Journal of Social Psychology*, 22, 303–313.

(1985). The methodological imperative in psychology. *Philosophy of the Social Sciences*, 15, 1–13.

(1990). *Constructing the subject: Historical origins of psychological research*. Cambridge University Press.

(1994). Does the history of psychology have a future? *Theory & Psychology*, 4, 467–484.

(1997a). The historical formation of selves. In Richard D. Ashmore & Lee Jussim (eds.), *Self and identity: Fundamental issues* (pp. 137–159). New York: Oxford University Press.

(1997b). *Naming the mind: How psychology found its language*. London: Sage.

(2001a). Sealing off the discipline: Wilhelm Wundt and the psychology of memory. In Christopher D. Green, Marlene Shore, & Thomas Teo (eds.), *The transformation of psychology: Influences of 19th century philosophy, technology, and natural science* (pp. 45–62). Washington, DC: American Psychological Association.

(2001b). The unknown Wundt: Drive, apperception and volition. In Robert W. Rieber & Daniel K. Robinson (eds.), *Wilhelm Wundt in history: The making of a scientific psychology* (pp. 95–120). New York: Kluwer/Plenum.

(2008). *Marking the mind: A history of memory*. Cambridge University Press.

Darwall, Stephen (2005). Berkeley's moral and political philosophy. In Kenneth P. Winkler (ed.), *The Cambridge companion to Berkeley* (pp. 311–338). Cambridge University Press.

Darwin, Charles (1871). *The descent of man, and selection in relation to sex*, vol. I. New York: Appleton.

(n.d.). *The voyage of the Beagle by Charles Darwin*. Ipswich, MA: eBook Collection (EBSCOhost), Project Gutenberg.

Daston, Lorraine, & Galison, Peter (2007). *Objectivity*. New York: Zone.

David, Henry P., & Buchanan, Joan (2003). International psychology. In Irving B. Weiner (ed.), *Handbook of psychology*, vol. I (pp. 509–533). New York: Wiley.

Davidson, Hugh M. (1983). *Blaise Pascal*. Boston, MA: Twayne.

Davis, Mike (2001). *Late Victorian holocausts: El Niño famines and the making of the third world*. London: Verso.

Davis, R. C. (1936). American psychology, 1800–1885. *Psychological Review*, 43, 471–493.

Davis, William C. (2006). *Thomas Reid's ethics: Moral epistemology on legal foundations*. London: Continuum.

Deely, John (2001). *Four ages of understanding: The first postmodern survey of philosophy from ancient times to the turn of the twenty-first century.* University of Toronto Press.

Dehue, Trudy (1995). *Changing the rules: Psychology in the Netherlands, 1900–1985.* Cambridge University Press.

(2000). From deception trials to control reagents: The introduction of the control group about a century ago. *American Psychologist*, 55, 264–268.

Dei, George, J. S. (1996). *Anti-racism education: Theory and practice.* Halifax, Nova Scotia: Fernwood Books.

Della Rocca, Michael (2008). *Spinoza.* London: Routledge.

Delprato, Dennis J., & Midgeley, Bryan D. (1992). Some fundamentals of B. F. Skinner's behaviorism. *American Psychologist*, 47, 1507–1520.

Descartes, René (1985). Meditations on first philosophy. In John Cottingham, Robert Stoothhoff, & Dugald Murdoch (trans.), *The philosophical writings of Descartes*, vol. II. Cambridge University Press. (Original work published in French 1641)

(1996). *Discourse on the method and meditations on First Philosophy*, ed. D. Weissmann. New Haven, CT: Yale University Press. (Original work published in French 1637–1641)

Dessoir, Max (1911). *Abriss einer Geschichte der Psychologie* [Outline of a history of psychology]. Heidelberg, Germany: Winter.

De Vos, Jan (2011). From La Mettrie's voluptuous machine man to the perverse core of psychology. *Theory & Psychology*, 21, 67–85.

Dewey, John (1896). The reflex arc concept in psychology. *Psychological Review*, 3, 357–370.

(1900). Psychology and social practice. In J. A. Boydston (ed.), *The middle works of John Dewey, 1899–1924*, vol. I (pp. 131–150). Carbondale, IL: Southern Illinois University Press.

(1909). *Moral principles in education.* New York: Greenwood Press.

(1916). *Democracy and education.* New York: Macmillan.

(1933). *Art as experience.* New York: Capricorn Books.

Dewsbury, Donald A. (2009). Charles Darwin and psychology at the bicentennial and sesquicentennial: An introduction. *American Psychologist*, 64(2), 67–74.

(1992). Comparative psychology and ethology: A reassessment. *American Psychologist*, 47, 208–215.

(2003). Comparative psychology. In Irving B. Weiner (series ed.) & Donald K. Freedheim (vol. ed.), *Handbook of psychology*, vol. I. *History of psychology* (pp. 67–84). Hoboken, NJ: Wiley.

Dicks, Henry Victor (1970). *Fifty years of the Tavistock Clinic.* London: Routledge & Kegan Paul.

Dilthey, Wilhelm (1957). Ideen über eine beschreibende und zergliedernde Psychologie [Ideas on a descriptive and analytical psychology]. In Wilhelm Dilthey (ed.), *Die geistige Welt: Einleitung in die Philosophie des Lebens (Gesammelte Schriften V. Band)* [The mental world: Introduction to the philosophy of life (Collected writings, vol. V)] (pp. 139–240). Stuttgart: Teubner. (Original work published 1894)

(1958). *Der Aufbau der geschichtlichen Welt in den Geisteswissenschaften (Gesammelte Schriften VII. Band)* [The construction of the historical world in the human sciences (Collected writings, vol. VII)]. Stuttgart: Teubner.

(1976). *Selected writings*, ed. and trans. H. P. Rickman. Cambridge University Press.

Dimidjian, Sona, & Hollon, Steven D. (2010). How would we know if psychotherapy were harmful? *American Psychologist*, 65, 21–33.

Dinwiddy, John (1989). *Bentham*. Oxford University Press.

Dixon, Thomas (2003). *From passions to emotions: The creation of a secular psychological category*. New York: Cambridge University Press.

Dobson, Keith (2002). A national imperative: Public funding of psychological services. *Canadian Psychology*, 43, 65–75.

Domjan, Michael (2005). Pavlovian conditioning: A functional perspective. *Annual Review of Psychology*, 56, 179–206.

Donald, Ian J., & Canter, David (1987). United Kingdom. In Albert R. Gilgen & Carol K. Gilgen (eds.), *International handbook of psychology* (pp. 502–533). New York: Greenwood Press.

Donaldson, Gail (1996). Between practice and theory: Melanie Klein, Anna Freud and the development of child analysis. *Journal of the History of the Behavioral Sciences*, 32, 160–176.

Downing, Lisa (2005). Berkeley's natural philosophy and philosophy of science. In Kenneth P. Winkler (ed.), *The Cambridge companion to Berkeley* (pp. 230–265). Cambridge University Press.

Drake, Stillman (1990). *Galileo: Pioneer scientist*. University of Toronto Press.

Drapeau, Martin (2012). Introduction to the special issue on sports and exercise psychology. *Canadian Psychology*, 53, 259–260.

Dreyfus, Stuart E. (2004). The five-stage model of adult skill acquisition. *Bulletin of Science, Technology, and Society*, 24, 177–181.

Dreier, Ole (2007). *Psychotherapy in everyday life*. Cambridge University Press.

Droysen, Johann G. (1868). *Grundriss der Historik* [Laying out historiography]. Leipzig: Veit.

Droysen, Johann G. (1967). *Outline of the principles of history*, trans. E. B. Andrews. New York: Fertig. (Original work published in German 1858)

Drunen, Peter van, & Jansz, Jeroen (2004a). Child-rearing and education. In Jeroen Jansz & Peter van Drunen (eds.), *A social history of psychology* (pp. 45–92). Oxford: Blackwell.
  (2004b). Introduction. In Jeroen Jansz & Peter van Drunen (eds.), *A social history of psychology* (pp. 1–11). Oxford: Blackwell.

Dryden, Windy, Mearns, Dave, & Thorne, Brian (2000). Counselling in the United Kingdom: Past, present and future. *British Journal of Guidance & Counselling*, 28(4), 467–483.

Duhem, Pierre (1954). *The aim and structure of physical theory*, trans. P. P. Wiener. Princeton University Press. (Original work published in French 1905)

Dumenil, Lynn (1995). *The modern temper: American culture and society in the 1920s*. New York: Hill and Wang.

Dunkel, Harold B. (1970). *Herbart and Herbartianism: An educational ghost story*. University of Chicago Press.

Dunker, Christian Ingo Lenz (2008). Psychology and psychoanalysis in Brazil: From cultural syncretism to the collapse of liberal individualism. *Theory & Psychology*, 18, 223–236.

Dzielska, Maria (1995). *Hypatia of Alexandria*, trans. F. Lyra. Cambridge, MA: Harvard University Press.

Eamon, William (1994). *Science and the secrets of nature: Books of secrets on medieval and early modern culture*. Princeton University Press.

Ebbinghaus, Hermann (1896). Übererklärende und beschreibende Psychologie [Concerning explanatory and descriptive psychology]. *Zeitschrift für Psychologie*, 9, 161–205.

Eckardt, Marianne Horney (2005). Karen Horney: A portrait. *The American Journal of Psychoanalysis*, 65, 95–101.

Edelman, Gerald (1991). *Bright air, brilliant fire: On the matter of the mind*. New York: Basic Books.

Eichenbaum, Luise, & Orbach, Susie (2003). Relational psychoanalysis and feminism: A crossing of historical paths. *Psychotherapy and Politics International*, 1, 17–26.

Eisold, Kenneth (2002). Jung, Jungians, and Psychoanalysis. *Psychoanalytic Psychology*, 19, 501–524.

   (2005). Psychoanalysis and psychotherapy: A long and troubled relationship. *Psychoanalytical Psychotherapy*, 86, 1175–1195.

Eldridge, Jennifer J., & Gluck, John P. (1996). Gender differences in attitudes toward animal research. *Ethics & Behavior*, 6, 239–256.

Eliot, Lise (2009). *Pink brain, blue brain: How small differences narrow into troublesome gaps – and what we can do about it*. New York: Houghton Mifflin Harcourt.

Ellenberger, Henri F. (1970). *The discovery of the unconscious: The history and evolution of dynamic psychiatry*. New York: Basic Books.

Elliott, Robert, Fischer, Constance T., & Rennie, David L. (1999). Evolving guidelines for publication of qualitative research studies in psychology and related fields. *British Journal of Clinical Psychology*, 38, 215–229.

Elms, Alan (2005). Jung's lives. *Journal of the History of the Behavioral Sciences*, 41, 331–346.

Ellwood, Robert (1999). *The politics of myth: A study of C. G. Jung, Mircea Eliade, and Joseph Campbell*. New York: SUNY Press.

Emery, Nathan J., & Clayton, Nicola S. (2009). Comparative social cognition. *Annual Review of Psychology*, 60, 87–113.

Engel, George, L. (1977). The need for a new medical model: A challenge for biomedicine. *Science*, 196, 129–136.

Enriquez, Virgilio G. (1992). *From colonial to liberation psychology: The Philippine experience*. Diliman, Quezon City: University of the Philippines Press.

Erdelyi, Matthew Hugh (2010). The ups and downs of memory. *American Psychologist*, 65, 623–633.

Erikson, Erik H. (1958). *Young man Luther: A study in psychoanalysis and history*. London: Faber and Faber.

   (1963). *Childhood and society*, 2nd edn. New York: Norton.

Erös, Ferenc (2003). The Ferenczi cult: Its historical and political roots. *International Forum of Psychoanalysis*, 13, 121–128.

Esterson, Allen (2002). The myth of Freud's ostracism by the medical community in 1896–1905: Jeffery Masson's assault on truth. *History of Psychology*, 5, 115–134.

Evans, Rand B. (1990a). Introduction. In Ruth Leys & Rand B. Evans (eds.), *Defining American psychology: The correspondence between Adolf Meyer and E. B. Titchener* (pp. 3–38). Baltimore, MD: Johns Hopkins University Press.

   (1990b). William James and his Principles. In Michael G. Johnson & Tracy B. Henley (eds.), *Reflections on* The Principles of Psychology: *William James after a century* (pp. 11–31). Hillsdale, NJ: Erlbaum.

   (1991). E. B. Titchener on scientific psychology and technology. In Gregory A. Kimble, Michael Wertheimer, & Charlotte L. White (eds.), *Portraits of pioneers in psychology*, vol. I (pp. 89–103). Washington, DC: American Psychological Association.

Eysenck, Hans J. (1953). *Uses and abuses of psychology*. Baltimore, MD: Penguin.

Fagan, Thomas K. (1992). Compulsory schooling, child study, clinical psychology, and special education: Origins of school psychology. *American Psychologist*, 47, 236–243.

Fancher, Raymond E. (1985). *The intelligence men: Makers of the IQ controversy*. New York: Norton.

(2000). *Psychoanalytic psychology: The development of Freud's thought*. New York: Norton.

Fancher, Raymond E., & Rutherford, Alexandra (2012). *Pioneers of psychology: A history*, 4th edn. New York: Norton.

Fanelli, Danielle (2009). How many scientists fabricate and falsify research? A systematic review and meta-analysis of survey data. *PLoS ONE* 4(5), e5738.

Fang, Ferric C., Steen, R. Grant, & Casadevall, Arturo (2012). Misconduct accounts for the majority of retracted scientific publications. *Proceedings of the National Academy of Sciences*, 109, 17028–17033.

Fanon, Frantz (1963). *The wretched of the earth*, trans. Constance Farrington. New York: Grove Press. (Original work published in French 1961)

(1967). *Black skin, white masks*, trans. C. L. Markmann. New York: Grove. (Original work published in French 1952)

Fara, Patricia (2004). *Pandora's breeches: Women, science and power in the Enlightenment*. London: Pimlico.

Farah, Martha J. (2012). Neuroethics: The ethical, legal, and societal impact of neuroscience. *Annual Review of Psychology*, 63, 571–591.

Farrell, Martin J. (2011). Space perception and William James's metaphysical presuppositions. *History of Psychology*, 14, 158–173.

Febbraro, Angela R. (1997). Gender, mentoring, and research practices: Social psychologists trained at the University of Michigan, 1949–1974. Unpublished doctoral dissertation, University of Guelph, Ontario.

Feest, Uljana (2005). Operationalism in psychology: What the debate is about, what the debate should be about. *Journal of the History of the Behavioral Sciences*, 41, 131–149.

Ferguson, Niall (ed.) (1997). *Virtual history: Alternatives and counterfactuals*. London: Picador.

Festinger, Leon (1957). *A theory of cognitive dissonance*. Stanford University Press.

Feyerabend, Paul (1975). *Against method: Outline of an anarchistic theory of knowledge*. London: New Left Books.

Finch, Sue, Thomason, Neil, & Cumming, Geoff (2002). Past and future American Psychological Association guidelines for statistical practice. *Theory & Psychology*, 12, 825–853.

Fine, Michelle (2006). Bearing witness: Methods for researching oppression and resistance (A textbook for critical research). *Social Justice Research*, 19(1), 83–108.

Finison, Lorenz (1976). Unemployment, politics, and the history of organized psychology. *American Psychologist*, 31, 747–755.

(1986). The psychological insurgency: 1936–1945. *Journal of Social Issues*, 42(1), 21–33.

Fink, Bruce (2007). *Fundamentals of psychoanalytic technique: A Lacanian approach for practitioners*. New York: Norton.

Finkelberg, Aryeh (1993). Anaximander's conception of the apeiron. *Phronesis*, 38, 229–256.

Finsen, Lawrence, & Finsen, Susan (1994). *The animal rights movement in America: From compassion to respect*. New York: Twayne.

Fisher, Celia B., & Fryberg, Denise (1994). Participant-partners: College students weigh the costs and benefits of deceptive research. *American Psychologist*, 49, 417–427.

Fiske, Susan T., & Taylor, Shelley E. (1982). *Social cognition*. New York: Random House.

Fitzgerald, Allan D. (ed.) (1999). *Augustine through the ages*. Cambridge: William B. Eerdmans.

Flanagan, Sabina (1998). *Hildegard of Bingen, 1098–1179: A visionary life*, 2nd edn. London: Routledge.

Flannery, Kevin L. (2003). The multifarious moral object of Thomas Aquinas. *The Thomist*, 67, 95–118.

Flax, Jane (2004). What is the subject? Review essay on psychoanalysis and feminism in postcolonial time. *Signs: Journal of Women in Culture and Society*, 29, 905–923.

Fleeson, William (2001). Toward a structure- and process-integrated view of personality: Traits as density distributions of states. *Journal of Personality and Social Psychology*, 80, 1011–1027.

Flynn, J. R. (2012). *Are we getting smarter? Rising IQ in the 21ˢᵗ century*. New York: Cambridge University Press.

Fodor, Jerry, & Piatelli Palmarini, Massimo (2010). *What Darwin got wrong*. New York: Farrar, Straus and Giroux.

Fogelin, Robert J. (2001). *Berkeley and the* Principles of Human Knowledge. London: Routledge.

Foglia, Marc (2010). Michel de Montaigne. In E. N. Zalta (ed.), *The Stanford encyclopedia of philosophy*. Retrieved from http://plato.stanford.edu/archives/win2010/entries/montaigne/

Fonagy, Peter (2003). Genetics, developmental psychopathology, and psychoanalytic theory: The case for ending our (not so) splendid isolation. *Psychoanalytic Inquiry*, 23, 218–247.

Foucault, Michel (1977). *Discipline and punish: The birth of the prison*, trans. A. Sheridan. London: Lane. (Original work published in French 1975)

   (1978). *The history of sexuality*, vol. I: *An introduction*, trans. R. Hurley. New York: Vintage Books. (Original work published in French 1976)

Foucault, Michel (1988). *Madness and civilization: A history of insanity in the age of reason*, trans. R. Howard. New York: Vintage Books. (Original work published in French 1965)

Fox, Dennis, Prilleltensky, Isaac, & Austin, Stephanie (eds.) (2009). *Critical psychology: An introduction*. London: Sage.

Foxhall, Lin (1989). Household, gender and property in classical Athens. *The Classical Quarterly*, n.s., 39, 22–44.

Frank, Joseph (1986). *Dostoevsky: The stir of liberation*. Princeton University Press.

Frankl, Viktor E. (1992). *Man's search for meaning: An introduction to logotherapy*, 4th edn. Boston, MA: Beacon Press. (Original work published 1946)

Franklin, Allan (1990). *Experiment, right or wrong*. Cambridge University Press.

Franks, Peter E. (1975). A social history of American social psychology up to the Second World War. Unpublished PhD dissertation, State University of New York, Stony Brook.

Freire, Paulo (1997). *Pedagogy of the oppressed*, new revised 20th-anniversary edition, trans. M. Bergman Ramos. New York: Continuum. (Original work published in Portuguese 1968)

Freud, Sigmund (1910). The origin and development of psychoanalysis. *American Journal of Psychology*, 21, 181–218.

   (1955). *Group psychology and the analysis of the ego*. New York: Boni and Liveright. (Original work published in German 1921)

Frie, Roger (1997). *Subjectivity and intersubjectivity in modern philosophy and psychoanalysis: A study of Sartre, Binswanger, Lacan, and Habermas*. Lanham, MD: Rowman & Littlefield.

Fromm, Erich (1955). *The sane society*. New York: Holt, Rinehart, and Winston.

   (1961). *Marx's concept of man*. New York: Frederick Ungar.

Frosh, Stephen (1999). *The politics of psychoanalysis: An introduction to Freudian and post-Freudian theory*. New York University Press.

   (2002). *Key concepts in psychoanalysis*. New York University Press.

   (2006). *For and against psychoanalysis*, 2nd edn. New York: Routledge.

Frosh, Stephen, & Baraitser, Lisa (2008). Psychoanalysis and psychosocial studies. *Psychoanalysis, Culture & Society*, 13, 346–365.

Frost, Samantha (2008). *Lessons from a materialist thinker: Hobbesian reflections on Ethics and politics*. Stanford University Press.

Fuchs, Alfred H. (2000). The psychology of Thomas Upham. In Gregory A. Kimble & Michael Wertheimer (eds.), *Portraits of pioneers in psychology*, vol. IV (pp. 1–13). Washington, DC: American Psychological Association.

Furumoto, Laurel (1988). Shared knowledge: The experimentalists, 1904–1929. In Jill G. Morawski (ed.), *The rise of experimentation in American psychology* (pp. 94–113). New Haven, CT: Yale University Press.

(1989). The history of psychology. In T. S. Cohen (ed.), *The G. Stanley Hall lecture series*, vol. IX (pp. 9–34). Washington, DC: American Psychological Association.

(1991). From "paired associates" to a psychology of the self: The intellectual odyssey of Mary Whiton Calkins. In Gregory A. Kimble, Michael Wertheimer, & Charlotte L. White (eds.), *Portraits of pioneers in psychology*, vol. I (pp. 57–72). Washington, DC: American Psychological Association.

Furumoto, Laurel, & Scarborough Elizabeth (1986). Placing women in the history of psychology: The first American women psychologists. *American Psychologist*, 41, 35–42.

Gabbey, Alan (1996). Spinoza's natural science and methodology. In Don Garrett (ed.), *The Cambridge companion to Spinoza* (pp. 142–191). Cambridge University Press.

Gadamer, Hans-Georg (1997). *Truth and method*, trans. J. Weinsheimer & D. G. Marshall. New York: Continuum. (Original work published in German 1960)

Galison, Peter, & Hevly, Bruce (eds.) (1992). *Big science: The growth of large scale research*. Stanford University Press.

Garber, Daniel (2001). *Descartes embodied: Reading Cartesian philosophy through Cartesian science*. Cambridge University Press.

Gardner, Howard (1985). *The mind's new science: A history of the cognitive revolution*. New York: Basic Books.

(1993). *Multiple intelligences: The theory in practice*. New York: Basic Books.

Gaukroger, Stephen (1995). *Descartes: An intellectual biography*. Oxford: Clarendon Press.

(2001). *Francis Bacon and the transformation of early-modern philosophy*. Cambridge University Press.

Gay, Peter (1988). *Freud: A life for our time*. New York: Norton.

Gazzaniga, Michael S. (2011). *Who's in charge? Free will and the science of the brain*. New York: HarperCollins.

Geison, Gerald L. (1995). *The private science of Louis Pasteur*. Princeton University Press.

Gellner, Ernest (1985). *The psychoanalytic movement: The cunning of unreason*. London: Paladin.

Gemignani, Marco, & Giliberto, Massimo (2005). Counseling and psychotherapy in Italy: A profession in constant change. *Journal of Mental Health Counseling*, 27, 168–184.

Gentner, Dedre, & Grudin, Jonathan (1985). The evolution of mental metaphors in psychology: A 90-year retrospective. *American Psychologist*, 40, 181–192.

Gergen, Kenneth J. (1982). *Transformation in social knowledge*. New York: Springer.

(1985). The social constructionist movement in modern psychology. *American Psychologist*, 40, 266–275.

(1990). *Metaphor, metatheory, and the social world*. In D. Leary (ed.), *Metaphors in the history of psychology* (pp. 267–299). Cambridge University Press.

(1994). Exploring the postmodern: Perils or pitfalls? *American Psychologist*, 49, 412–416.

(2001). Psychological science in a postmodern context. *American Psychologist*, 56, 808–813.

(2009). *Relational being: Beyond self and community*. New York: Oxford University Press.

(2010). The acculturated brain. *Theory & Psychology*, 20, 795–816.

Gergen, Kenneth J., Gulerce, Aydan, Lock, A., & Misra, Girishwar (1996). Psychological science in cultural context. *American Psychologist*, 51, 496–503.

Gergen, Mary (2001). *Feminist reconstructions in psychology: Narrative, gender, and performance*. Thousand Oaks, CA: Sage.

Gerson, Lloyd P. (ed.) (1996). *The Cambridge companion to Plotinus*. Cambridge University Press.

Gert, Bernard (1996). *Hobbes's psychology*. In Tom Sorrell (ed.), *The Cambridge companion to Hobbes* (pp. 157–174). Cambridge University Press.

Geuter, Ulfried (1992). *The professionalization of psychology in Nazi Germany*, trans. Richard J. Holmes. Cambridge University Press. (Original work published in German 1984)

Ghaemi, Nassir S. (2007). Existence and pluralism: The rediscovery of Karl Jaspers. *Psychopathology*, 40, 75–82.

Ghobari, Bagher, & Bolhari, Jafar (2001). The current state of medical psychology in Iran. *Journal of Clinical Psychology in Medical Settings*, 8, 39–43.

Gibby, Robert E., & Zickar, Michael J. (2008). A history of the early days of personality testing in American industry: An obsession with adjustment. *History of Psychology*, 11, 164–184.

Gigerenzer, Gerd (1987). Probabilistic thinking and the fight against subjectivity. In Lorenz Krueger, Gerd Gigerenzer, & Mary Morgan (eds.), *The probabilistic revolution: Ideas in the sciences*, vol. II (pp. 7–33). Cambridge, MA: MIT Press.

(1989). *The empire of chance: How probability changed science and everyday life*. Cambridge University Press.

Gilbert, Nigel, & Mulkay, Michael (1981). Contexts of scientific discourse: Social accounting and experimental papers. In Karin D. Knorr, Roger Krohn, & Richard Whitley (eds.), *The social process of scientific investigation* (pp. 269–296). Dordrecht: D. Reidel.

Gilgen, Albert R. (1982). *American psychology since World War II: A profile of the discipline*. Westport, CT: Greenwood Press.

Gilgen, Albert R., & Gilgen, Carol K. (eds.) (1987). *International handbook of Psychology*. New York: Greenwood Press.

Gillespie, Richard (1988). The Hawthorne experiments and the politics of experimentation. In Jill G. Morawski (ed.), *The rise of experimentation in American psychology* (pp. 114–137). New Haven, CT: Yale University Press.

Gillham, Nicholas Wright (2001). *A life of Sir Francis Galton: From African exploration to the birth of eugenics*. New York: Oxford University Press.

Gilligan, Carol (1982). *In a different voice: Psychological theory and women's development*. Cambridge, MA: Harvard University Press.

Giorgi, Amedeo (1970). *Psychology as a human science: A phenomenologically based approach*. New York: Harper & Row.

Gleick, James (1988). *Chaos: Making a new science*. New York: Penguin.

Gleitman, Henry (1991). Edward Chace Tolman: A life of scientific and social purpose: In Gregory A. Kimble, Michael Wertheimer, & Charlotte L. White (eds.), *Portraits of pioneers in psychology* (pp. 227–241). Washington, DC: American Psychological Association.

Glickman, Stephen E. (1996). *Donald Olding Hebb: Returning the nervous system to psychology*. In Gregory A. Kimble, Charles A. Bonneau, & Michael Wertheimer (eds.), *Portraits of pioneers in psychology*, vol. II (pp. 227–244). Washington, DC: American Psychological Association.

Götzl, Herbert (2003). *Wolfgang Metzger: Perspectives on his life and work*. In Gregory A. Kimble & Michael Wertheimer (eds.), *Portraits of pioneers in psychology*, vol. V (pp. 277–191). Washington, DC: American Psychological Association.

Goertz, Hans-Jürgen (1993). *Thomas Müntzer: Apocalyptic mystic and revolutionary*, trans. J. Jaquiery, ed. P. Matheson. Edinburgh, Scotland: T&T Clark. (Original work published in German 1989)

Goertzen, Jason R. (2008). On the possibility of unification: The reality and nature of the crisis in psychology. *Theory & Psychology*, 18, 829–852.

Goldberg, Arnold (1998). Self psychology since Kohut. *Psychoanalytic Quarterly*, 67, 240–255.

Goldenfeld, Nigel, & Woese, Carl (2007). Biology's next revolution. *Nature*, January 25.

Goldman, Steven L. (ed.) (1989). *Science, technology, and human progress*. Bethlehem, PA: Lehigh University Press.

Goleman, Daniel (1995). *Emotional intelligence*. New York: Bantam.

Gombrich, Ernst H. (2006). *The story of art*. London: Phaidon.

Goodall, Jane (1990). *Through a window*. Boston, MA: Houghton Mifflin.

Goodman, David M. (2012). *The demanded self: Levinasian ethics and identity in psychology*. Pittsburgh, PA: Duquesne University Press.

Goodwin, C. James (2005). Reorganizing the Experimentalists: The origins of the Society of Experimental Psychologists. *History of Psychology*, 8, 347–361.

Gould, Stephen J. (1996). *The mismeasure of man*, rev. edn. New York: Norton.

Graham, Daniel, W. (2011). Heraclitus. In E. N. Zalta (ed.), *The Stanford encyclopedia of philosophy*. Retrieved from http://plato.stanford.edu/archives/sum2011/entries/heraclitus/

Grant, Michael (1971). *Cicero: On the good life*. New York: Penguin.

Gray, Jeffrey A. (1979). *Pavlov*. Hassocks: Harvester Press.

Green, Christopher D. (1998). The thoroughly modern Aristotle: Was he really a functionalist? *History of Psychology*, 1, 8–20.

(2001). Charles Babbage, the Analytical Engine, and the possibility of a 19th-century cognitive science. In Christopher D. Green, Marlene Shore & Thomas Teo (eds.), *The transformation of psychology: Influences of 19th-century philosophy, technology, and natural science* (pp. 133–152). Washington, DC: American Psychological Association.

(2003). Psychology strikes out: Coleman R. Griffith and the Chicago Cubs. *History of Psychology*, 6, 267–283.

(2009). Darwinian theory, functionalism, and the first American psychological revolution. *American Psychologist*, 64(2), 75–83.

Green, Christopher D., Shore, Marilyn, & Teo, Thomas (eds.) (2001). *The transformation of psychology: Influences of 19th-century philosophy, technology, and natural science*. Washington, DC: American Psychological Association.

Greenway, A. P. (1973). The incorporation of action into associationism: The psychology of Alexander Bain. *Journal of the History of the Behavioural Sciences*, 9, 42–52.

Greenwood, John D. (1999). Understanding the cognitive revolution in psychology. *Journal of the History of the Behavioral Sciences*, 35, 1–22.

(2004). *The disappearance of the social in American social psychology*. Cambridge University Press.

(2009). Materialism, strong psychological continuity, and American scientific psychology. *Theory & Psychology*, 19, 545–564.

Gribbin, John (2002). *Science: A history, 1543–2001*. London: Allen Lane.

Griffin, Donald R. (1976). *The question of animal awareness: Evolutionary continuity of mental experience*. New York: Rockefeller University Press.

Gross, Alan G. (1990). *The rhetoric of science*. Cambridge, MA: Harvard University Press.

Grossman, William I., & Silverman, Doris K. (2002). History of the vicissitudes in the application of psychoanalytic method during the last fifty years. *International Journal of Psychoanalysis*, 83, 496–500.

Gruber, Howard E. (1981). *Darwin on man*. University of Chicago Press.

Grünbaum, Adolf (1984). *The foundations of psychoanalysis: A philosophical critique*. Berkeley, CA: University of California Press.

(1993). *Validation in the clinical theory of psychoanalysis: A study in the philosophy of psychoanalysis*. Madison, CT: International Universities Press.

Grusec, Joan E. (1992). Social learning theory and developmental psychology: The legacies of Robert Sears and Albert Bandura. *Developmental Psychology*, 28, 776–786.

Guillin, Vincent (2004). Theodule Ribot's ambiguous positivism: Philosophical and epistemological strategies in the founding of French scientific psychology. *Journal of the History of the Behavioural Sciences*, 40, 165–181.

Gundlach, Horst (2004). Reine Psychologie, angewandte Psychologie und die Institutionalisierung der Psychologie [Pure psychology, applied psychology, and the institutionalization of psychology]. *Zeitschrift fur Psychologie*, 212(4), 183–199.

Gusfield, Joseph (1976). The literary rhetoric of science: Comedy and pathos of drinking driver research. *American Sociological Review*, 47, 16–33.

Guthrie, Robert V. (1998). *Even the rat was white: A historical view of psychology*, 2nd edn. Boston, MA: Allyn and Bacon.

Haakonssen, Knud (1990). Introduction. In Knud Haakonssen (ed.), *Thomas Reid: Practical ethics* (pp. 1–89). Princeton University Press.

Habermas, Jürgen (1972). *Knowledge and human interest*, trans. J. J. Shapiro. Boston, MA: Beacon Press. (Original work published in German 1968)

(1984). *The theory of communicative action*, vol. I: *Reason and the rationalization of society*, trans. Thomas McCarthy. Boston, MA: Beacon Press. (Original work published in German 1981)

(1988). *On the logic of the social sciences*, trans. Shierry Weber Nicholsen & Jerry A. Stark. Cambridge, MA: MIT Press. (Original work published in German 1967)

Hacking, Ian (1988). Telepathy: Origins of randomization in experimental design. *Isis*, 79, 427–451.

(1994). The looping effects of human kinds. In D. Sperber, D. Premack, & A. J. Premack (eds.), *Causal cognition: A multi-disciplinary approach* (pp. 351–382). Oxford: Clarendon Press.

(1995). *Rewriting the soul: Multiple personality and the sciences of memory*. Princeton University Press.

Hagen, Edward H. (2005). Controversial issues in evolutionary psychology. In David M. Buss (ed.), *The handbook of evolutionary psychology* (pp. 145–173). New York: Wiley.

Haidt, Jonathan (2006). *The happiness hypothesis: Finding modern truth in ancient wisdom*. New York: Basic Books.

Hale, Matthew (1980). *Human science and social order: Hugo Münsterberg and the origins of applied psychology*. Philadelphia, PA: Temple University Press.

Hallie, Philip P. (1959). *Maine de Biran*. Cambridge, MA: Harvard University Press.

Hallman, David (1992). *A place in creation: Ecological visions in science, religion, and economics*. Toronto: United Church Publishing House.

Hambridge, John, & Baker, Amanda (2001). Medical psychology in Australia. *Journal of Clinical Psychology in Medical Settings*, 8, 3–7.

Hamilton, Edith, & Cairns, Huntington (eds.) (1961). *The collected dialogues of Plato*. Princeton University Press. (Original work published in Greek c. 380 BCE)

Hardin, Russell (2007). *David Hume: Moral and political theorist*. Oxford: Oxford University Press.

Harding, Sandra G. (1986). *The science question in feminism*. Ithaca, NY: Cornell University Press.

(1998). *Is science multicultural? Post-colonialisms, feminisms, and epistemologies*. Bloomington, IN: Indiana University Press.

(2008). *Sciences from below: Feminisms, postcolonialities, and modernities*. Durham, NC: Duke University Press.

Harlow, Harry F. (1958). The nature of love. *American Psychologist*, 13, 673–685.

Harré, Rom, & Gillett, Grant (1994). *The discursive mind*. London: Sage.

Harrington, Austin (2000). In defence of Verstehen and Erklären: Wilhelm Dilthey's *Ideas Concerning a Descriptive and Analytical Psychology*. *Theory and Psychology*, 10, 435–451.

Harris, Benjamin (1979). Whatever happened to Little Albert? *American Psychologist*, 34, 151–160.

(1986). Reviewing 50 years of the psychology of social issues. *Journal of Social Issues*, 42(1), 1–20.

(1996). Psychology and Marxist politics in the United States. In Ian Parker & Russell Spears (eds.), *Psychology and society: Radical theory and practice* (pp. 64–78). London: Pluto.

(2011). Arnold Gesell's progressive vision: Child hygiene, socialism and eugenics. *History of Psychology*, 14, 311–334.

Harris, Benjamin, & Nicholson, Ian A. M. (1998). Toward a history of psychological expertise. *Journal of Social Issues*, 54, 1–5.

Hartelius, Glenn, Caplan, Mariana, & Rardin, Mary Anne (2007). Transpersonal psychology: Defining the past, divining the future. *The Humanistic Psychologist*, 35, 1–26.

Hartley, David (1966). *Observations on man, his frame, his duty, and his expectations*. Gainesville, FL: Scholars' Facsimiles and Reprints. (Original work published 1749)

Hartsock, Nancy C. M. (1985). *Money, sex, and power: Toward a feminist historical materialism*. Boston, MA: Northeastern University Press.

Hasse, Dag Nikolaus (2008). Influence of Arabic and Islamic philosophy on the Latin West. In E. N. Zalta (ed.), *The Stanford encyclopedia of philosophy*. Retrieved from plato.stanford. edu/archives/fall2008/entries/arabic-islamic-influence/

Hatfield, Gary (1992). Descartes' physiology and its relation to his psychology. In John Cottingham (ed.), *The Cambridge companion to Descartes* (pp. 335–370). Cambridge University Press.

(1995). Remaking the science of mind: Psychology as natural science. In Christopher Fox, Roy Porter, & Robert Wokler (eds.), *Inventing human science: Eighteenth-century domains* (pp. 184–231). Berkeley, CA: University of California Press.

Haupt, Edward J. (1998). Origins of American psychology in the work of G. E. Mueller: Classical psychophysics and serial learning. In Robert W. Rieber & Kurt Salzinger (eds.), *Psychology: Theoretical-historical perspectives*, 2nd edn. (pp. 17–72). Washington, DC: American Psychological Association.

Hawkins, Mike (1997). *Social Darwinism in European and American thought, 1860–1945: Nature as a model and nature as a threat*. Cambridge University Press.

Healy, David (2002). *The creation of psychopharmacology*. Cambridge, MA: Harvard University Press.

Hearnshaw, L. S. (1964). *A short history of British psychology: 1840–1940*. New York: Barnes & Noble.

Hebb, Donald O. (1949). *The organization of behavior: A neuropsychological theory*. New York: Wiley.

   (1958). *Biological and biochemical bases of behavior*, 2nd edn. Madison, WI: University of Wisconsin Press.

Hegel, Georg W. F. (1966). *Hegel's science of logic*, trans. W. H. Johnston & L. G. Struthers. London: Allen & Unwin. (Original work published in German 1812–1816)

   (1991). *The encyclopaedia logic (with the Zusätze): Part I of the Encyclopaedia of philosophical sciences with the Zusätze*, trans. T. F. Geraets, W. A. Suchting, & H. S. Harris. Indianapolis, IN: Hackett. (Original work published in German 1830)

Heidbreder, Edna (1972). Mary Whiton Calkins: A discussion. *Journal of the History of the Behavioral Sciences*, 8, 56–68.

Heidegger, Martin (1962). *Being and time*, trans. John MacQuarrie & Edward Robinson. New York: Harper. (Original work published in German 1927)

Heilbroner, Robert L. (1999). *The worldly philosophers*, 7th edn. New York: Simon & Schuster.

Held, Barbara S. (2007). *Psychology's interpretive turn: The search for truth and agency in theoretical and philosophical psychology*. Washington, DC: American Psychological Association.

Hempel, Carl G., & Oppenheim, Paul (1948). Studies in the logic of explanation. *Philosophy of science*, 15, 135–175.

Henle, Mary (1978). Gestalt psychology and Gestalt therapy. *Journal of the History of the Behavioral Sciences*, 14, 23–32.

Henley, Tracy B., Johnson, Michael G., Jones, Elizabeth M., & Herzog, Harold A. (1989). Definitions of psychology. *Psychological Record*, 39, 143–151.

Henrich, Josephe, Heine, Steven J., & Norenzayan, Ara (2010). The weirdest people in the world? *Behavioral and Brain Sciences*, 33, 61–83.

Hepburn, Alexa, & Wiggins, Sally (2007). Discursive research: Themes and debates. In Alexa Hepburn & Sally Wiggins (eds.), *Discursive research in practice: New approaches to psychology and interaction* (pp. 1–28). New York: Cambridge University Press.

Herbert, Gary B. (1989). *Thomas Hobbes: The unity of scientific and moral wisdom*. Vancouver, BC: University of British Columbia Press.

Herman, Ellen (1995). *The romance of American psychology: Political culture in the age of experts*. Berkeley, CA: University of California Press.

Hermans, Hubert, J. M., & Hermans-Konopka, Agnieszka (2010). *Dialogical self theory: Positioning and counter-positioning in a globalized society*. New York: Cambridge University Press.

Hersch, Edwin L. (2003). *From philosophy to psychotherapy: A phenomenological model for psychology, psychiatry, and psychoanalysis*. University of Toronto Press.

Highhouse, Scott (1999). The brief history of personnel counselling in industrial-organizational psychology. *Journal of Vocational Behavior*, 55, 318–336.

Hilgard, Ernest R. (1987). *Psychology in America: A historical survey*. San Diego, CA: Harcourt Brace Jovanovich.

Hobbes, Thomas (1962). *Leviathan*, ed. John Plamenatz. London: Collins. (Original work published 1651)

Hobbs, Nicholas (1965). Ethics in clinical psychology. In Benjamin B. Wolman (ed.), *Handbook of clinical psychology*. New York: McGraw-Hill.

Hobsbawm, Eric J. (1996). *The age of extremes: A history of the world, 1914–1991*. New York: Vintage Books.

Hoff, Tory L. (1992). Psychology in Canada one hundred years ago: James Mark Baldwin at the University of Toronto. *Canadian Psychology*, 33, 683–694.

Hoffman, Robert R., Bringmann, Wolfgang, Bamberg, Michael, & Klein, Richard (1987). Some historical observations on Ebbinghaus. In David S. Gorfein & Robert R. Hoffman (eds.), *Memory and learning: The Ebbinghaus centennial conference* (pp. 57–76). Hillsdale, NJ: Erlbaum.

Hogan, Robert, Harkness, Allan R., & Lubinski, David (2000). Personality and individual differences. In Kurt Pawlik & Mark R. Rosenzweig (eds.), *International handbook of psychology* (pp. 283–304). London: Sage.

Holdstock, Len T. (2000). *Re-examining psychology: Critical perspectives and African insights*. London: Routledge.

Holzkamp, Klaus (1972). *Kritische Psychologie: Vorbereitende Arbeiten* [Critical psychology: Preparatory works]. Frankfurt am Main: Fischer.

(1983). *Grundlegung der Psychologie* [Laying the foundations for psychology]. Frankfurt am Main: Campus.

Holzman, Lois (2000). Performative psychology: An untapped resource for educators. *Educational and Child Psychology*, 17, 86–100.

Hook, Derek (ed.) (2004). *Critical psychology.* Lansdowne, Zambia: UCT Press.

(2005). A critical psychology of the postcolonial. *Theory & Psychology*, 15, 475–503.

(2007). *Foucault, psychology, and the analytics of power*. New York: Palgrave Macmillan.

(2008). Postcolonial psychoanalysis. *Theory & Psychology*, 18, 269–283.

Horgan, John (1999). *The undiscovered mind: How the human brain defies replication, medication, and explanation*. New York: Free Press.

Horkheimer, Max (1992). Traditional and critical theory. In D. Ingram & J. Simon-Ingram (eds.), *Critical theory: The essential readings* (pp. 239–254). New York: Paragon House. (Original work published in German 1937)

Horkheimer, Max, & Adorno, Theodor W. (1982). *Dialectic of enlightenment*. New York: Continuum. (Original work published in German 1947)

Hornstein, Gail A. (1988). Quantifying psychological phenomena: Debates, dilemmas, and implications. In Jill G. Morawski (ed.), *The rise of experimentation in American psychology* (pp. 1–34). New Haven, CT: Yale University Press.

(1992). The return of the repressed: Psychology's problematic relations with psychoanalysis, 1909–1960. *American Psychologist*, 47, 254–263.

Horowitz, Frances Degen (1992). John B. Watson's legacy: Learning and environment. *Developmental Psychology*, 28, 360–367.

Horowitz, Irving (1974). *The rise and fall of Project Camelot: Studies in the relationship between social science and practical politics*. Cambridge, MA: MIT Press. (Original work published 1967)

Horst, Frank, C. P. van der, & Veer, René van der (2010). The ontology of an idea: John Bowlby and contemporaries on mother–child separation. *History of Psychology*, 13, 25–45.

House, Richard (1996). The professionalization of counselling: A coherent "case against"? *Counselling Psychology Quarterly*, 9, 343–358.

House, Richard, & Totten, Nick (eds.) (1997). *Implausible professions: Arguments for pluralism and autonomy in psychotherapy and counselling*. Ross-on-Wye: PCCS Books.

Huffman, Carl (2011). Pythagoras. In E. N. Zalta (ed.), *The Stanford encyclopedia of philosophy*. Retrieved from plato.stanford.edu/archives/fall2011/entries/pythagoras/

Huizinga, Johan (1956). *The waning of the Middle Ages*. Garden City, NY: Doubleday.

Hull, Clark L. (1943). *Principles of behavior*. New York: Appleton-Century-Crofts.

Hume, David (1977). *An enquiry concerning human understanding*, ed. Edward Steinberg. Indianapolis, IN: Hackett Publishing. (Original work published 1748)

Hunt, Lynn (ed.) (1989). *The new cultural history: Essays*. Berkeley, CA: University of California Press.

Hunt, Morton (2007). *The story of psychology*, 2nd edn. New York: Anchor.

Hunter, Lynette, & Hutton, Sarah (1997). *Women, science and medicine: 1500–1700*. Phoenix Mill, Gloucestershire: Sutton.

Hursthouse, Rosalind (1999). *On virtue ethics*. Oxford University Press.

Husserl, Edmund (1977). *Phenomenological psychology. Lectures, summer semester, 1925*, trans. J. Scanlon. The Hague: Martin Nijhoff. (Original work published in German 1962)
   (1996). *Die Krisis der europäischen Wissenschaften und die transzendentale Phänomenologie* [The crisis of the European sciences and transcendental phenomenology]. Hamburg: Meiner. (Original work published 1936)

Hwang, Kwang Kuo (2012). *Foundations of Chinese psychology: Confucian social relations*. New York: Springer.

Hyde, Janet S. (2005). The gender similarities hypothesis. *American Psychologist*, 60, 581–592.

Iggers, Georg G. (1997). *Historiography in the 20th century: From scientific objectivity to the postmodern challenge*. Hanover, NH: University Press of New England.

Illich, Ivan (1976). *Limits to medicine. Medical nemesis: The expropriation of health*. Toronto: Bantam.

Inhelder, Bärbel (1998). Genetic epistemology and developmental psychology. In Robert W. Rieber & Kurt Salzinger (eds.), *Psychology: Theoretical-historical perspectives* (pp. 411–421). Washington, DC: American Psychological Association.

Innis, Nancy K. (1992). Tolman and Tryon: Early research on the inheritance of the ability to learn. *American Psychologist*, 47, 190–197.
   (2003). William McDougall: "A major tragedy"? In Gregory A. Kimble & Michael Wertheimer (eds.), *Portraits of pioneers in psychology*, vol. V (pp. 91–108). Washington, DC: American Psychological Association.

Institoris, Heinrich & Sprenger, Jakob (2006). *Malleus maleficarum*, ed. and trans. Christopher S. Mackay. Cambridge University Press. (Original work published in Latin 1486–7)

Isaac, Joel (2011). Introduction: The human science and cold war America. *Journal of the History of the Behavioral Sciences*, 47, 225–231.

Iwahara, Shinkuro (1976). Japan. In Virginia S. Sexton & Henryk Misiak (eds.), *Psychology around the world* (pp. 242–258). Monterey, CA: Brooks/Cole.

Izard, Carroll E. (2009). Emotion theory and research: Highlights, unanswered questions, and emerging issues. *Annual Review of Psychology*, 60, 1–25.

Jackson, John P., Jr. (2006). Kenneth B. Clark: The complexities of activist psychology. In Donald A. Dewsbury, Ludy T. Benjamin Jr., & Michael Wertheimer (eds.), *Portraits of pioneers in psychology*, vol VI (pp. 273–286). Washington, DC: American Psychological Association.

Jackson, John P., & Weidman, Nadine M. (2004). *Race, racism, and science: Social impact and interaction*. Santa Barbara, CA: ABC-Clio.

Jacobsen, Erik (1986). The early history of psychotherapeutic drugs. *Psychopharmacology*, 89, 138–144.

Jacoby, Rebecca (2001). Medical psychology in Israel. *Journal of Clinical Psychology in Medical Settings*, 8, 45–50.

Jaeger, Siegfried (1982). Origins of child psychology: William Preyer. In William R. Woodward & Mitchell G. Ash (eds.), *The problematic science: Psychology in nineteenth-century thought* (pp. 300–321). New York: Praeger.

Jahoda, Gustav (2007). *A history of social psychology: From the eighteenth-century Enlightenment to the Second World War*. Cambridge University Press.

James, Jon L. (2007). *Transcendental phenomenological psychology: Introduction to Husserl's psychology of human consciousness*. Oxford: Trafford.

James, William (1890). *The principles of psychology*. New York: Holt.
  (1892). *Psychology: A briefer course*. New York: Holt.

James, William (1902). *The varieties of religious experience*. London: Fontana.

Janaway, Christopher (2010). The real essence of human beings: Schopenhauer and the unconscious will. In Angus Nicholls & Martin Liebscher (eds.), *Thinking the unconscious: Nineteenth-century German thought* (pp. 140–155). New York: Cambridge University Press.

Jansz, Jeroen, & van Drunen, Peter (eds.) (2004). *A social history of psychology*. Oxford: Blackwell.

Jarrett, Charles (2007). *Spinoza: A guide for the perplexed*. London: Continuum.

Jaspers, Karl (1997). *General psychopathology* (2 vols.), trans. J. Hoenig & M. W. Hamilton. Baltimore, MD: Johns Hopkins University Press. (Original work published in German 1913)

Jenkins, Keith (1991). *Re-thinking history*. London: Routledge.

Jensen, Arthur R. (2000). Hans Eysenck: Apostle of the London School. In Gregory A. Kimble & Michael Wertheimer (eds.), *Portraits of pioneers in psychology*, vol. IV (pp. 339–357). Washington, DC: American Psychological Association.

John, Leslie, Loewenstein, George, & Prelec, Drazen (2012). Measuring the prevalence of questionable research practices with incentives for truth-telling. *Psychological Science*, 23, 524–532.

Johnson, Norine (2003). Psychology and health research, practice and policy. *American Psychologist*, 58, 670–677.

Johnston, Elizabeth, & Johnson, Ann (2008). Searching for the second generation of American women psychologists. *History of Psychology*, 11, 40–72.

Jolley, Nicholas (1999). *Locke: His philosophical thought*. Oxford University Press.
  (2005). *Leibniz*. New York: Routledge.

Joncich, Geraldine (1968). *The sane positivist: A biography of Edward L. Thorndike*. Middletown, CT: Wesleyan University Press.

Jones, Dai, & Elcock, Jonathan (2001). *History and theories of psychology*. New York: Oxford University Press.

Jones, Glen A., McCarney, Patricia L., & Skolnik, Michael L. (2005). *Creating knowledge, strengthening nations: The changing role of higher education*. University of Toronto Press.

Jonte-Pace, Diane (2006). Psychoanalysis, colonialism, and modernity: Reflections on Brickman's aboriginal populations in the mind. *Religious Studies Review* 32, 1–4.

Joravsky, David (1989). *Russian psychology: A critical history*. Oxford: Blackwell.

Jordanova, Ludmilla (2000). *History in practice*. London: Arnold.

Joseph, Jay (2004). *The gene illusion: Genetic research in psychiatry and psychology under the microscope*. New York: Algora.

Joseph, Stephen (2007). Agents of social control? *The Psychologist*, 20, 429–431.

Joshi, Mohan C. (1992). India. In Virginia Staudt Sexton & John D. Hogan (eds.), *International psychology: Views from around the world* (pp. 206–219). Lincoln, NE: University of Nebraska Press.

Juhasz, Joseph B. (1971). Greek theories of imagination. *Journal of the History of the Behavioural Sciences*, 7, 39–58.

Jung, Carl Gustav (1970). After the catastrophe. In H. Read, M. Fordham, G. Adler, & W. McGuire (eds.) & R. F. C. Hull (trans.), *The collected works of C. G. Jung*, vol. X: *Civilization in transition*, 2nd edn. (pp. 194–217). Princeton University Press. (Original work published in German 1945)

Kabat-Zinn, Jon (1990). *Full catastrophe living: Using the wisdom of your body and mind to face stress, pain, and illness*. New York: Bantam Dell.

Kagan, Jerome (2007). *What is emotion? History, measures, and meanings*. New Haven, CT: Yale University Press.

(2009). *The three cultures: Natural sciences, social sciences, and the humanities in the 21st century. Revisiting C. P. Snow*. New York: Cambridge University Press.

(2010). *The temperamental thread: How genes, culture, time and luck make us who we are*. New York: Dana Press.

Kakar, Sudhir (1990). Stories from Indian psychoanalysis – Context and text. In J. Stigler, R. Shweder, & G. Herdt (eds.), *Cultural psychology* (pp. 427–445). New York: Cambridge University Press.

Kaneko, Takayoshi (1987). Japan. In Albert R. Gilgen & Carol K. Gilgen (eds.), *International handbook of psychology* (pp. 274–296). New York: Greenwood Press.

Kant, Immanuel (1970). *Metaphysical foundations of natural science*, trans. James Ellington. Indianapolis, IN: Bobbs-Merrill. (Original work published in German 1786)

(1998). *Critique of pure reason*, ed. and trans. Paul Guyer & Allen W. Wood. Cambridge University Press. (Original work published in German 1781)

Kanter, Joel (2000). The untold story of Donald and Clare Winnicott: How social work influenced modern psychoanalysis. *Clinical Social Work*, 28, 245–261.

Karier, Clarence J. (1986). *Scientists of the mind: Intellectual founders of modern Psychology*. Urbana and Chicago: University of Illinois Press.

Katz, Daniel, Johnson, Blair T., & Nichols, Diana R. (1998). Floyd Henry Allport: Founder of social psychology as a behavioural science. In Gregory A. Kimble & Michael Wertheimer (eds.), *Portraits of pioneers in psychology*, vol. III (pp. 121–142). Washington, DC: American Psychological Association.

Kazdin, Alan E. (2009). Psychological science's contributions to a sustainable environment: Extending our reach to a grad challenge of society. *American Psychologist*, 64, 339–356.

Keller, Evelyn F. (1983). *A feeling for the organism: The life and work of Barbara McClintock*. San Francisco, CA: Freeman.

(1985). *Reflections on gender and science*. New Haven, CT: Yale University Press.

Keller, Heidi (2000). Developmental psychology I: Prenatal to adolescence. In Kurt Pawlik & Mark R. Rosenzweig (eds.), *International handbook of psychology* (pp. 235–260). London: Sage.

Kelly, George A. (1955). *The psychology of personal constructs*. New York: Norton.

Kemp, Simon (1998). Medieval theories of mental representation. *History of Psychology*, 1, 275–288.

Kerber, Linda K. (1988). Separate spheres, female worlds, woman's place; the rhetoric of women's history. *The Journal of American History*, 75, 9–39.

Kidd, Sean A. (2002). The role of qualitative research in psychological journals. *Psychological Methods*, 7, 126–138.

Kidder, Louise H., & Fine, Michelle (1997). Qualitative inquiry in psychology: A radical tradition. In Dennis Fox & Isaac Prilleltensky (eds.), *Critical psychology: An introduction* (pp. 34–50). Thousand Oaks, CA: Sage.

Kim, Uichol, Yang, Guoshu, & Hwang, Kwang-kuo (eds.) (2006). *Indigenous and cultural psychology: Understanding people in context*. New York: Springer.

Kimble, Gregory A. (1991a). Psychology from the standpoint of a mechanist: An appreciation of Clark L. Hull. In Gregory A. Kimble, Michael Wertheimer, & Charlotte L. White (eds.), *Portraits of pioneers in psychology*, vol. I (pp. 209–225). Washington, DC: American Psychological Association.

(1991b). The spirit of Ivan Petrovich Pavlov. In Gregory A. Kimble, Michael Wertheimer, & Charlotte A. White (eds.), *Portraits of pioneers in psychology*, vol. I (pp. 27–40). Washington, DC: American Psychological Association.

(1996). Ivan Michalovich Sechenov: Pioneer in Russian reflexology. In Gregory A. Kimble, C. Alan Boneau, & Michael Wertheimer (eds.), *Portraits of pioneers in psychology*, vol. II (pp. 33–45). Washington, DC: American Psychological Association.

Kirk, Geoffrey Stephen, & Raven, John Earle (1957). *The presocratic philosophers*. Cambridge University Press.

Kite, Mary E., Russo, Nancy Felipe, Brehm, Sharon Stephens, Fouad, Nadya A., Iijima-Hall, Christine C., Hyde, Janet Shibley, & Keita, Gwendolyn Puryear (2001). Women psychologists in academe: Mixed progress, unwarranted complacency. *American Psychologist*, 56, 1080–1098.

Klein, Ann G. (2002). *A forgotten voice: A biography of Leta Stetter Hollingworth*. Scottsdale, AZ: Great Potential Press.

Klein, Melanie (1959). Our adult world and its roots in infancy. *Human Relations*, 12, 291–303.

Kneller, Kane (2006). Kant on sex and marriage right. In Paul Guyer (ed.), *The Cambridge companion to Kant and modern philosophy* (pp. 447–476). Cambridge University Press.

Knobe, Joshua, Buckwalter, Wesley, Nichols, Shaun, Robbins, Philip, Sarkissian, Hagop, & Sommers, Tamler (2012). Experimental philosophy. *Annual Review of Psychology*, 63, 81–99.

Koch, Sigmund (1981). The nature and limits of psychological knowledge: Lessons of a century qua "science." *American Psychologist*, 36, 257–269.

Koffka, Kurt (1935). *Principles of Gestalt psychology*. New York: Harcourt Brace.

Kögler, Hans H. (1999). *The power of dialogue: Critical hermeneutics after Gadamer and Foucault*. Cambridge, MA: MIT Press.

Köhler, Wolfgang (1959). Gestalt psychology today. *American Psychologist*, 14, 727–734.

Konstan, David (2008). *A life worthy of the gods: The materialist psychology of Epicurus*, revised and expanded edn. Las Vegas, NV: Parmenides Publishing.

Koppes, Laura (1997). American female pioneers of industrial and organizational psychology during the early years. *Journal of Applied Psychology*, 82, 500–515.

Korn, James H. (1988). Students' roles, rights, and responsibilities as research participants. *Teaching of Psychology*, 15, 74–78.

Kors, Alan Charles, & Korshin, Paul J. (eds.) (1987). *Anticipations of the Enlightenment in England, France, and Germany*. Philadelphia: University of Pennsylvania Press.

Kovel, Joel (1991). *History and spirit: An inquiry into the philosophy of liberation*. Boston, MA: Beacon Press.

Kozulin, Alex (1984). *Psychology in utopia: Toward a social history of Soviet psychology*. Cambridge, MA: MIT Press.

   (1985). Georgy Chelpanov and the establishment of the Moscow Institute of Psychology. *Journal of the History of the Behavioral Sciences*, 21, 23–32.

   (1992). Union of Soviet Socialist Republics. In Virginia Staudt Sexton & John D. Hogan (eds.), *International psychology: Views from around the world* (pp. 390–402). Lincoln, NE: University of Nebraska Press.

Kraut, Richard (2008). *How to read Plato*. London: Granta.

Krech, David (1962). Cortical localization of function. In Leo Postman (ed.), *Psychology in the making* (pp. 31–72). New York: Kropf.

Kristeller, Paul Oskar (1979). *Renaissance thought and its sources*. New York: Columbia University Press.

Kuder, George Frederic (1964). *Kuder DD occupational interest survey*. Chicago, IL: Science Research Associates.

Kuehn, Manfred (2001). *Kant: A biography*. Cambridge University Press.

   (2009). Aristotelianism in the Renaissance. In E. N. Zalta (ed.), *The Stanford encyclopedia of philosophy*. Retrieved from http://plato.stanford.edu/archives/spr2009/entries/aristotelianism-renaissance/

Kuhn, Thomas S. (1962). *The structure of scientific revolutions*. University of Chicago Press.

Kupisiewicz, Czeslaw (1993). Jan Wladyslaw Dawid (1859–1914). *Prospects: The Quarterly Review of Comparative Education*, 23, 235–247.

Kuppuswamy, Bangalore (1990). *Elements of ancient Indian psychology*. Delhi: Konark Publishers.

Kurzweil, Edith (1995). *Freudians and feminists*. Boulder, CO: Westview.

Kusch, Martin (1995). Recluse, interlocutor, interrogator: Natural and social order in turn-of-the-century psychological research schools. *Isis*, 86, 419–433.

   (1999). *Psychological knowledge: A social history and philosophy*. London: Routledge.

Kvale, Steinar (2003). The church, the factory and the market: Scenarios for psychology in a postmodern age. *Theory & Psychology*, 13, 579–603.

Laar, Tjeerd van de, & Regt, Herman de (2008). Is cognitive science changing its mind? Introduction to embodied embedded cognition and neurophenomenology. *Theory & Psychology*, 18, 291–296.

Ladd-Franklin, Christine (1929). *Colour and colour theories*. New York: Harcourt Brace Jovanovich.

Lagerlund, Henrik (2011). Mental representation in medieval philosophy. In E. N. Zalta (ed.), *The Stanford encyclopedia of philosophy*. Retrieved from http://plato.stanford.edu/archives/spr2011/entries/representation-medieval/

Lamiell, James T. (1996). William Stern: "More than the IQ guy". In Gregory A. Kimble, C. Alan Boneau, & Michael Wertheimer (eds.), *Portraits of pioneers in psychology*, vol. II (pp. 73–85). Washington, DC: American Psychological Association.

Landes, David S. (1983). *Revolution in time: Clocks and the making of the modern world.* Cambridge, MA: Harvard University Press.

Landrum, R. Eric, & Chastain, Garvin (1999). Subject pool policies in undergraduate-only departments: Results from a nationwide survey. In Garvin Chastain & R. Eric Landrum (eds.), *Protecting human subjects: Departmental subject pools and institutional review boards* (pp. 25–42). Washington, DC: American Psychological Association.

Landy, Frank J. (1992). Hugo Münsterberg: Victim or visionary? *Journal of Applied Psychology,* 77, 787–802.

Lange, Friedrich A. (1950). *The history of materialism and criticism of its present importance,* trans. E. C. Thomas, 3rd edn. (This translation first published in three volumes in 1877, 1890, and 1892.) New York: The Humanities Press. (Original work published in German 1866)

Langford, Peter E. (2005). *Vygotsky's developmental and educational psychology.* New York: Psychology Press.

Lapointe, François H. (1970). Origin and evolution of the term "psychology." *American Psychologist,* 25, 640–646.

Larkin, Michael, Eatough, Virginia, & Osborn, Mike (2011). Interpretive phenomenological analysis and embodied, active, situated cognition. *Theory & Psychology,* 21, 318–337.

Larner, Glenn (2001). The critical-practitioner model in therapy. *Australian Psychologist,* 36, 36–43.

Lashley, Kurt S. (1930). Basic neural mechanisms in behavior. *Psychological Review,* 37, 1–24.

Latour, Bruno, & Woolgar, Stephen (1979). *Laboratory life: The social construction of scientific facts.* Beverly Hills, CA: Sage.

Lawson, Russell M. (2004). *Science in the ancient world: An encyclopedia.* Santa Barbara, CA: ABC-CLIO.

Layard, Richard (2005). *Happiness: Lessons from a new science.* New York: Penguin.

Leahey, Thomas H. (1992). The mythical revolutions of American psychology. *American Psychologist,* 47, 308–318.

(2003). Cognition and learning. In Irving B. Weiner (series ed.) & Donald K. Freedheim (vol. ed.), *Handbook of psychology,* vol. I: *History of psychology* (pp. 109–133). Hoboken, NJ: Wiley.

Leary, David E. (1977). Berkeley's social theory: Context and development. *Journal of the History of Ideas,* 38, 635–649.

(1978). The philosophical development of the conception of psychology in Germany. *Journal of the History of the Behavioural Sciences,* 14, 113–121.

(1980). The historical foundation of Herbart's mathematization of psychology. *Journal of the History of the Behavioural Sciences,* 16, 150–163.

(1982). Immanuel Kant and the development of modern psychology. In William R. Woodward & Mitchell G. Ash (eds.), *The problematic science: Psychology on nineteenth-century thought* (pp. 17–42). New York: Praeger.

(1987). Telling likely stories: The rhetoric of the new psychology, 1880–1920. *Journal of the History of the Behavioral Sciences,* 23, 315–331.

(1990a). Psyche's muse: The role of metaphor in the history of psychology. In David E. Leary (ed.), *Metaphors in the history of psychology* (pp. 1–78). Cambridge University Press.

(1990b). William James on the self and personality: Clearing the ground for subsequent theorists, researchers, and practitioners. In Michael G. Johnson & Tracy B. Henley (eds.), *Reflections on The Principles of Psychology: William James after a century* (pp. 101–137). Hillsdale, NJ: Erlbaum.

(1992). William James and the art of human understanding. *American Psychologist*, 47, 152–160.

(2003). A profound and radical change: How William James inspired the reshaping of American psychology. In Robert J. Sternberg (ed.), *The anatomy of impact: What makes the great works of psychology great* (pp. 19–42). Washington, DC: American Psychological Association.

Lechte, John (2008). *Fifty key contemporary thinkers*, 2nd edn. New York: Routledge.

Lehrer, Keith (1989). *Thomas Reid*. London: Routledge.

Lenrow, Peter, & Cowden, Peter (1980). Human services, professionals, and the paradox of institutional reform. *American Journal of Community Psychology*, 8, 463–484.

Lerman, Hannah, & Porter, Natalie (1990). *Feminist ethics in psychotherapy*. New York: Springer.

Lerner, Gerda (1993). *The creation of feminist consciousness from the Middle Ages to eighteen-seventy*. New York: Oxford University Press.

Levinas, Emmanuel (1996). *Emmanuel Levinas: Basic philosophical writings*, ed. Adriaan T. Peperzak, Simon Critchley, & Robert Bernasconi. Bloomington, IN: Indiana University Press.

Lewin, Kurt, Lippitt, Ronald, & White, Ralph K. (1939). Patterns of aggressive behaviour in experimentally created social climates. *Journal of Social Psychology*, 10, 271–299.

Lewontin, Richard C. (2000) *The triple helix; Gene, organism, and environment*. Cambridge, MA: Harvard University Press.

Lilienfeld, Scott O. (2012). Public skepticism of psychology: Why many people perceive the study of human behavior as unscientific. *American Psychologist*, 67, 111–129.

Lindberg, David C. (1992). *The beginnings of Western science: The European scientific tradition and philosophical, religious, and institutional context, 600 B.C. to A.D. 1450*. University of Chicago Press.

Linden, David J. (2009). *Accidental mind: How brain evolution has given us love, memory, dreams, and God*. Cambridge, MA: Harvard University Press.

Lindenfield, David (1978). Oswald Külpe and the Wuerzburg school. *Journal of the History of the Behavioral Sciences*, 14, 132–141.

Lindsay, R. C. & Holden, Ronald R. (1987). The introductory psychology subject pool in Canadian universities. *Canadian Psychology*, 28, 45–52.

Line, William (1951). Psychology. In *Royal commission studies on national development in the arts, letters and sciences*. Ottawa: E. Clouthier, King's Printer.

Lipsey, Richard G., Carlaw, Kenneth, & Bekar, Clifford (2005). *Economic transformations: General purpose technologies and long term economic growth*. New York: Oxford University Press.

Lloyd, A. C. (1985). *The self in Berkeley's philosophy*. In John Foster & Howard Robinson (eds.), *Essays on Berkeley: A tercentennial Celebration* (pp. 187–209). Oxford: Clarendon Press.

Locke, John (1924). *An essay concerning human understanding*, ed. A. S. Pringle-Pattison. London: Oxford University Press. (Original work published 1689)

(1996). *An essay concerning human understanding*. Indianapolis, IN: Hackett. (Original work published in 1689)

Logan, Cheryl A. (2002). When scientific knowledge becomes scientific discovery: The disappearance of classical conditioning before Pavlov. *Journal of the History of the Behavioral Sciences*, 38(4), 393–403.

Lomov, Boris F. (1987). Soviet Union. In Albert R. Gilgen & Carol K. Gilgen (eds.), *International handbook of psychology* (pp. 418–439). New York: Greenwood Press.

London, Ivan D. (1949). A historical survey of psychology in the Soviet Union. *Psychological Bulletin*, 46, 241–277.

Lorenz, Hendrik (2009). Ancient theories of soul. In E. N. Zalta (ed.), *The Stanford encyclopedia of philosophy*. Retrieved from http://plato.stanford.edu/archives/sum2009/entries/ancient-soul/

Lösel, Friedrich, Bender, Doris, & Bliesener, Thomas (eds.) (1992). *Psychology and law: International perspectives*. New York: Walter de Gruyter.

Lourenco, Orlando, & Machado, Amando (1996). In defense of Piaget's theory: A reply to 10 common criticisms. *Psychological Review*, 103, 143–164.

Lovejoy, Arthur O. (1948). On the discrimination of romanticisms. In *Essays in the history of ideas*. Baltimore, MD: Johns Hopkins University Press.

Lovelock, James (2006). *The revenge of Gaia: Why the Earth is fighting back–and how we can still save humanity*. London: Penguin.

Lovett, Benjamin J. (2006). The new history of psychology: A review and critique. *History of Psychology*, 9, 17–37.

Lowry, Robert (1970). The reflex model in psychology: Origins and evolution. *Journal of the History of the Behavioral Sciences*, 6, 64–69.

Lunt, Ingrid (1999). The professionalization of psychology in Europe. *European Psychologist*, 4, 240–247.

(2004). Psychology in the United Kingdom. In Michael J. Stevens & Danny Wedding (eds.), *Handbook of international psychology* (pp. 371–385). New York: Brunner-Routledge.

Luria, Alexander R. (1980). *Higher cortical functions in man*, 2nd edn. New York: Basic Books.

Lyotard, Jean-François (1984). *The postmodern condition: A report on knowledge*, trans. Geoff Bennington & Brian Massumi. Manchester University Press. (Original work published in French 1979)

Maccoby, Eleanor E. (2000). Parenting and its effects on children: On reading and misreading behavior genetics. *Annual Review of Psychology*, 51, 1–27.

Maccoby, Michael (1976). *The gamesman: The new corporate leaders*. New York: Simon and Schuster.

Machover, Peter (1998). Introduction. In Peter Machover (ed.), *The Cambridge companion to Galileo* (pp. 1–26). Cambridge University Press.

Mack, Wolfgang G. (1997). The Würzburg school of psychology. In Wolfgang G. Bringmann, Helmut E. Lück, Robert Miller, & Charles E. Early (eds.), *A pictorial history of psychology* (pp. 177–181). Chicago, IL: Quintessence Publishing.

Madigan, Robert, Johnson, Susan, & Linton, Patricia (1995). The language of psychology: APA style as epistemology. *American Psychologist*, 50, 428–436.

Madigan, Stephen, & O'Hara, Ruth (1992). Short-term memory at the turn of the century: Mary Whiton Calkins's memory research. *American Psychologist*, 47, 170–174.

Madill, Anna, & Gough, Brendan (2008). Qualitative research and its place in psychological science. *Psychological Methods*, 13, 254–271.

Malone, Kareen Ror (2008). Psychoanalysis: Formalization and logic and the question of speaking and affect. *Theory & Psychology*, 18, 179–193.

Mandler, George (2002). Psychologists and the National Socialist access to power. *History of Psychology*, 5, 190–200.

Manganyi, N. Chabani, & Louw, Johann (1986). Clinical psychology in South Africa: A comparative study of emerging professional trends. *Professional Psychology: Research and Practice*, 17, 171–178.

Manicas, Peter T. (2002). John Dewey and American psychology. *Journal for the Theory of Social Behavior*, 32, 267–294.

Manicas, Peter T., & Secord, Paul F. (1983). Implications for psychology of the new philosophy of science. *American Psychologist*, 38, 399–413.

Marchel, Carol, & Owens, Stephanie (2007). Qualitative research in psychology: Could William James get a job? *History of Psychology*, 10, 301–324.

Marcuse, Herbert (1964). *One dimensional man: Studies in the ideology of advanced industrial society*. Boston, MA: Beacon Press.

Marecek, Jeanne (2001). After the facts: Psychology and the study of gender. *Canadian Psychology*, 42, 254–267.

Marecek, Jeanne, & Hare-Mustin, Rachel (1990). *Making a difference: Psychology and the construction of gender*. New Haven, CT: Yale University Press.

(2009). Clinical psychology; The politics of madness. In Dennis Fox, Issac Prilleltensky, & Stephanie Austin (eds.), *Critical psychology: An introduction*, 2nd edn. (pp. 75–92). Thousand Oaks, CA: Sage.

Martin, Jack, & Sugarman, Jeff (2001). Interpreting human kinds: Beginnings of a hermeneutic psychology. *Theory and Psychology*, 11, 193–207.

(2009). Does interpretation in psychology differ from interpretation in natural science? *Journal for the Theory of Social Behaviour*, 39, 19–37.

Martin, Jack, Sugarman, Jeff, & Hickinbottom, Sarah (2010). *Persons: Understanding psychological selfhood and agency*. New York: Springer.

Martin, Mabel F. (1940). The psychological contributions of Margaret Floy Washburn. *American Journal of Psychology*, 53, 7–18.

Martín-Baró, Ignacio (1994). *Writings for a liberation psychology*, ed. A. Aron & S. Corne. Cambridge, MA: Harvard University Press.

Martinich, Aloysius P. (1999). *Hobbes. A biography*. Cambridge University Press.

Marx, Karl (1983). *The portable Karl Marx, selected, translated in part, and with an introduction by Eugene Kamenka*. New York: Penguin.

Marx, Karl, & Engels, Friedrich (1964). *The German ideology*. Moscow: Progress. (Original work written German 1845–1846; first published in 1932)

(1968). *The communist manifesto*. New York: Modern Reader Paperbacks. (This translation first published 1888; original work published 1848)

Mashoura, George A., Walker, Erin E., & Martuza, Robert L. (2005). Psychosurgery: Past, present, and future. *Brain Research Reviews* 48, 409–419.

Masling, Joseph (1966). Role-related behavior of the subject and psychologist and its effects upon psychological data. *Nebraska Symposium on Motivation*, 14, 67–103.

Maslow, Abraham (1969). The farther reaches of human nature. *Journal of Transpersonal Psychology*, 1, 1–9.

Masson, Jeffrey (1984). *The assault on truth: Freud's suppression of the seduction theory*. New York: Farrar, Straus & Giroux.

(1988). *Against therapy: Emotional tyranny and the myth of psychological healing*. New York: Atheneum.

Masson, J. Moussaieff, & McCarthy, Susan (1995). *When elephants weep: The emotional lives of animals*. New York: Delacorte.

May, Gita (1991). Diderot, Denis. In John W. Yolton, Roy Porter, Pat Rogers, & Maria Stafford (eds.), *The Blackwell companion to the Enlightenment* (pp. 126–128). Oxford: Blackwell.

May, Rollo (1958). *Existence: A new dimension in psychiatry and psychology*. New York: Basic Books.

(1961). *Existential psychology*. New York: Random House.

Mayer, Susan Jean (2005). The early evolution of Jean Piaget's clinical method. *History of Psychology*, 8, 362–382.

Mayhauser, Richard von (1992). The mental testing community and validity: A prehistory. *American Psychologist*, 47, 244–253.

Mays, Daniel, & Franks, Cyril (eds.) (1985). *Above all do not harm: Negative outcome in psychotherapy and what to do about it*. New York: Springer.

McAdams, Dan P., & Olson, Bradley D. (2010). Personality development: Continuity and change over the life course. *Annual Review of Psychology*, 61, 517–542.

McCann, Edwin (1993). Locke's philosophy of body. In Vere Chappell (ed.), *The Cambridge companion to Locke* (pp. 56–88). Cambridge University Press.

McCoy, Alfred (2006). *A question of torture: CIA interrogation from the cold war to the war on terror*. New York: Metropolitan Books.

McHugh, Kathryn R., & Barlow, David H. (2010). The dissemination and implementation of evidence-based psychological treatments: A review of current efforts. *American Psychologist*, 65, 73–84.

McInerny, Ralph, & O'Callaghan, John (2010). Saint Thomas Aquinas. In E. N. Zalta (ed.), *The Stanford encyclopedia of philosophy*. Retrieved from http://plato.stanford.edu/archives/win2010/entries/aquinas/

McLeod, John, & Balamoutsou, Sophia (2001). A method for qualitative narrative analysis of psychotherapy transcripts. *Psychologische Beitrage*, 43, 128–152.

McMahon, Ciarán (2008). The origins of the psychological "interior." *Journal of the History of the Behavioral Sciences*, 22, 19–37.

McNeill, Dan, & Freiberger, Paul (1993). *Fuzzy logic*. New York: Simon & Schuster.

McRae, Robert (1995). The theory of knowledge. In Nicholas Jolley (ed.), *The Cambridge companion to Leibniz* (pp. 176–198). Cambridge University Press.

Meehl, Paul E. (1978). Theoretical risks and tabular asterisks: Sir Karl, Sir Ronald, and the slow progress of soft psychology. *Journal of Consulting and Clinical Psychology*, 46, 806–834.

Melling, David J. (1987). *Understanding Plato*. Oxford University Press.

Melzer, David, Fryers, Tom, & Jenkins, Rachel (eds.) (2004). *Social inequalities and the distribution of the common mental disorders*. Hove, East Sussex: Psychology Press.

Mendelson, Michael (2010). Saint Augustine. In E. N. Zalta (ed.), *The Stanford encyclopedia of philosophy*. Retrieved from http://plato.stanford.edu/archives/win2010/entries/augustine/

Mercer, Jean (2011). Attachment theory and its vicissitudes: Toward an updated theory. *Theory & Psychology*, 21, 25–45.

Merchant, Carolyn (2008). Secrets of nature: The Bacon debates revisited. *Journal of the History of Ideas*, 69, 147–162.

Merleau-Ponty, Maurice (1962). *Phenomenology of perception*, trans. C. Smith. London: Routledge & Kegan Paul. (Original work published in French 1945)

Milgram, Stanley (1974). *Obedience to authority: An experimental view*. New York: Harper & Row.

Miller, Arden (1981). A survey of introductory psychology subject pool practices among leading universities. *Teaching of Psychology*, 8, 211–213.

Miller, Arthur G. (ed.) (1972). *The social psychology of psychological research*. New York: Free Press.

Miller, George A. (1969). Psychology as a means of promoting human welfare. *American Psychologist*, 24, 1063–1075.

(2003). The cognitive revolution: A historical perspective. *Trends in Cognitive Sciences*, 7, 141–145.

Miller, George A., Galanter, Eugene H., & Pribram, Karl H. (1960). *Plans and the structure of behavior*. New York: Holt, Rinehart, and Winston.

Miller, Peter, & Rose, Nikolas (1994). On therapeutic authority: Psychoanalytical expertise under advanced liberalism. *History of the Human Sciences*, 7, 29–64.

Mischel, Walter (2004). Toward an integrative science of the person. *Annual Review of Psychology*, 55, 1–22.

Mishler, Elliott (1996). Missing persons: Recovering developmental stories/histories. In Richard Jessor, Anne Colby, & Richard A. Shweder (eds.), *Ethnography and human development: Context and meaning in social inquiry* (pp. 73–99). University of Chicago Press.

Misumi, Gyuji, & Peterson, Mark F. (1990). Psychology in Japan. *Annual Review of Psychology*, 41, 213–241.

Mitchell, Joel (2002). The quantitative imperative: Positivism, naïve realism and the place of qualitative methods in psychology. *Theory & Psychology*, 13, 5–31.

Mitchell, Juliet (1974). *Psychoanalysis and feminism*. New York: Pantheon.

Mitchell, Stephen A. & Black, Margaret J. (1995). *Freud and Beyond. A history of modern psychoanalytic thought*. New York: Basic Books.

Moghaddam, Fathali M. (1987). Psychology in the three worlds as reflected by the crisis in social psychology and the move toward indigenous third-world psychology. *American Psychologist*, 42, 912–920.

Moghaddam, Fathali, & Taylor, Donald (1986). What constitutes an appropriate psychology for the developing world? *International Journal of Psychology*, 21, 253–267.

Moi, Toril (2004). From femininity to finitude: Freud, Lacan, and feminism, again. *Signs: Journal of Women in Culture and Society*, 29, 841–878.

Montero, Maritza (2003). Relatedness as the basis for liberation. *Critical Psychology*, 61–74.

Moore, Francis Charles Timothy (1970). *The psychology of Maine de Biran*. London: Oxford University Press.

Moore, Thomas (1992). *Care of the soul: A guide for cultivating depth and sacredness in everyday life*. New York: HarperCollins.

Moran, Dermot (2000). *Introduction to phenomenology*. New York: Routledge.

Morawski, Jill G. (1982). Assessing psychology's moral heritage through our neglected utopias. *American Psychologist*, 37, 1082–1095.

(1986). Psychologists for society and societies for psychologists: SPSSI's place among professional organizations. *Journal of Social Issues*, 42(1), 111–126.

(ed.) (1988). *The rise of experimentation in American psychology*. New Haven, CT: Yale University Press.

(2007). Scientific selves: Discerning the subject and the experimenter in experimental psychology in the United States, 1900–1935. In Mitchell G. Ash & Thomas Sturm (eds.), *Psychology's territories: Historical and contemporary perspectives from different disciplines* (pp. 129–148). Mahwah, NJ: Erlbaum.

(2011). Our debates: Finding, fixing, and enacting reality. *Theory & Psychology*, 21, 260–274.

Morawski, Jill G., & Bayer, Betty M. (2003). Social psychology. In Irving B. Weiner (series ed.) & Donald K. Freedheim (vol. ed.), *Handbook of psychology*, vol. I: *History of psychology* (pp. 223–247). Hoboken, NJ: Wiley.

Morawski, Jill G., & St. Martin, Jenna (2011). The evolving vocabulary of the social sciences: The case of "socialization." *History of Psychology*, 14, 1–25.

Morgan, Christiana, & Murray, Henry A. (1935). A method for investigating fantasies: The Thematic Apperception Test. *Archives of Neurology and Psychiatry*, 34, 289–306.

Morgan, Robert (ed.) (1983). *The iatrogenics handbook: A critical look at research and practice in the helping professions*. Toronto: IPI Publishing.

Moriarty, Michael (2006). *Fallen nature, fallen selves: Early modern French thought II*. Oxford University Press.

Morse, Jane Fowler (2002). Ignored but not forgotten: The work of Helen Bradford Thompson. *NWSA Journal*, 14, 121–147.

Mos, Leendert P. (1998). On methodological distinctions: Nomothetic psychology, or historical understanding. *Theory & Psychology*, 8(1), 39–57.

Moskowitz, Debbie S. (2008). Coming full circle: Conceptualizing the study of interpersonal behaviour. *Canadian Psychology*, 50, 33–41.

Mowbray, Richard (1995). *The case against psychotherapy registration: A conservation issue for the human potential movement*. London: Trans Marginal Press.

Mueller-Vollmer, Kurt (ed.) (1985). *The hermeneutic reader: Texts of the German tradition from the Enlightenment to the Present*. New York: Continuum.

Münsterberg, Hugo (1899). Psychology and history. *Psychological Review*, 6, 1–31.
    (1908/1925). On the witness stand: Essays on psychology and crime. *Classics in the History of Psychology*. Retrieved from http://psychclassics.yorku.ca/Munster/Witness/

Murphy, Gardner (1949). *Historical introduction to modern psychology*, rev. edn. New York: Harcourt, Brace and Company.

Murray, Charles A., & Herrnstein, Richard J. (1994). *The bell curve: Intelligence and class structure in American life*. New York: Free Press.

Murray, David J. (1988). *A history of Western psychology*, 2nd edn. Englewood Cliffs, NJ: Prentice Hall.

Murray, David J., Kilgour, Andrea R., & Wasylkiw, Louise (2000). Conflicts and missed signals in psychoanalysis, behaviorism, and gestalt psychology. *American Psychologist*, 55, 422–426.

Murray, Henry A. (1938). *Explorations in personality: A clinical and experimental study of fifty men of college age*. New York: Oxford University Press.

Napoli, Donald S. (1981). *Architects of adjustment: The history of the psychological profession in the United States*. Port Washington: Kennikat Press.

Needleman, Jacob (1982). *The heart of philosophy*. New York: Knopf.

Neisser, Ulric (1967). *Cognitive psychology*. New York: Appleton-Century-Crofts.

Newman, Barbara (1987). *Sister of wisdom: St. Hildegard's theology of the feminine*. Berkeley, CA: University of California Press.

Newnes, Craig (2002). The rhetoric of evidence-based practice. *Ethical Human Sciences & Services*, 4, 121–130.

Nichols, Ryan (2007). *Thomas Reid's theory of perception*. Oxford: Clarendon Press.

Nicholson, Ian A. M. (2001). "Giving up maleness": Abraham Maslow, masculinity, and the boundaries of psychology. *History of Psychology*, 4, 79–91.

(2003). *Inventing personality: Gordon Allport and the science of selfhood*. Washington, DC: American Psychological Association.

(2007). Baring the soul: Paul Bindrim, Abraham Maslow and "nude psychotherapy." *Journal of the History of the Behavioral Sciences*, 43, 337–359.

(2011). "Torture at Yale": Experimental subjects, laboratory torment and the "rehabilitation" of Milgram's "Obedience to Authority." *Theory & Psychology*, 21, 737–761.

Nicolas, Serge, & Murray, David J. (1999). Theodule Ribot (1839–1916), founder of French psychology: A biographical introduction. *History of Psychology*, 2, 277–301.

Nietzsche, Friedrich (1983). *Untimely meditations,* trans. R. J. Hollingdale. Cambridge University Press. (Original work published in German 1873–1876)

(2007). *On the genealogy of morality*, trans. Carol Diethe, ed. K. Ansell-Pearson. New York: Cambridge University Press. (Original work published in German 1887)

Nisbett, Richard E. (2000). Stanley Schacter (1922–1997). *American Psychologist*, 55, 1505–1506.

(2009). *Intelligence and how to get it: Why schools and culture count*. New York: Norton.

Noone, Tim, & Houser, R. E. (2010). Saint Bonaventure. In E. N. Zalta (ed.), *The Stanford encyclopedia of philosophy*. Retrieved from http://plato.stanford.edu/archives/win2010/entries/bonaventure/

Norman, Donald (1980). Twelve issues for cognitive science. *Cognitive Science*, 4, 1–33.

Nussbaum, Martha C. (1986). *The fragility of goodness*. Cambridge University Press.

(2001). *Upheavals of thought: The intelligence of emotions*. Cambridge University Press.

O'Connell, Agnes N., & Russo, Nancy Felipe (eds.) (1991). Women's heritage in psychology: Special centennial issue. *Psychology of Women Quarterly*, 15, 491–678.

O'Donnell, John M. (1985). *The origins of behaviorism: American psychology, 1870–1920*. New York: New York University Press.

Okie, Susan (2005). Glimpses of Guantánamo – Medical ethics and war on terror. *The New England Journal of Medicine*, 353, 2529–2534.

Olfson, Mark, Marcus, Steven, Druss, Benjamin, Elinson, Lynn, Tanielian, Terri, & Pincus, Harold Alan (2002). National trends in the outpatient treatment of depression, *Journal of the American Medical Association*, 287, 203–209.

Olton, David S. (1992). Tolman's cognitive analyses: Predecessors of current approaches in psychology. *Journal of Experimental Psychology: General*, 121, 427–428.

Ormiston, Gayle L., & Schrift, Alan D. (eds.) (1990). *The hermeneutic tradition: From Ast to Ricoeur*. Albany, NY: State University of New York Press.

Orne, Martin T. (1962). On the social psychology of the psychological experiment: With particular reference to demand characteristics and their implications. *American Psychologist*, 17, 776–783.

Osbeck, Lisa M. (2009). Transformations in cognitive science: Implications and issues posed. *Journal of Theoretical and Philosophical Psychology*, 29, 16–33.

Osler, Margaret J. (2000). The canonical imperative: Rethinking the Scientific Revolution. In Margaret J. Osler (ed.), *Rethinking the Scientific Revolution* (pp. 2–22). Cambridge University Press.

Outram, Dorinda (2005). *The Enlightenment*. Cambridge University Press.

Owens, Carol (2009). "Lacan for critics!" *Annual Review of Critical Psychology*, 7, 1–4 http://www.discourseunit.com/arcp/7.htm

Painter, Desmond, Marvakis, Athanasios, & Mos, Leendert (2009). German critical psychology: Interventions in honor of Klaus Holzkamp. *Theory & Psychology*, 19, 139–147.

Palmer, John (2012). Parmenides. In E. N. Zalta (ed.), *The Stanford encyclopedia of philosophy.* Retrieved from http://plato.stanford.edu/archives/spr2012/entries/parmenides/

Paloutzian, Raymond F., & Park, Crystal L. (2005). *Handbook of the psychology of religion and spirituality.* New York: Guilford Press.

Pancer, S. Mark (1997). Social psychology: The crisis continues. In Dennis Fox & Issac Prilleltensky (eds.), *Critical psychology: An introduction* (pp. 150–165). Thousand Oaks, CA: Sage.

Pandora, Katherine (1997). *Rebels within the ranks: Psychologists' critique of scientific authority and democratic realities in New Deal America.* Cambridge University Press.

Paranjpe, Anand C. (1998). *Self and identity in modern psychology and Indian thought.* New York: Plenum.

(2006). From tradition through colonialism to globalization: Reflections on the history of psychology in India. In Adrian Brock (ed.), *Internationalizing the history of psychology* (pp. 56–74). New York University Press.

Park, Katherine (1988). The organic soul. In Charles B. Schmitt, Quentin Skinner, Eckhard Kessler, & Jill Kraye (eds.), *The Cambridge history of Renaissance philosophy*, vol. I (pp. 464–484). Cambridge University Press.

Park, Katherine, & Kessler, Eckhard (1988). The concept of psychology. In Charles B. Schmitt, Quentin Skinner, Eckhard Kessler, & Jill Kraye (eds.), *The Cambridge history of Renaissance philosophy*, vol. I (pp. 455–463). Cambridge University Press.

Parke, Ross D., & Clarke-Stewart, K. Alison (2003). Developmental psychology. In Irving B. Weiner (series ed.) & Donald K. Freedheim (vol. ed.), *Handbook of psychology*, vol. I: *History of psychology* (pp. 205–221). Hoboken, NJ: Wiley.

Parker, Ian (2002). *Critical discursive psychology.* New York: Palgrave Macmillan.

(2003). Jacques Lacan, barred psychologist. *Theory & Psychology*, 13, 95–115.

(2008). Psychoanalytic theory and psychology: Conditions of possibility for clinical and cultural practice. *Theory & Psychology*, 18, 147–165.

(2009). Critical psychology and revolutionary Marxism. *Theory & Psychology*, 19, 71–92.

Parker, Ian, & Spears, Russell (eds.) (1996). *Psychology and society: Radical theory and practice.* London: Pluto Press.

Parkovnick, Sam (2000). Contextualizing Floyd Allport's social psychology. *Journal of the History of the Behavioural Sciences*, 36, 429–441.

Pascual-Leone, Antonio, Singh, Terence, & Scoboria, Alan (2010). Using deception ethically: Practical research guidelines for researchers and reviewers. *Canadian Psychology*, 51, 241–248.

Pavlov, Ivan P. (1928). *Lectures on conditioned reflexes: Twenty-five years of objective study of the higher nervous activity (behaviour) of animals*, trans. W. Horsley Gantt. London: Charles Griffin & Company. (Original work published in Russian 1926)

(1932). The reply of a physiologist to psychologists. *Psychological Review*, 39, 91–127.

Penelhum, Terence (2000). *Themes in Hume: The self, the will, religion.* Oxford: Clarendon Press.

Pepitone, Albert (1981). Lessons from the history of social psychology. *American Psychologist*, 36, 972–985.

Perez-Ramos, Antonio (1996). Bacon's legacy. In Markku Peltonen (ed.), *The Cambridge companion to Bacon* (pp. 311–334). Cambridge University Press.

Pert, Candace (1997). *Molecules of emotion: Why you feel the way you feel.* New York: Scribner.

Pettifor, Jean (1996). Ethics: Virtue and politics in the science and practice of psychology. *Canadian Psychology*, 37, 1–12.

Pettigrew, Thomas F. (1999). Gordon Willard Allport: A tribute. *Journal of Social Issues*, 55, 415–427.

Pettit, Michael (2010). The problem of raccoon intelligence in behaviourist America. *British Journal for the History of Science*, 43, 391–421.

Petrie, Trent A., & Diehl, Nancy, S. (1995). Sport psychology in the profession of psychology. *Professional Psychology: Research and Practice*, 26, 288–291.

Petzold, Matthias (1987). The social history of Chinese psychology. In Mitchell G. Ash & William R. Woodward (eds.), *Psychology in twentieth-century thought and society* (pp. 213–231). Cambridge University Press.

Phelps, Elizabeth A. (2006). Emotion and cognition: Insights from studies of the human amygdala. *Annual Review of Psychology*, 57, 27–53.

Phillips, Patricia (1990). *The Scientific Lady: A social history of women's scientific interests*. New York: St. Martin's Press.

Piaget, Jean (1952). Autobiography. In Edward G. Boring (ed.), *A history of psychology in autobiography*, vol. IV. Worcester, MA: Clark University Press.

(1971). *Structuralism*, trans. Chaninah Maschler. New York: Harper. (Original work published in French 1968)

Pick, Herbert L., Jr. (1992). Eleanor J. Gibson: Learning to perceive and perceiving to learn. *Developmental Psychology*, 28, 787–794.

Pickren, Wade E. (2000). A whisper of salvation: American psychologists and religion in the popular press. *American Psychologist*, 55, 1022–1024.

(2007). Tension and opportunity in post-World War II American psychology. *History of Psychology*, 10, 279–299.

Pickren, Wade E., & Rutherford, Alexandra (2010). *A history of modern psychology in context*. Hoboken, NJ: Wiley.

Plath, Ingrid, & Eckensberger, Lutz H. (2004). Psychology in Germany. In Michael J. Stevens & Danny Wedding (eds.), *Handbook of international psychology* (pp. 331–349). New York: Brunner-Routledge.

Plotinus (1991). *The Enneads*, trans. S. MacKenna. London: Penguin. (Original work published Greek 250)

Plotkin, Henry (2004). *Evolutionary thought in psychology: A brief history*. Malden, MA: Blackwell.

Plotkin, Mariano (ed.) (2003). *Argentina on the couch: Psychiatry, state, and society, 1880 to the present*. Albuquerque, NM: University of New Mexico.

Plous, Scott (1996a). Attitudes toward the use of animals in psychological research and education: Results from a national survey of psychologists. *American Psychologist*, 51, 1167–1180.

(1996b). Attitudes toward the use of animals in psychological research and education: Results from a national survey of psychology majors. *Psychological Science*, 7, 352–358.

Politzer, George (1994). *Critique of the foundations of psychology: The psychology of psychoanalysis*. Pittsburgh, PA: Duquesne University Press. (Original work published 1928)

Polkinghorne, Donald E. (1988). *Narrative knowing and the human sciences*. Albany, NY: State University of New York Press.

Pongratz, Ludwig J. (1976). Germany. In Virginia S. Sexton & Henryk Misiak (eds.), *Psychology around the world* (pp. 154–181). Monterey, CA: Brooks/Cole.

(1984). *Problemgeschichte der Psychologie* (2., durchges. u. überarbeitete Aufl.) [History of problems of psychology (2nd edn.)]. Munich: Francke.

Pope, Kenneth, Keith-Spiegel, Patricia, & Tabachnik, Barbara (1986). Sexual attraction to clients: The human therapist and the (sometimes) inhuman training system. *American Psychologist*, 41, 147–158.

Pope, Kenneth, & Vetter, Valerie (1992). Ethical dilemmas encountered by members of the American Psychological Association: A national survey. *American Psychologist*, 47, 397–411.

Popper, Karl (1959). *The logic of scientific discovery*. London: Hutchinson.

Porter, Roy, & Teich, Mikulas (eds.) (1992). *The scientific revolution in national context*. Cambridge University Press.

Porter, Theodore M. (1995). *Trust in numbers: The pursuit of objectivity in science and public life*. Princeton University Press.

Posner, Michael I., & Rothbart, Mary K. (2007). Research on attention networks as a model for the integration of psychological science. *Annual Review of Psychology*, 58, 1–23.

Postman, Leo (1969). Hermann Ebbinghaus. *American Psychologist*, 24, 149–157.

Prasadarao, P. S. D. V., & Matam Sudhir, Paulomi (2001). Clinical psychology in India. *Journal of Clinical Psychology in Medical Settings*, 8, 31–38.

Prentice, Ernest D., Reitemeier, Paul. J., Antonson, D. L., Kelso, Timothy K., & Jameton, Andrew (1993). Bill of rights for research subjects. *IRB: A Review of Human Subjects Research*, 15(2), 7–9.

Prilleltensky, Isaac (1992). Humanistic psychology, human welfare and the social order. *The Journal of Mind and Behaviour*, 13, 315–327.

Prilleltensky, Isaac, & Nelson, Geoffrey (2002). *Doing psychology critically: Making a difference in diverse settings*. New York: Palgrave Macmillan.

(2009). Community psychology: Advancing social justice. In Dennis Fox, Issac Prilleltensky, & Stephanie Austin (eds.), *Critical psychology: An introduction*, 2nd edn. (pp. 126–143). Thousand Oaks, CA: Sage.

Prilleltensky, Isaac, Rossiter, Amy, & Walsh-Bowers, Richard (1996). Preventing harm and promoting ethical discourse in the helping professions: Conceptual, research, analytical, and action frameworks. *Ethics & Behavior*, 6, 287–306.

Probst, Paul (1997). The beginnings of educational psychology in Germany. In Wolfgang G. Bringmann, Helmut E. Lück, Robert Miller, & Charles E. Early (eds.), *A pictorial history of psychology* (pp. 315–321). Chicago, IL: Quintessence Publishing.

Prokop, Charles, K., Bradley, Laurence, A., Burish, Thomas, G., Anderson, Karen, O., & Fox, Judith, E. (1991). *Health psychology: Clinical methods and research*. New York: Macmillan.

Puente, Antonio E. (2000). Roger W. Sperry: Nobel laureate, neuroscientist, and psychologist. In Gregory A. Kimble & Michael Wertheimer (eds.), *Portraits of pioneers in psychology*, vol. IV (pp. 321–336).Washington, DC: American Psychological Association.

Pyke, Sandra W. (2001). Feminist psychology in Canada: Early days. *Canadian Psychology*, 42, 268–275.

Pyke, Sandra, & Agnew, Neil M. (1991). *The science game: An introduction to research in the social sciences*, 5th edn. Englewood Cliffs, NJ: Prentice Hall.

Quine, Willard V. (1969). *Ontological relativity and other essays*. New York: Columbia University Press.

Rachman, Arnold W. M. (1988). The rule of empathy: Sandor Ferenczi's pioneering contributions to the empathic method in psychoanalysis. *Journal of the American Academy of Psychoanalysis*, 16, 1–27.

Rakos, Richard F. (1992). Achieving the just society in the 21st century: What can Skinner contribute? *American Psychologist*, 47, 1499–1506.

Randall, Lisa (2005). *Warped passages*. New York: Ecco.

Raphael-Leff, Joan (2001). Women in the history of psychoanalysis. *Psychoanalysis & Psychotherapy*, 18, 113–131.

Ravetz, Jerome R. (2005). *The no-nonsense guide to science*. Toronto: New Internationalist Between the Lines.

Rayner-Canham, Marlene F. (1992). *Harriet Brooks: Pioneer nuclear scientist*. Montreal: McGill-Queen's University Press.

Rebick, Judy (2005). *Ten thousand roses: The making of a feminist revolution*. Toronto: Penguin Books Canada.

Reich, Wilhelm (1973). *The function of the orgasm*, trans. V. R. Carfagno. New York: Noonday. (Original work published in German 1942)

Reich Rubin, Lore (2003). Wilhelm Reich and Anna Freud: His expulsion from psychoanalysis. *International Forum of Psychoanalysis*, 12, 109–117.

Reiff, Robert (1970). Psychology and public policy. *Professional Psychology*, 1, 315–324.

Rennie, David L. (2007). Methodical hermeneutics and humanistic psychology. *The Humanistic Psychologist*, 35, 1–14.

Rennie, David L., Watson, Kimberly D., & Monteiro, Althea M. (2002). The rise of qualitative research in psychology. *Canadian Psychology*, 43, 179–189.

Rescorla, Robert A. (1988). Pavlovian conditioning: It's not what you think it is. *American Psychologist*, 43, 151–160.

Reuchlin, M. (1965). The historical background for national trends in psychology: France. *Journal of the History of the Behavioral Sciences*, 1, 115–123.

Revenson, Tracey A., & Seidman, Edward (2002). Looking backward and moving forward: Reflections on a quarter century of community psychology. In Tracey A. Revenson (ed.), *A quarter century of community psychology: Readings from the American Journal of Community Psychology* (pp. 3–31). New York: Kluwer/Plenum.

Revonsuo, Antti (2001). Can functional brain imaging discover consciousness? *Journal of Consciousness Studies*, 8, 3–23.

Richards, Graham (1995). "To know our fellow men to do them good": American psychology's enduring moral project. *History of the Human Sciences*, 8, 1–24.

(2010). *Putting psychology in its place*, 3rd edn. New York: Routledge.

(2011). *Psychology, religion, and the nature of the soul*. New York: Springer.

(2012). *"Race," racism and psychology: Towards a reflexive history*, 2nd edn. London: Routledge.

Richards, Robert J. (1987). *Darwin and the emergence of evolutionary concepts of mind and behaviour*. University of Chicago Press.

Richardson, Frank C., Fowers, Blaine J., & Guignon, Charles B. (1999). *Re-envisioning psychology: Moral dimensions of theory and practice*. San Francisco: Jossey-Bass.

Rickman, Hans Peter (1988). *Dilthey today: A critical appraisal of the contemporary relevance of his work*. New York: Greenwood Press.

Ricoeur, Paul (1970). *Freud and philosophy.* New Haven, CT: Yale University Press.

Rieber, Robert W. (1998). Americanization of psychology before William James. In Robert W. Rieber & Kurt Salzinger (eds.), *Psychology: Theoretical-historical perspectives*, 2nd edn. (pp. 191–215). Washington, DC: American Psychological Association.

Rieber, Robert W., & Robinson, David (eds.) (2001). *Wilhelm Wundt in history: The making of a scientific psychology.* New York: Kluwer Academic / Plenum.

Riegel, Klaus F. (1978). *Psychology, mon amour: A countertext.* Boston, MA: Houghton Mifflin.

Riger, Stephanie (1992). Epistemological debates, feminist voices: Science, social values, and the study of women. *American Psychologist*, 47, 730–740.

Rimer, Sara (2005). For women in sciences, slow progress in academia. *New York Times*, April 12.

Roback, A. A. & Kiernan, Thomas (1969). *Pictorial history of psychology and psychiatry.* New York: Philosophical Library.

Roberts, Andrew (ed.) (2004). *What might have been: Imaginary history from twelve leading historians.* London: Weidenfeld & Nicolson.

Robins, Richard W., Gosling, Samuel D., & Craik, Kenneth H. (1999). An empirical analysis of trends in psychology. *American Psychologist*, 54, 117–128.

Robinson, Daniel N. (1976). *An intellectual history of psychology.* New York: Macmillan.
  (1985). *Philosophy of psychology.* New York: Columbia University Press.
  (1986). The Scottish Enlightenment and its mixed bequest. *Journal of the History of the Behavioral Sciences*, 22, 171–177.
  (1995). *An intellectual history of psychology*, 3rd edn. Madison, WI: University of Wisconsin Press.
  (2010). Consciousness: The first frontier. *Theory & Psychology*, 20, 781–793.

Robinson, David K. (2010). Fechner's "inner psychophysics." *History of Psychology*, 13, 424–433.

Robinson, Forrest G. (1992). *Love's story told: A life of Henry A. Murray.* Cambridge, MA: Harvard University Press.

Roderick, Rick (1986). *Habermas and the foundations of critical theory.* New York: St. Martin's Press.

Roediger, Henry L. (2000). Sir Frederic Charles Bartlett: Experimental and applied psychologist. In Gregory A. Kimble & Michael Wertheimer (eds.), *Portraits of pioneers in psychology*, vol. IV (pp.149–161). Washington, DC: American Psychological Association.

Rogers, Ben (2003). Pascal's life and times. In Nicholas Hammond (ed.), *The Cambridge companion to Pascal* (pp. 4–19). Cambridge University Press.

Rogers, Carl R. (1942). *Counseling and psychotherapy.* Boston, MA: Houghton Mifflin.
  (1951). *Client-centered therapy: Its current practice, implications, and theory.* Boston: Houghton Mifflin.

Rogers, Tim B. (1995). *The psychological testing enterprise: An introduction.* Pacific Grove, CA: Brooks/Cole.
  (1997). Extending the CPA code of ethics: A research participant's Bill of Rights. *History and Philosophy of Psychology Bulletin*, 9, 3–15.

Rogers, Wendy Stainton (2009). Research methodology. In Dennis Fox, Isaac Prilleltensky, & Stephanie Austin (eds.), *Critical psychology: An introduction*, 2nd edn. (pp. 335–354). Los Angeles, CA: Sage.

Rollins, Wayne G. (1999). *Soul and psyche: The Bible in psychological perspective.* Minneapolis, MN: Fortress Press.

Rose, Hilary, & Rose, Steven (eds.) (2001). *Alas, poor Darwin*. New York: Vintage.

Rose, Nikolas (1979). The psychological complex: Mental measurement and social administration. London: LSE Research Online. Retrieved from http://eprints.lse.ac.uk/622/1/NikRose_I_C_5.pdf

(1985). *The psychological complex: Psychology, politics and society in England, 1869–1939*. London: Routledge & Kegan Paul.

(1996). A critical history of psychology. In Nikolas Rose (ed.), *Inventing ourselves: Psychology, power, and personhood* (pp. 41–66). New York: Cambridge University Press.

(2008). Psychology as a social science. *Subjectivity*, 25, 446–462.

Rosenau, Pauline M. (1992). *Post-modernism and the social sciences: Insights, inroads, and intrusions*. Princeton University Press.

Rosenbaum, Philip J., & Valsiner, Jaan (2011). The un-making of a method: From rating scales to the study of psychological processes. *Theory & Psychology*, 21, 67–85.

Rosenberg, Milton J. (1969). The conditions and consequences of evaluation apprehension. In Robert Rosenthal & Robert L. Rosnow (eds.), *Artifact in behavioral research* (pp. 280–349). New York: Academic Press.

Rosenberg, Rosalind (1982). *Beyond separate spheres: Intellectual roots of modern feminism*. New Haven, CT: Yale University Press.

Rosenberg, Sheldon (1993). Chomsky's theory of language: Some recent observations. *Psychological Science*, 4, 15–19.

Rosenblum, Bruce, & Kuttner, Fred (2006). *Quantum enigma: Physics encounters consciousness*. New York: Oxford University Press.

Rosenthal, Robert (1969). Interpersonal expectations. In Robert Rosenthal & Robert L. Rosnow (eds.), *Artifact in behavioral research* (pp. 182–277). New York: Academic Press.

(1994). Science and ethics in conducting, analyzing, and reporting psychological research. *Psychological Science*, 5, 127–134.

Rosenzweig, Saul (1933). The experimental situation as a psychological problem. *Psychological Review*, 40, 337–354.

Rosnow, Ralph L. (1997). Hedgehogs, foxes, and the evolving social contract in psychological science: Ethical challenges and methodological opportunities. *Psychological Methods*, 2, 345–356.

Rosnow, Ralph L., Rotheram-Borus, Mary Jane, Ceci, Stephen J., Blanck, Peter D., & Koocher, Gerald P. (1993). The institutional review board as a mirror of scientific and ethical standards. *American Psychologist*, 48, 821–826.

Ross, Barbara (1991). William James: Spoiled child of American psychology. In Gregory A. Kimble, Michael Wertheimer, & Charlotte L. White (eds.), *Portraits of pioneers in psychology*, vol. I (pp. 13–25). Washington, DC: American Psychological Association.

Ross, Dorothy (1972). *G. Stanley Hall: The psychologist as prophet*. University of Chicago Press.

Rossetti, Livio (ed.) (2004). *Greek philosophy in the new millennium*. Sankt Augustin: Academia Verlag.

Rossi, Paolo (1996). Bacon's ideal of science. In Markku Peltonen (ed.), *The Cambridge companion to Bacon* (pp. 25–46). Cambridge University Press.

Rossiter, Amy, Walsh-Bowers, Richard, & Prilleltensky, Isaac (2002). Ethics as a located story: A comparison of North American and Cuban clinical ethics. *Theory & Psychology*, 12, 533–556.

Rossiter, Margaret (1982). *Women scientists in America: Struggles and strategies to 1940.* Baltimore, MD: Johns Hopkins University Press.

Roszak, Theodore, Gomes, Mary E., & Kanner, Allen D. (eds.). (1995). *Ecopsychology: Restoring the earth, healing the mind.* San Francisco, CA: Sierra Club Books.

Roth, Wolff-Michael, & Lee, Yew-Jin (2007). "Vygotsky's neglected legacy": Cultural-historical activity theory. *Review of Educational Research*, 77(2), 186–232.

Rowbotham, Sheila (2010). *Dreamers of a new day: Women who invented the twentieth century.* New York: Verso.

Rozin, Paul (2007). Exploring the landscape of modern academic psychology: Finding and filling the holes. *American Psychologist*, 62, 754–766.

Ruether, Rosemary Radford (1983). *Sexism and god-talk: Toward a feminist theology.* Boston, MA: Beacon Press.

Rusbult, Caryl E., & Van Lange, Paul A. M. (2003). Interdependence, interaction, and relationships. *Annual Review of Psychology*, 54, 351–375.

Rushton, J. Philippe (1994). *Race, evolution, and behaviour: A life history perspective.* New Brunswick, NJ: Transaction Publishers.

Rushton, J. Philippe, & Jensen, Arthur R. (2005). Thirty years of research on race differences in cognitive ability. *Psychology, Public Policy, and Law*, 11, 235–294.

Russell, Bertrand (1945). *A history of Western philosophy.* New York: Simon and Schuster.

Rutherford, Alexandra (2009). *Beyond the box: B. F. Skinner's technology of behavior from laboratory to life, 1950s–1970s.* University of Toronto Press.

Rutherford, Alexandra, Capdevila, Rose, Undurti, Vindhya, & Palmary, Ingrid (eds.) (2011). *Handbook of international feminisms: Perspectives on psychology, women, culture, and rights.* New York: Springer.

Rutherford, Alexandra, Vaughn-Blount, Kelly, & Ball, Laura C. (2010). Responsible opposition, disruptive voices: Science, social change, and the history of feminist psychology. *Psychology of Women Quarterly*, 34(4), 460–473.

Rychlak, Joseph F. (1993). William James and the concept of free will. In Margaret E. Donnelly (ed.), *Reinterpreting the legacy of William James* (pp. 323–338). Washington, DC: American Psychological Association.

Said, Edward W. (1978). *Orientalism.* New York: Random House.

Sampson, Edward E. (1981). Cognitive psychology as ideology. *American Psychologist*, 36, 730–743.

(1991). The democratization of psychology. *Theory & Psychology*, 1, 275–298.

Samuels, Andrew (1993). *The political psyche.* New York: Routledge.

Sanches, Aderito Alain (1992). France. In Virginia Staudt Sexton & John D. Hogan (eds.), *International psychology: Views from around the world* (pp. 136–148). Lincoln, NE: University of Nebraska Press.

Sandoval, Chela (2000). *Methodology of the oppressed.* Minneapolis, MN: University of Minnesota Press.

Sanford, Nevitt (1970). Whatever happened to action research? *Journal of Social Issues*, 26(4), 3–23.

Sannino, Annalisa, & Sutter, Berthel (2011). Cultural-historical activity theory and interventionist methodology: Classical legacy and contemporary developments. *Theory & Psychology*, 21, 557–570.

Sapp, Jan (2009). *The new foundations of evolution: On the tree of life.* New York: Oxford University Press.

Sarasohn, Lisa T. (2006). *The scientific revolution*. Boston, MA: Houghton Mifflin.

Sarason, Seymour B. (1981). *Psychology misdirected*. New York: Free Press.

Sartre, Jean-Paul (1956). *No exit, and three other plays*, trans. Stuart Gilbert. New York: Vintage Books. (Original work published in French 1949)

Sayre, Ann (1975). *Rosalind Franklin and DNA*. New York: Norton.

Scarborough, Elizabeth (1992). Women in the American Psychological Association. In Evans, Rand B., Sexton, Virginia Staudt, & Cadwallader, Thomas C. (eds.), *The American Psychological Association: A historical perspective* (pp. 303–323). Washington, DC: American Psychological Association.

Scarborough, Elizabeth, & Furumoto, Laurel (1987). *Untold lives: The first generation of American women psychologists*. New York: Columbia University Press.

Schachter, Stanley, & Singer, Jerome E. (1962). Cognitive, social and physiological determinants of emotional state. *Psychological Review*, 69, 379–399.

Schiebinger, Londa (1989). *The mind has no sex? Women in the origins of modern science*. Cambridge, MA: Harvard University Press.

  (2002). European women in science. *Science in Context*, 15, 473–481.

Schiller, Francis (1992). *Paul Broca: Founder of French anthropology, explorer of the brain*. New York: Oxford University Press.

Schmidt, Frank L. (1992). What do data really mean? Research findings, meta-analysis and cumulative knowledge in psychology. *American Psychologist*, 47, 1173–1181.

Schmidt, Hans-Dieter (1987). German Democratic Republic. In Albert R. Gilgen & Carol K. Gilgen (eds.), *International handbook of psychology* (pp. 222–238). New York: Greenwood Press.

Schmit, David (2005). Re-visioning antebellum American psychology: The dissemination of mesmerism, 1836–1854. *History of Psychology*, 8(4), 403–434.

Schultz, Duane P. (1969). The human subject in psychological research. *Psychological Bulletin*, 72, 214–228.

Schure, Marc B., Christopher, John, & Christopher, Suzanne (2008). Mind-body medicine and the art of self-care: Teaching mindfulness to counseling students through yoga, meditation, and Qigong. *Journal of Counseling & Development*, 86, 47–56.

Schuster, John A., & Yeo, Richard R. (1986). Introduction. In John A. Schuster & Richard R. Yeo (eds.), *The politics and rhetoric of scientific method* (pp. ix–xxxvii). Dordrecht: Reidel.

Searle, John R. (1992). *The rediscovery of the mind*. Cambridge, MA: MIT Press.

Segal, Gideon (2000). Beyond subjectivity: Spinoza's cognitivism of the emotions. *British Journal for the History of Philosophy*, 8, 1–19.

Seligman, Martin E. P. (1975). *Helplessness: On depression, development, and death*. New York: W. H. Freeman

  (1991). *Learned optimism: How to change your mind and your life*. New York: Knopf.

Seligman, Martin E. P., & Csikszentmihalyi, Mihaly (2000). Positive psychology: An introduction. *American Psychologist*, 55, 5–14.

Seth, Anil, Baars, Bernard, & Edelman, David (2005). Criteria for consciousness in humans and other mammals. *Consciousness and Cognition*, 14, 119–139.

Seto, Michael (1995). Sex with therapy clients: Its prevalence, potential consequences, and implications for professional training. *Canadian Psychology*, 36, 70–86.

Sexton, Virginia Staudt, & Hogan, John D. (eds.) (1992). *International psychology: Views from around the world*. Lincoln, NE: University of Nebraska Press.

Shamdasani, Sonu (2003). *Jung and the making of modern psychology: The dream of a science.* New York: Cambridge University Press.

(ed.) (2009). *The red book: Liber novas: C. G. Jung.* New York: Philemon Series & Norton.

Shapiro, Kenneth J. (1998). *Animal models of human psychology: Critique of science, ethics, and policy.* Seattle, WA: Hogrefe & Huber.

Sharma, Dinesh (2000). Psychoanalysis and sociocultural change in India: A conversation with Suhir Kakar. *International Journal of Group Tensions*, 29, 253–283.

Shedler, Jonathan (2010). The efficacy of psychodynamic psychotherapy. *American Psychologist*, 65, 98–109.

Shercliffe, Regan J., Stahl, William, & Tuttle, Megan P. (2009). The use of meta-analysis in psychology: A superior vintage or old wine in new bottles? *Theory & Psychology*, 19, 413–430.

Sherrill, Robert, Jr. (1991). Natural wholes: Wolfgang Koehler and Gestalt theory. In Gregory A. Kimble, Michael Wertheimer, & Charlotte L. White (eds.), *Portraits of pioneers in psychology* (pp. 257–273). Washington, DC: American Psychological Association.

Sherry, David F. (2006). Neuroecology. *Annual Review of Psychology*, 57, 167–197.

Shields, Christopher (2011). Aristotle's psychology. In E. N. Zalta (ed.), *The Stanford encyclopedia of philosophy.* Retrieved from plato.stanford.edu/archives/spr2011/entries/aristotle-psychology/

Shields, Stephanie A. (1975). Functionalism, Darwinism, and the psychology of women. *American Psychologist*, 30, 739–753.

(2006). Magda B. Arnold: Pioneer in research on emotion. In Donald A. Dewsbury, Ludy T. Benjamin Jr., & Michael Wertheimer (eds.), *Portraits of pioneers in psychology*, vol. VI (pp. 223–237). Washington, DC: American Psychological Association.

(2007). Passionate men, emotional women: Psychology constructs gender difference in the late 19th century. *History of Psychology*, 10, 92–110.

Shields, Stephanie A., & Bhatia, Sunil (2009). Darwin on race, gender, and culture. *American Psychologist*, 64, 111–119.

Shingu, Kazushige & Funaki, Tetsuo (2008). "Between two deaths": The intersection of psychoanalysis and Japanese Buddhism. *Theory & Psychology*, 18, 253–267.

Sieber, Joan E. (1992). *Planning ethically responsible research: A guide for students and internal review boards.* Newbury Park, CA: Sage.

(1999). What makes a subject pool (un)ethical? In Garvin Chastain & R. Eric Landrum (eds.), *Protecting human subjects: Departmental subject pools and institutional review boards* (pp. 43–64). Washington, DC: American Psychological Association.

Sieber, Joan E., & Saks, Michael J. (1989). A census of subject pool characteristics and policies. *American Psychologist*, 44, 1053–1061.

Siegler, Robert (1992). The other Alfred Binet. *Developmental Psychology*, 28, 179–190.

Simon, Bennett (1972). Models of mind and mental illness in ancient Greece: II. The Platonic model. *Journal of the History of the Behavioural Sciences*, 8, 389–404.

(1973). Models of mind and mental illness in ancient Greece: II. The Platonic model: Section 2. *Journal of the History of the Behavioural Sciences*, 9, 3–17.

Simon, Bennett, & Weiner, Herbert (1966). Models of mind and mental illness in ancient Greece: I. The Homeric model. *Journal of the History of the Behavioural Sciences*, 2, 303–314.

Simons, Herbert W. (1993). The rhetoric of the scientific research report: "Drug-pushing" in a medical journal article. In Richard H. Roberts & James M. M. Good (eds.), *The recovery of rhetoric: Persuasive discourse and disciplinarity in the human sciences* (pp. 148–163). Charlottesville, VA: University Press of Virginia.

Simons, Jon (2002). Immanuel Kant (1724–1804). In Jon Simons (ed.), *From Kant to Levi-Strauss: The background to contemporary critical theory* (pp. 17–32). Edinburgh University Press.

Simonton, Dean K. (1994). *Greatness: Who makes history and why.* New York: Guilford Press.

Sinclair, Carole, & Pettifor, Jean (eds.) (2001). *Companion manual to the Canadian Code of ethics for psychologists*, 3rd edn. Ottawa, ON: Canadian Psychological Association.

Sinha, Durganand (1987). India. In Albert R. Gilgen & Carol K. Gilgen (eds.), *International handbook of psychology* (pp. 239–257). New York: Greenwood Press.

Skinner, B. F. (1948). *Walden Two.* New York: Macmillan.

  (1953). *Science and human behavior.* New York: Macmillan.

  (1957). *Verbal behavior.* New York: Appleton-Century-Crofts.

  (1971). *Beyond freedom and dignity.* New York: Knopf.

Skitka, Linda J., & Sargis, Edward G. (2006). The internet as psychological laboratory. *Annual Review of Psychology*, 57, 529–555.

Slife, Brent D., & Reber, Jeff. S. (2009). Is there a pervasive implicit bias against theism in psychology? *Journal of Theoretical and Philosophical Psychology*, 29, 63–79.

Slife, Brent D., Reber, J. S., & Richardson, Frank C. (2005). *Developing critical thinking about psychology: Hidden assumptions and plausible alternatives.* Washington, DC: American Psychological Association.

Slife, Brent, & Richardson, Frank (2008). Problematic ontological underpinnings of positive psychology: A strong relational alternative. *Theory & Psychology*, 18, 699–723.

Sloan, Richard P. (2006). *Blind faith: The unholy alliance between medicine and religion.* New York: St. Martin's Press.

Sloan, Tod (1997). Theories of personality: Ideology and beyond. In Dennis Fox & Isaac Prilleltensky (eds.), *Critical psychology: An introduction* (pp. 87–103). Thousand Oaks, CA: Sage.

  (ed.) (2000). *Critical psychology: Voices for change.* London: Macmillan.

Smith, C. U. M. (1987). David Hartley's Newtonian neuropsychology. *Journal of the History of the Behavioral Sciences*, 23, 123–136.

Smith, Daniel B. (2009). The Doctor is IN. *The American Scholar*, Autumn. Retrieved from www.theamericanscholar.org/the-doctor-is-in/#more-5299

Smith, Joseph Carman (1990). *Psychoanalytic roots of patriarchy: The neurotic foundations of social order.* New York University Press.

Smith, Laurence D., Best, Lisa A., Cylke, Virginia A., & Stubbs, D. Alan (2000). Psychology without p values: Data analysis at the turn of the 19th century. *American Psychologist*, 55, 260–263.

Smith, Roger (1997). *The Norton history of the human sciences.* New York: Norton.

  (2005). The history of psychological categories. *Studies in History and Philosophy of Biological and Biomedical Sciences*, 36, 55–94.

Smits, Harry (2011). Conflicts in our mind. *Theory & Psychology*, 21, 377–395.

Sohn, David (1996). Meta-analysis and science. *Theory & Psychology*, 6, 229–246.

Sokal, Michael M. (1982). James McKeen Cattell and the failure of anthropometric mental testing, 1890–1901. In William R. Woodward & Mitchell G. Ash (eds.), *The problematic science: Psychology in nineteenth-century thought* (pp. 322–345). New York: Praeger.

(1984). The Gestalt psychologists in behaviorist America. *American Historical Review*, 89, 1240–63.

(1992). Origins and early years of the American Psychological Association, 1880–1906. *American Psychologist*, 47, 111–122.

Soldz, Stephen (2006). A profession struggles to save its soul: Psychologists, Guantánamo, and torture. *Counterpunch*, August 1. Retrieved from www.counterpunch.org/soldz08012006.html

(2008). Healers or interrogators: Psychology and the United States torture regime. *Psychoanalytic Dialogues* [Special Issue: *Coercive interrogations and the mental health profession*], 18, 592–613.

Solomon, Barbara M. (1985). *In the company of educated women: A history of women and higher education in America*. New Haven, CT: Yale University Press.

Sorrell, Tom (1986). *Hobbes*. London: Routledge & Kegan Paul.

(1987). *Descartes: A very short introduction*. Oxford University Press.

Soueif, Moustafa, & Ahmed, Ramadan (2001). Psychology in the Arab world: Past, present, and future. *International Journal of Group Tensions*, 3, 211–240.

Spade, Paul Vincent (2010). Medieval philosophy. In E. N. Zalta (ed.), *The Stanford encyclopedia of philosophy*. Retrieved from plato.stanford.edu/archives/sum2010/entries/medieval-philosophy/

Spade, Paul Vincent, & Panaccio, Claude (2011). William of Ockham. In E. N. Zalta (ed.), *The Stanford encyclopedia of philosophy*. Retrieved from plato.stanford.edu/archives/fall2011/entries/ockham/

Spaulding, John, & Balch, Philip (1983). A brief history of primary prevention in the twentieth century: 1908 to 1980. *American Journal of Community Psychology*, 11, 59–80.

Spender, Dale (1983). *Women of ideas and what men have done to them*. London: Ark Paperbacks.

Sperry, Roger W. (1988). Psychology's mentalist paradigm and the religion/science tension. *American Psychologist*, 43, 607–613.

Spilka, Bernard (1987). Religion and science in early American psychology. *Journal of Psychology and Theology*, 15, 3–9.

Spivak, Gayatri C. (1988). Can the subaltern speak? In C. Nelson & L. Grossberg (eds.), *Marxism and the interpretation of culture* (pp. 271–313). Urbana, IL: University of Illinois Press.

(1999). *A critique of postcolonial reason: Toward a history of the vanishing present*. Cambridge, MA: Harvard University Press.

Spranger, Eduard (1928). *Types of men: The psychology and ethics of personality*, trans.Paul J. W. Pigors. Halle: Max Niemeyer. (Original work published in German 1914)

(1929). *Psychologie des Jugendalters. Elfte Auflage* [Psychology of youth, 11th edn.]. Leipzig: Quelle & Meyer.

Sprung, Helga, & Sprung, Lothar (2000a). Carl Stumpf: Experimenter, theoretician, musicologist, and promoter. In Gregory A. Kimble & Michael Wertheimer (eds.), *Portraits of pioneers in psychology*, vol. IV (pp. 51–69). Washington, DC: American Psychological Association.

Sprung, Lothar, & Sprung, Helga (2000b). Georg Elias Müller and the beginnings of modern psychology. In Gregory A. Kimble & Michael Wertheimer (eds.), *Portraits of pioneers in psychology*, vol. IV (pp. 71–91). Washington, DC: American Psychological Association.

Stachel, John (ed.) (2005). *Einstein's miraculous year: Five papers that changed the face of physics*. Princeton University Press.

Staeuble, Irmingard (2004). De-centering Western perspectives: Psychology and the disciplinary order in the first and third world. In Adrian C. Brock, Johann Louw, & Willem Van Hoorn (eds.), *Rediscovering the history of psychology: Essays inspired by the work of Kurt Danziger* (pp. 183–205). New York: Kluwer Academic / Plenum Press.

Stam, Henderikus J., & Kalmanovitch, Tanya (1998). E. L. Thorndike and the origins of animal psychology: On the nature of the animal in psychology. *American Psychologist*, 53, 1135–1144.

Stanley, Barbara H., Sieber, Joan E., & Melton, Gary B. (eds.) (1996). *Research ethics: A psychological approach*. Lincoln, NE: University of Nebraska Press.

Stark, Laura (2010). The science of ethics: Deception, the resilient self, and the APA code of ethics, 1966–1973. *Journal of the History of the Behavioral Sciences*, 46, 337–370.

Staum, Martin S. (1980). *Cabanis*. Princeton University Press.

(2007). Ribot, Binet, and the emergence from the anthropological shadow. *Journal of the History of the Behavioural Sciences*, 43, 1–18.

Sternberg, Robert J. (2003). Intelligence. In Irving B. Weiner (series ed.) & Donald K. Freedheim (vol. ed.), *Handbook of psychology*, vol. I: *History of psychology* (pp. 135–156). Hoboken, NJ: Wiley.

Sternberg, Robert J., & Jarvin, Linda (2003). Alfred Binet's contributions as a paradigm for impact in psychology. In R. J. Sternberg (ed.), *The anatomy of impact: What makes the great works of psychology great* (pp. 89–107). Washington, DC: American Psychological Association.

Stevens, S. S. (1935). The operational basis of psychology. *American Journal of Psychology*, 47, 323–330.

Stewart, Abigail J., & McDermott, Christa (2004). Gender in psychology. *Annual Review of Psychology*, 55, 519–544.

Stewart, Matthew (2006). *The courtier and the heretic: Leibniz, Spinoza, and the fate of God in the modern world*. New York: Norton.

Stigler, Stephen M. (1999). *Statistics on the table: The history of statistical concepts and methods*. Cambridge, MA: Harvard University Press.

Stocking, George S., Jr. (1965). On the limits of "presentism" and "historicism" in the historiography of the behavioral sciences. *Journal of the History of the Behavioral Sciences*, 1, 211–218.

Stoerring, Gustav (1923). Ernst Meumann 1862–1915. *American Journal of Psychology*, 34, 271–274.

Stolte-Heiskanen, Veronica (1991). Introduction. In Veronica Stolte-Heiskanen (ed.), *Women in science: Token women or gender equality?* (pp. 1–8). Providence, RI: Berg.

Strack, Fritz, & Schwarz, Norbert (2007). Asking questions: Measurement in the social sciences. In Mitchell G. Ash & Thomas Sturm (eds.), *Psychology's territories: Historical and contemporary perspectives from different disciplines* (pp. 225–250). Mahwah, NJ: Erlbaum.

Stricker, George (2000). The scientist-practitioner model. *American Psychologist*, 55, 253–254.

(2010). *Psychotherapy integration*. Washington, DC: American Psychological Association.

Strien, Pieter J. van (1997). Psychology in the Netherlands. In Wolfgang G. Bringmann, Helmut E. Lück, Rudolf Miller, & Charles E. Early (eds.), *A pictorial history of psychology* (pp. 541–547). Chicago, IL: Quintessence Publishing.

(1998). Early applied psychology between essentialism and pragmatism: The dynamics of theory, tools, and clients. *History of Psychology*, 1, 205–234.

Strong, Edward K., & Campbell, David P. (1974). *Strong-Campbell interest inventory (test): Merged form of the Strong vocational interest blank*. Stanford University Press.

Sturm, Thomas (2006). Is there a problem with mathematical psychology in the eighteenth century? A fresh look at Kant's old argument. *Journal of the History of the Behavioural Sciences*, 42, 353–377.

Sturm, Thomas, & Ash, Mitchell G. (2009). Roles of instruments in psychological research. *History of Psychology*, 8, 3–34.

Sudokov, K. V. (2001). The development of the scientific ideas of I. P. Pavlov on the goal reflex in studies of the mechanisms of biological motivation. *Neuroscience and Behavioral Psychology*, 31, 87–94.

Sullivan, Edmund V. (1984). *A critical psychology: Interpretation of the personal world*. New York: Plenum Press.

Sundararajan, Louise (2005). Happiness donut: A Confucian critique of positive psychology. *Journal of Theoretical and Philosophical Psychology*, 25, 35–60.

Sweeney, Gerald (2001). *"Fighting for the good cause": Reflections on Francis Galton's legacy to American hereditarian psychology*. Independence Square, PA: American Philosophical Society.

Swim, Janet K., Stern, Paul C., Doherty, Thomas J., Clayton, Susan, Reser, Joseph P., Weber, Elke U., Gifford, Robert, & Howard, George S. (2011). Psychology's contribution to understanding and addressing global climate change. *American Psychologist*, 66, 241–250.

Szasz, Thomas, S. (1970). *The Manufacture of madness: A comparative study of the inquisition and the mental health movement*. New York: Harper & Row.

Tanner, Michael (2000). *Nietzsche: A very short introduction*. New York: Oxford University Press.

Tattersall, Ian, & DeSalle, Rob (2011). *Race? Debunking a scientific myth*. College Station: Texas A&M University Press.

Taylor, Charles (1985). *Philosophy and the human sciences: Philosophical papers 2*. Cambridge University Press.

(1989). *Sources of the self: The making of the modern identity*. Cambridge, MA: Harvard University Press.

Taylor, Charles Alan (1996). *Defining science: A rhetoric of demarcation*. Madison, WI: University of Wisconsin Press.

Taylor, Eugene (1990). New light on the origin of William James's experimental psychology. In Michael G. Johnson & Tracy B. Henley (eds.), *Reflections on The Principles of Psychology: William James after a century* (pp. 33–61). Hillsdale, NJ: Erlbaum.

(1996). The new Jung scholarship. *The Psychoanalytic Review*, 83, 547–568.

(1998). William James on the demise of positivism in American psychology. In Robert W. Rieber & Kurt Salzinger (eds.), *Psychology: Theoretical-historical perspectives*, 2nd edn. (pp. 101–132). Washington, DC: American Psychological Association.

(2000). Psychotherapeutics and the problematic origins of clinical psychology in America. *American Psychologist*, 55, 1029–1033.

(2010). Who was Frederic William Henry Myers? *Journal of Consciousness Studies*, 17(11–12), 153–171.

Taylor, Shelley (1998). The social being in social psychology. In *Daniel Gilbert*, Susan T. Fiske, & Gardner Lindzey (eds.), *The handbook of social psychology*, 4th edn., vol. I (pp. 58–95). Boston, MA: McGraw-Hill.

Tedeschi, Richard G., & McNally, Richard J. (2011). Can we facilitate posttraumatic growth in combat veterans? *American Psychologist*, 66, 19–24.

Tell, Hakan (2007). Sages and games: Intellectual displays and dissemination of wisdom in ancient Greece. *Classical Antiquity*, 26, 249–275.

Teo, Thomas (1999a). Functions of knowledge in psychology. *New Ideas in Psychology*, 17, 1–15.

(1999b). Methodologies of critical psychology: Illustrations from the field of racism. *Annual Review of Critical Psychology*, 1, 119–134.

(2001). Karl Marx and Wilhelm Dilthey on the socio-historical conceptualization of the mind. In Christopher D. Green, Marlene Shore & Thomas Teo (eds.), *The transformation of psychology: Influences of 19th-century philosophy, technology, and natural science* (pp. 195–218). Washington, DC: American Psychological Association.

(2002). Friedrich Albert Lange on neo-Kantianism, socialist Darwinism, and a psychology without a soul. *Journal of the History of the Behavioral Sciences*, 38, 285–301.

(2004). The historical problematization of "mixed race" in psychological and human-scientific discourses. In A. Winston (ed.), *Defining difference: Race and racism in the history of psychology* (pp. 79–108). Washington, DC: American Psychological Association.

(2005). *The critique of psychology: From Kant to post-colonial theory*. New York: Springer.

(2007). Local institutionalization, discontinuity, and German textbooks of psychology, 1816–1854. *Journal of the History of the Behavioral Sciences*, 43(2), 135–157.

(2008). From speculation to epistemological violence in psychology: A critical-hermeneutic reconstruction. *Theory & Psychology*, 18, 47–67.

(2009). Philosophical concerns in critical psychology. In D. Fox, I. Prilleltensky & S. Austin (eds.), *Critical psychology: An introduction*, 2nd edn. (pp. 36–53). London: Sage.

Teo, Thomas & Febbraro, Angela (2002). Attribution errors in the postmodern landscape. *American Psychologist*, 57, 458–460.

(2003). Ethnocentrism as a form of intuition in psychology. *Theory & Psychology*, 13, 673–694.

Thelen, Esther, & Adolph, Karen E. (1992). Arnold L. Gesell: The paradox of nature and nurture. *Developmental Psychology*, 28, 368–380.

Thompson, Jon, Baird, Patricia, & Downey, Jocelyn (2001). *Report of the Committee of Inquiry on the case involving Dr. Nancy Olivieri, the Hospital for Sick Children, and Apotex Inc.* Toronto: Canadian Association of University Teachers.

Thompson, Richard F., & Zola, Stuart M. (2003). Biological psychology. In Irving B. Weiner (series ed.) & Donald K. Freedheim (vol. ed.), *Handbook of psychology*, vol. I: *History of psychology* (pp. 47–66). Hoboken, NJ: Wiley.

Thomson, Robert (1968). *The Pelican history of psychology*: Harmondsworth: Penguin.

Thorndike, Edward L. (1931). *Human learning*. New York: Century.

(1991). Edward L. Thorndike: A professional and personal appreciation. In G. A. Kimble, M. Wertheimer, & C. White (eds.), *Portraits of pioneers in psychology* (pp. 139–151). Washington, DC: American Psychological Association.

Tiefer, Leonore (1991). A brief history of the Association for Women in Psychology: 1969–1991. *Psychology of Women Quarterly*, 15, 635–649.

Titchener, E. B. (1909). *A text-book of psychology*. New York: Macmillan.

Todd, Janet (2000). *Mary Wollstonecraft: A revolutionary life*. New York: Columbia University Press.

Todes, Daniel P. (1997). From the machine to the ghost within: Pavlov's transition from digestive physiology to conditional reflexes. *American Psychologist*, 52, 947–955.

(2001). *Pavlov's physiology factory: Experiment, interpretation, laboratory enterprise.* Baltimore, MD: Johns Hopkins University Press.

Tolman, Charles W. (1994). *Psychology, society, and subjectivity: An introduction to German Critical Psychology.* London: Routledge.

(2001). Philosophical doubts about psychology as a natural science. In Christopher D. Green, Marlene Shore & Thomas Teo (eds.), *The transformation of psychology: Influences of 19th-century philosophy, technology, and natural science* (pp. 175–193). Washington, DC: American Psychological Association.

(2009). Holtzkamp's critical psychology as a science from the standpoint of the human subject. *Theory and Psychology*, 19, 149–160.

Tolman, E. C. (1948). Cognitive maps in rats and men. *Psychological Review*, 55, 189–208.

Tomlinson, Stephen (1997). Edward Lee Thorndike and John Dewey on the science of education. *Oxford Review of Education*, 23, 365–383.

Tooby, John, & Cosmides, Leda (2005). Conceptual foundations of evolutionary psychology. In David M. Buss (ed.), *The handbook of evolutionary psychology* (pp. 5–67). New York: Wiley.

Toulmin, Stephen (1972). *Human understanding.* Princeton University Press.

Toulmin, Stephen, & Leary, Daniel E. (1985). The cult of empiricism in psychology, and beyond. In S. Koch & D. E. Leary (eds.), *A century of psychology as science* (pp. 594–617). New York: McGraw-Hill.

Treisman, Michel (1996). Why Goethe rejected Newton's theory of light. *Perception*, 25(10), 1219–1222.

Trendler, Güntler (2009). Measurement theory, psychology and the revolution that cannot happen. *Theory & Psychology*, 19, 579–599.

Triandis, Harry C., & Suh, Eunkook M. (2002). Cultural influences on personality. *Annual Review of Psychology*, 53, 133–160.

Triplet, Rodney G. (1992). Henry A. Murray: The making of a psychologist? *American Psychologist*, 47, 299–307.

Trognon, Alain (1987). France. In Albert R. Gilgen & Carol K. Gilgen (eds.), *International handbook of psychology* (pp. 184–207). New York: Greenwood Press.

Tuana, Nancy (ed.) (1994). *Feminist interpretations of Plato.* University Park, PA: Pennsylvania State University Press.

Tuck, Richard (1989). *Hobbes.* Oxford University Press.

Tucker, William H. (1994). *The science and politics of racial research.* Urbana, IL: University of Illinois Press.

(2007). Burt's separated twins: The larger picture. *Journal of the History of the Behavioral Sciences*, 43, 81–86.

Turner, R. Steven (1977). Hermann von Helmholtz and the empiricist vision. *Journal of the Behavioral Sciences*, 13, 48–58.

(1994). *In the eye's mind: Vision and the Helmholtz–Hering controversy.* Princeton University Press.

Tutty, Leslie (1990). The response of community mental health professionals to clients' rights: A review and suggestions. *Canadian Journal of Community Mental Health*, 9, 5–22.

Tweney, Ryan D. (1987). Programmatic research in experimental psychology: E. B. Titchener's laboratory investigations, 1891–1927. In Mitchell G. Ash & William R. Woodward (eds.), *Psychology in twentieth-century thought and society* (pp. 35–57). Cambridge University Press.

(1997). Edward Bradford Titchener (1867–1927). In Wolfgang G. Bringmann, Helmut E. Lück, Robert Miller, & Charles E. Early (eds.), *A pictorial history of psychology* (pp. 153–161). Chicago, IL: Quintessence Publishing.

Undeutsche, Udo (1992). Highlights of the history of forensic psychology in Germany. In Friedrich Lösel, Doris Bender & Thomas Bliesener (eds.), *Psychology and law: International perspectives* (pp. 509–518). New York: Walter de Gruyter.

Unger, Rhoda (2001). Marie Jahoda (1907–2001). *American Psychologist*, 56, 1040–1041.

Urbach, Peter (1987). *Francis Bacon's philosophy of science: An account and a reappraisal*. La Salle, IL: Open Court.

Ussher, Jane (ed.) (1997). *Body talk: The material and discursive regulation of sexuality, madness and reproduction*. London: Routledge.

Valentine, Elizabeth R. (2005). *Beatrice Edgell: Pioneer woman psychologist*. Hauppauge, NY: Nova Science Publishers.

Vasilyeva, Nina (2000). Psychoanalysis in Russia: The past, the present, and the future. *American Imago*, 57, 5–24.

Vassilieva, Julia (2010). Russian psychology at the turn of the 21st century and post-Soviet reforms in the humanities disciplines. *History of Psychology*, 13, 138–159.

Vicedo, Marga (2009). Mothers, machines, and morals: Harry Harlow's work on primate love from lab to legend. *Journal of the History of the Behavioral Sciences*, 45, 193–218.

Vigneault, Jacques (2005). Canada. *International Dictionary of Psychoanalysis*, ed. Alain de Mijolla. Gale Cengage, eNotes.com. 2006. Retrieved 31 May, 2010, www.enotes.com/psychoanalysis-encyclopedia/canada

Viner, Russell (1996). Melanie Klein and Anna Freud: The discourse of the early dispute. *Journal of the History of the Behavioral Sciences*, 32, 4–15.

Viney, Wayne, & Burlingame-Lee, Laura (2003). Margaret Floy Washburn: A quest for the harmonies in the context of a rigorous scientific framework. In Gregory A. Kimble & Michael Wertheimer (eds.), *Portraits of pioneers in psychology*, vol. V (pp. 73–88). Washington, DC: American Psychological Association.

Vogt, Katja (2010). Ancient scepticism. In E. N. Zalta (ed.), *The Stanford encyclopedia of philosophy*. Retrieved from http://plato.stanford.edu/archives/win2011/entries/skepticism-ancient/

Vygotsky, Lev S. (1978). *Mind in society: The development of higher psychological processes*, trans. Alexander Luria; ed. Michael Cole, Vera John-Steiner, Sylvia Scribner, & Ellen Souberman. Cambridge, MA: Harvard University Press.

Wachtel, Paul L. (1977). *Psychoanalysis and behavior therapy: Toward an integration*. New York: Basic Books.

Wade, Nicholas J., & Brozek, Josef (2001). *Purkinje's vision: The dawning of neuroscience*. Mahwah, NJ: Erlbaum.

Waithe, Mary Ellen (ed.) (1987). *A history of women philosophers*, vol. I: *Ancient women philosophers, 600 B.C.–500 A.D.* Dordrecht: Kluver Academic.

Walkderdine, Valerie (ed.) (2002). *Challenging subjects: Critical psychology for a new millennium*. New York: Palgrave Macmillan.

(2008). Contextualizing debates about psychosocial studies. *Psychoanalysis, Culture & Society*, 13, 341–345.

Wallace, B. Alan, & Shapiro, Shauna L. (2006). Mental balance and well-being: Building bridges between Buddhism and Western psychology. *American Psychologist*, 61, 690–701.

Waller, John C. (2001). Gentlemanly men of science: Sir Francis Galton and the professionalization of the British life-sciences. *Journal of the History of Biology*, 34, 83–114.

Wallerstein, Robert S., & Fonagy, Peter (1999). Psychoanalytic research and the IPA: History, present status and future potential. *International Journal of Psychoanalysis*, 80, 91–109.

Walls, Joan (1982). The psychology of David Hartley and the root metaphor of mechanism: A study in the history of psychology. *The Journal of Mind and Behavior*, 3, 259–274.

Walsh, Richard T. (1987). The evolution of the research relationship in community psychology. *American Journal of Community Psychology*, 15, 773–788.

(1989). Do research reports in mainstream feminist psychology journals reflect feminist values? *Psychology of Women Quarterly*, 13, 433–444.

Walsh-Bowers, Richard (1995). The reporting and ethics of the research relationship in areas of interpersonal psychology, 1939–89. *Theory & Psychology*, 5, 233–250.

(1998). Community psychology in the Canadian psychological family, *Canadian Psychology*, 39, 280–287.

(1999). Fundamentalism in psychological science: The publication manual as Bible. *Psychology of Women Quarterly*, 23, 375–393.

(2000). A personal sojourn to spiritualize community psychology. *Journal of Community Psychology*, 28, 221–236.

(2002). Constructing qualitative knowledge in psychology: Students and faculty negotiate the social context of inquiry. *Canadian Psychology*, 43, 163–178.

(2004). Expanding the terrain of Kurt Danziger's *Constructing the subject*: The research relationship in psychology. In Adrian C. Brock, Johann Louw, & Willem van Hoorn (eds.), *Rediscovering the history of psychology: Essays inspired by the work of Kurt Danziger* (pp. 97–118). Dordrecht: Kluwer Academic.

(2006). A theatre acting perspective on the dramaturgical metaphor and the postmodern self. *Theory & Psychology*, 16, 661–690.

(2007). The research relationship in English-language European psychology journals: Forty years of American scientific colonization? *Social Practice/Psychological Theorizing* (pp. 35–50). Retrieved November 5, 2007 from http://sppt-gulerce.boun.edu.tr.html

(2010). Some social-historical issues underlying psychology's fragmentation. *New Directions in Psychology*, 28, 244–252.

Walsh-Bowers, Richard, & Johnson, Pam (2002). Introducing mainstream psychology to Native students whose feet are in two vessels. *Canadian Journal of Native Studies*, 22, 121–135.

Wang, Zhong-Ming (1993). Psychology and China: A review dedicated to Li Chen. *Annual Review of Psychology*, 44, 87–116.

Ward, Stephen C. (2002). *Modernizing the mind: Psychological knowledge and the remaking of society*. Westport, CT: Praeger.

Warren, Mark E. (1988). *Nietzsche and political thought*. Cambridge, MA: MIT Press.

Wartofsky, Marx (1973). Action and passion: Spinoza's construction of a scientific psychology. In Marjorie Grene (ed.), *Spinoza: A collection of critical essays* (pp. 328–353). Notre Dame, IN: University of Notre Dame Press.

Washburn, Jennifer (2005). *University, Inc.: The corporate corruption of higher education*. New York: Basic Books.

Washburn, Margaret F. (1916). *Movement and mental imagery: Outlines of a motor theory of the complex mental processes*. Boston, MA: Houghton Mifflin.

(1936). *The animal mind: A text-book of comparative psychology*, 4th edn. New York: Macmillan.

Watkins, Mary, & Shulman, Helene (2008). *Toward psychologies of liberation*. Basingstoke: Palgrave Macmillan.

Watson, John B. (1913). Psychology as the behaviorist views it. *Psychological Review*, 20, 158–177.

(1928). *Psychological care of the infant and child*. New York: Norton.

Watson, John B., & Rayner, Rosalie (1920). Conditioned emotional reactions. *Journal of Experimental Psychology*, 3, 1–14.

Watson, Robert I. (1977). In Josef Brozek & Rand B. Evans (eds.), *R. I. Watson's selected papers on the history of psychology* (pp. 224–229). Hanover, NH: University Press of New England.

Watson, Robert I., & Evans, Rand B. (1991). *The great psychologists: A history of psychological thought*, 5th edn. New York: HarperCollins.

Watts, Roderick J. (1992). Elements of a psychology of human diversity. *Journal of Community Psychology*, 20, 116–131.

Weasel, Lisa (1996). The cell in relation: An ecofeminist revision of cell and molecular biology. *Women's Studies International Forum*, 20, 49–59.

Weidman, Nadine M. (1999). *Constructing scientific psychology: Karl Lashley's mind-brain debate*. New York: Cambridge University Press.

Weimer, Walter B. (1974). The history of psychology and its retrieval from historiography: I. The problematic nature of history. *Science Studies*, 4, 235–258.

Weisberg, Robert W. (2006). *Creativity: Understanding innovation in problem solving, science, invention, & the arts*. Hoboken, NJ: Wiley.

Weizmann, Frederic (2010). From "The Village of a Thousand Souls" to "Race Crossing in Jamaica": Arnold Gesell, eugenics and child development. *Journal of the History of the Behavioral Sciences*, 46, 263–275.

Wellman, Henry A. (2006). Theory of mind: A core human cognition. In Qicheng Jing, Mark R. Rosenzweig, Gery d'Ydewalle, Houcan Zhang, Hisuan-Chi Chen, & Kan Zhang (eds.), *Progress in psychological science around the world*, vol. I (pp. 503–526). New York: Psychology Press.

Wentworth, Phyliss. A. (1999). The moral of her story: Exploring the philosophical and religious commitments in Mary Whiton Calkins's self-psychology. *History of Psychology*, 2, 119–131.

Wertheimer, Michael (1991). Max Wertheimer: Modern cognitive psychology and the Gestalt problem. In Gregory A. Kimble, Michael Wertheimer, & Charlotte L. White (eds.), *Portraits of pioneers in psychology* (pp. 189–207). Washington, DC: American Psychological Association.

Westfall, Richard (1980). *Never at rest*. Cambridge University Press.

Westkott, Marcia (1986). *The feminist legacy of Karen Horney*. New Haven, CT: Yale University Press.

Wetherell, Margaret (2008). Subjectivity or psychodiscursive practices? Investigating complex intersectional identities. *Subjectivity*, 22, 73–81.

Whaley, Leigh Ann (2003). *Women's history as scientists: A guide to the debates*. Santa Barbara, CA: ABC-CLIO.

Wheen, Francis (2006). *Marx's Das Kapital: A biography*. New York: Atlantic Monthly Press.

White, Stephen H. (1992). G. Stanley Hall: From philosophy to developmental psychology. *Developmental Psychology*, 28, 25–34.

Whitney, Charles (1986). *Francis Bacon and modernity*. New Haven, CT: Yale University Press.

Wiggins, Jerry S. (2003). *Paradigms of personality assessment*. New York: Guilford Press.

Wilber, Ken (2007). *The integral vision: A very short introduction to the revolutionary integral approach to life, God, the universe, and everything*. Boston, MA: Shambhala.

Wilkinson, Leland, & the Task Force on Statistical Inference (1999). Statistical methods and psychology journals: Guidelines and explanations. *American Psychologist*, 54, 594–604.

Wilkinson, Sue (2001). Theoretical perspectives on women and gender. In Rhoda K. Unger (ed.), *Handbook of the psychology of women and gender* (pp. 17–28). New York: Wiley.

Williams, Thomas (2010). John Duns Scotus. In E. N. Zalta (ed.), *The Stanford encyclopedia of philosophy*. Retrieved from http://plato.stanford.edu/archives/spr2010/entries/duns-scotus/

Willy, Rudolf (1899). *Die Krisis in der Psychologie* [The crisis in psychology]. Leipzig: Reisland.

Wilson, Catherine (2007). The moral epistemology of Locke's Essay. In Lex Newman (ed.), *The Cambridge companion to Locke's "Essay concerning Human Understanding"* (pp. 381–405). Cambridge University Press.

Wilson, Eric G. (2008). *Against happiness*. New York: Sarah Crichton Books.

Windelband, Wilhelm (1998). History and natural science, trans. J. T. Lamiell. *Theory & Psychology*, 8, 5–22. (German original work published 1894)

Windholz, George (1997). Ivan P. Pavlov: An overview of his life and psychological work. *American Psychologist*, 52, 941–946.

Winston, Andrew S. (2001). Cause into function: Ernst Mach and the reconstruction of explanation in psychology. In Christopher D. Green, Marlene Shore, & Thomas Teo (eds.), *The transformation of psychology: Influences of 19th-century philosophy, technology, and natural science* (pp. 107–131). Washington, DC: American Psychological Association.

(2004a). Controlling the metalanguage: Authority and acquiescence in the history of method. In Adrian C. Brock, Johann Louw, & Willem van Hoorn (eds.), *Rediscovering the history of psychology: Essays inspired by the work of Kurt Danziger* (pp. 53–73). Dordrecht: Kluwer Academic.

(ed.) (2004b). *Defining difference: Race and racism in the history of psychology*. Washington, DC: American Psychological Association.

Wise, Steven M. (2000). *Rattling the cage: Toward legal rights for animals*. Cambridge, MA: Perseus Books.

Wolf, Theta Holmes (1973). *Alfred Binet*. University of Chicago Press.

Wolpe, Joseph, & Plaude, Joseph J. (1997). Pavlov's contributions to behavior therapy. *American Psychologist*, 52, 966–972.

Wolterstorff, Nicholas (2001). *Thomas Reid and the story of epistemology*. Cambridge University Press.

Wood, Neal (1983). *The politics of Locke's philosophy: A social study of "An Essay concerning Human Understanding."* Berkeley, CA: University of California Press.

Woodward, William R. (1972). Fechner's panpsychism: A scientific solution to the mind-body problem. *Journal of the History of the Behavioral Sciences*, 8, 367–386.

(1982). Wundt's program for the new psychology: Vicissitudes of experiment, theory, and system. In W. R. Woodward & M. G. Ash (eds.), *The problematic science: Psychology in nineteenth-century thought* (pp. 167–197). New York: Praeger.

Woodworth, Robert S. (1924). Four varieties of behaviorism. *Psychological Review*, 31, 257–264.

Woolfolk, Robert, L. (2002). The power of negative thinking: Truth, melancholia, and the tragic sense of life. *Journal of Theoretical and Philosophical Psychology*, 22, 19–27.

Wozniak, Robert H. (1998). Thought and things: James Mark Baldwin and the biosocial origins of mind. In R. W. Rieber & K. Salzinger (eds.), *Psychology: Theoretical-historical perspectives*, 2nd edn. (pp. 429–453). Washington, DC: American Psychological Association.

Wright, Mary J. (1996). William Emet Blatz: A Canadian pioneer. In Gregory A. Kimble, C. Alan Boneau, & Michael Wertheimer (eds.), *Portraits of pioneers in psychology* (pp. 199–211). Washington, DC: American Psychological Association.

Wright, Mary J., & Myers, C. Roger (eds.) (1982). *History of academic psychology in Canada*. Toronto: C. J. Hogrefe.

Wrightsman, Lawrence (1992). *Assumptions about human nature: Implications for researchers and practitioners*, 2nd edn. Newbury Park, CA: Sage.

Wundt, Wilhelm (1896). *Grundrisse der Psychologie* [Outlines of psychology]. Leipzig: Engelmann.

   (1897). *Outlines of psychology*, trans. Charles H. Judd. Leipzig: Englemann.

   (1910). *Principles of physiological psychology*, trans. Edward Bradford Titchener. London: Sonnenschein. (First English edition 1904; Original work published in German 1874)

Wynne, Clive D. L. (2001). *Animal cognition: The mental lives of animals*. New York: Palgrave/ St. Martin's.

Xie, Yu, & Shauman, Kimberlee A. (2003). *Women in science: Career processes and outcomes*. Cambridge, MA: Harvard University Press.

Yaroshevski, Mikhail G. (1968). I. M. Sechenov: The founder of objective psychology. In Benjamin B. Wolman (ed.), *Historical roots of contemporary psychology* (pp. 77–110). New York: Harper & Row.

Yaroschevskii, Mikhail Grigorevitch (1982). The logic of scientific development and the scientific school: The example of Ivan Michalovich Sechenov. In William R. Woodward & Mitchell G. Ash (eds.), *The problematic science: Psychology in nineteenth-century thought* (pp. 231–254). New York: Praeger.

Yasnitsky, Anton, & Ferrari, Michel (2008). Rethinking the early history of post-Vygotskian psychology: The case of the Kharkov School. *History of Psychology*, 11, 101–121.

York, Geoffrey (1989). *The dispossessed: Life and death in native Canada*. Toronto: Lester & Orpen Dennys.

Young, Robert J. C. (2001). *Postcolonialism: A historical introduction*. Malden, MA: Blackwell.

Young, Robert M. (1970). *Mind, brain and adaptation in the nineteenth century: Cerebral localization and its biological context from Gall to Ferrier*. Oxford University Press.

Young-Bruehl, Elisabeth & Dunbar, Christine (2009). *One hundred years of psychoanalysis a timeline: 1900–2000*. Toronto: Caversham.

Youniss, James (2006). G. Stanley Hall and his times: Too much so, yet not enough. *History of Psychology*, 9, 224–235.

Yovel, Yirmiyahu (1989). *Spinoza and other heretics: The adventures of immanence*. Princeton University Press.

Yu, Jiyuan (2004). The Chinese encounter with Greek philosophy. In L. Rossetti, (ed.), *Greek philosophy in the new millennium* (pp. 187–198). Sankt Augustin: Academia.

Yuan, Teresa (2002). Psychoanalysis in China. *International Journal of Psychoanalysis*, 83, 516–517.

Zaretsky, Eli (2004). *Secrets of the soul: A social and cultural history of psychoanalysis*. New York: Knopf.

Zebian, Samar, Alamuddin, Rayane, Maalouf, Mariane, & Chatila, Yasmine (2007). Developing an appropriate psychology through culturally sensitive research practices in the Arabic-speaking world: A content analysis of psychological research published between 1950 and 2004. *Journal of Cross-Cultural Psychology*, 38, 91–122.

Zhang, Hou-can (1987). People's Republic of China. In Albert R. Gilgen & Carol K. Gilgen (eds.), *International handbook of psychology* (pp. 109–123). New York: Greenwood Press.

Zhang, Jingyuan (2003). Psychoanalysis in the Chinese context. *International Institute for Asian Studies*, 30, 8–9.

Zinn, Howard (2005). *A people's history of the United States*. New York: Harper Perennial.

NAME INDEX

SUBJECT INDEX